Create Value

The set of value proposition **benefits** that you **design** to attract customers.

DEF·I·NI·TION
VALUE PROPOSITION
Describes the benefits customers can
expect from your products and services.

Observe Customers

The set of customer **characteristics** that you **assume, observe, and verify** in the market.

Value Map

The Value (Proposition) Map describes the features of a specific value proposition in your business model in a more structured and detailed way. It breaks your value proposition down into products and services, pain relievers, and gain creators.

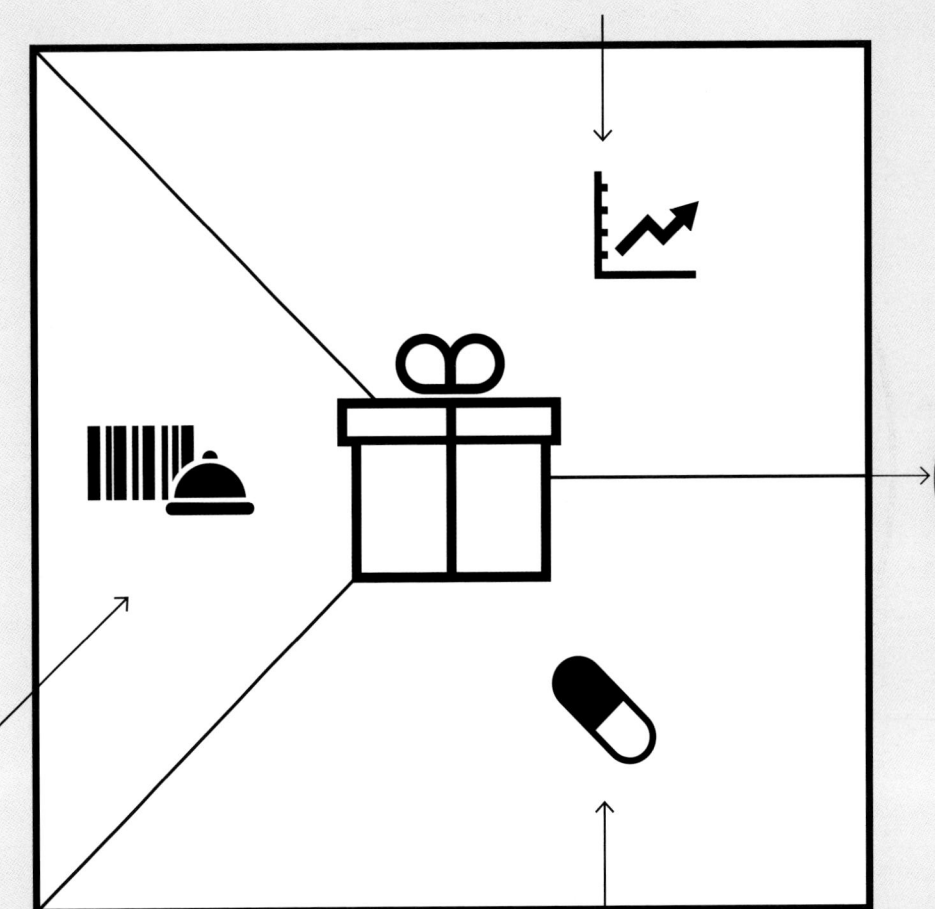

Gain Creators describe how your products and services create customer gains.

This is a list of all the **Products and Services** a value proposition is built around.

Pain Relievers describe how your products and services alleviate customer pains.

Gains describe the outcomes customers want to achieve or the concrete benefits they are seeking.

Customer Profile

The Customer (Segment) Profile describes a specific customer segment in your business model in a more structured and detailed way. It breaks the customer down into its jobs, pains, and gains.

Customer Jobs describe what customers are trying to get done in their work and in their lives, as expressed in their own words.

Pains describe bad outcomes, risks, and obstacles related to customer jobs.

You achieve **Fit** when your value map meets your customer profile—when your products and services produce pain relievers and gain creators that match one or more of the jobs, pains, and gains that are important to your customer.

1.1

Customer Profile

Customer Jobs

Jobs describe the things your customers are trying to get done in their work or in their life. A customer job could be the tasks they are trying to perform and complete, the problems they are trying to solve, or the needs they are trying to satisfy. Make sure you take the customer's perspective when investigating jobs. What you think of as important from your perspective might not be a job customers are actually trying to get done.*

Distinguish between three main types of customer jobs to be done and supporting jobs:

Functional jobs

When your customers try to perform or complete a specific task or solve a specific problem, for example, mow the lawn, eat healthy as a consumer, write a report, or help clients as a professional.

Social jobs

When your customers want to look good or gain power or status. These jobs describe how customers want to be perceived by others, for example, look trendy as a consumer or be perceived as competent as a professional.

Personal/emotional jobs

When your customers seek a specific emotional state, such as feeling good or secure, for example, seeking peace of mind regarding one's investments as a consumer or achieving the feeling of job security at one's workplace.

Supporting jobs

Customers also perform supporting jobs in the context of purchasing and consuming value either as consumers or as professionals. These jobs arise from three different roles:

- BUYER OF VALUE: jobs related to buying value, such as comparing offers, deciding which products to buy, standing in a checkout line, completing a purchase, or taking delivery of a product or service.

- COCREATOR OF VALUE: jobs related to cocreating value with your organization, such as posting product reviews and feedback or even participating in the design of a product or service.

- TRANSFERRER OF VALUE: jobs related to the end of a value proposition's life cycle, such as canceling a subscription, disposing of a product, transferring it to others, or reselling it.

*The jobs to be done concept was developed independently by several business thinkers including Anthony Ulwick of the consulting firm Strategyn, consultants Rick Pedi and Bob Moesta, and Professor Denise Nitterhouse of DePaul University. It was popularized by Clay Christensen and his consulting firm Innosight and Anthony Ulwick's Strategyn.

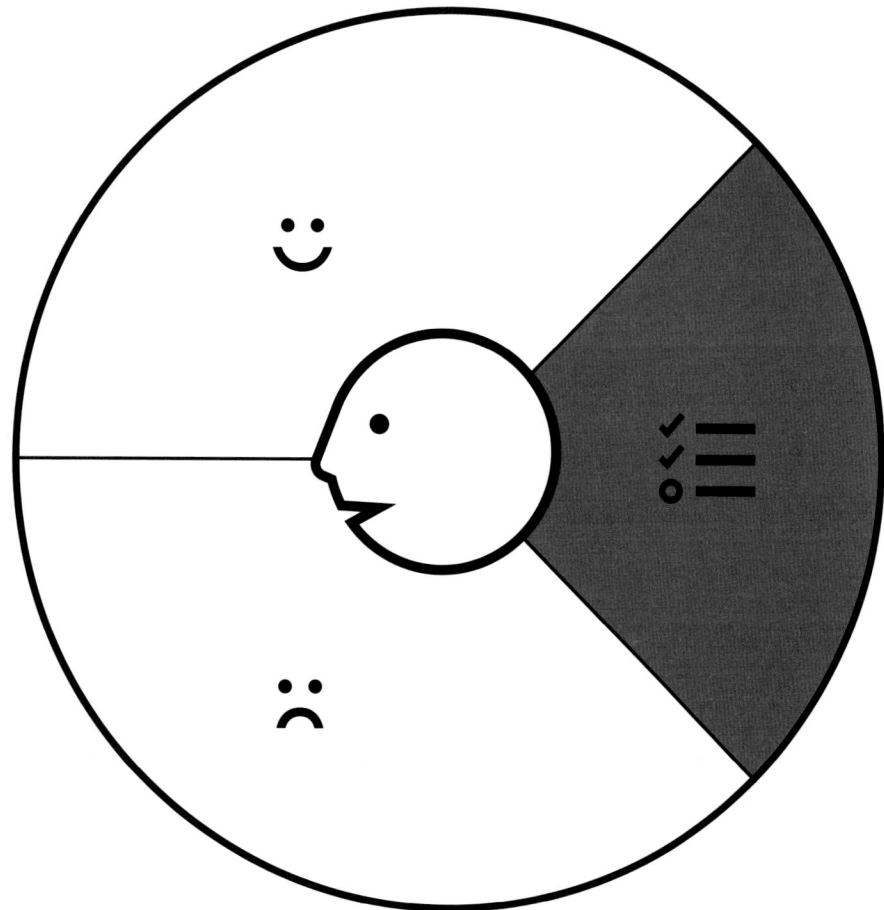

Job context

Customer jobs often depend on the specific context in which they are performed. The context may impose certain constraints or limitations. For example, calling somebody on the fly is different when you are traveling on a train than when you are driving a car. Likewise, going to the movies with your kids is different than going with your partner.

Job importance

It is important to acknowledge that not all jobs have the same importance to your customer. Some matter more in a customer's work or life because failing to get them done could have serious ramifications. Some are insignificant because the customer cares about other things more. Sometimes a customer will deem a job crucial because it occurs frequently or because it will result in a desired or unwanted outcome.

+
Important

↑
↓

Insignificant
−

 Download trigger questions to help find customer jobs

Customer Pains

Pains describe anything that annoys your customers before, during, and after trying to get a job done or simply prevents them from getting a job done. Pains also describe risks, that is, potential bad outcomes, related to getting a job done badly or not at all.

Seek to identify three types of customer pains and how severe customers find them:

Undesired outcomes, problems, and characteristics

Pains are functional (e.g., a solution doesn't work, doesn't work well, or has negative side effects), social ("I look bad doing this"), emotional ("I feel bad every time I do this"), or ancillary ("It's annoying to go to the store for this"). This may also involve undesired characteristics customers don't like (e.g., "Running at the gym is boring," or "This design is ugly").

Obstacles

These are things that prevent customers from even getting started with a job or that slow them down (e.g., "I lack the time to get this job done accurately," or "I can't afford any of the existing solutions").

Risks (undesired potential outcomes)

What could go wrong and have important negative consequences (e.g., "I might lose credibility when using this type of solution," or "A security breach would be disastrous for us").

Pain severity

A customer pain can be extreme or moderate, similar to how jobs can be important or insignificant to the customer.

Tip: Make pains concrete.

To clearly differentiate jobs, pains, and gains, describe them as concretely as possible. For example, when a customer says "waiting in line was a waste of time," ask after how many minutes exactly it began to feel like wasted time. That way you can note "wasting more than *x* minutes standing in line." When you understand how exactly customers measure pain severity, you can design better pain relievers in your value proposition.

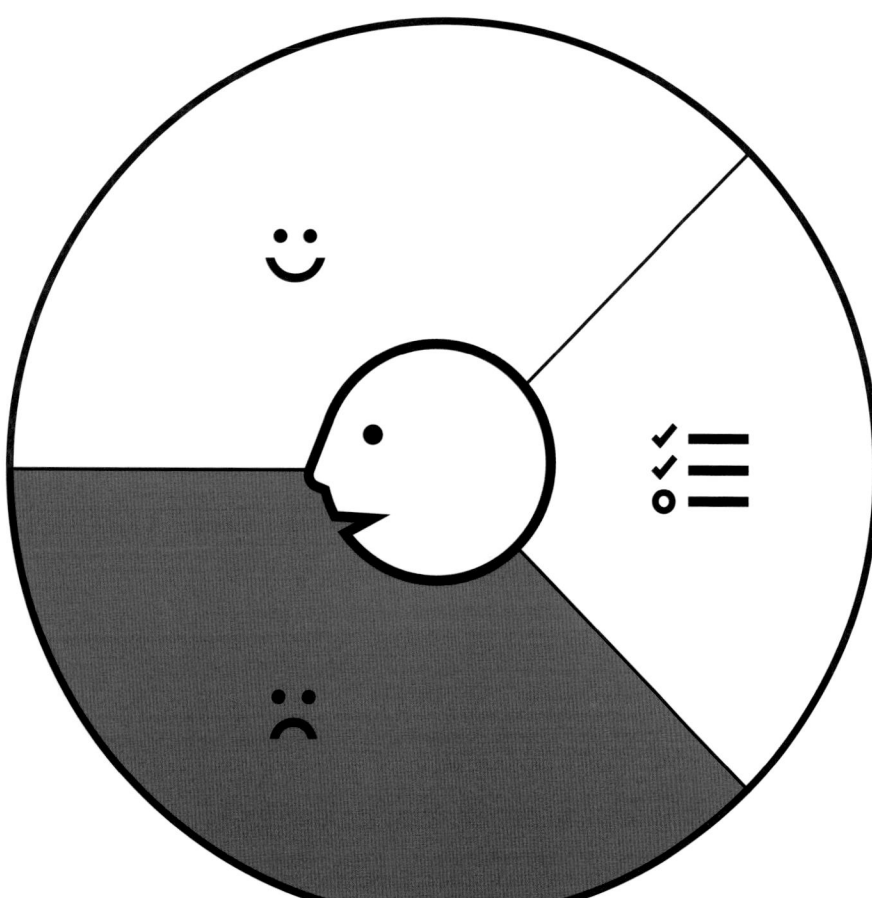

The following list of trigger questions can help you think of different potential customer pains:

- How do your customers define too costly? Takes a lot of time, costs too much money, or requires substantial efforts?
- What makes your customers feel bad? What are their frustrations, annoyances, or things that give them a headache?
- How are current value propositions underperforming for your customers? Which features are they missing? Are there performance issues that annoy them or malfunctions they cite?
- What are the main difficulties and challenges your customers encounter? Do they understand how things work, have difficulties getting certain things done, or resist particular jobs for specific reasons?
- What negative social consequences do your customers encounter or fear? Are they afraid of a loss of face, power, trust, or status?
- What risks do your customers fear? Are they afraid of financial, social, or technical risks, or are they asking themselves what could go wrong?
- What's keeping your customers awake at night? What are their big issues, concerns, and worries?
- What common mistakes do your customers make? Are they using a solution the wrong way?
- What barriers are keeping your customers from adopting a value proposition? Are there upfront investment costs, a steep learning curve, or other obstacles preventing adoption?

 Download trigger questions

Customer Gains

Gains describe the outcomes and benefits your customers want. Some gains are required, expected, or desired by customers, and some would surprise them. Gains include functional utility, social gains, positive emotions, and cost savings.

Seek to identify four types of customer gains in terms of outcomes and benefits:

Required gains

These are gains without which a solution wouldn't work. For example, the most basic expectation that we have from a smartphone is that we can make a call with it.

Expected gains

These are relatively basic gains that we expect from a solution, even if it could work without them. For example, since Apple launched the iPhone, we expect phones to be well-designed and look good.

Desired gains

These are gains that go beyond what we expect from a solution but would love to have if we could. These are usually gains that customers would come up with if you asked them. For example, we desire smartphones to be seamlessly integrated with our other devices.

Unexpected gains

These are gains that go beyond customer expectations and desires. They wouldn't even come up with them if you asked them. Before Apple brought touch screens and the App Store to the mainstream, nobody really thought of them as part of a phone.

Gain relevance

A customer gain can feel essential or nice to have, just like pains can feel extreme or moderate to them.

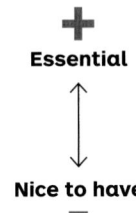

Essential

Nice to have

Tip: Make gains concrete.

As with pains, it's better to describe gains as concretely as possible to clearly differentiate jobs, pains, and gains from one another. Ask how much they'd expect or dream of when a customer indicates "better performance" as a desired gain. That way you can note "would love an increased performance of more than *x*." When you understand how exactly customers measure gains (i.e., outcomes and benefits), you can design better gain creators in your value proposition.

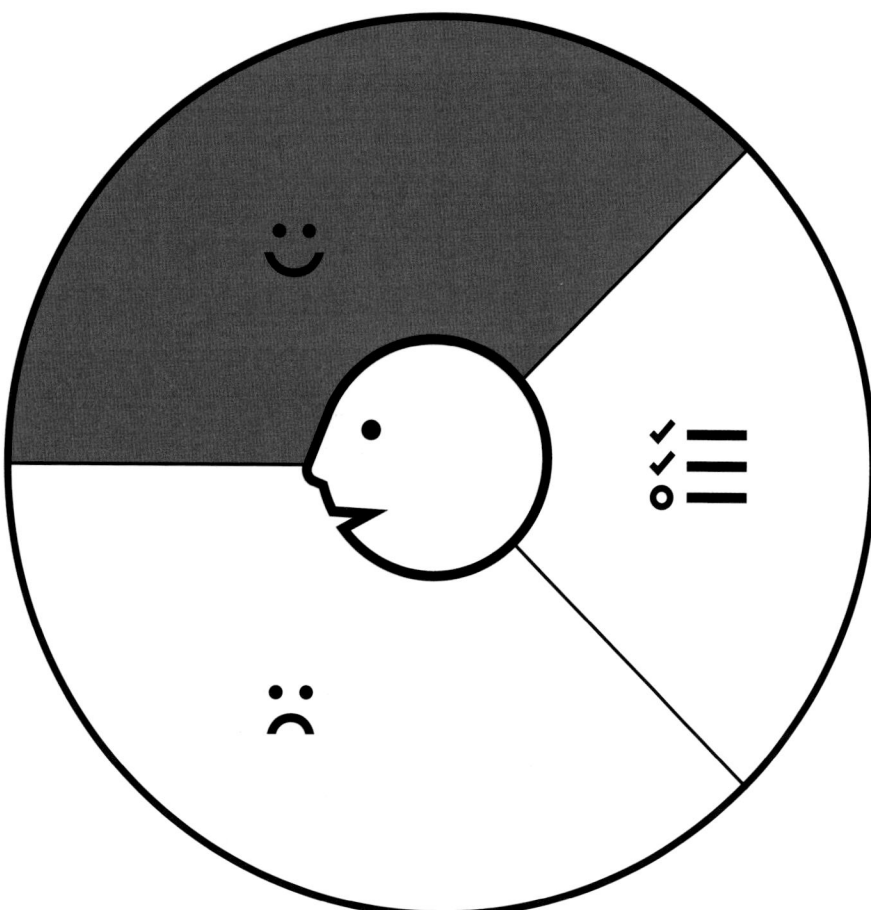

The following list of trigger questions can help you think of different potential customer gains:

- Which savings would make your customers happy? Which savings in terms of time, money, and effort would they value?
- What quality levels do they expect, and what would they wish for more or less of?
- How do current value propositions delight your customers? Which specific features do they enjoy? What performance and quality do they expect?
- What would make your customers' jobs or lives easier? Could there be a flatter learning curve, more services, or lower costs of ownership?
- What positive social consequences do your customers desire? What makes them look good? What increases their power or their status?
- What are customers looking for most? Are they searching for good design, guarantees, specific or more features?
- What do customers dream about? What do they aspire to achieve, or what would be a big relief to them?
- How do your customers measure success and failure? How do they gauge performance or cost?
- What would increase your customers' likelihood of adopting a value proposition? Do they desire lower cost, less investment, lower risk, or better quality?

 *Download trigger questions*

Profile of a "Business Book Reader"

We chose to use potential readers of this book to illustrate the customer profile. We deliberately went beyond jobs, pains, and gains merely related to reading books, since we intended to design an innovative and more holistic value proposition for businesspeople in general.

The customer profile sketched out on the right is informed by several interviews we conducted and thousands of interactions we had with workshop participants. However, it is not mandatory to start with preexisting customer knowledge. You may begin exploring ideas by sketching out a profile based on what you believe your potential customers look like. This is an excellent starting point to prepare customer interviews and tests regarding your assumptions about customer jobs, pains, and gains.

Gains are benefits, results, and characteristics that customers require or desire. They are outcomes of jobs or wanted characteristics of a value proposition that help customers get a job done well.

The more tangible and specific you make pains and gains, the better. For example, "examples from my industry" is more concrete than "relevant to my context." Ask customers how they measure gains and pains. Investigate how they measure success or failure of a job they want to get done.

Make sure you deeply understand your customer. If you have only a few sticky notes on your profile, that probably indicates a lack of customer understanding. Unearth as many jobs, pains, and gains as you can. Search beyond those directly related to your value proposition.

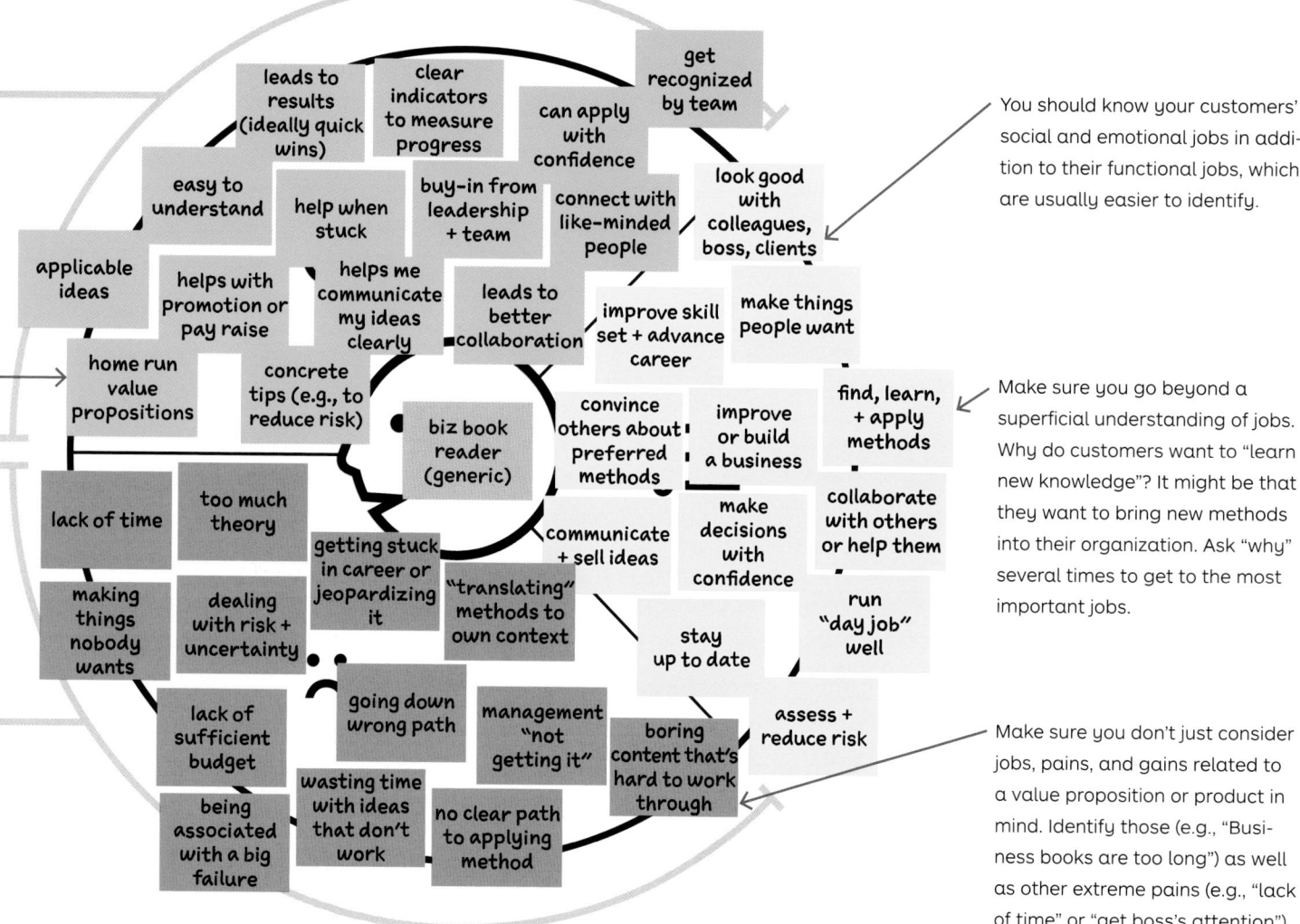

get recognized by team

leads to results (ideally quick wins)

clear indicators to measure progress

can apply with confidence

easy to understand

help when stuck

buy-in from leadership + team

connect with like-minded people

look good with colleagues, boss, clients

applicable ideas

helps with promotion or pay raise

helps me communicate my ideas clearly

leads to better collaboration

improve skill set + advance career

make things people want

home run value propositions

concrete tips (e.g., to reduce risk)

biz book reader (generic)

convince others about preferred methods

improve or build a business

find, learn, + apply methods

lack of time

too much theory

getting stuck in career or jeopardizing it

communicate + sell ideas

make decisions with confidence

collaborate with others or help them

making things nobody wants

dealing with risk + uncertainty

"translating" methods to own context

stay up to date

run "day job" well

lack of sufficient budget

going down wrong path

management "not getting it"

boring content that's hard to work through

assess + reduce risk

being associated with a big failure

wasting time with ideas that don't work

no clear path to applying method

You should know your customers' social and emotional jobs in addition to their functional jobs, which are usually easier to identify.

Make sure you go beyond a superficial understanding of jobs. Why do customers want to "learn new knowledge"? It might be that they want to bring new methods into their organization. Ask "why" several times to get to the most important jobs.

Make sure you don't just consider jobs, pains, and gains related to a value proposition or product in mind. Identify those (e.g., "Business books are too long") as well as other extreme pains (e.g., "lack of time" or "get boss's attention").

Ranking Jobs, Pains, and Gains

Although individual customer preferences vary, you need to get a sense of customer priorities. Investigate which jobs the majority consider important or insignificant. Find out which pains they find extreme versus merely moderate. Learn which gains they find essential and which are simply nice to have.

Ranking jobs, pains, and gains is essential in order to design value propositions that address things customers really care about. Of course, it's difficult to unearth what really matters to customers, but your understanding will improve with every customer interaction and experiment.

It doesn't matter if you start out with a ranking that is based on what you think is important to your potential customers as long as you strive to test that ranking until it truly reflects priorities from the customer's perspective.

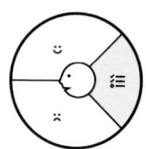

Job importance

Rank jobs according to their importance to customers.

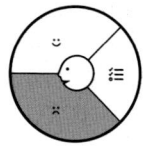

Pain severity

Rank pains according to how extreme they are in the customers' eyes.

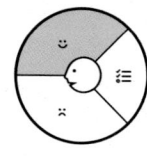

Gain relevance

Rank gains according to how essential they are in the customers' eyes.

+ Important

- improve skill set + advance career
- run "day job" well
- improve or build a business
- assess and reduce risk
- collaborate with others or help them
- find, learn, + apply methods

- look good with colleagues, boss, clients
- make decisions with confidence
- communicate + sell ideas
- make things people want
- convince others about preferred methods
- stay up to date

Insignificant

+ Extreme

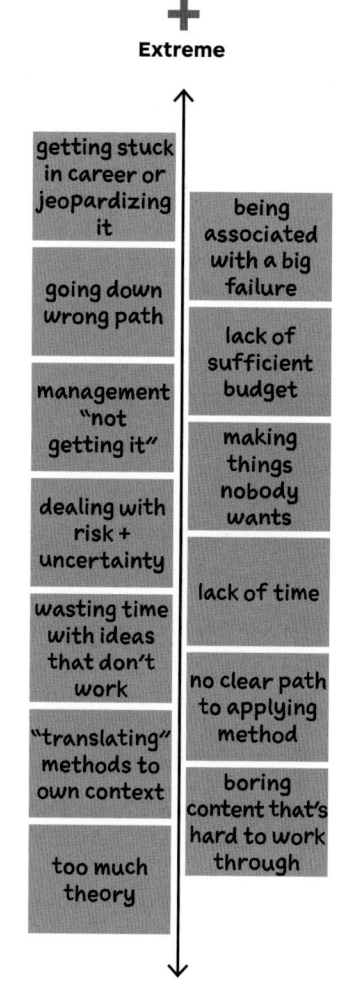

- getting stuck in career or jeopardizing it
- going down wrong path
- management "not getting it"
- dealing with risk + uncertainty
- wasting time with ideas that don't work
- "translating" methods to own context
- too much theory

- being associated with a big failure
- lack of sufficient budget
- making things nobody wants
- lack of time
- no clear path to applying method
- boring content that's hard to work through

Moderate

+ Essential

- helps with promotion or pay raise
- buy-in from leadership + team
- get recognized by team
- help when stuck
- applicable ideas
- can apply with confidence
- easy to understand

- home run value propositions
- leads to results (ideally quick wins)
- helps me communicate my ideas clearly
- clear indicators to measure progress
- connect with like-minded people
- leads to better collaboration
- concrete tips (e.g., to reduce risk)

Nice to have

Step into Your Customers' Shoes

OBJECTIVE
Visualize what matters to your customers in a shareable format

OUTCOME
One page actionable customer profile

How good is your understanding of your customers' jobs, pains, and gains? Map out a customer profile.

Instructions

Map the profile of one of your currently existing customer segments to practice using the customer profile. If you are working on a new idea, sketch out the customer segment you intend to create value for.

1. Download the Customer Profile Canvas.
2. Grab a set of small sticky notes.
3. Map out your customer profile.

   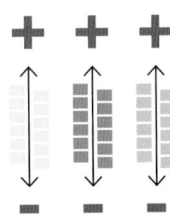

1
Select customer segment.
Select a customer segment that you want to profile.

2
Identify customer jobs.
Ask what tasks your customers are trying to complete. Map out all of their jobs by writing each one on an individual sticky note.

3
Identify customer pains.
What pains do your customers have? Write down as many as you can come up with, including obstacles and risks.

4
Identify customer gains.
What outcomes and benefits do your customers want to achieve? Write down as many gains as you can come up with.

5
Prioritize jobs, pains, and gains.
Order jobs, pains, and gains in a column, each with the most important jobs, most extreme pains, and essential gains on top and the moderate pains and nice-to-have gains at the bottom.

 Do this exercise online

Customer Profile

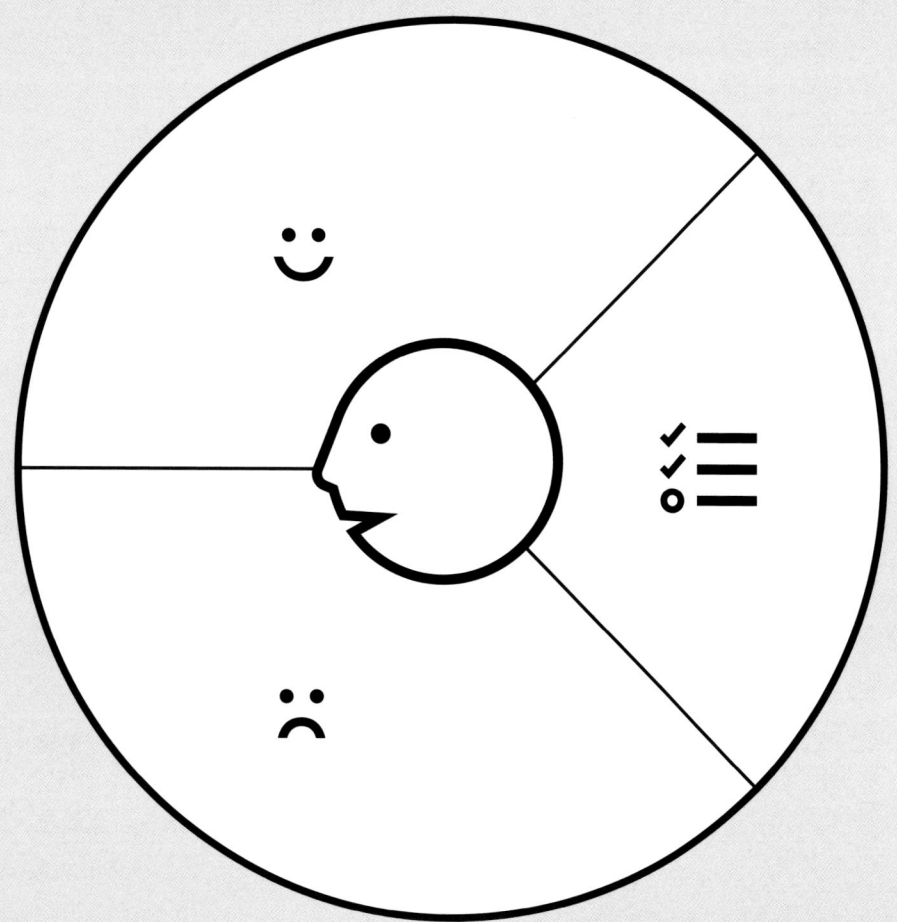

 **Strategyzer**

Download the Customer Profile pdf

Best Practices for Mapping Jobs, Pains, and Gains

Avoid frequently committed mistakes when profiling a customer, and instead follow these best practices.

✖ Common Mistakes

Mixing several customer segments into one profile.

Mixing jobs and outcomes.

Focusing on functional jobs only and forgetting social and emotional jobs.

Listing jobs, pains, and gains with your value proposition in mind.

Identifying too few jobs, pains, and gains.

Being too vague in descriptions of pains and gains.

✔ Best Practices

Make a Value Proposition Canvas for every different customer segment. If you sell to companies, ask yourself if you have different types of customers within each company (e.g., users, buyers).

Jobs are the tasks customers are trying to perform, the problems they are trying to solve, or the needs they are trying to satisfy, whereas gains are the concrete outcomes they want to achieve—or avoid and eliminate in the case of pains.

Sometimes social or emotional jobs are even more important than the "visible" functional jobs. "Looking good in front of others" might be more important than finding a great technical solution that helps complete the job effectively.

When you map your customer, you should proceed like an anthropologist and "forget" what you are offering. For example, a business publisher should not map jobs, pains, and gains merely related to books, because a reader has the choice between business books, consultants, YouTube videos, or even completing an MBA program or training. Go beyond the jobs, pains, and gains you intend or hope to address with your value proposition.

A good customer profile is full of sticky notes, because most customers have a lot of pains and expect or desire a lot of gains. Map out all your (potential) customers' important jobs, extreme pains, and essential gains.

Make pains and gains tangible and concrete. Rather than just writing "salary increase" in gains, specify how much of an increase a customer is seeking. Rather than writing "takes too long" in pains, indicate how long "too long" actually is. This will allow you to understand how exactly customers measure success and failure.

Pains vs. Gains

When you get started with the customer profile, you might simply put the same ideas in pains and gains as opposites of each other. For example, if one of the customers' jobs to be done is "earn more money," you might start by adding "salary increase" to gains and "salary decrease" to pains.

Here's a better way to do it:

- Find out precisely how much more money the customer expects to earn so it feels like a gain and investigate what decrease would feel like a pain.

- In the pains, add the barriers that prevent or make it difficult to get a job done. In our example the pain might be "my employer doesn't give raises."

- In the pains, add the risks related to not getting the job done. In our example the pain could be "might not be able to afford my child's future college tuition."

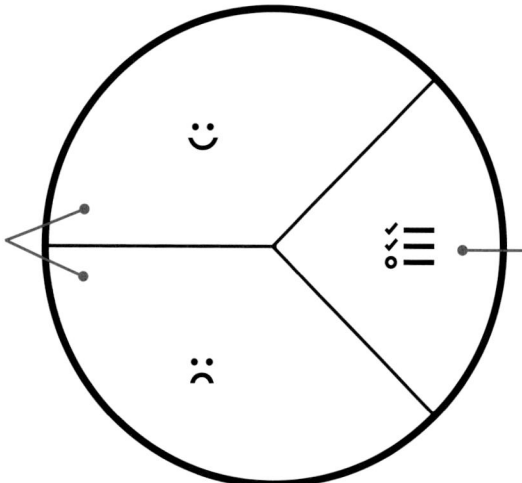

Ask "why" several times until you really understand your customers' jobs to be done.

Another issue when you get started with the customer profile is that you might settle with a superficial understanding of your customer's jobs. To avoid this, you need to ask yourself why a customer wants to perform a certain job to dig deeper toward the real motivations.

For example, why might a customer want to learn a foreign language? Maybe because the "real" customer job to be done is to improve his CV. Why does he want to improve his CV? Maybe because he wants to earn more money.

Don't settle until you really understand the underlying jobs to be done that really drive customers.

1.2

Value Map

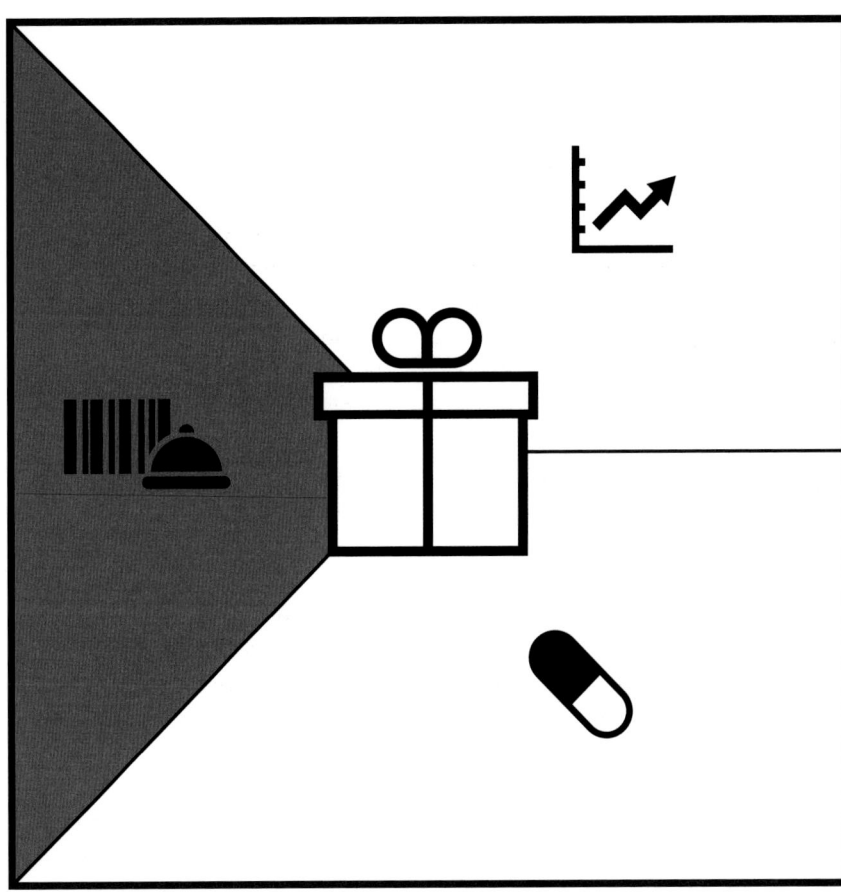

Products and Services

This is simply a list of what you offer. Think of it as all the items your customers can see in your shop window —metaphorically speaking. It's an enumeration of all the products and services your value proposition builds on. This bundle of products and services helps your customers complete either functional, social, or emotional jobs or helps them satisfy basic needs. It is crucial to acknowledge that products and services don't create value alone— only in relationship to a specific customer segment and their jobs, pains, and gains.

Your list of products and services may also include supporting ones that help your customers perform the roles of buyer (those that help customers compare offers, decide, and buy), co-creator (those that help customers co-design value propositions), and transferrer (those that help customers dispose of a product).

Your value proposition is likely to be composed of various types of products and services:

Physical/tangible
Goods, such as manufactured products.

Intangible
Products such as copyrights or services such as after-sales assistance.

Digital
Products such as music downloads or services such as online recommendations.

Financial
Products such as investment funds and insurances or services such as the financing of a purchase.

Relevance
It is essential to acknowledge that not all products and services have the same relevance to your customers. Some products and services are essential to your value proposition; some are merely nice to have.

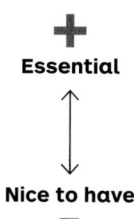

Essential

Nice to have

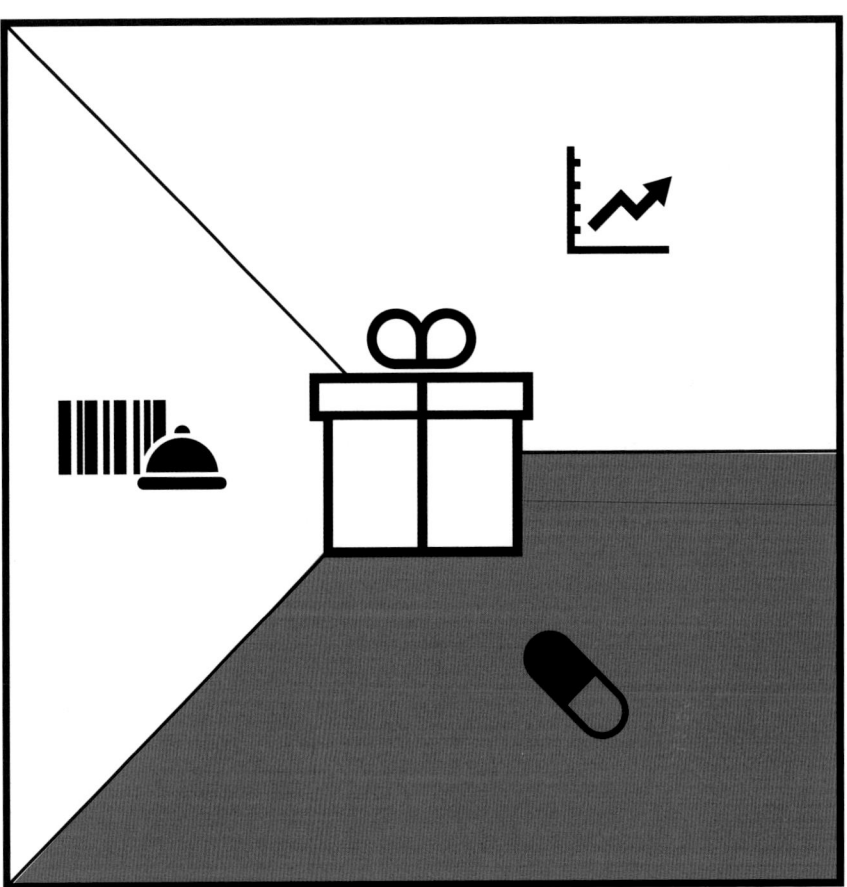

Pain Relievers

Pain relievers describe how exactly your products and services alleviate specific customer pains. They explicitly outline how you intend to eliminate or reduce some of the things that annoy your customers before, during, or after they are trying to complete a job or that prevent them from doing so.

Great value propositions focus on pains that matter to customers, in particular extreme pains. You don't need to come up with a pain reliever for every pain you've identified in the customer profile—no value proposition can do this. Great value propositions often focus only on few pains that they alleviate extremely well.

The following list of trigger questions can help you think of different ways your products and services may help your customers alleviate pains.

Ask yourself: Could your products and services...

- produce savings? In terms of time, money, or efforts.
- make your customers feel better? By killing frustrations, annoyances, and other things that give customers a headache.
- fix underperforming solutions? By introducing new features, better performance, or enhanced quality.
- put an end to difficulties and challenges your customers encounter? By making things easier or eliminating obstacles.
- wipe out negative social consequences your customers encounter or fear? In terms of loss of face or lost power, trust, or status.
- eliminate risks your customers fear? In terms of financial, social, technical risks, or things that could potentially go wrong.
- help your customers better sleep at night? By addressing significant issues, diminishing concerns, or eliminating worries.
- limit or eradicate common mistakes customers make? By helping them use a solution the right way.
- eliminate barriers that are keeping your customer from adopting value propositions? Introducing lower or no upfront investment costs, a flatter learning curve, or eliminating other obstacles preventing adoption.

Relevance

A pain reliever can be more or less valuable to the customer. Make sure you differentiate between essential pain relievers and ones that are nice to have. The former relieve extreme issues, often in a radical way, and create a lot of value. The latter merely relieve moderate pains.

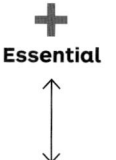

Essential

Nice to have

Download trigger questions

Gain Creators

Gain creators describe how your products and services create customer gains. They explicitly outline how you intend to produce outcomes and benefits that your customer expects, desires, or would be surprised by, including functional utility, social gains, positive emotions, and cost savings.

As with pain relievers, gain creators don't need to address every gain identified in the customer profile. Focus on those that are relevant to customers and where your products and services can make a difference.

The following list of trigger questions can help you think of different ways your products and services may help your customers obtain required, expected, desired, or unexpected outcomes and benefits.

Ask yourself: Could your products and services...

- create savings that please your customers? In terms of time, money, and effort.
- produce outcomes your customers expect or that exceed their expectations? By offering quality levels, more of something, or less of something.
- outperform current value propositions and delight your customers? Regarding specific features, performance, or quality.
- make your customers' work or life easier? Via better usability, accessibility, more services, or lower cost of ownership.
- create positive social consequences? By making them look good or producing an increase in power or status.
- do something specific that customers are looking for? In terms of good design, guarantees, or specific or more features.
- fulfill a desire customers dream about? By helping them achieve their aspirations or getting relief from a hardship?
- produce positive outcomes matching your customers' success and failure criteria? In terms of better performance or lower cost.

- help make adoption easier? Through lower cost, fewer investments, lower risk, better quality, improved performance, or better design.

Relevance

A gain creator can produce more or less relevant outcomes and benefits for the customer just like we have seen for pain relievers. Make sure you differentiate between essential and nice to have gain creators.

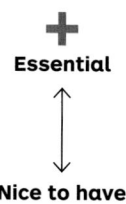

Essential

Nice to have

Download trigger questions

34

Mapping the Value Proposition of Value Proposition Design

Remarkable value propositions focus on jobs, pains, and gains that matter to customers and achieve those exceedingly well. Again, you should not try to address all customer pains and gains. Focus on those that will make a difference for your customer.

It's okay to aggregate several value propositions into one.

"Naked" list of the products and services that your value proposition builds on to target a specific customer segment.

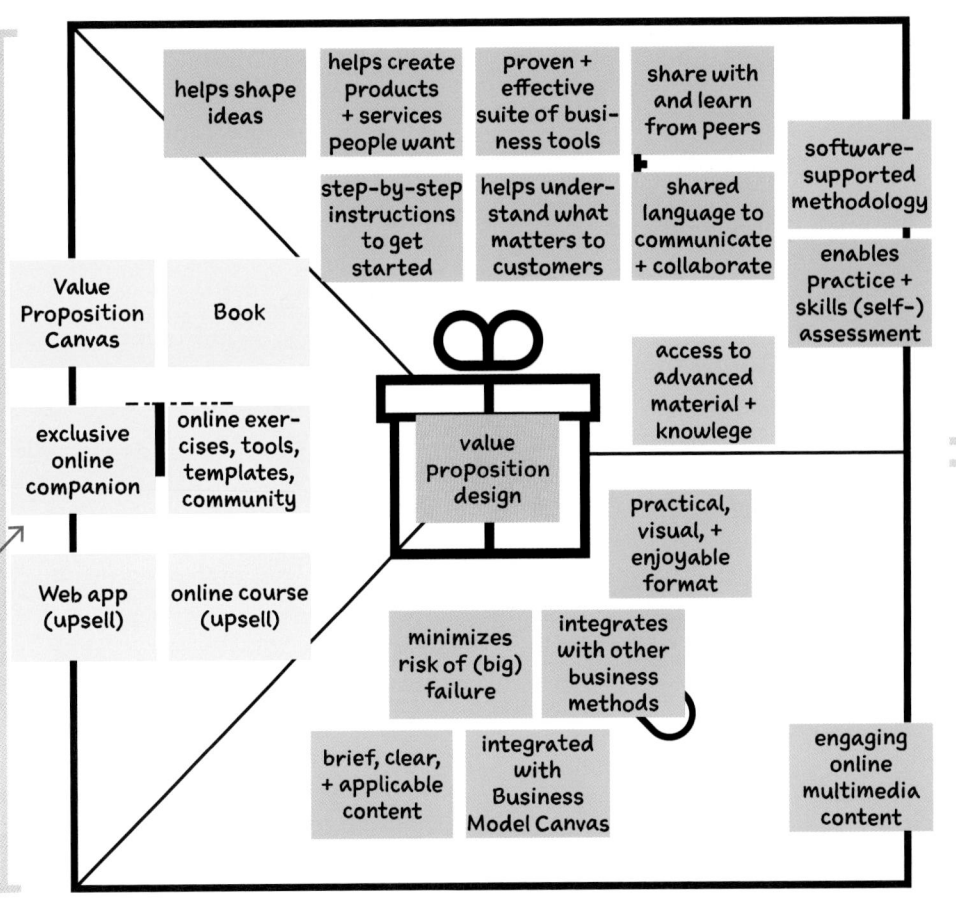

Pain relievers outline how exactly your products and services kill customer pains. Each pain reliever addresses at least one or more pains or gains. Don't add products or services here.

Gain creators highlight how exactly your products and services help customers achieve gains. Each gain creator addresses at least one or more pains or gains. Don't add products or services here.

Formal Map
of how we believe
the products and
services around this
book create value
for customers

Map How Your Products and Services Create Value

OBJECTIVE
Describe explicitly how your products and services create value

OUTCOME
1 page map of value creation

Instructions

Sketch out the value map of one of your existing value propositions. For example, use one that targets the customer segment you profiled in the previous exercise. It's easier to get started with an existing value proposition. However, if you don't have one yet, sketch out how you intend to create value with a new idea. We will cover the creation of new value propositions more specifically later on in this book.

For now:

1. Grab the customer profile you previously completed.
2. Download the value map.
3. Grab a set of small sticky notes.
4. Map out how you create value for your customers.

Download the Value Map pdf

The Value Map

Strategyzer

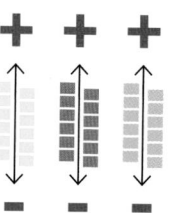

1

List products and services.

List all the products and services of your existing value proposition.

2

Outline pain relievers.

Outline how your products and services currently help customers alleviate pains by eliminating undesired outcomes, obstacles, or risks. Use one sticky note per pain reliever.

3

Outline gain creators.

Explain how your products and services currently create expected or desired outcomes and benefits for customers. Use one sticky note per gain creator.

4

Rank by order of importance.

Rank products and services, pain relievers, and gain creators according to how essential they are to customers.

Do this exercise online

Pain relievers vs. Gain creators

Pain relievers and gain creators both create value for the customer in different ways. The difference is that the former specifically addresses pains in the customer profile, while the latter specifically addresses gains. It is okay if either of them addresses pains and gains at the same time. The main goal of these two areas is to make the customer value creation of your products and services explicit.

What is the difference with the pains and gains in the customer profile?

Pain relievers and gain creators are distinctly different from pains and gains. You have control over the former, whereas you don't have control over the latter. You decide (i.e., design) how you intend to create value by addressing specific jobs, pains, and gains. You don't decide over which jobs, pains, and gains the customer has. And no value proposition addresses all of a customer's jobs, pains, and gains. The best ones address those that matter most to customers and do so extremely well.

Best Practices for Mapping Value Creation

 ## Common Mistakes

List all your products and services rather than just those targeted at a specific segment.

Add products and services to the pain reliever and gain creator fields.

Offer pain relievers and gain creators that have nothing to do with the pains and gains in the customer profile.

Make the unrealistic attempt to address all customer pains and gains.

 ## Best Practices

Products and services create value only in relationship to a specific customer segment. List only the bundle of products and services that jointly form a value proposition for a specific customer segment.

Pain relievers and gain creators are explanations or characteristics that make the value creation of your products and services explicit. Examples include "helps save time" and "well-designed."

Remember that products and services don't create value in absolute terms. It is always relative to customers' jobs, pains, and gains.

Realize that great value propositions are about making choices regarding which jobs, pains, and gains to address and which to forgo. No value proposition addresses all of them. If your value map indicates so, it's probably because you're not honest about all the jobs, pains, and gains that should be in your customer profile.

1.3

Fit

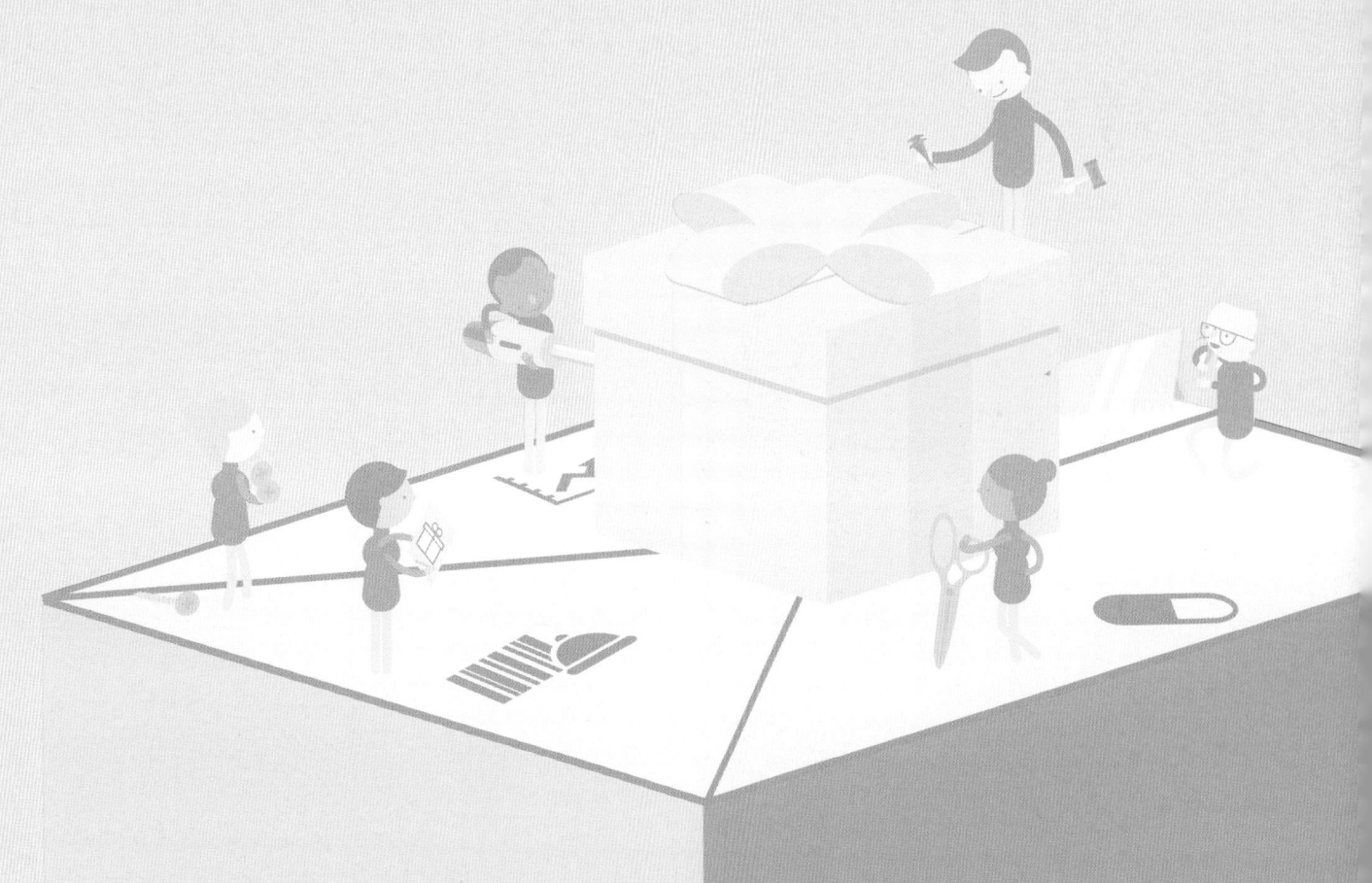

Fit

You achieve fit when customers get excited about your value proposition, which happens when you address important jobs, alleviate extreme pains, and create essential gains that customers care about. As we will explain throughout this book, fit is hard to find and maintain. Striving for fit is the essence of value proposition design.

Customers expect and desire a lot from products and services, yet they also know they can't have it all. Focus on those gains that matter most to customers and make a difference.

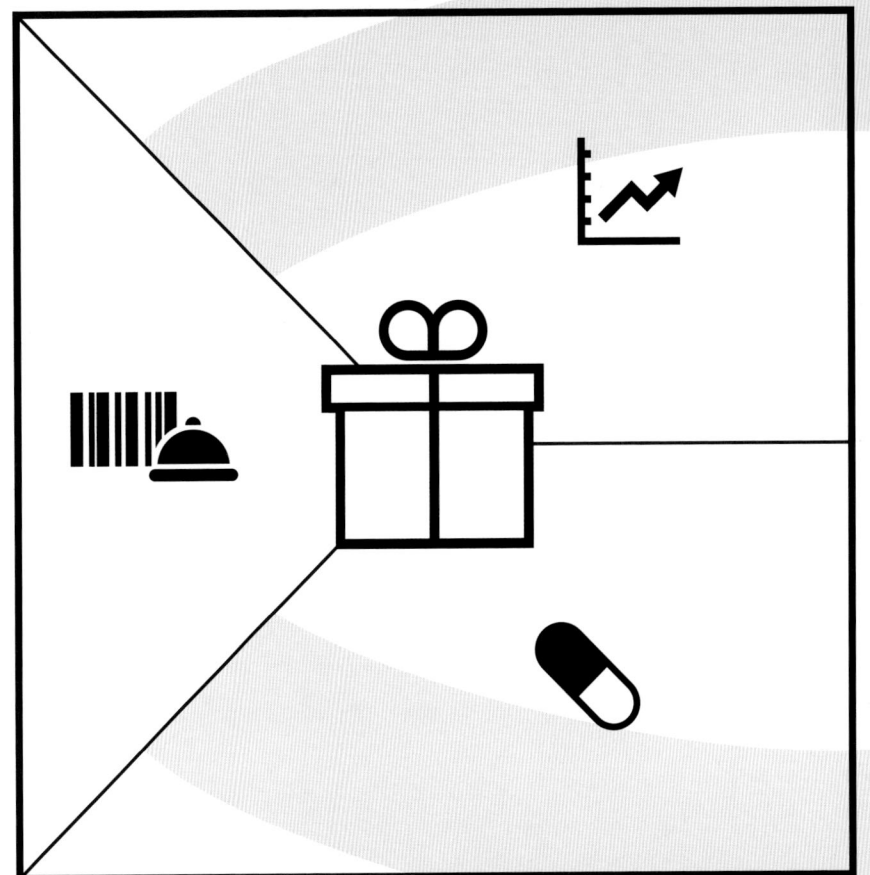

Customers have a lot of pains. No organization can reasonably address all of them. Focus on those headaches that matter most and are insufficiently addressed.

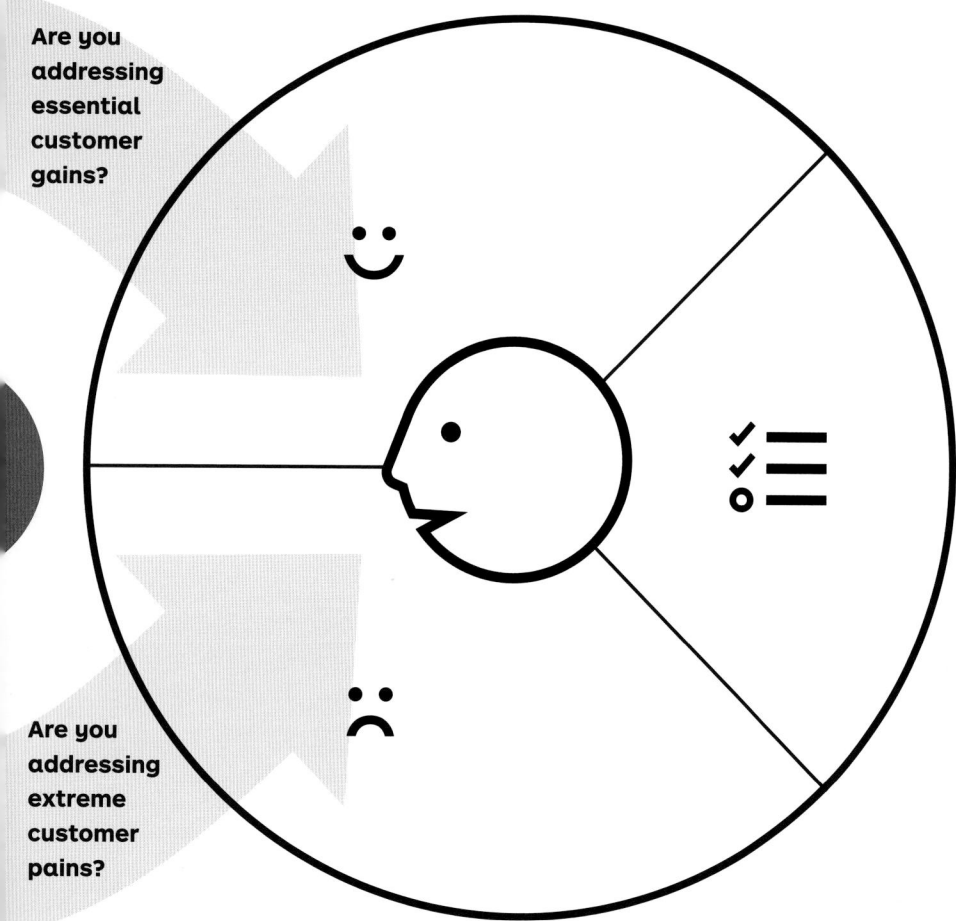

Are you addressing essential customer gains?

Are you addressing extreme customer pains?

Your customers are the judge, jury, and executioner of your value proposition. They will be merciless if you don't find fit!

Fit?

When we designed the value proposition for this book, we strived to address some of the most important jobs, pains, and gains that potential customers have and that are insufficiently addressed by current business book formats.

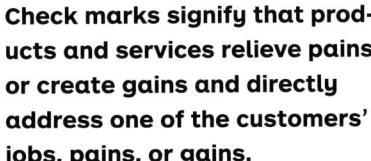

Check marks signify that products and services relieve pains or create gains and directly address one of the customers' jobs, pains, or gains.

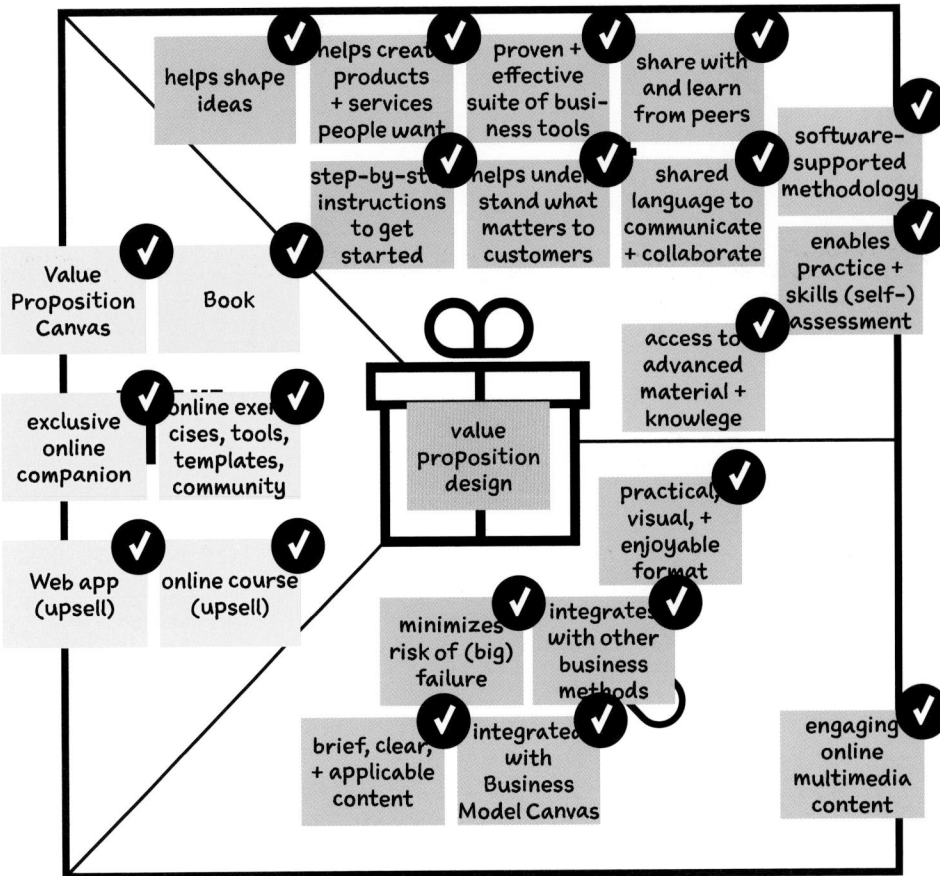

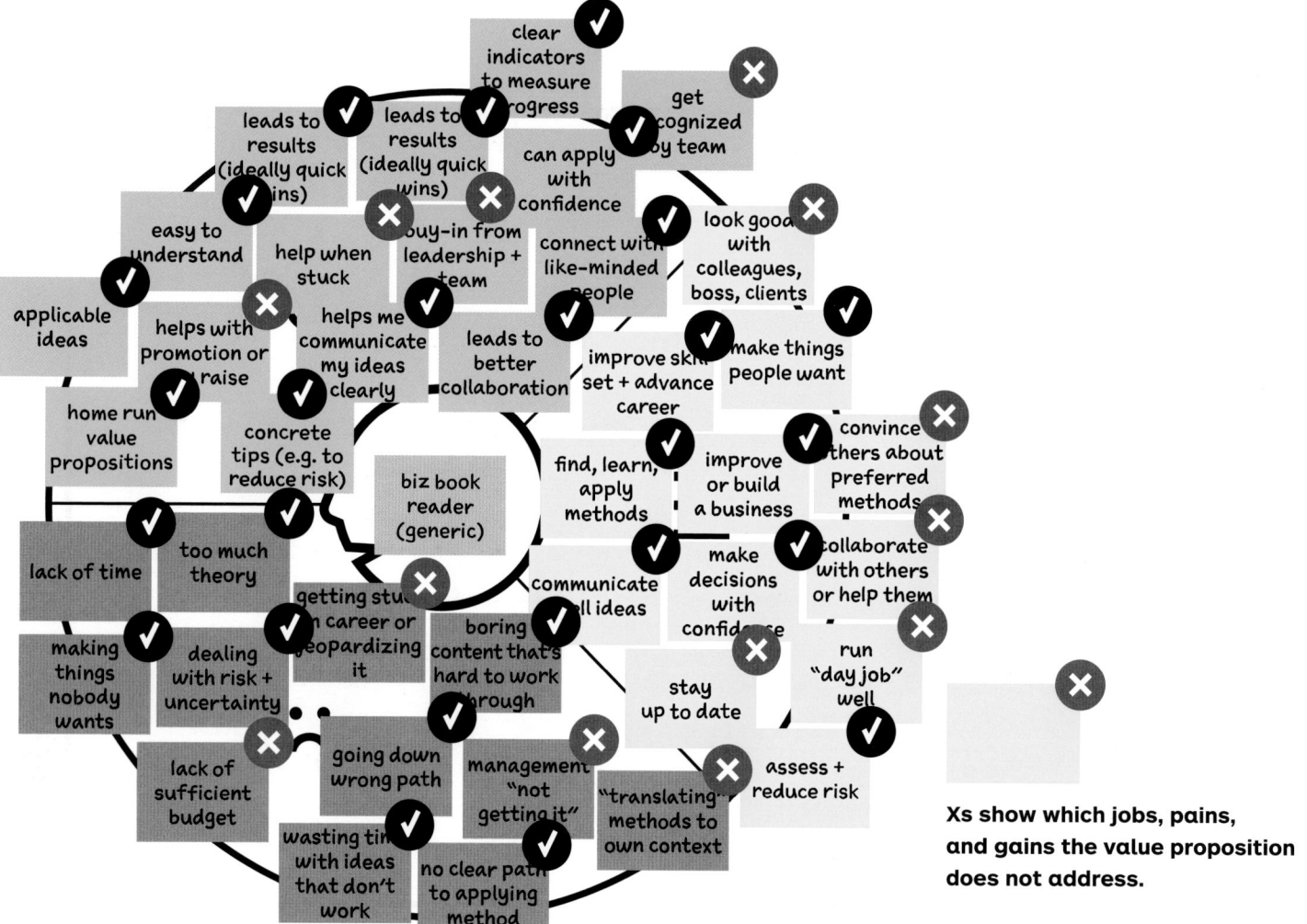

Xs show which jobs, pains, and gains the value proposition does not address.

clear indicators to measure progress ✓

get recognized by team ✗

leads to results (ideally quick wins) ✓

leads to results (ideally quick wins) ✓

can apply with confidence ✓

buy-in from leadership + team ✗

connect with like-minded people ✓

look good with colleagues, boss, clients ✗

easy to understand ✓

help when stuck

helps me communicate my ideas clearly ✓

leads to better collaboration ✓

improve skill set + advance career ✓

make things people want ✓

applicable ideas ✓

helps with promotion or raise ✓

concrete tips (e.g. to reduce risk) ✓

improve or build a business ✓

convince others about preferred methods ✓

home run value propositions ✓

biz book reader (generic)

find, learn, apply methods ✓

make decisions with confidence ✓

collaborate with others or help them ✗

lack of time ✓

too much theory ✓

getting stuck in career or jeopardizing it ✗

communicate ill ideas ✓

run "day job" well ✓

making things nobody wants ✓

dealing with risk + uncertainty ✓

boring content that's hard to work through ✓

stay up to date ✗

assess + reduce risk ✗

lack of sufficient budget ✗

going down wrong path ✓

management "not getting it" ✗

"translating" methods to own context ✗

wasting time with ideas that don't work ✓

no clear path to applying method ✓

✗

Check Your Fit

OBJECTIVE
Verify if you are addressing what matters to customers

OUTCOME
Connection between your products and services and customer jobs, pains, and gains

 Do this exercise online

1

Instructions

Bring in the Value Proposition Map and Customer Segment Profile you completed earlier. Go through pain relievers and gain creators one by one, and check to see whether they fit a customer job, pain, or gain. Put a check mark on each one that does.

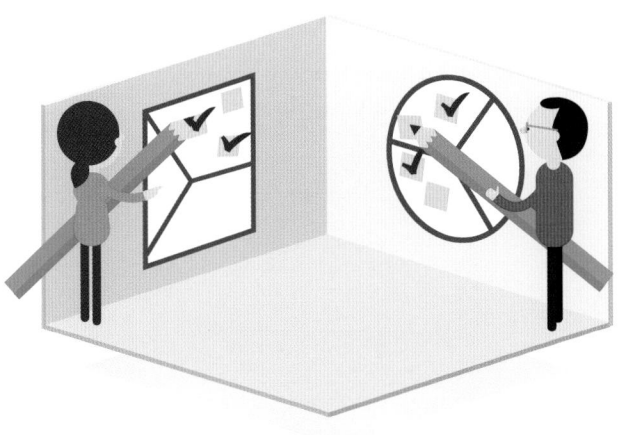

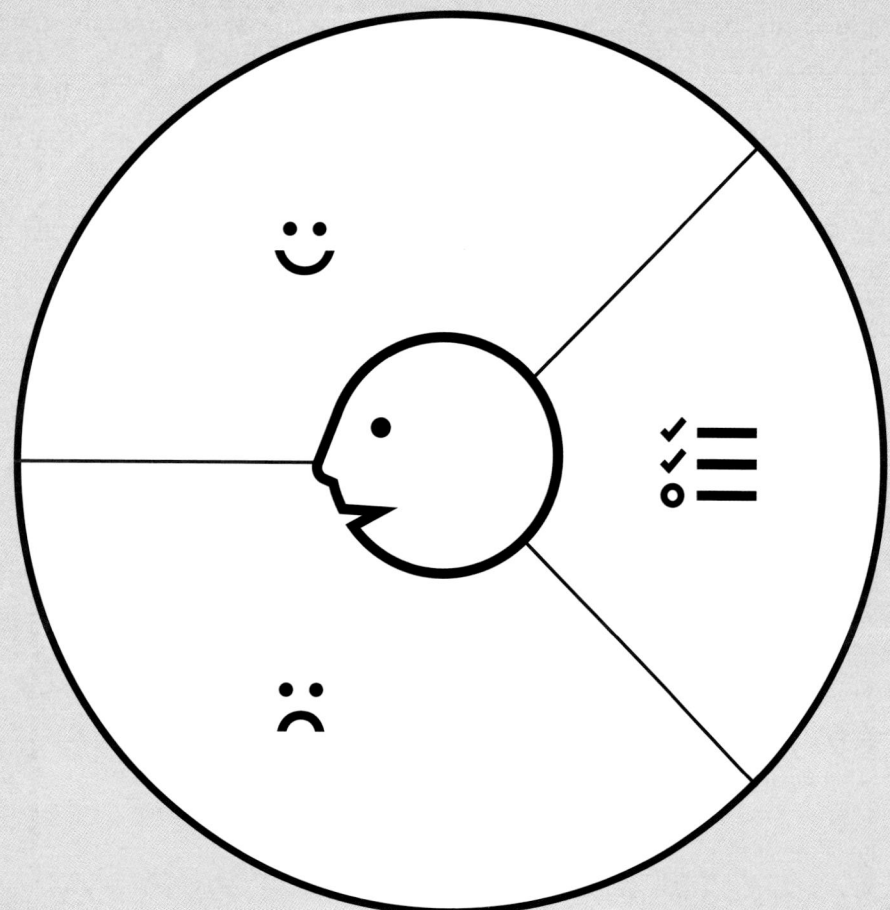

2

Outcome

If a pain reliever or gain creator doesn't fit anything, it may not be creating customer value. Don't worry if you haven't checked all pains/gains—you can't satisfy them all. Ask yourself, how well does your value proposition really fit your customer?

⊙ *Download the Value Proposition Canvas pdf*

Three Kinds of Fit

Searching for Fit is the process of designing value propositions around products and services that meet jobs, pains, and gains that customers really care about. Fit between what a company offers and what customers want is the number one requirement of a successful value proposition.

Fit happens in three stages. The first occurs when you identify relevant customer jobs, pains, and gains you believe you can address with your value proposition. The second occurs when customers positively react to your value proposition and it gets traction in the market. The start-up movement calls these problem-solution fit and product-market fit, respectively. The third occurs when you find a business model that is scalable and profitable.

 *Get "Fit" poster*

3
Business Model Fit

2
Product-Market Fit

1
Problem-Solution Fit

On Paper $\longrightarrow$

1. Problem-Solution Fit

Problem-solution fit takes place when you

- Have evidence that customers care about certain jobs, pains, and gains.
- Designed a value proposition that addresses those jobs, pains, and gains.

At this stage you don't yet have evidence that customers actually care about your value proposition.

    This is when you strive to identify the jobs, pains, and gains that are most relevant to customers and design value propositions accordingly. You prototype multiple alternative value propositions to come up with the ones that produce the best fit. The fit you achieve is not yet proven and exists mainly on paper. Your next steps are to provide evidence that customers care about your value proposition or start over with designing a new one.

In the Market $\longrightarrow$

2. Product-Market Fit

Product-market fit takes place when you

- Have evidence that your products and services, pain relievers, and gain creators are actually creating customer value and getting traction in the market.

During this second phase, you strive to validate or invalidate the assumptions underlying your value proposition. You will inevitably learn that many of your early ideas simply don't create customer value (i.e., customers don't care) and will have to design new value propositions. Finding this second type of fit is a long and iterative process; it doesn't happen overnight.

In the Bank$\longrightarrow$

3. Business Model Fit

Business model fit takes place when you

- Have evidence that your value proposition can be embedded in a profitable and scalable business model.

A great value proposition without a great business model may mean suboptimal financial success or even lead to failure. No value proposition—however great—can survive without a sound business model.

    The search for business model fit entails a laborious back and forth between designing a value proposition that creates value for customers and a business model that creates value for your organization. You don't have business model fit until you can generate more revenues with your value proposition than you incur costs to create and deliver it (or "them" in the case of platform models with more than one interdependent value propositions).

Customer Profiles in B2B

Value propositions in business-to-business (B2B) transactions typically involve several stakeholders in the search, evaluation, purchase, and use of a product or service. Each one has a different profile with different jobs, pains, and gains. Stakeholders can tilt the purchasing decision in one direction or another. Identify the most important ones and sketch out a Value Proposition Canvas for each one of them.

Profiles vary according to the sector and size of organization, but they typically include the following roles:

+Unbundled

Value propositions to stakeholders *within* the business

Influencers   Recommenders   Economic buyers   Decision makers   End users   Saboteurs

Aggregated

Value Proposition   Business Segment

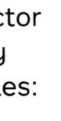

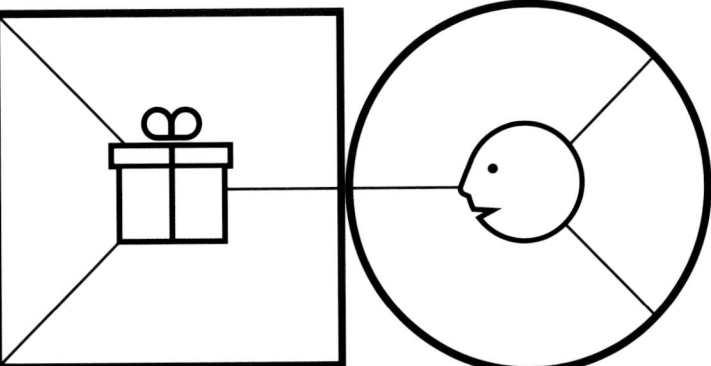

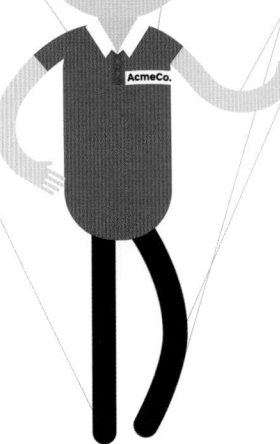

Organizations are customers that are composed of different stakeholders who all have different jobs, pains, and gains. Consider making a Value Proposition Canvas for each one.

Adapted from Steve Blank, The Four Steps to the Epiphany, 2006.

Influencers

Individuals or groups whose opinions might count and whom the decision maker might listen to, even in an informal way.

Recommenders

The people carrying out the search and evaluation process and who make a formal recommendation for or against a purchase.

Economic Buyers

The individual or group who controls the budget and who makes the actual purchase. Their concerns are typically about financial performance and budgetary efficiency.

In some cases, the economic buyer may sit outside an organization, such as a government paying for the basic medical supply in nursing homes for elderly citizens.

Decision Makers

The person or group ultimately responsible for the choice of a product/service and for ordering the purchase decision. Decision makers usually have ultimate authority over the budget.

End Users

The ultimate beneficiaries of a product or service. For a business customer, end users can either be within their own organization (a manufacturer buying software for its designers), or they can be external customers (a device manufacturer buying chips for the smartphones it sells to consumers). End users may be passive or active, depending on how much say they have in the decision and purchase process.

Saboteurs

The people and groups who can obstruct or derail the process of searching, evaluating, and purchasing a product or a service.

Decision makers typically sit inside the customer's organization, whereas Influencers, recommenders, economic buyers, end users, and saboteurs can sit inside or outside the organization.

Unbundling the Family

Value propositions to the consumer may also involve several stakeholders in the search, evaluation, purchase, and use of a product or service. For example, consider a family that intends to buy a game console. In this situation, there is also a difference between the economic buyer, the influencer, the decision maker, the users, and the saboteurs. It therefore makes sense to sketch out a different Value Proposition Canvas for each stakeholder.

Multiple Fits

Some business models work only with a combination of several value propositions and customer segments. In these situations, you require fit between each value proposition and its respective customer segment for the business model to work.

Two common illustrations of multiple fits are *intermediary* and *platform* business models.

Intermediary

When a business sells a product or service through an intermediary, it effectively needs to cater to two customers: the end customer and the intermediary itself. Without a clear value proposition to the intermediary, the offer might not reach the end customer at all, or at least not with the same impact.

Chinese firm Haier sells home appliances and electronics to households globally. It does this largely through retailers such as Carrefour, Walmart, and others. To be successful, Haier needs to craft an appealing value proposition both to households (the end customer) and to intermediary distributors.

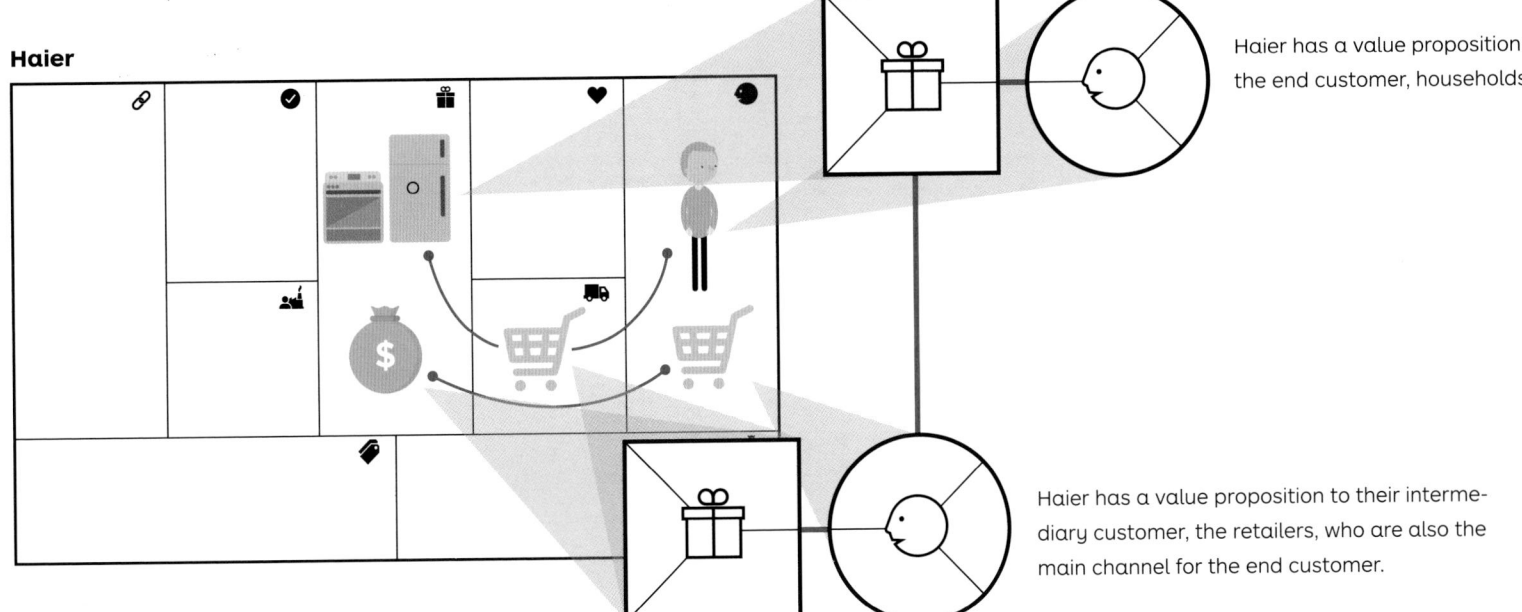

Haier

Haier has a value proposition to the end customer, households.

Haier has a value proposition to their intermediary customer, the retailers, who are also the main channel for the end customer.

Platforms

Platforms function only when two or more actors interact and draw value within the same inter-dependent business model. Platforms are called double-sided when there are two such actors and multisided when there are more than two. A platform exists only when all sides are present in the model.

Airbnb is an example of a double-sided platform. It is a website that connects local residents with extra space to rent out and travelers looking for alternatives to hotels as a place to stay. In such a case, the business model needs to hold two value propositions, one for local residents (called hosts) and one for travelers.

Airbnb

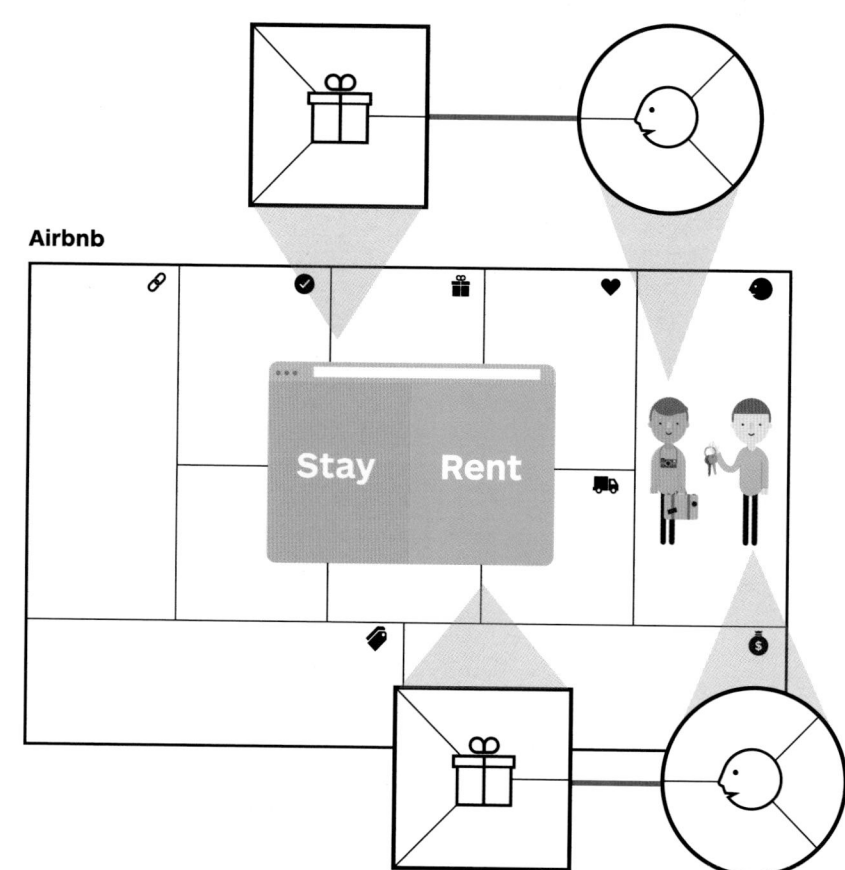

Going to the Movies

Let us walk through the concepts of the Value Proposition Canvas with another simple example. Imagine the owner of a movie theater chain wants to design new value propositions for his customers.

He could start with the value proposition's features and get excited about the latest generation of big screens, state-of-the-art display technologies, tasty snacks, social happenings, urban experiences, and so on. But, of course, those only really matter if customers care about them. So he sets out to better understand what his customers truly want.

Traditionally he'd sketch out psychodemographic profiles of his customer segments. But this time he decides to complement this type of segmentation with customer profiles that highlight a customer's jobs, pains, and gains.

54

What drives the moviegoer?

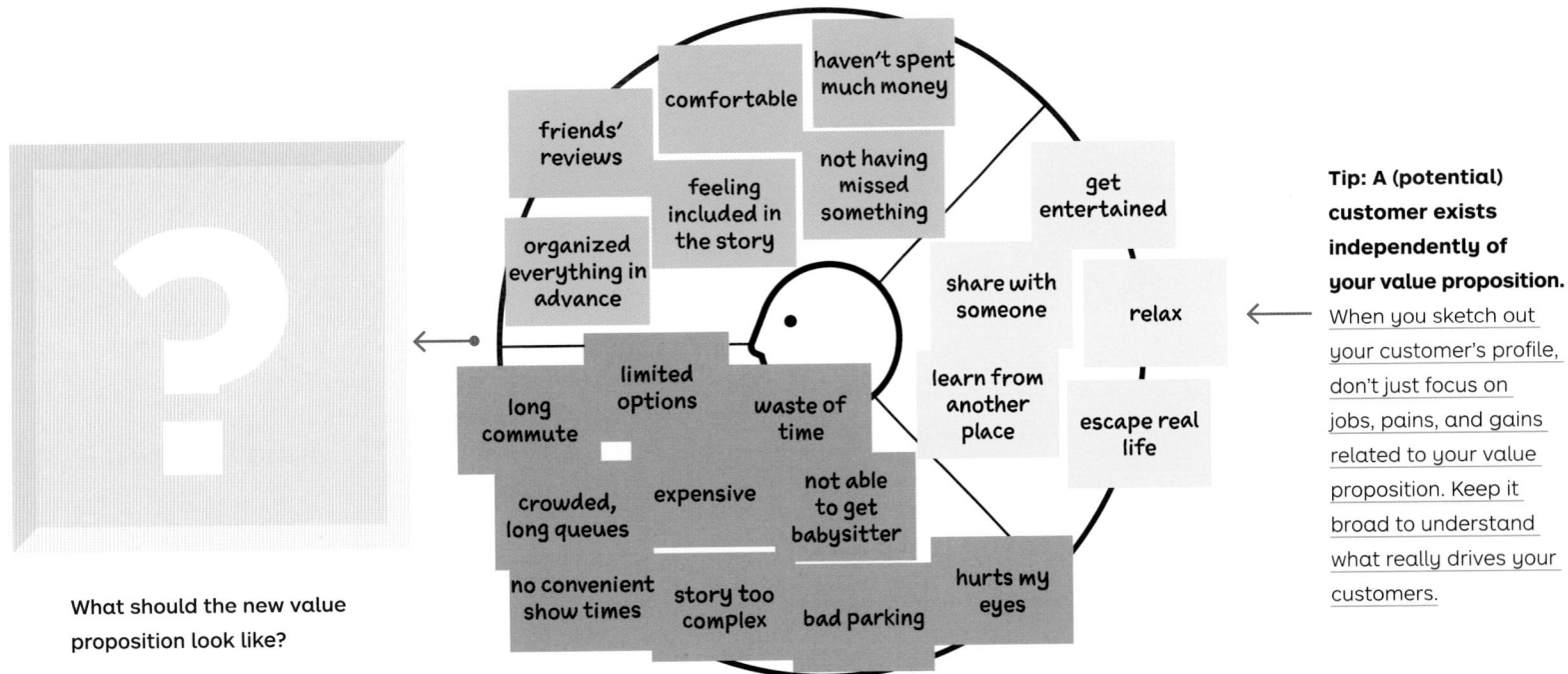

haven't spent much money
comfortable
friends' reviews
feeling included in the story
not having missed something
organized everything in advance
get entertained
share with someone
relax
learn from another place
escape real life
limited options
long commute
waste of time
crowded, long queues
expensive
not able to get babysitter
no convenient show times
story too complex
bad parking
hurts my eyes

What should the new value proposition look like?

Tip: A (potential) customer exists independently of your value proposition. When you sketch out your customer's profile, don't just focus on jobs, pains, and gains related to your value proposition. Keep it broad to understand what really drives your customers.

A Movie Theater's Business Model

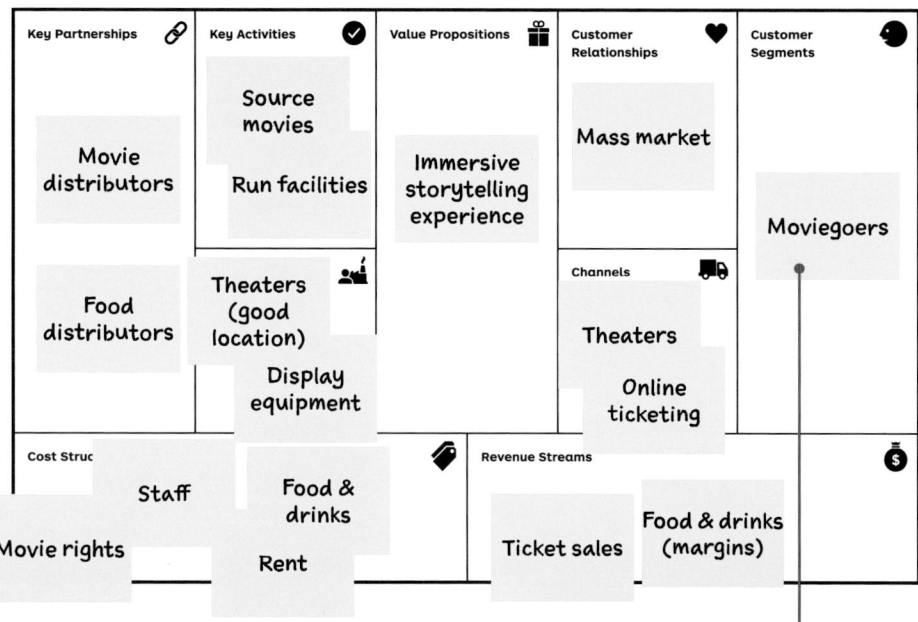

Key Partnerships	Key Activities	Value Propositions	Customer Relationships	Customer Segments
Movie distributors	Source movies / Run facilities	Immersive storytelling experience	Mass market	Moviegoers
Food distributors	Theaters (good location) / Display equipment		Channels: Theaters / Online ticketing	

Cost Structure	Revenue Streams
Staff / Food & drinks / Movie rights / Rent	Ticket sales / Food & drinks (margins)

The new approach: *focusing on the jobs, pains, and gains that drive customers*

By sketching out a customer profile, you aim to uncover what really drives people, rather than just describing their socioeconomic characteristics. You investigate what they're trying to achieve, their underlying motives, their objectives, and what's holding them back. Doing so will broaden your horizon and likely uncover new or better opportunities to satisfy customers.

The traditional approach: *psychodemographic profiles*

Traditional psychodemographic profiles group consumers into categories that have the same socioeconomic characteristics.

JANE MOVIEGOER
20-30 years old
Upper middle class
Earns $100K/year
Married, 2 children

Movie Behavior:
- Prefers action movies
- Likes popcorn and soda
- Does not like waiting in line
- Buys tickets online
- Goes once a month

Same Customer, Different Contexts

Priorities change depending on a customer's context. Taking this context into account before you think of a value proposition for that customer is crucial.

With the jobs-to-be-done approach, you uncover the motivations of different customer segments. Yet, depending on the context, some jobs will become more important or matter less than others.

In fact, the context in which a person finds himself or herself often changes the nature of the jobs that the person aims to accomplish.

For example, the clientele of a restaurant is likely to use very different criteria to evaluate their dining experience at lunch versus at dinner. Likewise a mobile phone user will have different job requirements when using the phone in a car, in a meeting, or at home. Hence, the features of your value proposition will be different depending on which context(s) you are focusing.

In our example, the context in which our moviegoer finds herself will influence which jobs matter more or less to her.

Add contextual elements to your customer profiles if necessary. They might serve as constraints for designing value propositions later on.

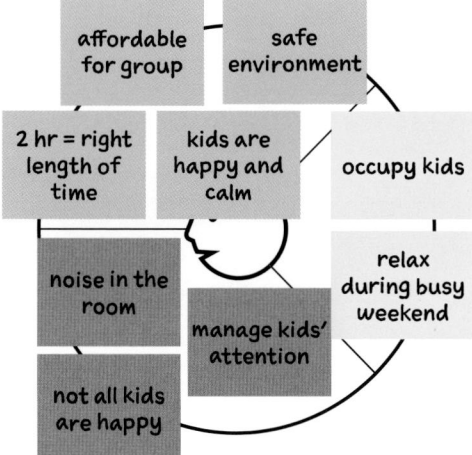

- affordable for group
- safe environment
- 2 hr = right length of time
- kids are happy and calm
- occupy kids
- noise in the room
- relax during busy weekend
- manage kids' attention
- not all kids are happy

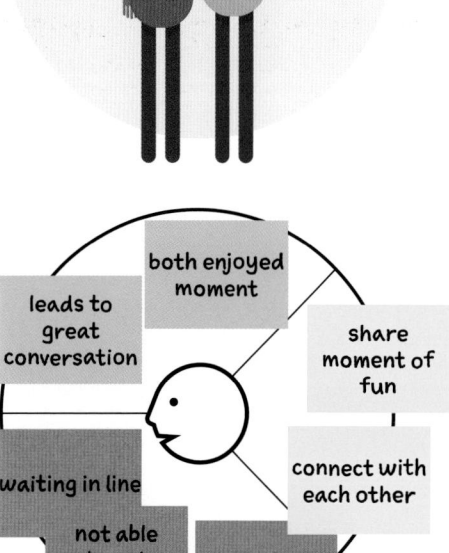

- both enjoyed moment
- leads to great conversation
- share moment of fun
- waiting in line
- connect with each other
- not able to get babysitter
- not intimate enough

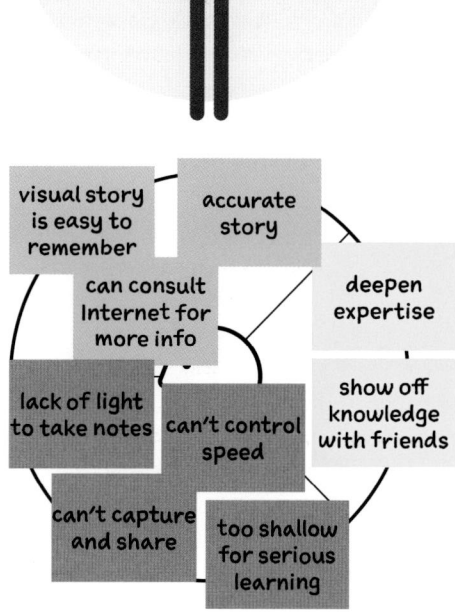

- visual story is easy to remember
- accurate story
- can consult Internet for more info
- deepen expertise
- lack of light to take notes
- can't control speed
- show off knowledge with friends
- can't capture and share
- too shallow for serious learning

The kids' afternoon off

When? Wednesday afternoon

Where? Leaving from home

With whom? Kids and maybe their friends

Constraints? After school, before dinner time

Date night

When? Saturday evening

Where? Leaving from home

With whom? Partner

Constraints? Kids taken care of (if parents)

Personal research

When? Any time

Where? Leaving from home

With whom? Alone

Constraints? Needs to be able to take notes

Same Customer, Different Solutions

58

In today's hypercompetitive world, customers are surrounded by an ocean of tempting value propositions that all compete for the same limited slots of attention.

Very different value propositions may address similar jobs, pains, and gains. For example, our movie theater chain competes for customer attention not only with other movie theaters but also with a broad range of alternative options: renting a movie at home, going out to dinner, visiting a spa, or maybe even attending an online virtual art exhibit with 3D glasses.

Strive to understand what your customers really care about. Investigate their jobs, pains, and gains beyond what your own value proposition directly addresses in order to imagine totally new or substantially improved ones.

Understand your customers beyond your solution. Unearth the jobs, pains, and gains that matter to them in order to understand how to improve your value proposition or invent new ones.

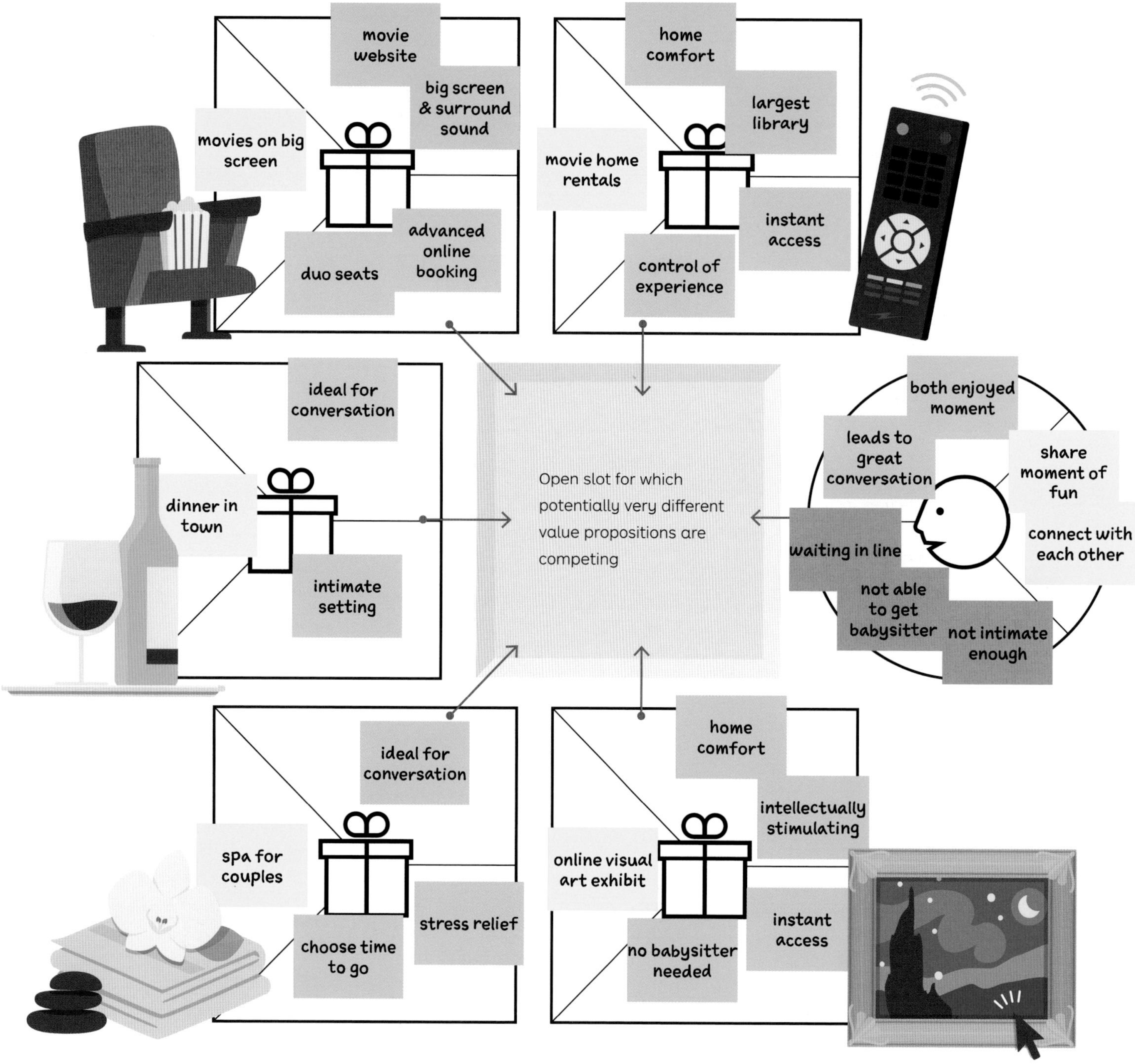
movie website
big screen & surround sound
movies on big screen
advanced online booking
duo seats
home comfort
largest library
movie home rentals
instant access
control of experience
ideal for conversation
dinner in town
intimate setting
Open slot for which potentially very different value propositions are competing
both enjoyed moment
leads to great conversation
share moment of fun
connect with each other
waiting in line
not able to get babysitter
not intimate enough
ideal for conversation
spa for couples
stress relief
choose time to go
home comfort
intellectually stimulating
online visual art exhibit
instant access
no babysitter needed

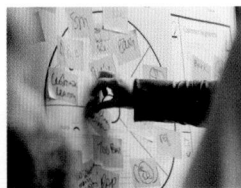
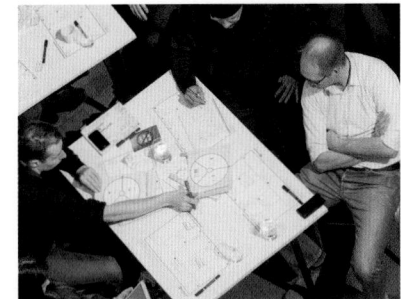
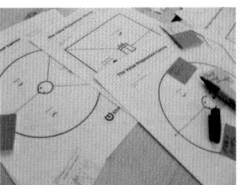

Lessons Learned

Customer Profile

Use the customer profile to visualize what matters to customers. Specify their jobs, pains, and gains. Communicate the profile across your organization as a one-page actionable document that creates a shared customer understanding. Apply it as a "scoreboard" to track if assumed customer jobs, pains, and gains exist when you talk to real customers.

Value Map

Use the value map to make explicit how you believe your products and services will ease pains and create gains. Communicate the map across your organization as a one-page document that creates a shared understanding of how you intend to create value. Apply it as a "scoreboard" to track if your products actually ease pains and gains when you test them with customers.

Fit

Problem-solution fit: Evidence that customers care about the jobs, pains, and gains you intend to address with your value proposition. Product-market fit: Evidence that customers want your value proposition. Business model fit: Evidence that the business model for your value proposition is scalable and profitable.

The Value Proposition Canvas

Value Proposition

Customer Segment

Gain Creators

Products & Services

Pain Relievers

Gains

Customer Job(s)

Pains

Strategyzer
strategyzer.com

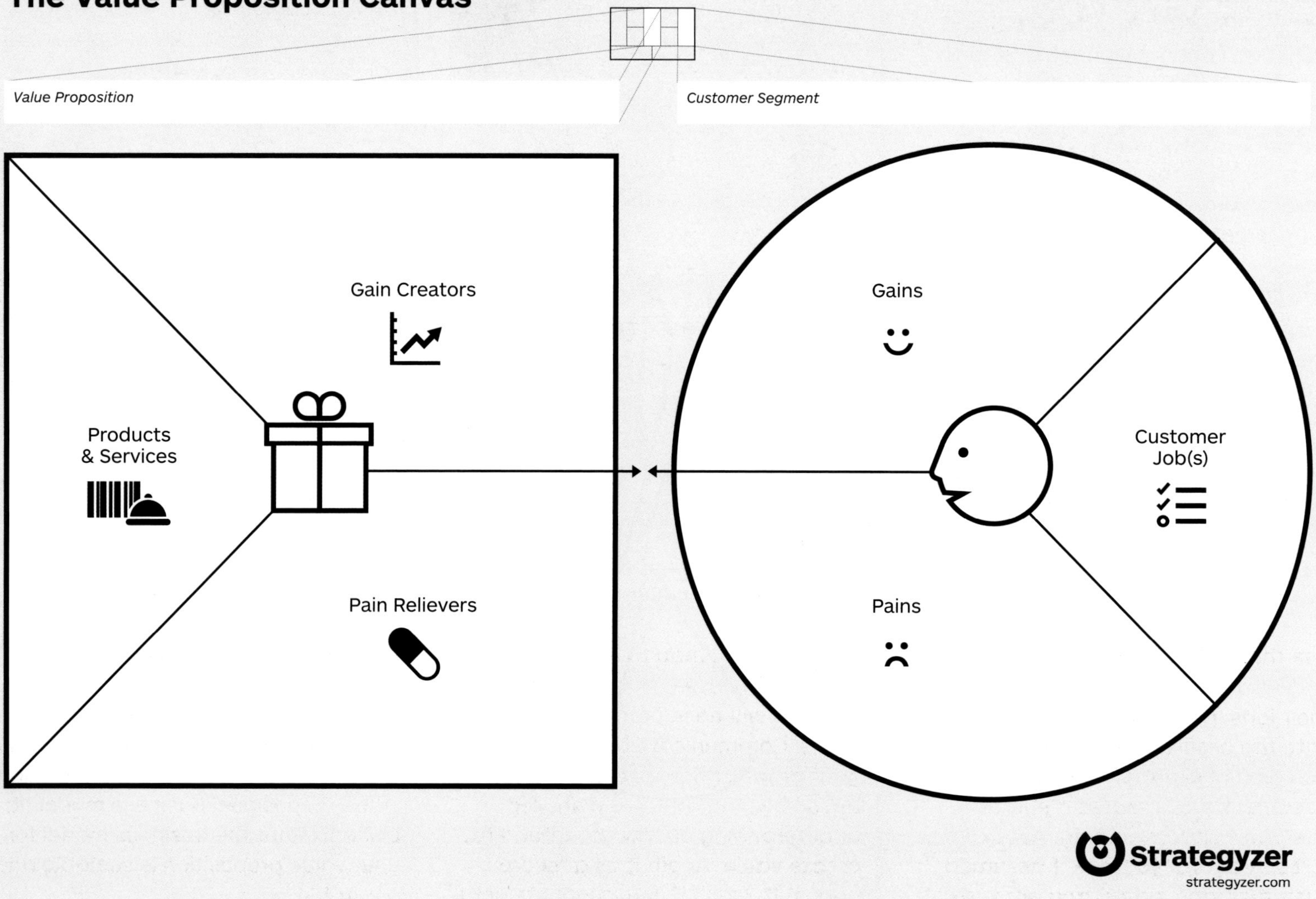

 Download the Value Proposition Canvas pdf

Design, Test, Repeat

The search for value propositions that meet customer jobs, pains, and gains is a continuous back and forth between designing prototypes and testing them. The process is iterative rather than sequential. The goal of *Value Proposition Design* is to test ideas as quickly as possible in order to learn, create better designs, and test again.

design

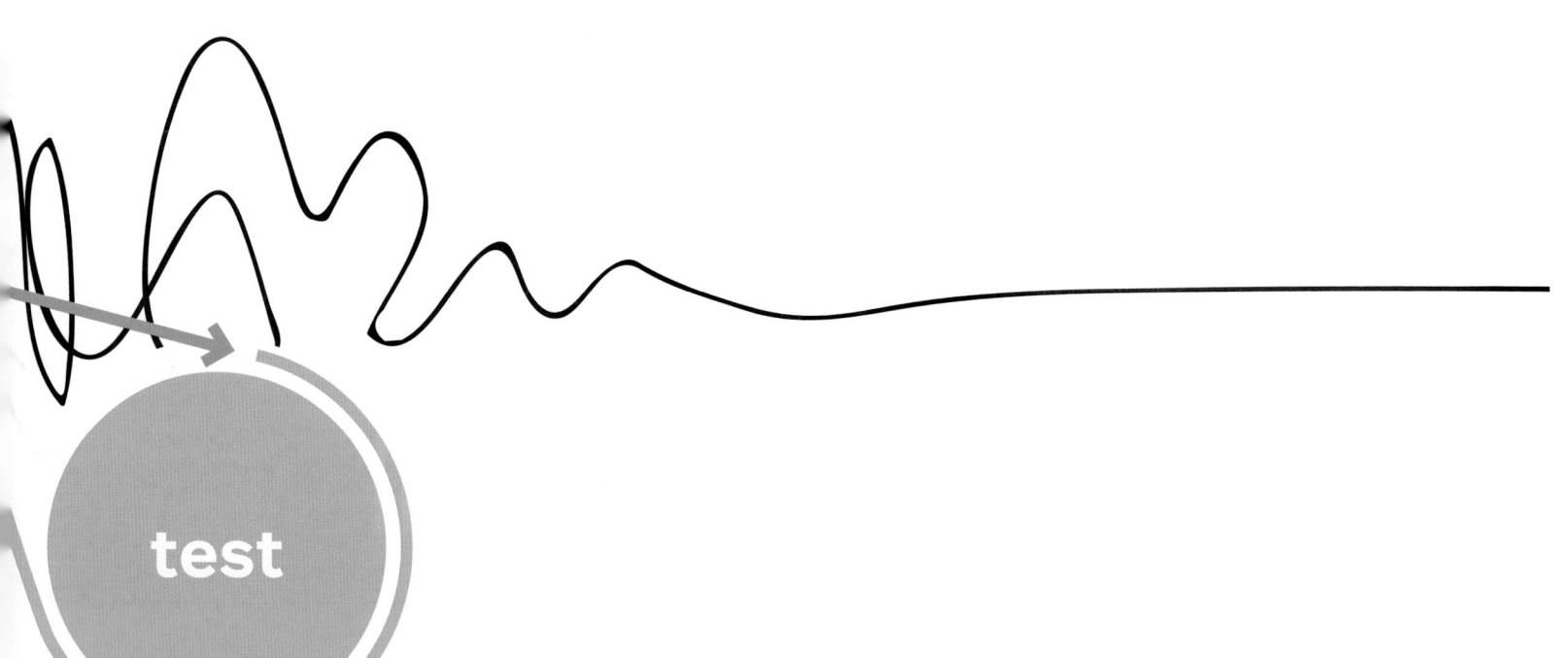

test

des

ign

2

Kick-start value proposition design with **Prototyping Possibilities** p. 74 for one of your **Starting Points** p. 86. Shape your value propositions by **Understanding Customers** p. 104, then select which ones you want to further explore by **Making Choices** p. 120 and **Finding the Right Business Model** p. 142. If you are an existing company, discover the particularities of **Designing in Established Organizations** p. 158.

Shaping Your Ideas

Design is the activity of turning your ideas into value proposition prototypes. It is a continuous cycle of prototyping, researching customers, and reshaping your ideas. Design may start with prototyping or with customer discovery. The design activity feeds into the testing activity that we explore in the next chapter (see section 3. Test, ❷ p. 172).

Ideas, Starting Points, and Insights
❷ p. 86

Starting points for new or improved value propositions may come from anywhere. It could be from your customer insights ❸ p. 116, from exploration of prototypes ❸ p. 76, or from many other sources ❸ p. 88. Be sure not to fall in love with your early ideas, because they are certain to transform radically during prototyping ❸ p. 76, customer research ❸ p. 104, and testing ❸ p. 172.

Prototype Possibilities
❷ p. 74

Shape your ideas with quick, cheap, and rough prototypes. Make them tangible with napkin sketches ❸ p. 80, ad-libs ❸ p. 82, and Value Proposition Canvases ❸ p. 84. Don't get attached to a prototype too early. Keep your prototypes light so you can explore possibilities, easily throw them away again, and then find the best ones that survive a rigorous testing process with customers ❸ p. 240.

Understand Customers
❷ p. 104

Inform your ideas and prototypes with early customer research. Plough through available data ❸ p. 108, talk to customers ❸ p. 110, and immerse yourself in their world ❸ p. 114. Don't show customers your value proposition prototypes too early. Use early research to deeply understand your customers' jobs, pains, and gains. Unearth what really matters to them to prototype value propositions that are likely to survive rigorous testing with customers ❸ p. 172.

Prototyping Possibilities

Ideas and Starting Points

Understanding Customers

10 Characteristics of Great Value Propositions

 Stop for an instant and reflect on the characteristics of great value propositions before reading about how to design them in this chapter. We offer 10 characteristics to get you started. Don't hesitate to add your own. Great Value Propositions...

Get "10 Characteristics of Great Value Propositions" poster

72

1
Are embedded in great business models

2
Focus on the jobs, pains, and gains that matter most to customers

3
Focus on unsatisfied jobs, unresolved pains, and unrealized gains

4
Target few jobs, pains, and gains, but do so extremely well

5
Go beyond functional jobs and address emotional and social jobs

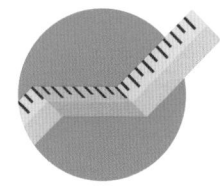

6

Align with how customers measure success

7

Focus on jobs, pains, and gains that a lot of people have or that some will pay a lot of money for

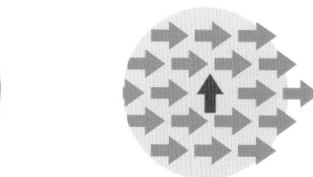

8

Differentiate from competition on jobs, pains, and gains that customers care about

SCORE

9

Outperform competition substantially on at least one dimension

10

Are difficult to copy

2.1

Prototyping Possibilities

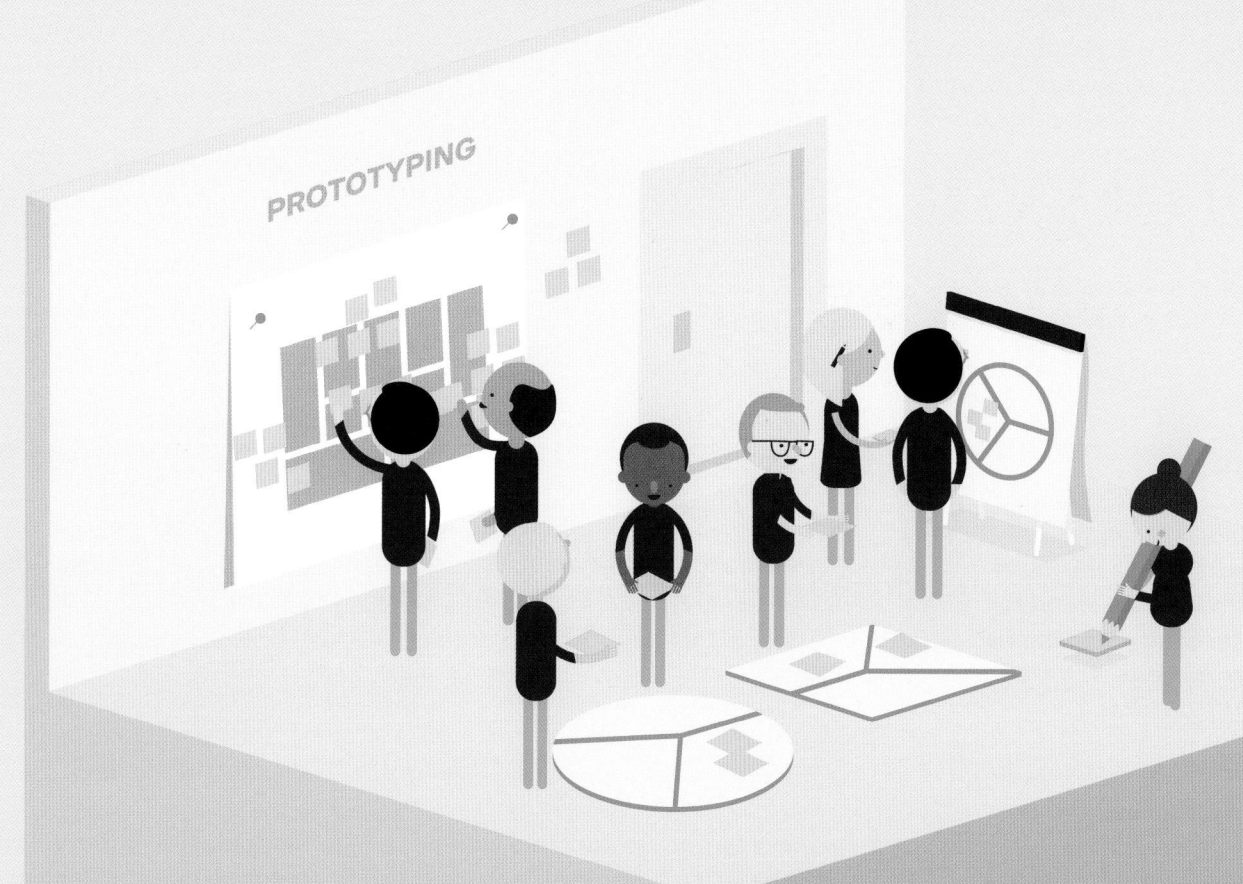

What's Prototyping?

Use the activity of making quick and rough study models of your idea to explore alternatives, shape your value proposition, and find the best opportunities. Prototyping is common in the design professions for physical artifacts. We apply it to the concept of value propositions to rapidly explore possibilities before testing and building real products and services.

DEF·I·NI·TION
Prototyping
The practice of building quick, inexpensive, and rough study models to learn about the desir-ability, feasibility, and viability of alternative value propositions and business models.

Quickly explore radically different directions for the same idea with the following prototyping techniques before refining one in particular.

Napkin Sketches
⊘ p. 80

Make alternatives tangible with napkin sketches. Use a single sketch for every potential direction your idea could take.

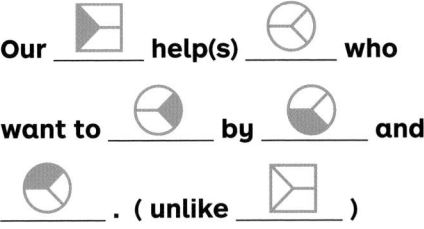

Ad-libs
⊘ p. 82

Pinpoint how different alternatives create value by filling in the blanks in short ad-libs.

- Spend a maximum of 5 to 15 minutes on sketching out your early prototypes.
- Always use a visible timer and stick to a predefined time frame.
- Don't discuss too long which one of several possible directions to prototype. Prototype several of them quickly and then compare.
- Remember constantly that prototyping is an exploratory tool. Don't spend time on the details of a prototype that is likely to change radically anyway.

Value Proposition Canvases
⊖ p. 84

Flesh out possible directions with the Value Proposition Canvas. Understand which jobs, pains, and gains each alternative is addressing.

Representation of a Value Proposition
⊖ p. 234

Help customers and partners understand potential value propositions by bringing them to life without building them.

Minimum Viable Product
⊖ p. 222

Build a minimum feature set that brings your value proposition to life and allows testing it with customers and partners.

More in section 3. Test, ⊕ p. 172

10 Prototyping Principles

Unlock the power of prototyping. Resist the temptation of spending time and energy refining one direction only. Rather, use the principles described here to explore multiple directions with the same amount of time and energy. You will learn more and discover better value propositions.

 Get "10 Prototyping Principles" poster

1
Make it visual and tangible.

These kinds of prototypes spark conversations and learning. Don't regress into the land of blah blah blah.

2
Embrace a beginner's mind.

Prototype "what can't be done." Explore with a fresh mind-set. Don't let existing knowledge get in the way of exploration.

3
Don't fall in love with first ideas— create alternatives.

Refining your idea(s) too early prevents you from creating and exploring alternatives. Don't fall in love too quickly.

4
Feel comfortable in a "liquid state."

Early in the process the right direction is unclear. It's a liquid state. Don't panic and solidify things too early.

5
Start with low fidelity, iterate, and refine.

Refined prototypes are hard to throw away. Keep them rough, quick, and cheap. Refine with increasing knowledge about what works and what doesn't.

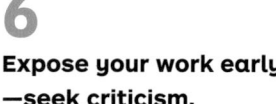
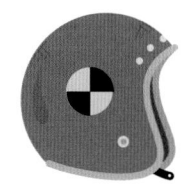

6
Expose your work early —seek criticism.
Seek feedback early and often before refining. Don't take negative feedback personally. It's worth gold to improve your prototype.

7
Learn faster by failing early, often, and cheaply.
Fear of failure holds people back from exploring. Overcome that with a culture of rough and quick prototyping that keeps failure cheap and leads to faster learning.

8
Use creativity techniques.
Use creativity techniques to explore groundbreaking prototypes. Dare to break out of how things are usually done in your company or industry.

9
Create "Shrek models."
Shrek models are extreme or outrageous prototypes that you are unlikely to build. Use them to spark debate and learning.

10
Track learnings, insights, and progress.
Keep track of all your alternative prototypes, learnings, and insights. You might use earlier ideas and insights later in the process.

Make Ideas Visible with Napkin Sketches

STRATEGYZER.COM / VPD / DESIGN / 2.1

OBJECTIVE
Quickly visualize ideas for value propositions

OUTCOME
Alternative prototypes in the form of napkin sketches

80

Napkin sketches are a rough representation of a value proposition or business model and highlight only the core idea, not how it works. They are rough enough to fit on the back of a napkin and still communicate the idea. Use them early in your prototyping process to explore and discuss alternatives.

What is a napkin sketch?

Napkin sketches are a cheap way to make your ideas more tangible and shareable. They avoid going into the details of how an idea works to steer clear of getting hung up with implementation issues.

What is it used for?

Use napkin sketches to quickly share and evaluate ideas during the early value proposition design process. Their roughness is deliberate so you can throw ideas away without regret and explore alternatives. You may also use them to gather early feedback from customers.

Caveat

Make sure people understand that napkin sketches are an exploratory tool. You will kill or transform many of the sketched out ideas during the prototyping and testing process.

The best napkin sketches...

Contain only one core idea or direction (ideas can be merged later).

Explain what an idea is about, not how it will work (no processes or business models yet!).

Keep things simple enough to get it in a glance (details are for more refined prototypes later on).

Can be pitched in 10 to 30 seconds.

The Self-Service Shop of _____

our clients get individual components from our shop and assemble the product later on themselves

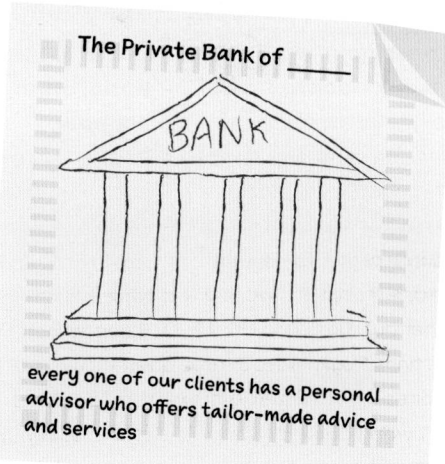

The Private Bank of _____

every one of our clients has a personal advisor who offers tailor-made advice and services

4
Display

All napkin sketches are exposed in a sort of gallery on the wall. You should now have a nice diversity of alternative directions.

3
Pitch · 30 sec per group

One team member of each break-out group takes the stage and pitches the (large) napkin sketches. Each pitch should be no longer than 30 seconds—just enough to outline what the idea is about, not to explain how it works! Make sure there is sufficient diversity across the groups or else send everybody back to the drawing board.

5
Dotmocracy · 10–15 min (ideally over a break)

Participants get 10 stickers to vote for their favorite ideas. They can give all votes to one idea or distribute them among several napkin sketches. This is not a decision-making mechanism. It is a process that highlights the ideas that participants are most excited about. p. 138

1
Brainstorm · 15–20 min

Use different brainstorming techniques, such as trigger questions ⊕ p. 15, 17, 31, 33 or "what if" questions to generate a large quantity of possible directions for interesting value propositions. Don't worry about choice at this stage. Quantity is better than quality. These are quick and dirty prototypes that will change inevitably.

2
Draw · 12–15 min

Participants split into break-out groups, and each group quickly picks three ideas for three alternative value propositions. They draw a napkin sketch for each one on a flip chart. Making two or three sketches increases diversity and reduces the risk of endless discussions.

6
Prototype

Break-out groups continue by sketching out a value proposition canvas for the one napkin sketch out of their three that got most votes. Potentially redistribute the napkin sketches that got most votes among the different groups.

Create Possibilities Quickly with Ad-Libs

OBJECTIVE
Quickly shape potential value proposition directions

OUTCOME
Alternative prototypes in the form of "pitchable" sentences

Ad-libs are a great way to quickly shape alternative directions for your value proposition. They force you to pinpoint how exactly you are going to create value. Prototype three to five different directions by filling out the blanks in the ad-lib below.

 *Download the template*

Our  _____ **help(s)**  _____ **who**

products and services   *customer segment*

want to  _____ **by**  _____ **and**

jobs to be done   *your own verb (e.g., reducing, avoiding)*

 _____ **. (** **Tip** Add at the beginning or end of sentence: **unlike** 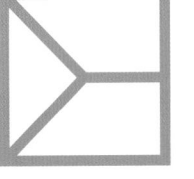 _____ **)**

your own verb (e.g., increasing, enabling)   *competing value proposition*

Our _____ `book` help(s) _____ `business professionals` who

want to _____ `improve or build a business` by _____ `avoiding` `making stuff nobody wants` and

`creating` `clear indicators to measure progress` _____ .

Flesh out Ideas with Value Proposition Canvases

OBJECTIVE
Sketch explicitly how different ideas create customer value

OUTCOME
Alternative prototypes in the form of Value Proposition Canvases

Use the Value Proposition Canvas to sketch out quick alternative proto-types, just like you would with napkin sketches or ad-libs. Don't just work with the canvas to refine final ideas, but use it as an exploratory tool until you find the right direction.

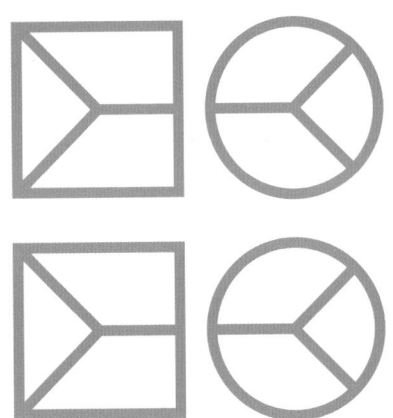
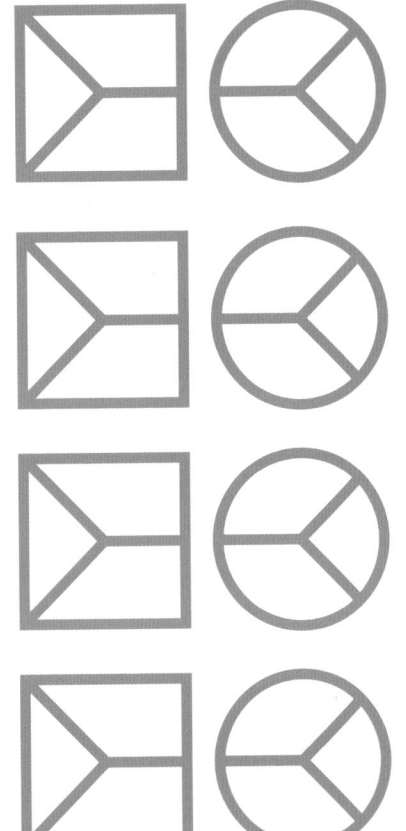
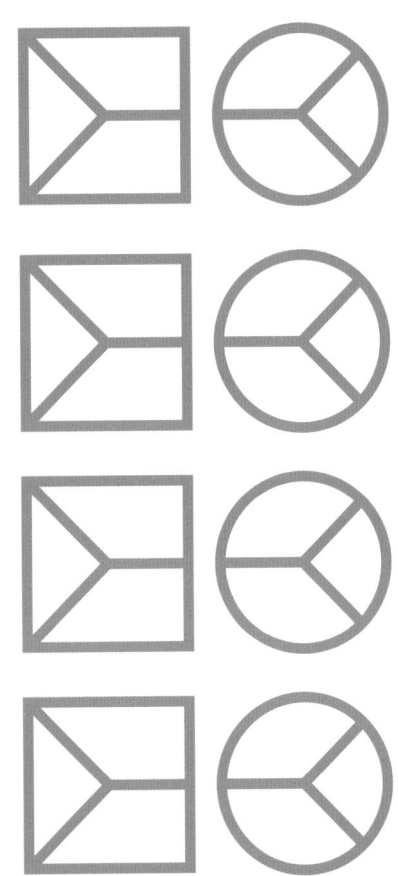

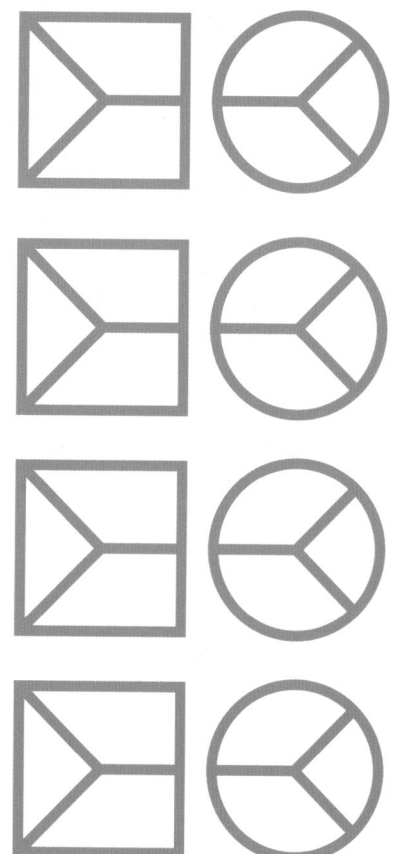

Use a visible timer to constrain the time you spend working on a specific prototype. Keep early prototypes short.

Don't be afraid to prototype radical directions, even if you know you are unlikely to pursue them. Explore and learn.

2.2
Starting Points

Where to Start

Contrary to popular belief, great new value propositions don't always have to start with the customer. They do, however, always have to end with addressing jobs, pains, or gains that customers care about.

On this spread we offer 16 trigger areas to get started with new or improved value propositions. They start from either the customer, your existing value propositions, your business models, your environment, or business models and value propositions from other industries and sectors.

 Get "Innovation Starting Points" poster

Zoom out

Could you...

Imitate and "import" a pioneering model from another sector or industry?

Create value based on a new technology trend or turn a new regulation to your advantage?

Come up with a new value proposition that your competitors can't copy?

Come up with a new value proposition based on a new partnership?

Build on your existing activities and resources, including patents, infrastructure, skills, user base?

Dramatically alter your cost structure to lower your prices substantially?

Create a new gain creator for a given customer profile?

Imagine a new product or service?

Create a new pain reliever for a given customer profile?

Zoom in

Your Business Model Environment

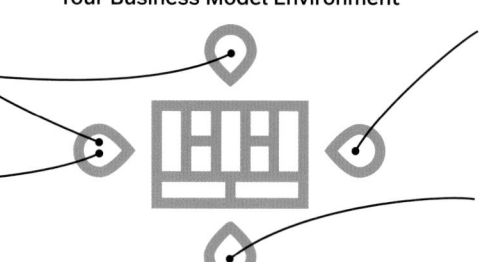

Adapt your value proposition to a new or underserved segment such as the rising middle class in emerging markets?

Design a value proposition for a new macroeconomic trend such as rising healthcare costs in the Western hemisphere?

Your Current Business Model(s)

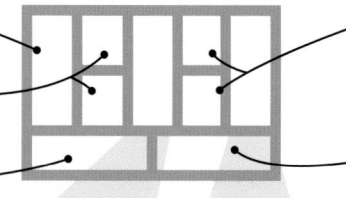

♥🚚 Leverage your existing relationships and channels to offer customers a new value proposition?

💰 Give away your core product for free or increase your prices by a multiple?

Your Value Proposition(s)

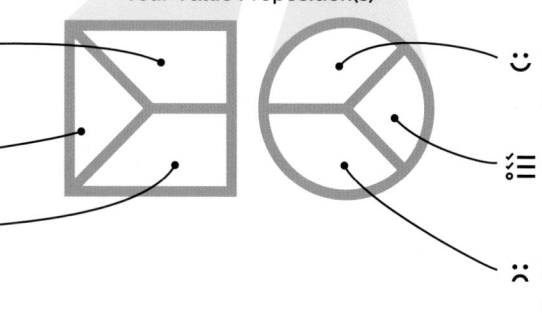

☺ Focus on your customers' most essential unrealized gain?

≣ Uncover a new unsatisfied job?

☹ Solve your customers' most extreme unresolved pain?

Spark Ideas with Design Constraints

Use design constraints to force people to think about innovative value propositions embedded in great business models. We outline five constraints of businesses whose value proposition and business model you can copy into your own arena. Don't hesitate to come up with other ones.

OBJECTIVE
Force yourself to think outside of the box

OUTCOME
Ideas that differ from your "usual" value propositions and business models

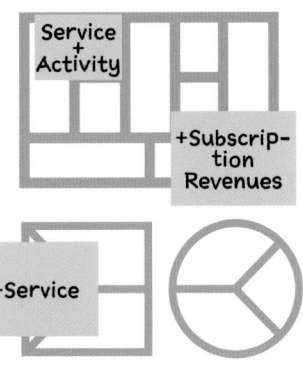

HILTI

Servitization

Constraint: Transform from selling a product-based value proposition to a service-based one that generates revenues from a subscription model.

Hilti shifted from selling machine tools to builders to leasing fleet management services to managers at construction companies.

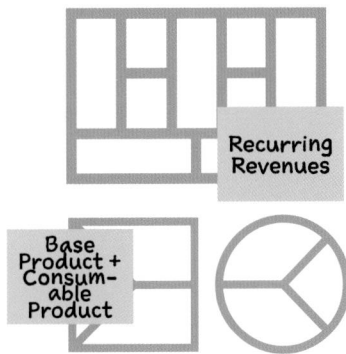

NESPRESSO.

Razor Blade

Constraint: Create a value proposition composed of a base product and a consumable product that generates recurring revenues.

Nespresso transformed the sales of espresso from a transactional business to one with recurring revenues based on consumable pods for its espresso machine.

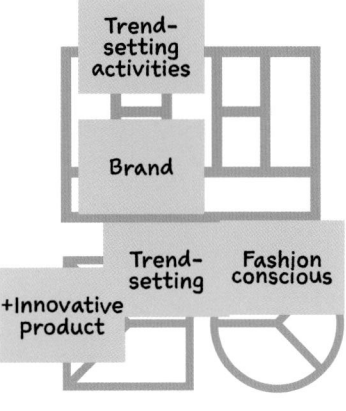

swatch+

Trendsetter

Constraint: Transform a technology (innovation) into a fashionable trend.

Swatch conquered the world by turning a plastic watch that could be made cheaply due to a reduced number of pieces and innovative production technology into a global fashion trend.

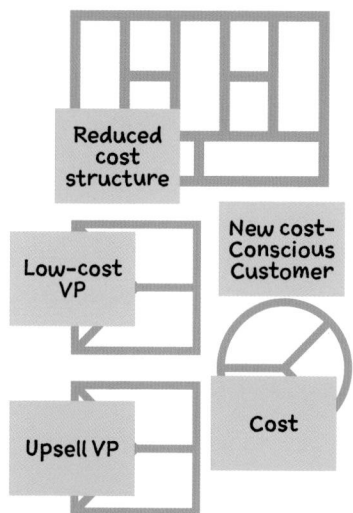

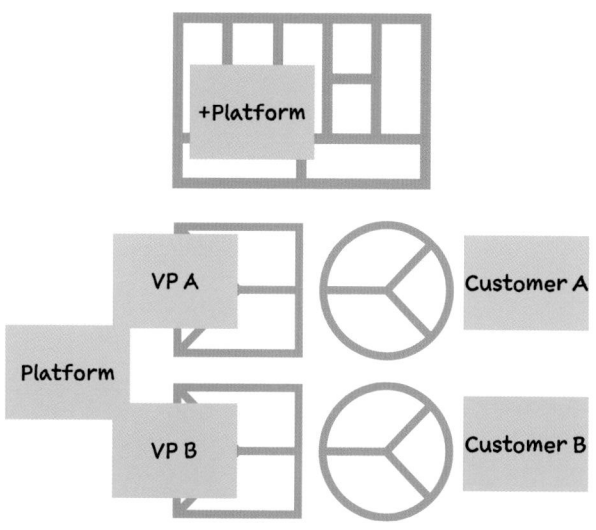

Low-Cost

Constraint: Reduce the core value proposition to its basic features, target an unserved or under-served customer segment with a low price and sell everything else as an additional value proposition.

Southwest became the largest low-cost airline by stripping down the value proposition to its bare minimum, travel from point A to point B, and offering low prices. They opened up flying to a new segment.

Platform

Constraint: Build a platform model that connects several actors with a specific value proposition for each.

Airbnb made private homes around the world accessible to travelers by connecting them with people who seek to rent out their apartments short term.

Tips

- Assign different constraints to different working groups if you have the opportunity to do so. It allows you to explore alternatives in parallel.

- Use constraints that represent the challenges in your arena, such as free value propositions, decreasing margins, and so on.

 Download Constraint Cards

Invite Big Ideas to the Table with Books and Magazines

92

OBJECTIVE
Broaden horizon and generate fresh ideas

OUTCOME
Ideas that build on relevant topics and integrate latest trends

Use best-selling books and magazines to generate fresh ideas for new and innovative value propositions and business models. It's a quick and effective way to immerse yourself in various relevant and popular topics and build on current trends.

Bringing books into a workshop is like inviting the world's best thinkers to brainstorm. This way you can afford a lot more of them at the same time.

1

Select books.

Prepare a series of books and magazines representing a trend, important topic, or big idea on a large table. Ask workshop participants to pick up a book each.

E-retailers grow in power

Climate change awareness affects consumer behavior

Rise of the "sharing economy"

Mass-collab. changes how value is created

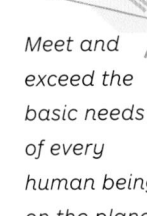

WIRED

FAST COMPANY

WHAT'S MINE IS YOURS

HERE COMES EVERYBODY

Abundance

MAKERS

Black Swan Green
David Mitchell
The Economist

What Would Google Do?

Harvard Business Review

BIG DATA

grown up digital

Recoil

Meet and exceed the basic needs of every human being on the planet

How the digital generation ticks differently

Surge of the maker movement

2

Browse and extract.

Participants browse their book and capture the best ideas on sticky notes. (45 min)

Tribes

Tips

- Select books about society, technology, and environment that push participants outside of their comfort zone.
- Avoid complicated business theories or methods.
- Mix in YouTube videos of keynote talks by the authors.
- Use napkin sketches to share your value proposition ideas.

3

Share and discuss.

Participants share their highlights in groups of four or five people and capture their insights on a board. (20 min)

5

Pitch.

Each group shares their alternative value propositions with the other groups.

4

Brainstorm possibilities.

Each group generates three new value proposition ideas based on their discussions. (30 min)

 Download "Big Idea Book List"

Push vs. Pull

The push versus pull debate is a common one. *Push* indicates that you're starting the design of your value proposition from a technology or innovation you possess, whereas *pull* means you're beginning with a manifest customer job, pain, or gain. These are two common starting points, many of which we outlined previously ➜ p. 88. Consider both as viable options depending on your preferences and context.

Technology Push

Start from an invention, innovation, or (technological) resource for which you develop a value proposition that addresses a customer job, pain, and gain. In simple terms, this is a solution in search of a problem.

Explore value proposition prototypes that are based on your invention, innovation, or technological resource with potentially interested customer segments. Design a dedicated value map for each segment until you find problem-solution fit. Read more about the build, measure, learn cycle on ➜ p. 186.

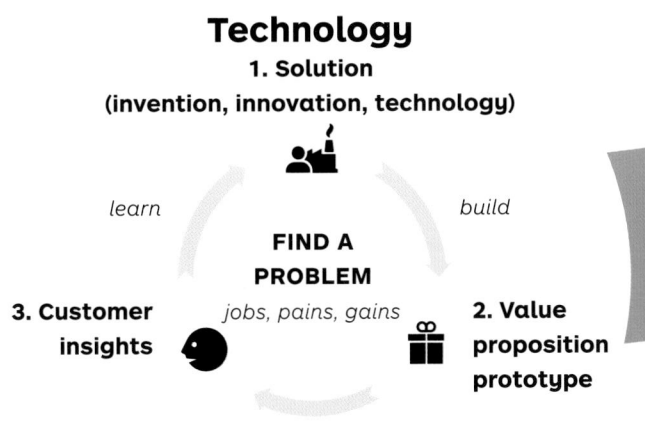

Technology

1. Solution
(invention, innovation, technology)

learn   *build*

FIND A PROBLEM
jobs, pains, gains

3. Customer insights   **2. Value proposition prototype**

measure

Key Partnerships 🔗	Key Activities ✓	Value
	Key Resources 🏭	
	technological resources	
Cost Structure		

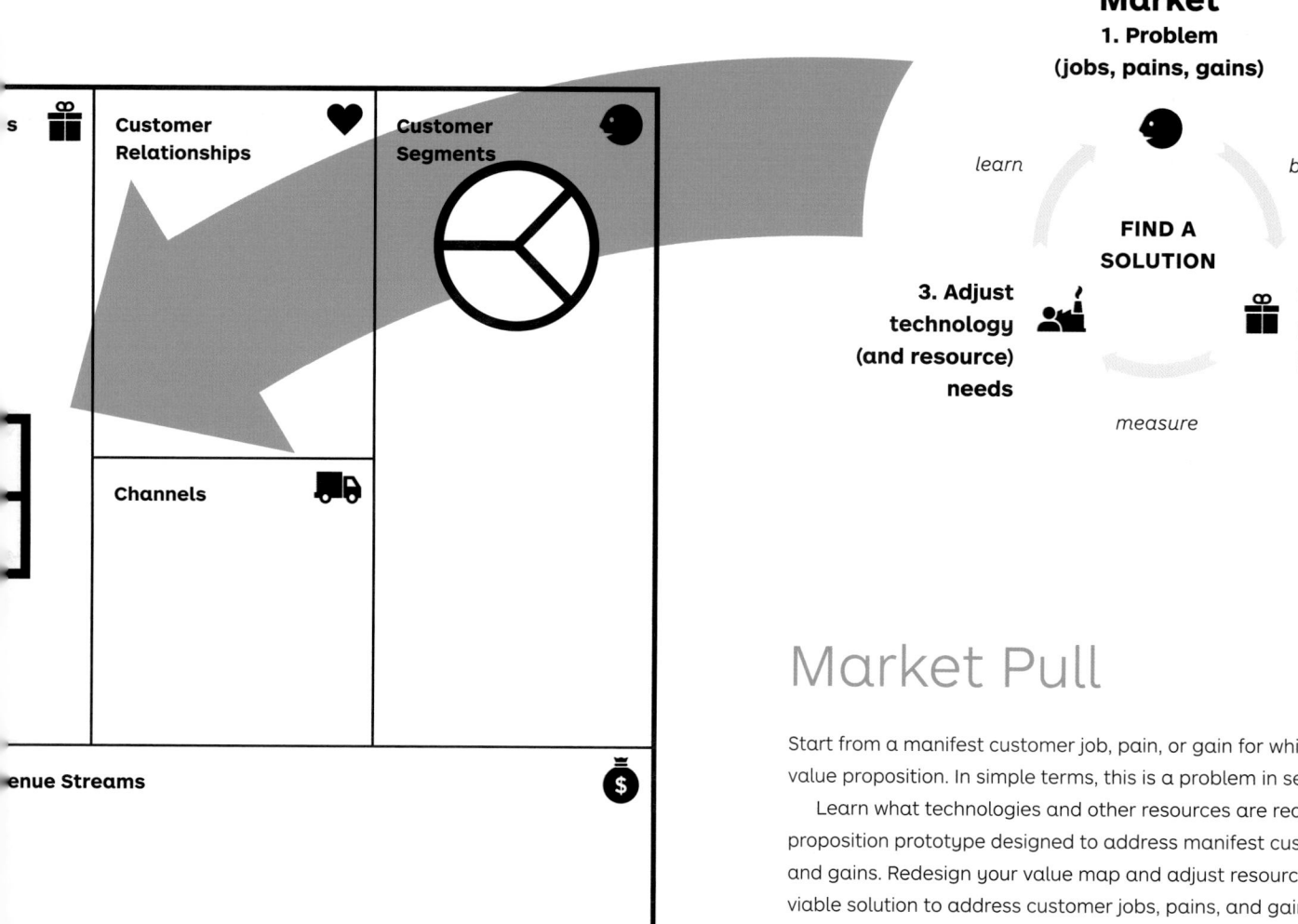

Market

**1. Problem
(jobs, pains, gains)**

learn   *build*

**FIND A
SOLUTION**

**3. Adjust
technology
(and resource)
needs**

**2. Value
proposition
prototype**

measure

Market Pull

Start from a manifest customer job, pain, or gain for which you design a value proposition. In simple terms, this is a problem in search of a solution.

Learn what technologies and other resources are required for each value proposition prototype designed to address manifest customer jobs, pains, and gains. Redesign your value map and adjust resources until you find a viable solution to address customer jobs, pains, and gains. More about the build, measure, learn cycle on p. 186.

Customer
Relationships

Customer
Segments

Channels

enue Streams

Push: Technology in Search of Jobs, Pains, and Gains

OBJECTIVE
Practice the technology-driven approach with no risk

OUTCOME
Improved skills

 This push exercise starts with the solution

1

Design.
Design a value proposition based on the technology outlined in the press excerpt from the Swiss Federal Institute of Technology in Lausanne (EPFL) by targeting a customer segment that might be interested in adopting this technology.

2

?

Ideate.
Come up with an idea for a value proposition using the compressed air energy storage.

3

?

Segment.
Select a customer segment that could be interested in this value proposition and would be ready to pay for it.

The Business Model Canvas

Key Partnerships 🔗	Key Activities ✔	Value Propositions 🎁	Customer Relationships ♥	Customer Segments ●
	Key Resources 🏭 compressed air energy storage		**Channels** 🚚	

Cost Structure 🏷	Revenue Streams 💰

ⓦ **Strategyzer**

"Solar and aeolian sources are great candidates for the electricity generation of the future... However, solar and wind sources' peak availability takes place at times that do not usually correspond to peak demand hours. Therefore, a way must be devised to store and later reuse the energy generated.

EPFL has worked for over ten years on an original storage system: compressed air. The use of a hydraulic piston delivers the best system performance... The obtained high pressure air can be safely stored in bottles without losses until it is necessary to generate new electricity by expanding the gas in the cylinder. One of the advantages of our system is that it does not require rare materials.

A spin-off has been created to develop this principle and create 'turnkey' electrical energy storage and retrieval units. In 2014, a 25 kW pilot will be installed at a photovoltaic park in Jura.... In the future, there will be 250 kW installations at first and 2,500 kW ones afterwards."

Continued on ➔ p. 152

Tips

- Add design constraints to technology push exercises. Your organization might not want to address certain customer segments (e.g., B2B, business-to-consumer [B2C], specific regions, etc.). Or you might prefer certain strategic directions, for example, licensing rather than building solutions.
- Follow up on your customer assumptions by researching customers ➔ p. 104 and producing evidence ➔ p. 172 once you've selected a potentially interested segment.

6

Assess.

Assess the fit between the customer profile and the designed value proposition.

Zoom in

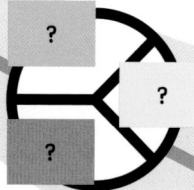

4

Profile.

Sketch out the customer's profile. Make assumptions about jobs to be done, pains, and gains.

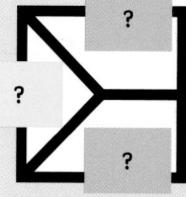

5

Sketch.

Refine the value proposition by sketching out how it will kill customer pains and create gains.

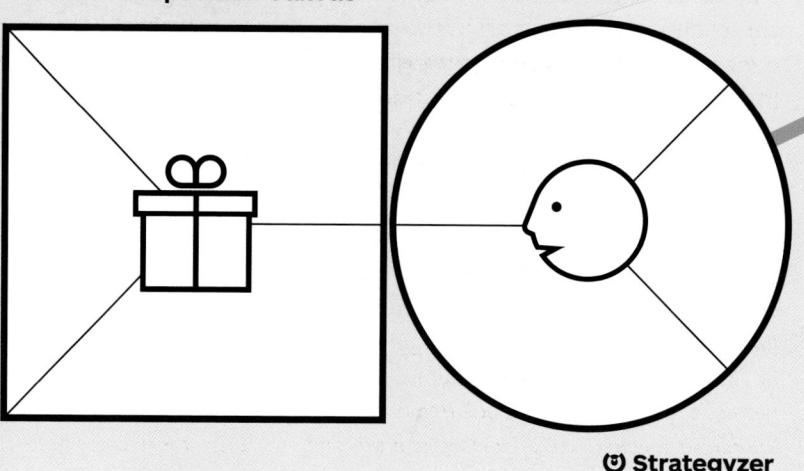
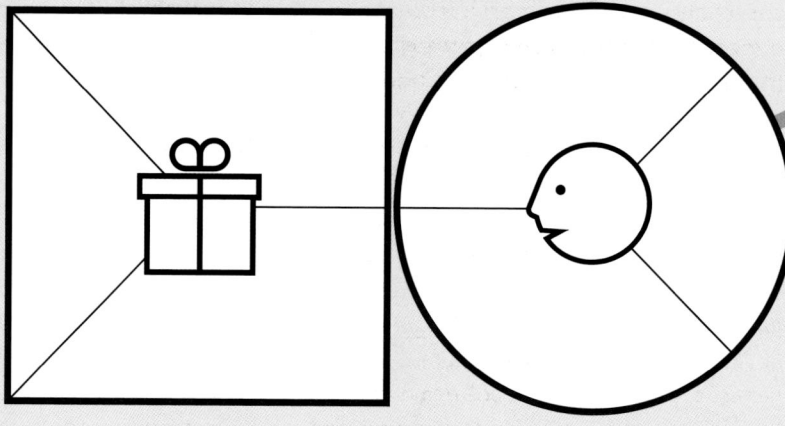

The Value Proposition Canvas

ⓦ **Strategyzer**

Pull: Identify High-Value Jobs

Great value proposition creators master the art of focusing on the jobs, pains, and gains that matter. How will you know which of these jobs, pains, and gains to focus on? Identify high-value jobs by asking if they are important, tangible, unsatisfied, and lucrative.

High-value jobs are characterized by pains and gains that are...

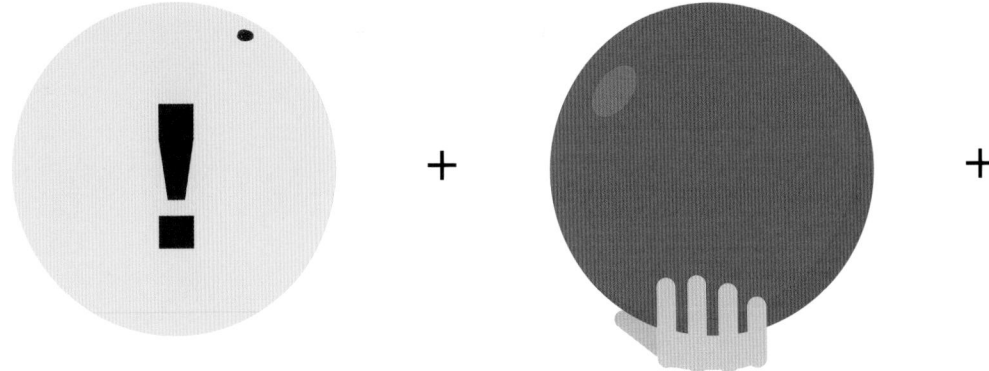

+   +

Important

When the customer's success or failure to get the job done leads to essential gains or extreme pains, respectively.

- Does failing the job lead to extreme pains?
- Does failing the job lead to missing out on essential gains?

Tangible

When the pains or gains related to a job can be felt or experienced immediately or often, not just days or weeks later.

- Can you feel the pain?
- Can you see the gain?

Unsatisfied   + Lucrative   = High-value jobs

When current value propositions don't help relieve pains or create desired gains in a satisfying way or simply don't exist.

- Are there unresolved pains?
- Are there unrealized gains?

When many people have the job with related pains and gains or a small number of customers are willing to pay a premium.

- Are there many with this job, pain, or gain?
- Are there few willing to pay a lot?

Focus on the highest-value jobs and related pains and gains.

Based on initial work by consultancy, Innosight.

Pull: Job Selection

STRATEGYZER.COM / VPD / DESIGN / 2.2

OBJECTIVE
Identify high-value customer jobs that you could focus on

OUTCOME
Ranking of customer jobs from your perspective

This pull exercise starts with the customer.

Imagine your customers are chief information officers (CIOs) and you have to understand which jobs matter most to them. Do this exercise to prioritize their jobs or apply it to one of your own customer profiles.

Tips

- This exercise helps you prioritize jobs from mainly your perspective. It doesn't mean you have to mandatorily address the most important ones in your value proposition; those might be outside your scope. However, make sure your value proposition does address jobs that are highly relevant to customers.
- Great value proposition creators often focus on only few jobs, pains, and gains, but do that extremely well.
- Complement this exercise with getting customer insights from the field ➔ p. 106 and experiments that produce evidence ➔ p. 216.

Customer Profile
Synthesized customer profile of a CIO

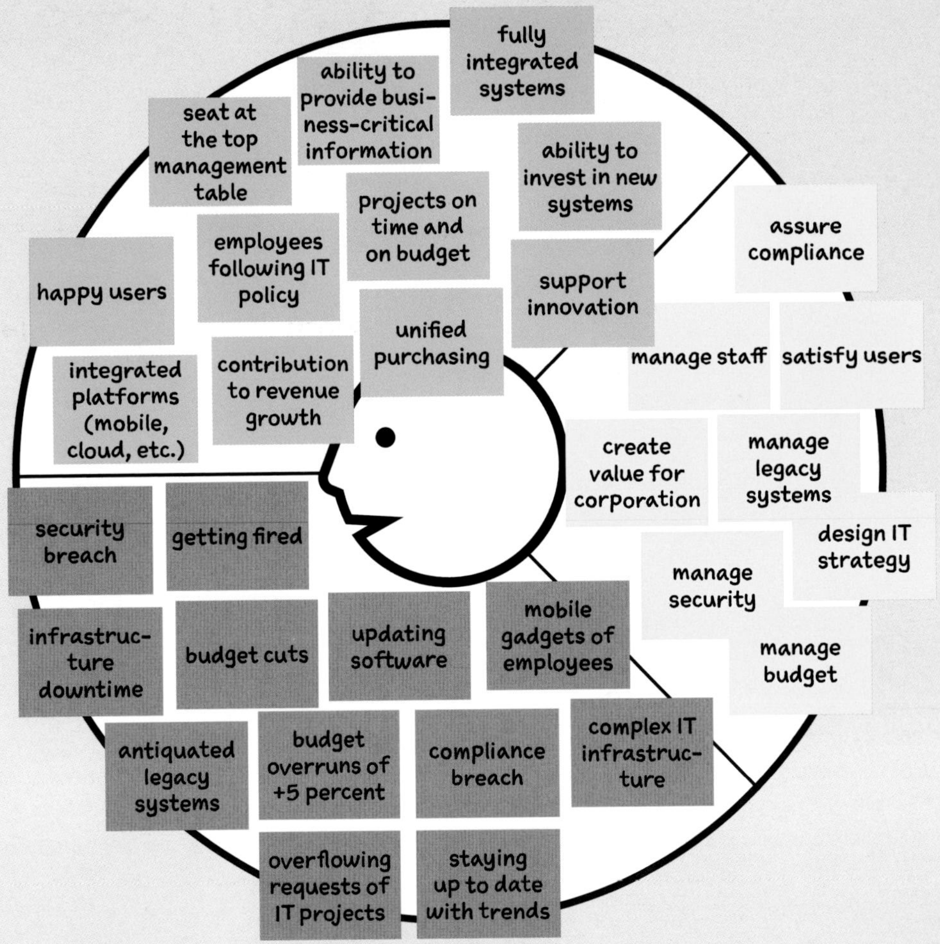

- fully integrated systems
- ability to provide business-critical information
- seat at the top management table
- ability to invest in new systems
- assure compliance
- projects on time and on budget
- employees following IT policy
- support innovation
- happy users
- unified purchasing
- manage staff
- satisfy users
- integrated platforms (mobile, cloud, etc.)
- contribution to revenue growth
- create value for corporation
- manage legacy systems
- design IT strategy
- security breach
- getting fired
- manage security
- manage budget
- infrastructure downtime
- budget cuts
- updating software
- mobile gadgets of employees
- antiquated legacy systems
- budget overruns of +5 percent
- compliance breach
- complex IT infrastructure
- overflowing requests of IT projects
- staying up to date with trends

⊙ Strategyzer

- Does failing the job lead to extreme pains?
- Does failing the job lead to missing out on essential gains?

- Can you feel the pain?
- Can you see the gain?

- Are there unresolved pains?
- Are there unrealized gains?

- Are there many with this job, pain, or gain?
- Are there few willing to pay a lot?

Focus on the highest value jobs and related pains and gains.

Jobs	Important	Tangible	Unsatisfied	Lucrative	High-value jobs
create value for corporation	•••	•	•••	••	= 9
design IT strategy	••	•	••	••	= 7

Scoring scale: • (low) to •••• (high)

Based on initial work by consultancy, Innosight.

Six Ways to Innovate from the Customer Profile

You've mapped your customer profile. What to do from here?
Here are six ways to trigger your next value proposition move.

Can you...

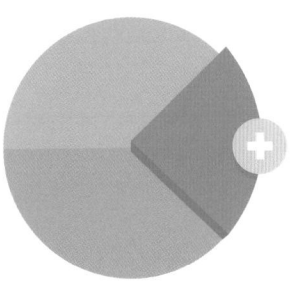

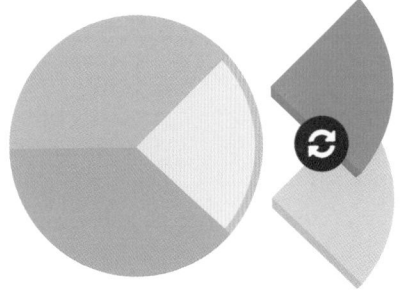

Address more jobs?

Switch to a more important job?

Go beyond functional jobs?

Address a more complete set of jobs, including related and ancillary jobs.

With the iPhone, Apple not only reinvented the mobile phone but enabled us to store and play music and browse the web on one device.

Help customers do a job that is different from what most value propositions currently focus on.

Hilti, the machine tool manufacturer, understood that construction managers needed to keep schedules to avoid penalties, not only drill holes. Their fleet management solution addressed the former in addition to the latter.

Look beyond functional jobs and create new value by fulfilling important social and emotional jobs.

Mini Cooper created a car that became as much a means of transport as a statement of identity.

Download trigger questions

Help a lot more customers get a job done?

Help more people do a job that was otherwise too complex or too expensive.

High-end web data storage and computing power used to be reserved to big companies with large IT budgets. Amazon.com made it available to companies of any size and budget with Amazon Web Services.

Get a job done incrementally better?

Help customers better do a job by making a series of microimprovements to an existing value proposition.

German engineering and electronics multi-national Bosch improved on a wide range of features of its circular saw that really mattered to customers and outperformed competition.

Help a customer get a job done radically better?

This is the stuff of new market creation, when a new value proposition dramatically outper-forms older ways of helping a customer get a job done.

The first spreadsheet called VisiCalc not only introduced a new market for such tools but also ushered a whole new realm of possibili-ties across industries powered by easy, visual calculations.

2.3

Understanding Customers

Six Techniques to Gain Customer Insights

Understanding the customer's perspective is crucial to designing great value propositions. Here are six techniques that will get you started. Make sure you use a good mix of these techniques to understand your customers deeply.

The Data Detective

Build on existing work with (desk) research. Secondary research reports and customer data you might already have provide a great foundation for getting started. Look also at data outside your industry and study analogs, opposites, or adjacencies.

Difficulty level: ★

Strength: great foundation for further research

Weakness: static data from a different context

➲ p. 108 for more

The Journalist

Talk to (potential) customers as an easy way to gain customer insights. It's a well-established practice. However, customers might tell you one thing in an interview but behave differently in the real world.

Difficulty level: ★★

Strength: quick and cheap to get started with first learnings and insights

Weakness: customers don't always know what they want and actual behavior differs from interview answers

➲ p. 110 for more

The Anthropologist

Observe (potential) customers in the real world to get good insights into how they really behave. Study which jobs they focus on and how they get them done. Note which pains upset them and which gains they aim to achieve.

Difficulty level: ★★★

Strength: data provide unbiased view and allow discovering real-world behavior

Weakness: difficult to gain customer insights related to new ideas

➲ p. 114 for more

The Impersonator

"Be your customer" and actively use products and services. Spend a day or more in your customer's shoes. Draw from your experience as an (unsatisfied) customer.

Difficulty level: ★★

Strength: firsthand experience of jobs, pains, and gains

Weakness: not always representative of your real customer or possible to apply

The Cocreator

Integrate customers into the process of value creation to learn with them. Work with customers to explore and develop new ideas.

Difficulty level: ★★★★★

Strength: the proximity with customers can help you gain deep insights

Weakness: may not be generalized to all customers and segments

The Scientist

Get customers to participate (knowingly or unknowingly) in an experiment. Learn from the outcome.

Difficulty level: ★★★★

Strength: provides fact-based insights on real-world behavior; works particularly well for new ideas

Weakness: can be hard to apply in existing organizations because of strict (customer) policies and guidelines

➲ p. 216 for more

The Data Detective: Get Started with Existing Information

Never before have creators had more access to readily available information and data inside and outside their companies before even getting started with designing value. Use available data sources as a launching pad to getting started with customer insights.

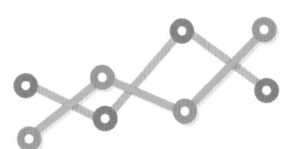

Google Trends

Compare three search terms representing three different trends related to your idea.

Google Keyword Planner

Learn what's popular with potential customers by finding the top five search terms related to your idea. How often are they searched for?

Government Census Data, World Bank, IMF, and more

Identify the (government) data that are relevant to your idea and at your fingertips via the web.

Third-Party Research Reports

Identify three readily available research reports that can serve you as a starting point to prepare your own customer and value proposition research.

Social Media Analytics

Existing companies and brands should:

- Identify the shakers and movers related to their brand on social media?
- Spot the 10 most frequently mentioned positive and negative things said about them on social media.

Customer Relationship Management (CRM)

- List the top three questions, complaints, and requests that you are getting from your daily interactions with customers (e.g., support).

Tracking Customers on Your Website

- List the top three ways customers reach your site (e.g., search, referrals).
- Find the 10 most and least popular destinations on your website.

Data Mining

Existing company should mine their data to:

- Identify three patterns that could be useful to their new idea.

Source: Siegel & Davenport, *Predictive Analytics: The Power to Predict Who Will Click, Buy, Lie, or Die*, 2013.

The Journalist:
Interview Your Customers

110

OBJECTIVE
Gain a better customer understanding

OUTCOME
First lightly validated customer profile(s)

Talk to customers to gain insights relevant to your context. Use the Value Proposition Canvas to prepare interviews and organize the chaotic mass of information that will be coming at you during the interview process.

2
Create an interview outline.
Ask yourself what you want to learn. Derive the interview questions from your customer profile. Ask about the most important jobs, pains, and gains.

1
Create a customer profile.
Sketch out the jobs, pains, and gains you believe characterize the customer you are targeting. Rank jobs, pains, and gains in order of importance.

5
Review the interview.
Assess if you need to review the interview questions based on what you learned.

Tip
Capture your biggest insights from all the interviews.

3

Conduct the interview.

Conduct the interview by following the interview ground rules outlined on the next page.

7

Synthesize.

Make a separate synthesized customer profile for every customer segment that emerges from all your interviews. Write down your most important insights on sticky notes.

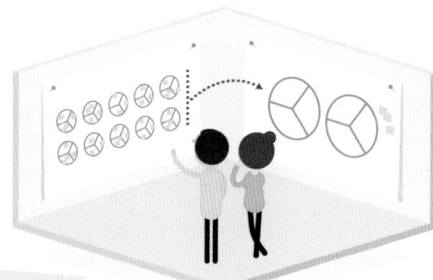

4

Capture.

Map out the jobs, pains, and gains you learned about in the interview on an empty customer profile.

Make sure you also capture business model learnings. Write down your most important insights.

6

Search for patterns.

Can you discover similar jobs, pains, and gains? What stands out? What is similar or different among interviewees?

Why are they similar or different? Can you detect specific (recurring) contexts that influence jobs, pains, and gains?

Ground Rules for Interviewing

It is an art to conduct good interviews that provide relevant insights for value proposition design. Make sure you focus on unearthing what matters to (potential) customers rather than trying to pitch them solutions. Follow the rules on this spread to conduct great interviews.

⚙ Get "Ground Rules for Interviewing" poster

Rule 1
Adopt a beginner's mind.
Listen with a "fresh pair of ears" and avoid interpretation. Explore unexpected jobs, pains, and gains in particular.

Rule 2
Listen more than you talk.
Your goal is to listen and learn, not to inform, impress, or convince your customer of anything. Avoid wasting time talking about your own beliefs, because it's at the expense of learning about your customer.

Rule 3
Get facts, not opinions.
Don't ask, "Would you...?"
Ask, "When is the last time you have...?"

Rule 4
Ask "why" to get real motivations.
Ask, "Why do you need to do...?"
Ask, "Why is ___ important to you?"
Ask, "Why is ___ such a pain?"

Rule 5

The goal of customer insight interviews is not selling (even if a sale is involved); it's about learning.

Don't ask, "Would you buy our solution?" Ask "what are your decision criteria when you make a purchase of...?"

Rule 6

Don't mention solutions (i.e., your prototype value proposition) too early.

Don't explain, "Our solution does..."
Ask, "What are the most important things you are struggling with?"

Rule 7

Follow up.

Get permission to keep your interviewee's contact information to come back for more questions and answers or testing prototypes.

Rule 8

Always open doors at the end.

Ask, "Who else should I talk to?"

Tips

- Interviews are an excellent starting point to learn from customers, but typically they don't provide enough or sufficiently reliable insights for making critical decisions. Complement your interviews with other research, just like a good journalist does further research to find the real story behind what people tell. Add real-world observations of customers and experiments that produce hard data to your research mix.

- Conduct interviews in teams of two people. Decide in advance who will lead the interview and who will take notes. Use a recording device (photo, video, or other) if possible, but be aware that interviewees might not answer the same way with a recording device on the table.

Fitzpatrick, The Mom Test, 2013.

The Anthropologist: Dive into Your Customer's World

Dive deep into your (potential) customers' worlds to gain insights about their jobs, pains, and gains. What customers do on a daily basis in their real settings often differs from what they believe they do or what they will tell you in an interview, survey, or focus group.

B2C: Stay with the family.
Stay at one of your potential customers' home for several days and live with the family. Participate in daily routines. Learn about what drives that person.

B2C: Observe shopping behavior.
Go to a store where your (potential) customers shop and observe people for 10 hours. Watch. Can you detect any patterns?

B2B: Work alongside/consult.
Spend time working with or alongside a (potential) customer (e.g., in a consulting engagement). Observe. What keeps the person up at night?

B2B/B2C?
How could you immerse yourself in your (potential) customer's life? Be creative! Go beyond the usual boundaries.

B2C: Shadow your customer for a day.
Be your (potential) customer's shadow and follow him or her for a day. Write down all the jobs, pains, and gains you observe. Time stamp them. Synthesize. Learn.

A Day in the Life Worksheet

OBJECTIVE
Understand your customer's world in more detail

OUTCOME
Map of your customer's day

Capture the most important jobs, pains, and gains of the customer you shadowed.

Tips

- Observe and take notes. Hold back with interpretation based on your own experience. Stay nonjudgmental! Work like an anthropologist and watch with "fresh" eyes and an open mind-set.
- Pay attention to both what you see and what you don't see.
- Capture not only what you can observe but also what is not talked about such as feelings or emotions.
- Develop customer empathy as a critical mind-set to perform this type of contextual inquiry effectively.

Time	Activity (what I see)		Notes (what I think)
7 pm	brush kid's teeth before bed		parents annoyed by water splashing everywhere

Download "A Day in the Life" worksheet

Identify Patterns in Customer Research

OBJECTIVE
Crystallize your customer

OUTCOME
Synthesized Customer Profile(s)

Analyze your data and try to detect patterns once you have a good amount of customer research gathered. Search for customers with similar jobs, pains, or gains or customers that care about the same jobs, pains, or gains and make separate customer profiles.

1
Display.
Display all the customer profiles from your research on a large wall.

2
Group and segment.
Group similar customer profiles in to one or more separate segments if you can identify patterns in the jobs, pains, and gains.

3
Synthesize.
Synthesize the profiles from each segment into a single master profile. Identify the most common jobs, pains, and gains and use separate labels to describe them in the master profile.

4
Design.
Get started with proto-typing value propositions after finishing your first attempt at customer segmentation. Design one or more value prop-osition prototypes with confidence, based on the newly identified patterns in the master profile.

Synthesis Example: Master profile of a business professional / book reader

To establish a master profile of book readers, we looked at the jobs, pains, and gains of the different customer profiles from our interviews. We synthesized the most frequent ones into the master profile by using representative labels.

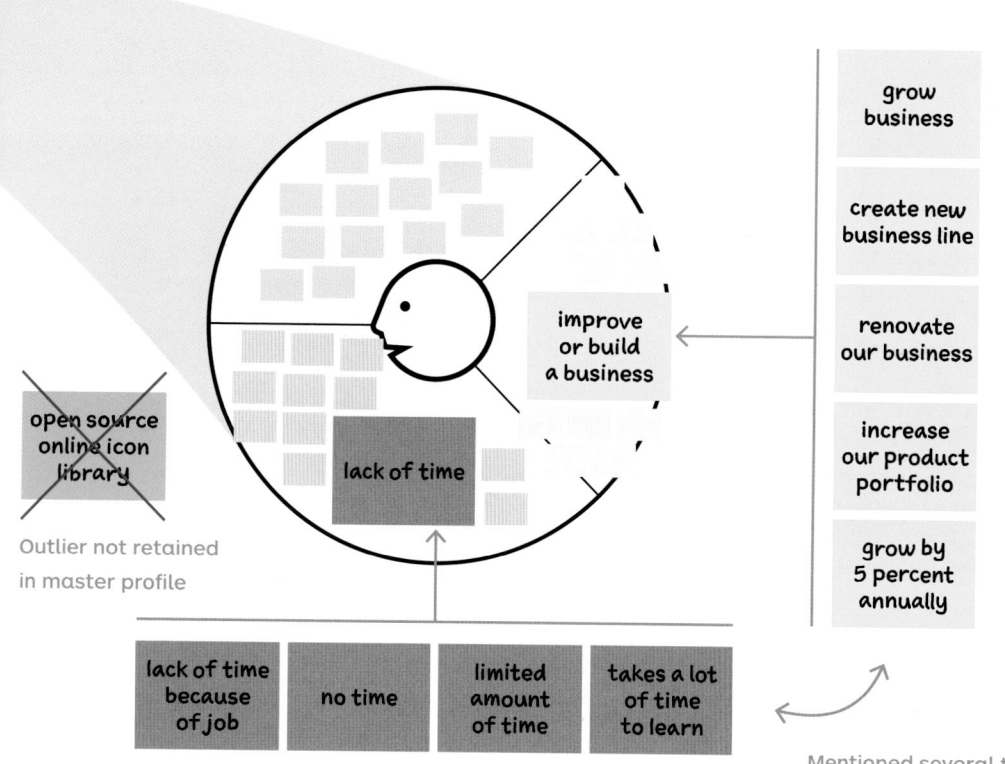

grow business

create new business line

renovate our business

increase our product portfolio

grow by 5 percent annually

improve or build a business

lack of time

open source online icon library

Outlier not retained in master profile

lack of time because of job

no time

limited amount of time

takes a lot of time to learn

Mentioned several times

Tips

- Pay special attention to outlier profiles. They might be irrelevant, but they could represent a special learning opportunity. Sometimes the best discoveries lie at the edges.
- Ask yourself if an outlier might be a bellwether and a sign of things to come that you should pay attention to. Or maybe an outlier is different by positive deviance. It may simply be a better solution to jobs, pains, and gains than peers offer.

118

Find Your Earlyvangelist

Pay attention to earlyvangelists when researching potential customers and looking for patterns. The term was coined by Steve Blank* to describe customers who are willing and able to take a risk on a new product or service. Use earlyvangelists to build a foothold market and shape your value propositions via experimentation and learning.

5
Has or can acquire a budget.
The customer has committed or can quickly acquire a budget to purchase a solution.

4
Has put together solution out of piece parts.
The job is so important that the customer has cobbled together an interim solution.

3
Is actively looking for a solution.
The customer is searching for a solution *and* has a timetable for finding it.

2
Is aware of having a problem.
The customer understands that there is a problem or job.

1
Has a problem or need.
In other words, there is a job to be done.

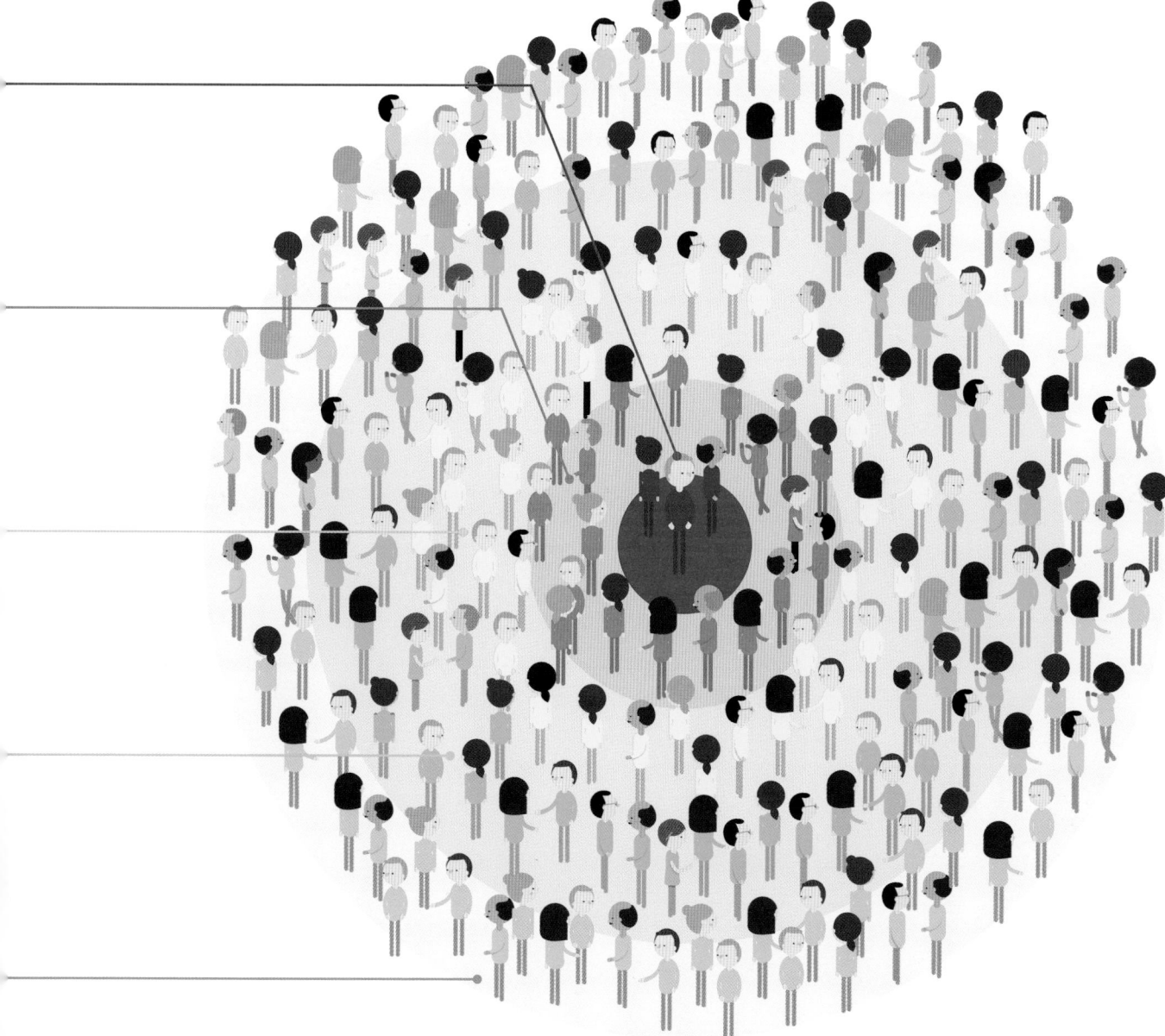

STRATEGYZER.COM / VPD / DESIGN / 2.3

Steve Blank, Bob Dorf, The Start-up Owner's Manual, 2012.

2.4

Making Choices

10 Questions to Assess Your Value Proposition

STRATEGYZER.COM / VPD / DESIGN / 2.4

OBJECTIVE
Unearth potential to improve your value proposition

OUTCOME
Value proposition assessment

122

Use the 10 questions of great value propositions we presented previously to constantly assess the design of your value propositions. Draw on them to integrate your customer insights. Integrate them when you decide which prototypes to explore further and test with customers.

 Do this exercise online

1
Is it embedded in a great business model?

2
Does it focus on the most important jobs, most extreme pains, and most essential gains?

3
Does it focus on unsatisfied jobs, unresolved pains, and unrealized gains?

4
Does it concentrate on only a few pain relievers and gain creators but does those extremely well?

5
Does it address functional, emotional, and social jobs all together?

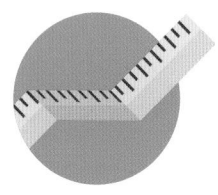

6

Does it align with how customers measure success?

7

Does it focus on jobs, pains, or gains that a large number of customers have or for which a small number are willing to pay a lot of money?

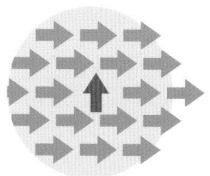

8

Does it differentiate from competition in a meaningful way?

9

Does it outperform competition substantially on at least one dimension?

10

Is it difficult to copy?

Simulate the Voice of the Customer

OBJECTIVE
Stress-test your value proposition "in the meeting room"

OUTCOME
More robust value proposition before validating it "in the market"

Use role-playing to bring the voice of the customer and other stakeholder perspectives "into the room" long before you test your value propositions in the real world.

The success of your value proposition typically depends on a number of key stakeholders. Customers are the obvious one, but there are many others (e.g., stakeholders inside your company). Pick the most important ones, and organize role-plays to stress test your value proposition from the perspective of these stakeholders.

Tips

- Make sure you choose the person who plays the stakeholder wisely. Who best represents the voice of the customer? Is it sales, customer support, field engineering, or somebody else who is close to the buyer?
- Role-plays don't replace testing your value propositions in the real world with customers and stakeholders, but they help evolve your ideas by taking a stakeholder's perspective into consideration.
- Role-plays can be an effective way to bring in the voice of the customer after you intensively analyzed customer behavior.

Two workshop participants engage in a role-playing game in which one person plays a company sales rep and the other, a stakeholder, for example, the customer. A third person takes notes.

The salesperson

The note taker

The (critical) customer

Quickly evaluate your ideas with role-playing by simulating the voices of key players.

Customers

Take the customers' point of view and focus on customer jobs, pains, and gains and competing value propositions. In a B2B context think of end users, influencers, economic buyers, decision makers, and saboteurs.

Chief executive officer (CEO), senior leaders, and board members

Take the company leadership's point of view (e.g., CEO, chief financial officer [CFO], chief operations officer [COO]). Give feedback from the perspective of the company's vision, direction, and strategy.

Other internal stakeholders

Who else's buy-in in the company do you need for your idea to succeed? Does production play a role? Do you need to convince sales or marketing?

Strategic partners

Your value proposition may rely on the collaboration with strategic partners. Are you offering them value?

Government officials

What role does the government play? Is it an enabler or a barrier?

Investors/shareholders

Will they support or resist your ideas?

Local community

Are they affected by your ideas?

The planet!

What effect does your value proposition have on the environment?

Understand the Context

126

Value propositions and business models are always designed in a context. Zoom out from your models to map the environment in which you are designing and making choices about the prototypes to pursue. The environment is made up of competition, technology change, legal constraints, changing customer desires, and other elements. Learn more with the illustration on this spread or read more in *Business Model Generation*.

Zoom out

Industry Forces

Key actors in your space, such as competitors, value chain actors, technology providers, and more

Macroeconomic Forces

Macro trends, such as global market conditions, access to resources, commodities prices, and more

Key Trends

Key trends shaping your space, such as technology innovations, regulatory constraints, social trends, and more

Market Forces

Key customer issues in your space, such as growing segments; customer switching costs; changing jobs, pains, and gains; and more

Zoom in

Osterwalder & Pigneur, Business Model Generation, 2010.

Participatory TV

Imagine you are a player in the movie industry. So far, you have been making movies and TV series with leading actors for cinema and home viewers globally. But you'd like to explore new avenues.

There is one idea that your innovation teams want to explore more closely: participatory TV—enabling viewers to crowdsource the plot of a TV series.

Illustration:
Participatory TV

Sketch out your environment and ask which elements look like...

- an opportunity that strengthens the case for your value proposition (in **green**)
- a threat or a constraint that undermines or limits it (in **red**)

Social media is a powerful marketing channel for passionate viewers.

+

Democra-
tization of
distribution

–

Size doesn't matter anymore—anybody can get access to millions of users.

Web tools make it easier for anyone to participate.

+

Democra-
tization of
production

–

User-led content can be a disruptor to professionally produced content.

Integration of TV and web will enable high-engagement experiences.

+

Connected
TV + www

User-generated content is less prone to piracy.

+

Piracy

–

Piracy is on the rise.

– It is difficult to get viewers to leave established platforms such as Netflix or Apple.

Platform
fidelity

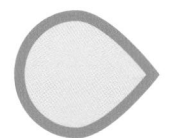

–

Gaming
industry

Actors in the gaming industry might be better equipped to succeed with a partici-patory value proposition.

Cost of talent is dropping.

+

Cost of
star talent

Subscription
pricing

+

Pricing models that produce recurring revenues (subscription) fit well with a commu-nity of cocreators.

Web
generation

+

The generation of users who grew up with the Internet participates online on a daily basis.

Value Proposition Design vs. Competitors

128

Let's focus on one element of your design and decision making environment: your competitors. Assess how your value proposition performs against those of your competition by comparing them on a Strategy Canvas, a graphical tool from the *Blue Ocean Strategy* book. This is a simple but powerful way to visualize and compare how the "benefits" of your value proposition perform.

On this spread we compare the performance of *Value Proposition Design* to the performance of executive education and massive open online courses (so-called MOOCs). We do so by drawing a Strategy Canvas with a number of competitive factors on the *x*-axis and then plot how the different competitors perform on each one of these factors. We selected the competitive factors from our value map and complemented them with elements from our competitors' value maps.

Value Proposition (VP) Design

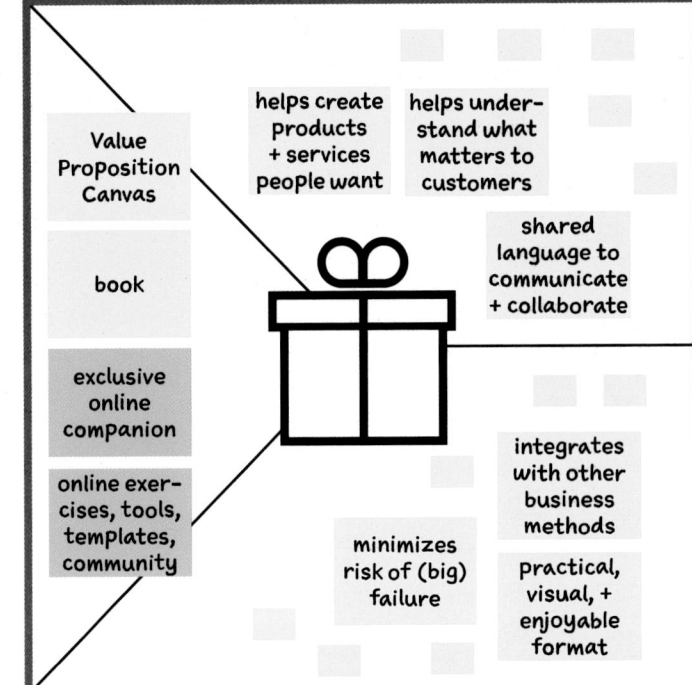

Select the most important features from your VP to use on the Strategy Canvas as factors of competition.

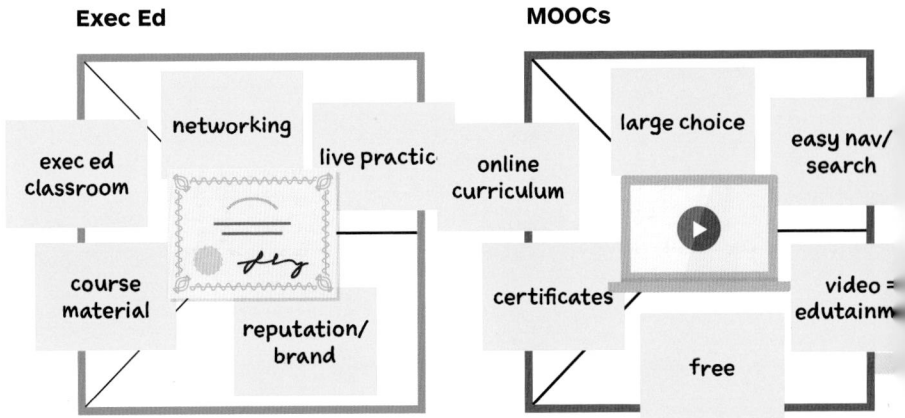

Kim & Mauborgne, Blue Ocean Strategy, 2005.

Strategy Canvas

Value proposition of <u>this book</u> vs. <u>executive education</u> vs. <u>MOOCs</u>
as compared with each other

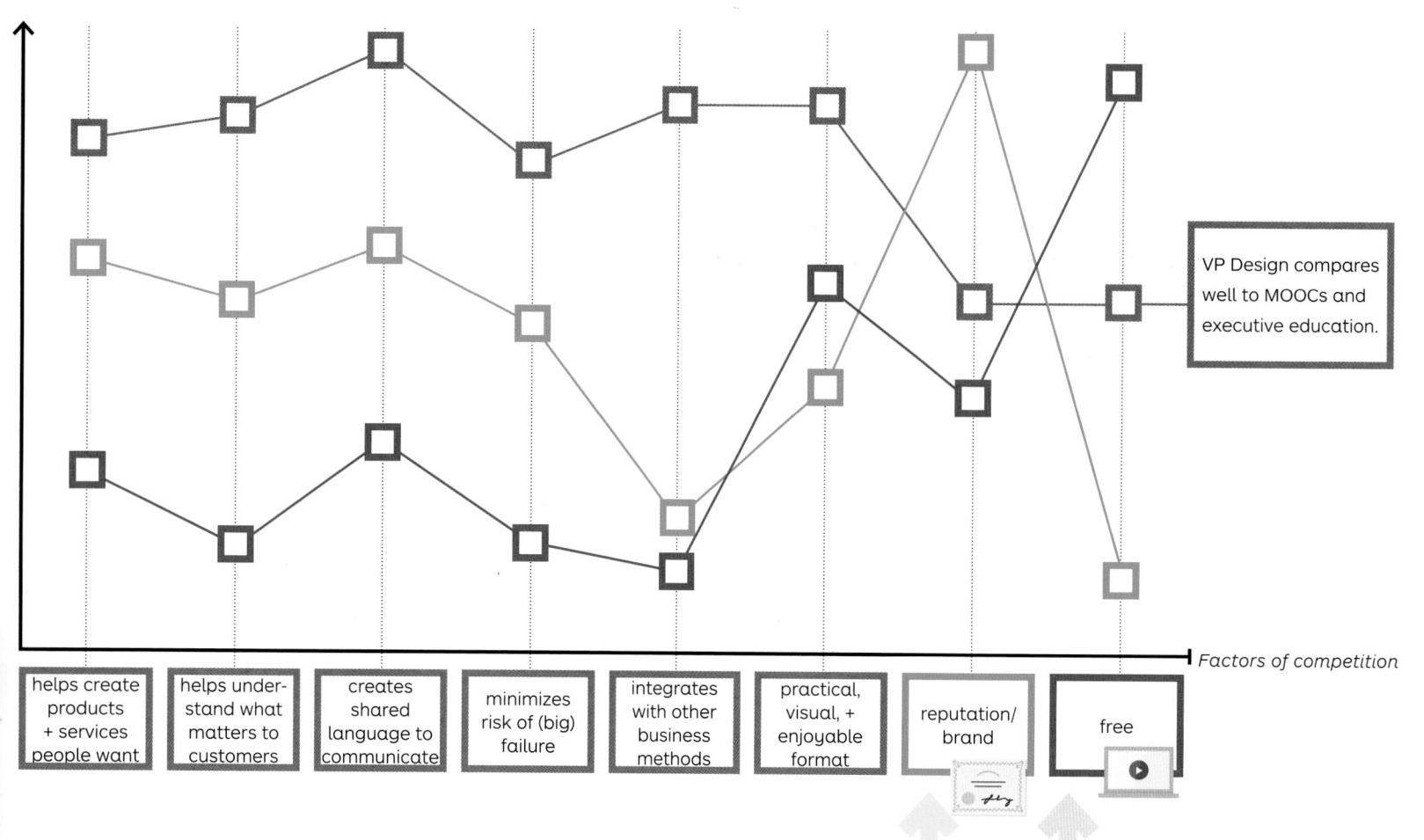

VP Design compares well to MOOCs and executive education.

Factors of competition

| helps create products + services people want | helps under-stand what matters to customers | creates shared language to communicate | minimizes risk of (big) failure | integrates with other business methods | practical, visual, + enjoyable format | reputation/ brand | free |

Compare Your Value Proposition with Competitors

OBJECTIVE	OUTCOME
Understand how you are performing compared to others	Visual comparison with competitors

Use the Strategy Canvas from the *Blue Ocean Strategy* book to plot the performance of your value proposition against those of your competitors. Then compare the curves to assess how you are differentiating.

Instructions

Draw a Strategy Canvas step by step and compare your value proposition with those of your competitors.

1. Prepare or pick a value map for this exercise.
2. Grab a big sheet of paper or use a whiteboard.
3. Follow the steps.

1

Select a value proposition.

Select the value proposition (prototype) you want to compare.

2

Select factors of competition.

Draw a horizontal axis (x-axis). Pick the pain relievers and gain creators you want to compare with competition. Place them on the axis. These are the factors of competition of your Strategy Canvas.

Tip

You can also add pains and gains if you feel like they better describe important factors of competition.

3

Score your value proposition.

Draw a vertical axis (y-axis) to represent the performance of a value proposition. Add a scale from low to high or from 0 to 10. Plot how your value proposition performs on each factor of competition on the x-axis (i.e., the pain relievers and gain creators you chose).

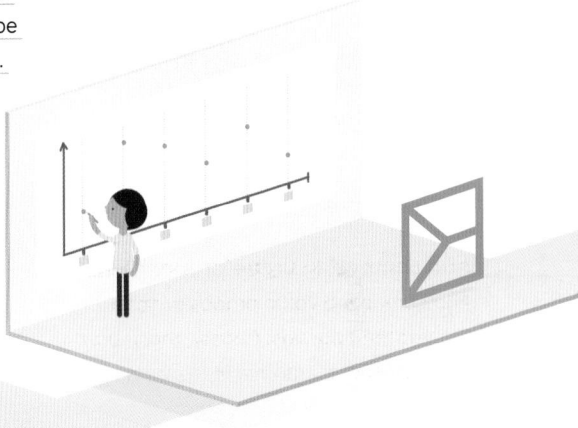

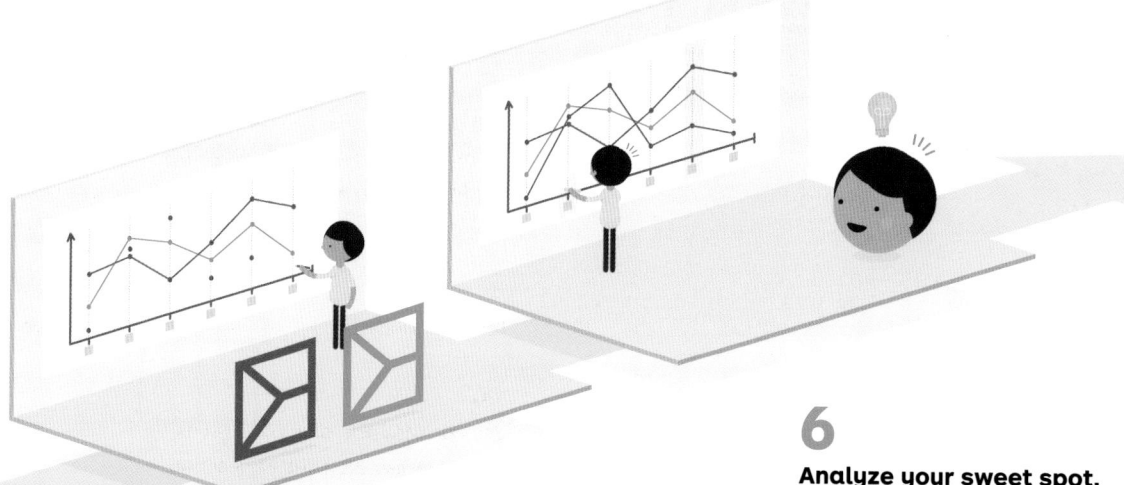

6

Analyze your sweet spot.

Analyze the curves and uncover opportunities. Ask yourself if and how you are differentiating from competitors with your value proposition.

Tip

Make sure the factors of competition that you compare align with the top jobs, pains, and gains in the customer profile. Normally that should be the case, because pain relievers and gain creators are designed to match relevant jobs, pains, and gains.

5

Score competing value propositions.

Plot how competing value propositions perform, just as you did for your own.

Tip

Use this tool to compare the performance of alternative value propositions you might be considering.

4

Add competing value propositions.

Add competing value propositions to the Strategy Canvas. Choose those that are most representative of the competition out there. Add pain relievers and gain creators from their value proposition to the factors of competition on the x-axis if necessary.

Tip

Consider competing value propositions beyond traditional industry boundaries. Don't just compare value propositions based on products and services that are similar to yours.

Avoid Cognitive Murder to Get Better Feedback

Present your value proposition to others to gather feedback, get buy-in, and complement the more "analytical assessment" that we looked at up to this point and the experiments we will study in the testing chapter.

Make sure you get the best from presenting your ideas by explaining them with disarming simplicity and coherence. It would be a waste of time and resources to put all your energy into designing remarkable value propositions only to fail to present them in a convincing way when it matters.

Presenting your ideas and canvases in a clear and tangible way is critical throughout the design process. Present early and rough prototypes before refining to get buy-in from different stakeholders. Only work on more refined presentations later in the design process.

One of the most important aspects of presenting value propositions is to convey messages with customer jobs, pains, and gains in mind. Never just pitch features; instead, think about how your value proposition helps get important jobs done, kills extreme pains, and creates essential gains.

Use low-fidelity prototypes to make your ideas tangible.

Always refer back to customer jobs, pains, and gains in your presentation.

Best Practices for Presenters

√ DOS	× DON'TS
Simple	Complex
Tangible	Abstract
Presenting only what matters	Presenting all you know
Customer-centric	Feature-centric
1 piece of info after the other	All information at once
The right media support	No visual support
Storyline	Random flow of information

1. Start with an empty canvas. Make sure listeners were given at least a short introduction to the canvas.

2. Begin your presentation wherever it makes most sense. You can start with products or with jobs.

3. Put up one sticky note after the other progressively to explain your value proposition so your audience doesn't experience cognitive murder. Synchronize what you say and what you put up. Tell a story of value creation by connecting products and services with customer jobs, pains, and gains.

Canvases to be implemented

High-fidelity prototypes

Testing data

Customer interviews and videos

Tested Canvases

Untested Canvases

Low-fidelity prototypes (e.g., product box)

Napkin sketches

What to present and when

Present different types of prototypes depending on how far you are into the design and testing process.

Master the Art of Critique

Practice the art of feedback to help ideas evolve rather than stall. This goes for feedback receivers who present ideas, as well as for feedback providers who give input on ideas.

Learn from the design professions, where people are trained to present ideas early and feedback providers are trained to provide effective design critiques. This contrasts with feedback providers in business who are often leaders in steering boards or advisory committees. They are trained to decide rather than to give feedback. If they cannot get to decisions fast, they often get nervous or become unsatisfied.

Teach feedback providers how to help ideas evolve (rather than to decide on them). Get them to understand that value proposition prototypes are still rough and evolving during the design and testing phase. Prototypes may radically change, in particular based on market facts that matter more than the opinion of feedback providers.

Teach feedback receivers that feedback providers are not as important as customers, however powerful they might be. Listening to feedback providers more than to customers and market facts only postpones failure.

(꙰) *Get "Master the Art of Critique" poster*

In a great feedback culture...

People feel comfortable presenting (bold) new ideas early, knowing that they will evolve substantially, maybe into something very different.

Present early.

Distinguish between Three Types of Feedback

		+	−
OPINION	*"If we added ____ I believe we'd have a better chance to make it work."*	Logical reasoning can help improve ideas.	It can lead to pursuing pet ideas of people with more power.
EXPERIENCE	*"When we did ____ in our last project, we learned that..."*	Past experiences provide valuable learning that can help prevent costly mistakes.	Failing to realize that different contexts lead to different results.
(MARKET) FACTS	*"We interviewed people about this and learned that ____ percent struggled with..."*	This provides input that reduces uncertainty and (market) risk.	Measuring the wrong data or simply bad data can lead to missing out on a big opportunity.

Don't judge.   **Listen.**   **Evolve ideas.**

Leaders and decision makers are trained to give feedback on early ideas to help them evolve. They know their opinion can be trumped by market facts and they're comfortable with that.

Don't ✗	Shoot people down for presenting new (bold) ideas.	Present only refined ideas to leadership and decision makers.	Have long, unstructured, free-flowing, time-consuming discussions.	Allow for proliferation of pure opinion.	Create a context that enables politics and personal agendas to supersede value creation.	Create negative vibes that destroy positive creative energy.	Foster culture in which feedback destroys big ideas because they're hard to implement.	Just ask "why?"
Do ✓	Create a safe environment in which people feel comfortable to present (bold) ideas.	Foster a culture of early feedback on rapidly evolving ideas.	Run facilitated, structured feedback processes.	Provide feedback based on experience or (market) facts.	Encourage a customer-centered feedback culture that neutralizes politics.	Bring in fun and productive feedback processes.	Draw a distinction between hard to do and worth doing.	Ask, "Why not?" "What if?" and "What else?"

Collect Efficient Feedback with de Bono's Thinking Hats

Collect feedback on ideas, value propositions, and business models using Edward de Bono's thinking hats. This method is very effective—especially in large groups—and helps you avoid losing time in endless discussions.

OBJECTIVE
Collect feedback effectively and avoid lengthy discussions

OUTCOME
Understanding of what's good or bad about ideas and how they can be improved

Workshop participants put on a metaphorical colored hat that symbolizes a certain type of thinking. This technique allows you to quickly collect different types of feedback and avoid having an idea shot down for purely political reasons. Use four of de Bono's six thinking hats to gather feedback.

1
Pitch
3–15 min depending on stage of idea
The design team presents their idea and value proposition and/or Business Model Canvas.

2
White hat
Information and data; neutral and objective
2–5 min depending on stage of idea
"Audience" members ask clarifying questions to fully understand the idea.

3a
Black hat
Difficulties, weaknesses, dangers; spotting the risks
1 min to write down
Participants write down why it's a bad idea on a sticky note.

3b
3 min to collect feedback
The facilitator rapidly collects one feedback after the other on a flip chart, while participants read it out loud.

Tips

- This exercise requires strong facilitation skills. Make sure people don't voice opinions when it's time for the white hat to ask clarifying questions.
- Make sure that regardless of whether people hate or love an idea, everybody puts on all hats, white, black, yellow, and green.
- Use the black hat before the yellow hat to neutralize extremely negative people. Once they voiced their feedback, they might even think positively.
- De Bono's Thinking Hats also works well in small groups or individually to help people come up with all the reasons why an idea might fail or succeed.

4a
Yellow hat
Positives, plus points; why an idea is useful

1 min to write down
Participants write down why it's a good idea on a sticky note.

4b

3 min to collect feedback
The facilitator rapidly collects one feedback after the other on a flip chart, while participants read it out loud.

5
Green hat
Ideas, alternative, possibilities; solutions to black hat problems

5–15 min of open discussion
The floor is opened to discussion. Participants bring in suggestions regarding how to evolve the ideas that were presented.

6
Evolve
The presenting team evolves their idea equipped with the white, black, yellow, and green hat feedback.

Edward de Bono, Six Thinking Hats, 1985.

Vote Visually with Dotmocracy

OBJECTIVE
Visualize the preferences of a group and avoid lengthy discussions

OUTCOME
Quick selection of ideas

Use Dotmocracy to quickly visualize the preferences of a group, in particular in large workshop settings. This is a simple and speedy technique to prioritize among different value propositions and business model options. It helps to prevent lengthy discussions.

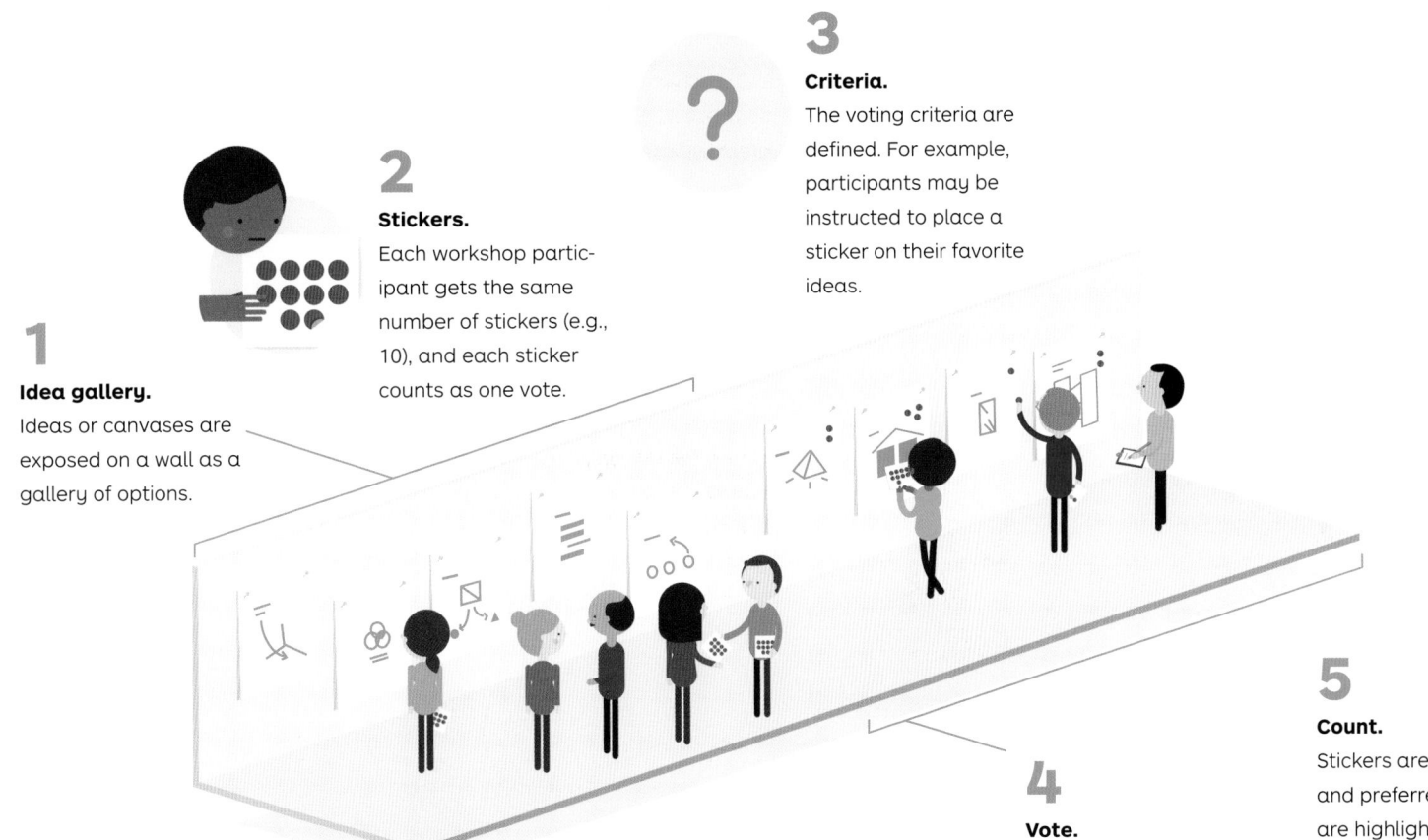

1
Idea gallery.
Ideas or canvases are exposed on a wall as a gallery of options.

2
Stickers.
Each workshop participant gets the same number of stickers (e.g., 10), and each sticker counts as one vote.

3
Criteria.
The voting criteria are defined. For example, participants may be instructed to place a sticker on their favorite ideas.

4
Vote.
Participants can put all their stickers on one idea or distribute them across several ideas.

5
Count.
Stickers are counted, and preferred ideas are highlighted.

Value Propositions

IDEAS	GROWTH	RISK
• Free		
• Partnership with Supplier		
• Emerging Markets Push		
Sustainability Focused		

Multicriteria

Use a table when you want to use several criteria to select among alternative value propositions and business models.

Dotmocracy is used to select ideas based on internal criteria, such as growth potential, risk, and differentiation potential. Apply this technique during the design process to choose among several alternatives before you test them in the real world.

Define Criteria and Select Prototypes

OBJECTIVE
Select among a range of alternatives

OUTCOME
Ranking of prototypes

Decide which criteria are most important to you and your organization and select value propositions and business models accordingly during the design process. You need to prioritize among (hopefully attractive) alternatives, even if your customer is the final judge of your ideas later on in the process.

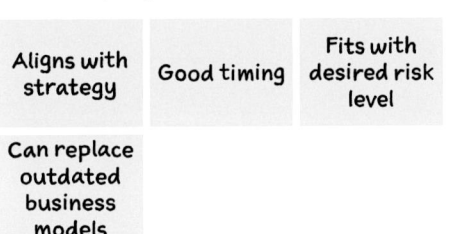

1

Brainstorm criteria.
Come up with as many criteria as you can to assess the attractive-ness of your prototypes.

Use the following themes and criteria as an input for your own selection criteria.

Fit with Strategy
How the idea fits with the overall direction of the company

Aligns with strategy	Good timing	Fits with desired risk level
Can replace outdated business models		

Fit with Customer Insights
How the idea relates to the first customer insights gained during first market research

Important job	No good solution exists	Visible and tangible pain
Strong customer evidence		

Competition and Environment
How the idea allows the company to position itself related to the competition

Provides competitive advantage	Fits with tech and other trends	Allows differentia-tion

Relation to Current Business Model
How the idea builds or doesn't build on the current business model

Fit with brand	Fits current business model	Builds on strengths	Plugs weaknesses
Disrupts current cash cows			

Financials and Growth
What potential each idea has related to growth and financials

Market size	Revenue potential	Market growth	Margins

Implementation Criteria
How difficult it is to implement the idea from design to market

Time to market	Cost to build	Do we have right team and skills	Access to target customers
Technology risk	Implementa-tion risk	Risk of management resistance	

2
Select criteria.
Select the criteria that are most important for your team and organization.

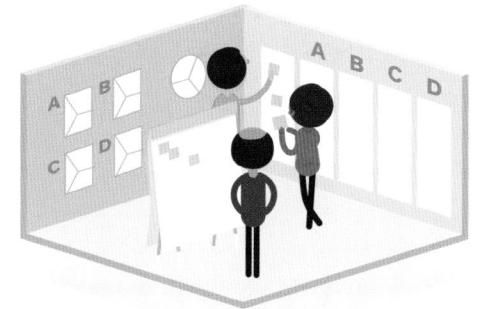

Criteria	Prototype A: **36**	Prototype B: **32**	Prototype C: **12**	Prototype D: **42**
Allows differentiation				
Builds on strengths				
Market growth				

3
Score prototypes (0 [low] – 10 [high]).
Score each idea on the criteria you chose.

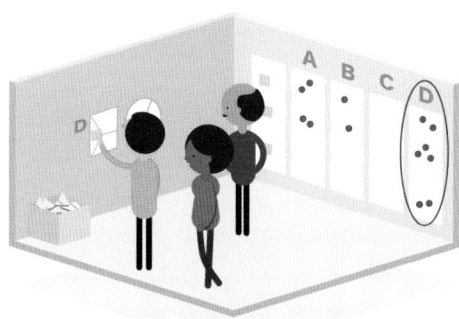

4
Evolve prototype and explore with market.
Evolve your prototype (e.g., based on the scores it got), and test it in the market to learn if it really has potential.

2.5

Finding the Right Business Model

Create Value for
Your Customer
and Your Business

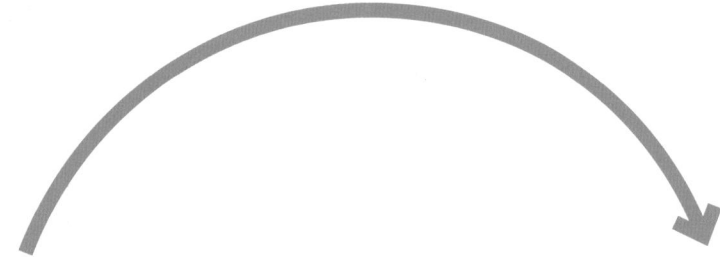

To create value for your business, you need to create value for your customer.

To sustainably create value for your customer, you need to create value for your business.

A business that generates fewer revenues than it incurs costs will inevitably disappear, even with the most successful value proposition. This section shows how getting both the business model and the value proposition right is a process of back and forth until you nail it.

Are you creating value for your business?

The Business Model Canvas makes explicit how you are creating and capturing value for your business.

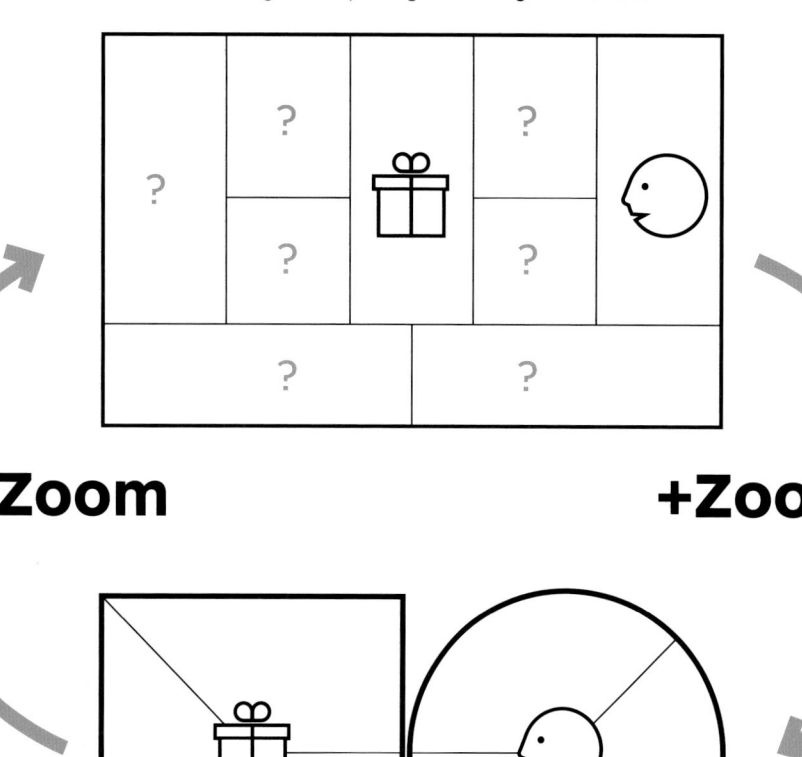

-Zoom

+Zoom

Zoom out to the bigger picture to analyze if you can profitably create, deliver, and capture value around this particular customer value proposition.

Zoom in to the detailed picture to investigate if the customer value proposition in your business model really creates value for your customer.

Are you creating value for your customer?

The Value Proposition Canvas makes explicit how you are creating value for your customers.

Azuri (Eight19): Turning a Solar Technology into a Viable Business

1

Initial idea

An opportunity.

Developing low-cost solar technology and providing low-income people with access to electricity.

1.6 billion people in the world still live without electricity. Could innovative value propositions and business models around new technology offer answers?

Simon Bransfield-Garth founded Eight19 based on a printed plastic technology originating from Cambridge University. The technology is designed to deliver low-cost solar cells. In 2012 Eight19 launched Azuri to commercialize the technology and bring electricity to off-grid customers in rural emerging markets.

Finding the right value propositions and business models in such a context is not easy. We illustrate how it is a continuous back and forth between both on the following pages.

Azuri Business Model: version 0

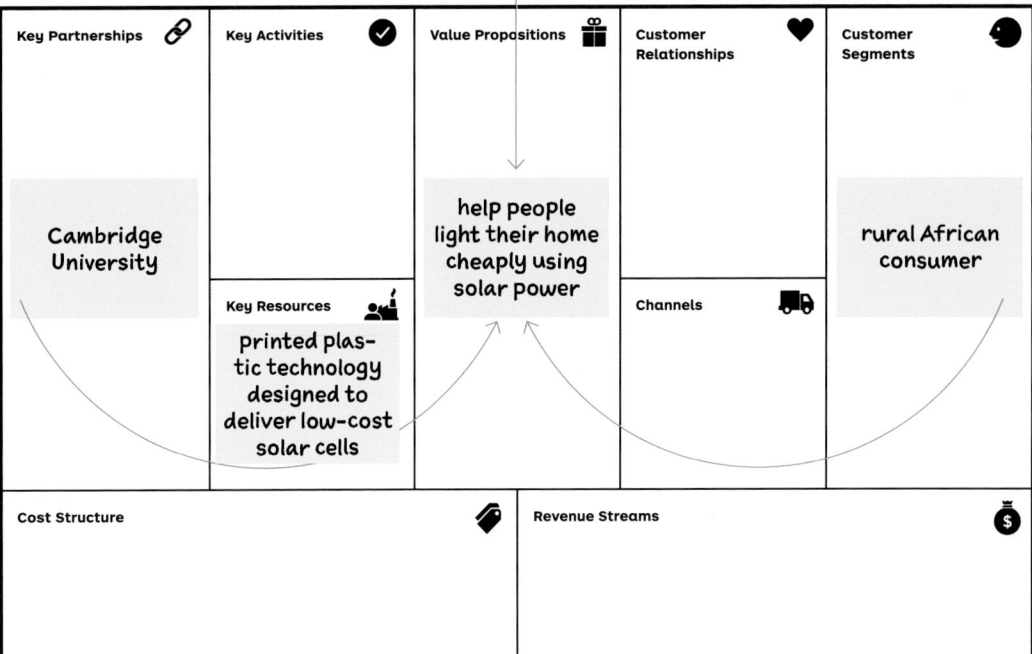

Key Partnerships	Key Activities	Value Propositions	Customer Relationships	Customer Segments
Cambridge University		help people light their home cheaply using solar power		rural African consumer
	Key Resources printed plastic technology designed to deliver low-cost solar cells		Channels	

Cost Structure	Revenue Streams

Case adopted in accordance with Azuri.

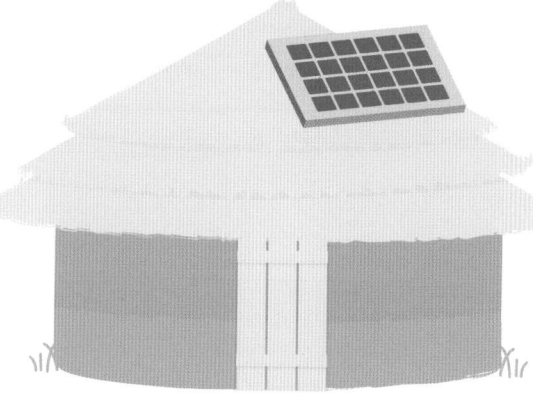

Zoom in

$70

2

Observe

The Cost Barrier.

"A rural farmer on $3 per day struggles to afford a $70 solar power system."

FREE

3

Design

What If?

Give the solar installations away for free to eliminate the hurdle of upfront investment.

Azuri Value Proposition: version 0

Rural African consumer

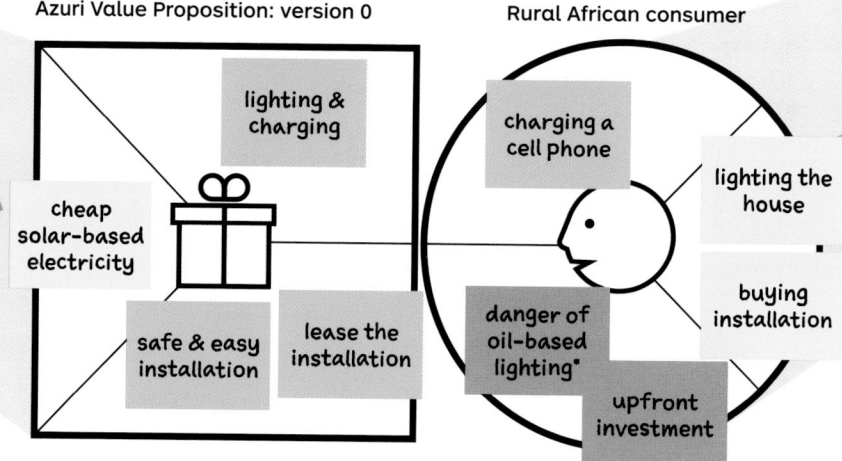

An alternative for lighting is burning oil, which is dangerous and expensive.

4

Iteration 2

**Idea for
Business Model.**

Lease the solar instal-
lations and collect
regular subscription fees;
it works just fine with
conventional panels; get
resources and partner-
ships for financing the
installations.

Zoom out

Azuri Business Model: version 1

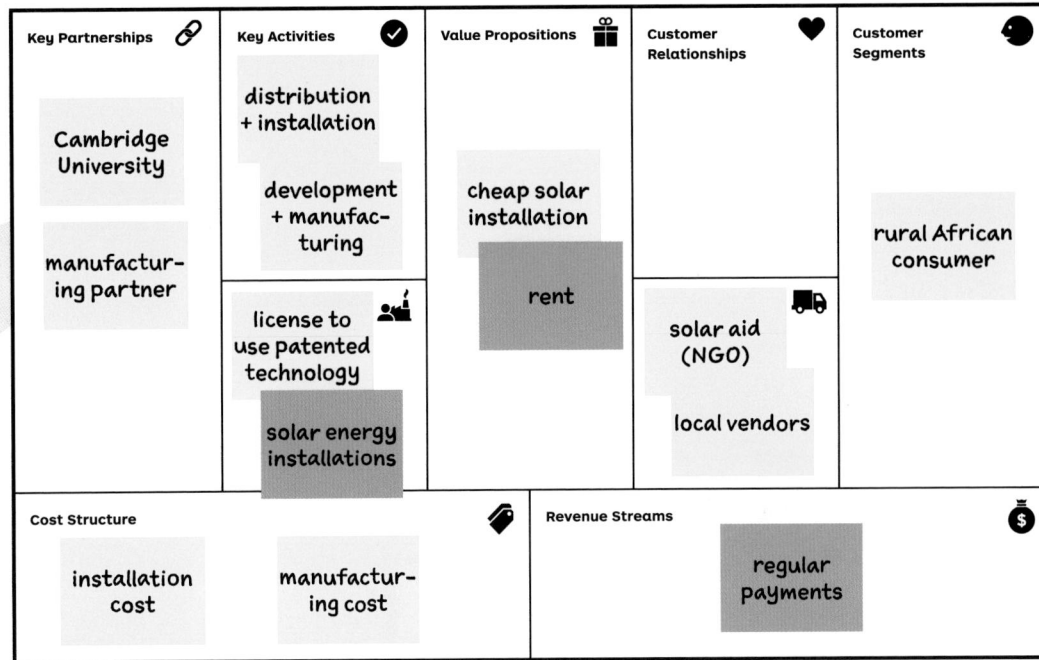

091-6135-926208

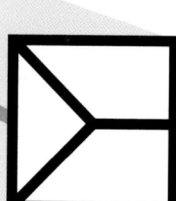

Zoom in

5

Observe

The no-banking barrier.

How can regular payments be recovered without any efficient banking system?

6

Design

Low-tech solution.

Combine mobile phone and solar technology with scratch cards to access electricity over a period of time.

Azuri Value Proposition: version 1

Rural African consumer

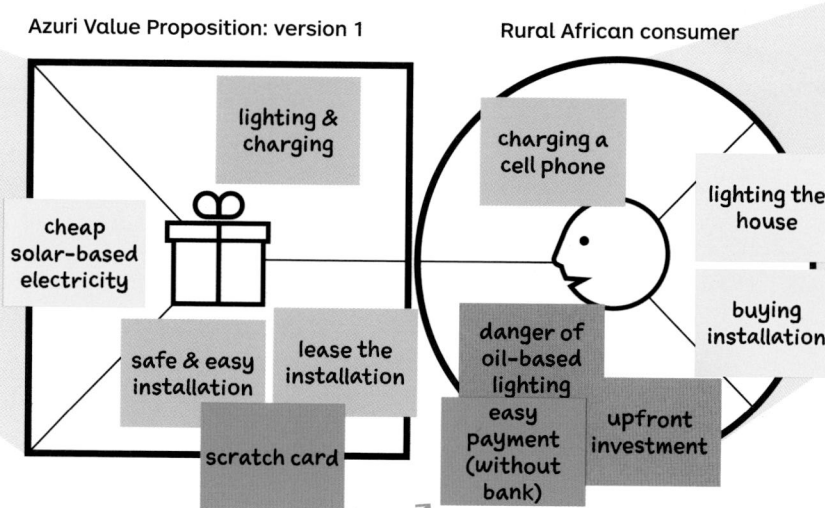

cheap solar-based electricity

lighting & charging

safe & easy installation

lease the installation

scratch card

charging a cell phone

lighting the house

buying installation

danger of oil-based lighting

easy payment (without bank)

upfront investment

7

Iteration 3

Idea for the Azuri Business Model.

150

Azuri provides solar-as-a-service, with *Indigo*, a pay-as-you-go lighting and charging system for which customers purchase weekly scratch cards: adapt the revenue model accordingly.

Zoom out

Azuri Business Model: version 2

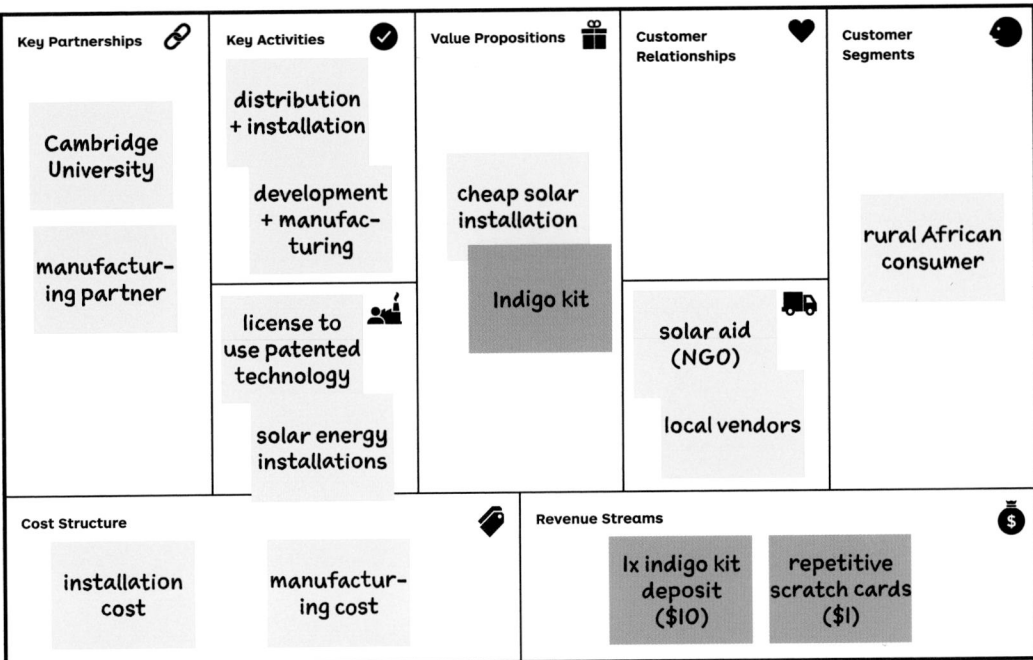

Key Partnerships 🔗	Key Activities ✓	Value Propositions 🎁	Customer Relationships ♥	Customer Segments
Cambridge University manufacturing partner	distribution + installation development + manufacturing license to use patented technology solar energy installations	cheap solar installation Indigo kit	solar aid (NGO) local vendors	rural African consumer

Cost Structure 🏷	Revenue Streams 💲
installation cost manufacturing cost	1x indigo kit deposit ($10) repetitive scratch cards ($1)

Affordable scratch cards make it possible to slowly cover the installation fees.

So...

How does the *Indigo* value proposition
look for a customer?

$10

$1

free

upgrade

Time

**Buy the Indigo kit
(solar panel, lamps, charger).**

**Buy scratch cards, use SMS
from a mobile phone, enter
the resulting passcode into
the *Indigo* unit, and use the
installation for a period of
time (typically a week).**

**Own your box after 80 scratch
cards, or...**

**Escalate to a larger system
and access more energy;
continue to buy scratch cards.**

From Value Proposition to Business Model...

OBJECTIVE
Practice the connection between value proposition and business model with no risk

OUTCOME
Improved skills

◁ From p. 96

A1

Front Stage.

Prototype a revenue model, select distribution channels, and define the relationships that could be adopted with customers.

The Business Model Canvas

Key Partnerships 🔗	Key Activities ✓	Value Propositions 🎁	Customer Relationships ♥	Customer Segments ●
	Key Resources 🏭	Your idea from page 96	Channels 🚚	Your Idea from page 96
Cost Structure 🏷			Revenue Streams 💰	

?

?

ⓒ Strategyzer

Part A

Design the Full Business Model.
On page 96 you imagined a value proposition to commercialize an innovative compressed air energy storage technology. Now map out the remaining business model elements and sketch out the rough numbers (part A).

A2

Backstage.

Add the Key Resources, Key Activities, and Partners required for the model to work and use that to estimate the cost structure.

A3

Assessment.

Assess your prototype and detect possible weaknesses of the business model ➔ p. 156.

...and Back Again

Part B

Revisiting the Value Proposition
Assess the weaknesses of your first full business model prototype (from part A). Ask yourself how you could improve or change your initial value proposition, maybe by shifting to an entirely different segment by considering the following five questions:

Tip
Follow up on your new customer assumptions by researching customers ➔ p. 106 and producing evidence ➔ p. 216.

Zoom in

B1
New VP?
Could there be another radically different value proposition for the same technology?

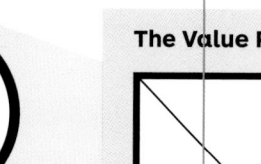

B2
New segment?
Will you keep the same customer segment, or will you shift to an entirely different, maybe larger, market segment?

B4
Change or clear your benefits?
Do you need to change or clear the benefits your value proposition created because the customer profile changed?

B5
Got fit?
Do you have fit between your new customer profile and the newly designed value proposition?
➔ p. 40 on fit

B3
Refine or clear your profile?
Could you refine your customer profile, or do you need to describe an entirely new one because you switched customer segments?

◀ *Repeat Step A if required.*

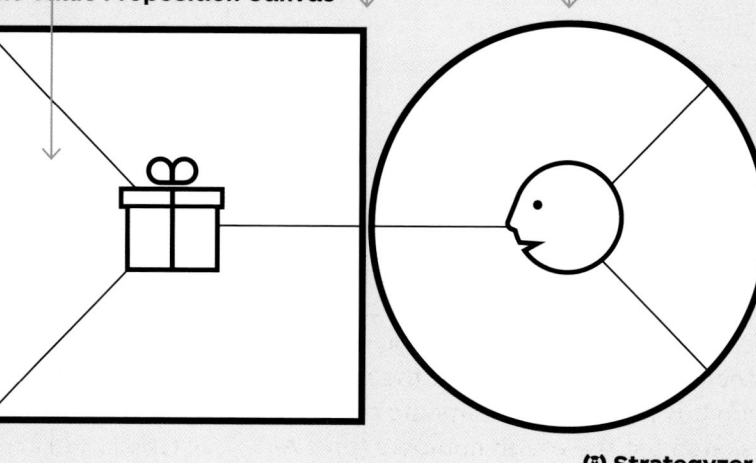

The Value Proposition Canvas

🐦 **Strategyzer**

Stress Testing with Numbers: A MedTech Illustration

A great value proposition without a financially sound business model is not going to get you very far. In the worst case you will fail because your business model incurs more costs than it produces revenues. But even business models that work can produce substantially different results.

Play with different business models and financial assumptions to find the best one. We illustrate this with the medical technology illustration on this spread. We sketched out two models both starting from the same technology that enables building a cheap diagnostic device.

Prototype 1 generates $5.5 million in revenues and a profit of $0.5 million. Prototype 2 starts from the same technology but produces more than $30 million in revenues and a profit of $23 million with a different value proposition and business model.

Only the market can judge if either model could work, but you certainly want to explore and test the best options.

Medtech Prototype 1

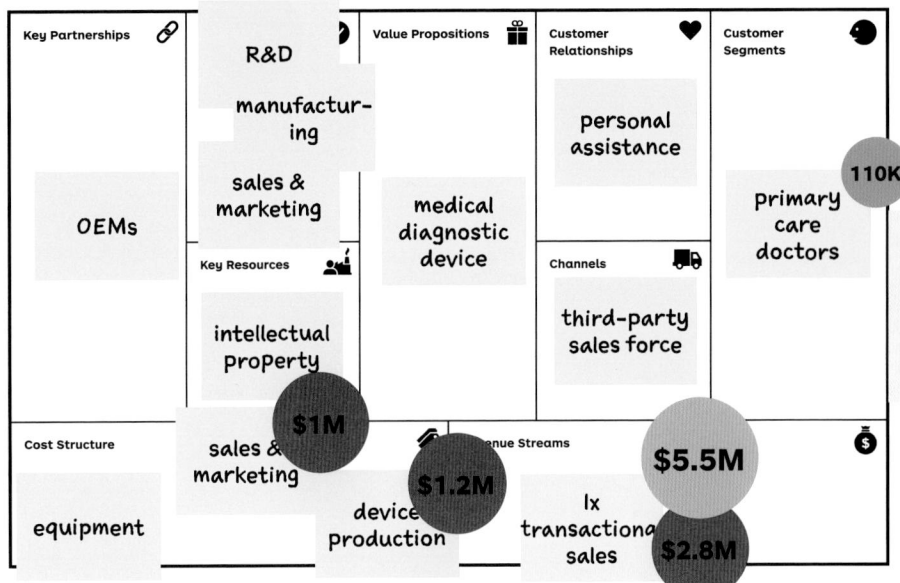

VS.

Medtech Prototype 2

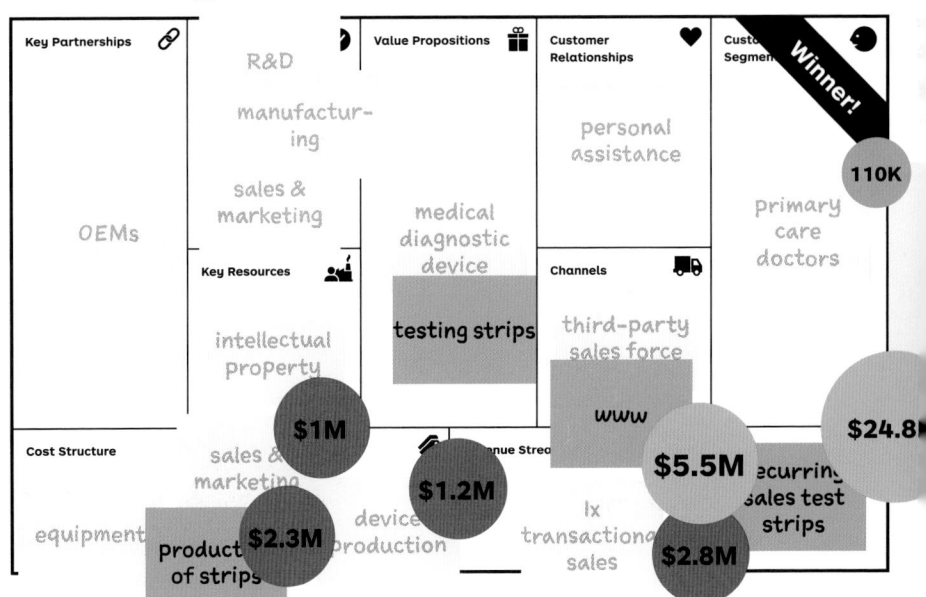

Model 1: Sales of Medical Diagnostic Device

- 1× transactional sales of device to primary care doctors in the United States for $1,000/device
- 5 percent market share
- Sales via third-party sales force -50 percent commission
- Variable production costs of $225/device
- Fixed marketing expenses of $1 million

Costs	Revenues
Device Production, 1.2M	Device Sales, 5.5M
Sale & Marketing, 1M	
Sales Commission, 2.8M	
Profit 0.5M	

Profit

A quick sketch of the numbers provides us with a sanity check that this model is not very profitable, so we should go back and explore changes to the business model.

$0.5M

Value Prop Model 1

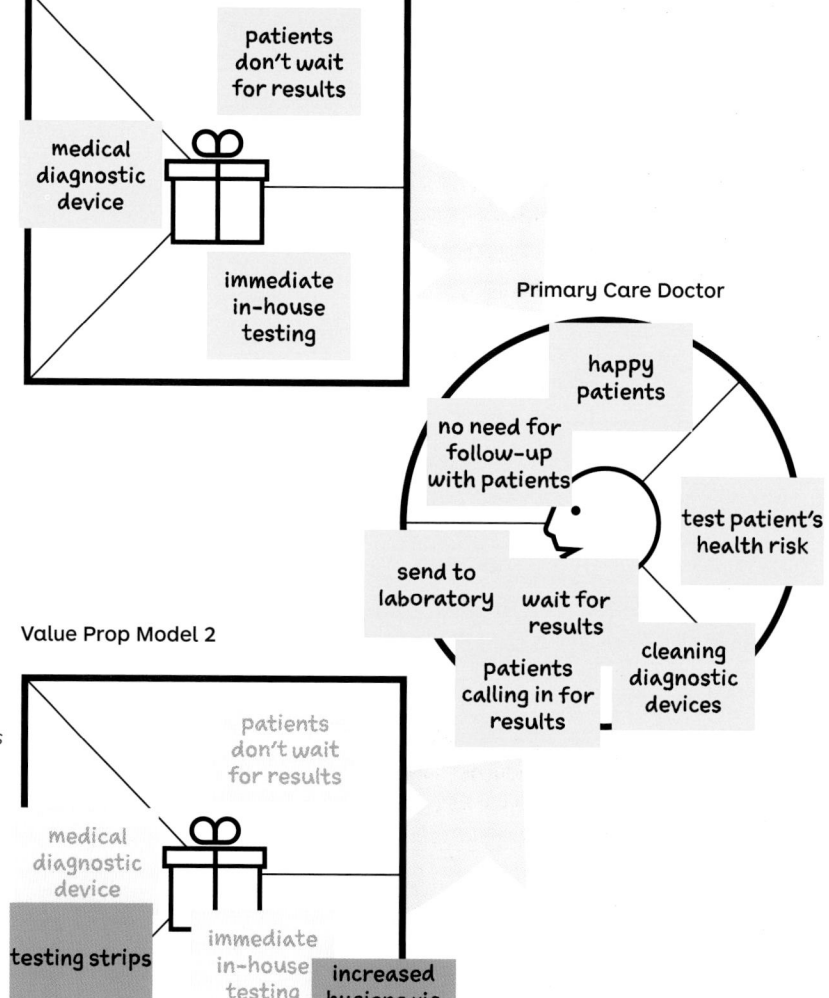

Primary Care Doctor

Model 2: Recurring Revenues from Consumable Testing Strips

- Each diagnosis requires a consumable testing strip
- Recurring revenues from selling an average of 5 strips/month/device for $75 each
- Variable production costs of testing strips of $7/strip

Costs	Revenues
Device Production, 1.2M	Device Sales, 5.5M
Sale & Marketing, 1M	Testing Strip Sales, 24.8M
Sales Commission, 2.8M	
Testing Strips Prod., 2.3M	
Profit, 23M	

Profit

The same technology with a different business model now yields a much larger potential profit. Although these numbers aren't validated, it's clearly the more interesting prototype to take to the testing stage.

$23M

Value Prop Model 2

Seven Questions to Assess Your Business Model Design

STRATEGYZER.COM / VPD / DESIGN / 2.5

OBJECTIVE
Unearth potential to improve your business model

OUTCOME
Business Model Assessment

Great value propositions should be embedded in great business models. Some are better than others by design and will produce better financial results, will be more difficult to copy, and will outperform competitors.

Score your business model design by answering these seven questions:

1. Switching Costs.
How easy or difficult is it for customers to switch to another company?

2. Recurring Revenues.
Is every sale a new effort or will it result in quasi-guaranteed follow-up revenues and purchases?

My customers are locked in for several years.

10
○
○
○
○
○
○
○
○
○
0

Nothing holds my customers back from leaving me.

100 percent of my sales lead to automatically recurring revenues.

10
○
○
○
○
○
○
○
○
○
0

100 percent of my sales are transactional.

Apple's iPod got people to copy their entire music library into the iTunes software, which made switching more difficult for customers.

Nespresso turned the transactional industry of selling coffee into one with recurring revenues by selling single-portioned pods that fitted only into their machines.

 Download "Seven Questions to Assess Your Business Model"

   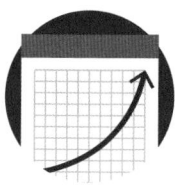 

3. Earnings vs. Spending.

Are you earning revenues before you are incurring costs?

4. Game-changing Cost Structure.

Is your cost structure substantially different and better than those of your competitors?

5. Others Who Do the Work.

How much does your business model get customers or third parties to create value for you for free?

6. Scalability.

How easily can you grow without facing roadblocks (e.g., infrastructure, customer support, hiring)?

7. Protection from Competition.

How much is your business model protecting you from your competition?

3. Earnings vs. Spending	4. Game-changing Cost Structure	5. Others Who Do the Work	6. Scalability	7. Protection from Competition
I earn 100 percent of my revenues before incurring costs of goods & services sold (COGs).	My cost structure is at least 30 percent lower than my competitors.	All the value created in my business model is created for free by external parties.	My business model has virtually no limits to growth.	My business model provides substantial moats that are hard to overcome.
10	10	10	10	10
○	○	○	○	○
○	○	○	○	○
○	○	○	○	○
○	○	○	○	○
○	○	○	○	○
○	○	○	○	○
○	○	○	○	○
○	○	○	○	○
○	○	○	○	○
○	○	○	○	○
0	0	0	0	0
I incur 100 percent of my costs of COGs before earning revenues.	My cost structure is at least 30 percent higher than my competitors.	I incur costs for all the value created in my business model.	Growing my business model requires substantial resources and effort.	My business model has no moats, and I'm vulnerable to competition.

Personal computers (PCs) used to be produced well ahead of selling them at the risk of inventory depreciation until Dell disrupted the industry, sold directly to consumers, and earned revenue before assembling PCs.

Skype and WhatsApp disrupted the telecom industry by using the Internet as a free infrastructure for calls and messages, while telecoms incurred heavy capital expenditures.

Most of the value in Facebook's business model comes from content produced for free by more than 1 billion users. Similarly, merchants and shoppers create value for free for credit card companies.

Licensing and franchising are extremely scalable, as are platforms like Facebook or WhatsApp that serve hundreds of millions of users with few employees. Credit card companies are also an interesting example of scalability.

Powerful business models are often hard to compete with. Ikea has found few imitators. Similarly, platform models like Apple with the App Store provide powerful moats.

2.6

Designing in Established Organizations

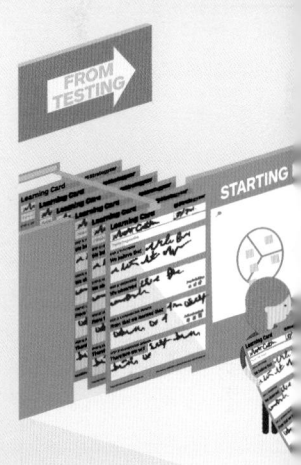

Adopt the Right Attitude to Invent or Improve

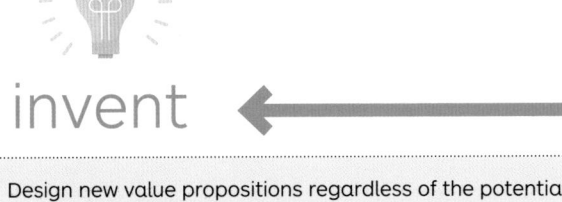

invent

Existing organizations need to improve existing value propositions and create new ones proactively. Make sure you understand on which end of the spectrum you are at the beginning of a particular project, because each requires a different attitude and process. Great companies will have a balanced portfolio of projects covering the entire spectrum from improve to invent.

Objective	Design new value propositions regardless of the potential constraints given by existing value propositions and business models (although leadership may define other constraints).
Helps With	• Proactive bet on the future • Take on a crisis • Emergence of a game-changing technology, regulation, etc. • Response to a disruptive value proposition of a competitor
Financial Goals	At least 50 percent annual revenue growth (caveat: company-specific)
Risk and Uncertainty	High
Customer Knowledge	Low, potentially nonexistent
Business Model	Requires radical adaptions or changes
Attitude to Failure	Part of learning and iteration process
Mind-set	Open to exploring new possibilities
Design Approach	Radical/disruptive change to value proposition (and business model)
Main Activities	Search, test, and evaluate
Examples	*Amazon Web Services* Design of a new IT infrastructure value proposition targeted at a new customer segment. Builds on existing key resources and activities but requires a substantial expansion of Amazon.com's business model.

improve

Improve your existing value proposition(s) without radically changing or affecting the underlying business model(s).

- Renew outdated products and services.
- Ensure or maintain fit.
- Improve profit potential or cost structure.
- Keep growth going.
- Address customer complaints.

0 to15 percent annual revenue increase or more (caveat: company-specific)

Low

High

Little change

Not an option

Focused on making one or several aspects better

Incremental change and tweaks to existing value proposition

Refine, plan, and execute

Amazon Prime

Introduce a membership with special benefits targeted at frequent users of Amazon.com.

In between: Extend

A common situation in the Improve-Invent spectrum is the need to find new growth engines without investing in substantial changes to the existing business model. This is often required to monetize investments in existing models and platforms.

The objective is to search for new value propositions that substantially extend the existing underlying business model, without modifying too many aspects of it.

For example, with the introduction of the Kindle, Amazon created a new channel to extend its digital offering to Amazon.com customers. Although this presents a great new value proposition to its customers, it remains to a large extent within the parameters of its successfully established and well-mastered e-commerce business model.

Tip

Great companies manage a portfolio of value propositions and business models that cover the entire invent-improve spectrum and make synergies and competitive conflicts explicit. They are proactive and invent while they are still successful, rather than wait for a crisis.

The Business Book of the Future

Imagine if you were a business book publisher. How could you improve your present offering and invent the business book of the future, which might not even be a book anymore? We sketched out three ideas along the invent-improve spectrum.

invent

The YouTube of business education

An online platform matching videos from business experts with customers who are looking for answers to their problems. This would require a substantial extension or reinvention of the business model of publishing books.

The 1-800-Business-Book hotline

A hotline number extending physical business books and offering on-demand answers. This would build on the existing business model but require an extension from a sales to a service model.

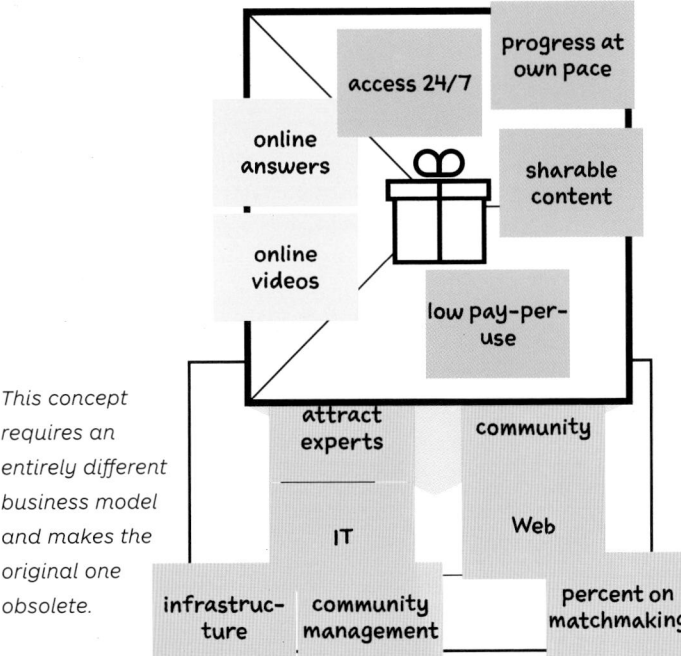

This concept requires an entirely different business model and makes the original one obsolete.

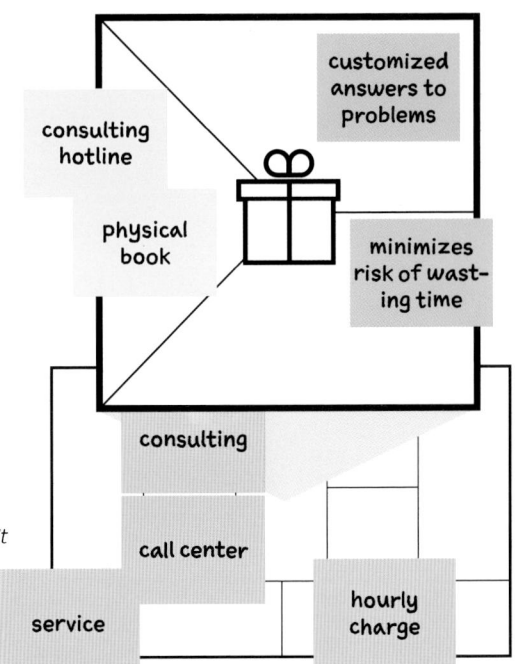

An additional service capability adds a layer to the business model but doesn't transform it.

improve

The practical business book

Improve business books by making them more visual and applicable without altering the core business model behind it substantially.

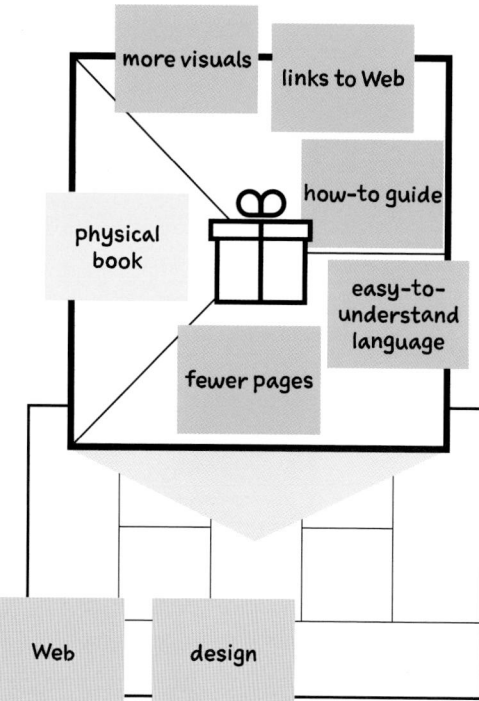

Improvements add to the value proposition and require only minor tweaks to the business model.

The more you move toward the invent end of the spectrum, the more your new value proposition will differ from your existing ones. Inventing new value propositions provides an opportunity to more closely address jobs that really matter to customers (in this case, getting answers to business questions).

Our three-tier value proposition consists of a physical book, sharable practical content online, and advanced learning through our online course. It is our attempt to push the boundaries of business learning and doing.

The value proposition of this book combined with online exercises and material on Strategyzer.com is our attempt to more closely address the jobs we believe matter to our readers.

Reinvent by Shifting from Products...

Construction equipment manufacturer Hilti reinvented its value proposition and business model by shifting from products to services. Its move from selling branded machine tools to guaranteeing timely access to them required a substantial overhaul not just of their value proposition but also of their business model. Let's learn how Hilti did it.

Many organizations aspire to regain a competitive advantage by transforming from a product manufacturer into a service provider. This requires a substantial reinvention.

An Expired Model

Hilti's old model focused mainly on selling high-quality machine tools directly to builders. They were known for breaking less often, lasting longer, and overall being less costly by minimizing time loss. Hilti tools also have a reputation for being particularly safe and enjoyable to work with.

Unfortunately, this old model was one of decreasing margins and subject to competition from lower-cost competitors.

Read more about Hilti in Johnson, Seizing the Whitespace, 2010.

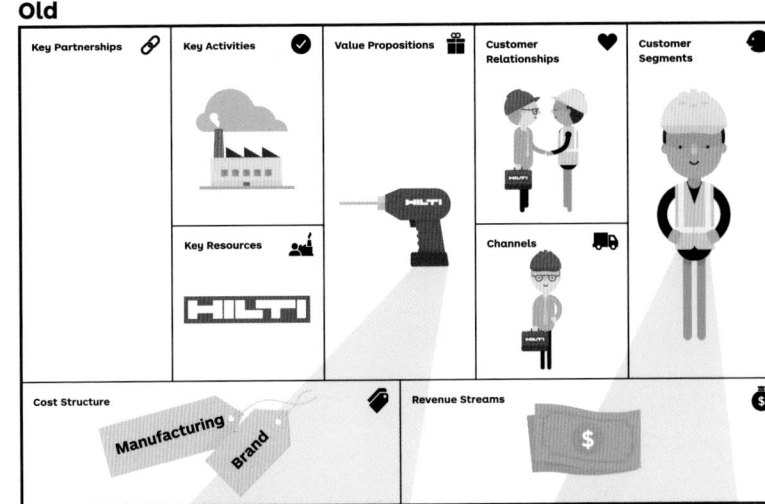

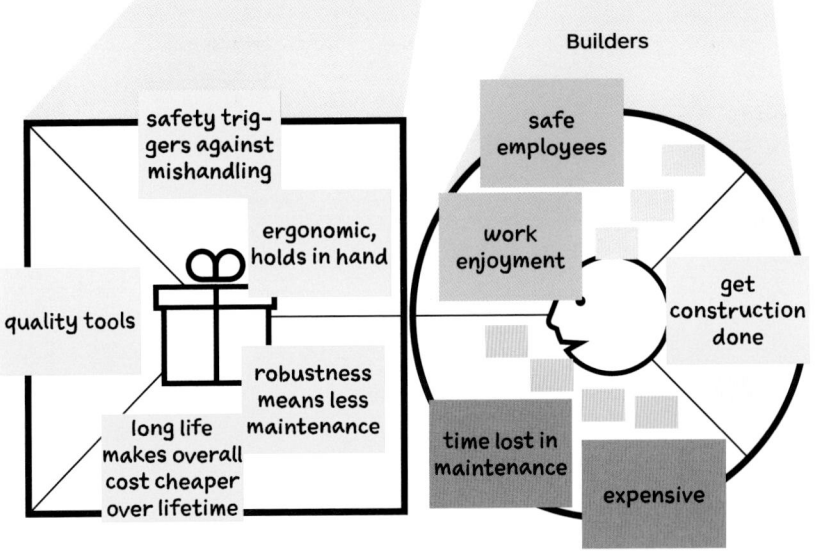

New

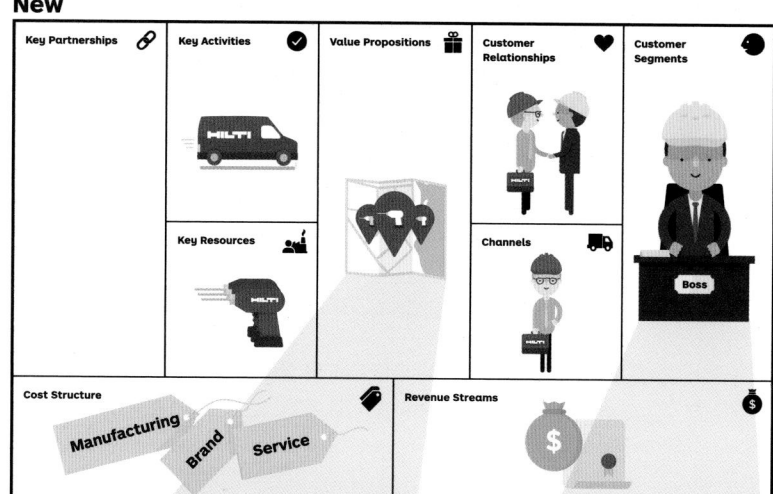

Key Partnerships 🔗	Key Activities ✓	Value Propositions 🎁	Customer Relationships ♥	Customer Segments 👁
				Boss
	Key Resources		Channels 🚚	

Cost Structure
Manufacturing · Brand · Service

Revenue Streams 💰
$

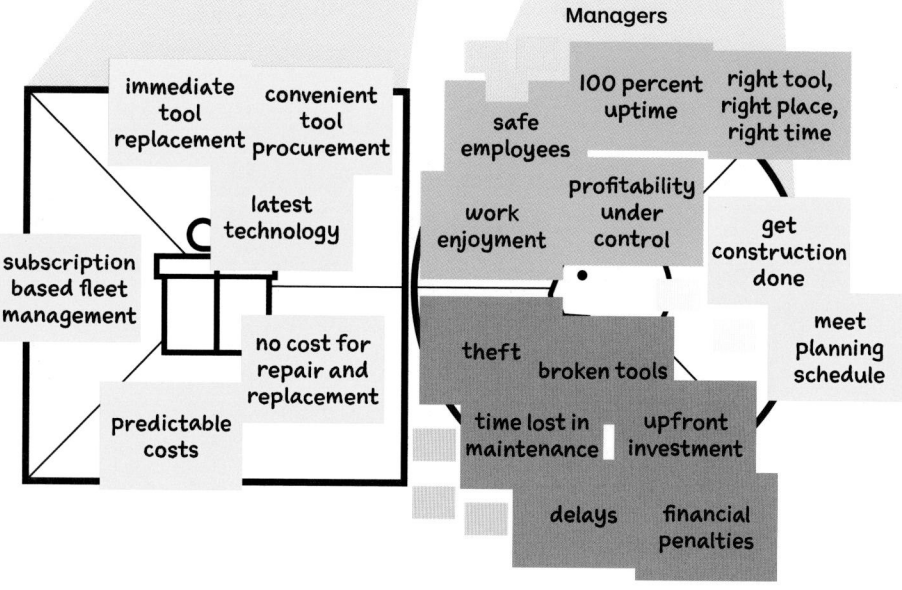

Managers

immediate tool replacement · convenient tool procurement

latest technology

subscription based fleet management

no cost for repair and replacement

predictable costs

safe employees

100 percent uptime · right tool, right place, right time

work enjoyment · profitability under control · get construction done

theft · broken tools · meet planning schedule

time lost in maintenance · upfront investment

delays · financial penalties

New service created: monthly subscriptions to fleet management utility

"New" customer, more important job identified: delivering on time!

...to Services

Hilti focused on a new job to be done after discovering that its tools were related to a more important customer job: that of delivering projects on time to avoid financial penalties. They learned that broken, malfunctioning, or stolen tools could lead to major delays and penalties. From there, Hilti moved toward a new value proposition, offering services around machine tools.

A Fresh Start

Hilti used its new service-based value proposition to create more value for construction companies by ensuring that they had the right tools at the right place at the right time. This would help construction companies achieve a much more predictable cost management and keep operations profitable.

Impact on the Business Model

Moving from products to services sounds like an easy and obvious value proposition shift, but it requires substantially reengineering the business model. Hilti had to add substantial new service resources and activities in addition to manufacturing. But it was worth it. With their new value proposition, Hilti achieves higher margins, recurring revenues, and better differentiation.

165

STRATEGYZER.COM / VPD / DESIGN / 2.6

The Perfect
Workshop Setting

Workshops are an important part of value proposition design in established organizations. Great workshops can make a big difference in the design process and lead to better results. The questions below will help you create the perfect setting.

Use thick markers so ideas are visible from afar.

Use wall-sized posters to sketch out big ideas.

Use sticky notes to move ideas around—ideally in several colors for color-coding.

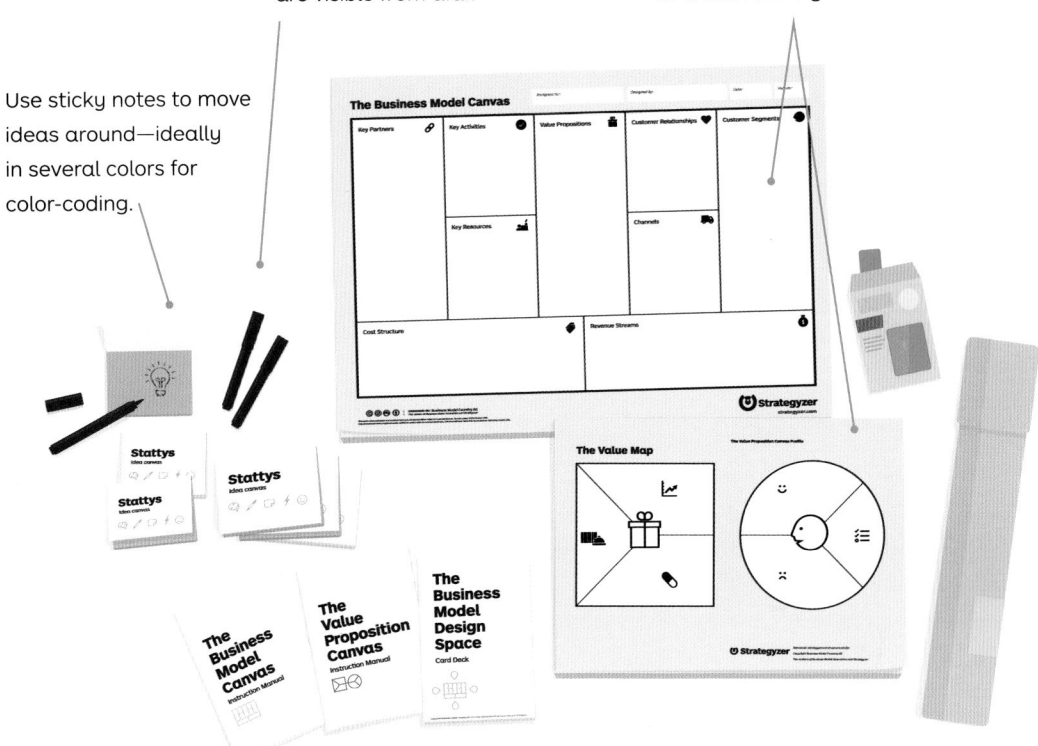

Who should join?

Invite people with different backgrounds, especially when you know there will be a substantial effect on the business model. Their buy-in is crucial. Get customer-facing staff to participate to leverage their knowledge. Customers or partners may also be a good addition to help evaluate value propositions.

What should the format be?

As a rule of thumb, more viewpoints are generally better than fewer at the early stages of value proposition design. With 10 participants or more, you can explore several alternatives in parallel by working in groups of five. Smaller teams need to explore alternatives sequentially. At the later stages of developing and refining value propositions, fewer participants are usually better.

How can space be used as an instrument?

Great workshop spaces are an often-overlooked instrument to create outstanding workshops with exceptional outcomes. Choose a space that is sufficiently large and offers large walls or working areas. Set up the space to support creation, collaboration, and productivity. For breakthrough results, choose an unusual and inspiring venue.

What tools and materials are needed?

Prepare a self-service area with canvas posters, sticky notes, paper, blue tack, markers, and other tools so participants can help themselves with what they need.

Check readily available workshop material

Work-in-Progress Gallery/Inspiration Wall

Set up an area where you can expose canvases and other work in progress. Add an "inspiration wall" with content that participants can draw from, such as reference models, examples, and models of competitors.

Projector and Screen

This is used to show slides or customer videos. It should be easily viewable by all.

Small Group Areas

This is where work gets done. Four or five people per group is best. Do not use chairs or tables unless required for specific work. Keep working groups in the same room rather than a break-out room to retain high energy levels throughout the workshop.

Room Control

This space should be set aside for the facilitator and team to access computer, sound system, Wi-Fi, and maybe a printer.

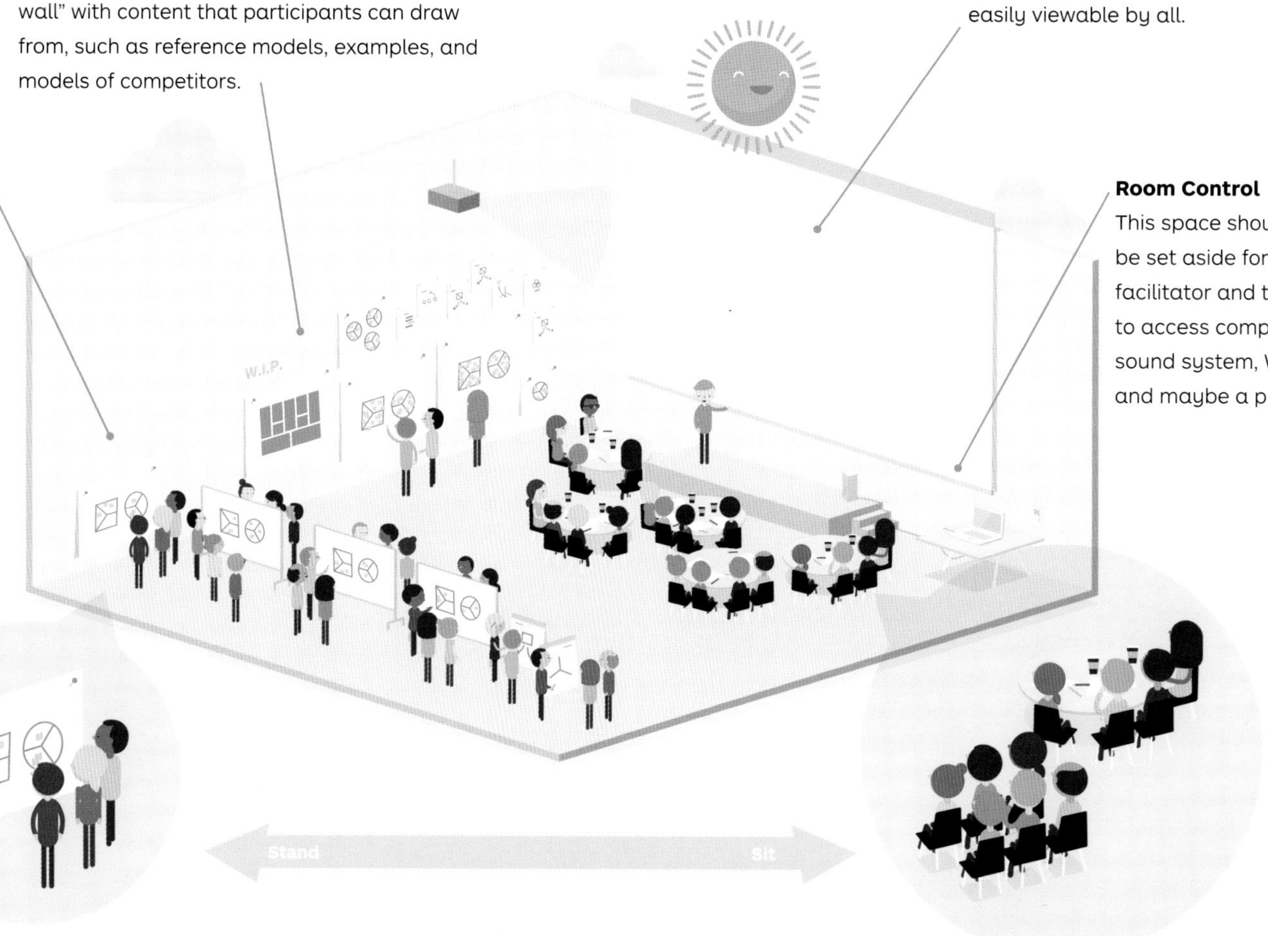

Walls

Large vertical surfaces are indispensable, whether movable or part of the building. Make sure you can stick large posters, sticky notes, and flip chart paper on them.

Venue Size, Look, and Feel

As a rule of thumb, calculate 50m² per 10 participants. Favor inspiring venues over boring hotel meeting rooms.

Plenary Space

Everyone can meet here for plenary presentations and discussions. It can be set up with or without tables.

Compose Your Workshop

A great workshop produces tangible and actionable outcomes. Use the tools and processes from this book to start designing a draft workshop outline that leads to great results.

Design Principles for a Great Workshop

- Create a workshop agenda with a clear thread that shows participants how the new or improved value proposition(s) or business model(s) will emerge.
- Take participants on a journey of many steps by focusing on one simple task (module) at a time.
- Avoid "blah blah blah" and favor structured interactions with tools like the canvases or processes like the thinking hats.
- Alternate between work in small groups (4–6 people) and plenary sessions for presentations and integration.
- Strictly manage time for each module, in particular for prototyping. Use a timer visible to all participants.
- Design the agenda as a series of iterations for the same value proposition (or business model). Design, critique, iterate, and pivot.
- Avoid slow activities after lunch.

Day 1

9 AM

10 AM

11 AM

12 PM

1 PM

2 PM

3 PM

4 PM

5 PM

Day 2

9 AM

10 AM

11 AM

12 PM

1 PM

2 PM

3 PM

4 PM

5 PM

Use the modules below as a menu of options to draft a workshop agenda.

Before Your Workshop

Do your homework and gather customer insights ⊕ p. 106.

After Your Workshop

Get going with testing your value propositions and business models in the real world ⊕ p. 172.

Get Online For:

- sample agendas
- templates and instructions
- all-in-one material package

Prototype Possibilities

Trigger Questions — ⊕ p. 15, 17, 31, 33

CS Mapping — ⊕ p. 22

VP Mapping — ⊕ p. 36

Napkin Sketches — ⊕ p. 80

Ad libs — ⊕ p. 82

Flesh out Ideas with VPC — ⊕ p. 84

Constraints — ⊕ p. 90

New Ideas with Books — ⊕ p. 92

Push / Pull Exercise — ⊕ p. 94

Six Ways to Innovate — ⊕ p. 102

Making Choices

Rank Jobs, Pains, and Gains — ⊕ p. 20

Check Your Fit — ⊕ p. 94

'Job' Selection — ⊕ p. 100

10 Questions — ⊕ p. 122

Voice of Customer — ⊕ p. 124

Assess against Environment — ⊕ p. 126

Differentiate from Competition — ⊕ p. 128

De Bono's Hats — ⊕ p. 136

Dotmocracy — ⊕ p. 138

Selecting Prototype — ⊕ p. 140

Back and Forth with Business Model

Back and Forth Iteration — ⊕ p. 152

Numbers Projections — ⊕ p. 154

7 BM Questions — ⊕ p. 156

Preparing Tests

Extracting Hypotheses — ⊕ p. 200

Prioritizing Hypotheses — ⊕ p. 202

Test Design — ⊕ p. 204

Choose a Mix of Experiments — ⊕ p. 216

Test Road Map — ⊕ p. 242–245

Breaks

Lunch

Coffee and snacks

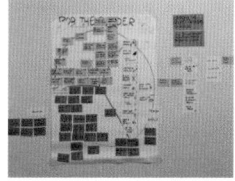

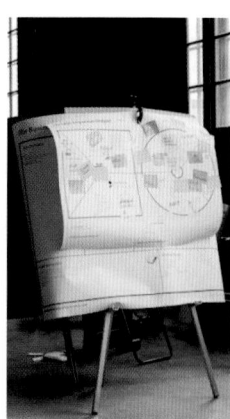

Lessons Learned

Prototyping Possibilities

Rapidly prototype alternative value propositions and business models. Don't fall in love with your first ideas. Keep your early models rough enough to throw away without regret so that they can evolve and improve.

Understanding Customers

Imagine, observe, and understand your customers. Put yourself in their shoes. Learn what they are trying to get done in their work and in their lives. Understand what prevents them from getting this done well. Unearth which outcomes they are looking for.

Finding the Right Business Model

Search for the right value proposition embedded in the right business model, because every product, service, and technology can have many different models. Even the best value propositions can fail without a sound business model. The right business model can be the difference between success and failure.

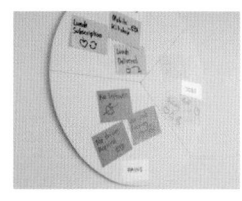

te

st

Reduce the risk and uncertainty of your ideas for new and improved value propositions by deciding **What to Test** p. 188. Then, get started with **Testing Step-by-Step** p. 196 and drawing from the **Experiment Library** p. 214 before **Bringing It All Together** p. 238 and measuring your progress.

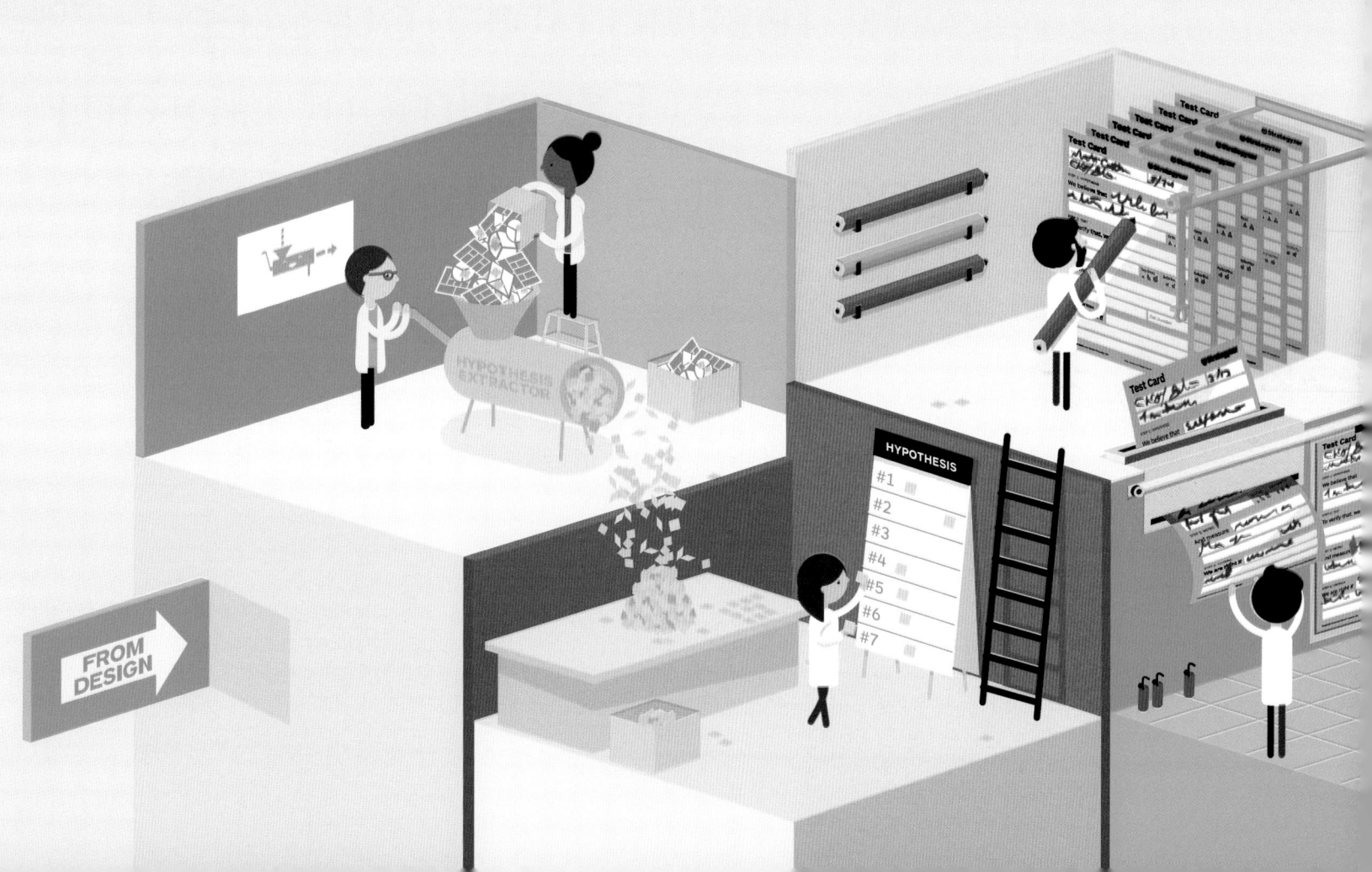

FROM DESIGN

HYPOTHESIS EXTRACTOR

HYPOTHESIS
#1
#2
#3
#4
#5
#6
#7

Test Card

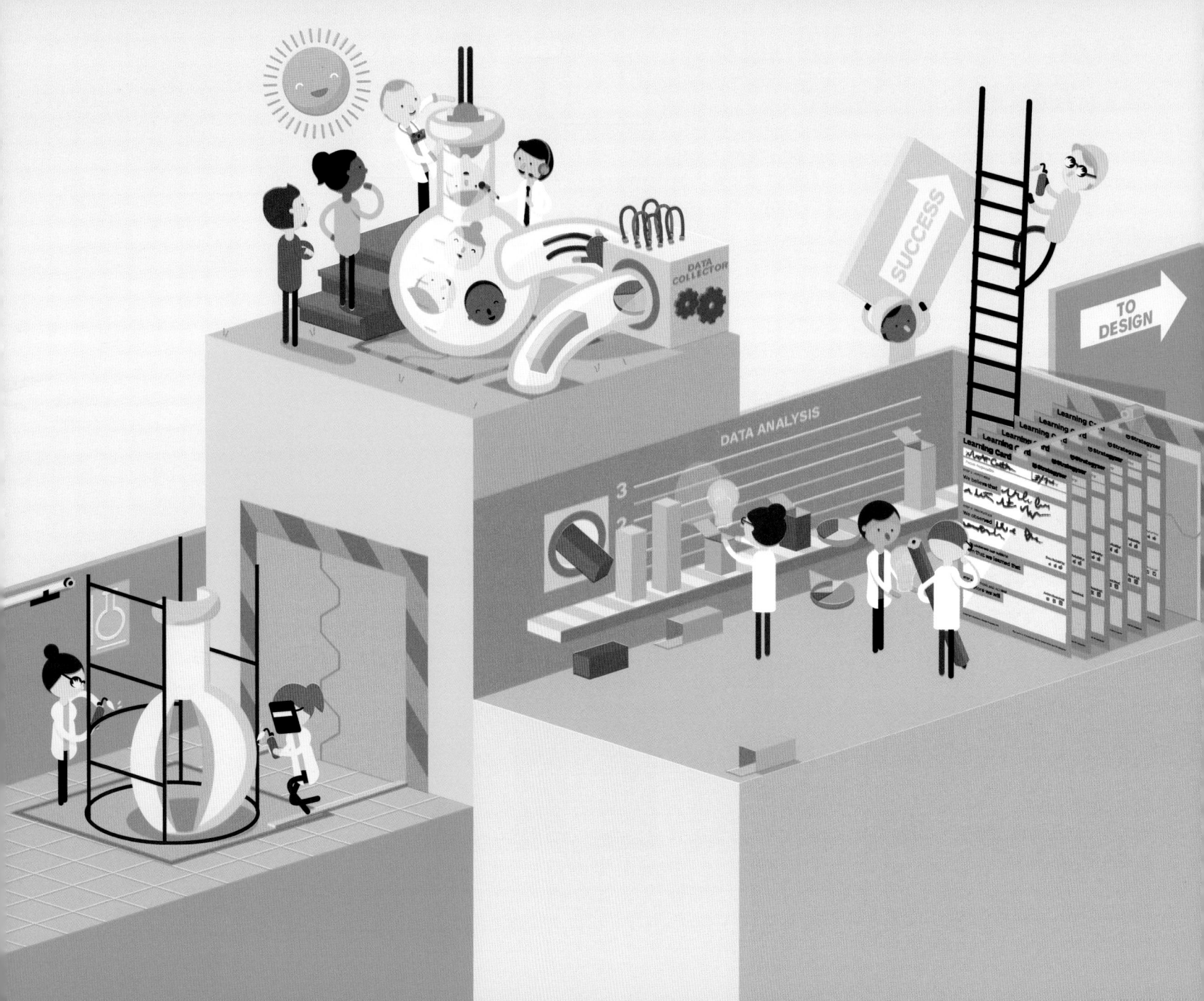

Start Experimenting to Reduce Risk

When you start exploring new ideas, you are usually in a space of maximum uncertainty. You don't know if your ideas will work. Refining them in a business plan won't make them more likely to succeed. You are better off testing your ideas with cheap experiments to learn and systematically reduce uncertainty. Then increase spending on experiments, proto-types, and pilots with growing certainty. Test all aspects of your Value Proposition and Business Model Canvases, all the way from customers to partners (e.g., channel partners).

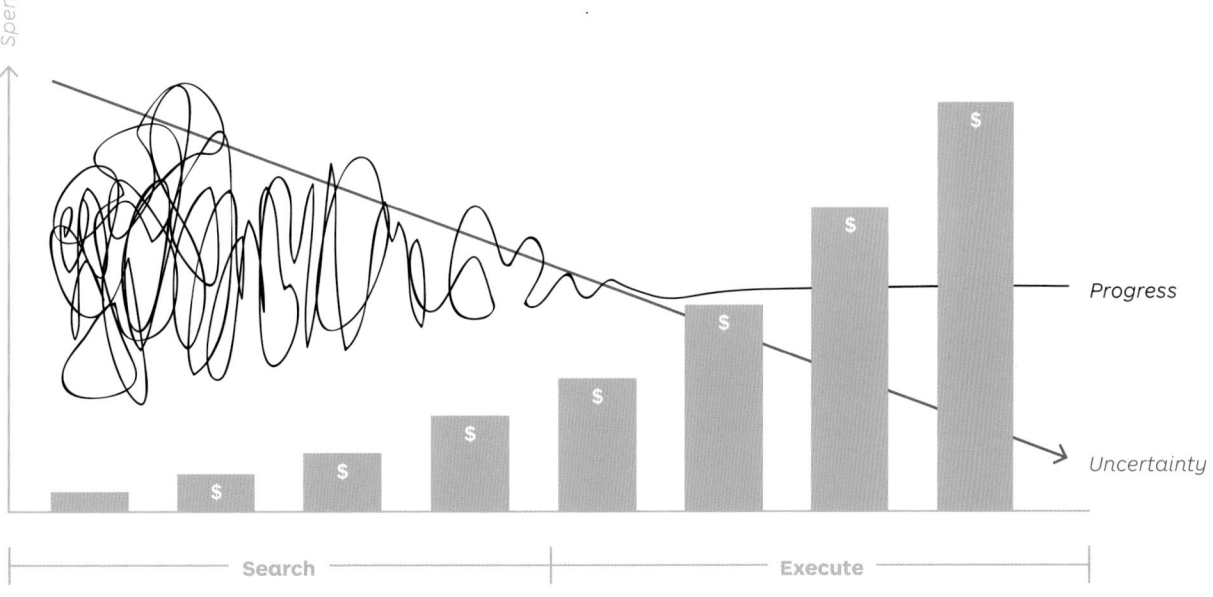

Spending

Progress

Uncertainty

Search — Execute

Business Plans vs. Experimentation Processes

The first step in any venture used to be writing a business plan. We now know better. Business plans are great execution documents in a known environment with sufficient certainty. Unfortunately, new ventures often take place under high uncertainty. Therefore, systematically testing ideas to learn what works and what doesn't is a far better approach than writing a plan. One might even argue that plans maximize risk. Their refined and polished nature gives the illusion that with great execution little can go wrong. Yet ideas dramatically change from inception to market readiness and often die along the way. You need to experiment, learn, and adapt to manage this change and progressively reduce risk and uncertainty. This process of experimentation, which we will explore on the following pages, is known as customer development and lean start-up.

Business Planning ⟵⟶ Experimentation

Applied to New Ventures

Business Planning		Experimentation
We know	**Attitude**	Our customers and partners know
Business plan	**Tools**	Business Model and Value Proposition Canvas
Planning	**Process**	Customer development and lean start-up
Inside the building	**Where**	Outside the building
Execution of a plan	**Focus**	Experimentation and learning
Historical facts from past success	**Decision basis**	Facts and insights from experiments
Not addressed adequately	**Risk**	Minimized via learnings
Avoided	**Failure**	Embraced as means to learn and improve
Masked via detailed plan	**Uncertainty**	Acknowledged and reduced via experiments
Granular documents and spreadsheets	**Detail**	Dependent on level of evidence from experiments
Assumptions	**Numbers**	Evidence-based

10 Testing Principles

Apply these 10 principles when you start testing your value proposition ideas with a series of experiments. A good experimentation process produces evidence of what works and what doesn't. It also will enable you to adapt and change your value propositions and business models and systematically reduce risk and uncertainty.

🏫 *Get "10 Testing Principles" poster*

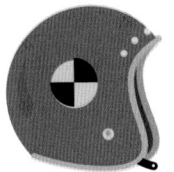

1

Realize that evidence trumps opinion.

Whatever you, your boss, your investors, or anybody else thinks is trumped by (market) evidence.

2

Learn faster and reduce risk by embracing failure.

Testing ideas comes with failure. Yet failing cheaply and quickly leads to more learning, which reduces risk.

3

Test early; refine later.

Gather insights with early and cheap experiments before thinking through or describing your ideas in detail.

4

Experiments ≠ reality.

Remember that experiments are a lens through which you try to understand reality. They are a great indicator, but they differ from reality.

5

Balance learnings and vision.

Integrate test outcomes without turning your back on your vision.

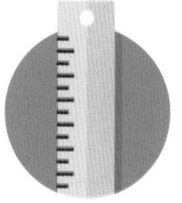

6
Identify idea killers.
Begin with testing the most important assumptions: those that could blow up your idea.

7
Understand customers first.
Test customer jobs, pains, and gains before testing what you could offer them.

8
Make it measurable.
Good tests lead to measurable learning that gives you actionable insights.

9
Accept that not all facts are equal.
Interviewees might tell you one thing and do another. Consider the reliability of your evidence.

10
Test irreversible decisions twice as much.
Make sure that decisions that have an irreversible impact are particularly well informed.

Introducing the Customer Development Process

Customer development is a four-step process invented by Steve Blank, serial entrepreneur turned author and educator. The basic premise is that there are no facts in the building, so you need to test your ideas with customers and stakeholders (e.g., channel partners or other key partners) before you implement them. In this book we use the customer development process to test the assumptions underlying Value Proposition and Business Model Canvases.

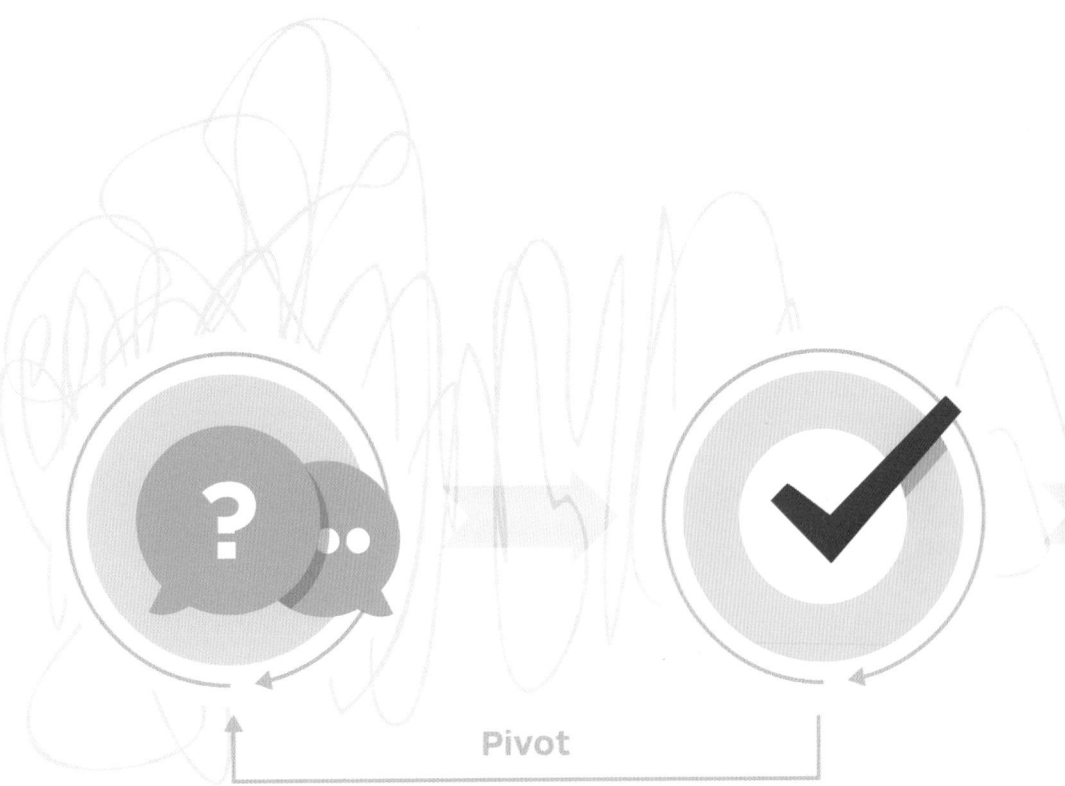

Pivot

Customer Discovery

Get out of the building to learn about your customers' jobs, pains, and gains. Investigate what you could offer them to kill pains and create gains.

Customer Validation

Run experiments to test if customers value how your products and services intend to alleviate pains and create gains.

Search

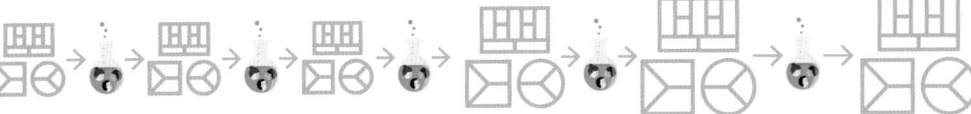

Search vs. Execute

The goal of the search phase is to experiment and learn which value propositions might sell and which business models could work. Your canvases will radically change and constantly evolve during this phase while you test every critical hypothesis. Only when you have validated your ideas do you get into the execution mode and scale. At the early stages of the process, your canvases change rapidly; they will stabilize with increasing knowledge from your experiments.

Customer Creation

Start building end user demand. Drive customers to your sales channels and begin scaling the business.

Company Building

Transition from a temporary organization designed to search and experiment to a structure focused on executing a validated model.

Tip

Capture every hypothesis, everything you tested, and everything you learned. Use the Value Proposition and Business Model Canvases to track your progress from initial idea and starting point toward a viable value proposition and business model. Keeping track of your progress and evidence produced along the way allows you to refer back to it if necessary.

Execute

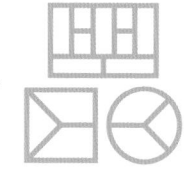

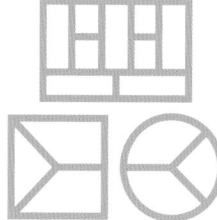

Blank & Dorf, The Startup Owner's Manual, 2012.

Integrating Lean Start-up Principles

Eric Ries launched the Lean Startup movement based on Steve Blank's customer development process. The idea is to eliminate slack and uncertainty from product development by continuously building, testing, and learning in an iterative process. Here we apply the three steps in combination with the canvases and customer development to test ideas, assumptions, and so-called minimum viable product (MVPs).

184

Zoom in

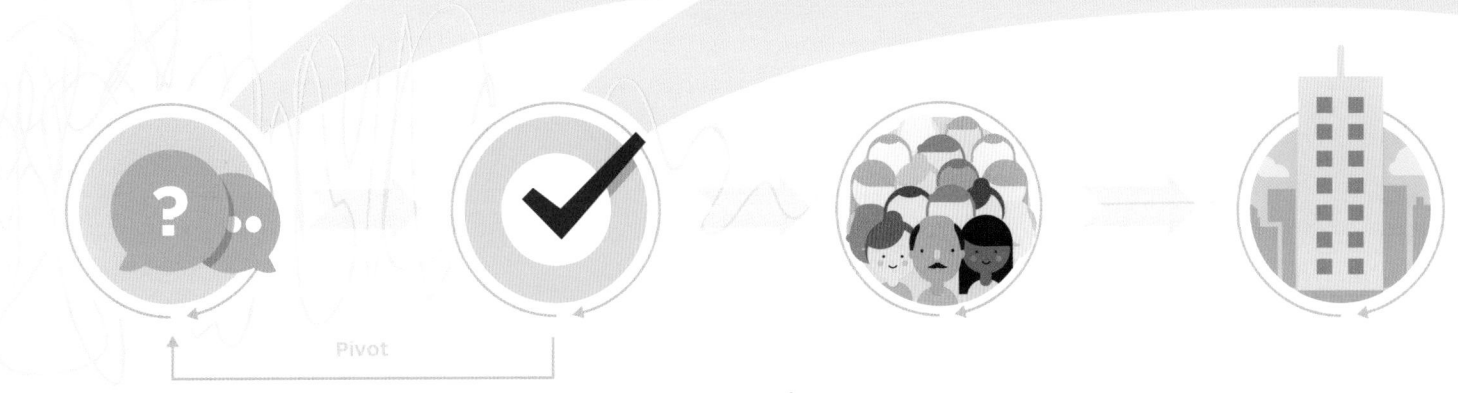

Pivot

———————— Search ————————

———————— Execute ————————

Customer Discovery   **Customer Validation**   **Customer Creation**   **Company Building**

1. Design/build.

Design or build an artifact specifically conceived to test your hypotheses, gain insights, and learn. This could be a conceptual prototype, an experiment, or simply a basic prototype (MVP) of the products and services you intend to offer.

0. Generate a hypothesis.

Start with the Value Proposition and Business Model Canvases to define the critical hypotheses underlying your ideas in order to design the right experiments.

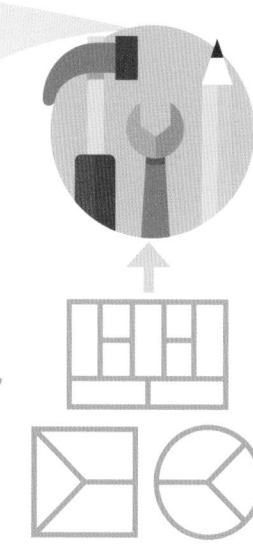
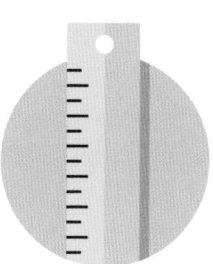

3. Learn.

Analyze the performance of the artifact, compare to your initial hypotheses, and derive insights. Ask what you thought would happen. Describe what actually happened. Then outline what you will change and how you will do so.

2. Measure.

Measure the performance of the artifact you designed or built.

Ries, The Lean Startup, 2011.

Apply Build, Measure, Learn

Apply the Lean Startup circle to more than just products and services. Use the same three steps of designing/building, testing/measuring, and learning with all the artifacts you create in *Value Proposition Design*. Apply design/build, test/measure, learn to your...

Conceptual Prototypes

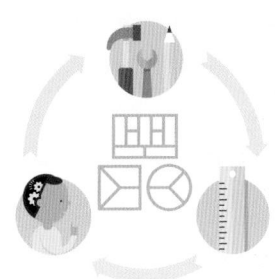

Design rapid conceptual prototypes to shape your ideas, figure out what could work, and identify which hypotheses need to be true to succeed. Use these prototypes as a tangible way to clearly map, track, iterate, and share your ideas and hypotheses.

Hypotheses

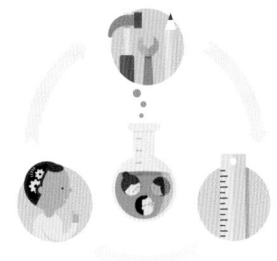

Design and build experiments to test the hypotheses that need to be true for your idea to succeed. Start with the most critical hypotheses that could kill your idea.

Products and services

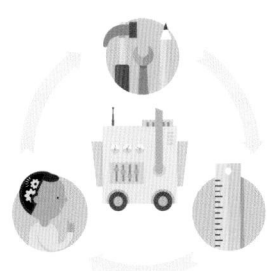

Build so-called MVPs to test your value propositions. These are prototypes with a minimum feature set specifically designed to learn rather than to sell.

Design/Build	Measure	Learn
Business Model and/or Value Proposition Canvases to shape your ideas throughout the process	Performance of conceptual prototype: fit between customer profile and value map, ballpark figures, design assessment with 7 business model questions	If and why you need to adapt your conceptual prototypes Assumed financial performance of your business model Assumed fit Which hypotheses you need to test
Interviews, observations, and experiments to test initial value proposition and business model assumptions derived from conceptual prototyping	What actually happens in your experiments compared with what you thought would happen (i.e., your hypotheses)	If and why you need to change any of the building blocks of your Business Model or Value Proposition Canvas
MVPs with the benefits and features you want to test	If your products and service actually relieve pains and create gains for customers	If and why you need to change the products and services in your value proposition Which pain relievers and gain creators work and which ones don't

I present Shrek models, that's a Yiddish expression for making people nervous.
Frank Gehry, Architect

There are no facts in the building... So get the hell out and talk to customers.
Steve Blank, Entrepreneur & Educator

Fail early to succeed sooner.
David Kelley, Designer

3.1

What to Test

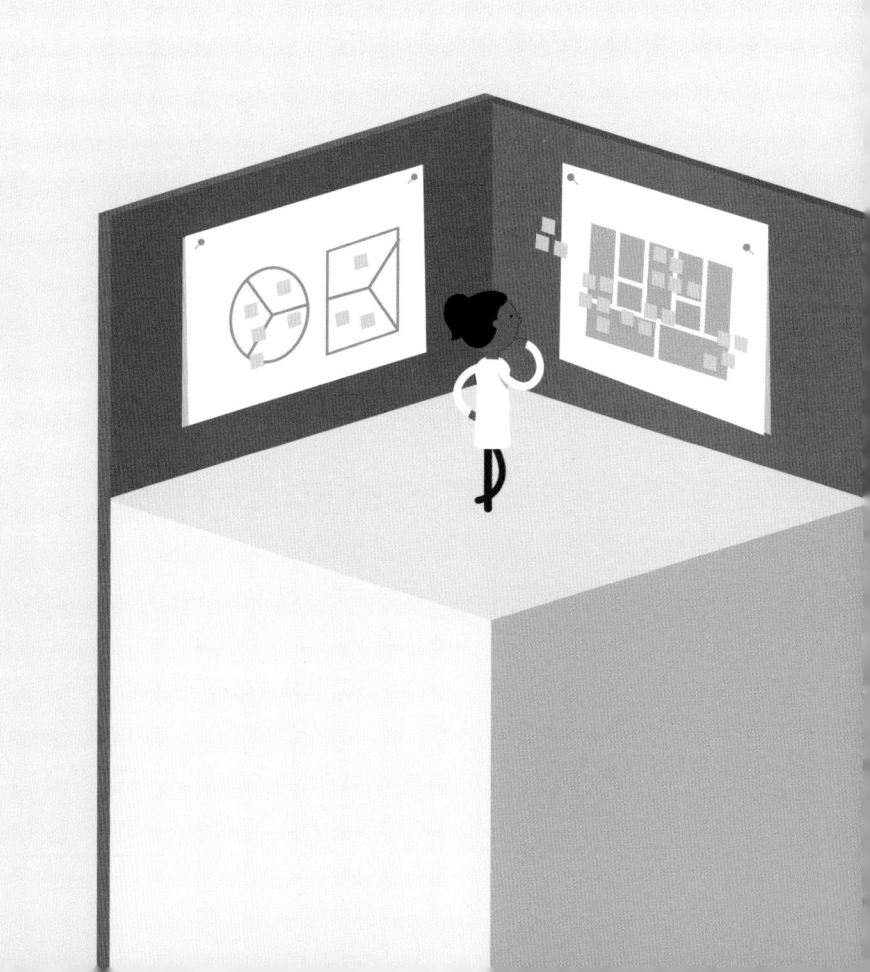

Testing
the Circle

Prove which jobs, pains, and gains matter to customer most by conducting experiments that produce evidence beyond your initial customer research. Only after this has been done should you get started with your value proposition. This will prevent you from wasting time with products and services customers don't care about.

Provide evidence showing what customers care about (the circle) before focusing on how to help them (the square).

Start with jobs, pains, and gains

In the design section we looked at a series of techniques to better understand customers. In this chapter we go a step further. The objective of "testing the circle" is to confirm with evidence that our profile sketches, our initial research, our observations, and our insights from interviews were correct. We aim to know with more certainty which jobs, pains, and gains customers really care about.

Possessing evidence about customer jobs, pains, and gains before you focus on your value proposition is very powerful. If you start by testing your value proposition, you never know if customers are rejecting your value proposition or if you are simply addressing irrelevant jobs, pains, or gains. This is less likely to happen if you have evidence about which jobs, pains, and gains matter to customers.

Of course, this means you need to find creative ways to test customer preferences without already drawing on the use of minimum viable products (MVPs). We show how to do so with the tools in the testing library ➔ p. 214.

- Which gains matter to your customers?
- Which ones are most essential?

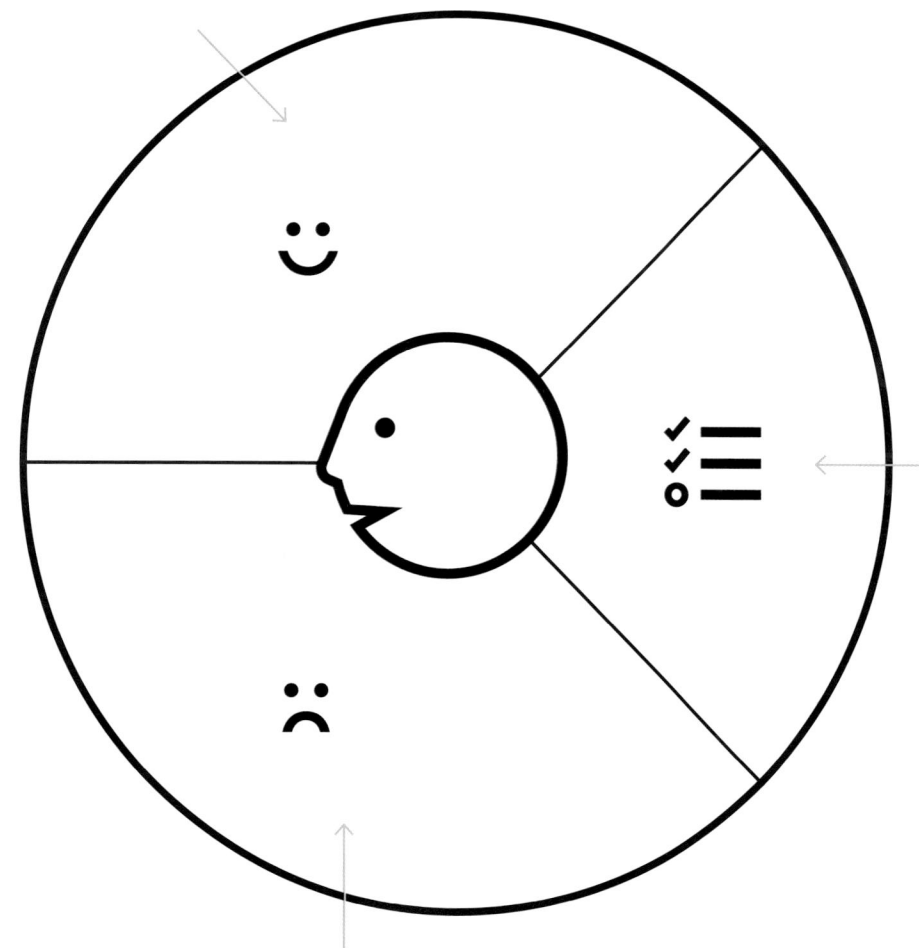

Do you
have evidence
showing...

- Which jobs matter to your customers?
- Which ones matter most?

- Which pains matter to your customers?
- Which ones are most extreme?

Testing the Square

Test if and how much your customers care about how you intend to help them. Design experiments that produce evidence showing that your products and services kill pains and create gains that matter to customers.

Do you have evidence showing...

- Which one of your gain creators customers really need or desire?
- Which ones they crave most?

- Which one of your products and services customers really want?
- Which ones they want most?

- Which one of your pain relievers helps your customers with their headaches?
- Which ones they long for most?

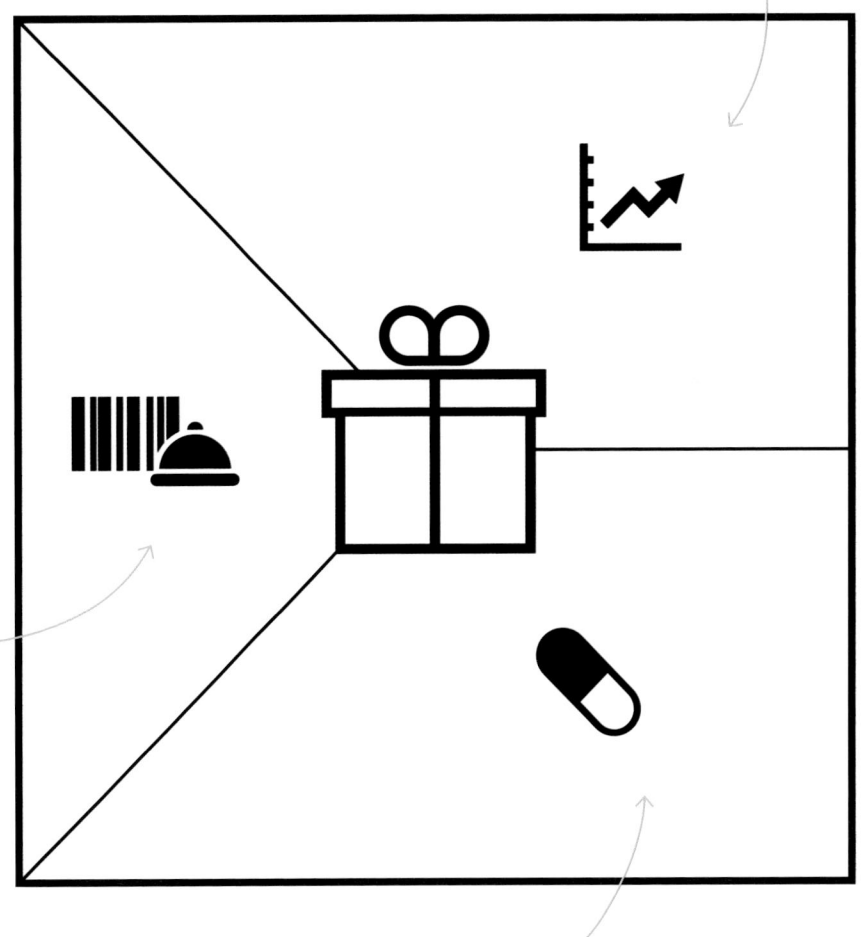

Provide evidence showing that your customers care about how your products and services kill pains and create gains.

The Art of Testing Value Propositions

It is an art to test how much your customers care about your value proposition because the goal is to do so as cheaply and quickly as possible without implementing the value proposition in its entirety.

You need to test your customers' taste for your products and services one pain reliever and gain creator at a time by designing experiments that are measurable, provide insights, and allow you to learn and improve ➔ p. 214.

Make sure your experiments allow you to understand which aspects of your products and services customers appreciate, so that you can avoid offering anything unnecessary. In other words, remove any features or efforts that don't contribute directly to the learning you seek.

Always make sure you aim to find the simplest, quickest, and cheapest way to test a pain reliever or gain creator before you start prototyping products and services.

Testing the Rectangle

Test the most critical assumptions underlying the business model your value proposition is embedded in. Remember, even great value propositions can fail without a sound business model. Provide evidence showing that your business model is likely to work, will generate more revenue than costs, and will create value not only for your customers but for your business.

Provide evidence showing that the way you intend to create, deliver, and capture value is likely to work.

Don't neglect testing your business model

You can fail even with a successful value proposition if your business model generates less revenue than it incurs costs. Many creators are so focused on designing and testing products and services that they sometimes neglect this obvious equation (profit = revenues - costs) resulting from the building blocks of the Business Model Canvas.

A value proposition that customers want is worth little if you don't have the channels to reach customers in a way they want to be reached. Likewise, a business model that spends more money on acquiring customers than it will earn from revenue from those same customers won't survive over the long term. Similarly, a company will obviously go out of business if resources and activities required to create value are more costly than the value they capture. In some markets you might need access to key partners who might not be interested in working with you.

Design experiments that address the most important things that have to be true for your business model to work. Testing such critical assumptions will prevent you from failing with a great value proposition that customers actually want.

Do you have evidence showing...

- That you will have access to the partners required for your model to work?

- That you will be able to perform the activities required to create value?

- How you will succeed in acquiring and retaining customers?

- That you will have access to the resources required to create value?

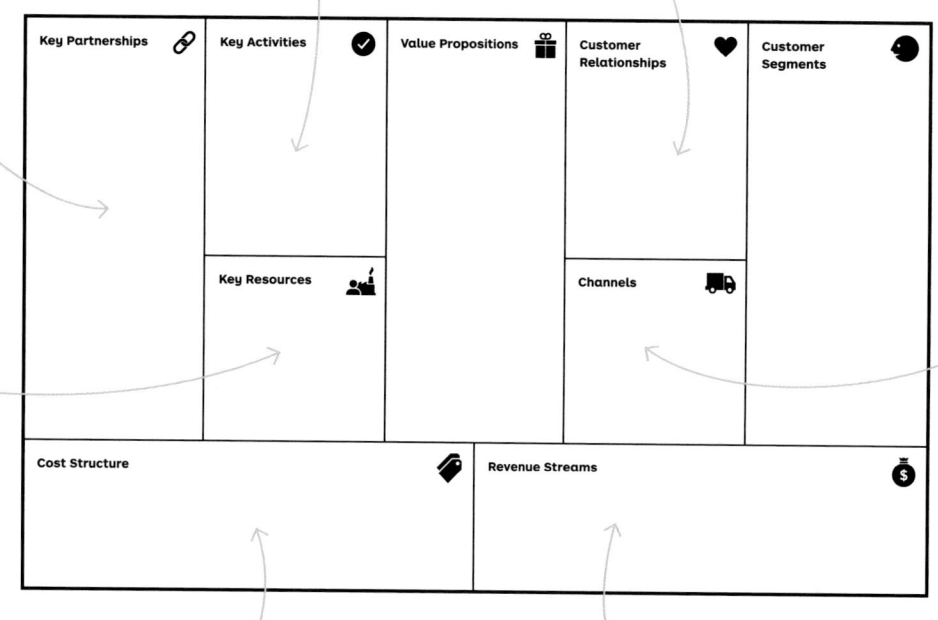

Key Partnerships	Key Activities	Value Propositions	Customer Relationships	Customer Segments
	Key Resources		Channels	
Cost Structure		Revenue Streams		

- Through which channels will you be able to reach customers?

- That you can generate more revenue than costs incurred?

- How you will generate revenues from customers?

3.2

Testing Step-by-Step

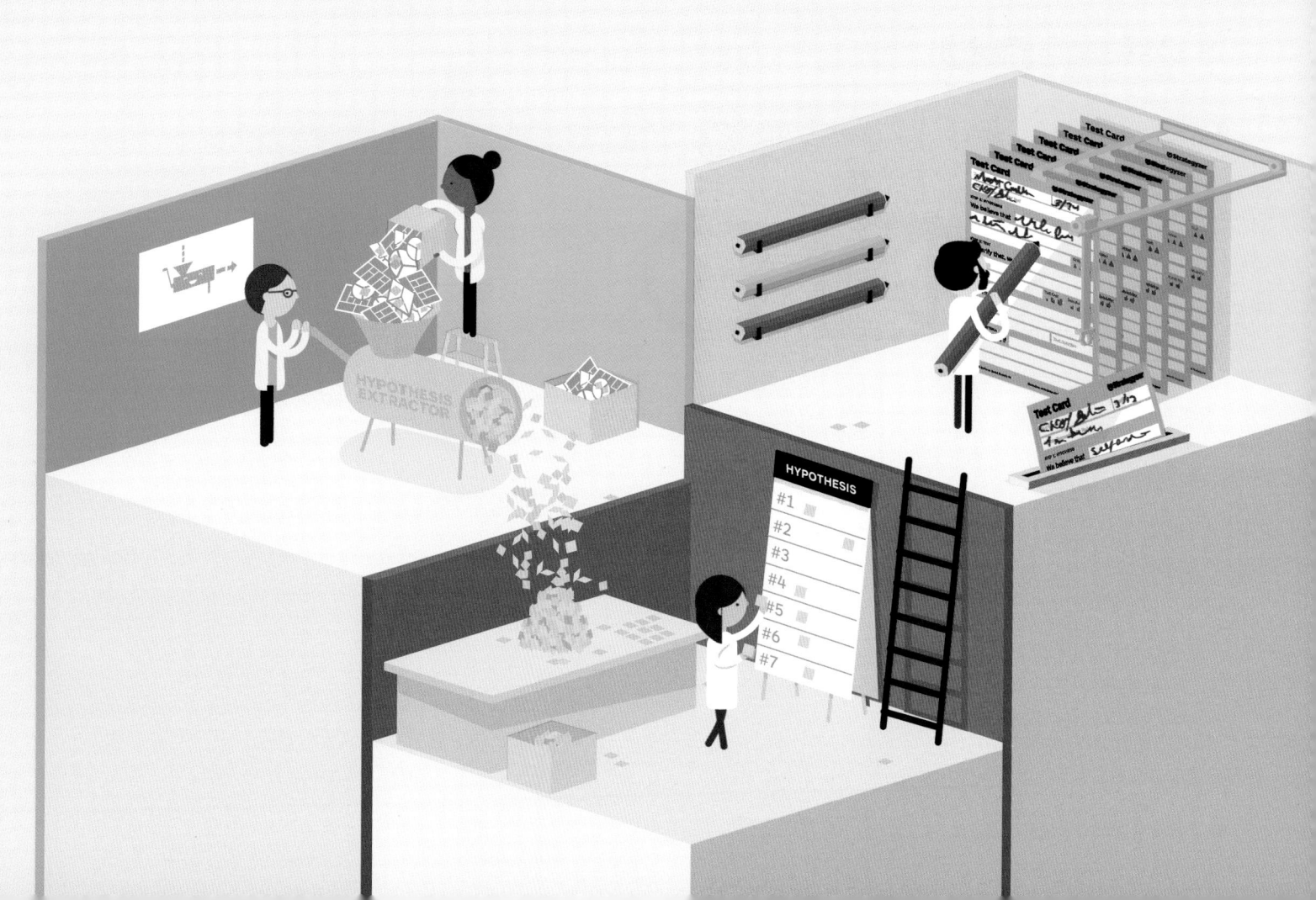

Overview of the Testing Process

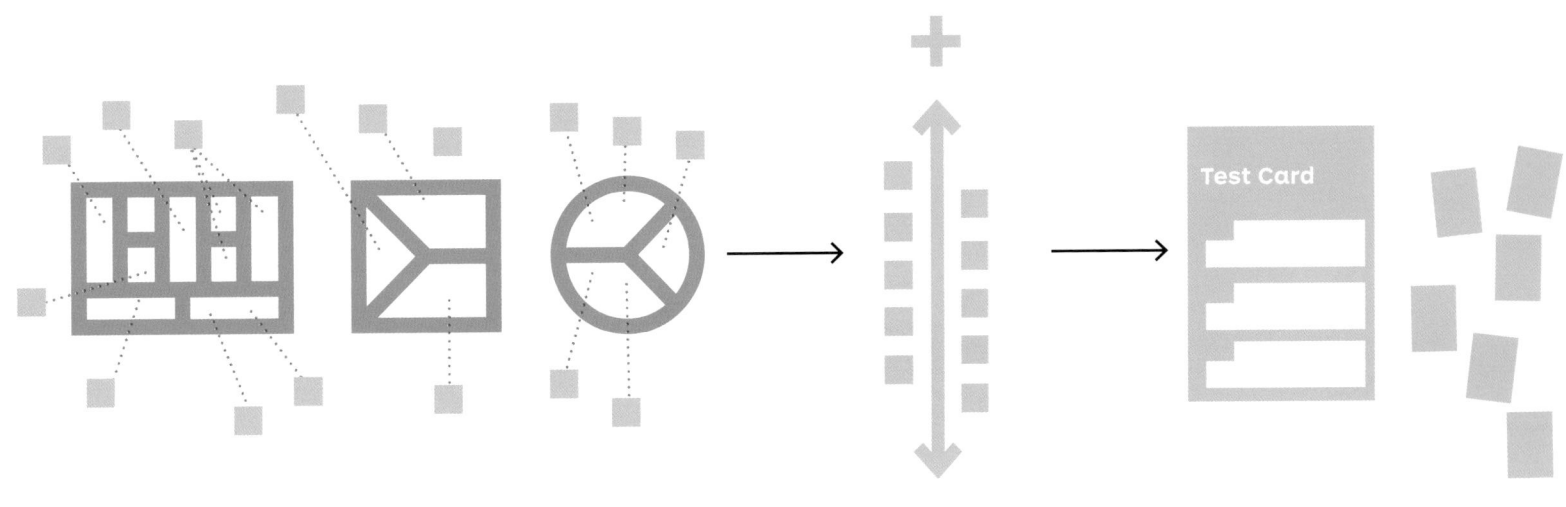

Extract Hypotheses
→ p. 200

Prioritize Hypotheses
→ p. 202

Design Tests
→ p. 204

■ Design ■ Testing

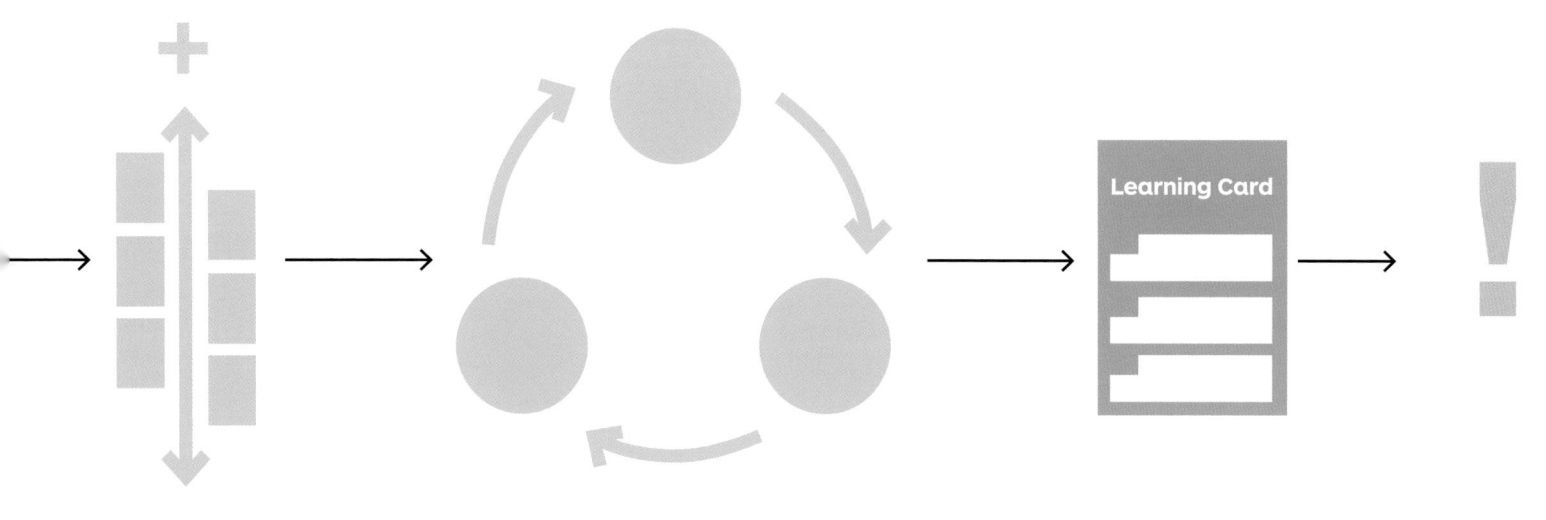

Prioritize Tests
⊕ p. 205

Run Tests
⊕ p. 205

Capture Learnings
⊕ p. 206

Make Progress
⊕ p. 242–245

Get "Testing Process Overview" poster

Extract Your Hypotheses: What Needs to Be True for Your Idea to Work?

200

Use the Value Proposition and Business Model Canvases to identify what to test before you "get out of the building." Define the most important things that must be true for your idea to work.

Do the exercise online

we can produce a best seller

readers sign up for free online content

people are interested in this topic

Wiley is the right publishing partner

people will find our book

our dev team can handle the challenge

retailers will acquire, stock, and display book

we can attract a top-tier publisher

Key Partnerships	Key Activities	Value Propositions	Customer Relationships	Customer Segments
Wiley	content creation	book		reader
	Key Resources	online	Channels	retail
	platform	Web app	retail	Wiley
			strategyzer.com	

Cost Structure	Revenue Streams
IT content	percent royalties course fee app subscription

cost structure can be supported by revenues

people will buy our book

some people convert to paid services

To succeed, ask yourself what needs to be true about...

 **...your business model?**

DEF·I·NI·TION
Business Hypothesis
Something that needs to be true for your idea to work partially or fully but that hasn't been validated yet.

▢ Hypotheses

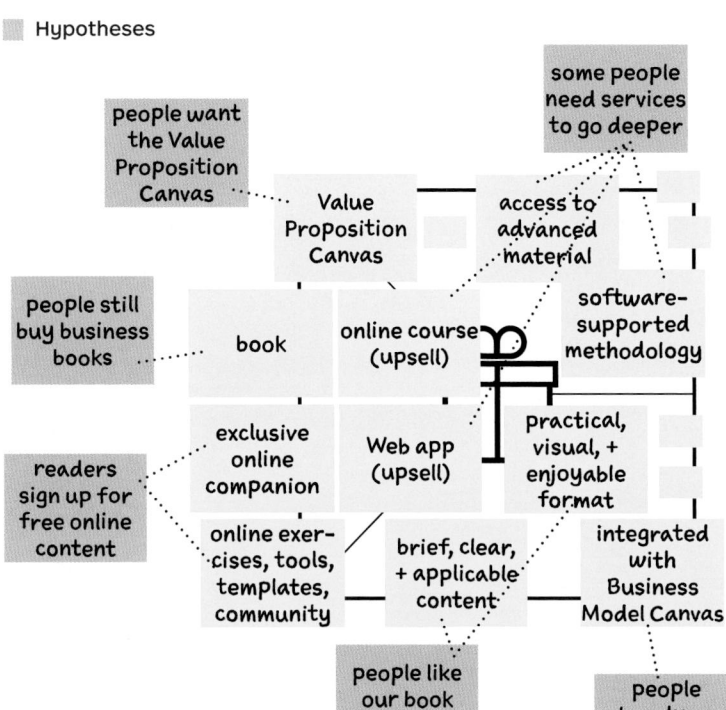

people want the Value Proposition Canvas

people still buy business books

readers sign up for free online content

some people need services to go deeper

Value Proposition Canvas

access to advanced material

book

online course (upsell)

software-supported methodology

exclusive online companion

Web app (upsell)

practical, visual, + enjoyable format

online exercises, tools, templates, community

brief, clear, + applicable content

integrated with Business Model Canvas

people like our book format

people already use Business Model Canvas

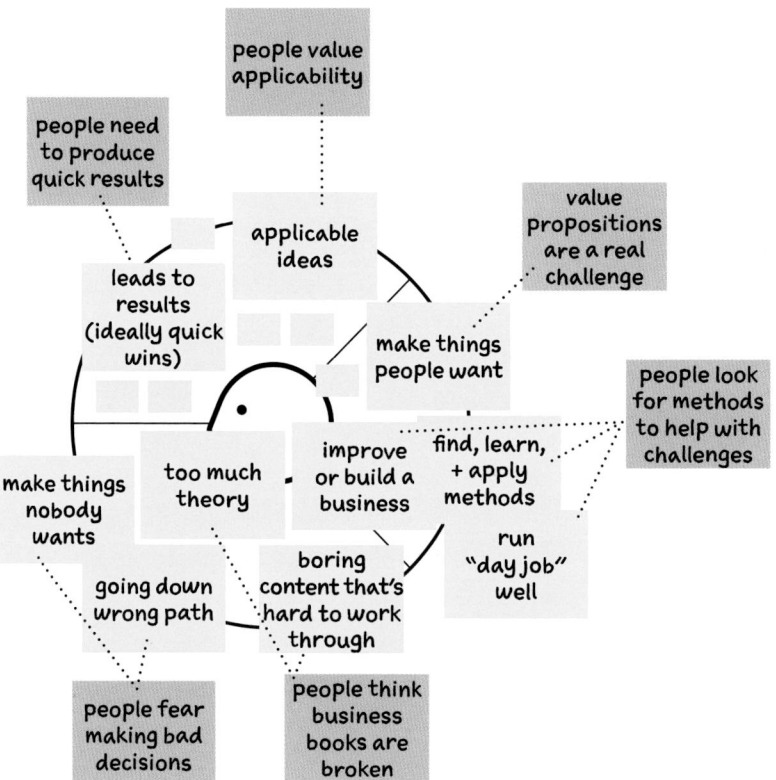

people value applicability

people need to produce quick results

applicable ideas

value propositions are a real challenge

leads to results (ideally quick wins)

make things people want

people look for methods to help with challenges

make things nobody wants

too much theory

improve or build a business

find, learn, + apply methods

going down wrong path

boring content that's hard to work through

run "day job" well

people fear making bad decisions

people think business books are broken

➤ **...your value proposition?** **...your customer?**

Prioritize Your Hypotheses: What Could Kill Your Business

Not all hypotheses are equally critical. Some can kill your business, whereas others matter only once you get the most important hypotheses right. Start prioritizing what's critical to survival.

Identify the business killers. These are the hypotheses that are critical to the survival of your idea. Test them first!

There is no basis for our idea if people aren't making or don't fear making bad business decisions (in particular regarding products and services) or if they aren't looking for methods to help them with such issues.

People are interested in this topic

duplicate hypothesis—eliminate one sticky note

There is no foundation for our idea if people don't buy business books anymore and we can't produce a best seller in a format they like.

It's critical that we can get people to use **strategyzer.com** so we can upsell to those interested in more services.

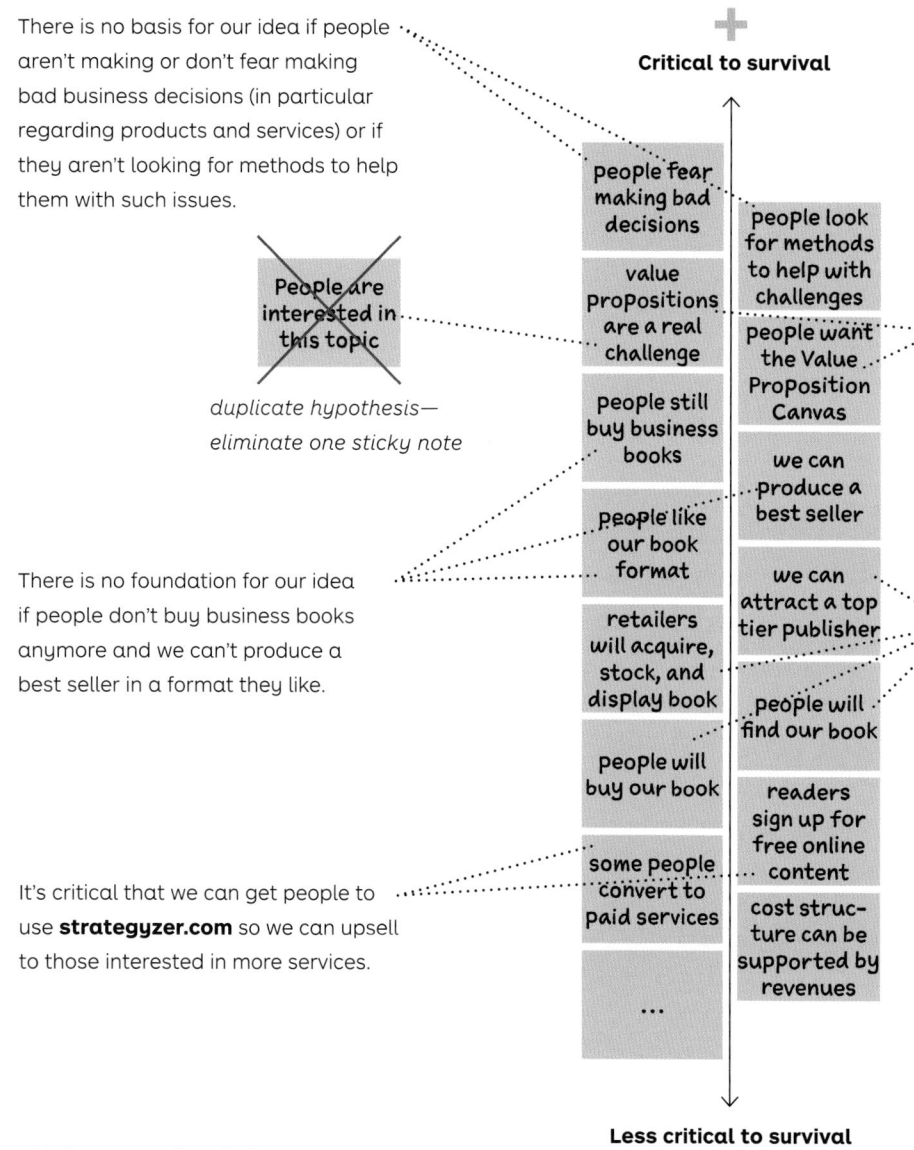

Critical to survival

people fear making bad decisions

value propositions are a real challenge

people still buy business books

people like our book format

retailers will acquire, stock, and display book

people will buy our book

some people convert to paid services

people look for methods to help with challenges

people want the Value Proposition Canvas

we can produce a best seller

we can attract a top tier publisher

people will find our book

readers sign up for free online content

cost structure can be supported by revenues

...

Less critical to survival

If people don't struggle with value propositions and if they don't see the Value Proposition Canvas as a helpful tool, there is no opportunity for our ideas.

It's critical that people like or love our book, but that's only the start. If they can't find it or don't know about it, they won't be able to buy it even if they potentially would have liked it.

What priorities matter most?

Design Your Experiments with the Test Card

Structure all of your experiments with this simple Test Card. Start by testing the most critical hypotheses.

1

Design an experiment.
Describe the hypothesis that you want to test.

Outline the experiment you are going to design to verify if the hypothesis is correct or needs to be rejected and revised.

Define what data you are going to measure.

Define a target threshold to validate or invalidate the tested hypothesis.
Caveat: Consider following up with additional experiments to increase certainty.

How will I learn?

⊙ Download the Test Card and do the exercise online

Test Card   ⊙ Strategyzer

| AdWords campaign | May 1, 2014 |
| Natasha Hanshaw | 2 weeks |

STEP 1: HYPOTHESIS

We believe that businesspeople are looking for methods to help them design better value propositions.

Critical: ⚠ ⚠ ⚠

STEP 2: TEST

To verify that, we will launch a Google AdWords campaign around the search term "value proposition."

Test Cost: 🪙🪙🪙   Data Reliability: 👍👍👍

STEP 3: METRIC

And measure how the advertising campaign performs in terms of clicks.

Time Required: 🕐🕐🕐

STEP 4: CRITERIA

We are right if we can achieve a click-through rate (CTR) of at least 2 percent (number of clicks divided by total impressions of ad).

Copyright Business Model Foundry AG   *The makers of Business Model Generation and Strategyzer*

Name the test, set a due date, and list the person responsible.

Indicate how critical this hypothesis is for the entire idea to work.

Indicate how costly this test will be to execute.

Indicate how reliable the measured data are.

Indicate how long it takes until this test produces results.

4

Run experiments.

Start performing the experiments at the top of your list.

Caveat: If your first experiments invalidate your initial hypotheses, you might have to go back to the drawing board and rethink your ideas. This might render the remaining Test Cards in your list irrelevant.

Critical to survival

Less critical to survival

2

Design a series of experiments for the most critical hypotheses.

Tip

Consider testing the most critical hypotheses with several experiments. Start with cheap and quick tests. Then follow up with more elaborate and reliable tests if necessary. Thus, you may create several Test Cards for the same hypotheses.

3

Rank Test Cards.

Prioritize your Test Cards. Rank the most critical hypotheses highest, but prioritize cheap and quick tests to be done early in the process, when uncertainty is at its maximum. Increase your spending on experiments that produce more reliable evidence and insights with growing certainty.

Repeat.

Where can I get the most learning the fastest?

Capture Your Insights with the Learning Card

Structure all of your insights with this simple Learning Card.

Describe the hypothesis that you tested.

Outline the outcomes of your experiment(s) in terms of data and results. A Learning Card may aggregate the observations from several Test Cards.

Explain what conclusions and insights you derived from the test results.

Describe what actions you will take based on your insights.

 Download the Learning Card

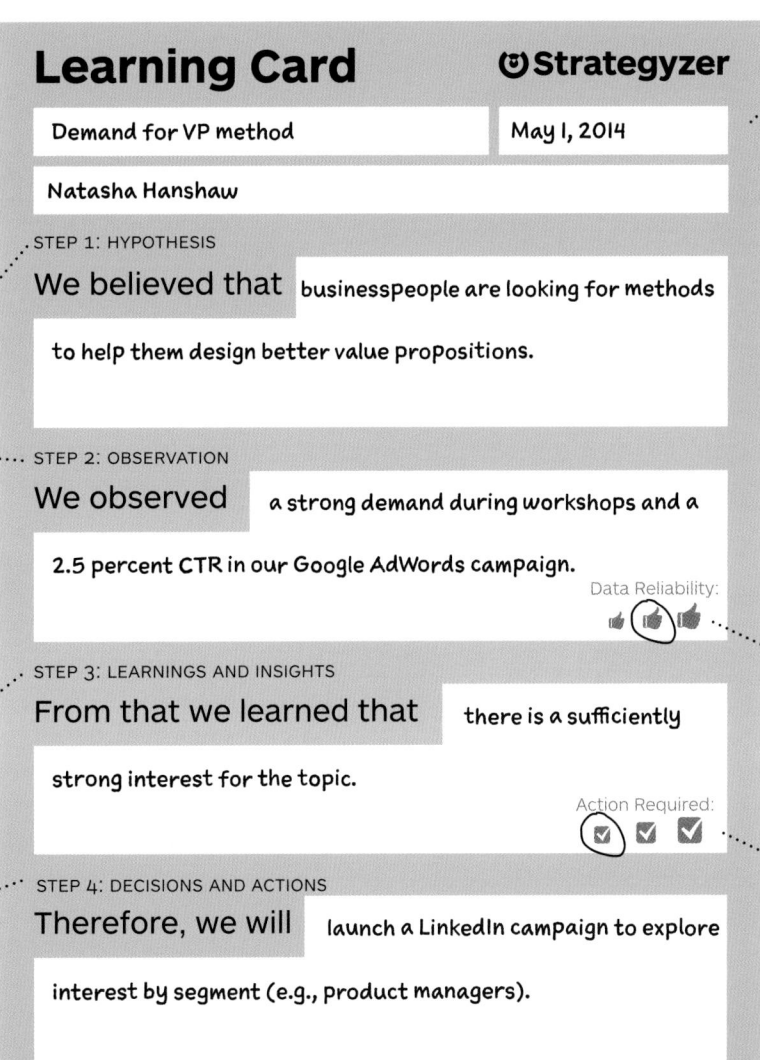

Name the insight, the date of learning, and the person responsible.

Note how reliable the data measured are.

Highlight how dramatic the actions required are based on what you learned.

Learning Card — Strategyzer

Demand for VP method | **May 1, 2014**

Natasha Hanshaw

STEP 1: HYPOTHESIS

We believed that businesspeople are looking for methods to help them design better value propositions.

STEP 2: OBSERVATION

We observed a strong demand during workshops and a 2.5 percent CTR in our Google AdWords campaign.

Data Reliability:

STEP 3: LEARNINGS AND INSIGHTS

From that we learned that there is a sufficiently strong interest for the topic.

Action Required:

STEP 4: DECISIONS AND ACTIONS

Therefore, we will launch a LinkedIn campaign to explore interest by segment (e.g., product managers).

Copyright Business Model Foundry AG   *The makers of Business Model Generation and Strategyzer*

Invalidated

Get back to the drawing board: pivot.
Find new alternative segments, value propositions, or business models to make your ideas work when your tests invalidate your first attempts.

For example, when you have invalidated customer interest for your value proposition around a novel technology, search for new potential customers, value propositions, and business models.

Learn more

Seek confirmation.
Design and conduct further tests when quick and early experiments based on a small amount of data indicate the need for drastic actions.

For example, if interviews with potential customers show a strong interest for a service that requires heavy investments to launch, follow up with research and experiments that produce more reliable data validating customer interest.

Deepen your understanding.
Design and conduct further tests to understand why a trend is taking place once you discovered that it is taking place.

For example, if the quantitative data of an experiment show that potential customers are not interested, follow up with qualitative interviews to understand why they are uninterested.

Validated

Expand to next building block.
Move on to test your next important hypothesis when you are satisfied with your insights and the data reliability.

For example, when you have validated customer interest for a product, follow up with experiments that validate the willingness of channel partners to stock and promote your product.

Execute.
When you are satisfied with the quality of your insights and the reliability of the data, you may directly start executing based on your findings.

For example, when you have learned and validated exactly what it takes to get channel partners interested in reselling your value proposition, start scaling up sales efforts by hiring salespeople or designing dedicated marketing material.

You experimented and learned. Now what?

How Quickly Are You Learning?

The only thing standing between you and finding out what customers and partners really want is the consistency and speed with which you and your team can propel yourself through the design/build, measure, learn cycle. This is called cycle time.

The speed at which you learn is crucial, especially during the early phases of value proposition design. When you start out, uncertainty is at its maximum. You don't know if customers care about the jobs, pains, and gains you intend to address, let alone if they're interested in your value proposition.

Therefore, it is critical that your early experiments be extremely fast and produce a maximum of learning so you can adapt rapidly. This is why writing a business plan or conducting a large third-party market study is the wrong thing to start with, although it can make sense later in the process.

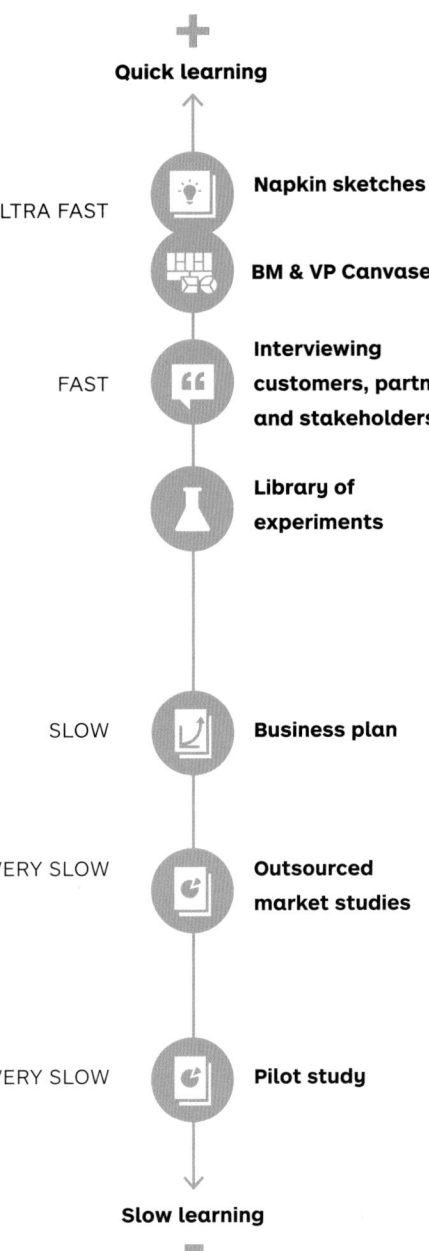

Quick learning

ULTRA FAST — **Napkin sketches**

BM & VP Canvases

FAST — **Interviewing customers, partners, and stakeholders**

Library of experiments

SLOW — **Business plan**

VERY SLOW — **Outsourced market studies**

VERY SLOW — **Pilot study**

Slow learning

Learning Instruments

Quickly shape your ideas to share, challenge, or iterate them and to generate hypotheses to test.

Quickly gain first market insights. Keep the effort in-house so learnings remain fresh and relevant and so you can move fast and act upon insights.

Use the whole range of experiments from the experiment library ⊕ p. 214. Start with quick ones when uncertainty is high. Continue with more reliable, slower ones, when you have evidence about the right direction.

Business plans are more refined documents and usually more static. Write one only when you have clear evidence and are approaching the execution phase.

Market studies are often costly and slow. They are not an optimal search tool because they don't allow you to adapt to circumstances rapidly. They make most sense in the context of incremental changes to a value proposition.

A pilot study is often the default way to test an idea inside a corporation. However, they should be preceded by quicker and cheaper learning tools, because most pilots are based on relatively refined value propositions that involve substantial time and cost.

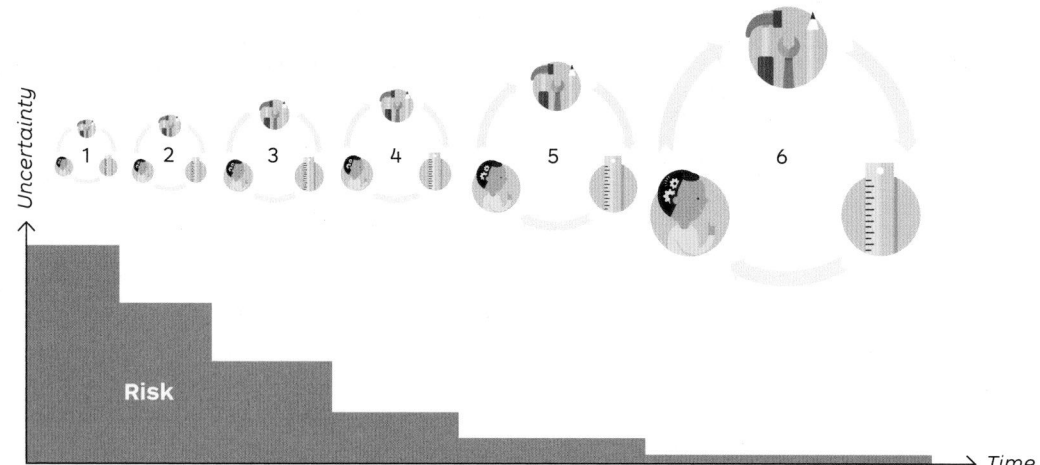

Six rapid iteration cycles based on quick experiments produce more learning than three long iteration cycles based on slower experiments. The faster approach will produce knowledge more quickly and thus reduce risk and uncertainty more substantially than the latter.

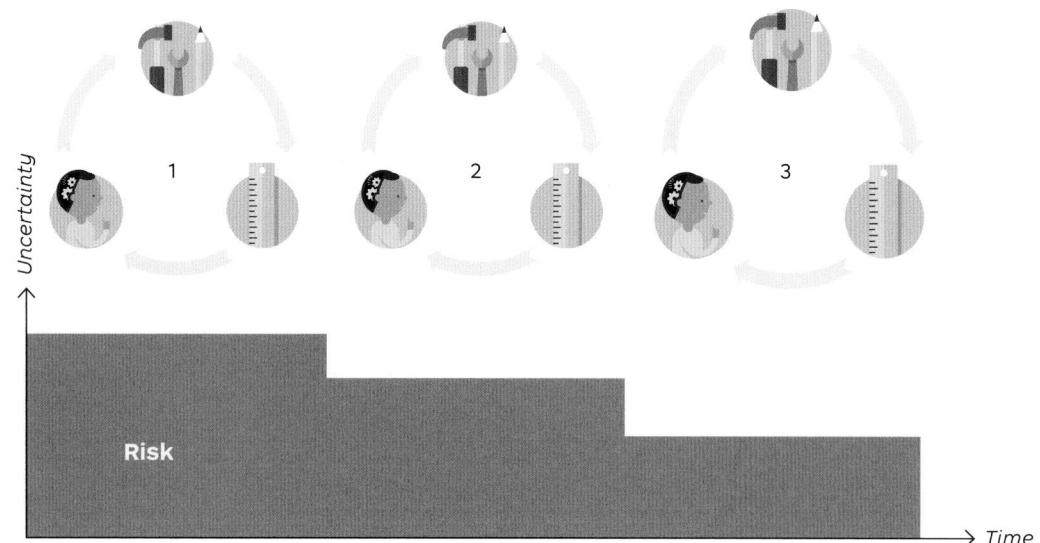

The faster you iterate, the more you learn and the faster you succeed.

Don't waste your time!

Imagine spending a week, a month, or more on refining and perfecting your idea. Imagine spending all that time thinking hard about what you'd need to do to produce great growth numbers only to find out that your customers and partners don't really care. That's wasted time!

Five Data Traps to Avoid

Avoid failure by thinking critically about your data. Experiments produce valuable evidence that can be used to reduce risk and uncertainty, but they can't predict future success with 100 percent accuracy. Also, you might simply draw the wrong conclusions from your data. Avoid the following five traps to ensure you successfully test your ideas.

False-Positive Trap

Risk: Seeing things that are not there.
Occurs: When your testing data mislead you to conclude, for example, that your customer has a pain when in fact it is not true.

Tips

- Test the circle before you test the square. Understand what's relevant to customers to avoid being misled by positive signals for irrelevant value propositions.
- Design different experiments for the same hypothesis before making important decisions.

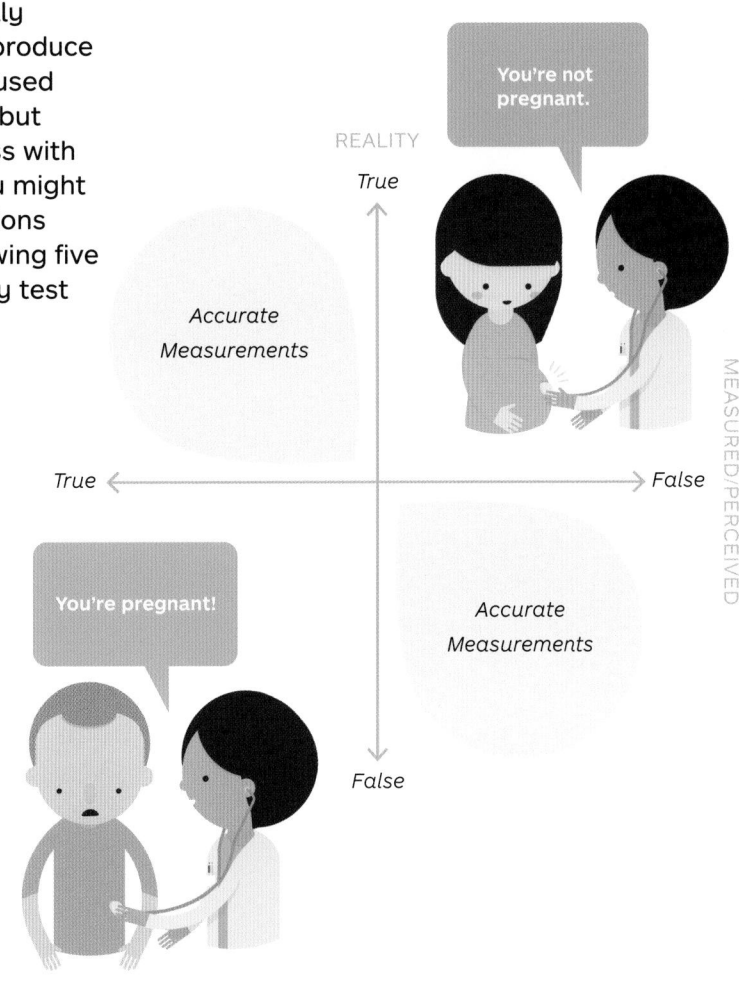

REALITY

True

True ⟵⟶ False

MEASURED/PERCEIVED

False

Accurate Measurements

Accurate Measurements

You're not pregnant.

You're pregnant!

False-Negative Trap

Risk: Not seeing things that are there.
Occurs: When your experiment fails to detect, for example, a customer job it was designed to unearth.

Tips

Make sure your test is adequate. Dropbox, a file hosting service, initially tested customer interest with Google AdWords. They invalidated their hypotheses, because the ads didn't perform. But the reason people didn't search was because it was a new market, not because there was a lack of interest.

The "Local Maximum" Trap

Risk: Missing out on the real potential.

Occurs: When you conduct experiments that optimize around a local maximum while ignoring the larger opportunity. For example, positive testing feedback might result in you sticking with a much less profitable model when a more profitable one exists.

Tip

Focus on learning rather than optimizing. Don't hesitate to go back to designing better alternatives if the testing data are positive but the numbers feel like they should be better (e.g., larger market, more revenues, better profit).

The "Exhausted Maximum" Trap

Risk: Overlooking limitations (e.g., of a market).

Occurs: When you think an opportunity is larger than it is in reality. For example, when you think you are testing with a sample of a large population but the sample is actually the entire population.

Tip

Design tests that prove the potential beyond the immediately addressed test subjects.

The Wrong Data Trap

Risk: Searching in the wrong place.

Occurs: When you abandon an opportunity because you are looking at the wrong data. For example, you might drop an idea because the customers you are testing with are not interested and you don't realize that there are people who are interested.

Tip

Go back to designing other alternatives before you give up.

Test Card

⊚ Strategyzer

Test Name	Deadline
Assigned to	Duration

STEP 1: HYPOTHESIS

We believe that

Critical:

⚠ ⚠ ⚠

STEP 2: TEST

To verify that, we will

Test Cost: Data Reliability:

👍 👍 👍

STEP 3: METRIC

And measure

Time Required:

🕐 🕐 🕐

STEP 4: CRITERIA

We are right if

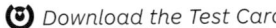 *Download the Test Card*

Learning Card

☺Strategyzer

Insight Name

Date of Learning

Person Responsible

STEP 1: HYPOTHESIS

We believed that

STEP 2: OBSERVATION

We observed

Data Reliability:
👍 👍 👍

STEP 3: LEARNINGS AND INSIGHTS

From that we learned that

Action Required:
☑ ☑ ☑

STEP 4: DECISIONS AND ACTIONS

Therefore, we will

Copyright Business Model Foundry AG   *The makers of Business Model Generation and Strategyzer*

 Download the Learning Card

3.3

Experiment Library

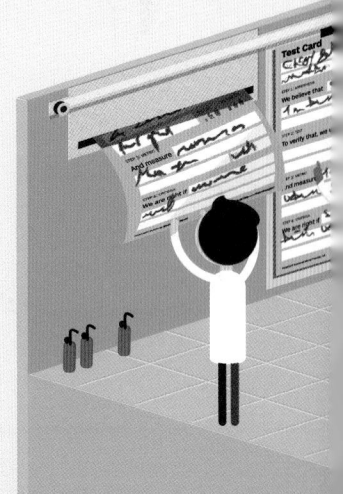

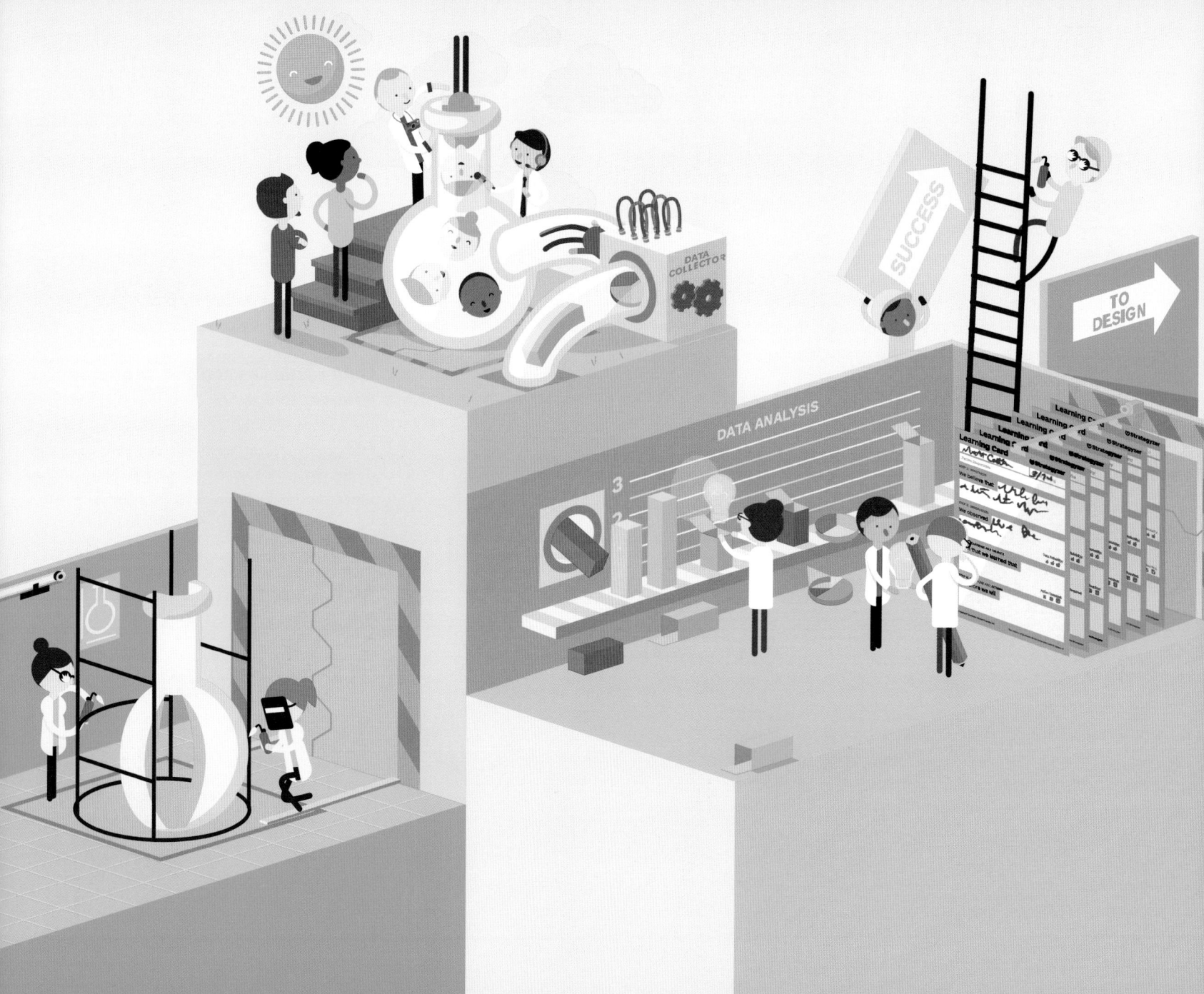

Choose a Mix of Experiments

Every experiment has strengths and weaknesses. Some are quick and cheap but produce less reliable evidence. Some produce more reliable evidence but require more time and money to execute.

Consider cost, data reliability, and time required when you design your mix of experiments. As a rule of thumb, start cheap when uncertainty is high and increase your spending on experiments with increasing certainty.

DEF·I·NI·TION
Experiment
A procedure to validate or invalidate a value proposition or business model hypothesis that produces evidence.

Select a series of tests by drawing from our experiment library or by using your imagination to invent new experiments. Keep two things in mind when you compose your mix:

What customers say and do are two different things.
Use experiments that provide verbal evidence from customers as a starting point. Get customers to perform actions and engage them (e.g., interact with a prototype) to produce stronger evidence based on what they do, not what they say.

Customers behave differently when you are there or when you are not.
During direct personal contact with customers, you can learn why they do or say something and get their input on how to improve your value proposition. However, your presence might lead them to behave differently than if you weren't there.

In an indirect observation of customers (on the web, for example) you are closer to a real-life situation that isn't biased by your interaction with customers. You can collect numerical data and track how many customers performed an action you induced.

Tip

Use these techniques to verify whether customers really mean what they say. Produce evidence that the jobs, pains, and gains they mention are real and that they are seriously interested in your products and services.

DIRECT CONTACT with customers

Learn why and how to improve

INDIRECT OBSERVATION of customers

Learn how many and how much

WHAT CUSTOMERS DO
Observe their behaviors

Lab studies
- Learning prototype/MVP ➔ p. 222
- Life-size prototypes ➔ p. 226
- Wizard of Oz ➔ p. 223

Anthropologist ➔ p. 114
For field studies

Sale actions
- Mock sales ➔ p. 236
- Presales ➔ p. 237
- Crowdfunding ➔ p. 237

Tracking actions
- Ad and link tracking ➔ p. 220
- Landing page ➔ p. 228
- Split testing ➔ p. 230

WHAT CUSTOMERS SAY
Observe their attitudes

Participatory design and evaluation
- Illustrations, storyboards, and scenarios ➔ p. 224
- Speedboat ➔ p. 233
- Product box ➔ p. 234
- Buy a feature ➔ p. 235

Journalist ➔ p. 110
For interviews

Detective ➔ p. 108
For data analysis

Tip

Use these techniques to understand how customers interact with your prototypes. Investments are usually higher but produce concrete and actionable feedback.

Tip

Use these techniques at the early stages of the design process, because investment is low and they produce quick insights.

Inspired by the work in user experience by Christian Rohner (NN).

Produce Evidence with a Call to Action

Use experiments to test if customers are interested, what preferences they have, and if they are willing to pay for what you have to offer. Get them to perform a call to action (CTA) as much as possible in order to engage them and produce evidence of what works and what doesn't.

The more a customer (test subject) has to invest to perform a CTA, the stronger the evidence that he or she is really interested. Clicking a button, answering a survey, providing a personal e-mail, or making a prepurchase are different levels of investments. Select your experiments accordingly.

CTAs with a low level of investment are appropriate at the beginning of value proposition design. Those requiring a high level of investment make more sense later in the process.

DEF·I·NI·TION
Call to Action (CTA)
Prompts a subject to perform an action; used in an experiment in order to test one or more hypotheses.

Use experiments to test...

interest and relevance

Prove that potential customers and partners are genuinely interested and don't just tell you so. Show that your ideas are relevant enough to them to get them to perform actions that go beyond lip service (e.g., e-mail sign-ups, meetings with decision makers and budget holders, letters of intent, and more).

priorities and preferences

Show which jobs, pains, and gains your potential customers and partners value most and which ones they value least. Provide evidence that indicates which features of your value proposition they prefer. Prove what really matters to them and what doesn't.

willingness to pay

Provide evidence that potential customers are interested enough in the features of your value proposition to pay. Deliver facts that show they will put their money where their mouth is.

Ad Tracking

Use ad tracking to explore your potential customers' jobs, pains, gains, and interest—or lack of it—for a new value proposition. Ad tracking is an established technique used by advertisers to measure the effectiveness of ad spending. You can use the same technique to explore customer interest even before a value proposition exists.

Test customer interest with Google AdWords

We use Google AdWords to illustrate this technique because it's particularly well suited for testing based on its use of search terms for advertising (other services such as LinkedIn and Facebook also work well).

1. **Select search terms.**
   Select search terms that best represent what you want to test (e.g., the existence of a customer job, pain, or gain or the interest for a value proposition).

2. **Design your ad/test.**
   Design your test ad with a headline, link to a landing page, and blurb. Make sure it represents what you want to test.

3. **Launch your campaign.**
   Define a budget for your ad/testing campaign and launch it. Pay only for clicks on your ad, which represent interest.

4. **Measure clicks.**
   Learn how many people click on your ad. No clicks may indicate a lack of interest.

Where to apply?

Test interest early in the process to learn about the existence of customer jobs, pains, gains, and interest for a particular value proposition.

Unique Link Tracking

Set up unique link tracking to verify potential customers' or partners' interest beyond what they might tell you in a meeting, interview, or call. It's an extremely simple way to measure genuine interest.

Where to apply?

This works anywhere but is particularly interesting in industries where building MVPs is difficult, such as in industrial goods and medical devices.

221

STRATEGYZER.COM / VPD / TEST / 3.3

1
"Fabricate" a unique link.

Make a unique and trackable link to more detailed information about your ideas (e.g., a download, landing page) with a service such as goo.gl.

2
Pitch and track.

Explain your idea to a potential customer or partner. During or after the meeting (via e-mail), give the person the unique link and mention it points to more detailed information.

3
Learn about genuine interest.

Track if the customer used the link or not. If the link wasn't used, it may indicate lack of interest or more important jobs, pains, and gains than those that your idea addresses.

MVP Catalog

MVP stands for minimum viable product, a concept popularized by the lean start-up movement to efficiently test the interest in a product before building it entirely. Rather than coining a new term we stick to this established one and adapt it to testing value propositions.

Make it "real" with a representation of a value proposition.

Use the following techniques to make your value propositions feel real and tangible before implementing anything when you test them with potential customers and partners.

What's an MVP in this book?

A representation or prototype of a value proposition designed specifically to test the validity of one or more hypotheses/ assumptions.

The goal is to do so as quickly, cheaply, and efficiently as possible. MVPs are mainly used to explore potential customer and partner interest.

Tip

Start cheaply, even in large companies with big budgets. For example, use your smartphone to make and test reactions to a video before you bring in a video crew to "professionalize" videos and expand testing.

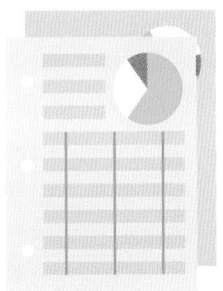

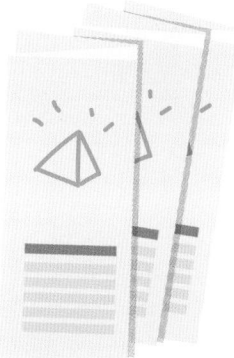

Data Sheet

Specs of your imagined value proposition
Requirements:
Word processor

Brochure

Mocked-up brochure of your imagined value proposition
Requirements:
Word processor and design skills

Storyboard

Illustration of a customer scenario showcasing your imagined value proposition
Requirements:
Sketch artist

Landing Page

Website outlining your imagined value proposition (mostly with a CTA).
Requirements:
Web designer

Product Box

Prototype packaging of your imagined value proposition
Requirements:
Packaging designer and prototype implementation

Video

Video showcasing your imagined value proposition or explaining how it works
Requirements:
Video crew

Learn with Functional MVPs

Use prototypes designed specifically to learn from experiments with potential customers and partners.

Learning Prototype

Functioning prototype of your value proposition with the most basic feature set required for learning
Requirements:
Product development

Wizard of Oz

Set up a front that looks like a real working value proposition and manually carry out the tasks of a normally automated product or service
Requirements:
Getting your hands dirty

Illustrations, Storyboards, and Scenarios

Share illustrations, storyboards, and scenarios related to your value proposition ideas with your potential customers to learn what really matters to them. These types of Illustrations are quick and cheap to produce and make even the most complex value propositions tangible.

Tips

- In a business-to-business (B2B) context think of value propositions for each important customer segment, such as users, budget owners, decision makers, and so on.
- For existing organizations, make sure to include customer-facing staff in the process, notably to get buy-in and gain access to customers to present the illustrations.
- Complement the illustrations with mock data sheets, brochures, or videos to make your ideas even more tangible.
- Run A/B tests with slightly different scenarios to capture which variations get most traction.
- Four or five meetings per customer segment are typically sufficient to generate meaningful feedback.
- Leverage the customer relationship and repeat the process later on with more sophisticated prototypes.

Process adapted from Christian Doll, bicdo.de.

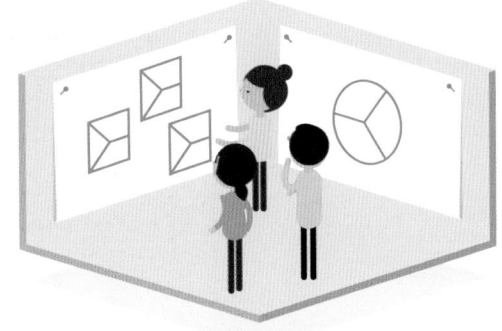

1
Prototype alternative value propositions.
Come up with several alternative prototypes for the same customer segment. Go for diversity (i.e., 8-12 radically different value propositions) and variations (i.e., slightly different alternatives).

2
Define scenarios.
Sketch out scenarios and storyboards that describe how a customer will experience each value proposition in a real-world setting.

3
Create compelling visuals.
Use an illustrator to consolidate your sketches into compelling visuals that make the customer experience clear and tangible. Use single illustrations for each value proposition or entire story boards.

Questions to ask customers:

Which value propositions really create value for you?

Which ones should we keep and move forward with, and which ones should we abandon?

Dig deeper for each value proposition; pay attention to jobs, pains, and gains; and inquire:

· What is missing?

· What should be left aside?

· What should be added?

· What should be reduced?

· Always ask why to capture qualitative feedback.

4

Test with customers.

Meet customers and present the different illustrations, scenarios, and storyboards to start a conversation, provoke reactions, and learn what matters to them. Get customers to rank value propositions from most valuable to least helpful.

5

Debrief and adapt.

Use the insights from your meetings with customers. Decide which value propositions you will continue exploring, which ones you will abandon, and which ones you will adapt.

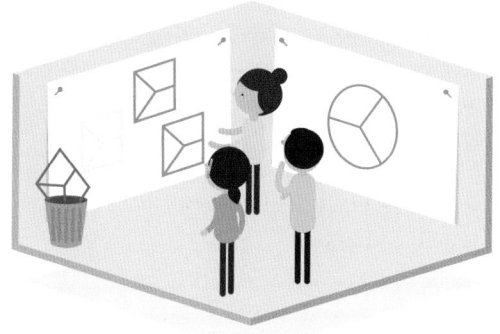

Life-Size Experiments

Get your customers to interact with life-size prototypes and real-world replicas of service experiences. Stick to the principles of rapid, quick, and low-cost prototyping to gather customer insights despite the more sophisticated set-up. Add a CTA to validate interest.

Concept Cars and Life-Size Prototypes

These are cars made to showcase new designs and technologies. Their purpose is get reactions from customers rather than to go into mass production directly.

Lit Motors used lean start-up principles to prototype and test a fully electric, gyroscopically stabilized two-wheel drive with customers. Because this type of vehicle represents a completely new concept, it was essential for Lit Motors to understand customer perception and acceptance from the very beginning.

In addition, Lit Motors added a CTA to validate customer interest beyond initial interactions with the prototype. Customers can prereserve a vehicle with a deposit ranging from $250 to $10,000. Deposits go into a holding account until vehicles are ready, with higher deposits moving customers to the front of the waiting list.

Prototype Spaces

These are spaces to cocreate products and service experiences with customers and/or observe their behavior to gain new insights. Invite potential customers to create their own perfect experience. Include industry experts to help build and test new concepts and ideas.

Hotel chain Marriott built a prototyping space in its headquarters' basement called the Underground. Guests and experts are invited to create the hotel experience of the future by cocreating hotel rooms and other spaces. Guests are invited to add furniture, electricity outlets, electronic gadgets, and more, to hotel room replicas that can easily be reconfigured.

Tips

- Make sure you validate life-size prototypes and service experiences with a CTA. Customers will always be tempted to create the perfect experience in a prototype setting, whereas they might not be willing to pay for it in real life.
- Use quicker and cheaper validation methods before you draw on life-size prototypes and real-world replicas of service experiences.
- Don't let the costs for this type of prototyping get out of hand. Stick to the principles of rapid, quick, and low-cost prototyping as much as possible, while offering a close-to-life experience to test subjects.

Landing Page

The typical landing page MVP is a single web page or simple website that describes a value proposition or some aspects of it. The website visitor is invited to perform a CTA that allows the tester to validate one or more hypotheses. The main learning instrument of a landing page MVP is the conversion rate from the number of people visiting the site to visitors performing the CTA (e.g., e-mail sign-up, simulated purchase).

"The goal of a landing page MVP is to validate one or more hypotheses, not to collect e-mails or sell, which is a nice by-product of the experiment."

When?

Test early to learn if the jobs, pains, and gains you intend to address and/or your value proposition are sufficiently important to your customer for them to perform an action.

Variations

Combine with split testing to investigate preferences or alternatives that work better than others. Measure click activity with so-called heat maps to learn where visitors click on your page.

Use your value map to craft the headline and text that describes your value proposition on the landing page.

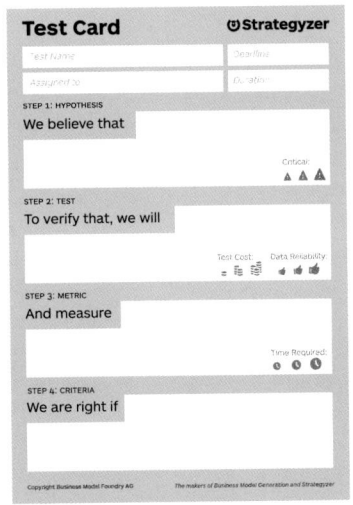

Design your landing page, traffic generation, and CTA based on your learning goals.

Traffic

Generate traffic to your landing page MVP with ads, social media, or your existing channels. Make sure you address the target customers you want to learn about, not just anybody.

Headline

Craft a headline that speaks to your potential customers and introduces the value proposition.

Value Proposition

Use the previously described techniques to make your value proposition clear and tangible to potential customers.

Call to Action

Get website visitors to perform an action that you can learn from (e.g., e-mail sign-up, surveys, fake purchase, prepurchase). Limit your CTAs to optimize learning.

Outreach

Reach out to people who performed your CTA and investigate why they were motivated enough to perform the action. Learn about their jobs, pains, and gains. Of course, this requires collecting contact information during the CTA.

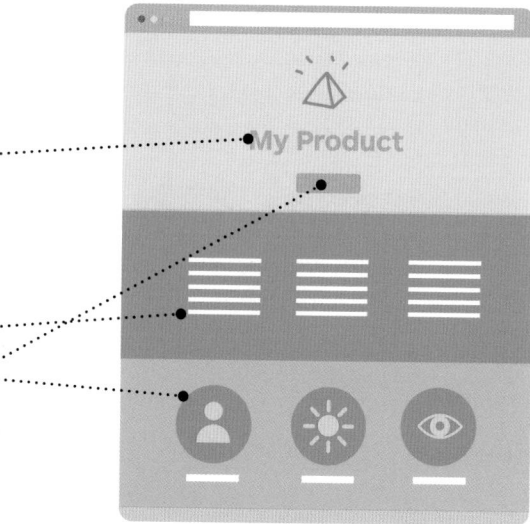

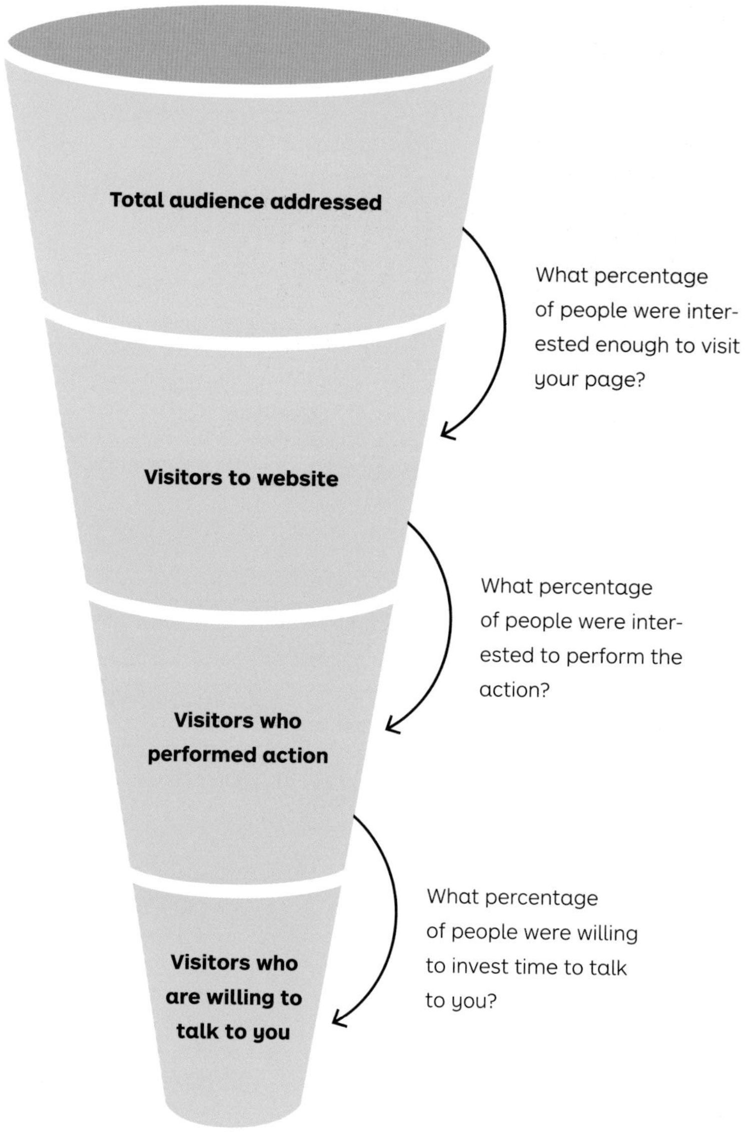

Tips

- Consider building a landing page MVP that gives the illusion that a value proposition exists even if doesn't yet. Your insights from a CTA closer to reality (e.g., simulated sales) will provide more realistic evidence than, for example, the e-mail sign-up to a planned value proposition or a prepurchase of it.
- Be transparent with your test subjects after a concluded experiment if you, for instance, "fake" the existence of a value proposition. Consider offering them a reward for participating in the experiment.
- A landing page MVP can be set up as a standalone web page or within an existing website.

Total audience addressed

Visitors to website

Visitors who performed action

Visitors who are willing to talk to you

What percentage of people were interested enough to visit your page?

What percentage of people were interested to perform the action?

What percentage of people were willing to invest time to talk to you?

Split Testing

Split testing, also known as A/B testing, is a technique to compare the performance of two or more options. In this book we apply the technique to compare the performance of alternative value propositions with customers or to learn more about jobs, pains, and gains.

Control

8%

Send the same amount of people to the different options you want to test.

Compare how each option performs regarding your CTA.

Challenge

20%

Conducting Split Tests

The most common form of split test is to test two or more variations of a web page or a purpose-built landing page (e.g., the variations may have design tweaks or outline slightly or entirely different value propositions). This technique was popularized by companies such as Google and LinkedIn, as well as the 2008 Obama campaign. Split tests can also be conducted in the physical world. The main learning instrument is to compare if conversion rates regarding a specific call to action differ between competing alternatives.

What to Test?

Here are some elements that you can easily test with A/B testing

- Alternative features
- Pricing
- Discounts
- Copy text
- Packaging
- Website variations
- …

Call to Action

How many of the test subjects perform the CTA?

- Purchase
- E-mail sign-up
- Click on button
- Survey
- Completion of any other task

Split testing the title of this book

For this book we performed several split tests. For example, we redirected traffic from businessmodelgeneration.com to test three different book titles. We tested the titles with more than 120,000 people over a period of 5 weeks.

There were several CTAs. The first one was to simply click on a button labeled "learn more." Then people could sign up with their e-mail for the launch of the book. In the last CTA, we asked them to fill out a survey to learn more about their jobs, pains, and gains. As a small reward we showed people a video explaining the Value Proposition Canvas.

Tips

- Test a single variation in the challenging option if you want to clearly identify what leads to a better performance.
- Use so-called multivariate testing to test several combined elements to figure out which combination creates the highest impact.
- Use Google AdWords or other options to attract test subjects.
- Make sure you reach a statistical significance of greater than 95 percent
- Use tools such as Google Website Optimizer, Optimizely, or others to easily perform split tests.

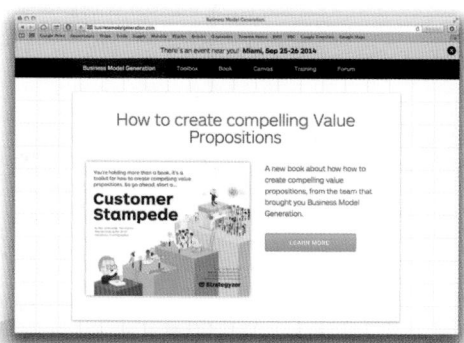

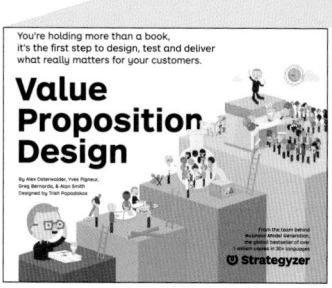

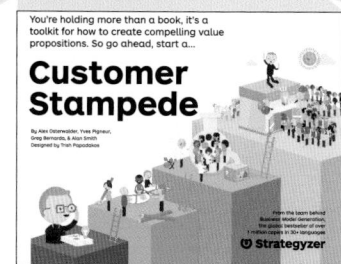

Conversion rates: 8.51 percent   6.62 percent   8.21 percent

Innovation Games®

Innovation Games is a methodology popularized by Luke Hohmann to help you design better value propositions by using collaborative play with your (potential) customers. The games can be played online or in person. We present three of them.

All three Innovation Games we present can be used in various ways. We outline three specific tasks they can help us with when it comes to the Value Proposition Canvas and related hypotheses.

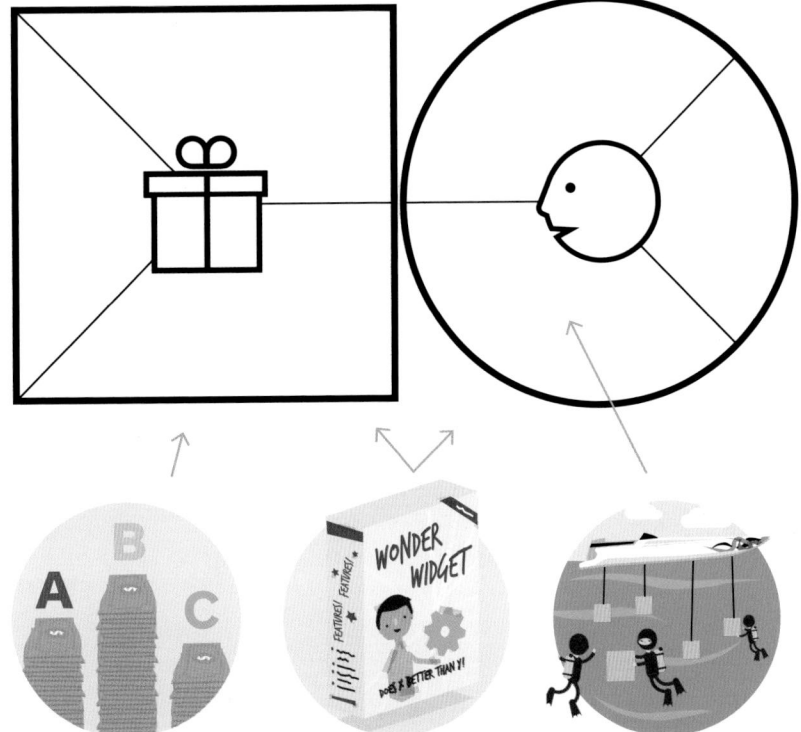

Buy a Feature

Task: Prioritize which features customers want most.

Product Box

Task: Understand your customers' jobs, pains, and gains and the value propositions they'd like.

Speed Boat

Task: Identify the most extreme pains holding customers back from completing their jobs to be done.

Hohmann, Innovation Games, 2006.

Speed Boat

This is a simple but powerful game to help you verify your understanding of customer pains. Get your customers to explicitly state the problems, obstacles, and risks that are holding them back from successfully performing their jobs to be done by using the analogy of a speed boat held back by anchors.

1

Set-up.

Prepare a large poster with a speed-boat floating at sea.

2

Identify pains.

Invite customers to identify the problems, obstacles, and risks that are preventing them from success-fully performing their jobs. Each issue should go on a large sticky note. Ask them to place each sticky as anchors to the boat—the lower the anchor, the more extreme the pain.

3

Analysis.

Compare the outcomes of this exercise with your previous understanding of what is holding customers back from performing their jobs to be done.

Tips

- This exercise can be used during the design phase to identify customer pains or during testing to verify your existing understanding.
- Use a sailing boat with anchors and sails if you want to work on pains and gains simultaneously. The sails allow you to ask, "What makes the boat faster," in addition to using the anchors to symbolize what holds people back.

Product Box

In this game, you ask customers to design a product box that represents the value proposition they'd want to buy from you. You'll learn what matters to customers and which features they get excited about.

1

Design.

Invite customers to a workshop. Give them a cardboard box and ask them to literally design a product box that they would buy. The box should feature the key marketing messages, main features, and key benefits that they would expect from your value proposition.

2

Pitch.

Ask your customers to imagine they're selling your product at a tradeshow. Pretend you're a skeptical prospect and get your customer to pitch the box to you.

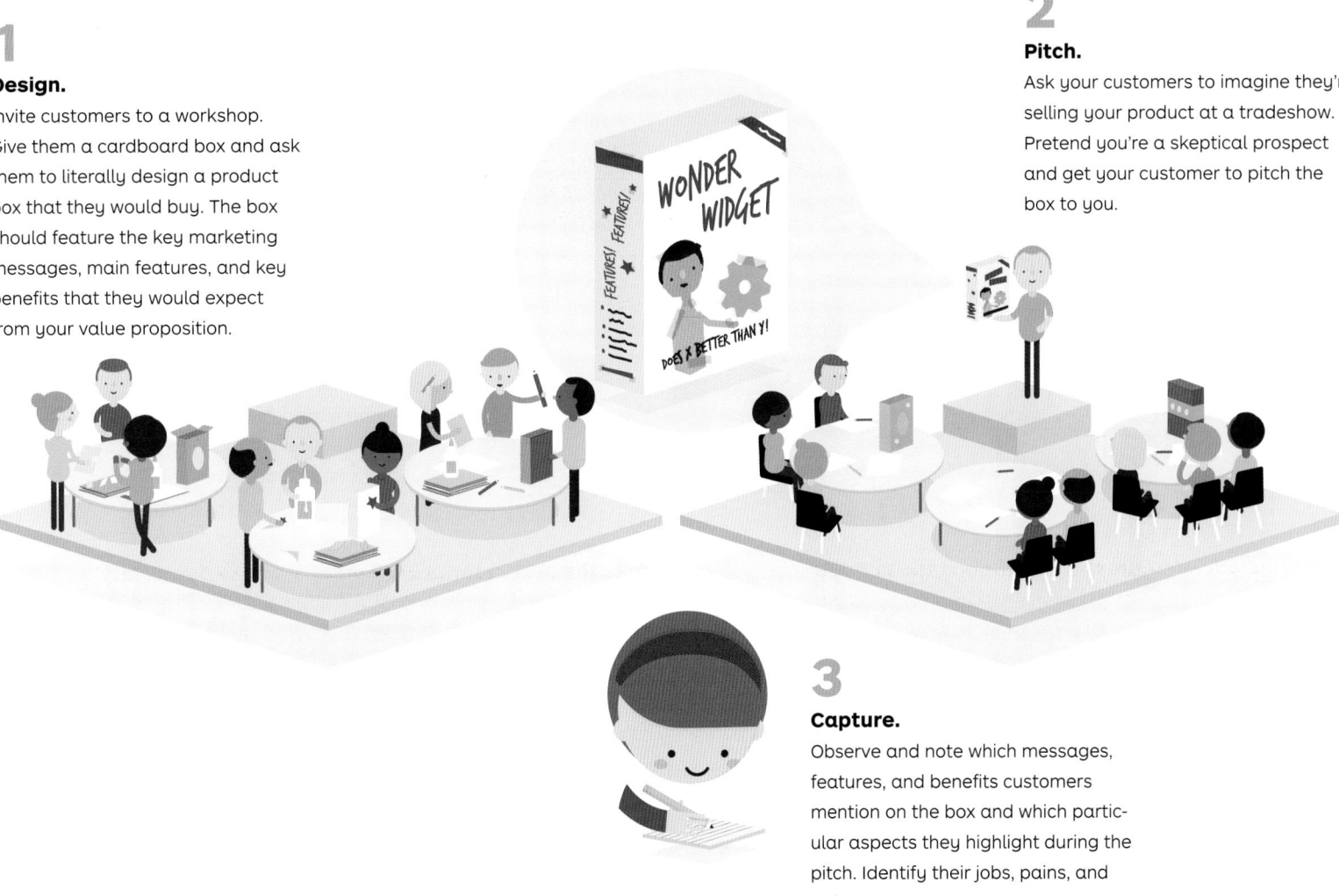

3

Capture.

Observe and note which messages, features, and benefits customers mention on the box and which particular aspects they highlight during the pitch. Identify their jobs, pains, and gains.

Buy a Feature

This is a sophisticated game to get customers to prioritize among a list of predefined (but not yet existing) value proposition features. Customers get a limited budget of play money to buy their preferred features, which you price based on real-world factors.

Features	Price	$35	$35	$35	Total Required	Bought?
	$35	20	0	10	-5	No
	$50	5	0	0	-45	No
	$70	10	35	25	0	Yes

1
Select and price features.

Select the features for which you want to test customer preferences. Price each one based on development cost, market price, or other factors that are important to you.

2
Define the budget.

Participants buy features as a group, but each participant gets a personal budget that he or she can allocate individually. Make sure the personal budget forces participants to pool resources, and the overall budget forces them to make hard choices among the features they want.

3
Have the participants buy.

Invite participants to allocate their budget among the features they want. Instruct them to collaborate with others to get more features.

4
Analyze outcomes.

Analyze which features get most traction and are bought and which ones are not.

Mock Sales

A great way to test sincere customer interest is to set up a mock sale before your value proposition even exists. The goal is make your customers believe they are completing a real purchase. This is easily done in an online context but can also be done in a physical one.

Online

Test different levels of customer commitment with these three experiments:

Learn about customer interest by measuring how many people click on a simple "buy now" button.

Learn how pricing influences customer interest. Combine with A/B testing (see p. 230) to learn more about demand elasticity and the optimal price point.

Get hard data by simulating a transaction with the customer's credit card information. This is the strongest evidence of customer demand (see tips to manage customer perception, p. 237).

Physical World

Mock sales are not limited to online. Here's what retailers do to test customer interest and pricing in the real world:

Introduce products that don't exist yet in a limited number of (mail order) catalogs.

Sell a product in one retail location only for a limited amount of time (different from a pilot, which typically covers an entire market).

Presales

The main objective of this type of presales is to explore customer interest; it is not to sell. Customers make a purchase commitment and are aware of the fact that your value proposition does not yet fully exist. In case of a lack of interest, the sale is canceled and the customer reimbursed.

Tips

Don't fear that mock sales might alienate customers and negatively affect your brand. Manage customer perception well, and mock sales can be turned into an advantage. Build on these best practices:

- Explain that you were performing a test after the customer completes the mock purchase.
- Be transparent about which information you keep or erase.
- Always erase credit card information in a fake purchase.
- Offer a reward for participating in the test (e.g. goodies, discounts).

You will turn test subjects into advocates for your brand rather than alienate them if you manage customer perception well.

Attention

Remember that successful presales are only an indicator. Ouya, an Android-based video game console, raised millions on Kickstarter but later failed to attract a large base of customers or design a scalable business model.

Online

Platforms such as Kickstarter made preselling popular. They allow you to advertise a project, and if customers like it, they can pledge money. Projects receive funds only if they reach their predefined funding goals. If you are up for building the required infrastructure you can also set up your own presales process.

Physical World

Pledges, letters of intent, and signatures, even if not legally binding, are a powerful technique to test potential customers' willingness to buy. This is also easier to apply in a B2B context.

3.4
Bringing It All Together

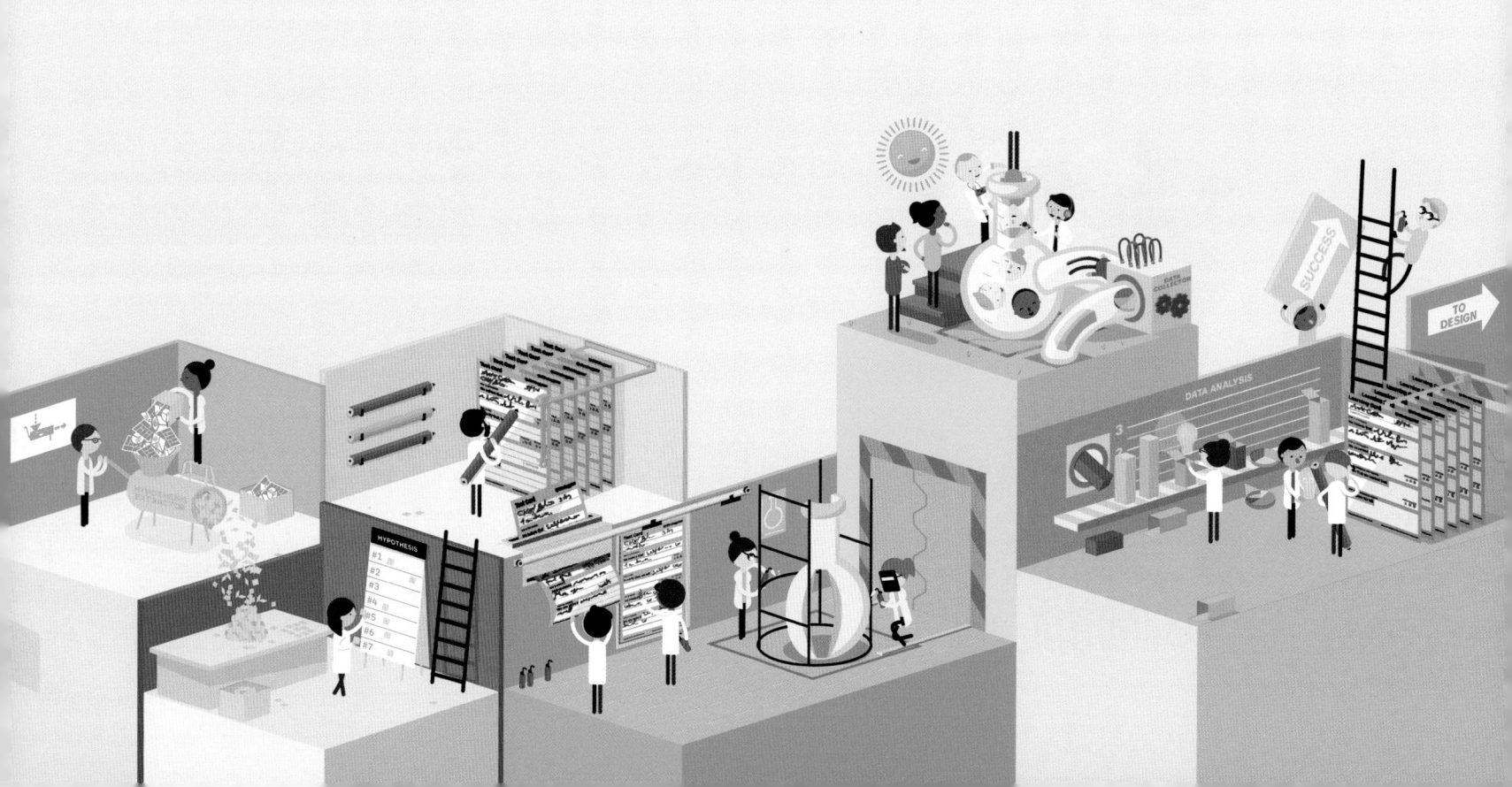

The Testing Process

Use all the tools you learned about to describe what you need to test and how you will do so in order to turn your idea into reality.

What to Test

With the Value Proposition and Business Model Canvases, you map out how you believe your idea could become a success. This foundation allows you to easily make the hypotheses explicit that need to be true for your idea to work. Start by testing the most important ones with a series of experiments.

How to Test

With the testing card, you describe how exactly you will verify your most important hypotheses and what you will measure. After one or more completed experiments, you use the learning card to capture your insights and indicate whether you need to learn more, iterate, pivot, or move on to test the next important hypothesis.

What's Next

Keep your eyes on the prize, and make sure you are progressing. Track whether you are advancing from your initial idea toward a profitable and scalable business via problem-solution fit, product-market fit, and business model fit.

1
**(re)Shape
your ideas.**

(6)

2
**Extract
your
hypotheses.**

5A
INVALIDATED
iterate or pivot

5B
UNCERTAIN
test more

Build

Learning Card

5
**Capture
learnings
and next
actions.**

5C
VALIDATED
*progress toward
next element*

Learn

4
**Enter the
learning loop.**

Measure

Test Card

3
**Design
your
tests.**

6
**Measure
progress.**

**Customer
Discovery**

Pivot

**Customer
Validation**

**Customer
Creation**

**Company
Building**

242

Measure Your Progress

The testing process allows you to continuously reduce uncertainty and gets you closer to turning your idea into a real business. Measure your progress toward this goal by tracking the activities you've done and the results you've achieved. We designed this spread that allows you to understand if you're progressing based on Steve Blank's Investment Readiness Thermometer.

Download Progress Indicators

Blank, Investment Readiness Thermometer, 2013, http://steveblank.com/2013/11/25/its-time-to-play-moneyball-the-investment-readiness-level/.

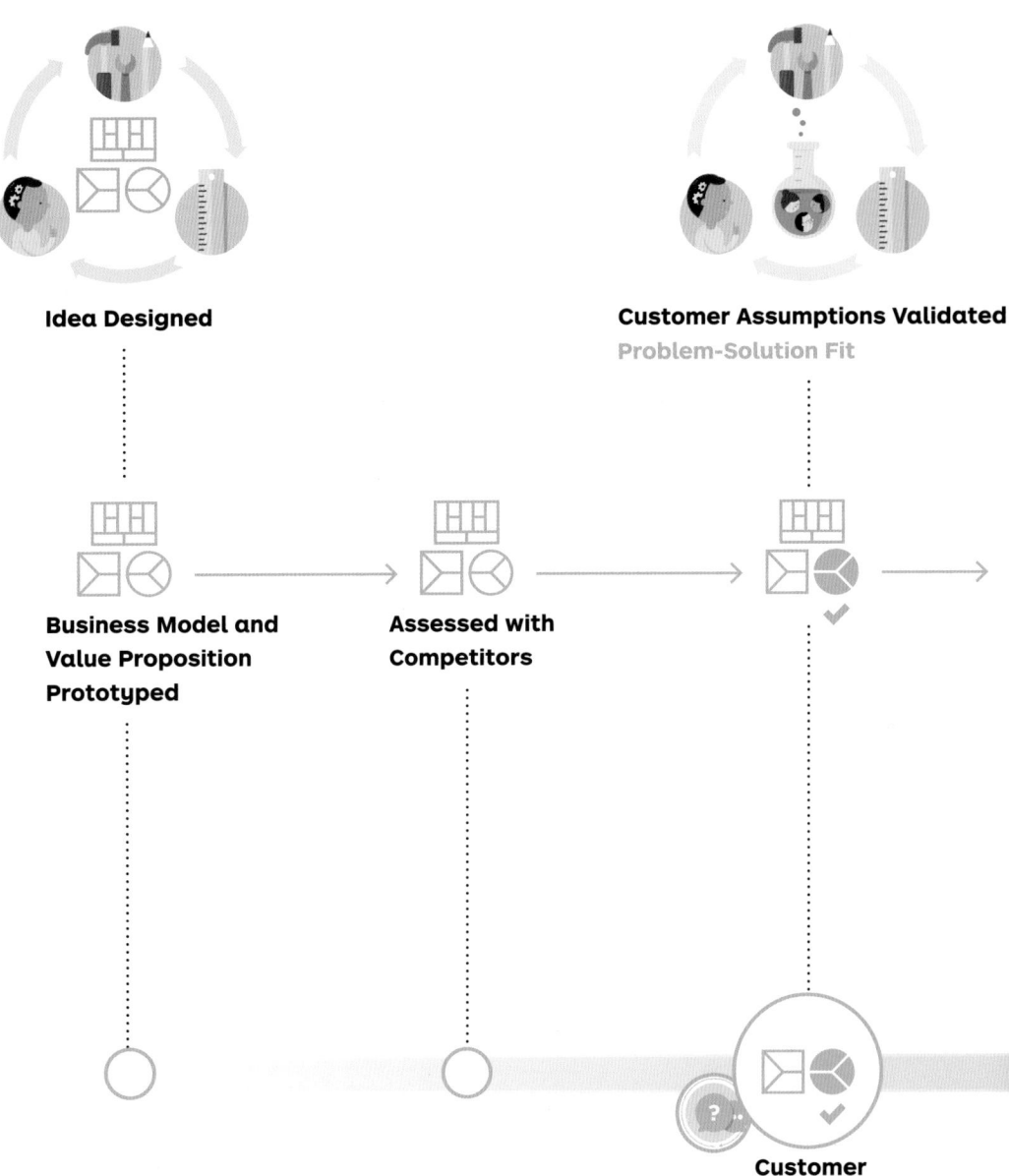

Idea Designed

Customer Assumptions Validated
Problem-Solution Fit

Business Model and Value Proposition Prototyped

Assessed with Competitors

Customer Discovery

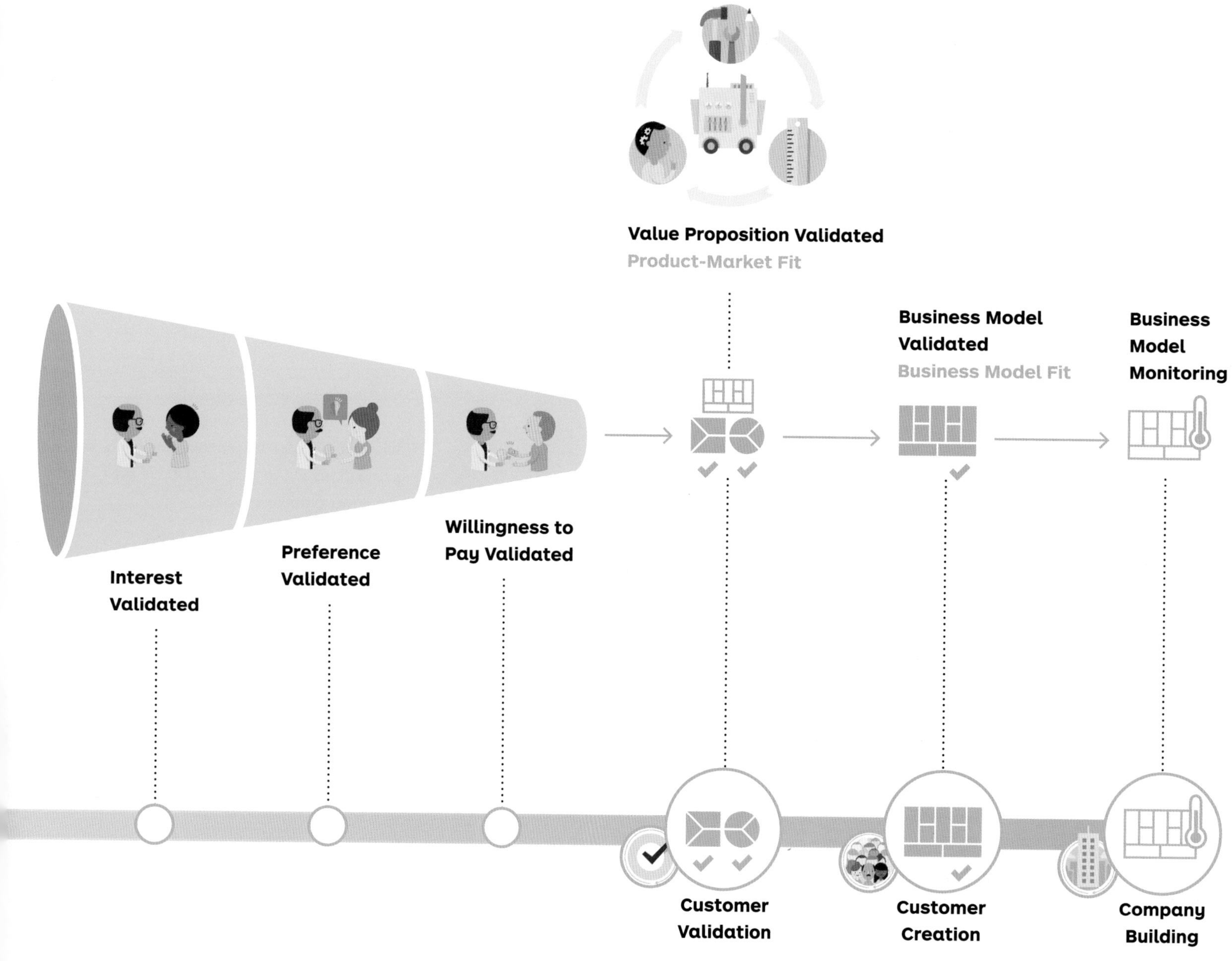

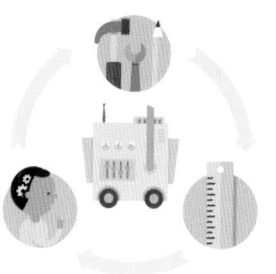

Value Proposition Validated
Product-Market Fit

Business Model Validated
Business Model Fit

Business Model Monitoring

Interest Validated

Preference Validated

Willingness to Pay Validated

Customer Validation

Customer Creation

Company Building

The Progress Board

Use the progress board to manage and monitor your tests and assess how much progress you are making toward success.

🦉 *Get Progress Board poster*

What did I test already?

Use the Value Proposition and Business Model Canvases to track which elements you have tested, validated, or invalidated.

What am I testing, and what did I learn?

Track the tests you are planning, building, measuring, and digesting to learn and make your insights and follow-up actions explicit.

How much progress did I make?

Keep score of how much progress you are making.

1
(re)Shape your ideas.

(6)

2
Extract your hypotheses.

back to the drawing board: iterate or pivot your design

3
Design your tests.

5A
INVALIDATED

5
Insights and Actions

5B
LEARN MORE

4
Tests

backlog → build → measure → learn → done

5C
VALIDATED

advance to next step: move on in your quest to turn your idea into reality

6
Measure progress.

Owlet: Constant Progress with Systematic Design and Testing

Wireless monitoring of babies' blood oxygen, heart rate, and sleep data.*

Owlet Business Model: version 0

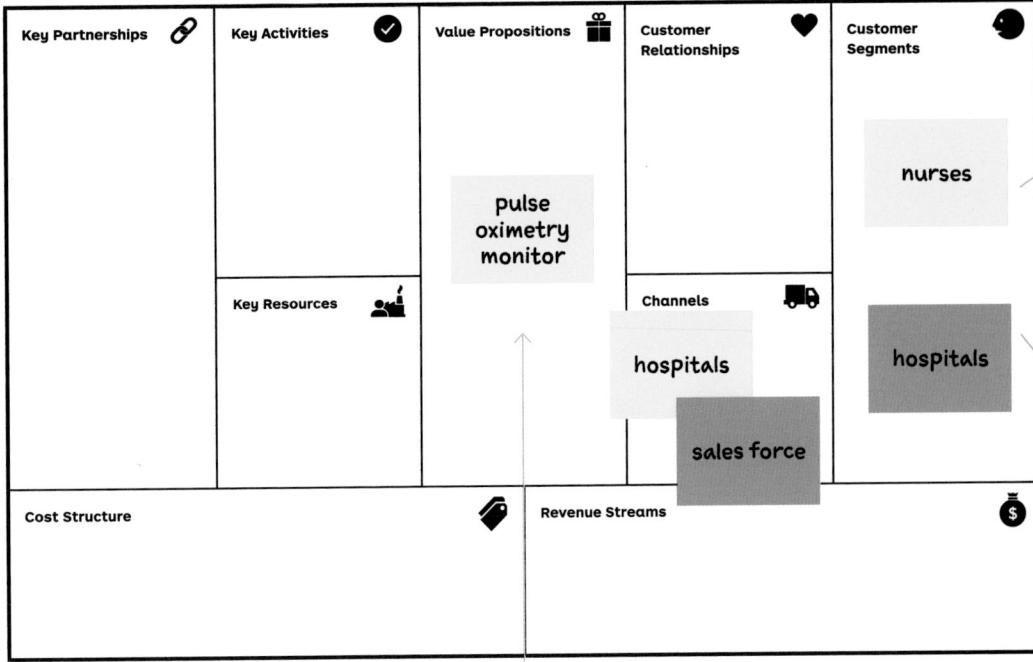

1

Initial idea

An opportunity

Monitoring pulse oximetry could be easier without the cord between the device and the monitor display.

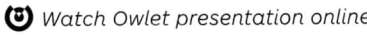 *Watch Owlet presentation online*

Test 1A: Nurse Interviews

HYPOTHESIS: Wireless pulse oximetry is more convenient

METRIC: Percentage of positive feedback

TEST: Interview nurses

DATA: Of 58 nurses interviewed, 93 percent prefer the wireless monitoring.

Validated: 1 week, $0

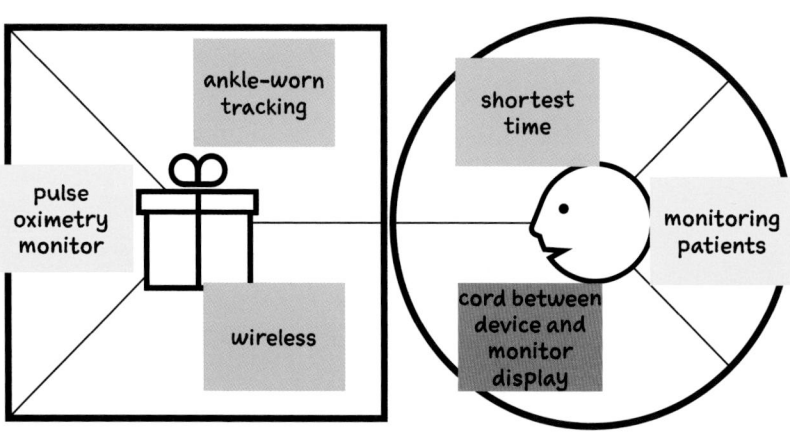

Nurses

Test 1B: Hospital Administrator Interviews

HYPOTHESIS: Wireless pulse oximetry is more convenient.

METRIC: Percentage of positive feedback

TEST: Interview hospital administrators

DATA: 0 percent ready to pay more for wireless "ease of use is not a pain, if not cost-effective."

Unvalidated: 1 week, $0

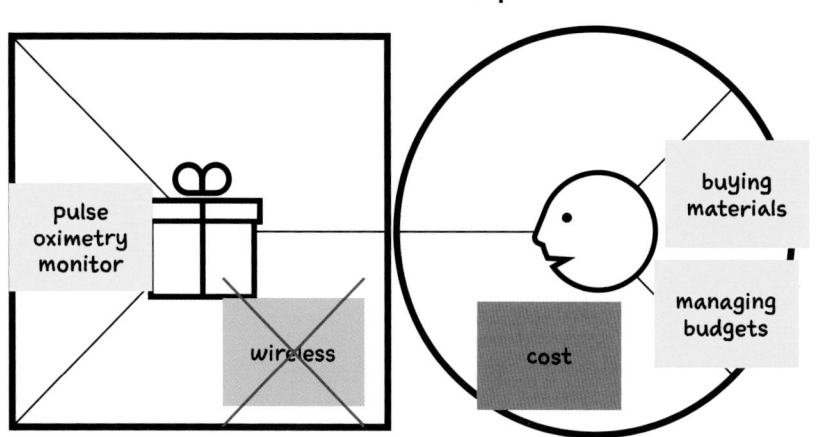

Hospital administrators

Pivot:
change the customer segment

Owlet Business Model: version 2

Key Partnerships 🔗	Key Activities ✓	Value Propositions 🎁	Customer Relationships ♥	Customer Segments ◐
		baby alarm		**parents**
	Key Resources 🏭		Channels 🚚	
			baby stores	
Cost Structure 🏷			Revenue Streams 💰	
			<$200 price	

DATA: Sudden infant death syndrome (SIDS) is the leading cause of infant deaths.

a first pivot after one week

Pivot:
Change the customer segment from nurses and hospitals to worried parents.

2
Iteration
Peace of mind for parents

A wireless monitor that collects the baby's heart rate, oxygen level, and sleep pattern and sends them via Bluetooth to the parents' smartphone with alerts; distributed by baby stores.

Test 2: Parent interviews

HYPOTHESIS: Parents are ready to adopt
and buy a wireless baby alarm.
METRIC: Percentage of adopting parents
TEST: Interview mothers
DATA: Of 105 mothers interviewed, 96 percent
adopt the wireless monitoring.
"Awesome. I want to buy now!"
Validated

Test 3: MVP Landing page

HYPOTHESIS: A smart bootie is convenient and
easy to use for monitoring.
METRIC: Number of positive comments
TEST: An MVP, with a video on a website
DATA: 17,000 views, 5,500 shares of Facebook,
500 positive comments by parents, distributors,
and research organizations
Validated, 2 weeks, $220

Test 4: A/B Price test

HYPOTHESIS: Rental versus sale at $200+
sale price
METRIC: Percentage for a sale price
TEST: A/B testing, 3 rounds, on the website
DATA: 1,170 people tested, $299 the best price
Validated, 8 weeks, $30

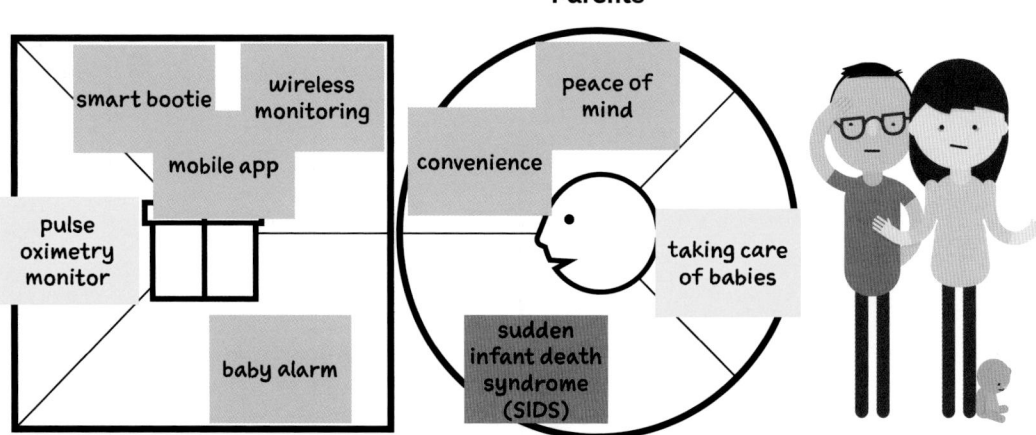

seems to be
a promising
business
but...

Owlet Business Model: version 3

Key Partnerships 🔗	Key Activities ✓	Value Propositions 🎁	Customer Relationships ♥	Customer Segments
		baby alarm		worried parents
	Key Resources 🏭		Channels 🚚	
	FDA clearance	infant health tracker	baby stores	less worried parents

Cost Structure 🏷	Revenue Streams 💰
	<$200 price

after 24 weeks, and $1,150 for the tests, including a technical proof of concept

Need to be revalidated...

3
Iteration

Peace of mind, but for less worried parents

Running lean

based on experts, a Food and Drug Administration (FDA) clearance for a baby alarm is one year, $120,000–$200,000

With a more minimal, less risky product, an infant health tracker (heart rate, oxygen levels, and sleep patterns), but without alarm, for another customer segment: the less worried parents.

Test 5: Interview/Proposition: "Owlet Challenge"

HYPOTHESIS: Less worried parents are ready to adopt and buy a wireless baby health tracker, without alarm.

METRIC: Percentage of parents adopting the no-alarm tracker

TEST: Interview at retail locations, having to choose between the Owlet tracker and other similar systems (video, sound, and movement)

DATA: Of 81 people interviewed, 20 percent adopted the Owlet tracker.

Validated, 3 weeks, $0

Less worried parents

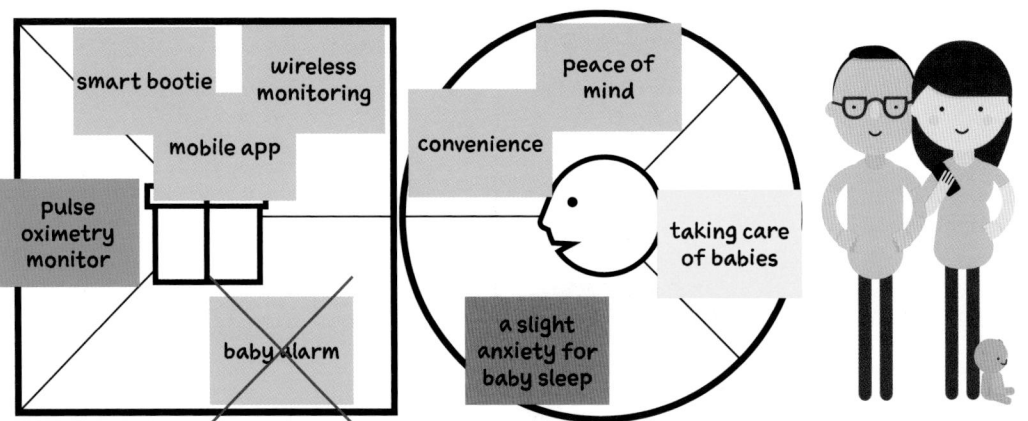

Owlet decided to start first with the baby health tracker and to come later with the baby alarm, after FDA clearance.

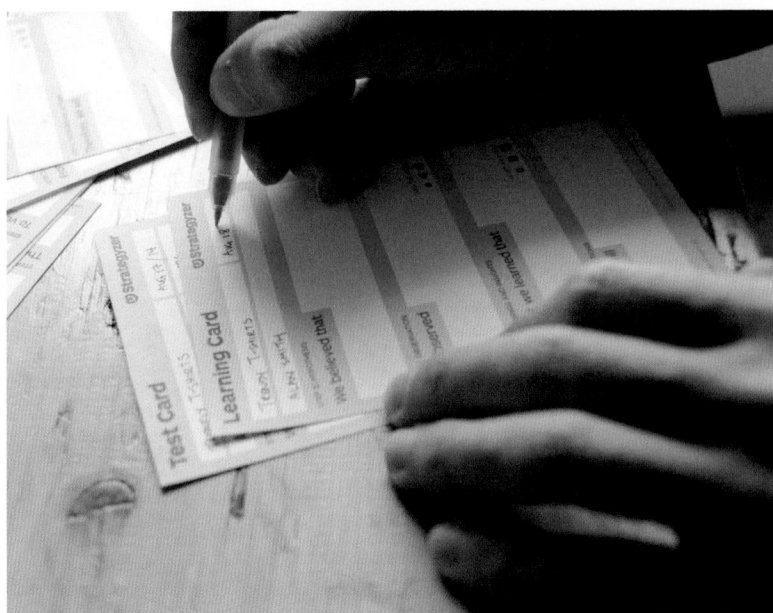

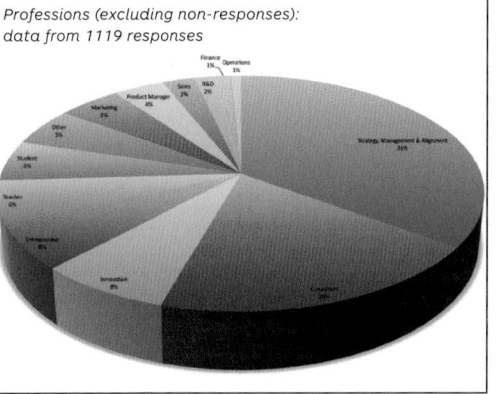

Professions (excluding non-responses): data from 1119 responses

Lessons Learned

Testing Step-by-Step

Your customers are the judge, jury, and executioner of your value proposition, so get outside of the building and test your ideas with the customer development and lean start-up process. Make sure you start with quick and cheap experiments to test the assumptions underlying your ideas when uncertainty is at its maximum.

Experiment Library

What your customers say might wildly differ from what they do in reality. Go beyond talking to customers and conduct a series of experiments. Get them to perform actions that provide evidence of their interest, their preferences, and their willingness to pay.

Bringing It All Together

Launching ideas without testing is wishful thinking. Testing ideas without launching is just a pastime. Launching tested ideas can change your life as an entrepreneur. Measure your progress from idea to real business step by step.

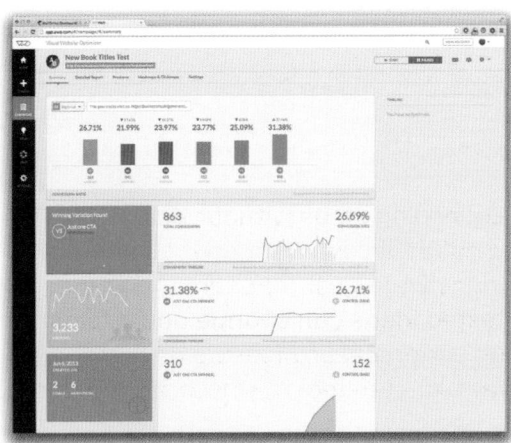

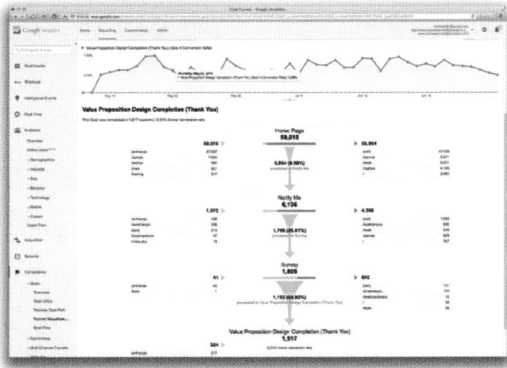
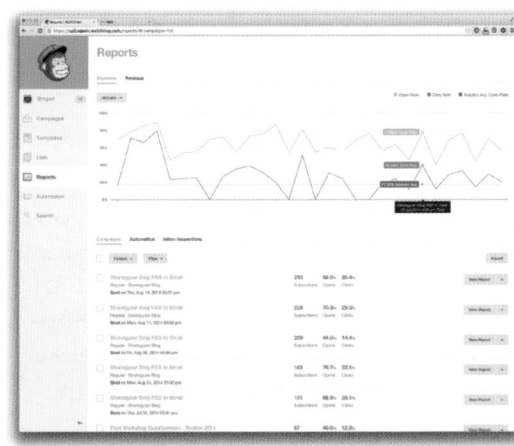

evo

lve

4

Use the Value Proposition and Business Model Canvas as a shared language to **Create Alignment** p. 260 throughout every part of your organization while it continuously evolves. Make sure you constantly **Measure and Monitor** p. 262 your value propositions and business models in order to **Improve Relentlessly** p. 264 and **Reinvent Yourself Constantly** p. 266.

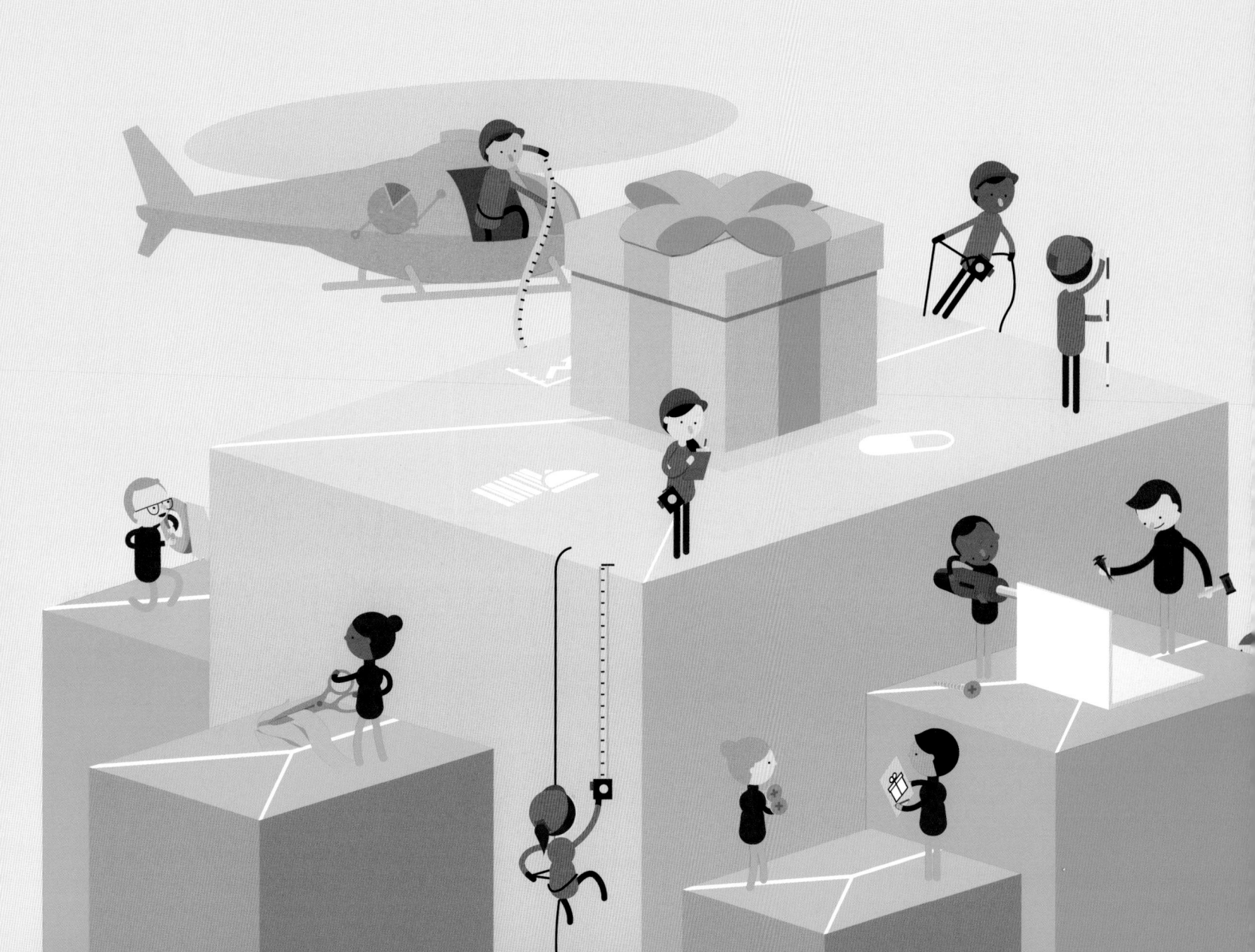

Create Alignment

The Value Proposition Canvas is an excellent alignment tool. It helps you communicate to different stakeholders which customer jobs, pains, and gains you are focusing on and explains how exactly your products and services relieve pains and create gains.

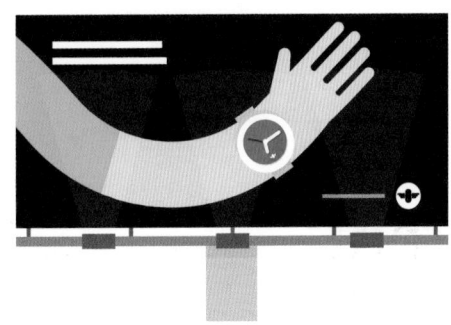

Packaging

Advertising

Explainer Videos

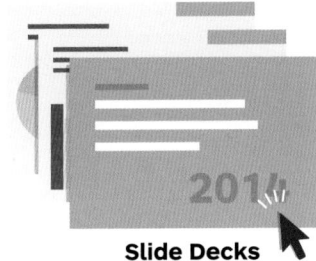

Slide Decks

Sales Scripts

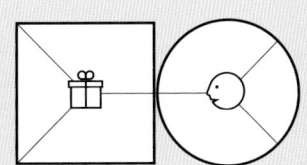

Craft aligned messages.

Align internal and external stakeholders.

Marketing

Craft marketing messages based on the jobs, pains, and gains your products and services are helping with. Align customer-facing messaging all the way from advertising to package design. Point out which pain relievers and gain creators to focus on.

(Channel) Partners

Bring (channel) partners on board, and explain your value proposition. Help them understand why customers will love your products and services by highlighting pain relievers and gain creators.

Employees

Help all employees understand which customers you are targeting and which jobs, pains, and gains you are addressing, and outline how exactly your products and services will create value for customers. Explain how the value proposition fits into the business model.

Sales

Help sales understand which segments to target and what customers' jobs, pains, and gains are. Highlight which attributes of your value proposition are most likely to sell by relieving pains and creating gains. Align sales scripts and pitch decks.

Shareholders

Explain to your shareholders how exactly you intend to create value for your customers. Clarify how the (new or improved) value proposition will bolster your business model and create a competitive advantage.

Measure
and Monitor

Use the Value Proposition and Business Model Canvases to create and monitor performance indicators once your value proposition is operational in the market. Track the performance of your business model, your value proposition, and your customers' satisfaction.

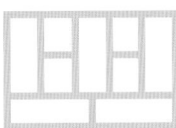

Business Model Performance

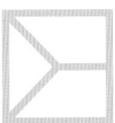

Value Proposition Performance
(Quantitative Facts)

Customer Satisfaction
(Perception)

BUILD
indicators

Investigate Change

Δ **MONITOR**
indicator/target

Track

MEASURE
(continuously)

Performance

Threshold

Indicator

Time

Target

50%

25%

★★★★⯪

80% satisfied
with balance

Indicator

\# workshop guide
downloads by readers
who signed up online

rating on
Amazon.com

conversion rate from
book to online sign-up

\# of readers who feel
theory/practice is
good

Building Block

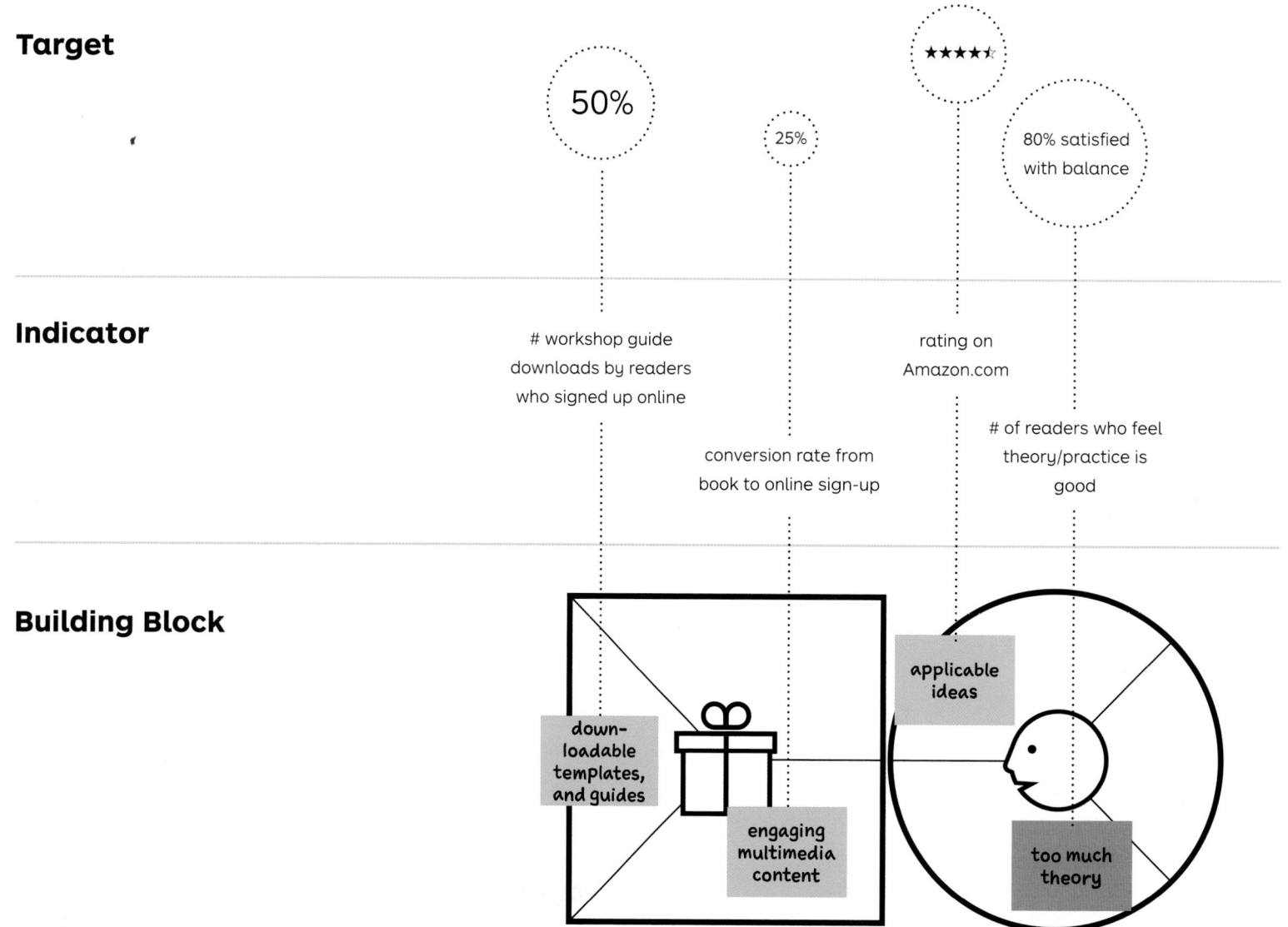

down-
loadable
templates,
and guides

engaging
multimedia
content

applicable
ideas

too much
theory

Improve Relentlessly

Value Proposition Performance
(Quantitative Facts)

Customer Satisfaction
(Perception)

Build

5C
INVALIDATED
no impact on customer satisfaction

5A
UNCERTAIN
test more

Learning Card

Test Card

Learn

Measure
measure causal effect on customer satisfaction

5B
VALIDATED
improved customer satisfaction

Use the same tools and processes from testing and monitoring to improve your value proposition once it's in the market. Continuously test "what if" improvement scenarios, and measure their impact on customer satisfaction.

Performance

Time

Customer Satisfaction

Hilti

Construction Companies

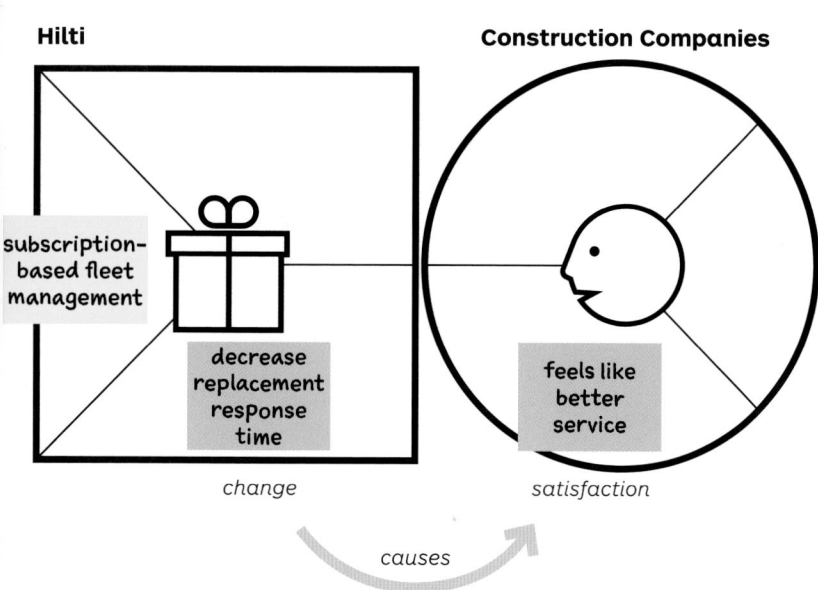

subscription-based fleet management

decrease replacement response time

change

feels like better service

satisfaction

causes

Test Card ⓤ**Strategyzer**

Test Name | *Deadline*
Assigned to | *Duration*

STEP 1: HYPOTHESIS

We believe that **if we decrease the response time to replace broken tools, customers feel like they are getting a better service.**

Critical: ▲ ▲ ⚠

STEP 2: TEST

To verify that, we will **decrease response time for one client** by 25% on average.

Test Cost: 🪙🪙🪙 Data Reliability: 👍👍

STEP 3: METRIC

And measure **customer satisfaction at the beginning and the end of the experiment.**

Time Required: 🕐🕐🕐

STEP 4: CRITERIA

We are right if **customer satisfaction increases by x%.**

Copyright Business Model Foundry AG   The makers of Business Model Generation and Strategyzer

Value Proposition Design

Readers

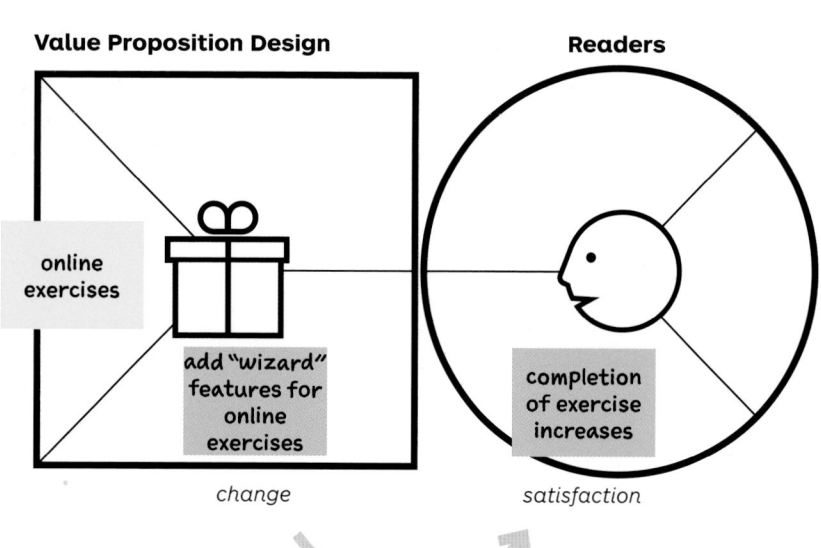

online exercises

add "wizard" features for online exercises

change

completion of exercise increases

satisfaction

causes

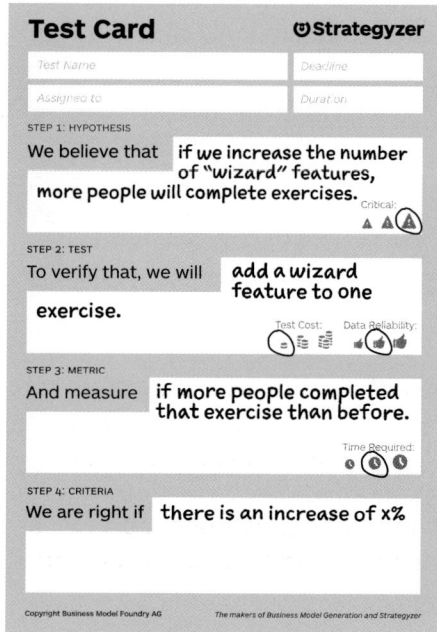

Test Card ⓤ**Strategyzer**

Test Name | *Deadline*
Assigned to | *Duration*

STEP 1: HYPOTHESIS

We believe that **if we increase the number of "wizard" features, more people will complete exercises.**

Critical: ▲ ▲ ⚠

STEP 2: TEST

To verify that, we will **add a wizard feature to one exercise.**

Test Cost: 🪙🪙🪙 Data Reliability: 👍👍

STEP 3: METRIC

And measure **if more people completed that exercise than before.**

Time Required: 🕐🕐🕐

STEP 4: CRITERIA

We are right if **there is an increase of x%**

Copyright Business Model Foundry AG   The makers of Business Model Generation and Strategyzer

Reinvent Yourself Constantly

Successful companies create value propositions that sell embedded in business models that work. Outstanding companies do so continuously. They create new value propositions and business models while they are successful.

Today's enterprise must be agile and develop what Columbia Business School Professor Rita McGrath calls transient advantages in her book *The End of Competitive Advantage*. She argues that companies must develop the ability to rapidly and continuously address new opportunities, rather than search for increasingly unsustainable long-term competitive advantages.

Use the tools and processes of *Value Proposition Design* to continuously reinvent yourself and create new value propositions embedded in great business models.

Five things to remember when you build transient advantages:

· Take the exploration of new value propositions and business models just as seriously as the execution of existing ones.

· Invest in continuously experimenting with new value propositions and business models rather than making big bold uncertain bets.

· Reinvent yourself while you are successful; don't wait for a crisis to force you to.

· See new ideas and opportunities as a means to energize and mobilize employees and customers rather than a risky endeavor.

· Use customer experiments as a yardstick to judge new ideas and opportunities rather than the opinions of managers, strategists, or experts.

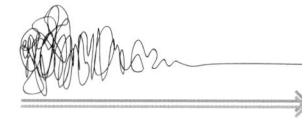

Continuously ask yourself...

What elements in your environment are changing? What do market, technology, regulatory, macroeconomic, or competitive changes mean for your value propositions and business models? Do those changes offer an opportunity to explore new possibilities or could they be a threat that might disrupt you?

Is your business model expiring? Do you need to add new resources or activities? Do the existing ones offer an opportunity to expand your business model? Could you bolster your existing business model or should you build completely new ones? Is your business model portfolio fit for the future?

Is your value proposition still compelling to your customers? How are your customer's jobs, pains, and gains evolving? Can you build on your existing value proposition or do you need to revisit it entirely? Is there a new potential customer or a new segmentation emerging? What is happening in your business that creates the basis for new value propositions to existing or new customers?

Taobao: Reinventing (E-)Commerce

Taobao is the Chinese e-commerce phenomenon, part of the Alibaba Group. It is credited with ushering in a new wave of commerce in China by using the Internet to create an ecosystem where trusted commercial exchanges could take place. In 10 years it evolved its business models three times. It proactively embraced the changes taking place on its platform and in the wider Chinese economy and turned them into an opportunity.

Check out the full Taobao case online

2003

A new Consumer-to-Consumer (C2C) Platform

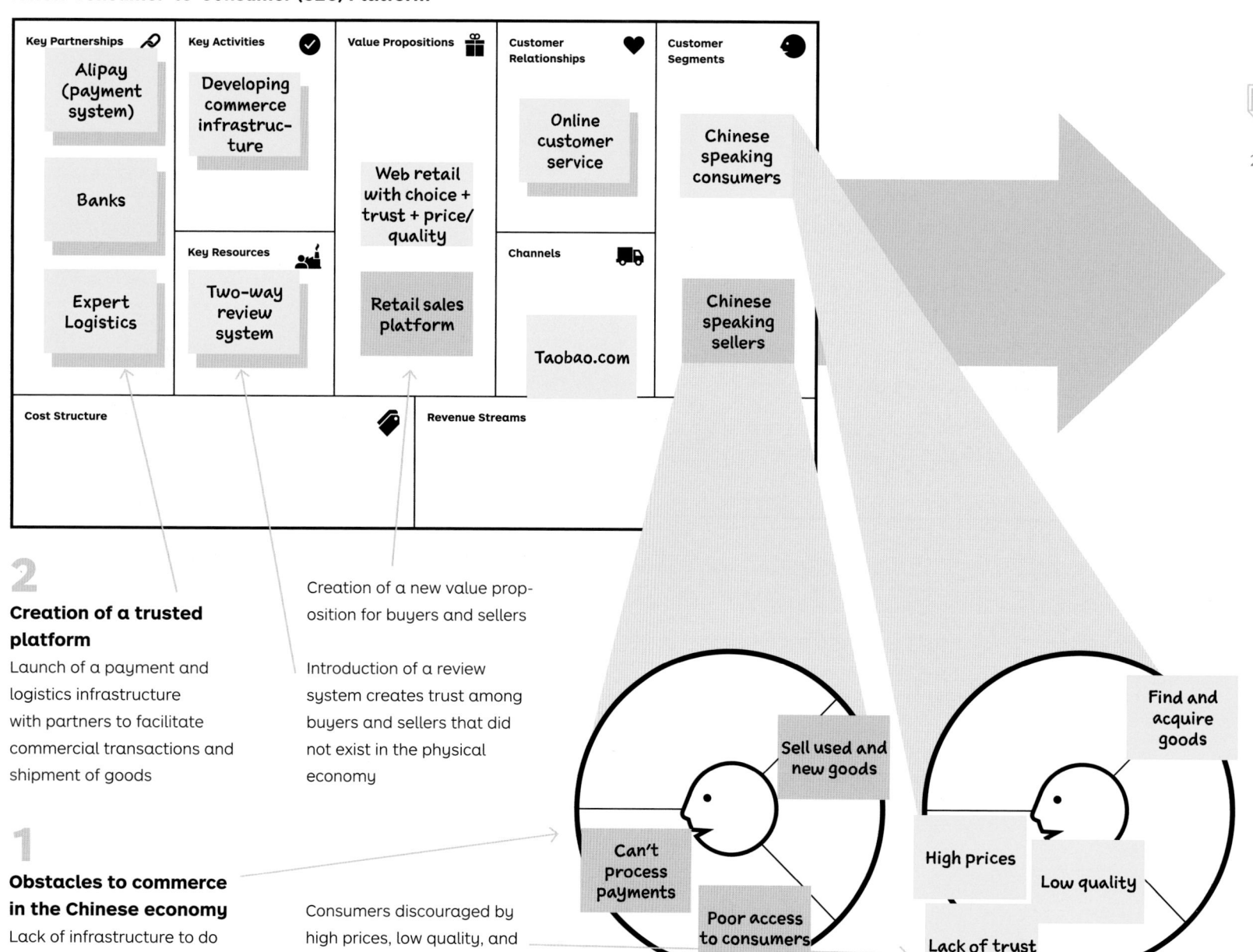

Key Partnerships 🔖

Alipay (payment system)

Banks

Expert Logistics

Key Activities ✓

Developing commerce infrastructure

Key Resources 🏭

Two-way review system

Value Propositions 🎁

Web retail with choice + trust + price/quality

Retail sales platform

Customer Relationships ♥

Online customer service

Channels 🚚

Taobao.com

Customer Segments

Chinese speaking consumers

Chinese speaking sellers

Cost Structure 🏷

Revenue Streams

2

Creation of a trusted platform

Launch of a payment and logistics infrastructure with partners to facilitate commercial transactions and shipment of goods

Creation of a new value proposition for buyers and sellers

Introduction of a review system creates trust among buyers and sellers that did not exist in the physical economy

1

Obstacles to commerce in the Chinese economy

Lack of infrastructure to do business

Consumers discouraged by high prices, low quality, and lack of trust.

Sell used and new goods

Can't process payments

Poor access to consumers

Find and acquire goods

High prices

Low quality

Lack of trust

270

2006
Taobao — Small Business-to-Consumer (B2C)

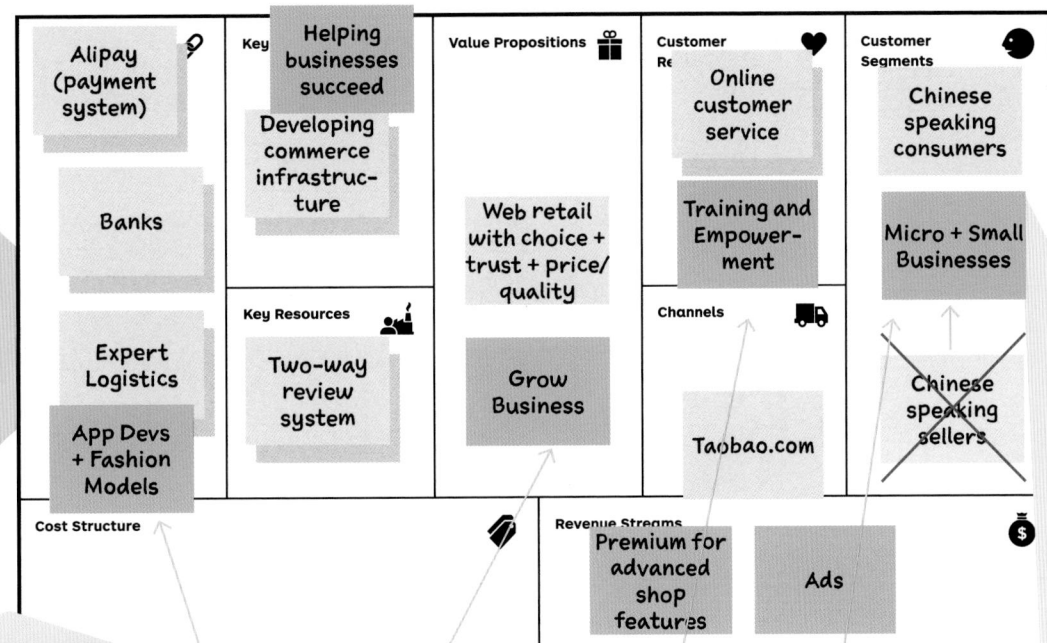

Key Partners

Alipay (payment system)

Banks

Expert Logistics

App Devs + Fashion Models

Key Activities

Helping businesses succeed

Developing commerce infrastructure

Key Resources

Two-way review system

Value Propositions

Web retail with choice + trust + price/quality

Grow Business

Customer Relationships

Online customer service

Training and Empowerment

Channels

Taobao.com

Customer Segments

Chinese speaking consumers

Micro + Small Businesses

Chinese speaking sellers

Cost Structure

Revenue Streams

Premium for advanced shop features

Ads

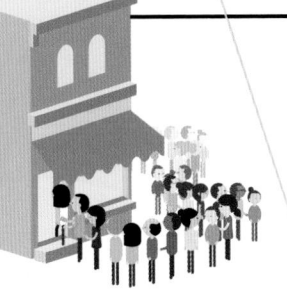

2
Pivot toward micro-entrepreneurs
Taobao shifts focus and builds on this trend by catering to micro-entrepreneurs

Inclusion of third-party service providers to strengthen the value proposition

1
Birth of micro-entrepreneurs
The Taobao platform becomes so popular that millions of sellers see an opportunity to become micro-entrepreneurs

Creation of the 'Taobao University' to help entrepreneurs navigate the platform and learn about business

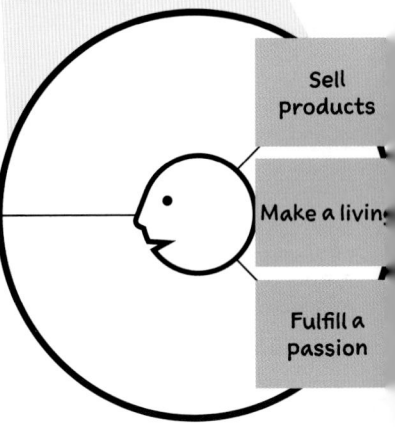

Sell products

Make a living

Fulfill a passion

2008
Taobao — Big Business-to-Consumer (B2C)

Key Partners
- Alipay (payment system)
- Banks
- Expert Logistics
- App Devs
- Fashion Models

Key Activities
- Helping businesses succeed
- Developing commerce infrastructure

Key Resources
- Millions of Chinese consumers
- 2-way review system

Value Propositions
- One-stop presence
- Web retail with choice + trust + price/quality
- Grow Business

Customer Relationships
- Online customer service
- Training and Empowerment

Channels
- Tmall.com
- Taobao.com

Customer Segments
- Chinese speaking consumers
- Micro + Small Businesses
- Big brands

Cost Structure

Revenue Streams
- Premium for advanced shop features
- Ads
- Membership fees
- 2-5% Sales commission

Creation of new Revenue Streams

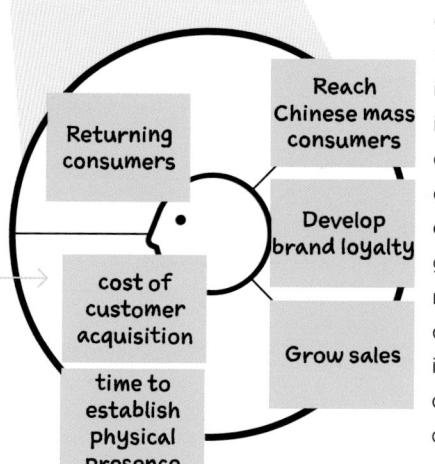

2013
Taobao — ?

271

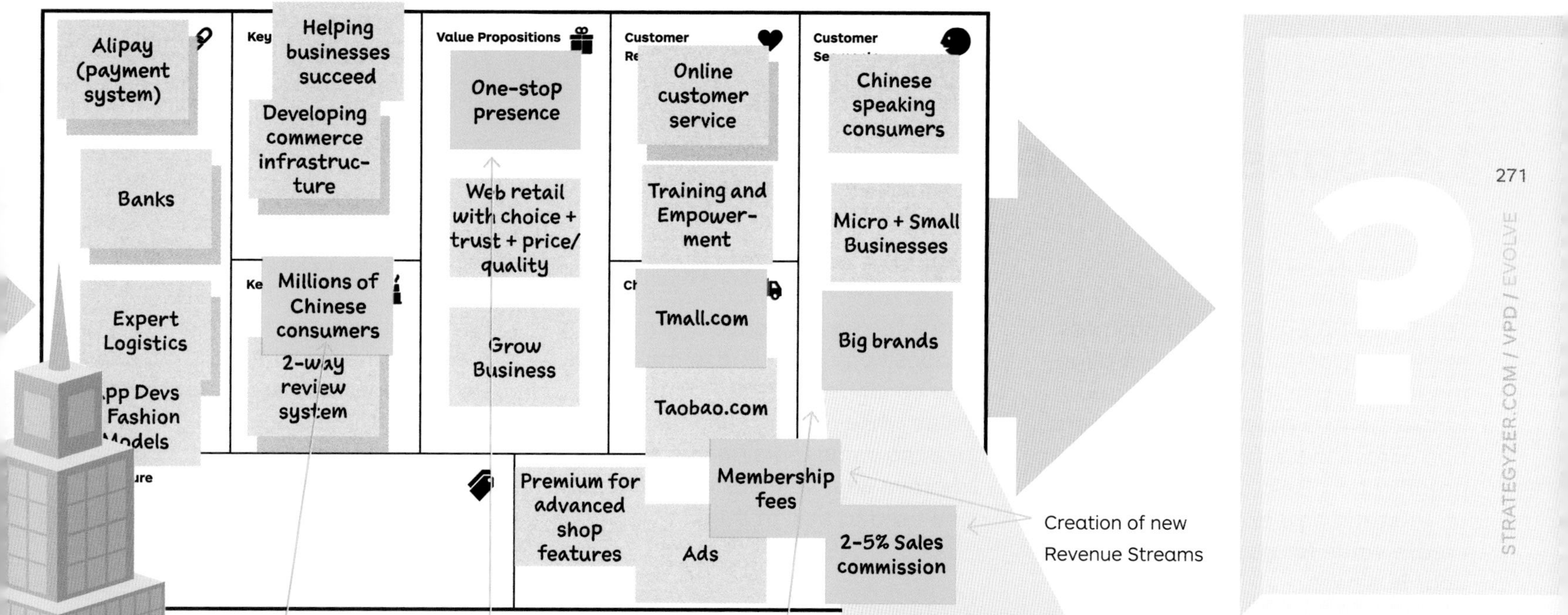

1

A new asset is revealed
Taobao realizes that its business model possesses an incredible asset: hundreds of millions of Chinese consumers.

2

Launch of a new business
The "new" asset becomes the basis of a new value proposition

...for a new customer (big brands)...

...helping them reach Chinese consumers much faster than through the opening of physical stores.

- Returning consumers
- Reach Chinese mass consumers
- Develop brand loyalty
- cost of customer acquisition
- time to establish physical presence
- Grow sales

Taobao went from a simple e-commerce platform to complex ecosystem in 10 years. It achieved this by improving and reinventing its value propositions and business models on the way. With new developments in mobile, gaming, messaging, and more, however, the company can't rest on its laurels. Taobao is constantly challenged to continue its evolution.

Lessons Learned

Create Alignment

The Value Proposition and Business Model Canvases are excellent alignment tools. Use them as a shared language to create better collaboration across the different parts of your organization. Help every stakeholder understand how exactly you intend to create value for your customers and your business.

Measure, Monitor, Improve

Track the performance of your value propositions over time to make sure you continue to create customer value while market conditions change. Use the same tools and processes to improve your value propositions, which you used to design them.

Reinvent While Successful

Don't wait with reinventing your value propositions and business models. Do so before before market conditions force you to, because it might be too late. Create organizational structures that allow you to improve existing value propositions and business models and invent new ones at the same time.

after

word

Glossary

(Business) Hypothesis

Something that needs to be true for your idea to work partially or fully but that hasn't been validated yet.

Business Model

Rationale of how an organization creates, delivers, and captures value.

Business Model Canvas

Strategic management tool to design, test, build, and manage (profitable and scalable) business models.

Call to Action (CTA)

Prompts a subject to perform an action; used in an experiment in order to test one or more hypotheses.

Customer Development

Four-step process invented by Steve Blank to reduce the risk and uncertainty in entrepreneurship by continuously testing the hypotheses underlying a business model with customers and stakeholders.

Customer Gains

Outcomes and benefits customers must have, expect, desire, or dream to achieve.

Customer Insight

Minor or major breakthrough in your customer understanding helping you design better value propositions and business models.

Customer Pains

Bad outcomes, risks, and obstacles that customers want to avoid, notably because they prevent them from getting a job done (well).

Customer Profile

Business tool that constitutes the right-hand side of the Value Proposition Canvas. Visualizes the jobs, pains, and gains of a customer segment (or stakeholder) you intend to create value for.

Environment Map

Strategic foresight tool to map the context in which you design and manage value propositions and business models.

Evidence

Proves or disproves a (business) hypothesis, customer insight, or belief about a value proposition, business model, or the environment.

Experiment/Test

A procedure to validate or invalidate a value proposition or business model hypothesis that produces evidence.

Fit

When the elements of your value map meet relevant jobs, pains, and gains of your customer segment and a substantial number of customers "hire" your value proposition to satisfy those jobs, pains, and gains.

Gain Creators

Describes how products and services create gains and help customers achieve the outcomes and benefits they require, expect, desire, or dream of by getting a job done (well).

Jobs to Be Done

What customers need, want, or desire to get done in their work and in their lives.

Lean Start-up

Approach by Eric Ries based on the Customer Development process to eliminate waste and uncertainty from product development by continuously building, testing, and learning in an iterative fashion.

Learning Card

Strategic learning tool to capture insights from research and experiments.

Minimum Viable Product (MVP)

A model of a value proposition designed specifically to validate or invalidate one or more hypotheses.

Pain Relievers

Describes how products and services alleviate customer pains by eliminating or reducing bad outcomes, risks, and obstacles that prevent customers from getting a job done (well).

Products and Services

The items that your value proposition is based on that your customers can see in your shop window—metaphorically speaking.

Progress Board

Strategic management tool to manage and monitor the business model and value proposition design process and track progress toward a successful value proposition and business model.

Prototyping (low/high fidelity)

The practice of building quick, inexpensive, and rough study models to learn about the desirability, feasibility, and viability of alternative value propositions and business models.

Test Card

Strategic testing tool to design and structure your research and experiments.

Value Map

Business tool that constitutes the left-hand side of the Value Proposition Canvas. Makes explicit how your products and services create value by alleviating pains and creating gains.

Value Proposition

Describes the benefits customers can expect from your products and services.

Value Proposition Canvas

Strategic management tool to design, test, build, and manage products and services. Fully integrates with the Business Model Canvas.

Value Proposition Design

The process of designing, testing, building, and managing value propositions over their entire lifecycle.

🐤 *Get Glossary pdf*

Core Team

Yves Pigneur
Supervising Author

Trish Papadakos
Designer

Tegan Mierle   **Sarah Kim**

Brandon Ainsley   **Matt Mancuso**

Greg Bernarda
Author

Alex Osterwalder
Lead Author
Strategyzer Cofounder

Alan Smith
Author + Creative Director
Strategyzer Cofounder

Pilot Interactive
Illustration Team

Strategyzer Content Team
Benson Garner, Nabila Amarsy

Strategyzer Product Team
Dave Lougheed, Tom Phillip, Joannou Ng, Chris Hopkins,
Matt Bullock, Federico Galindo

Prereaders

We practice what we preach and tested our ideas before releasing them. More than 100 selected people from around the world participated as prereaders to scrutinize our raw creations. More than 60 actively contributed by reviewing ideas, concepts, and spreads. They offered suggestions, meticulously proofread, and pointed out flaws and inconsistencies without pity. We iterated the book title several times with prereaders before testing various alternatives in the market.

Gabrielle Benefield

Phil Blake

Jasper Bouwsma

Frederic Briguet

Karl Burrow

Manuel Jose Carvajal

Pål Dahl

Christian Doll

Joseph Dougherty

Todd Dunn

Reinhard Ematinger

Sven Gakstatter

Jonas Giannini

Claus Gladyszak

Boris Golob

Dave Gray

Gaute Hagerup

Natasha Hanshaw

Chris Hill

Luke Hohmann

Jay Jayaraman

Shyam Jha

Greg Judelman

James King

Hans Kok

Ryuta Kono

Jens Korte

Jan Kyhnau

Michael Lachapelle

Ronna Lichtenberg

Justin Lokitz

Ranjan Malik

Deborah Mills-Scofield

Nathan Monk

Mario Morales

Fabio Nunes

Jan Ondrus

Aloys Osterwalder

Matty Paquay

Olivier Perez Kennedy

Johan Rapp

Christian Saclier

Andrea Schrick

Gregoire Serikoff

Aron Solomon

Peter Sonderegger

Lars Spicker Olesen

Matt Terrell

James Thomas

Paris Thomas

Patrick Van Der Pijl

Emanuela Vartolomei

Mauricio

Reiner Walter

Matt Wanat

Lu Wang

Marc Weber

Judith Wimmer

Shin Yamamoto

Bios

Alex Osterwalder

Dr. Alexander Osterwalder is the lead author of the international bestseller *Business Model Generation*, passionate entrepreneur, and demanded speaker. He cofounded Strategyzer, a software company specializing in tools and content for strategic management and innovation. Dr. Osterwalder invented the Business Model Canvas, the strategic management tool to design, test, build, and manage business models, which is used by companies like Coca Cola, GE, P&G, Mastercard, Ericsson, LEGO, and 3M. He is a frequent keynote speaker in leading organizations and top universities around the world, including Stanford, Berkeley, MIT, IESE, and IMD. Follow him online @alexosterwalder.

Yves Pigneur

Dr. Yves Pigneur is coauthor of *Business Model Generation* and a professor of management and information systems at the University of Lausanne. He has held visiting professorships in the United States, Canada, and Singapore. Yves is a frequent guest speaker on business models in universities, large corporations, entrepreneurship events, and international conferences.

Greg Bernarda

Greg Bernarda is a thinker, creator, and facilitator who supports individuals, teams, and organizations with strategy and innovation. He works with inspired leaders to (re)design a future which employees, customers, and communities can recognize as their own. His projects have been with the likes of Colgate, Volkswagen, Harvard Business School, and Capgemini. Greg is a frequent speaker; he cofounded a series of events on sustainability in Beijing; and is an advisor at Utopies in Paris. Prior to that, he was at the World Economic Forum for eight years setting up initiatives for members to address global issues. He holds an MBA (Oxford Saïd) and is a Strategyzer certified business model coach.

Alan Smith

Alan is obsessed with design, business, and the ways we do them. A design-trained entrepreneur, he has worked across film, television, print, mobile, and web. Previously, he cofounded The Movement, an international design agency with offices in London, Toronto, and Geneva. He helped create the Value Proposition Canvas with Alex Osterwalder and Yves Pigneur, and the breakthrough design for *Business Model Generation*. He cofounded Strategyzer, where he builds tools and content with an amazing team; helping businesspeople make stuff customers want. Follow him online @thinksmith.

Trish Papadakos

Trish is a designer, photographer, and entrepreneur. She holds a Masters in Design from Central St. Martins in London and Bachelor of Design from the York Sheridan Joint Program in Toronto. She teaches design at her alma mater, has worked with award-winning agencies, launched several businesses, and is collaborating for the third time with the Strategyzer team. Follow her photography on Instagram @trishpapadakos.

Index

282

A

A/B testing, 230–231

ad-libs, for Prototyping, 76, 82–83

Ad Tracking (Experiment Library), 220

AirBnB, 91

Alibaba Group, 268–271

alignment, creating, 260–261

Anthropologist, 106, 114–115, 217

Apple, 156, 157

App Store (Apple), 157

assessment
  Business Model and, 156–157
  of competitors, 128–129, 130–131
  of skills for Value Proposition Design, xxii–xxiii
  of Value Proposition, 122–123

Azuri, 146–151

B

best practices
  for mapping customers' jobs, pains, and gains, 24–25 (*See also* Customer Gains; Customer Pains; Jobs to be Done)
  for mapping value creation, 30

Blank, Steve, 118, 182–183

Blue Ocean Strategy, 130

books, as Starting Points, 92–93

brainstorming
  defining criteria with, 140
  possibilities for, 92–93
  See also Starting Points

Bransfield-Garth, Simon, 146

brochures, creating, 222

Build, Measure, Learn Circle, 94, 95

Business Hypothesis
  defined, 201
  extracting, 200–201
  Lean Startup and, 185, 186–187
  prioritizing, 202–203

Business Model, 142–157
  assessing, 156–157
  Azuri example, 146–151
  compressed air energy storage example, 152–153
  creating value for customers and, 144–145
  Fit and, 48–49, 52–53
  platform Business Models, 52–53
  stress testing, 154–155
  testing, 194–195

Business Model Canvas
  defined, xv
  illustrated, xvii

Business Model Generation (Osterwalder), xiv, xvi

business plans, experimentation processes *versus*, 179

business-to-business (B2B) transactions, 50–51

Buy a Feature (Experiment Library), 235

Buyer of Value (customer role), 12

C

Call to Action (CTA), 218–219

Canvas
    Customer Profile and, 3–5, 9, 10–25
    Fit and, 3–5, 40–59
    identifying stakeholders with, 50–51
    moviegoing example, 54–55
    observing customers, 7
    summarized, 60
    Value Map and, 3–5, 8, 26–39
    Value Proposition, defined, 6
    See also Business Model Canvas; Customer Profile; Fit; Value Map; Value
        Proposition; Value Proposition Canvas

change. *See* Evolve

channels, defined, xvi

characteristics, of customers, 14–15

Choices, 120–141
    competitors and, 128–129, 130–131
    context and, 126–127
    defining criteria and selecting prototypes, 140–141
    feedback and, 132–133, 134–135, 136–137
    role-playing and, 107, 124–125
    tips for, 124, 131, 137
    Value Proposition assessment, 122–123
    visualization and, 138–139

Circle, Testing the, 190–191

Cocreator (for Customer Insight), 107

Cocreator of Value (customer role), 12

colleagues, Value Proposition Design for, xxiv–xxv

Company Building (Customer Development process), 183

competitors, assessing, 128–129, 130–131

compressed air energy storage example
    Business Model, 152–153
    Prototyping, 96–97

context
    Jobs to be Done, 13
    understanding, 126–127

cost structure, defined, xvi

Creation (Customer Development process), 183

criteria, defining, 140–141

Customer Development process, 182–183

Customer Gains
    best practices for mapping, 24–25
    checking Fit and, 46–47
    defined, 16–17
    psychodemographic profile approach *versus*, 54–55
    ranking, 20–21
    as Starting Point, 88–89
    Testing the Circle objective, 190–191
    See also Gain Creators

Customer Insight, 104–119
    Anthropologist, 106, 114–115, 217
    choosing mix of experiments for, 216–217 (*See also* Experiment Library)
    Cocreator, 107
    creating value for, 144–145 (*See also* Business Model)
    customer relationship management (CRM), xvi, 109
    Data Detective, 106, 108–109, 217

284   gaining, 106–107

identifying patterns in, 111, 116–119

Impersonator, 107, 124–125

Journalist, 106, 110–113, 217, 225

Scientist, 107

shaping ideas and, 70–71

tips for, 113, 115, 117

Customer Pains

best practices for mapping, 24–25

checking Fit and, 46–47

defined, 14–15

psychodemographic profile approach *versus*, 54–55

ranking, 20–21

as Starting Point, 88–89

Testing the Circle objective, 190–191

See also Pain Relievers

Customer Profile, 10–25

best practices for mapping jobs, pains, and gains, 24–25

business-to-business (B2B) transactions, 50–51

Customer Gains, defined, 16–17

Customer Pains, defined, 14–15

customer's context and, 56–57

customer segments, xvi, 116

defined, 9

different solutions for same customers, 58–59

identifying high-value jobs, 100–101

innovating from, 102–103

jobs, pains, and gains as new approach, 54–55

Jobs to be Done, defined, 12–13

ranking jobs, pains, and gains, 20–21

sketching, 18–19

understanding customer perspective for, 22–23

use of, 60–61

See also Jobs to be Done; Starting Points

D

Data Detective, 106, 108–109, 217

data mining, 109

data sheets, creating, 222

data traps, avoiding, 210–211

Day in the Life, A (worksheet), 115–116

de Bono, Edward, 136–137

decision makers, 50–51

Dell, 157

Design, 64–170

characteristics of great Value Propositions, 72–73

constraints, 90–91

design/build (Lean Startup), 185, 186–187

in established organizations, 158–187 (*See also* established organizations)

finding the right Business Model, 142–157 (*See also* business model)

making choices for, 120–141 (*See also* Choices)

overview, 67

Prototyping possibilities, 70–71, 74–85 (*See also* Prototyping)

shaping ideas with, 70–71

Starting Points, 70–71, 86–103 (*See also* Starting Points)

summarized, 170

understanding customers, 70–71, 104–119 (*See also* Customer Insight)

discovery (Customer Development process), 182

Dotmocracy, 138–139

Dropbox, 210

E

Earlyvangelists, 118

economic buyers, 50–51

Eight19 (Azuri), 146–151

emotional jobs, of customers, 12

end users, 50–51. See also Customer Insight

Environment Map, v, xv

EPFL, 96–97

established organizations, 158–169
    inventing and improving, 160–161, 162–163
    reinventing, 164–165
    Value Proposition Design for, xix
    workshops for, 166–167, 168–169

Evidence
    Call to Action (CTA) and, 218–219
    need for, 190–195
    producing, 97, 216
    See also Test

Evolve, 254–272
    creating alignment and, 260–261
    improvement and, 264–265
    measuring and monitoring, 262–263
    overview, 257
    reinventing and, 266–267, 268–271
    summarized, 272

"exhausted maximum" trap, 211

experience, as feedback, 134

Experiment Library, 214–237
    Ad Tracking, 220
    Buy a Feature, 235

Call to Action (CTA), 218–219

choosing mix of experiments, 216–217

experiment, defined, 216

experiment design and, 204–205

experimenting to reduce risk, 178–179

Illustrations, Storyboards, and Scenarios, 222, 224–225

Innovation Games, 232

Landing Page MVP, 228–229

Life-Size Experiments, 226–227

Minimum Viable Product (MVP), 222–223, 228–229

Mock Sales, 236–237

Pre Sales, 237

Product Box, 234

Speed Boat, 233

Split Testing, 230–231

tips for, 217, 222, 224, 227, 229, 231, 233, 237

Unique Link Tracking, 221

See also Test

F

Facebook, 157

facts, as feedback, 134

false-negative/false-positive traps, 210

Federal Institute of Technology (Switzerland), 96–97

feedback, 132–133, 134–135, 136–137

financial issues
    cost structure, defined, xvi
    generating revenue, 144–145
    profit, defined, xvi

286   revenue streams, defined, xvi

stress testing, 154–155

testing customers' willingness to pay, 219

    (*See also* Experiment Library)

See also Business Model

Fit, 40–59

    addressing customers' jobs, pains, and gains with, 44–45

    checking for, 46–47

    Customer Profile and customer context, 56–57

    Customer Profile and Value Map as two sides of, 3–5

    Customer Profile *versus* psychodemographic profile approach, 54–55

    different solutions for same customers, 58–59

    multiple Fit, 52–53

    stages of, 48–49

    striving for, 42–43

    use of, 60–61

functional jobs, of customers, 12

G

Gain Creators

    Fit and, 9, 47

    Pain Relievers *versus*, 38

    Products and Services as, 33

    Value Map and, 33–34

gains. *See* Customer Gains

Google

    AdWords, 220

    searches, 108

government census data, 108

H

Hilti, 90

Hohmann, Luke, 232

hypothesis. *See* Business Hypothesis

I

Ikea, 157

Illustrations, Storyboards, and Scenarios (Experiment Library), 222, 224–225

Impersonator, 107

improvement

    for established organizations, 160–161, 162–163

    as relentless, 264–265

    See also Evolve

Indigo, 150–151

influencers, 50–51

Innovation Games, 232

intermediary Fit, 52–53

interviewing, of customers, 106, 110–113, 217, 225

iPod (Apple), 156

J

Jobs to be Done

    best practices for mapping, 24–25

    defined, 12–13

    identifying high-value jobs, 98–99, 100–101

    psychodemographic profile approach *versus*, 54–55

ranking, 20–21
as Starting Point, 88–89
Testing the Circle objective, 190–191
Journalist, 106, 110–113, 217, 225

K

key activities, defined, xvi
key partnerships, defined, xvi
key resources, defined, xvi

L

Landing Page MVP (Experiment Library), 228–229
Lean Startup, 184–185, 186–187
Learning Cards, 206–207, 213
learning (Lean Startup), 185, 186–187
Life-Size Experiments (Experiment Library), 226–227
listening, 112
Lit Motors, 226
"local maximum" trap, 211

M

magazines, as Starting Points, 92–93
market pull, 95
Marriott, 227

measurement

Evolve and, 262–263
Lean Startup feature, 185, 186–187
See also Test
MedTech, 154–155
Minimum Viable Product (MVP)
Lean Start-up with, 184
Prototyping and, 77
testing with, 222–223, 228–229
Mock Sales (Experiment Library), 236–237

N

napkin sketch, for Prototyping, 76, 80–81
Nespresso, 90, 156
new ventures, Value Proposition Design for, xviii

O

observation, of customers, 106, 114–115, 216–217. *See also* Experiment Library
obstacles, of customers, 14–15. *See also* Customer Pains
opinion, as feedback, 134
Osterwalder, Alexander, xiv, xvi
outcomes
Customer Gains as, 16–17
undesired, by customers, 14–15
Owlet, 246–251

P

288

Pain Relievers
    Fit and, 9, 47
    Gain Creators *versus*, 38
    Products and Services as, 31–32
    Value Map and, 33–34
"participatory tv," for understanding context, 126, 127
patterns, identifying, 111, 116–119
personal jobs, of customers, 12
perspective, of customers, 22–23. *See also* Customer Insight
platform Business Models, 52–53
Pre Sales (Experiment Library), 237
prioritization, 202–203, 219.
    See also Experiment Library
problems, of customers, 14–15.
    See also Customer Pains
Problem-Solution Fit, 48–49
Product Box (Experiment Library), 234
Product-Market Fit, 48–49
Products and Services
    meeting customer expectations with, 31–32
    multiple Fit for, 52–53
    Testing the Square objective, 192–193
    types of, 29–30
    value of, to customers, 31–32
profit, defined, xvi
Progress Board, 242–243, 244–245
Prototyping, 74–85
    ad-libs for, 76, 82–83
    defined, 76

    napkin sketch for, 76, 80–81
    packaging and, 223, 234
    principles of, 78–79
    selecting prototypes, 140–141
    shaping ideas with, 70–71
    spaces for, 227
    tips for, 77
    Value Proposition Canvas for, 77, 84–85
    See also Experiment Library
psychodemographic profiles, as traditional approach, 54–55
push *versus* pull debate, 94–95, 96–97, 98–99, 100–101

R

ranking, for customer jobs/pains/gains, 20–21
recommenders, 50–51
Rectangle, Testing the, 194–195
reinventing, to Evolve, 266–267, 268–271
required gains, of customers, 16
research, about customers. *See* Customer Insight
revenue streams, defined, xvi
Ries, Eric, 184–185
risks, customers and, 14–15
role-playing, 107, 124–125

S

saboteurs, 50–51
Scientist, 107

segmentation, xvi, 116

services. See Products and Services

Skype, 157

social jobs, of customers, 12

social media analytics, 109

Southwest, 91

Speed Boat (Experiment Library), 233

Split Testing (Experiment Library), 230–231

Square, Testing the, 192–193

stakeholders

    identifying, 50–51

    role-playing and, 107, 124–125

Starting Points, 86–103

    addressing customer concerns with, 88–89

    books and magazines for, 92–93

    design constraints and, 90–91

    innovation with Customer Profile, 102–103

    push *versus* pull debate, 94–95, 96–97, 98–99, 100–101

    shaping ideas with, 70–71

    tips for, 93, 97

start-ups, Value Proposition Design for, xviii

Step-by-Step Testing, 196–213

    avoiding data traps, 210–211

    extracting hypothesis, 200–201

    Learning Cards for insight, 206–207, 213

    learning speed and, 208–209

    overview, 198–199

    prioritizing hypothesis, 202–203

    Test Cards for experiment design, 204–205, 212

    tips for, 210

Strategy Canvas, 129, 130

Strategyzer logo, explained, x

stress testing, 154–155

supporting jobs, of customers, 12

Swatch, 90

synthesis, 116, 117

T

Taobao, 268–271

technology push, 94, 96–97

Test, 172–252

    Customer Development process, 182–183

    experimenting to reduce risk, 178–179

    Experiment Library for, 214–237

        (See also Experiment Library)

    Lean Startup, applying, 186–187

    Lean Startup movement, 184–185

    principles, 180–181

    Progress Board, 242–243, 244–245

    step-by-step, 196–213

        (See also Step-by-Step Testing)

    systematic design and testing example, 246–251

    testing process, summarized, 240–241, 252

    Testing the Circle objective, 190–191

    Testing the Rectangle objective, 194–195

    Testing the Square objective, 192–193

    tips for, 183

Test Cards, 204–205, 212

thinking hats (de Bono), 136–137

290 third-party research reports, 108

Transferrer of Value (customer role), 12

U

unique link tracking (Experiment Library), 221

V

validation (Customer Development process), 182

Value Map, 26–39
  best practices for mapping value creation, 30
  Gain Creators and, 33–34
  mapping how products and services create value, 36–38
  mapping value propositions, 34–35
  Pain Relievers, 31–32
  Products and Services, 29–30
  use of, 60–61

Value Proposition
  assessing competitors and, 128–129, 130–131
  assessment, 122–123
  Business Model connection to, 152–153
  defined, vi, xvi, 6
  See also Value Proposition Canvas; Value Proposition Design

Value Proposition Canvas
  characteristics of great value propositions, 72–73 (See also Design)

for Prototyping, 77, 84–85

Value Proposition Design
  book organization and online companion, x
  Business Model Canvas, defined, xv (See also Business Model Canvas)
  competitors versus, 128–129
  Environment Map and, v, xv
  for established organizations, xix
  to overcome problems, vi–vii
  selling colleagues on, xxiv–xxv
  skills needed for, xxii–xxiii
  for start-ups, xviii
  successful use of, viii, xi
  tools and process of, xii–xiii (See also Canvas; Design; Evolve; Test)
  uses of, xx–xxi
  Value Proposition Canvas, defined, xiv, xv (See also Value Proposition Canvas)

visualization, 138–139

W

website
  tracking customers on, 109
  Value Proposition Design Online Companion, explained, x
websites
  landing pages of, 223, 228–229
WhatsApp, 157
workshops, for established organizations, 166–167, 168–169

Don't risk wasting your time, energy, and money working on products and services nobody wants—
Flip the book over!

The Value Proposition Canvas has two sides. With the **Customer Profile** ^{p. 10} you clarify your customer understanding. With the **Value Map** ^{p. 26} you describe how you intend to create value for that customer. You achieve **Fit** ^{p. 40} between the two when one meets the other.

vas

can

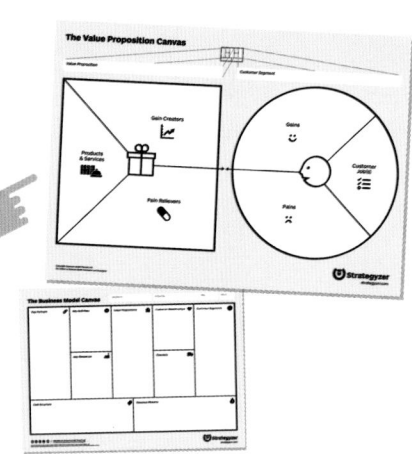

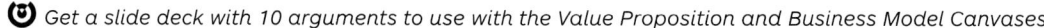

Get a slide deck with 10 arguments to use with the Value Proposition and Business Model Canvases

Sell Your Colleagues on Value Proposition Design

I am...

worried that we focus too much on products and features instead of creating value for customers.

astonished at how poorly aligned product development, sales, and marketing are when it comes to developing new value propositions.

concerned that we don't have a methodology to track our progress on the development of that new value proposition and business model.

surprised at how often we make stuff nobody wants, despite our good ideas and good intentions.

really disappointed by how much we talked about value propositions and business models at our last meeting without really getting tangible results.

blown away by how unclear that last presentation on that new value proposition and business model was.

amazed by how many resources we wasted when that great idea in that last business plan turned out to be a flop because we didn't test it.

concerned that our product development process doesn't use a more customer-focused methodology.

surprised that we invest so much in research and development (R&D), but fail to invest in developing the right value propositions and business models.

not sure if everybody in our team has a shared understanding of what a good value proposition actually is.

Design Thinking Skills

You explore multiple alternatives before picking and refining a particular direction. You are comfortable with the nonlinear and iterative nature of value creation.

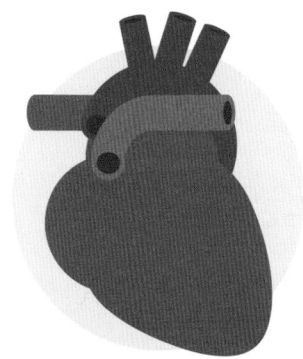

Customer Empathy

You relentlessly take a customer perspective and are even better at listening to customers than selling to them.

Experimentation Skills

You systematically seek evidence that supports your ideas and tests your vision. You experiment at the earliest stages to learn what works and what doesn't.

Assess
Your Value
Proposition
Design Skills

Complete our online test and assess whether you have the attitude and skills required to systematically be successful at value proposition design. Take the test before and after working through *Value Proposition Design* to measure your progress.

Take your skills test online

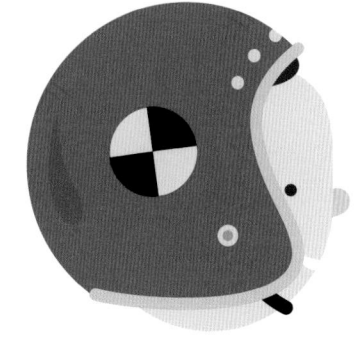

Entrepreneurial Knowledge

You enjoy trying out new things. You don't see the risk of failing as a threat but an opportunity to learn and progress. You easily navigate between the strategic and the tactical.

Tool Skills

You systematically use the Value Proposition Canvas, Business Model Canvas, and other tools and processes in your search for great value propositions and business models.

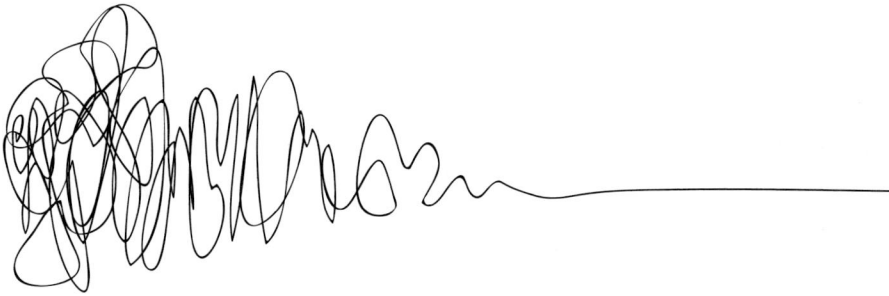

Improve

Manage, measure, challenge, improve, and renew
existing value propositions and business models.

Use *Value Proposition Design* to...

invent and improve value propositions. The tools we will study work for managing and renewing value propositions (and business models) just as much as for creating new ones. Put the value proposition and business model to work to create a shared language of value creation in your organization. Use them to continuously invent and improve value propositions that meet customer profiles, which is an undertaking that never ends.

Invent

Invent new value propositions that people want with business models that work.

Established Organizations

Teams within existing companies setting out to improve or invent value propositions and business models

Get "Innovating in Established Organizations" poster

Main opportunities

- Build on existing value propositions and business models.
- Leverage existing assets (sales, channels, brand, etc.).
- Build portfolios of business models and value propositions.

Main challenges

- Get buy-in from top management.
- Get access to existing resources.
- Manage cannibalization.
- Overcome risk aversion.
- Overcome rigid and slow processes.
- Produce big wins to move the needle.
- Manage career risk of innovators.

Value Proposition Design works for...

Are you creating something from scratch on your own or are you part of an existing organization? Some things will be easier and some harder depending on your strategic playground.

A start-up entrepreneur deals with different constraints than a project leader for a new venture within an existing organization. The tools presented in this book apply to both contexts. Depending on your starting point you will execute them in a different way to leverage different strengths and overcome different obstacles.

New Ventures

Individuals or teams setting out to create a great value proposition and business model from scratch

Main challenges

- Produce proof that your ideas can work on a limited budget.
- Manage involvement of investors (if you scale your ideas).
- Risk running out of money before finding the right value proposition and business model.

Main opportunities

- Use speedy decision making and agility to your advantage.
- Leverage the motivation of owner- ship as a driver for success.

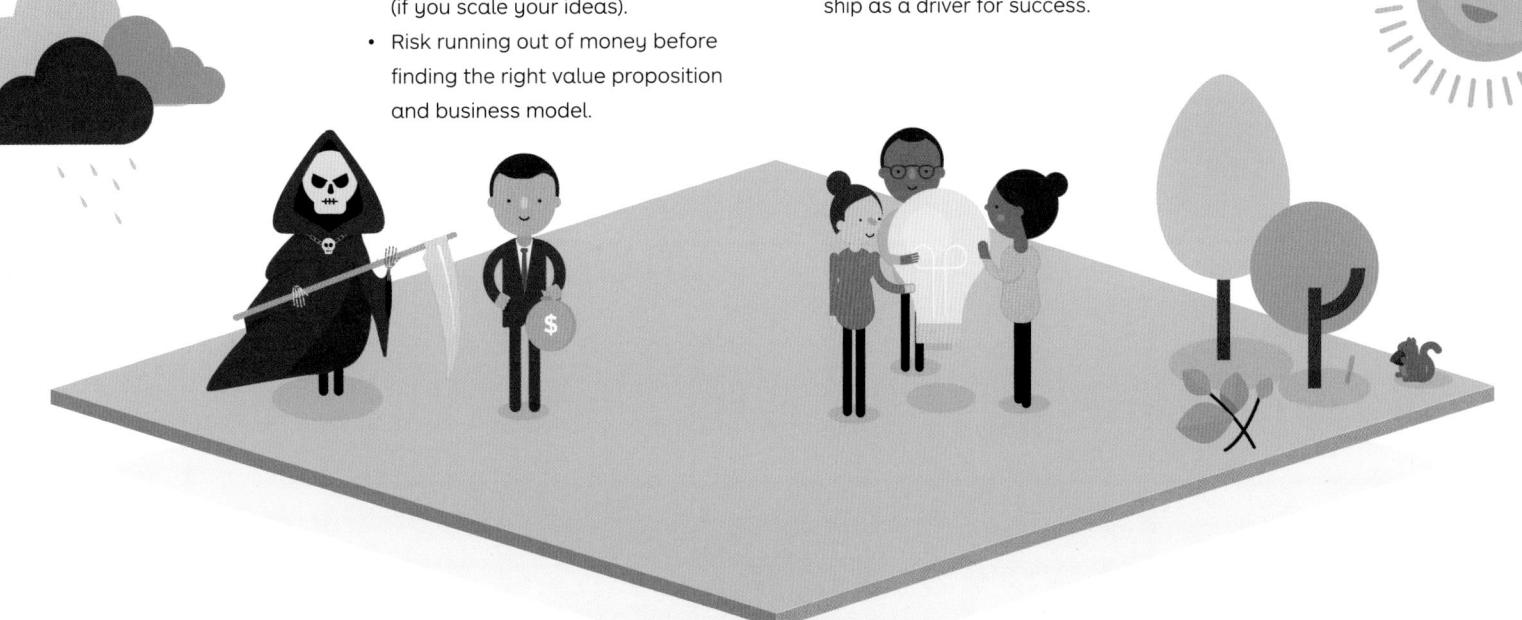

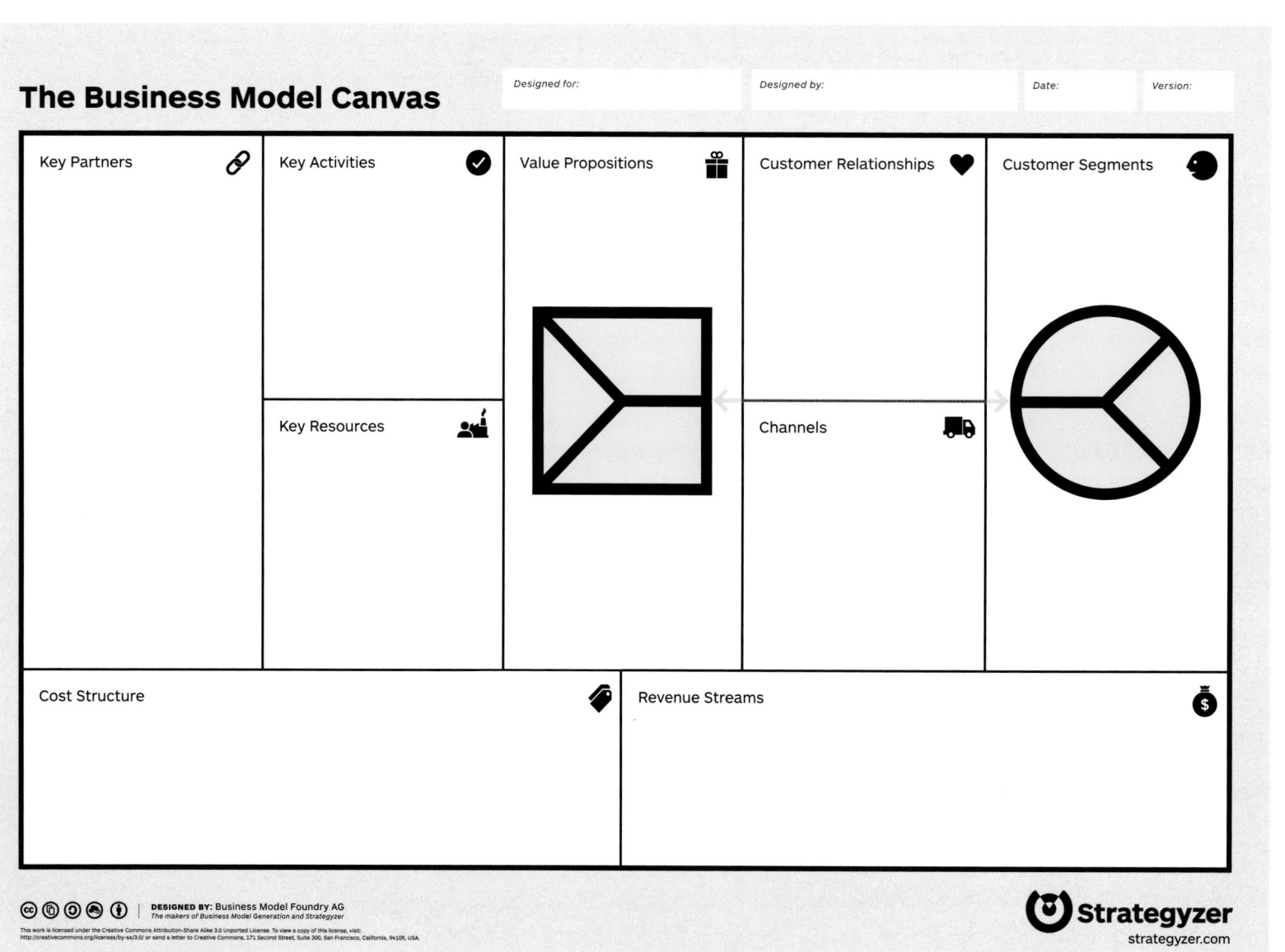

The Business Model Canvas

Designed for:

Designed by:

Date:

Version:

Key Partners	Key Activities	Value Propositions	Customer Relationships	Customer Segments
	Key Resources		Channels	

Cost Structure

Revenue Streams

Strategyzer

strategyzer.com

Download detailed Business Model Canvas Explanation and the Business Model Canvas pdf

Refresher: The Business Model Canvas

Embed your value proposition in a viable business model to capture value for your organization. To do so, you can use the Business Model Canvas, a tool to describe how your organization creates, delivers, and captures value. The Business Model Canvas and Value Proposition Canvas perfectly integrate, with the latter being like a plug-in to the former that allows you to zoom into the details of how you are creating value for customers.

The refresher of the Business Model Canvas on this spread is sufficient to work through this book and create great value propositions. Go to the online resources if you are interested in more or get *Business Model Generation,** the sister publication to this book.

Customer Segments
are the groups of people and/or organizations a company or organization aims to reach and create value for with a dedicated value proposition.

Value Propositions
are based on a bundle of products and services that create value for a customer segment.

Channels
describe how a value proposition is communicated and delivered to a customer segment through communication, distribution, and sales channels.

Customer Relationships
outline what type of relationship is established and maintained with each customer segment, and they explain how customers are acquired and retained.

Revenue Streams
result from a value proposition successfully offered to a customer segment. It is how an organization captures value with a price that customers are willing to pay.

Key Resources
are the most important assets required to offer and deliver the previously described elements.

Key Activities
are the most important activities an organization needs to perform well.

Key Partnerships
shows the network of suppliers and partners that bring in external resources and activities.

Cost Structure
describes all costs incurred to operate a business model.

Profit
is calculated by subtracting the total of all costs in the cost structure from the total of all revenue streams.

**Business Model Generation, Osterwalder and Pigneur, 2010.*

The
Environment Map
helps you *understand the context
in which you create.*

The
Business Model Canvas
helps you
create value for your business.

The
Value Proposition Canvas
helps you
create value for your customer.

An Integrated Suite of Tools

The Value Proposition Canvas is the tool at the center of this book. It makes value propositions visible and tangible and thus easier to discuss and manage. It perfectly integrates with the Business Model Canvas and the Environment Map, two tools that are discussed in detail in *Business Model Generation*,* the sister book to this one. Together, they shape the foundation of a suite of business tools.

The Value Proposition Canvas zooms into the details of two of the building blocks of the Business Model Canvas.

Business Model Generation, Osterwalder and Pigneur, 2010.

Zoom out

Zoom in

The heart of *Value Proposition Design* is about applying **Tools** to the messy **Search** for value propositions that customers want and then keeping them aligned with what customers want in **Post search**.

Value Proposition Design shows you how to use the **Value Proposition Canvas** to Design and Test great value propositions in an iterative search for what customers want. Value proposition design is a never-ending process in which you need to Evolve your value proposition(s) constantly to keep it relevant to customers.

Progress

Manage the messy and nonlinear process of value proposition design and reduce risk by systematically applying adequate tools and processes.

Evolve

Post search

Design Squiggle adapted from Damien Newman, Central

The Tools and Process of *Value Proposition Design*

Zoom out

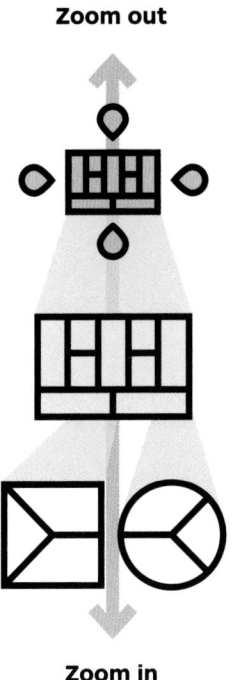

Zoom in

Canvas

Tools

Design / Test

Search

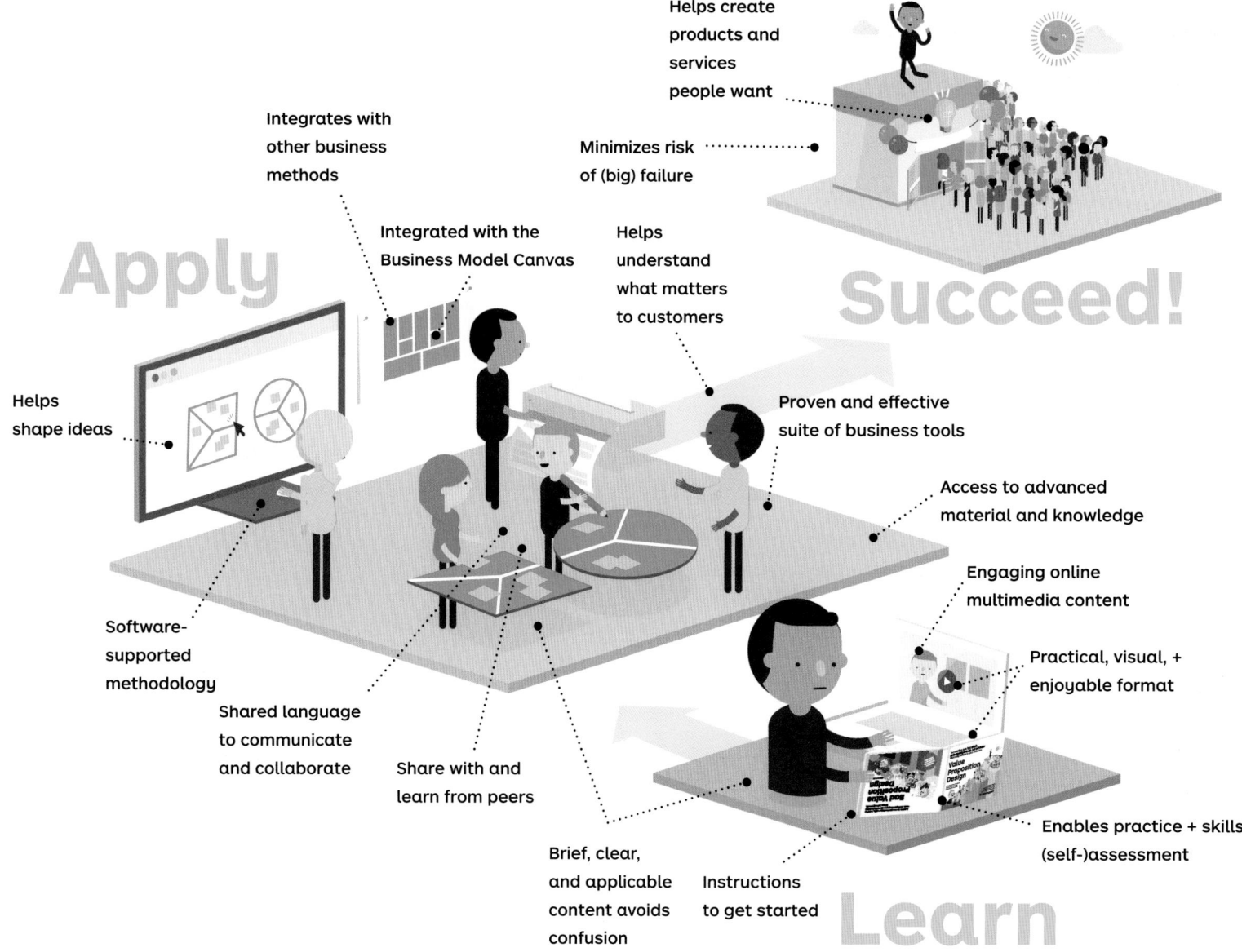

Apply

Helps shape ideas

Integrates with other business methods

Integrated with the Business Model Canvas

Helps understand what matters to customers

Minimizes risk of (big) failure

Helps create products and services people want

Succeed!

Software-supported methodology

Shared language to communicate and collaborate

Share with and learn from peers

Brief, clear, and applicable content avoids confusion

Instructions to get started

Proven and effective suite of business tools

Access to advanced material and knowledge

Engaging online multimedia content

Practical, visual, + enjoyable format

Enables practice + skills (self-)assessment

Learn

Our Value Proposition to You

The links you see on the side of every page point to resources in the online companion.

Watch for the ☺Strategyzer logo and follow the link to 🏃online exercises, ⚲tools/templates, 🗊posters, and more.

Note: To gain access to these exclusive online portions of *Value Proposition Design*, you'll need to prove you own the book. Keep the book near you to help you answer the secret questions and verify your ownership!

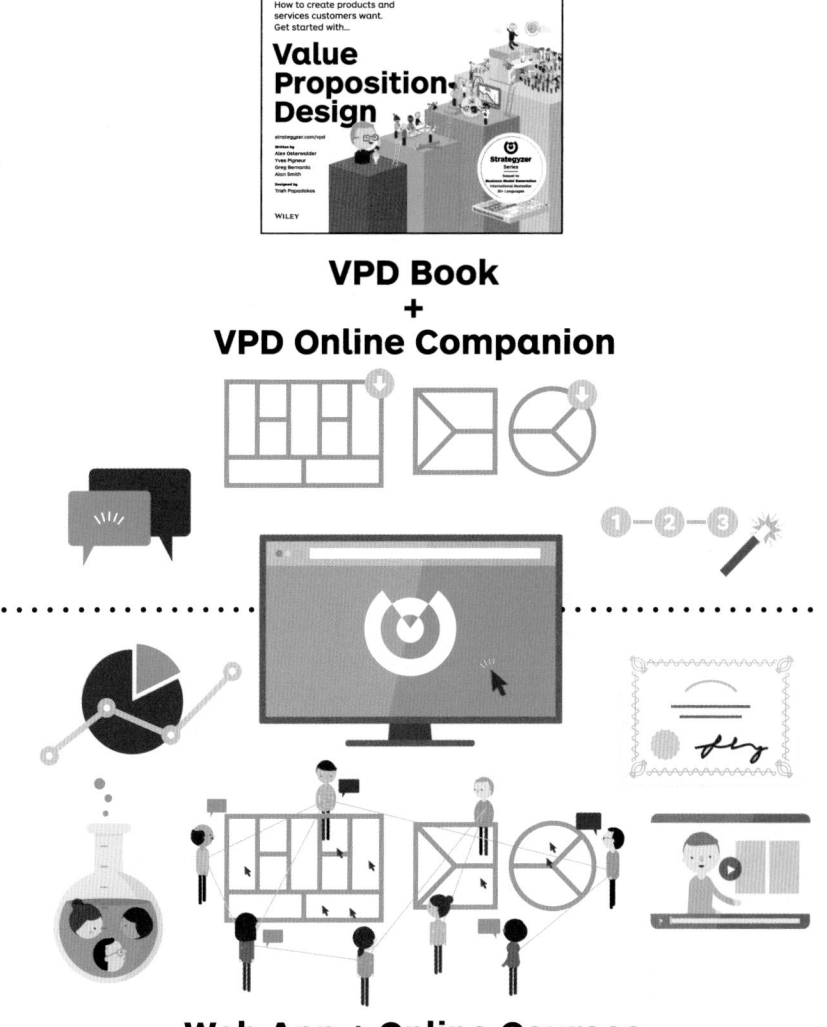

VPD Book
+
VPD Online Companion

Web App + Online Courses
Go further with pro tools and courses

Avoid wasting time with ideas that won't work

Relentlessly test the most important hypotheses underlying your business ideas in order to reduce the risk of failure. This will allow you to pursue big bold ideas without having to break the bank. Your processes to shape new ideas will be fit for the task and complement your existing processes that help you run your business.

Minimize the risk of a flop.

Design, test, and deliver what customers want.

Get "From Failure to Success" poster

Value Proposition Design will help you successfully...

Understand the patterns of value creation

Organize information about what customers want in a simple way that makes the patterns of value creation easily visible. As a result, you will more effectively design value propositions and profitable business models that directly target your customers' most pressing and important jobs, pains, and gains.

Gain clarity.

Leverage the experience and skills of your team

Equip your team with a shared language to overcome "blah blah blah," conduct more strategic conversations, run creative exercises, and get aligned. This will lead to more enjoyable meetings that are full of energy and produce actionable outcomes beyond a focus on technology, products, and features toward creating value for your customers and your business.

Get your team aligned.

Involved in bold shiny projects that blew up

You have seen projects that...

- Were big bold bets that failed and wasted a lot money.
- Put energy into polishing and refining a business plan until it perpetuated the illusion that it could actually work.
- Spent a lot of time building detailed spreadsheets that were completely made up and turned out to be wrong.
- Spent more time developing and debating ideas rather than testing them with customers and stakeholders.
- Let opinions dominate over facts from the field.
- Lacked clear processes and tools to minimize risk.
- Used processes suited for running a business rather than ones for developing new ideas.

Disappointed by the failure of a good idea.

Get "From Failure to Success" poster

You'll love *Value Proposition Design* if you've been...

Overwhelmed by the task of true value creation

Sometimes you feel like...

- There should be better tools available to help you create value for your customers and your business.
- You might be pursuing the wrong tasks and you feel insecure about the next steps.
- It's difficult to learn what customers really want.
- The information and data you get from (potential) customers is overwhelming and you don't know how to best organize it.
- It's challenging to go beyond products and features toward a deep understanding of customer value creation.
- You lack the big picture of how all the puzzle pieces fit together.

Frustrated by unproductive meetings and misaligned teams

You have experienced teams that...

- Lacked a shared language and a shared understanding of customer value creation.
- Got bogged down by unproductive meetings with tons of unstructured "blah blah blah" conversations.
- Worked without clear processes and tools.
- Were focused mainly on technologies, products, and features rather than customers.
- Conducted meetings that drained energy and ended without a clear outcome.
- Were misaligned.

3. Test

3.1 What to Test *188*
3.2 Testing Step-by-Step *196*
3.3 Experiment Library *214*
3.4 Bringing It All Together *238*

4. Evolve

Create Alignment *260*
Measure & Monitor *262*
Improve Relentlessly *264*
Reinvent Yourself Constantly *266*
Taobao: Reinventing (E-)Commerce *268*

Glossary *276*
Core Team *278*
Prereaders *279*
Bios *280*
Index *282*

1. Canvas

1.1 Customer Profile *10*
1.2 Value Map *26*
1.3 Fit *40*

2. Design

2.1 Prototyping Possibilities *74*
2.2 Starting Points *86*
2.3 Understanding Customers *104*
2.4 Making Choices *120*
2.5 Finding the Right Business Model *142*
2.6 Designing in Established Organizations *158*

How to create products and
services customers want.
Get started with...

Value
Proposition
Design

strategyzer.com/vpd

Written by
Alex Osterwalder
Yves Pigneur
Greg Bernarda
Alan Smith

Designed by
Trish Papadakos

Cover image: Pilot Interactive

Cover design: Alan Smith and Trish Papadakos

This book is printed on acid-free paper. ∞

Published by John Wiley & Sons, Inc., Hoboken, New Jersey.

Published simultaneously in Canada.

For general information about our other products and services, please contact our Customer Care Department within the United States at (800) 762-2974, outside the United States at (317) 572-3993 or fax (317) 572-4002.

Wiley publishes in a variety of print and electronic formats and by print-on-demand. Some material included with standard print versions of this book may not be included in e-books or in print-on-demand. If this book refers to media such as a CD or DVD that is not included in the version you purchased, you may download this material at http://booksupport.wiley.com. For more information about Wiley products, visit www.wiley.com.

ISBN 978-1-118-96805-5 (paper); ISBN 978-1-118-96807-9 (ebk); ISBN 978-1-118-96806-2 (ebk); ISBN 978-1-118-97310-3 (ebk)

Printed in the United States of America

SKY10065176_011724

Value Proposition Design

The
Invincible
Company

For general information on our other products and services or for technical support, please contact our Customer Care Department within the United States at (800) 762-2974, outside the United States at (317) 572-3993 or fax (317) 572-4002.

Wiley publishes in a variety of print and electronic formats and by print-on-demand. Some material included with standard print versions of this book may not be included in e-books or in print-on-demand. If this book refers to media such as a CD or DVD that is not included in the version you purchased, you may download this material at http://booksupport.wiley.com. For more information about Wiley products, visit www.wiley.com.

ISBN 978-1119523963 (Paperback)
ISBN 978-1119523987 (ePDF)
ISBN 978-1119523932 (ePub)

Cover image: Alan Smith
Cover design: Alan Smith

Printed in the United States of America
V10016957_022820

You're holding a guide to the world's best business models.
Use it to inspire your own portfolio of new ideas and reinventions.
Design a culture of innovation and transformation to become...

The Invincible Company

strategyzer.com/invincible

Written by

Alex Osterwalder

Yves Pigneur

Fred Etiemble

Alan Smith

Designed by

Chris White

Trish Papadakos

WILEY

The Invincible Company

An organization that constantly reinvents itself before it becomes obsolete. The Invincible Company explores the future, while excelling at exploiting the present. It cultivates an innovation and execution culture that lives in harmony under the same roof. It competes on superior business models and transcends traditional industry boundaries.

How to become
an Invincible Company...

Constantly Reinvent Yourself

To stay ahead of everybody else and beat disruption you need to constantly reinvent yourself. Business Models expire faster than ever before and you don't want to become obsolete alongside their decline. Competition increasingly comes from unexpected places like insurgent startups in addition to traditional incumbent rivals. Invincible Companies constantly reinvent who they are and where and how they compete in order to stay relevant and ahead.

Discover how to manage and improve what you have and simultaneously explore the future with business model portfolios.

Design, implement, and manage an innovation culture to constantly feed your innovation funnel and stay relevant.

Compete on Superior Business Models

It is increasingly a rat race to compete on new products, services, price, and technologies alone. Leave competitors behind and maximize market opportunities, new customer needs, and emerging technologies by embedding them in superior business models. Design, test, and build superior business models that disrupt others and are hard to disrupt.

Discover how to design, test, and manage superior business models.

Apply business model patterns to make the best out of market opportunities, new technologies, and product and service innovations.

Transcend Industry Boundaries

The most successful organizations aren't confined by industry boundaries or industry forces. In fact, they often crush industry boundaries and disrupt others. Their business model or portfolio of businesses is not the result of the area they work in; it comes from an organization that constantly explores new ways to create value around market opportunities.

Discover how to create and manage an ambidextrous organization that is capable of improving your core business and exploring completely new opportunities beyond traditional industry boundaries.

Learn how the Chinese company Ping An evolved from a traditional banking and insurance conglomerate to a technology group that competes in five distinct arenas and became one of the world's largest companies.

...and create more value

For Society
Small and large companies that constantly reinvent themselves have an enormously positive impact on society. They provide economic growth and potentially game-changing innovations. The best of them put environmental and societal impacts at the center of their endeavors to change the world for the better. On the other hand, the decline or death of companies can be devastating for cities and entire regions that will suffer from economic decline.

For Customers
Companies that constantly innovate and explore new business models, constantly create new and better value propositions at more attractive prices. Some innovations may be banal and just lead to more consumption. Yet, many will create substantial value for customers in the form of convenience, entertainment, well-being, and fulfillment.

For the Team
Invincible Companies thrive over centuries and provide long-term job security, while others that fail to reinvent themselves have to let go of thousands of employees. Invincible Companies provide a home for execution and innovation talent alike and they feature world-class organizational structures and processes that are fit for the challenges of the 21st century.

For Owners
Owners of Invincible Companies benefit from long-term growth, reduced disruption risk, and the attraction of world class execution and innovation talent. Invincible Companies thrive over the long term, because they harvest the fruits of managing the present, while already sowing the seeds for tomorrow's business. Their ability to exploit and explore simultaneously substantially reduces the risk of disruption and obsolescence and attracts the best talent.

ix

From Business Model Generation to Invincible Company

The Invincible Company is the fourth in the series of Strategyzer books. It complements the previous books and addresses a number of jobs-to-be-done for innovation teams, entrepreneurs, and senior leaders who manage entire organizations.

x

The new content is based on what we've learned from working with leading organizations around the world and from studying the world's few Invincible Companies.

strategyzer.com/books

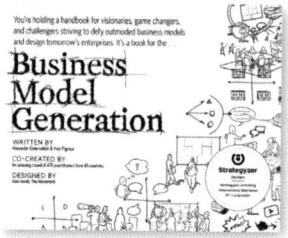

	Job-to-be-Done	Key Question	Key Tool and Process	Books
Innovate and Design *Invent and Improve*	Map your business, idea, or innovation	How do you create sustainable profits and value for your organization?	Business Model Canvas (BMC) or Mission Model Canvas (MMC)	*Business Model Generation* (2009)
	Map your product and service	How do you create value for your customers?	Value Proposition Canvas (VPC)	*Value Proposition Design* (2014)
	Maximize opportunities and compete on business models	How do I maximize opportunities and improve my business with the best business model design?	Business Model Patterns (invent patterns and shift patterns)	*The Invincible Company* (2020), *Business Model Generation* (2009)
Test and De-Risk	Test and de-risk your idea	How do you reduce the risk of pursuing a business idea that won't work?	Customer Development (Steve Blank) and Agile Engineering/ Lean Startup (Eric Ries), Test Card, Learning Card	*The Startup Owner's Manual* (Steve Blank, 2012), *Lean Startup* (Eric Ries, 2011), *Value Proposition Design* (2014)
	Pick the right experiments to test your idea	What are the most appropriate experiments to test and de-risk your ideas?	Experiment Library	*Testing Business Ideas* (2019)
	Measure the reduction of risk and uncertainty	Am I making progress from idea to realistic business model?	Strategyzer Innovation Metrics	*The Invincible Company* (2020)
Design Innovation Culture and Manage Portfolio	Stay ahead of competition and become invincible	How do you prevent disruption and constantly reinvent yourself?	Portfolio Map, Portfolio Actions	*The Invincible Company* (2020)
	Create an (innovation) culture	How do you design, test, and manage an innovation culture?	Culture Map (CM), Innovation Culture Assessment	*The Invincible Company* (2020)
	Invest in the best ideas	Which ideas and teams should I invest in?	Strategyzer Growth Funnel (SGF), Innovation Project Scorecard (IPS)	*The Invincible Company* (2020)
	Align (innovation) teams	How do you pull through execution and keep teams aligned?	Team Alignment Map (TAM)	*The Team Alignment Map* (2020)

How to Read This Book

Senior Leader

Innovation Leader and Teams

Entrepreneurs

As a business leader you establish the conditions to keep your organization humming and growing. You need transparency to understand which parts of your business have further potential to grow, which parts need renovation, and which parts are at substantial risk of disruption. You need to understand which initiatives have the potential to define tomorrow's business. You aim to make sound investments in the future, while consciously managing risk.

Use the **PORTFOLIO MAP (p. 10)**, *to design, test, and* **MANAGE (p. 49)** *your business portfolio. Create GUIDANCE to lead your teams in the right direction and transparency for everybody to manage the present and invest in the future.*

Create the conditions for success to establish an **INNOVATION CULTURE (p. 306)**. *Complement your core execution culture with a world class innovation culture.*

Ask the right **QUESTIONS FOR LEADERS (p. 212)** *to help your teams explore new opportunities and compete on superior business models.*

As an innovation leader and team you help your organization de-risk ideas that keep it growing and improving. You put the tools, processes, and metrics in place that help manage innovation. You understand how to enhance innovation opportunities by embedding them in sound business models in order to disrupt entire arenas or renovate your company's declining business models.

Use the **PATTERN LIBRARY (p. 130)** *to enhance market opportunities, new technologies, and other innovations. Apply Business Model Patterns to design superior business models.*

Use the **PORTFOLIO MAP (p. 42)** *to create the transparency your senior leaders need to make sound investment decisions. Show where the opportunities are. Learn how to* **MANAGE (p. 49)** *your business portfolio.*

Help your senior leaders implement an **INNOVATION CULTURE (p. 296)**. *Understand the key enablers that foster innovation and blockers that prevent innovation.*

xiii

As an entrepreneur your only goal is to de-risk your idea and turn it into a real business. You understand that the hard part of entrepreneurship is to constantly test and adapt your idea based on input from the real world. You know that superior business models—rather than technology or product innovation alone—will allow you to disrupt entire industries and build a more sustainable business.

 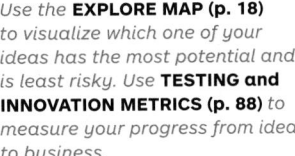 

Use the **EXPLORE MAP (p. 18)** *to visualize which one of your ideas has the most potential and is least risky. Use* **TESTING and INNOVATION METRICS (p. 88)** *to measure your progress from idea to business.*

Use the **PATTERN LIBRARY (p. 130)** *to enhance market opportunities, new technologies, and other innovations. Apply Business Model Patterns to design superior business models.*

Establish the kind of **ENTREPRENEURIAL LEADERSHIP & TEAM (p. 310)** *that will help you succeed. Understand the key characteristics of winning teams.*

Contents

1

Tool

The Portfolio Map
p. 10

Explore Portfolio
p. 14

Exploit Portfolio
p. 27

Explore and Exploit
p. 37

2

Manage

Strategic Guidance
p. 50

Explore Portfolio
Management
p. 70

Exploit Portfolio
Management
p. 109

3

**Invent
Pattern Library**

Frontstage Disruption
p. 142

Backstage Disruption
p. 162

Profit formula Disruption
p. 188

Assessment Questions
for Leaders
p. 212

4

**Improve
Pattern Library**

Value Proposition Shifts
p. 230

Frontstage Driven Shifts
p. 242

Backstage Driven Shifts
p. 254

Profit Formula
Driven Shifts
p. 266

Questions for Leaders
p. 280

5

Culture

The Culture Map
p. 296

Designing an
Exploration Culture
p. 308

Innovation Culture
Readiness Assessment
p. 314

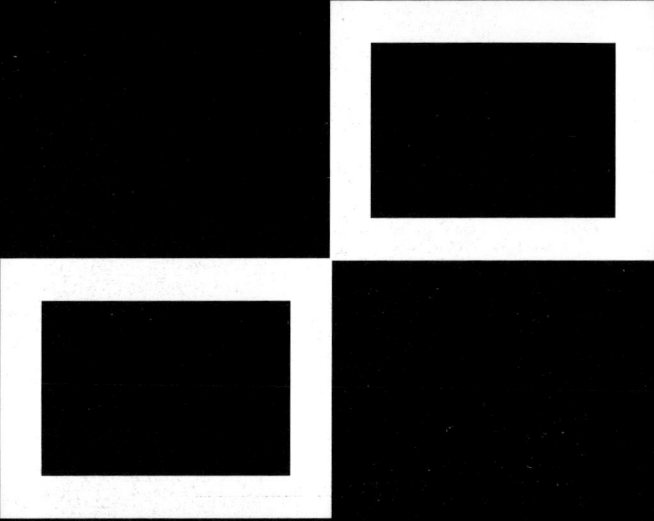

Business Model Portfolio

The collection of existing business models a company exploits and the new business models it explores in order to avoid disruption and ensure longevity.

Chasing Invincibility

No company is invincible. Those that come closest are the ones that constantly reinvent themselves in the face of disruption. These companies manage a portfolio of existing business models that they exploit and continuously improve. Simultaneously, they manage a portfolio of new business models that they explore to systematically produce new growth engines.

PORTFOLIO MAP

A strategic management tool to simultaneously visualize, analyze, and manage the business models you are improving and growing and the future business models you are searching for and testing.

PORTFOLIO DICHOTOMY

We believe great business model portfolios are actually composed of two distinct portfolios with a completely different logic: the Exploit portfolio and the Explore portfolio. The former includes existing businesses, value propositions, products, and services that you are managing and growing. The latter includes all your innovation projects, new business models, new value propositions, new products, and services that you are testing.

Portfolio Management

Designing and maintaining a strong business model portfolio requires three main activities: visualize, analyze, manage.

VISUALIZE

The starting point for any good discussion, meeting, or workshop about your business model portfolio is a shared language to visualize it. You need a shared understanding of which business models you have and which ones you are exploring.

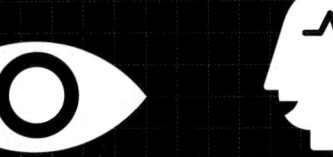

ANALYZE

A shared understanding of your business model portfolio allows you to identify if you are at risk of disruption and if you are doing enough against it. This includes analyzing which of your business models are most profitable, which ones are most at risk, and which ones you are exploring to ensure your future growth.

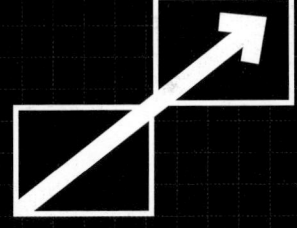

MANAGE

Good portfolio management includes taking action to design and maintain a balanced portfolio that protects you from disruption. This includes continuously growing and improving existing business models by shifting outdated ones to new business models and protecting those that are established. It also includes exploring completely new business models of which many will fail, but some will produce outsized returns and ensure your future.

Explore

Exploit

The Explore/ Exploit Continuum

Invincible Companies do *not* prioritize exploitation over exploration. They are world class at simultaneously managing the entire continuum from exploring new businesses to exploiting existing ones. They keep a culture of "day one," maintaining a start-up spirit, while managing thousands or even hundreds of thousands of people and multibillion-dollar businesses. Increasingly, this ability to manage exploration and exploitation is not just limited to large established companies. It is also a matter of survival for SMEs and start-ups with the shortening lifespan of business models across industries.

8

Explore		Exploit
Search and breakthrough	**Focus**	Efficiency and growth
High	**Uncertainty**	Low
Venture-capital style risk-taking, expecting few outsized winners	**Financial Philosophy**	Safe haven with steady returns and dividends
Iterative experimentation, embracing speed, failure, learning, and rapid adaptation	**Culture & Processes**	Linear execution, embracing planning, predictability, and minimal failure
Explorers who excel in uncertainty, are strong at pattern recognition, and can navigate between big picture and details	**People & Skills**	Managers who are strong at organizing and planning and can design efficient processes to deliver on time and budget

Explore
High uncertainty

Exploit
Low uncertainty

GROW

Scaling new businesses
and improving or reinventing
established ones

SEARCH

Turning business ideas
into value propositions
that matter to customers,
embedded in scalable
and profitable
business models

The Portfolio Map

A strategic management tool to simultaneously visualize, analyze, and manage the business models you are improving and growing and the future business models you are searching for and testing.

Explore Portfolio

Your portfolio of innovation projects, new business models, new value propositions, and new products and services, all mapped out in terms of **Expected Return** and **Innovation Risk**.

Exploit Portfolio

Your portfolio of existing businesses, value propositions, products, and services, all mapped out in terms of **Return** and **Death and Disruption Risk**.

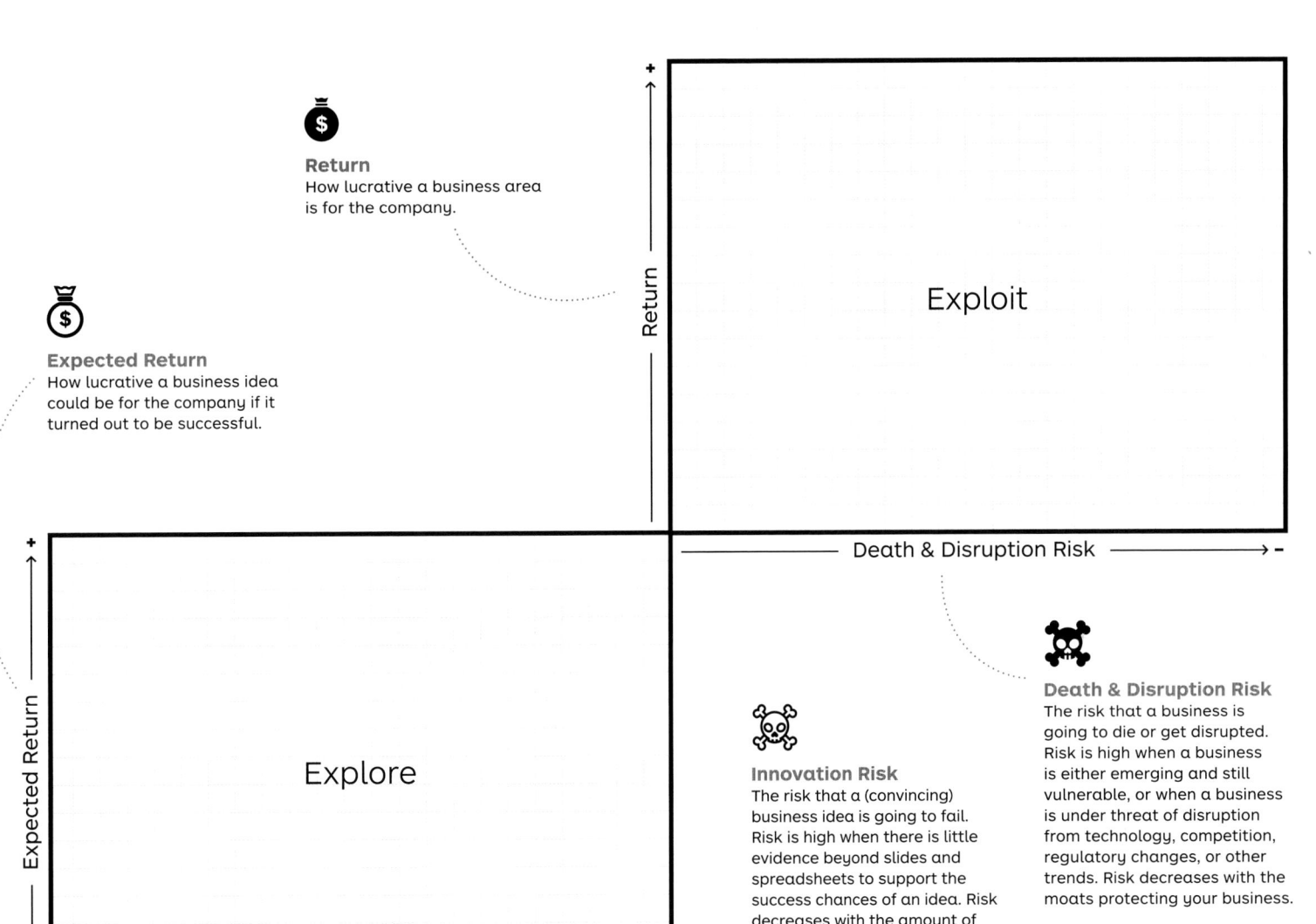

Return
How lucrative a business area is for the company.

Expected Return
How lucrative a business idea could be for the company if it turned out to be successful.

Return

Exploit

Death & Disruption Risk

Expected Return

Explore

Innovation Risk

Innovation Risk
The risk that a (convincing) business idea is going to fail. Risk is high when there is little evidence beyond slides and spreadsheets to support the success chances of an idea. Risk decreases with the amount of evidence that supports the desirability, feasibility, viability, and adaptability of a business idea.

Death & Disruption Risk
The risk that a business is going to die or get disrupted. Risk is high when a business is either emerging and still vulnerable, or when a business is under threat of disruption from technology, competition, regulatory changes, or other trends. Risk decreases with the moats protecting your business.

Portfolio Management

Explore: search

The Explore portfolio is all about the search for new ideas, value propositions, and business models to ensure the future of your company. Search involves maximizing expected returns and minimizing innovation risk. You improve the expected return by working on your business model design. You decrease the risk of working on an idea that might fail by testing and adapting it.

Exploit: grow

The Exploit portfolio is all about keeping your existing business models on a growth trajectory. This includes scaling emerging business models, renovating declining ones, and protecting successful ones. You ensure growth by improving returns and minimizing disruption risk. This is best achieved by shifting all of your business models from outdated ones to stronger ones.

Exploit Portfolio

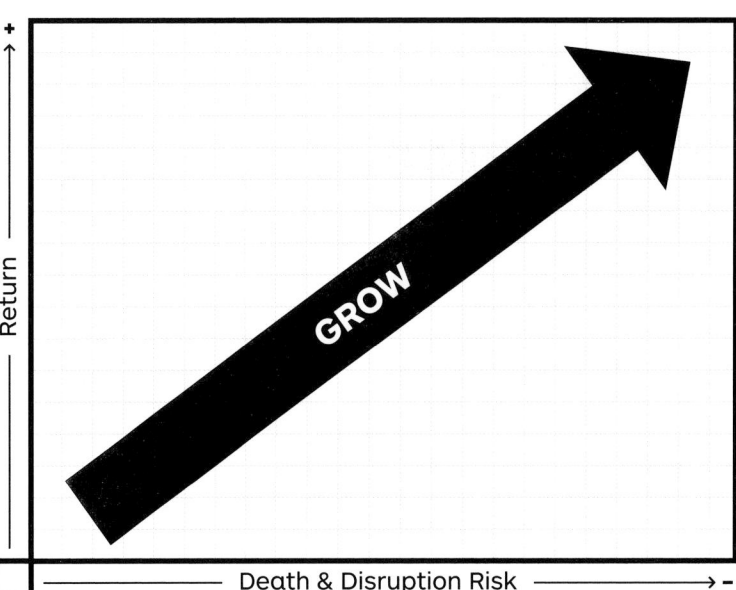

Return → +

Death & Disruption Risk ⟶ -

GROW

Explore Portfolio

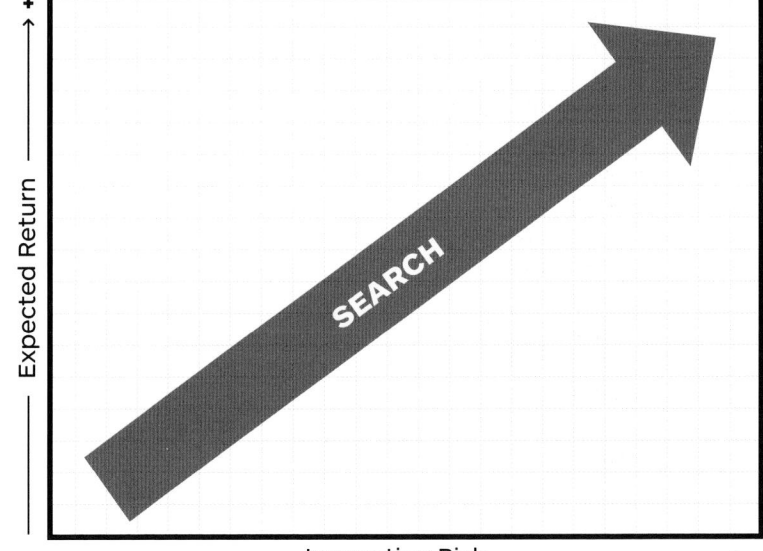

Expected Return → +

Innovation Risk ⟶ -

SEARCH

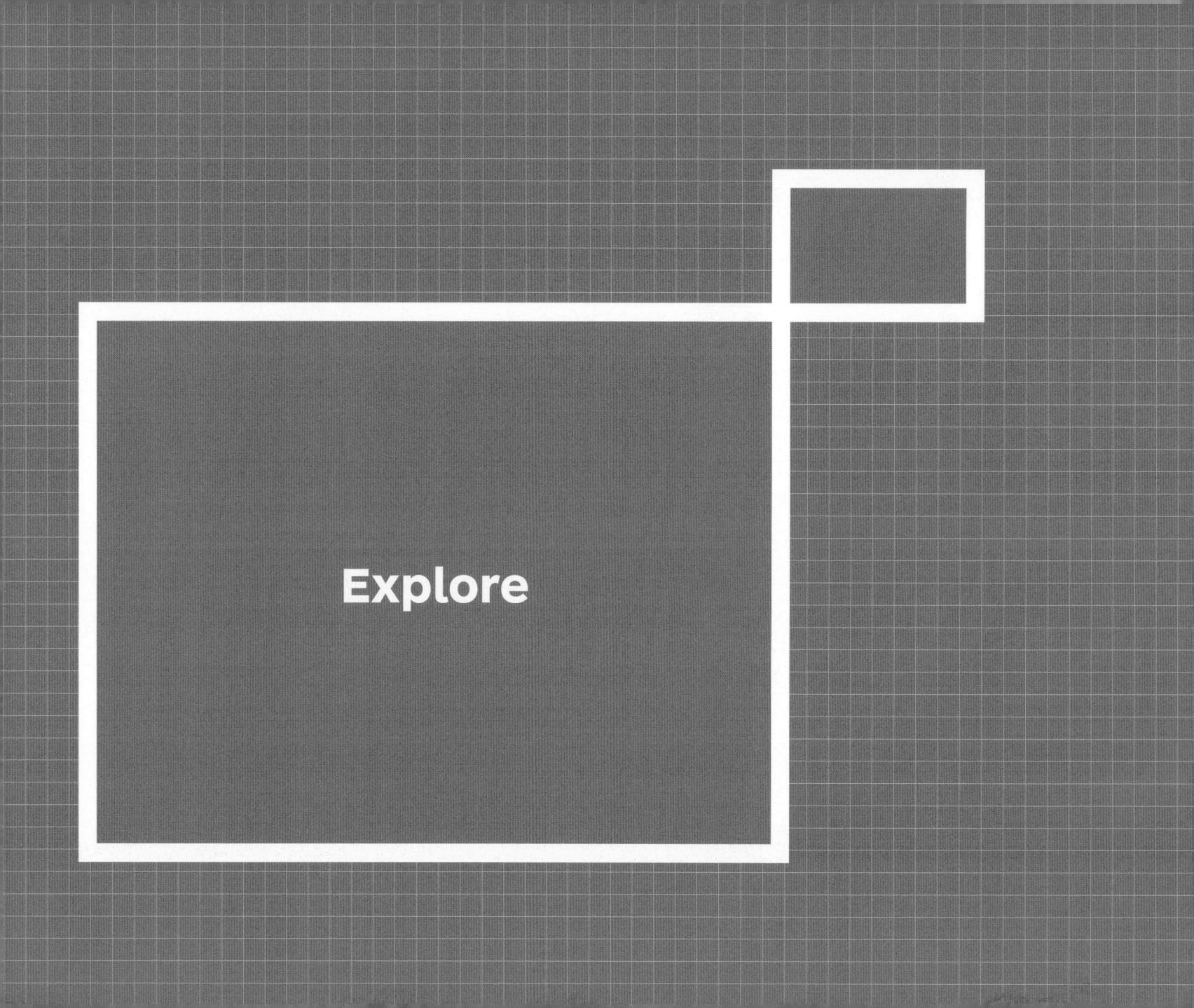

The Innovation Journey

Exploit

Explore

Five Innovation Journey Myths

The journey of exploring new business ideas is not a linear one and differs radically from managing an existing business. We outline five myths regarding the innovation and entrepreneurship journey that may prevent you from turning an idea into a real business.

Myth #1: **The most important part of the innovation and entrepreneurship journey is to find and execute the perfect idea.**
Reality: **The innovation and entrepreneurship journey is about turning ideas into value propositions that customers care about and business models that can scale.**
Ideas are easy but they are just a starting point. The hard part is to constantly test and adapt ideas that look great in theory until you have sufficient evidence that they will work in reality. The exploration journey is all about adapting ideas iteratively until you find a value proposition that customers really want and a business model that can scale profitably.

Myth #2: **The evidence will show you a clear path forward when you systematically test ideas. The solution will magically emerge if you just test and adapt your idea often enough.**
Reality: **Innovation and entrepreneurship is about making informed decisions based on incomplete and potentially contradictory evidence. And sometimes killing an idea is the healthy thing to do.**
Turning an idea into a real business will always remain an art, even with the most rigorous testing process. It is rare that the evidence shows you an obvious path forward. Evidence allows you to detect patterns and make informed decisions that are less risky than opinion-based bets. Also, make sure you don't get stuck in testing or evidence analysis. Decide to persevere, pivot, or abandon an idea based on the evidence at hand.

Myth #3: **A small number of big bets will lead to a large return.**
Reality: **Exploration requires making a large number of small bets that you gradually reduce over time, based on evidence.**
In the early stages of innovation, it's impossible to know which ideas will work and which ones won't. Start out by investing small amounts of money and time in a large number of ideas and projects. Give ideas and projects that can provide real evidence follow-up investments. The best ideas and teams with the most promising returns will emerge if you do this systematically over several rounds.

Myth #4: **The skills required to explore a new business and to manage an existing one are pretty similar. Business is business.**
Reality: **Exploration and exploitation are two radically different professions that require a different skill set and different experience.**
Testing and adapting a business idea until it works requires a radically different skill set than managing a business. In innovation and entrepreneurship you deal with high uncertainty. You need to detect patterns in the data you gather from testing and transform that into something that can scale profitably. You get better at exploration the more experience you have, just like you get better at management over time.

Myth #5: **Innovation teams are renegades or pirates that are out to disrupt the old business. They need to operate in stealth mode to survive inside a company.**
Reality: **Innovators need to be seen as partners who are essential for the future of the company. Otherwise, any meaningful innovation is unlikely to emerge on a large scale.**
Innovation teams that are seen as renegades have a hard time accessing company resources like access to clients, brand, prototyping, and so on. They need to be seen as partners who have the mandate to create a company's future in order to operate successfully.

Exploit

Potential Steps in the Exploration Journey

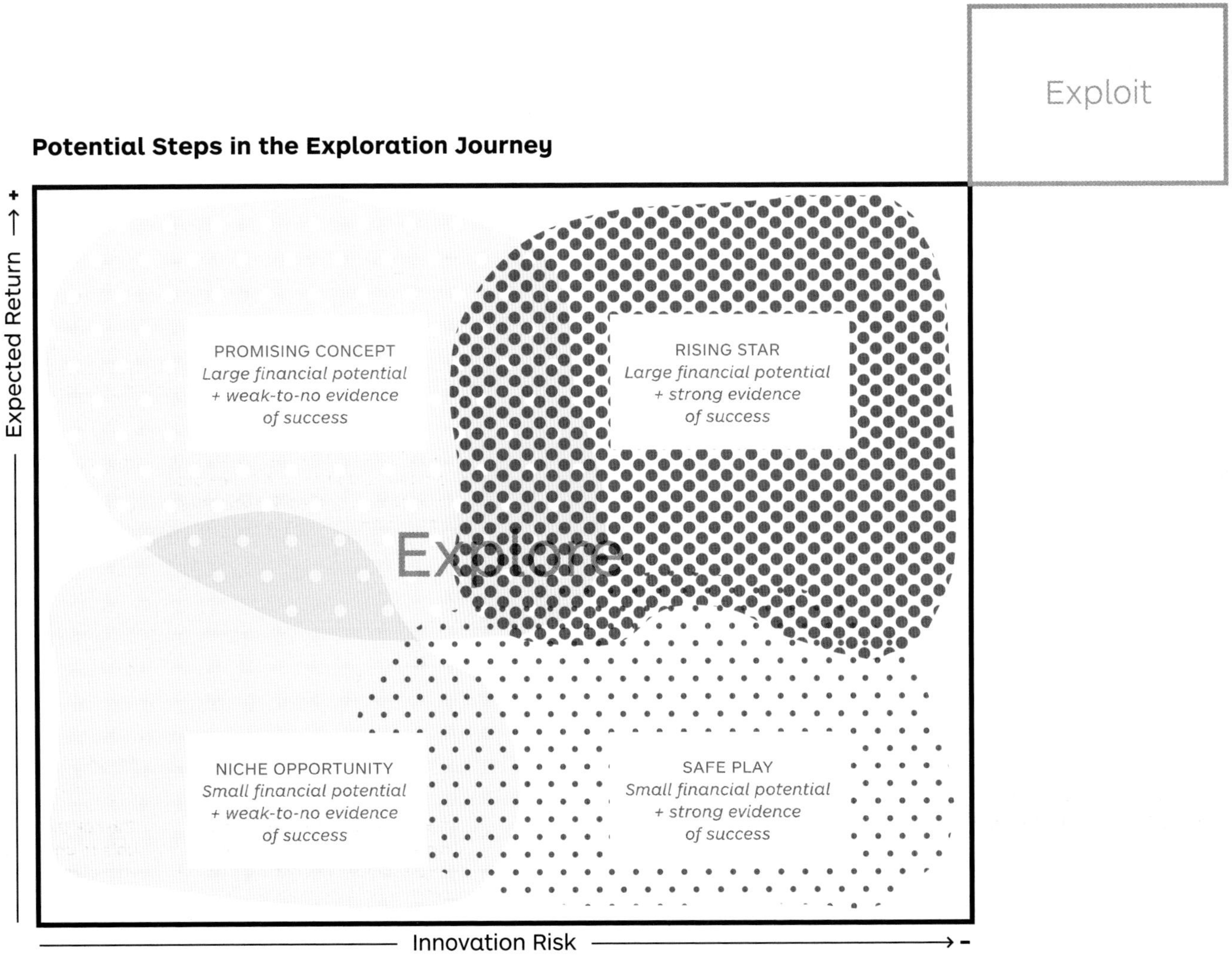

Expected Return → +

Innovation Risk → -

Explore

PROMISING CONCEPT
*Large financial potential
+ weak-to-no evidence
of success*

RISING STAR
*Large financial potential
+ strong evidence
of success*

NICHE OPPORTUNITY
*Small financial potential
+ weak-to-no evidence
of success*

SAFE PLAY
*Small financial potential
+ strong evidence
of success*

Expected Return and Innovation Risk

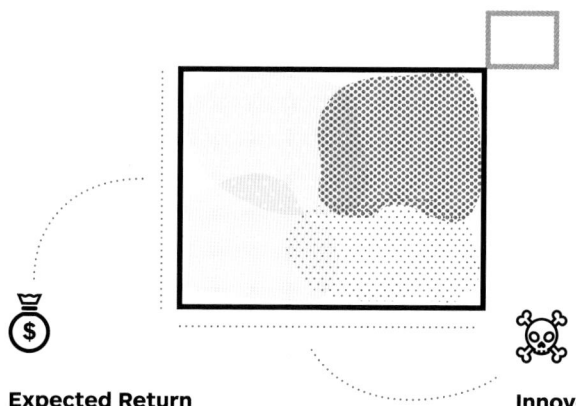

Expected Return

The financial potential (or impact) of a business idea if it is successful. You can pick how you define expected return according to your preferences. This may be profitability, revenue potential, growth potential, margins, or any other financial metric that allows you to evaluate the financial potential of an idea. Alternatively, you may focus on the social or environmental return, rather than the financial return.

Innovation Risk

There are four types of innovation risks that might kill a business idea: Desirability Risk, Viability Risk, Feasibility Risk, and Adaptability Risk.

Desirability Risk
Customers aren't interested.

The risk that the market a business is targeting is too small, that too few customers want the value proposition, or that the company can't reach, acquire, and retain targeted customers.

Viability Risk
We can't earn enough money.

The risk that a business can't generate successful revenue streams, that customers are unwilling to pay (enough), or that the costs are too high to make a sustainable profit.

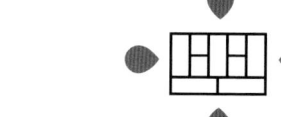

Feasibility Risk
We can't build and deliver.

The risk that a business can't manage, scale, or get access to key resources (technology, IP, brand, etc.), key activities, or key partners.

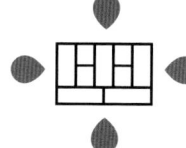

Adaptability Risk
External factors are unfavorable.

The risk that a business won't be able to adapt to the competitive environment, technology, regulatory, social, or market trends, or that the macro environment is not favorable (lacking infrastructure, recession, etc.).

This icon is the Business Model Canvas; see p. 78 for an introduction.

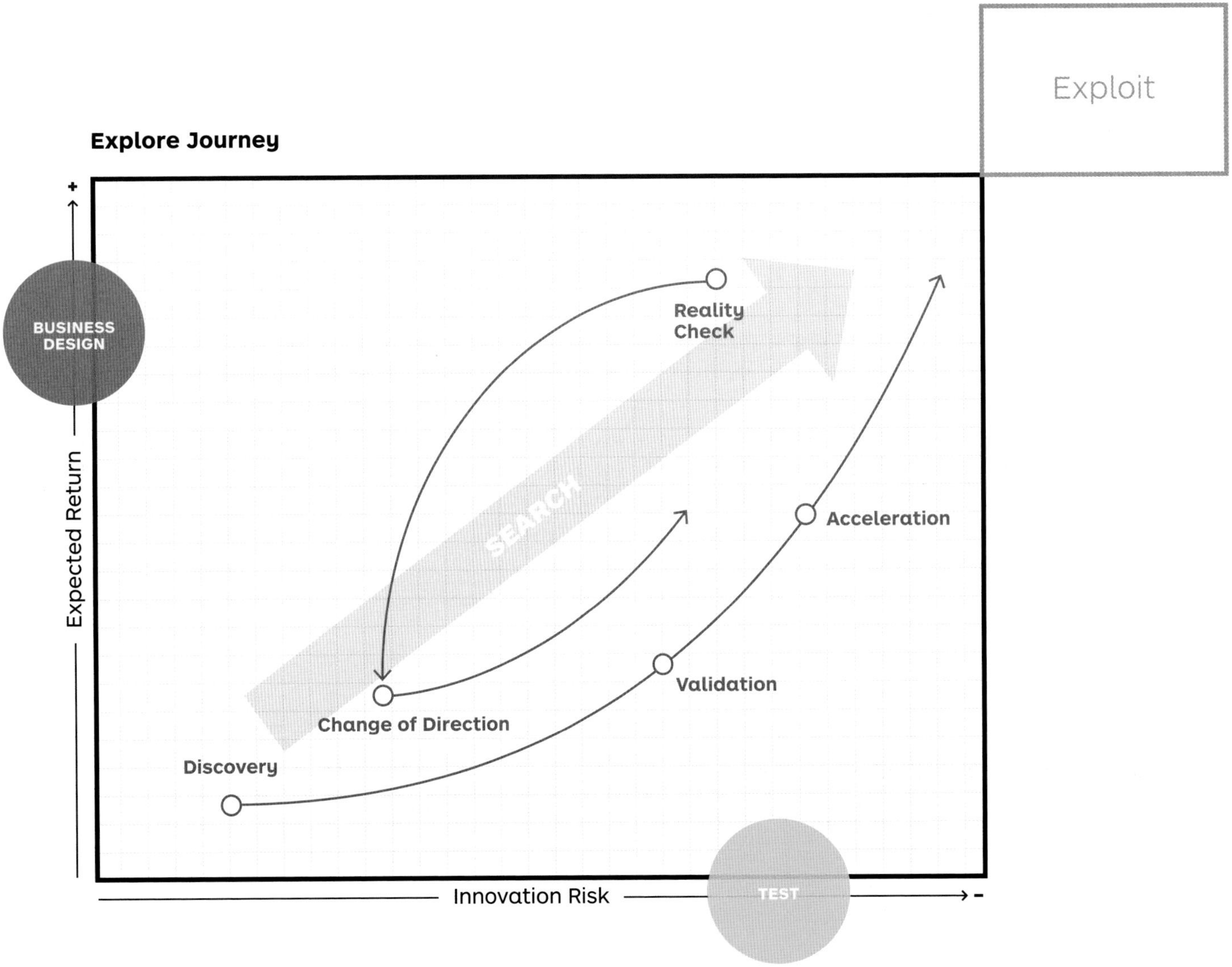

Explore Journey

Exploit

+

BUSINESS DESIGN

Expected Return

SEARCH

○ Reality Check

○ Acceleration

○ Validation

○ Change of Direction

Discovery ○

Innovation Risk ——— **TEST** → -

Search and Pivot

The journey in the Explore portfolio is one of search and pivot until you have enough evidence that a new business idea will work. The search for ideas, value propositions, and business models that will work consists of two main activities that continuously nourish each other:

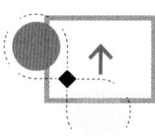

Business Design

Design is the activity of turning vague ideas, market insights, and evidence from testing into concrete value propositions and solid business models. Good design involves the use of strong business model patterns to maximize returns and compete beyond product, price, and technology.

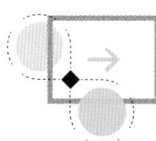

Test

Testing is the activity of reducing the risk of pursuing ideas that look good in theory, but won't work in reality. You test ideas by defining critical hypotheses, conducting rapid experiments, and learning from the evidence. The evidence may support or refute the value propositions and business models you are exploring.

Search Trajectory

Discovery
Customer understanding, context, and willingness to pay

This is where you begin to reduce risk through testing. Initial evidence indicates that customers care about what you intend to address (desirability). Further evidence typically indicates customer willingness to pay (viability). Discovery prototypes at this stage do not need technical skills. Examples are storyboards, videos, and mock brochures.

Validation
Proven interest and indications of profitability

At this stage you search for more solid evidence that shows interest for your products and services (desirability). First mock sales or letters of intent signal how much customers will pay (viability). First evidence of the required cost structure indicates expected profitability (viability). Technical prototypes suggest that you can manage activities and resources (feasibility).

Acceleration
Proven model at limited scale

At this stage you aim for a working prototype or first products and services to test your value proposition in a limited market. You search for evidence that shows that you can create and deliver customer value at a limited scale and with a profit. You search for evidence to justify larger investments to scale customer acquisition and retention, and test profitability at scale.

Pivot Trajectory

Reality Check
Failure of initial trajectory

A reality check is needed when new evidence indicates that the idea you've been testing is unlikely to work despite earlier promising evidence. It might lead you to question your entire business model or certain aspects of it. It requires rethinking which parts of your initial idea and business model you will keep and which ones you will abandon.

Change of Direction
Testing a new direction

At this stage you've pivoted from an initial trajectory to a new one. You have made significant changes to one or more elements of your business model. This means you need to reconsider the hypotheses underlying your new direction. You need to analyze which evidence is still relevant and which evidence isn't. A change of direction usually requires re-testing elements of your business model that you've already tested.

See p. 76 in Manage for more on the design-test loop.

See p. 128 in Invent Patterns for more on designing powerful business models.

Potential Actions in the Explore Portfolio

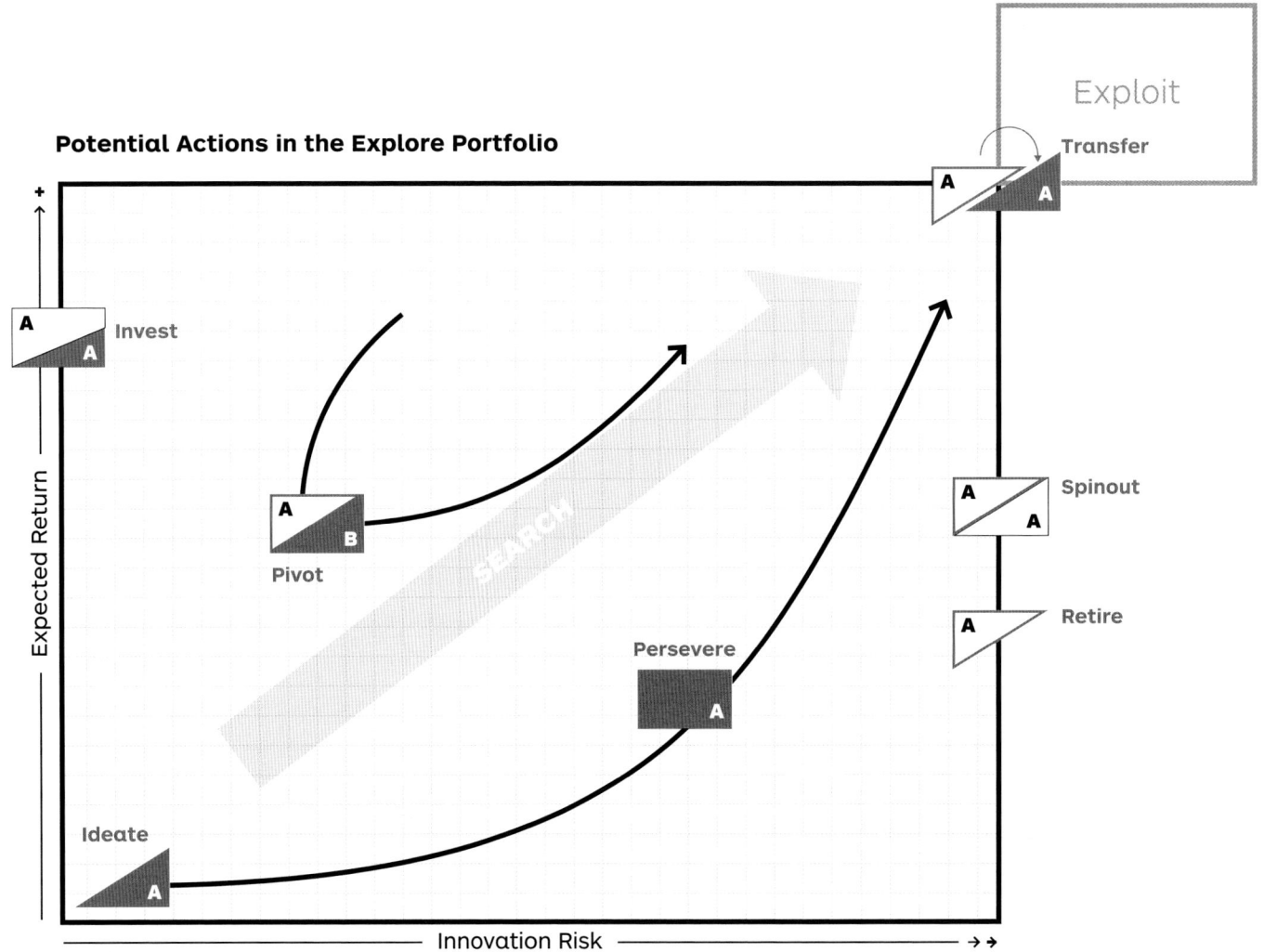

Invest

Transfer

Exploit

Spinout

Retire

Pivot

SEARCH

Persevere

Ideate

Expected Return

Innovation Risk

Explore Actions

There are seven actions you perform in your Explore portfolio. All of them are related to shaping and testing new business ideas in order to improve their return and reduce their innovation risk. The exploration of new ideas may include everything from radically new business models all the way to testing incremental improvements of existing business models in the Exploit portfolio.

The idea to visualize actions with a triangle emerged after a discussion with Luis Felipe Cisneros. See p. 96 in Manage for more on Explore portfolio actions.

Ideate
A still exists but outside the portfolio
↓
A belongs to the portfolio

The activity of turning market opportunities, technologies, products, or services into first business model and value proposition prototypes. This typically happens in a workshop setting. At this stage, there is no real evidence that significantly reduces innovation risk, only assumptions that you plan to test. You capture results in slides and spreadsheets.

Invest
A exists, outside the portfolio
↓
A partly belongs to the portfolio

The decision to invest fully or partially in an outside start-up or exploration project to bolster your portfolio of internal projects.

Persevere
A belongs to the portfolio
↓
A is unchanged, inside the portfolio

The decision to continue testing an idea based on evidence. This typically happens after gaining insights you feel confident about from the analysis of the evidence. You persevere by further testing the same hypothesis with a stronger experiment or by moving on to your next important hypothesis.

Pivot
A belongs to the portfolio
↓
A is changed into **B**, inside the portfolio

The decision to make a significant change to one or more elements of your business model. This typically happens after learning that the idea you've been testing won't work in reality without major modifications. A pivot often means that some of your earlier evidence may be irrelevant to your new trajectory. It usually requires re-testing elements of your business model that you've already tested.

Retire
A belongs to the portfolio
↓
A is killed

The decision to kill a search project based on evidence or lack of strategic fit. The evidence might show that an idea won't work in reality or that the profit potential is insufficient.

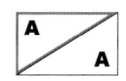

Spinout
A belongs to the portfolio
↓
A still exists but outside the portfolio

The decision to spin out rather than to kill a promising idea. This can either be in the form of selling it to another company, to investors, or to the team that explored the idea. The company might invest in the spinout or buy it back at a later, less-risky stage.

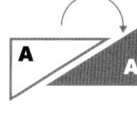

Transfer
A belongs to the Explore portfolio
↓
A is transferred to the Exploit portfolio

The decision to move a business model idea from exploration to exploitation based on strong evidence. This typically happens once you've produced strong evidence of desirability, feasibility, viability, and adaptability. Transferring requires finding a good home in the exploit portfolio. This may be as part of an existing business or as a new stand-alone business.

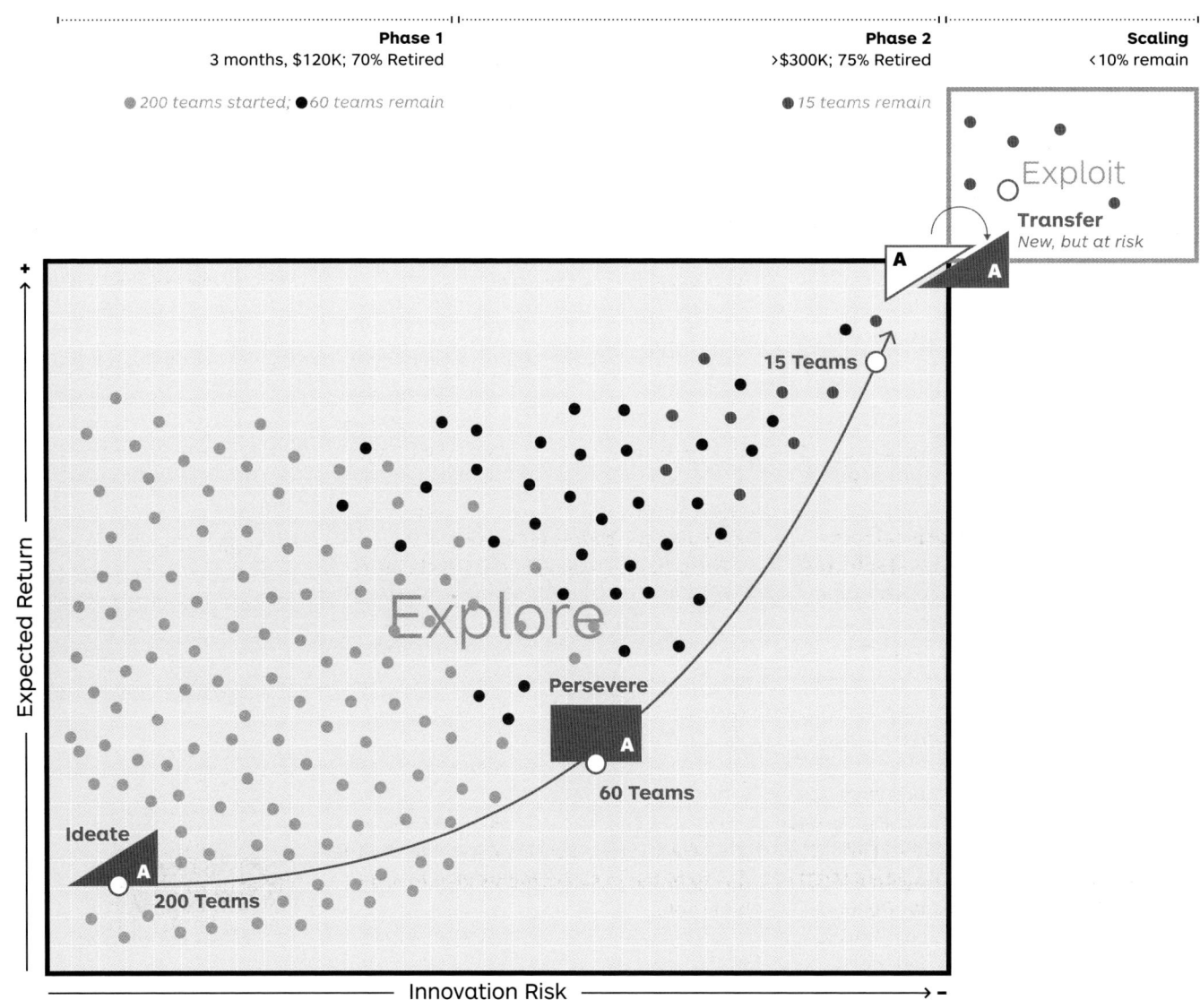

Phase 1
3 months, $120K; 70% Retired

Phase 2
>$300K; 75% Retired

Scaling
<10% remain

● 200 teams started; ● 60 teams remain

● 15 teams remain

Exploit

Transfer
New, but at risk

15 Teams

Explore

Persevere

A

60 Teams

Ideate

A

200 Teams

Expected Return

Innovation Risk

Bosch

To illustrate the Explore portfolio we use Bosch, the German multinational engineering and technology company founded in 1886. This illustration is based on anonymized data from the Bosch Accelerator Program between 2017 and 2019.

The Bosch Group employs 410,000 associates worldwide with annual sales of €78.5 billion (2018).[1]

Bosch has four core business sectors: Mobility Solutions (hardware and software), Consumer Goods (household appliances and power tools), Industrial Technology (including drive and control), and Energy and Building Technology.

From Products and Technology to Business Models

Since its beginnings, Bosch has been a driving force in technological innovation. Its R&D led to successes such as the diesel injection pump and the antilock brake system (ABS).

In 2014, Bosch's CEO, Volkmar Denner, sent out a communication to spur business model innovation. Bosch needed to maintain its technology and product focus but simultaneously turn more of its attention to new types of business models.

In 2015, Bosch created the Business Model Innovation Department to complement its innovation process with business model development capabilities. Bosch saw a need to create an ecosystem dedicated to exploring, nurturing, and facilitating growth innovation, moving beyond product innovation.

Bosch Accelerator Program

As part of their service portfolio Bosch's Business Model Innovation Department has created the Accelerator Program.

Teams going through the program explore either a new idea or explore a concept originating in an existing business. The program teams perform a business model deep dive and refine, test, and adapt ideas systematically over the course of two phases.

The program management selects an initial cohort of 20 to 25 teams from all over the world that work together for 2 to 10 months. Teams receive an initial funding of €120,000 and get two months to test whether their business-model ideas can scale. Depending on the results, teams can obtain an additional €300,000 or more during Phase 2 of the program. With this additional funding, teams can test minimum viable products (MVPs) with customers and demonstrate the ability of the business model idea to scale profitably.

After the successful completion of the Bosch Accelerator Program, only the teams with the best evidence move on to the incubation phase.

Since 2017, Bosch has invested in more than 200 teams. From these teams, 70% retired their projects after the first investment round and 75% of the remaining teams stopped after the second. With this process, 15 teams have successfully transferred their projects to scale with follow-on funding.

The Bosch Accelerator Program has become Bosch's global standard for validating new business ideas with batches in Europe, Asia, North America, and South America.

"The Bosch Accelerator Program has allowed Bosch to implement a fast, structured, and capital-efficient process for validating business models at scale and has led to the establishment of a Bosch-wide innovation portfolio."

DR. UWE KIRSCHNER
VP Business Model Innovation, Bosch Management Consulting

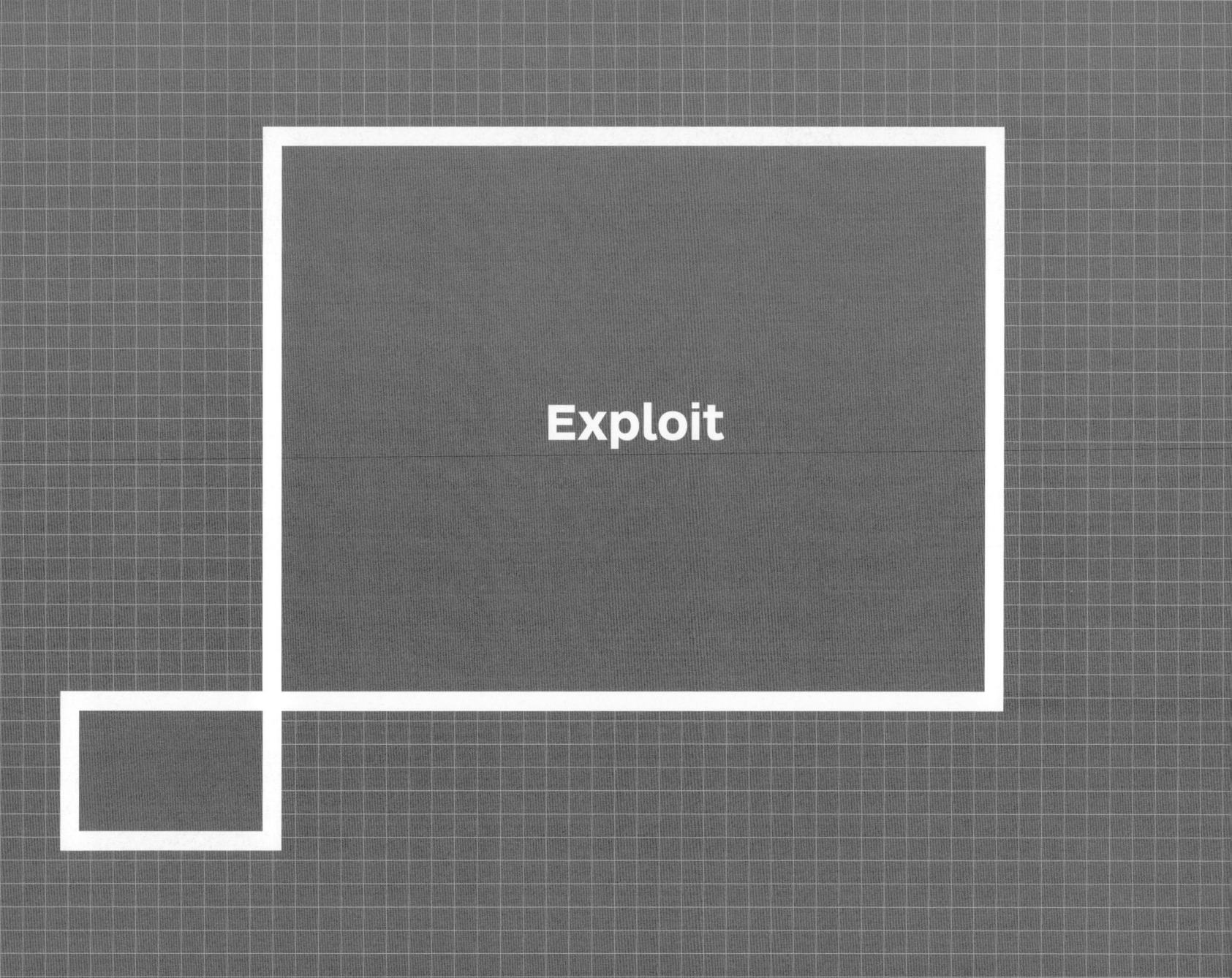

Return and Death and Disruption Risk

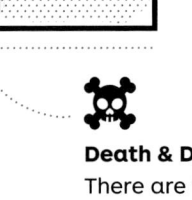

Return

The financial return (or impact) of an existing business. You can pick how you define the financial return according to your preferences. This may be based on profitability, revenue, revenue growth, margins, or any other financial metric that allows you to evaluate the financial return of a business. Alternatively, you may focus on the social or environmental return rather than the financial return.

Death & Disruption Risk

There are two types of death and disruption risks that might kill a business:

Internal Business Model Design Risk
Weaknesses

A business model can be more or less vulnerable to disruption based on its design. For example, a company that competes mainly on products, services, or price is easier to disrupt than a company that is protected by strong business model moats. The Invent and Improve sections of this book outline how you can compete with better business models.

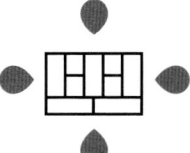

External Business Model Disruption Risk
Threats

Even the most powerful business models may be disrupted by external forces. Disruption can come from four different areas: shifting markets, disruptive trends (technological, social, environmental, regulatory), changing supply chains and competition, and changing macroeconomic circumstances.

Possible Risk Areas in Exploit Portfolio

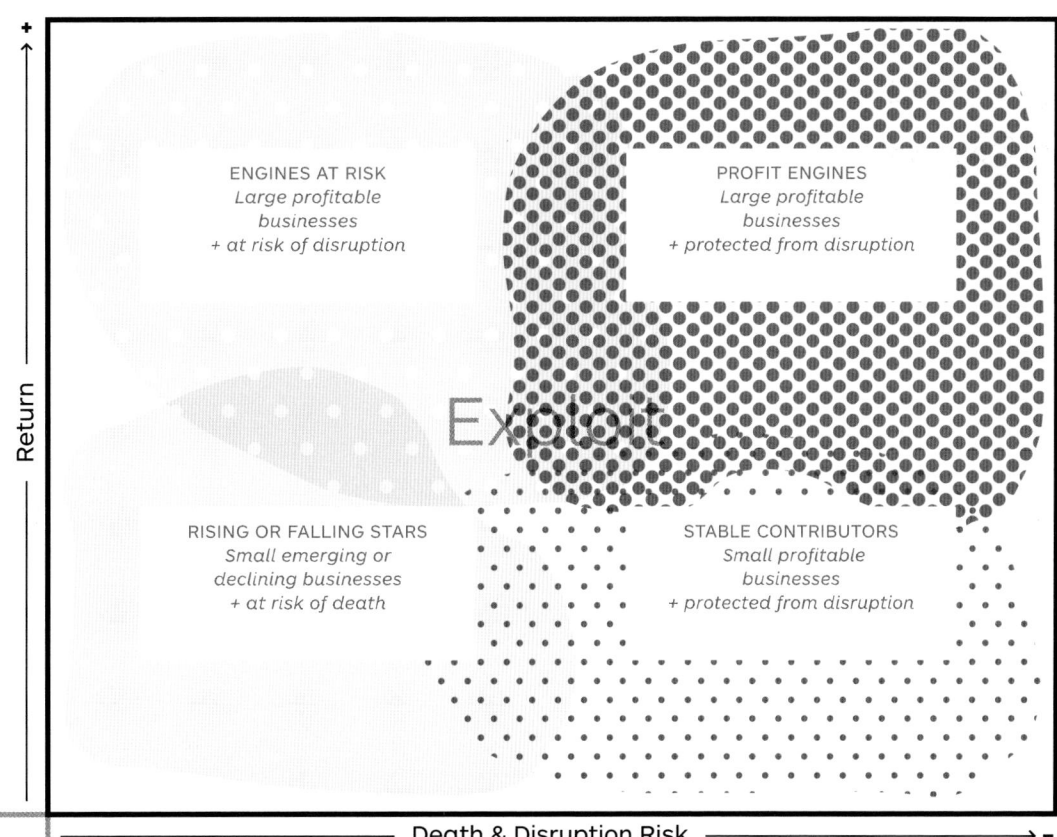

Return

ENGINES AT RISK
Large profitable businesses + at risk of disruption

PROFIT ENGINES
Large profitable businesses + protected from disruption

Exploit

RISING OR FALLING STARS
Small emerging or declining businesses + at risk of death

STABLE CONTRIBUTORS
Small profitable businesses + protected from disruption

+ ← Death & Disruption Risk → -

Explore

Growth and Decline Trajectories

The journey in the Exploit portfolio is one of growth and decline of a business. The aim is to continuously prevent existing business models from declining by protecting, improving, and reinventing them.

See p. 124 in Manage for more on testing business model shifts. See p. 228–229 in Improve for more on shifting old business models to new ones.

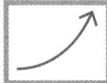

Growth Trajectory

Scale
Get the business off the ground

This is the first growth phase, when you turn a proven and promising opportunity into a real business. Main activities consist of scaling customer acquisition, retention, and product/service delivery. The entire team is focused on expansion on all fronts, including infrastructure and human resources.

Boost
Bolster the performance of an established business

In this phase you boost and maintain the growth of your proven business model with sustaining innovation. You bolster your business model with new product innovations, new channels, and the exploration of adjacent markets.

Protect
Make a business more efficient and protect it from disruption

In this phase you focus on maintaining the strong position of your business by protecting it from competition and by increasing its efficiency. Efficiency innovation usually dominates this phase. At this stage your business is large and profitable, but growth tends to stagnate.

Decline Trajectory

Disruption
Emergence of external forces that threaten your business

In this phase changes in the external environment make your business vulnerable and threaten it. Disruption may come from shifting markets; technological, social, environmental, or regulatory trends; shifting supply chains; competition; new entrants; or a changing macro-economic environment. At this stage your business is still large and profitable, but at risk.

Crisis
External forces disrupt your business and trigger decline

Your business is disrupted by external forces and is in rapid decline. At this stage you are still heavily invested in the old business model, yet your outdated business model needs major changes to avoid obsolescence.

Shift & Reemergence
Substantial business model shift and renewed growth

You succeed in the shift from an outdated disrupted business model to a renewed one. The new business model initiates a new era of growth.

Exploit Portfolio Journey

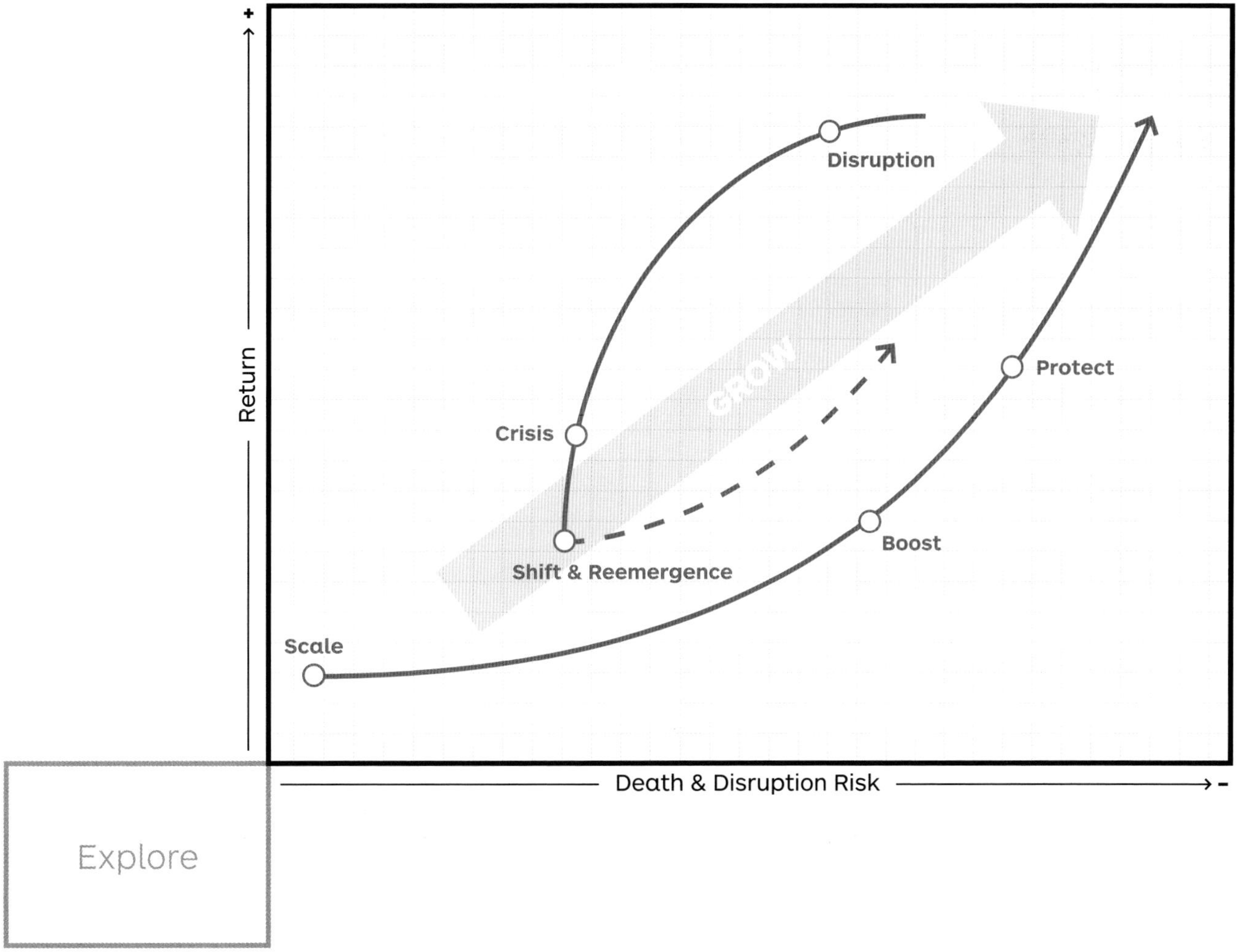

Return (vertical axis, +)

Death & Disruption Risk (horizontal axis)

GROW

- Scale
- Crisis
- Shift & Reemergence
- Disruption
- Boost
- Protect

Explore

Exploit Actions

There are seven actions you can perform in your Exploit portfolio. All of them are related to managing your existing business models and aligning it with your corporate identity. This may include everything from adding new businesses all the way to getting rid of some that don't fit anymore. It also includes improving existing business models incrementally or radically, which you will indicate in your Exploit portfolio in order to reduce disruption risk. However, you will test this improvement in your Explore portfolio, in order to reduce the innovation risk.

See p. 110 in Manage for more on Exploit portfolio actions.

Acquire

A exists, outside the portfolio
↓
A belongs to the portfolio

The activity of buying an outside business to either create a new stand-alone business or to merge it with one of your existing businesses.

Partner

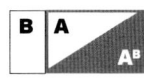

A belongs to the portfolio,
B exists outside the portfolio
↓
A still belongs to the portfolio, reinforced by **B**,
B exists outside the portfolio

The activity of partnering with an outside business to strengthen one or more of your business models.

Invest

A exists, outside the portfolio
↓
A partly belongs to the portfolio

The decision to invest fully or partially in an outside business to bolster your portfolio.

Improve

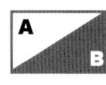

A belongs to the portfolio
↓
A is transformed into **B**,
inside the portfolio

The activity of renovating an outdated business model to shift it toward a new, more competitive business model.

Merge

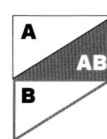

A exists, outside the portfolio,
B exists inside the portfolio
↓
A is acquired and merged with **B**, inside the portfolio

The activity of merging an acquired outside or owned inside business with one or several owned businesses.

Divest

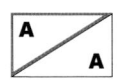

A belongs to the portfolio
↓
A still exists but outside the portfolio

The activity of disengaging from one of your business models. This can either be in the form of selling it to another company, to investors, or to the current management (management buyout).

Dismantle

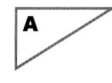

A belongs to the portfolio
↓
A is killed

The activity of ending and disintegrating a business.

Potential Actions in the Exploit Portfolio

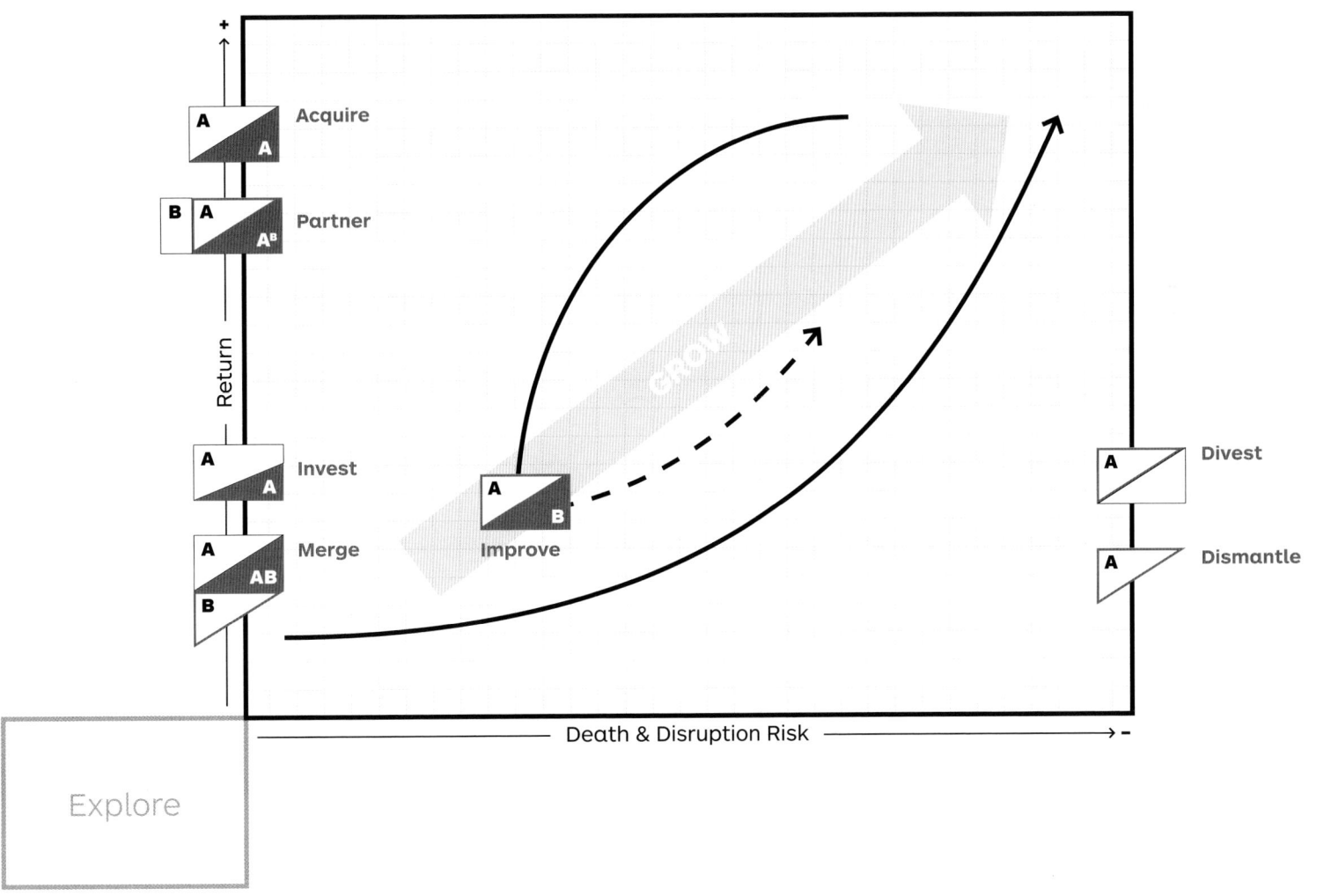

Nestlé

To illustrate the use of the Exploit portfolio, we outline how Swiss food company Nestlé managed its portfolio of existing businesses over the course of 2017 and 2018. This illustration is based on CEO Ulf Mark Schneider's annual investor day presentation on February 14, 2019. Schneider had joined Nestlé in January 2017 as the first outside CEO at Nestlé since 1922.

34

TOOL

We positioned Nestlé's main business categories vertically, based on size of total revenues of each category. Alternatively you could choose to organize the information by profitability, margins, or any other financial indicator your company uses to assess financial returns.

In the absence of clear information on death and disruption risk, we did not position Nestlé's main business categories based on risk. In his investor day presentation CEO Ulf Mark Schneider did mention, however, individual businesses and brands that were being fixed or which were under strategic review. We positioned those brands in the improve area of the portfolio map.

Acquire, Invest, Partner

Nestlé expanded its portfolio across categories by acquiring, investing in, or partnering with outside companies.

In beverages, Nestlé acquired a perpetual global license from Starbucks to market Starbucks products to consumers through retail. Previously, Nestlé acquired a majority stake in the San Fransisco–based coffee-chain start-up Blue Bottle Coffee.

In health science, Nestlé expanded with the acquisition of Atrium Innovations.

In petcare, Nestlé Purina acquired a majority stake in tails.com.

In prepared dishes, Nestlé acquired Sweet Earth, a plant-based foods manufacturer in California.[2]

Improve

Over the course of 2017 and 2018 Nestlé improved its Gerber baby food brand, Chinese food brand Yinlu, and Nestlé Skin Health. It placed Nestlé Skin Health and the food brand Herta under strategic review to potentially sell them.

Divest

Nestlé adapted its portfolio with several divestitures. It sold its U.S. confectionery business to Ferrero for $2.8 billion in cash in 2018.

It sold its Gerber Life Insurance Company ("Gerber Life"), to Western & Southern Financial Group for $1.55 billion in cash.[2]

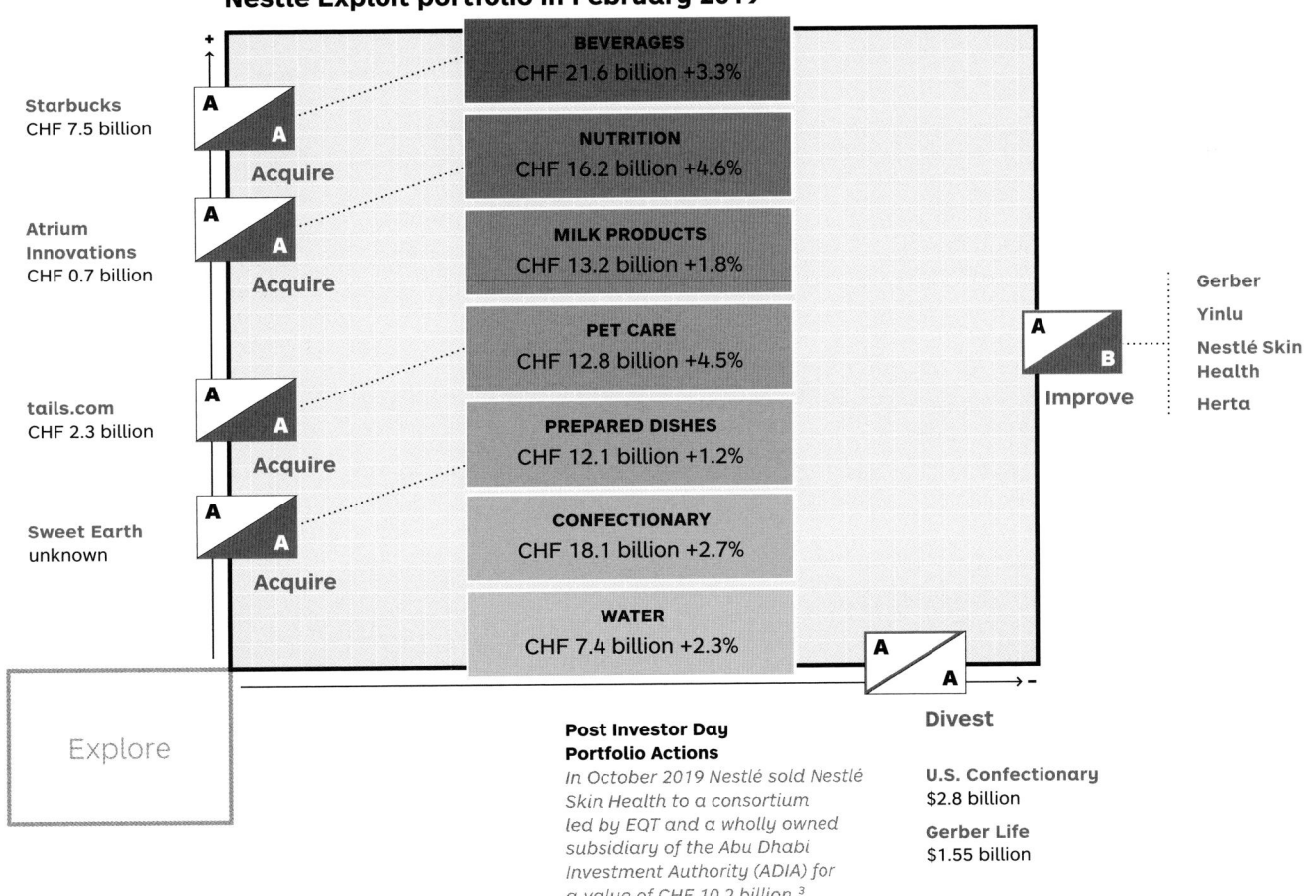

Main Business Categories

Nestlé breaks out its results in seven main business categories. Each of those business categories holds several brands and may cover several different business models. Nestlé does not break out its results in terms of individual business models, which may differ substantially (e.g., Nespresso and Dolce Gusto both sell portioned coffee, but with radically different business models and under different brands).

Nestlé Exploit portfolio in February 2019

Starbucks
CHF 7.5 billion

Atrium Innovations
CHF 0.7 billion

tails.com
CHF 2.3 billion

Sweet Earth
unknown

Acquire

BEVERAGES CHF 21.6 billion +3.3%
NUTRITION CHF 16.2 billion +4.6%
MILK PRODUCTS CHF 13.2 billion +1.8%
PET CARE CHF 12.8 billion +4.5%
PREPARED DISHES CHF 12.1 billion +1.2%
CONFECTIONARY CHF 18.1 billion +2.7%
WATER CHF 7.4 billion +2.3%

Improve

Gerber
Yinlu
Nestlé Skin Health
Herta

Divest

Explore

Post Investor Day Portfolio Actions
In October 2019 Nestlé sold Nestlé Skin Health to a consortium led by EQT and a wholly owned subsidiary of the Abu Dhabi Investment Authority (ADIA) for a value of CHF 10.2 billion.[3]

U.S. Confectionary
$2.8 billion

Gerber Life
$1.55 billion

Exploit Portfolio

Explore Portfolio

Types of Innovation

Not all innovations are equal. Different types of innovations require different skills, resources, experience levels, and support from the organization. Ideally, they also live in different parts of the organization and have different degrees of autonomy in order to succeed. We distinguish between three different types of innovation heavily borrowed from Harvard professor Clayton Christensen: efficiency, sustaining, and transformative innovation.

Explore ⟷ Exploit

Transformative

Transformative innovation is the most diffi-cult innovation. It's about exploring oppor-tunities outside of the traditional field of a company. This type of innovation usually requires a radical change or expansion of a company's business model(s). It includes opportunities that help a company expand and create new growth, but also covers opportunities that disrupt the existing busi-ness(es). Transformative innovation helps position a company for the long term.

Advantage
Positions the company for the long-term; offers pro-tection from disruption.

Disadvantage
High risk and uncertainty; rarely quick returns.

Home
Dedicated and autonomous innovation teams outside of business units, with access to skills and resources from operating businesses.

Sustaining

Sustaining innovation is about exploring opportunities that build on top of a compa-ny's existing business model(s) to strengthen it/them and keep it/them alive. Typical examples of sustaining innovation are new products and services, new distribution channels, new support and production tech-nologies, or geographical expansions.

Advantage
Low risk and uncertainty, immediate impact, pre-dictability; covers the entire range from small to large financial impact, depending on innovation.

Disadvantage
No protection from disruption; doesn't help position the company for the future.

Home
Across the organization and at every level, ideally with the support of professional innovators.

Efficiency

Efficiency innovation is about exploring opportunities that improve operational aspects of a company's existing business model(s). They don't change the business model in a substantial way. Typical exam-ples include technologies that improve oper-ations, distribution, or support, and process innovations that make an organization more effective.

Advantage
Low risk and uncertainty, immediate impact, pre-dictability; covers the entire range from small to large financial impact, depending on innovation.

Disadvantage
No protection from disruption; doesn't help position the company for the future.

Home
Across the organization and at every level, ideally with the support of professional innovators.

Gore

We use W. L. Gore & Associates to illustrate a balanced Explore and Exploit portfolio. Gore is an American multinational engineering and technology company founded in 1958 by husband and wife team Bill and Vieve Gore.

Gore specializes in material science and is known for creating innovative, technology-driven solutions that range from medical devices that treat aneurysms to high-performance GORE-TEX® Fabrics found in casual and professional clothing.

Gore's three main areas of focus are industrial and electronics, performance fabrics, and implantable medical devices. It has an annual revenue of $3.7 billion and is one of the 200 largest privately held companies in the United States. The company employs 10,500-plus associates in 50 facilities around the world.[4]

Trigger

Traditionally, Gore's revenue growth relied heavily on adding new divisions. It started out with insulated wire and cables, then added electronics in 1970, medical devices in 1975, and wearable fabrics in 1976. In the last decade, however, the markets for Gore's most successful products have matured. This, along with competitive, cheap alternatives, triggered Gore to be more ambitious with their innovation strategy. The organization decided to launch innovation initiatives for their core businesses, but also to explore potential future businesses.

Innovation Funnel

In 2015, Gore launched an initiative to grow its innovation funnel to explore, test, and adapt new ideas. The goal was to build a process-driven ecosystem that allowed for continuous generation and testing of potential new growth engines, while also looking for ways to constantly improve the existing businesses.

In fall of that year, the first cohort of six teams of internal entrepreneurs started their innovation journey. By the end of 2019, 12 cohorts of 103 teams in total will have been through the innovation funnel.

The process is made up of two major phases. During the first phase, called Concept Development, the teams are expected to provide evidenced based recommendations for each component of the Business Model Canvas. In the second phase, called Product Development, teams tackle the main technical and market uncertainties to reduce risk and uncertainty.

Teams are made up of engineers and other associates who dedicate 100% of their time to their internal start-up for each phase. Gore wants to build a pool of internal entrepreneurs that the organization can draw on for future exploration.

For Gore, innovation is an ongoing activity with an end-to-end process and a continuous pipeline of exploration.

"We innovate by fostering genuine curiosity, deep imagination, and courage to take risks. Our innovative culture and advanced materials expertise enables us to find the possibilities where none presently exist."

GREG HANNON
Chief Technology Officer

GORE-TEX® INFINIUM THERMIUM footwear

One of the first tested and validated products to come out of the innovation funnel was GORE-TEX® INFINIUM THERMIUM footwear. The team took an existing technology and turned it into a footwear technology that customers want. It provides the warmth of an insulated winter boot without the bulk. The launch of GORE-TEX® INFINIUM THERMIUM footwear in 2018 included multiple styles of women's footwear available through ECCO® and FRAU® with additional brands utilizing the technology in their 2019 collections.

GORE® Thermal Insulation

One innovation team spoke to over 80 industry contacts in the mobile electronics supply chain to conduct a value proposition deep dive. This resulted in an extensive collaboration with DELL to use GORE® Thermal Insulation in their latest XPS Laptops to prevent devices from overheating.

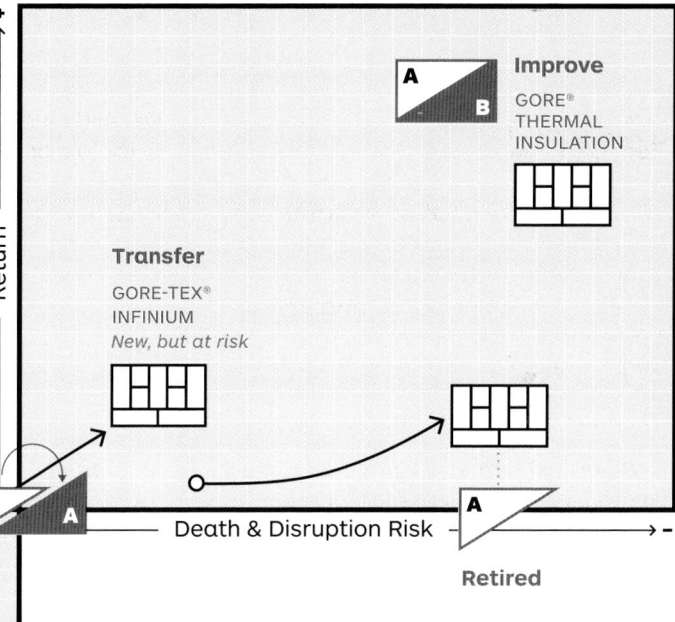

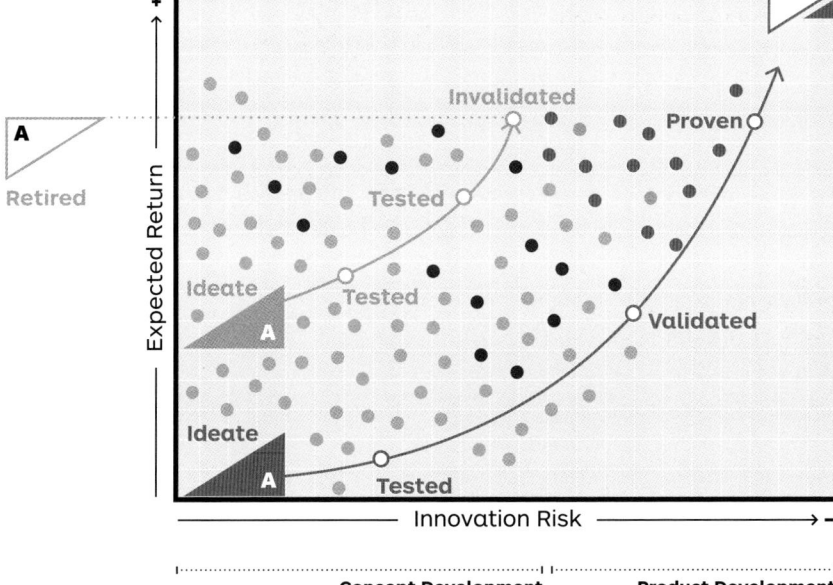

Concept Development
66% Retired

Product Development
57% Retired

● 103 teams started ● 35 teams remain   ● 15 teams remain

From niche to mass market

One team explored how to potentially expand sales of an existing product from a premium market into a mid-tier segment. The hypothesis was that this new segment would value the differentiation this product provided. However, evidence from customer interviews proved them wrong and showed low demand and perceived value from end users. The idea was shelved without wasting a lot of time and energy on something that wouldn't work in the market.

Using the Portfolio Map

Use the Portfolio Map to visualize, analyze, and manage your existing businesses and the new ideas you are exploring.

TOOL

	Entrepreneurs	Corporate Innovation Teams	Senior Leaders
VISUALIZE	Map all the ideas you are exploring according to expected return and innovation risk profile.	Gather all innovation leads in your organization and map the innovation projects according to expected return and innovation risk (based on evidence).	Gather your senior leadership team and map all your existing businesses (categories, units, business models, products, brands) according to return and death and disruption risk.
ANALYZE	Evaluate all ideas and identify the most promising one based on your ambitions and risk appetite.	Evaluate whether your exploration portfolio is likely to generate the returns you expect. Ask if you're exploring enough ideas and if you are de-risking them sufficiently.	Evaluate both your explore and exploit portfolios. Determine if you are exploring a sufficiently large number of new innovation projects to compensate for established businesses at risk of disruption.
MANAGE	Continue to test and de-risk your most promising idea and improve the business model to optimize the expected return.	Expand your exploration portfolio if you need to increase the expected return. Intensify testing if the majority of your projects haven't been able to reduce risk and uncertainty.	Invest more in exploration if you are at high risk of disruption. Expand or prune your exploit portfolio based on your vision and improve your businesses that are at risk.

The Portfolio Map

Business:

By:

Date:

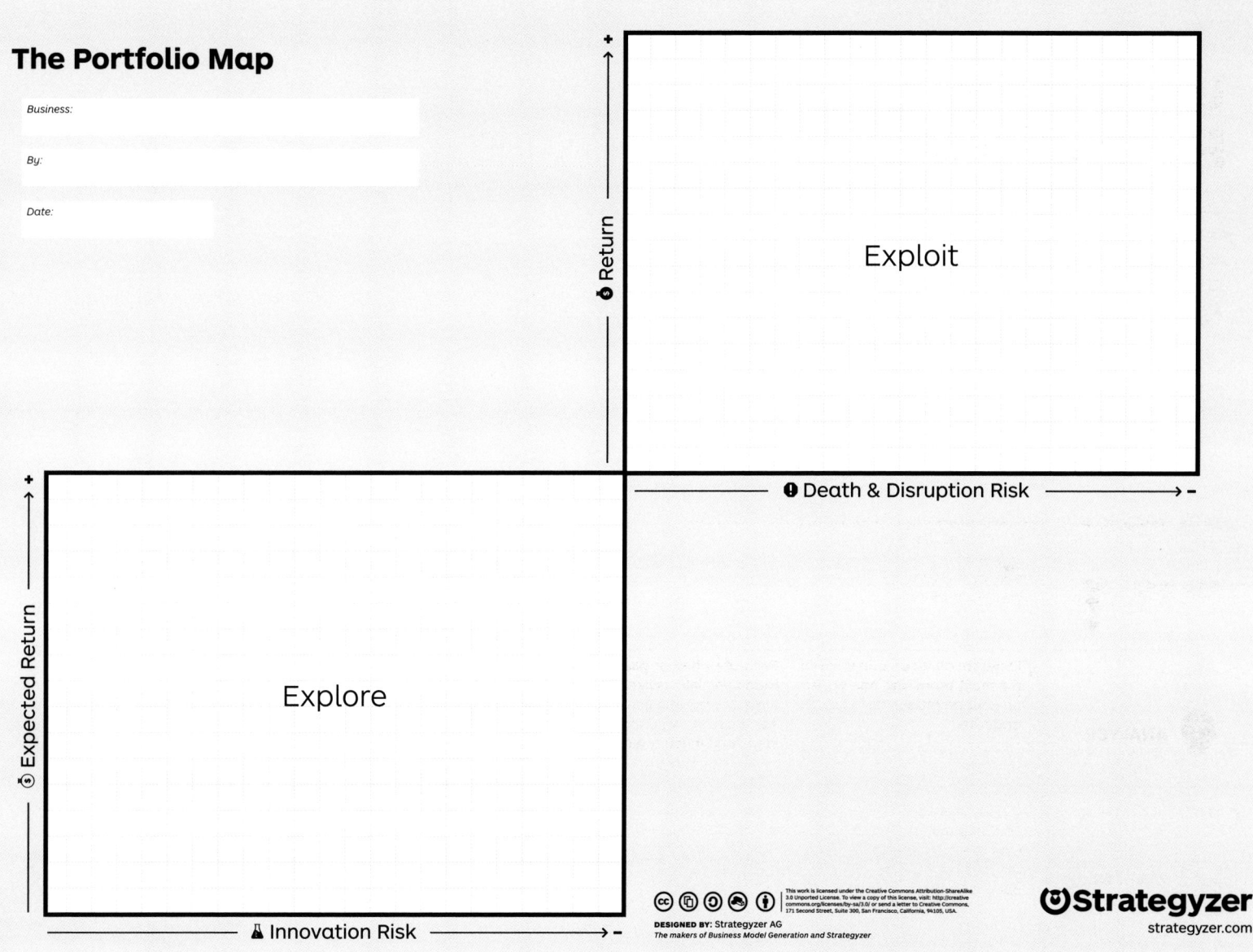

Exploit

⊕ Return

❶ Death & Disruption Risk →

Explore

⊕ Expected Return

⚗ Innovation Risk →

DESIGNED BY: Strategyzer AG
The makers of Business Model Generation and Strategyzer

Ⓢ**Strategyzer**
strategyzer.com

CREATE TRANSPARENCY TO SEE EYE TO EYE WITH YOUR FUTURE

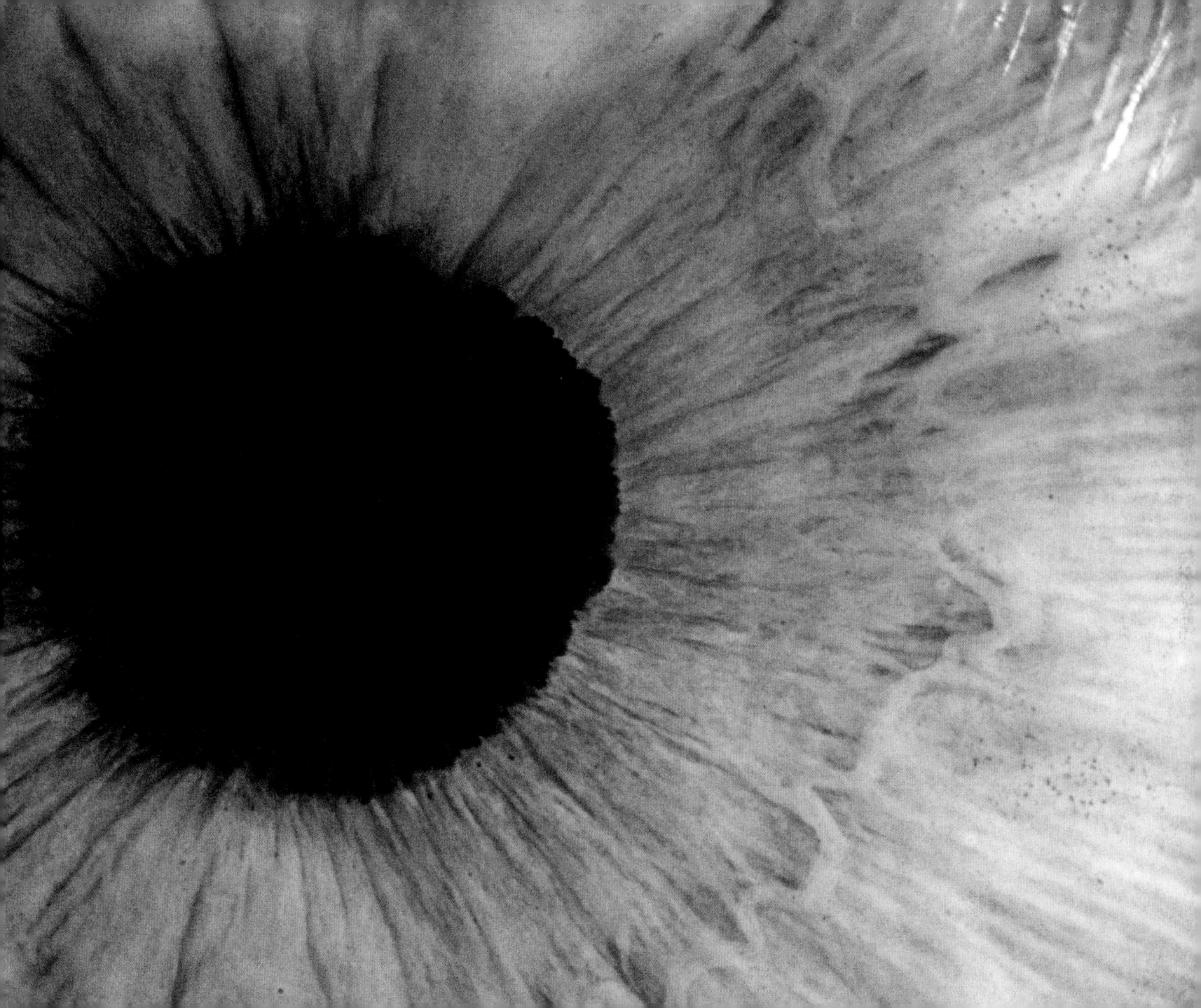

Manage

Manage Your Portfolio

Invincible Companies strategically guide, diversify, measure, and act upon their portfolio of existing and potential new businesses simultaneously.

GUIDE

Provide strategic portfolio guidance to make clear what type of projects, innovations, improvements, and portfolio actions are in or out.

DIVERSIFY

Create an innovation funnel, spread bets to minimize innovation risk. Let the best projects and teams emerge. Incrementally invest in teams with evidence.

MEASURE

Systematically measure and visualize innovation and disruption risk of all businesses and opportunities. Understand how fit your portfolio is for the future.

ACT

Use the full range of portfolio actions to optimize your portfolio. Grow businesses in-house, make acquisitions and divestitures, or do both depending on context.

Guidance

You need to provide a clear direction in order to design and maintain a strong portfolio. We call this strategic guidance and it consists of outlining your strategic direction, the required organizational culture, and the corporate image you would like to project to the outside world. Once you have defined this strategic portfolio guidance, you will have all you need to determine your portfolio actions.

Strategic Direction
Why you do what you do

Defines your aspirations for your organization. Here you make explicit where you want to play and what kind of financial performance you hope to achieve. Strategic direction is about defining what type of company you want to build or become.

Corporate Indentity
Who we are

Organizational Culture
How your values guide you

Brand Image
What you say about what you do

Defines the key behaviors people in your company need to exhibit in order to implement the strategic direction you outlined for your organization. Here you describe which enablers you will put in place to facilitate the culture you want.

Defines how you want the outside world to perceive you. This includes customers, stakeholders, shareholders, and media. Your desired external image should be aligned with your strategic direction and organizational culture.

Portfolio Guidance

Your strategic guidance provides a clear context for portfolio management. It helps you define the portfolio guidance for resource allocation and portfolio actions. Portfolio guidance provides explicit boundaries to understand what to focus on and what not to, where to invest and where to divest, or what to explore and what not to explore.

OVERALL GUIDANCE

Define...

☐ financial performance philosophy (e.g., safe dividends, growth performance, etc.)

☐ arenas to play in the long term (e.g., markets, geographies, technologies, etc.)

☐ strategic key resources and capabilities to develop (e.g., tech resources, business model foundations, etc.)

EXPLOIT GUIDANCE

☐ short term financial performance targets

☐ business model improvement targets (e.g., technology investments, business model shifts)

☐ how to develop or improve value propositions for the existing portfolio

Return

Death & Disruption Risk ⟶ -

EXPLORE GUIDANCE

☐ performance guidelines to prioritize explore projects (e.g., size of opportunity, size of markets, size cost savings, etc.)

☐ exploration boundaries and strategic fit (e.g., new arenas or not, new business models or not, new technologies or not, etc.)

☐ key resources and capabilities to prioritize (e.g., tech resources, business model foundations, etc.)

TRANSFER GUIDANCE

Define...

☐ governance of how explore projects will be integrated into existing profit and loss divisions or how new ones will be set up

☐ governance of how explore projects will be protected from being swallowed up by dominant established business models

Expected Return

Innovation Risk ⟶ -

Portfolio Funnel Quiz

In how many project teams would a company have to invest $100,000 in order to produce at least one outsized success (e.g., a new $500+ million business)?

MANAGE

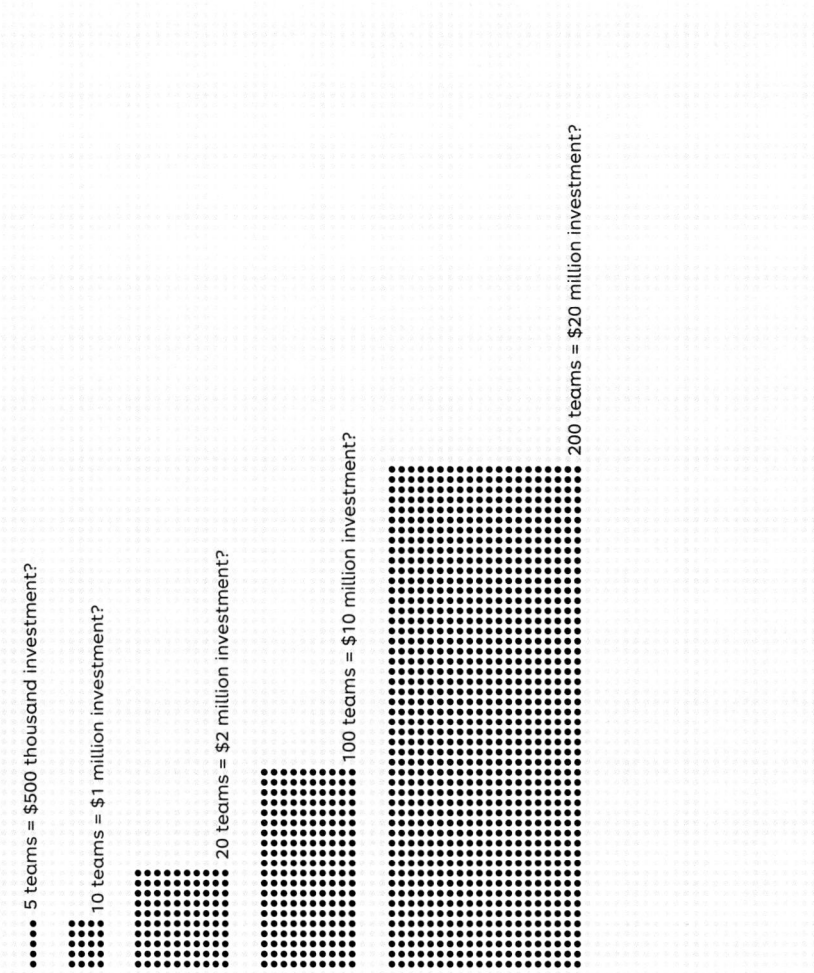

2 teams = $200 thousand investment?

5 teams = $500 thousand investment?

10 teams = $1 million investment?

20 teams = $2 million investment?

100 teams = $10 million investment?

200 teams = $20 million investment?

10,000 teams = $10 billion investment?

If we invest into _____ projects of $100K each, ^A _____ will fail, ^B _____ will find some success, and ^C _____ will become a new growth engine.

Answer on the following page →

Exploit

Return

Death & Disruption Risk ———————→ -

Explore

Expected Return

Innovation Risk ———————→ -

You Can't Pick the Winner

The statistics on this page stem from early-stage venture capital investments into start-ups. This data provides a very good proxy to estimate the order of magnitude regarding the success/failure ratio in established organizations. The ratio might be even more extreme if we assume that established companies are often less innovative and more risk averse than start-ups.

MANAGE

Return Distribution in U.S. Venture Captial

2004–2013

Statistics from early-stage venture capital investment show that the majority of early-stage investments won't return capital or will only provide small returns.

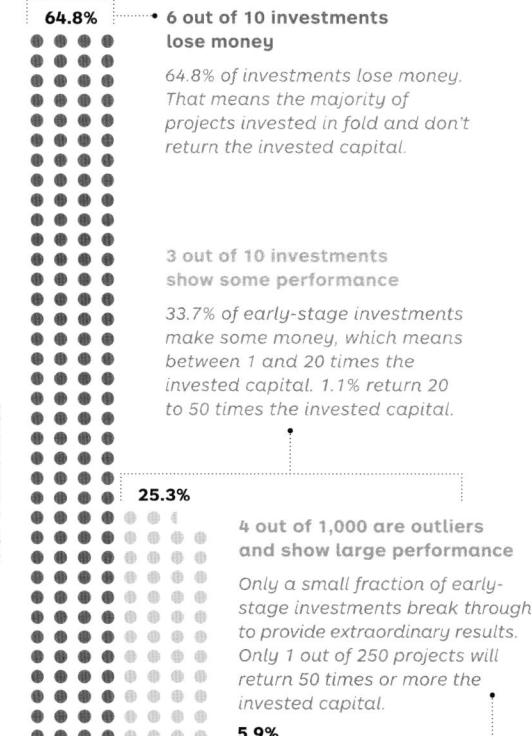

6 out of 10 investments lose money

64.8% of investments lose money. That means the majority of projects invested in fold and don't return the invested capital.

3 out of 10 investments show some performance

33.7% of early-stage investments make some money, which means between 1 and 20 times the invested capital. 1.1% return 20 to 50 times the invested capital.

4 out of 1,000 are outliers and show large performance

Only a small fraction of early-stage investments break through to provide extraordinary results. Only 1 out of 250 projects will return 50 times or more the invested capital.

64.8%

25.3%

5.9%

2.5%

1.1%

0.4%

% OF FINANCINGS

| 0–1x | 1–5x | 5–10x | 10–20x | 20–50x | 50x+ |

RETURN GROUPINGS

Lessons Learned

You can't pick the winner without investing in projects that will fail. The larger the return you expect, the more projects you need to invest small sums in.

If we invest into _250_ projects of $100K each, A _162_ will fail, B _87_ will find some success, and C __1__ will become a new growth engine.

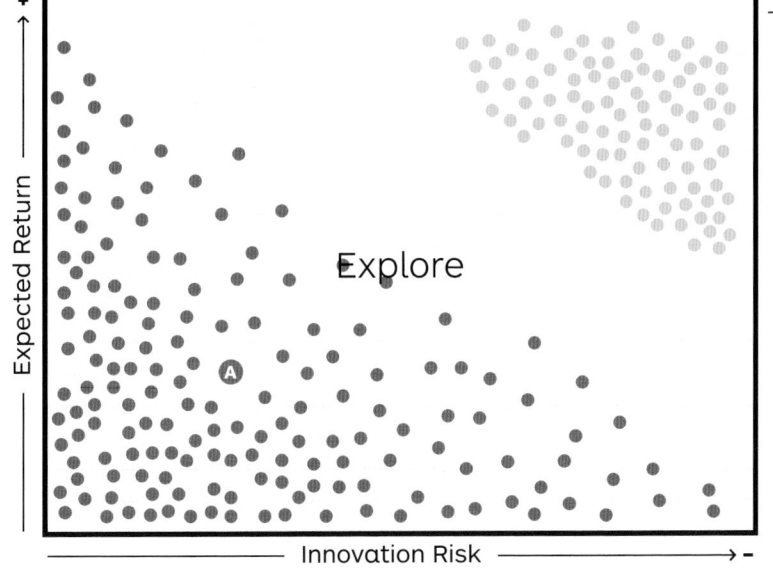

Innovation Funnel

Return

Exploit

C

Death & Disruption Risk

Expected Return

Explore

A

Innovation Risk

B

Metered Funding

The traditional investment process of established corporations equips teams with a large budget upfront to implement a full project. This leads to large risky bets with unproven ideas. In innovation you can't know what will work.

In the start-up and venture world risk and uncertainty are acknowledged and investments are spread over a portfolio of projects. This is combined with metered funding that equips teams with capital over a series of rounds. Only ideas with traction are retained and get follow-up funding to continue. In other words, a large number of ideas obtain small amounts of money to get started. Of all those ideas only those with sufficient traction and evidence receive follow-up funding. Ideas that don't work or project teams that don't have it in them are weeded out.

Smaller Outcome, Fewer Bets

Not every investment needs to produce outliers.
A small- or medium-size company (SME), for
example, will be happy with a new business that
is in line with its current revenues and profits.
Or, a division or business unit of an established
company will not need to produce the growth
expectations the overall company might have.
What remains constant, however, is that you can't
pick the winner. You have to invest in at least four
projects, if you want to see any kind of return
beyond the invested capital. The statistics would
predict a return between 1x to 5x. Only 6 out of
100 will produce a 5x to 10x return.

If we invest into __10__ projects of $100K each, A __6__ will fail, B __3__ will find some success, and C __1__ will become a new growth engine.

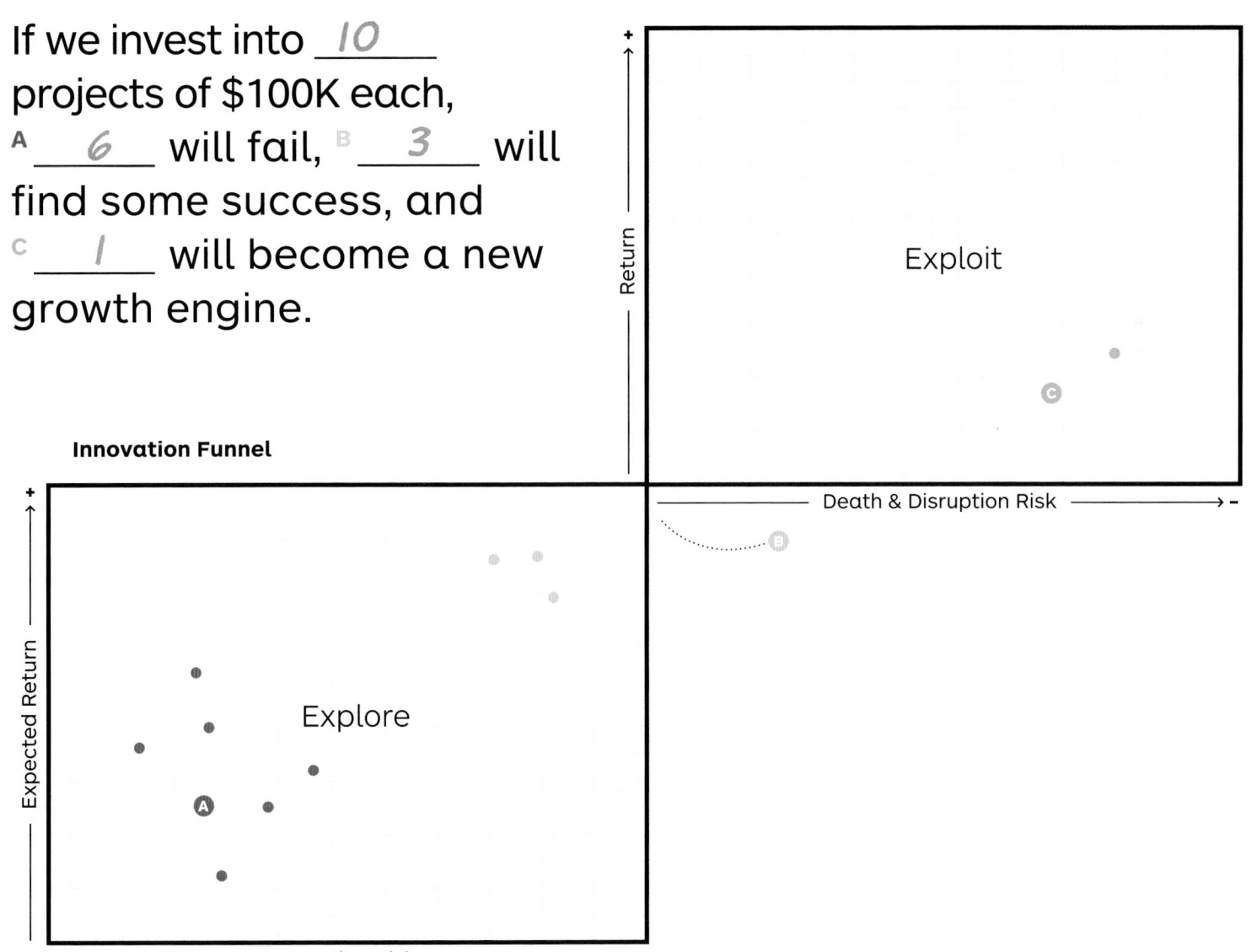

Innovation Funnel

Return

Exploit

— Death & Disruption Risk ——→ -

Expected Return

Explore

—— Innovation Risk ——→ -

ALL YOU TOUCH WILL NOT TURN TO GOLD

MAKE MANY SMALL BETS TO CATCH ONE SUCCESS

Amazon

"Failure and invention are inseparable twins," says Amazon CEO Jeff Bezos. Mistakes are where learning comes from and understanding this has been at the heart of Amazon's rampant success. Amazon has been able to build their entire organization's culture through embracing failure from leadership and incentivizing experimentation from every single employee.

Bezos understands the road to success is scattered with failures. What's clever about Amazon's strategy is its ability to create value out of a culture of failure. Externally, it has accustomed investors to its many costly failures so that the company's value is not tied to its losses but to its potential successes. Internally, it has rewarded employees who take initiative to pursue something that is far from a sure thing by making it completely "acceptable to take a risk, try hard, and fail."

Bezos has also indicated that the larger Amazon becomes, the larger its failures will be. In order for an organization to truly push its innovative boundaries, smaller "safe" failures won't really move the needle. Making a lot of mistakes, even disastrous failures (writing off $170 million for the Fire Phone), is what will keep Amazon relevant in the future.[1]

Read more about Amazon's culture of innovation on p. 302.

✔ **Amazon Marketplace**

2007

✔ **Amazon Web Service**

Launches Fulfilmentby Amazon (FBA)

Launches Amazon AWS

2005

Satellite hub sets up
in South Africa

Launches free shipping
on orders over $99

2003

Dedicates team of 57 to build
"infrastructure of the world"

Auctions shuts down

Multiple vendors exit Auctions;
confusion over retail vs auctions

Bezos issues mandate for tech to
be "good enough for outside use"

Launches Marketplace

zShops shuts down

2001

Issues with timely
tech/infrastructure deployment

Launches zShops mini-shops
for other retailers
within the Amazon site

Creates a joint auction site for
high end products with Sotheby's

Builds merchant.com for 3rd party
seller to build online site

Purchases LiveBid to allow
the broadcast of auctions live

Amazon Auctions launches

1999

Secret project to build an auction
site from scratch to take on eBay

Embrace Failure to Let Winners Emerge

This is a selection of businesses that
Amazon has explored and retired since 2001.

JEFF BEZOS

Amazon founder & CEO

*"The big winners pay for
thousands of failed experiments."*

✕ Amazon Wallet

✕ Endless.com

✕ Amazon
Music Importer

✕ Amazon Destination

✕ Amazon
Local Register

✕ zShops

✕ Kozmo.com

✕ Amazon Spark

✕ Askville

✕ Instant Pickup

✕ Amazon Local

✕ Dash Buttons

✕ Testdrive

✕ Auctions

✕ Quidsi

✕ Storybuilder

✕ Webpay

✕ Fire Phone

✕ Amazon Webstore

✕ Amazon Restaurants

Ping An

In 2008, Peter Ma, founder of Ping An Insurance (Group) Company of China, Ltd., starts shifting the company from a financial conglomerate to become a technology company. Ping An builds an innovation funnel to transcend industry boundaries and compete in five distinct arenas beyond banking and insurance.

Ping An Insurance Company of China, Ltd., founded in 1988 by Peter Ma, is a Chinese financial conglomerate whose subsidiaries mainly deal with insurance, banking, and financial services. By 2007 it was China's second largest insurance provider.

In 2008, Peter Ma started Ping An's transformation from a financial institution to a technology company. Ping An built an innovation funnel to transcend industry boundaries and compete in five distinct arenas beyond banking and insurance.

In 2008, Ping An was ranked 462 on the *Fortune* Global 500 list. In 2019, it was ranked 29th and was the third most valuable global financial services company in the world.[2]

62

MANAGE

Pre-Empt Disruption

The global financial crisis of 2008 made Ping An realize how vulnerable it was to disruptions. The company decided to shift its strategic direction and business models to build resilience into the system.

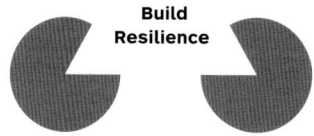

Build Resilience

PETER MA

Founder and CEO of Ping An Insurance

Strategic Direction

In 2008 Ping An shifts its strategic direction from a financial conglomerate to a tech company where their capabilities can be used a cross industries, moving from a single- to multiple-ecosystem strategy: finance, healthcare, auto services, real estate, and smart-city ecosystems.

Organizational Culture

To be a tech giant, Ping An understands they need to think and act like a start-up, prioritizing the tech start-ups in their ecosystem—now worth one-third of the company value. They even hired a Co-CEO, Jessica Tan, tasked with driving Ping An's technology transformation and dedicated to ideating and managing the start-ups in Ping An's portfolio.

Just like a start-up, Ping An acknowledges there are many areas where they have no experience, but they are not afraid of giving it a go. Ping An has founded start-ups in new sectors that have failed very quickly, learned from their mistakes, and evolved these failed start-ups into more successful versions.

Brand Image

Ping An no longer sees the company as a financial services provider; rather, it is evolving to an organization with adaptable skill sets and capabilities that can problem solve across any sector. Ping An wants to redefine industry lines and be seen as a tech company leader across an array of industries such as real estate, auto services, and even entertainment. Just like other tech start-ups, Ping An measures success in terms of online active users.

Exploit Guidance

In the last decade, Ping An has invested $7 billion into Ping An Technology, developing the four core technologies believed to be critical to the future of financial services:[3] cognitive recognition, AI, blockchain, and cloud. These technologies are breathing new life into Ping An's core financial services, increasing profits while lowering disruption risk.

Existing Businesses Change in Revenue From 2008–2018

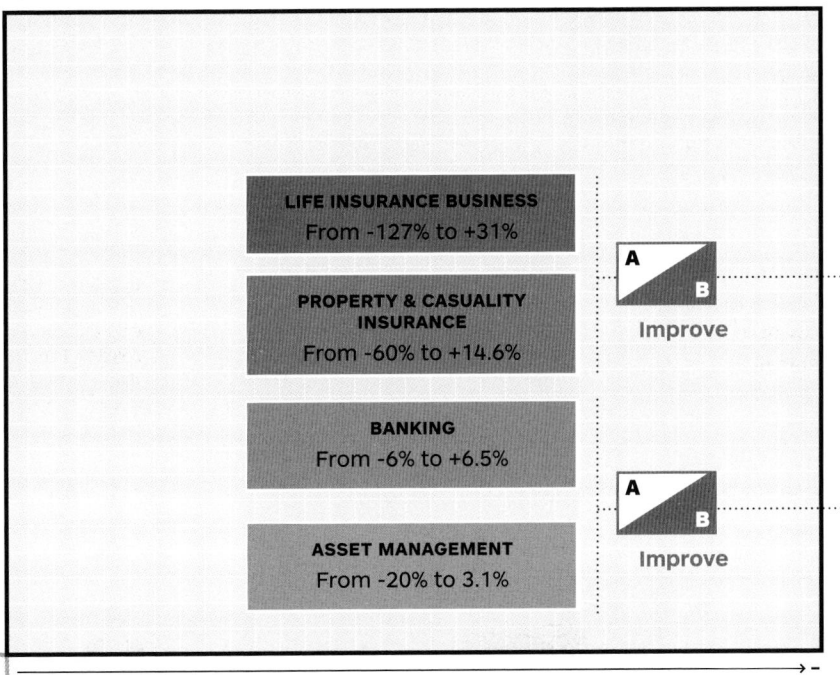

LIFE INSURANCE BUSINESS
From -127% to +31%

PROPERTY & CASUALITY INSURANCE
From -60% to +14.6%

A / B
Improve

BANKING
From -6% to +6.5%

ASSET MANAGEMENT
From -20% to 3.1%

A / B
Improve

Explore

In 2014 **Ping An Property & Casualty Insurance** develops the Ping An Auto Owner app, using AI and telematics to track driver behavior in order to tailor policy pricing and risk selection. This redefines their relationship with customers by turning a passive product into a responsive personalized good that rewards good behavior. Through the app, Ping An can shorten the average turnaround time of a single claim to 168 seconds, with no back-end manual operation involved. As of 2019, the app has 16 million monthly active users, topping the list of auto service apps in China.[4]

Ping An spent four years developing proprietary technology using AI for loan application and fraud detection. By 2017 the program can read micro-expressions of applicants with 90% accuracy in detecting lies. This is used in loan approval instead of credit scores, giving Ping An access to a new customer segment: 40% of Chinese consumers who currently do not have a credit score. This technology can help reduce credit losses by 60%, with accuracy being much higher than other approaches.[5,6]

Exploring in the Future

Since Ping An's strategic shift in 2008 they have committed to spending 1% of revenue on R&D (~10% of profit) every year.[7] This was to establish Ping An Technology as the technology incubator arm of Ping An Group. Ping An Technology has been responsible for seeding the group's most successful start-ups while revolutionizing Ping An's existing financial services. By 2028, Ping An expects to have spent $21 billion in R&D to support their strategic direction of evolving into a tech giant.[8]

This steadfast commitment to R&D investment, along with an agile "can do" culture, has enabled Ping An to have a strong innovation pipeline resulting in a diverse explore portfolio that is now worth one-third of the company's brand value. These include 11 start-ups in tech. Two are listed (Lufax, Autohome) and four are valued at more than $1 billion (Lufax, Good Doctor, Autohome and OneConnect).[9]

JESSICA TAN

Ping An Group Co-CEO

Measuring Success

Ping An's most successful platforms are the ones that have fully embraced their ecosystem strategy of being a "one-stop shop" for their customers, continuously improving online user experience, and aligning use cases with user needs. Ping An tracks user engagement to measure the success of their business. In 2019, yearly active users reached 269 million, translating to 2.49 online services per user.[9]

Good Doctor (2014)
Ping An realized the medical needs in China were woefully underserved and saw an opportunity to use its capabilities to bolster the ecosystem. Good Doctor was developed by Wang Tao, previously VP of Alibaba group. He joined in 2013 as the new CEO of Ping An Health, with the objective of building China's largest medical app. Good Doctor is now the largest online health-care platform in China, with over 265 million users. It provides users with comprehensive 24/7 online consultation through their AI doctor services. Good Doctor went public in 2018 with a $1.12 billion IPO.[11]

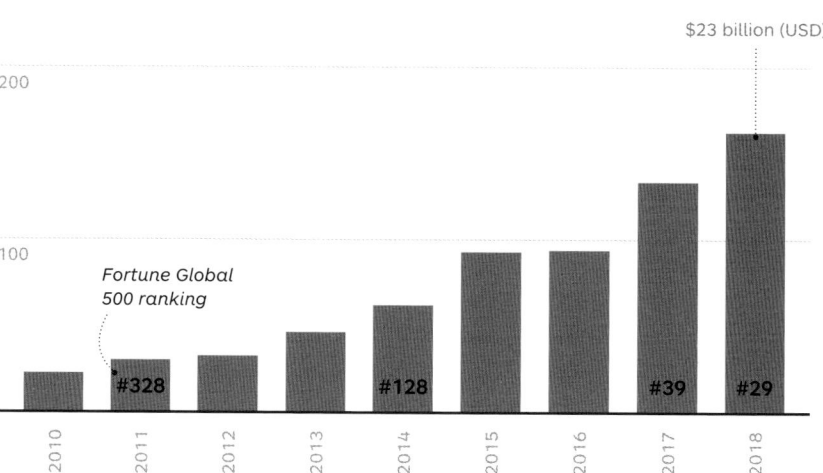

Ping An Net Profit Growth (2010–2018)
In billions (Yuan)

$23 billion (USD)

200

100

Fortune Global 500 ranking

#328   #128   #39   #29

2010 2011 2012 2013 2014 2015 2016 2017 2018

Oneconnect (2015)

Ping An's proprietary technology has become so advanced that they have now bundled it up into a cloud platform known as OneConnect, providing fintech solutions to other financial institutions. As of 2018 OneConnect had provided services for 3,289 financial institutions, including 590 banks, 72 insurers and 2,627 non-bank financial institutions across China. It is now rolling out into the rest of Asia and Europe as well.

Autohome (2016)

Ping An then took a majority stake ($1.6 billion) in Autohome, an Australian O2O platform. Ping An made significant improvements to the platform by integrating data products including smart recommendation, smart online sales, and smart marketing to help auto manufacturers and dealers increase conversion rates.[15]

Autohome (2019)

It is now valued at $10 billion. In the first half of 2019, Autohome recorded rapid business growth with revenue totaling RMB3,921 million, up 24.2% year on year. The app has an average of 38 million daily unique visitors in 2019.[12, 13]

Good Doctor (2019)

62.7 million monthly active users.

Oneconnect (2019)

Risk management products used 721 million times.

Lufax (2019)

11.58 million active investor users.

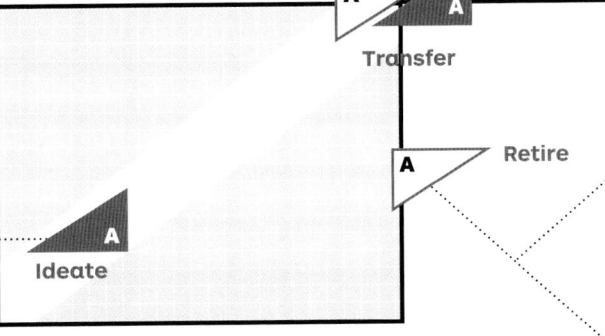

Exploit 2019

Invest

Explore 2008–2018

Transfer

Retire

Ideate

Ping HaoChe (2013–2016)

O2O secondhand car sales platform connecting car manufacturers and dealer partnerships. A year after launch, and $200 million in sunk costs later, it was quickly scaled back.[14]

Lufax

Lufax is an example of how Ping An has been able to provide financial services to a segment of the market it was unable to access until it made the transition to a tech company. It matches borrowers and lenders by providing the middle class with over 5,000 financial products for investments of as little as $1,000. Lufax uses AI (robo-advisor) to cut operating costs and optimize interactions, opening up a whole new market of investors to Ping An. Lufax is currently valued at $5 billion, with Ping An owning 41%.[10]

Ping Haufang (2014–2018)

A one-stop shop for home sales, rental, real estate investing and property developments. It failed because it was unable to capture the complexity of the real estate industry, an ecosystem Ping An does not have any experience in. Yet they were very much willing to give it a go.

Business R&D

Innovation is a young, emerging profession that substantially differs from managing a business and is not the same as traditional R&D. Because it's such a young discipline, some misconceptions persist that, unfortunately, prevent organizations from investing in innovation the right way. We outline five misconceptions that we've seen senior leaders falling for.

66

MANAGE

Misconception #1

Innovation = new technologies and R&D.

Reality

Technology may or may not play a role in a particular innovation.

Innovation is first and foremost about exploring novel ways to create value for customers and your organization. That is broader than just technology-based innovation. The Nintendo Wii, for example, was an inferior technological platform when it launched, yet it disrupted the gaming industry. (cf p. 240).

Misconception #2

Innovation = find the perfect idea.

Reality

Good ideas are easy.

The hard part of innovation is the search and iteration process of shaping and adapting ideas until you find a concrete value proposition that customers care about, embedded in a business model that can scale profitably. Finally, to reduce risk you should not bet on a few bold ideas that look good, but create a portfolio in which you explore many ideas, so the best ones emerge.

Successful Innovation = (R&D)* + Business + Execution[16]

R&D

invention
optional

Customer Value   Business Model

Misconception #3
Innovation = build products (and services) customers love.
Reality
Products, services, and value propositions customers care about are a pillar of innovation, yet insufficient on their own.

Without a business model that can scale profitably, even the best products will die. All types of innovations, from efficiency to transformative innovation, require a sustainable business model.

Misconception #4
Innovation = creative genius that can't be learned.
Reality
Innovation is not black magic that depends on creative genius.

Turning innovative ideas into a business result is an art and a science that can be learned. Some aspects, like the tools, business model patterns, or testing can be learned "in the classroom." Other aspects, like turning evidence from testing into better value propositions and business models, are more an "art" (i.e., pattern recognition) and come from experience.

Misconception #5
Innovation = business and strategy as usual.
Reality
Most organizations have done traditional R&D for decades.

However, what worked in the past isn't fit for the future. Business models and value propositions are expiring faster than ever before, industry boundaries are disappearing, and competitors increasingly come from unexpected places. It's time for a new type of business R&D on the strategic agenda.

Guidance

The activities a company undertakes to spot, create, test, de-risk, and invest in a portfolio of novel business opportunities. Opportunities range from improving the existing business(es) to exploring radically new ones. The heart of business R&D is the art and science of shaping value propositions and business models and the identification and testing of desirability, feasibility, viability, and adaptability risks for each opportunity. It complements traditional technology and product R&D, which mainly focus on feasibility.

Innovation Performance and R&D spending

According to a 2018 study by Strategy& of PwC there is no strong direct link between innovation success and R&D spending. For example, the car manufacturer Volkswagen spent $15.8 billion on R&D and was the third largest spender in the study, yet didn't make the top 10 innovators. Tesla spent $1.5 billion on R&D or 7% of revenues and ranked fifth among the study's most innovative companies.[17]

The top two in that list also look pretty different. Top ranked Apple is only the seventh largest R&D spender with $11.6 billion or 5.1% of revenues. Second ranked Amazon is the number one R&D spender with $22.6 billion or 12.7% of revenues. Pharmaceutical companies like Roche, Johnson & Johnson, Merck, Novartis, Pfizer, and Sanofi are all top 20 spenders (14% to 25% of revenues), yet none of them made the top 10 innovators.

The Strategy& study shows that the 10 most innovative companies outperformed the 10 biggest R&D spenders on revenue growth, gross margin, and market cap growth.

Innovating vs. Spending[17]

Top 10 innovators — Top 10 spenders

Companies selected by Strategy& study respondents as the most innovative, outperformed the biggest R&D spenders.

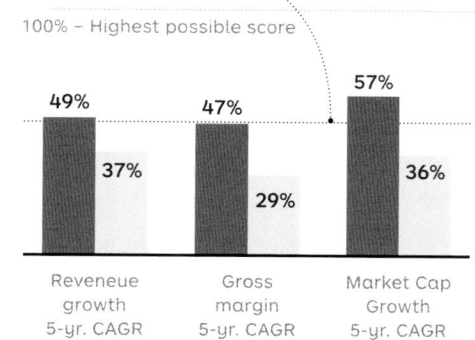

100% – Highest possible score

| | 49% | 47% | 57% |
| Revenue growth 5-yr. CAGR | 37% | 29% (Gross margin 5-yr. CAGR) | 36% (Market Cap Growth 5-yr. CAGR) |

MANAGE

Business R&D in Action

Business R&D doesn't replace traditional technology and product R&D. It's complementary. Its purpose is to create, explore, and research new value propositions and business models and reduce the risk for the business hypotheses underlying them. Business R&D may draw on traditional R&D, which focuses more on the technological aspects of feasibility.

Main Business R&D tasks include:

1) Identification of Opportunities

This is the activity of scanning the environment for promising opportunities to improve the existing business or explore completely new ones. Opportunities may come from shifting customer needs, technology innovations, regulatory changes, societal trends, and more. It may also include the acquisition of competitors, start-ups, or complementary organizations.

2) Shaping, Testing, and Adapting Value Propositions and Business Models

The majority of Business R&D is dedicated to testing opportunities and turning them into real businesses. This consists of shaping, testing, and adapting value propositions and business models, until customers care and evidence shows you can build and scale the business model profitably.

3) Portfolio Management

This last activity of Business R&D consists of protecting your company from disruption by maintaining a business (model) portfolio. This includes spreading your innovation bets across all types of innovation projects and incrementally investing in those that produce evidence, while shelving those that don't. This diversifies risk and lets the best ideas and teams emerge.

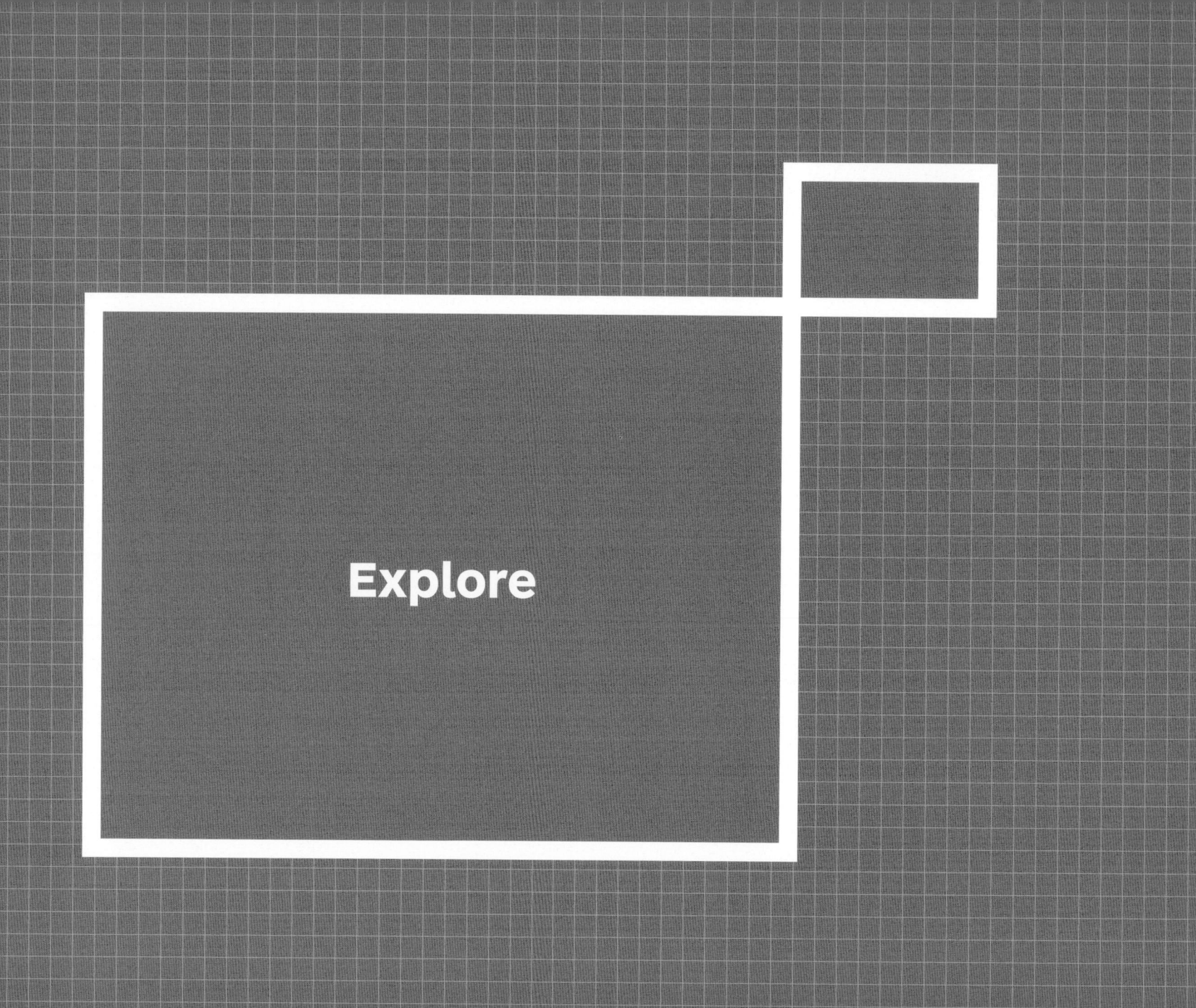

Explore

Exploration Portfolio

Your exploration portfolio serves to develop new growth engines for the future and protects you from outside disruption. It helps you either derisk new business areas you hope to develop and implement yourself or it equips you with sufficient insights to make better acquisitions.

For all your exploration projects work through two main iteration loops: the improvement of your business design to maximize expected returns and the reduction of risk and uncertainty to avoid investing in projects that won't hold up to the real world.

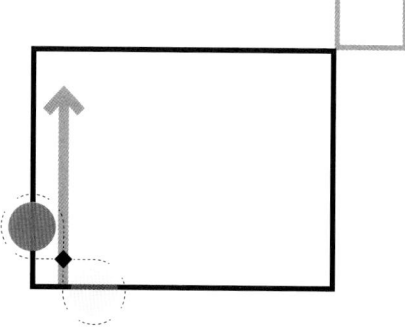

Business Design
Increase Expected Return

In the business design loop teams shape and reshape their business ideas to turn them into business models with the best possible expected return. First iterations are based on intuition and starting points (product ideas, technologies, market opportunities, etc.). Subsequent iterations are based on evidence and insights from the testing loop.

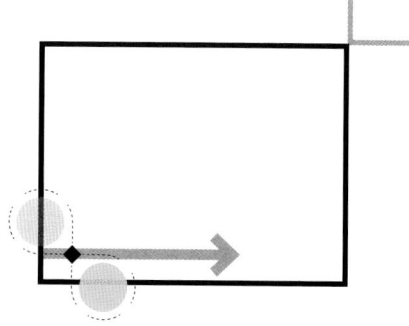

Test
Reduce Innovation Risk

In the test loop teams test and retest the hypotheses underlying their business ideas until they have sufficiently reduced the risk and uncertainty of an idea to justify larger investments. First iterations are often based on quick and cheap experiments (e.g., interviews and surveys to gauge customer interest). Subsequent, more sophisticated experiments help confirm initial insights.

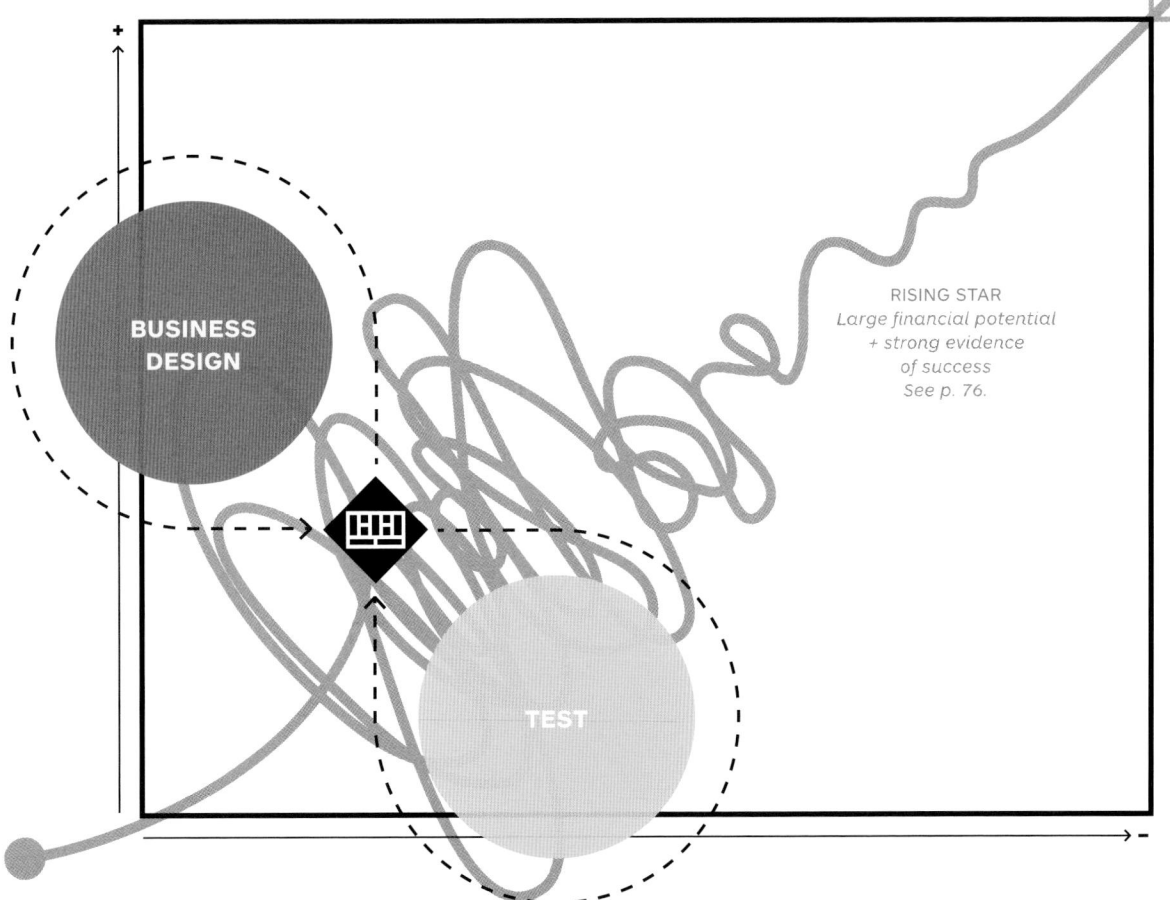

A strong business model design "on paper" does not mean an idea is necessarily going to work. To figure out if your idea is going to work, you need to test your business model design "in the real world." Business design and testing are two loops that continuously feed each other.

Exploit

BUSINESS DESIGN

TEST

RISING STAR
Large financial potential + strong evidence of success
See p. 76.

MANAGE

Business Model Design Performance

Good business model design is about competing beyond superior or innovative products, services, and lower prices. It is about creating business models that beat or even disrupt competition, based on superior profitability and protectability. At every stage of your innovation journey you should ask yourself how you can create a better business model, based on what you learn from the market.

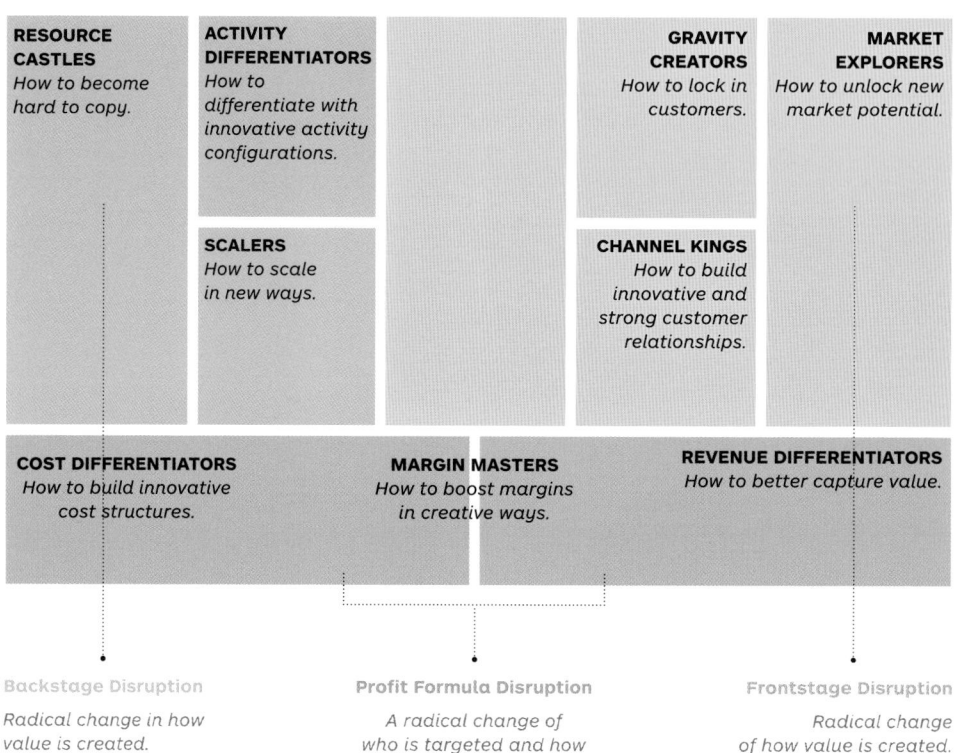

RESOURCE CASTLES
How to become hard to copy.

ACTIVITY DIFFERENTIATORS
How to differentiate with innovative activity configurations.

SCALERS
How to scale in new ways.

GRAVITY CREATORS
How to lock in customers.

MARKET EXPLORERS
How to unlock new market potential.

CHANNEL KINGS
How to build innovative and strong customer relationships.

COST DIFFERENTIATORS
How to build innovative cost structures.

MARGIN MASTERS
How to boost margins in creative ways.

REVENUE DIFFERENTIATORS
How to better capture value.

Backstage Disruption

Radical change in how value is created.

Profit Formula Disruption

A radical change of who is targeted and how value is delivered.

Frontstage Disruption

Radical change of how value is created.

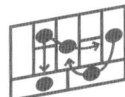

Business Model Pattern Library

To help you boost your business model performance, see the library of nine business model patterns in chapter 3. These patterns serve as a reference library or inspiration to help you compete beyond products, services, and price.

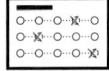

Assess Your Design

We also introduce an assessment sheet on p. 213-214 to evaluate the current design of your business model idea, existing business, or business unit. A high score indicates a strong business model. A low score indicates strong potential for improvement. You can also use this score to evaluate existing and new competitors in the market. Caveat: Good design DOES NOT EQUAL "it's going to work."

Design–Test

To explore ideas systematically, work through two iterative loops: shape ideas with business design and reduce risk with testing.

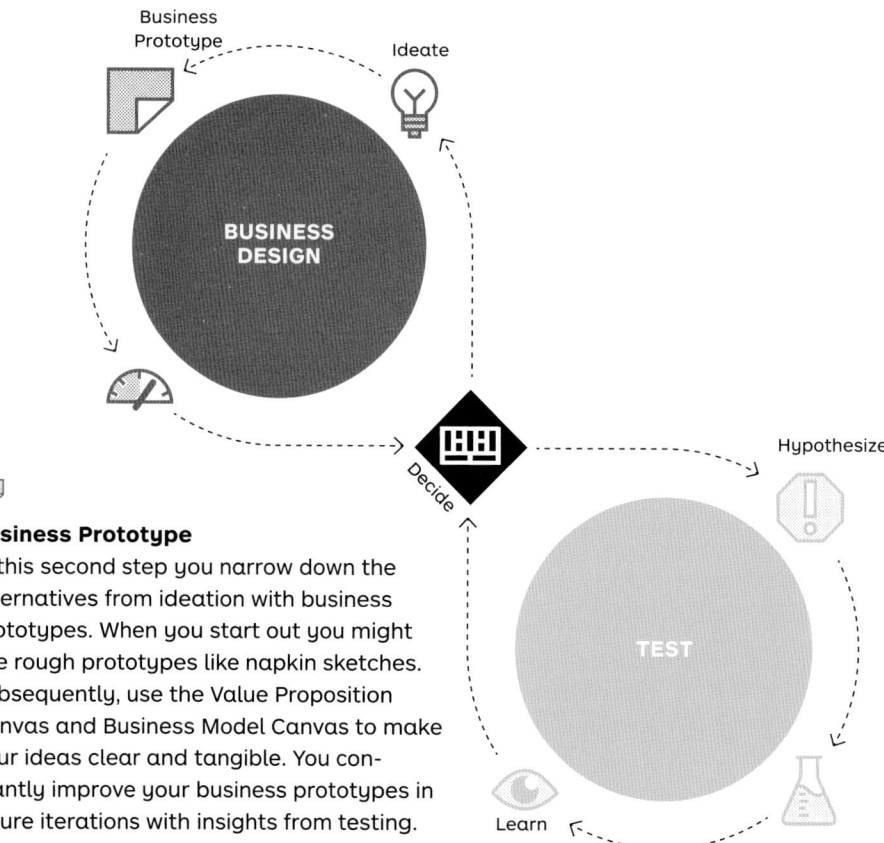

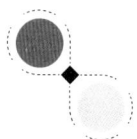

Business Design Loop

In the design loop you shape and reshape your business idea to turn it into the best possible business model. Your first iterations are based on your intuition and starting point (product idea, technology, market opportunity, etc.). Subsequent iterations are based on evidence and insights from the testing loop.

Ideate

In this first step you try to come up with as many alternative ways as possible to use your initial intuition or insights from testing to turn your idea into a stronger business. At this stage it's important to not fall in love with your first ideas.

Business Prototype

In this second step you narrow down the alternatives from ideation with business prototypes. When you start out you might use rough prototypes like napkin sketches. Subsequently, use the Value Proposition Canvas and Business Model Canvas to make your ideas clear and tangible. You constantly improve your business prototypes in future iterations with insights from testing.

Assess

In this last step of the design loop you assess the design of your business prototypes with the assessment sheet on p. 110. Once you are satisfied with the design of your business prototypes you start testing in the field or go back to testing if you are working on subsequent iterations.

STEVE BLANK

*Inventor of Customer
Development and Godfather
of the Lean Startup Movement*

*"No business plan survives
first contact with customers."*

Testing Loop

Every (radically) new business idea, product, service, value proposition, business model, or strategy requires a leap of faith. If proven false, these important and yet unproven aspects of your idea can make or break your business.

That's why it's important to break down your idea into smaller chunks that you can test. You achieve this by making the uncertainty and assumptions underlying your idea explicit in the form of hypotheses. Then you prioritize these hypotheses to test the most important ones.

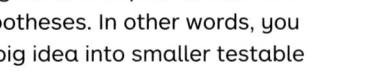

Hypothesize

The first step of testing a business idea is to understand the risks and uncertainty of an idea. Ask: "What are all the things that need to be true for this idea to work?" This question allows you to make the assumptions underlying an idea explicit in the form of testable hypotheses. In other words, you break down a big idea into smaller testable pieces.

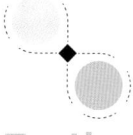

Experiment

To reduce the risk and uncertainty of your ideas it's not sufficient to make your hypotheses explicit. Don't make the mistake of executing business ideas without evidence. Test your ideas thoroughly with experiments, regardless of how great they may seem in theory. This second step will prevent you from pursuing ideas that look good in theory, but won't work in reality.

Learn

In this last step of the testing process you analyze the evidence from experiments in order to support or refute your hypotheses. Your insights will inform your decision to persevere with, pivot, or kill your idea.

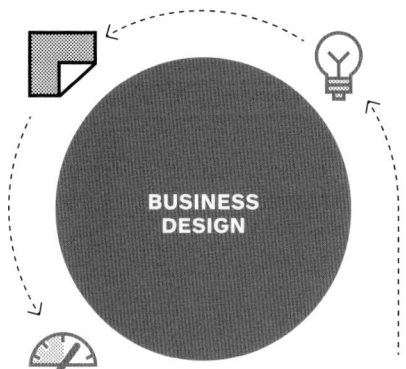

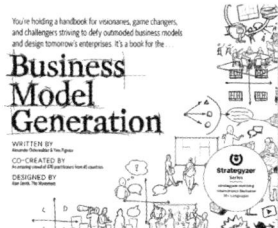

The Business Model Canvas

MANAGE

You don't have to be a master of the Business Model Canvas to use this book, but you can use it to shape ideas into a business model so you can define, test, and manage risk. In this book, we use the Business Model Canvas to define the desirability, feasibility, and viability of an idea. If you'd like to go deeper than the synopsis of the Business Model Canvas, we recommend reading *Business Model Generation* or going online to learn more.

Customer Segments

Describe the different groups of people or organizations you aim to reach and serve.

Value Propositions

Describe the bundle of products and services that create value for a specific customer segment.

Channels

Describe how a company communicates with and reaches its customer segments to deliver a value proposition.

Customer Relationships

Describe the types of relationships a company establishes with specific customer segments.

Revenue Streams

Describe the cash a company generates from each customer segment.

Key Resources

Describe the most important assets required to make a business model work.

Key Activities

Describe the most important things a company must do to make its business model work.

Key Partners

Describe the network of suppliers and partners that make the business model work.

Cost Structure

Describe all costs incurred to operate a business model.

The Business Model Canvas

Key Partners 🔗	Key Activities ✔	Value Propositions 🎁	Customer Relationships ♥	Customer Segments ⬤
	Key Resources 🏭		Channels 🚚	

Designed for: Designed by: Date: Version:

Cost Structure 🏷	Revenue Streams 💰

⊛ **Strategyzer**
strategyzer.com

To learn more about the Business Model Canvas visit
strategyzer.com/books/business-model-generation.

How to create products and
services customers want.
Get started with...

Value Proposition Design

⊛ Strategyzer
WILEY

The Value Proposition Canvas

Much like the Business Model Canvas, the same goes for the Value Proposition Canvas. You'll get value from this book without having a proficiency in using it, but we do reference it for framing your experimentation, especially with regard to understanding the customer and how your products and services create value. If you'd like to go deeper than the synopsis of the Value Proposition Canvas, we recommend reading *Value Proposition Design* or going online to learn more.

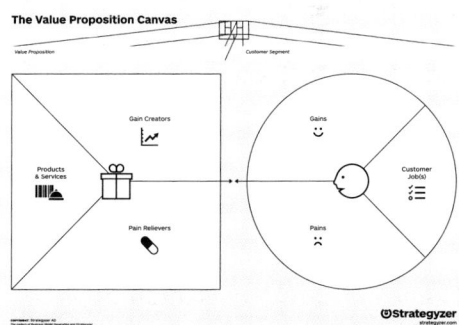

To learn more about the Value Proposition Canvas visit
strategyzer.com/books/value-proposition-design.

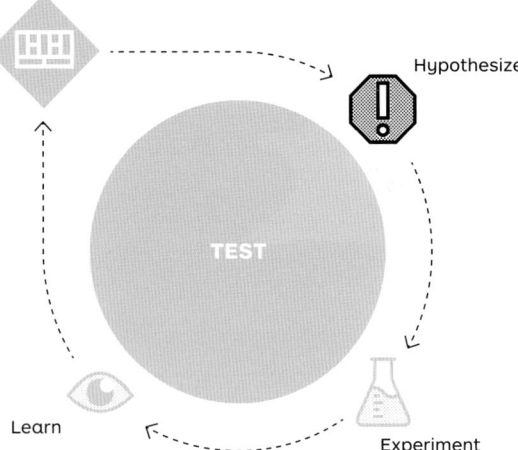

Hypothesize

TEST

Learn

Experiment

MANAGE

TESTING

Hypothesize

The first step of the testing loop is to identify and prioritize the critical hypotheses underlying your business idea. This allows you to make the most important risks of your idea explicit so that you can test them.

Definition

- *an assumption that your value proposition, business model, or strategy builds on.*
- *what you need to learn about to understand if your business idea might work.*
- *linked to the desirability, feasibility, viability, or adaptability of a business idea.*
- *formulated so that it can be tested and supported (validated) or refuted (invalidated) based on evidence and guided by experience.*

Identify the Four Types of Hypotheses

To understand the risk and uncertainty of your idea you need to ask: "What are all the things that need to be true for this idea to work?" This will allow you to identify all four types of hypotheses underlying a business idea: desirability, feasibility, viability, and adaptability.

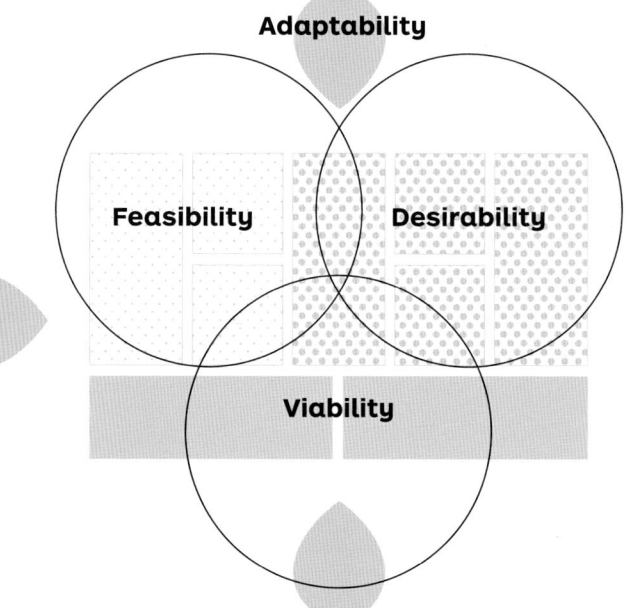

Adaptability

Feasibility   Desirability

Viability

Prioritize Your Hypotheses

Not all hypotheses are equal. It is important to identify the most important hypotheses for which you have no evidence, in order to test them first. You achieve this by using a tool called the Assumptions Map that uses the following two dimensions:

Desirability

Does the market want this idea?

Use the Value Proposition Canvas and the frontstage of the Business Model Canvas to identify desirability hypotheses.

Feasibility

Can we deliver at scale?

Use the backstage of the Business Model Canvas to identify feasibility hypotheses.

Viability

Is the idea profitable enough?

Use the revenue streams and cost structure in the Business Model Canvas to identify viability hypotheses.

Adaptability

Can the idea survive and adapt in a changing environment?

Use the environment surrounding your business model to identify adaptability hypotheses.

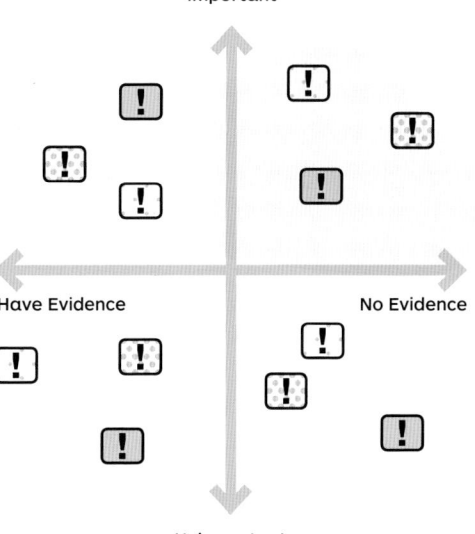

Importance

Ask how critical a hypothesis is for your business idea to succeed. In other terms, if that hypothesis is proven wrong, your business idea will fail, and all other hypotheses become irrelevant.

Existence of Evidence

Ask how much observable and recent firsthand evidence you have—or don't have—to support or refute a specific hypothesis.

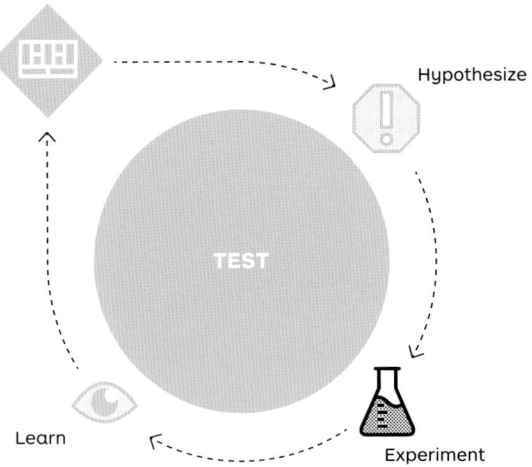

Hypothesize

TEST

Learn

Experiment

82

MANAGE

Experiment

Reducing the Risk of Your Ideas with Experiments

To avoid building something nobody wants you need to test your ideas thoroughly with business experiments. Test your most important hypotheses first and continue until you are sufficiently confident that your idea will work.

Definition

- *a procedure to reduce the risk and uncertainty of a business idea.*
- *produces weak or strong evidence that supports or refutes a hypothesis.*
- *can be fast/slow and cheap/expensive to conduct.*

There are a multitude of experiments to test your ideas. We describe 44 different business experiments at length in our book *Testing Business Ideas* (strategyzer.com/test). Experiments can range from simple interviews over discussion prototypes, all the way to simulated sales, working prototypes (so-called minimum viable products, [MVP]), and co-creation with customers. In general, we have observed that most teams don't sufficiently test their ideas and barely go beyond interviews. We'd like to invite you to more thoroughly test your ideas over three phases before you transfer them to your execution portfolio and scale them.

To learn more about Testing Business Ideas visit strategyzer.com/test.

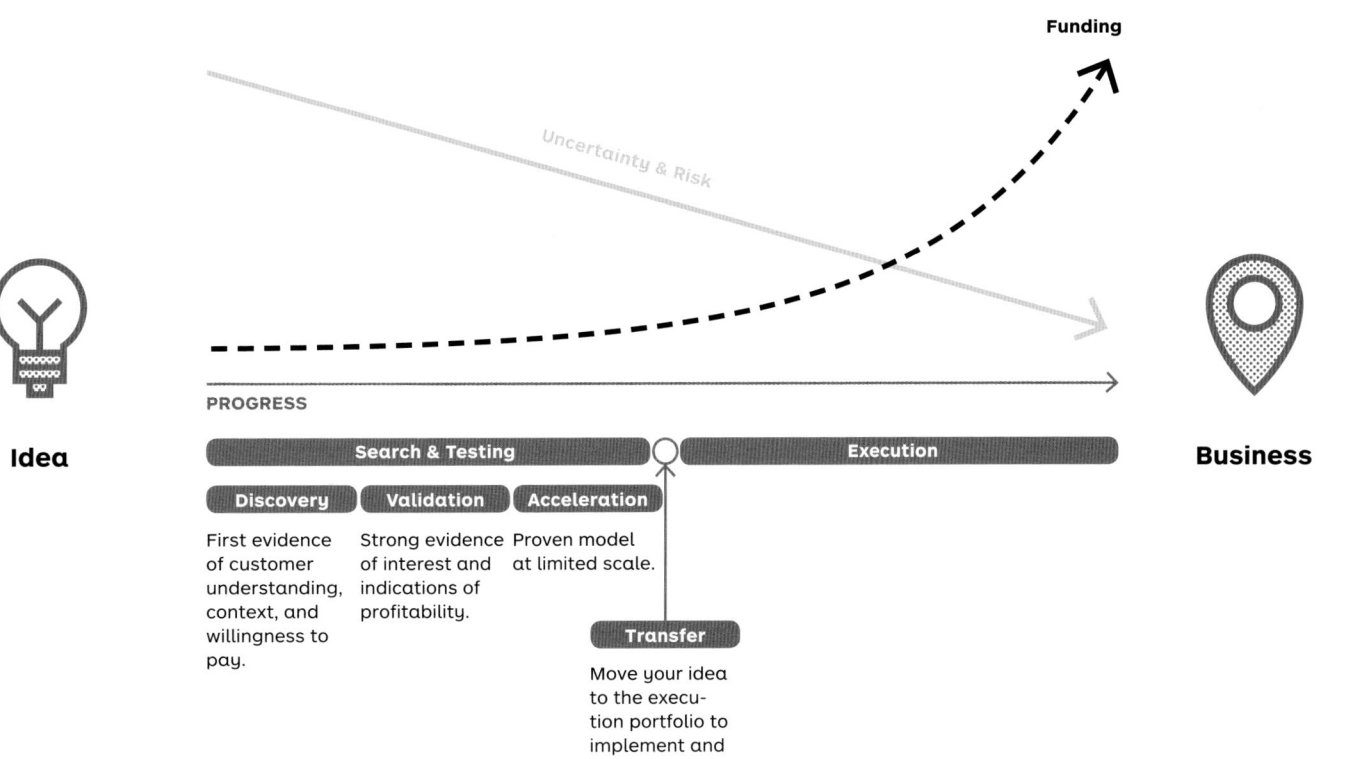

Funding

Uncertainty & Risk

PROGRESS

Idea

Business

Search & Testing

Execution

Discovery | Validation | Acceleration

First evidence of customer understanding, context, and willingness to pay.

Strong evidence of interest and indications of profitability.

Proven model at limited scale.

Transfer

Move your idea to the execution portfolio to implement and scale.

Here are four rules of thumb that we describe in Testing Business Ideas *to pick the right experiments to test your business ideas.*

1. **Go cheap and fast at the beginning.**

   Early on, you generally know little. Stick to cheap and quick experiments to detect the right direction. You can afford starting out with weaker evidence, because you will test more later. Ideally, you select an experiment that is cheap and fast, yet still produces strong evidence.

2. **Increase the strength of evidence with multiple experiments for the same hypothesis.**

   Run several experiments to support or refute a hypothesis. Try to learn about a hypothesis as fast as possible, then run more experiments to produce stronger evidence for confirmation. Don't make important decisions based on one experiment or weak evidence.

3. **Always pick the experiment that produces the strongest evidence, given your constraints.**

   Always select and design the strongest experiment you can, while respecting the context. When uncertainty is high you should go fast and cheap, but that doesn't necessarily mean you can't produce strong evidence.

4. **Reduce uncertainty as much as you can before you build anything.**

   People often think they need to build something to start testing an idea. Quite the contrary. The higher the cost to build something, the more you need to run multiple experiments to show that customers actually have the jobs, pains, and gains you think they have.

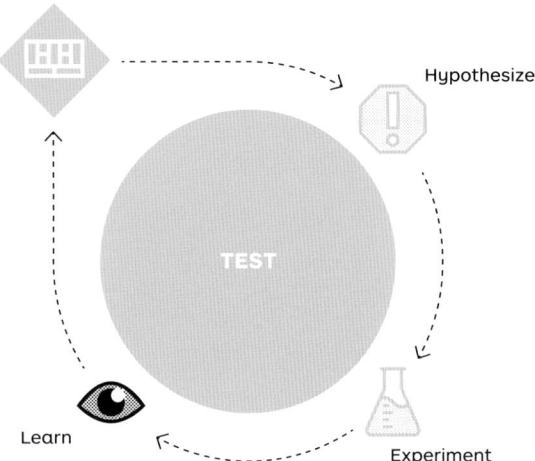

Hypothesize

TEST

Learn

Experiment

84

MANAGE

Learn

The last step of the Testing Loop is about learning if your evidence from testing supports or refutes your business hypotheses. It's the analysis of evidence to detect patterns and gain insights. The more experiments you run, the more evidence you have, the stronger it is, the more confident you can be about your insights.

Evidence

Evidence is what you use to support or refute the hypotheses underlying your business idea. It is data that you get from research or generate from business experiments. Evidence can come in many different forms, ranging from weak to strong.

Definition

- *data generated from an experiment or collected in the field.*
- *fact(s) that support or refute a hypothesis.*
- *can be of different nature (e.g., quotes, behaviors, conversion rates, orders, purchases, etc.) and can be weak/strong.*

Evidence Strength

The strength of a piece of evidence determines how reliably the evidence helps support or refute a hypothesis. You can evaluate the strength of evidence by checking four areas.

Weak	Strong(er)
Opinions (beliefs)	Facts (events)
What people say	What people do
Lab settings	Real-world settings
Small investments	Large investments

Confidence Level

Your confidence level indicates how much you believe that your evidence is strong enough to support or refute a specific hypothesis.

Not Confident at All   *Very Confident*

Support   Unclear   Refute

Insights

Insights are what you learn from studying the evidence. You need to search for patterns that either support or refute the hypotheses you have been testing.

Definition
- *what you learn from studying the evidence.*
- *learning related to the validity of hypotheses and potential discovery of new directions.*
- *foundation to make informed business decisions and take action.*

Very Confident
You can be very confident if you've run several experiments of which at least one is a call-to-action test that produced very strong evidence.

Somewhat Confident
You can be somewhat confident if you've run several experiments that produce strong evidence or a particularly strong call-to-action experiment.

Not Really Confident
You need to run more and stronger experiments if you've only done interviews or surveys in which people say what they will do. They might behave differently in reality.

Not Confident at All
You need to experiment more if you've only run one experiment that produces weak evidence, such as an interview or survey.

AVOID BIG FAILURES, OR YOU'RE DEAD

EMBRACE SMALL FAILURES, OR YOU'RE DEAD

Innovation Metrics

In innovation, the main task is not to measure if you are on time and on budget, which are key metrics in an execution project. In innovation and exploration it is crucial to measure whether you are reducing the risk and uncertainty of new business ideas before you invest big and scale.

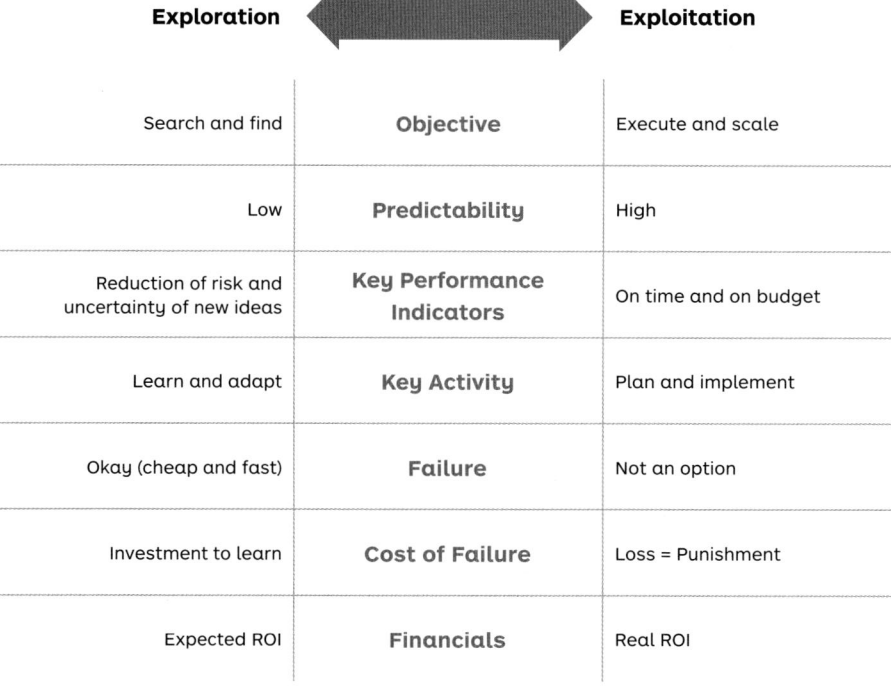

Exploration	Objective	Exploitation
Search and find	**Objective**	Execute and scale
Low	**Predictability**	High
Reduction of risk and uncertainty of new ideas	**Key Performance Indicators**	On time and on budget
Learn and adapt	**Key Activity**	Plan and implement
Okay (cheap and fast)	**Failure**	Not an option
Investment to learn	**Cost of Failure**	Loss = Punishment
Expected ROI	**Financials**	Real ROI

For every exploration project you need to track four main key performance indicators (KPIs):

- *Risk and Uncertainty*
  How much have you de-risked an idea so far? How much risk remains?
- *Expected Profitability*
  How big might the idea be in financial terms?
- *Learning Velocity and Time Spent*
  How much time have you spent so far? How much have you learned during this time?
- *Cost*
  How much have you spent to test this idea?

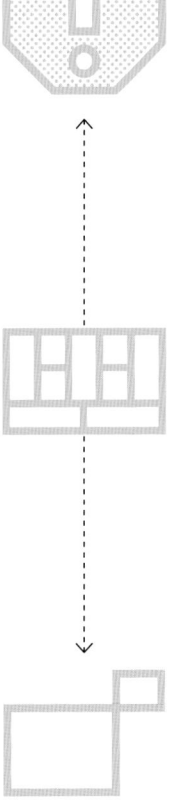

Risk and uncertainty are measured at three different levels:

1. Hypothesis Level

By breaking down an idea into smaller chunks you can understand and test risk at a more granular level. We call this the hypotheses underlying your idea. In other words, the most important things that need to be true for your idea to work. If you don't have recent evidence to support or refute a hypothesis, you need to test to reduce risk and uncertainty.

2. Business Model Level

At the business model level you look at all the important hypotheses underlying your idea. The more unproven hypotheses you have, the riskier your idea. To de-risk an idea you need to test the most important hypotheses until you are confident that the idea could work.

3. Portfolio Level

At the portfolio level you look at all the ideas you currently have and how much you've de-risked them so far. You also look at the financial potential of each one.

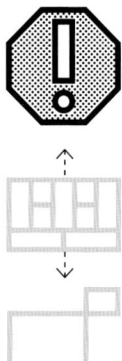

INNOVATION METRICS

Hypothesis Level

At the hypothesis level you capture everything related to a specific hypothesis in terms of experiments conducted and insights gained.

	Hypothesis	Experiment Log
Data	Hypothesis statement	• Experiment description • Success metric • Success criteria
Types	• Desirability • Feasibility • Viaibility	• Lab vs. real world • Say vs. do
Metrics	Status	• Cost • Time running
Example	*HYPOTHESIS I:* *WE BELIEVE* *PEOPLE WILL BUY* *SHOES ONLINE* *(DESIRABILITY I)*	*EXPERIMENT I : LANDING PAGE* *MEASURE : % OF CLICKS ON "BUY SH* *BUTTON* *SUCCESS : % OF CLICKS ON "BUY SHO* *BUTTON > I0% OF VISITOR* *COST: $200*

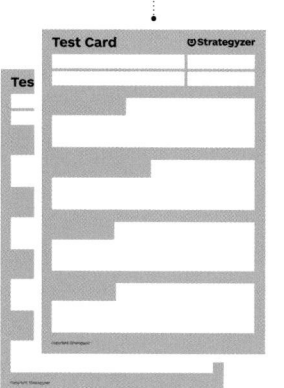

Experiment Log

Here you log all the experiments you have conducted to either support or refute a specific hypothesis. For each experiment you capture the experiment type, what you measured, the success criteria, how much time each experiment took, and what it cost.

Learning Log

Action

- Evidence

Insight

Confidence Level

- Pivot
- Shelve
- Persevere
- Test Again

Support   Unclear   Refute

- Low/medium/high strength

(0) (0.1) (0.2) (0.3) (0.4) (0.5) (0.6) (0.7) (0.8) (0.9) (1.0)

Not Confident at All   *Very Confident*

- Number of data points

EVIDENCE STRENGTH:
HIGH
NUMBER OF DATA POINTS:
10,000+
RESULTING EV. QUALITY:
STRONG

√ SUPPORT HYPOTHESIS I

.75 CONFIDENT

PERSEVERE

MANAGE

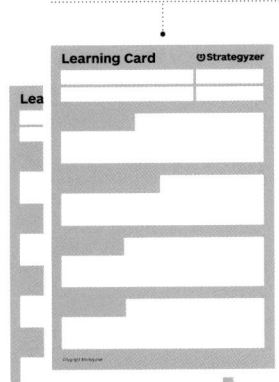

Learning Log

Here you log what you have learned from the evidence to support or refute a specific hypothesis. You specifically capture all the evidence gathered, the number of data points, the strength of the evidence, and how confident you are that your insights are true.

Insight

Indicates if we support (√) or refute (×) a hypothesis, or if it's still unclear (?).

Confidence Level

Indicates how confident you are that the evidence is strong enough to support the insight (0 = no confidence to 1 = absolute confidence).

Action

Indicates if you kill the project, persevere and test the next hypothesis, or pivot the idea.

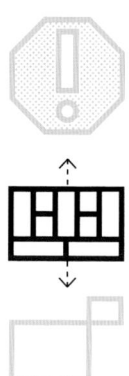

INNOVATION METRICS

Business Model Level

At the business model level, aggregate all hypotheses related to a particular project. Estimate how much risk each individual hypothesis represents of the overall risk and uncertainty of an idea. This allows you to track how much you have de-risked an idea over the course of a project.

At the aggregate project level you can now see:

- **Innovation risk level**: indicates how much you reduced the risk of the idea and how risky it still is.
- **Expected profitability**: highlights the financial opportunity of the idea.
- **Project duration**: shows how much time you've spent on testing this idea.
- **Overall cost**: outlines how much you spent to test this idea. This may or may not include the salaries of the team members.

Risk Reduction
Multiplies the percentage of risk that the hypothesis represents with the confidence level to ascertain how much you actually reduced risk for this specific hypothesis.

Once you've captured all the data, you can easily plot the change of the risk level over time and how much you have been spending to test the idea.

Pivots
Each pivot means you decided to change your previous idea. This usually leads to an increase in risk for your idea, because some of the hypotheses you already tested and de-risked are no longer relevant for your new direction. A new direction also leads to new hypotheses that you need to test again to reduce risk and uncertainty.

Cost Increase
In general, the duration and cost of your experiments will rise with the reduction of risk, because it becomes less risky to conduct expensive experiments. Later on in the life of a project, you need to produce stronger evidence and even build parts of your idea to continue to reduce risk and uncertainty. This usually increases the cost of experimentation.

Project Metrics

	Name	Start Date	Project Duration
	PROJECT A	9/12/2020	8 weeks

Hypotheses Log		Experiment Log		Learning Log			Actions
Name	**Risk** %	**Name**	**Cost** $	**Insight** ✓ ? ✗	**Confidence** #0–1	**Risk Reduction** = Risk x Confidence	Re-test, Shelve, Perservere, Pivot
Desirability							
HYPOTHESIS 1	10%	EXP. 1	$0.2K	✓	0.75	10% x 0.75 = 7.5%	Persevere
HYPOTHESIS 2	7.5%	EXP. 2	$0.5K	✗	1	0%	Pivot
HYPOTHESIS 3	7.5%	EXP. 3, EXP. 4	$1.2K	✓	1	7.5% x 1 = 7.5%	Persevere
Feasibility							
HYPOTHESIS 7	15%	EXP. 9, EXP. 10	$0.2K	✓	0.5	15% x 0.5 = 7.5%	Persevere
HYPOTHESIS 8	10%	EXP. 11	$1K	?		0%	Re-test
Viability							
HYPOTHESIS 4	15%	EXP. 5	$1.3K	✗	1	0%	Pivot
HYPOTHESIS 5	10%	EXP. 6, EXP. 7	$0.5K	✓	0.5	10% x 0.5 = 5%	Persevere
Adaptability							
HYPOTHESIS 6	15%	EXP. 8	$0.2K	?		0%	Re-test
HYPOTHESIS 9	10%	EXP. 12	$0.7K	✓	0.25	10% x 0.25 = 2.5%	Persevere

Expected Return

Revenue Potential
$1 billion

Cost Structure
$250 million

Overall Cost $

$5,800

Innovation Risk Level %

 70%

Expected Return $

 $750 million

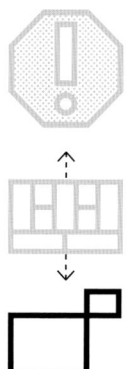

INNOVATION METRICS

Portfolio Level

You can visualize the state of your Explore portfolio once you get your teams to track the KPIs of their individual explore project. This gives you a powerful overview of the financial potential of your ideas in exploration and their current risk level. Equipped with this data and overview you can make better investment decisions and decide which projects to fund and support and which projects to retire.

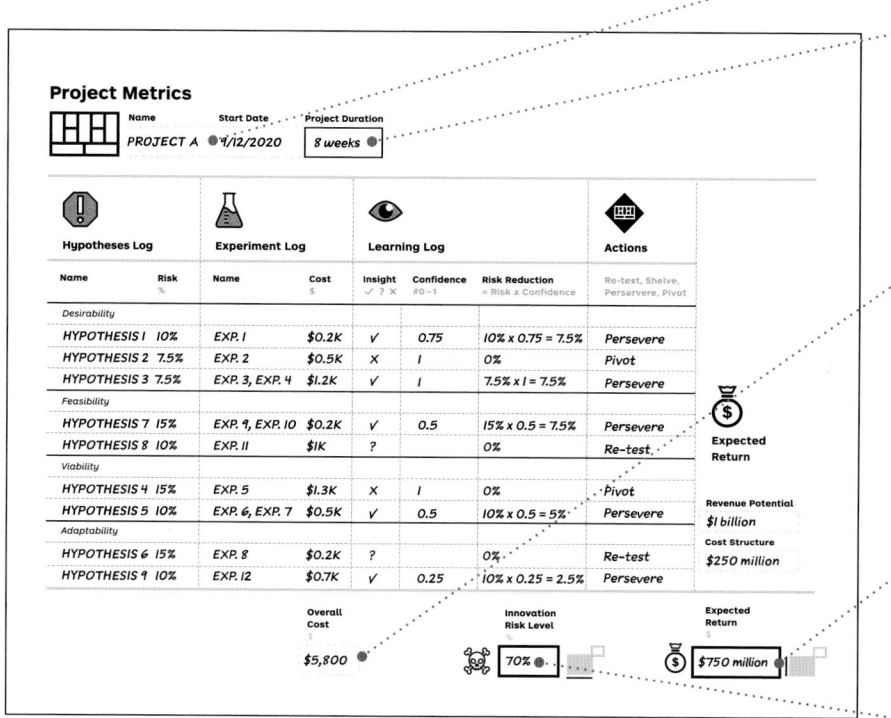

Project Metrics

Name	Start Date	Project Duration
PROJECT A	4/12/2020	8 weeks

Hypotheses Log		**Experiment Log**		**Learning Log**			**Actions**
Name	Risk %	Name	Cost $	Insight ✓ ? ✗	Confidence #0–1	Risk Reduction = Risk x Confidence	Re-test, Shelve, Perservere, Pivot
Desirability							
HYPOTHESIS 1	10%	EXP. 1	$0.2K	✓	0.75	10% x 0.75 = 7.5%	Persevere
HYPOTHESIS 2	7.5%	EXP. 2	$0.5K	✗	1	0%	Pivot
HYPOTHESIS 3	7.5%	EXP. 3, EXP. 4	$1.2K	✓	1	7.5% x 1 = 7.5%	Persevere
Feasibility							
HYPOTHESIS 7	15%	EXP. 9, EXP. 10	$0.2K	✓	0.5	15% x 0.5 = 7.5%	Persevere
HYPOTHESIS 8	10%	EXP. 11	$1K	?		0%	Re-test
Viability							
HYPOTHESIS 4	15%	EXP. 5	$1.3K	✗	1	0%	Pivot
HYPOTHESIS 5	10%	EXP. 6, EXP. 7	$0.5K	✓	0.5	10% x 0.5 = 5%	Persevere
Adaptability							
HYPOTHESIS 6	15%	EXP. 8	$0.2K	?		0%	Re-test
HYPOTHESIS 9	10%	EXP. 12	$0.7K	✓	0.25	10% x 0.25 = 2.5%	Persevere

Expected Return

Revenue Potential
$1 billion

Cost Structure
$250 million

Overall Cost	Innovation Risk Level	Expected Return $
$5,800	70%	$750 million

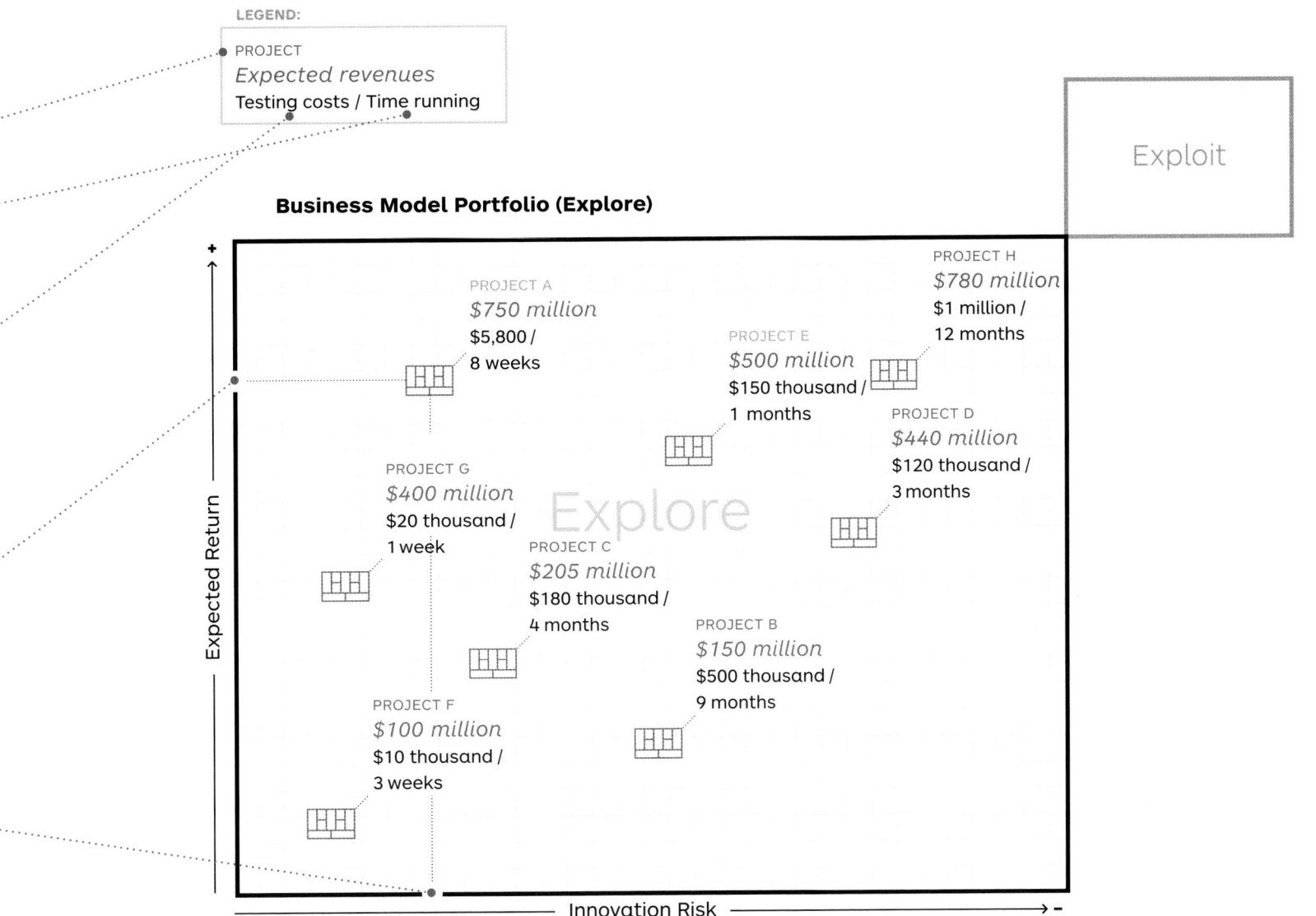

LEGEND:

PROJECT
Expected revenues
Testing costs / Time running

Exploit

Business Model Portfolio (Explore)

Expected Return

Innovation Risk

Explore

PROJECT A
$750 million
$5,800 /
8 weeks

PROJECT H
$780 million
$1 million /
12 months

PROJECT E
$500 million
$150 thousand /
1 months

PROJECT D
$440 million
$120 thousand /
3 months

PROJECT G
$400 million
$20 thousand /
1 week

PROJECT C
$205 million
$180 thousand /
4 months

PROJECT B
$150 million
$500 thousand /
9 months

PROJECT F
$100 million
$10 thousand /
3 weeks

Decisions and Actions

We developed the innovation project scorecard to systematically assess the progress that innovation and exploration teams are making in their quest to find business ideas that work. The assessment helps make better investment decisions.

The scorecard has three dimensions based on the innovation metrics and portfolio guidelines outlined previously:

Strategic Fit

The first dimension is about fit. Projects need to demonstrate they fit the vision, culture, and image of the company. They also need to fit the company's portfolio guidance and demonstrate leadership support.

Risk Reduction

The second dimension is the most important one. It is about assessing if a team is making progress in reducing the risk and uncertainty of the business idea. Teams need to produce strong evidence, beyond spreadsheets and PowerPoint slides, that their idea is likely to work in the real world.

Size of Opportunity

The third dimension is about financial fit. Teams need to show a clear understanding of the financial opportunity and provide evidence from experiments that their financial estimations are not just fantasies.

The innovation project scorecard is used by:

Leaders

- *To evaluate a pitch asking for investment.*
- *To ask better questions and guide teams.*

Teams

- *To evaluate their own progress during sprints and stand-ups.*

Leaders and teams

- *To benchmark the current status of an innovation project.*
- *To decide next steps for testing.*

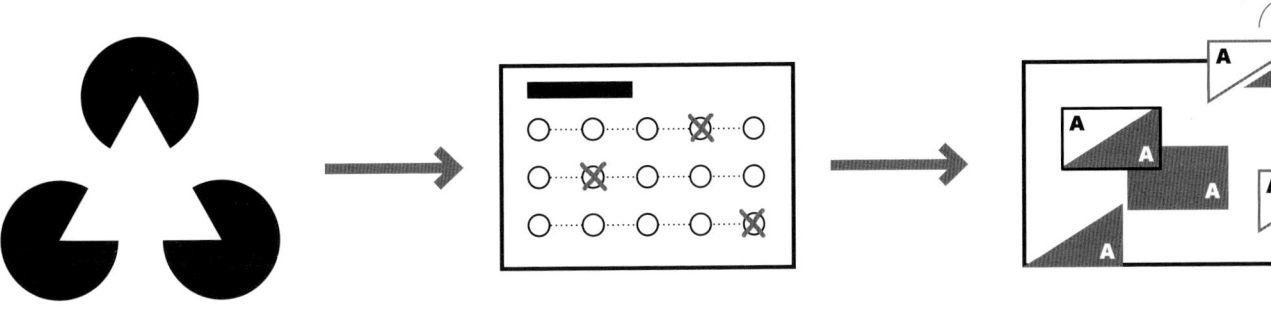

Strategic Fit
p. 50

Project Scorecard
p. 98

Explore Actions
p. 23 and 100

Project Scorecard

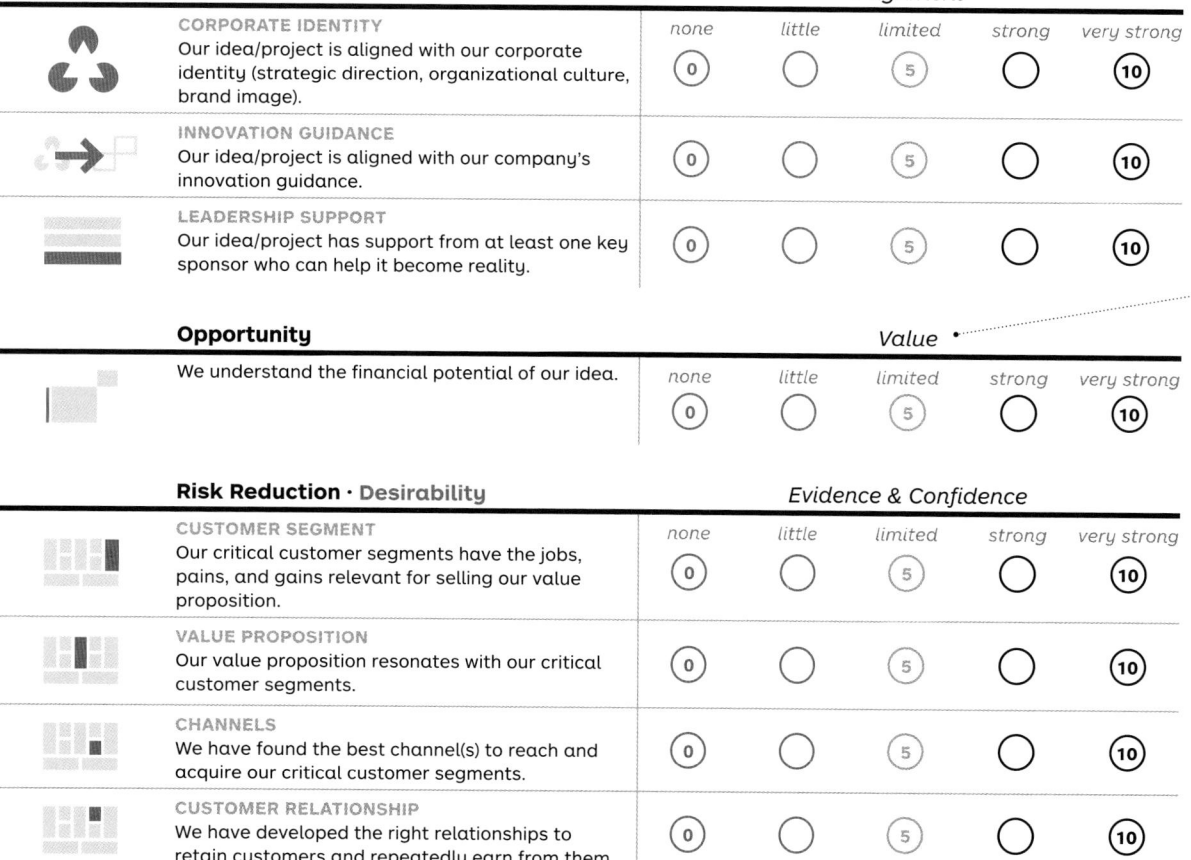

Strategic Fit   *Alignment*

		none	little	limited	strong	very strong
	CORPORATE IDENTITY Our idea/project is aligned with our corporate identity (strategic direction, organizational culture, brand image).	0		5		10
	INNOVATION GUIDANCE Our idea/project is aligned with our company's innovation guidance.	0		5		10
	LEADERSHIP SUPPORT Our idea/project has support from at least one key sponsor who can help it become reality.	0		5		10

Opportunity   *Value* •

		none	little	limited	strong	very strong
	We understand the financial potential of our idea.	0		5		10

Risk Reduction · Desirability   *Evidence & Confidence*

		none	little	limited	strong	very strong
	CUSTOMER SEGMENT Our critical customer segments have the jobs, pains, and gains relevant for selling our value proposition.	0		5		10
	VALUE PROPOSITION Our value proposition resonates with our critical customer segments.	0		5		10
	CHANNELS We have found the best channel(s) to reach and acquire our critical customer segments.	0		5		10
	CUSTOMER RELATIONSHIP We have developed the right relationships to retain customers and repeatedly earn from them.	0		5		10

Some companies sort opportunity by the geographical reach of the value created:

- *little opportunity would be an opportunity that impact a local team only*
- *very strong opportunity would be an opportunity with global impact*

Other companies sort opportunity by $ value:

- *little opportunity would be < $100 thousands*
- *very strong opportunity would be > $100 millions*

Risk Reduction · Feasibility

Evidence & Confidence

	KEY RESOURCES	none	little	limited	strong	very strong
	We have the right technologies and resources to create our value proposition.	0	○	5	○	10
	KEY ACTIVITIES We have the right capabilities to handle the most critical activities for creating our value proposition.	0	○	5	○	10
	KEY PARTNERS We have found the right key partners who are willing to work with us to create and deliver our value proposition.	0	○	5	○	10

Risk Reduction · Viability

Evidence & Confidence

	REVENUES	none	little	limited	strong	very strong
	We know how much our customers are willing to pay us and how they will pay.	0	○	5	○	10
	COSTS We know our costs for creating and delivering the value proposition.	0	○	5	○	10

Risk Reduction · Adaptability

Evidence & Confidence

	INDUSTRY FORCES	none	little	limited	strong	very strong
	Our idea/project is well positioned to succeed against established competitors and new emerging players.	0	○	5	○	10
	MARKET FORCES Our idea/project takes known and emerging market shifts into account.	0	○	5	○	10
	KEY TRENDS Our idea/project is well positioned to benefit from key technology, regulatory, cultural, and societal trends.	0	○	5	○	10
	MACROECONOMIC FORCES Our idea/project is adapted to known and emerging macroeconomic and infrastructure trends.	0	○	5	○	10

*e.g. **limited** would be evidence from only one experiment, **strong** would be evidence from one experiment with very strong confidence, **very strong** would be evidence from several experiments.*

From Risk Assessment to Action

We introduced Explore portfolio actions on p. 96. Here we further develop the topic to highlight decision-making in the context of exploration. In fact, there are two entities that make decisions in the context of exploration:

Teams: Teams need to constantly evaluate and reevaluate their business model and value propositions based on evidence from the testing process. Every week the team should decide about staying the course (persevere), substantially changing aspects of the idea (pivot), or killing the idea altogether.

Committee: A decision or investment committee should meet every couple of months to decide which teams and ideas to invest in and which ideas to kill. The Innovation Project Scorecard and evidence from testing should be the main drivers for decision-making. The committee should trust the process and not interfere with teams between committee meetings.

MANAGE

Action	Innovation Team/Entrepreneur	Committee
Ideate	Teams don't just ideate at the beginning of a project. During the whole journey there should be mini-ideations to create a more powerful business model and better value proposition. Ideally, ideation is based on evidence from testing.	The committee's role during the initial ideation phase is to set the exploration guidelines. It should help teams understand how to evaluate strategic fit in terms of size and direction. The committee should support the exploration of several ideas in parallel.
Invest	Based on evidence from testing, a team might suggest investing in a startup* or acquiring a technology rather than building in-house.	The committee should always ask if it's more appropriate to invest externally or explore internally. Also, internal testing leads to better investments.
Persevere	At every stage of the journey the team should evaluate evidence to justify staying the course. The stronger the evidence, the more confidently a team can persevere.	The committee should only make persevere, pivot, kill, or spinout recommendations on predefined dates. The committee's role is to support teams to make evidence-based decisions on their own, between committee meeting dates.

All recommendations by the committee should be evidence-based, rather than opinion-based, and grounded in strategic fit. Recommendations should be made in the context of all teams exploring. Teams exploring strategic ideas, but incapable of producing sufficient evidence, should only rarely be encouraged to persevere. |
Pivot	The team should consider slightly or radically changing course when the evidence doesn't support your initial direction. Make sure your evidence is strong enough before you pivot.	
Retire	Sometimes pivoting doesn't make sense and the best option is to kill an idea. Remember you are saving money, time, and energy by killing an idea that won't work.	
Spinout	Teams may suggest a spinout if it believes a project could be successful, but not fit the company's portfolio guidance.	
Transfer	A team should recommend to scale and execute an idea when it is sufficiently confident that the idea will work based on strong evidence from many experiments.	The committee should move an idea from exploration to execution, if one of the teams shows strong evidence that the idea will succeed.

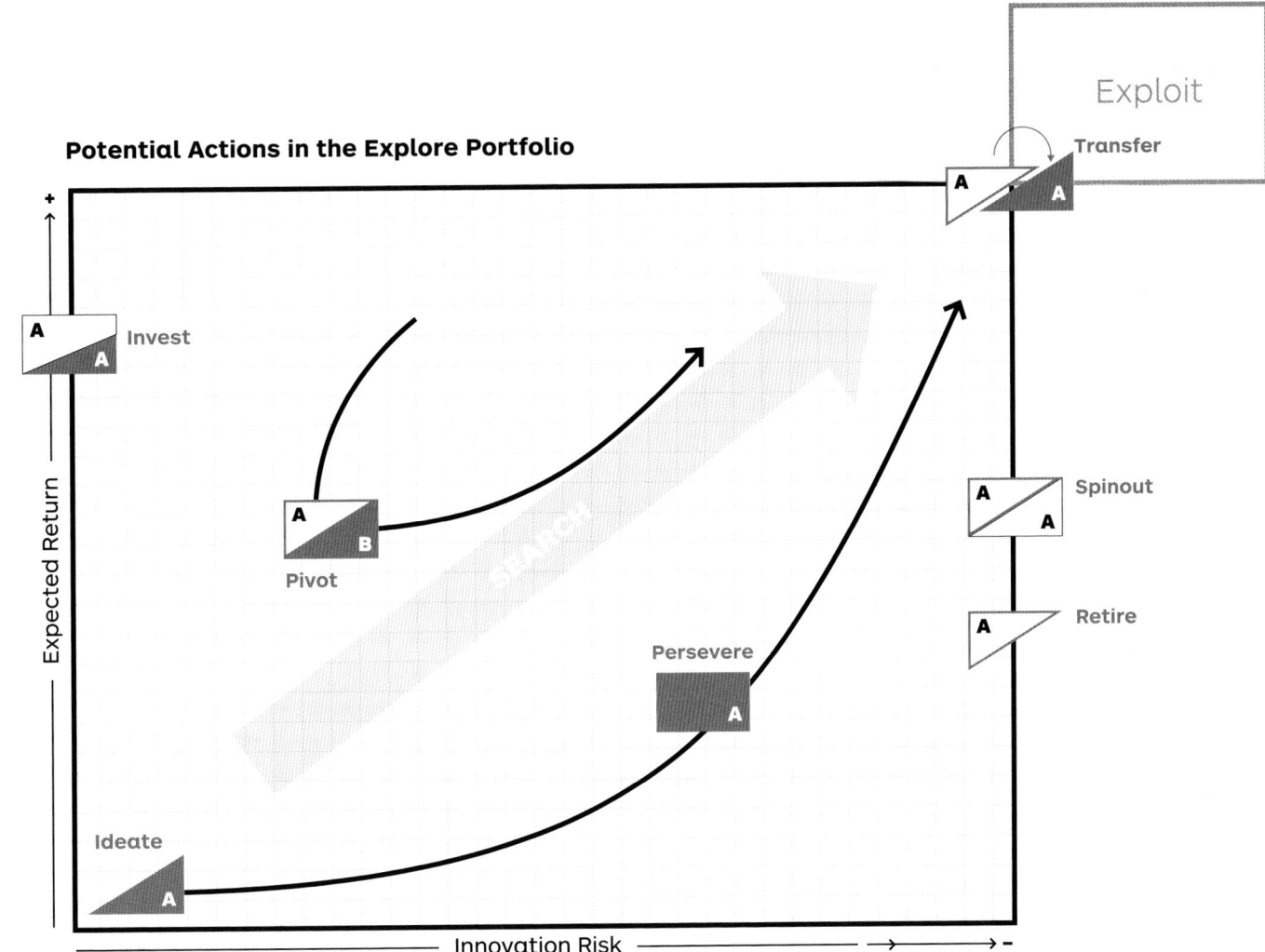

Potential Actions in the Explore Portfolio

Exploit

Transfer

Invest

Expected Return

Pivot

Spinout

Retire

Persevere

Ideate

Innovation Risk

Invest Like a Venture Capitalist

For exploration, adopt a more venture capital-style investment approach, as opposed to the relatively rigid annual budgeting cycles practiced in Exploit projects.

The Enemy of Innovation: The Business Plan

Companies that still require business plans from project teams maximize the risk of failure. The business plan is a document that describes an idea and its execution in detail. This maximizes the risk of executing an unproven idea that looks good on paper and in spreadsheets. Innovation is about admitting risk and uncertainty. It is about iterating and adapting ideas based on evidence from experiments until they are likely to work. This minimizes the risk of executing a flawed idea.

This requires the following four principles:

1. Invest in a portfolio of projects rather than individual projects to spread your bets and manage risk (see "You Can't Pick the Winner," p. 54).

2. Start with small bets (i.e., investments/funding), while risk and uncertainty of project success are high.

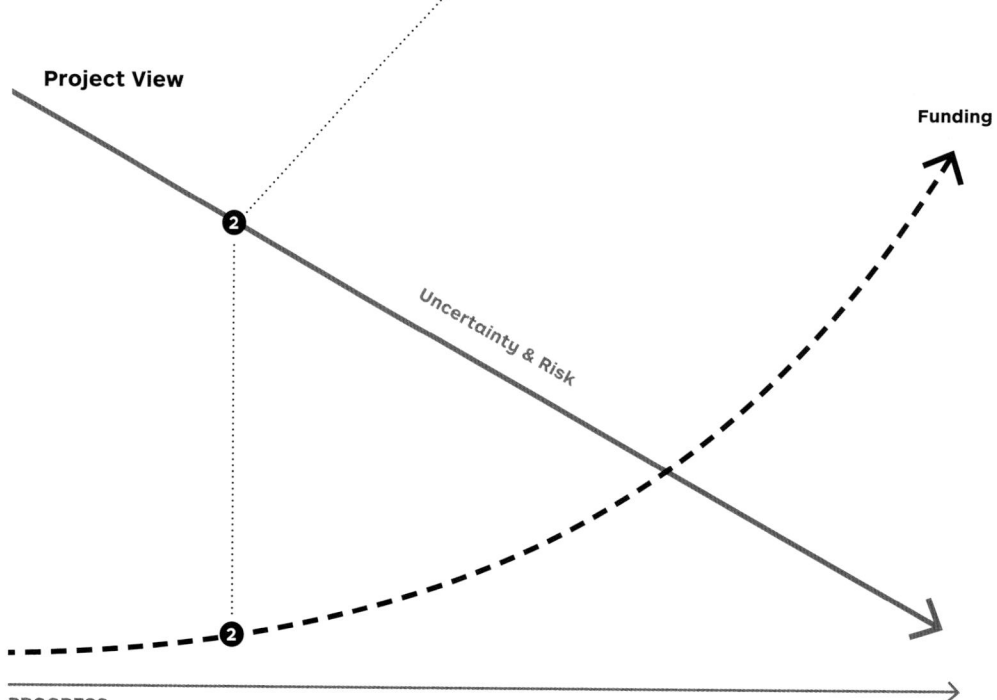

Project View

Funding

Uncertainty & Risk

PROGRESS

102

MANAGE

3. Increase your bets incrementally and provide follow-up
   funding when evidence and
   traction from experiments
   suggest risk reduction and
   real-world project potential.

4. Manage return on portfolio,
   not return on individual projects.

Return

Death & Disruption Risk ⟶ -

Portfolio View

Expected Return

Innovation Risk ⟶ -

Portfolio Return

Because of the high uncertainty of innovation
projects, you need to settle with the fact that
you can't pick the winners. Instead of focusing on the return of individual projects, you
need to focus on the return of your portfolio.

You diversify portfolio risks by spreading
your bets and by investing in different types
of innovation. Spreading your bets allows
the best teams and ideas to emerge, based
on evidence and performance. Investing
across all three types of innovation, namely,
efficiency, sustaining, and transformative
innovation, spreads bets across different
levels of risk and return.

Growth and Innovation Investment Committee

An important aspect of funding like a venture capitalist is the constitution of an investment committee dedicated to growth and innovation. It's crucial to create a dedicated committee, because the investment logic and investment style substantially differ from investments in execution projects.

The committee is composed of a small number of leaders who have decision-making authority when it comes to budget. Ideally, it includes members who are fully dedicated to exploration, as well as members who are more preoccupied with exploitation. Investment decisions usually take place every 3 to 6 months, depending on the type of organization. Investments are mainly in internal teams, but may also include start-ups.

Project guidance and investment guidelines

Communicate portfolio guidance. Clarify which types of projects are in and which ones are out. Highlight financial expectations. Outline how teams can get initial discovery funding and what type of evidence is required to qualify for follow-up validation and acceleration investments.

Portfolio management

Maintain a balanced portfolio with the right number of projects in discovery, validation, and acceleration. Make sure your pipeline is full of projects to improve existing businesses before they are at severe risk of disruption or decline. Make sure you invest in a sufficiently large number of exploration projects of which some will be the foundation of the future of your organization.

Evidence-based Investments

Invest in projects that deliver evidence from testing, rather than ideas that look irresistible in PowerPoint presentations and spreadsheets. Make sure you give teams a chance to explore ideas, because you can't know which ones will excel. Let the best teams and ideas emerge through the process, rather than trying to pick them upfront.

Project team support and protection

Help project teams get to the next level by asking them how they might improve their business models. Help them qualify for follow-up funding by suggesting how they might further test their ideas to generate the required evidence. Protect projects from company forces that make exploration and testing difficult.

Encourage innovation behavior, not just outcomes

Make sure all teams that test their ideas feel valued, not just those that get follow-up investment. Encourage innovators and teams that show strong testing skills to come back with new ideas and projects after every failure.

MANAGE

Metered Funding

To fund Explore projects you should apply the metered funding practiced by venture capitalists, as opposed to the annual entitlement budgeting practiced in Exploit projects. Incrementally increase your investments in projects that produce evidence from testing and shelve those that don't. In the discovery phase you invest small amounts of money in a large number of tiny teams to explore ideas. In validation you increase your investment in those 30% to 50% of the teams that produced evidence during discovery. In acceleration you continue to trim your portfolio and again invest in only 30% to 50% of the teams.

Combining portfolio management and metered funding increases your chances to find outliers that will create exceptionally large returns and substantially reduces the risk you'd incur by making 1 to 2 large bets in bold ideas.

10x Rule of Thumb
Success is unpredictable and depends on organization and context. However, from experience, we recommend the 10x rule of thumb: invest 1 million into your portfolio to create 10 million in new revenue or costs savings. For example, invest $20,000 in 10 small teams. Make a $50,000 follow-up investment in the 5 teams that produce the best evidence. Finally, invest around $500 thousand, in the team with the best evidence. For a billion dollar success, invest $100 million into a much larger portfolio of projects.

	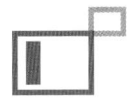 Discover	 Validate	 Accelerate
Funding	Less than $50,000	$50,000–$500,000	$500,000+
Team Size	1–3	2–5	5+
Time per Team Member	20–40%	40–80%	100%
Number of Projects	High	Medium	Low
Objectives	Customer understanding, context, and willingness to pay	Proven interest and indications of profitability	Proven model at limited scale
KPIs	• Market size • Customer evidence • Problem/solution fit • Opportunity size	• Value proposition evidence • Financial evidence • Feasibility evidence	• Product/market fit • Acquisition and retention evidence • Business model fit
Experiment Themes	50–80% 0–10% 10–30% 0–10%	30–50% 10–40% 20–50% 0–10%	10–30% 40–50% 20–50%

Legend:

- DESIRABILITY
- FEASIBILITY
- VIABILITY
- ADAPTABILITY

Sony Startup Acceleration Program

In 2014, Sony establishes the Sony Startup Accelerator Program (SSAP) to ideate, commercialize, and scale business ideas that live outside of Sony's traditional business units. It reports directly to the CEO.

KAZUO HIRAI
President and CEO of Sony Corporation 2012–2018

Sony, founded in 1943 by Masaru Ibuka and Akio Morita, is a Japanese multinational conglomerate with business divisions in electronics, gaming, motion pictures, music, and financial services.

In 2012 Kazuo Hirai took over as CEO and under his guidance, Sony experienced a resurgence in the 2010s. Under Hirai's One Sony policy, poorer performing divisions like mobile were downsized while the company advocated a deeper focus on products. This allowed Sony to streamline and focus on its core competencies.

As a part of this strategy, Sony created the Startup Accelerator Program (SSAP), which reports directly to the CEO. Hirai took ownership of SSAP as he envisioned a sustained innovation engine as paramount to the future of Sony. Having the CEO (and not a business division) take responsibility of SSAP ensured a long-term objective for Sony's innovation funnel and made it less prone to short-term business volatilities. In 2019, Sony brought in ¥8.66 trillion in revenue, reporting its best year ever in terms of profit in its 73-year history.[18]

Sony Startup Accelerator Program
Established in 2014 and led by Shinji Odashima, SSAP is an internal program for Sony employees to ideate, commercialize, and scale business ideas that live outside of Sony's traditional business units. Since then, SSAP has ideated over 750 business ideas and incubated 34. Out of those, 14 businesses have been successfully created.

Of the 14 businesses launched: six have continued their scaling phase under SSAP, five have moved into existing business units, two are now subsidiaries under Sony Group, and one has become wholly independent and its own company. Allowing for a variety of exit strategies means SSAP is not limited to the scope of ideas possible and is willing to accept most that can prove profitability.

Open Innovation
After five years, in 2019, the program transformed from an internal incubator to being open externally, helping anyone incubate their idea. This is because SSAP sees innovation as a numbers game. Based on their previous experience they knew the chance of success for any idea was very small (1.85%). Consequently, the more ideas running through the accelerator program, the higher the number of successes.

SSAP is also a vehicle for Sony to collaborate and partner with outside entities without disrupting its core businesses. In 2014, Sony partnered with VC firm WiL to create Qrio, a smart lock that can be easily installed in any existing door.

Crowdfunding campaigns have become a core part of SSAP testing strategy. The best way to ensure product market fit is by getting your customers to preemptively pay for it.

14 Businesses Transferred
6 continued to scale
5 merged into existing business units
2 new subsidiaries under Sony Group
1 spinout independent company

Merge

A
AB
B

Transfer

A
A

Perservere
34 business incubated

A
A

Spinout

Ideate
750 ideas created

A

A10 Lab
Independent and its own company
A10 Lab helps companies improve their customer lifetime value by building consumer loyalty through gamification. A10 Lab became an independent entity as A10 Lab Co., Ltd. in February 2017.

FES Watch
Move into existing business units
FES Watch U is an e-paper fashion watch that allows its wearer to change its design at any given moment. The project was initially going to be retired, since the material did not match Sony's high quality product, but the CEO protected the project, seeing it as a way for Sony to tap into a new consumer segment: young fashionistas.

MESH
Move into existing business units
MESH is a next-generation Internet of Things (IoT) block. Each block is a sensor with built-in functions to make it easy to prototype and build projects for the IoT. It is now a part of Sony Business Solutions Corporation.

SRE Holdings
Become a subsidiary of an existing business units
SRE Holdings offers comprehensive real estate services such as real estate brokerage, loan management, and renovations. SRE Holdings became a separate entity and listed on the Tokyo Stock Exchange in December 2019.

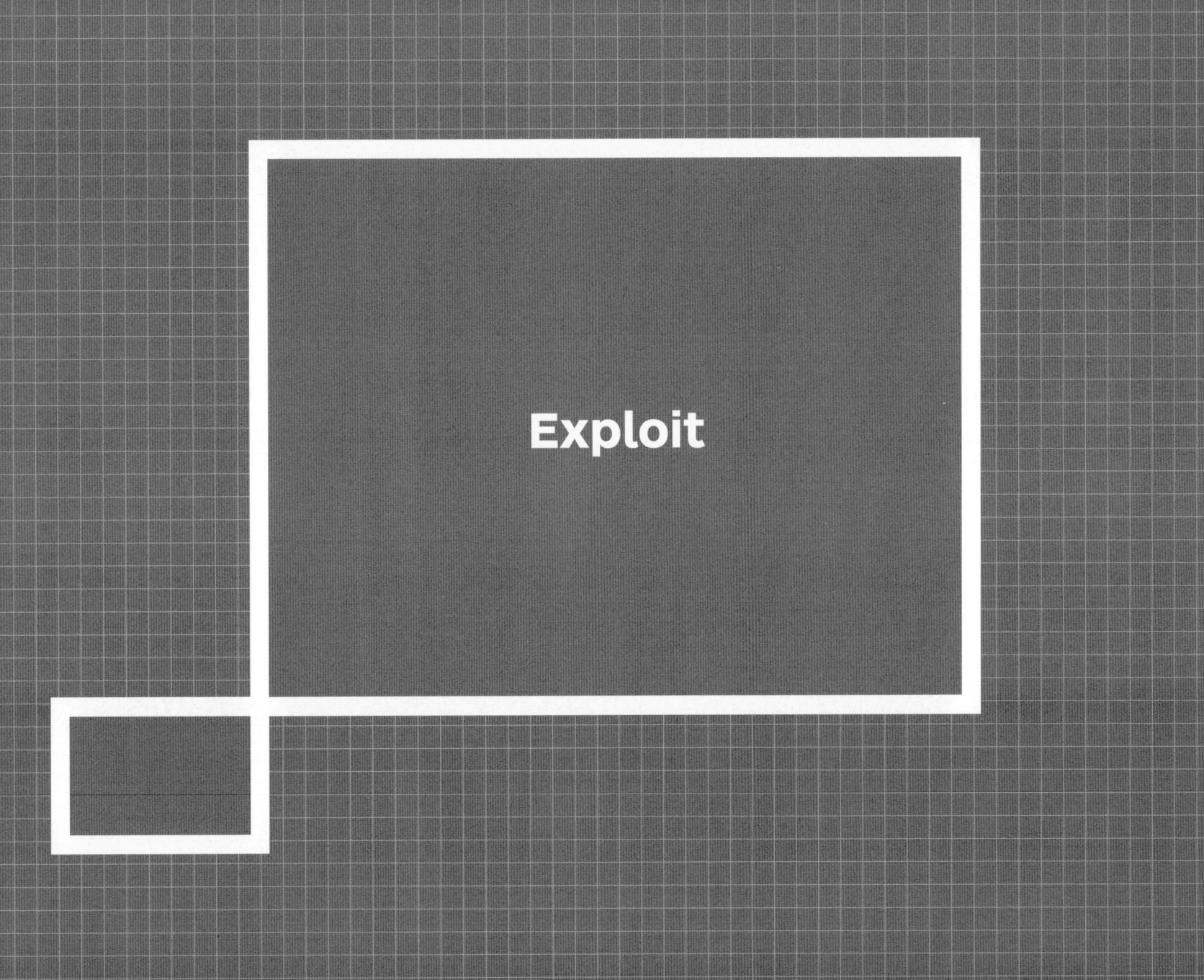

Exploit

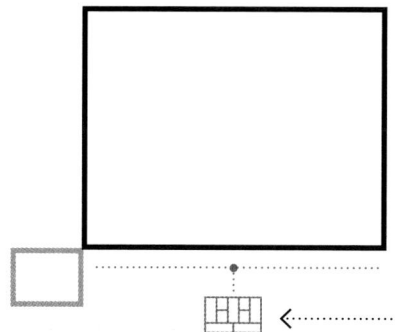

110

MANAGE

DEATH AND DISRUPTION METRICS

Performance Assessment

The disruption risk assessment helps identify how healthy or at risk a business model in your portfolio actually is and how much attention it needs to be improved and de-risked. The assessment includes two dimensions:

1. **Business model performance**
   strengths and weaknesses
   reveals positioning on Exploit portfolio *x*-axis

2. **Business model trend**
   opportunities and threats
   indicates likely future positioning on *x*-axis

Business Model Performance
Strength and Weakness Assessment
This assessment reveals how healthy or at risk a business model is based on recent performance. It assesses the strengths and weaknesses of the frontstage, backstage, and profit formula of a model. The resulting score ranges from -5 (highly at risk) to +5 (low risk), and allows you to place each business model on the *x*-axis of the Exploit portfolio.

Score and Positioning
The score from the business model performance assessment indicates the health of a business model based on its performance. The assessment looks at the frontstage, backstage, and profit formula of a business model. The score allows you to position each business model on the *x*-axis of the Exploit portfolio in terms of their death and disruption risk. Poorly performing business models at risk go on the left half of the Exploit portfolio. Healthy business models go on the right half of the Exploit portfolio.

Frontstage

		Negative				Positive			
VP	Our products and services perform worse than those of our competition.	-3	-2	-1	0	+1	+2	+3	Our products and services are highly differentiated and loved by our customers.
CS	We lost over 20% of our customer base in the last six months.	-3	-2	-1	0	+1	+2	+3	We increased our customer base by at least 50% over the last six months.
CH	We are 100% dependent on intermediaries to get products and services to customers and they are making market access difficult.	-3	-2	-1	0	+1	+2	+3	We have direct market access and fully own the relationship with the customers of our products and services.
CR	All our customers could theoretically leave us immediately, without incurring direct or indirect switching costs if they left.	-3	-2	-1	0	+1	+2	+3	All our customers are locked in for several years and they would incur significant direct and indirect switching costs if they left.

Backstage

KR	Our key resources are significantly inferior to those of our competitors and they have deteriorated over the last six months. New entrants compete with new, better, or cheaper resources.	-3	-2	-1	0	+1	+2	+3	Our key resources can't easily be copied or emulated for the next couple of years and they give us a competitive advantage (e.g., intellectual property, brand, etc.).
KA	The performance of our key activities is significantly inferior to that of our competitors and has deteriorated over the last six months. New entrants compete with new, better, or cheaper activities.	-3	-2	-1	0	+1	+2	+3	Our key activities can't easily be copied or emulated for the next couple of years and they give us a competitive advantage (e.g., cost effectiveness, scale etc.).
KP	Over the last six months we lost access to key partners.	-3	-2	-1	0	+1	+2	+3	Our key partners are locked in for years to come.

Profit Formula

RS	We lost over 20% of our revenues in the last six months.	-3	-2	-1	0	+1	+2	+3	We doubled our revenues over the last six months and are growing significantly faster than our competitors.
CS	Our cost structure grew faster than revenues and is significantly less effective than that of our competitors.	-3	-2	-1	0	+1	+2	+3	Our cost structure shrunk compared to revenue growth and is significantly more effective than that of our competitors.
Mar	Our margins shrunk by over 50% in the last six months and/or are significantly lower than those of our competition (e.g., over 50% lower).	-3	-2	-1	0	+1	+2	+3	Our margins increased by at least 50% in the last six months and/or are significantly higher than those of our competition (e.g., over 50% higher).

Trend Assessment

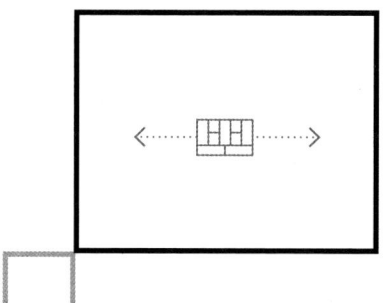

Business Model Trend

Opportunities and Threats Assessment

This assessment uncovers how a business model is trending in terms of risks coming from your external environment. It assesses how external forces represent opportunities or threats for the frontstage, backstage, and profit formula of a business model. The resulting score ranges from -5 (trending left on the risk axis) to +5 (trending right on the risk axis) and indicates how a business model is likely to perform in the future.

Score and Direction

The score from the business model trend assessment indicates in which direction a business model is likely to move based on external factors and what future performance might look like. The assessment looks at how external forces may impact and disrupt the frontstage, backstage, and profit formula of a business model. The score shows if a business model is likely to move to the left (higher death and disruption risk) or to the right (lower death and disruption risk) in the Exploit portfolio in the future.

Adding Impact Weighting

Increase the accuracy of how external forces may impact your business model by weighting each force in terms of likelihood to occur and severity of impact. For example, ask how likely new regulations are and how severely they would impact a business model. Or ask how likely new entrants are to gain traction and how severely that would impact a business model.

Trends Impact on Frontstage

		Negative	Scale	Positive
VP	New entrants are gaining traction with cheaper, better, or substitute products and services that may make our business model obsolete.	(-3) (-2) (-1) (0) (+1) (+2) (+3)		Competition for our products and services is shrinking and our products and services are likely to gain traction and benefit from that.
CS	The markets in which we are active are projected to shrink significantly over the coming years.	(-3) (-2) (-1) (0) (+1) (+2) (+3)		The markets in which we are active are projected to grow significantly over the coming years.
CR	Various trends (tech, cultural, demographics) are reducing the friction for our customers to leave us and never come back.	(-3) (-2) (-1) (0) (+1) (+2) (+3)		Various trends are making it harder for our customers to desert us and the friction for them to leave is increasing.
VP/CS	Social and cultural trends that are projected to grow are driving customers away from us (e.g., sustainability, fashion, etc.).	(-3) (-2) (-1) (0) (+1) (+2) (+3)		Various trends are making it harder for our customers to desert us and the friction for them to leave is increasing.

Trends Impact on Backstage

KR	Technology trends that substantially undermine our business model or make it obsolete are gaining traction.	(-3) (-2) (-1) (0) (+1) (+2) (+3)	Technology trends that substantially strengthen our business model are gaining traction.
KR/KA	New regulations make our business model significantly more expensive or impossible to operate and give our competitors an advantage.	(-3) (-2) (-1) (0) (+1) (+2) (+3)	New regulations make our business model significantly cheaper or easier to operate and give us a competitive advantage over our competitors.
KR/KA	Suppliers and value chain actors are changing in a way that puts our business model at risk.	(-3) (-2) (-1) (0) (+1) (+2) (+3)	Suppliers and value chain actors are changing in a way that radically strengthens our business model.

Trends Impact on Profit Formula

ECONOMIC	An economic downturn in the next six months would be lethal to our business model (e.g., due to high cost structure, debt obligations, etc.).	(-3) (-2) (-1) (0) (+1) (+2) (+3)	Our business model is resilient and would even benefit if an economic downturn happened in the next six months (e.g., due to weak competitors).
GEOPOLITICAL	Our business model depends on key resources or other factors that may be affected by geopolitical or other external forces (e.g., commodity prices, trade wars, etc.).	(-3) (-2) (-1) (0) (+1) (+2) (+3)	Our business model does not depend on key resources or other factors that are affected by geopolitical or other external forces (e.g., commodity prices, trade wars, etc.).
VC FUNDING	There are a significant amount of venture capital funding start-ups in our arena and this has grown over the last six months.	(-3) (-2) (-1) (0) (+1) (+2) (+3)	There are little to no venture capital funding start-ups in our arena.

From Risk Assessment to Action

We introduced Exploit Portfolio Actions on p. 109. Much has been written about the topic in other books already. The main contribution here consists of unifying the vocabulary and creating a shared language for all actions in the context of managing a portfolio of existing businesses.

Acquire

Acquiring outside companies or business units helps boost an existing portfolio by either plugging a hole or by strengthening an existing internal business. You may either organizationally integrate an acquired business with an existing business (merge) or offer it organizational independence.

Improve

When one of your businesses is suffering decline you may decide to renovate it by substantially changing its business model. This requires testing the new business model, while operating the existing one (see p. 124). There are two types of renovation. The first consists of renovating the business to maintain it as a pillar of your portfolio. The second consists of renovating the business to divest at an attractive price.

Divest

You divest when a business does not fit your portfolio guidelines anymore in terms of fit or performance. Divestiture can be immediate by closing a business down (dismantle), or by selling it to another company, investors, or the current management (management buyout). You may also divest over time after revamping the business first to make it more attractive to potential buyers.

Invest

Sometimes you are not prepared to or simply can't fully acquire an outside business. In that case, you may build up an investment stake to take advantage of its success. A joint venture is a particular type of investment where two or more companies set up a separate business and own it together.

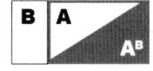

Partner

Some types of partnerships are so important that they merit mentioning at the portfolio level rather than just within a particular business model. These are partnerships that are strategic and impact several of the businesses in your portfolio in significant ways.

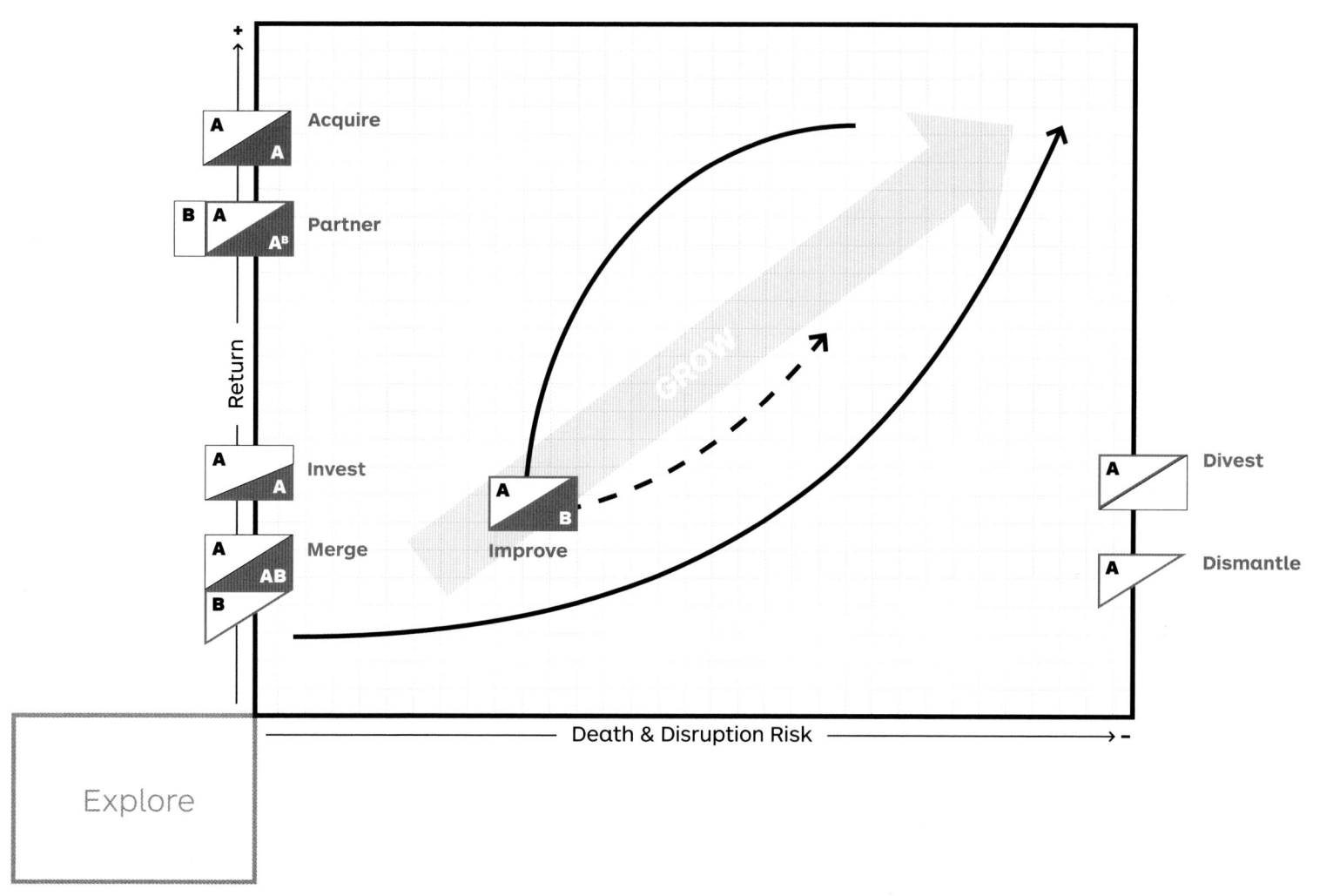

+

Acquire

Return

Partner

Invest

Merge

Improve

GROW

Death & Disruption Risk

–

Divest

Dismantle

Explore

Microsoft

Satya Nadella becomes CEO of Microsoft in 2014 and radically repositions the company away from the Windows operating system to focus on enterprise users and the cloud. Nadella understands the next phase of Microsoft's growth will require an open mindset and collaboration with partners.

Microsoft was founded in 1975 by Bill Gates and Paul Allen. The company's meteoric growth came from its operating system, Windows, which came preinstalled on the majority of PCs sold. Microsoft also expanded into software and hardware that was centered around its proprietary operating system.

In 2014, Satya Nadella became Microsoft's CEO and took over from Steve Ballmer, who had led and grown the company for over a decade. Nadella profoundly changed the company's strategy to reposition it for the future. He de-emphasized the role of proprietary Windows, which was traditionally the heart and foundation of Microsoft.

Nadella focused Microsoft on enterprise users and the cloud. To accomplish that shift he established an open and collaborative mindset, a radical change from the

Demote Company's Historic Growth Engine

By 2010, the invention of the smartphone and tablet were contributing to the irreversible decline of the PC market. At that point, Windows made up 54% of Microsoft's operating income. The company needed to transform, and to do it quickly.

Growth Mindset

SATYA NADELLA
Microsoft CEO

company's traditionally closed and proprietary attitude. Nadella wanted Microsoft's technology to be running on all platforms, rather than waiting for it to "catch up" to its competitors. Technology should work with Windows, not have to be on Windows.

Strategic Direction
The Productivity and Platform Company

Ⓐ Accelerate its efforts to unchain products and services to be platform agnostic for wider adoption.

Ⓑ Be an industry leader in cloud platform technology to facilitate open source collaboration across platforms.

Ⓒ Help enterprise users do more and achieve more.

Organizational Culture
Collaborative and Customer Focused

Nadella shifts Microsoft's culture from a fixed to growth mindset, where leadership must be "boundary-less and globally minded in seeking solutions." This comes with the understanding that if you really want to give your customers the best products you can, then you can't do it alone.

Brand Image
Open Innovation

Ⓓ Microsoft is building partnerships with "competitors" like Amazon and Sony to provide consumers with greater products and connectivity, making their software available on more platforms.

Microsoft also joins networks like Linux Foundation (2016) and Open Innovation Network (2018) to cement their commitment to open source collaboration. Developers in these networks are now able to use Microsoft's 60,000 issued patents royalty free and on any platform.[19]

D GitHub (2018, $7.5 billion)
GitHub is the cross-platform framework that developers can use to build for any platform and deploy to devices, the cloud, or IoT scenarios. Microsoft soon becomes one of the largest contributors to the platform.[23]

LinkedIn (2016, $26.2 billion)
Talent Solutions, Marketing, and Premium Subscriptions.[24]

B Cloud companies (2013–2018)
Microsoft acquires 23 cloud-related companies to build out their intelligent cloud division.[25]

A Windows / Office
By 2013, Windows revenue falls into third place behind office and service.[27] Consumers are choosing simpler devices like smartphones and tablets over traditional PCs. Recognizing this, one of Nadella's first tasks as CEO is to bring Office to Android and iOS, even offering free apps, including Word and Excel.[28]

2019 End of Year Results

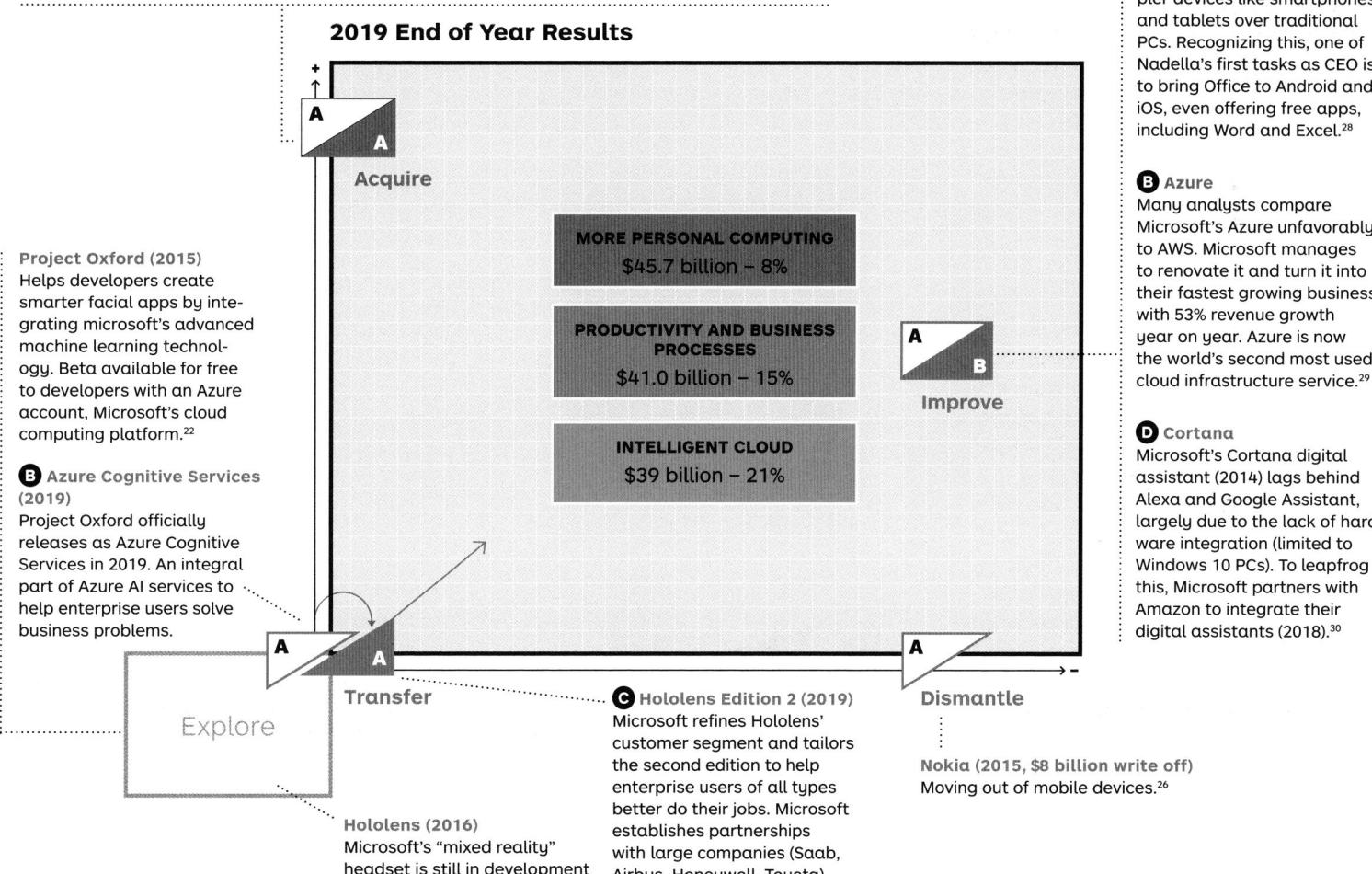

A Acquire

Project Oxford (2015)
Helps developers create smarter facial apps by integrating microsoft's advanced machine learning technology. Beta available for free to developers with an Azure account, Microsoft's cloud computing platform.[22]

B Azure Cognitive Services (2019)
Project Oxford officially releases as Azure Cognitive Services in 2019. An integral part of Azure AI services to help enterprise users solve business problems.

MORE PERSONAL COMPUTING
$45.7 billion – 8%

PRODUCTIVITY AND BUSINESS PROCESSES
$41.0 billion – 15%

INTELLIGENT CLOUD
$39 billion – 21%

A B Improve

B Azure
Many analysts compare Microsoft's Azure unfavorably to AWS. Microsoft manages to renovate it and turn it into their fastest growing business with 53% revenue growth year on year. Azure is now the world's second most used cloud infrastructure service.[29]

D Cortana
Microsoft's Cortana digital assistant (2014) lags behind Alexa and Google Assistant, largely due to the lack of hardware integration (limited to Windows 10 PCs). To leapfrog this, Microsoft partners with Amazon to integrate their digital assistants (2018).[30]

A Transfer

Explore

A Dismantle

C Hololens Edition 2 (2019)
Microsoft refines Hololens' customer segment and tailors the second edition to help enterprise users of all types better do their jobs. Microsoft establishes partnerships with large companies (Saab, Airbus, Honeywell, Toyota) to optimize their production processes.[21]

Hololens (2016)
Microsoft's "mixed reality" headset is still in development phase. Sales reach 50,000 units sold by May 2018.[20]

Nokia (2015, $8 billion write off)
Moving out of mobile devices.[26]

Unilever

Paul Polman joins Unilever as CEO in 2010 and repositions Unilever to become a purpose-driven company. He believes most consumers are willing to switch their purchase to a brand that supports sustainable living—and he thinks that, as a company, you can do well by doing good.

Unilever, founded in 1929, is a British-Dutch transnational company producing products in food and beverage, home care, and personal care. Unilever now owns over 400 brands, with a turnover in 2018 of €51 billion. It has grown to be one of the most recognizable brands in the world.

By the 2000s, Unilever was struggling to overcome rising commodity prices and the financial crisis (of 2008). In 2010, Unilever picked an outsider as CEO in an effort to increase communication and transparency with the marketplace.

Paul Polman believed in focusing on the long term and set ambitious sustainability goals for Unilever, all the while doubling its business. He believed that a company's growth can decouple from its environmental impact; products with a purpose can create higher consumer demand and better constructed supply chains will be more sustainable, long term.

Incorporate Sustainability

Unilever is struggling in the 2000s to overcome rising commodity prices and then the financial crisis of 2008. When Paul Polman takes over as CEO, he creates the Sustainable Living Plan, "defining a new era of responsible capitalism."

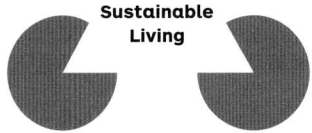

Sustainable Living

PAUL POLMAN
Unilver CEO

In 2019, Paul Polman stepped down as CEO and was replaced by Alan Jope. Jope pledged to push Unilever's sustainability objectives even further by making every one of their brands purpose led.

Strategic Direction
Make Sustainable Living Commonplace
Unilever will make all 400+ of its brands purpose led by reducing their environmental footprint, while increasing positive social impact.

Sustainability and Profits
Unilever wants to double its revenue by moving from low- to high-margin goods while halving the environmental impact of its products. These ambitious targets prove you can both do good and do well.

Long-Term Planning
Banning quarter reporting and scaling back hedge fund shareholdings reduces share price fluctuations. This, in turn, creates a more stable environment to plan for long-term growth over short-term returns.

Organizational Culture
Purposeful and Principled
At Unilever, success is defined as having "the highest standards of corporate behavior towards everyone we work with, the communities we touch, and the environment on which we have an impact." Everyone is expected to conduct operations with integrity and with respect for the many people, organizations, and environments the business touches.

Brand Image
Purpose Driven not Profit Driven
"Over 90% of millennials say they would switch brands for one which champions a cause." Unilever wants to be perceived as a company driven by the desire to act responsibly—and, to prove that sustainability is good for business.

Comfort One Rinse
A newly released version of the fabric conditioner uses 20% less water then previous editions, saving 10 million Olympic-sized pools' worth of water a year.

Lifebuoy
Creates the Handwashing Programme to prevent 600,000 child deaths every year from respiratory infections and diarrheal disease.

Dove
Dove creates the Self-Esteem Project, to ensure the next generation grow up feeling confident about the way they look—to help them reach their full potential. Since 2005, The educational tool has been improving self-esteem in more than 35 million young people.

TG Tips
In 2018 introduces fully biodegradable tea bags made with plant-based material, significantly improving their environmental impact.

Domestos
In 2017 launches Flush Less spray to market in South Africa, in response to the water shortages affecting the area.

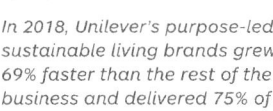

In 2018, Unilever's purpose-led, sustainable living brands grew 69% faster than the rest of the business and delivered 75% of the company's growth.[31]

Schmidt's Natural (2017, Sustainability)
Natural, chemical-free deodorants

Living Proof (2016, Premium)
Premium hair care products

Mae Terra (2016, Sustainbility)
Natural and organic food business

GRAZE (2019, Sustainbility)
Healthy subscription-based snacking

Seventh Generation (2016, Sustainability)
Eco-friendly cleaning products

The Laundress (2019, Premium)
High-end, eco-friendly laundry and household cleaning products

Explore

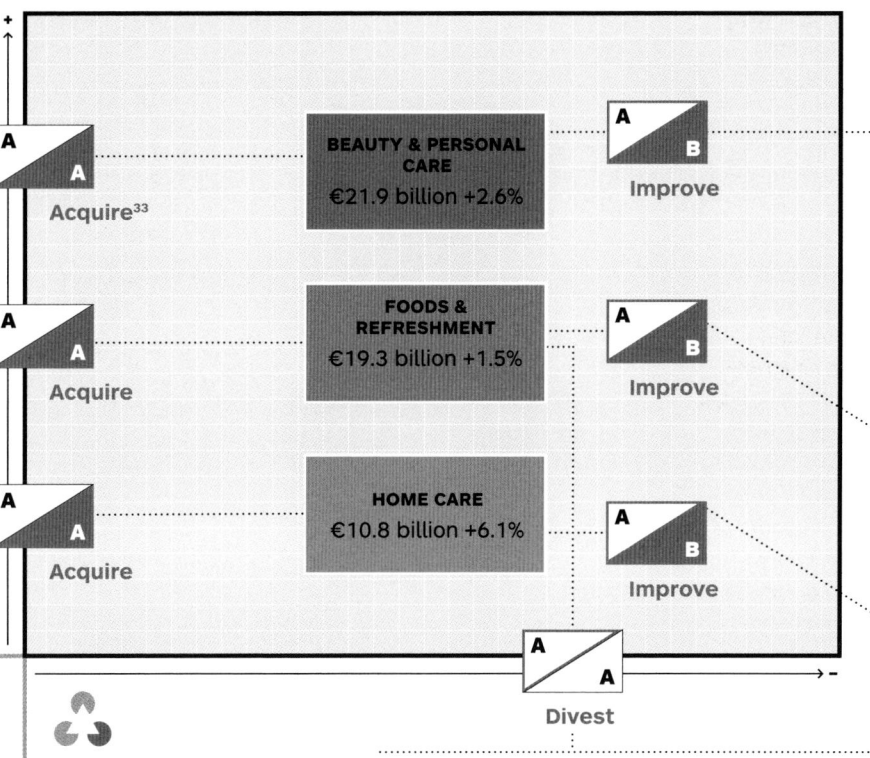

2019 End of Year Results

A — Acquire[33]

A — Acquire

A — Acquire

BEAUTY & PERSONAL CARE
€21.9 billion +2.6%

FOODS & REFRESHMENT
€19.3 billion +1.5%

HOME CARE
€10.8 billion +6.1%

A B — Improve

A B — Improve

A B — Improve

A A — Divest

119

MANAGE

Unilever has indicated it will drop brands that do not "contribute meaningfully to the world," even if it affects their bottom line. These include much loved brands like Marmite, Magnum, and Pot Noodle.[34]

Purpose-led
In 2014, sells SlimFast to Kaios Group. SlimFast makes shakes, snacks, and other dietary supplement foods that promote diets and weight-loss plans.[32]

Profit-led
Unilever sells off many of their food brands to make the shift to a higher-margin portfolio mix.

In 2013 sells Wish-Bone salad dressing to for $580 million and Skippy peanut butter for $700 million. In 2014, sells pasta sauce brand, Ragu for £1.26 billion.

Logitech

In 2013 Bracken Darrell takes the helm of Logitech. He unlocks growth by moving the company away from the declining PC market. Logitech builds a portfolio of design-focused consumer and enterprise accessories that benefit from the growth of the cloud.

Logitech was founded in 1981 in Switzerland. It rapidly grew, based on its innovative computer peripherals, like advanced versions of the PC mouse. Logitech came under pressure with the decline of the PC market and a $100 million failure with Google TV in 2012.[35]

Bracken Darrell re-focused the company's portfolio on consumer and enterprise accessories that would benefit from the growth of the cloud and connected devices. Logitech acquired several brands to expand its portfolio, particularly in music and gaming. Logitech, traditionally an engineering-focused company, put design at the center of the company and its portfolio. In 2013 it hired Allistair Curtis, former head of design for Nokia, to help build a design-led organization.

Revive Entrepreneurship

In 2012 the PC market started an irreversible decline and moved toward mobile, tablets, and the cloud. Logitech, which traditionally relied on the growth in the PC industry, had to dramatically change.

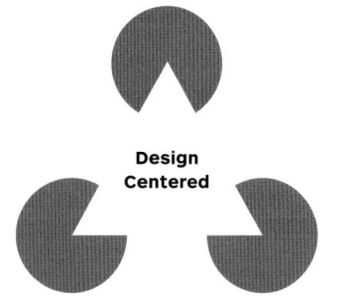

Design Centered

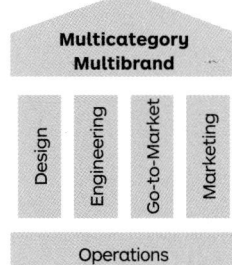

Multicategory Multibrand

Design | Engineering | Go-to-Market | Marketing

Operations

From Logitech's presentation

Strategic Direction
The Leading Cloud Peripheral Player

A Be a big fish in many small ponds and avoid giants like Apple, Google, and Amazon.

B Reinvest profits in growth, assure growth across major categories, and improve margins to high end of range.

Become a "design company."

Organizational Culture
Entrepreneural and Design Driven

Revive entrepreneurial culture where people are willing to try new things and maintain entrepreneurial independence of acquisitions.

Expand core capabilities, in particular, in-house design and customer obsession.

Design for cost early on in the process to increase operational efficiency.

Brand Image
High End Design

A Multibrand company that brings people together through music, gaming, video, and computing.

Known for innovating for the customer, to deliver exactly what they want with high-end design.

Logitech's Fiscal Year 2019 vs. 2013[36]

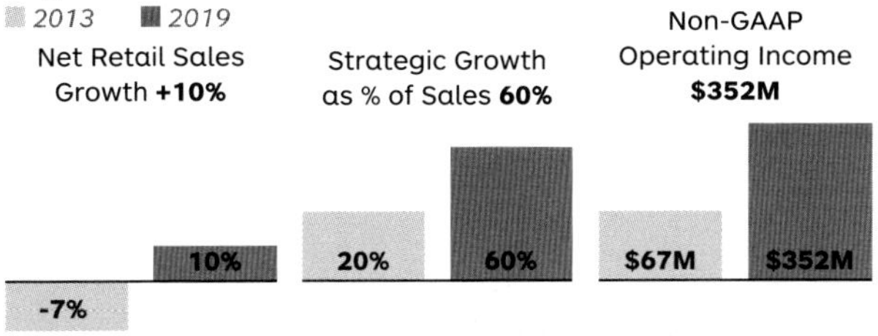

■ 2013 ■ 2019

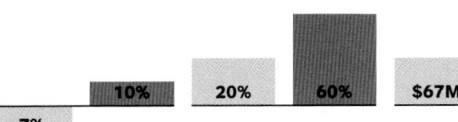

Net Retail Sales Growth +10%	Strategic Growth as % of Sales 60%	Non-GAAP Operating Income $352M
-7% / 10%	20% / 60%	$67M / $352M

2019 End of Year Results

Saitek Pro Flight (2016)[37]
Advanced manufacturer of flight simulation controllers

ASTRO Gaming (2017)
Leading console gaming accessory brand for professional gamers and enthusiasts

Beyond Entertainment (2018)
Online platform that offers the latest news from the console industry

Jaybird (2016)
Leader in wireless audio wearables for sports and active lifestyles

Blue Microphones (2018)
Microphones for audio professionals, musicians, and consumers

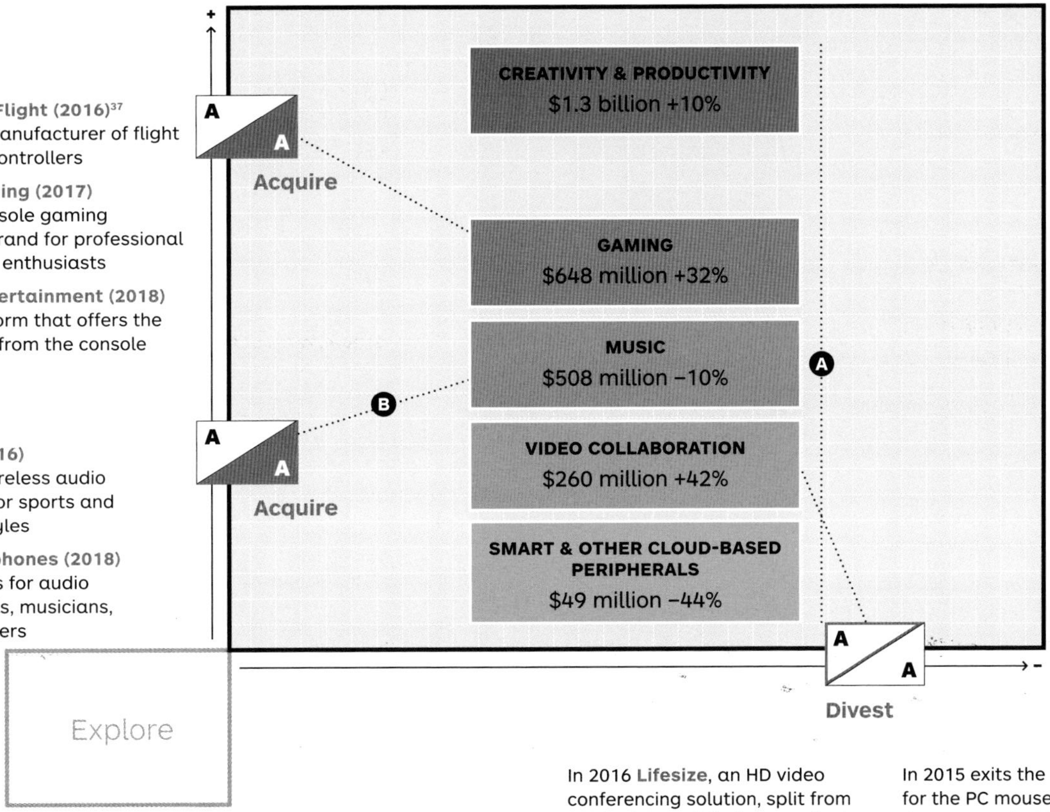

A — **Acquire**

A B — **Acquire**

CREATIVITY & PRODUCTIVITY
$1.3 billion +10%

GAMING
$648 million +32%

MUSIC
$508 million −10%

VIDEO COLLABORATION
$260 million +42%

SMART & OTHER CLOUD-BASED PERIPHERALS
$49 million −44%

A A — **Divest**

Explore

$2.79
Billion
Total sales

BRACKEN DARRELL
Logitech CEO

In 2016 **Lifesize**, an HD video conferencing solution, split from Logitech as a fully independent company.[39]

In 2015 exits the **OEM** Business for the PC mouse, which for a long time accounted for a large portion of Logitech's revenue.[38]

FUJIFILM Holdings

In 2003 Shigetaka Komori is appointed CEO of Fujifilm. He understands for the company to survive the digital disruption of analog film, it has to completely restructure and reinvent itself as a technology player.

Fujifilm, founded in 1934, was Japan's first producer of photofilm. By the mid-80s it dominated the industry together with Kodak. However, in the early 2000s, the digitization of film made the industry virtually irrelevant.

In 2004, CEO Shigetaka Komori came up with a 5-year medium-term management plan to "save Fujifilm from disaster and ensuring its viability as a leading company." Komori decided to downsize the photofilm business and cut almost 5,000 jobs worldwide all the while building a $400 million research facility to venture into new markets.[40] Before then, Fujifilm spent 1.5 years taking stock of their technical inventory to find a renewed appreciation of Fujifilm's capabilities nurtured in photofilm.

The new business unit Healthcare and Material Solutions now makes up 43% of total revenue and photofilms accounts for less than 1% of its revenue.[41]

MANAGE

122

Fight Disruption

By the mid 2000s, the digitization of photography had made photo film imaging virtually irrelevant. Komori understood he needed a plan to dramatically change the direction of the company, in order to ensure its survival.

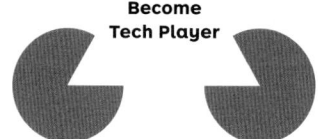

Become Tech Player

Strategic Direction
The three strategic directions outlined in Komori's 5-year plan are:

- Implementing structural reforms for cost reduction
- Building new growth strategies through a diversified portfolio
- Enhancing consolidated management for faster decision making

Organizational Culture
To ensure Fujifilm could make the rapid transformation in time, Komori understood the organization needed to create the right structure:

- Stronger individuals with greater autonomy and role flexibility that could take initiative and be more entrepreneurial
- Lean and decisive corporate leadership with rapid decision-making process[42]

Brand Image
Fujifilm is known to the world over for their state-of-the-art technology, delivering top-quality products. They want the brand image and trust they built with film to carry over to an array of care products as they make a leap to other industries.

"Fujifilm had, until then, been one of the leading companies in the photographic products industry and had continually produced big profits. I wanted to make sure it stayed that way into and through the next century. Figuring out how to do it was my job as CEO."

SHIGETAKA KOMORI
FUJIFILM Holdings Chairman and CEO

Fujifilm acquires two companies (**Diosynth RTP LLC and MSD Biologics (UK) Limited**) and renames them to Fujifilm Diosynth Biotechnologies. This is to enter into the biopharmaceutical contract development and manufacturing organization business to expand their Healthcare & Material Solutions.

The Acquisition of **Toyama Chemical** (currently Fujifilm Toyama Chemical) in 2008 signals Fujifilm's full scale entry into the pharmaceutical business.

In 2001, Fujifilm purchases an additional 25% share of **Fuji Xerox**, a joint venture with Xerox. Making it a consolidated subsidiary. The Document Solutions division now makes up 41% of annual revenue.

By 2006, the digital transformation of photography was well on its way and Fujifilm knew it had to dramatically restructure its film ecosystem, by downsizing its photographic film business. This frees up much-needed resources to fulfil their diversification plan. In 2019, **photo film** accounts for less than 1% of its annual revenue.

Building a Diversified Portfolio 2004–2019

+

A **A**
Acquire

A **A**
Invest

HEALTHCARE & MATERIAL
¥1039 billion +43%

DOCUMENT SOLUTIONS
¥1006 billion +41%

IMAGING SOLUTIONS
¥387 billion +16%

A
B
Improve

-

Explore

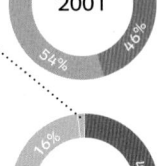

2001
54%   46%

2019
16%   41%
43%

123

MANAGE

HEALTH CARE & MATERIAL SOLUTIONS
Health care & Material, Highly Functional Materials, Recording Media, Graphic Systems/Inkjet Display Materials

DOCUMENT SOLUTIONS
Office Products & Printers, Production Services, Solutions & Services

IMAGING SOLUTIONS
Photo Imaging, Electronic Imaging, Optical Devices

Fujifilm makes a bold decision to invest in LCD films, predicting the boom of LCD screens. Fujifilm invests over ¥150 billion in new facilities to manufacture **FUJITAC**, a high-performance film essential for making LCD panels for TV, computers, and smartphones.

Fujifilm's understanding of how photos fade and oxidizes over time helped them make the leap into the functional cosmetic realm, as the human skin ages in a similar manner. In 2007, the skincare line **Astalift** was founded.

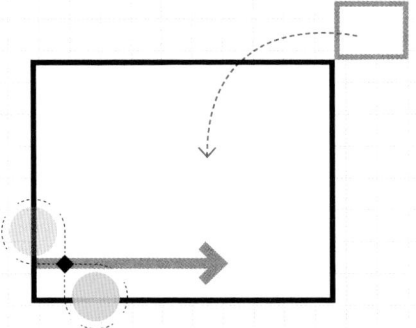

Business Model Shifts

A company needs to apply the processes and metrics of the Explore portfolio when it decides to renovate one of its expiring business models in order to shift to a new one. More precisely, it needs to continue to operate the expiring business model, while simultaneously exploring and testing the shift to a new one. This is a challenging endeavor, but you will only succeed if you apply an exploration rather than an execution mindset to the testing of a potential new business model. This will reduce the risk that you shift to a new business model that won't work.

Testing Your Shift

Shifting to a new business model is very risky, because uncertainty whether it will work is high. However, if you apply the testing process and principles from the Explore portfolio you can substantially reduce the risk of shifting toward something that won't work. The main difference is that you build on top of an existing business. That has advantages and disadvantages. The main advantage is that you are likely to know customers, market, and technologies well. The disadvantage is that you might prioritize running the business as is at the expense of testing the hypotheses underlying the business model shift.

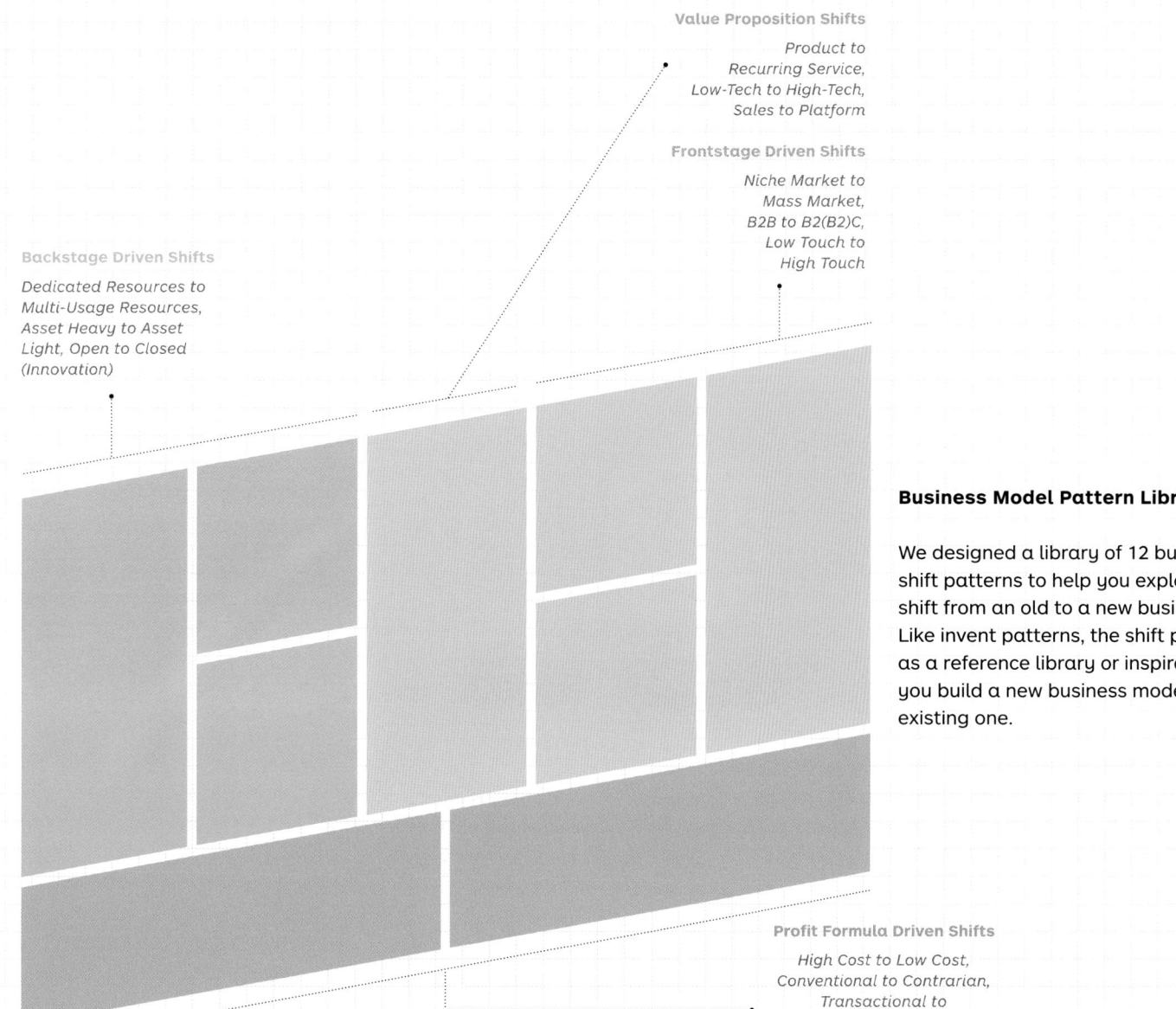

Value Proposition Shifts

Product to Recurring Service, Low-Tech to High-Tech, Sales to Platform

Frontstage Driven Shifts

Niche Market to Mass Market, B2B to B2(B2)C, Low Touch to High Touch

Backstage Driven Shifts

Dedicated Resources to Multi-Usage Resources, Asset Heavy to Asset Light, Open to Closed (Innovation)

Profit Formula Driven Shifts

High Cost to Low Cost, Conventional to Contrarian, Transactional to Recurring Revenue

Business Model Pattern Library

We designed a library of 12 business model shift patterns to help you explore how to shift from an old to a new business model. Like invent patterns, the shift patterns serve as a reference library or inspiration to help you build a new business model on top of an existing one.

Patt

erns

Business Model Patterns

A repeatable configuration of different business model building blocks to strengthen an organization's overall business model.

Help new ventures develop a competitive advantage beyond technology, product, service, or price.

Help established companies shift from an outdated to more competitive business model.

A single business model can incorporate several patterns.

Pattern Library

In the following pages we outline a pattern library that is split into two categories of patterns: invent patterns to enhance new ventures and shift patterns to substantially improve an established but deteriorating business model to make it more competitive.

Invent Patterns

Codify aspects of a superior business model. Each pattern helps you think through how to compete on a superior business model, beyond the traditional means of competition based on technology, product, service, or price. The best business models incorporate several patterns to outcompete others.

Exploit

Explore

Shift Patterns

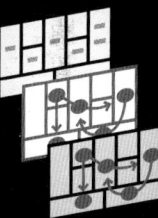

Codify the shift from one type of business model to another. Each pattern helps you think through how you could substantially improve your current business model by shifting it from a less competitive one to a more competitive one.

Applying Patterns

Understand business model patterns to better
perform the following business model activities:

Design and Assess

Use patterns to design better business models around market opportunities, technology innovations, or new products and services. Use them to assess the competitiveness of an existing business model. (p. 229)

Disrupt and Transform

Use patterns as an inspiration to transform your market. In the following pages, we provide a library of companies that disrupted entire industries. They were the first to introduce new business model patterns in their arena.

Question and Improve

Use patterns to ask better business model questions, beyond the traditional product, service, pricing, and market-related questions. Regardless of whether you are a senior leader, innovation lead, entrepreneur, investor, or faculty, you can help develop superior business models based on better questions.

THE BIGGEST THREAT TO INCUMBENTS

IS THE UPSTARTS

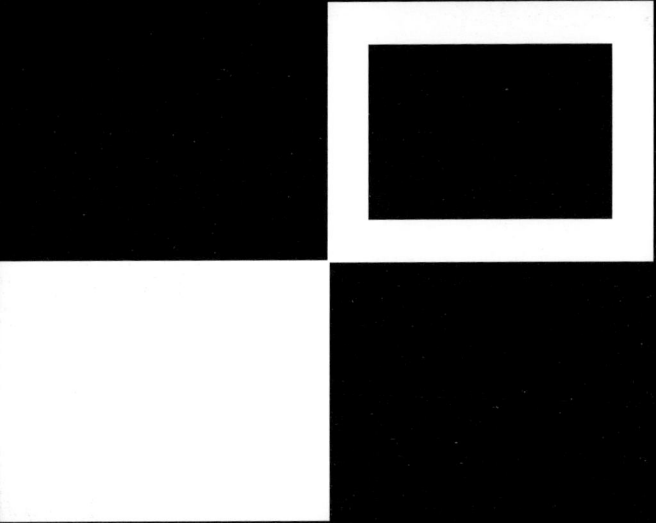

Epicenters

Business model patterns
can originate in the
frontstage (customer-driven),
backstage (resource-driven),
or profit formula (finance-driven)
of a business model.

Backstage Disruption
*Radical change
of how value is created.*

Profit Formula Disruption
*A radical change of
who is targeted and how
value is delivered.*

Frontstage Disruption
*Radical change of how
value is created.*

Invent Pattern Library

Frontstage Disruption

p. 144   Market Explorers

p. 145   Visionaries
p. 145   Repurposers
p. 145   Democratizers

p. 150   Channel Kings

p. 151   Disintermediators
p. 151   Opportunity Builders

p. 156   Gravity Creators

p. 157   Stickiness Scalers
p. 157   Superglue Makers

Backstage Disruption

p. 164   Resource Castles

p. 165   User Base Castles
p. 165   Platform Castles
p. 165   IP Castles
p. 165   Brand Castles

p. 172   Activity Differentiators

p. 173   Efficiency Disruptors
p. 173   Speed Masters
p. 173   Sustainability Masters
p. 173   Build-to-Order

p. 178   Scalers

p. 179   Delegators
p. 179   Licensors
p. 179   Franchisors

Profit Formula Disruption

p. 190   Revenue Differentiators

p. 191   Recurring Revenue
p. 191   Bait & Hook
p. 191   Freemium Providers
p. 191   Subsidizers

p. 198   Cost Differentiators

p. 199   Resource Dodgers
p. 199   Technologists
p. 199   Low Cost

p. 204   Margin Masters

p. 205   Contrarians
p. 205   High Ender

Invent Patterns

Greenfield

The companies we portray in this section all started from a blank sheet. They built business models from scratch around a technology, market opportunity, or trend. They all disrupted an industry by applying powerful business model patterns unheard of in that industry.

Pattern

We highlight nine different invent patterns with 27 flavors that new ventures and established companies can apply to build better, more competitive business models. We describe each pattern so that you can make use of it as a reference library.

Flavor
Each pattern has two or more different flavors. These are variations of a particular pattern to help you understand different ways to apply the pattern in question.

Case Illustration

Each case serves to highlight a pattern in action. We don't outline the company's entire business model—just show how it applied a particular pattern to build a more competitive business model. In reality, an entire business model might combine several patterns.

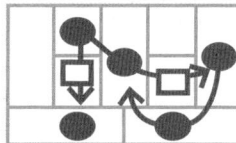

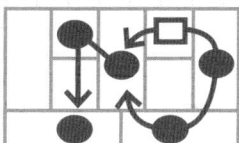

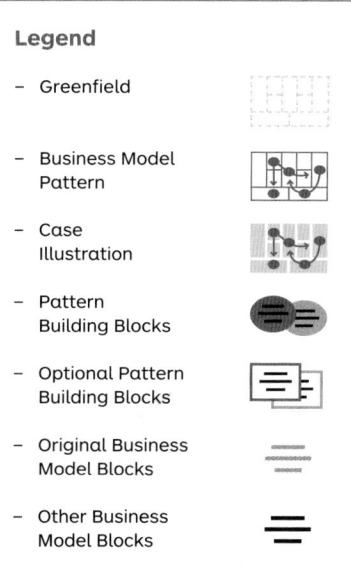

Legend

- Greenfield

- Business Model Pattern

- Case Illustration

- Pattern Building Blocks

- Optional Pattern Building Blocks

- Original Business Model Blocks

- Other Business Model Blocks

141

Frontstage Disruption

Market Explorers

p.146	**Visionaries**	Tesla Motors
p.148	**Repurposers**	M-Pesa
p.149	**Democratizers**	Sears, Roebuck and Co.

Channel Kings

| p.152 | **Disintermediators** | Dollar Shave Club |
| p.154 | **Opportunity Builders** | Tupperware |

Gravity Creators

| p.158 | **Stickiness Scaler** | Microsoft Windows |
| p.159 | **Superglue Makers** | Microsoft Xbox |

A radical change of who is targeted and how value is delivered.

Market Explorers

Unlock Markets

Develop innovative value propositions that create, unleash, or unlock completely new, untapped, or underserved markets with large potential. Be a pioneer and unearth new revenue potential through market exploration.

144

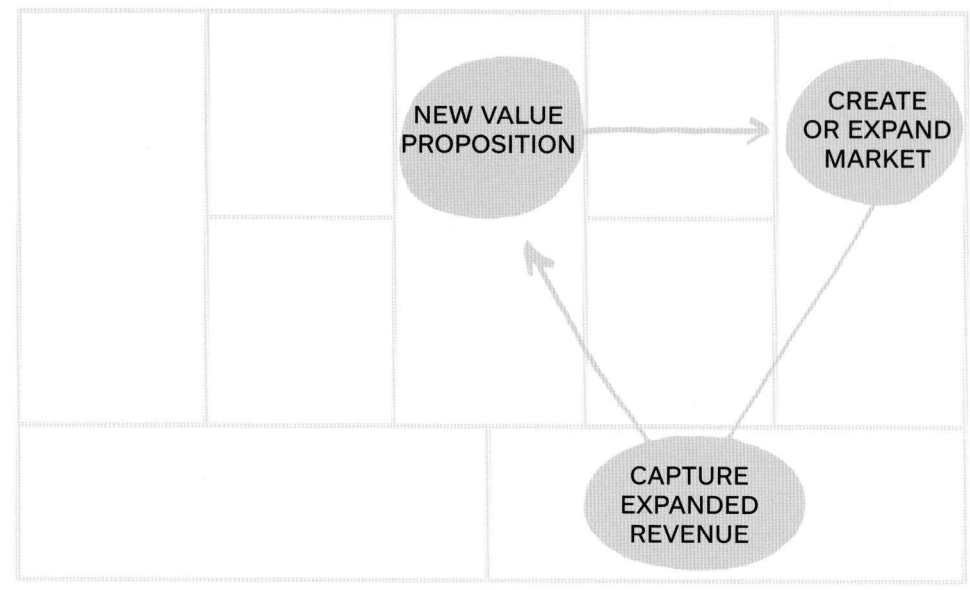

TRIGGER QUESTION
How could we tap into new, untapped, or underserved markets with large potential?

Assessment Question
How large and attractive is the untapped market potential we are going after?

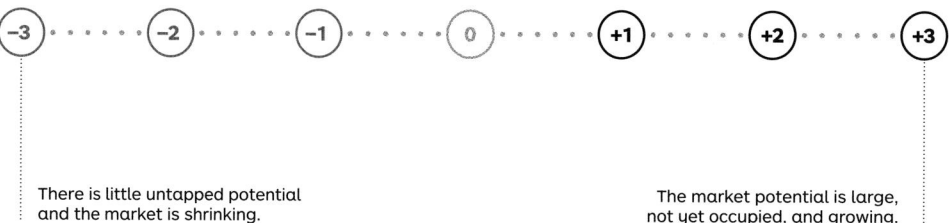

There is little untapped potential and the market is shrinking.

The market potential is large, not yet occupied, and growing.

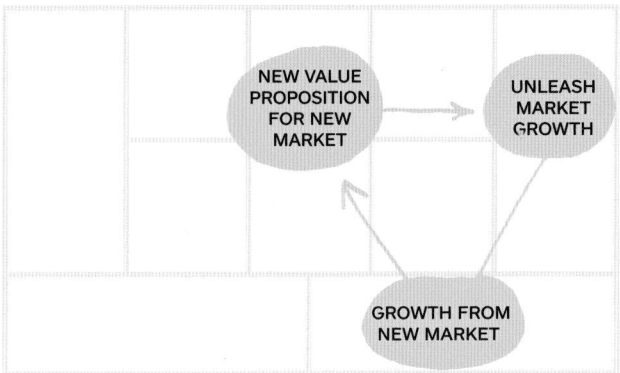

Visionaries – Use imagination to see a large market potential where others don't. Unleash growth by *exploring unproven needs* that you satisfy with a new value proposition.

EXAMPLES
Tesla, iPhone, Nintendo Wii

TRIGGER QUESTION
Which unproven needs of a large market might be worth exploring?

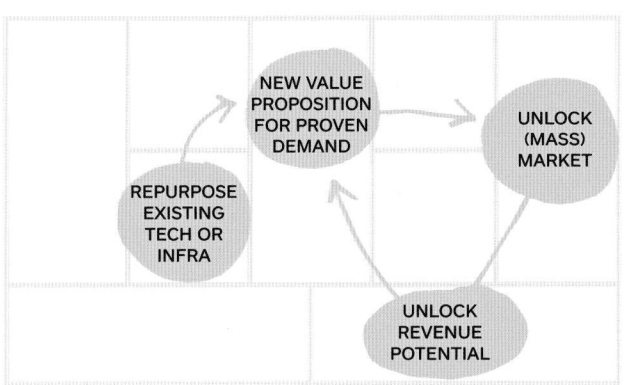

Repurposers – Find innovative ways to tap into proven market demand by *repurposing existing technology and infrastructure* that previously served other ends.

EXAMPLES
M-Pesa, AWS

TRIGGER QUESTION
How could we repurpose an existing technology or infrastructure to unlock proven, but so far inaccessible, customer needs?

145

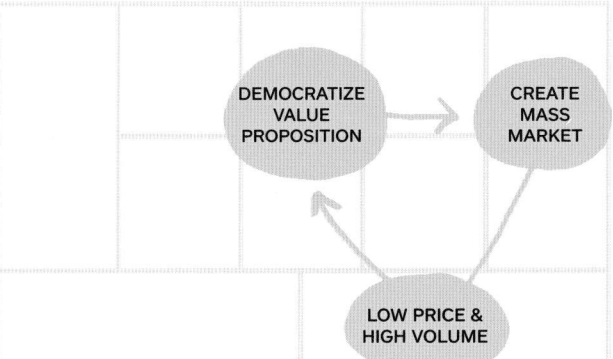

Democratizers – Find innovative ways to *democratize access to products, services, and technologies* that were previously only accessible to a small number of high-end customers.

EXAMPLES
Sears, Azuri, M-Pesa, AWS

TRIGGER QUESTION
How could we unlock products, services, and technologies that are limited to a niche market and make them more widely available for a mass market?

Tesla Motors

In 2012 Tesla envisions a large untapped market (high-end electric vehicles) where nobody else sees one. With the Model S they create the right value proposition to unlock the opportunity.

Tesla was founded in 2003 with the goal of commercializing electric vehicles, starting with luxury sports cars and then moving on to affordable, mass market vehicles. In 2008, Tesla began selling its Roadster. Its first breakthrough was in 2012 when it launched the Model S. Tesla's first "affordable" car, the Model 3, was announced in 2015 and produced in 2017.

Prior to Tesla, the market for electric vehicles was relatively insignificant and was served by utilitarian and unremarkable models. Tesla was the first car manufacturer to view the market for electric vehicles differently: Tesla saw a significant opportunity by focusing on performance and the high end of the market.

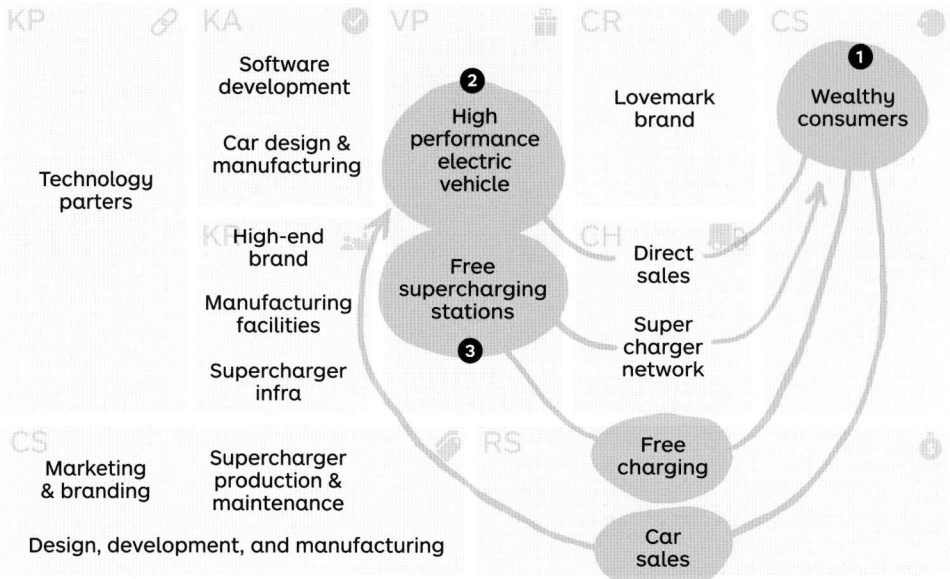

1 Envision a Large, Untapped Market, Where Nobody Sees One

Tesla identifies a potential market of environmentally conscious, wealthy consumers who are interested in electric vehicles, but not at the expense of comfort, performance, and design.

2 Create Customer Gains in New Ways

With the Model S, Tesla taps into the aspirations of its initial customer segment. In 2013, it is called the "best car ever tested," and becomes the best selling car in eight of America's 25 wealthiest zip codes.[1]

3 Relieve Customer Pains in New Ways

Tesla recognizes its customers' fears over battery range. It substantially improves the speed of charging and creates its own network of free superchargers in high traffic areas.

+ Lovemark Brand

Tesla built up a lovemark brand in record time. It inspired significant brand loyalty because of its dedication to saving the planet, high-quality vehicles, and personal customer service. In 2014, the Tesla Model S was voted the "most loved car in America."

+ Direct Distribution

From the start Tesla sold its cars directly (through the Internet, gallery-like stores in urban malls, and its owner loyalty program) to educate customers on the cars' features.

From Hardware to Software and Data

Tesla is not just a car manufacturer, it is truly a software company. Its cars run on sophisticated software that updates wirelessly. Self-driving software that constantly learns from the data of its community of drivers is introduced in 2014. Software drives the entire user experience of owning a Tesla.

Building the Backstage for Disruption

To enable its vision of unleashing the electric vehicle market, Tesla bolsters its portfolio of key resources and key activities with technology partners like Toyota, Mercedes, and Panasonic. It also manages to overcome substantial manufacturing challenges for Tesla's first affordable car, the Model 3.

14,000 Superchargers were deployed globally at 1,261 stations, as of September 2019.[3]

276 thousand Model 3 preorders in its first two days, worth more than $10 billion for Tesla as of April 2, 2016.[4]

Tesla Strategy Canvas[2]
Comparing electric cars

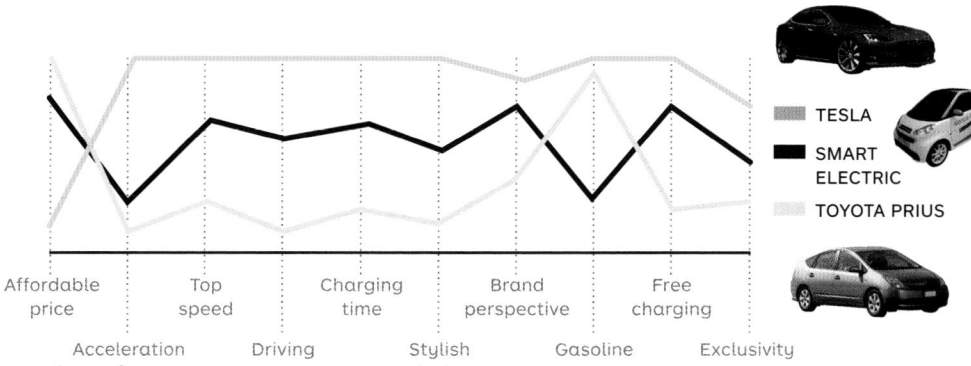

TESLA
SMART ELECTRIC
TOYOTA PRIUS

Affordable price · Acceleration for performance · Top speed · Driving range · Charging time · Stylish design · Brand perspective · Gasoline usage · Free charging · Exclusivity

Global Electric Vehicle Sales in 2019[5]

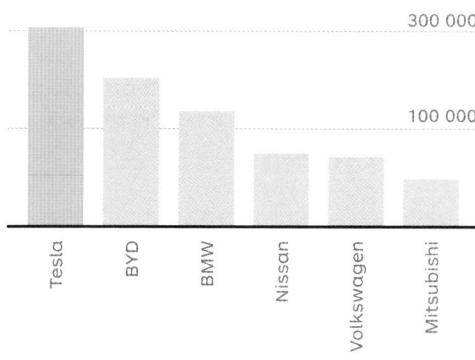

300 000

100 000

Tesla · BYD · BMW · Nissan · Volkswagen · Mitsubishi

M-Pesa

In 2007, Safaricom repurposes its telecom network to create M-Pesa, a reliable money transfer solution for the masses.

Safaricom is the biggest telecom operator in Kenya. In 2007, it decided to use its telecom infrastructure to build M-Pesa, a simple mobile money transfer system. It tapped into the proven demand for mobile payments from millions of Kenyans with a mobile phone.

Existing financial services were expensive and inappropriate for small transactions. In 2009, there were only 352 ATMs and 491 bank branches in the entire country (with a population of 39 million). Most money transfers were in cash, which was expensive, unreliable, and sometimes dangerous.

M-Pesa changed that. Within two years of its introduction, M-Pesa saw 10,000 new registrant applications daily.[6] In 2010, it processed over 90% of all mobile money transactions in Kenya, and had a 70% market share of all mobile money subscribers.[7]

M-Pesa also had an impact on a national scale in Kenya with studies crediting M-Pesa for lifting an estimated 2% of Kenyan households out of extreme poverty.[8]

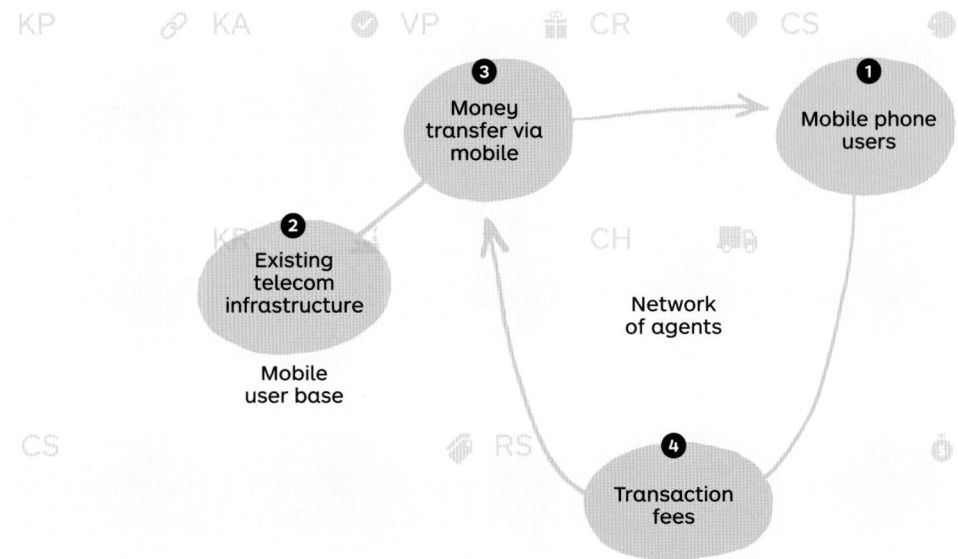

1. Identify a Proven Demand You May Unlock Based on Your Resources

Safaricom has evidence for market demand: some of their mobile customers hack their own digital payment solution by using SMS messages to share mobile airtime as a means of e-currency.

2 Repurpose Your Key Resources to Enable the New Value Proposition

In 2007, Safaricom imagines how it could repurpose its telecom network to create a reliable money transfer solution with M-Pesa. As the dominant telecom operator in Kenya, it already has a relationship with millions of Kenyans.

3 Differentiate from Competition

In the mid-2000s, financial services are expensive and do not cater to irregular and small transactions. Only a minority of Kenyans are using the banking system. With M-Pesa's affordable money transfers, Safaricom opens up the financial system to the previously unbanked.

4 Enjoy the New Revenue Stream

M-Pesa generates a new revenue stream for Safaricom reaching Sh62.9 billion ($625 million equivalent), that is, 28% of Safaricom total revenues in 2018.[9] Revenues come from small transaction fees on money transfers and other financial services.

+ Network of Agents

Through 2018, M-Pesa builds a distribution network of 110,000 agents across Kenya, allowing Kenyans to exchange cash for virtual currency and vice versa.[10] This includes small shops, gas stations, post offices, and even traditional bank branches and is 40 times the number of bank ATMs in Kenya.

INVENT PATTERNS

23
million Kenyans
used the system by 2013
which is equivalent to

74%
of the adult
population.[11]

M-Pesa Active Customers[12]
In millions as of 2019

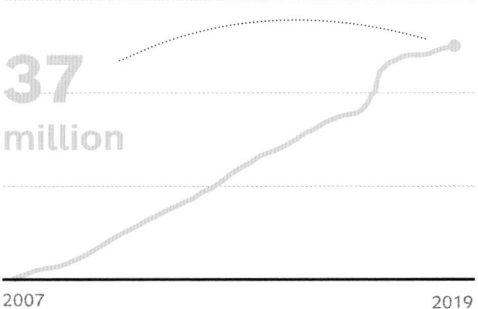

37
million

2007   2019

43% of Kenya's GDP was transferred per month over the system in 2013, up from 10% in 2009.[13]

Sears, Roebuck and Co.

In the late 1800s, Sears, Roebuck and Co. ("Sears") democratizes access to mass market retail with the Sears mail order catalog. By leveraging the growth in U.S. mail and delivery services, Sears was able to distribute its products to all rural areas throughout the United States.

HISTORICAL CASE

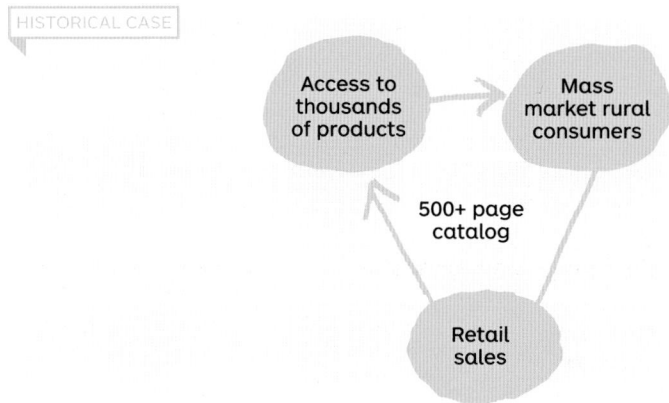

The Sears mail order catalog gave isolated settlers in the west access to a variety of low-price everyday goods that were previously inaccessible to them. By 1895 the catalog was more than 500 pages long, bringing in $750 thousand in annual sales ($23 million equivalent today).

The first Sears retail store opened in 1925 in Chicago, and Sears remained the U.S.'s top retailer until 1991. The catalog was discontinued in 1993, after over a century of use.

$23
million

Amount of sales (in today's dollars) brought in by the catalog in 1895.[14]

Channel Kings

Access Customers

Radically change how to reach and acquire a large number of customers. Pioneer innovative new channels that haven't been used in your industry before.

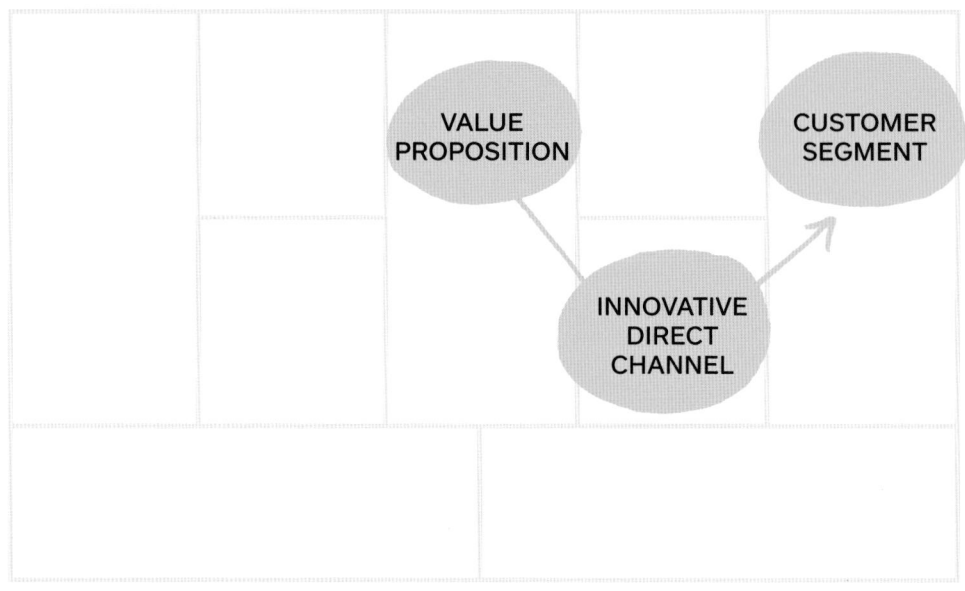

TRIGGER QUESTION

How could we increase market access and build strong and direct channels to our end customers?

Assessment Question

Do we have large-scale and, ideally, direct access to our end customer?

We have limited market access and depend on intermediaries to get our products and services to customers and interact with them.

We have large-scale market access and own the channel(s) and relationships with end users of our products and services.

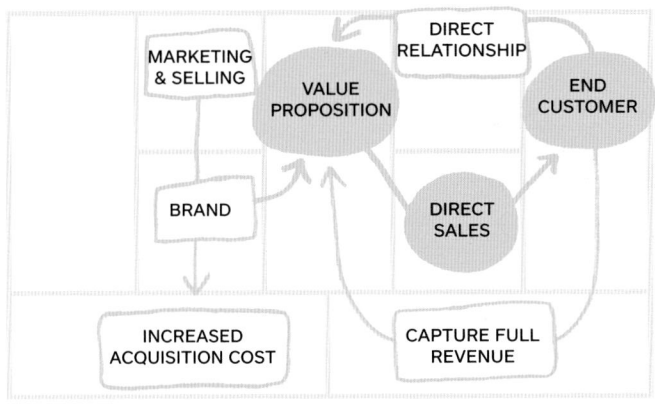

Disintermediators – Establish direct channels to customers where intermediaries previously dominated market access. Replace the reach of intermediaries with your own (often creative) marketing, customer acquisition activities, and strong brand. Develop a better market understanding, build stronger customer relationships, and capture the full revenue, which you previously shared with intermediaries.

EXAMPLES
Dollar Shave Club (DSC), Nespresso, Gore-Tex

TRIGGER QUESTION
How could we cut out the middleman and create a direct access to our end-customers?

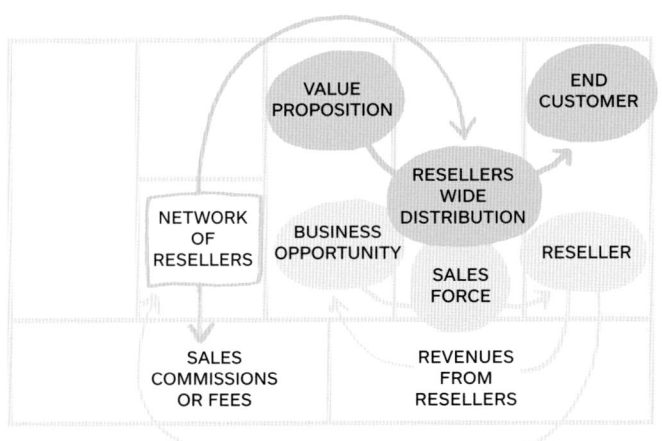

Opportunity Builders – Create business opportunities for others to sell the company's products and services. Help others make money and/or gain status, which is a powerful incentive to help you increase your market reach.

EXAMPLES
Tupperware, Grameen Phone, J. Hilburn

TRIGGER QUESTION
How could we make it attractive for a large number of people or third-party businesses to sell our products and services?

Dollar Shave Club

In 2012, Dollar Shave Club (DSC) launches with a viral marketing campaign and disrupts the market for men's shaving products by selling directly to consumers.

Dollar Shave Club spotted consumer inconveniences, where most saw an over-served market. In the shaving market, men had to choose between (supposedly) high-tech razors or low-cost, low-functionality tools. DSC aimed to change this by providing an end-to-end customer experience with affordable shaving products.

In 2012, DSC launched its online store and quickly disrupted the overpriced men's razor blade market. It purchased its products from wholesalers, removed the traditional physical retail channel, and sold razors and blades online at a lower price.

DSC focused heavily on online marketing to replace the reach of the eliminated middleman. Its launch video with founder Michael Dubin showcased the brand's sense of humor and went viral. Editorial content accompanies each delivery, often with a humorous twist.

The company was acquired by Unilever in 2016 for approximately $1 billion.[15]

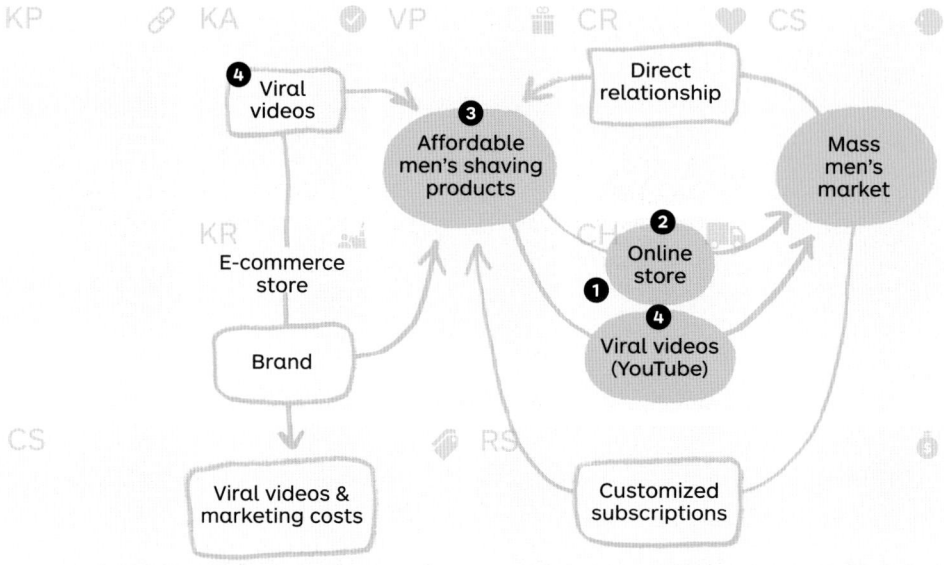

1 Eliminate (or Go Around) the Middleman

DSC cuts out retail stores to sell directly. On the upside, this means saving margins traditionally paid to retailers. On the downside, it means losing the broad market reach of retailers.

2 Build an Optimized Direct Channel

The company launches its online store in 2012, which gives it full control over the customer experience, relationships, and data. DSC uses this channel to continuously test its product line and optimize its value proposition.

3 Differentiate Your Value Proposition

DSC competes on an end-to-end customer buying experience with affordable products. Its flexible subscription plans allow members to buy their first product for just $1 and then choose the products and shipping frequency.

4 Replace the Reach of the "Historic" Middleman with Innovative Marketing

Because DSC can't rely on the reach of a retailer, it creates visibility and brand recognition with its viral videos. DSC keeps consumers coming back with educational videos and editorial content delivered with its unique brand voice.

DollarShaveClub.com - Our Blades Are F***ing Great

Published on Mar 6, 2012   👍 133K   👎 2.6K   ➤ SHARE   ☰+ SAVE   •••

As of November 2019
Dollar Shave Club's first video has

26,525,768
views[16]

69%
retention
rate

Portion of customers
that come back
and transact
in the first month
after making
an initial purchase.[17]

Disruptive Direct to Consumer Brands

Brands with a singular product focus and an elevated customer experience have led the recent growth in direct-to-consumer (DTC) brands.

DTC companies have used disintermediation to become successful by controlling: (1) their relationship with the customer, (2) the presentation of their products whether online or instore, (3) the collection of customer data, and (4) the speed to market of new products.

Increasingly, DTCs are also moving out of an online-only presence into physical stores (Warby Parker, Bonobos, and Glossier, for instance). These physical stores further cement the brand relationship (customers can actually try before they buy) and allow the brands to tailor a physical experience.

Incumbent	Product and Global Market Size (USD)	D2C Brand
Nike	SNEAKERS $62.5 billion	Allbirds
Colgate	ORAL CARE $28 billion	Quip
Luxottica	EYEWEAR $123.58 billion	Warby Parker

Tupperware

In 1948, Tupperware takes off when it starts selling through Tupperware Home Parties, empowering women to sell to other women, using their social networks.

Although Earl Tupper invented his now-ubiquitous Wonderlier Bowl in 1946, it wasn't until he partnered with Brownie Wise to create Tupperware Home Parties in 1948 that the innovative, bell-shaped plastic containers took off.

Brownie Wise pioneered the Hostess Group Demonstrations (aka Tupperware Parties) in order to tap into the power of women's social networks for personalized, in-home demonstrations.

Tupperware turned the initial challenge of selling plastics into an opportunity for women to make money independently from their husbands. The independent dealers were so successful that Tupperware abandoned in-store sales completely in 1951.

Tupperware was a women-focused business, empowering women to sell to other women, using their social networks as a means of expanding their reach and building trust.

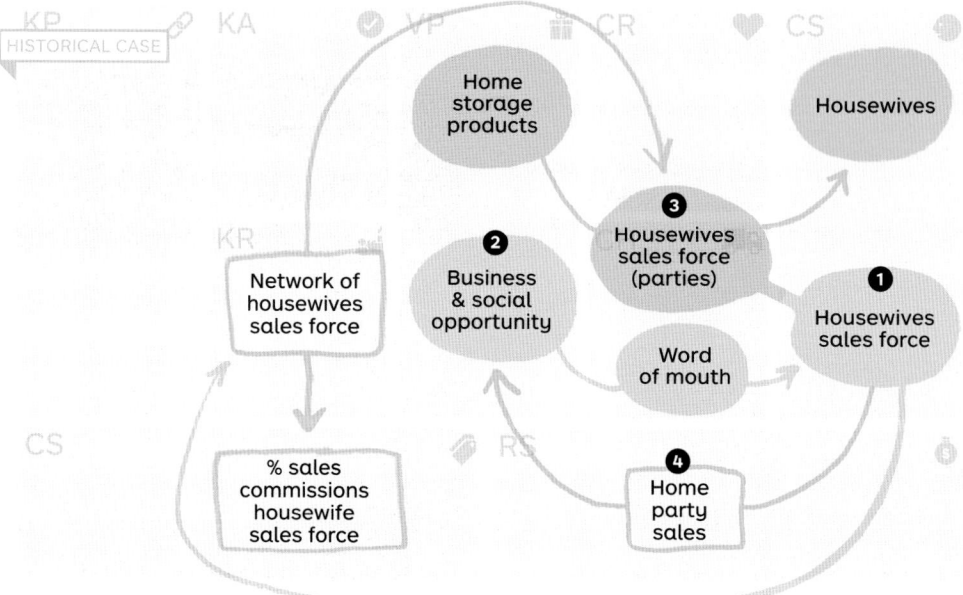

1 Identify Who You Can Create an Opportunity for to Help You Sell

After their contribution to the WW2 war effort, women are often told to go back to the kitchen. Brownie Wise sees how Tupperware can offer housewives an opportunity to become independent Tupperware dealers.

3 Develop the Channel

By 1954 there are 20,000 people in the network of dealers and none of them are employees of Tupperware: they are private contractors who collectively act as the channel between the company and the consumer.[18]

2 Design the Opportunity

Wise pioneers Tupperware Parties, where a hostess opens up her social network and the Tupperware dealer demonstrates the products. Hostesses receive products as a reward for hosting, and dealers get a cut of the sales.

4 Earn from Helping Others

Women are convinced of the utility of the product by seeing it in person and by receiving persuasive recommendations from friends. This channel is so successful that Tupperware decides to abandon in-store sales completely in 1951.

70%

In the 1950s, 70% of U.S. homes included a working husband and a stay-at-home wife.[19]

Sales Force Growth[20]
Tupperware dealer growth during 1954

20,000

7,000

January   December

$233 million

Tupperware sales of home storage products soar and hit $25 million in 1954 (more than $233 million in 2019's money), driven entirely by the sales efforts of Tupperware dealers.[21]

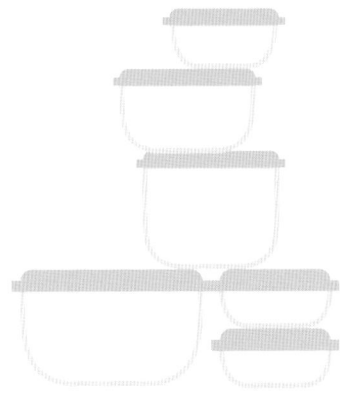

By the 1990s, the percentage of U.S. homes that owned at least one item of Tupperware was[22]

90%

A Tupperware Career

Rita Richardson receives her Pontiac, presented by Tupperware Sales Counselor Homer Wilson.

Peggy Allison shows delight as Brownie awards her a new Ford, at Tupperware's Jubilee.

Ruth Acker and her distributor Leonard Kopowski admire her new Ford, awarded by Tupperware.

"I'll never forget my first Tupperware Party! I was nervous, of course, but thrilled to find I was really a Tupperware dealer at last. It's wonderful to be a part of our national 'family' and yet be in business for myself!"

Fleda Segraves receives a $5,000 mink coat from Brownie.

Put yourself in the Tupperware Picture

Natura

The modern-day version of Tupperware is Natura, one of the largest cosmetics companies in Latin America. It has been using a direct selling model called Selling through Relationships since 1974.

1.7 Million

number of sales consultants in the Natura network[23]

Hundreds of thousands of female entrepreneurs act as brand ambassadors and beauty advisors and sell Natura products. In 2005, Natura expanded to retail stores with its first boutique in Paris, France. In 2012, it added a digital platform to support sales consultants globally, with online courses and support features.

In May 2019, Natura agreed to purchase Avon, its largest direct selling competitor, in a share swap.

Gravity Creators

Lock In Customers

Make it difficult for customers to leave or switch to competitors. Create switching costs where previously there were none and turn transactional industries into ones with long-term relationships.

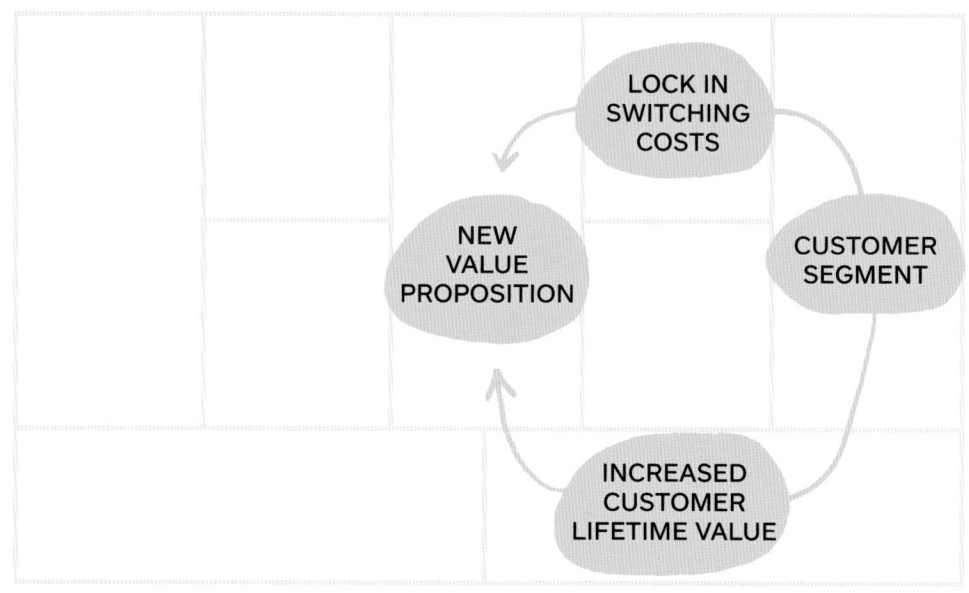

TRIGGER QUESTION

How could we make it difficult for customers to leave and increase switching costs in a positive way?

Assessment Question
How easy or difficult is it for our customers to leave or switch to another company?

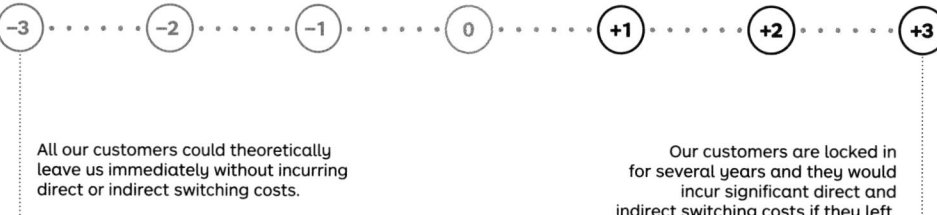

All our customers could theoretically leave us immediately without incurring direct or indirect switching costs.

Our customers are locked in for several years and they would incur significant direct and indirect switching costs if they left.

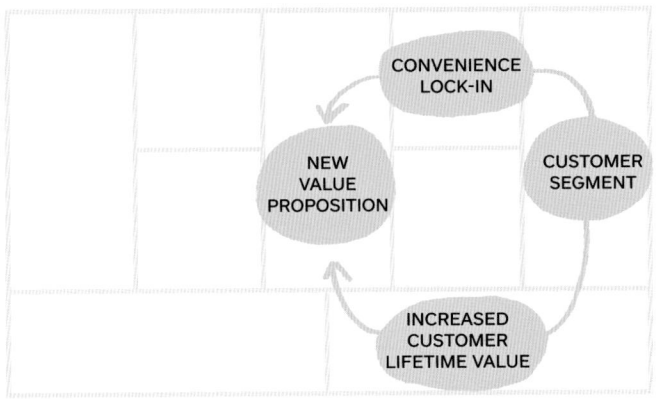

Stickiness Scalers – Increase stickiness by making it inconvenient for customers to leave. Inconvenience may be related to the difficulty of transferring data, steep learning curves, onerous departure procedures, or other customer pains if they decide to leave.

EXAMPLE
Microsoft Windows

TRIGGER QUESTION
How can we increase customer stickiness?

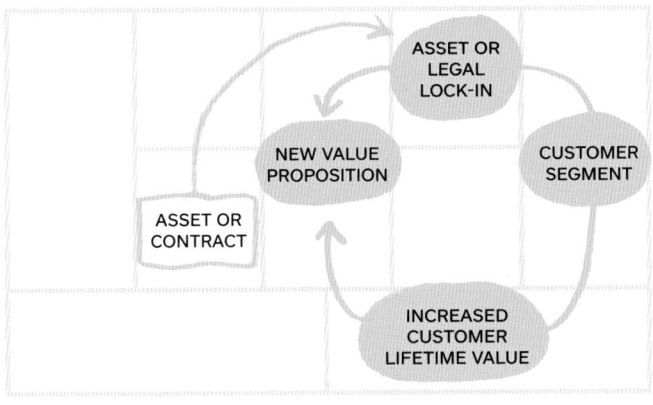

Superglue Makers – Make it difficult for customers to leave by locking them in. Lock-in may occur based on multiyear contracts, upfront sunk costs, cancellation fees, elimination of alternatives, and other techniques.

EXAMPLES
Microsoft Xbox, Nespresso

TRIGGER QUESTION
How can we lock in customers?

Microsoft Windows

In 1990 Microsoft got 30 PC manufacturers to preinstall Windows 3.0 on their machines. That move effectively locked in millions of users into the Microsoft ecosystem and generated recurring revenues for over two decades.

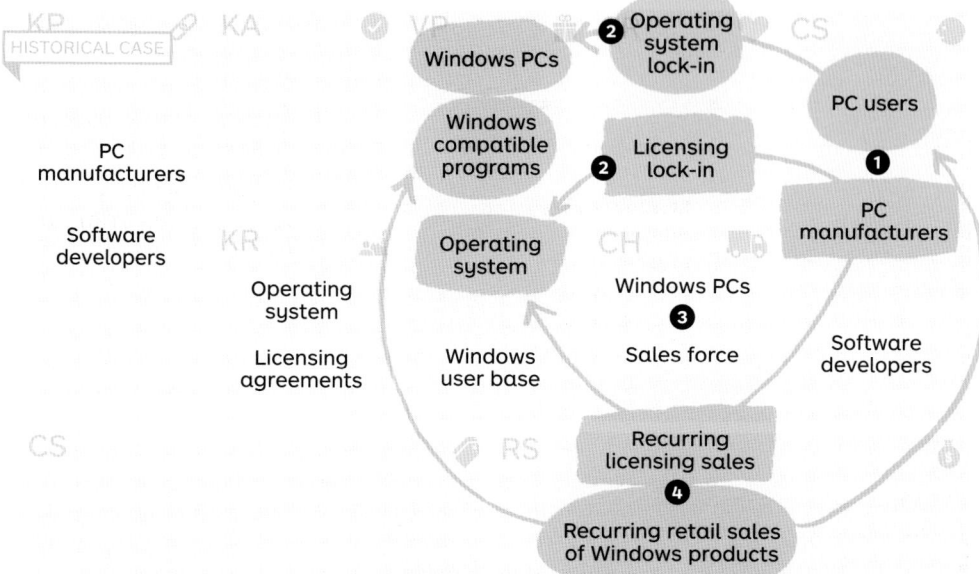

Microsoft originally launched Windows in 1985 as an add-on to MS-DOS, the original operating system of the PC. However, in 1990, when Microsoft launched Windows 3.0, it leveraged its relationships with PC manufacturers to preinstall the operating system (rather than shipping it separately). More than 30 manufacturers agreed to include the program for free and preinstalled it with every machine. As a result Windows rapidly gained in popularity—shipping over one million copies just two months after launch.[24]

Once consumers had learned how to use Windows and compatible programs, most of them were reluctant to invest the time, cost, and effort to learn a new operating system and new programs. PC users effectively got themselves locked into the Microsoft ecosystem once they purchased their first Windows-equipped PC.

1 Spot a Market with Low Switching Costs for Customers

The early computer market is rather fragmented, and each computer manufacturer operates their own unique operating system. At this time it is relatively easy for customers to switch from one system to another.

2 Create a Value Proposition That Locks Customers In

Windows 3.0 increases switching costs in three ways: (1) PC manufacturers preinstall Windows, increasing the effort needed to switch, (2) the graphical interface and new features steepen the learning curve, (3) Microsoft builds an ecosystem of Windows-compatible software to lock customers in via interoperability.

3 Focus on Scaling First-Time Customer Acquisition

Microsoft scales first-time customer acquisition of Windows 3.0 users in 1990 by getting 30 of the main PC manufacturers to preinstall Windows 3.0 and sign long-term licensing agreements. That puts Windows in the hands of millions of users and effectively locks them in.

4 Enjoy the Benefits of Lock-in

Due to the learning curve and software compatibility advantages, customers continuously come back to buy Windows PCs. This lock-in guarantees recurring licensing royalties from PC manufacturers and Windows sales to retail customers for over two decades.

+ Boost Windows Compatible Software

A key component of Microsoft's lock-in strategy is to boost acquisition of developers to quickly increase the number of software applications available for the Windows ecosystem: Windows-compatible software rises from 700 before the launch of 3.0 to 1,200 one year later, and 5,000 by 1992.[25]

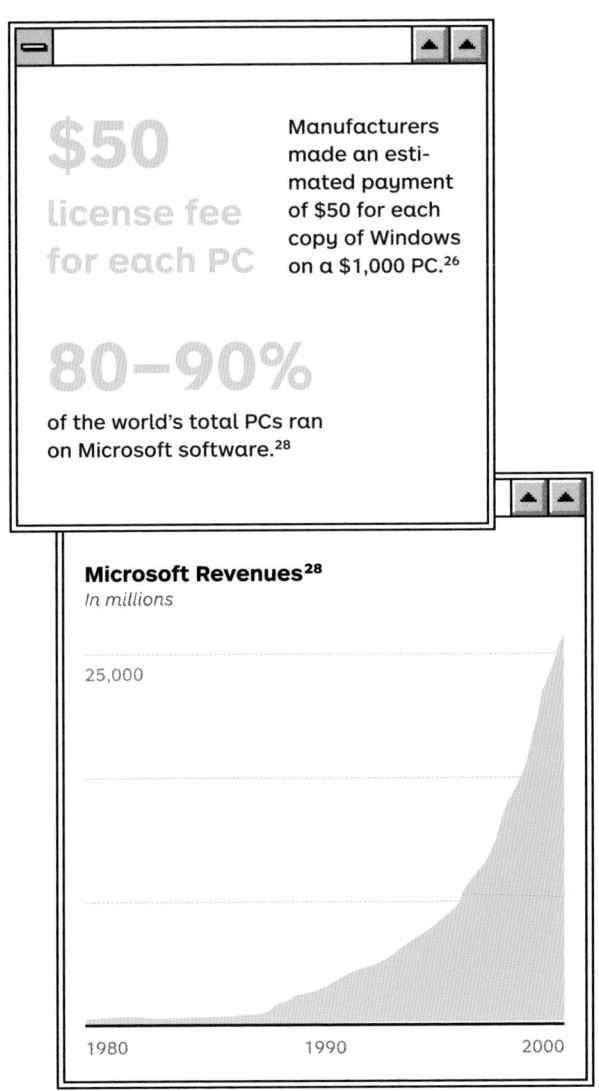

$50
license fee
for each PC

Manufacturers made an estimated payment of $50 for each copy of Windows on a $1,000 PC.[26]

80–90%

of the world's total PCs ran on Microsoft software.[28]

Microsoft Revenues[28]
In millions

Microsoft Xbox

In 2001, Microsoft makes its first foray into the living room and releases the original Xbox game console. The subsidized console locks gamers in and increases their lifetime value from game sales and royalty payments from third-party game developers.

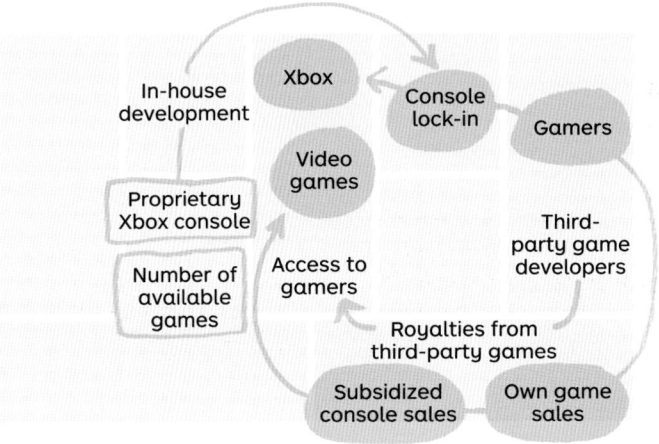

Microsoft developed the Xbox in 2001 as a closed-system gaming console. They attracted and locked in a large number of gamers by subsidizing console sales. Microsoft monetized the Xbox by selling exclusive in-house games like *Halo* and from royalties paid by third-party game developers for every game sold. Gamers have been unlikely to switch due to their upfront investment in the console and the library of games they purchased for the platform. Microsoft successfully adopted this business model from the competing Sony PlayStation 2.

$5
billion

The *Halo* franchise has made in games and hardware sales as of 2015.[29]

Questions
for Leaders

Market Explorers

How could we tap into new, untapped, or underserved markets with large potential?

Assessment Question
How large and attractive is the untapped market potential we are going after?

There is little untapped potential and the market is shrinking.

The market potential is large, not yet occupied, and growing.

Channel Kings

TRIGGER QUESTION

How could we increase market access and build strong and direct channels to our end customers?

Assessment Question
Do we have large-scale and, ideally, direct access to our end customers?

We have limited market access and depend on intermediaries to get our products and services to customers and interact with them.

We have large-scale market access and own the channel(s) and relationships with end-users of our products and services.

Gravity Creators

TRIGGER QUESTION

How could we make it difficult for customers to leave and increase switching costs in a positive way?

Assessment Question
How easy or difficult is it for our customers to leave or switch to another company?

All our customers could theoretically leave us immediately without incurring direct or indirect switching costs.

Our customers are locked in for several years and they would incur significant direct and indirect switching costs if they left.

Backstage Disruption

Resource Castles

p.166	**User Base Castles**	Waze
p.168	**Platform Castles**	DiDi
p.170	**IP Castles**	Dyson
p.171	**Brand Castles**	Wedgwood

Activity Differentiators

p.174	**Efficiency Disruptors**	Ford Model T
p.175	**Speed Masters**	Zara
p.176	**Sustainability Masters**	Patagonia
p.177	**Build-to-Order**	Dell Computers

Scalers

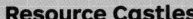

p.180	**Delegators**	IKEA
p.182	**Licensors**	ARM
p.184	**Franchisors**	Harper

A radical change in how value is created.

Resource Castles

Build Moats

Build a competitive advantage with key resources that are difficult or impossible for competitors to copy.

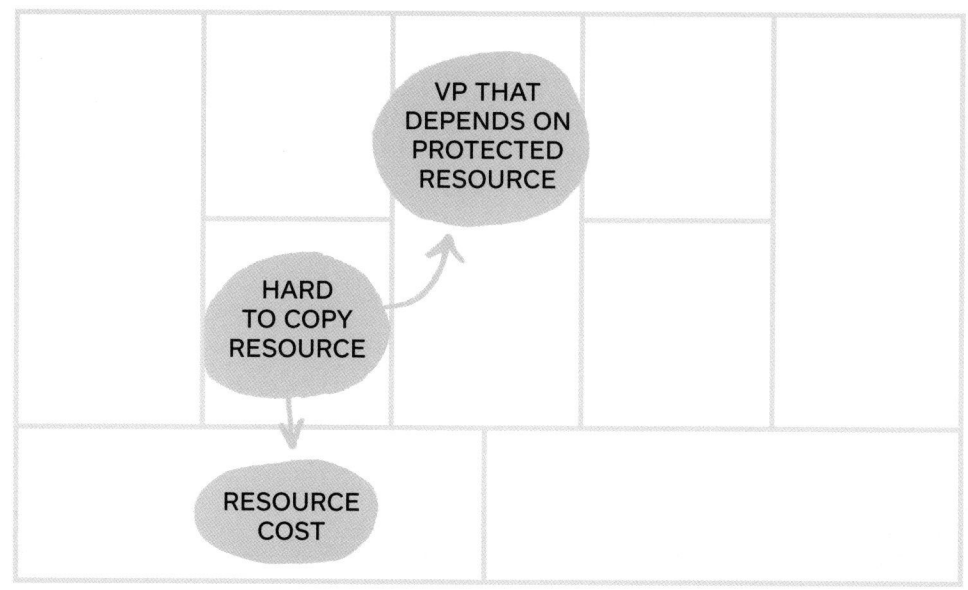

TRIGGER QUESTION
How could we make difficult-to-copy resources a key pillar of our business model?

Assessment Question
Do we own key resources that are difficult or impossible to copy and which give us a significant competitive advantage?

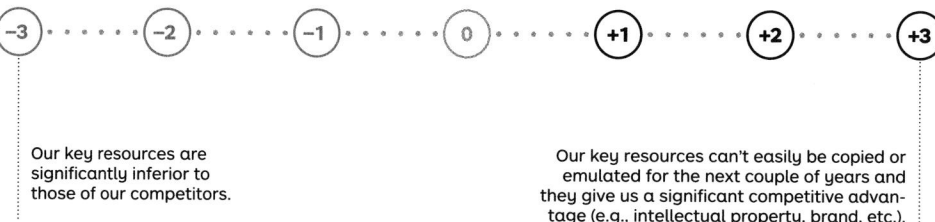

Our key resources are significantly inferior to those of our competitors.

Our key resources can't easily be copied or emulated for the next couple of years and they give us a significant competitive advantage (e.g., intellectual property, brand, etc.).

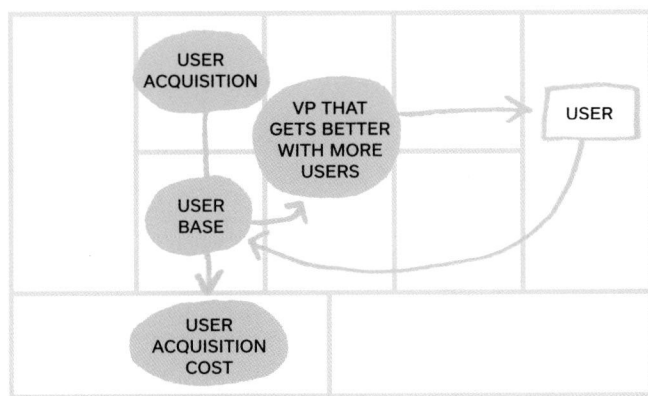

User Base Castles – Create a business model with network effects in which a large number of users equals the relative value for other users. Acquire a large user base to establish a competitive advantage that makes it hard for anybody else to catch up.

TRIGGER QUESTION
How could we establish a competitive advantage rooted in a large user base and network effects in our value proposition?

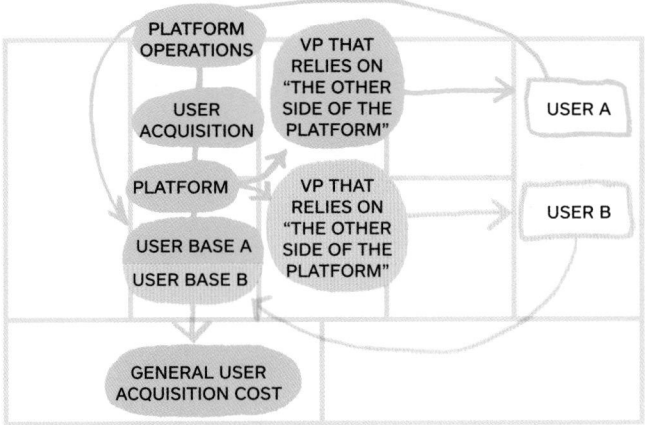

Platform Castles – Create a business model with network effects in which a large number of users represents value to one or more other distinct sets of users, and vice versa. That makes it hard for anybody else with fewer users to compete or to catch up.

TRIGGER QUESTION
How could we create a multisided platform that depends on the existence of two or more large user bases?

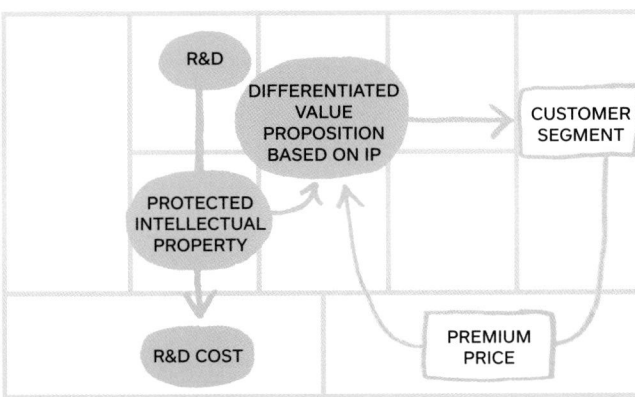

IP Castles – Use protected intellectual property (IP) to outcompete others. Offer distinct value propositions that are hard or impossible to copy if you don't own the IP.

TRIGGER QUESTION
How could we use protected intellectual property as a competitive advantage (in arenas where it hasn't mattered before)?

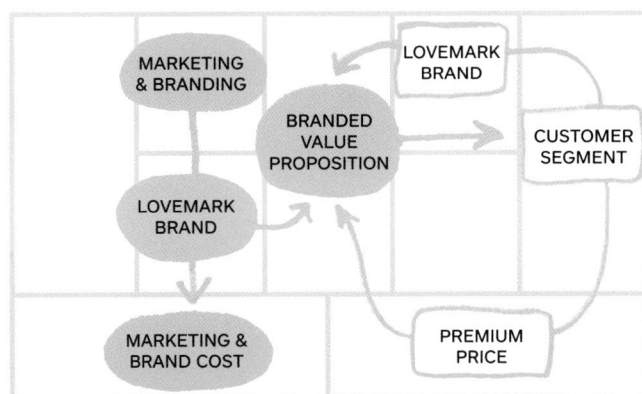

Brand Castle – Use a strong brand to outcompete others. Focus on value propositions in which a strong brand is an essential component.

TRIGGER QUESTION
How could we make brand a relevant competitive advantage (in an area where it hasn't been so far)?

Waze

In 2008, Waze develops a traffic navigation system that gets better with every additional user. Real-time information from users helps shorten commutes and reduce traffic congestion.

Ehud Shabtai, Amir Shinar, and Uri Levine founded Waze in 2008. The business idea originated from a crowdsourced project developed by Ehud Shabtai in 2006. The project aimed to create a free digital map of Israel with free updates and distribution.

Waze then evolved into a traffic navigation app that combines the reach of a social network with GPS data to shorten the commutes of its users and reduce traffic congestion globally. It's a great example of network effects, where the service becomes more valuable as more people use it.

Waze had more than 50 million users globally when Google purchased it in 2013 for $966 million, to improve its mapping service.[30]

INVENT PATTERNS

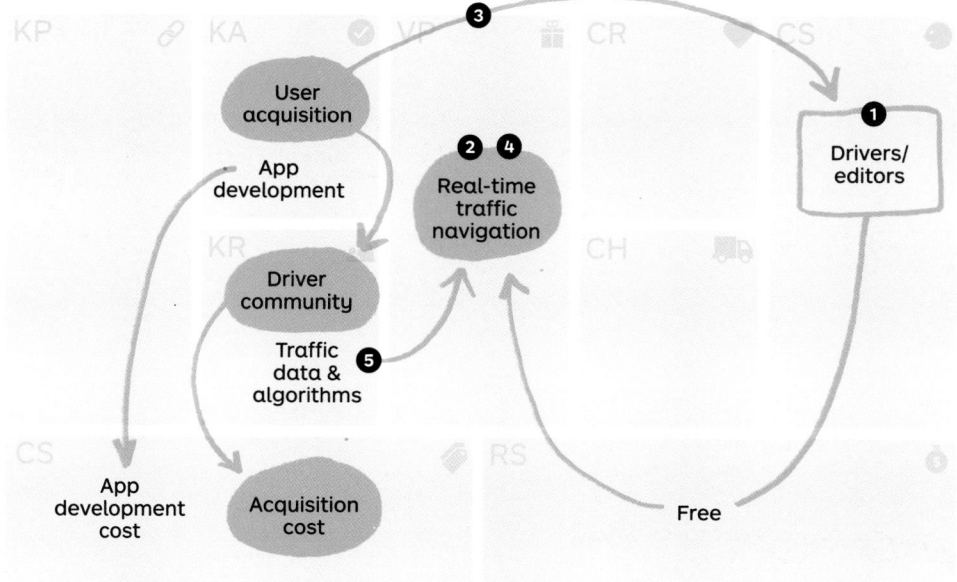

1 Identify User Base for Competitive Advantage

Waze identifies its users as a critical resource to improve its digital maps. They instrumentalize users by collecting the data they generate and by asking them to actively help improve maps.

2 Solve Pains and Create Gains for Those Users

Waze is not just a voice navigation system. Its traffic algorithm optimizes routes to help users avoid congestion and solves the pain of long delays in commutes for millions of drivers globally.

3 Acquire Users Aggressively

To build its user base quickly, Waze makes the strategic choice to offer the app for free. Users are drawn to the free tool and then stay for the steadily improving value proposition (i.e., the effectiveness of the algorithm).

4 Use Users in Your Value Proposition

Users contribute in three ways: (1) Waze collects driving times and GPS data from all users, (2) active users post traffic updates, and (3) a volunteer army of editors update maps and translate them into other languages.

5 Reap Competitive Advantage

With every new user, Waze algorithms become smarter, creating an even more attractive value proposition to existing and new users. Waze's large and active global user base is difficult to replicate by a competitor.

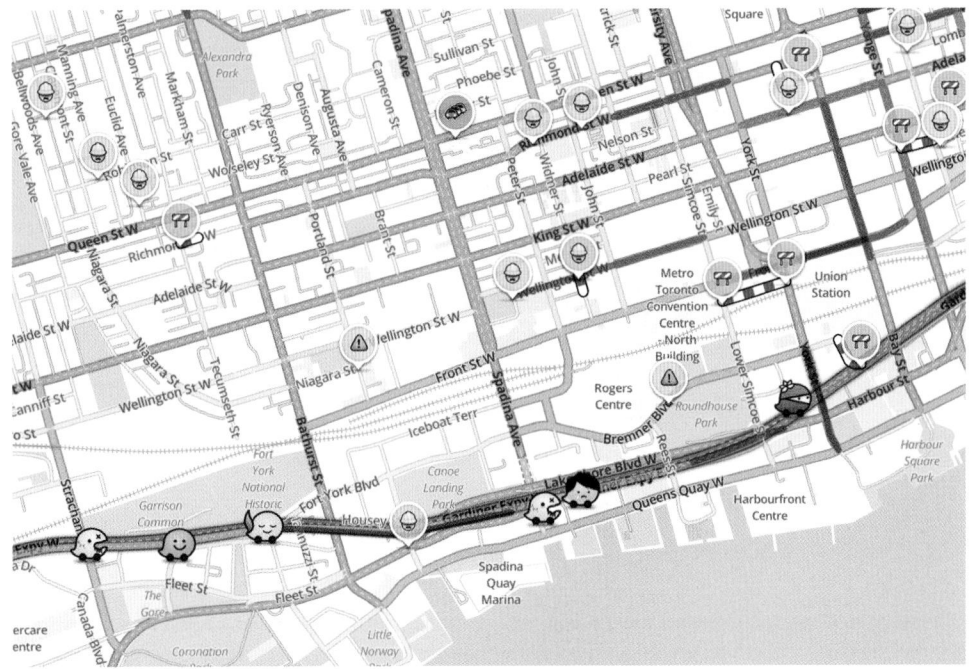

Example of a live Waze map of Toronto, generated from information reported by their user base.

Waze User Base [31]
In millions

```
120

80

40

     2011  2012  2013  2017  2018  2019
```

130 million

monthly active users in 2019. Waze's user base has grown from 7 million in 2011.[32]

Volunteer editors Waze counted in 2016:

420 thousand[33]

Network Effects

A network effect occurs when a product or service becomes more valuable to its users as more people use it.
A *direct network effect* occurs when the increase in the user base of a product or service creates more value based on the increased number of direct connections between these users. Examples include the telephone, WhatsApp, Skype, or Facebook.

2 Active Users
= 1 Connection

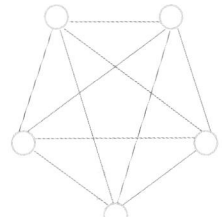

5 Active Users
= 10 Connections

12 Active Users
= 66 Connections

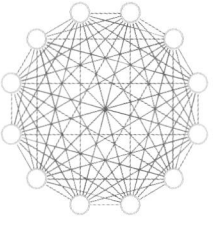

Adapted from Andreessen Horowitz

BACKSTAGE DISRUPTION

DiDi

In 2012, DiDi launches a ride-hailing service and rapidly acquires the largest pool of drivers and passengers in the industry, making it hard for anyone else to compete in this space.

DiDi—the Chinese equivalent to America's Uber—was born out of the desire to fix the enormous traffic congestion and transportation problem in Beijing. Prior to the introduction of ride-hailing services in China, passenger brawls over taxis and exorbitant fares charged by illegal taxis were commonplace in crowded, urban centers. China had a unique problem: a massive population that was already connected through mobile combined with highly congested cities in need of traffic relief.

The word *DiDi* itself means "honk honk" in Chinese, a nod to the perpetual traffic congestion. While it was founded as a taxi-hailing service, it rapidly transformed to a ride-hailing platform.

DiDi's dominance is the result of an aggressive strategy of acquisitions. DiDi purchased its two main rivals (Uber China and Kuaidi Dache) and now matches the largest base of connected passengers with the biggest pool of drivers.

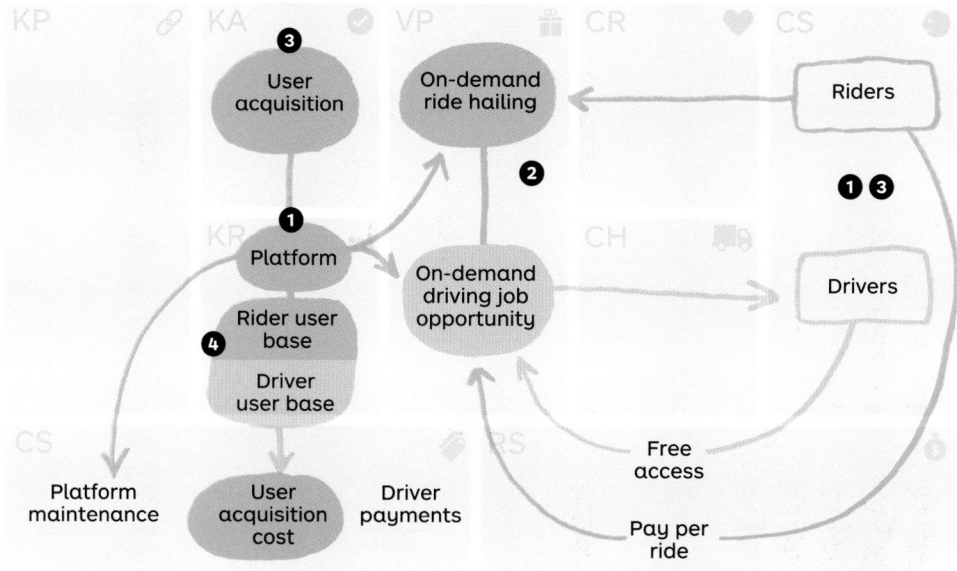

1 Identify How You Can Connect Two Groups via a Platform

DiDi identified the opportunity of improving personal mobility by matching riders and drivers. Originally, DiDi started as a taxi-hailing service, but rapidly expanded to occasional drivers to expand its available cars.

2 Create the Value Proposition for Each Group

DiDi attracts passengers with its large pool of drivers, consistent pricing, reduced wait times, and WeChat and Alipay integrations. It attracts drivers with a large pool of passengers, reduced idle time, and discounts (e.g., gas, insurance, etc.).

3 Aggressively Acquire Both Groups

DiDi pursued a very aggressive strategy to grow its passenger and driver pools, in particular, by purchasing its two main rivals (Uber China and Kuaidi Dache). As of January 2019, DiDi had more than 31 million drivers servicing 550 million registered passengers.

4 Reap Competitive Advantage

The sheer size of the two interdependent customer groups has created a competitive advantage for DiDi, which makes it hard for anyone else to compete in the transportation sector in China.

INVENT PATTERNS

550
million registered users[35]

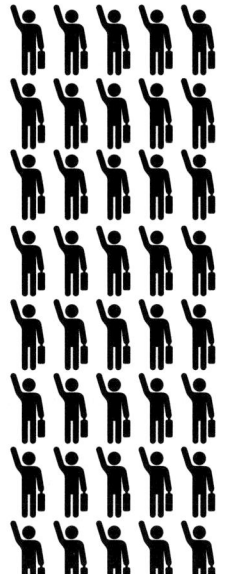

👤 = 13.75 million users

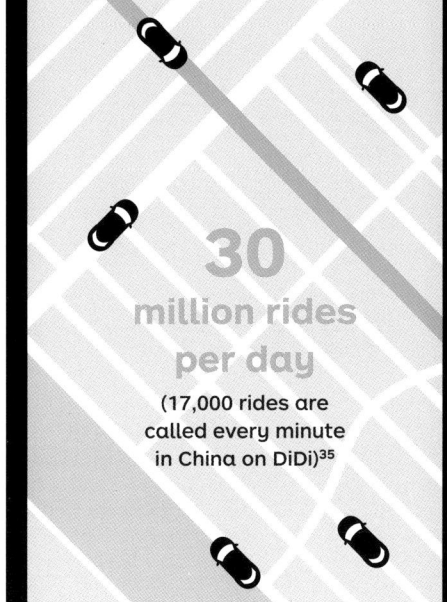

30
million rides per day

(17,000 rides are called every minute in China on DiDi)[35]

Network Effects

Two-sided network effects occur when increases in usage by one set of users increases the value of a complementary product to another distinct set of users. Examples include DiDi, Uber, Open Table, Airbnb, eBay, and Craigslist.

23 million
Private cars

3 million
Carpooling

3 million
Taxis

340 thousand
Chauffeured rides

31
million registered drivers[36]

11
billion rides

In 2018 DiDi handled an estimated 11 billion rides — up from 7.4 billion in 2017.[34]

48.8
billion km

DiDi users traveled in 2018, of which...

800
million km

...800 million kilometers on pooled trips, saving 43 million liters of fuel and 97,000 tons of CO_2 emissions.[36]

Dyson

Starting with a vacuum in 1993, Dyson tackles a wide range of product engineering challenges with an ingenious approach. It invests heavily in R&D to launch innovative, best-in-class products that it sells at a premium and protects with patents.

In the 1980s, James Dyson developed revolutionary, bagless, cyclonic vacuum technology. He attempted to license it to vacuum manufacturers, but the companies rejected his ideas. The technology was indeed better but this product would remove the recurring revenues from bag and filter sales.

Dyson didn't give up and manufactured his own vacuum in 1993, fighting off several patent infringement lawsuits along the way. Subsequently, Dyson's business portfolio grew by continuing to manufacture superior products from patented IP. The company expanded into hand dryers, fans, air purifiers, hair dryers, robot vacuums, and even electric cars. Each product is the result of a leap in technology (with patented IP).

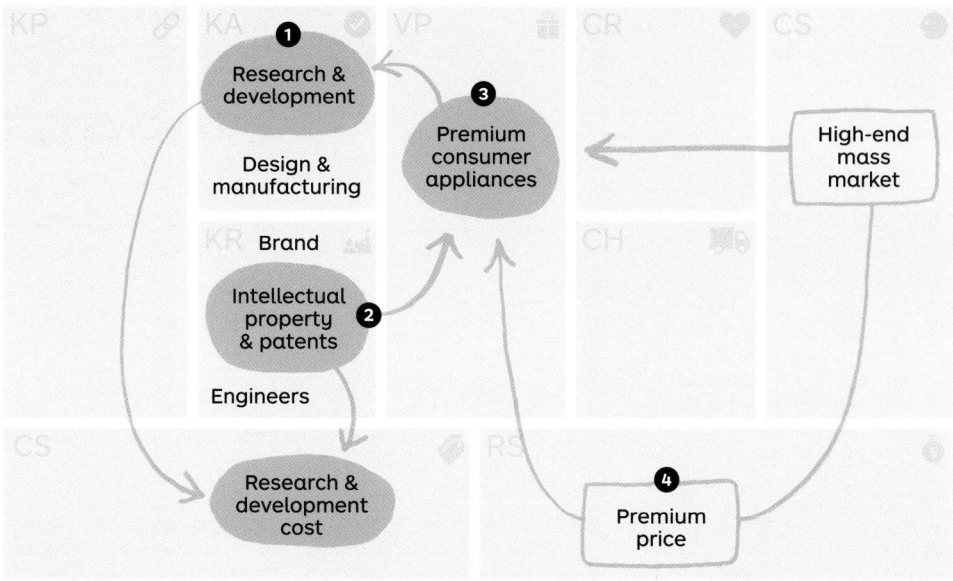

1 Invest Heavily in R&D

Dyson's ambition is to produce the best in class or nothing in each product range it enters. The company reinvests approximately 20% of its earnings into research and development.

2 Patent Aggressively

Dyson protects its product innovations with many patents. For the development of the Supersonic Hair Dryer, Dyson spent $71 million and filed 100 patent applications. The company reportedly spends over $6.5 million per year on patent litigation.[37]

3 Differentiate with the Best Products and Services

Dyson uses its IP to create the best product within each category it competes. Its vacuums, for instance, include technologies that have never been incorporated into its competitors' products.

4 Sell at a Premium

Dyson sells its home appliances at a premium price point. With a $700 price tag for its upright vacuum, Dyson is the most expensive vacuum on the market, with the cheapest alternative selling for $40.

+ Brand

Dyson developed a strong brand by transforming the sleepy home appliance market into one filled with cutting edge technology and sleek industrial design. Dyson has often been dubbed the "Apple of home appliances," as the company strives for perfection before releasing a product.

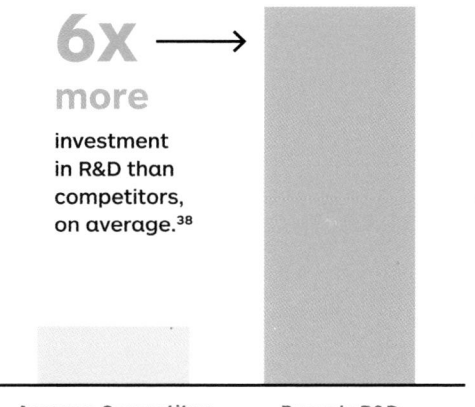

6x →

more

investment in R&D than competitors, on average.[38]

Average Competitor Investment	Dyson's R&D Investment

100 million machines

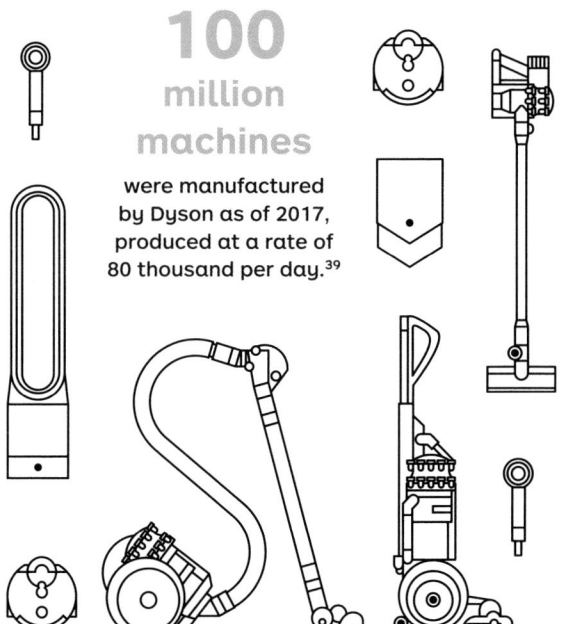

were manufactured by Dyson as of 2017, produced at a rate of 80 thousand per day.[39]

Wedgwood

In 1765, Josiah Wedgwood wins a royal pottery competition and is declared Her Majesty's Potter. He uses that recognition to build a strong and defensible brand, markets his pieces as Queensware, and generates a fortune of $3.4 billion in today's market value.

HISTORICAL CASE

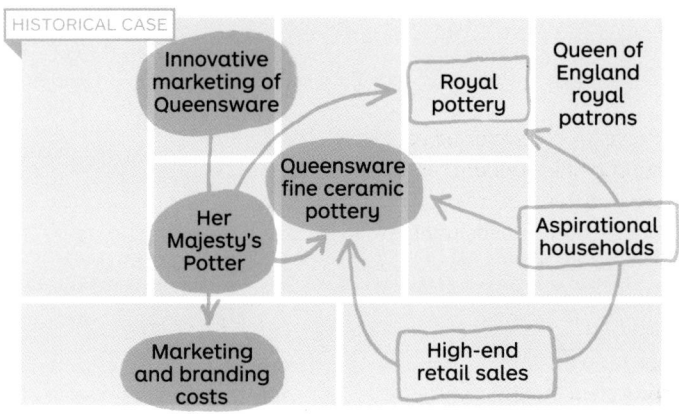

Wedgwood used his royal recognition to target aspirational consumers who wanted to drink tea like the upper class, but could not necessarily afford expensive porcelain. He created a brand in an area where there was none previously. Wedgwood also convinced consumers to buy pottery for display rather than use and used the strength of his brand to protect his business from competition for decades.

245 years

Wedgwood's Jasper vases have stayed in continuous production since 1774.[40]

BACKSTAGE DISRUPTION

Activity Differentiators

Better Configure Activities

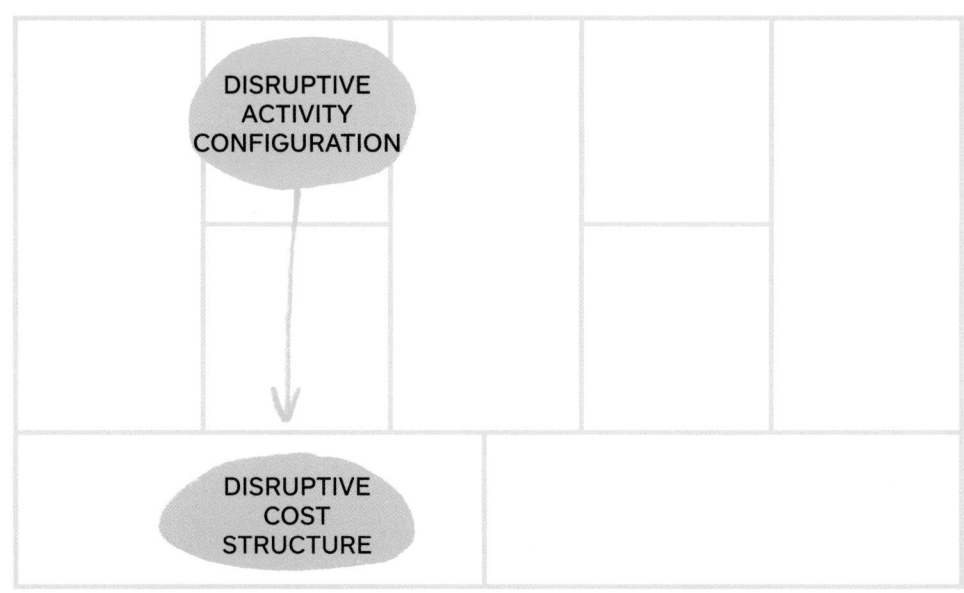

Radically change which activities they perform and how they combine them to create and deliver value to customers. Create innovative value propositions based on activity differentiation.

TRIGGER QUESTION
Could we create (significantly more) value for customers by performing new activities or configuring activities in innovative ways?

Assessment Question

Do we create significant value for customers because we perform and configure activities in disruptively innovative ways?

We operate conventional activities that perform similarly or worse than comparable organizations.

Our key activities can't easily be copied or emulated for the next couple of years and they give us a significant competitive advantage (e.g., cost effectiveness, scale, etc.).

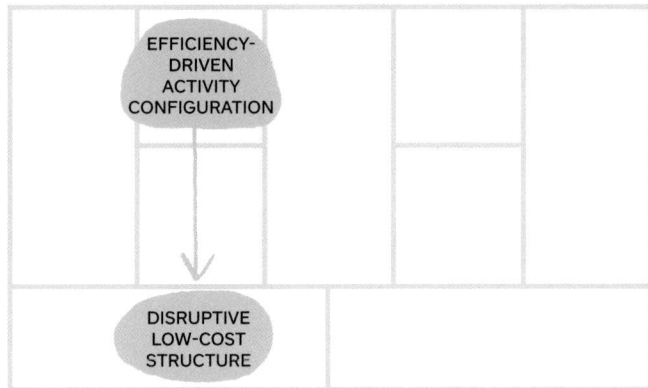

Efficiency Disruptors – Substantially change which activities you perform and how you configure them in order to become radically more efficient. Use this to create a disruptively low cost structure. You may or may not pass the cost savings onto customers.

TRIGGER QUESTION
How can we radically change the configuration of our activities to compete with a disruptive cost structure?

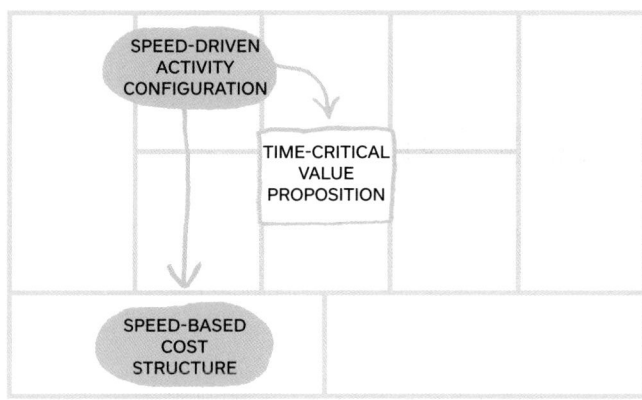

Speed Masters – Build radically new activity configurations focused on speed. Create new, time-critical value propositions and accelerate time to market.

TRIGGER QUESTION
How might we put speed at the center of our activity configuration to develop new, time-critical value propositions?

173

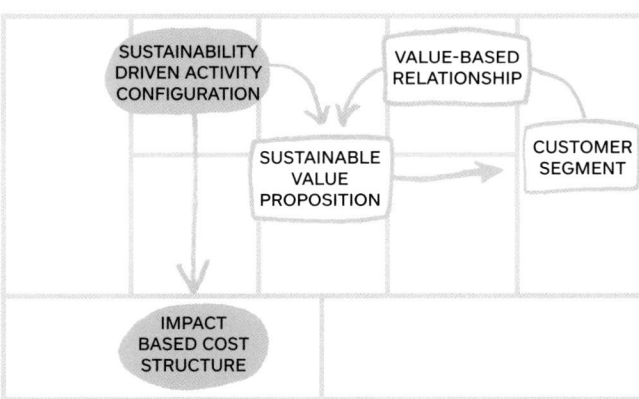

Sustainability Masters – Adjust activities such that they are environmentally friendly and positively impact society, even if it may lead to higher costs. Cut out activities that hurt the planet and society while engaging in those that add benefits.

TRIGGER QUESTION
How might we reconfigure our activities to have a positive environmental and social impact?

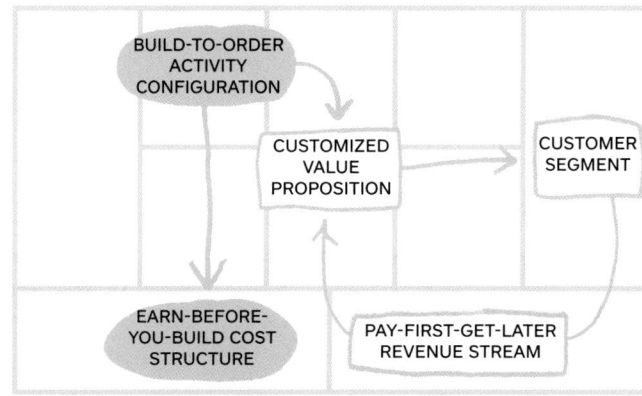

Build-to-Order – Configure products or services to match the exact specifications of customers. Adjust activities such that they only go into motion when an order is received.

TRIGGER QUESTION
How might we reconfigure our activities to build to order and only start building after order confirmation and payment?

Ford Model T

In 1913, Henry Ford introduces the assembly line to automobile production, slashes the cost of production by a factor of three, and disrupts the industry in the process.

In the early 1900s, automobiles were considered toys for the rich, and they were often overly complicated, requiring a trained chauffeur. Henry Ford was determined to build a safe, affordable automobile for the masses, and he sought any production efficiency to deliver it. Ford looked outside of his own industry, which led him to invent the assembly line.

The introduction of the assembly line reduced the time to assemble each car from over 12 hours to about 90 minutes. Training employees on just one task in the assembly line also allowed Ford to hire lower-skilled workers and further slash costs. Model T production went from 100 cars a day to up to 1,000—which is similar to a modern factory—and enabled a price drop from $850 to $300.[41]

After just 10 years of using the assembly line, Ford's 10 millionth Model T rolled off the line.[42]

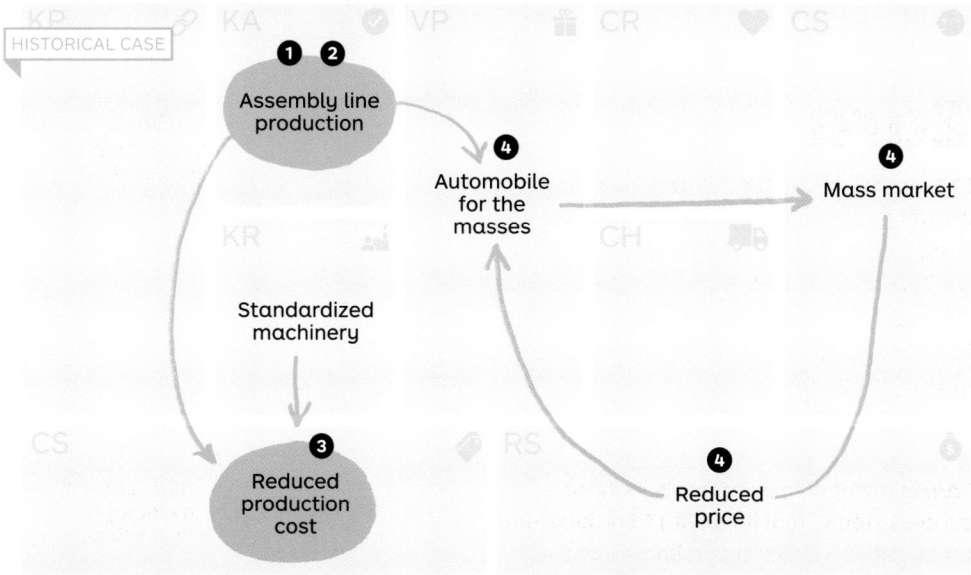

HISTORICAL CASE

1 Scout Other Industries for Innovative Efficiency-Driven Activity Configurations

Ford is inspired by the continuous-flow production methods used by flour mills, breweries, canneries, and meat packers of the time. He believes he can adapt these activity configurations to the automobile industry.

2 Adapt Outside Ideas to Your Industry

Ford introduces the assembly line to the automobile industry. The car assembly process is standardized and broken into 84 steps.[44] Workers remain at one station and focus on one task while the car moves down a mechanized line—as opposed to working in a team to assemble each car.

3 Reap the Benefits

Rapidly, car production costs go down with this new way of working, while productivity goes up. Standardized machines lead to higher quality and more reliable production cost. Workers can now assemble a car in about 90 minutes compared to over 12 hours previously.[43]

4 Disrupt Your Industry

In 1914 Ford's 13,000 workers build around 300,000 cars—more than his nearly 300 competitors manage to build with 66,350 employees.[45] As he lowers production costs, he lowers the price of an automobile from $850 to less than $300 and disrupts the car industry.

Zara

In the 1980s Zara disrupts the fashion industry by radically reconfiguring the supply chain and creating the fast-fashion category. It is able to almost instantly react to fashion trends by vertically integrating its supply chain.

Zara is a global fashion retailer whose success stems from its ability to reduce lead times and react to trends almost instantaneously. Zara is owned by Inditex, the world's biggest fashion group.

The company was not afraid to go against conventional wisdom, vertically integrate its supply chain, and move its production to Europe (near-shoring), while many players in the fashion industry chose to outsource production to lower-cost factories in Asia.

Zara disrupted the fashion industry by shortening the time to market to less than three weeks from inspiration to retail. Zara created a new category of affordable fast fashion. This model allowed the company to become a heavyweight in the highly competitive fashion industry: as of 2018, Zara was active online and in 96 countries, managed 2,238 physical stores and €18.9 billion annual revenue.[46]

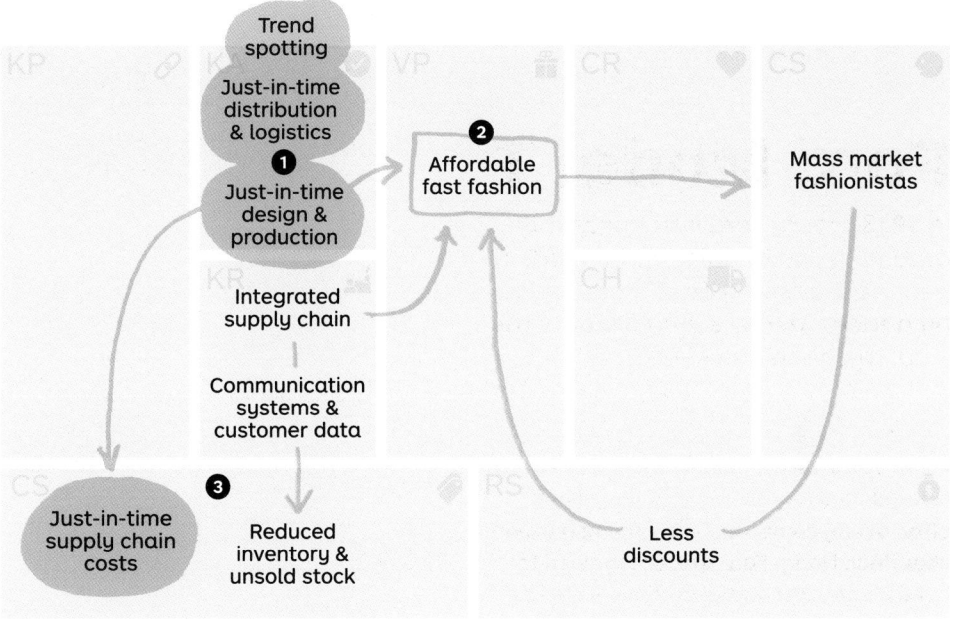

1 Radically Reconfigure Activities for Speed

Zara decides to produce more than half its fashion items locally and in its own facilities to achieve speed. At the time, most large fashion players rely on outsourcing production to Asia for cost reasons. This activity differentiation allows Zara to effectively react with lightning speed to fashion trends.

2 Develop Time-Critical Value Proposition

Zara's value proposition focuses on keeping up with fast-changing fashion trends. Its activity configuration allows it to spot trends and launch new pieces in less than three weeks. Competitors show two collections per year and take over nine months to get items to stores. Zara ships only a few items in each style to its stores, so inventory is always scarce. This leads to constantly changing collections and customers tend to "buy it when they see it," because the clothes won't be around for long.

3 Embrace a New Cost Structure

Higher labor cost was the price to pay for flexibility, full control, and the required speed in its design and production processes. Zara reserves 85% of its factory capacity for in-season adjustments and over 50% of its clothes are designed and manufactured mid-season.[47]

+ Trends, Data, and Communication

Zara trains its retail employees to relay customers' preferences and real-time sales data to designers through effective communication systems. The latest designs and production forecasts are adjusted accordingly. Because Zara manufactures only a limited supply of items, it doesn't have to deal with excess inventory or constant markdowns.

+ Pricing Power

Each store has a limited inventory of items in each style that are replenished based on demand. New styles based on latest trends arrive constantly. As a consequence Zara rarely discounts clothes, contrary to most fashion houses.

Sustainability Master
1973 ~~~ 2019

Patagonia

In 1973, Yvon Chouinard creates an outdoor apparel company whose activities are configured through the lens of environmental protection.

Patagonia was founded by Yvon Chouinard in 1973 to make clothing and equipment for rock climbers. Chouinard was an avid climber who believed in clean climbing with little impact on the outdoors.

From the start Patagonia had a clear focus on environmental protection that reflected the personal ethics of its founder. It was the first California company to use renewable energy sources to power its buildings and one of the first to print its catalogs on recycled paper. Patagonia switched to 100% organically grown cotton in 1994 and removed chlorine from its wool products.

Patagonia's commercial success enabled it to become a visibly activist company. In 2018 it changed its mission statement to "We're in business to save our home planet." It also provides tools and funding to grassroots organizations.

Growth is not the ultimate goal for Patagonia, yet their differentiation and environmental focus has helped them grow sustainably.

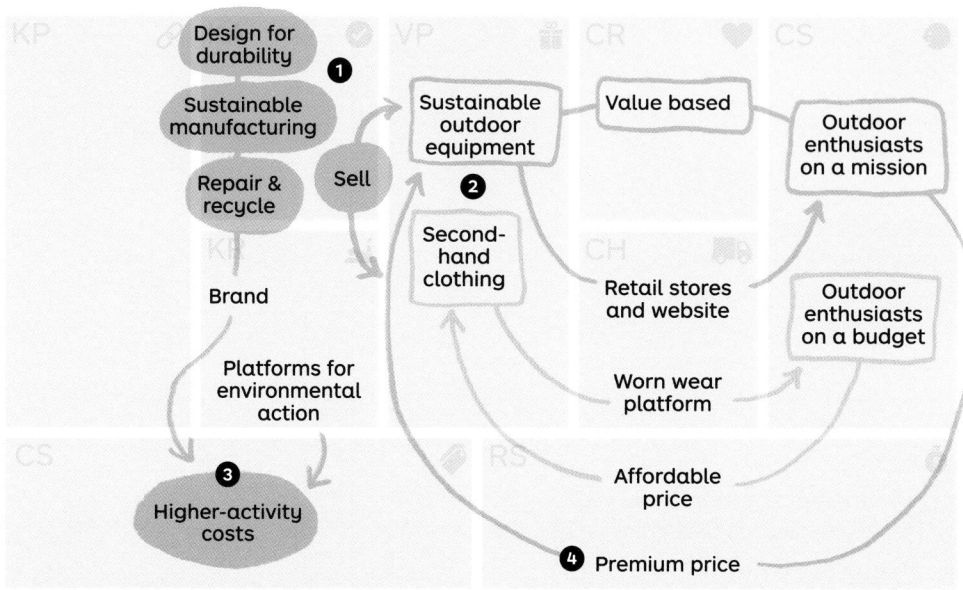

1 Align Activities to Environmental Objectives

Patagonia makes durability a strong constraint in the design and manufacturing of its outdoor clothing equipment, in order to align with its environmental objectives. The goal is to reduce consumption and waste. In addition, the company limits its environmental impact by maximizing the use of organic and recycled materials, by repairing damaged clothes, and by complying with strong environmental protection standards for its entire supply chain.

2 Develop Sustainable Value Propositions

Patagonia makes customers feel they are contributing to protecting the environment by extending its value proposition beyond the functional value proposition of high quality outdoor clothing and equipment. By buying Patagonia products, customers feel they are contributing to the highest environmental standards. Patagonia even launches a second-hand clothing value proposition to limit its environmental footprint and make its products accessible to a larger market.

3 Accept Higher Activity Costs

Patagonia's high sustainability standards lead to higher costs. It uses more costly organic cotton, develops the infrastructure to recycle materials, and educates the public (Footprint Chronicles). It also bears the cost of making its supply chain more environmentally friendly by educating suppliers on sustainable practices.

4 Apply Premium Pricing

Patagonia can charge a premium, because customers accept that environmental friendly production comes at a cost. The company's customers are more environment-conscious than price-conscious.

INVENT PATTERNS

Build-to-Order
1984 ~~~ 2007

Dell Computers

In 1984, Dell disrupts the personal computer market with high quality, low-cost machines that are built-to-order and sold directly to customers.

In 1984, Michael Dell launched his company out of his college dorm room. He recognized that sophisticated computer buyers wanted customized, high quality, technical machines at an affordable cost. This is not something they could get from IBM, which dominated the market at the time.

Dell targeted users by offering customized machines that were built-to-order. Customers would simply dial a toll-free number, place a customized order, and wait for their computer to be delivered by mail.

Dell turned the traditional PC sales model on its head with build-to-order and direct sales. He disrupted the PC industry with customized, high quality, affordable PCs by avoiding retail locations, high-touch sales, and minimizing inventory and inventory depreciation costs.

Dell grew from PCs assembled in a dorm room in 1984 to a $300 million business just five years later.[48]

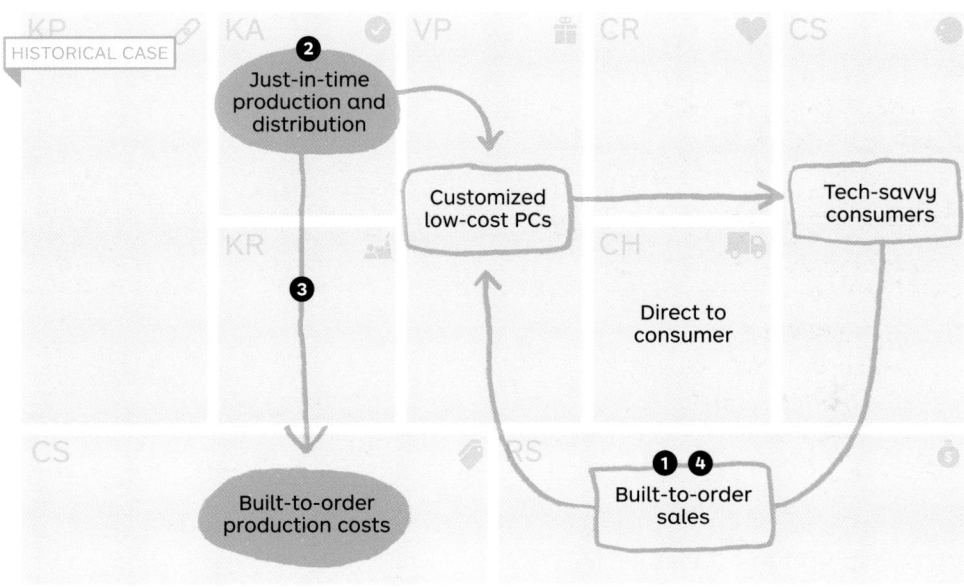

1 Take Customized Orders and Get Paid

In 1984 Dell begins to take customized PC orders over the phone. Buyers determine their exact specifications and pick from a variety of PC components. In 1996, the company brings its direct model to the Web and automates build-to-order.

2 Build the Product

Dell purchases components from PC equipment wholesalers and builds the customized machine himself (just-in-time production) based on the customer's order. He is able to keep the cost of his machines under $1,000.

3 Manage Your Just-in-Time Supply Chain

Contrary to a traditional PC manufacturer, Dell stays away from heavy costs of inventory management, retail, and logistics. Products are built-to-order. This requires Dell to develop excellence around a new set of activities: just-in-time supply chain and production.

4 Pass on Cost Savings to Customers and Disrupt the Market

Dell's build-to-order model avoids unsold PCs and value depreciation. In addition, Dell's direct model and wholesale component purchases further reduce production and distribution costs. This allows him to pass on cost savings in the form of disruptive prices for high quality PCs.

Scalers

Grow Faster

Find radically new ways to scale where others stay stuck in conventional nonscalable business models.

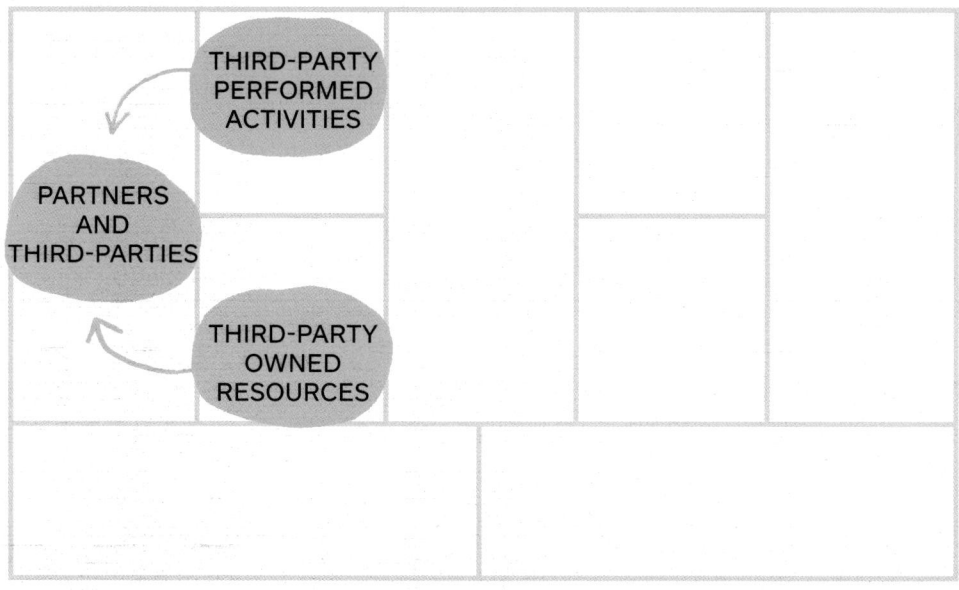

What could we do differently to make our business model more scalable (e.g., eliminate resource and activity bottlenecks)?

Assessment Question

How rapidly and how easily can we grow our business model without substantial additional resources and activities (e.g. building infrastructure, finding talent)?

Growing our business and customers is resource intensive (e.g. more people) and requires a lot of effort (e.g., nonscalable activities).

Our revenues and customer base can easily grow and scale without a lot of additional resources and activities.

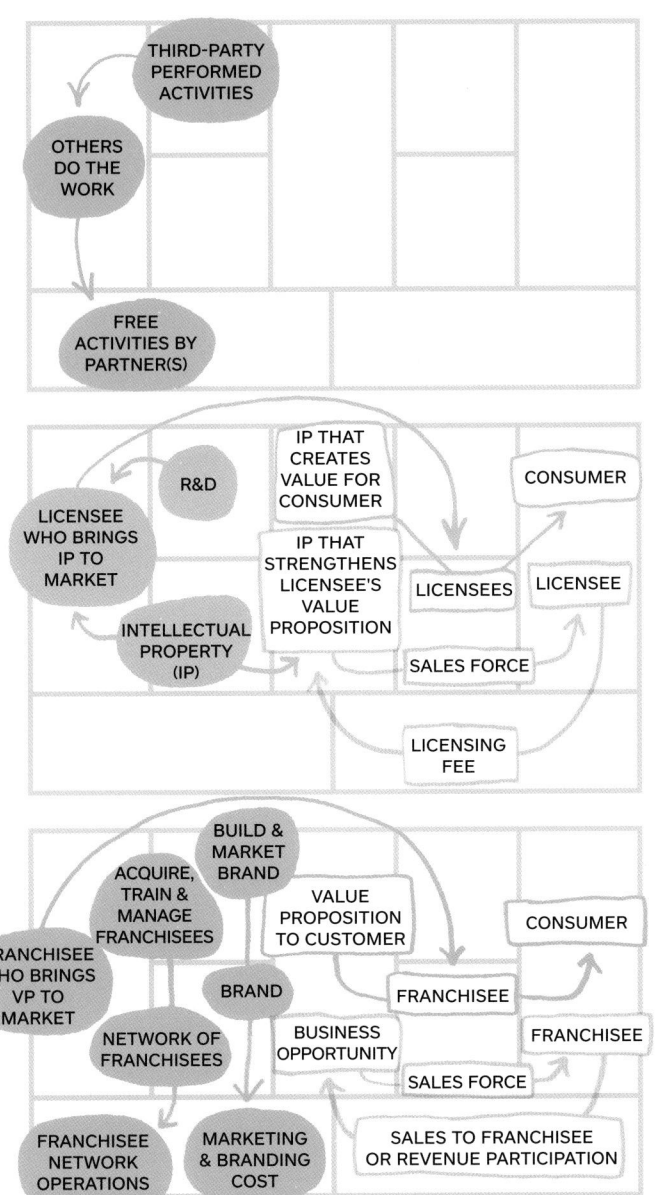

Delegators – Increase scalability by getting others to do some of the key activities (for free) that you have previously performed internally yourself.

EXAMPLES
IKEA, Facebook, Twitter, Instagram, Red Hat, Zinga

TRIGGER QUESTION
In which areas could we leverage customers or third parties to help us create value for free?

Licensors – Increase scalability by getting licensees to perform the bulk of value-creating activities like product manufacturing and commercialization.

EXAMPLES
ARM, Disney

TRIGGER QUESTION
How could we use licensing to make our business model more scalable and/or monetize intellectual property (e.g., brand, patents, etc.)?

Franchisors – Create scalability by licensing your business concept, trademarks, products, and services to franchisees who run franchise locations.

EXAMPLES
Harper, Ritz Carlton, McDonald's

TRIGGER QUESTION
How could we use franchising to make our business model more scalable and increase our market reach?

IKEA

In 1956, IKEA introduces "flatpacking" and turns customers into a free workforce that takes over part of the traditional furniture manufacturing value chain. Customers buy furniture in pieces in stores and assemble it in a DIY fashion at home.

IKEA was founded in 1943 on a vision of offering "a wide range of well-designed, functional home furnishing products at prices so low, that as many people as possible will be able to afford them."

In 1956, the stores introduced furniture through the "flatpacking" method: furniture was sold in pieces and customers assembled it at home. By reducing transportation, assembly, and inventory costs, IKEA was able to scale aggressively, locating wherever it had willing customers.

IKEA's ability to leverage the work done by its customers enabled it to grow to 433 stores in 49 global markets, serving more than 957 million customers for a retail revenue of €41.3 billion in 2019.[49, 50]

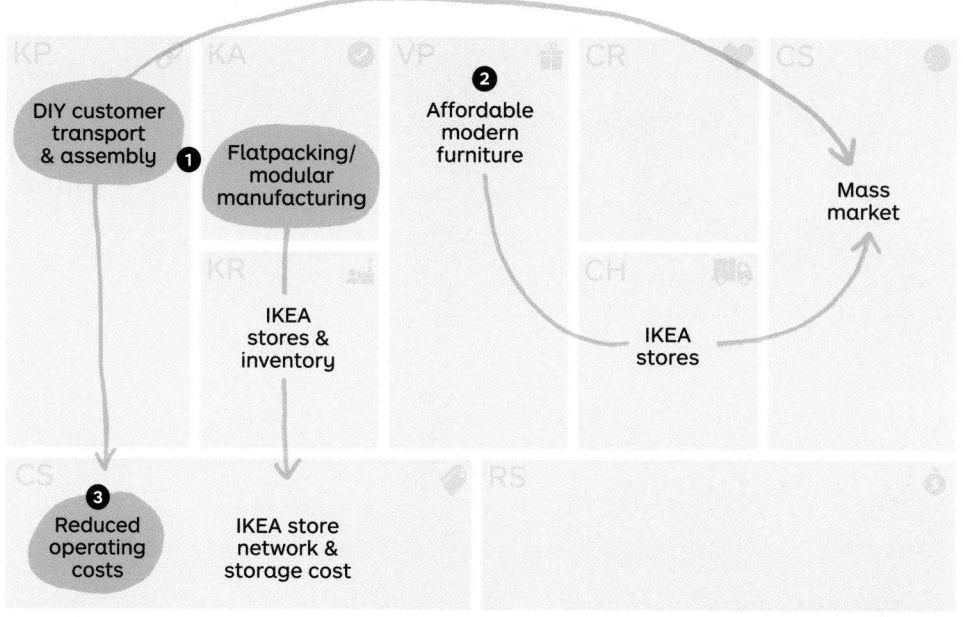

1 Identify How Others Can Create Value for You for Free

In 1956 IKEA adopts flat-pack, ready-to-assemble furniture that is easier and cheaper to transport from factory to retail centers. The company sees an opportunity in getting the customer to take over that part of the value chain.

2 Develop a Value Proposition

Because of flatpacking, IKEA can keep more furniture in stock and offer more affordable prices than competitors. Customers find the modular pieces they want to purchase in IKEA's open storerooms, then transport and assemble them at home.

3 Reap the Operational Savings from Getting Others to Do the Work

IKEA reaps substantial operational cost savings from getting customers to perform part of the work. Since storerooms also act as warehouses, customers select furniture, pick up the flatpacks, then transport and assemble them all at their own cost.

+ Modular Design and Manufacturing

Flatpacking, price differentiation, and customer assembly encourage IKEA to embrace a very modular, simple, clean, and minimalist design for which the company is known globally, which also simplifies manufacturing.

+ Overall Savings from Flatpacking

Flatpacking doesn't just enable cost savings from enlisting customers to do part of the work: it leads to overall cost savings in the manufacturing, storage, and mass transportation of furniture from factories to retail centers.

$500

The cost of shipping a sofa in the U.S. depending upon the size and distance traveled.

$20

The cost of shipping a truckload of IKEA couches can be as low as $20 for each sofa.[51]

Red Hat

Red Hat launched in 1993 as a software company. Its main value proposition builds on the freely available Linux open-source operating system. The particularity of open-source software like Linux is that it is created by a community of developers and made available to anybody for free.

Red Hat found a way to create a business model on top of Linux, as the operating system became more complicated. It recognized that there were significant barriers to its adoption by enterprise customers. It made Linux more accessible to the enterprise by offering them a subscription for the testing, certification, and support of Linux.

Red Hat found a way to effectively monetize the work done by the Linux developer community in a way that was mutually beneficial to Red Hat and the developer community.

In 2019, IBM completed its acquisition of Red Hat for $34 billion.[54]

In 2010 IKEA changed the design of its Ektorp sofa, reducing the size of the flatpack by

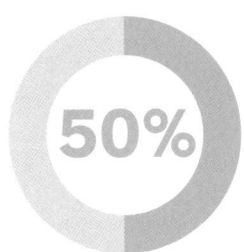

50%

and charging a 14% lower retail price.[52]

16% of surveyed U.S. homeowners have purchased more than

1/4 of their furniture from IKEA in the last 10 years.[53]

ARM

In 1990, ARM launched as a spinoff of a computer manufacturer to focus entirely on designing and licensing intellectual property for silicon chips. Today, almost all of the world's smartphones and tablets contain ARM designs.

ARM Holdings develops intellectual property (IP) used in silicon chips. It was founded in 1990 as a spinoff of British computer manufacturer Acorn Computers. The first time ARM designs were used in a cell phone was in 1994 for the Nokia 6110.

Semiconductor manufacturers combine ARM IP with their own IP to create complete chip designs. Chips containing ARM IP power most of today's mobile devices, due to their low power consumption. In 2014, 60% of the world's population used a device with an ARM chip on a daily basis.[55] In 2012, 95% of the chips found in smartphones and tablets were ARM designs.[56]

ARM licenses IP to over 1,000 global partners (including Samsung, Apple, Microsoft). The company doesn't manufacture or sell chips, unlike semiconductor manufacturers such as Intel or AMD.

SoftBank purchased ARM in 2016 for £24.3 billion.[57]

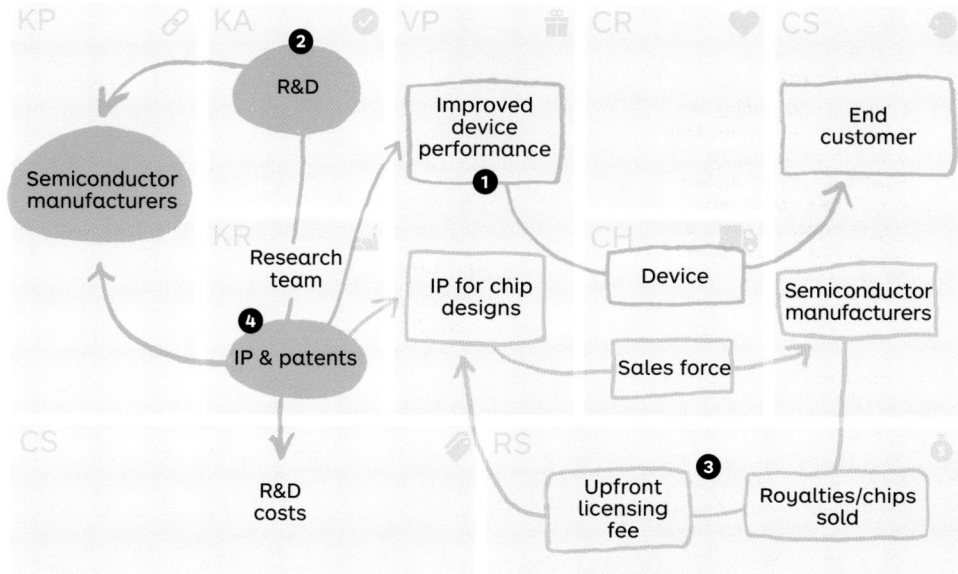

1 Detect and Solve Difficult Problems

ARM recognizes that tablets, laptops, and smartphones are the next wave of technology. To create attractive chips and intellectual property for portable devices, ARM focuses on faster processing speeds, lower power consumption, and lower costs.

2 Invest Heavily in R&D

In 2018, ARM invests $773 million in R&D (42% of 2018 revenues).[58] ARM is able to incur R&D costs many years before revenue starts (eight years on average). In 2008, ARM's R&D expenditure was £87 million or 29% of revenues. Expenditures continue to grow over time.[59]

3 License Intelligently

ARM earns fixed upfront license fees when they deliver IP to partners and variable royalties from partners for each chip they ship that contains ARM IP. The licensing fees vary between an estimated $1 million to 10 million. The royalty is usually 1 to 2% of the selling price of the chip.

4 Scale without Manufacturing

Licensing enables ARM to scale the business efficiently. Designs can be sold multiple times and reused across multiple applications (e.g., mobile, consumer devices, networking equipment, etc.). ARM has no manufacturing costs.

INVENT PATTERNS

+ Growing Base Yield Royalties Over a Long Period

Licensing and royalty fees earn revenues over multiple years. In particular, the sales-dependent royalties constitute a sort of recurring revenue. License and royalty from new IP build on top of existing ones, creating a powerful long-term revenue engine.

+ Growth of the Smartphone Industry

ARM-based chip architectures are particularly suited for mobile devices, because of their low power consumption. That allows ARM to surf the exponential growth of the mobile industry.

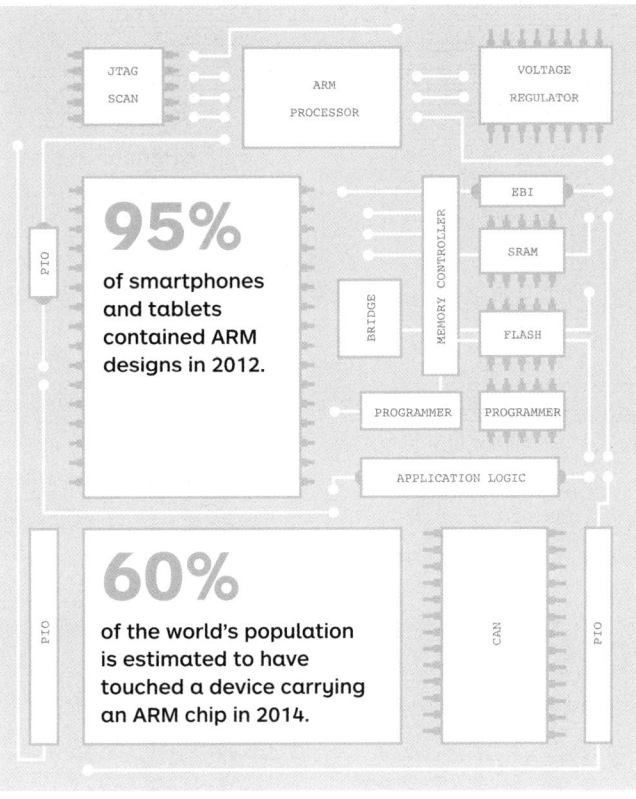

95%
of smartphones and tablets contained ARM designs in 2012.

60%
of the world's population is estimated to have touched a device carrying an ARM chip in 2014.

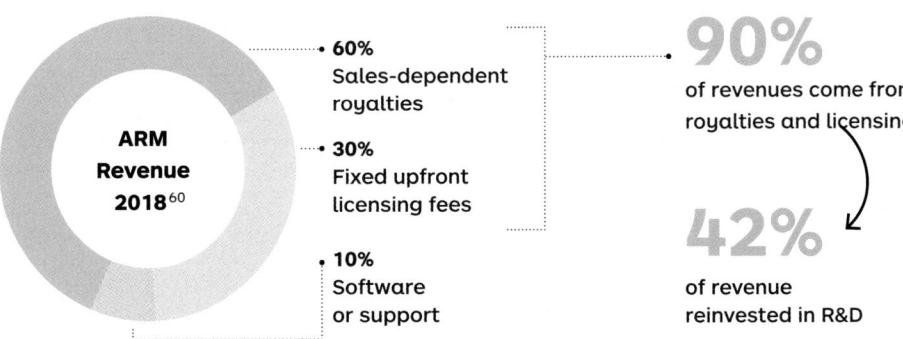

ARM Revenue 2018[60]

- **60%** Sales-dependent royalties
- **30%** Fixed upfront licensing fees
- **10%** Software or support

90%
of revenues come from royalties and licensing

42%
of revenue reinvested in R&D

Disney

Walt Disney created Mickey Mouse in 1928, and quickly licensed the iconic character in 1930 for the cover of a writing tablet. In 1929, Disney created Walt Disney Enterprises for the purpose of separating merchandising from studio productions.

6 out of 10

The Walt Disney Company had 6 of the top 10 entertainment merchandising franchises in the world in 2017.[61]

Disney began by licensing toys, dolls, and watches. Then in 1934, Mickey Mouse became the first licensed character on a cereal box. Walt Disney Enterprises effectively became the precursor to Disney Consumer Products.

Disney Consumer Products continues to grow, especially through its Princess franchises (established in 1999). Licensing today is not limited to traditional kids, toys and books. Disney sells food, apparel, home goods, targeting "children of all ages."

Harper

In 1891, Martha Matilda Harper creates the modern franchising system, empowering female entrepreneurs to run their own beauty salons under the Harper brand.

Martha Matilda Harper opened her first beauty salon in 1888, and her focus on customer service and pampering led to the initial success of her business. Harper created the modern franchising system by creating a network of salons in order to scale her business while empowering female entrepreneurs.

Harper's clients were both suffragettes and socialites, and word of mouth helped to build her market reach. Soon women were asking her to open satellite salons across the country.

Harper was determined to create a network of franchises owned and operated by working-class women like herself. By 1891, the first two franchise salons had opened. In the 1930s, Harper scaled to 500 active salons across the globe, along with a chain of training schools.[62]

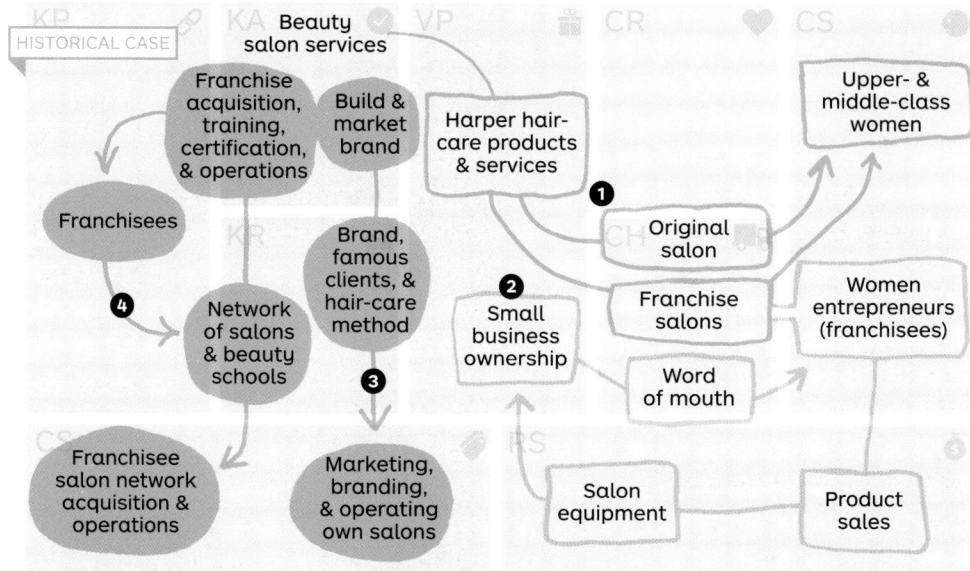

1 Create a Successful Reference Business and Value Proposition

Harper starts with a single salon where she offers hair-care services and products. The initial salon is a success and demand develops rapidly for other salons.

2 Create a Franchising Opportunity for Entrepreneurs

Harper uses this demand to grow a network of salons operated by working-class women like herself. She supports these franchise owners with start-up loans, marketing support, and training in the Harper Method of beauty.

3 Invest in Your Brand

The Harper brand becomes famous thanks to the publicity around the faithful clientele of high caliber politicians, Hollywood stars, and the British royal family. To assure brand consistency, Harper asks franchises to go through salon inspections and continual refresher courses.

4 Scale through Franchisees

With the franchising model Harper is able to scale rapidly. To generate revenues she sells her hair-care products and salon equipment to 500 salons across the globe at the height of her business in the 1930s.

+ Innovative in Hair Care

Harper disrupts existing habits and social norms around hair care. She introduces the scientific approach to hair care. Her invention of the reclining salon chair and her focus on customer service also remove some stigma around getting one's hair done outside of the home and triggers the expansion of the beauty salon market.[63]

$360

Life savings to open
first store in 1888.[64]

Harper grew up as a poor servant girl
and her clients include significant women
in the suffragist movement. She decides
that her first 100 salons should be opened
and operated by women like herself to
empower them. She provides them with
start-up loans and training on her hair-care
method and customer service.[65]

Profile of Harper's Franchisees

Jobs:
- Achieve financial independence
- Obtain a skilled job outside the
  home or factory

Pains:
- Lack of skills and education
- Lack of job opportunities

Gains:
- Empowerment
- Financial independence

Harper used her famously long tresses as
a marketing tool to demonstrate the health
of her hair and the efficacy of her products.

500
Salons Worldwide

Harper grew her network of salons
to 500 across the globe at the
height of her success in the 1930s.

Franchising

Franchising has remained a popular
tool for scaling across industry sectors
and geographies. In 2018, in the U.S.
alone, there are close to 740 thousand
franchises employing 7.6 million people and putting over $800 billion into
the economy.[66]

Franchises are a substantial source
of economic growth and stability.
During the first five years 50% of new
businesses fail, whereas franchises are
much more likely to be operating after
five years.

Number of Franchises
in U.S. since 1900

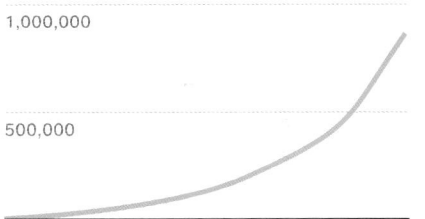

1,000,000

500,000

1900   2018

| 750 Thousand | 7.6 Million | $800 Billion |
| Establishments | Jobs | Output |

Questions for Leaders

Resource Castles

TRIGGER QUESTION
How could we make difficult-to-copy resources a key pillar of our business model?

Assessment Question

Do we own key resources that are difficult or impossible to copy and which give us a significant competitive advantage?

Our key resources are significantly inferior to those of our competitors.

Our key resources can't easily be copied or emulated for the next couple of years and they give us a significant competitive advantage (e.g., intellectual property, brand, etc.).

Activity Differentiators

TRIGGER QUESTION
Could we create (significantly more) value for customers by performing new activities or configuring activities in innovative ways?

Assessment Question

Do we create significant value for customers because we perform and configure activities in disruptively innovative ways?

We operate conventional activities that perform similarly or worse than comparable organizations.

Our key activities can't easily be copied or emulated for the next couple of years and they give us a significant competitive advantage (e.g., cost effectiveness, scale etc.).

Scalers

TRIGGER QUESTION
What could we do differently to make our business model more scalable (e.g., eliminate resource and activity bottlenecks)?

Assessment Question

How rapidly and how easily can we grow our business model without substantial additional resources and activities (e.g., building infrastructure, finding talent)?

Growing our business and customers is resource intensive (e.g., more people) and requires a lot of effort (e.g., nonscalable activities).

Our revenues and customer base can easily grow and scale without a lot of additional resources and activities.

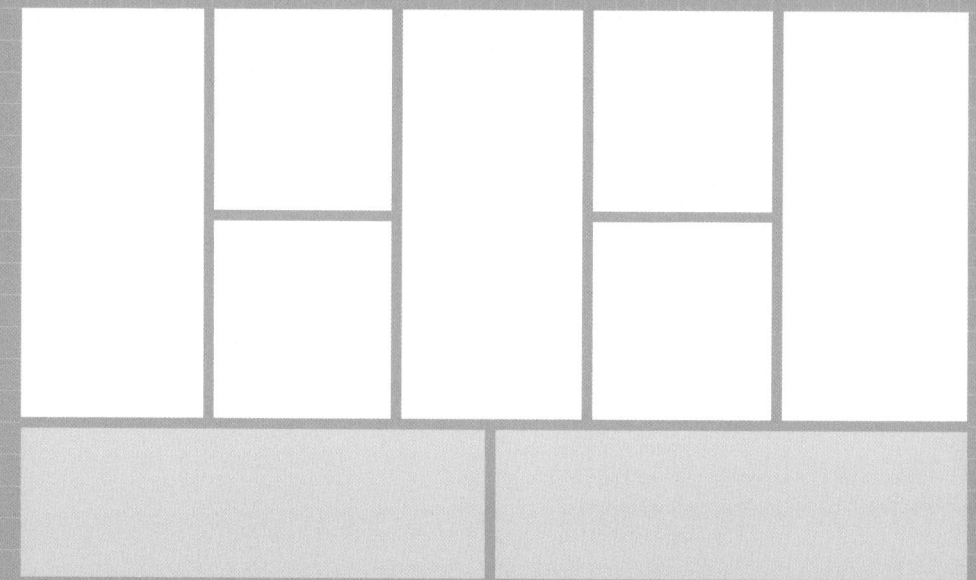

Profit Formula Disruption

Revenue Differentiators

p. 192	**Recurring Revenue**	Xerox
p. 194	**Bait & Hook**	Kodak
p. 196	**Freemium Providers**	Spotify
p. 197	**Subsidizers**	Fortnite

Cost Differentiators

p. 200	**Resource Dodgers**	Airbnb
p. 202	**Technologists**	WhatsApp
p. 203	**Low Cost**	easyJet

Margin Masters

| p. 206 | **Contrarians** | CitizenM |
| p. 208 | **High Enders** | iPhone |

A radical change in how profits are made in terms of revenues and costs.

Revenue Differentiators

Boost Revenues

Find innovative ways to capture value, unlock previously unprofitable markets, and/or substantially increase revenues.

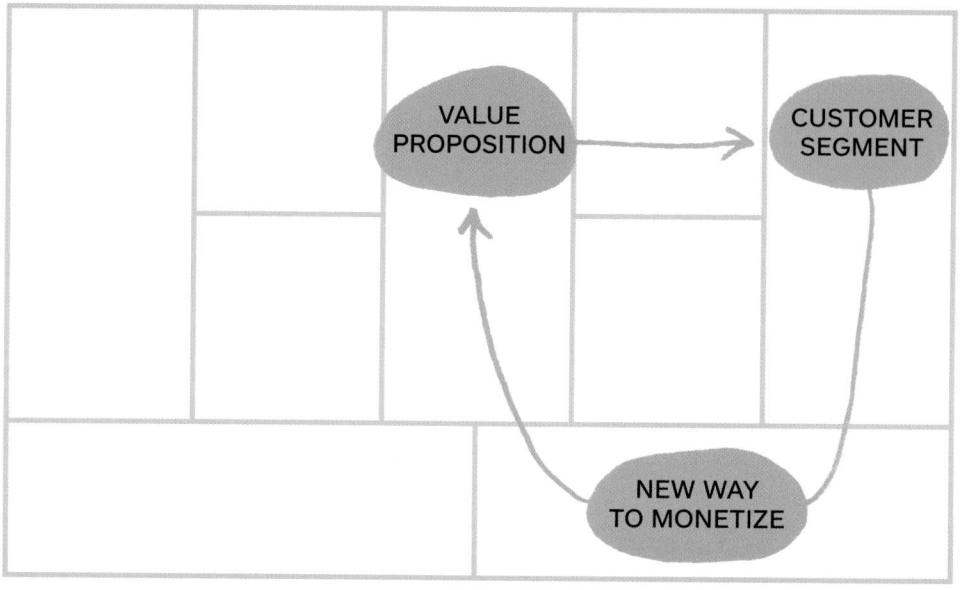

Which new revenue streams or pricing mechanisms could we introduce to capture more value from our customers or unlock unprofitable markets?

Assessment Question
Do we use strong revenue streams and pricing mechanisms to monetize value creation for customers?

We mainly have unpredictable and transactional revenues that require constant cost of sales.

We have predictable and recurring revenues where one sales leads to several years of revenue.

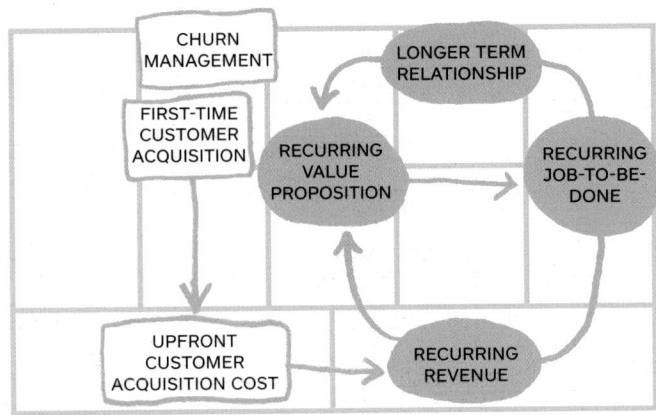

Recurring Revenue – Generate recurring revenues from one-time sales. Advantages include compound revenue growth (new revenues stack up on top of existing revenues), lower cost of sales (sell once and earn recurrently), and predictability.

TRIGGER QUESTION
How could we generate long-term recurring revenues rather than transactional ones?

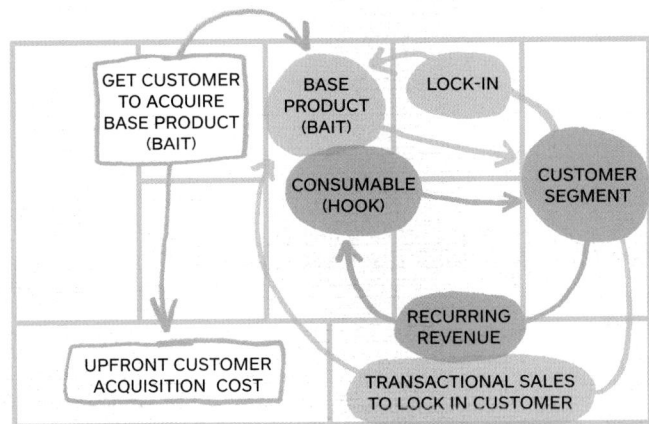

Bait & Hook – Lock customers in with a base product (the bait) in order to generate recurring revenues from a consumable (the hook) that customers need recurrently to benefit from the base product.

TRIGGER QUESTION
How could we create recurring revenues with a base product or service and a consumable?

191

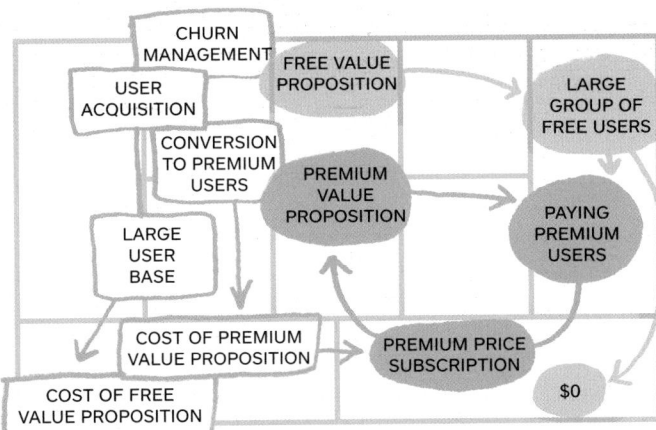

Freemium Providers – Offer basic products and services free of charge and premium services and advanced product features for a fee. The best freemium models acquire a large customer base and excel in converting a substantial percentage to paid users.

TRIGGER QUESTION
How could we split our value proposition into a free and a premium offer?

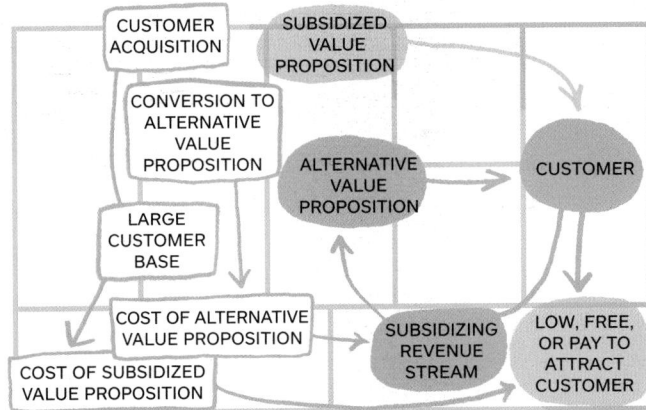

Subsidizers – Offer the full value proposition for free or cheaply by subsidizing it through a strong alternative revenue stream. This differs from freemium, which only gives free access to a basic version of products and services.

TRIGGER QUESTION
How could we give away our main value proposition for free by generating sufficient alternative revenue streams?

Xerox

In 1959, Xerox launches the first plain paper photocopier, the Xerox 914. Rather than just selling the machine, they generate long-term, recurring revenues from each photocopy made.

In 1959, Xerox revolutionized access to information by inventing and commercializing the first plain paper photocopy machine, the Xerox 914. The 914 took over a decade and a significant R&D budget to develop.

The machine was revolutionary: averaging 2,000 copies a day or 100 times more than the average business copier at the time.[67]

Because the 914 was expensive, it adopted a leasing model to make it more affordable. Customers were able to cancel the lease with only 15 days' notice, demonstrating Xerox's confidence in its value proposition.

Xerox added a pay-per-copy plan in order to monetize what they believed would become a copy addiction, but included the the first 2,000 copies for free. It's thanks to this innovative business model that earnings from the technology far exceeded earnings had they just sold the machine.

By 1962, the commercial copying business was worth $400 million, up from $40 million a decade before. By then the Xerox name had become synonymous with photocopying.[68]

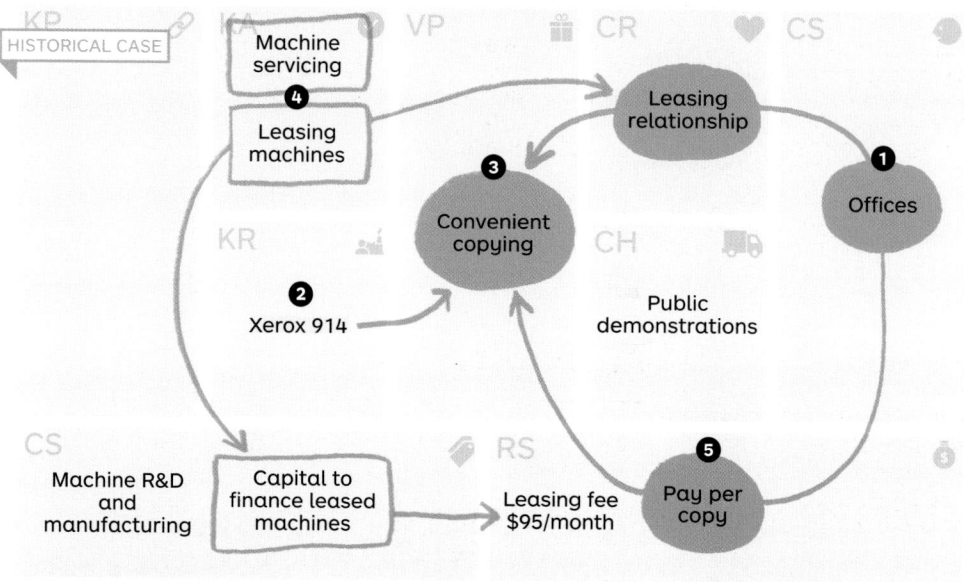

HISTORICAL CASE

1 Identify Recurring Job-to-Be-Done

Chester Carlson, a patent office employee, struggles with the cumbersome job of copying documents. At the time, the average business copier produces 15 to 20 copies per day.

2 Create Asset to Monetize Continuously

To address the challenge, Carlson invents and patents a new technique called xerography. Together with what later becomes Xerox, he develops the first plain paper photocopying machine, the Xerox 914, which averages 2,000 copies per day.

3 Design the Value Proposition

Xerox believes that once workers become familiar with the power of photocopies, they will be addicted to the convenience and copy more than ever before. Xerox offers the first 2,000 copies for free and a pay-per-copy plan after that.

4 Acquire Customers

Xerox recognizes that its copier is too expensive and new for mass adoption. It adopts a leasing model to make the machine affordable and get it into offices. Instead of Xerox selling it for $29,500, customers lease it for $95 a month.[69]

5 Earn Recurring Revenue

Each machine is fitted with a counter to tally the monthly usage. After the first 2,000 copies, customers pay 4 cents a copy. This allows Xerox to continuously monetize its value proposition through recurring revenue.

+ Public Demonstrations to Boost Adoption

The Model 914 is large and difficult to transport, and the technology has to be seen to be believed. Rather than using a traditional sales model, Xerox chooses to hold public demonstrations (including in NYC's Grand Central Terminal). These events help exhibit the machine's productivity and spur adoption.

100
thousand

The average monthly copy volume of the 914, which was originally designed to produce an average monthly copy volume of 10 thousand copies.[70]

$12.5
million

Development cost of the 914 (the equivalent of $110 million today). That was more than the company's total earnings from 1950 to 1959.[71]

650 lbs.

The weight of the original Model 914, which had to be tilted and squeezed through most office doors.[71]

Xerox Revenue[72]
In millions of U.S. dollars

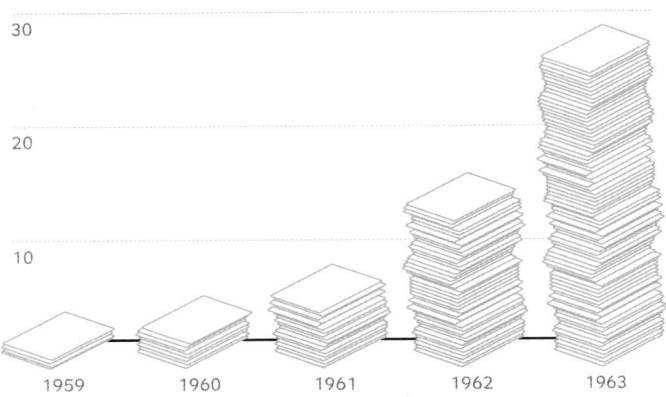

| 1959 | 1960 | 1961 | 1962 | 1963 |

The Rise of Recurring Revenue through Subscriptions

A more conventional way to generate recurring revenues is through subscriptions. Historically popularized through newspaper subscriptions, the model has spread to countless domains.

15% product subscriptions

15% of online shoppers have signed up for one or more subscriptions to receive products on a recurring basis.[73]

In particular, with the rise of the Internet, the subscription model has boomed. In 2018 Interbrand attributed 29% of the total value of the top 100 brands to subscription-based businesses versus 18% in 2009.[74]

Customers can subscribe to countless replenishment or curation services (food, clothing, etc.), or subscribe to services where access replaces ownership (e.g., software-as-a-service [SaaS], clothing, entertainment). The subscription model has conquered not just the consumer market, but also business-to-business and industrial markets.

Kodak

In 1900, Kodak "baits" consumers with cheap cameras to generate significant follow-on revenues from selling high margin film and photo processing.

George Eastman founded Kodak in 1888 with a goal of making "the camera as convenient as the pencil." One can argue that he succeeded with the introduction of the Brownie, an inexpensive camera, in 1900. With the Brownie, Kodak made cameras accessible to the masses: affordable, portable, and easy to use.

Kodak created the amateur photography market and held a dominant position through most of the twentieth century. Only the introduction of the digital camera in 1999—which it helped invent—triggered the end of Kodak's dominance over photography.

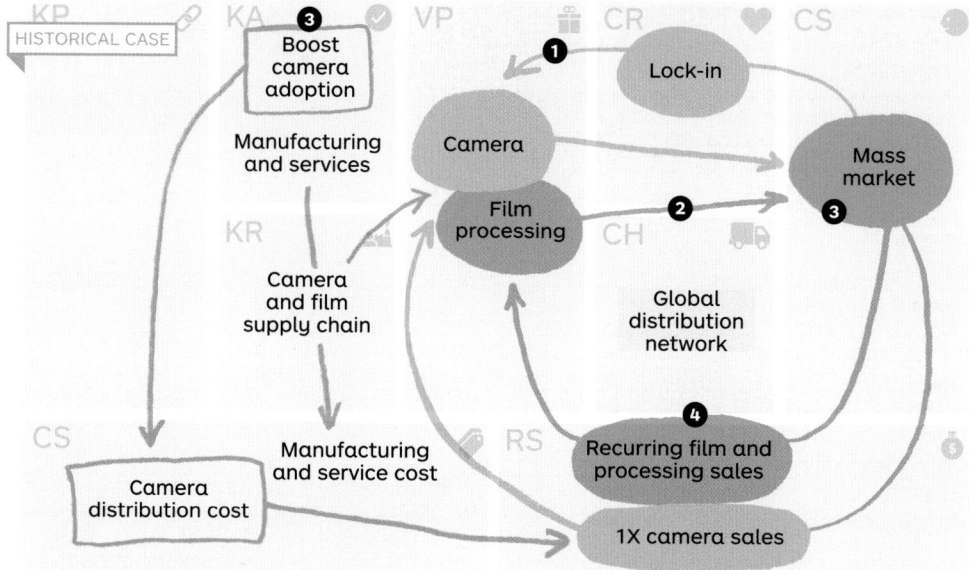

1 "Bait" and Lock In Customer with Base Product

In 1900, Kodak introduces the Brownie, the first mass market camera. It sells for only $1 (equivalent to $30 in 2019) and introduces amateur photography to the masses.[75]

2 "Hook" Customers with a Consumable Product and Service

The Brownie comes preloaded with film. Once the film is used, amateur photographers send the film back to Kodak for processing. Photographers get hooked and need to come back if they want to continue their hobby.

3 Acquire Customers

In 1900 photography is very new. Kodak uses low pricing for the Brownie and extensive marketing campaigns targeted at amateur photographers, including women and children, to spur customer acquisition. It sells 250,000 cameras the first year.[76]

4 Enjoy Recurring Revenues from Consumable

At the time, film costs 15¢ a roll. For an extra 10¢ a photo plus 40¢ for developing and postage, users can send their film to Kodak for development. Repeat purchases of film and processing generate significant recurring revenues for Kodak.

Building the Backstage for Film and Processing

Kodak builds up a backstage to support the complex process of manufacturing film. Kodak owns most of its supply chain, including raw materials such as processing chemicals, which create significant barriers to entry.

Distribution and Brand

Over the decades, Kodak establishes a global distribution network of dealers, which it supports with a strong brand and substantial marketing investments.

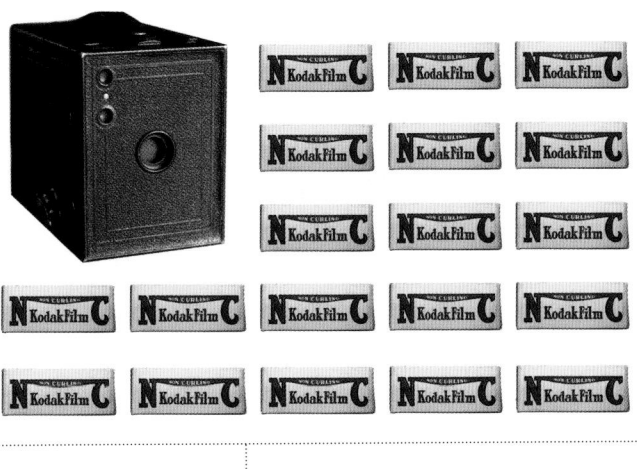

5th

most valuable
brand globally
(in 1996).[79]

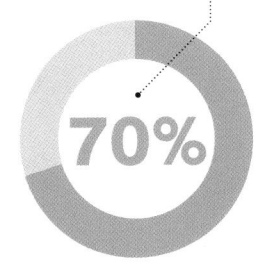

70%

profit margin on film Kodak
enjoyed in the 1980s.[77]

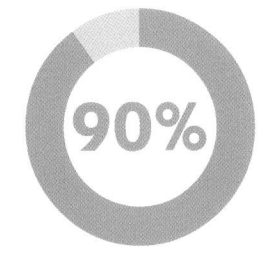

90%

of film sales in the U.S.
were by Kodak in 1976.[78]

Disruption of an Innovator

Kodak filed for bankruptcy in 2012 due to the disruption of Kodak's business model by digital cameras and smartphones. They made Kodak's major revenue engine (analog film) obsolete. Ironically, Kodak engineer Steven Sasson invented the first digital camera in 1975.

Kodak failed to adapt its camera, and film-based business model to the digital world. In 2001, it acquired a photo-sharing site called Ofoto. Instead of using an advertising-based business model (like Facebook), Kodak positioned Ofoto to attract more people to print digital images, when the printing market was already highly competitive and in decline.

Photo Prints by U.S. Consumers
▬▬ Digital Prints   ▬▬ Film Prints

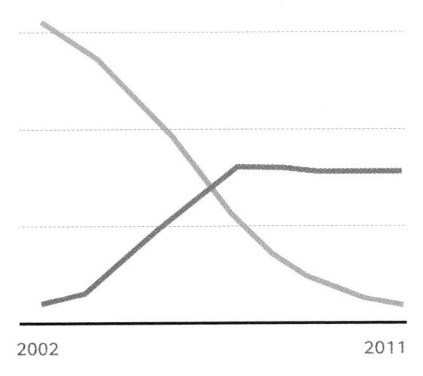

2002   2011

Photos Taken Each Year
▬▬ All Photos   ▬▬ Analog Photos

The Rise

2000

The Decline

1826   1918   2011

Spotify

In 2006, Spotify launches a free online music service to compete against freely available, pirated music. Its main revenue source comes from users upgrading to a premium subscription.

Spotify is a music streaming platform that gives users access to a large catalog of music. It uses a freemium revenue model that offers a basic, limited, ad-supported service for free and an unlimited premium service for a subscription fee.

Spotify relies heavily on its music algorithms and its community of users and artists to keep its premium experience delightful. Its premium subscriber base has grown from 10% of total users in 2011 to 46% in 2018.[80]

From the start Spotify saw itself as a legal alternative to pirated music and paid song purchases on iTunes. Spotify pays a significant portion of its revenue in the form of royalties to music labels. It has paid close to $10 billion in royalties since its launch in 2006.[81]

The company accelerated the shift from music downloads to streaming and disrupted Apple iTunes in the process.

For the first time in company history, Spotify made a profit in 2019.[82]

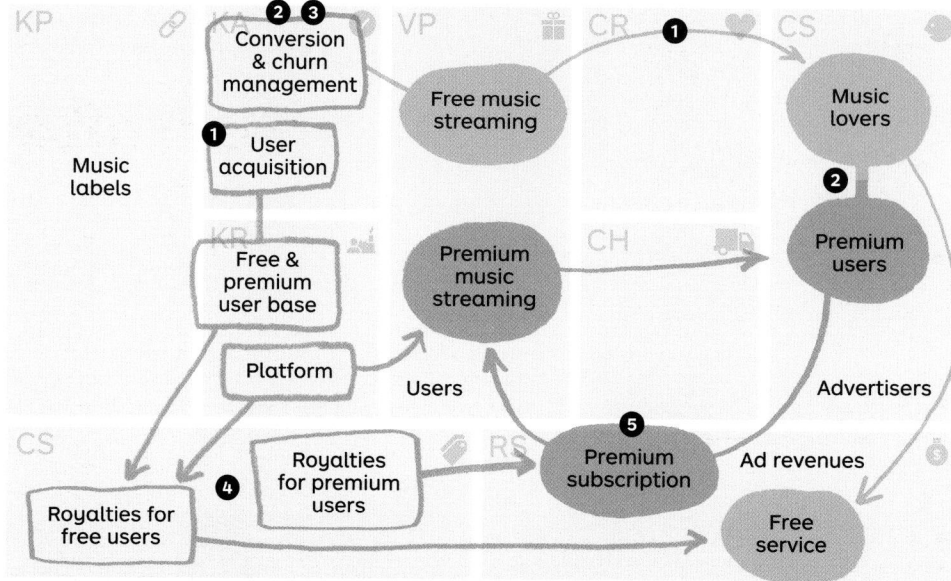

1 Attract a Large Base of Users with a Free Service

Spotify's free music streaming service gives users access to a catalog of millions of songs. The free service has basic functionality and users have to listen to messages from advertisers that partially subsidize the free service.

2 Convert Free Users to a Premium Value Proposition

Spotify has been extremely successful at converting free users to paid users. Its premium service has additional features and it removes advertising. In 2018, 46% of Spotify's users are premium users, who generate 90% of its total revenues.

3 Manage Retention and Churn

Like in any subscription model a user's lifetime value (LTV)—how much Spotify can earn from a user over time—increases the longer the company can retain users. This is called managing customer churn. In the first half year of 2019, Spotify's premium subscriber churn rate fell to a record low of 4.6%.[83]

4 Balance Cost of Free and Premium

Spotify pays record labels close to 52% of the revenue generated by each stream. Over 85% of music streamed from Spotify belongs to four record labels: Sony, Universal, Warner, and Merlin. In 2018, Spotify pays €3.5 billion in royalties for premium users and €0.5 billion for free users, which equates to 74% of overall costs.[84]

5 Finance It All with Your Revenue Stream from Premium

The particularity of the freemium model is that you need to be able to cover the costs of free and paying users. Spotify's user base grows to over 248 million users in 2019 for which it needs to pay royalties. Of those users, 54% consume (limited) music for free.[85]

#1

most downloaded music streaming app

in the United States on the App Store in 2018.[86]

U.S. On-Demand Audio Song Streams[87]
In billions

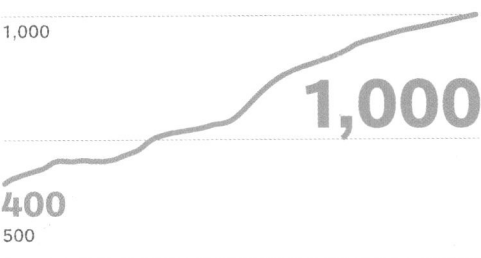

1,000

1,000

400

500

2017   2019

46% conversion rate to paid services

compared to 30% for Slack, 4% for Evernote, 4% for Dropbox, and 0.5% for Google Drive.[88]

Fortnite

In 2017, Epic Games releases *Fortnite: Battle Royale*, a completely free, multiplatform, online video game that is subsidized by in-app purchases for digital goods.

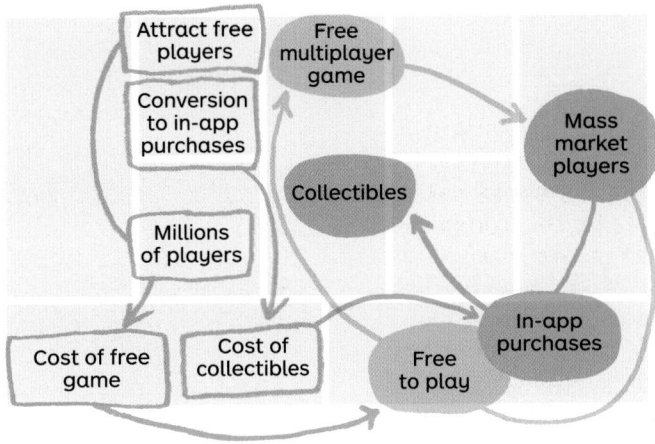

Fortnite: Battle Royale became a cultural phenomenon after its release. It is a free-to-play, multiplayer video game where hundreds of players fight to the death on an island.

Epic Games monetizes through in-app purchases, allowing players to buy collectibles like fashion statements or dance moves, but which provide no strategic edge to advance in the game. *Fortnite* was originally released as a paid version for $40 in July 2017 before switching to a free version subsidized by in-app purchases.[89]

Festivals

Festivals often use subsidizer mechanics. For some festivals, the sale of food and drinks subsidizes the festival free-entry fee. In other instances, a paid festival can subsidize an off or free festival such as the Montreux Jazz Festival in Switzerland.

Cost Differentiators

Kill Costs

Build a business model with a game-changing cost structure, not just by streamlining activities and resources, but by doing things in disruptive new ways.

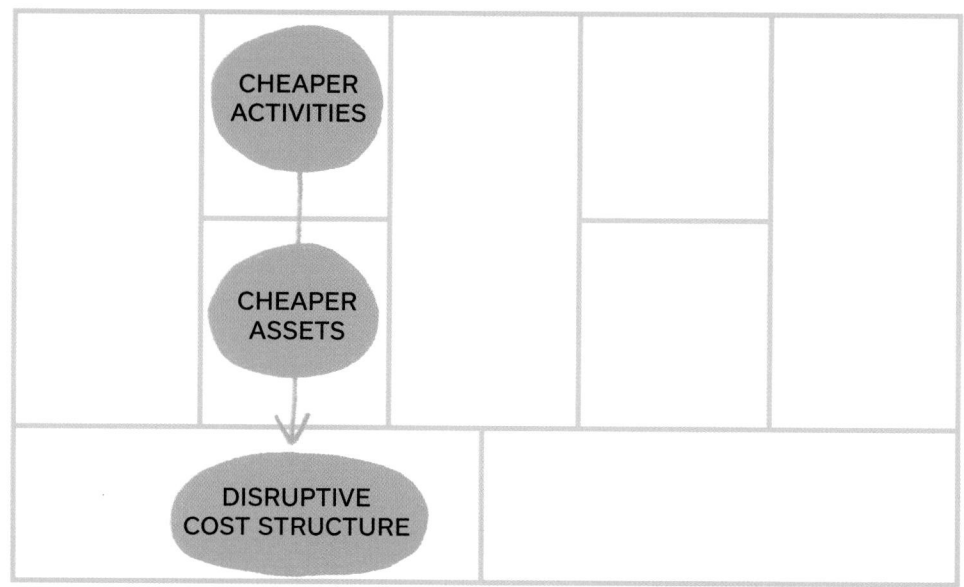

Could we change our cost structure significantly by creating and delivering value with different and differently configured resources and activities?

Assessment Question
Is our cost structure conventional or disruptive?

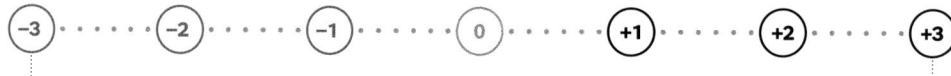

We have a conventional cost structure that performs similarly or worse than comparable organizations (e.g., worse by a factor of two).

We have a game-changing disruptive cost structure that performs differently and substantially better than comparable organizations (e.g., better by a factor of two).

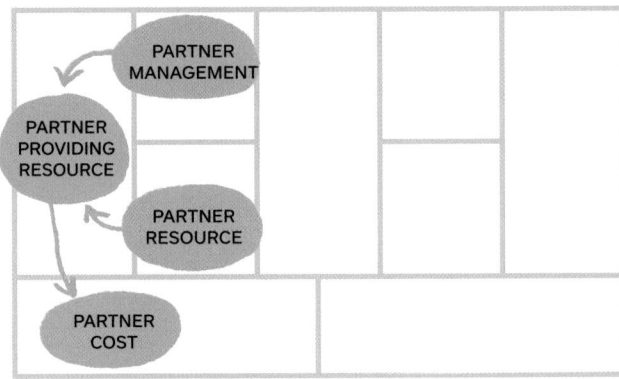

Resource Dodgers – Eliminate the most costly and capital-intensive resources from your business model to create a game-changing cost structure.

EXAMPLES
Airbnb, Uber, Bharti Airtel

TRIGGER QUESTION
How could we create a resource-light business model and get rid of the most costly and capital intensive resources?

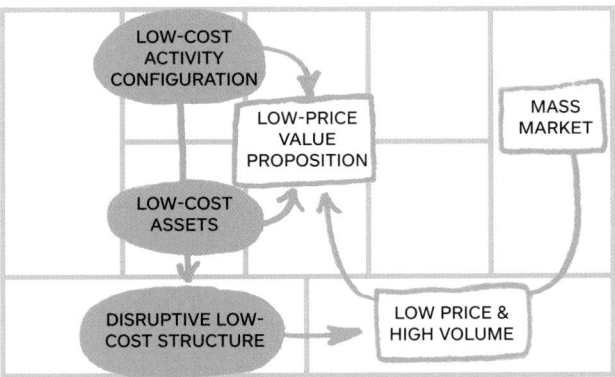

Technologists – Use technology in radically new ways to create a game-changing cost structure.

EXAMPLES
WhatsApp, Skype

TRIGGER QUESTION
How could we use technology to replace activities and resources to create a game-changing cost structure?

Low Cost – Combine activities, resources, and partners in radically new ways to create a game-changing cost structure with disruptively low prices.

EXAMPLES
easyJet, Ryanair, Trader Joe's

TRIGGER QUESTION
How could we radically recombine activities, resources, and partners to significantly lower costs and pricing?

Airbnb

In 2008, Airbnb launches a platform that feels like a hotel chain but owns no properties. It connects travelers with owners of idle assets.

Airbnb was founded in 2008 as an online marketplace to connect travelers looking for an authentic, unique place to stay with hosts that had extra room to rent. Airbnb operates as an intermediary, matching these two distinct customer segments.

The company has a radically lighter cost structure than the hotel chains with which it competes, because it does not own any of the rooms it lists on its website, nor does it manage a large hospitality staff. Airbnb's main costs are platform management and marketing, which explains how they have scaled so quickly.

The success of Airbnb's business model is based on a resource-light cost structure. It found an innovative way to partner with owners of idle assets (empty rooms) and help them monetize those assets via their matchmaking platform.

Airbnb differs from other matchmaking sites like booking.com or hotels.com, in that travelers associate the listed properties and rooms with the Airbnb brand as if it was a traditional hotel chain.

INVENT PATTERNS

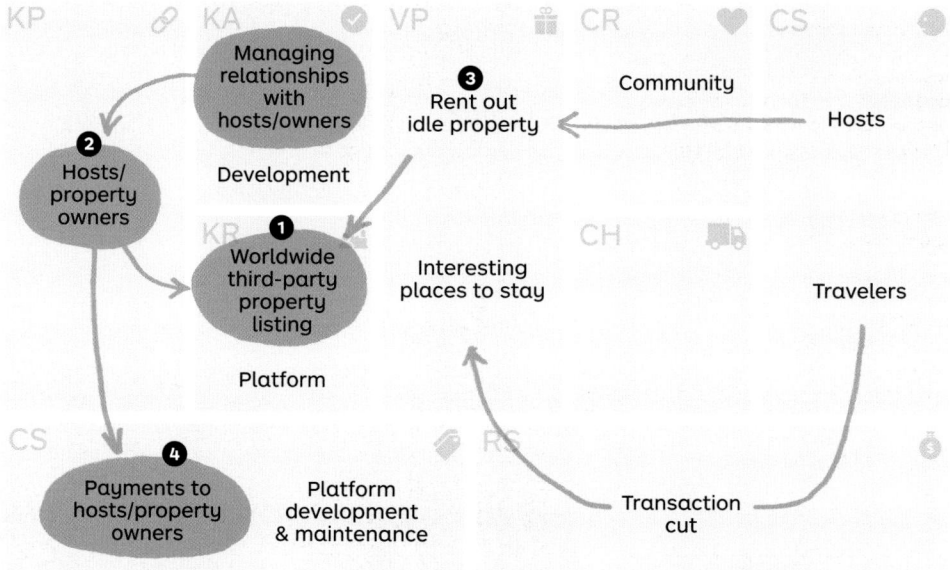

1 Identify the Most Costly Resource in your Business Model or Industry

The most costly elements in the hotel industry are the properties, their mainte-nance, staff, and services. Also, when hotel rooms are not rented out on a given night, they are a sunk cost. The hotel industry is very capital intensive.

2 Identify Asset Owners That Could Provide You with the Required Resource

Airbnb recognizes that many property owners have idle assets (unused bedrooms, apartments, beach houses, etc.) that are relatively difficult for an individual to rent out con-tinuously for short periods of time.

3 Develop an Innovative Value Proposition to Acquire Resources from Partners

Airbnb offers property owners the opportunity to become hosts to generate extra income (average $924/month in 2017).[90] Airbnb gives hosts access to a pool of travelers through the platform and relieves one of the biggest pains for property owners.

4 Compete on a New Cost Structure

Airbnb competes on a much lighter cost struc-ture than hotels, because it owns no hotels, nor employs cleaning or service staff. Airbnb's operational costs are mostly platform manage-ment, marketing and promotion, and other host and traveler support activities.

+ Double-Sided Platform

For Airbnb to be attractive to hosts, it needs a large pool of travelers. Developing this "other side of its platform" is a key success factor in the value proposition to hosts.

+ Lovemark Brand

Airbnb develops a very strong brand for this particular type of travel experience. It deeply changes social norms and habits. While it is commonplace now, in 2008 it is unheard of to be willing to sleep in a stranger's home.

+ The Importance of Community and the Sharing Economy

Airbnb fosters the connection of hosts and travelers on a more personal level than what they'd experience at a hotel, in order to build a global Airbnb community. This type of connectivity gives rise to the sharing economy, also known as collaborative consumption.

7
million global listings

Airbnb indicates 7 million global active listings on its platform in early 2019, which was more rooms than the top 5 hotel rooms combined.[91]

2
million+

Average number of people staying in an Airbnb per night in 2019.[91]

Zero

Number of properties Airbnb owns.

Share of Travelers Using Airbnb[92]
Percentage of leisure and business travelers in the U.S. and Europe

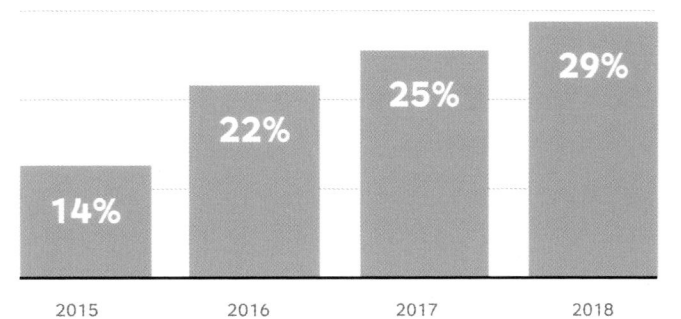

2015	2016	2017	2018
14%	22%	25%	29%

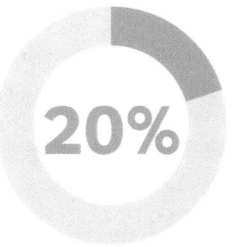

20%

Airbnb's 2018 percentage of U.S. consumer spending for lodging.[93]

WhatsApp

In 2009, WhatsApp launches a device-agnostic free messaging service and platform that disrupts SMS and free desktop messaging.

WhatsApp was originally, in 2009, a status update app before it transformed into a free, unlimited messaging service. The company targeted anyone with a smartphone and an Internet connection, regardless of device and location.

When WhatsApp launched, it disrupted a very competitive messaging market. Text messaging was dominated by paid SMS services by telecom operators and free desktop messaging like Yahoo! Messenger, MSN Messenger, and Skype.

WhatsApp used software and the Internet to externalize the hardware and proprietary infrastructure costs that telecom operators bear in order to offer SMS services. This allowed them to benefit from the growth of smartphone users globally, operate at a radically lower cost structure, and pass on cost savings to users in the form of a free service. In February 2013, WhatsApp serviced 200 million active users with only 50 staff members. By December that year, it had 400 million users.[94, 95]

In 2014, Facebook acquired WhatsApp for more than $19 billion.[96]

INVENT PATTERNS

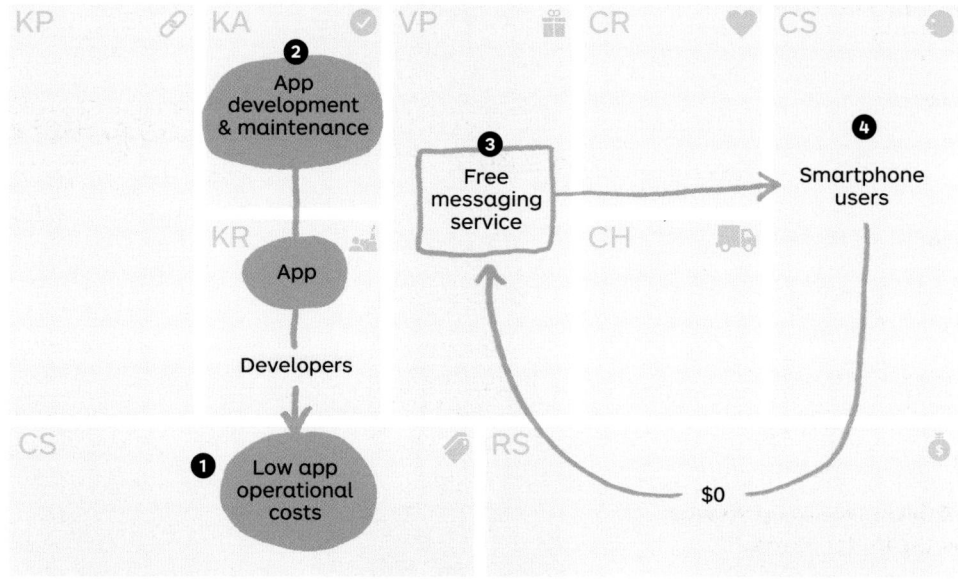

1 Identify an Industry Cost and Revenue Structure That You Can Disrupt with Tech

Telecom operators charge an estimated 6,000% markup for SMS messages. WhatsApp disrupts this revenue stream with a free service.[97]

2 Build the Technology

In early 2009 Jan Koum starts working on a new type of Internet-based iPhone messaging app. Unlike SMS messages, which use a telecom operator's network infrastructure, WhatsApp piggybacks on a user's smartphone connection to deliver messaging for free.

3 Disrupt with a Radically Different Cost Structure

WhatsApp incurs no variable or fixed costs for messages sent by users. Its main costs are in software development, not infrastructure. With only a few software developers, it serves millions of users and destroys billions of dollars of lucrative SMS revenues for telecom operators in the process.

4 Reap the Benefits

WhatsApp grows at a breathtaking speed without having to grow its cost structure substantially. In December 2013 WhatsApp claims they've reached 400 million active users with only 35 engineers.

+ Smartphone Growth

WhatsApp focuses on mobile first and benefits from the rapid growth of the smartphone market. WhatsApp expands to multiple platforms and devices, but contrary to their free, desktop messaging competitors (like Yahoo! Messenger, MSN Messenger, and Skype) WhatsApp's primary focus always remains mobile.

Monthly active users
In millions

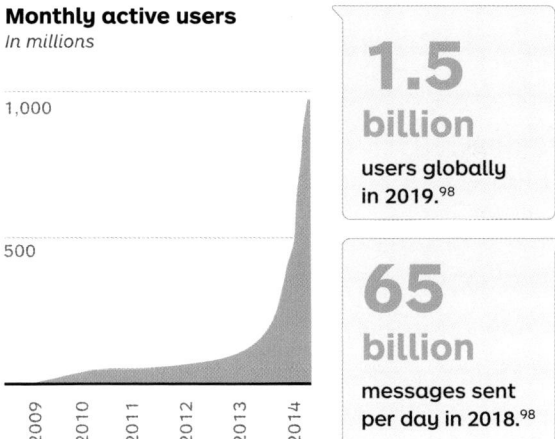

1,000

500

2009 2010 2011 2012 2013 2014

1.5 billion
users globally in 2019.[98]

65 billion
messages sent per day in 2018.[98]

Mobile Messaging Volume in the United States[99]
In billions

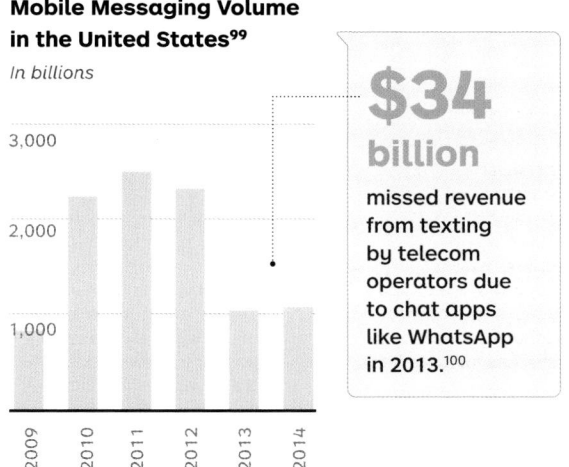

3,000

2,000

1,000

2009 2010 2011 2012 2013 2014

$34 billion
missed revenue from texting by telecom operators due to chat apps like WhatsApp in 2013.[100]

$19 billion
Amount Facebook paid to acquire WhatsApp in February 2014, five years after launch.

easyJet

In 1995, easyJet disrupts European travel with a low-cost, no frills air travel experience.

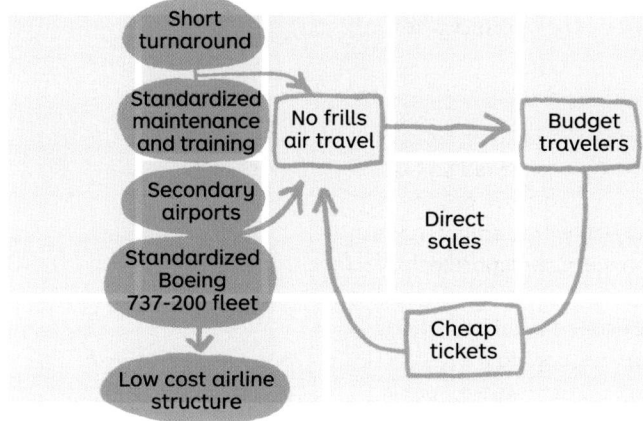

easyJet launched in 1995, popularizing the low-cost carrier model in the European market. easyJet's business model applies the following low-cost blueprint until it diversifies in 2002:

- No-frills airline experience for budget travelers.
- **Secondary airports**: often land in secondary airports that charge lower fees.
- **Fleet standardization:** one model of aircraft with simple cabin configuration to reduce maintenance and training costs.
- **Short turnaround times:** minimizing the time aircraft are on the ground not generating revenues.
- **Direct sales:** selling directly to customers to bypass travel agent fees.

Margin Masters

Boost Margins

Achieve significantly higher margins than competitors by focusing on what customers are willing to pay for most, while keeping your cost structure in check. Prioritize profitability over market share.

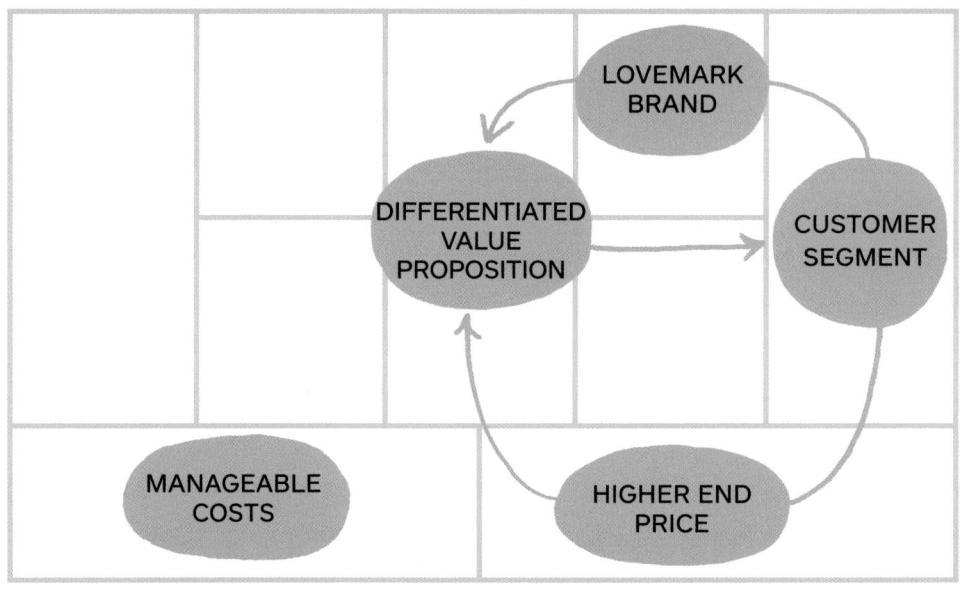

TRIGGER QUESTION

How could we find innovative ways to eliminate the most costly aspects of our business model, while focusing on value that matters to customers most and which they are willing to pay a high price for?

Assessment Question

Do we have strong margins from low costs and high prices?

| –3 | –2 | –1 | 0 | +1 | +2 | +3 |

We have very thin margins due to our cost structure and weak pricing power (e.g., we perform worse than comparable organizations by at least 50%).

We have very strong margins from an optimized management of costs and strong pricing power (e.g., we perform better than comparable organizations by at least 50%).

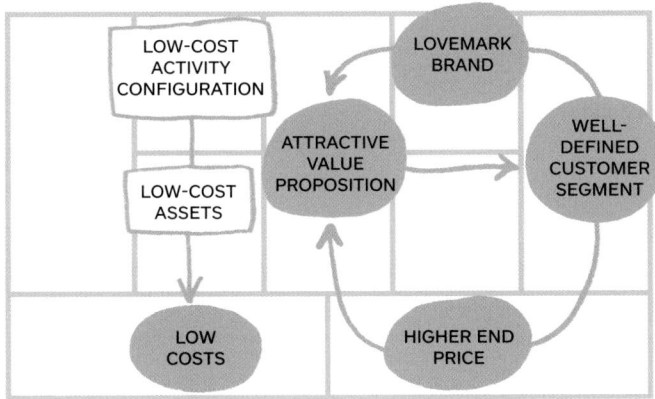

Contrarians – Significantly reduce costs and increase value at the same time. Eliminate the most costly resources, activities, and partners from your business model, even if that means limiting the value proposition. Compensate by focusing on features in the value proposition that a well-defined customer segment loves and is willing to pay for, but which are relatively cheap to provide.

EXAMPLES
CitizenM, Cirque de Soleil, Nintendo Wii

TRIGGER QUESTION
Which costly elements of our business model and value proposition could we eliminate and make up for with extremely valuable but affordable elements?

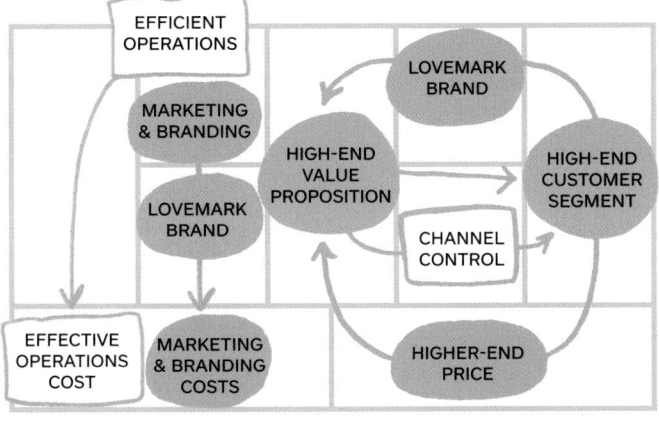

High Enders – Create products and services at the high end of the market spectrum for a broad range of high-end customers. Use these to maximize margins and avoid the small size and extreme cost structure of a luxury niche.

EXAMPLE
iPhone

TRIGGER QUESTION
What could we modify in our business model to significantly increase customer value and price without substantially increasing our cost structure?

citizenM

In 2005, citizenM launches a hotel concept with reduced costs but increased value for "mobile citizens."

In 2005, the founders of citizenM realized that the modern hotel industry hadn't changed in decades, despite the changing tastes and habits of the global traveler.

citizenM focused on the "mobile citizen"— the person who travels often and depends upon mobile technology. citizenM recognized that global travelers have a few essential conveniences and luxuries that they are willing to pay for, while other traditional amenities are not always necessary.

Based on these insights, the founders launched a hotel concept at Schiphol Airport in Amsterdam that minimized costs and maximized value for the mobile citizen without making it feel cheap. citizenM found a way to create more for less and was able to maintain high profit margins per room.

In 2019, the privately owned citizenM operated 20 hotels in 13 cities on three continents with an additional 10 hotels planned.

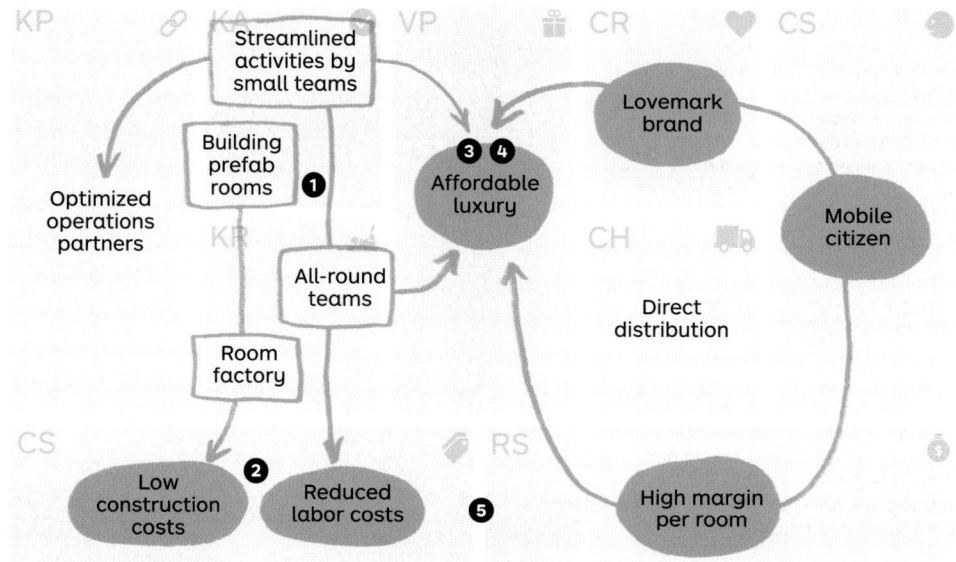

1 Eliminate Most Costly, Desirable Elements, Yet Not Essential to Customers

citizenM launches in Amsterdam in 2008. It removes the most costly elements of a high-end hotel, not essential to the mobile citizens it targets: no fine dining, no spa or sophisticated gym, no mini-bar, and no room service.

2 Reduce Costs without Making It Feel Cheap

citizenM drastically reduces construction and maintenance costs by building highly standardized 14-square-meter rooms in a room factory, which are then stacked like shipping containers to form the hotel.[101] It reduces HR costs by working with small, cross-functional teams.

3 Increase Value That Customers Care about at Low Cost

citizenM focuses on what really matters to mobile citizens: great mattresses, pillows, and sound-proof rooms. Its small staff has only one task: make customers happy. The lobby is vibrant, equipped with designer furniture, and 24-hour food and drinks.

4 Create New Elements That Boost Value at Less Cost

CitizenM launches its own room factory to fuel low-cost expansion from Amsterdam to New York and Taipei. It streamlines cleaning and linens with new operations partners.[102] Rooms are equipped with free broadband WiFi and movies-on-demand.

5 Reap Benefits of Creating More Value at Less Cost

citizenM's profitability per square meter is twice that of comparable upscale hotels.[103] It achieves that by eliminating the most costly elements from the hotel business without making it feel cheap for its customer, the mobile citizen.

Optimized for Mobile Citizens

From the start, citizenM optimizes its hotel experience for the mobile citizen: travelers who visit a city for 1 to 3 days for culture, shopping, entertainment, or work. They mainly use the hotel as a base to sleep and roam the city. They don't need many of the services embedded in other hotels.

Empowered Employees, Strong Customer Relationship, and Lovemark Brand

citizenM hires people who are highly customer oriented and then gives them the autonomy to deliver a great guest experience. It has one of the lowest staff turnovers in the industry. In addition, citizenM encourages teams to establish a strong customer relationship in order to establish a lovemark brand.

A. Build

99%
of each room is finished at the factory.[104]

2x profitability

CitizenM's profitability per square meter is twice that of comparable upscale hotels.

B. Assemble

C. Enjoy

7,000
rooms in

30
hotels on

3
continents[105]

iPhone

In 2007, Apple launches the iPhone and combines an Internet browser, a music player, and a mobile phone in one high-end, multitouch device without a keyboard. It ushers in the era of the smartphone.

In 2007, Apple founder Steve Jobs famously introduced the iPhone at the Macworld 2007 convention as a revolutionary device that "would change everything." Its initial selling price was a hefty $499, but 270 thousand units sold its first weekend and 6 million units in its first year of production.[107, 106]

Apple's iPhone ushered in the era of the smartphone, the world of mobile-first and constant connection, leading the way for mobile technology to dominate and reform day-to-day existence. Apple's iPhone has consistently been more expensive than competing devices. However, Apple continually packs new features and technology into its iPhone in order to keep its products from seeming like a commodity.

Despite high prices, Apple maintains a high degree of control over production costs in its supply chain. This combination of controlled costs, high-end positioning, and continuous technology innovation have resulted in gross margins of 60 to 70% in the last 10 years.[108]

INVENT PATTERNS

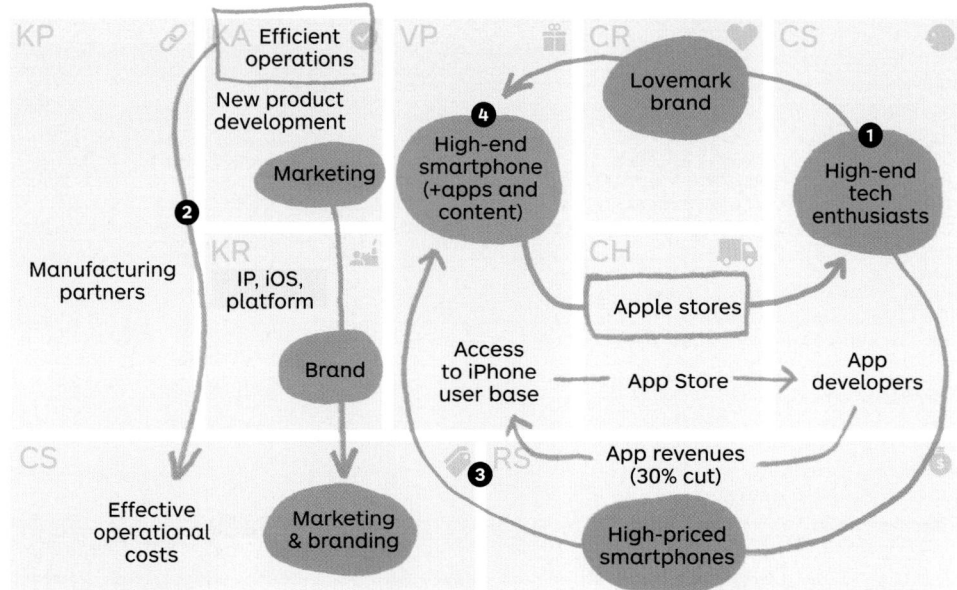

1 Delight and Surprise the High End of the Market

Apple positions the iPhone at the high end of the spectrum, knowing that the price will put it out of reach for the majority of the market. The phone combines an aspiration feel with design, technology, and simplicity, and capitalizes on its lovemark brand.

2 Control Costs

Apple does not manufacture the iPhone, but keeps its production costs low by controlling its supply chain. Due to the popularity of the device, Apple forces its suppliers to keep costs low as well as maintain privacy and secrecy over their devices.

3 Maximize Margins and Profits from High End Market Share

The iPhone's profit margins have remained between 60 to 70% over the past 10 years. At its peak, Apple captured 94% of the smartphone industry's profits, despite only accounting for 14.5% of sales.[109]

4 Continuously Reinvent and Surprise the High End of the Market

Since 2007, Apple has released 12 generations of iPhones. While Apple isn't always the first to develop many of the iPhone's technological innovations, it often delivers the best: multitouch screen, dual cameras, Apple Pay, Siri, iMessage, FaceTime, facial recognition.

+ The App Store

The iPhone initially launched without the App Store, which was opened in 2008 with 500 applications. As of 2019, the store featured over 1.8 million apps. The available applications and number of developers provide Apple with an additional competitive advantage as described in the Resource Castle Platform (p. 164).[110]

2.2
billion

iPhones sold as
of November 2018.[111]

60–70%
profit margins

on iPhones in the
past 10 years.

14% Despite only
accounting
for 14.5% of
all sales...

Total
smartphone
sales

94% ...at its peak
in 2015, Apple
captured 94%
of smartphone
profits in the
industry.

Total
smartphone
profits

The Cost of iPhones (USD)[108]
Bill of materials   Retail cost

$1,000	100%

% Profit
margin

$600 — 60%

$200 — 20%

| iPhone 2007 | iPhone 3G 2008 | iPhone 3GS 2009 | iPhone 4 2010 | iPhone 4S 2011 | iPhone 5C 2013 | iPhone 6 2014 | iPhone 6S 2015 | iPhone SE 2016 | iPhone 7 2016 | iPhone 8 2017 | iPhone X 2017 | iPhone XS 2018 |

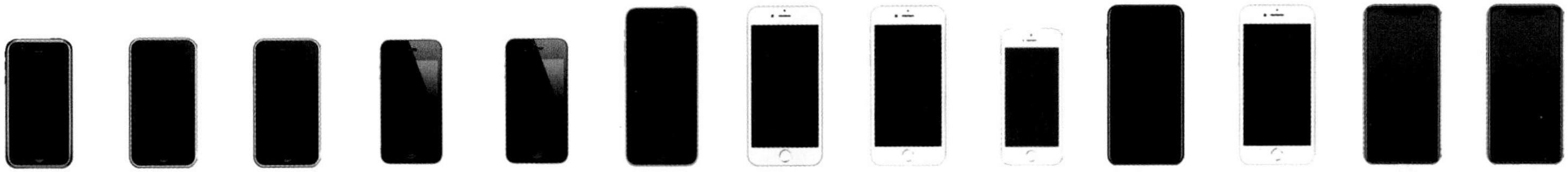

209

PROFIT FORMULA DISRUPTION

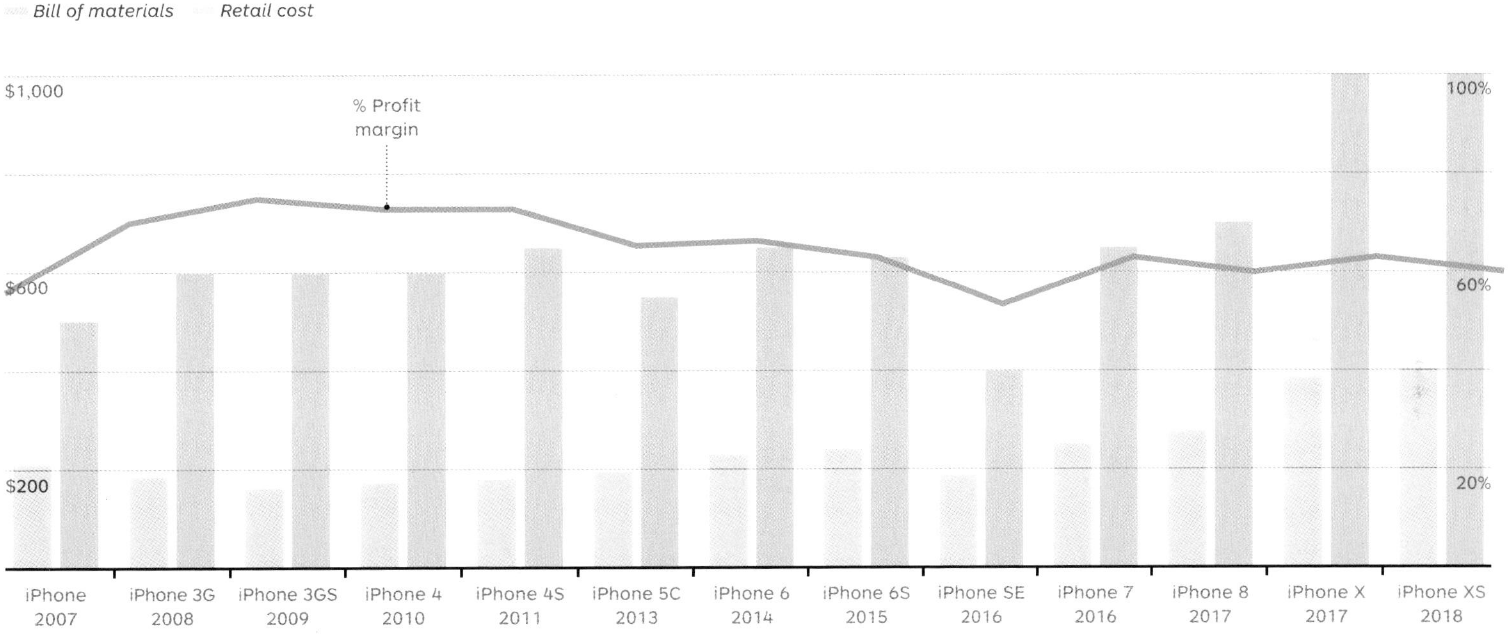

Questions
for Leaders

Revenue Differentiators

TRIGGER QUESTION
Which new revenue streams or pricing mechanisms could we introduce to capture more value from our customers or unlock unprofitable markets?

Assessment Question: Do we use strong revenue streams and pricing mechanisms to monetize value creation for customers?

We mainly have unpredictable and transactional revenues that require constant cost of sales.

We have predictable and recurring revenues where one sale leads to several years of revenue.

Cost Differentiators

TRIGGER QUESTION
Could we change our cost structure significantly by creating and delivering value with different and differently configured resources and activities?

Assessment Question: Is our cost structure conventional or disruptive?

Our cost structure is significantly less effective than that of our competitors (e.g., by a factor of two).

Our cost structure is significantly more effective than that of our competitors (e.g., by a factor of two).

Margin Masters

TRIGGER QUESTION
How could we find innovative ways to eliminate the most costly aspects of our business model, while focusing on value that matters to customers most and which they are willing to pay a high price for?

Assessment Question: Do we have strong margins from low costs and high prices?

We have very thin margins due to our cost structure and weak pricing power (e.g., we perform worse than comparable organizations by at least 50%).

We have very strong margins from an optimized management of costs and strong pricing power (e.g., we perform better than comparable organizations by at least 50%).

Assessment Questions for Leaders

Assess your existing and new business models with the Assessment Questions for Leaders. Visualize your strengths and weaknesses and unearth opportunities with the resulting score. No business model achieves a perfect score. Simply be conscious about where you score well and where you don't and use the trigger questions continuously to spark ideas for improvements.

Assessment Questions for Leaders

Frontstage

		-3	-2	-1	0	+1	+2	+3
	Market Explorers: How large and attractive is the untapped market potential we are going after?	(−3)	(−2)	(−1)	(0)	(+1)	(+2)	(+3)
	Channel Kings: Do we have large-scale and, ideally, direct access to our end-customer?	(−3)	(−2)	(−1)	(0)	(+1)	(+2)	(+3)
	Gravity Creators: How easy or difficult is it for our customers to leave or switch to another company?	(−3)	(−2)	(−1)	(0)	(+1)	(+2)	(+3)

Backstage

		-3	-2	-1	0	+1	+2	+3
	Resource Castles: Do we own key resources that are difficult or impossible to copy and which give us a significant competitive advantage?	(−3)	(−2)	(−1)	(0)	(+1)	(+2)	(+3)
	Activity Differentiators: Do we create significant value for customers because we perform and configure activities in disruptively innovative ways?	(−3)	(−2)	(−1)	(0)	(+1)	(+2)	(+3)
	Scalers: How rapidly and how easily can we grow our business model without substantial additional resources and activities (e.g., building infrastructure, finding talent)?	(−3)	(−2)	(−1)	(0)	(+1)	(+2)	(+3)

Profit Formula

		-3	-2	-1	0	+1	+2	+3
	Revenue Differentiators: Do we use strong revenue streams and pricing mechanisms to monetize value creation for customers?	(−3)	(−2)	(−1)	(0)	(+1)	(+2)	(+3)
	Cost Differentiators: Is our cost structure conventional or disruptive?	(−3)	(−2)	(−1)	(0)	(+1)	(+2)	(+3)
	Margin Monsters: Do we have strong margins from low costs and high prices?	(−3)	(−2)	(−1)	(0)	(+1)	(+2)	(+3)

CitizenM

citizenM streamlined its entire hotel experience to focus on what it calls mobile citizens, the short-term business, party, culture, or shopping traveler visiting a city. It performed the remarkable feat of substantially reducing costs and simultaneously increasing customer satisfaction.

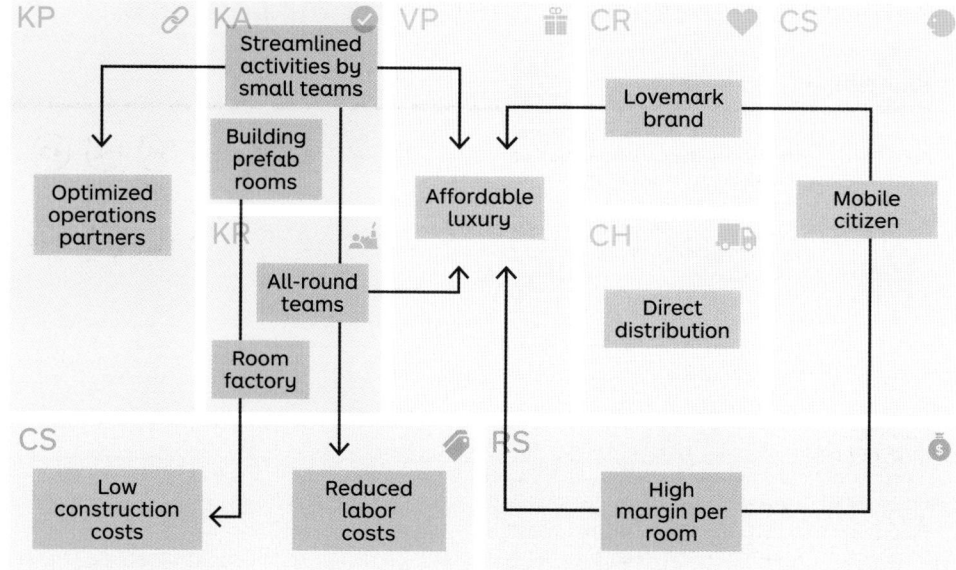

citizenM Business Model

Assessment

The citizenM business model performs extremely well on cost differentiation and does well on revenue differentiation, which leads to an overall extremely high margin business model. The weak spots are the business model's low customer switching costs and slow scalability, due to large capital and construction requirements. The low switching costs and heavy capital requirements mean that citizenM has to carefully monitor customer satisfaction to keep its business model in shape.

Four Actions Framework
Adapted from Blue Ocean Strategy

Eliminate (–)

– Minibar and room service

– Fine-dining table-seated restaurant

– Focus on traditional star rating

– Fitness, wet areas, spa

Raise (↗)

– Occupancy rate and revenue per room

– Effective use of space

– Focus on narrow customer segment

– Margins

– Customer satisfaction and service ratings

– Level of standardization

– Free broadband WiFi and video-on-demand

Reduce (↘)

– Construction costs

– Maintenance costs

– HR and operations costs

Create (+)

– Empowered all-round staff

– New segment: mobile citizens

– Room factory and prefab construction

Assessment Questions for Leaders

Frontstage

▦	**Market Explorers:** How large and attractive is the untapped market potential we are going after?	(-3) (-2) ⊗ (0) (+1) (+2) (+3)
▦	**Channel Kings:** Do we have large-scale and, ideally, direct access to our end-customer?	(-3) (-2) (-1) (0) (+1) ⊗ (+3)
▦	**Gravity Creators:** How easy or difficult is it for our customers to leave or switch to another company?	(-3) ⊗ (-1) (0) (+1) (+2) (+3)

Backstage

▦	**Resource Castles:** Do we own key resources that are difficult or impossible to copy and which give us a significant competitive advantage?	(-3) (-2) (-1) (0) ⊗ (+2) (+3)
▦	**Activity Differentiators:** Do we create significant value for customers because we perform and configure activities in disruptively innovative ways?	(-3) (-2) (-1) (0) (+1) ⊗ (+3)
▦	**Scalers:** How rapidly and how easily can we grow our business model without sub-stantial additional resources and activities (e.g., building infrastructure, finding talent)?	(-3) (-2) ⊗ (0) (+1) (+2) (+3)

Profit Formula

▦	**Revenue Differentiators:** Do we use strong revenue streams and pricing mechanisms to monetize value creation for customers?	(-3) (-2) (-1) (0) (+1) ⊗ (+3)
▦	**Cost Differentiators:** Is our cost structure conventional or disruptive?	(-3) (-2) (-1) (0) (+1) (+2) ⊗
▦	**Margin Monsters:** Do we have strong margins from low costs and high prices?	(-3) (-2) (-1) (0) (+1) (+2) ⊗

citizenM performs poorly on locking in customers. Little prevents them from switching to another hotel chain. Investment in hotel city plots and construction costs make the business model relatively difficult to scale.

citizenM's high occupancy rate and effective use of space lead to higher revenues per room and square meter than those of their competitors.[112]

Due to an innovative activity configuration and extremely high level of standardization, citizenM is able to keep construction and maintenance costs extremely low.[113] A small, empowered, and all-round hotel staff magically keeps HR costs low, despite high customer service ratings.[114]

The combination of lower costs and higher revenues per room leads to a margin level unheard of in the hotel industry.

OneConnect

In 2015 the financial service conglomerate Ping An launches OneConnect to sell the technology it uses internally to other financial institutions.

OneConnect is a subsidiary of China's largest banking and insurance conglomerate. It launched OneConnect as an internal start-up to market cutting edge end-to-end financial technology solutions to small and medium-sized financial institutions. As of June 30, 2019, OneConnect has served over 600 banks and 80 insurance companies in China.[115]

The technology and platform that OneConnect sells to clients was initially developed for PingAn's internal use. OneConnect prides itself on being an industry leader in terms of technical capabilities, with a focus on preparing its clients for the ensuing digital transformation in the financial sector. Solutions range from credit checks and interbank transactions to biometric services, product sales, and mobile retail banking applications.

After a successful launch in China, in 2018, OneConnect established subsidiaries in Hong Kong, Singapore, and Indonesia to service local financial institutions. OneConnect[116] also partners with other fintech institutions to offer its software-as-a-service (SaaS) to the global market.[117]

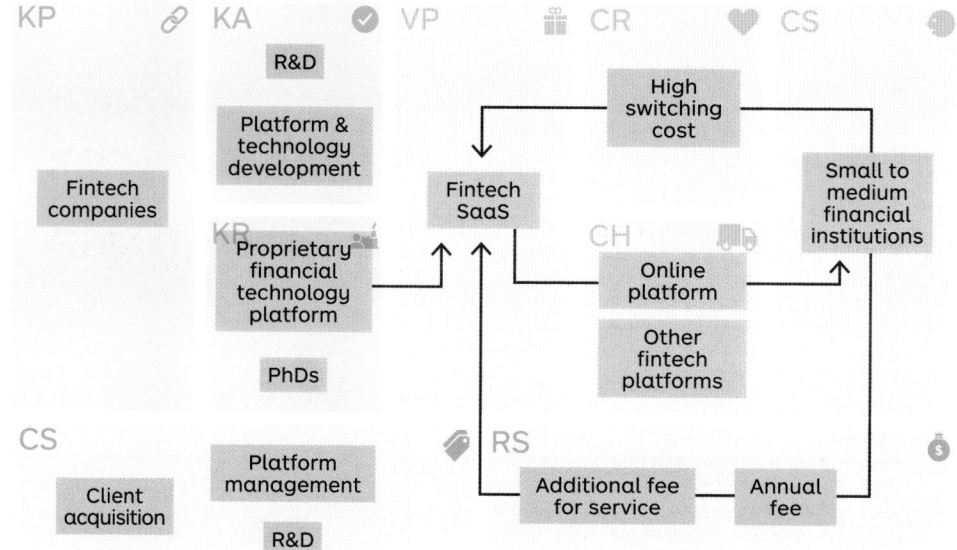

OneConnect Business Model

Assessment

OneConnect built a powerful SaaS business model that performs well on several dimensions. The substantial investments in hiring top developers, conducting fintech R&D, and building and maintaining its platform are compensated by customer lock-in, scalability of its services, recurring revenues, and strong protection of its business model.

Assessment Questions for Leaders

Frontstage

	Market Explorers: How large and attractive is the untapped market potential we are going after?	(−3) (−2) (−1) ⊗ (+1) (+2) (+3)
	Channel Kings: Do we have large-scale and, ideally, direct access to our end-customer?	(−3) (−2) (−1) (0) (+1) ⊗ (+3)
	Gravity Creators: How easy or difficult is it for our customers to leave or switch to another company?	(−3) (−2) (−1) (0) (+1) (+2) ⊗

Backstage

	Resource Castles: Do we own key resources that are difficult or impossible to copy and which give us a significant competitive advantage?	(−3) (−2) (−1) (0) (+1) (+2) ⊗
	Activity Differentiators: Do we create significant value for customers because we perform and configure activities in disruptively innovative ways?	(−3) (−2) (−1) (0) (+1) ⊗ (+3)
	Scalers: How rapidly and how easily can we grow our business model without sub-stantial additional resources and activities (e.g., building infrastructure, finding talent)?	(−3) (−2) (−1) (0) (+1) (+2) ⊗

Profit Formula

	Revenue Differentiators: Do we use strong revenue streams and pricing mechanisms to monetize value creation for customers?	(−3) (−2) (−1) (0) (+1) ⊗ (+3)
	Cost Differentiators: Is our cost structure conventional or disruptive?	(−3) (−2) (−1) ⊗ (+1) (+2) (+3)
	Margin Monsters: Do we have strong margins from low costs and high prices?	(−3) (−2) (−1) ⊗ (+1) (+2) (+3)

Financial institutions that adopt the OneConnect technology platform incur significant switching costs if they leave. Moving to another platform could create substantial downtime and re-training costs for clients.[118] Like for any SaaS, provider lock-in can be substantial. In the finance industry it is even higher, due to security reasons, data confidentiality, and regulation.

OneConnect's proprietary technology is very hard to copy and it constantly innovates. The initial platform was built for Ping An before the organization decided to leverage it for external clients through OneConnect's services. This expansion allowed OneConnect to invest substantially in advanced intellectual property and infrastructure, because its investments serve hundreds of financial institutions, including its owner Ping An.

The company employs legions of data scientists and holds thousands of patents. It constantly develops and updates its technology and platform in order to stay ahead of the curve. OneConnect has one of the most accurate biometric identification systems in the world with 99.8% accuracy.[119]

The SaaS business model requires substantial upfront investments to put the platform in place. However, after this initial investment phase, OneConnect can easily expand into new geographical territories with relatively low investments. OneConnect's hundreds of products can be deployed anywhere around the world.[120]

Salesforce

In 1999 Salesforce.com disrupts the customer relationship management (CRM) arena by offering CRM-as-a-service over the Internet. Salesforce unlocks a new market and continuously strengthens its business model with new innovations.

Salesforce.com was founded in 1999 with the goal of "making enterprise software as easy to use as a website like amazon .com." Salesforce pioneered the software-as-a-service (Saas) for customer relationship management tools. The company didn't stop there and has constantly improved its services and business model. We distinguish between two, nonexhaustive, business model phases: the early business model in 1999 and extensions starting in 2005.

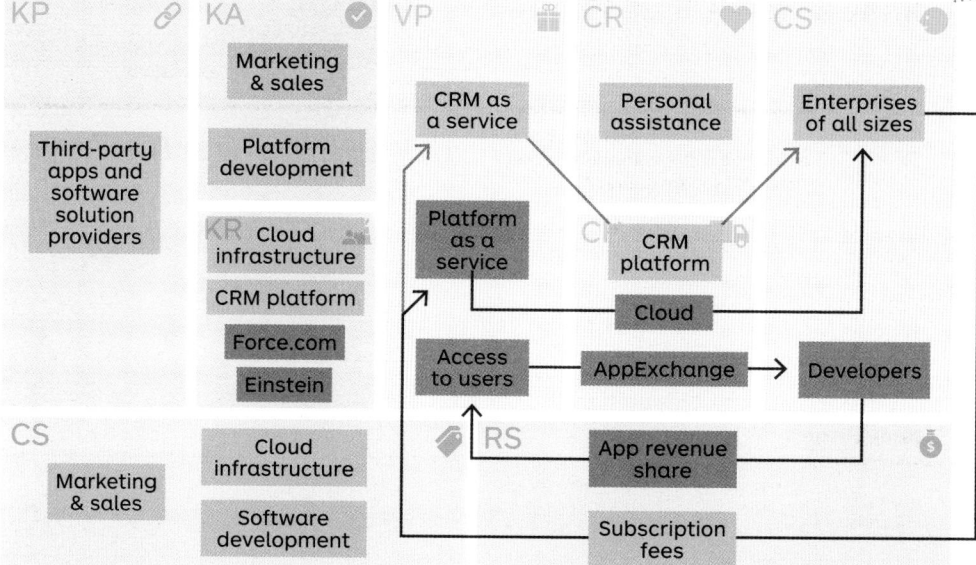

Salesforce.com Business Model

Assessment

Salesforce pioneered the SaaS model, which performs well on several business model dimensions that largely compensate for some of its shortcomings. Once its platform is in place it can scale its services easily and maintain a constant and direct relationship with its customers. The subscription model leads to predictable and recurring revenues and higher customer lifetime value. This compensates for the lower margins due to infrastructure costs.

Salesforce expands its business model in 2005, which addresses some of its initial weaknesses like relatively low switching costs and low protectability of its business model.

Early Business Model (1999) – No Software

Salesforce's platform was unique to the CRM world in that its services could be deployed rapidly without infrastructure investments. Customers didn't require hardware investments and software installations like incumbent CRM providers. Salesforce customers accessed the CRM service through the cloud and payed a recurring subscription fee.

Business Model Extensions – AppExchange, Force.com, and Einstein

Salesforce didn't stop at trailblazing the software-as-a-service model. The company continuously evolved and strengthened their business model over time.

Assessment Questions for Leaders

✗ = Early business model

✗ = Business model extensions

Frontstage

		-3	-2	-1	0	+1	+2	+3
	Market Explorers: How large and attractive is the untapped market potential we are going after?	(−3)	(−2)	(−1)	(0)	(+1)	(+2)	(✗3)
	Channel Kings: Do we have large-scale and, ideally, direct access to our end-customer?	(−3)	(−2)	(−1)	(0)	(+1)	(✗2)	(+3)
	Gravity Creators: How easy or difficult is it for our customers to leave or switch to another company?	(−3)	(−2)	(−1)	(✗)	(+1)	(+2)	(**✗**)

Backstage

		-3	-2	-1	0	+1	+2	+3
	Resource Castles: Do we own key resources that are difficult or impossible to copy and which give us a significant competitive advantage?	(−3)	(−2)	(−1)	(✗)	(+1)	(+2)	(**✗**)
	Activity Differentiators: Do we create significant value for customers because we perform and configure activities in disruptively innovative ways?	(−3)	(−2)	(−1)	(0)	(+1)	(✗2)	(**✗**)
	Scalers: How rapidly and how easily can we grow our business model without sub-stantial additional resources and activities (e.g., building infrastructure, finding talent)?	(−3)	(−2)	(−1)	(0)	(+1)	(+2)	(**✗**)

Profit Formula

		-3	-2	-1	0	+1	+2	+3
	Revenue Differentiators: Do we use strong revenue streams and pricing mechanisms to monetize value creation for customers?	(−3)	(−2)	(−1)	(0)	(+1)	(✗2)	(+3)
	Cost Differentiators: Is our cost structure conventional or disruptive?	(−3)	(−2)	(−1)	(✗)	(+1)	(+2)	(+3)
	Margin Monsters: Do we have strong margins from low costs and high prices?	(−3)	(−2)	(✗)	(0)	(**✗**)	(+2)	(+3)

Salesforce was visionary in predicting the potential of the cloud. A pioneer of SaaS, it opens up CRM services from Fortune 500 companies to the wider market of organizations of all sizes.

Since customers access Salesforce directly via the cloud, the company maintains a permanent customer relationship. Salesforce can continuously push upgrades and new functionalities to its entire customer base.

Because Salesforce provides its service in the cloud it can easily scale and with minimal cost.

Salesforce shifts the transactional license sales models of incumbents to recurring revenues from a service subscription. It increases the customer lifetime value of each customer.

Salesforce's net margins are significantly lower than those of its incumbent competitors. Offering CRM-as-a-service requires investments in hosting, monitoring, customer support, and account management. However, strengths in other areas largely compensate for this weakness.

In 2008 Salesforce releases Force.com (now called Lightning Platform) that allows customers to build their own custom applications on the platform. This substantially scales stickiness and increases switching costs. It extends stickiness by launching Einstein, a service that delivers artificial intelligence (AI) capabilities and allows developers to build apps.

In 2005, Salesforce launches AppExchange, a platform for third-party software that integrates with its CRM. It builds up a large library of hard-to-copy third-party software and shifts from a simple service provider to a platform castle.

Industry	Disruptor
Messaging	**WhatsApp, WeChat**
Auto	**Tesla**
Retail	**Amazon, Alibaba**
Hotel	**Airbnb**
Taxi	**Uber, DiDi**
TV & movie	**Netflix**
Mobile phones	**Apple, Xiaomi**
Music	**Spotify**
Telecommunications	**Skype**
Recruitment	**LinkedIn**
Travel booking	**Expedia**
Venture Capital	**Andreessen Horowitz**

...to be disrupted

Banking
Pharmaceuticals
Legal services
Education
Manufacturing
Healthcare
Insurance
Real estate
Construction
Energy production and distribution
Transport and delivery

What about your industry?

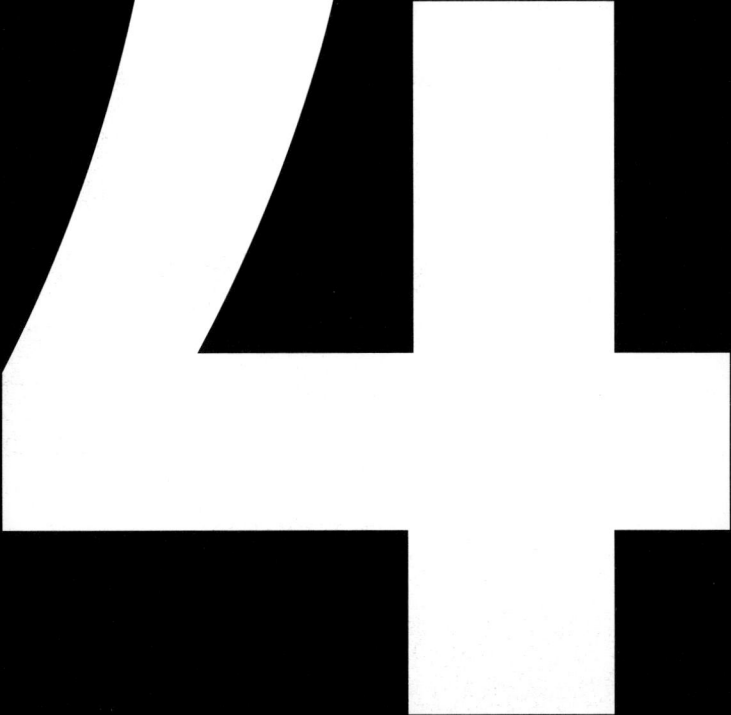

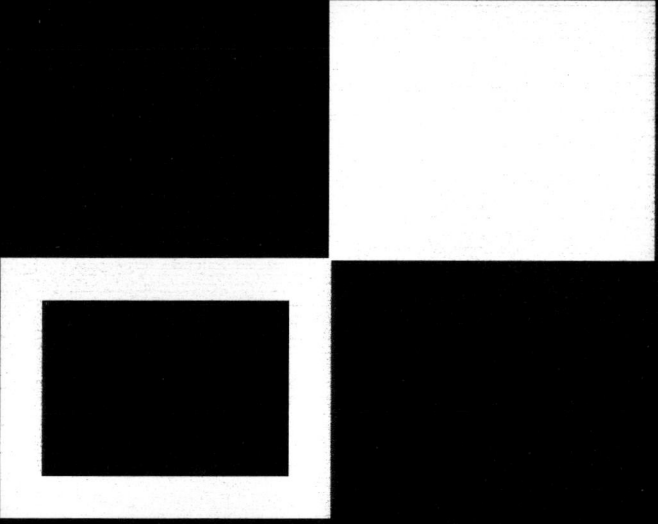

Business Model Shifts

A business model shift describes an organization's transformation from a declining business model to a more competitive one. For example, the shift from product to service. However, in some contexts, the reverse shift, from service to product, might make just as much sense.

Shift Pattern Library

Value Proposition Shifts

p. 231   **From Product to Recurring Service**

p. 234   **From Low Tech to High Tech**

p. 235   **From Sales to Platform**

Frontstage Driven Shifts

p. 243   **From Niche Market to Mass Market**

p. 246   **From B2B to B2(B2)C**

p. 247   **From Low Touch to High Touch**

Backstage Driven Shifts

p. 255   **From Dedicated Resources to Multi-Usage Resources**

p. 258   **From Asset Heavy to Asset Light**

p. 259   **From Closed to Open (Innovation)**

Profit Formula Driven Shifts

p. 267   **From High Cost to Low Cost**

p. 270   **From Transactional to Recurring Revenue**

p. 271   **From Conventional to Contrarian**

From Original Business Model

Apply New Business Model Pattern

Shift to New Business Model

228

Shift
Patterns

From Original Business Model...

The companies we portray in this section all started from an existing business model. This existing business model is often outdated and in decline and requires an overhaul.

Apply New Business Model Pattern

Twelve different shift patterns that established companies can apply to substantially improve and boost an existing business model are highlighted. We describe each pattern so that you can make use of it as a reference library.

...Shift to New Business Model

Each case serves to highlight a pattern in action. The company's entire business model isn't outlined, we just show how it applied a particular pattern to shift from an old business model to a new, more competitive business model. In reality, an entire business model has many more building blocks that we omit to focus on the shift.

Legend

- From Original Business Model

- Apply New Business Model Pattern

- Shift to New Business Model

- Pattern Building Blocks

- Optional Pattern Building Blocks

- Original Business Model Blocks

- Other Business Model Blocks

From Product to Recurring Service

p. 232   Hilti

From Low Tech to High Tech

p. 236   Netflix

From Sales to Platform

p. 238   The App Store

230

Value Proposition Shifts

A radical shift of the value created for customers

From Product to Recurring Service

is the shift from manufacturing (and/or buying) and selling products toward providing a recurring service. Selling products on a transactional basis requires a continuous effort for every sale and it is often unpredictable. Recurring services require upfront customer acquisition costs that lead to recurring revenues. Revenues become more predictable and grow exponentially, because you build on top of a continuously growing base of customers.

231

STRATEGIC REFLECTION
How might we grow recurring and predictable revenues by providing a recurring service, rather than selling a product?

Upfront acquisition costs per customer might be higher, but revenues become more predictable and the lifetime value of customers often increases. Product and/or technology innovation can often provide the foundation for new services.

EXAMPLE
HILTI

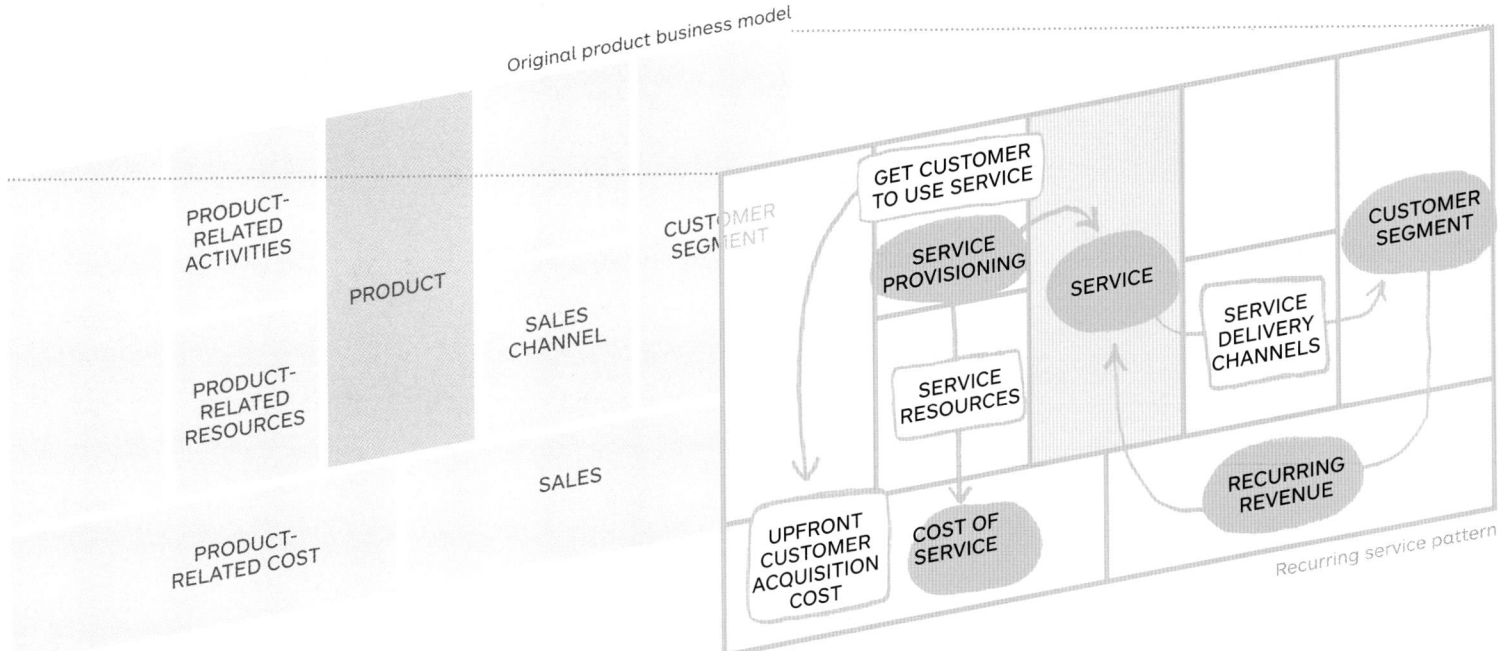

Original product business model

PRODUCT-RELATED ACTIVITIES

PRODUCT

PRODUCT-RELATED RESOURCES

SALES CHANNEL

PRODUCT-RELATED COST

SALES

CUSTOMER SEGMENT

GET CUSTOMER TO USE SERVICE

SERVICE PROVISIONING

SERVICE

SERVICE RESOURCES

SERVICE DELIVERY CHANNELS

CUSTOMER SEGMENT

UPFRONT CUSTOMER ACQUISITION COST

COST OF SERVICE

RECURRING REVENUE

Recurring service pattern

Hilti

Hilti shifts from selling high quality tools to selling tool fleet management services to construction companies, after a key customer requests a holistic tool management system to increase productivity.

In 2000, one of Hilti's customers asked for a holistic tool management solution. That made Hilti realize that customers didn't want to own tools, but always wanted their workers to work productively. Hilti began an initial pilot program for tool fleet management in Switzerland and eventually rolled out the service worldwide in 2003.

With tool fleet management, Hilti became more relevant to construction companies by reducing nonproductive time for workers and adding a gain of taking on more customer jobs (e.g., tool repair).

Hilti also discovered that customers were willing to lease more tools than they had ever purchased. Some even asked Hilti to include non-Hilti tools in the service to completely prevent nonproductive time due to broken tools.

When the 2008 financial crisis hit the construction sector, many stopped purchasing new equipment. Yet Hilti's business model shift from a product to a recurring service allowed it to overcome the crisis and it has continued to grow since.

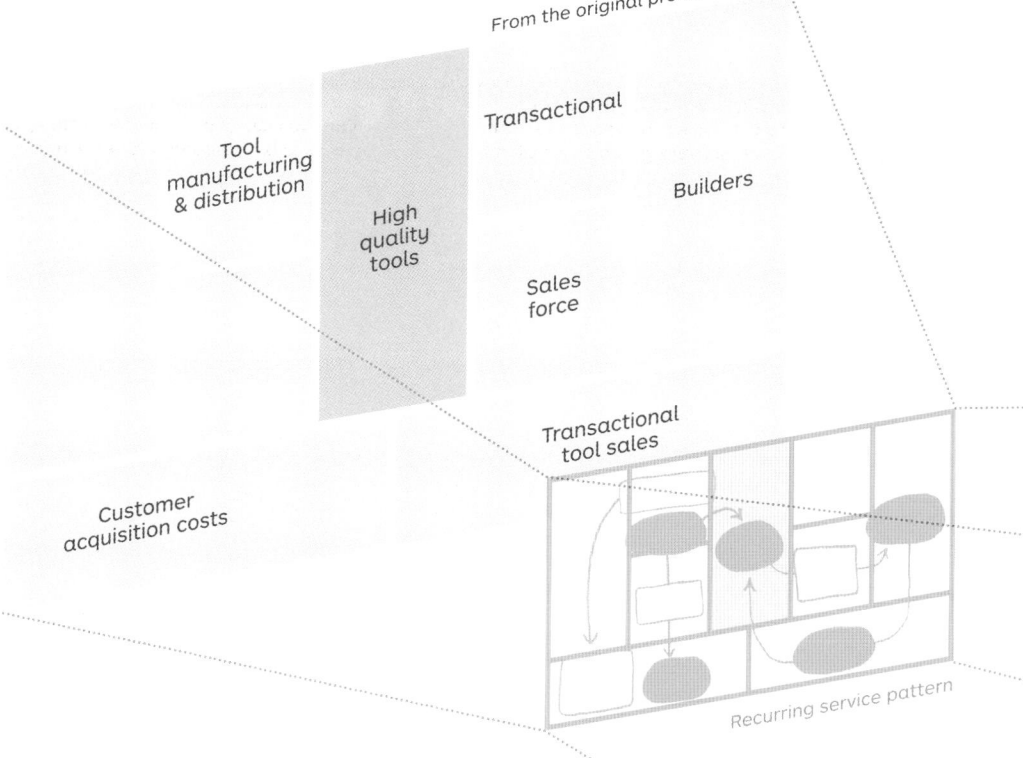

1 From Product to Recurring Service and Revenues

Managers of building companies have a lot more to worry about than just buying tools. Hilti recognizes that in 2000 and starts offering to track, repair, replace, and upgrade the whole tool fleet for their clients. This increases their productivity by ensuring they always have the right tools, properly maintained and reliable at all times. Hilti allows customers to lease the tools through a monthly subscription rather than paying for them upfront – enabling predictability of costs for building company managers and recurring revenues for Hilti.

2 From Product-Related Activities to Service Provisioning

Hilti evolves its key activities from its core of manufacturing and sales to fleet management activities that enable tool tracking, repairing, replacement, and upgrading.

IMPROVE PATTERNS

3 From Sales Channel to Service Delivery Channels

Hilti retrains its sales force to speak to executives rather than project managers, and about logistics and efficiency rather than tools. It adds new online service channels to the traditional sales channel, raising awareness about the service, helping fleet customers access their inventory online, and enabling them to access Hilti easily in case of a problem with their tools.

4 From a Product to a Service Cost Structure

Hilti's cost structure adapts to this new service orientation with new fleet management costs. To date, this shift has added over CHF1 billion worth of receivable volume to Hilti's balance sheet. Even customer acquisition costs (CAC) increase, due to the longer sales and contracting process with building company managers. The CAC, however, is now a one-time cost, leading to recurring revenues and opportunities for additional revenues with the long-term relationship.

1.5
million tools

Hilti had 1.5 million tools under fleet management in 2015.[1]

2
billion CHF

Total contract value of all tools under fleet management in 2018.[2]

"The big benefit of recurring service revenues helped us to stabilize our business during the [global financial] crisis—a time when most contractors wouldn't purchase new equipment"

—DR. CHRISTOPH LOOS

CEO of Hilti

233

VALUE PROPOSITION SHIFTS

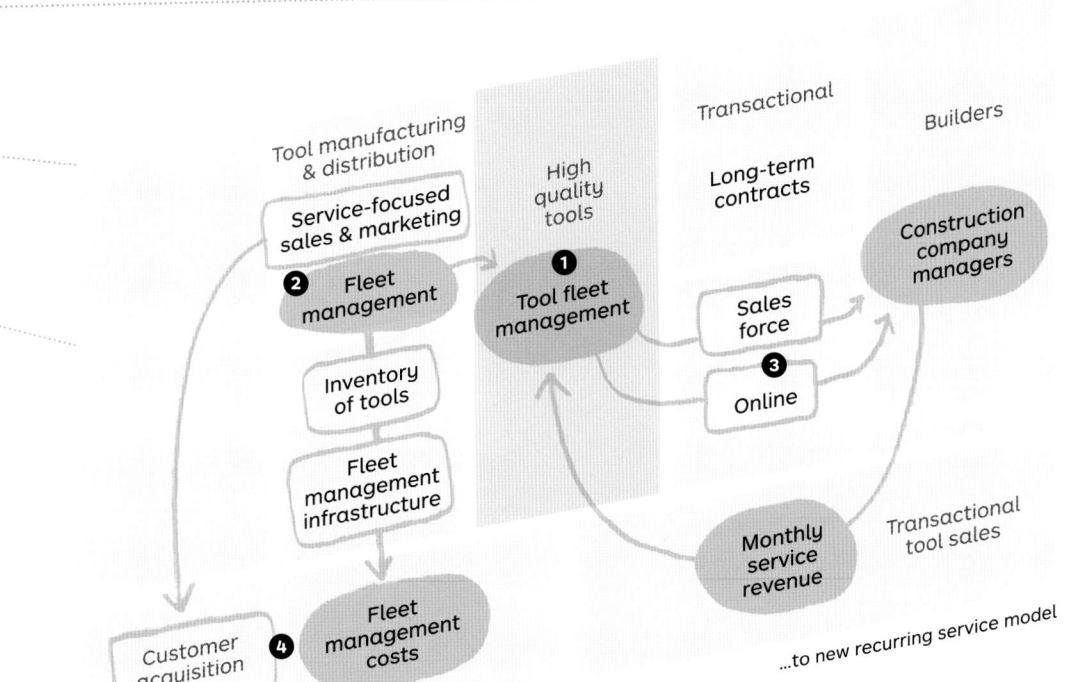

...to new recurring service model

From Low Tech to High Tech

STRATEGIC REFLECTION
How might we scale our reach, increase price, and boost revenues by transforming a low-tech value proposition into a high-tech value proposition? Which new technology activities, skills, and resources are required to accomplish this shift? Which new tech costs does this create? How attractive are the resulting margins?

EXAMPLE
Netflix

is the shift from basic, often labor-intensive, low-tech value propositions toward technology-based value propositions. This shift allows scaling reach and increasing price, which leads to a boost in revenues. The increase in price and revenues compensates for new technology-related costs and often leads to higher margins.

234

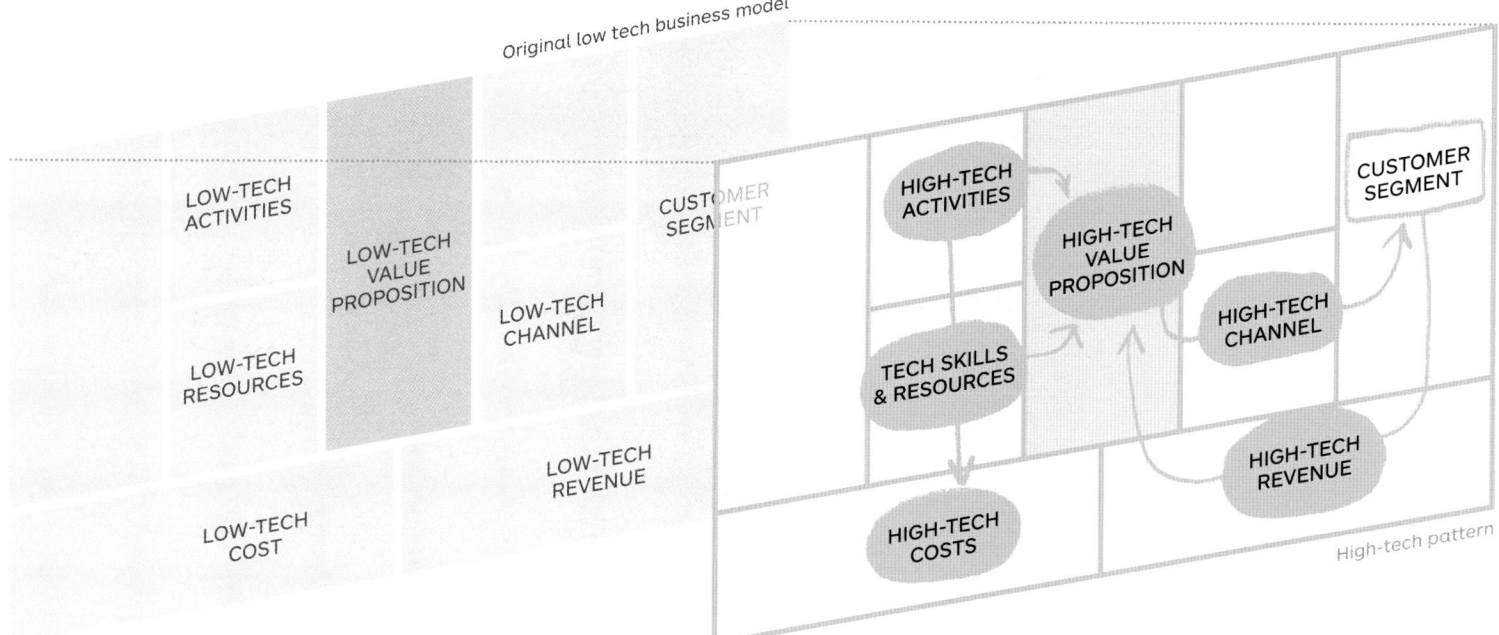

Original low tech business model

LOW-TECH ACTIVITIES

LOW-TECH VALUE PROPOSITION

CUSTOMER SEGMENT

LOW-TECH CHANNEL

LOW-TECH RESOURCES

LOW-TECH REVENUE

LOW-TECH COST

HIGH-TECH ACTIVITIES

HIGH-TECH VALUE PROPOSITION

CUSTOMER SEGMENT

HIGH-TECH CHANNEL

TECH SKILLS & RESOURCES

HIGH-TECH REVENUE

HIGH-TECH COSTS

High-tech pattern

From Sales to Platform

STRATEGIC REFLECTION
How might we gain a competitive advantage by establishing ourselves as the platform connecting our customers with third-party products and service providers?

This will allow us to increase value for our customers and build an ecosystem of third-party product and service providers. Platform ecosystems are harder to replicate than copying products.

EXAMPLE
iPhone & App Store

is the shift from value-chain activities and selling products toward products that become a platform for third-party products and value-added services. Value increases for customers because they don't just purchase a product, but buy into a platform ecosystem. The value for third-party product and service providers is access to a customer base. Platforms are harder to disrupt than simple products because they create resource castles network effects (see p. 164).

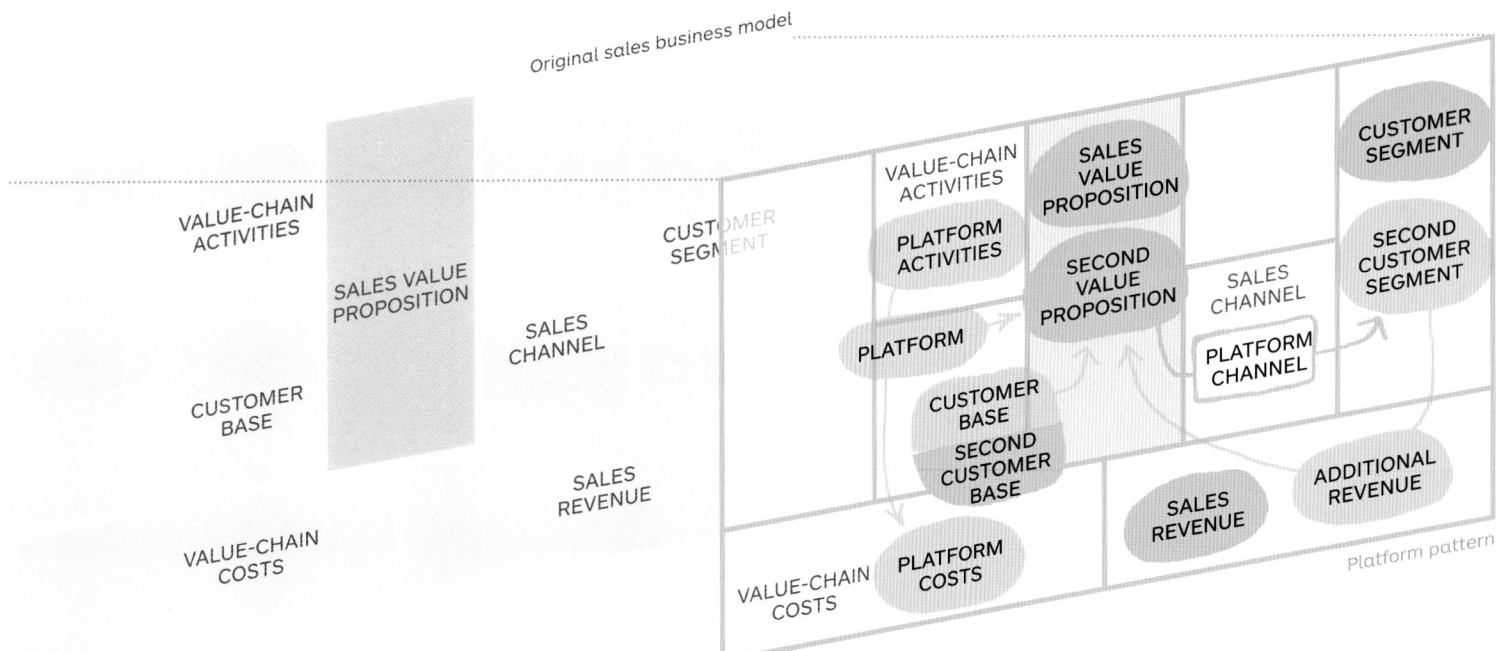

Original sales business model

VALUE-CHAIN ACTIVITIES

SALES VALUE PROPOSITION

CUSTOMER BASE

CUSTOMER SEGMENT

SALES CHANNEL

SALES REVENUE

VALUE-CHAIN COSTS

VALUE-CHAIN ACTIVITIES

PLATFORM ACTIVITIES

PLATFORM

SALES VALUE PROPOSITION

SECOND VALUE PROPOSITION

CUSTOMER BASE

SECOND CUSTOMER BASE

VALUE-CHAIN COSTS

PLATFORM COSTS

SALES CHANNEL

PLATFORM CHANNEL

SALES REVENUE

CUSTOMER SEGMENT

SECOND CUSTOMER SEGMENT

ADDITIONAL REVENUE

Platform pattern

Netflix

Netflix shifts from a mail order DVD rental company to an online streaming platform in 2007 when Internet speeds and consumer devices align with Reed Hastings's vision of "movies on the Internet."

In 1998 Reed Hastings and Marc Randolph launched Netflix as an online DVD rental service. They believed it was the right product and service for the Internet at the time.

Yet from the start the founders had a vision of a video streaming platform. Netflix invested 1 to 2% of its revenue in downloading services, waiting patiently to transform its business model toward streaming with increasing Internet bandwidth.[3]

In 2007, Netflix successfully shifted from low tech to high tech, replacing physical DVDs with online streaming as its main source of revenue.

Revenues grew tenfold in the following decade, with physical DVD shipping no longer constraining scalability. By 2018, 96% of revenue came from streaming.

Netflix adapted its business model again in 2013 and began producing original content. In 2019, Netflix spent an estimated $15 billion on content.[4]

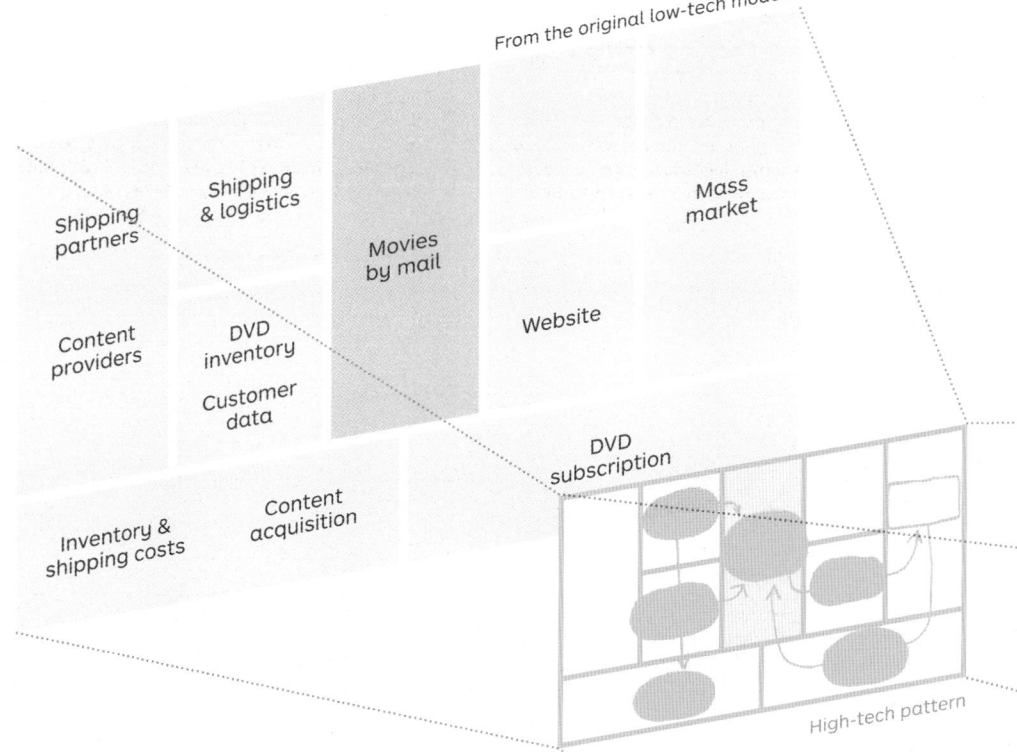

From the original low-tech model...

High-tech pattern

1 From Low-Tech to High-Tech Value Proposition

Netflix launches as an online DVD rental business in 1998, with the vision to move to streaming as soon as Internet speeds permit. In 2007 it makes that vision a reality and shifts to streaming content online.

2 From Low-Tech to High-Tech Activities

To deliver streaming Netflix executes a major shift in key activities. They move from labor-intensive activities such as shipping and logistics to tech activities such as streaming platform development and maintenance. Netflix also expands into licensing and producing content.

3 From Low-Tech to High-Tech Skills and Resources

Streaming results in major changes to key resources, with the streaming platform replacing the DVD inventory. Software and network engineering skills become central. Customer-viewing data and recommendation algorithms gain even more importance with the shift to streaming. Data drives content investment decisions and helps customers find relevant content.

4 From Low-Tech to High-Tech Costs

With the major shift in activities and resources Netflix's cost structure evolves from that of a logistics company to one of a software and platform company. Main costs are now platform development and maintenance. In the future Netflix will also increase its investments in content licensing and their own production.

5 From Low-Tech to High-Tech Revenues

Netflix experiments with several subscription plans. To boost growth in 2007 it lowers the price of its streaming plan to $9.99 per month (compared to its DVD subscription of $19.95 per month in 2004). While revenue per customer declines, the ease of access and global reach leads to high customer growth and subsequently greater revenues from its high-tech streaming value proposition.

10%
of U.S. TV viewing

Netflix now accounts for 10% of U.S. TV viewing time. Netflix says it streams 100 million hours a day to TV screens in the United States.[5]

158
million

Paid subscribers globally as of September 2019.[6]

...to new high-tech model

"DVDs will continue to generate big profits in the near future. Netflix has at least another decade of dominance ahead of it. But movies over the Internet are coming, and at some point it will become big business."

—REED HASTINGS IN 2005,
Netflix founder

The App Store

With the release of the App Store in 2008, Apple shifts its business model from selling hardware and music to a platform business connecting millions of app developers with iPhone users. This shift significantly increases customer value, creates a lock-in, and produces strong network effects.

238

Apple launched the iPhone in 2007 and the App Store, its platform for smartphone apps, in 2008.

Steve Jobs was initially hesitant to let third-party developers in the App Store but changed his mind as it ultimately fit into his vision of adding value to the iPhone. The App Store became a compelling, complementary value proposition to the iPhone. The two were promoted as one, with the memorable 2009 tagline: "There's an App for That."

The App Store enabled Apple to shift its business model from selling a phone to managing a platform. This platform became so powerful that in 2019, the U.S. Supreme Court allowed an antitrust lawsuit against Apple to proceed (based on the premise that Apple has an effective monopoly over the App Store).

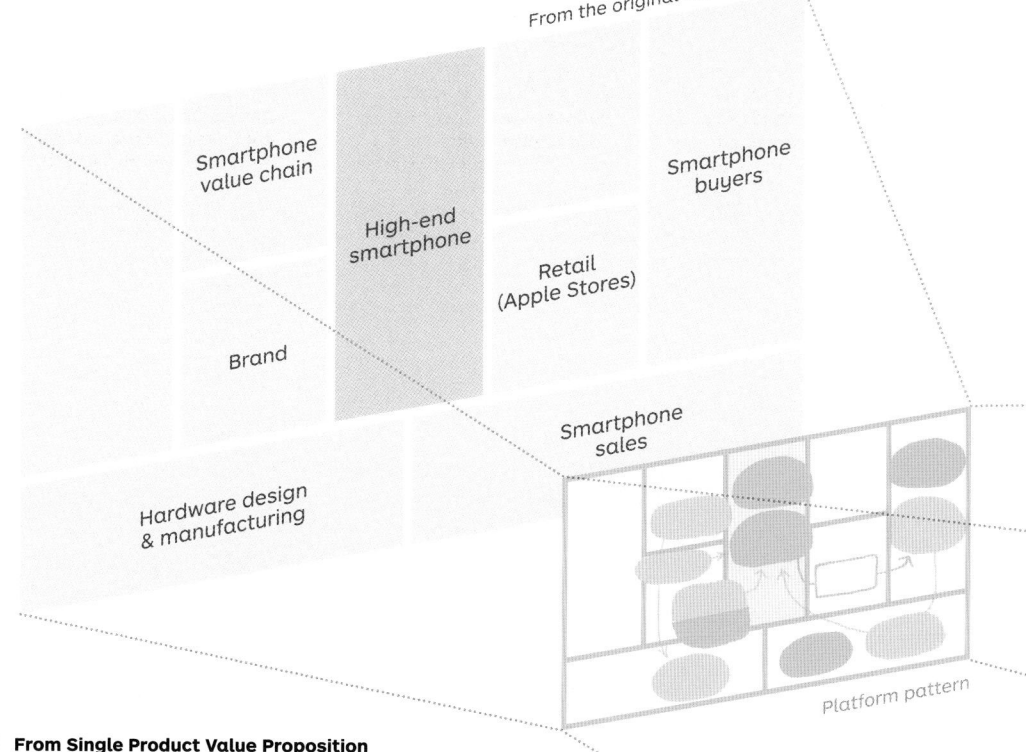

From the original sales model...

Smartphone value chain

High-end smartphone

Smartphone buyers

Retail (Apple Stores)

Brand

Smartphone sales

Hardware design & manufacturing

Platform pattern

1 From Single Product Value Proposition for One Segment to Second Platform Value Proposition to Another Segment

One year after launching the iPhone, Apple releases the App Store, shifting from just selling phones to becoming a platform. This has two consequences:

1. The attractiveness of the iPhone grows with every additional game, utility, and entertainment app added to the App Store.

2. Apple's mass of iPhone users willing to pay for apps becomes an alluring value proposition to attract app developers.

Apple is the first mobile phone manufacturer to shift toward becoming a mobile-first platform that connects consumers with app developers on a large global scale.

2 From Sales Channel to Platform as a Channel

Apple also extends its channels with the shift from sales to platform. The App Store becomes a continuous platform channel that connects iPhone owners with app developers. Retail and Apple Stores where buyers get their phones is a much more transactional sales channel.

IMPROVE PATTERNS

3 From Value Chain Activities to Platform Activities

Apple continues to manage value chain activities for its smartphones, yet adds key activities such as App Store development and maintenance to enable its platform business.

4 From Nonexistent to Strong Network Effects

The App Store becomes a significant part of Apple's business model and creates strong network effects. The more iPhone users, the more attractive the value proposition for app developers becomes. The more app developers, the more apps on the platform and, subsequently the more attractive the value proposition for iPhone buyers.

5 From Sales to Additional Revenue Stream

The App Store generates a new source of revenue for Apple—taking a 15 to 30% commission on every app and subscription purchased within the App Store. Later in Apple's history this recurring revenue helps Apple diversify away from a purely transactional, hardware sales model toward more service revenues.

2 million

The App Store launched with 552 apps and has grown to 2 million with over 180 billion apps downloaded in the past decade.[7]

$120 billion

Amount Apple has paid developers since the App Store launched.[8]

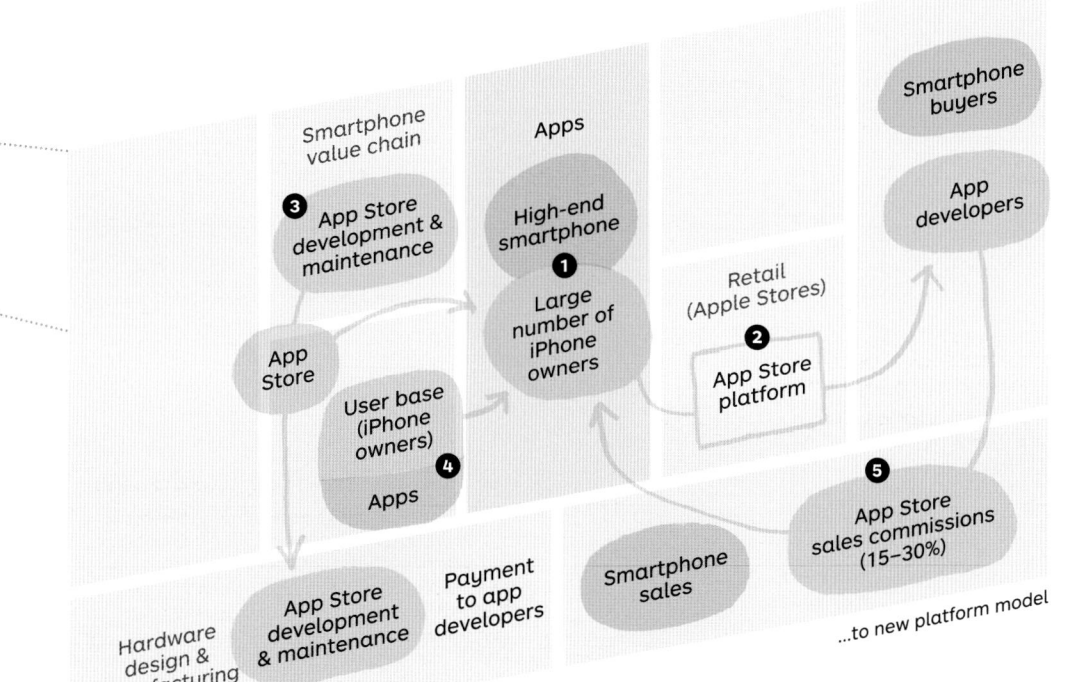

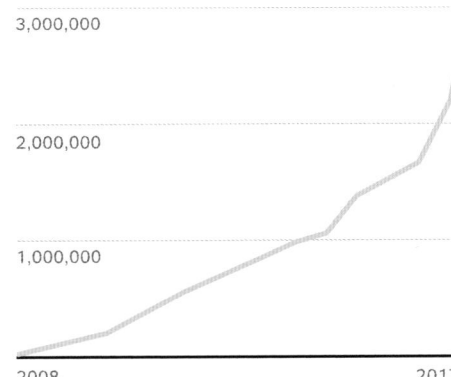

Number of Available Apps in the Apple App Store[9]

3,000,000

2,000,000

1,000,000

2008   2017

From High Tech to Low Tech
2003 ～～ 2006

REVERSE

Nintendo Wii

In the early 2000s, Nintendo no longer has the means to compete on high-tech gaming consoles. In 2006, it turns a weakness into an opportunity and releases the Wii. The Wii features inferior technology but is an instant success with casual gamers.

In 2003, the profits of the Japanese game and console developer Nintendo fell by 38%. Several major game developers pulled their support for the GameCube, Nintendo's main console at the time. The company was in a "state of crisis." It had to react and decided to take a different approach.

Nintendo refocused on its core mission of play over power. It acknowledged that it could no longer compete in the race to build the most powerful console with the best graphics at the lowest cost. It sidestepped competition and released the Wii in 2006—a simplified console targeted at the mass market of casual gamers.

Nintendo sold five times more Wii than GameCube consoles. It regained market leadership for the next few years by shifting from high-tech to low-tech consoles with off-the-shelf components.[10]

IMPROVE PATTERNS

240

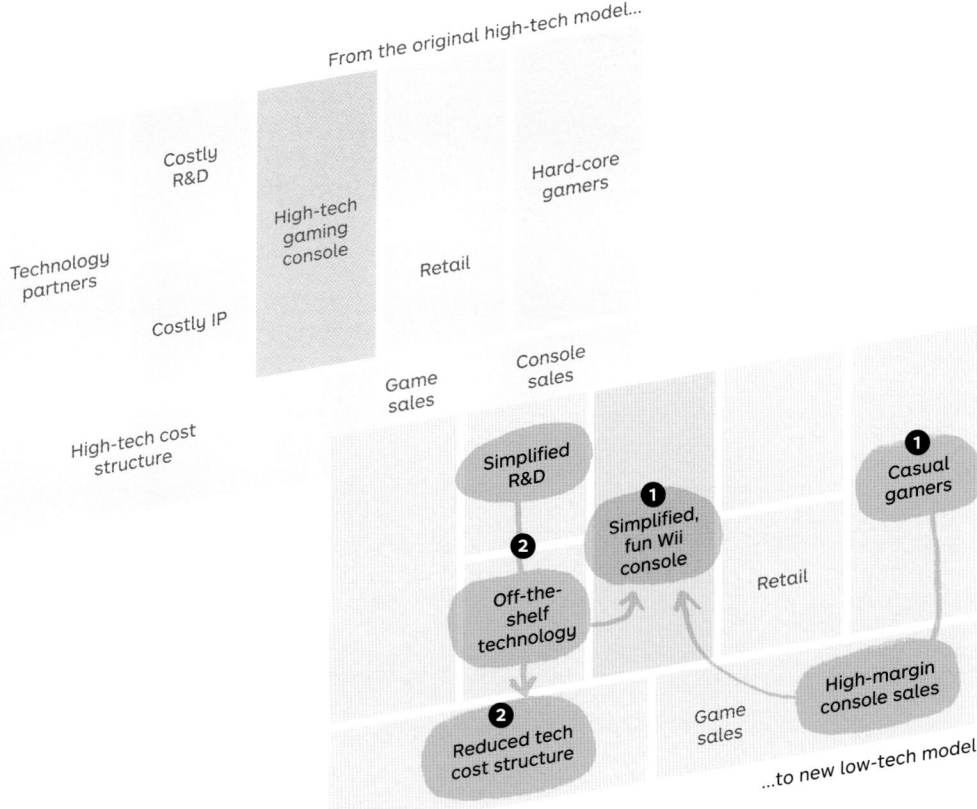

From the original high-tech model...

...to new low-tech model

1 From High Tech for Traditional Customer Segment to Low Tech for Untapped Customer Segment

With the Wii, Nintendo decides to break the rules of competition in the game console market. It shifts from competing on technology performance for hardcore gamers to fun gameplay and motion control for casual gamers, all enabled by cheap, off-the-shelf technology. The Wii's main competitors at the time, the Xbox 360 from Microsoft and PS3 from Sony, have 20 times more graphic processing power and more than four times as much computing power. Yet the unique low-tech Wii resonates with the large and untapped market of casual gamers.

2 From High-Tech Cost Structure to Low-Tech Cost Structure

Nintendo shifts from costly high-tech activities and resources to lower-cost ones, because the Wii makes do with less processing power and lower quality graphics. Manufacturing the Wii is much simpler and cheaper because it uses off-the-shelf components. The significant changes in the cost structure allow Nintendo to make a profit on every Wii sold, as compared to Sony and Microsoft, who need to subsidize their consoles.

Amazon Private Label

In 2009, Amazon expands from platform to sales by launching Amazon private labels. It copies third-party sellers who created successful businesses by sourcing products absent from Amazon's platform. Amazon sees this as an opportunity to create its own line of products.

In 1999 Amazon launched its third-party seller marketplace and established itself as an incredibly successful e-commerce platform for other retailers. In 2007 Amazon began to use its platform to sell its own electronic devices (Kindle e-reader) and expanded to private label products under the AmazonBasics brand.

While many companies aim to shift from sales to platform, Amazon executed a reverse shift from platform to sales. With its private label business Amazon started to compete with third-party suppliers who are also customers of its e-commerce business.

Amazon continuously expanded its private label product catalog with a wide selection (from electronics to clothing and everyday accessories) and lower prices.

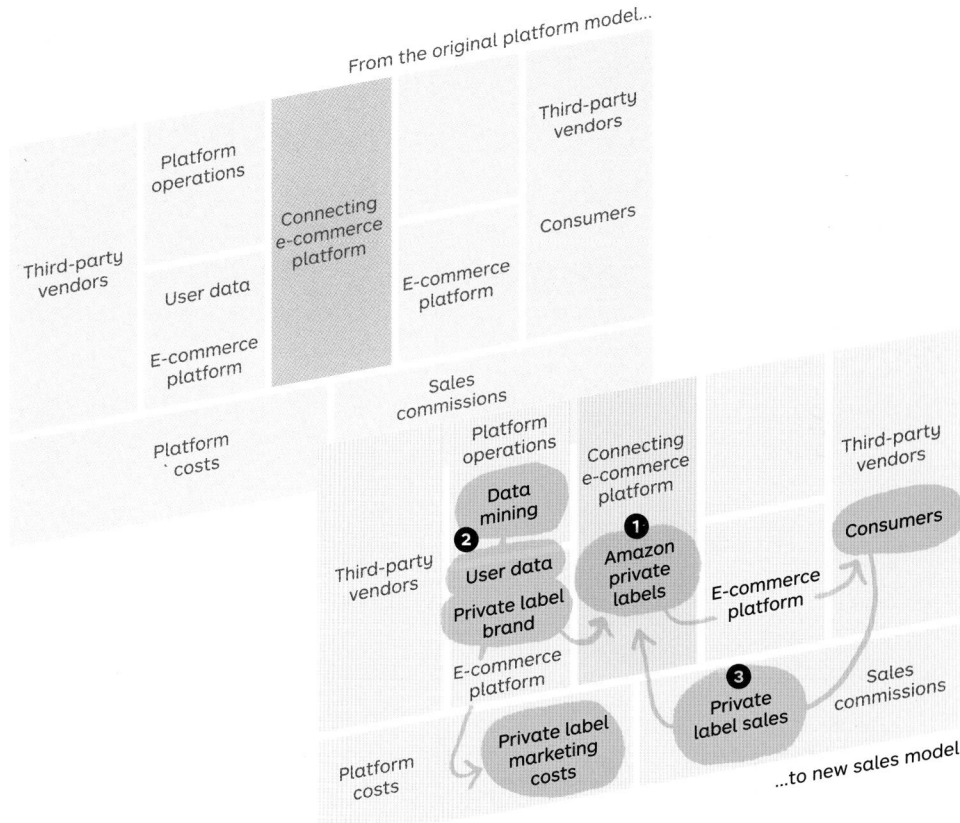

From the original platform model...

...to new sales model

241

VALUE PROPOSITION SHIFTS

1 From Platform Value Proposition to Sales Value Proposition

With Amazon marketplace the company built the leading e-commerce platform for third-party products. In 2007 Amazon decides to shift towards also selling its own branded products. The Kindle e-reader is the first. In 2009 Amazon launches its private label business under the AmazonBasics name. It expands from selling charging cables and batteries to thousands of everyday items.

2 From Platform Activities to Sales-Focused Activities

Amazon uses the consumer data from its platform business to identify product candidates for its private label business. Amazon markets successful product candidates under the AmazonBasics brand. It purchases products in bulk from retailers already transacting on its platform, rebrands them and sells them as recommended products on its e-commerce platform.

3 From Platform Revenues to Sales Revenues

Amazon expands its revenue streams from transaction commissions to sales margins with the shift from platform to sales. Revenues from selling its own private label products are an attractive addition to a pure commission-based model.

From Niche Market to Mass Market

p. 244   TED

From B2B to B2(B2)C

p. 248   Intel Inside

From Low Touch to High Touch

p. 250   Apple Genius Bar

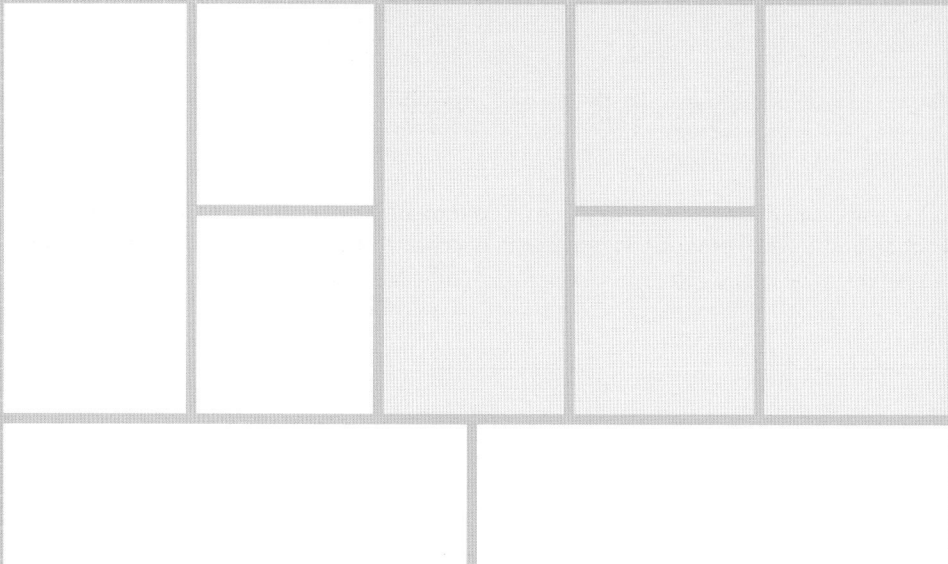

242

Frontstage Driven Shifts

A radical shift of who is targeted and how products and services are delivered

From Niche Market to Mass Market

is the shift from niche market player to mass market player. This often requires a simplification of the value proposition to cater to a larger market. The lower price that such a simplified value proposition commands is compensated by a larger volume of revenues from the mass market. This shift requires marketing activities, channels, and a brand that are tailored to the mass market.

STRATEGIC REFLECTION
How might we simplify our value proposition to break out of a niche market and cater to a mass market? How might we change marketing and brand to reach a mass market? How can we compensate for lower prices and increased marketing costs with more revenues from a larger mass market?

EXAMPLE
TED

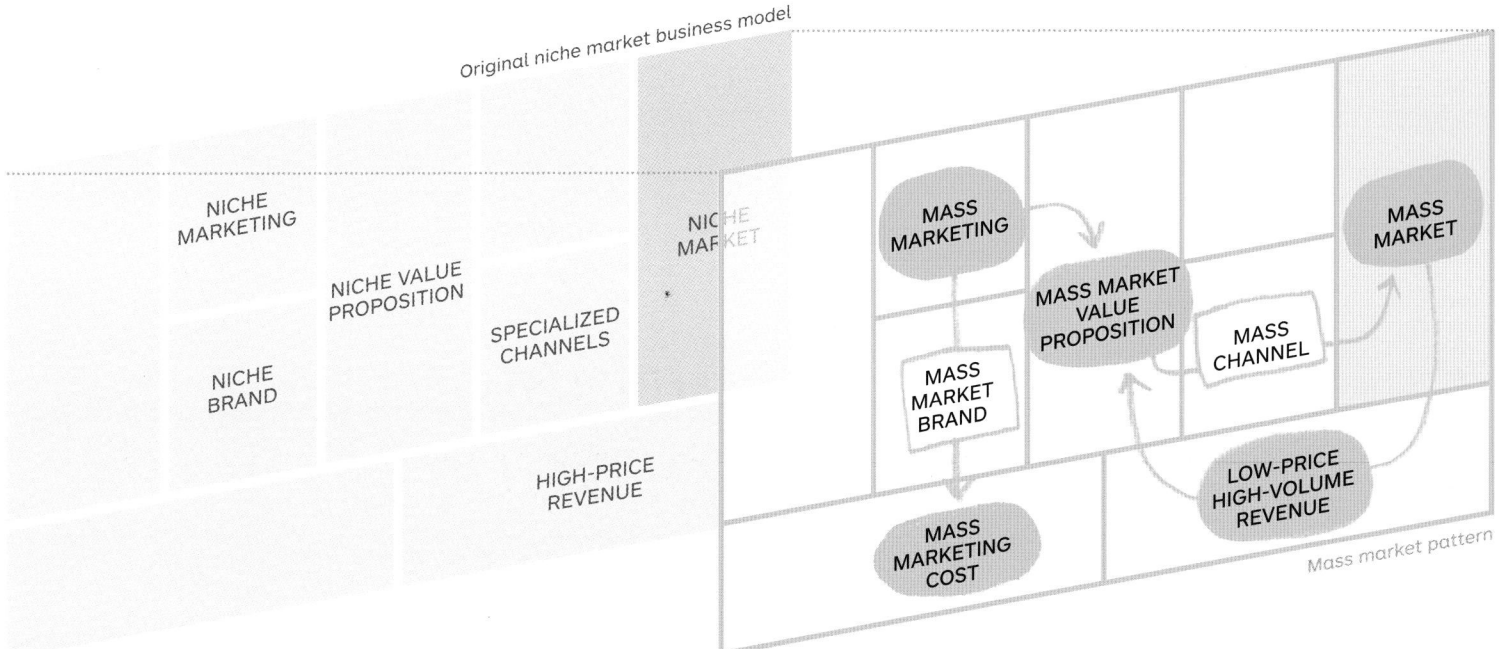

Original niche market business model

NICHE MARKETING

NICHE VALUE PROPOSITION

SPECIALIZED CHANNELS

NICHE MARKET

NICHE BRAND

HIGH-PRICE REVENUE

MASS MARKETING

MASS MARKET VALUE PROPOSITION

MASS CHANNEL

MASS MARKET

MASS MARKET BRAND

LOW-PRICE HIGH-VOLUME REVENUE

MASS MARKETING COST

Mass market pattern

TED

TED puts six TED Talks online in 2006 and the success is overwhelming. TED transforms from an invite-only, niche conference to a mass, online destination for the intellectually curious.

TED launched in 1984 as a conference for the intellectually curious on the topics of technology, entertainment, and design. The first conference in California lost money and the event wasn't held again until 1990. From then on, it became an annual event.

In 2001, a nonprofit acquired TED with a renewed commitment to seek "out the most interesting people on Earth and let them communicate their passion." It wasn't until six TED Talks were posted online (for free) in 2006 that TED became a mass market, viral sensation.

After one million views within three months TED relaunched its website to focus on videos. By 2012, TED Talks reached its one billionth view.[11]

TED continues to reinject profits from conferences and sponsored grants into its online platform, content development, and mass marketing activities. This way ideas shared in local TED conferences continue to be available to the masses via the recorded TED Talks.

IMPROVE PATTERNS

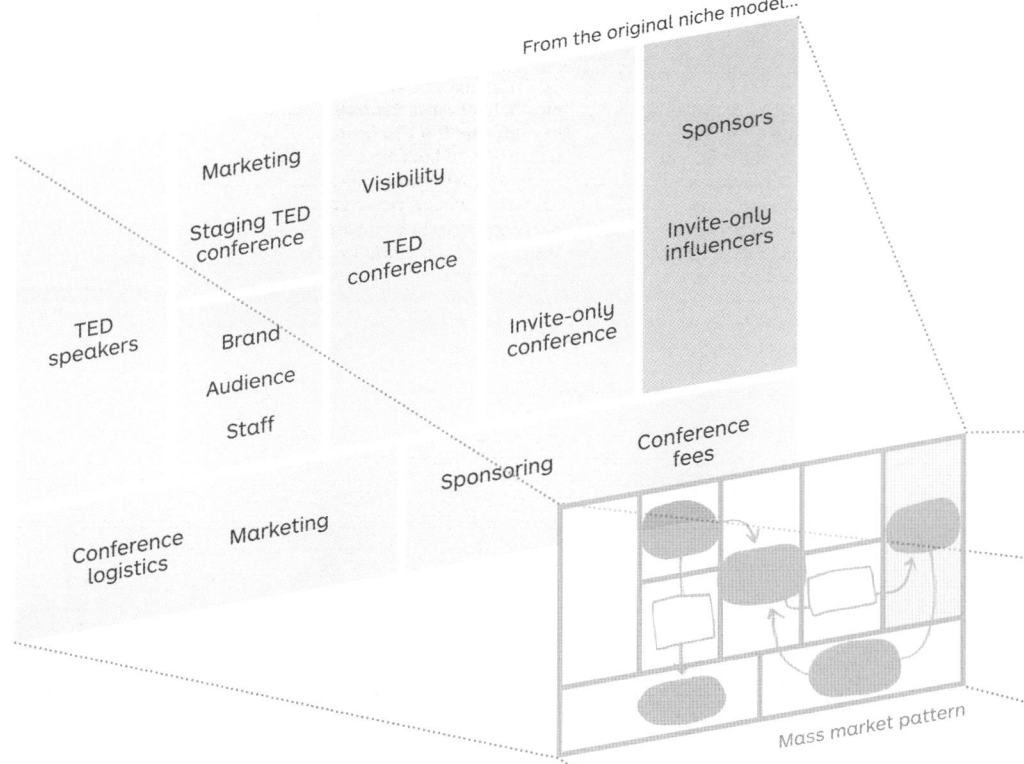

1 From Niche to Mass Market

After the success of posting videos of a few talks online, TED decides to shift from an exclusive conference, once a year in California, to providing video content of all its talks online. TED shifts from locally impacting 800 people per year to reaching millions of people every day.

2 From Specialized Channels to Mass Channel

Historically TED used local channels to sell their invite-only tickets for their conference. With the success of TED Talks, TED develops a digital infrastructure to reach the masses. TED Talks are distributed globally through its website.

3 From Niche Activities to Mass Marketing

Historically TED's activities focused on the organization and sales of the yearly conference. TED evolves its activities to reach as many viewers as possible with its slogan "ideas worth spreading." It also expands its activities to world-class video production in order to capture and broadcast world-class content.

4 From Niche to Mass Brand

TED Talks have more than nine million views per day in 2018, and the TED brand has grown to become a mass market brand well-known to curious individuals and attractive to sponsors that are required to fund TED's growth.

1
million views

The first six TED Talks posted online reached 1 million views within three months.[12]

3,200+
TED Talks online

As of December 2019, 3,200 TED talks are posted online for free.[13]

6,000

New video views per minute.[14]

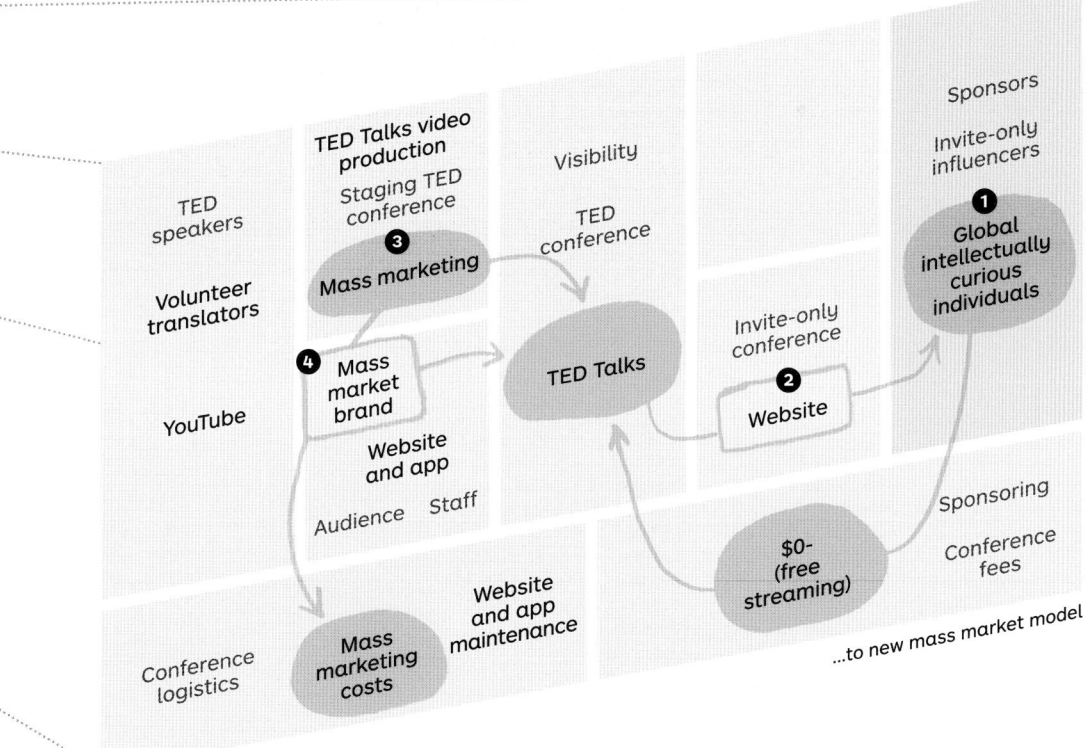

...to new mass market model

"When we first put up a few of the talks as an experiment, we got such impassioned responses that we decided to flip the organization on its head and think of ourselves not so much as a conference but as 'ideas worth spreading,' building a big website around it. The conference is still the engine, but the website is the amplifier that takes the ideas to the world."

—CHRIS ANDERSON, MARCH 2012
Curator of TED

FRONSTAGE DRIVEN SHIFTS

From B2B to B2(B2)C

is the shift from a B2B supplier that's invisible to the consumer toward a brand that matters to the consumer. This doesn't necessarily require a shift toward cutting out the middleman completely and going it alone. It's often a brand shift toward becoming more relevant to the consumer and includes increased consumer marketing and B2C brand development or extension.

STRATEGIC REFLECTION
How might we increase revenues by becoming more relevant to consumers if we are a "hidden" B2B supplier? How might we position ourselves to create value for consumers? How will that positioning make us more attractive to our B2B customer and incentivize them to make our brand visible in their product and/or service?

EXAMPLE
Intel Inside

246

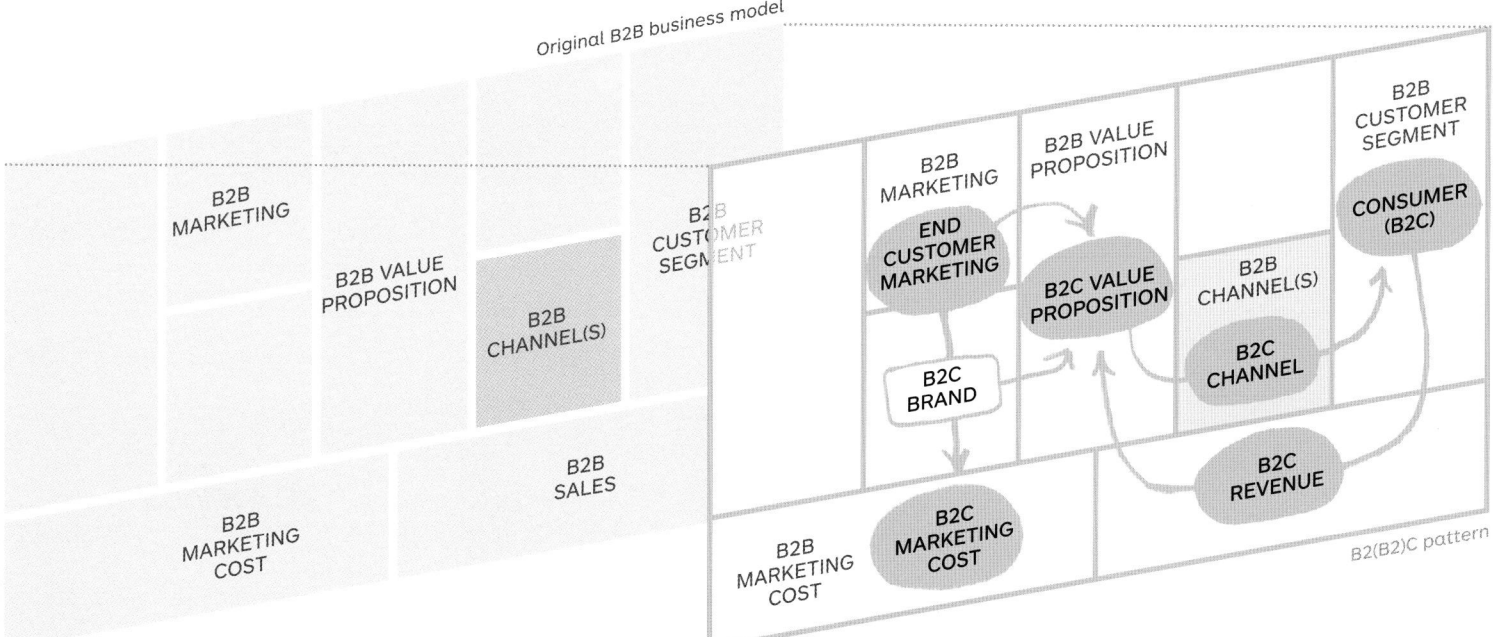

Original B2B business model

- B2B MARKETING
- B2B VALUE PROPOSITION
- B2B CHANNEL(S)
- B2B CUSTOMER SEGMENT
- B2B MARKETING COST
- B2B SALES

B2B MARKETING
B2B VALUE PROPOSITION
B2B CUSTOMER SEGMENT
END CUSTOMER MARKETING
B2C VALUE PROPOSITION
B2B CHANNEL(S)
CONSUMER (B2C)
B2C BRAND
B2C CHANNEL
B2B MARKETING COST
B2C MARKETING COST
B2C REVENUE

B2(B2)C pattern

From Low Touch to High Touch

is the shift from standardized, low-touch value propositions toward customized, high-touch value propositions. This shift normally requires new human-based activities, which increase labor costs. However, high-touch value propositions command premium prices and lead to increased revenues.

How might we increase price and revenues by turning a standardized low-touch value proposition into a high-touch value proposition? How can we best maintain the scale benefits of standardization without incurring all of the scale limitations of a high-touch approach?

EXAMPLE
Apple Genius Bar

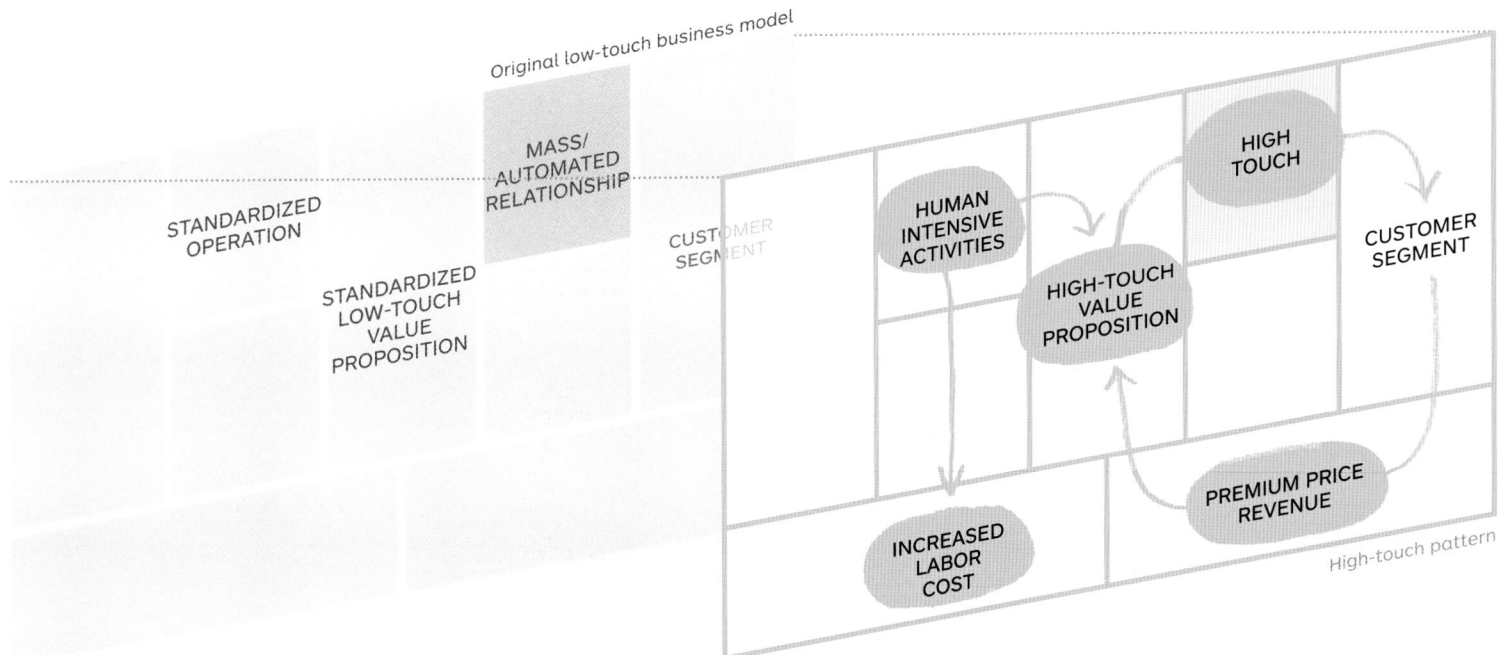

Original low-touch business model

STANDARDIZED OPERATION

STANDARDIZED LOW-TOUCH VALUE PROPOSITION

MASS/ AUTOMATED RELATIONSHIP

CUSTOMER SEGMENT

HUMAN INTENSIVE ACTIVITIES

HIGH-TOUCH VALUE PROPOSITION

HIGH TOUCH

CUSTOMER SEGMENT

INCREASED LABOR COST

PREMIUM PRICE REVENUE

High-touch pattern

Intel Inside

In the 1990s, PCs and the components within them are rapidly commoditizing. To respond to this threat, Intel launches the Intel Inside campaign to shift from a behind-the-scenes business-to-business microchip supplier to a trusted business-to-consumer brand.

Intel created the Intel Inside marketing campaign in 1991 as a means to differentiate its microprocessors (and the PCs that contained them) from other, lower-quality PCs on the market. Previously, Intel had no direct relationship with the PC consumer—it was merely a producer of the component yet integral part of the PC, and Intel dealt only with the PC manufacturers.

Intel decided to split the cost of advertising with the PC manufacturers if they agreed to affix the Intel Inside logo and sticker on the PCs and their packaging.

The Intel Inside sticker became a "seal of approval"—consumers might not know what a processor did but they knew it meant quality, reliability, and performance.

Intel effectively transformed from an engineering company manufacturing a computer component to a consumer product company guaranteeing a level of performance.

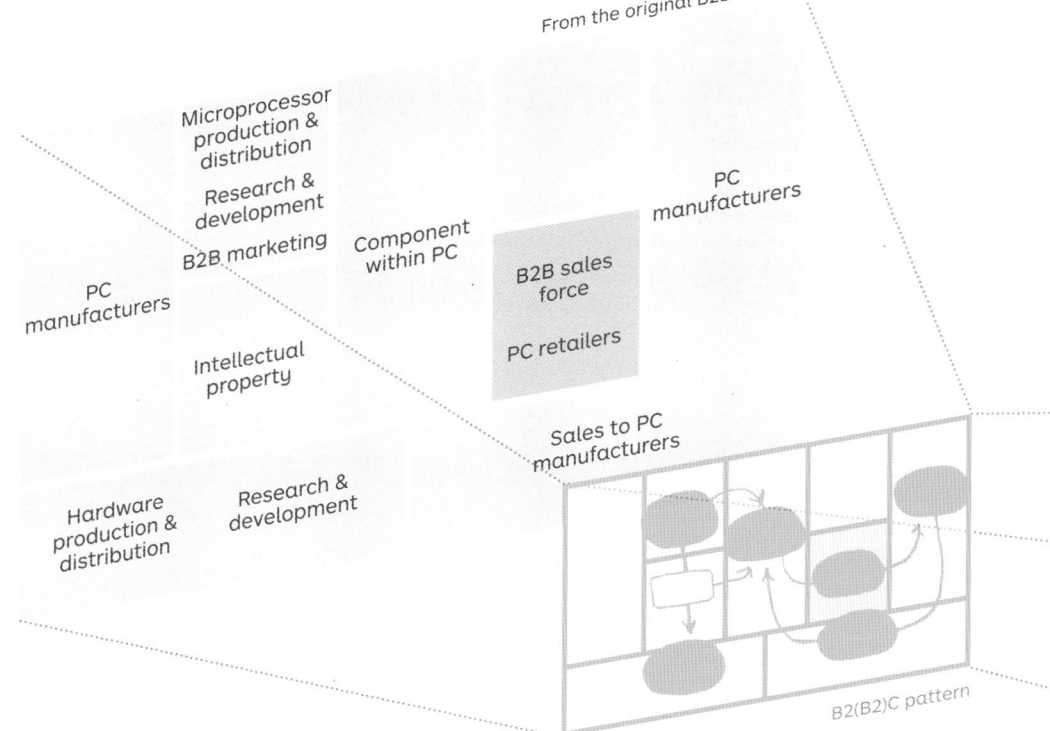

1 From B2B to B2C Channel

In 1991, Intel launches the Intel Inside advertising campaign as a B2C channel to reach consumers directly. It drastically increases its visibility. Intel also convinces PC manufacturers to add the Intel Inside logo on their PCs, external packaging, and advertising in return for heavily contributing to marketing costs. Intel shifts from a behind-the-scenes B2B microchip supplier to a B2C brand with direct consumer access.

2 From B2B Marketing to End-Customer Marketing

Marketing mattered little when Intel was an engineering-driven B2B player. With the shift toward consumers, Intel needs to develop new end-customer marketing skills and a strong B2C brand. It succeeds and builds a consumer staple associated with quality, reliability, and performance.

248

IMPROVE PATTERNS

3 From Less to More B2B Sales Thanks to B2C Brand as a Revenue Multiplier

The power of its newly gained B2C mass-market brand helps Intel differentiate itself from no-name microchip suppliers. PC manufacturers start to rely on Intel's trusted brand as a differentiator to charge higher premiums to the end customer. This leads to higher sales and revenues for PC manufacturers that multiply Intel's revenues from microprocessors.

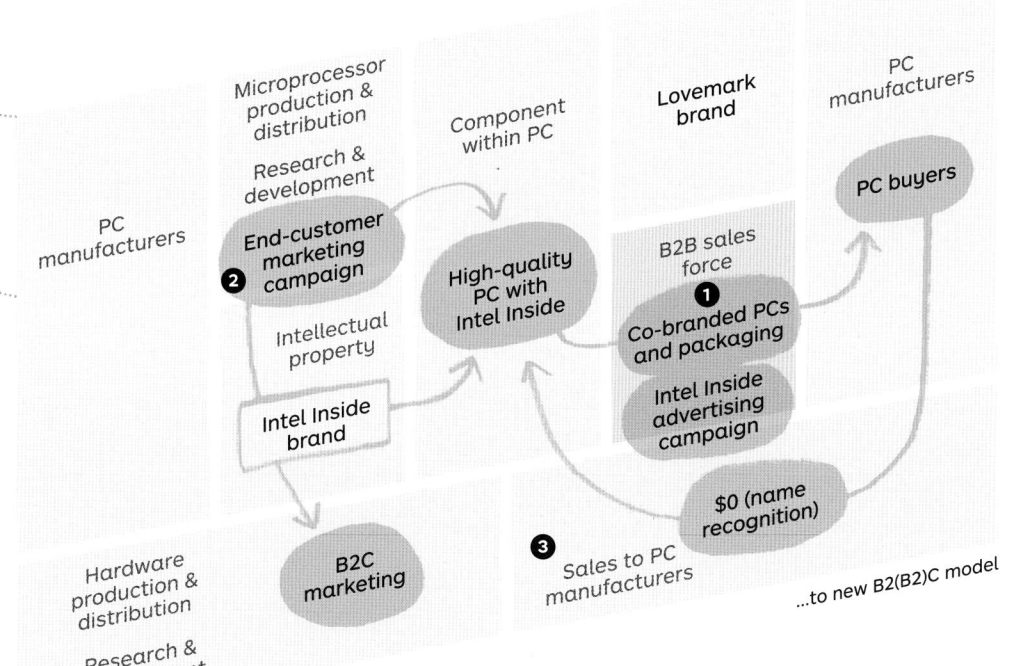

$110 million

Cost of advertising campaign over the first three years.[15]

#1

Market leader in semiconductor sales from 1992–2016 with 10 to 15% market share.[16]

3,000

In its first year (1991), the Intel Inside logo appeared on over 3,000 pages of its customers' (OEM) advertising.[17]

133 thousand

By 1993, 133 thousand PC advertisements were using the Intel Inside Logo and 1,400 OEMs had signed on to the program.[15]

$1 billion

Intel's net income topped $1 billion for the first time in 1992, following the Intel Inside campaign[18]

Apple Genius Bar

In 2001, Apple launches the Genius Bar as a key component of the Apple Store. They turn an undifferentiated and intimidating PC buying and support experience into a true, high-touch and high-value concierge-style service for customers.

Before Apple Stores, Apple used third-party retailers for both sales and technical support. This led to inconsistencies in customer experience both during and after sales.

In 2001, Apple launched the Apple Store with the Genius Bar embedded, as a key component of its retail strategy.

The Genius Bar provided personalized, friendly technical support, as well as product demos and training workshops. Geniuses used a high-touch, human-centred approach to make customers feel like true masters of their devices. The Genius Bar made going to the Apple Store and asking for support a lot less intimidating for customers.

IMPROVE PATTERNS

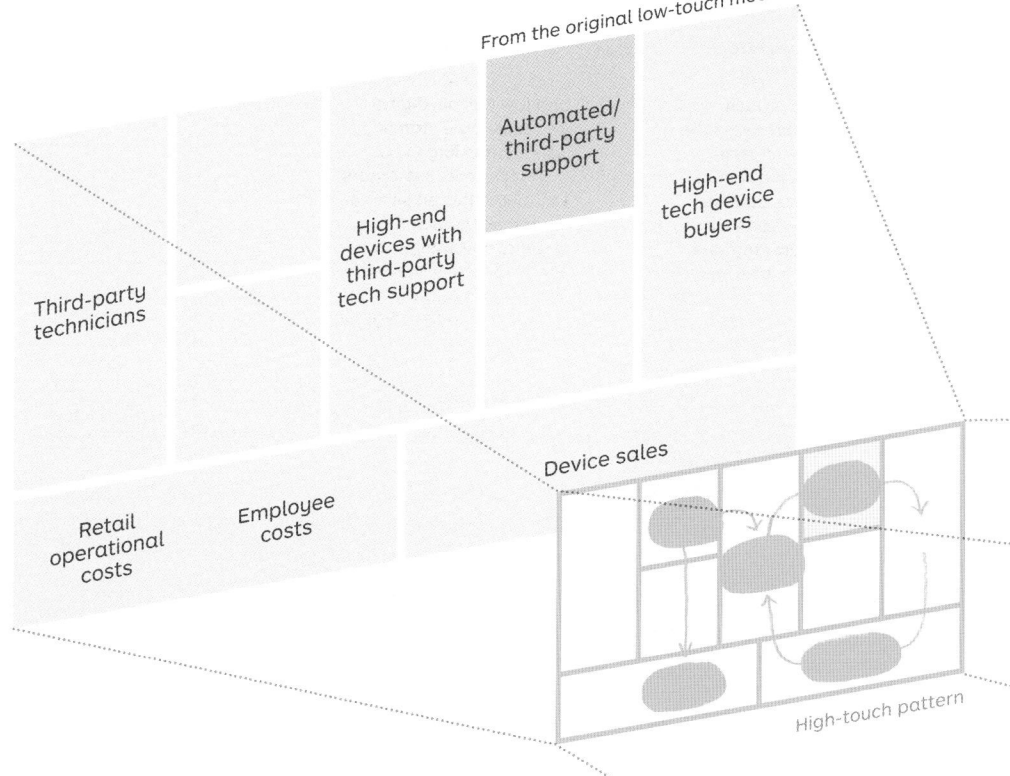

From the original low-touch model...

Automated/third-party support

High-end devices with third-party tech support

High-end tech device buyers

Third-party technicians

Retail operational costs

Employee costs

Device sales

High-touch pattern

1 From Mass Automated to High-Touch Relationship

What happens when customers experience an issue with a device? They usually have to call a third-party call center, or go through a painful repair process via a partner (mass, undifferentiated approach). In 2001 Apple launches the Genius Bar, inside of its new Apple Stores, to control the entire customer experience over the lifetime of a product. If customers have an issue or even a question about their Apple devices, they can head to the Genius Bar in the nearest Apple Store.

2 From Standardized Operations to Human-Intensive Activities

Apple shifts from standardized, back office type support structure, often involving third parties, to new customer-facing activities. The Genius Bar provides face-to-face tech support, on-site repairs, as well as software training and workshops. To enable the shift, Apple trains and certifies a new breed of employees: the Geniuses. They are modeled after high-end hotel concierges who provide personalized services. They focus on building relationships, not upselling.

3 Increased Labor Cost

As a consequence of its high-touch approach, Apple accepts an increase in the cost of labor and retail operations of the Genius Bar. Apple considers the additional created value more important than the retail costs incurred.

4 Premium Price Revenue

In a sea of undifferentiated and low margin digital devices, Apple stands out by providing expert guidance to its customers. This personalized service reinforces the perceived benefits of Apple products and its brand. It ultimately helps justify Apple's premium prices and margins.

"I'm there to help the customer and their product have the best relationship they possibly can."

—LEAD GENIUS AT APPLE'S PALO ALTO STORE (2014)

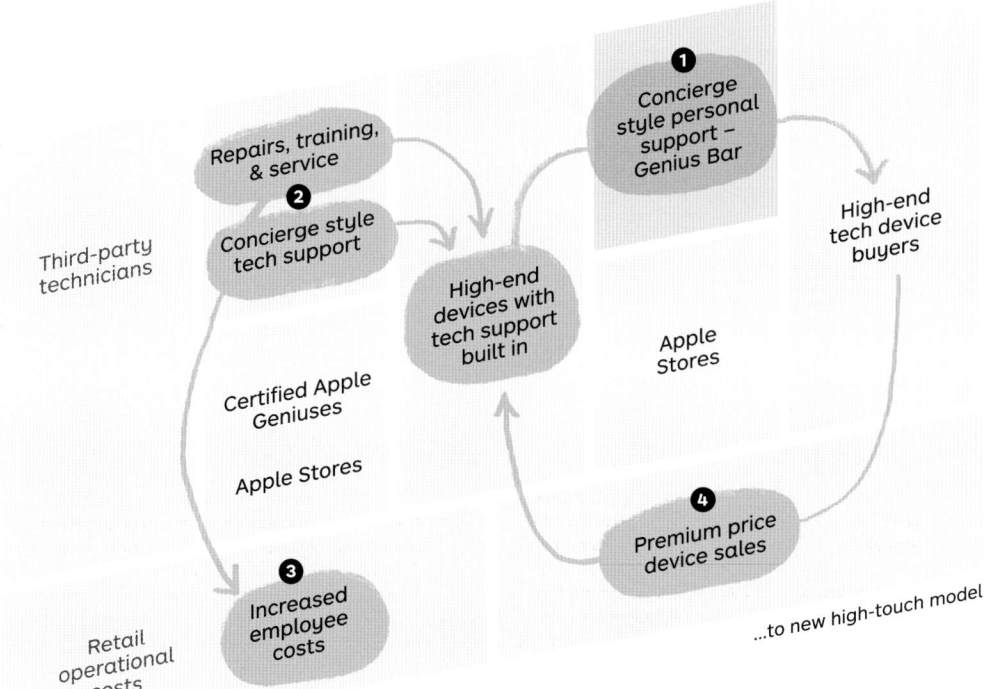

1 Concierge style personal support – Genius Bar

Repairs, training, & service

2 Concierge style tech support

Third-party technicians

High-end devices with tech support built in

High-end tech device buyers

Apple Stores

Certified Apple Geniuses

Apple Stores

4 Premium price device sales

3 Increased employee costs

Retail operational costs

...to new high-touch model

50
thousand

Genius Bar appointments scheduled each day in 2014.[19]

Direct to Consumer Trend

Apple Stores

Apple launches it own retail stores in 2001 in order to control the entire customer experience. Previously, Apple had never sold through its own physical stores to consumers. It had always used third-party, retail locations. Apple Stores instantly become a hit with a very distinct experience from that of traditional computer retailers. Apple Stores are bright, open spaces. Customers come to engage with the devices and interact at the Genius bar. Training workshops and events turn Apple Stores into much more than a sales floor.

Nespresso Boutiques

Nespresso, a high-end coffee brand known for single-portioned coffee, opens its first boutique in 2000 in Paris as a concept store. At the time, Nespresso was already operating a successful e-commerce business, but needed a physical presence to cement Nespresso's position as a high-end brand. It steadily opened an increasing number of Nespresso boutiques to showcase the "ultimate coffee experience" to its customers and deliver on its brand promise. By the end of 2017, there are more than 700 Nespresso boutiques in prime locations in large cities around the globe.

Audemars Piguet

In 2013, Francois-Henry Bennahmias, CEO of Audemars Piguet (AP), the Swiss watch manufacturer, decides to move away entirely from third-party retailers. AP expects to remove all its multibrand retail partners completely by 2024. This radical shift helps AP regain control over the customer experience, customer data, and the customer relationship with the brand. The purchasing experience becomes highly personalized and uses more intimate locations than stores (its Lounges), like high-end apartments in major cities. In addition, cutting out the retail intermediary allows AP to capture the full margin on its retail sales.

Rise of Niche

Craft Beer

The craft beer movement has been on the rise over the last couple of decades—even forcing traditional incumbents to purchase or distribute craft beers.

For example, by the 1980s, beer in United States had become a mass-produced commodity with little or no character, tradition, or culture. Consumers started to turn to fuller-flavored beers created by small, regional brewers. As a result, industry heavyweights jumped into the market. AB Inbev (maker of Budweiser) purchased 10 formerly independent U.S. craft breweries between 2011–2017.

Co-Branded or Affinity Credit Cards

Credit cards used to mean Visa, Mastercard, or American Express. Today, the bank or financial lender is secondary to the retailer, offering benefits for card membership and usage. Retailers have issued their own cards since the 1980s but co-branding has hit new niche extremes: Starbucks, Uber, and Amazon Prime all offer Visa reward cards, for instance. Co-branded credit cards covered 41% of the U.S. consumer and small business credit card purchase value in 2017 and over $990 billion in purchase value in 2018 (Packaged Facts).

Exclusive Sneaker Drops

Nike and Adidas have taken niche to an entirely new level—limited, exclusive releases that drop on a weekly basis at specific times and exclusive retailers. The sneakers, which are produced in amounts ranging from the hundreds to hundred thousands, are targeted to sneakerheads looking for an exclusive fashion statement or a collectible (for online resale). Shoes that originally sell for $120 can balloon to over $4 thousand on the secondary market depending on rarity and prestige.

**From Dedicated Resources
to Multi-Usage Resources**

p. 256   Fujifilm

From Asset Heavy to Asset Light

p. 260   Bharti Airtel

From Closed to Open (Innovation)

p. 262   Microsoft

254

Backstage Driven Shifts

*A radical shift of
how value is created*

From Dedicated Resources to Multi-Usage Resources

STRATEGIC REFLECTION
How might we monetize one of our most important key resources with a new value proposition for a new customer segment? How might the synergies with our existing business allow us to disrupt that new market we are targeting?

EXAMPLE
Fujifilm

is the shift from using a resource for one value proposition toward using the same resource for a completely different value proposition—which targets a new customer. This leads to substantial synergies, while opening up an entirely new revenue stream.

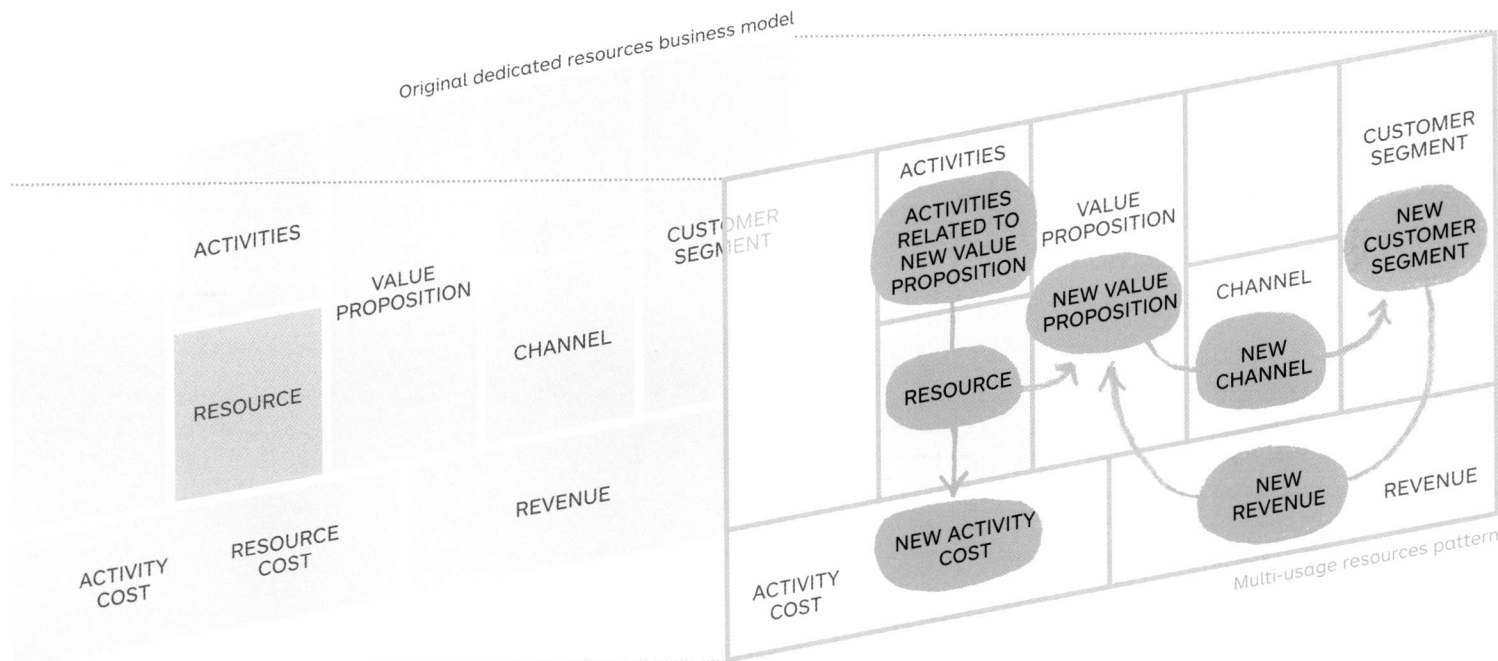

Original dedicated resources business model

Multi-usage resources pattern

Fujifilm

With the digitization of photography in the 2000s, Fujifilm realizes that it can no longer rely on continued revenue from analog film. Chairman Shigetaka Komori starts a period of transformation for Fujifilm with the VISION 75 plan. In 2006, Fujifilm puts its photographic film expertise to new use in cosmetics and launches Astalift skincare.

As part of the VISION 75 plan, Fujifilm created the Advanced Research Laboratories (R&D) to look for innovative uses of its technology in 2006. Fujifilm soon developed Astalift skincare and leveraged its brand name to market the new cosmetics line. By building a successful new business model around an existing key resource, Fujifilm was able to bounce back from the sharp decline of film, unlike its former competitor, Kodak.

This success became a launchpad to explore other businesses (e.g., functional materials, medical devices, etc.) and Fujifilm transformed into a diversified technology conglomerate. Fujifilm's Imaging Solutions Division accounted for 54% of the firm's revenue in 2001 versus just 15% in 2017.

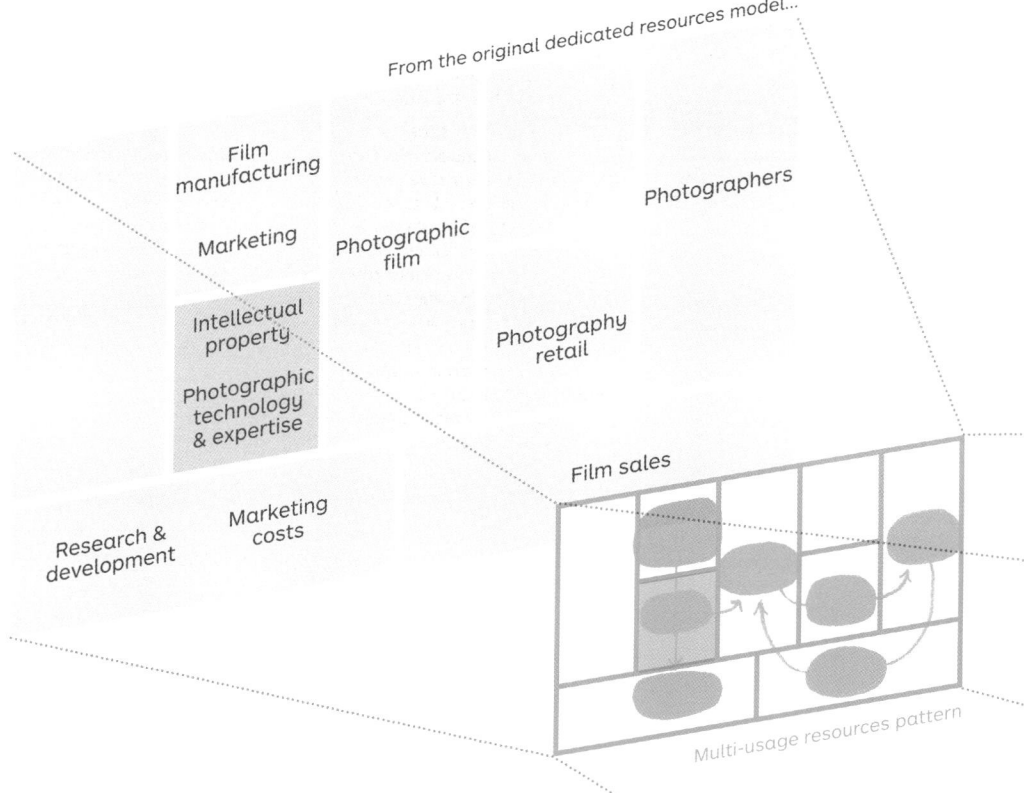

**1 From Dedicated to Multi-Usage
of a Key Resource**

Fujifilm realizes that collagen is a major component of both film and skin, and that it can apply its photographic technology and expertise in film manufacturing to skincare production. Over the years, Fujifilm has developed 20,000 chemical compounds in its chemical library, originally for use with photographic film, and now applicable to pharmaceuticals and skincare.

**2 From One Value Proposition
to a New Value Proposition
for a New Customer Segment**

Fujifilm operates a radical shift from its original photographic film value proposition for photographers worldwide. It now targets Asian women with its Astalift, high-end skincare value proposition.

3 From Traditional Channel to New Channel

Photographic film and high-end skincare don't use the same retail channels, so Fujifilm opens up new retail channels dedicated to cosmetics for the Astalift business.

4 From Traditional Activities to New Activities and Costs Related to a New Value Proposition

Fujifilm creates the Advanced Research Laboratories to look for innovative uses of its photographic technology. It invests in the skincare business and backs up Astalift with a significant marketing campaign, as cosmetics require a strong brand. It then builds the skincare manufacturing and distribution infrastructure to support the new value proposition.

5 From Revenue to New Revenue

From its peak in 2001, demand for photographic film drops rapidly, almost disappearing in less than 10 years. To compensate for declining film revenues, Fujifilm creates a new revenue stream with high-end skincare and supplements that contribute to the growth of its healthcare division from 2006.

2x

Astalift helps double Fujifilm's Healthcare business from ¥288 billion revenues in 2008 to ¥484 billion in 2018. Fujifilm's Astalift revenues are included in the healthcare division.[20, 21]

20,000
Chemical compounds

Fujifilm had developed 20 thousand chemical compounds in its chemical library, originally all for use for photographic film, but now used for pharmaceuticals.[22]

Film manufacturing

Marketing

Photographic film

Photographers

Skincare manufacturing & marketing

❶ Intellectual property

Cosmetics brand

❶ Photographic technology & expertise

❷ Skincare products (Astalift)

❸ Cosmetics retail

Asian cosmetic buyers

Photography retail

❹

❺ Skincare product sales

Film sales

Marketing costs

Cosmetic manufacturing & marketing costs

Research & development

...to new multi-usage resources model

Fujifilm vs. Kodak Revenue[23]
In millions USD

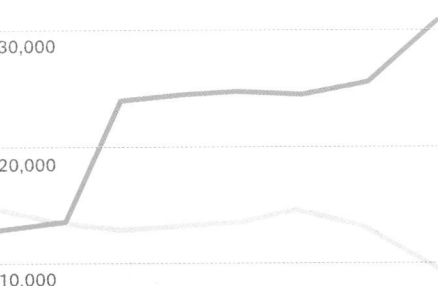

— Fujifilm   — Kodak

30,000

20,000

10,000

2000 2001 2002 2003 2004 2005 2006 2007

From Asset Heavy to Asset Light

STRATEGIC REFLECTION
How might we free up capital and energy from building and maintaining assets toward focusing on service provisioning and customer acquisition? How might that shift help us scale our customer base and increase revenues?

EXAMPLE
Bharti Airtel

is the shift from a business model based on high fixed costs and high capital expenditures toward an asset-light business with variable costs. This shift allows focusing on service provisioning and customer acquisition rather than building and maintaining assets. The freed-up capital and energy are invested in boosting growth and increasing revenues. In addition, third-party providers can often split the cost of building and maintaining assets between multiple clients. This leads to lower unit cost than if the company built and maintained the assets themselves.

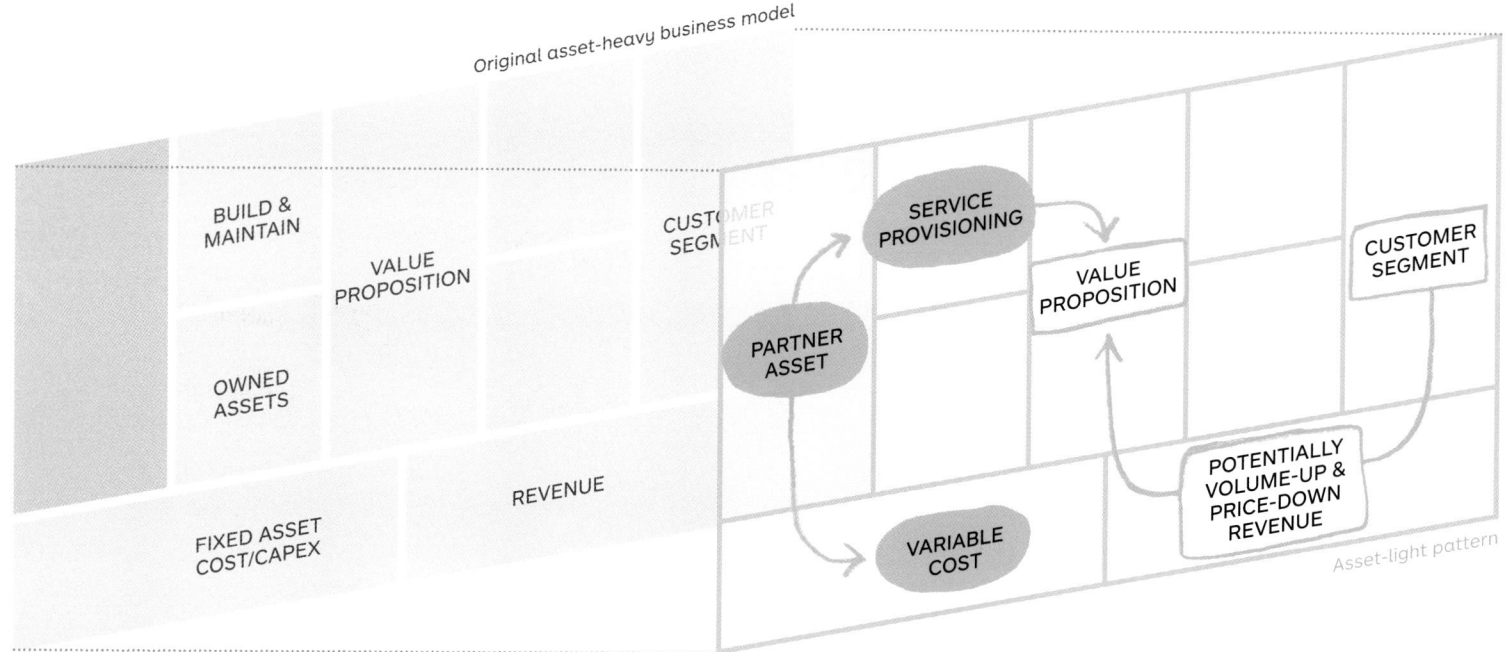

From Closed to Open (Innovation)

is the shift from a closed approach to developing new value propositions toward an open approach to developing new value propositions. This outside-in approach (to innovation) is based on external R&D and intellectual property (IP). A similar type of shift is from the tight protection of internal R&D and IP toward an inside-out approach of sharing R&D and IP with outside partners.

STRATEGIC REFLECTION
How might we make more usage of external R&D and IP (outside-in) or share internal R&D and IP with outside partners (inside-out)? Both should lead to a higher return on R&D through new revenues.

EXAMPLE
Microsoft

Bharti Airtel

In the early 2000s, Airtel lacks the required capital to grow its telecom infrastructure. It decides to explore an unprecedented strategy in the telecom industry. Airtel outsources its entire network infrastructure and most of its operations to compete on service provisioning instead of infrastructure development.

INVENT PATTERNS

In the early 2000s, Bharti Airtel wanted to capture the lion's share of the Indian telecom market growth. However, it didn't have the capital to invest in the infrastructure required.

Instead of competing on infrastructure like everybody else, Airtel decided to get rid of this costly asset and compete on services.

In 2003, Airtel was the first major telecom company to outsource its infrastructure and most of its business operations to partners. Massive capital costs disappeared from their business model. This shift transformed capital expenditures into variable operating expenses based on customer usage. Airtel channeled savings from this shift back into price cuts and new value propositions that sustained the rapid growth of its subscriber base.

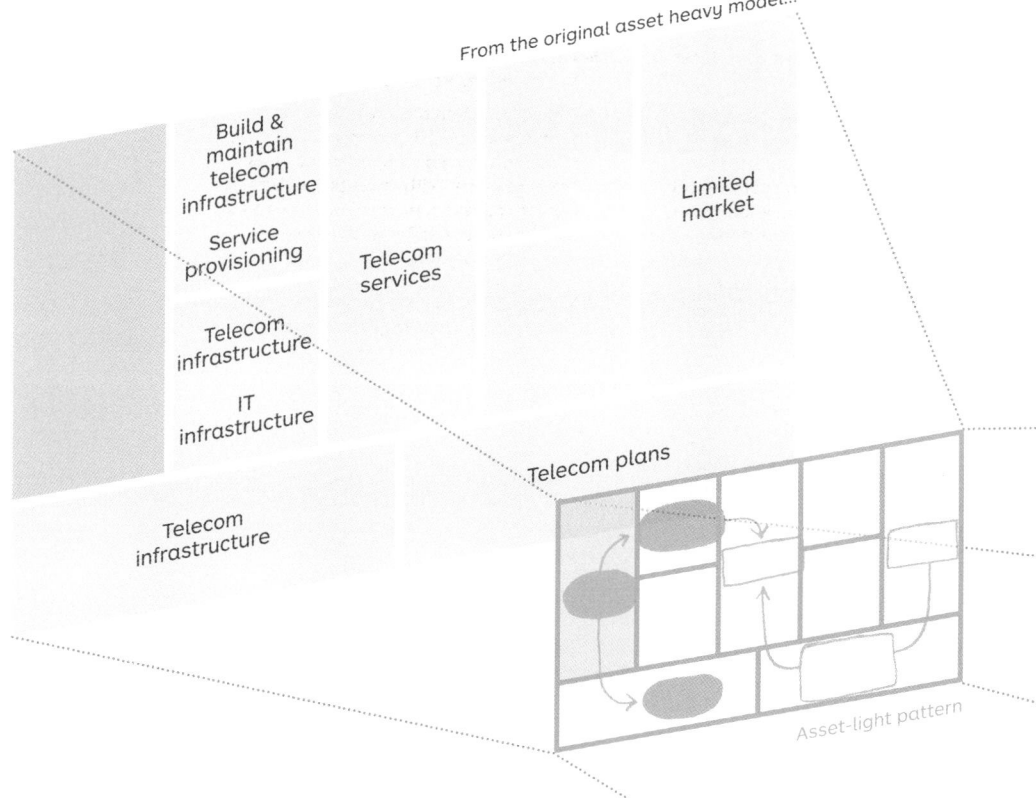

1 From Owned Key Assets to Partner Assets

In 2003–2004, Airtel makes the radical decision to outsource the operations and maintenance of the physical telecom infrastructure and most of its IT system in a multi-year deal with four global vendors. This is an unprecedented move for telecom operators who see their network as the main competitive advantage.

2 From Build and Maintain Activities to Service Provisioning Activities

Airtel reallocates the freed-up financial resources to expand sales, marketing, and customer service. Those activities enable faster customer growth and better service provisioning.

3 From a Fixed to a Variable Cost Structure

Airtel no longer has to spend on telecom equipment and own its infrastructure (fixed costs). Airtel negotiates a payment model with its partners that is based on usage and quality of service (variable costs).

4 From Baseline Revenues to Lower Price, Higher Volume Revenues

Airtel decides to pass on the savings from outsourcing its infrastructure to its customers by reducing the price of its telecom plans. With lower prices Airtel is able to achieve a much higher volume of sales and tap into the rapidly growing Indian telecom market. Because its growth is no longer constrained by its infrastructure, Airtel can quickly expand its customer base after the shift.

#3
in India

Third largest mobile operator in India in 2019.[24]

325
million

subscribers in India in 2019.[24]

27.5%
market share

of all Indian wireless subscriptions in 2019.[24]

120%
growth

120% compounded annual growth in sales revenues between 2003 and 2010 and growth in net profits of 282% per year.[25]

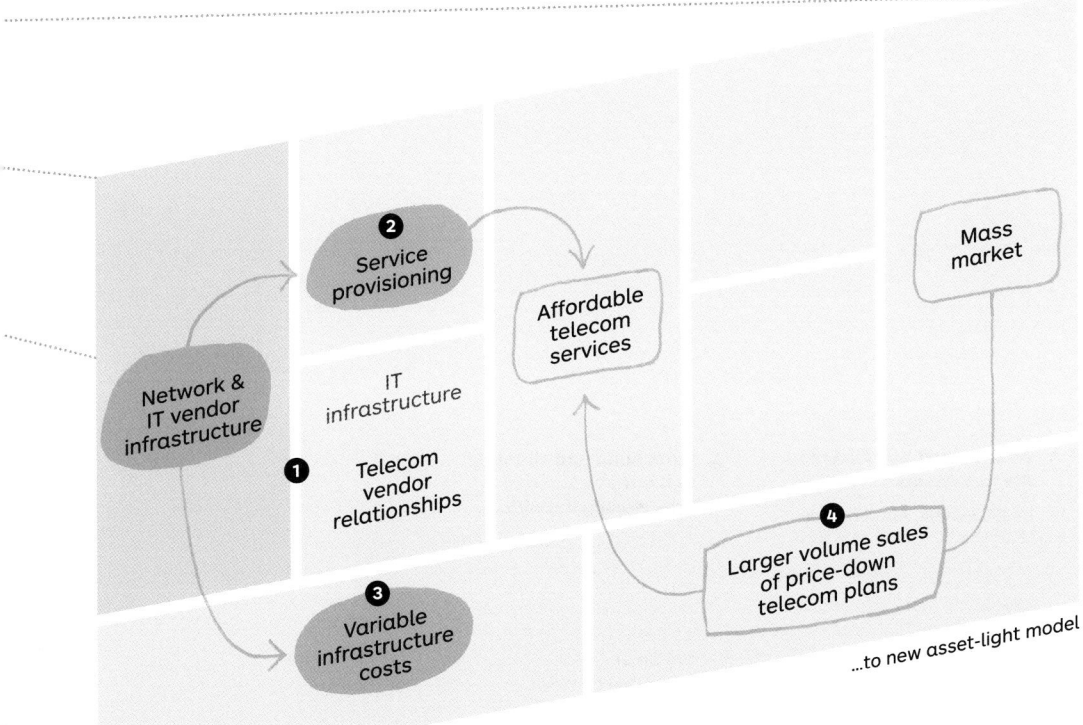

2 Service provisioning

Network & IT vendor infrastructure

1 Telecom vendor relationships

IT infrastructure

Affordable telecom services

Mass market

3 Variable infrastructure costs

4 Larger volume sales of price-down telecom plans

...to new asset-light model

From Closed to Open Innovation

2012 ～～ 2018

Microsoft

Enterprise users and developers no longer want to be tied to an operating system. To overcome this, Microsoft starts embracing open source. Microsoft shifts from calling open source a cancer in 2001 to joining its community in 2014.

In the Steve Ballmer era, Microsoft had been notoriously outspoken against open source. Patent litigation and overt threats against the theft of intellectual property were common. In 2012, Microsoft first experimented with open source with the creation of Microsoft Open Technologies in 2012.

In 2014, new CEO Satya Nadella radically sped up that shift toward an open approach. He moved Microsoft's focus away from proprietary Windows toward operating-system agnostic cloud solutions to satisfy enterprise users and developers.

To meet the needs of enterprise customers, Microsoft shifted from closed to open innovation. It no longer relied only on proprietary software development and opened up to the open source community. Microsoft made it easier for developers to work on its software and improved its Azure Cloud service offerings.

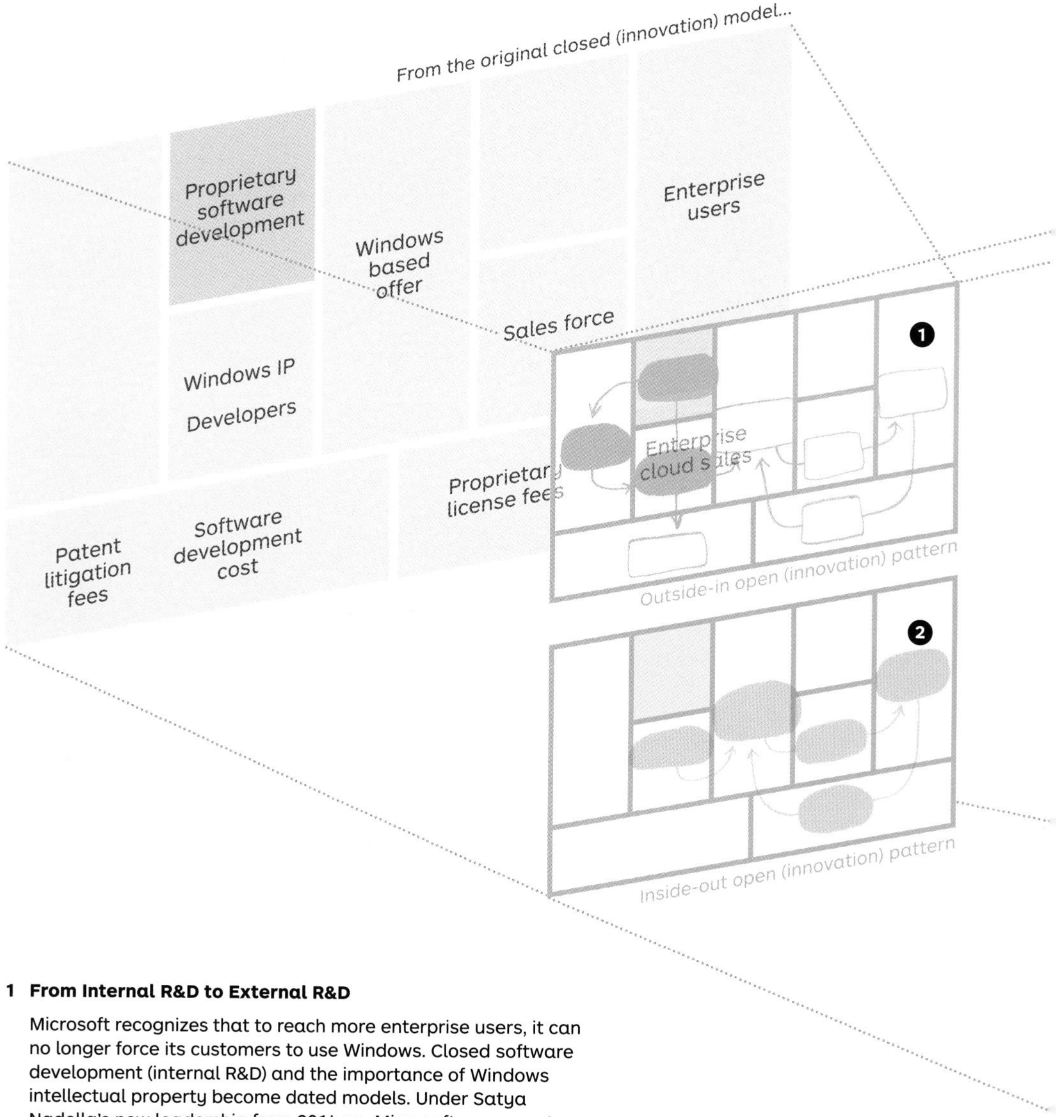

262

INVENT PATTERNS

From the original closed (innovation) model…

Proprietary software development

Windows based offer

Enterprise users

Sales force

Windows IP

Developers

Enterprise cloud sales

❶

Proprietary license fees

Patent litigation fees

Software development cost

Outside-in open (innovation) pattern

❷

Inside-out open (innovation) pattern

1   From Internal R&D to External R&D

Microsoft recognizes that to reach more enterprise users, it can no longer force its customers to use Windows. Closed software development (internal R&D) and the importance of Windows intellectual property become dated models. Under Satya Nadella's new leadership from 2014 on, Microsoft opens up to contributions from the open source community. It incorporates more and more open source code (external R&D) in its Azure cloud services to meet the needs of enterprise users.

❶ ...to new outside-in open (innovation) model

Proprietary software development

Open source community relationship management

Windows-based offer

Azure platform agnostic enterprise cloud

Enterprise users

Open source community

Open source code

Windows IP
GitHub
Developers

Sales force

Software development cost

Reduced development cost

Proprietary license fees

Enterprise cloud sales

❷ ...to new inside-out open (innovation) model

Proprietary software development

Open source software development

Windows-based offer

Open source contribution

Enterprise users

Open source community

Open source code

Windows IP
GitHub
Developers

Open Innovation Network (OIN)

$0

Software development cost

Proprietary license fees

60
thousand
patents

In 2018, Microsoft open sourced 60 thousand patents when it joined the OIN.[26]

$7.5
billion paid
for GitHub

Microsoft purchases GitHub, the world's leading open software development platform in 2018.[27]

#1

Microsoft is the leading contributor to GitHub, with over 4,550 employees contributing in 2018.[28]

2 From Proprietary IP to New IP-Based Value Proposition

Microsoft joins the Linux Foundation in 2016. The Linux Foundation is an open technology consortium promoting open source development. In 2018 it also joins the Open Innovation Network (or OIN, a patent consortium). Microsoft opens over 60 thousand patents (proprietary IP) to the community upon membership to OIN.

In 2018, Microsoft purchases GitHub. GitHub is a platform for collaboration and software version control for the open source community. Microsoft soon becomes one of the largest contributors to the platform (new IP-based value proposition).

REVERSE

From Dedicated Resources to Multi-Usage Resources

2006 ~~~ 2019

Big Data Trends: 23andMe

Big data, the analysis of extremely large data sets, opens up many opportunities for new growth using the "from dedicated to multi-usage" pattern, as illustrated by 23andMe.

1 From Dedicated Usage: Genetic Testing

23andMe begins selling direct-to-consumer DNA testing kits in 2006. They offer both an ancestry report and a health analysis. 23andMe asks consumers buying their kits to opt into its research "to become part of something bigger." On average 80% of users accept. With every new sale, 23andMe grows its database of users, DNA information, and self-reported behavioral data.

2 To Multi-Usage: Access to Database

23andMe knows its database will become a key resource for scientific research. 23andMe anonymizes the data and sells access to the database to researchers (in medical, government, and educational fields). In 2018, more than four million of 23andMe's customers have agreed to let their DNA be used in research. The average 23andMe customer contributes to more than 230 studies.

3 To Multi-Usage: Drug Discovery

This wealth of data also enables 23andMe to enter the field of drug discovery. They explore this new field both on their own and through partnerships with leading pharmaceuticals companies. At the start of 2020, 23andMe, for the first time, has sold the rights to a new drug that it has developed using its customers' data. This paves the way for substantial new revenue streams.

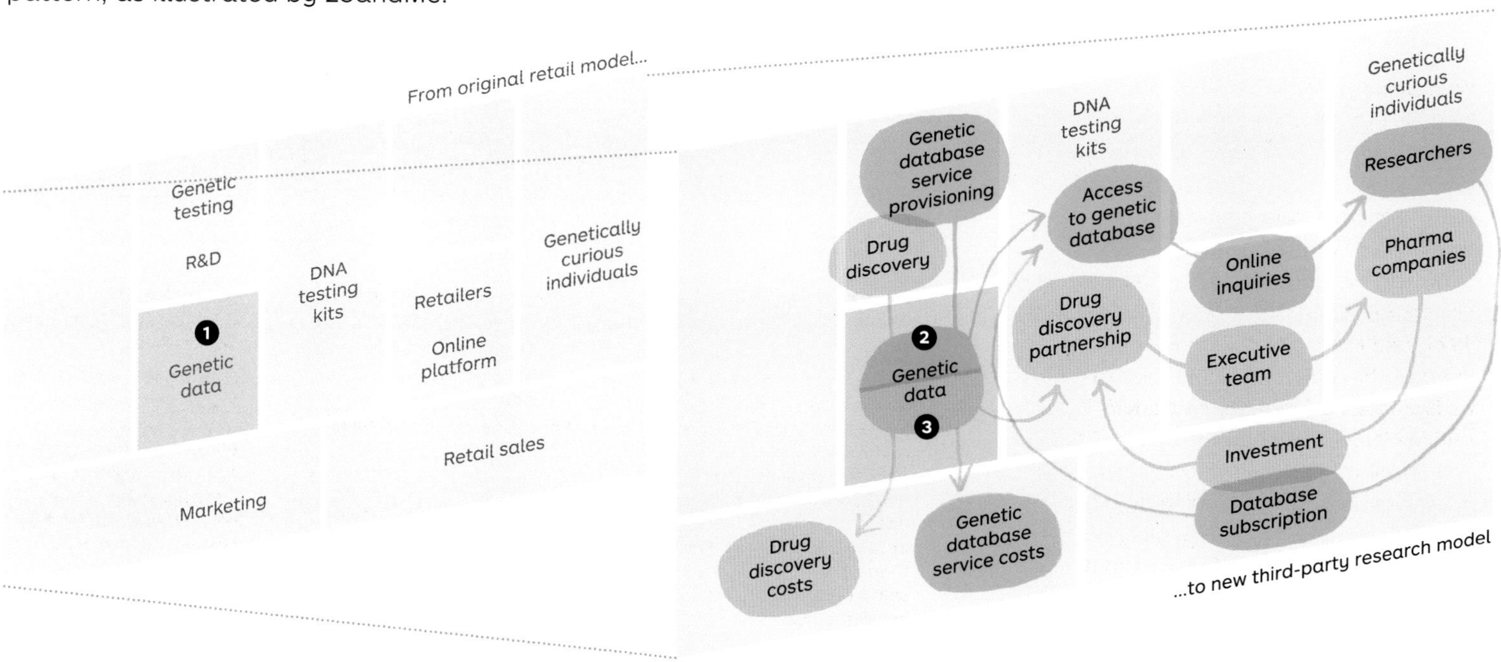
From original retail model...
Genetic testing
R&D
1
Genetic data
DNA testing kits
Retailers
Online platform
Genetically curious individuals
Marketing
Retail sales
Genetic database service provisioning
Drug discovery
2
Genetic data
3
DNA testing kits
Access to genetic database
Drug discovery partnership
Online inquiries
Executive team
Genetically curious individuals
Researchers
Pharma companies
Investment
Database subscription
Drug discovery costs
Genetic database service costs
...to new third-party research model

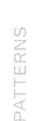

From Asset Light to Asset Heavy

1928 ~~~ 1955

Disney Parks & Resorts

In the 1930s, Disney founder Walt Disney dreams of giving families a magical experience both on screen and in real life. Following the success of his movies (light assets), he expands into theme parks in 1955 and resorts (heavy assets).

Walt Disney released his first Mickey Mouse cartoon in 1928. Four years later he began sketching his idea for a family-friendly amusement park. In 1955, Disneyland opened in California, and within its first 10 weeks, it attracted one million visitors. By 1960, that number would rise to five million visitors per year. Disney World followed in 1971, and both resorts opened hotels to support the tourists. In 1983, Disney opened its first international theme park in Tokyo, and in 1996 it launched the Disney Cruise Line. Disney's continual growth and investment into heavy assets has paid off. It built a profitable hospitality business next to its media empire. And Disney continues to be the most valuable media brand in the world. Another $24 billion is expected to be invested in theme parks through 2023.[29]

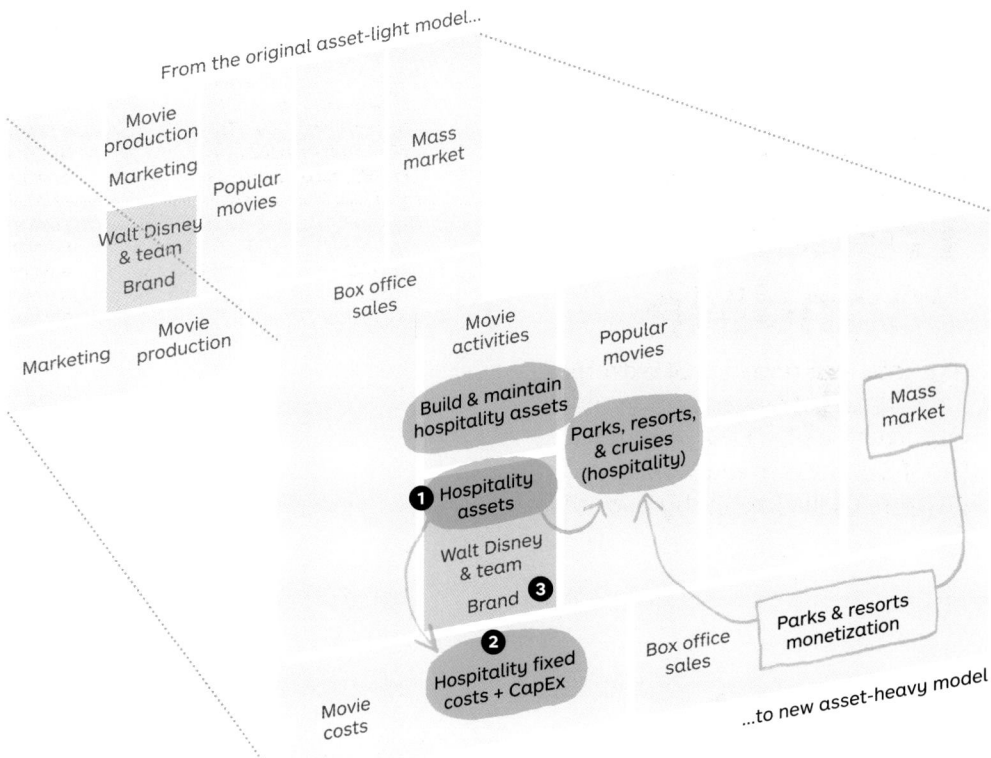

1 From Asset Light to Asset Heavy

Disney's movie business requires few assets beyond Walt Disney and his creative team. When Disney decides to shift to creating real world experiences, it accepts that it needs to invest in heavy hospitality assets. Disney opens its first park, Disneyland, in 1955 and adds another 11 theme parks, 51 resorts, 4 cruise ships, and 1 private island to its key resources.

2 From Asset-Light to Asset-Heavy Cost Structure

Movie	Park
Lady and the Tramp $38.1 million	Disneyland $162 million
The Jungle Book $30.6 million	Disney World $2.02 billion
The Little Mermaid $82 million	Disney Hollywood Studios $824 million

3 Asset Light and Asset Heavy Mutually Reinforce Each Other.

Disney uses its movie franchises and brand to market parks, resorts, cruises, and other products. At the same time, parks and resorts become a channel to reinforce the customer connection with the Disney brand.

From High Cost to Low Cost

p. 268   Dow Corning Xiameter

**From Transactional
to Recurring Revenue**

p. 272   Adobe

From Conventional to Contrarian

p. 274   Apple iMac

Profit Formula Driven Shifts

*A radical change of how profits are
made in terms of revenues and costs*

From High Cost to Low Cost

is the shift toward a more efficient activity and resource configuration in order to substantially decrease the cost structure and offer price-conscious customers a low-price value proposition. This shift allows for the conquering of new customer segments that might have not had access to such a value proposition previously.

STRATEGIC REFLECTION
Which new, price-conscious customer segment might we conquer with a low-price value proposition? How might we reconfigure activities and resources to disrupt our cost structure and make that low price possible?

EXAMPLE
Dow Corning Xiameter

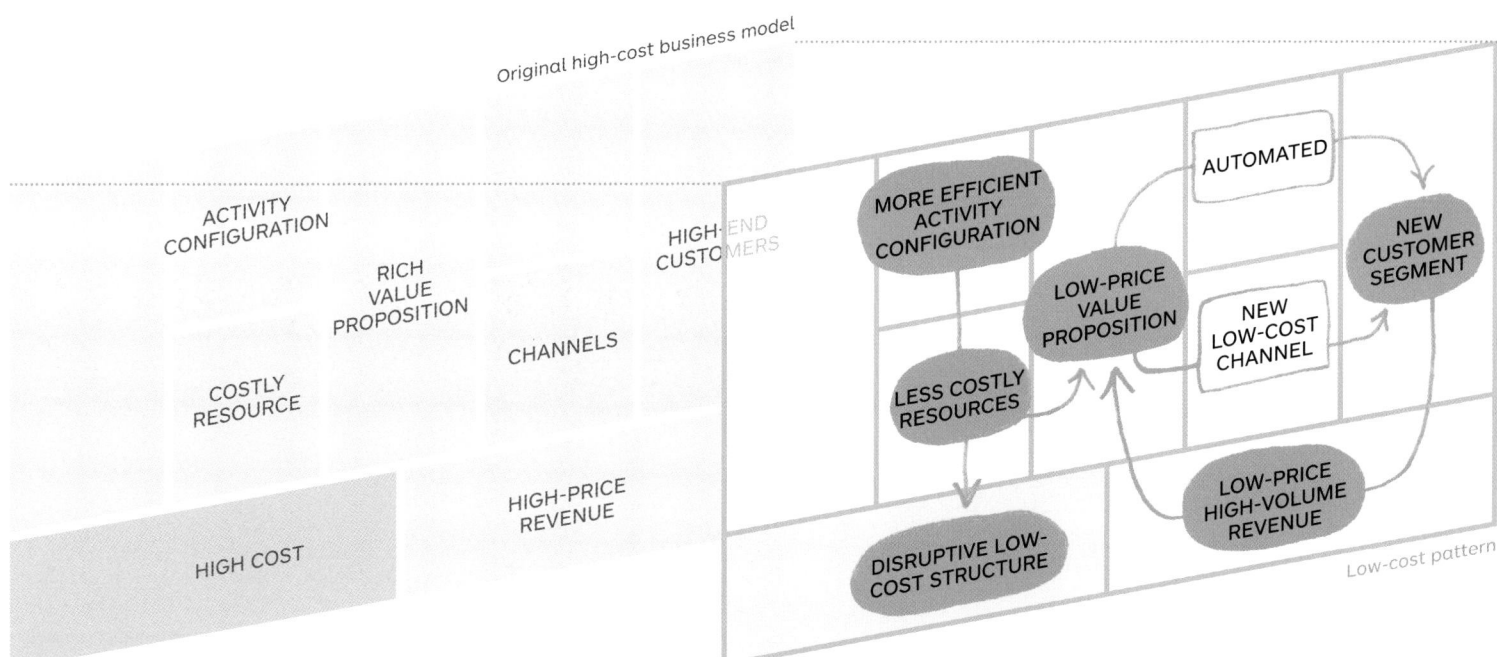

Dow Corning Xiameter

Silicone is becoming a commodity in the late 1990s, and Dow Corning's specialty silicone business is under threat. To respond, Dow Corning creates Xiameter in 2002, a no-frills standard silicone offering, sold online to price-sensitive manufacturers.

In the 1990s, silicone was becoming a commodity and Dow Corning could have given up the low end of the silicone market. Instead it took on the challenge of designing a business that could offer silicone at a 15% lower price point. This led to the launch of Xiameter in 2002: an online-only distribution platform for standard silicone products.

Dow Corning maintained its high-cost speciality silicone business alongside the low-cost Xiameter standard silicone business. Both business models successfully co-existed and helped the company overcome the threat of silicone commoditization.

Dow Corning was acquired by the Dow Chemical company in 2016.

INVENT PATTERNS

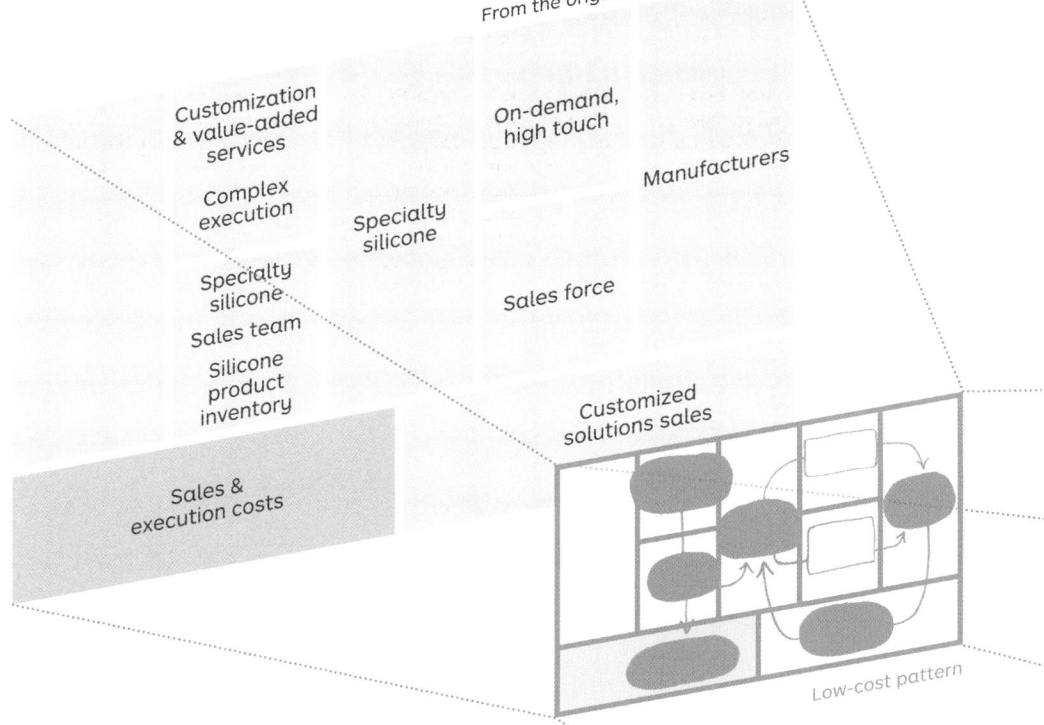

From the original high-cost model...

Customization & value-added services

Complex execution

Specialty silicone

Specialty silicone

Sales team

Silicone product inventory

On-demand, high touch

Manufacturers

Specialty silicone

Sales force

Sales & execution costs

Customized solutions sales

Low-cost pattern

1 From High Cost to Disruptive Low-Cost Structure

Xiameter radically changes its cost structure from its Dow Corning parent. It achieves a disruptive low-cost structure thanks to less costly resources, less complex activities, and standardized sales.

2 From Costly to Less Costly Resources and Activities

Xiameter eliminates the most costly resources of Dow Corning's traditional business model. This includes the elimination of specialty silicone resources to reduce inventory and the elimination of a dedicated sales team. It also reduces the complexity of activities, such as customization of silicone products, value-added services, or specific contract terms. The new business model is designed for standardized sales and online execution.

3 From a Specialty Value Proposition to a Low-Price Value Proposition

The less costly resources and more efficient activity configuration allow Xiameter to offer a lower priced value proposition. It sells standard silicone online at a lower price point than Dow Corning. This value proposition attracts a new customer segment of price-sensitive manufacturers willing to forego specialty, high-touch sales activities in exchange for speed, convenience, and price.

4 From Traditional (Offline) Channels to New (Online) Channel

The original Dow Corning business depends completely on a dedicated sales team and has no online presence. Xiameter creates an e-commerce platform and introduces a new online channel to reach its customers.

5 From High-Price Revenues to Low-Price, High-Volume Revenues

Dow Corning sells its speciality silicone products at a high price. Xiameter aims for a 15% lower price. In exchange, customers have to purchase large-volume orders and agree to standard credit terms and lead times. Xiameter sales grow from 0 to 30% of Dow Corning total sales in less than 10 years.

20%
cheaper

price differential between Dow Corning and Xiameter.[30]

"Our two-brand strategy offers the choices and solutions that customers need to help them solve problems and seize opportunities."

—DONALD SHEETS

Chief financial officer and Americas area president, Dow Corning

0% to 30%
online sales in less than 10 years

30% of Dow's sales were online in 2011 vs. 0% prior to the launch of Xiameter in 2002.[31]

13%
sales growth

Peak in sales growth in 2006 and double digit growth every year since introduction in 2002.[32]

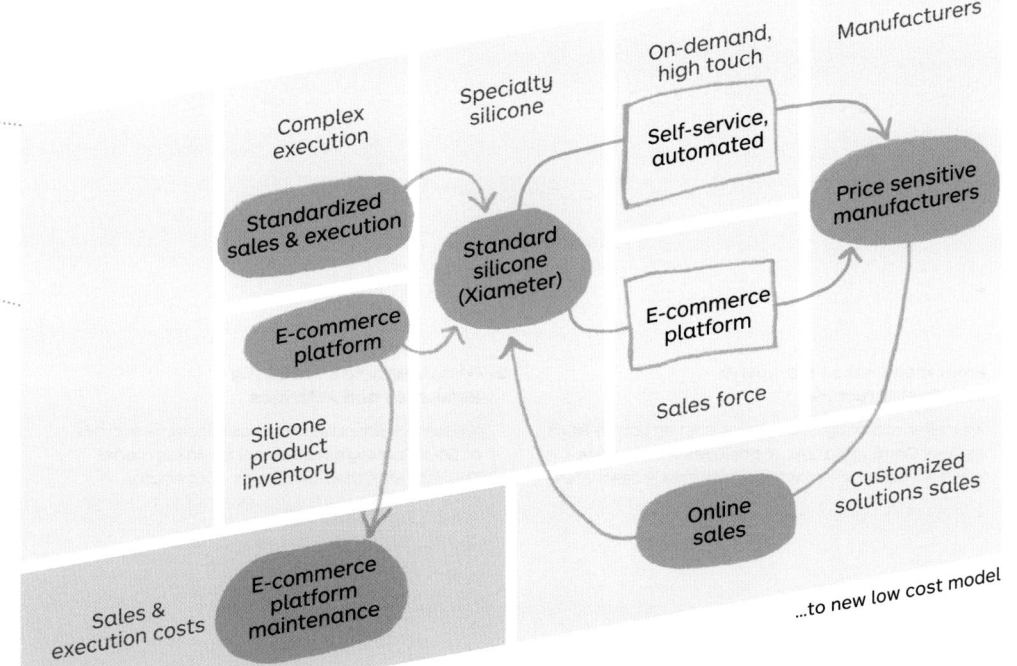

Adapted from Seizing the White Space, *by Mark W. Johnson*

From Transactional to Recurring Revenue

270

STRATEGIC REFLECTION
Which recurring customer job-to-be-done might allow us to create a recurring value proposition with a long-term relationship and recurring revenues?

EXAMPLE
Adobe

is the shift from having to sell again and again with continuous cost of sales toward acquiring customers/users once to then earn recurring revenues. This shift requires identifying a recurring customer job-to-be-done that you can address with a recurring value proposition. Because of the increased customer lifetime value from recurring revenues you can afford a higher upfront acquisition cost than in a transactional model. Advantages of recurring revenues include compound revenue growth and more revenue predictability.

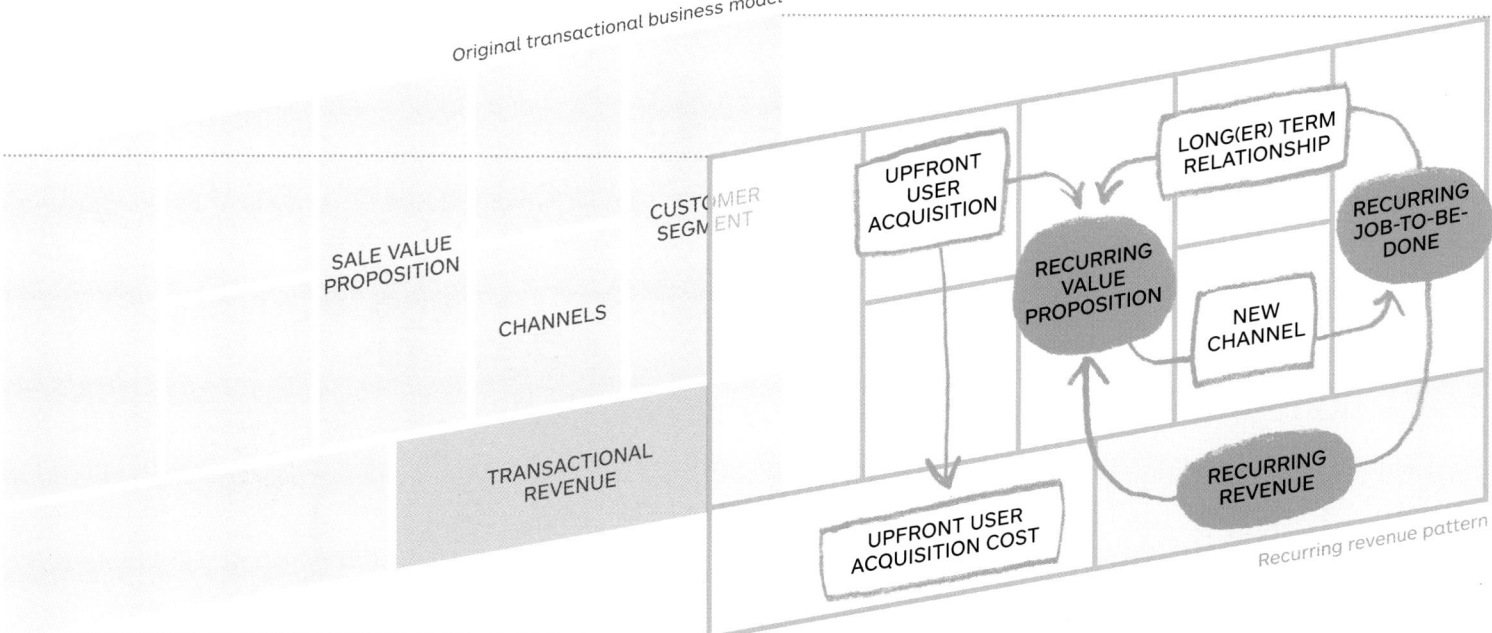

Original transactional business model

Recurring revenue pattern

From Conventional to Contrarian

is the shift to significantly reduce costs and increase value at the same time. Contrarians eliminate the most costly resources, activities, and partners from their business model, even if that means limiting the value proposition. They compensate by focusing on features in the value proposition that a well-defined customer segment loves and is willing to pay for, but which are relatively cheap to provide.

STRATEGIC REFLECTION
Which of the most costly activities and resources might we eliminate or reduce, even if they create value for customers? How might we we replace that lost (expensive) value by augmenting our value proposition with cheap value creators that matter to customers most?

EXAMPLE
Apple iMac

271

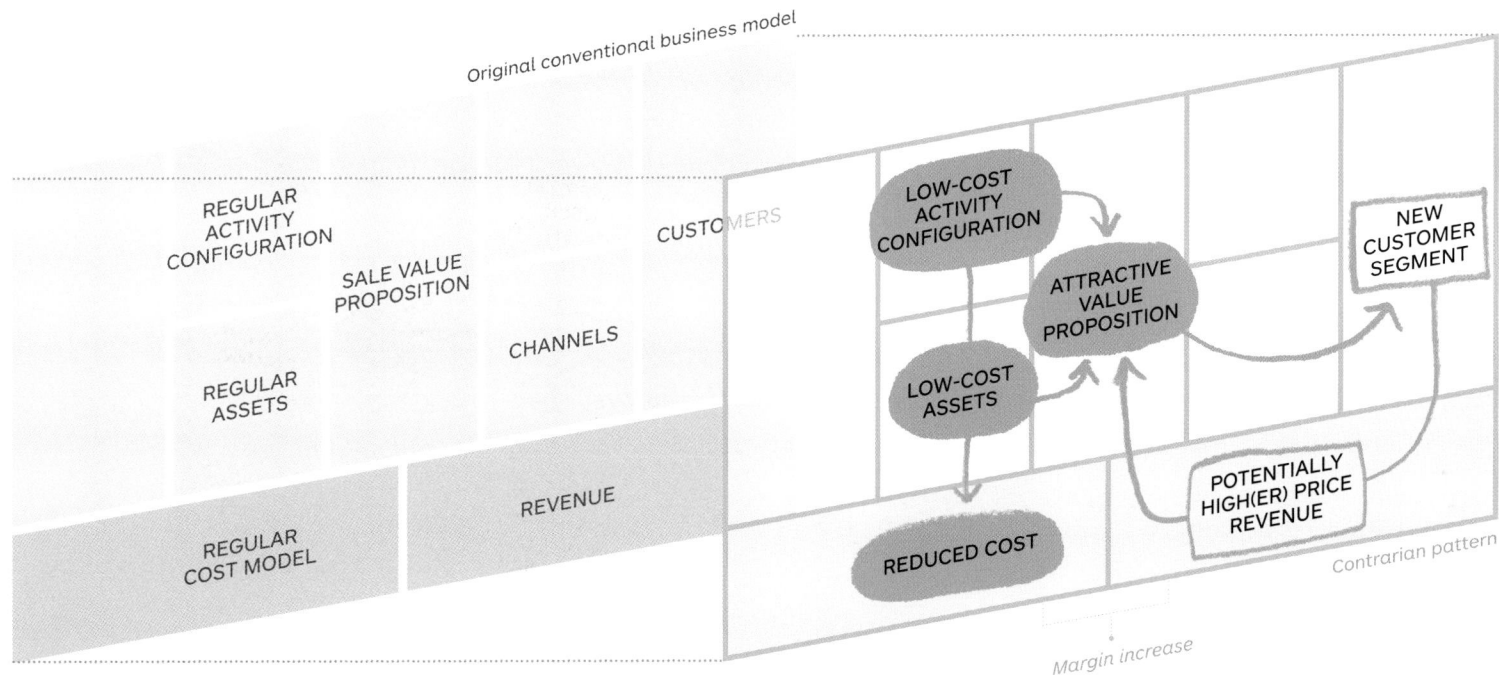

Original conventional business model

REGULAR ACTIVITY CONFIGURATION

SALE VALUE PROPOSITION

CUSTOMERS

CHANNELS

REGULAR ASSETS

REVENUE

REGULAR COST MODEL

LOW-COST ACTIVITY CONFIGURATION

ATTRACTIVE VALUE PROPOSITION

NEW CUSTOMER SEGMENT

LOW-COST ASSETS

POTENTIALLY HIGH(ER) PRICE REVENUE

REDUCED COST

Contrarian pattern

Margin increase

Adobe

In the 2010s, software distribution over the Internet becomes possible and the software industry starts shifting toward software as a service (SaaS). Adobe seizes the opportunity early and switches from transactional sales of software to a cloud subscription service in 2012.

Adobe historically earned revenues from transactional sales of perpetual licenses to its software. Every few years it had to convince customers to upgrade to a new version.

In 2012, Adobe launched its Creative Cloud and joined a growing number of software providers selling software as a service (SaaS). Customers then received access to a full suite of products that were continuously upgraded and supported through the cloud.

In 2013, Adobe stopped selling its Creative Suite as a stand-alone, software product. Adobe's revenue dipped initially as it shifted from transactional to recurring revenues. But recurring revenues started to grow dramatically with the adoption of the Creative Cloud by the mass market.

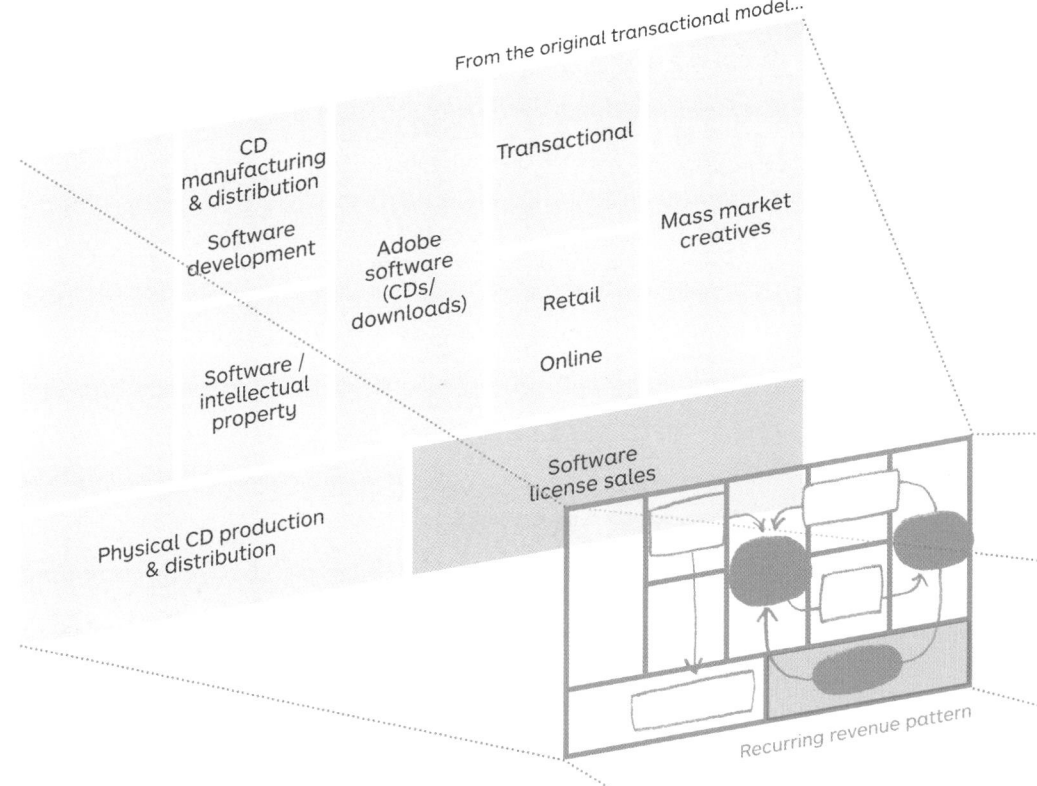

From the original transactional model...

Recurring revenue pattern

1 From Transactional to Recurring Revenues

Adobe decides to shift from offering perpetual software licenses to a monthly subscription service in 2012. At the time Adobe's complete Master Software Collection costs $2,500, versus a monthly $50 subscription for the entire Creative Cloud.

2 From Sales to Recurring Value Proposition

Prior to 2012, Adobe customers purchase a perpetual license that requires seasonal upgrades in order to get access to the latest software. Of course, customers want access to the best and latest software and features all the time, not once every few years. The shift to the Creative Cloud satisfies that recurring need with automatic updates, technical support, online storage, publishing capability, and file sharing.

3 From Transactional to Long-Term Relationship

The shift to the Creative Cloud effectively means transforming a transactional relationship with customers into a long-term one. Adobe invests heavily in creating an online user community. This leads to open discussions on the value and benefits of the new subscription model.

4 From Continuous Customer Acquisition Every Few Years to Important First-Time Customer Acquisition

Prior to 2012, Adobe bears the activity and cost of customer acquisition for every new software sale and every subsequent upgrade. With the shift from transactional to recurring revenue, Adobe invests in acquiring customers once, upfront, in order to collect subscription revenues over their lifetime.

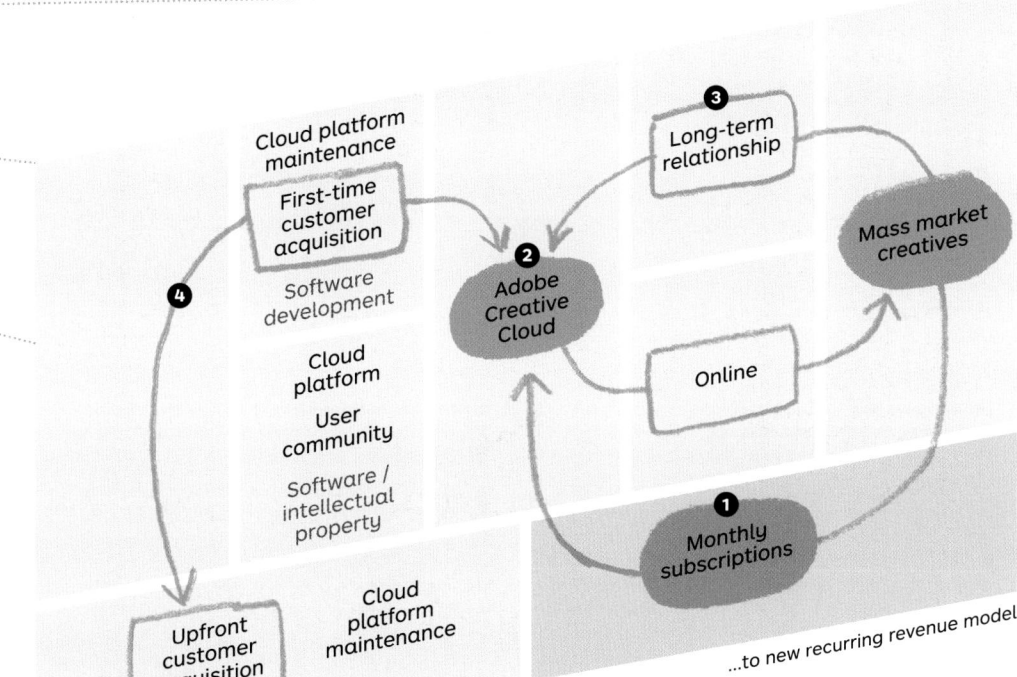

...to new recurring revenue model

Adobe Net Profit Margin[33]

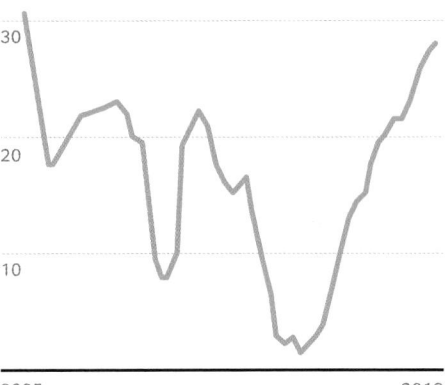

Adobe Revenues by Segment[34]
as a percentage of total revenues

Product ▬ *Subscription*

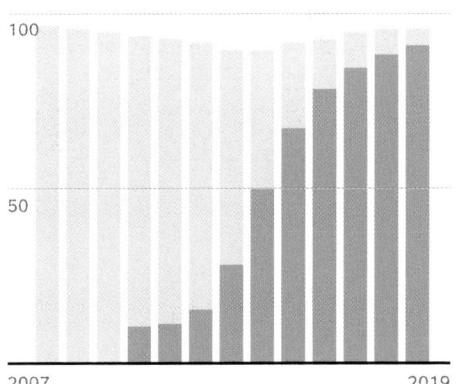

273

PROFIT FORMULA DISRUPTION

Apple iMac

In 1997, Steve Jobs returns to Apple, which is in a dire financial situation. Jobs significantly reduces operating costs, while focusing Apple's new desktop computer value proposition on exactly what design-sensitive consumers want with the iMac.

In late 1996 Apple acquired NeXT, the company launched by Apple founder Steve Jobs after resigning from Apple. Apple, which was close to bankruptcy, put Steve Jobs in charge to turn around the company. Jobs also acted swiftly on the product side and killed more than 70% of Apple's hardware and software portfolio to focus on very few projects. This decision resulted in the layoffs of over 3,000 employees, but allowed Apple to focus on reinventing the home computer. Newly appointed head of design Jonathan Ive was tasked with this reinvention. He designed the iconic iMac with its translucent Bondi blue casing. A year later Apple was back to profitable figures and the success of the iMac paved the way for future game-changing Apple products (iPod, iPhone, iPad). Its new operating system, Mac OS X, which was launched in 2001, also originated in the NeXT acquisition.

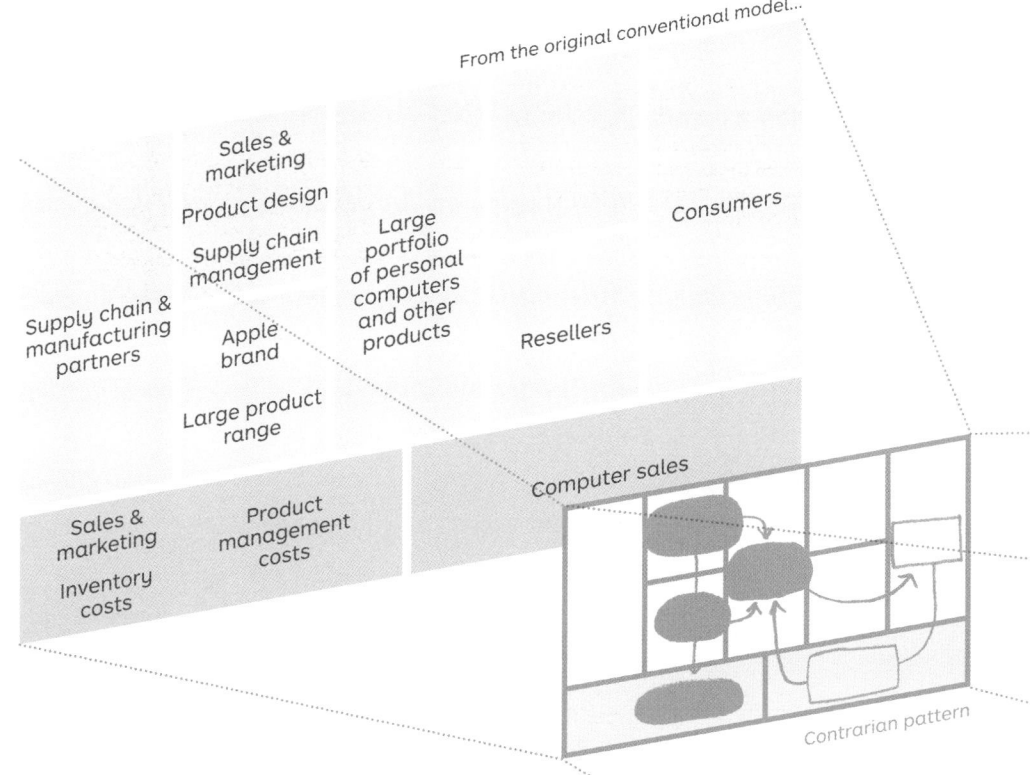

From the original conventional model...

Contrarian pattern

1 From Conventional Activities and Resources to Low-Cost Activity Configuration and Reduced Asset Costs

Apple shifts from costly and diversified activities and resources driven by an unnecessarily extensive product portfolio to a focused and trimmed cost structure. Steve Jobs eliminates product customizations for different resellers and reduces operating costs by killing 70% of Apple hardware and software developments. In parallel, Tim Cook leads the transformation of Apple's supply chain, which results in a significant reduction of inventory costs.

2 From Conventional to Attractive New Value Proposition for New Design-Sensitive Customer Segments and Apple Fans

Apple launches the iMac and breaks the beige or grey computer dogma in the PC market. The iMac is dramatically different from any previous computer: Apple increases both power and ease of use, especially to access the now popular Internet. Apple also creates a completely new aesthetic with the iMac's curvy, colorful design. Reasonably priced at $1,299, the iMac resonates immediately with a new segment of design-sensitive consumers.

3 From a Loss-Making to a High-Margin Business

Apple simplifies its product portfolio, ups its game in supply chain management, and focuses design efforts in the desktop computer for consumers segment on the new iMac. Within a year Apple returns to making profits.

$309
million profit in 1998

vs.

$1,045
million loss in fiscal year 1997[35]

800,000
iMacs sold

within the first 140 days of release. An iMac was sold every 15 seconds.[36]

31 to 6
days, worth of supply held in inventory

In fiscal year 1997, Apple had $437 million tied up in inventory, or a full month's supply on the books. But by the close of fiscal year 1998, the company had slashed inventory levels by 80%, to just six days.[37]

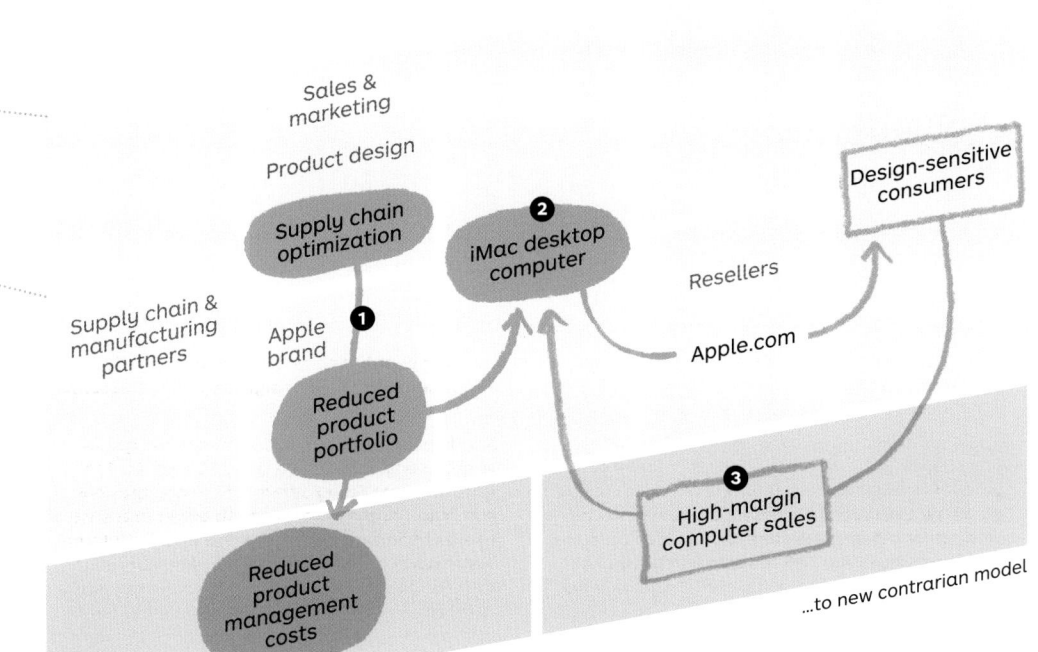

Sales & marketing

Product design

Supply chain & manufacturing partners

Supply chain optimization

2 iMac desktop computer

Resellers

Design-sensitive consumers

Apple.com

Apple brand

1 Reduced product portfolio

Reduced product management costs

3 High-margin computer sales

...to new contrarian model

Ørsted

In 2012, new CEO Henrik Poulsen leads the transformation of Ørsted from a fossil fuel energy producer and distributor to an exclusively green energy powerhouse. The shift comes after falling gas prices trigger a debt crisis.

Ørsted was established in the 1970s as DONG Energy, a Danish state-owned business that built coal-fired plants and offshore oil and gas rigs around Europe.

In 2009 DONG Energy decided to dramatically shift toward green energy. It announced targets to reduce the use of fossil fuels from 85% to 15% by 2040. This shift was supported by the Danish government, which started subsidizing renewable energy production.

In 2012, falling gas prices led to a debt crisis at DONG Energy and Henrik Poulsen was brought on as new CEO. Under his leadership, DONG Energy accelerated its shift to green energy. In 2019, it was the world's largest offshore wind farm developer.

In 2016, DONG Energy went public in a $15 billion IPO. In 2017, the company formally abandoned fossil fuels when it sold its oil and gas business and changed its name to Ørsted.[38]

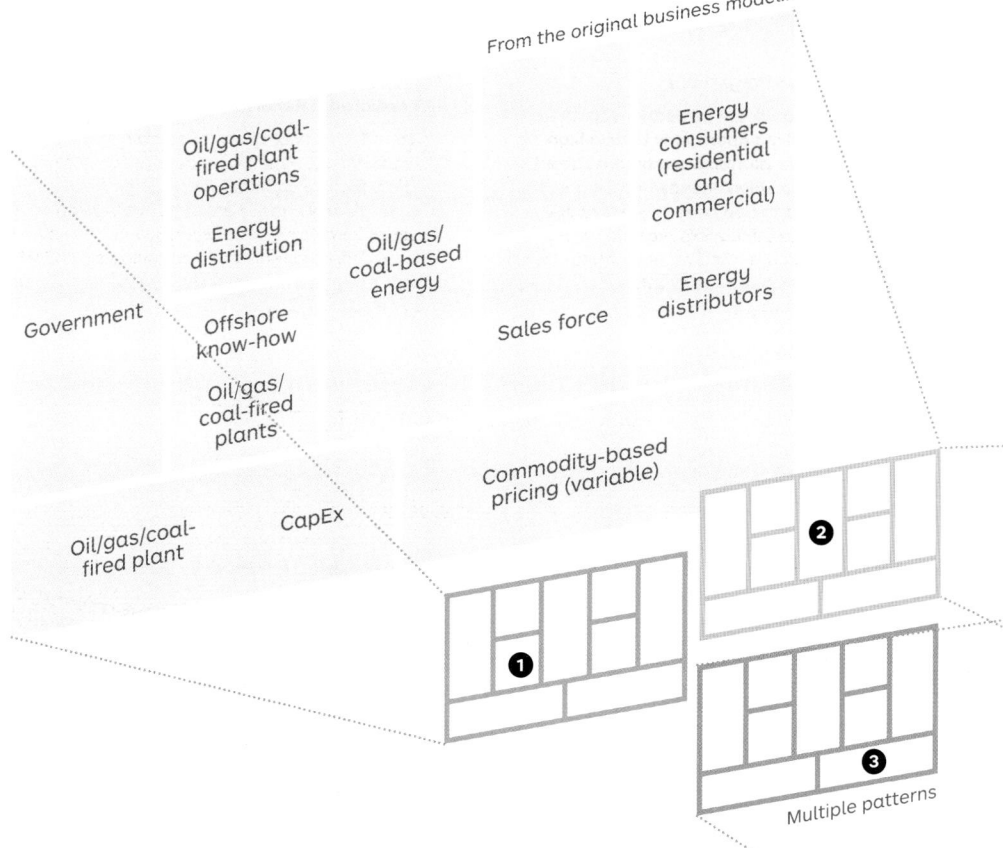

Ørsted's transformation toward becoming a sustainable business combines several shifts:

1 From Dedicated to Multi-Usage of a Key Resource

When Ørsted starts its transformation it applies its offshore know-how from years of North Sea drilling operations to building offshore wind farms. This facilitates the radical shift from its original focus on fossil fuel energy to the new focus on renewable energy.

2 From Low Tech to High Tech

Ørsted incurs significant investment costs to shift from its drilling operations to new high-tech green power plants. Government subsidies facilitate the transition. Meanwhile, oil and gas drilling in the North Sea becomes relatively expensive due to the basin's maturity, making Ørsted's transition to wind technology and wind farms operations highly relevant.

3 From Volatile Transactional Revenues to Predictable Recurring Revenues

Ørsted's traditional revenues from fossil fuels were highly volatile and prices depended on geo-political factors and fluctuating commodity prices. Ørsted's wind-based energy prices, however, are set at long-term, fixed prices due to government subsidies (and renewable certificates). In 2007, only 13% of Ørsted's production is based on fixed prices versus 81% in 2018.

75%
of energy produced from renewables
Green share of generation increased from 64% to 75% in 2018.[39]

81%
reduction in CO_2 emissions
Reduced carbon emissions from 18 million tons in 2006 to 3.4 million tons in 2018.[39]

87%
of capital invested in renewables. In 2007, 16% of total capital employed was invested in renewables. In 2018, the share of renewables had increased to 87%.[39]

Government

Energy distribution

Wind farm production and operations

Value-based relationship (sustainability)

Energy consumers (residential and commercial)

2 Renewable energy (wind farms)

Energy distributors

Wind turbine manufacturers

Offshore know-how

Sales force

1

Wind farms

Reduced cost due to government subsidies

Wind farm operations

CapEx

Fixed pricing for renewable energy **3** Higher prices (green energy premium)

...to new business model

Rolls-Royce

Rolls-Royce launches TotalCare© in the late 1990s. It is the first jet engine manufacturer to shift from selling an engine (product) to selling care for every stage of the product lifecycle (service).

Rolls-Royce's civil aerospace business recognized in the 1990s that its business model was misaligned with its airline and business aviation customers: in order to generate a new sale, Rolls-Royce engines had to break or malfunction.

In 1999, American Airlines asked Rolls-Royce to deliver not only a large engine order but also all after-sales services related to repair, maintenance, transportation, and peripheral supplies. TotalCare service was born out of this initial request.

TotalCare transferred the risk of managing a jet engine over its lifetime from the customer to Rolls-Royce. TotalCare realigned Rolls-Royce's incentives with those of its customers with a recurring revenue model where Rolls-Royce gets paid by the flying hour of its jet engine.

With TotalCare, Rolls-Royce has shifted from a product to a recurring service business model. Its jet engines are sold at a loss and Rolls-Royce recoups losses with the service contract over time.

14.3 million charged hours

14.3 million large engine invoiced flying hours in 2018.[40]

90% of fleet covered

90% of the 2018 Rolls-Royce widebody fleet is covered by TotalCare service agreements.[40]

The Washington Post

Jeff Bezos purchases the *Washington Post* in 2013 in order to transform the niche local newspaper into a national, digital, mass-media powerhouse.

In 2103, Jeff Bezos purchased the *Washington Post* (*The Post*) for $250 million. *The Post* was struggling to survive as a print publication, hyper-focused on Washington politics. Bezos used his Internet expertise to transform the newspaper into a global, digital media company focused on a mass market, leveraging the free distribution of the Internet.

The Post kept the integrity of its editorial, investigative journalism while also making a broad outreach to additional readers. It installed a paywall to increase its subscriber revenues and it created a platform for aggregating news across platforms, reaching more journalists and more readers.

1.7 million digital subscriptions

From 484,000 print subscribers and 28,000 digital subscriptions in 2012 to over 1.7 million digital subscriptions in 2019.[41,42]

87 million unique visitors

in March 2019 with an increase of 84% in three years (vs. 28 million in 2010, 41 million in 2012).[43]

GORE-TEX

In 1989, W.L. Gore launches the "guaranteed to keep you dry" promise on products using its Gore-Tex fabrics. That allows Gore to shift from a behind-the-scenes B2B fabric manufacturer to a trusted B2C brand.

Gore-Tex was developed by W.L. Gore in 1969 as the world's first waterproof and breathable fabric. The company received its first commercial Gore-Tex order in 1976 to develop rainwear and tents for an outdoor company.

In 1989, Gore-Tex introduced the Guaranteed to Keep You Dry \ promise on its waterproof products, which included a lifetime product warranty. W.L. Gore, which doesn't manufacture the final product, convinced clothing and outdoor brands to market this guarantee with hang tags on the garments using its fabrics. This gave consumers an extra sense of quality and peace of mind and made Gore-Tex a ubiquitous brand by piggybacking established clothing manufacturers.

Although Gore didn't manufacture the end garments, the supplier extended its promise to consumers. If consumers weren't "completely satisfied" with their garment, Gore would take care of it. Gore used its logo and its Gore-Tex label to show end consumers that their garments could be trusted regardless of the manufacturer.

> *"It is one thing for a company to guarantee what it makes. It is quite another for it to guarantee what others make. But that is exactly what they do."*
>
> —THE GORE-TEX PROMISE

Delta Airlines

In 1996 Delta Airlines puts its SkyMiles to new use and resells them to American Express for their loyalty program.

Delta Airlines created its SkyMIles frequent flier program in 1981. SkyMiles were a key resource in Delta's air travel business model—to rewarding its loyal customers.

In 1996, Delta Airlines realized it could reuse that key resource for another value proposition. It started selling SkyMiles to a new customer, American Express (AmEx) who would distribute these SkyMiles to their own customers, AmEx credit card holders.

This partnership allowed AmEx to target high-end travelers interested in earning SkyMiles with their credit card spending and allowed Delta to find another usage for its SkyMiles.

35%
of Delta's income ($3.4 billion of value) came from selling miles to American Express in 2018.[44]

2x
Delta expects its benefit from the relationship to double to nearly $7 billion by 2023.[45]

Questions for Leaders

Value Proposition Shifts

Shift	How might we...
From ⟶ To **Product** ⟷ **Service** To ⟵ From	...shift to a business business model built around a recurring service that provides predictable and recurring revenues? ...add scalable products to our services to increase the share of wallet and lifetime value of each customer and boost overall revenues?
From ⟶ To **Low Tech** ⟷ **High Tech** To ⟵ From	...leverage technology activities or resources to transform our value proposition, radically modify our cost structure, or dramatically extend our reach? ...leverage low-tech activities or resources to provide value to customers that they really appreciate, but that doesn't cost much to provide or that technology can't offer?
From ⟶ To **Platform** ⟷ **Sales** To ⟵ From	...turn a product or service into a valuable platform that connects users with third-party product and service providers and vice-versa? ...add our own scalable products and services to our platform to increase the lifetime value of each customer and boost overall revenues?

Frontstage Driven Shifts

Shift	How might we...
From ⟶ To **Niche Market** ⟷ **Mass Market** To ⟵ From	...modify our value proposition, adapt our marketing and branding, and extend our reach to shift from a niche market to a mass market? ...create niche value propositions for a series of niche segments with specific needs? How would that affect our marketing and branding and distribution strategy?
From ⟶ To **B2B** ⟷ **B2C** To ⟵ From	...become relevant and visible to our end customers, the consumers? How would we have to modify our value proposition to our direct customers (B2B) and consumers (B2C) to make that happen? ...use our B2C customer experience and relationships, infrastructure, resources, activities, and expertise, to create value for B2B customers and even competitors?
From ⟶ To **High Touch** ⟷ **Low Touch** To ⟵ From	...create a high-touch experience, improve our value proposition, and increase price and revenues, while maintaining the advantages of standardization and scale? ...create or maintain customer value, while shifting from a high-touch to a low-touch experience? Which aspects of high touch do customers not value as much as the price of providing them?

Backstage Driven Shifts

Shift	How might we...
From ⟶ **To** **Dedicated Resources** ⟷ **Multi-Usage Resources** **To** ⟵ **From**	...monetize one of our key resources to create a new value proposition for a completely new customer segment? How might our key resources enable us to provide a better value proposition than competitors?
	...trim our business model by refocusing resources used to serve several value propositions and dedicate them to one only? How might that help us improve our profit formula?
From ⟶ **To** **Asset Heavy** ⟷ **Asset Light** **To** ⟵ **From**	...free up capital and energy from building and maintaining assets toward focusing on client-related activities? How might we better put that available capital to use and improve our profit formula?
	...leverage our light assets like IP and brand to invest in heavy assets? How might that help us create a competitive advantage, make us difficult to copy, or create barriers to market entry?
From ⟶ **To** **Closed** ⟷ **Open** **To** ⟵ **From**	... leverage the strengths of our business model to use external R&D, IP, and resources (outside-in) or share internal R&D, IP, and resources with outside partners (inside-out)? How might that lead to a higher return on R&D or capital invested?
	...create a competitive advantage by internalizing R&D, IP, resources, and activities? How might that create cost, knowledge, or profit efficiencies? How might we stop sharing R&D, IP, resources, and activities with outside partners?

Profit Formula Driven Shifts

Shift	How might we...
From ⟶ **To** **High Cost** ⟷ **Low Cost** **To** ⟵ **From**	...create value for price-conscious customer segments? How might we reconfigure activities and resources to disrupt our cost structure and make that low price possible?
	...create value for price-insensitive customer segments? How might we leverage our resources and activities to create a high-value, high-price value proposition?
From ⟶ **To** **Transactional Revenue** ⟷ **Recurring Revenue** **To** ⟵ **From**	...focus on recurring customer jobs-to-be-done in order to create a recurring value proposition with a long-term relationship and recurring revenues?
	...add transactional revenues to our recurring revenues in order to improve customer share of wallet and boost our overall revenues?
From ⟶ **To** **Conventional** ⟷ **Contrarian** **To** ⟵ **From**	...eliminate or reduce costly activities and resources, even if they create value for customers? How might we replace that lost value with less costly value creators that matter most to customers?
	...add costly resources and activities to our business model to substantially increase value, price, and luxury feel? Or, conversely, how might we strip our business model to shift to a pure low-cost model?

Invincible Companies Transcend Industry Boundaries

Tencent social networks, online gaming, online advertising, content production, financial services, software, music...

Apple smartphones, personal computers, tablets, wearables, software, music, movies, health, photography, personal productivity, credit cards, mobile payments...

Ping An banking, insurance, healthcare, auto services, real estate, smart cities...

Amazon retail, logistics, electronics, streaming, IT infrastructure, publishing, e-commerce infrastructure, online advertising, SMB loans...

You...

Design Your Culture

To build an Invincible Company you need to create, manage, and harmonize two completely antagonistic cultures under one roof—and they both have an important role to play. You need to explore and exploit simultaneously.

Explore

Your **exploration culture** cultivates the creation, discovery, validation, and acceleration of completely new ideas that are foreign to an organization.

Exploit

Your exploitation culture cherishes the management, systematic improvement, and growth of existing businesses.

Cultivate Explore and Exploit Under One Roof

Invincible Companies design, manage, and maintain both a strong Explore and a strong Exploit culture. They cherish operational excellence, planning, and constant improvements when managing the present. Yet, they know they can't cost cut themselves into the future. They simultaneously embrace risk, experimentation, failure, and adaptation when exploring ideas for the coming years and decades. However successful today, they don't rest on their laurels; they already work on tomorrow.

290

GROW
Culture supports scaling new emerging businesses and improving or reinventing established ones to reposition them.

Explore
High uncertainty

Exploit
Low uncertainty

SEARCH
Culture supports business model design and testing in the search for new potential businesses.

Explore		Exploit
Explore ←————————————→ **Exploit**		
We admit that we don't know and adopt a beginner's mindset. We search for a solution and accept that not all projects will succeed.	**What's the mindset?**	We rely on our experience and adopt our expert's mindset. We plan and execute and believe failure is not an option.
We embrace risk and uncertainty. We manage them by experimenting, learning, and adapting. We make many small bets to find winners.	**How do we deal with risk and uncertainty?**	We shun risk and uncertainty. We minimize them by planning, executing, and managing. We make few and well-calculated bets on winners.
We work iteratively and make rough prototypes.	**How do we work?**	We work sequentially with high fidelity.
Failure is an inevitable side product of exploration. We embrace, manage, and learn from failure and minimize the cost of it by making many small bets.	**What's our attitude toward failure?**	Failure is unacceptable. We avoid and punish it. It can be avoided through careful planning and sound execution.
We define hypotheses to make risk explicit. Then we measure the reduction of risk of a new idea.	**How do we measure progress and success?**	We define milestones to make progress steps explicit. We measure whether we are on time and on budget.
We reward people for trying, learning, and reducing the risk of new ideas.	**What do we reward people for?**	We reward people for planning, executing, and staying on time and on budget.
We move fast on reversible decisions and test them as quickly and cheaply as possible to produce real-world evidence.	**What's our attitude toward speed of decision-making?**	We take time to carefully analyze, think through, and plan irreversible decisions with large sunk costs.
We make small bets when risk and uncertainty are high. We increase our investments based on the strength of the evidence.	**How do we invest?**	We take time to plan a project and release funds based on reaching milestones.
We value the ability to deal with ambiguity, to move fast and adapt, and to test ideas and reduce their risk.	**What do we value?**	We value rigor, the ability to plan and execute, the skill to design processes, and reliable delivery.

How It Fits Together

Your corporate identity defines who you want to be and sets the context for everything else. It allows you to specify the guidance that will shape your entire portfolio. Your portfolio is a reflection of who you are in terms of businesses you own (Exploit), and who you are trying to become in terms of businesses you are exploring (Explore).

In order to smoothly manage this type of dual portfolio you need to put in place a so-called ambidextrous culture that is world-class at both exploration and exploitation. This entire chapter describes how to achieve that by eliminating blockers and implementing enablers that will facilitate your cultural transformation.

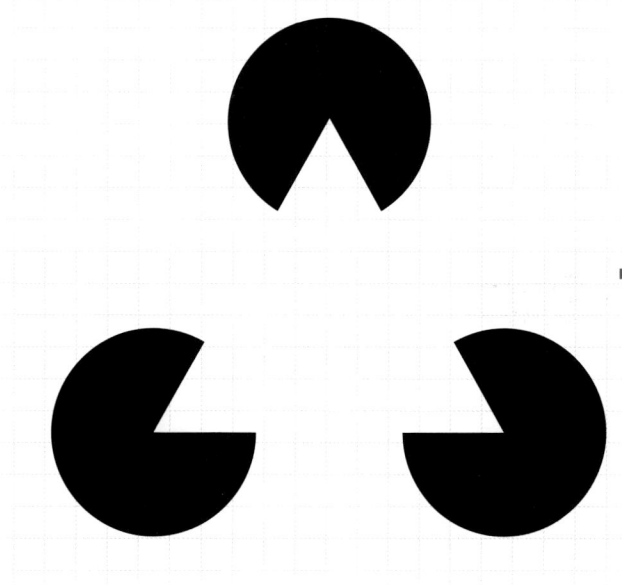

Corporate Identity

WHO WE ARE

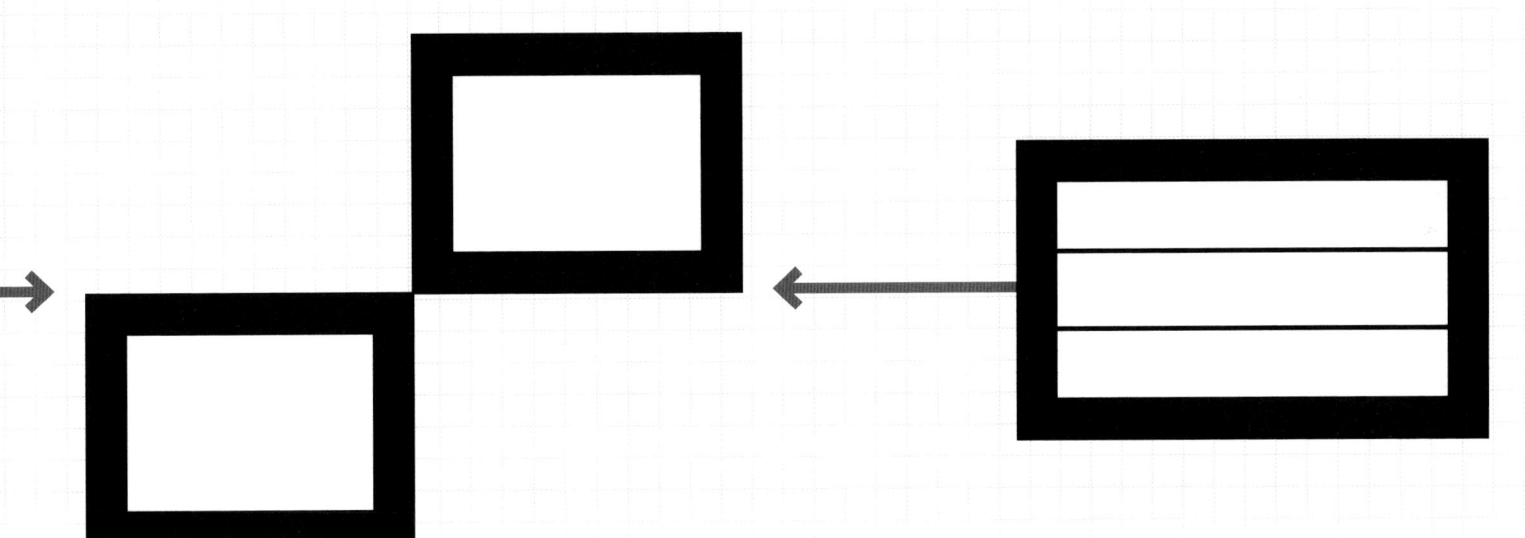

Portfolio Map

WHAT WE'RE DOING

Culture Map

HOW WE'LL DO IT

293

Every company has a corporate culture.

Yet, too many companies let culture just happen.
Invincible Companies actively understand, design,
and manage culture. They create world-class
innovation and execution cultures that live in harmony. In this section we outline how you can map
corporate culture and what it takes to create a
world-class innovation culture.

What are our desired outcomes?
What behaviors will allow us to achieve our desired outcomes?
What enables and blocks us from our goals?

The Culture Map

Together with Dave Gray, Strategyzer developed the Culture Map as a tool to design better-performing companies. The Culture Map is a practical, simple, and visual tool to understand, design, test, and manage the corporate culture you want to bring to fruition in your organization. In this book we use the Culture Map to map and design an innovation culture.

DAVE GRAY
Author and entrepreneur

"If you want to understand culture, you need to map it."

CULTURE

Outcomes
The concrete positive or negative consequences resulting from people's behavior.

Behaviors
How do individual and teams act or conduct themselves within the company? What do they do or say? How do they interact? What patterns do you notice?

Enablers/Blockers
The levers that lead to positive or negative behaviors inside your company. These could be formal policies, processes, and reward systems, or informal rituals and actions that influence people's behaviors and, ultimately, influence a company's outcomes.

The Culture Map Beta

A Change Management Tool

Designed for:	Designed by:	Date:	Iteration:

Outcomes

Behaviors

Enablers/Blockers

Strategyzer

strategyzer.com

LEADERS DON'T CREATE GROWTH

LEADERS CREATE CONDITIONS FOR GROWTH

Cultivate corporate culture like a garden.

You can't mechanistically design a corporate culture like you'd — for example — design a car. An organization is a social system that is infinitely more complex than a car. That doesn't mean you shouldn't design the aspects of your organization that are under your control. We really like Dave Gray's analogy of designing culture like you'd design and cultivate a garden.

The **outcomes** in your culture are the fruits. These are the things you want your culture to achieve, or what you want to "harvest" from your garden.

The **behaviors** are the heart of your culture. They're the positive or negative actions people perform every day that will result in a good or bad harvest.

The **enablers and blockers** are the elements that allow your garden to flourish or not. Some are under your control, like sufficient water or fertilizer. You need to take care of the soil, seeds, and the young plants for your garden to flourish. Other elements, like the weather, are not under your control and you can only prepare your garden to minimize the damage or maximize the positive impact.

Culture Map

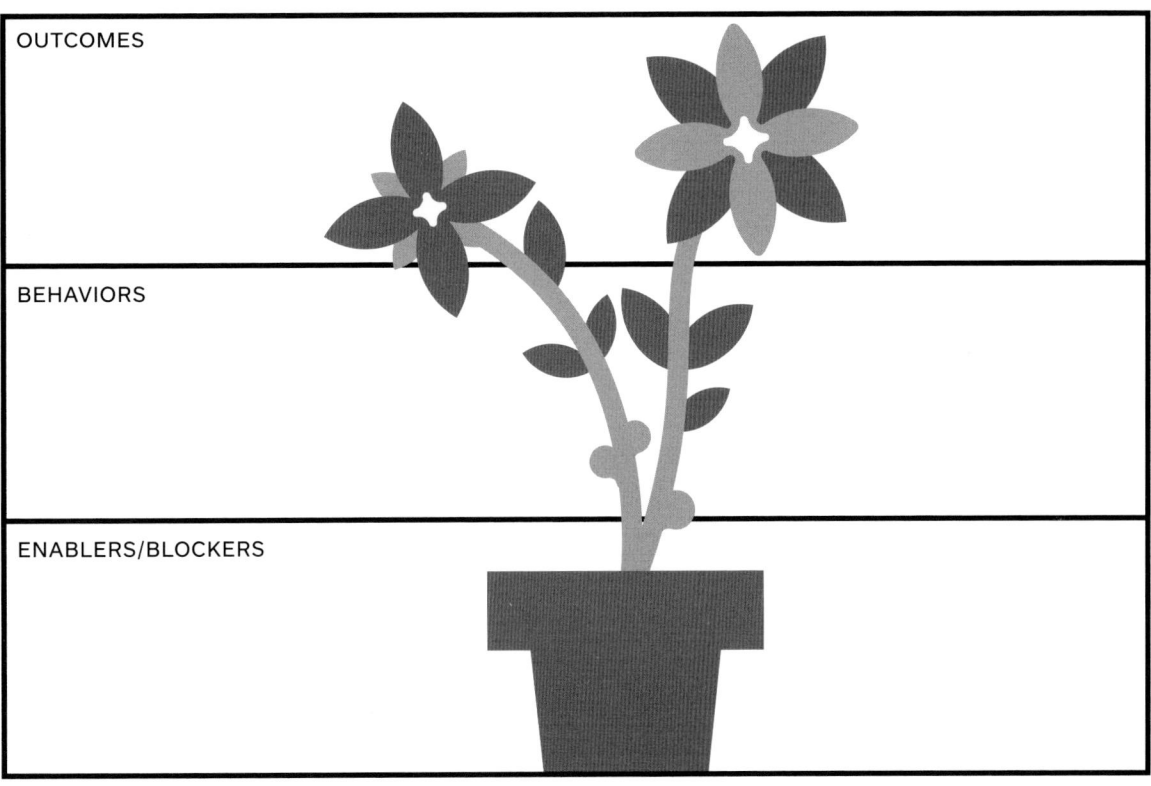

OUTCOMES

BEHAVIORS

ENABLERS/BLOCKERS

Amazon's Innovation Culture

Amazon's stellar growth and constant reinvention aren't magic, they're ingrained in the company culture. Read Jeff Bezos's letters to shareholders to understand how Amazon built a company culture that constantly pioneers in new spaces.

"We want to be a large company that's also an invention machine [...] with the speed of movement, nimbleness, and risk-acceptance mentality normally associated with entrepreneurial start-ups."

JEFF BEZOS
Amazon founder & CEO

amazon.com

1997 LETTER TO SHAREHOLDERS
(Reprinted from the 1997 Annual Report)

To our shareholders:

Amazon.com passed many milestones in 1997: by year-end, we had served more than 1.5 million customers, yielding 838% revenue growth to $147.8 million, and extended our market leadership despite aggressive competitive entry.

But this is Day 1 for the Internet and, if we execute well, for Amazon.com. Today, online commerce saves customers money and precious time. Tomorrow, through personalization, online commerce will accelerate the very process of discovery. Amazon.com uses the Internet to create real value for its customers and, by doing so, hopes to create an enduring franchise, even in established and large markets.

We have a window of opportunity as larger players marshal the resources to pursue the online opportunity and as customers, new to purchasing online, are receptive to forming new relationships. The competitive landscape has continued to evolve at a fast pace. Many large players have moved online with credible offerings and have devoted substantial energy and resources to building awareness, traffic, and sales. Our goal is to move quickly to solidify and extend our current position while we begin to pursue the online commerce opportunities in other areas. We see substantial opportunity in the large markets we are targeting. This strategy is not without risk: it requires serious investment and crisp execution against established franchise leaders.

It's All About the Long Term

We believe that a fundamental measure of our success will be the shareholder value we create over the *long term*. This value will be a direct result of our ability to extend and solidify our current market leadership position. The stronger our market leadership, the more powerful our economic model. Market leadership can translate directly to higher revenue, higher profitability, greater capital velocity, and correspondingly stronger returns on invested capital.

Our decisions have consistently reflected this focus. We first measure ourselves in terms of the metrics most indicative of our market leadership: customer and revenue growth, the degree to which our customers continue to purchase from us on a repeat basis, and the strength of our brand. We have invested and will continue to invest aggressively to expand and leverage our customer base, brand, and infrastructure as we move to establish an enduring franchise.

Because of our emphasis on the long term, we may make decisions and weigh tradeoffs differently than some companies. Accordingly, we want to share with you our fundamental management and decision-making approach so that you, our shareholders, may confirm that it is consistent with your investment philosophy:

- We will continue to focus relentlessly on our customers.
- We will continue to make investment decisions in light of long-term market leadership considerations rather than short-term profitability considerations or short-term Wall Street reactions.
- We will continue to measure our programs and the effectiveness of our investments analytically, to jettison those that do not provide acceptable returns, and to step up our investment in those that work best. We will continue to learn from both our successes and our failures.

- We will make bold rather than timid investment decisions where we see a sufficient probability of gaining market leadership advantages. Some of these investments will pay off, others will not, and we will have learned another valuable lesson in either case.
- When forced to choose between optimizing the appearance of our GAAP accounting and maximizing the present value of future cash flows, we'll take the cash flows.
- We will share our strategic thought processes with you when we make bold choices (to the extent competitive pressures allow), so that you may evaluate for yourselves whether we are making rational long-term leadership investments.
- We will work hard to spend wisely and maintain our lean culture. We understand the importance of continually reinforcing a cost-conscious culture, particularly in a business incurring net losses.
- We will balance our focus on growth with emphasis on long-term profitability and capital management. At this stage, we choose to prioritize growth because we believe that scale is central to achieving the potential of our business model.
- We will continue to focus on hiring and retaining versatile and talented employees, and continue to weight their compensation to stock options rather than cash. We know our success will be largely affected by our ability to attract and retain a motivated employee base, each of whom must think like, and therefore must actually be, an owner.

We aren't so bold as to claim that the above is the "right" investment philosophy, but it's ours, and we would be remiss if we weren't clear in the approach we have taken and will continue to take.

With this foundation, we would like to turn to a review of our business focus, our progress in 1997, and our outlook for the future.

Obsess Over Customers

From the beginning, our focus has been on offering our customers compelling value. We realized that the Web was, and still is, the World Wide Wait. Therefore, we set out to offer customers something they simply could not get any other way, and began serving them with books. We brought them much more selection than was possible in a physical store (our store would now occupy 6 football fields), and presented it in a useful, easy-to-search, and easy-to-browse format in a store open 365 days a year, 24 hours a day. We maintained a dogged focus on improving the shopping experience, and in 1997 substantially enhanced our store. We now offer customers gift certificates, 1-Click℠ shopping, and vastly more reviews, content, browsing options, and recommendation features. We dramatically lowered prices, further increasing customer value. Word of mouth remains the most powerful customer acquisition tool we have, and we are grateful for the trust our customers have placed in us. Repeat purchases and word of mouth have combined to make Amazon.com the market leader in online bookselling.

By many measures, Amazon.com came a long way in 1997:

- Sales grew from $15.7 million in 1996 to $147.8 million – an 838% increase.
- Cumulative customer accounts grew from 180,000 to 1,510,000 – a 738% increase.
- The percentage of orders from repeat customers grew from over 46% in the fourth quarter of 1996 to over 58% in the same period in 1997.
- In terms of audience reach, per Media Metrix, our Web site went from a rank of 90th to within the top 20.
- We established long-term relationships with many important strategic partners, including America Online, Yahoo!, Excite, Netscape, GeoCities, AltaVista, @Home, and Prodigy.

Amazon

Each Culture Map is based on an analysis of Jeff Bezos's letters to shareholders between 1997 and 2018. We captured the main outcomes, behaviors, enablers, and blockers related to innovation that Bezos mentions in his letters and visualized them in a Culture Map.

2005

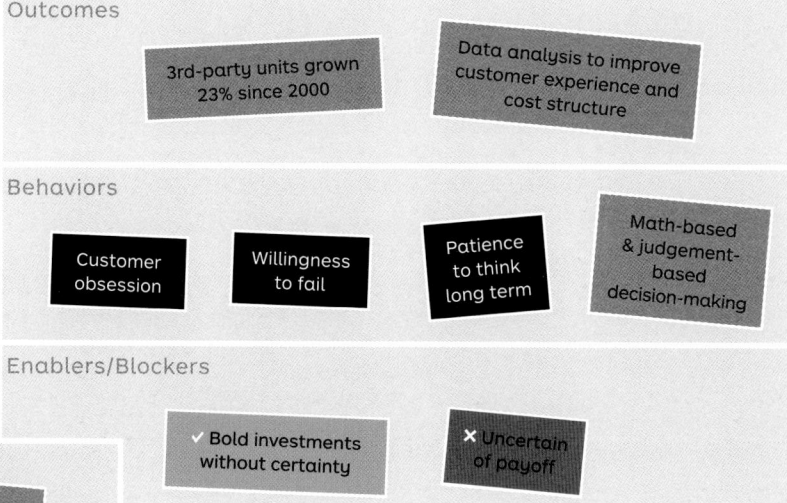

Outcomes

3rd-party units grown 23% since 2000

Data analysis to improve customer experience and cost structure

Behaviors

Customer obsession

Willingness to fail

Patience to think long term

Math-based & judgement-based decision-making

Enablers/Blockers

✔ Bold investments without certainty

✘ Uncertain of payoff

1997

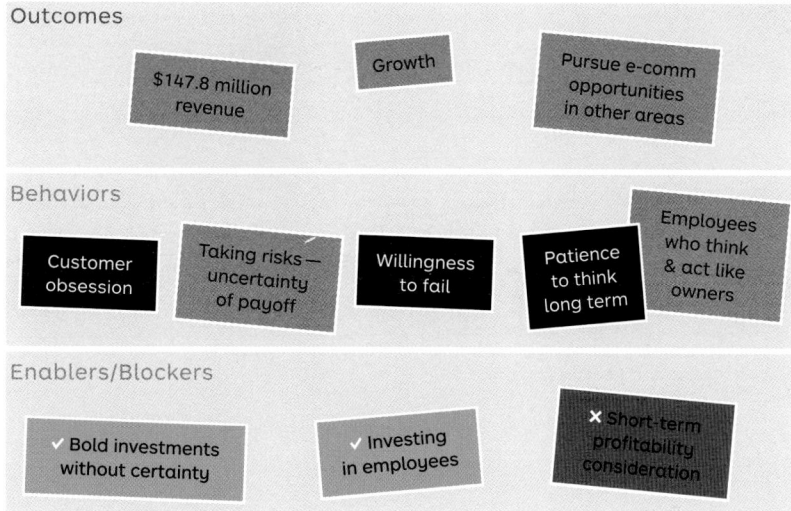

Outcomes

$147.8 million revenue

Growth

Pursue e-comm opportunities in other areas

Behaviors

Customer obsession

Taking risks — uncertainty of payoff

Willingness to fail

Patience to think long term

Employees who think & act like owners

Enablers/Blockers

✔ Bold investments without certainty

✔ Investing in employees

✘ Short-term profitability consideration

The foundation of Amazon's corporate culture was laid out in Bezos's 1997 letter to shareholders in the first annual report. The pillars of this culture (customer obsession, willingness to fail, patience to think long term) remain fundamentally unchanged and a copy of the 1997 letter has been attached to every subsequent annual report. We analyzed the annual shareholder letters for you to visualize and highlight the consistency of its innovation culture and show the progression of results and outcomes.

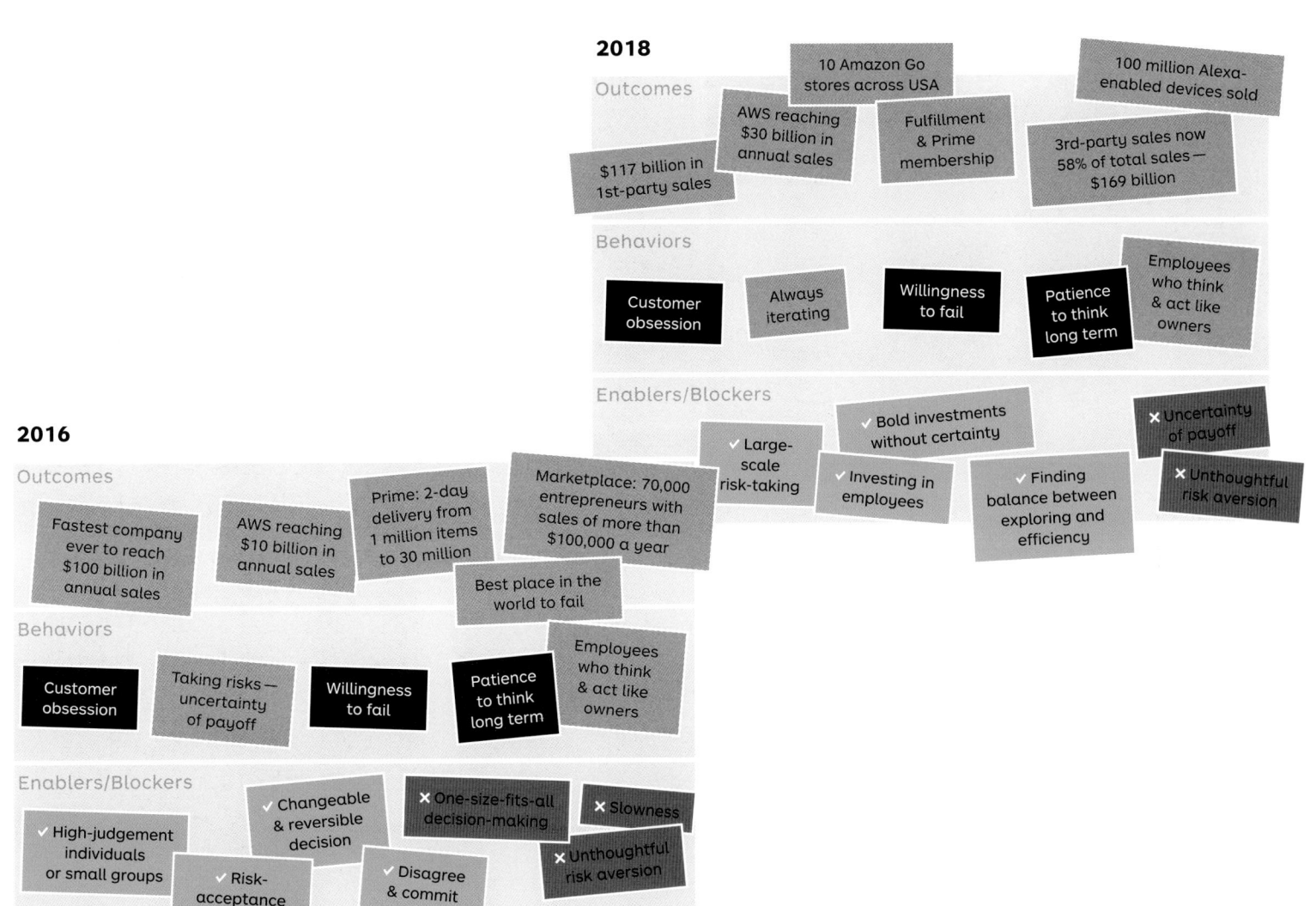

2018

Outcomes
- 10 Amazon Go stores across USA
- 100 million Alexa-enabled devices sold
- AWS reaching $30 billion in annual sales
- Fulfillment & Prime membership
- $117 billion in 1st-party sales
- 3rd-party sales now 58% of total sales — $169 billion

Behaviors
- Customer obsession
- Always iterating
- Willingness to fail
- Patience to think long term
- Employees who think & act like owners

Enablers/Blockers
- ✓ Bold investments without certainty
- ✗ Uncertainty of payoff
- ✓ Large-scale risk-taking
- ✓ Investing in employees
- ✓ Finding balance between exploring and efficiency
- ✗ Unthoughtful risk aversion

2016

Outcomes
- Fastest company ever to reach $100 billion in annual sales
- AWS reaching $10 billion in annual sales
- Prime: 2-day delivery from 1 million items to 30 million
- Marketplace: 70,000 entrepreneurs with sales of more than $100,000 a year
- Best place in the world to fail

Behaviors
- Customer obsession
- Taking risks — uncertainty of payoff
- Willingness to fail
- Patience to think long term
- Employees who think & act like owners

Enablers/Blockers
- ✓ High-judgement individuals or small groups
- ✓ Changeable & reversible decision
- ✗ One-size-fits-all decision-making
- ✗ Slowness
- ✓ Risk-acceptance mentality
- ✓ Disagree & commit
- ✗ Unthoughtful risk aversion

Applying the Culture Map

From existing culture to desired culture. Of course it's up to you to decide if your session should start top down by tackling outcomes and then the associated behaviors, enablers, and blockers. Practice shows that starting with behaviors is an easy place to get going.

CULTURE

Current State Innovation Culture

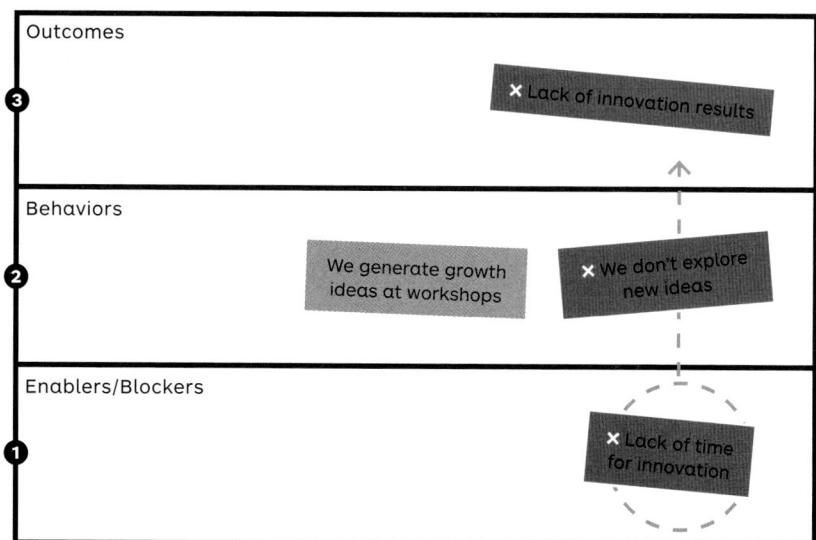

1. Start with Mapping Behaviors

There can be a tendency to describe behaviors in an abstract way, like "We don't innovate." Make sure you use specific examples and get into the habit of mapping behavior based on evidence, not opinion. For example, "Last year we conducted two workshops to develop new growth ideas, but nobody made time to explore them after we left the workshop." Make sure you capture positive and negative behaviors alike. Behave like an anthropologist who neutrally captures what's going on in your team or organization.

2. Capture Resulting Outcomes

Now continue with capturing the positive and negative outcomes resulting from the behaviors you just mapped out. Ask which behaviors you missed, if new outcomes arise that are not related to the already mapped behaviors. Again, remain neutral and make sure you capture both the positive and the negative.

3. Identify Enablers and Blockers

Now that you've captured behaviors and outcomes ask yourself what led to them. Ask "What are the enablers that made good or bad behaviors possible?" and "What are the blockers that prevented good or bad behaviors to emerge?" Make sure you identify formal enablers and blockers, like processes and incentive systems, and informal ones, like meeting rituals or lack of knowledge. Take note that behaviors, such as those of leaders, can also be enablers and blockers.

4. Design Your Desired Culture

When you've completed the Culture Map of your existing culture it's time to dream up your desired state. Design the desired outcomes, the required behaviors, and the enablers and blockers that will make that culture possible.

Desired Innovation Culture

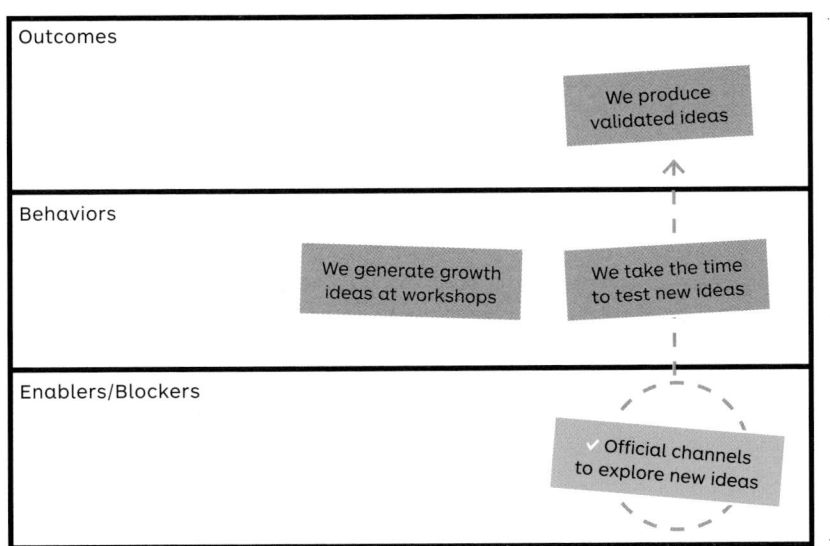

CULTURE

Tips & Tricks

Create a Safe Space
Designing an innovation culture without the buy-in of leadership is likely to fail. Make sure leaders are genuinely interested in creating an innovation culture. Show leadership the current state Culture Map to get them interested.

Blockers and Enablers Only
Consider working on the blockers and enablers only. First identify the blockers holding you back from innovating. Then brainstorm which enablers could boost innovation and how blockers could be eliminated. Categorize ideas into buckets of what can be done immediately, within a month, quarter, or year, or what's practically impossible to achieve.

Display Desired Culture
Prominently display the culture you want to establish. Place the map in a space where everyone can see it and is reminded of the tasks ahead. Put it up in meeting rooms so decisions can be made inline with the information on your Culture Map.

Invincible Companies build a strong exploration and exploitation culture under the same roof.
In this book we mainly outline how to build a strong exploration culture, since most companies already have a pretty strong exploitation culture.
We believe there are three main levers that you can work on to create an exploration culture.

Designing an Exploration Culture

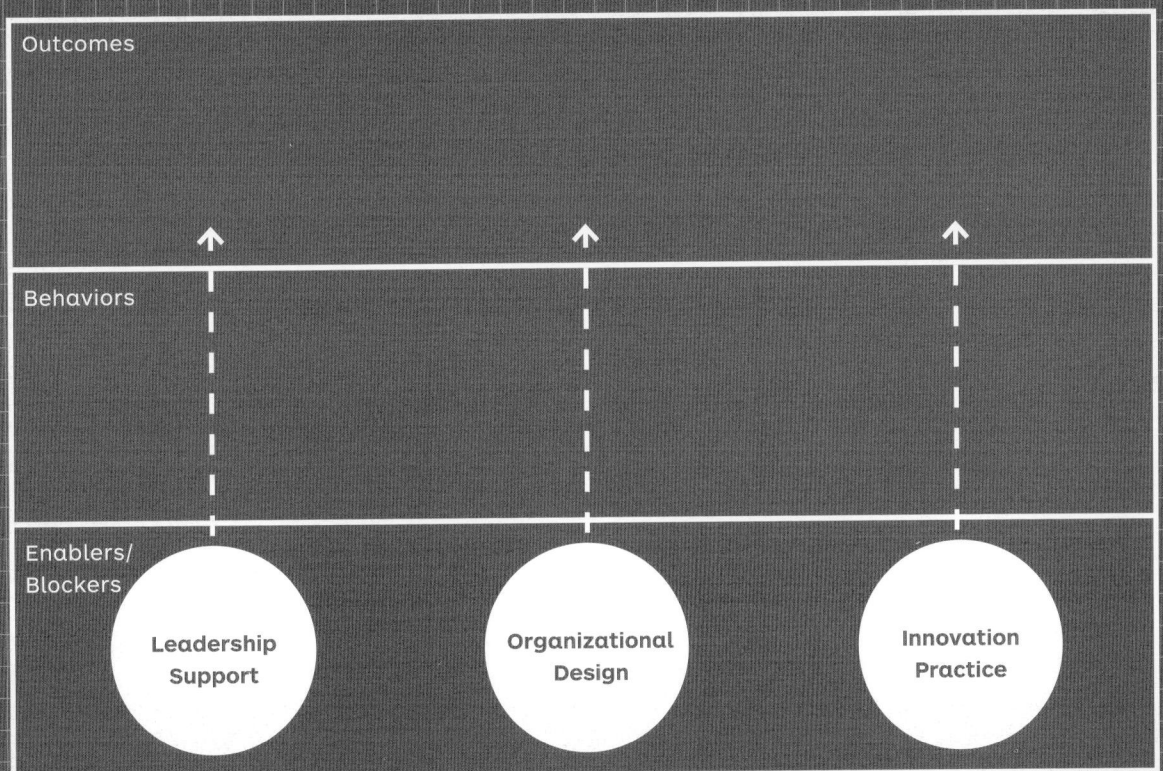

309

Innovation Behaviors and Outcomes

Invincible Companies design great enablers and eliminate the blockers in each one of these three areas: leadership support, organizational design, and innovaton practice. This leads to the following innovation behaviors that you can observe:

✓ Leadership Behavior

Leaders understand how innovation works and they invest a substantial amount of their time into innovation. They provide clear strategic guidance for innovation projects and they regularly review a company-wide Exploit and Explore portfolio. They are eager to explore new growth opportunities and they understand how the related risk is managed.

✓ Organizational Behavior

In organizations with an exploration culture, nobody gets fired for experimenting with new growth opportunities that fit the strategy. You find innovation on the agenda of the most important meetings and people choose innovation as a career path. Innovators understand the constraints of leaders and managers of the exisitng business and they, in return, do their best to help innovators. Exploration and execution form a true partnership to manage the present and explore the future.

✓ Innovation Team Behavior

Innovators pursue ideas based on evidence from experiments, not their opinions or their boss's opinions. Risk and uncertainty of ideas are systematically measured and projects start with cheap and quick experiments. Experiment time and costs increase with increasing evidence and decreasing uncertainty. People accumulate skills over years of practice and learn and grow from failures in any project.

Culture Map: Innovation Culture Blockers

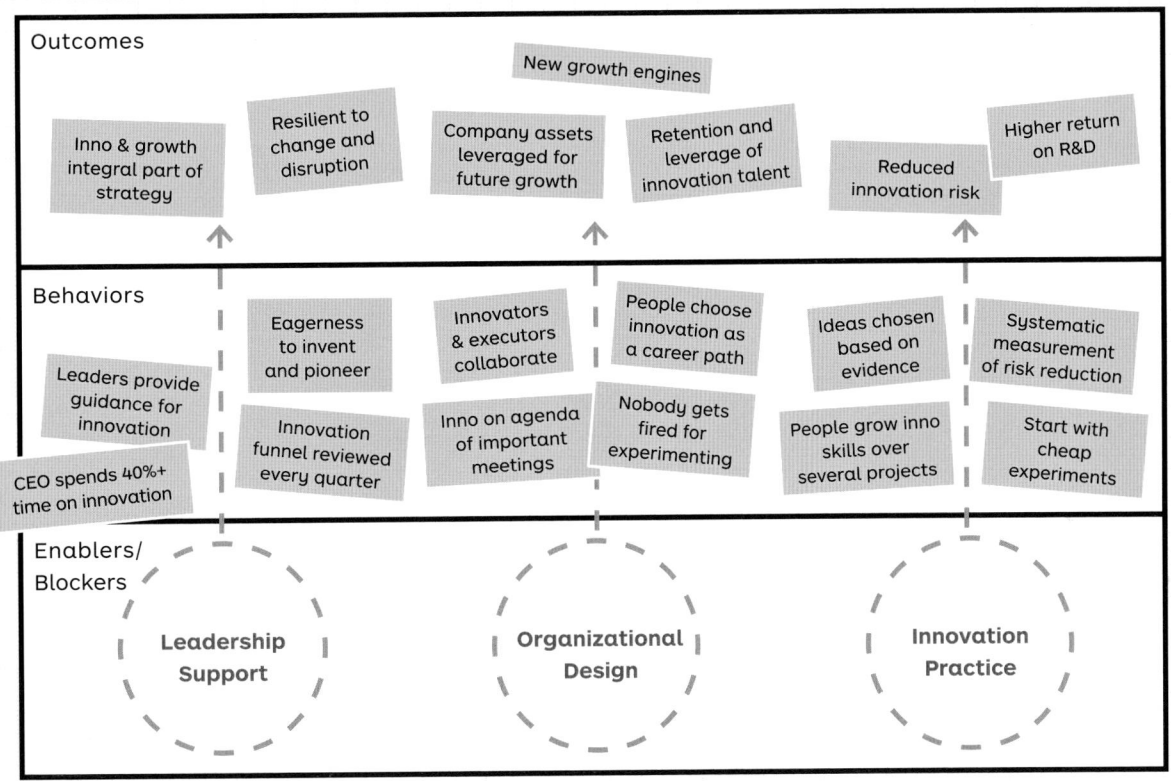

Outcomes

- New growth engines
- Inno & growth integral part of strategy
- Resilient to change and disruption
- Company assets leveraged for future growth
- Retention and leverage of innovation talent
- Reduced innovation risk
- Higher return on R&D

Behaviors

- Leaders provide guidance for innovation
- Eagerness to invent and pioneer
- Innovators & executors collaborate
- People choose innovation as a career path
- Ideas chosen based on evidence
- Systematic measurement of risk reduction
- CEO spends 40%+ time on innovation
- Innovation funnel reviewed every quarter
- Inno on agenda of important meetings
- Nobody gets fired for experimenting
- People grow inno skills over several projects
- Start with cheap experiments

Enablers/ Blockers

- Leadership Support
- Organizational Design
- Innovation Practice

Innovation Culture Blockers

In companies that lack innovation you can find at least some of the following innovation show stoppers:

✕ Leadership Support

Leaders focus predominantly on quarterly results and see innovation as a black box. There is no explicit innovation strategy, nor overall long-term innovation portfolio management. The management is locked into the current business model and exploring new directions is not part of the regular leadership discussion.

✕ Organizational Design

The reward system is geared toward managing and improving the existing business model. Failure is not an option, which is mandatory for world-class operations management, but lethal for experimenting with new ideas. Innovation teams have little autonomy and are slowed down by operational processes, and it's difficult for them to access customers and resources to experiment (e.g. brand, prototyping resources, other expertise).

✕ Innovation Practice

Innovation is a profession in itself, just like finance, marketing, or operations. You don't get good at it overnight, but with experience over time. Not having a substantial team with innovation as their sole job description will prevent an organization from developing a world-class innovation practice. Just like finance, sales, or operations, innovation needs its own processes, key performance indicators (KPIs), and culture.

Culture Map: Innovation Culture Blockers

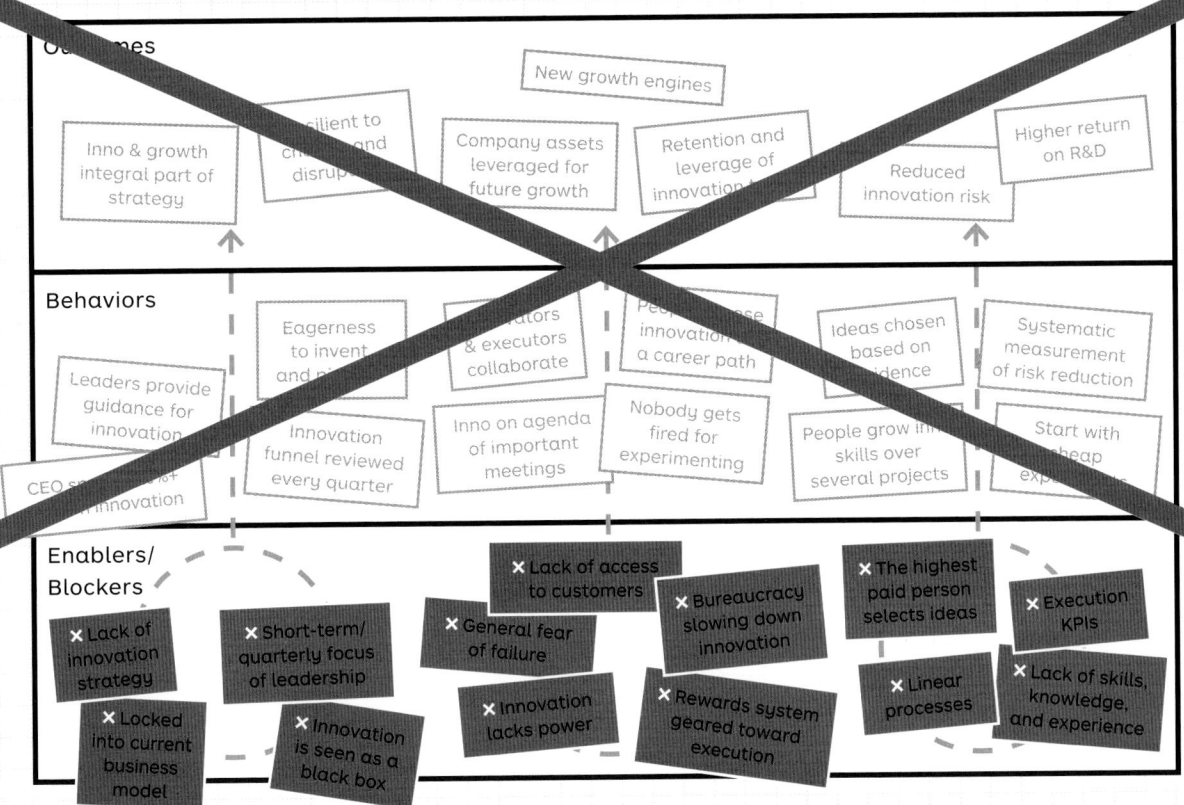

Innovation Culture Assessment

In the previous sections we showed you how Invincible Companies behave and how most companies still block innovation. Now let us show you how you can assess your innovation culture readiness with a scorecard we co-developed with Tendayi Viki, author of *The Corporate Startup.* Then we will help you reflect on how you can move toward becoming an Invincible Company by putting the right enablers in place.

To build an Invincible Company there are three main categories with three enablers each that you need to work on:

Leadership Support
• **Strategic Guidance:** a clear and explicitly communicated innovation strategy that is an important part of the overall strategy. It defines where to play, what's in, and what's out.
• **Resource Allocation:** an institutionalized allocation of resources available for innovation, which differs from the R&D budget. It includes a budget, time, and everything required to test business ideas.
• **Portfolio Management:** the exploration of the whole innovation spectrum from efficiency innovations, to sustaining innovations, to radical growth innovations with new business models. This includes a broad innovation funnel.

Organizational Design
• **Legitimacy and Power:** the status that growth and innovation and teams working on that topic have within the organization.
• **Bridge to the Core:** the access that growth and innovation has to resources and skills from the core business and the partnership that existing businesses build with innovation teams.
• **Rewards and Incentives**: a dedicated reward system that differs from management and operations and is tailored for experimentation around growth and innovation.

Innovation Practice
• **Innovation Tools:** the application and mastery of state-of-the art innovation concepts and tools that are practiced across leading organizations.
• **Process Management:** dedicated innovation processes and metrics that measure the reduction of risk and uncertainty from idea to scalable business.
• **Skills Development:** the existence of world-class innovation skills and experience across your organization, from professional innovation teams to existing business units.

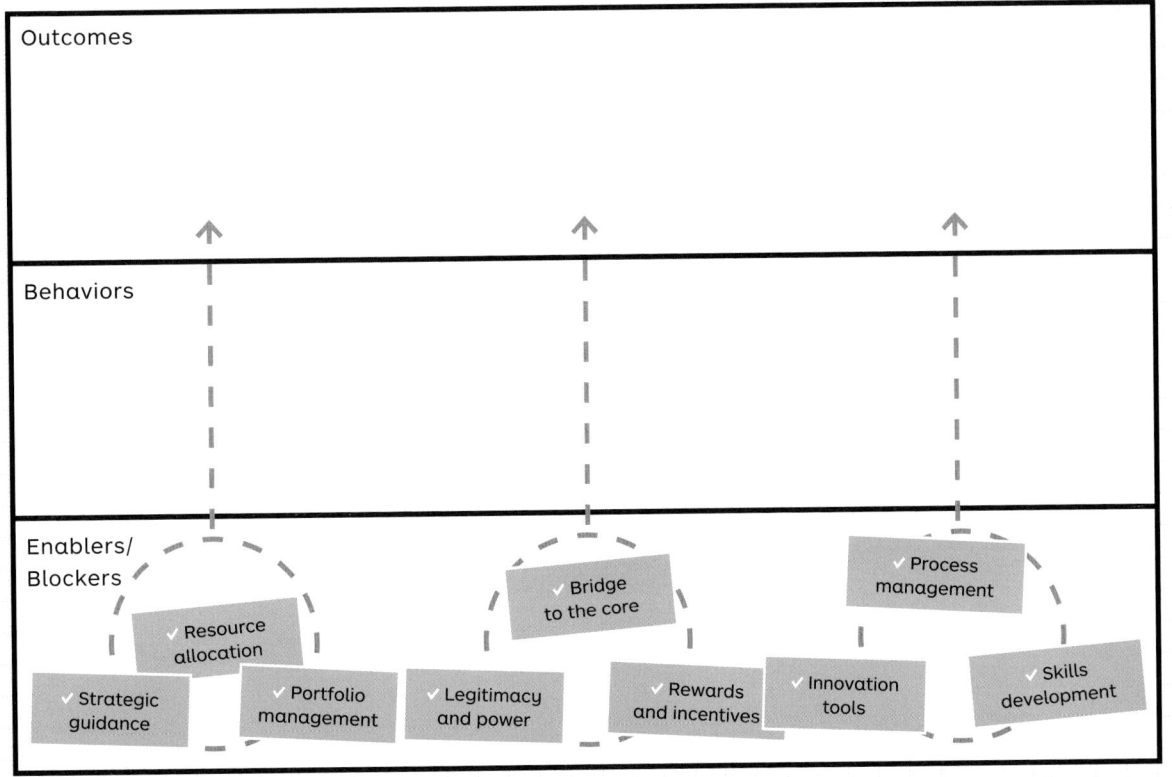

315

Leadership Support

Strategic Guidance

In companies with clear strategic innovation guidance, leadership communicates the strategy at important meetings at least once a quarter. The innovation guidance is completely aligned with the overall strategy and is widely understood across the organization. Good examples of clear guidance are Amazon and Ping An.

Resource Allocation

In Invincible Companies resources for innovation are institutionalized and leaders commit an important proportion of their time to innovation. Resources include:

- Leadership Time: In companies that innovate the CEO or a co-CEO invests 50% to 100% of his or her time to innovation. A great example is Bracken Darrell, CEO of Logitech or Ping An's co-CEO Jessica Tan.

- Innovation Funds: Money that is invested in internal and external innovation teams that start with small bets and get follow-up investments based on evidence. These funds differ from R&D investments.

- Innovation Core Team: A team of professional and experienced innovators who lead projects or coach project teams across an organization.

- Time: One of the scarcest resources in organizations is time. Systematically testing and de-risking ideas requires a substantial time investment from project teams.

- Prototyping Resources: Innovation teams run experiments and need access to resources for physical or digital prototypes, graphic design, videographers, and so on.

- Access to Customers, Brand, and Skills: Innovation teams need access to resources controlled by the core business. Testing requires access to customers, the use of the company brand, and often other skills and resources of the core business.

Portfolio Management

In Invincible Companies leadership is eager to pioneer. Leaders invest in a large innovation pipeline of small bets of which the best get follow-up investments. The portfolio covers the whole range of exploration, from efficiency innovation to breakthrough growth innovation.

Culture Map: Innovation Culture Enablers

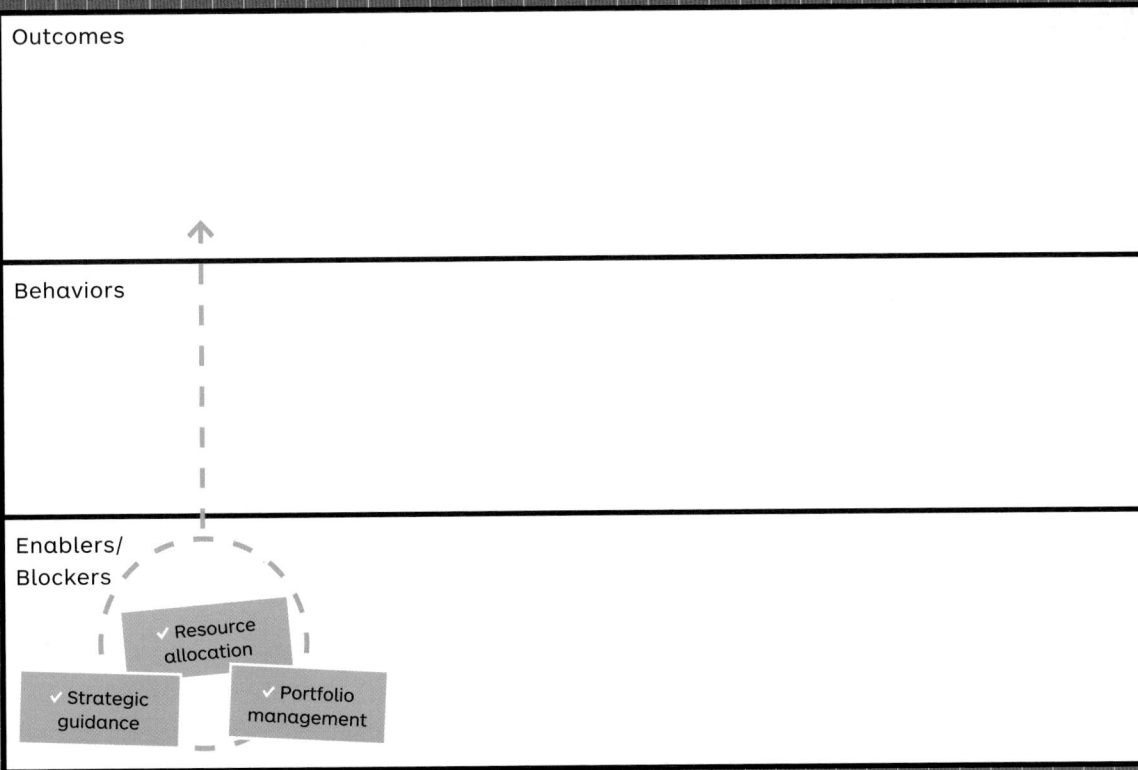

Outcomes

Behaviors

Enablers/
Blockers

✔ Resource
allocation

✔ Strategic
guidance

✔ Portfolio
management

- ☐ Give your company a score from 1 to 5 for each area.
- ☐ Define which area you'd like to improve over the next 12 and 36 months.
- ☐ Eliminate the blockers and implement the enablers that will help you achieve your improvement goals.

		BEGINNER *We have little to no experience with this topic*	*We have some experience*	INTERMEDIATE *We regularly work this way, but not systematically*	*We frequently work this way*	WORLD CLASS *Our practice is used as a case study for others to learn from*
Score Your Leadership Support	**Strategic Guidance**	**1** Leadership does not provide explicit strategic guidance for innovation	**2**	**3** There is some strategic guidance for innovation but not everybody in the company knows it	**4**	**5** Leadership provides strategic innovation guidance at important meetings and everybody knows it
	Resource Allocation	**1** Resources for innovation are bootstrapped or on an ad-hoc project basis	**2**	**3** Resources for innovation are available, but they are not substantial and not protected	**4**	**5** Resources for innovation are institutionalized and leaders commit at least 40% of their time to innovation
	Portfolio Management	**1** Leadership is mainly focused on improving the core business	**2**	**3** We make some investments to explore the future and new business models, but it's not systematic	**4**	**5** Leadership is eager to pioneer and invests in a large innovation pipeline of small bets of which the best get follow-up investments

Culture Map: Innovation Culture Enablers

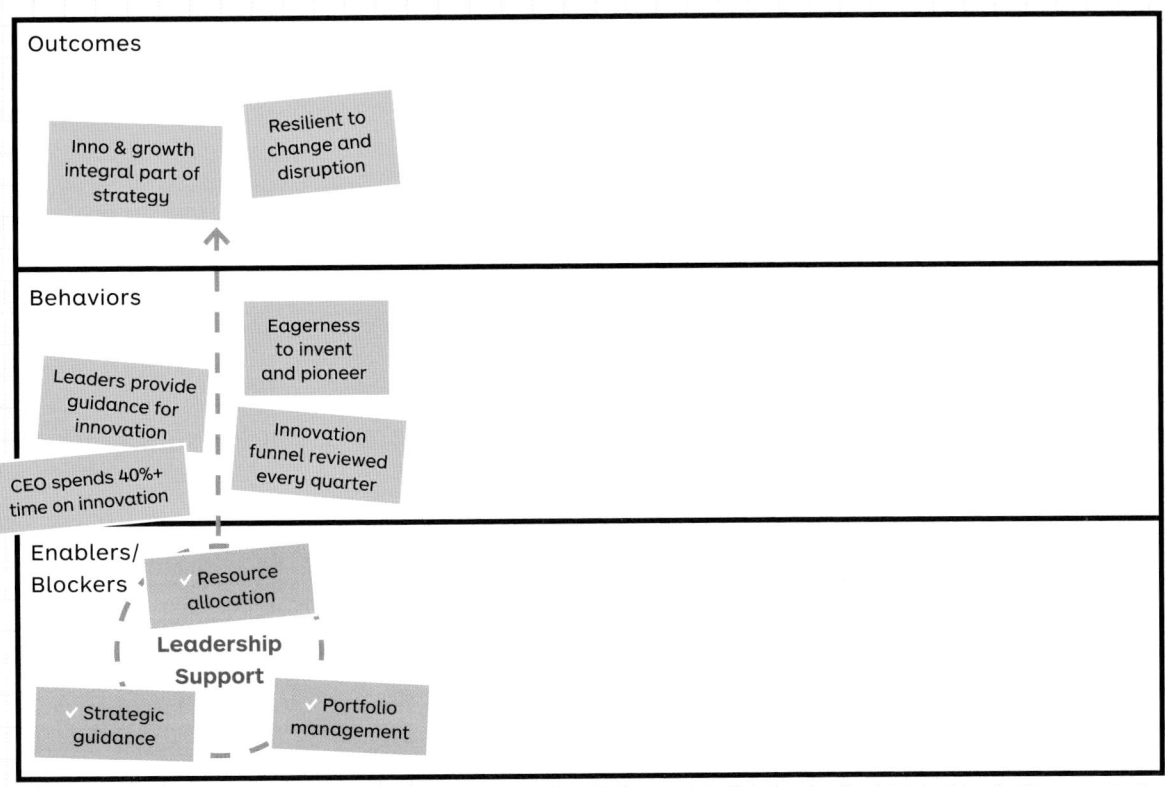

Organizational Design

Legitimacy and Power

Invincible Companies like Amazon or Ping An give innovation power and legitimacy. To have an impact, innovation needs to feature in the organizational chart and at the very top. Either the CEO, a co-CEO, or somebody reporting directly to the board needs to be responsible for growth and innovation and spend serious bandwidth, time, and energy on it. Talking about it at the top level is not enough.

Unfortunately, innovation still lacks legitimacy and power in most organizations. We see a lot of heads of innovation who are two to three levels down in the org chart. They are the sub-department of a leader who is the sub-department of another leader — guess how much impact that creates.

When growth and innovation lack power and legitimacy that sends a very strong signal to the company and often leads to severe consequences with long-term impact:

1. Innovation is not prestigious and it's not seen as a priority, so everybody puts it at the bottom of their to-do list.
2. People avoid exploring new ideas, because they fear taking risks and damaging their careers.
3. Promising innovation projects remain vulnerable and get killed by the antibodies in the organization, because innovation is not perceived as crucial. Few of them get scaled, because the short-term agenda prevails.
4. Your best talent doesn't choose innovation as a career path and either leaves to go to the competition or to start-ups.

Bridge to the Core

In Invincible Companies, Explore and Exploit operate as equal partners that live in harmony. There are clear policies that help innovation teams and the core business collaborate. Innovators get easy access to valuable resources from the core.

When there is no clear bridge to the core, innovation teams have only limited, conflicting, or no access to customers, resources, and skills of the core business. In the worst case, innovation projects are blocked from getting access to what they need to explore and test ideas. They basically have to operate like a start-up in chains: with the same limited resources as start-ups, but without the impetus. We therefore advocate for a so-called Chief Internal Ambassador and a supporting team who explicitly manage the relationship between Exploit and Explore on behalf of the CEO or the board (p. 322).

Rewards and Incentives

In our advisory work we often hear that the drive to innovate is intrinsic to innovators and entrepreneurs. Now imagine an innovator who gets punished every time he/she tries something out that was not in the plan. Or imagine an innovator who repeatedly creates new multimillion-dollar businesses for an organization and gets rewarded with promotions and pay raises. Will they perform to the very best of their innovation talent? Will they stay at your organization?

We argue that a dual strategy to rewards and incentives works best. First and foremost, eliminate all the downsides that prevent innovators from innovating in your organization. Once you've achieved that, develop a reward system for innovation.

Culture Map: Innovation Culture Enablers

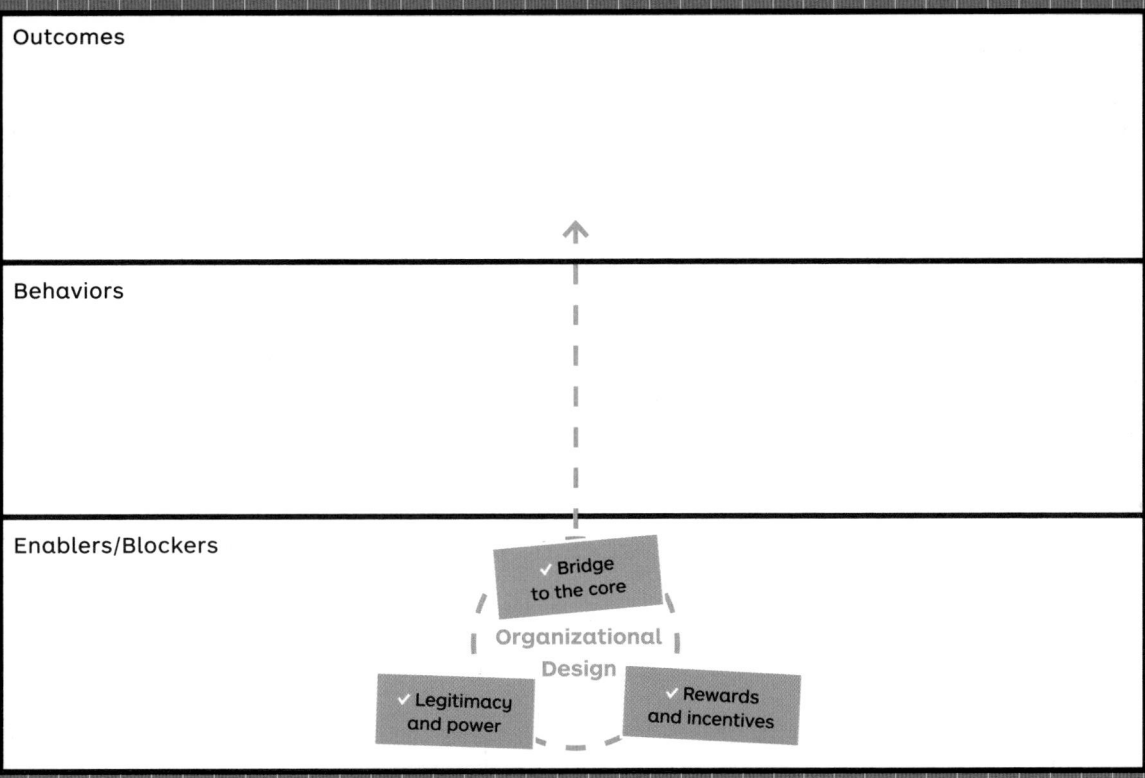

Outcomes

Behaviors

Enablers/Blockers

✓ Bridge to the core

Organizational Design

✓ Legitimacy and power

✓ Rewards and incentives

321

Legitimacy, Power, and Bridge to the Core

CEOs and the traditional leadership staff are generally excellent at growing and running a company within a known business model. But they often fall short at the task of innovating future growth engines. To create and manage new growth, companies need a Chief Entrepreneur with a dedicated staff. This new team is responsible for creating the future of the company while traditional executives take care of the existing business. Of course, they need to operate in harmony.

Chief Entrepreneur: The Chief Entrepreneur is responsible for managing a portfolio of entrepreneurs who experiment with new business models and value propositions. This is someone with a track record and passion for taking calculated risks to create new growth. The Chief Entrepreneur needs to be as powerful as the CEO. In fact, in some organizations like Amazon, the CEO is the Chief Entrepreneur. In others, there is a co-CEO who focuses on the future, like Jessica Tan at Ping An.

Chief Portfolio Manager: The Chief Portfolio Manager makes sure the company looks at a range of opportunities and business models that generate future growth. Some of those opportunities will be risky, some less so. Some will have a potential return, while others will have a guaranteed return. It is the Chief Portfolio Manager's job to establish and manage a portfolio that positions the company for the future.

Chief Venture Capitalist: The Chief Venture Capitalist (VC) allocates budgets and manages financing rounds for internal and external teams. A project won't get full funding right away, but it receives money in instalments. The Chief VC provides angel investments to fund early, cheap experiments. When those experiments succeed and produce evidence, the VC invests more. The Chief VC mirrors the role of the CFO in an established business. The CFO allocates budgets to the existing business, while the Chief VC allocates money to the discovery of a future business.

Chief Risk Officer: Some of the experiments a team will conduct may be detrimental to the brand and could carry legal liabilities. Legal can be a big constraint to experimentation in a company. The Chief Risk Officer is there to enable teams. The CRO helps entrepreneurs understand how to run experiments without putting the company at risk.

Chief Internal Ambassador: The Chief Internal Ambassador (CIA) is a trusted person with clout who knows everything going on on both sides of the company. The CIA and her team know all of the resources, activities, and patents that exist in the execution arm of the organization, and also have the trust of the powerful people that manage them. The CIA makes sure the Chief Entrepreneur and his team benefit from the strengths of the existing company by negotiating access to elements like clients, the salesforce, the brand, the supply chain, and other skills and knowledge. The CIA establishes and maintains a partnership between existing businesses and innovation. We've seen most success when this person is at the summit of their career and has nothing else to prove nor any political games to play to advance their career.

Entrepreneurs: The Entrepreneurs are internal and external people who build the businesses, with each one responsible for a particular project as its leader. This role is a lot stronger than your regular product or project manager: these are real entrepreneurs with clear incentives and a stake in the projects.

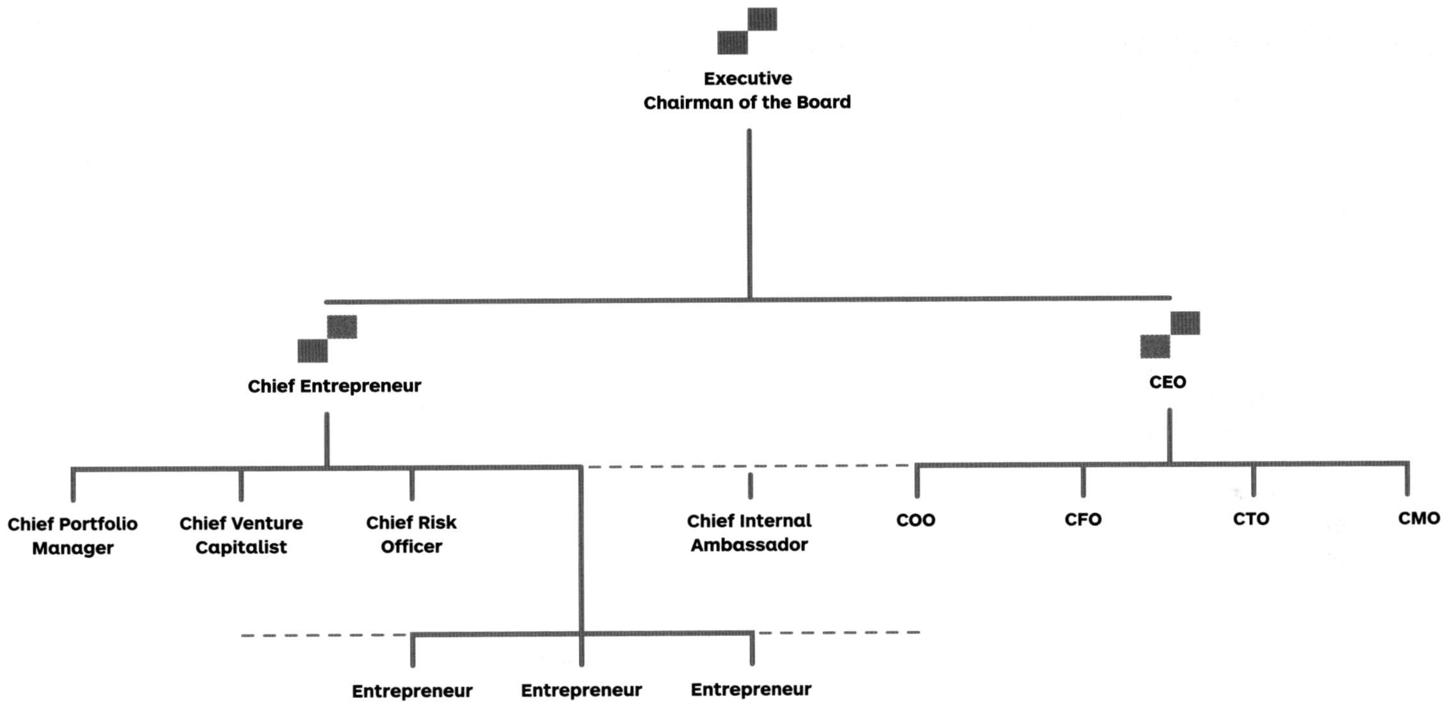

Executive
Chairman of the Board

Chief Entrepreneur

CEO

Chief Portfolio
Manager

Chief Venture
Capitalist

Chief Risk
Officer

Chief Internal
Ambassador

COO

CFO

CTO

CMO

Entrepreneur

Entrepreneur

Entrepreneur

Chief Entrepreneur Head Hunting

Fortune 50 company seeks a Chief Entrepreneur who will build the future. The Chief Entrepreneur will be responsible for managing a portfolio of entrepreneurs experimenting with new business models and value propositions. The candidate is someone with a passion for taking calculated risks. This is not a CTO role or a role that reports to the CEO. The Chief Entrepreneur is an executive as powerful as the CEO, with clear leadership over radical innovation within the company.

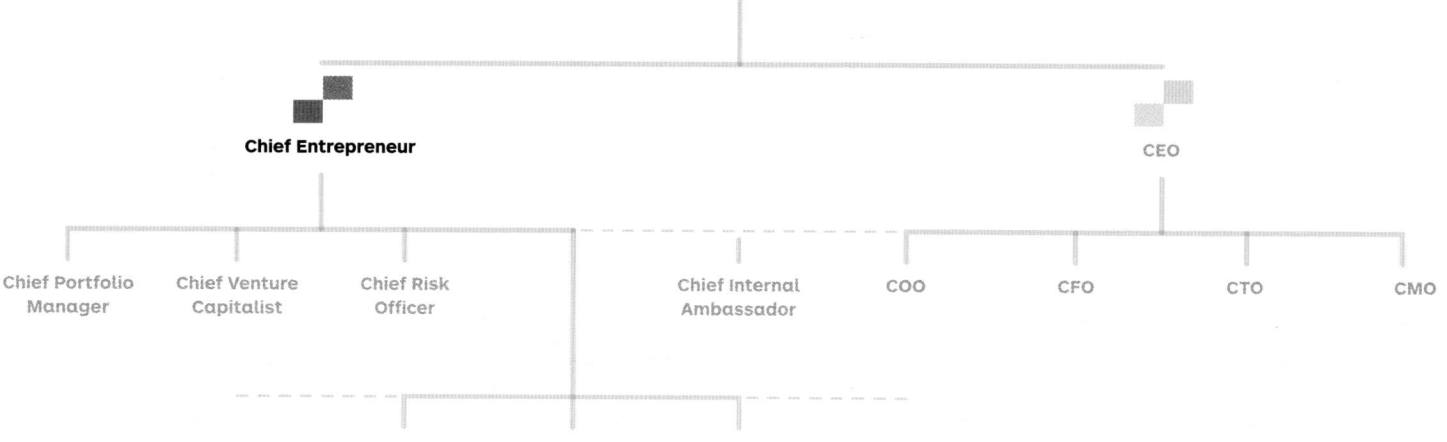

CULTURE

We are looking for an individual who...

- **Is passionate about building businesses.**
  You produce growth engines with calculated bets, not "wild-ass gambles."

- **Believes anything is possible.**
  You persevere. You have the charm, charisma, enthusiasm, work ethic, and marketing mind to encourage and drive your teams to think anything is possible.

- **Has built a $1 billion+ business from nothing.**
  You're especially valuable if you've met these figures in a large corporation.

- **Is comfortable with uncertainty.**
  You don't fear failure. You see failure as an opportunity to learn and iterate toward a solution.

- **Is tremendously diplomatic.**
  You address conflict head-on with one focus in mind: secure the money and resources you need to test your ideas.

Sound like you?
OK, now let's consider
your day-to-day tasks.

The Chief Entrepreneur's Responsibilities

☐ Build the future for the company. We cannot stress this enough. The Chief Entrepreneur is responsible for developing new business models and value propositions for the company's future growth.

☐ Guide and support your own team of entrepreneurs. You've been here before and you have knowledge to share. Your team will be searching for and validating business models and value propositions around opportunities for growth. This means managing entrepreneurs who can navigate trends and market behaviors.

☐ Design and maintain a space for invention. You are responsible for creating the habitat for your team to experiment, fail, and learn. This is an additional culture where ideas can be thoroughly tested. You must defend the culture, processes, incentives, and metrics that are born in this space.

☐ Introduce innovation metrics. You must develop a new process that measures whether you're making progress in building new businesses. How are your experiments helping your team to learn, reduce uncertainty and risk, and move forward?

☐ Establish and nurture a partnership with the CEO. You will have to work with the CEO to ensure resources and assets are available to validate or invalidate your ideas. You will be responsible for building a partnership to discuss progress and share new ideas. Communication will be key to this partnership because the CEO is the person who can help finance your future experiments. You will also recognize the importance of handing over a validated business model that demonstrates opportunities to scale.

☐ Report your progress directly to the Executive Chairman of the Board of Directors. You do not work for the CEO, or alongside the CTO, CIO, and CFO. These roles are mandated to keep the existing business in good shape. If the CE reported to the CEO, then the CEO could veto potential ideas in order to reserve resources and safeguard the company against failure.

Where Does Innovation Live?

Sometimes leaders say that everybody needs to be an innovator. That is true and silly at the same time. There are different types of innovation that require different skills, processes, and mindsets.

We distinguish between three types of innovation, heavily leaning on the work of Harvard professor Clayton Christensen. We distinguish between efficiency innovation, sustaining innovation, and transformative innovation, which often happens to be disruptive.

Explore ← → Exploit

Transformative

This type of innovation is the most radical and includes substantially new business models that a company is not familiar with. It may — but doesn't necessarily — include the cannibalization of the established business model. Transformative innovation has the largest long-term growth potential and helps position the company for the future. It requires the most advanced testing and requires the exploration of a broad portfolio of projects, because of high uncertainty.

Financial impact *Substantial in the long term*

Protection from disruption *Very strong*

Home *Outside the core established businesses to ensure survival*

Protagonists *Professional innovators with support from the core business for specific skills and resources*

Uncertainty *Maximum — because it explores uncharted territory*

Testing *Desirability, viability, feasibility, and adaptability*

Sustaining

With sustaining innovation you improve and expand your proven business model. Here uncertainty is higher because it may involve new market segments, new value propositions, or new channels. As a consequence you may also have to master new activities and resources. This type of innovation also includes business model shifts and can have a substantial impact on the longevity of a company's business model.

Financial impact *Potentially substantial — rarely immediate*

Protection from disruption *Limited*

Home *Inside the core established businesses, potentially outside*

Protagonists *Staff from the core businesses with support from professional innovators*

Uncertainty *Medium — because innovations build on top of the proven business model*

Testing *Desirability, viability, feasibility, and adaptability depending on the nature of the innovation*

Efficiency

This type of innovation is all about improving how smoothly your existing business models run. Uncertainty is relatively low, since it's about improving your proven business model. However, efficiency innovation may involve highly sophisticated technology innovations with high feasibility risk. Efficiency innovation may also include desirability risk, as when you create digital tools for internal stakeholders, like sales, customer support, marketing, finance, or operations. The immediate financial impact of efficiency innovations can be very high, for example, in the form of expanded margins.

Financial impact *From small to extremely large — often immediate*

Protection from disruption *None*

Home *Inside the core established businesses*

Protagonists *Staff from the core businesses*

Uncertainty *Low*

Testing *Mainly feasibility, some internal desirability, potentially cost savings or revenue impact*

Eliminate the Downside

Blockers	Don't...	Provide...
Barriers to Starting	...make it difficult, in the form of bureaucracy or other hurdles, for innovators to try out new ideas.	...easy access and small time or financial budgets for anybody who wants to start testing an idea. Provide follow-up funding for ideas that show traction.
Business Plan/Cases	...force innovators to write detailed business plans that make ideas look good in spreadsheets, but will mask the true risk of new ideas.	...process guidelines to test ideas and measure the reduction of risk and uncertainty. Judge evidence from testing, rather than good-looking ideas in PowerPoint presentations.
Execution-Focused KPIs	...reward innovators for execution only, because it will prevent them from experimenting and reducing innovation risk.	...KPIs specifically designed for innovators who experiment with new ideas. These must differ from KPIs for people who execute projects and must deliver on time and on budget.
Lack of Autonomy	...ask innovation teams to ask for approval for every experiment and every decision to adapt their idea, which reduces speed and adaptability.	...autonomy to test ideas, find evidence, and adapt ideas as long as they don't put the organization at risk.
Lack of Access	...make it difficult for innovators to access the resources they need to try out new ideas (customers, brand, prototyping, leadership support, etc.).	...infrastructure and support to help innovators rapidly, cheaply, and painlessly test ideas with appropriate experiments.
Lack of Skills	...confuse managerial and innovation/entrepreneurial skills. It's a whole different ball game to explore and adapt new ideas.	...innovation and entrepreneurship training. Avoid using good managers to explore new ideas without equipping them with the right skills and mindset to test new ideas.
Career Risk	...make failure from experimenting with new ideas a career-limiting move.	...visibility and promotions for people who have tried out new ideas throughout their career, even if those experiments failed.

Rewards and Incentives

Kill Blockers

In many organizations going into innovation equals career suicide. It doesn't have to be that way. On this page we outline how to remove the downside for people when they innovate in your organization. In discussion with fellow innovation expert Scott Anthony, from Innosight, we realized that this will already go a long way to boost innovation activities, even before putting in place formal rewards.

Create Enablers

Focus on the upside, once you've eliminated the downside. Design a reward system that incentivizes people to innovate. Make sure you don't just award successful outcomes, because many, many failed experiments allow you to detect the outliers that will succeed big. Reward good innovation behavior just as much as outcomes. Results will follow naturally. Finally, make sure you focus on impact, which is a crucial reward to attract and retain the best innovation talent.

Reward the Upside

Reward	Find Creative Ways to...	Incentives
Behavior *Make Innovation Sexy*	...make innovation just as prestigious at your organization as managing large teams and huge budgets. Promote people not just for their management merits, but for their courage to try out new ideas, even if they fail. Reward innovation, not just innovation outcomes. Reward the entire portfolio of innovation projects, not just the few big winners.	• Career promotions • Prestigious innovation rewards (for behavior, not just outcomes) • Company-wide visibility and recognition • Visibility with top management • Access to new exciting projects • Rewards at every stage of the innovation funnel, even for failure
Outcomes *Entrepreneurial Participation*	...allow innovators to participate in the financial upside of new ideas. Do so through internal mechanisms or through corporate venture capital. Allow people or teams to explore their ideas outside the organization with the option to invest and potentially buy back the venture.	• Financial stake in an idea • Success-dependent bonuses (e.g., number of new products or services sold; revenue, margin, or profit thresholds; etc.) • Start-up capital or investments to explore an idea externally
Impact *Change the World*	...attract outside innovation talent with an appealing company mission. Show world-class innovators how joining your organization will allow them to make a difference in the universe and have a real impact on society. Highlight what makes your company more attractive than creating or joining a start-up or competitor.	• Work for a company that stands for something • Make a difference (societal impact) • Access to resources a start-up or competitors don't have (e.g., infrastructure, brand, IP, market reach, etc.)

- ☐ Give your company a score from 1 to 5 for each area.
- ☐ Define which area you'd like to improve over the next 12 and 36 months.
- ☐ Eliminate the blockers and implement the enablers that will help you achieve your improvement goals.

Score Your Organizational Design

		BEGINNER We have little to no experience with this topic	We have some experience	INTERMEDIATE We regularly work this way, but not systematically	We frequently work this way	WORLD CLASS Our practice is used as a case study for others to learn from
	Legitimacy and Power	(1) Innovation projects are skunk work and outside official channels	(2)	(3) Innovation is officially in the org chart, but lacks power and influence	(4)	(5) Innovation is at the very top of the org chart and has power and influence
	Bridge to the Core	(1) Innovation teams have limited or no access to customers, resources, and skills of the core business	(2)	(3) The core business and innovation teams collaborate, but there are conflicts	(4)	(5) There are clear policies that help innovation teams and the core business collaborate as equal partners
	Rewards and Incentives	(1) Innovation does not have a dedicated incentive system that differs from the core business	(2)	(3) We have some incentives in place to encourage innovation and reward it differently from execution	(4)	(5) Innovation has a dedicated incentive system that rewards experimentation and new value creation

Culture Map: Innovation Culture Enablers

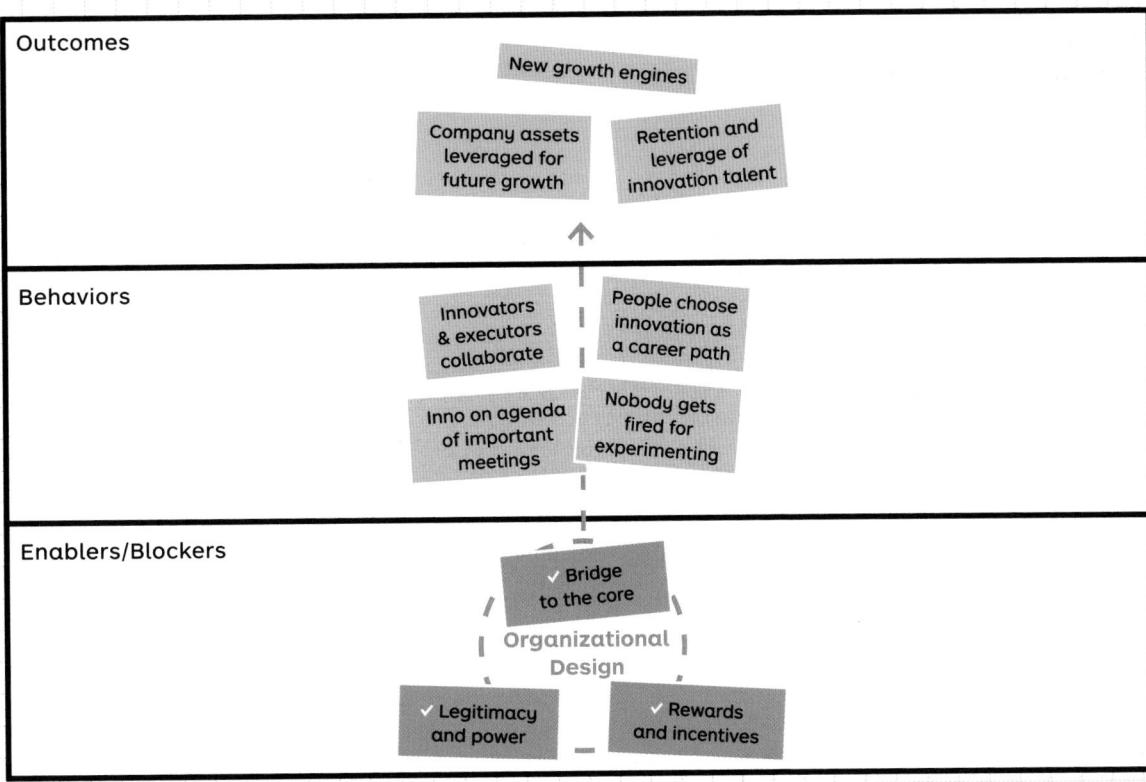

Outcomes

New growth engines

Company assets leveraged for future growth

Retention and leverage of innovation talent

Behaviors

Innovators & executors collaborate

People choose innovation as a career path

Inno on agenda of important meetings

Nobody gets fired for experimenting

Enablers/Blockers

✓ Bridge to the core

Organizational Design

✓ Legitimacy and power

✓ Rewards and incentives

Innovation Practice

Innovation Tools

Innovation professionals need to master a set of dedicated tools, just like a surgeon commands a set of surgical tools. We believe the quality of the innovation toolset you use has a substantial impact on the quality of your growth and transformation work. Tools are not neutral. They heavily influence the quality of your results. That's why it's incredibly important to carefully select the tools you use and learn how to apply them correctly.

Process Management

Invincible companies have dedicated processes and decision-making that are both optimized for innovation. They measure the systematic and effective reduction of risk in new ideas, rather than on-time and on-budget delivery, which are typical execution KPIs. We discussed the innovation process and innovation metrics intensely in Chapter 2: Manage.

Skills Development

Managing the existing and inventing the new are two fundamentally different professions. Innovators are typically comfortable with high uncertainty and radical pivots to adapt to the reality of new market insights. Invincible companies systematically develop world-class innovation talent with extensive innovation experience across the organization.

Culture Map: Innovation Culture Enablers

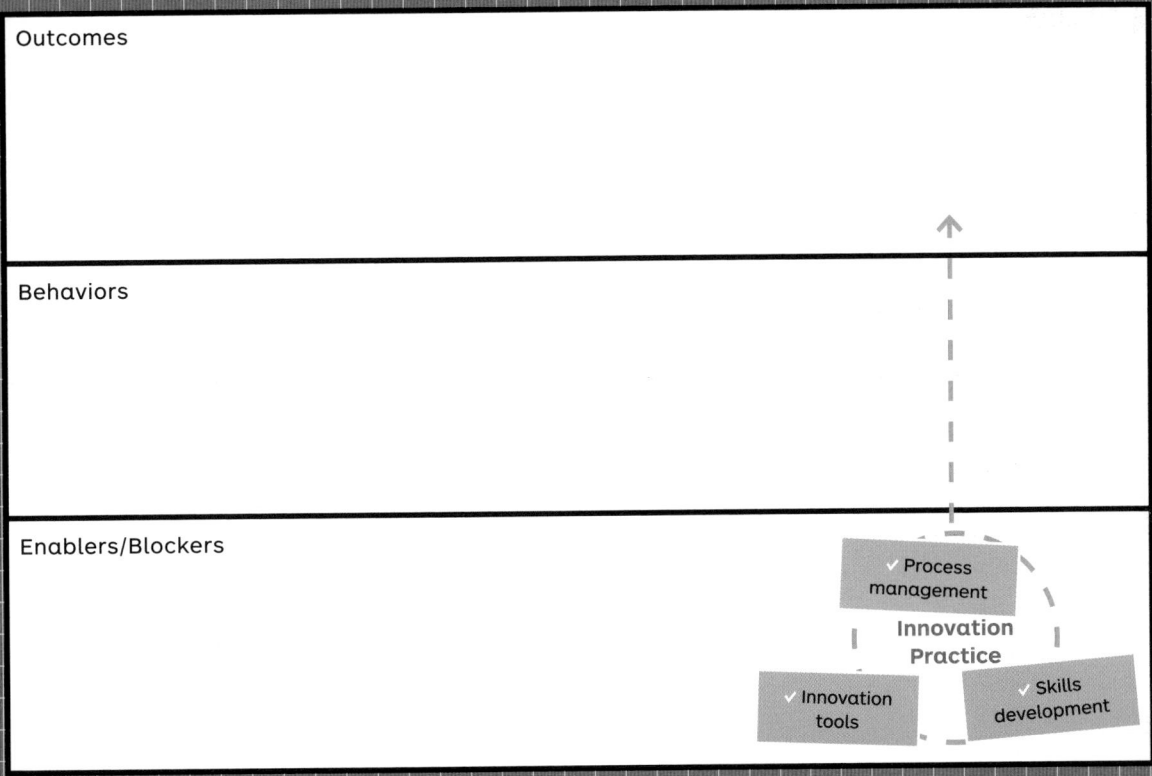

Outcomes

Behaviors

Enablers/Blockers

✓ Process management

Innovation Practice

✓ Innovation tools

✓ Skills development

Innovation Tools and Process

Mastering the tools of innovation radically facilitates the search for new growth engines. We suggest a toolbox of integrated tools to shape, test, and grow ideas in your organization.

CULTURE

Corporate Identity Triangle

A strategic management framework to make your corporate identity explicit in order to define your portfolio guidance.

Portfolio Guidance

The guidelines that define what types of innovations you want to pursue. They make explicit what is "in" and what is "out".

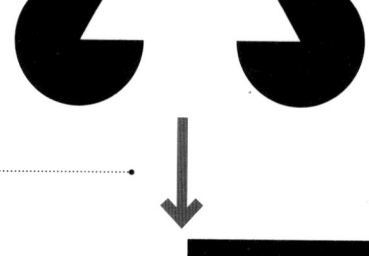

Portfolio Map

An analytical strategy tool to simultaneously visualize, analyze, and manage the business models you are improving and growing and future business models you are searching for and testing.

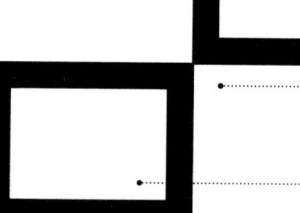

The Team Alignment Map
A project management tool to keep teams aligned over the course of an (innovation) project journey.

The Culture Map

A strategic management tool to help assess, design, implement, and transform a company's (innovation) culture.

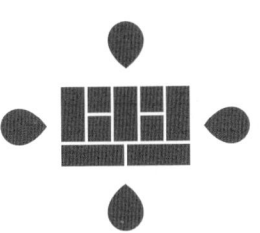

Business Design

Business Environment Map
A foresight and scanning tool to map the environment in which you conduct business. It captures the trends that might disrupt your organization or represent new opportunities for growth and transformation.

Business Model Canvas
A strategic management tool to make explicit how you create, deliver, and capture value. Used to improve existing business models or invent new ones. Serves as the foundation to identify hypotheses to test new business ideas.

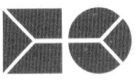

Value Proposition Canvas
A product management tool to make explicit how you create value for customers. Used to assess and improve existing value propositions or to invent new ones. Serves as the foundation to identify customer and product/ service hypotheses.

Testing

Strategyzer Innovation Metrics
A metrics system to measure the reduction of risk and uncertainty of new business ideas, visualize progress from idea to validated business case, and evaluate the disruption risk of a company's business portfolio.

Assumptions Map
A tactical tool to identify the hypotheses you need to test first.

Test Card
A tactical tool to design sound business experiments to test your business hypotheses.

Learning Card
A tactical tool to capture insights from your business experiments and define decisions and actions.

Skills Development

Among the many skills required in entrepreneurship and innovation there are three learnable ones that are crucial on your journey from big idea to real business:

1. Business Design (Different From Managing a Business):

The ability to shape and constantly adapt value propositions and business models to develop the most promising ones.

Master the value proposition canvas (VPC):
- Design value propositions that attract customers.
- Design value propositions that customers are willing to pay for.

Master the business model canvas (BMC):
- Design business models that are profitable and scalable.
- Design business models that are protectable.

2. Testing (and Learning):

The ability to break down big ideas into hypotheses you test in order to reduce the risk of pursuing ideas that won't work.

- Identify the most important hypotheses.
- Design and run experiments to support or refute your hypotheses.
- Detect patterns in the evidence.

3. Lead and Execute:

The ability to inspire a team and overcome the biggest obstacles.

- Lead and coordinate your team from idea to real business.
- Make sure every team member is always focused on what can best advance the team from idea to scalable business.
- Lead in the face of adversity and motivate the team to overcome the inevitable obstacles on the innovation journey.

□ **Skills Evolution from Idea to Business**
Over the course of a project journey the skills required by leadership and the team substantially change. Here are some of the key differences from discovery to execution and scaling.

	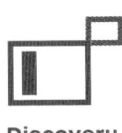 Discovery	 Validation	 Acceleration	 Execution and Scaling
Key Evidence	• Market size • Opportunity size $ • Customer jobs, pains, and gains • Problem/solution fit • Willingness to pay (basic evidence)	• Value proposition • Willingness to pay and pricing (strong evidence) • Feasibility (basic evidence)	• Product/market fit • Feasibility (strong evidence) • Acquisition and retention • Profitability	• Revenue (or user) growth
Key Questions	Is there an opportunity?	Can we create value in this market?	How can we best create demand and grow?	How can we scale our organization to satisfy demand?
Team size	1–3	3–8	8+	Unlimited
Key leadership skills	• Envision and motivate • Question fundamental assumptions • Pattern recognition • Pivot • Business model	• Envision and motivate • Pattern recognition • Pivot • Business model	• Envision and motivate • Lead domain matter experts • Business model	• Motivate and engage • Scale • Hire • Manage
Team skills	• Resourceful • Testing • Extreme adaptability • Perseverance	• Testing • Prototyping • Perseverance	• Domain matter expertise and building • Marketing • Perseverance	• Leadership, execution, and scaling • Deep domain matter expertise • Hiring • Functional expertise (marketing, finance, legal, etc.)

Entrepreneurial Leadership and Team

We believe that the most successful project teams in Invincible Companies are not led by project managers who manage several projects in parallel. They are led by people who see themselves as entrepreneurs. They are all in to bring an idea to fruition and behave like entrepreneurs even if they are actually employees on a company's payroll. Based on research from entrepreneurial performance labs we believe successful innovators and entrepreneurs and their teams have the following traits.

Innovators and entrepreneurs who lead teams and ventures are often...

Able to Create Reality Distortion Fields

- Gifted and captivating communicators who are able to mobilize resources and talent for their cause.
- Know what direction they want people to go and make stakeholders and team members believe the impossible.
- Create a compelling sense of "pull" to lead the team on a journey of discovery, validation, acceleration, and scaling.

Relentless and Resilient

- Yearn to overcome the status quo to improve things.
- Are action-biased, don't get stuck in analysis paralysis, and persevere in the face of adversity. They persistently work to overcome obstacles and are not easily derailed by setbacks.
- Display a crazy work ethic and set high standards for themselves and others, yet maintain mental and physical reserves necessary to deal with challenges.

Deeply Curious

- Some of their best ideas come from cross-fertilization of different domains and markets.
- Are incredibly agile intellectually (Jeff Bezos: from books to Amazon Web Services; Steve Jobs: from computers to music players to mobile phones; Elon Musk: from payment software to electric cars to rockets).

Independent

- Are willing or inclined to operate on their own with minimal support from others.
- Are comfortable standing apart from the herd.
- Prefer to control their environment and are likely to be dissatisfied working for someone else.

We believe great founding teams should display the following characteristics to complement the entrepreneurial leader. They are:

Inventive

- Generate ideas and explore new possibilities.
- Discern useful patterns from large amounts of information and are emergent learners, adapting through experience and experimentation.
- Easily navigate big-picture strategic questions and nitty-gritty experiments or domain matter expertise.

Risk Tolerant

- Break big ideas down into smaller testable hypotheses to test with business experiments.
- Feel comfortable making decisions with incomplete or contradicting information and skillfully deal with ambiguity and complexity.
- Are fearless and scared simultaneously, yet can distinguish between internal feelings of anxiety and more objective measures of actual risk.

Market Oriented

- See the market and financial potential of an opportunity, technology, or market need and turn that into concrete value propositions and business models.
- Constantly adapt business model and value propositions based on feedback from the field and evidence from experiments.
- Are opportunistic and pivot toward the most interesting direction.

Pragmatic and (Ideally) Experienced

- Understand which actions and decisions will substantially move the needle.
- Bring and apply valuable experience from previous innovation and entrepreneurship journeys.
- Have a strong 'no nonsense' radar.

Library of Congress, Prints and Photographs Division, NYWT&S Collection, [LC-USZ62-123247]

At the peak of her career, one of the wealthiest women in the world.

ELIZABETH ARDEN
Founded Elizabeth Arden Inc. in 1910

"Daniel Ek, CEO and Co-founder of Spotify" Stuart Isett/Fortune Brainstorm TECH/CC BY 2.0

Spotify has forever changed how consumers interact with music.

DANIEL EK
Founder of music streaming service Spotify

"Beech, Olive Ann" by San Diego Air and Space Museum Archive

Dubbed "The First Lady of Aviation" for being the first woman to lead a major aircraft company.

OLIVE ANN BEECH
Co-founder of Beech Aircraft Corporation

340

CULTURE

Jack Ma World Economic Forum/Ben Hider/ CC BY 2.0

Ranked 21st in the World's Most Powerful People of 2019 list by Forbes magazine.

JACK MA
Co-founder of Alibaba Group

"TechCrunch Disrupt SF 2017 - Day 2" by Techcrunch/CC BY 2.0

23andMe's DNA-testing kit was Time's 2008 Invention of the Year.

ANNE WOJKICKI
Co-founder of 23andme

"A photo of rock climber Yvon Chouinard." by Tom Frost/CC BY 2.0

One of the original pioneers of "do good to do well" business movement.

YVON CHOUINARD
Founder of sports apparel brand Patagonia

Ranked 33nd in Fortune magazine's World's Greatest Leaders list for 2017.

STRIVE MASIYIWA
Founder of media and tech company Econet Wireless

One of China's most powerful women in media and ranked 100 on the100 Most Powerful Women List of 2013 by Forbes.

YANG LAN
Co-founder of Sun Media Group

Considered "Japan's Thomas Edison," Kiichiro converted the family loom business into automobile manufacturing.

KIICHIRO TOYODA
Founder of Toyota Motor Corporation

Uses entrepreneurial approaches to address global poverty.

JACQUELINE NOVOGRATZ
Founder of Acumen Fund

Ranked 8th in the list of World's Billionaires by Forbes and considered the richest person in Latin America in 2019.

CARLOS SLIM
Founder of Grupo Carso conglomerate

Ranked 46th Most Powerful Woman in the World 2013 by Forbes.

CHER WANG
Co-founder of HTC Corporation

- ☐ Give your company a score from 1 to 5 for each area.
- ☐ Define which area you'd like to improve over the next 12 and 36 months.
- ☐ Eliminate the blockers and implement the enablers that will help you achieve your improvement goals.

Score Your Innovation Practice

		BEGINNER *We have little to no experience with this topic*	*We have some experience*	INTERMEDIATE *We regularly work this way, but not systematically*	*We frequently work this way*	WORLD CLASS *Our practice is used as a case study for others to learn from*
	Innovation Tools	① We do not use business model, lean startup, or design thinking tools for innovation	②	③ Business model, lean startup, or design thinking tools are used in pockets of the organization	④	⑤ Business model, lean startup, or design thinking tools are widely adopted and mastered
	Process Management	① Our processes are linear and require detailed business plans with financial projections	②	③ We occasionally use iterative processes and systematic business experiments to test business ideas	④	⑤ Our processes are optimized for innovation and we systematically measure the reduction of risk in new ideas
	Innovation Skills	① We don't hire for innovation skills and experience and don't develop them	②	③ We occasionally hire experienced innovation talent and train some specialized staff in innovation	④	⑤ We hire and develop world-class innovation talent with extensive experience across the organization

Culture Map: Innovation Culture Enablers

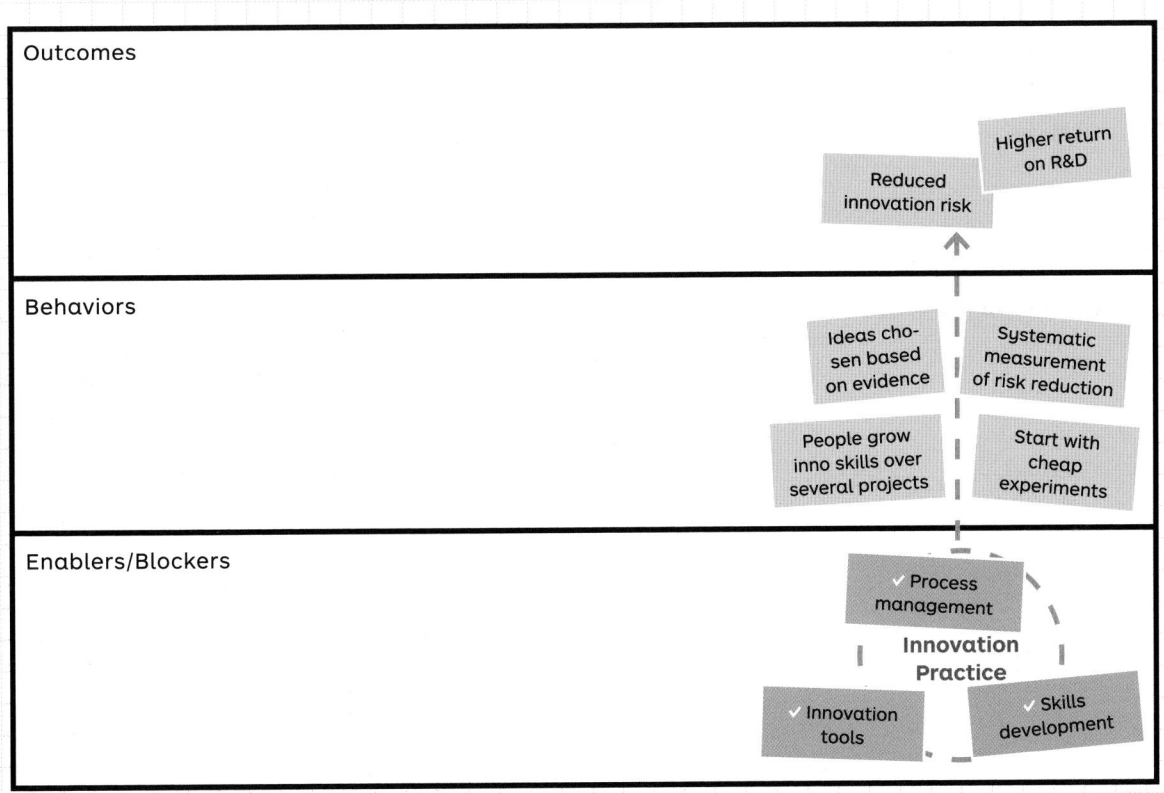

Innovation Culture Readiness

How ready are you to become an invincible company?

☐ Give your company a score from 1 to 5 for each area.

☐ Define which area you'd like to improve over the next 12 and 36 months.

☐ Eliminate the blockers and implement the enablers that will help you achieve your improvement goals.

CULTURE

Leadership Support

- Strategic Guidance
- Resource Allocation
- Portfolio Management

Organizational Design

- Legitimacy and Power
- Bridge to the Core
- Rewards and Incentives

Innovation Practice

- Innovation Tools
- Process Management
- Innovation Skills

BEGINNER *We have little to no experience with this topic*	*We have some experience*	INTERMEDIATE *We regularly work this way, but not systematically*	*We frequently work this way*	WORLD CLASS *Our practice is used as a case study for others to learn from*
① Leadership does not provide explicit strategic guidance for innovation	②	③ There is some strategic guidance for innovation but not everybody in the company knows it	④	⑤ Leadership provides strategic innovation guidance at important meetings and everybody knows it
① Resources for innovation are bootstrapped or on an ad-hoc project basis	②	③ Resources for innovation are available, but they are not substantial and not protected	④	⑤ Resources for innovation are institutionalized and leaders commit at least 50% of their time to innovation
① Leadership is mainly focused on improving the core business	②	③ We make some investments to explore the future and new business models, but it's not systematic	④	⑤ Leadership is eager to pioneer and invests in a large innovation pipeline of small bets of which the best get follow-up investments
① Innovation projects are skunk work and outside official channels	②	③ Innovation is officially in the org chart, but lacks power and influence	④	⑤ Innovation is at the very top of the org chart and has power and influence
① Innovation teams have limited or no access to customers, resources, and skills of the core business	②	③ The core business and innovation teams collaborate, but there are conflicts	④	⑤ There are clear policies that help innovation teams and the core business collaborate as equal partners
① Innovation does not have a dedicated incentive system that differs from the core business	②	③ We have some incentives in place to encourage innovation and reward it differently from execution	④	⑤ Innovation has a dedicated incentive system that rewards experimentation and new value creation
① We do not use business model, lean startup, or design thinking tools for innovation	②	③ Business model, lean startup, or design thinking tools are used in pockets of the organization	④	⑤ Business model, lean startup, or design thinking tools are widely adopted and mastered
① Our processes are linear and require detailed business plans with financial projections	②	③ We occasionally use iterative processes and systematic business experiments to test business ideas	④	⑤ Our processes are optimized for innovation and we systematically measure the reduction of risk in new ideas
① We don't hire for innovation skills and experience and don't develop them	②	③ We occasionally hire experienced innovation talent and train some specialized staff in innovation	④	⑤ We hire and develop world-class innovation talent with extensive experience across the organization

Afterword

Glossary

Adaptability Risk
The risk that a business won't be able to adapt to the competitive environment; technology, regulatory, social, or market trends; or that the macro environment is not favorable (lacking infrastructure, recession, etc.).

Business Design
Process to shape and reshape a business idea to turn it into the best possible business model and value proposition. Early iterations are based on intuition and starting point (product idea, technology, market opportunity, etc.). Subsequent iterations are based on evidence and insights from the testing.

Business Model
Rationale of how an organization creates, delivers, and captures value.

Business Model Canvas
Strategic management tool to describe how an organization creates, delivers, and captures value, initially presented in the book *Business Model Generation.*

Business Model Pattern
A repeatable configuration of different business model building blocks to strengthen an organization's overall business model. Helps new ventures develop a competitive advantage beyond technology, product, service, or price. Helps established companies shift from an outdated to more competitive business model. A single business model can incorporate several patterns.

Business Model Portfolio
The collection of existing business models a company exploits and the new business models it explores in order to avoid disruption and ensure longevity.

Business Model Shift
Describes an organization's transformation from a declining or expired business model to a more competitive one.

Business R&D
Activities a company undertakes to spot, create, test, de-risk, and invest in a portfolio of novel business opportunities. To improve existing business(es) and explore new ones. The heart of business R&D is the art and science of shaping value propositions and business models and testing risks. Complements traditional technology and product R&D, which mainly focus on feasibility.

Culture Map
Strategic management tool to understand, design, test, and manage the corporate culture you want to bring to fruition in your organization.

Death and Disruption Risk

The risk that a business is going to die or get disrupted. Risk is high when a business is either emerging and still vulnerable, or when a business is under threat of disruption from technology, competition, regulatory changes, or other trends. Risk decreases with the moats protecting your business.

Desirability Risk

The risk that the market a business is targeting is too small, that too few customers want the value proposition, or that the company can't reach, acquire, and retain targeted customers.

Evidence

Data generated from an experiment or collected in the field. Proves or disproves a (business) hypothesis, customer insight, or belief about a value proposition, business model, strategy, or the environment.

Expected Return

How lucrative a business idea could be for a company if it turned out to be successful.

Experiment

A procedure to validate or invalidate a value proposition or business model hypothesis that produces evidence. Used to reduce risk and uncertainty of a business idea.

Exploit Portfolio

Your portfolio of existing businesses, value propositions, products and services, all mapped out in terms of return and death and disruption risk.

Explore Portfolio

Your portfolio of innovation projects, new business models, new value propositions, new products and services, all mapped out in terms of expected return and innovation risk.

Feasibility Risk

The risk that a business can't manage, scale, or get access to key resources (technology, IP, brand, etc.), key activities, or key partners.

Grow

Activity of keeping your existing business models on a growth trajectory. Includes scaling emerging business models, renovating declining ones, and protecting successful ones. You ensure growth by improving returns and minimizing disruption risk.

Guidance

Context for portfolio management. Helps with resource allocation and portfolio actions. Provides explicit boundaries to understand what to focus on and what not to focus on, where to invest and where to divest, and what to explore and what not to explore.

Hypothesis

An assumption that your value proposition, business model, or strategy builds on. What you need to learn about to understand if your business idea might work. Relates to the desirability, feasibility, viability, or adaptability of a business idea.

Innovation Funnel

Mechanism to explore and test a constant stream of business ideas and innovation projects. The front of the funnel contains many ideas that you gradually reduce based on evidence from testing and then invest in the remaining projects with metered funding.

(Strategyzer) Innovation Metrics

A set of tools to measure the reduction of the risk and uncertainty of new business ideas before you invest big and scale.

Innovation Risk

The risk that a (convincing) business idea is going to fail. Risk is high when there is little evidence beyond slides and spreadsheets to support the success chances of an idea. Risk decreases with the amount of evidence that supports the desirability, feasibility, viability, and adaptability of a business idea.

Metered Funding
Funding practice, coming from the venture capital industry, where you incrementally increase investments in projects that produce evidence from testing and shelve those that don't.

Pivot
The decision to make a significant change to one or more elements of your business model and value proposition.

Portfolio Actions
The actions you perform in your EXPLORE portfolio (ideate, invest, persevere, pivot, retire, spinout, transfer) and your EXPLOIT portfolio (acquire, partner, invest, improve, merge, divest, dismantle).

Portfolio Map
A strategic management tool to simultaneously visualize, analyze, and manage the business models you are improving and growing and the future business models you are searching for and testing.

Return
How lucrative a business area is for a company.

Search
Search for new ideas, value propositions, and business models to ensure the future of your company. Involves maximizing expected returns and minimizing innovation risk.

Team Map
A visual tool created by Stefano Mastrogiacomo to boost alignment among team members for more effective meetings and conversations.

Test
Process of identifying and testing the most critical hypotheses underlying a business idea to make informed business design and investment decisions.

Types of Innovation
We distinguish between three different types of innovation heavily, borrowing from Harvard professor Clayton Christensen: efficiency, sustaining, and transformative innovation.

Viability Risk
The risk that a business can't generate successful revenue streams, that customers are unwilling to pay (enough), or that the costs are too high to make a sustainable profit.

Notes

TOOL

1. "The Bosch Group at a Glance," https://www.bosch.com/company/our-figures/.
2. Nestle, "Acquisitions and Disposals," https://www.nestle.com/investors/overview/mergers-and-acquisitions.
3. "Nestlé Closes the Sale of Nestlé Skin Health," October 02, 2019, https://www.nestle.com/media/pressreleases/allpressreleases/nestle-closes-sale-nestle-skin-health.
4. "The Gore Story," https://www.gore.com/about/the-gore-story.

MANAGE

1. Charles Arthur, "Amazon Writes Off $170M on Unsold Fire Phones," The Guardian, October 24, 2014. https://www.theguardian.com/technology/2014/oct/24/amazon-unsold-fire-phones.
2. "Ping An Tops Global Insurance Brands for the Third Consecutive Year," PR Newswire Asia, May 30, 2018, https://www.asiaone.com/business/ping-ranks-third-among-global-financial-services-companies-2018-brandztm-top-100-most.
3. Shu-Ching Jean Chen, "Chinese Giant Ping An Looks Beyond Insurance to a Fintech Future," June 2018, https://www.forbes.com/sites/shuchingjeanchen/2018/06/06/chinese-giant-ping-an-looks-beyond-insurance-to-a-fintech-future/.
4. Ping An 2019 Interim Report.
5. Ericson Chan, "FinTech, If It Doesn't Kill You, Makes You Stronger," April 13, 2018, https://www.youtube.com/watch?v=UixV7NNSgVl.
6. "Ping An to Employ Micro-Expression Technology to Deter Scammers," November 1, 2018, https://www.chinaknowledge.com/News/DetailNews/81721/Ping-An-to-employ-micro-expression-technology-to-deter-scammers.
7. Shu-Ching Jean Chen, "Chinese Giant Ping An Looks Beyond."
8. "Ping An Powering Ahead with World-Leading Fintech and Healthtech," PR News Asia, November 07, 2018, https://www.prnewswire.com/news-releases/ping-an-powering-ahead-with-world-leading-fintech-and-healthtech-300745534.html.
9. Ping An Annual Report 2018.
10. Kane Wu, "Ping An-Backed Lufax Raises $1.3 Billion at Lower Valuation: Sources," December 3, 2018, https://www.reuters.com/article/us-lufax-fundraising/ping-an-backed-lufax-raises-13-billion-at-lower-valuation-sources-idUSKBN1O20HG.
11. Laura He, "Ping An Good Doctor Prices US$1.12 Billion IPO at Top End Amid Retail Frenzy," April 27, 2018, https://www.scmp.com/business/companies/article/2143745/ping-good-doctor-prices-us112-billion-ipo-top-end-amid-retail.
12. Autohome Annual Report 2018.
13. "Autohome Inc. Announces Transaction between Shareholders and Board Change," February 22, 2017, https://www.globenewswire.com/news-release/2017/02/22/926600/0/en/Autohome-Inc-Announces-Transaction-Between-Shareholders-and-Board-Change.html.

14. Michael O'Dwyer, "China In-Depth: Digital Insurance Ecosystems," https://www.the-digital-insurer.com/china-in-depth-ecosystems-in-china/.

15. "Ping An to Buy Autohome Stake from Telstra for $1.6 Billion," April 15, 2016, https://www.bloomberg.com/news/articles/2016-04-15/ping-an-to-buy-stake-in-autohome-from-telstra-for-1-6-billion.

16. Tendayi Viki, "Innovation Versus R&D Spending," May 20, 2019, https://www.strategyzer.com/blog/innovation-versus-rd-spending.

17. Barry Jaruzelski, Robert Chwalik, and Brad Goehle, "What the Top Innovators Get Right," October 30, 2018, https://www.strategy-business.com/feature/What-the-Top-Innovators-Get-Right?gko=e7cf9.

18. Chris Wray, "Sony 2018-19 Financial Year Results – Most Profitable Year Ever," April 27, 2019, https://wccftech.com/sony-2018-19-financial-year-results/.

19. Steven J. Vaughan-Nichols, "What Does Microsoft Joining the Open Invention Network Mean for You?," October 11, 2018, https://www.zdnet.com/article/what-does-microsoft-joining-the-open-invention-network-mean-for-you/.

20. Surur, "Microsoft Finally Reveals How Many HoloLens Units Have Been Sold," April 25, 2018, https://mspoweruser.com/microsoft-finally-reveals-how-many-hololens-units-have-been-sold/.

21. Heather Kelly, "Microsoft's New $3,500 HoloLens 2 Headset Means Business," February 25, 2019, https://edition.cnn.com/2019/02/24/tech/microsoft-hololens-2/index.html.

22. Allison Linn, "Microsoft's Project Oxford Helps Developers Build More Intelligent Apps," May 1, 2015, https://blogs.microsoft.com/ai/microsofts-project-oxford-helps-developers-build-more-intelligent-apps/.

23. "Microsoft to Acquire GitHub for $7.5 Billion," June 4, 2018, https://news.microsoft.com/2018/06/04/microsoft-to-acquire-github-for-7-5-billion/.

24. Alex Hern and Jana Kasperkevic, "LinkedIn Bought by Microsoft for $26.2BN in Cash," June 13, 2016, London and New York, https://www.theguardian.com/technology/2016/jun/13/linkedin-bought-by-microsoft-for-262bn-in-cash.

25. "Microsoft Google Amazon Cloud Acquisitions," https://app.cbinsights.com/login?status=session&goto=https%3A%2F%2Fapp.cbinsights.com%2Fresearch%2Fmicrosoft-google-amazon-cloud-acquisitions-expert-intelligence%2F.

26. Tom Warren, "Microsoft Wasted at Least $8 Billion on Its Failed Nokia Experiment," May 25, 2016, https://www.theverge.com/2016/5/25/11766540/microsoft-nokia-acquisition-costs.

27. Paul Thurrott, "To Grow, Microsoft Must Deemphasize Windows," February 04, 2014, https://www.itprotoday.com/compute-engines/grow-microsoft-must-deemphasize-windows.

28. Daniel B. Kline, "What Declining PC Sales Mean for Microsoft," May 9, 2016, https://www.fool.com/investing/general/2016/05/09/what-declining-pc-sales-mean-for-microsoft.aspx.

29. Tom Krazit, "Azure Revenue Remains a Mystery, but Cloud Services Continue to Drive Microsoft Forward," April 24, 2019, https://www.geekwire.com/2019/azure-revenue-remains-mystery-cloud-services-continue-drive-microsoft-forward/.

30. Tom Warren, "Microsoft and Amazon Release Preview of Cortana and Alexa Integration," August 15, 2018, https://www.theverge.com/2018/8/15/17691920/microsoft-amazon-alexa-cortana-integration-preview-features.

31. "Unilever's Purpose-Led Brands Outperform," November 6, 2019, https://www.unilever.com/news/press-releases/2019/unilevers-purpose-led-brands-outperform.html.

32. "Unilever Tightens Belt with Slim-Fast Sale," *The Telegraph*, January 20, 2020 https://www.telegraph.co.uk/finance/newsbysector/retailandconsumer/10960347/Unilever-tightens-belt-with-Slim-Fast-sale.html.

33. Unilever, "Acquisitions and Disposals," https://www.unilever.com/investor-relations/understanding-unilever/acquisitions-and-disposals/.
34. Milly Vincent, "Marmite, Pot Noodles and Magnums Face Being Sold by Unilever If They Can't Prove They Make 'Meaningful' Impact on the Planet," July 27 2019, https://www.dailymail.co.uk/news/article-7291997/Marmite-favourites-like-Pot-Noodles-Magnums-face-sold-Unilever.html.
35. Lance Whitney, "Logitech Confesses to 'Gigantic' Mistake with Google TV, November 11, 2011, https://www.cnet.com/news/logitech-confesses-to-gigantic-mistake-with-google-tv/.
36. Logitech Annual Report 2019.
37. Logitech, "Acquisitions," https://www.crunchbase.com/organization/logitech/acquisitions/acquisitions_list#section-acquisitions.
38. "Lifesize Splits from Logitech," January 14, 2016, https://www.lifesize.com/en/company/news/in-the-news/2016/20160114-comms-business-lifesize-splits-from-logitech.
39. Anton Shilov, "Logitech Formally Exits OEM Mouse Market," January 22, 2016, https://www.anandtech.com/show/9984/logitech-exits-oem-mouse-market.
40. "Inside the Storm Ep 2: Fujifilm," Channel News Asia, February 1, 2017, https://www.channelnewsasia.com/news/video-on-demand/inside-the-storm-s2/fujifilm-7824486.
41. Fjuifilm Annual Report 2019.
42. "Medium Term Management Plan VISION 75 (2008)," April 28, 2008, https://www.fujifilmholdings.com/en/pdf/investors/ff_vision75_2008_001.pdf.

INVENT

1. Jessica Caldwell, "Drive by Numbers – Tesla Model S Is the Vehicle of Choice in Many of America's Wealthiest Zip Codes," October 31, 2013, Edmunds.com.
2. Blue Ocean Strategy.
3. Fred Lambert, "Tesla Is Accelerating Supercharger Deployment, 10 More V3 Stations Confirmed," September 25, 2019, https://electrek.co/2019/09/25/tesla-accelerating-supercharger-deployment-v3-stations-confirmed/.
4. Alex Hern, "Tesla Motors Receives $10BN in Model 3 Pre-Orders in Just Two Days," April 4, 2016, The Guardian, https://www.theguardian.com/technology/2016/apr/04/tesla-motors-sells-10bn-model-3-two-days.
5. "Global Top 20 November 2019," December 27, 2019, http://ev-sales.blogspot.com/2019/12/global-top-20-november-2019.html.
6. Kevin P. Donovan, "Mobile Money, More Freedom? The Impact of M-PESA's Network Power on Development as Freedom," University of Cape Town, International Journal of Communication 6 (2012): 2647–2669.
7. "The Mobile Money Revolution: M-Pesa," Ben & Alex, June 15, 2018, https://medium.com/@benandalex/the-mobile-money-revolution-m-pesa-f3fc8f86dbc9.
8. Rob Matheson, "Study: Mobile-Money Services Lift Kenyans Out of Poverty," MIT News Office, December 8, 2016, https://news.mit.edu/2016/mobile-money-kenyans-out-poverty-1208.
9. "M-Pesa Users Outside Kenya Hit 13.4 Million," Business Daily, January 29, 2019, https://www.businessdailyafrica.com/corporate/companies/M-Pesa-users-outside-Kenya-hit-13-4-million/4003102-4956208-16s8a9/index.html.
10. World Bank, "What Kenya's Mobile Money Success Could Mean for the Arab World," October 3, 2018, https://www.worldbank.org/en/news/feature/2018/10/03/what-kenya-s-mobile-money-success-could-mean-for-the-arab-world.
11. Leo Van Hove and Antoine Dubus, "M-PESA and Financial Inclusion in Kenya: Of Paying Comes Saving?," MDPI, January 22, 2019.
12. "What Is M-Pesa?," https://www.vodafone.com/what-we-do/services/m-pesa.
13. "Mobile Currency in Kenya: the M-Pesa," CPI, March 21, 2016, https://www.centreforpublicimpact.org/case-study/m-currency-in-kenya/.

14. Sears Archives, http://www.searsarchives.com/history/history1890s.htm.

15. John Murray Brown and Arash Massoudi, "Unilever Buys Dollar Shave Club for $1BN," Financial Times, July 20 2016, https://www.ft.com/content/bd07237e-4e45-11e6-8172-e39ecd3b86fc.

16. Youtube – Dollar Shave Club, https://www.youtube.com/watch?v=ZUG9qYTJMsI.

17. Barbara Booth, "What Happens When a Business Built on Simplicity Gets Complicated? Dollar Shave Club's Founder Michael Dubin Found Out," CNBC, March 24, 2019, https://www.cnbc.com/2019/03/23/dollar-shaves-dubin-admits-a-business-built-on-simplicity-can-get-complicated.html.

18. Kat Eschner, "The Story of Brownie Wise, the Ingenious Marketer behind the Tupperware Party," Smithsonian.com, April 10, 2018, https://www.smithsonianmag.com/smithsonian-institution/story-brownie-wise-ingenious-marketer-behind-tupperware-party-180968658/.

19. Bob Kealing, Life of the Party: The Remarkable Story of How Brownie Wise Built, and Lost ..., (New York: Crown/Archetype, 2008).

20. Dory Owens, "Tupperware Takes Its Parties into the Workplace," July 12, 1987, https://www.washingtonpost.com/archive/business/1987/07/12/tupperware-takes-its-parties-into-the-work-place/1cc29d20-49ff-4d63-94b4-32f46cbca15b/.

21. Kat Eschner, "The Story of Brownie Wise," https://www.smithsonianmag.com/smithsonian-institution/story-brownie-wise-ingenious-marketer-behind-tupperware-party-180968658/.

22. Avil Beckford, "Earl Tupper, Business Leader, Invented Tupperware, Air-Tight Plastic Containers," February 15, 2013, https://theinvisiblementor.com/earl-tupper-business-leader-invented-tupperware-air-tight-plastic-containers/.

23. Natura & Co. 2018 report, https://naturaeco.com/report_2018_en.pdf.

24. Microsoft Windows history, updated November 16, 2019 by Computer Hope, https://www.computerhope.com/history/windows.htm.

25. Amy Stevenson, "Windows History: Windows 3.0 Takes Off," January 25, 2018, https://community.windows.com/en-us/stories/story-of-windows3.

26. Emil Protalinski, "OEMs Pay Microsoft about $50 for Each Copy of Windows," September 17, 2009, https://arstechnica.com/information-technology/2009/09/microsoft-oems-pay-about-50-for-each-copy-of-windows/.

27. James Gleick, "Making Microsoft Safe for Capitalism," November 5, 1995, https://www.nytimes.com/1995/11/05/magazine/making-microsoft-safe-for-capitalism.html.

28. "Microsoft Revenue by Year – Fiscal 1990–2019," https://dazeinfo.com/2019/11/11/microsoft-revenue-worldwide-by-year-graphfarm/.

29. Jacob Kastrenakes, "The Halo Franchise Has Made More Than $5 Billion, November 4, 2015, https://www.theverge.com/2015/11/4/9668876/halo-franchise-5-billion-guardians-launch-sales.

30. "Police Urge Google to Turn Off 'stalking' Feature on Mobile App for Drivers," Associated Press, Washington, January 27, 2015, https://www.theguardian.com/technology/2015/jan/26/police-pressure-google-turn-off-waze-app-feature.

31. TechCrunch, "Waze." (No data available for 2014–2016.)

32. Aaron Pressman and Adam Lashinsky, "Why Waze Doesn't Share Traffic Data with Google Maps – Data Sheet," October 11, 2019, https://fortune.com/2019/10/11/waze-google-maps-how-it-works/.

33. Kristen Hall-Geisler, "Waze and Esri Make App-to-Infrastructure Possible," AEDT, October 12, 2016, https://techcrunch.com/2016/10/11/waze-and-ezri-make-app-to-infrastructure-possible/.

34. Zhou Xin, Ed., "DiDi Completes 7.43 Bln Rides in 2017," Xinhua, January 8, 2008, http://www.xinhuanet.com/english/2018-01/08/c_136880236.htm.

35. "Didi Now Serves 550M Users 30M Rides per Day, Growing against Meituan Challenges," June 7, 2018, https://kr-asia

.com/didi-now-serves-550m-users-30m-rides-per-day-growing-against-meituan-challenges.

36. Jane Zhang, "Didi by the Numbers: Ride-Hailing Firm Covered More Miles in 2018 Than 5 Earth-to-Neptune Round-Trips," January 23, 2019, https://www.scmp.com/tech/start-ups/article/2181542/didi-numbers-ride-hailing-firm-covered-more-miles-2018-5-earth.

37. Chloe Sorvino, "Inside Billionaire James Dyson's Reinvention Factory: From Vacuums to Hair Dryers and Now Batteries," September 13, 2016, https://www.forbes.com/sites/chloesorvino/2016/08/24/james-dyson-exclusive-top-secret-reinvention-factory/.

38. Michael Pooler and Peggy Hollinger, "Dyson's Perfectionists Invent a Future beyond Vacuum Cleaners, February 8, 2017, https://www.ft.com/content/2041b5b2-ec75-11e6-ba01-119a44939bb6.

39. Sophie Chapman, "Dyson Reaches Record Profits in 2017, Hitting £801MN," March 02, 2018, https://www.manufacturingglobal.com/leadership/dyson-reaches-record-profits-2017-hitting-ps801mn.

40. Brian Dolan, *Wedgwood: The First Tycoon* (New York : Viking, 2004).

41. "Model T," *Encyclopaedia Britannica*, December 5, 2019, https://www.britannica.com/technology/Model-T.

42. "Henry Ford with Ten-Millionth Ford Model T and 1896 Quadricycle, 1924," https://www.thehenryford.org/collections-and-research/digital-collections/artifact/276378/.

43. "100 Years of the Moving Assembly Line," https://corporate.ford.com/articles/history/100-years-moving-assembly-line.html.

44. "Ford's Assembly Line Starts Rolling," November 13, 2009, https://www.history.com/this-day-in-history/fords-assembly-line-starts-rolling.

45. "Ford's Assembly Line Turns 100: How It Changed Manufacturing and Society," *New York Daily News*, October 7, 2013, https://www.nydailynews.com/autos/ford-assembly-line-turns-100-changed-society-article-1.1478331.

46. Mary Hanbury, "We Went Inside One of the Sprawling Factories Where Zara Makes Its Clothes. Here's How the World's Biggest Fashion Retailer Gets It Done," October 29, 2018, https://www.businessinsider.com.au/how-zara-makes-its-clothes-2018-10?r=US&IR=T.

47. Seth Stevenson, "Polka Dots Are In? Polka Dots It Is!," June 21, 2012, https://slate.com/culture/2012/06/zaras-fast-fashion-how-the-company-gets-new-styles-to-stores-so-quickly.html.

48. Dell Inc. history, http://www.fundinguniverse.com/company-histories/dell-inc-history/.

49. Liam O'Connell, "Annual Revenue of IKEA worldwide from 2001 to 2019," October 15, 2019, https://www.statista.com/statistics/264433/annual-sales-of-ikea-worldwide/.

50. Liam O'Connell, "Number of Visits to IKEA Stores Worldwide from 2010 to 2019," October 15, 2019, https://www.statista.com/statistics/241828/number-of-visits-to-ikea-stores-worldwide/.

51. "Why Is IKEA So Successful?," July 12, 2018, https://furnitureblog.simplicitysofas.com/blog/why-is-ikea-so-successful/.

52. Jan-Benedict Steenkamp, Global Brand Strategy: World-Wise Marketing in the Age of Branding (New York: Springer 2017).

53. "Quantity of Furniture U.S. Homeowners Bought from IKEA in the Last Decade 2016, Statista Research Department, September 3, 2019, https://www.statista.com/statistics/618639/quantity-of-furniture-us-homeowners-bought-from-ikea-in-the-last-decade/.

54. IBM Newsroom, "IBM Closes Landmark Acquisition of Red Hat for $34 Billion; Defines Open, Hybrid Cloud Future, Armonk, NY and Raleigh, NC, July 9, 2019, https://newsroom.ibm.com/2019-07-09-IBM-Closes-Landmark-Acquisition-of-Red-Hat-for-34-Billion-Defines-Open-Hybrid-Cloud-Future.

55. Gary Sims, "ARM's Rise from a Small Acorn to a World Leader," May 19, 2014, https://www.androidauthority

.com/arms-rise-small-acorn-world-leader-376606/.

56. Kristin Bent, "ARM Snags 95 Percent of Smartphone Market, Eyes New Areas for Growth," July 16, 2012, https://www.crn.com/news/components-peripherals/240003811/arm-snags-95-percent-of-smartphone-market-eyes-new-areas-for-growth.htm.

57. Arash Massoudi, James Fontanella-Khan, and Richard Waters, "SoftBank to Acquire UK's ARM Holdings for £24.3BN," July 19 2016, https://www.ft.com/content/235b1af4-4c7f-11e6-8172-e39ecd3b86fc.

58. "Dan Swinhoe,"UK Government Gives £36 Million to ARM to Develop Secure Chips," October 24 2019, https://www.csoonline.com/article/3447856/uk-government-gives-36-million-to-arm-to-develop-secure-chips.html.

59. ARM Annual Report and Accounts 2009, http://www.annualreports.com/HostedData/AnnualReportArchive/a/LSE_ARM_2009.pdf.

60. ARM Annual Report and Accounts 2018.

61. Jenna Goudreau, "Disney Princess Tops List of the 20 Best-Selling Entertainment Products," https://www.forbes.com/sites/jennagoudreau/2012/09/17/disney-princess-tops-list-of-the-20-best-selling-entertainment-products/.

62. Victoria Sherrow, *Encyclopedia of Hair: A Cultural History* (Westport, CT: Greenwood Publishing Group, 2006).

63. Martha Matilda Harper, National Women's Hall of Fame, https://www.womenofthehall.org/inductee/martha-matilda-harper/.

64. "Martha Matilda Harper: Servant Girl to Beauty Entrepreneur," https://racingnelliebly.com/strange_times/servant-girl-beauty-entrepreneur/.

65. Jaimie Seaton, "Martha Matilda Harper, The Greatest Business Woman You've Never Heard Of," January 11, 2017, https://www.atlasobscura.com/articles/martha-matilda-harper-the-greatest-businesswoman-youve-never-heard-of.

66. "National Economic Impact of Franchising," International Franchise Association, https://franchiseeconomy.com/.

67. Clive Thompson, "How the Photocopier Changed the Way We Worked—and Played," March 2015, https://www.smithsonianmag.com/history/duplication-nation-3D-printing-rise-180954332/.

68. "Xerox Introduces the First Photocopier," November 28, 2019, https://www.encyclopedia.com/science/encyclopedias-almanacs-transcripts-and-maps/xerox-introduces-first-photocopier.

69. Daniel Gross, "Betting the Company: Joseph Wilson and the Xerox 914 from Forbes Greatest Business Stories of All Time," https://www.stephenhicks.org/wp-content/uploads/2012/01/forbes-xerox.pdf.

70. Alex Hutchinson, *Big Ideas: 100 Modern Inventions That Have Transformed Our World* (New York: Sterling Publishing, 2009).

71. "Xerox 914 Plain Paper Copier," National Museum of American History, https://americanhistory.si.edu/collections/search/object/nmah_1085916.

72. "The Story of Xerography," https://www.xerox.com/downloads/usa/en/s/Storyofxerography.pdf.

73. Louis Columbus, "The State of the Subscription Economy, 2018," Forbes, https://www.forbes.com/sites/louiscolumbus/2018/03/04/the-state-of-the-subscription-economy-2018/.

74. "Activating Brave," Intrabrand, https://www.interbrand.com/best-brands/best-global-brands/2018/articles/activating-brave/.

75. James Cowling, "Kodak: From Brownie and Roll Film to Digital Disaster," BBC News, January 20, 2012, https://www.bbc.com/news/business-16627167.

76. John McDonough and Karen Egolf, *The Advertising Age Encyclopedia of Advertising,* (Chicago, IL: Fitzroy Dearborn Publishers, 2002).

77. Jason Farago, "Our 'Kodak Moments' – and Creativity – Are Gone," August 23, 2013, https://www.theguardian.com/commentisfree/2013/aug/23/photography-photography.

78. David Usborne, "The Moment It All Went Wrong for Kodak," January 20, 2012, https://www.independent.co.uk/news/business/analysis-and-features/the-moment-it-all-went-wrong-for-kodak-6292212.html.

79. Jorn Lyseggen, *Outside Insight: Navigating a World Drowning in Data* (London: Penguin, 2016).

80. Mansoor Iqbal, "Spotify Usage and Revenue Statistics (2019)," May 10, 2019, https://www.businessofapps.com/data/spotify-statistics/.

81. Becky Peterson, "Spotify Has Spent $10 Billion on Music Royalties since Its Creation and It's a Big Part of Why It's Bleeding Money," March 1, 2018, https://www.businessinsider.com.au/spotify-has-spent-10-billion-on-music-licensing-and-revenue-since-it-started-2018-2?r=US&IR=T.

82. Monica Mercuri, "Spotify Reports First Quarterly Operating Profit, Reaches 96 Million Paid Subscribers," https://www.forbes.com/sites/monicamercuri/2019/02/06/spotify-reports-first-quarterly-operating-profit-reaches-96-million-paid-subscribers/.

83. "Spotify Technology S.A. Announces Financial Results for Second Quarter 2019," July 31, 2019, https://investors.spotify.com/financials/press-release-details/2019/Spotify-Technology-SA-Announces-Financial-Results-for-Second-Quarter-2019/default.aspx.

84. Mark Mulligan, "Spotify Q4 2018: Solid Growth with a Hint of Profitability but Longer Term Questions," February 14, 2019, https://www.midiaresearch.com/blog/spotify-q4-2018-solid-growth-with-a-hint-of-profitability-but-longer-term-questions/.

85. Paul Sawers, "Spotify Grows Users 30% in Q3 2019, Premium Subscribers Reach 113 Million," October 28, 2019, https://venturebeat.com/2019/10/28/spotify-grows-users-30-in-q3-2019-premium-subscribers-reach-113-million/.

86. Ariel, "Spotify Was Downloaded on 25 Million iPhones in the U.S. in 2018," October 23, 2018, https://blog.appfigures.com/pandora-chases-spotify-but-spotify-charges-ahead/.

87. Keith Caulfield, "2019 U.S. On-Demand Audio Streams Surpass Half-Trillion, Ariana Grande's 'Thank U, Next' First Album to Reach 2 Billion Streams This Year," September 21, 2019, https://www.billboard.com/articles/business/chart-beat/8530681/2019-on-demand-audio-streams-surpass-half-trillion-ariana-grande.

88. Kayleigh Vanandelmdy, "Case Study: How Spotify Achieves Astonishing 46% Conversion Rate from Free to Paid," October 08, 2019, https://growthhackers.com/articles/case-study-how-spotify-achieves-astonishing-46-conversion-rate-from-free-to-paid.

89. "Fortnite Phenomenon Turns a Game Developer into a Billionaire," July 24, 2018, https://adage.com/article/media/fortnite-phenomenon-turns-game-developer-into-a-billionaire/314357.

90. Catherine New, "How Much Are People Making from the Sharing Economy?," June 13, 2017, https://www.earnest.com/blog/sharing-economy-income-data/.

91. Airbnb Newsroom Fast Facts, https://news.airbnb.com/fast-facts/.

92. S. Lock, "Share of Leisure and Business Travelers using Airbnb in the United States and Europe from 2015 to 2018," January 16, 2019, https://www.statista.com/statistics/795675/travelers-using-airbnb/.

93. Zack Quaintance, "A First in 2018: American Consumers Spent More on Airbnb Than on Hilton," April 13, 2019, https://tophotel.news/a-first-in-2018-american-consumers-spent-more-on-airbnb-than-on-hilton/.

94. Parmy Olson, "Exclusive: The Rags-To-Riches Tale of How Jan Koum Built WhatsApp into Facebook's New $19 Billion Baby," February 19, 2014, forbes.com/sites/parmyolson/2014/02/19/exclusive-inside-story-how-jan-koum-built-whatsapp-into-facebooks-new-19-billion-baby/.

95. Ryan Bushey, "Texting App WhatsApp Now Has 400 Million People Using It Every Month," December 20, 2013, https://www.businessinsider.com.au/whatsapp-400-million-users-2013-12?r=US&IR=T.

96. Dominic Rushe, "WhatsApp: Facebook Acquires Messaging Service in $19BN Deal," February 20, 2014, https://www.theguardian.com/technology/2014/feb/19/facebook-buys-whatsapp-16bn-deal.

97. Diane Dragan, "10 Outrageous Markups You'd Never Guess You Were Paying," rd.com/advice/saving-money/10-outrageous-markups-youd-never-guess-you-were-paying/.

98. Mansoor Iqbal, "WhatsApp Revenue and Usage Statistics (2019)," February 19, 2019, https://www.businessofapps.com/data/whatsapp-statistics/.

99. "Mobile messaging volumes in the U.S. from 2004 to 2014," https://www.statista.com/statistics/215776/mobile-messaging-volumes-in-the-us/.

100. Charles Arthur, "App Messaging Damages Mobile Networks' Text Revenues," April 29, 2013, https://www.theguardian.com/technology/2013/apr/29/app-messaging-damages-mobile-text-revenues.

101. Citizen M Hotel Bankside London, https://archello.com/project/citizen-m-hotel-bankside-london.

102. Matylda Krzykowski, "CitizenM by Concrete," November 7, 2008, dezeen.com/2008/11/07/citizenm-by-concrete/.

103. W. Chan Kim and Renée Mauborgne, "How CitizenM Created New Market Space in the Hotel Industry," https://www.blueoceanstrategy.com/blog/citizenm-hotels-a-blue-ocean-chain-in-a-red-ocean-industry/.

104. "Hotels That Arrive Prebuilt: How CitizenM Manufactures Its Buildings," December 15, 2017, https://www.wired.co.uk/article/hotels-that-arrive-prebuilt.

105. "CitizenM Celebrates Yet Another Year of Affordable Luxury," https://www.citizenm.com/news/citizenm-celebrates-yet-another-year-of-affordable.

106. "A Million New iPhones Sold in the First Weekend," Reuters, July 15, 2008, https://www.nytimes.com/2008/07/15/technology/15apple.html.

107. Matthew Jones, "iPhone History: Every Generation in Timeline Order," September 14, 2014, https://historycooperative.org/the-history-of-the-iphone/.

108. Bill of Materials from Techinsights; Apple Product Announcements.

109. Chuck Jones, "Apple's iPhone: Why Care about Units When It Captures All the Profits," https://www.forbes.com/sites/chuckjones/2015/11/16/apples-iphone-why-care-about-units-when-it-captures-all-the-profits/.

110. J. Clement, "Number of Apps Available in Leading App Stores 2019," October 9, 2019, https://www.statista.com/statistics/276623/number-of-apps-available-in-leading-app-stores/.

111. Sam Costello, "How Many iPhones Have Been Sold Worldwide?," December 27, 2019, https://www.lifewire.com/how-many-iphones-have-been-sold-1999500.

112. How citizenM Created New Market Space in the Hotel Industry By W. Chan Kim & Renée Mauborgne https://www.blueoceanstrategy.com/blog/citizenm-hotels-a-blue-ocean-chain-in-a-red-ocean-industry/

113. CitizenM by Concrete Matylda Krzykowski | 7 November 2008 https://www.dezeen.com/2008/11/07/citizenm-by-concrete/ \h https://www.dezeen.com/2008/11/07/citizenm-by-concrete/

114. Innovation Management: Effective Strategy and Implementation By Keith Goffin, Rick Mitchell 2017 Palgrave

115. OneConnect moves up in the 2019 IDC Financial Insights FinTech Rankings Top 100 list October 11, 2019 https://finance.yahoo.com/news/oneconnect-moves-2019-idc-financial-130700278.html

116. Ping An Fintech Vehicle OneConnect Plans to List in New York by as Soon as September: Domestic Reports China Banking News http://www.chinabankingnews.com/2019/06/18/ping-ans-fintech-vehicle-oneconnect-plans-to-list-in-new-york-by-september-domestic-reports/

117. finleap connect partners with OneConnect to bring superior technology to Europe Aug 26, 2019, https://www.prnewswire.com/news-releases/finleap-connect-partners-with-oneconnect-to-bring-superior-technology-to-europe-300906797.html

118. Why banks can't delay upgrading core legacy banking platforms https://www.ey.com/en_gl/people/keith-pogson \h Keith Pogson 18 Jun 2019 https://www.ey.com/en_gl/banking-capital-markets/why-banks-can-t-delay-upgrading-core-legacy-banking-platforms

119. Ping An Accelerates Digital Transformation in Indonesia's Finance Industry 21 February 2019 https://www.bloomberg.com/press-releases/2019-02-20/ping-an-accelerates-digital-transformation-in-indonesia-s-finance-industry

120. An Overview of Pingan's OneConnect Will Huyler, May 20 2019 https://www.kapronasia.com/asia-banking-research-category/an-overview-of-pingan-s-oneconnect.html

IMPROVE

1. Ramon Casadesus-Masanell, Oliver Gassmann ,and Roman Sauer, "Hilti Fleet Management (A): Turning a Successful Business Model on Its Head," September 2018, https://www.hbs.edu/faculty/Pages/item.aspx?num=52550.

2. Dr. Christoph Loos, CEO of Hilti, correspondence.

3. Michelle Castillo, "Reed Hastings' Story about the Founding of Netflix Has Changed Several Times," May 23, 2017, https://www.cnbc.com/2017/05/23/netflix-ceo-reed-hastings-on-how-the-company-was-born.html.

4. Todd Spangler, "Netflix Spent $12 Billion on Content in 2018. Analysts Expect That to Grow to $15 Billion This Year," January 18, 2019, https://variety.com/2019/digital/news/netflix-content-spending-2019-15-billion-1203112090/.

5. Lauren Feiner, "Netflix Says It Has 10% of All TV Time in the US and Discloses Some Colossal Numbers for Its Shows," January 17, 2019, https://www.cnbc.com/2019/01/17/netflix-how-many-people-watch-bird-box.html.

6. Amy Watson, "Number of Netflix Paid Streaming Subscribers Worldwide 2011–2019," October 18, 2019, https://www.statista.com/statistics/250934/quarterly-number-of-netflix-streaming-subscribers-worldwide/.

7. J. Clement, "Number of Available Apps in the Apple App Store 2008–2017," September 12, 2018, https://www.statista.com/statistics/263795/number-of-available-apps-in-the-apple-app-store/.

8. Alex Guyot, "A Decade on the App Store: From Day One Through Today," July 11, 2018, https://www.macstories.net/news/a-decade-on-the-app-store-from-day-one-through-today/.

9. Mike Wuerthele, "Apple Has Paid Out $120 Billion to Developers since 2008," January 28, 2019, https://www.macstories.net/news/a-decade-on-the-app-store-from-day-one-through-today/.

10. Dedicated Video Games Sales Units, September 30, 2019, https://www.nintendo.co.jp/ir/en/finance/hard_soft/.

11. "TED Reaches Its Billionth Vdeo View!," November 13, 2012, https://blog.ted.com/ted-reaches-its-billionth-video-view/.

12. "History of TED," https://www.ted.com/about/our-organization/history-of-ted.

13. "TED," https://www.ted.com/talks.

14. "TED Opens Annual Conference in Vancouver as Media Platform Sees Record Global Audience Growth," April 10, 2018, https://blog.ted.com/ted-opens-annual-conference-in-vancouver-as-media-platform-sees-record-global-audience-growth/.

15. Intel Annual Report 1993, https://www.intel.com/content/www/us/en/history/history-1993-annual-report.html.

16. "Worldwide Semiconductor Revenue Grew 2.6 Percent in 2016," Stamford, CT, May 15, 2017, https://www.gartner.com/en/newsroom/press-releases/2017-05-15-worldwide-semiconductor-revenue-grew-2-percent-in-2016-according-to-final-results-by-gartner.

17. Intel Annual report 1991, https://www.intel.com/content/www/us/en/history/history-1991-annual-report.html.

18. Intel Corporation History, http://www.fundinguniverse.com/company-histories/intel-corporation-history/.

19. Jim Dalrymple, "Apple Stores See 300 Million Visitors in FY 2012, 50,000 Genius Bar Visits a Day," August 20, 2012, https://www.loopinsight.com/2012/08/20/apple-stores-see-300-million-visitors-in-2012-50000-genius-bar-visits-a-day/.

20. Fujifilm Annual report 2006.

21. Fujifilm Annual Report 2019.

22. "Inside the Storm Ep 2: Fujifilm," Channel News Asia, February 1, 2017, https://www.channelnewsasia.com/news/video-on-demand/inside-the-storm-s2/fujifilm-7824486.

23. Jake Nielson, "Story of Kodak: How They Could Have Saved the Business," August 22, 2014, https://www.ignitionframework.com/story-of-kodak/.

24. Telecom Regulatory Authority of India, New Delhi, December 30, 2019, https://main.trai.gov.in/sites/default/files/PR_No.128of2019.pdf.

25. Vijay Govindarajan, "Telecom's Competitive Solution: Outsourcing?," May 08, 2012, https://hbr.org/2012/05/telecoms-competitive-solution-outsourcing.

26. Steven J. Vaughan-Nichols, "What Does Microsoft Joining the Open Invention Network Mean for You?," October 11, 2018, https://www.zdnet.com/article/what-does-microsoft-joining-the-open-invention-network-mean-for-you/.

27. "Microsoft to Acquire GitHub for $7.5 Billion," June 4, 2018, https://news.microsoft.com/2018/06/04/microsoft-to-acquire-github-for-7-5-billion/.

28. "Microsoft Is the Largest Single Corporate Contributor to Open Source on Github," https://ballardchalmers.com/2018/05/07/microsoft-largest-single-corporate-contributor-open-source-github/.

29. Brooks Barnes, "Disney Is Spending More on Theme Parks Than It Did on Pixar, Marvel and Lucasfilm Combined," November 16, 2018, https://www.nytimes.com/interactive/2018/11/16/business/media/disney-invests-billions-in-theme-parks.html.

30. Linda Rosencrance, "Dow Corning Launches Business Unit, Xiameter," March 14, 2002, https://www.computerworld.com/article/2587477/dow-corning-launches-business-unit--xiameter.html.

31. Bruce Meyer, "Xiameter Business a Web Success Story," August 23, 2011, https://www.rubbernews.com/article/20110823/NEWS/308239996/xiameter-business-a-web-success-story.

32. "Two-Brand Strategy Spells Success for Dow Corning," Noria Corporation, https://www.reliableplant.com/Read/5144/two-br-strategy-spells-success-for-dow-corning.

33. "Adobe Profit Margin 2006–2019," https://www.macrotrends.net/stocks/charts/ADBE/adobe/profit-margins.

34. Itu Rathore, "Adobe Quarterly Subscription Revenue by Segment," November 7, 2019, https://dazeinfo.com/2019/11/07/adobe-quarterly-subscription-revenue-by-segment-graphfarm/.

35. John Markoff, "Company Reports; Apple's First Annual Profit Since 1995," October 15, 1998, https://www.nytimes.com/1998/10/15/business/company-reports-apple-s-first-annual-profit-since-1995.html.

36. "Apple Announces That 800,000 iMacs Sold/ 45% of Buyers New to Mac," January 6, 1999, https://www.macobserver.com/news/99/january/990106/800000imacs.html.

37. Doug Bartholomew, "What's Really Driving Apple's Recovery?," March 16, 1999, https://www.industryweek.com/leadership/companies-executives/article/21960994/whats-really-driving-apples-recovery.

38. "The Transformation 20: The Top Global Companies Leading Strategic Transformations," September 2019, https://www.innosight.com/insight/the-transformation-20/.

39. Ørsted ESG Performance Report 2018, https://orsted.com/-/media/Annual_2018/Orsted_ESG_performance_report_2018.ashx?la=en&hash=315A4E48E0AD794B64B9A-C56EE7ED2F1.

40. 2018 Annual Report Rolls-Royce Holdings PLC.

41. Amy Mitchell, Mark Jurkowitz, and Emily Guskin, "The Washington Post: By the Numbers," August 7, 2013, https://www.journalism.org/2013/08/07/the-washington-post-by-the-numbers/.

42. Joshua Benton, "The L.A. Times' Disappointing Digital Numbers Show the Game's Not Just about Drawing in Subscribers – It's about Keeping Them," July 31, 2019, https://www.niemanlab.org/2019/07/the-l-a-times-disappointing-digital-numbers-show-the-games-not-just-about-drawing-in-subscribers-its-about-keeping-them/.

43. "The Washington Post Records 86.6 Million Unique Visitors in March 2019," April 18, 2019, https://www.washingtonpost.com/pr/2019/04/17/washington-post-records-million-unique-visitors-march/.

44. Matthew Kazin, "Delta's American Express Credit Card Helps Boost Airline's Bottom Line," https://www.foxbusiness.com/markets/deltas-american-express-credit-card-helps-boost-airlines-bottom-line.

45. "American Express and Delta Renew Industry-Leading Partnership, Lay Foundation to Continue Innovating Customer Benefits," https://news.delta.com/american-express-and-delta-renew-industry-leading-partnership-lay-foundation-continue-innovating.

Image Credits

IMPROVE

Hilti–Courtesy of Hilti

Apple Genius Bar–"Genius Bar" by renatomitra / CC BY-SA 2.0, https://www.flickr.com/photos/33029569@N00/3554552146/

Direct to Consumer Trend

Apple Stores: "1373" by ptwo / CC BY 2.0, https://search.creativecommons.org/photos/45d908ee-a3d2-4ce4-85b9-babae4603d4a

Nespresso Boutique: Photo by Ayach Art on Pexels, https://www.pexels.com/photo/coffee-market-room-shop-453098/

Audemars Piguet: "Place de la Fusterie: magasin Audemars Piguet" by MHM55 / CC BY 4.0, https://commons.wikimedia.org/wiki/File:Place_de_la_Fusterie-03.jpg

Rise of Niche

Craft Beer: "Craft Beer Booze Brew Alcohol Celebrate Refreshment" / CC0 1.0, https://www.rawpixel.com/image/33597/premium-photo-image-beer-bar-alcohol

Co-branded credit card: "Amazon Prime Rewards Card" by Ajay Suresh / CC BY 2.0, https://commons.wikimedia.org/wiki/File:Amazon_Prime_Rewards_Card_(32861518627).jpg

Limited edition sneakers: Photo by Florian Olivo on Unsplash, https://unsplash.com/photos/5d4EhqeV0Og

Apple iMac–"Apple iMac G3 computer." by Musee Bolo / CC BY 2.0 France, https://upload.wikimedia.org/wikipedia/commons/2/22/IMac-IMG_7042.jpg

Orsted–Photo by Nicholas Doherty on Unsplash, https://unsplash.com/photos/pONBhDyOFoM

CULTURE

The Culture Map–Courtesy of David Gray

Amazon Innovation Culture–Courtesy of Amazon

Entrepreneurial Leadership and Team:

Elizabeth Arden–Library of Congress, Prints and Photographs Division, NYWT&S Collection, [LC-USZ62-123247] http://hdl.loc.gov/loc.pnp/cph.3c23247

Jack Ma–Jack Ma attends the 20th Anniversary Schwab Foundation Gala Dinner on September 23, 2018 in New York, NY USA. Copyright by World Economic Forum / Ben Hider / CC BY 2.0, https://commons.wikimedia.org/wiki/File:20th_Anniversary_Schwab_Foundation_Gala_Dinner_(44887783681).jpg

Anne Wojcicki–"TechCrunch Disrupt SF 2017 - Day 2" by Techcrunch / CC BY 2.0, https://www.flickr.com/photos/52522100@N07/36938473750/

Yvon Chouinard–"A photo of rock climber Yvon Chouinard." by Tom Frost / CC BY 2.0, https://commons.wikimedia.org/wiki/File:Yvon_Chouinard_by_Tom_Frost.jpg

Daniel Elk–Daniel Ek, CEO and Co-founder of Spotify, is interviewed by Andy Serwer of Fortune Magazine at Fortune Brainstorm TECH at the Aspen Institute Campus. Photograph by Stuart Isett/Fortune Brainstorm TECH / CC BY 2.0, https://commons.wikimedia.org/wiki/File:Fortune_Brainstorm_TECH_2011_(5961801428).jpg

Strive Masiyiwa–"Africa Progress Panel" by Rodger Bosch for APP / CC BY 2.0, https://www.flickr.com/photos/africaprogresspanel/8738568324/in/photostream/

Olive Ann Beech–"Beech, Olive Ann" by San Diego Air and Space Museum Archive, https://commons.wikimedia.org/wiki/File:Beech,_Olive_Ann.jpg

Cher Wang–"HTC Chairwoman, Cher Wang, shows off new mobile phone mother board" by Robert Scoble / CC BY 2.0, https://www.flickr.com/photos/scobleizer/2215637255

Carlos Slim–"Mexican businessman Carlos Slim Helú." by José Cruz/ABr / CC BY 3.0, https://commons.wikimedia.org/wiki/File:Carlos_Slim_Hel%C3%BA.jpg

Yang Lan–"Yang Lan" by World Economic Forum from Cologny, Switzerland / CC BY 2.0, https://zh.m.wikipedia.org/wiki/File:Yang_Lan_-_Annual_Meeting_of_the_New_Champions_2012.jpg

Kiichiro Toyoda–"Kiichiro Toyoda was an engineer in Japan.", https://de.m.wikipedia.org/wiki/Datei:Kiichiro_Toyoda.jpg

Jacqueline Novogratz–"Jacqueline Novogratz" by Acumen / CC BY 2.0, https://www.flickr.com/photos/acumenfund/38439020321/in/photostream/

Index

A

A10 Lab Co., Ltd., 107
Acceleration stage, 20–21, 83, 105, 337
Access, to innovation resources, 328
Acquire (action), 32–34, 114–115
Actions, Innovation Metrics and, 91, 93
Activities, key, *see* Key activities
Activity costs, 176
Activity Differentiators, 74, 139, 163,
    172–177, 187, 213
Acumen Fund, 341
Adaptability hypothesis, 80–81
Adaptability risk, 19, 99, 348
Adaptation, on innovation journey, 17
Adobe, 272–273
Affinity credit cards, 253
Agent network, 148
Airbnb, 200–201
Alibaba Group, 65, 340
Allen, Paul, 116
Amazon, 60–61, 68, 116, 241, 283, 302–305,
    320
Amazon Marketplace, 60
Amazon Private Label, 241
Amazon Web Service (AWS), 60
Ambidextrous culture, 292
Analysis, 4, 42
Anderson, Chris, 245

Apple, 68, 208, 238–239, 283. *See also*
    specific products and services
Apple Genius Bar, 250–251
Apple Store, 252
App Store, 208, 238–239
ARM Holdings, 182–183
Assess step, 76
Asset heavy—asset light pattern shifts, 227,
    254, 258, 260–261, 265, 281
Asset owners, 200
Assumptions Map, 81, 335
AstaLift, 123
ASTRO Gaming, 121
Atrium Innovations, 34, 35
Audemars Piguet (AP), 252
Autohome, 64, 65
Automation, 250
Autonomy, 328
Azure Cognitive Services, 117

B

B2B—B2(B2)C pattern shifts, 227, 242, 246,
    248–249, 279, 280
Backstage building, 195
Backstage disruption, 162–187
  for Activity Differentiators, 172–177
  assessment questions about, 187, 213
  defined, 74, 138, 163
  on disruption risk assessment, 111, 113
  for Resource Castles, 164–171
  for Scalers, 178–185
  types of, 139
Backstage driven shifts, 254–265
  asset heavy—asset light, 258, 260–261, 265

closed—open innovation, 259, 262–263
dedicated resources—multi-usage
    resources, 255–257, 264, 279
defined, 254
strategic reflections for leaders about,
    255, 258, 259, 281
testing, 125
types of, 227
Bait & Hook, 189, 191, 194–195
Ballmer, Steve, 116, 262
Barriers, to starting innovation, 328
Beech Aircraft Corporation, 340
Behaviors (Culture Map), 295–297, 300–301,
    306, 307, 310–311, 329
Bennahmias, Francois-Henry, 252
Beyond Entertainment, 121
Bezos, Jeff, 60–61, 278, 302–304
Bharti Airtel, 260–261
Big data, 264
Bland, David J., 82–83
Blank, Steve, 77
Blockers (Culture Map), 295–297
  and cultivating/designing culture, 300–
    301, 307
  eliminating, 328
  identifying, 295–297, 306
  innovation culture, 311–313
Blue Microphones, 121
Boost phase, 30–31
Bosch Group, 24–25
Bosh Accelerator Program, 24–25
Brand, access to, 316
Brand Castles, 163, 165, 171
Brand consistency, 184

Brand image, 50, 62, 116, 118, 120, 122
Branding, 170, 195
Brownie, 194
Build-to-Order, 163, 173, 177
Business design, 20–21, 336, 348
Business design loop, 72–73, 76, 78–79
Business Environment Map, 335
Business models:
 adapting/improving, 68, 133
 assessing, in terms of trends, 110, 112–113
 Business Model Patterns and, 129,
  132–133
 defined, 348
 Innovation Metrics related to, 89, 92–93
 of invincible companies, vii
 performance assessments for, 74–75,
  110–111, 133
 and shift patterns, 228–229
Business Model Canvas, 40, 76, 78–79
 and business design skills, 336
 defined, 348
 finding invent patterns with, 214, 216, 218
 as innovation tool, 335
Business model design assessment sheets,
 75
Business Model Generation (Osterwalder &
 Pigneur), 78
Business Model Pattern Library, xiii
 boosting model performance with, 75
 invent patterns in, 130–131, 138–139
 shift patterns in, 125, 130–131, 226–227
Business Model Patterns, 129–221
 applying, to business model activities,
  132–133

and business model design performance,
 74–75
 defined, 129, 348
 functions of, 129
 invent patterns, 130–131, 138–221
 shift patterns, 130–131, 226–281
Business Model Portfolio, 3–44
 defined, 3, 348
 examples, 24–25, 34–35, 40–41
 Exploit portfolio, 28–35
 explore/exploit continuum for, 8–9
 Explore portfolio, 16–25
 and innovation types, 38–39
 of invincible companies, 4
 portfolio management, 5, 12–13
 Portfolio Map, 10–13, 42–43
Business model shifts, 124–125, 225, 348
Business plans, for innovation projects,
 102–103, 328
Business Prototype step, 76
Business research and development
 (business R&D), 66–69, 348
Business strategy, 67

C

Career risk, 328
Carlson, Chester, 192
Case illustrations, 140–141
Change of Direction stage, 20–21
Channel Kings, 74, 139, 143, 150–155, 161,
 213
Channels:
 and backstage disruption, 184
 in backstage driven shifts, 257

on Business Model Canvas, 78–79
 and frontstage disruption, 152, 154, 158
 in frontstage driven shifts, 244, 245, 248,
  249
 on Innovation Project Scorecard, 98
 in profit formula driven shifts, 269
 in value proposition shifts, 233, 238, 239
Chief Entrepreneur, 322–325
Chief Internal Ambassador (CIA), 320,
 322–323
Chief Portfolio Manager, 322–323
Chief Risk Officer, 322–323
Chief Venture Capitalist, 322–323
Chouinard, Yvon, 176
Christensen, Clayton, 38
Churn, customer, 196, 197
CitizenM, 206–207, 214–215
Closed—open innovation pattern shifts, 227,
 254, 259, 262–263, 281
Co-branded credit cards, 253
Collaborative consumption, 201
Comfort One Rinse, 119
Communication, at Zara, 175
Community, Airbnb, 201
Confidence level, 85, 91
Consumable products, 194
Contrarian—conventional pattern shifts, 227,
 266, 271, 274–275, 281
Contrarians, 189, 205–207
Cook, Tim, 274
Core business, 314, 320–323, 330, 344–345
Corporate culture, *see* Culture(s)
Corporate identity, 50, 98, 292–293, 334
 The Corporate Startup (Viki), 314

Cost(s):
  at business model level, 92
  on Innovation Project Scorecard, 99
  as key performance indicator, 89
Cost Differentiators, 74, 139, 189, 198–203, 211, 213
Cost structure:
  and backstage disruption, 174–176, 180
  in backstage driven shifts, 261, 265
  on Business Model Canvas, 78–79
  in frontstage driven shifts, 251
  and profit formula disruption, 196, 200, 202, 206, 208
  in profit formula driven shifts, 268, 269
  in value proposition shifts, 233, 237, 240
Craft beer, 253
Creative genius, 67
Credit cards, affinity/co-branded, 253
Crisis phase, 30–31
Crowdfunding, 107
Culture(s), 50, 287–345
  corporate identity, Portfolio Map, and, 292–293
  creating, 294–295
  cultivating, 300–301
  and Culture Map, 296–307
  designing, 307
  examples of, 62, 116, 118, 120, 122, 302–305
  exploitation, 8, 288–291, 308
  exploration, 8, 288–291, 308–345
  at invincible companies, 287
Culture Map (CM), 296–307, 309–315, 334, 348

Curiosity, 339
Curtis, Allistair, 120
Customer acquisition, 192, 194, 273
Customer relationships:
  on Business Model Canvas, 78–79
  and frontstage disruption, 158
  in frontstage driven shifts, 250, 251
  on Innovation Project Scorecard, 98
  and profit formula disruption, 194, 196, 207
  in profit formula driven shifts, 273
Customers:
  access to, 316
  in business R&D, 67
  value creation for, ix
  as workforce, 180
Customer segments:
  and backstage disruption, 166, 168, 174
  on Business Model Canvas, 78–79
  and frontstage disruption, 146, 147, 154, 158
  in frontstage driven shifts, 244, 245
  on Innovation Project Scorecard, 98
  and profit formula disruption, 192, 194, 196, 202, 208
  in value proposition shifts, 240

D

Darrell, Bracken, 120, 121
Data transmission, at Zara, 175
Death and disruption risk, 10, 11, 28–29, 110–113, 349
Decision making, 17, 291
Decline trajectory, 30–31

Dedicated resources—multi-usage resources pattern shift, 227, 254–257, 264, 276, 277, 279, 281
Delegators, 163, 179–181
Dell, Michael, 177
Dell Computers, 177
Delta Airlines, 279
Democratizers, 143, 145, 149
Denner, Volkmar, 25
Desirability hypothesis, 80–81
Desirability risk, 19, 98, 349
DiDi, 168–169
Digital camera industry, 195
Diosynth RTP LLC, 123
Direct distribution, 146
Direct network effects, 167
Direct sales, 177, 203, 264
Direct-to-consumer (DTC) brands, 152, 153, 252
Discovery stage, 20–21, 83, 105, 337
Disintermediators, 143, 151–153
Dismantle (action), 32–33
Disney, Walt, 183, 265
Disney Consumer Products, 183
Disruption, 122–123, 133, 195, 220–221, 327. *See also specific types*
Disruption phase, 30–31
Disruption risk assessment, 110–113
Distribution network, 195
Diversification, 49, 103
Divest (action), 32–34, 114–115
Dollar Shave Club (DSC), 152–153
Domestos, 119
Double-sided platform, 200

Dove, 119
Dow Chemical Company, 268
Dow Corning, 268–269
Drug discovery, 264
Dubin, Michael, 152, 153
Dyson, 170–171
Dyson, James, 170

E
Eastman, George, 194
easyJet, 203
Econet Wireless, 341
Efficiency Disruptors, 163, 173, 174
Efficiency innovation, 39, 327
Electric vehicle sales, 147
Elizabeth Arden, Inc., 340
Enablers (Culture Map):
    creating, 329
    cultivating, 300–301
    described, 295–297
    designing desired, 307
    identifying, 306
    for innovation culture, 309–311, 314–343
    innovation practice, 309–311, 332–343
    leadership support, 309–311, 314–319
    organizational design, 309–311, 320–331
End-customer marketing, 248
Engines at Work, 29
Entrepreneurial leadership, xiii, 338–339
Entrepreneurs, xiii, 42, 100, 322–323
Entrepreneurship, 17, 120–121
Environmental objectives, 176
Epicenters, Business Model Pattern, 138
Epic Games, 197

Evidence, 81, 83, 84, 349
Evidence-based investments, 105
Execution, 17, 336, 337
Existence of Evidence dimension
    (Assumptions Map), 81
Expected profitability, 89, 92
Expected return, 10, 11, 18–19, 72, 349
Experience, of innovation team, 339
Experiments, 82–83, 105, 349
Experiment Log, 90, 93
Experiment step, 77, 82–83
Exploitation, 8–9, 17, 88
Exploitation culture, 288–291, 308
Exploit portfolio, 28–35
    death and disruption metrics for, 110–113
    defined, 349
    examples of, 34–35, 40–41, 116–123
    Explore portfolio vs., 8–9
    growth and decline trajectories with,
      30–31
    guidance for, 51
    of invincible companies, 4
    journey in, 30–31
    Portfolio Actions, 32–33, 114–115
    portfolio management, 12–13, 110–125
    Portfolio Map, 10–11
    return and death and disruption risk with,
      28–29
    shift patterns for, 131. See also Shift
      patterns
    testing shifts for, 124–125
    transfer to, 22–23, 100–101
Exploration, 8–9, 17, 88
Exploration culture, 308–345

    components of, 309
    cultivating exploitation culture and,
      290–291
    defined, 288
    designing, 308–343
    innovation behaviors and outcomes for,
      310–311
    and innovation culture blockers,
      312–313
    innovation practice for, 332–343
    of invincible companies, 8, 308
    leadership support for, 316–319
    organizational design for, 320–331
    readiness for, 314–315, 344–345
Explore Map, xiii
Explore portfolio, 16–25
    business design loop, 72–79
    defined, 349
    examples of, 24–25, 40–41, 106–107
    expected return and innovation risk with,
      18–19
    Exploit portfolio vs., 8–9
    guidance for, 51
    innovation journey with, 16–17
    Innovation Metrics for, 88–95
    invent patterns for, 131. See also Invent
      patterns
    of invincible companies, 4
    Portfolio Actions, 22–23, 96–105
    portfolio management, 12–13, 72–107
    Portfolio Map, 10–11
    search and pivot trajectories with, 20–21
    test loop, 72–73, 76–77, 80–85
External business model disruption risk, 28

F

Facts, as evidence, 84
Failure, 60–61, 87, 88, 291
Falling Stars, 29
Feasibility hypothesis, 80–81
Feasibility risk, 19, 99, 349
Festivals, 197
FES Watch U, 107
Financial impact, of innovation types, 327
Financial measures, for innovation, 88
Flatpacking, 180, 181
Flavors, Business Model Pattern, 141
Ford, Henry, 174
Ford Model T, 174
Fortnite: Battle Royale, 197
Four Actions Framework, 214
Franchises, 184, 185
Franchisors, 163, 179, 184–185
Freemium Providers, 189, 191, 196–197
Frontstage disruption, 142–161
    assessment questions about, 161, 213
    for Channel Kings, 150–155
    defined, 74, 138, 143
    on disruption risk assessment, 111, 113
    for Gravity Creators, 156–159
    for Market Explorers, 144–149
    types of, 139
Frontstage driven shifts, 242–253
    B2B—B2(B2)C, 246, 248–249, 279
    defined, 242
    and direct to consumer trend, 252
    low touch—high touch, 247, 250–251
    niche market—mass market, 243–245, 278
    and rise of niche markets, 253

strategic reflections for leaders about, 243, 246, 247, 280
    testing, 125
    types of, 227
FUJIFILM Holdings, 122–123, 256–257
FUJITAC, 123
Funding, metered, 55, 105, 350

G

Gates, Bill, 116
Gerber, 34, 35
GitHub, 117
Good Doctor, 64–65
Gore, Genevieve, 40
Gore, Wilbert, 40
GORE-TEX® Fabrics, 40, 279
GORE-TEX® INFINIUM, 41
GORE® Thermal Insulation, 41
Gravity Creators, 74, 139, 143, 156–159, 161, 213
Gray, Dave, 296
GRAZE, 119
Greenfields, 140–141
Growth, 9, 12, 13, 30–31, 290, 298–299, 349
Grupo Carso, 341

H

Hannon, Greg, 40
Harper (company), 184–185
Harper, Martha Matilda, 184–185
Hastings, Reed, 236, 237
Herta, 34, 35
High cost—low cost pattern shifts, 227, 266–269, 281

High Enders, 189, 205, 208–209
High-tech—low-tech pattern shifts, 227, 230, 234, 236–237, 240, 277, 280
High touch—low touch pattern shifts, 227, 242, 247, 250–251, 280
Hilti, 232–233
Hirai, Kazuo, 106
Hololens, 117
HTC Corporation, 341
Hypothesis(-es), 80–81, 83, 89–91, 349
Hypothesis Log, 90, 93
Hypothesize step, 77, 80–81

I

Ibuka, Masaru, 106
Ideate (action), 22–23, 100–101
Ideate step, 76
Identity, corporate, 50, 98, 292–293, 334
IKEA, 180–181
iMac, 274–275
Impact weighting, 112, 329
Importance dimension (Assumptions Map), 81
Improve (action), 32–34, 41, 114–115
In-app purchases, 197
Incentives, 314, 320, 328–330, 344–345
Incumbents, threat to, 134–135
Independence, of entrepreneurial leader, 339
Industry, vii, 99, 174, 220–221, 282–283
Innovation, 38–39, 66–68, 326–327, 350
Innovation behaviors, 105, 310–311
Innovation core team, 316

Innovation culture, xiii
  blockers of, 311–313
  innovation practice for, 332–343
  leadership support for, 316–319
  organizational design for, 320–331
Innovation Culture Assessment, 314–315,
  344–345
Innovation funds, 316
Innovation Funnel, 40, 54–57, 349
Innovation guidance, 98
Innovation Journey (Exploration Journey),
  16–21
Innovation Metrics, 88–95, 335, 349
Innovation practice, 332–345
  assessing your, 342, 344–345
  components of, 332–333
  culture blockers related to, 312
  for entrepreneurial leadership and team,
    338–341
  innovation tools for, 334–335
  skills development in, 336–337
Innovation process, 334–335
Innovation Project Scorecard (IPS), 96–99
Innovation risk, 10, 11, 18–19, 72, 92, 349
Innovation skills, 342, 344–345
Innovation teams, xiii, 17, 42, 96, 100, 105,
  310, 316, 339
Innovation team leaders, xiii, 96
Innovation tools, 314, 332, 334–335, 342,
  344–345
Insights, 85, 91
Intel, 248–249
Internal business model design risk, 28
Inventiveness, of team, 339

Invent patterns, 138–221
  assessment questions, see Pattern
    Assessment Questions for Leaders
  with backstage disruption, 162–187
  in Business Model Pattern Library,
    130–131, 138–139
  with frontstage disruption, 142–161
  greenfields and case illustrations for, 141
  with profit formula disruption, 188–211
Invest (action), 22–23, 32–33, 100–101,
  114–115
Investments, 17, 52–58, 88, 102–105, 291
Investment committees, 100, 104
Invincible company(-ies), v
  becoming a, vi–ix
  business model portfolio of, 4
  culture at, 287, 308, 320
  exploration and exploitation at, 8–9
  industry boundaries for, 282–283
  portfolio management for, 49
IP Castles, 163, 165, 170–171
iPhone, 208–209
Ive, Jonathan, 274

J
Jasper Vase, Wedgwood, 171
Jaybird, 121
Jobs, Steve, 238, 274
Just-in-time supply chain, 177

K
Key activities:
  and backstage disruption, 168, 170,
    174–177, 180, 182

  in backstage driven shifts, 257, 260, 261
  on Business Model Canvas, 78–79
  of exploration vs. exploitation, 88
  and frontstage disruption, 152
  in frontstage driven shifts, 245, 248–251
  on Innovation Project Scorecard, 99
  and profit formula disruption, 192, 194,
    196, 202, 206
  in profit formula driven shifts, 268
  in value proposition shifts, 232, 233, 236,
    237, 239–241
Key partners, 78–79, 99, 184, 200, 208,
  273
Key performance indicators (KPIs), 88, 89,
  105, 328
Key resources:
  and backstage disruption, 166, 168, 170,
    177, 182, 184
  in backstage driven shifts, 256, 257, 260,
    261, 264, 265
  on Business Model Canvas, 78–79
  and frontstage disruption, 148
  in frontstage driven shifts, 245
  on Innovation Project Scorecard, 99
  in multi-pattern shifts, 276, 277
  and profit formula disruption, 192, 200
  in profit formula driven shifts, 268, 274,
    275
  in value proposition shifts, 236, 237, 239
Key trends, on Innovation Project
  Scorecard, 99
Kindle e-reader, 241
Kirschner, Uwe, 25
Kodak, 194–195, 257

Komori, Shigetaka, 122, 256
Koum, Jan, 202

L
Labor costs, 251
The Laundress, 119
Leadership, entrepreneurial, xiii, 338–339
Leadership behavior, 310
Leadership buy-in, for culture, 307
Leadership skills, developing, 336
Leadership support, 98, 312, 316–319, 344–345
Leadership time, allocation of, 316
Learning Card, 335
Learning Log, 91, 93
Learning velocity, 89
Learn step, 77, 84–85
Legitimacy, team, 314, 320–323, 330, 344–345
Levine, Uri, 166
Licensing, 182, 183
Licensors, 163, 179, 182–183
Lifebuoy, 119
Lifesize, 121
Lifetime value (LTV), 196
LinkedIn, 117
Living Proof, 119
Lock-in strategy, 158
Logitech, 120–121
Long-term customer relationships, 272
Loos, Christoph, 233
Lope, Alan, 118
Lovemark brands, 146, 201, 207
Low Cost, 189, 199, 203

Low cost—high cost pattern shifts, 227, 266–269, 281
Low-tech—high-tech pattern shifts, 227, 230, 234, 236–237, 240, 277, 280
Low touch—high touch pattern shifts, 227, 242, 247, 250–251, 280
Lufax, 64, 65

M
Ma, Peter, 62
Macroeconomic forces, 99
Management, of business, 4, 42
Margin Masters, 74, 139, 189, 204–209, 211, 213
Market disruption, 177
Market Explorers, 74, 139, 143–149, 161, 213
Market forces, 99
Marketing, 245, 248
Market orientation, team, 339
Mass market—niche market pattern shifts, 41, 227, 242–245, 278, 280
Measurement, in portfolio management, 49
Merge (action), 32–33
MESH, 107
Metered funding, 55, 105, 350
Microsoft, 116–117, 157–159, 262–263. See also specific products
Mindset, culture and, 291
Mobile citizens, 206, 207
Model 3 (Tesla), 146, 147
Model 914 (Xerox), 193
Model S (Tesla), 146
Model T (Ford), 174
Modular design and manufacturing, 180

Monetization, 192
Morita, Akio, 106
M-Pesa, 148–149
MSD Biologics Limited, 123
Multiple shift patterns, 276–277
Multi-usage resources—dedicated resources pattern shifts, 227, 254–257, 264, 276, 277, 279, 281

N
Nadella, Satya, 116, 117, 262
Natura, 155
Nespresso, 252
Nestlé, 34–35
Nestlé Skin Health, 34, 35
Netflix, 236–237
Network effects, 167, 169, 239
New ventures, Business Model Patterns for, 129
NeXT, 274
Niche market—mass market pattern shifts, 41, 227, 242–245, 278, 280
Niche markets, rise of, 253
Niche Opportunities, 18
Nintendo, 240
Nokia, 117

O
Objectives, 88, 105
Odashima, Shinji, 106
Office (Microsoft), 117
OneConnect, 64, 216–217
Open—closed innovation pattern shifts, 227, 254, 259, 262–263, 281

370

Opinions, as evidence, 84
Opportunities, 68, 96, 99
Opportunities and threats assessment, 110, 112–113
Opportunity Builders, 143, 151, 154–155
Organizational behavior, 310
Organizational culture, see Culture(s)
Organizational design:
    assessing your, 330, 344–345
    Chief Entrepreneur and staff, 322–324
    components of, 320–321
    culture blockers related to, 312
    for exploration culture, 320–331
    and responsibility for innovation, 326–327
    rewards and incentives in, 328–329
Ørsted, 276–277
Osterwalder, Alexander, 78, 79, 82–83
Outcomes (Culture Map), 295–297, 300–301, 306, 307, 311, 329
Overall cost, in Innovation Metrics, 92
Owners, value creation for, ix

P
Partner (action), 32–33, 114–115
Partner assets, 260
Partners, key, 78–79, 99, 184, 200, 208, 273
Patagonia, 176, 340
Patents, 170
Pattern Assessment Questions for Leaders, xiii, 212–221
    about backstage disruption, 164, 172, 178, 187, 213
    about frontstage disruption, 144, 150, 156, 161, 213

about profit formula disruption, 190, 198, 204, 211, 213
    examples, 214–219
    finding invent pattern with, 213, 215, 217, 219
Persevere (action), 22–23, 100–101
Pigneur, Yves, 78
Ping An Insurance (Group) Company of China, Ltd., vii, 62–65, 216, 283, 320
Pivot (action), 22–23, 92, 100–101
Pivot trajectory, 20–21, 350
Platform Castles, 163, 165, 168–169
Platform—sales pattern shifts, 227, 230, 235, 238–239, 241, 280
Polman, Paul, 118
Portfolio Actions:
    defined, 350
    Exploit portfolio, 32–33, 114–115
    Explore portfolio, 22–23, 96–105
    and Innovation Project Scorecard, 96–99
    investment/funding types, 102–105
    in portfolio management, 49, 96–105, 114–115
    selecting, from risk assessment, 100–101
    types of, 22–23, 32–33
Portfolio Funnel Quiz, 52–57
Portfolio guidance, 50–69
    and business research and development, 66–69
    defined, 349
    examples, 60–65
    in innovation practice, 334
    by investment committee, 105
    Portfolio Funnel Quiz, 52–57

in portfolio management, 49
Portfolio level, of Innovation Metrics, 89, 94–95
Portfolio management, 49–125
    assessing your, 318, 344–345
    business design loop, 72–79
    business model portfolio, 5
    as business R&D activity, 68
    and business research and development, 66–69
    death and disruption metrics for, 110–113
    enabling innovation culture with, 314, 316
    examples of, 60–65, 106–107, 116–123
    for Exploit portfolio, 12–13, 110–125
    for Explore portfolio, 12–13, 72–107
    guidance for, 50–69
    innovation metrics for, 88–95
    by investment committee, 105
    for invincible companies, 49
    Portfolio Actions, 96–105, 114–115
    Portfolio Funnel Quiz, 52–57
    Portfolio Map for, 12–13
    and testing shifts, 124–125
    test loop, 72–73, 76–77, 80–85
Portfolio Map, xiii, 4, 10–13, 42–43, 292–293, 334, 350
Poulsen, Henrik, 276
Power, team, 314, 320–323, 330, 344–345
Pragmatism, of team, 339
Predictability, with exploration vs. exploitation, 88
Premium price point, 170, 176, 251
Premium service, 196, 197
Pricing power, at Zara, 175

Prius (Toyota), 147
Process management, 314, 332, 342, 344–345
Product—recurring service pattern shifts, 227, 230–233, 278, 280
Profitability, at CitizenM, 205, 206
Profit Engines, 29
Profit formula disruption, 188–211
    assessment questions about, 211, 213
    for Cost Differentiators, 198–203
    defined, 74, 138, 189
    on disruption risk assessment, 111, 113
    for Margin Masters, 204–209
    for Revenue Differentiators, 190–197
    types of, 139
Profit formula driven shifts, 266–279
    conventional—contrarian, 271, 274–275
    defined, 266
    high cost—low cost, 267–269
    with multiple shift patterns, 276–277
    product—recurring service, 278
    strategic reflections for leaders about, 267, 270, 271, 281
    testing, 125
    transactional—recurring revenue, 270, 272–273
    types of, 227
Project duration, in Innovation Metrics, 92
Promising Concepts, 18
Protect phase, 30–31
Prototyping resources, 316

Q

Qrio, 106
Questioning, pattern-based, 133

R

Ragu, 119
Randolph, Marc, 236
Reality Check stage, 20–21
Recurring revenue, 192–194
Recurring Revenue, 189, 191–193
Recurring service—product pattern shifts, 227, 230–233, 278, 280
Recurring—transactional revenue pattern shifts, 227, 266, 270, 272–273, 277, 281
Red Hat, 181
Reinvention, vii, 4
Relationships, customer, see Customer relationships
Relentlessness, 338
Repurposers, 143, 145, 148–149
Research and development (R&D), 66–69, 170, 182, 262, 263
Resilience, 62, 338
Resource allocation, 314, 316, 318, 344–345
Resource Castles, 74, 139, 164–171, 187, 213
Resource Dodgers, 189, 199–201
Resources, key, see Key resources
Retire (action), 22–23, 41, 100–101
Return:
    and death and disruption risk, 28–29
    defined, 11, 350
    expected, 10, 11, 18–19, 72, 349
    on EXPLOIT Portfolio Map, 10, 11
    for EXPLORE portfolio, 103
    on investments, 52–57
Revenue Differentiators, 74, 139, 189–197, 211, 213

Revenues, on Innovation Project Scorecard, 99
Revenue streams:
    and backstage disruption, 170, 174, 176, 177, 182
    in backstage driven shifts, 257, 261
    on Business Model Canvas, 78–79
    and frontstage disruption, 148, 154, 158
    in frontstage driven shifts, 249, 251
    in multi-pattern shifts, 277
    and profit formula disruption, 192, 194, 196
    in profit formula driven shifts, 272, 273, 275
    in value proposition shifts, 237, 239, 241
Rewards, 291, 314, 320, 328–330, 344–345
Rising Stars, 18, 29, 73
Risk. See also specific types
    as key performance indicator, 89
    reduction of, 92, 96, 98–99
Risk tolerance, of team, 339
Roadster (Tesla), 146
Rolls-Royce Civil Aerospace, 278
Royalties, 183

S

Safaricom, 148
Safe Plays, 18
Salek Pro Flight, 121
Salesforce.com, 218–219
Sales—platform pattern shifts, 227, 230, 235, 238–239, 241, 280
Sales value proposition, 272
Sasson, Steven, 195

Scale phase, 30–31, 337
Scalers, 74, 139, 163, 178–185, 187, 213
Scaling, 182, 184
Schmidt's Natural, 119
Schneider, Ulf Mark, 34
Search, 9, 12, 13, 20–21, 290, 350
Sears, Roebuck and Co., 149–150
Secondary airports, use of, 203
Senior leaders, xiii, 42, 66–67, 298–301
Service provisioning, 260
Seventh Generation, 119
Shabtai, Ehud, 166
Sharing economy, 201
Sheets, Donald, 269
Shift patterns, 226–283
    with backstage driven shifts, 254–265
    in Business Model Pattern Library, 125,
        130–131, 226–227
    and business models, 228–229
    with frontstage driven shifts, 242–253
    for invincible companies, 282–283
    with profit formula driven shifts, 266–279
    strategic reflections for leaders about,
        280–281
    with value proposition shifts, 230–241
Shift & Reemergence phase, 30–31
Shinar, Amir, 166
Skills:
    core business, 316
    development of, 314, 332, 336–337
    managerial vs. innovation, 328
Skippy, 119
Slimfast, 119
Smart Electric cars, 147

Smartphone industry, 183, 202
Sneakers, exclusive releases, 253
Society, value creation for, ix
Software, 147, 158
Sony Group, 106, 116
Sony Startup Accelerator Program (SSAP),
    106–107
Speed Masters, 163, 173, 175
Spending, on innovation, 68
Spinout (action), 22–23, 100–101
Spotify, 196–197, 340
SRE Holdings, 107
Stable Contributors, 29
Standardization, 203, 206, 250
Starbucks, 34, 35
Stickiness Scalers, 143, 157–159
Strategic direction, 50, 62, 116, 118, 120,
    122
Strategic fit, 96–98
Strategic guidance, 50–51, 314, 316, 318,
    344–345
Strategy&, 68
Strategyzer Innovation Metrics, see
    Innovation Metrics
Strengths and weaknesses assessment,
    110–111
Subscriptions, 193, 196
Subsidizers, 189, 191, 197
Success, in exploration vs. exploitation
    culture, 291
Sun Media Group, 341
Superglue Makers, 143, 157, 159
Sustainability, at Unilever, 118–119
Sustainability Masters, 163, 173, 176

Sustaining innovation, 39, 327
Sweet Earth, 34, 35

T
tails.com, 34, 35
Tan, Jessica, 64
Team, value creation for, ix. See also
    Innovation teams
Team Alignment Map, 334, 350
Technologists, 189, 199, 202–203
Technology, in business R&D, 66
TED, 244–245
10x Rule of Thumb, 105
Tencent, 283
Tesla Motors, 146–147
Test Card, 335
Testing, 17, 20–21, 68, 124–125, 327, 335,
    336, 350
Testing and Innovation Metrics, xiii
Testing Business Ideas (Bland and
    Osterwalder), 82–83
Testing loop, 72–73, 76–77, 80–85
TG Tips, 119
Time, allocation of, 316
Time spent, as KPI, 89
Toyama Chemical, 123
Toyota Motor Corporation, 341
Transactional—recurring revenue pattern
    shifts, 227, 266, 270, 272–273, 277, 281
Transfer (action), 22–23, 41, 51, 100–101, 107
Transformative innovation, 39, 133, 327
Transparency, 44
Trends, 99, 175
Tupper, Earl, 154

Tupperware, 154–155
Turnaround time, 203
23andMe, 264, 340
Two-sided network effects, 169

U
Uncertainty, 8, 83, 89, 291, 327
Unilever, 118–119
Upstarts, 134–135
User Base Castles, 163, 165–167

V
Validation stage, 20–21, 83, 105, 337
Value chain activities, 239
Value creation, viii–ix
Value proposition, 78–79
   adapting, in business R&D, 68
   and backstage disruption, 166, 168, 170,
      174–176, 180, 182, 184
   in backstage driven shifts, 256, 257, 262,
      263
   and frontstage disruption, 146, 147, 152,
      154
   on innovation journey, 17
   on Innovation Project Scorecard, 98
   in multi-pattern shifts, 277
   and profit formula disruption, 192, 194,
      200, 202, 206, 208

in profit formula driven shifts, 269,
   272–275
in value proposition shifts, 232, 233,
   236–241
Value Proposition Canvas, 76, 79, 335, 336
Value Proposition Design (Osterwalder,
   et al.), 79
Value proposition shifts, 230–241
   defined, 230
   low-tech—high-tech, 234, 236–237
   from low-tech to high-tech, 240
   product—recurring service, 231–233
   sales—platform, 235, 238–239
   from sales to platform, 241
   strategic reflections for leaders about,
      230, 234, 235, 280
   testing, 125
   types of, 227
Values, in exploration vs. exploitation
   culture, 291
Variable cost structure, 261
Venture capital investments, 54–55,
   102–105
Viability hypothesis, 80–81
Viability risk, 19, 99, 350
Viki, Tenday, 314
Visionaries, 143, 145–147
Visualization, 4, 42

W
Walt Disney Company, 265
Wang Tao, 65
Washington Post, 278
Waze, 166–167
Wedgwood, 171
Wedgwood, Josiah, 171
WhatsApp, 202–203
Wii (Nintendo), 240
WiL, 106
Windows (Microsoft), 116, 117, 158–159
Wise, Brownie, 154
Wish-Bone, 119
W.L. Gore, 40–41, 279

X
Xbox (Microsoft), 159
Xerox, 123, 192–193
Xiameter, 268–269

Y
Yang Lan, 341
Yinlu, 34, 35

Z
Zara, 175

Acknowledgments

This book would have been impossible to create without the love and support of our families, the Strategyzer team, the thinkers who inspired us, the practitioners who get things done, and everybody who gave us feedback.

We want to thank the core team who contributed to the book content and design, namely Lauren Cantor, Matt Woodward, and Erin McPhee.

A special thanks goes to all the thinkers and authors who inspired us, who we built upon, and many of whom gave us feedback. We'd like to particularly thank Dave Gray, Steve Blank, Rita McGrath, Roger Martin, Henry Chesbrough, Luis Felipe Cisneros Martinez, Scott Anthony, Bill Fischer, Saul Kaplan, and Marshall Goldsmith.

Several business and innovation leaders have taken time out of their agenda to contribute directly to case studies, namely Amy Calhoun, Bracken Darrell, Christoph Loos, Dave Liss, François-Henry Bennahmias, Uwe Kirschner, and Shinji Odashima.

The entire Strategyzer team has helped make this book possible and many projects had to take a step back to get this book done. The Strategyzer Advisory Team has put a particular effort into testing parts of the book. We thank Tendayi Viki, Shamira Miller, Paris Thomas, Greg Bernarda, Christian Doll, and Michael Wilkens.

We also thank the general community of Strategyzer coaches and innovation practitioners who helped test content, namely, Caroline Baumgart, Pete Cohen, Tim Daniel, Josie Gibson, John Hibble, and Nick Rakis.

We'd like to thank the executives who took time out of their agenda to test book content, namely, Sally Bateman, Vincent Besnard, Thierry Bonetto, Baudouin Corman, Carol Corzo, Eglantine Etiemble, Jay Jayamaran, Andrew Jenkin, Kate Koch, Tim Regan, Michel de Rovira, and Henning Trill.

Last but not least, we'd like to thank the entire Wiley team that has published all the books in the Strategyzer series, in particular, Richard Narramore, who took us on with *Business Model Generation*.

AUTHOR

Alex Osterwalder

Founder, Speaker, Business Thinker

Alex is a leading author, entrepreneur and in-demand speaker whose work has changed the way established companies do business and how new ventures get started. Ranked No. 4 of the top 50 management thinkers worldwide Alex also holds the Thinkers50 Strategy Award. Together with Yves Pigneur he invented the Business Model Canvas, Value Proposition Canvas, and Business Portfolio Map—practical tools that are trusted by millions of business practitioners.

@AlexOsterwalder
strategyzer.com/blog

COAUTHOR

Yves Pigneur

Professor, Business Thinker

Yves has been a professor at the University of Lausanne since 1984, and has held visiting professorships at Georgia State University, University of British Columbia, National University of Singapore, and HEC Montreal. Together with Alex Osterwalder, he invented the Business Model Canvas and co-authored the international bestselling books *Business Model Generation* and *Value Proposition Design*. Yves and Alex are ranked No. 4 among the Thinkers50's Most Influential Management Thinkers in the world and hold the Thinkers50 Strategy Award.

COAUTHOR

Fred Etiemble

Executive Advisor, Implementer

Fred is an executive advisor on strategy and innovation. He works with courageous leaders on how to develop an innovation culture, explore new growth engines, and transform their businesses. He has been working with or in large organizations for more than 20 years and knows their challenges from the inside. Fred co-creates tools and methodologies for strategy and innovation with other business thinkers and facilitates regular trainings on how to use them in Europe and Asia. Fred has been an associate at Strategyzer since 2017.

fredericetiemble.com

COAUTHOR
Alan Smith
Founder, Explorer, Designer

Alan uses his curiousity and creativity to ask questions and turn the answers into simple, visual, practical tools. He believes that the right tools give people confidence to aim high and build big meaningful things.

He cofounded Strategyzer with Alex Osterwalder, where he works with an inspired team to build great products. Strategyzer's books, tools, and services are used by leading companies around the world.

strategyzer.com

DESIGNER
Chris White
Designer, Art Director

Chris is a multidisciplinary designer who lives in Toronto. He has spent his time working on a number of business publications in various roles, most recently as Assistant Art Director at *The Globe and Mail,* focusing on presentation design for both print and online stories.

This is the first book he has collaborated on with the Stategyzer team.

DESIGNER
Trish Papadakos
Designer, Photographer, Creator

Trish holds a Master's in Design from Central St. Martins in London and a Bachelor's of Design from the York Sheridan Joint Program in Toronto.

She has taught design at her alma mater, worked with award-winning agencies, launched several businesses, and is collaborating for the fifth time with Strategyzer.

@trishpapadakos

CONTENT LEAD
Lucy Luo
Advisor, Problem Solver

Lucy is an innovation advisor to organizations large and small, helping them ideate and launch new products to seek breakthrough growth. She enjoys working with multinationals to build out and implement their innovation strategies as well as early-stage start-ups across Europe and Asia.

Lucy has a passion for addressing social and sustainability challenges through the use of innovation toolkits and has worked with a number of not-for-profit and social enterprise organizations such as the United Nations, the Atlantic Council, and World Economic Forum Global Shapers.

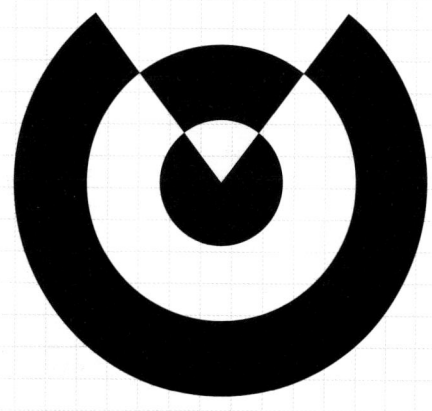

Strategyzer uses the best of
technology and coaching to
support your transformation
and growth challenges.

Discover what we can do
for you at Strategyzer.com

Create Change

Build skills at scale with the Strategyzer Cloud Academy course library and online coaching.

Mastering value propositions, mastering business models, mastering business testing, mastering culture, and mastering team alignment.

Create Growth

Systematize and scale your growth efforts, innovation culture, and business portfolio.

Innovation culture readiness assessment, growth strategy, growth funnel design and implementation, innovation management, coaching, and innovation metrics.

Business Model Generation

Business Model Generation

A Handbook for Visionaries, Game Changers, and Challengers

Written by
Alexander Osterwalder and Yves Pigneur

Design
Alan Smith, The Movement

Editor and Contributing Co-Author
Tim Clark

Production
Patrick van der Pijl

Co-created by an amazing crowd of
470 practitioners from 45 countries

WILEY

John Wiley & Sons, Inc.

Co-created by:

Ellen Di Resta	Matthew Milan	Karen Hembrough	Frank Camille Lagerveld	Peter Froberg	Jeroen de Jong
Michael Anton Dila	Ralf Beuker	Ronald Pilot	Andres Alcalde	Lino Piani	Gertjan Verstoep
Remko Vochteloo	Sander Smit	Yves Claude Aubert	Alvaro Villalobos M	Eric Jackson	Steven Devijver
Victor Lombardi	Norbert Herman	Wim Saly	Bernard Racine	Indrajit Datta Chaudhuri	Jana Thiel
Jeremy Hayes	Atanas Zaprianov	Woutergort	Pekka Matilainen	Martin Fanghanel	Walter Brand
Alf Rehn	Linus Malmberg	Fanco Ivan Santos Negrelli	Bas van Oosterhout	Michael Sandfær	Stephan Ziegenhorn
Jeff De Cagna	Deborah Mills-Scofield	Amee Shah	Gillian Hunt	Niall Casey	Frank Meeuwsen
Andrea Mason	Peter Knol	Lars Mårtensson	Bart Boone	John McGuire	Colin Henderson
Jan Ondrus	Jess McMullin	Kevin Donaldson	Michael Moriarty	Vivian Vendeirinho	Danilo Tic
Simon Evenblij	Marianela Ledezma	JD Stein	Mike	Martèl Bakker Schut	Marco Raaijmakers
Chris Walters	Ray Guyot	Ralf de Graaf	Design for Innovation	Stefano Mastrogiacoo	Marc Sniukas
Caspar van Rijnbach	Martin Andres Giorgetti	Lars Norrman	Tom Corcoran	Mark Hickman	Khaled Algasem
benmlih	Geert van Vlijmen	Sergey Trikhachev	Ari Wurmann	Dibrov	Jan Pelttari
Rodrigo Miranda	Rasmus Rønholt	Thomas	Antonio Robert	Reinhold König	Yves Sinner
Saul Kaplan	Tim Clark	Alfred Herman	Wibe van der Pol	Marcel Jaeggi	Michael Kinder
Lars Geisel	Richard Bell	Bert Spangenberg	paola valeri	John O'Connell	Vince Kuraitis
Simon Scott	Erwin Blom	Robert van Kooten	Michael Sommers	Javier Ibarra	Teofilo Asuan Santiago IV
Dimitri Lévita	Frédéric Sidler	Hans Suter	Nicolas Fleury	Lytton He	Ray Lai
Johan fflñrneblad	John LM Kiggundu	Wolf Schumacher	Gert Steens	Marije Sluis	Brainstorm Weekly
Craig Sadler	Robert Elm	Bill Welter	Jose Sebastian Palazuelos	David Edwards	Huub Raemakers
Praveen Singh	Ziv Baida	Michele Leidi	Lopez	Martin Kuplens-Ewart	Peter Salmon
Livia Labate	Andra Larin-van der Pijl	Asim J. Ranjha	jorge zavala	Jay Goldman	Philippe
Kristian Salvesen	Eirik V Johnsen	Peter Troxler	Harry Heijligers	Isckia	Khawaja M.
Daniel Egger	Boris Fritscher	Ola Dagberg	Armand Dickey	Nabil Harfoush	Jille Sol
Diogo Carmo	Mike Lachapelle	Wouter van der Burg	Jason King	Yannick	Renninger, Wolfgang
Marcel Ott	Albert Meige	Artur Schmidt	Kjartan Mjoesund	Raoef Hussainali	Daniel Pandza
Guilhem Bertholet	Pablo M. Ramírez	Slabber	Louis Rosenfeld	ronald van den hoff	Robin Uchida
Thibault Estier	Jean-Loup	Peter Jones	Ivo Georgiev	Melbert Visscher	Pius Bienz
Stephane Rey	Colin Pons	Sebastian Ullrich	Donald Chapin	Manfred Fischer	Ivan Torreblanca
Chris Peasner	Vacherand	Andrew Pope	Annie Shum	Joe Chao	Berry Vetjens
Jonathan Lin	Guillermo Jose Aguilar	Fredrik Eliasson	Valentin Crettaz	Carlos Meca	David Crow
Cesar Picos	Adriel Haeni	Bruce MacVarish	Dave Crowther	Mario Morales	Helge Hannisdal
Florian	Lukas Prochazka	Göran Hagert	Chris J Davis	Paul Johannesson	Maria Droujkova
Armando Maldonado	Kim Korn	Markus Gander	Frank Della Rosa	Rob Griffitts	Leonard Belanger
Eduardo Míguez	Abdullah Nadeem	Marc Castricum	Christian Schüller	Marc-Antoine Garrigue	Fernando Saenz-Marrero
Anouar Hamidouche	Rory O'Connor	Nicholas K. Niemann	Luis Eduardo de Carvalho	Wassili Bertoen	Susan Foley
Francisco Perez	Hubert de Candé	Christian Labezin	Patrik Ekström	Bart Pieper	Vesela Koleva
Nicky Smyth	Frans Wittenberg	Claudio D'Ipolitto	Greg Krauska	Bruce E. Terry	Martijn
Bob Dunn	Jonas Lindelöf	Aurel Hosennen	Giorgio Casoni	Michael N. Wilkens	Eugen Rodel
Carlo Arioli	Gordon Gray	Adrian Zaugg	Stef Silvis	Himikel - TrebeA	Edward Giesen

Marc Faltheim	Ricardo Dorado	Stephan Linnenbank	Jose Alfonso Lopez	Edwin Beumer	Manuel Toscano
Nicolas De Santis	John Smith	Liliana	Eric Schreurs	Dax Denneboom	John Sutherland
Antoine Perruchoud	Rod	Jose Fernando Quintana	Donielle Buie	Mohammed Mushtaq	Remo Knops
Bernd Nurnberger	Eddie	Reinhard Prügl	Adilson Chicória	Gaurav Bhalla	Juan Marquez
Patrick van Abbema	Jeffrey Huang	Brian Moore	Asanka Warusevitane	Silvia Adelhelm	Chris Hopf
Terje Sand	Terrance Moore	Gabi	Jacob Ravn	Heather McGowan	Marc Faeh
Leandro Jesus	nse_55	Marko Seppänen	Hampus Jakobsson	Phil Sang Yim	Urquhart Wood
Karen Davis	Leif-Arne Bakker	Erwin Fielt	Adriaan Kik	Noel Barry	Lise Tormod
Tim Turmelle	Edler Herbert	Olivier Glassey	Julián Domínguez Laperal	Vishwanath	Curtis L. Sippel
Anders Sundelin	Björn Kijl	Francisco Conde	Marco W J Derksen	Edavayyanamath	Abdul Razak Manaf
Renata Phillippi	Chris Finlay	Fernández	Dr. Karsten Willrodt	Rob Manson	George B. Steltman
Martin Kaczynski	Philippe Rousselot	Valérie Chanal	Patrick Feiner	Rafael Figueiredo	Karl Burrow
Frank	Rob Schokker	Anne McCrossan	Dave Cutherell	Jeroen Mulder	Mark McKeever
Bala Vaddi	Wouter Verwer	Larsen	Di Prisco	Emilio De Giacomo	Linda Bryant
Andrew Jenkins	Jan Schmiedgen	Fred Collopy	Darlene Goetzman	Franco Gasperoni	Jeroen Hinfelaar
Dariush Ghatan	Ugo Merkli	Jana Görs	Mohan Nadarajah	Michael Weiss	Dan Keldsen
Marcus Ambrosch	Jelle	Patrick Foran	Fabrice Delaye	Francisco Andrade	Damien
Jens Hoffmann	Dave Gray	Edward Osborn	Sunil Malhotra	Arturo Herrera Sapunar	Roger A. Shepherd
Steve Thomson	Rick le Roy	Greger Hagström	Jasper Bouwsma	Vincent de Jong	Morten Povlsen
Eduardo M Morgado	Ravila White	Alberto Saavedra	Ouke Arts	Kees Groeneveld	Lars Zahl
Rafal Dudkowski	David G Luna Arellano	Remco de Kramer	Alexander Troitzsch	Henk Bohlander	Elin Mørch Langlo
António Lucena de Faria	Joyce Hostyn	Lillian Thompson	Brett Patching	Sushil Chatterji	Xuemei Tian
Knut Petter Nor	Thorwald Westmaas	Howard Brown	Clifford Thompson	Tim Parsey	Harry Verwayen
Ventenat Vincent	Jason Theodor	Emil Ansarov	Jorgen Dahlberg	Georg E. A. Stampfl	Riccardo Bonazzi
Peter Eckrich	Sandra Pickering	Frank Elbers	Christoph Mühlethaler	Markus Kreutzer	André Johansen
Shridhar Lolla	Trond M Fflòvstegaard	Horacio Alvaro Viana	Ernest Buise	Iwan Schneider	Colin Bush
Jens Larsson	Jeaninne Horowitz Gassol	Markus Schroll	Alfonso Mireles	Michael Schuster	Alexander Korbee
David Sibbet	Lukas Feuerstein	Hylke Zeijlstra	Richard Zandink	Ingrid Beck	J Bartels
Mihail Krikunov	Nathalie Magniez	Cheenu Srinivasan	Fraunhofer IAO	Antti Äkräs	Steven Ritchey
Edwin Kruis	Giorgio Pauletto	Cyril Durand	Tor Rolfsen Grønsund	EHJ Peet	Clark Golestani
Roberto Ortelli	Martijn Pater	Jamil Aslam	David M. Weiss	Ronald Poulton	Leslie Cohen
Shana Ferrigan Bourcier	Gerardo Pagalday Eraña	Oliver Buecken	Kim Peiter Jørgensen	Ralf Weidenhammer	Amanda Smith
Jeffrey Murphy	Haider Raza	John Wesner Price	Stephanie Diamond	Craig Rispin	Benjamin De Pauw
Lonnie Sanders III	Ajay Ailawadhi	Axel Friese	Stefan Olsson	Nella van Heuven	Andre Macieira
Arnold Wytenburg	Adriana Ieraci	Gudmundur Kristjansson	Anders Stølan	Ravi Sodhi	Wiebe de Jager
David Hughes	Daniël Giesen	Rita Shor	Edward Koops	Dick Rempt	Raym Crow
Paul Ferguson	Erik Dejonghe	Jesus Villar	Prasert Thawat-	Rolf Mehnert	Mark Evans DM
Frontier Service Design, LLC	Tom Winstanley	Espen Figenschou- Skotterud	chokethawee	Luis Stabile	Susan Schaper
	Heiner P. Kaufmann		Pablo Azar	Enterprise Consulting	
Peter Noteboom	Edwin Lee Ming Jin	James Clark	Melissa Withers	Aline Frankfort	

Are you an entrepreneurial spirit?

yes ———— no ————

Are you constantly thinking about how to create value and build new businesses, or how to improve or transform your organization?

yes ———— no ————

Are you trying to find innovative ways of doing business to replace old, outdated ones?

yes ———— no ————

If you've answered "yes" to any of these questions, welcome to our group!

You're holding a handbook for visionaries, game changers, and challengers striving to defy outmoded business models and design tomorrow's enterprises. It's a book for the business model generation.

Today countless innovative business models are emerging. Entirely new industries are forming as old ones crumble. Upstarts are challenging the old guard, some of whom are struggling feverishly to reinvent themselves.

How do you imagine your organization's business model might look two, five, or ten years from now? Will you be among the dominant players? Will you face competitors brandishing formidable new business models?

This book will give you deep insight into the nature of business models. It describes traditional and bleeding-edge models and their dynamics, innovation techniques, how to position your model within an intensely competitive landscape, and how to lead the redesign of your own organization's business model.

Certainly you've noticed that this is not the typical strategy or management book. We designed it to convey the essentials of what you need to know, quickly, simply, and in a visual format. Examples are presented pictorially and the content is complemented with exercises and workshop scenarios you can use immediately. Rather than writing a conventional book about business model innovation, we've tried to design a practical guide for visionaries, game changers, and challengers eager to design or reinvent business models. We've also worked hard to create a beautiful book to enhance the pleasure of your "consumption." We hope you enjoy using it as much as we've enjoyed creating it.

An online community complements this book (and was integral to its creation, as you will discover later). Since business model innovation is a rapidly evolving field, you may want to go beyond the essentials in *Business Model Generation* and discover new tools online. Please consider joining our worldwide community of business practitioners and researchers who have co-created this book. On the Hub you can participate in discussions about business models, learn from others' insights, and try out new tools provided by the authors. Visit the Business Model Hub at www.BusinessModelGeneration.com/hub.

Business model innovation is hardly new. When the founders of Diners Club introduced the credit card in 1950, they were practicing business model innovation. The same goes for Xerox, when it introduced photocopier leasing and the per-copy payment system in 1959. In fact, we might trace business model innovation all the way back to the fifteenth century, when Johannes Gutenberg sought applications for the mechanical printing device he had invented.

But the scale and speed at which innovative business models are transforming industry landscapes today is unprecedented. For entrepreneurs, executives, consultants, and academics, it is high time to understand the impact of this extraordinary evolution. Now is the time to understand and to methodically address the challenge of business model innovation.

Ultimately, business model innovation is about creating value, for companies, customers, and society. It is about replacing outdated models. With its iPod digital media player and iTunes.com online store, Apple created an innovative new business model that transformed the company into the dominant force in online music. Skype brought us dirt-cheap global calling rates and free Skype-to-Skype calls with an innovative business model built on so-called peer-to-peer technology. It is now the world's largest carrier of international voice traffic. Zipcar frees city dwellers from automobile ownership by offering hourly or daily on-demand car rentals under a fee-based membership system. It's a business model response to emerging user needs and pressing environmental concerns. Grameen Bank is helping alleviate poverty through an innovative business model that popularized microlending to the poor.

But how can we systematically invent, design, and implement these powerful new business models? How can we question, challenge, and transform old, outmoded ones? How can we turn visionary ideas into game-changing business models that challenge the establishment—or rejuvenate it if we ourselves are the incumbents? *Business Model Generation* aims to give you the answers.

Since practicing is better than preaching, we adopted a new model for writing this book. Four hundred and seventy members of the Business Model Innovation Hub contributed cases, examples, and critical comments to the manuscript—and we took their feedback to heart. Read more about our experience in the final chapter of *Business Model Generation*.

Seven Faces of Business Model Innovation

The Senior Executive

Jean-Pierre Cuoni,

Chairman / EFG International

Focus: Establish a new business model in an old industry

Jean-Pierre Cuoni is chairman of EFG International, a private bank with what may be the industry's most innovative business model. With EFG he is profoundly transforming the traditional relationships between bank, clients, and client relationship managers. Envisioning, crafting, and executing an innovative business model in a conservative industry with established players is an art, and one that has placed EFG International among the fastest growing banks in its sector.

The Intrapreneur

Dagfinn Myhre,

Head of R&I Business Models / Telenor

Focus: Help exploit the latest techno-logical developments with the right business models

Dagfinn leads a business model unit at Telenor, one of the world's ten larg-est mobile telephone operators. The telecom sector demands continuous innovation, and Dagfinn's initiatives help Telenor identify and understand sustainable models that exploit the potential of the latest technological developments. Through deep analysis of key industry trends, and by develop-ing and using leading-edge analytical tools, Dagfinn's team explores new business concepts and opportunities.

The Entrepreneur

Mariëlle Sijgers,

Entrepreneur / CDEF Holding BV

Focus: Address unsatisfied customer needs and build new business models around them

Marielle Sijgers is a full-fledged entrepreneur. Together with her business partner, Ronald van den Hoff, she's shaking up the meeting, congress, and hospitality industry with innovative business models. Led by unsatisfied customer needs, the pair has invented new concepts such as Seats2meet.com, which allows on-the-fly booking of meetings in untraditional locations. Together, Sijgers and van den Hoff constantly play with new business model ideas and launch the most promising concepts as new ventures.

The Investor

Gert Steens, President & Investment Analyst / Oblonski BV

Focus: Invest in companies with the most competitive business models

Gert makes a living by identifying the best business models. Investing in the wrong company with the wrong model could cost his clients millions of euros and him his reputation. Understanding new and innovative business models has become a crucial part of his work. He goes far beyond the usual financial analytics and compares business models to spot strategic differences that may impart a competitive edge. Gert is constantly seeking business model innovations.

The Consultant

Bas van Oosterhout, Senior Consultant / Capgemini Consulting

Focus: Help clients question their business models, and envision and build new ones

Bas is part of Capgemini's Business Innovation Team. Together with his clients, he is passionate about boosting performance and renewing competitiveness through innovation. Business Model Innovation is now a core component of his work because of its high relevance to client projects. His aim is to inspire and assist clients with new business models, from ideation to implementation. To achieve this, Bas draws on his understanding of the most powerful business models, regardless of industry.

The Designer

Trish Papadakos, Sole Proprietor / The Institute of You

Focus: Find the right business model to launch an innovative product

Trish is a talented young designer who is particularly skilled at grasping an idea's essence and weaving it into client communications. Currently she's working on one of her own ideas, a service that helps people who are transitioning between careers. After weeks of in-depth research, she's now tackling the design. Trish knows she'll have to figure out the right business model to bring her service to market. She understands the client-facing part—that's what she works on daily as a designer. But, since she lacks formal business education, she needs the vocabulary and tools to take on the big picture.

The Conscientious Entrepreneur

Iqbal Quadir, Social Entrepreneur / Founder of Grameen Phone

Focus: Bring about positive social and economic change through innovative business models

Iqbal is constantly on the lookout for innovative business models with the potential for profound social impact. His transformative model brought telephone service to over 100 million Bangladeshis, utilizing Grameen Bank's microcredit network. He is now searching for a new model for bringing affordable electricity to the poor. As the head of MIT's Legatum Center, he promotes technological empowerment through innovative businesses as a path to economic and social development.

Table of Contents

The book is divided into five sections: ❶ The Business Model Canvas, a tool for describing, analyzing, and designing business models, ❷ Business Model Patterns, based on concepts from leading business thinkers, ❸ Techniques to help you design business models, ❹ Re-interpreting strategy through the business model lens, and ❺ A generic process to help you design innovative business models, tying together all the concepts, techniques, and tools in *Business Model Generation*. ⬤ The last section offers an outlook on five business model topics for future exploration. ◯ Finally, the afterword provides a peek into "the making of" *Business Model Generation*.

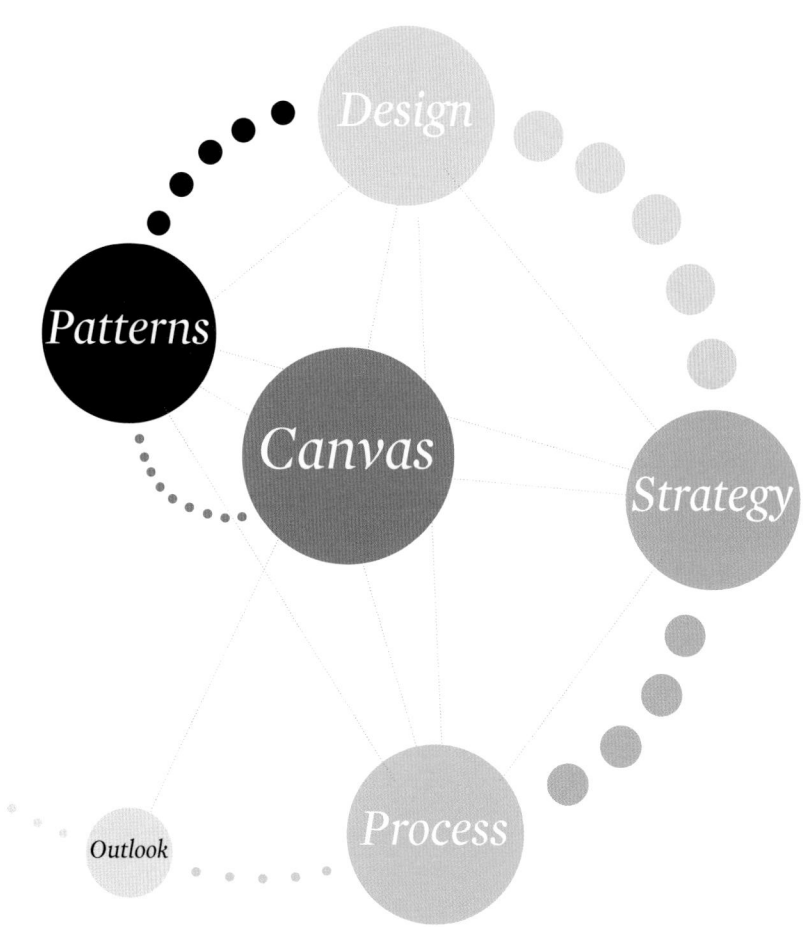

Design

Patterns

Canvas

Strategy

Afterword

Outlook

Process

❶ Canvas

14   Definition of a Business Model

16   The 9 Building Blocks

44   The Business Model Canvas

❷ Patterns

56   Unbundling Business Models

66   The Long Tail

76   Multi-Sided Platforms

88   FREE as a Business Model

108   Open Business Models

❸ Design

126   Customer Insights

134   Ideation

146   Visual Thinking

160   Prototyping

170   Storytelling

180   Scenarios

❹ Strategy

200   Business Model Environment

212   Evaluating Business Models

226   Business Model Perspective on Blue Ocean Strategy

232   Managing Multiple Business Models

❺ Process

244   Business Model Design Process

◉ Outlook

262   Outlook

○ Afterword

274   Where did this book come from?

276   References

Car

vas

The Business Model Canvas

A shared language for describing, visualizing, assessing, and changing business models

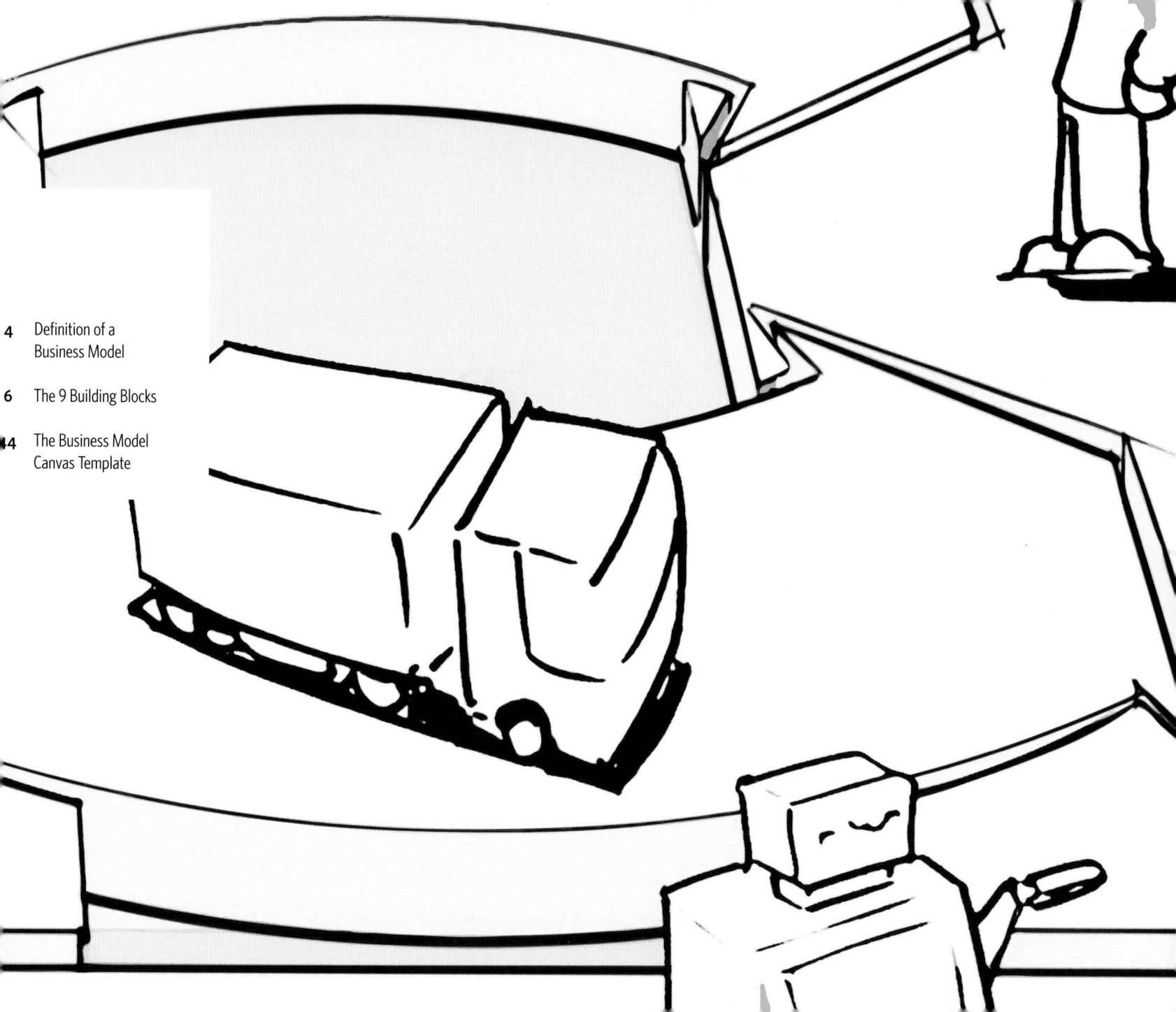

4   Definition of a
    Business Model

6   The 9 Building Blocks

44 The Business Model
    Canvas Template

Def_Business Model

A business model describes
the rationale of how an
organization creates, delivers,
and captures value

The starting point for any good discussion, meeting, or workshop on business model innovation should be a shared understanding of what a business model actually is. We need a business model concept that everybody understands: one that facilitates description and discussion. We need to start from the same point and talk about the same thing. The challenge is that the concept must be simple, relevant, and intuitively understandable, while not oversimplifying the complexities of how enterprises function.

In the following pages we offer a concept that allows you to describe and think through the business model of your organization, your competitors, or any other enterprise. This concept has been applied and tested around the world and is already used in organizations such as IBM, Ericsson, Deloitte, the Public Works and Government Services of Canada, and many more.

This concept can become a shared language that allows you to easily describe and manipulate business models to create new strategic alternatives. Without such a shared language it is difficult to systematically challenge assumptions about one's business model and innovate successfully.

We believe a business model can best be described through nine basic building blocks that show the logic of how a company intends to make money. The nine blocks cover the four main areas of a business: customers, offer, infrastructure, and financial viability. The business model is like a blueprint for a strategy to be implemented through organizational structures, processes, and systems.

The 9 Building Blocks

CS

1 Customer Segments

An organization serves one or several Customer Segments.

VP

2 Value Propositions

It seeks to solve customer problems and satisfy customer needs with value propositions.

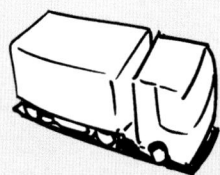

CH

3 Channels

Value propositions are delivered to customers through communication, distribution, and sales Channels.

CR

4 Customer Relationships

Customer relationships are established and maintained with each Customer Segment.

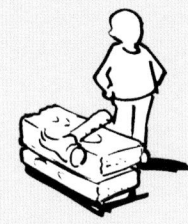

RS

Revenue Streams

Revenue streams result from value propositions successfully offered to customers.

KR 6

Key Resources

Key resources are the assets required to offer and deliver the previously described elements …

KA 7

Key Activities

… by performing a number of Key Activities.

KP 8

Key Partnerships

Some activities are outsourced and some resources are acquired outside the enterprise.

CS 9

Cost Structure

The business model elements result in the cost structure.

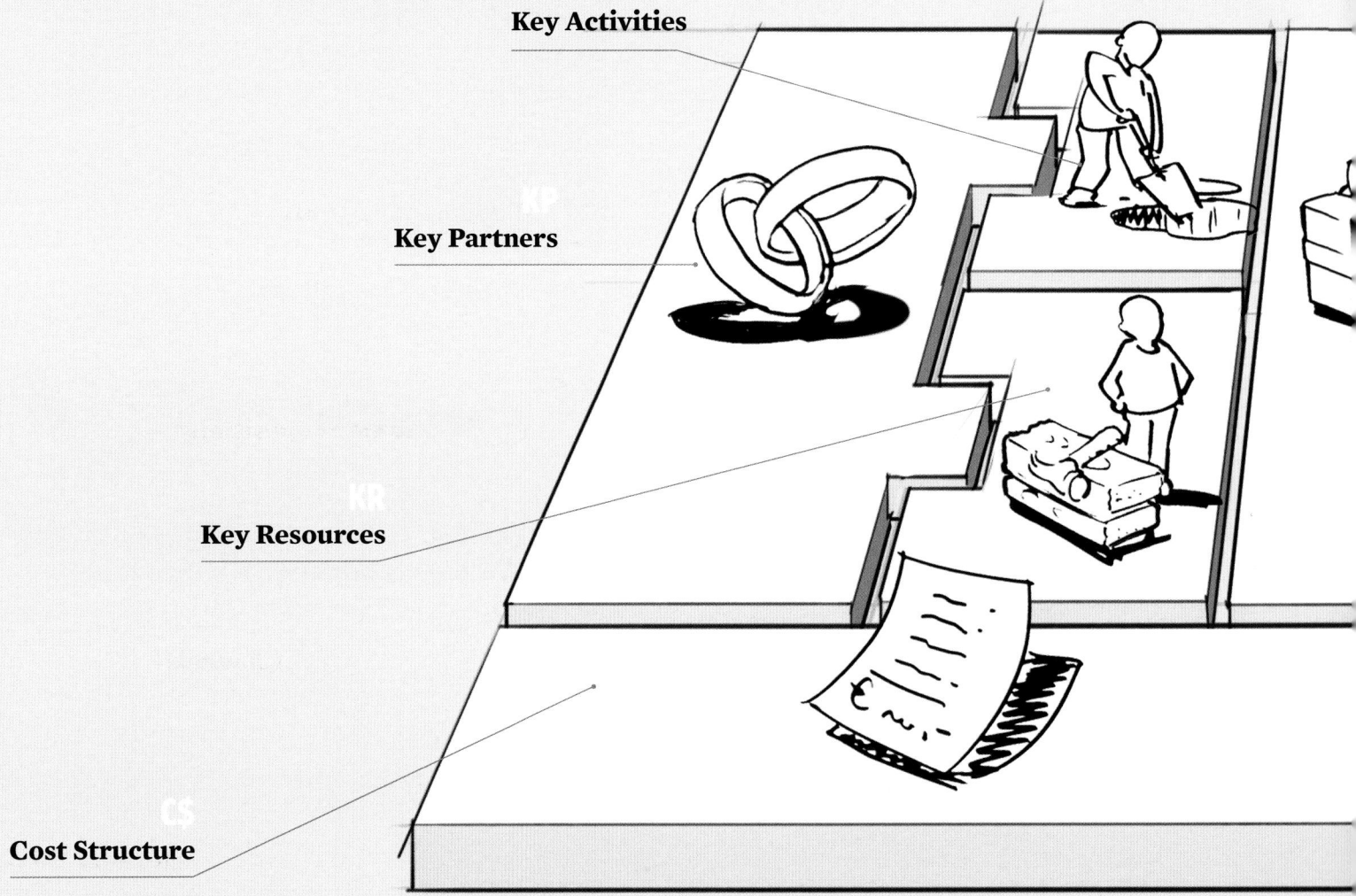

Key Activities

KA

KP

Key Partners

KR

Key Resources

C$

Cost Structure

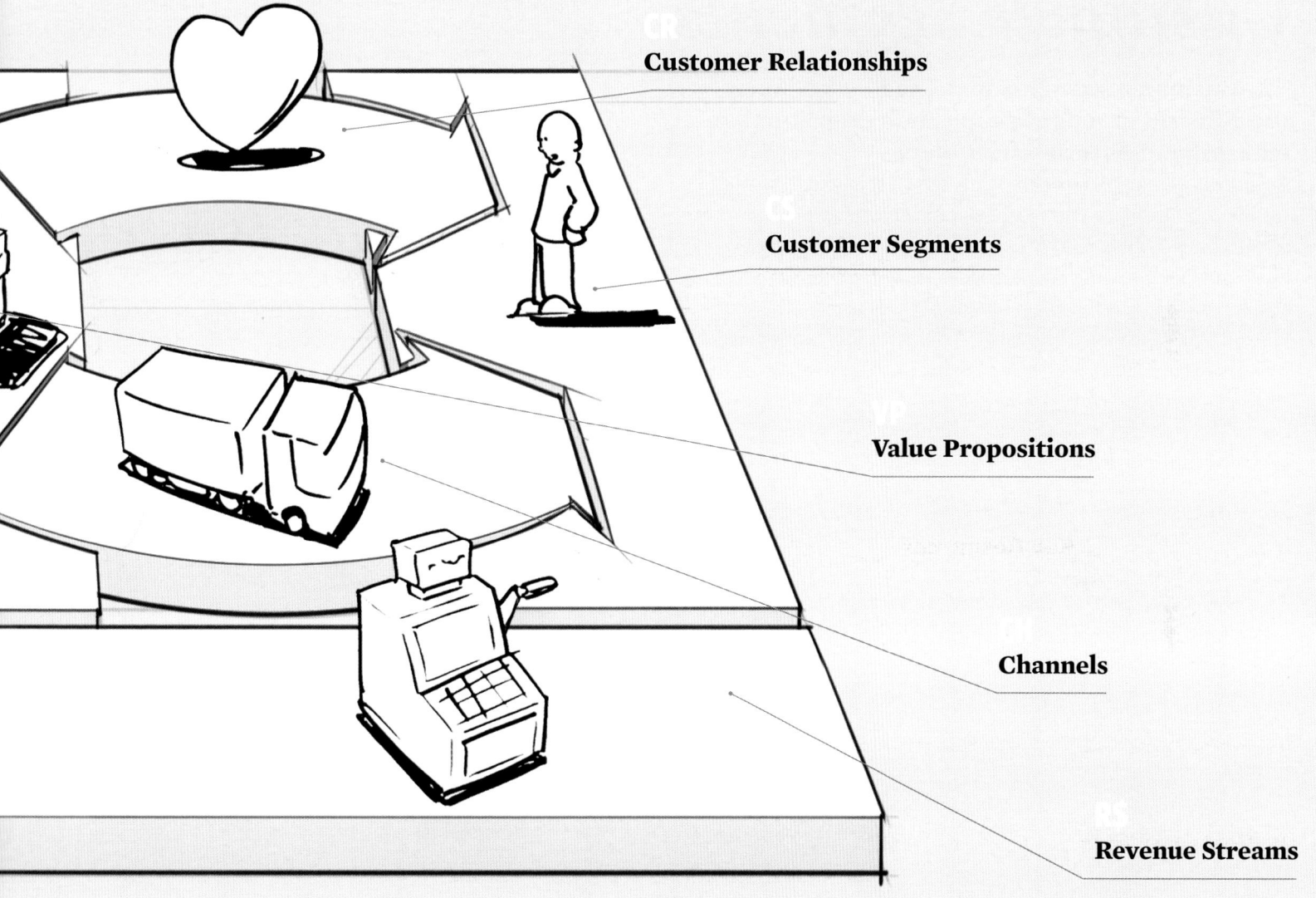

Customer Relationships

Customer Segments

Value Propositions

Channels

Revenue Streams

1 *Customer Segments*

The Customer Segments Building Block defines the different groups of people or organizations an enterprise aims to reach and serve

Customers comprise the heart of any business model. Without (profitable) customers, no company can survive for long. In order to better satisfy customers, a company may group them into distinct segments with common needs, common behaviors, or other attributes. A business model may define one or several large or small Customer Segments. An organization must make a conscious decision about which segments to serve and which segments to ignore. Once this decision is made, a business model can be carefully designed around a strong understanding of specific customer needs.

Customer groups represent separate segments if:
- *Their needs require and justify a distinct offer*
- *They are reached through different Distribution Channels*
- *They require different types of relationships*
- *They have substantially different profitabilities*
- *They are willing to pay for different aspects of the offer*

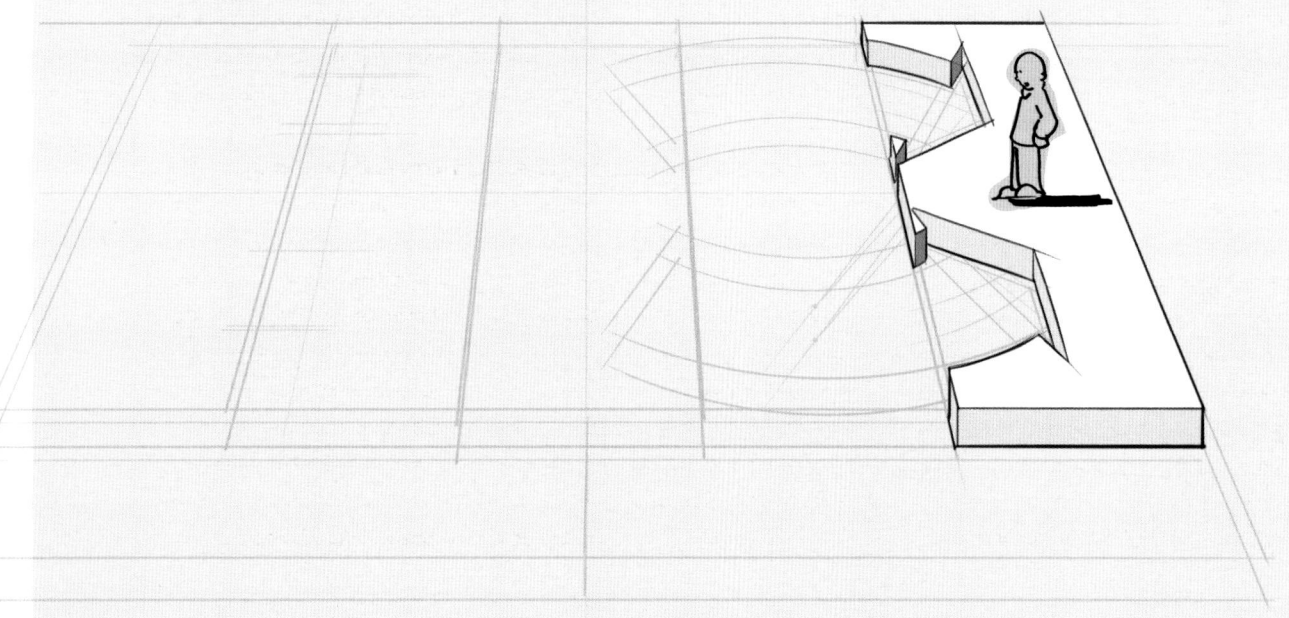

For whom are we creating value?
Who are our most important customers?

There are different types of Customer Segments.
Here are some examples:

Mass market

Business models focused on mass markets don't distinguish between different Customer Segments. The Value Propositions, Distribution Channels, and Customer Relationships all focus on one large group of customers with broadly similar needs and problems. This type of business model is often found in the consumer electronics sector.

Niche market

Business models targeting niche markets cater to specific, specialized Customer Segments. The Value Propositions, Distribution Channels, and Customer Relationships are all tailored to the specific requirements of a niche market. Such business models are often found in supplier-buyer relationships. For example, many car part manufacturers depend heavily on purchases from major automobile manufacturers.

Segmented

Some business models distinguish between market segments with slightly different needs and problems. The retail arm of a bank like Credit Suisse, for example, may distinguish between a large group of customers, each possessing assets of up to U.S. $100,000, and a smaller group of affluent clients, each of whose net worth exceeds U.S. $500,000. Both segments have similar but varying needs and problems. This has implications for the other building blocks of Credit Suisse's business model, such as the Value Proposition, Distribution Channels, Customer Relationships, and Revenue streams. Consider Micro Precision Systems, which specializes in providing outsourced micromechanical design and manufacturing solutions. It serves three different Customer Segments—the watch industry, the medical industry, and the industrial automation sector—and offers each slightly different Value Propositions.

Diversified

An organization with a diversified customer business model serves two unrelated Customer Segments with very different needs and problems. For example, in 2006 Amazon.com decided to diversify its retail business by selling "cloud computing" services: online storage space and on-demand server usage. Thus it started catering to a totally different Customer Segment—Web companies—with a totally different Value Proposition. The strategic rationale behind this diversification can be found in Amazon.com's powerful IT infrastructure, which can be shared by its retail sales operations and the new cloud computing service unit.

Multi-sided platforms (or multi-sided markets)

Some organizations serve two or more interdependent Customer Segments. A credit card company, for example, needs a large base of credit card holders and a large base of merchants who accept those credit cards. Similarly, an enterprise offering a free newspaper needs a large reader base to attract advertisers. On the other hand, it also needs advertisers to finance production and distribution. Both segments are required to make the business model work (read more about multi-sided platforms on p. 76).

2

Value Propositions

The Value Propositions Building Block describes the bundle of products and services that create value for a specific Customer Segment

The Value Proposition is the reason why customers turn to one company over another. It solves a customer problem or satisfies a customer need. Each Value Proposition consists of a selected bundle of products and/or services that caters to the requirements of a specific Customer Segment. In this sense, the Value Proposition is an aggregation, or bundle, of benefits that a company offers customers.

Some Value Propositions may be innovative and represent a new or disruptive offer. Others may be similar to existing market offers, but with added features and attributes.

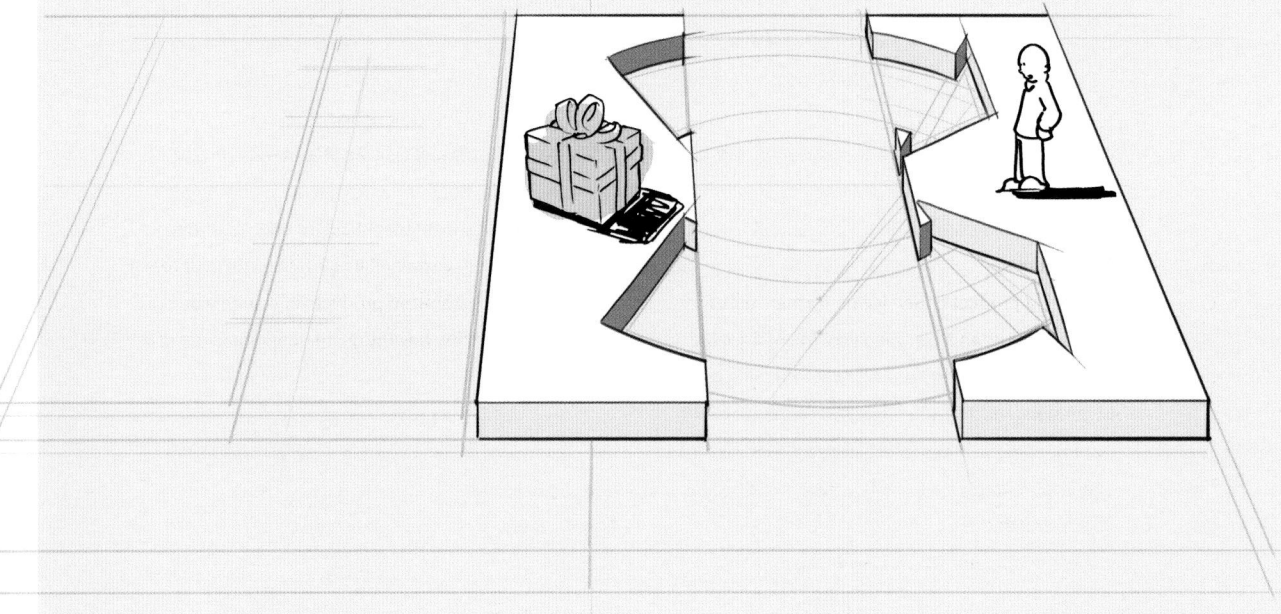

What value do we deliver to the customer? Which one of our customer's problems are we helping to solve? Which customer needs are we satisfying? What bundles of products and services are we offering to each Customer Segment?

A Value Proposition creates value for a Customer Segment through a distinct mix of elements catering to that segment's needs. Values may be quantitative (e.g. price, speed of service) or qualitative (e.g. design, customer experience).

Elements from the following non-exhaustive list can contribute to customer value creation.

Newness

Some Value Propositions satisfy an entirely new set of needs that customers previously didn't perceive because there was no similar offering. This is often, but not always, technology related. Cell phones, for instance, created a whole new industry around mobile telecommunication. On the other hand, products such as ethical investment funds have little to do with new technology.

Performance

Improving product or service performance has traditionally been a common way to create value. The PC sector has traditionally relied on this factor by bringing more powerful machines to market. But improved performance has its limits. In recent years, for example, faster PCs, more disk storage space, and better graphics have failed to produce corresponding growth in customer demand.

Customization

Tailoring products and services to the specific needs of individual customers or Customer Segments creates value. In recent years, the concepts of mass customization and customer co-creation have gained importance. This approach allows for customized products and services, while still taking advantage of economies of scale.

"Getting the job done"

Value can be created simply by helping a customer get certain jobs done. Rolls-Royce understands this very well: its airline customers rely entirely on Rolls-Royce to manufacture and service their jet engines. This arrangement allows customers to focus on running their airlines. In return, the airlines pay Rolls-Royce a fee for every hour an engine runs.

Design

Design is an important but difficult element to measure. A product may stand out because of superior design. In the fashion and consumer electronics industries, design can be a particularly important part of the Value Proposition.

Brand/Status

Customers may find value in the simple act of using and displaying a specific brand. Wearing a Rolex watch signifies wealth, for example. On the other end of the spectrum, skateboarders may wear the latest "underground" brands to show that they are "in."

Price

Offering similar value at a lower price is a common way to satisfy the needs of price-sensitive Customer Segments. But low-price Value Propositions have important implications for the rest of a business model. No frills airlines, such as Southwest, easyJet, and Ryanair have designed entire business models specifically to enable low cost air travel. Another example of a price-based Value Proposition can be seen in the Nano, a new car designed and manufactured by the Indian conglomerate Tata. Its surprisingly low price makes the automobile affordable to a whole new segment of the Indian population. Increasingly, free offers are starting to permeate various industries. Free offers range from free newspapers to free e-mail, free mobile phone services, and more (see p. 88 for more on FREE).

Cost reduction

Helping customers reduce costs is an important way to create value. Salesforce.com, for example, sells a hosted Customer Relationship management (CRM) application. This relieves buyers from the expense and trouble of having to buy, install, and manage CRM software themselves.

Risk reduction

Customers value reducing the risks they incur when purchasing products or services. For a used car buyer, a one-year service guarantee reduces the risk of post-purchase breakdowns and repairs. A service-level guarantee partially reduces the risk undertaken by a purchaser of outsourced IT services.

Accessibility

Making products and services available to customers who previously lacked access to them is another way to create value. This can result from business model innovation, new technologies, or a combination of both. NetJets, for instance, popularized the concept of fractional private jet ownership. Using an innovative business model, NetJets offers individuals and corporations access to private jets, a service previously unaffordable to most customers. Mutual funds provide another example of value creation through increased accessibility. This innovative financial product made it possible even for those with modest wealth to build diversified investment portfolios.

Convenience/Usability

Making things more convenient or easier to use can create substantial value. With iPod and iTunes, Apple offered customers unprecedented convenience searching, buying, downloading, and listening to digital music. It now dominates the market.

3 *Channels*

The Channels Building Block describes how a company communicates with and reaches its Customer Segments to deliver a Value Proposition

Communication, distribution, and sales Channels comprise a company's interface with customers. Channels are customer touch points that play an important role in the customer experience. Channels serve several functions, including:

- *Raising awareness among customers about a company's products and services*
- *Helping customers evaluate a company's Value Proposition*
- *Allowing customers to purchase specific products and services*
- *Delivering a Value Proposition to customers*
- *Providing post-purchase customer support*

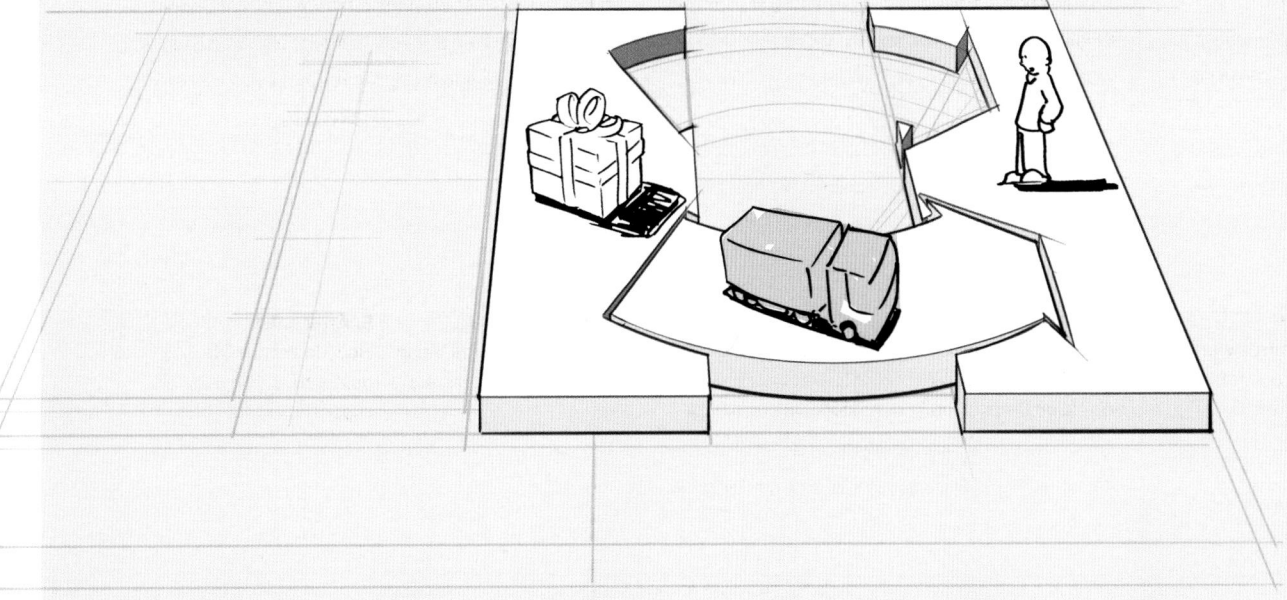

Through which Channels do our Customer Segments want to be reached? How are we reaching them now? How are our Channels integrated? Which ones work best? Which ones are most cost-efficient? How are we integrating them with customer routines?

Channels have five distinct phases. Each channel can cover some or all of these phases. We can distinguish between direct Channels and indirect ones, as well as between owned Channels and partner Channels.

Finding the right mix of Channels to satisfy how customers want to be reached is crucial in bringing a Value Proposition to market. An organization can choose between reaching its customers through its own Channels, through partner Channels, or through a mix of both. Owned Channels can be direct, such as an in-house sales force or a Web site, or they can be indirect, such as retail stores owned or operated by the organization. Partner Channels are indirect and span a whole range of options, such as wholesale distribution, retail, or partner-owned Web sites.

Partner Channels lead to lower margins, but they allow an organization to expand its reach and benefit from partner strengths. Owned Channels and particularly direct ones have higher margins, but can be costly to put in place and to operate. The trick is to find the right balance between the different types of Channels, to integrate them in a way to create a great customer experience, and to maximize revenues.

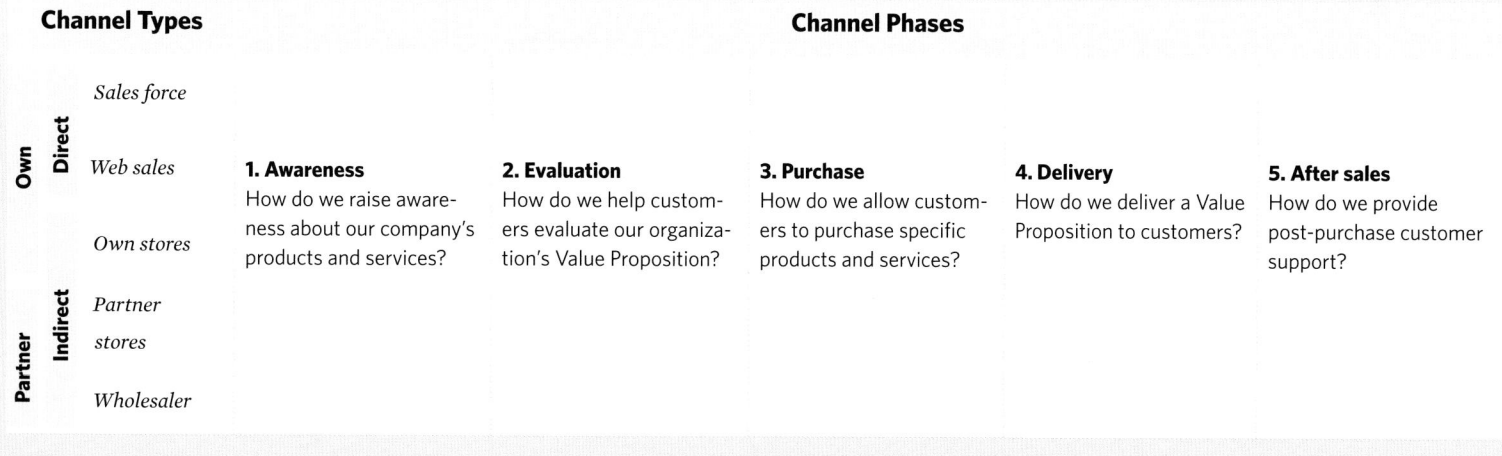

Channel Types

Own — Direct
- Sales force
- Web sales
- Own stores

Partner — Indirect
- Partner stores
- Wholesaler

Channel Phases

1. Awareness	2. Evaluation	3. Purchase	4. Delivery	5. After sales
How do we raise awareness about our company's products and services?	How do we help customers evaluate our organization's Value Proposition?	How do we allow customers to purchase specific products and services?	How do we deliver a Value Proposition to customers?	How do we provide post-purchase customer support?

4 | *Customer Relationships*

The Customer Relationships Building Block describes the types of relationships a company establishes with specific Customer Segments

A company should clarify the type of relationship it wants to establish with each Customer Segment. Relationships can range from personal to automated. Customer relationships may be driven by the following motivations:

- *Customer acquisition*
- *Customer retention*
- *Boosting sales (upselling)*

In the early days, for example, mobile network operator Customer Relationships were driven by aggressive acquisition strategies involving free mobile phones. When the market became saturated, operators switched to focusing on customer retention and increasing average revenue per customer.

The Customer Relationships called for by a company's business model deeply influence the overall customer experience.

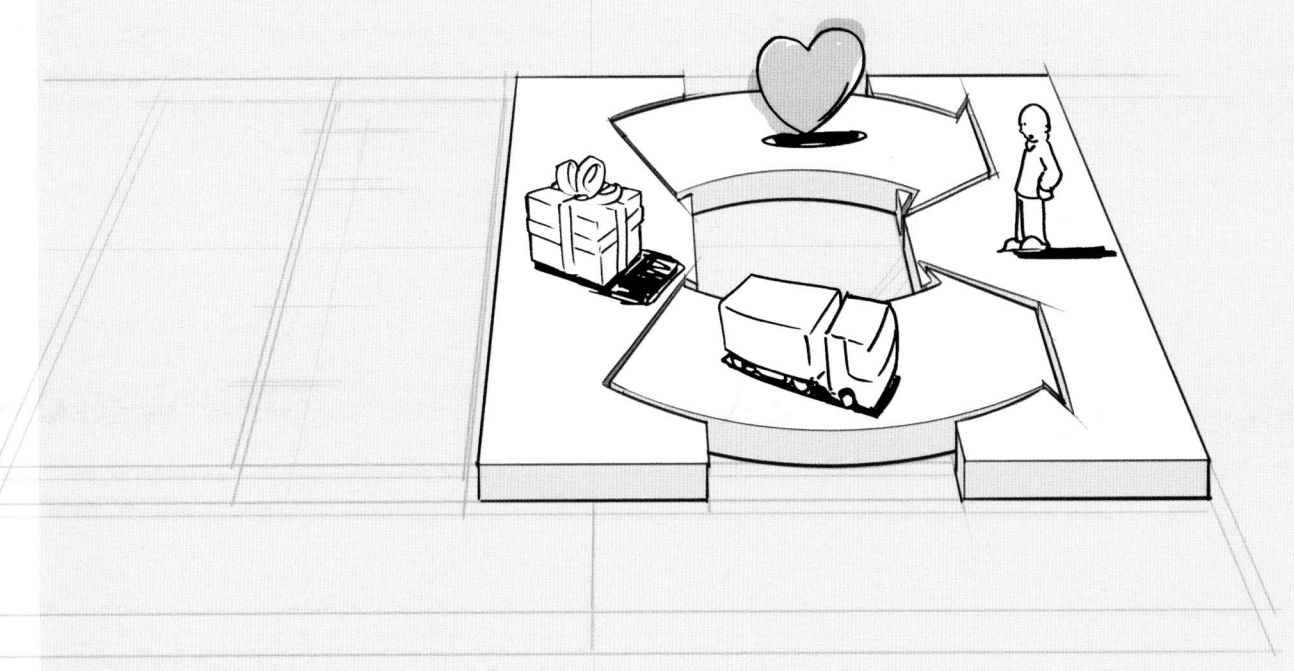

What type of relationship does each of our Customer Segments expect us to establish and maintain with them? Which ones have we established? How costly are they? How are they integrated with the rest of our business model?

We can distinguish between several categories of Customer Relationships, which may co-exist in a company's relationship with a particular Customer Segment:

Personal assistance

This relationship is based on human interaction. The customer can communicate with a real customer representative to get help during the sales process or after the purchase is complete. This may happen on-site at the point of sale, through call centers, by e-mail, or through other means.

Dedicated personal assistance

This relationship involves dedicating a customer representative specifically to an individual client. It represents the deepest and most intimate type of relationship and normally develops over a long period of time. In private banking services, for example, dedicated bankers serve high net worth individuals. Similar relationships can be found in other businesses in the form of key account managers who maintain personal relationships with important customers.

Self-service

In this type of relationship, a company maintains no direct relationship with customers. It provides all the necessary means for customers to help themselves.

Automated services

This type of relationship mixes a more sophisticated form of customer self-service with automated processes. For example, personal online profiles give customers access to customized services. Automated services can recognize individual customers and their characteristics, and offer information related to orders or transactions. At their best, automated services can simulate a personal relationship (e.g. offering book or movie recommendations).

Communities

Increasingly, companies are utilizing user communities to become more involved with customers/prospects and to facilitate connections between community members. Many companies maintain online communities that allow users to exchange knowledge and solve each other's problems. Communities can also help companies better understand their customers. Pharmaceutical giant GlaxoSmithKline launched a private online community when it introduced *alli*, a new prescription-free weight-loss product.

GlaxoSmithKline wanted to increase its understanding of the challenges faced by overweight adults, and thereby learn to better manage customer expectations.

Co-creation

More companies are going beyond the traditional customer-vendor relationship to co-create value with customers. Amazon.com invites customers to write reviews and thus create value for other book lovers. Some companies engage customers to assist with the design of new and innovative products. Others, such as YouTube.com, solicit customers to create content for public consumption.

5 | *Revenue Streams*

The Revenue Streams Building Block represents the cash a company generates from each Customer Segment (costs must be subtracted from revenues to create earnings)

If customers comprise the heart of a business model, Revenue Streams are its arteries. A company must ask itself, For what value is each Customer Segment truly willing to pay? Successfully answering that question allows the firm to generate one or more Revenue Streams from each Customer Segment. Each Revenue Stream may have different pricing mechanisms, such as fixed list prices, bargaining, auctioning, market dependent, volume dependent, or yield management.

A business model can involve two different types of Revenue Streams:

1. *Transaction revenues resulting from one-time customer payments*
2. *Recurring revenues resulting from ongoing payments to either deliver a Value Proposition to customers or provide post-purchase customer support*

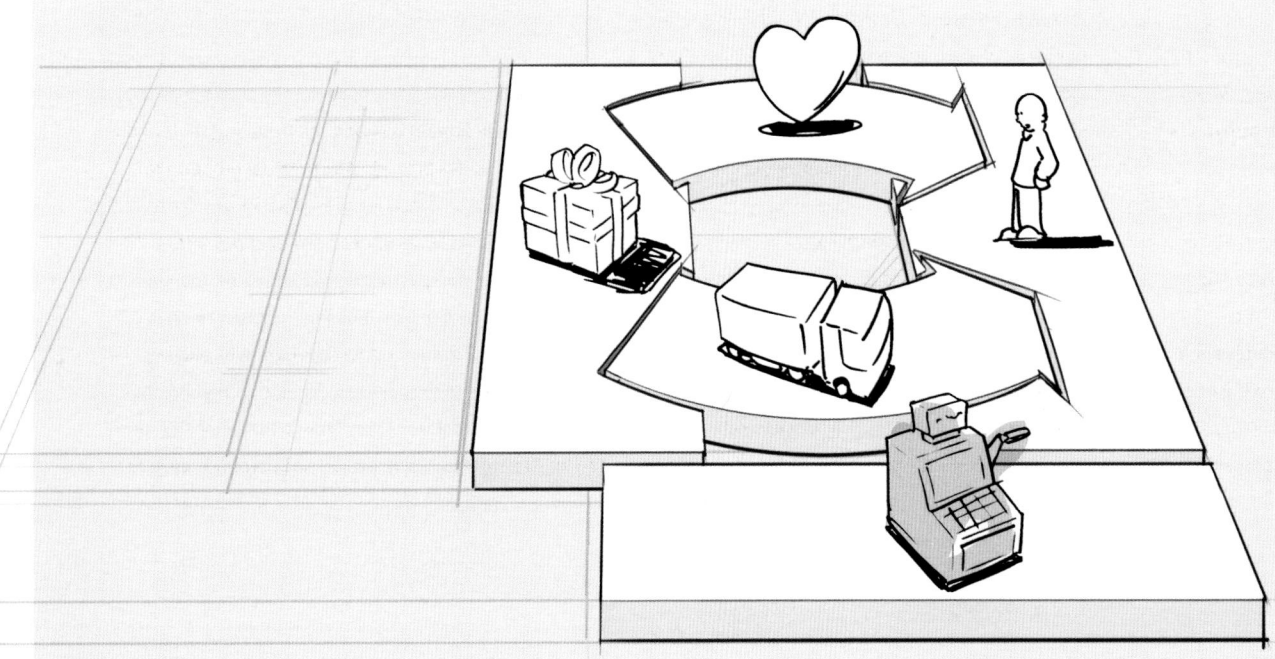

For what value are our customers really willing to pay? For what do they currently pay? How are they currently paying? How would they prefer to pay? How much does each Revenue Stream contribute to overall revenues?

There are several ways to generate Revenue Streams:

Asset sale

The most widely understood Revenue Stream derives from selling ownership rights to a physical product. Amazon.com sells books, music, consumer electronics, and more online. Fiat sells automobiles, which buyers are free to drive, resell, or even destroy.

Usage fee

This Revenue Stream is generated by the use of a particular service. The more a service is used, the more the customer pays. A telecom operator may charge customers for the number of minutes spent on the phone. A hotel charges customers for the number of nights rooms are used. A package delivery service charges customers for the delivery of a parcel from one location to another.

Subscription fees

This Revenue Stream is generated by selling continuous access to a service. A gym sells its members monthly or yearly subscriptions in exchange for access to its exercise facilities. World of Warcraft Online, a Web-based computer game, allows users to play its online game in exchange for a monthly subscription fee. Nokia's Comes with Music service gives users access to a music library for a subscription fee.

Lending/Renting/Leasing

This Revenue Stream is created by temporarily granting someone the exclusive right to use a particular asset for a fixed period in return for a fee. For the lender this provides the advantage of recurring revenues. Renters or lessees, on the other hand, enjoy the benefits of incurring expenses for only a limited time rather than bearing the full costs of ownership. Zipcar.com provides a good illustration. The company allows customers to rent cars by the hour in North American cities. Zipcar.com's service has led many people to decide to rent rather than purchase automobiles.

Licensing

This Revenue Stream is generated by giving customers permission to use protected intellectual property in exchange for licensing fees. Licensing allows rightsholders to generate revenues from their property without having to manufacture a product or commercialize a service. Licensing is common in the media industry, where content owners retain copyright while selling usage licenses to third parties. Similarly, in technology sectors, patentholders grant other companies the right to use a patented technology in return for a license fee.

Brokerage fees

This Revenue Stream derives from intermediation services performed on behalf of two or more parties. Credit card providers, for example, earn revenues by taking a percentage of the value of each sales transaction executed between credit card merchants and customers. Brokers and real estate agents earn a commission each time they successfully match a buyer and seller.

Advertising

This Revenue Stream results from fees for advertising a particular product, service, or brand. Traditionally, the media industry and event organizers relied heavily on revenues from advertising. In recent years other sectors, including software and services, have started relying more heavily on advertising revenues.

Each Revenue Stream might have different pricing mechanisms. The type of pricing mechanism chosen can make a big difference in terms of revenues generated. There are two main types of pricing mechanism: fixed and dynamic pricing.

Pricing Mechanisms

Fixed Menu Pricing
Predefined prices are based on static variables

List price — Fixed prices for individual products, services, or other Value Propositions

Product feature dependent — Price depends on the number or quality of Value Proposition features

Customer segment dependent — Price depends on the type and characteristic of a Customer Segment

Volume dependent — Price as a function of the quantity purchased

Dynamic Pricing
Prices change based on market conditions

Negotiation (bargaining) — Price negotiated between two or more partners depending on negotiation power and/or negotiation skills

Yield management — Price depends on inventory and time of purchase (normally used for perishable resources such as hotel rooms or airline seats)

Real-time-market — Price is established dynamically based on supply and demand

Auctions — Price determined by outcome of competitive bidding

6 | *Key Resources*

The Key Resources Building Block describes the most important assets required to make a business model work

Every business model requires Key Resources. These resources allow an enterprise to create and offer a Value Proposition, reach markets, maintain relationships with Customer Segments, and earn revenues. Different Key Resources are needed depending on the type of business model. A microchip manufacturer requires capital-intensive production facilities, whereas a microchip designer focuses more on human resources.

Key resources can be physical, financial, intellectual, or human. Key resources can be owned or leased by the company or acquired from key partners.

What Key Resources do our Value Propositions require? Our Distribution Channels? Customer Relationships? Revenue Streams?

Key Resources can be categorized as follows:

Physical

This category includes physical assets such as manufacturing facilities, buildings, vehicles, machines, systems, point-of-sales systems, and distribution networks. Retailers like Wal-Mart and Amazon.com rely heavily on physical resources, which are often capital-intensive. The former has an enormous global network of stores and related logistics infrastructure. The latter has an extensive IT, warehouse, and logistics infrastructure.

Intellectual

Intellectual resources such as brands, proprietary knowledge, patents and copyrights, partnerships, and customer databases are increasingly important components of a strong business model. Intellectual resources are difficult to develop but when success-fully created may offer substantial value. Consumer goods companies such as Nike and Sony rely heavily on brand as a Key Resource. Microsoft and SAP depend on software and related intellectual property developed over many years. Qualcomm, a designer and supplier of chipsets for broadband mobile devices, built its business model around patented microchip designs that earn the company substantial licensing fees.

Human

Every enterprise requires human resources, but people are particularly prominent in certain business models. For example, human resources are crucial in knowledge-intensive and creative industries. A phar-maceutical company such as Novartis, for example, relies heavily on human resources: Its business model is predicated on an army of experienced scientists and a large and skilled sales force.

Financial

Some business models call for financial resources and/or financial guarantees, such as cash, lines of credit, or a stock option pool for hiring key employ-ees. Ericsson, the telecom manufacturer, provides an example of financial resource leverage within a business model. Ericsson may opt to borrow funds from banks and capital markets, then use a portion of the proceeds to provide vendor financing to equipment customers, thus ensuring that orders are placed with Ericsson rather than competitors.

7 *Key Activities*

**The Key Activities Building Block describes
the most important things a company must do
to make its business model work**

Every business model calls for a number of Key Activities. These
are the most important actions a company must take to operate
successfully. Like Key Resources, they are required to create and
offer a Value Proposition, reach markets, maintain Customer
Relationships, and earn revenues. And like Key Resources, Key
Activities differ depending on business model type. For software
maker Microsoft, Key Activities include software development.

For PC manufacturer Dell, Key Activities include supply chain
management. For consultancy McKinsey, Key Activities include
problem solving.

What Key Activities do our Value Propositions require? Our Distribution Channels? Customer Relationships? Revenue Streams?

Key Activities can be categorized as follows:

Production

These activities relate to designing, making, and delivering a product in substantial quantities and/or of superior quality. Production activity dominates the business models of manufacturing firms.

Problem solving

Key Activities of this type relate to coming up with new solutions to individual customer problems. The operations of consultancies, hospitals, and other service organizations are typically dominated by problem solving activities. Their business models call for activities such as knowledge management and continuous training.

Platform/Network

Business models designed with a platform as a Key Resource are dominated by platform or network-related Key Activities. Networks, matchmaking platforms, software, and even brands can function as a platform. eBay's business model requires that the company continually develop and maintain its platform: the Web site at eBay.com. Visa's business model requires activities related to its Visa® credit card transaction platform for merchants, customers, and banks. Microsoft's business model requires managing the interface between other vendors' software and its Windows® operating system platform. Key Activities in this category relate to platform management, service provisioning, and platform promotion.

Key Partnerships

The Key Partnerships Building Block describes the network of suppliers and partners that make the business model work

Companies forge partnerships for many reasons, and partnerships are becoming a cornerstone of many business models. Companies create alliances to optimize their business models, reduce risk, or acquire resources.

We can distinguish between four different types of partnerships:

1. *Strategic alliances between non-competitors*
2. *Coopetition: strategic partnerships between competitors*
3. *Joint ventures to develop new businesses*
4. *Buyer-supplier relationships to assure reliable supplies*

Who are our Key Partners? Who are our key suppliers? Which Key Resources are we acquiring from partners? Which Key Activities do partners perform?

It can be useful to distinguish between three motivations for creating partnerships:

Optimization and economy of scale

The most basic form of partnership or buyer-supplier relationship is designed to optimize the allocation of resources and activities. It is illogical for a company to own all resources or perform every activity by itself. Optimization and economy of scale partnerships are usually formed to reduce costs, and often involve outsourcing or sharing infrastructure.

Reduction of risk and uncertainty

Partnerships can help reduce risk in a competitive environment characterized by uncertainty. It is not unusual for competitors to form a strategic alliance in one area while competing in another. Blu-ray, for example, is an optical disc format jointly developed by a group of the world's leading consumer electronics, personal computer, and media manufacturers. The group cooperated to bring Blu-ray technology to market, yet individual members compete in selling their own Blu-ray products.

Acquisition of particular resources and activities

Few companies own all the resources or perform all the activities described by their business models. Rather, they extend their own capabilities by relying on other firms to furnish particular resources or perform certain activities. Such partnerships can be motivated by needs to acquire knowledge, licenses, or access to customers. A mobile phone manufacturer, for example, may license an operating system for its handsets rather than developing one in-house. An insurer may choose to rely on independent brokers to sell its policies rather than develop its own sales force.

9 *Cost Structure*

The Cost Structure describes all costs incurred to operate a business model

This building block describes the most important costs incurred while operating under a particular business model. Creating and delivering value, maintaining Customer Relationships, and generating revenue all incur costs. Such costs can be calculated relatively easily after defining Key Resources, Key Activities, and Key Partnerships. Some business models, though, are more cost-driven than others. So-called "no frills" airlines, for instance, have built business models entirely around low Cost Structures.

What are the most important costs inherent in our business model? Which Key Resources are most expensive? Which Key Activities are most expensive?

Naturally enough, costs should be minimized in every business model. But low Cost Structures are more important to some business models than to others. Therefore it can be useful to distinguish between two broad classes of business model Cost Structures: cost-driven and value-driven (many business models fall in between these two extremes):

Cost-driven

Cost-driven business models focus on minimizing costs wherever possible. This approach aims at creating and maintaining the leanest possible Cost Structure, using low price Value Propositions, maximum automation, and extensive outsourcing. No frills airlines, such as Southwest, easyJet, and Ryanair typify cost-driven business models.

Value-driven

Some companies are less concerned with the cost implications of a particular business model design, and instead focus on value creation. Premium Value Propositions and a high degree of personalized service usually characterize value-driven business models. Luxury hotels, with their lavish facilities and exclusive services, fall into this category.

Cost Structures can have the following characteristics:

Fixed costs

Costs that remain the same despite the volume of goods or services produced. Examples include salaries, rents, and physical manufacturing facilities. Some businesses, such as manufacturing companies, are characterized by a high proportion of fixed costs.

Variable costs

Costs that vary proportionally with the volume of goods or services produced. Some businesses, such as music festivals, are characterized by a high proportion of variable costs.

Economies of scale

Cost advantages that a business enjoys as its output expands. Larger companies, for instance, benefit from lower bulk purchase rates. This and other factors cause average cost per unit to fall as output rises.

Economies of scope

Cost advantages that a business enjoys due to a larger scope of operations. In a large enterprise, for example, the same marketing activities or Distribution Channels may support multiple products.

The nine business model Building Blocks form the basis for a handy tool, which we call the *Business Model Canvas*.

The Business Model Canvas

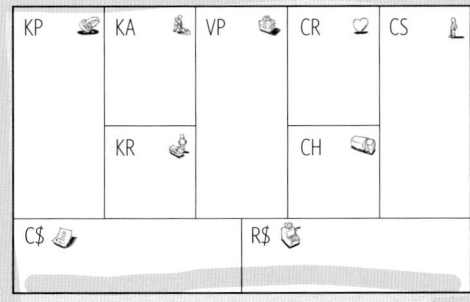

This tool resembles a painter's canvas—preformatted with the nine blocks—which allows you to paint pictures of new or existing business models. *The Business Model Canvas works best when printed out on a large surface so groups of people can jointly start sketching and discussing business model elements* with Post-it® notes or board markers. It is a hands-on tool that fosters understanding, discussion, creativity, and analysis.

43

The Business Model Canvas

Key Partners	Key Activities	Value Proposition	Customer Relationships	Customer Segments
	Key Resources		**Channels**	

Cost Structure	Revenue Streams

For a large poster-size version of The Business Model Canvas, visit www.businessmodelgeneration.com.

① PLOT THE CANVAS ON A POSTER

② PUT THE POSTER ON THE WALL

③ SKETCH OUT YOUR BUSINESS MODEL

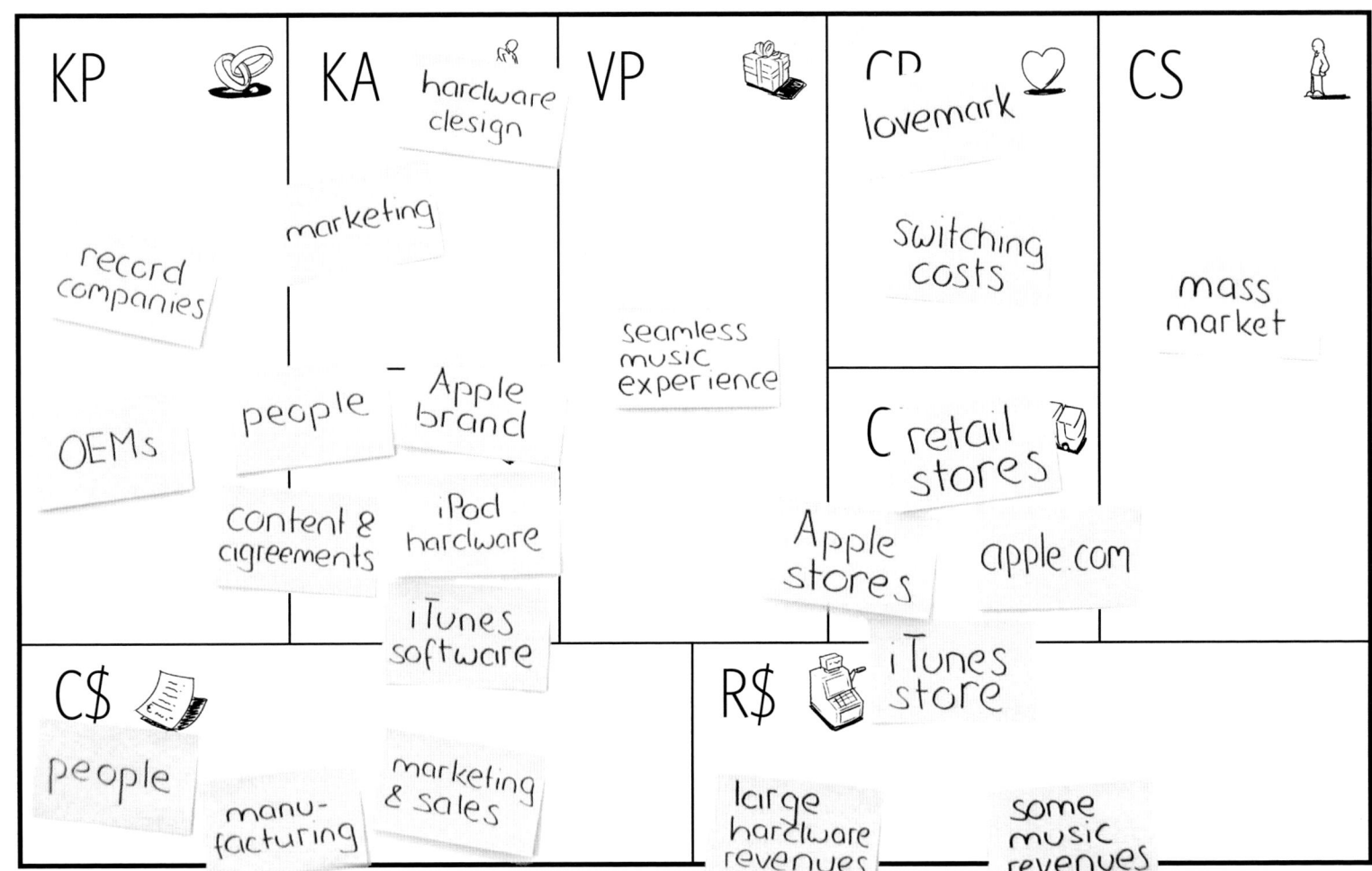

KP

record companies

OEMs

KA

hardware design

marketing

people — Apple brand

content & agreements

iPod hardware

iTunes software

VP

seamless music experience

CR

lovemark

switching costs

C retail stores

Apple stores

apple.com

iTunes store

CS

mass market

C$

people

manu- facturing

marketing & sales

R$

large hardware revenues

some music revenues

Example: Apple iPod/iTunes Business Model

In 2001 Apple launched its iconic iPod brand of portable media player. The device works in conjunction with iTunes software that enables users to transfer music and other content from the iPod to a computer. The software also provides a seamless connection to Apple's online store so users can purchase and download content.

This potent combination of device, software, and online store quickly disrupted the music industry and gave Apple a dominant market position. Yet Apple was not the first company to bring a portable media player to market. Competitors such as Diamond Multimedia, with its Rio brand of portable media players, were successful until they were outpaced by Apple.

How did Apple achieve such dominance? Because it competed with a better business model. On the one hand, it offered users a seamless music experience by combining its distinctively designed iPod devices with iTunes software and the iTunes online store. Apple's Value Proposition is to allow customers to easily search, buy, and enjoy digital music. On the other hand, to make this Value Proposition possible, Apple had to negotiate deals with all the major record companies to create the world's largest online music library.

The twist? Apple earns most of its music-related revenues from selling iPods, while using integration with the online music store to protect itself from competitors.

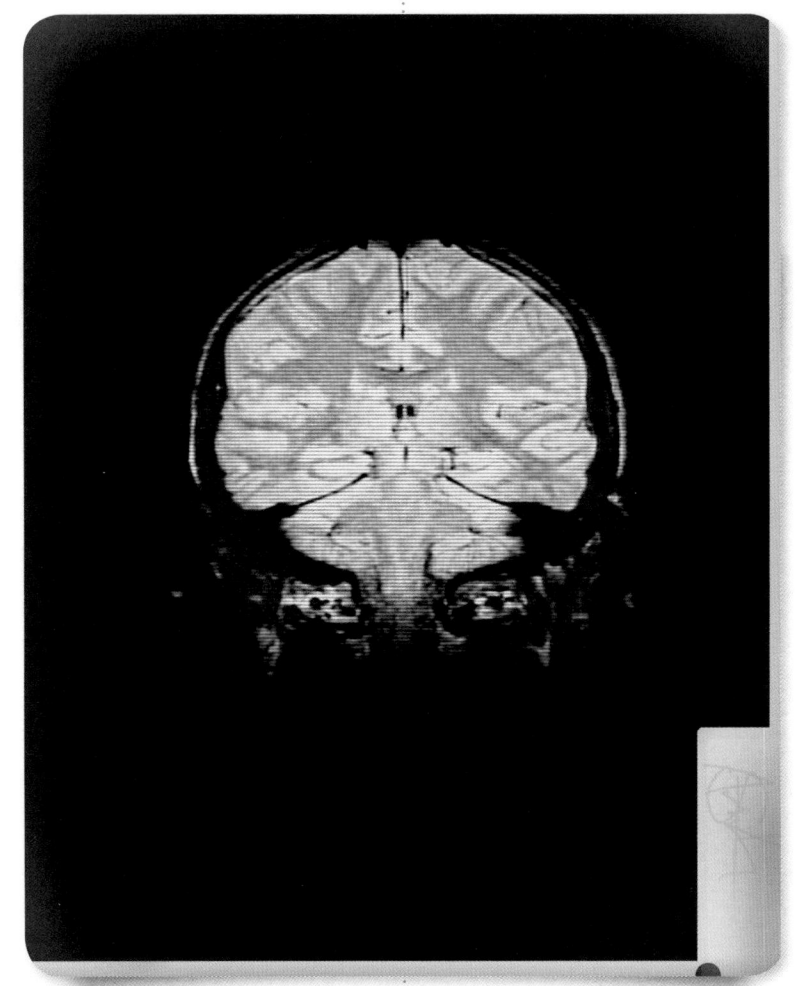

LEFT BRAIN
logic

RIGHT BRAIN
emotion

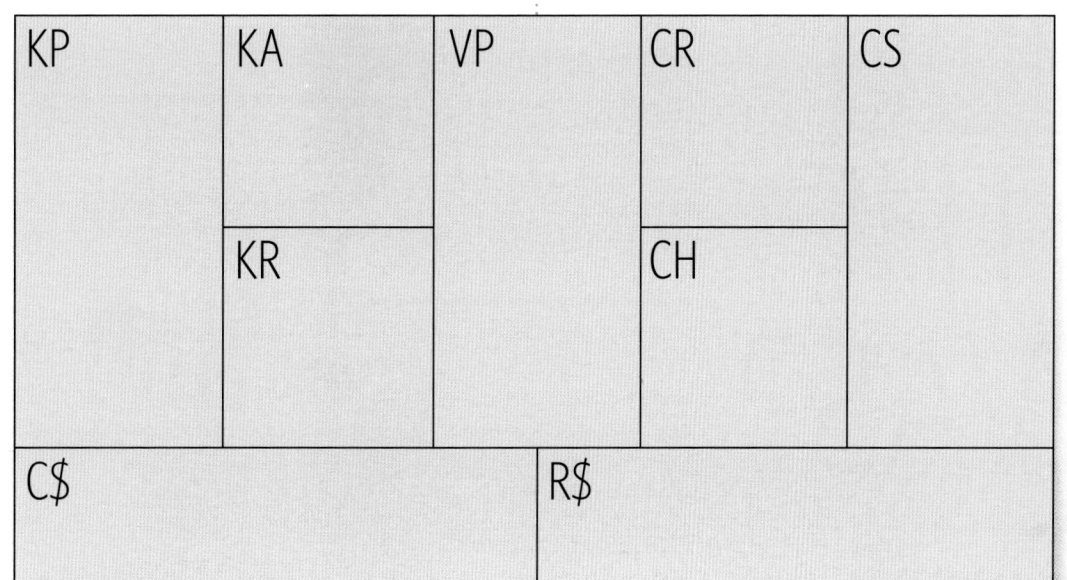

50

HOW DO YOU USE THE CANVAS?

The public sector is often challenged to implement private sector principles. I have used the Canvas to help a department view itself as a service-oriented business, **establishing externalized as-is and to-be business models.** It has created a whole new conversation around describing and innovating the business.
Mike Lachapelle, Canada

I consult with small companies on using the freemium business model. This model involves giving core products away for free, which is very counterintuitive to most businesspeople. Thanks to the Business Model Canvas, I can **easily illustrate how it makes financial sense.**
Peter Froberg, Denmark

I help business owners plan their transition and exit from their companies. Success depends on sustaining long-term company viability and growth. Key to this is a business model innovation program. The Canvas helps us identify and innovate their business models.
Nicholas K. Niemann, United States

I'm using the Business Model Canvas in Brazil to help artists, cultural producers, and game designers to envision innovative business models for the Cultural and Creative Industries. I apply it in the Cultural Production MBA at FGV and in the Innovation Games Lab at COPPE/UFRJ Business Incubator.
Claudio D'Ipolitto, Brazil

When you typically think of a business model, the conclusion is that it is a 'for profit' business. However, I found that the Canvas is also very effective in the non-profit sector. We used it to **DESIGN + ALIGN** members of the leadership team during the formation of a new non-profit program. The Canvas was flexible enough to take into account the goals of this social entrepreneurial venture, and bring clarity to the true Value Proposition of the business and how to make it sustainable.
Kevin Donaldson, United States

I wish I had known the Canvas years ago! With a particular tough and complicated print-to-digital project within the publishing industry it would have been so helpful to **show all project members in this visual way both the big picture, their (important) own roles in it and the inter-dependencies.** Hours of explaining, arguing, and misunderstanding could have been saved.
Jille Sol, Netherlands

A close friend was looking for a new job. **I used the Business Model Canvas in order to assess her personal business model.** Her core competences and Value Proposition were outstanding but she failed to leverage her strategic partners and develop appropriate Customer Relationships. This adjusted focus opened new opportunities.
Daniel Pandza, Mexico

Imagine 60 first-year students, knowing nothing about entrepreneurship. In less than five days, thanks to the Business Model Canvas, they were able to pitch a viable idea with conviction and clarity. They used it as a tool to cover all the startup-building dimensions.

Guilhem Bertholet, France

I use the Business Model Canvas to teach early stage entrepreneurs across a wide range of industries as a much better way to

TRANSLATE THEIR BUSINESS **PLANS** INTO THE BUSINESS **PROCESSES**

that they (will) need to operate their businesses and to ensure that they are focused properly on being customer-centric in a way that makes the business as highly profitable as it can be.

Bob Dunn, United States

I have used the Canvas with a co-founder to **design a business plan** for a national level contest held by *The Economic Times, India*. The Canvas enabled me to think through all the aspects of the startup and put together a plan that VCs might find well thought out and attractive to fund.

Praveen Singh, India

We were asked to redesign the language service of an international NGO. The Business Model Canvas was especially helpful to **show the links between the needs of people's day-to-day work and a service** that was felt too specialized, considered only as an afterthought, and far away from their priorities.

Paola Valeri, Spain

As a startup coach I support teams to create new products and design their businesses. The Business Model Canvas does a great job assisting me to

remind the teams to think holistically about their business and prevents them from getting stuck on details. This helps to

make their new venture a success.

Christian Schüller, Germany

The Business Model Canvas has allowed me to establish a common language and framework with colleagues.

I've used the Canvas to explore new growth opportunities, assess uses of new business models by competitors, and to communicate across the organization how we could accelerate technology, market, and business model innovations.

Bruce MacVarish, United States

The Business Model Canvas has helped several health care organizations in the Netherlands to **make the move from a budget driven governmental institution to an entrepreneurial value-adding organization.**

Huub Raemakers, Netherlands

I used the Canvas with senior managers of a public company to help them restructure their value chain due to changes in sector regulation. The key success factor was to understand which new Value Propositions could be offered to their clients and then translated into internal operations.

Leandro Jesus, Brazil

WE USED 15,000 POST-ITS AND MORE THAN 100 METERS OF BROWN PAPER

to design a future organizational structure in a global manufacturing company. The key of all activities was, however, the Business Model Canvas. It convinced us by its practical applicability, simplicity, and logical cause-and-effect relationships.

Daniel Egger, Brazil

I used the Canvas to do a

REALITY CHECK

for my new startup Mupps, a platform where artists can make their own music apps for iPhone and Android phones in minutes. You know what? The Canvas made me even surer of the possible success! So I gotta go, work to do!

Erwin Blom, Netherlands

The Business Model Canvas has proven to be a very useful tool for capturing ideas and solutions for e-commerce projects. Most of my clients are SMEs and the Canvas helps them to

clarify their current business models and

understand and focus on the impact of e-commerce on their organizations.

Marc Castricum, Netherlands

I applied the Canvas to help a company align key staff in order to determine shared goals and strategic priorities, which were used during the planning process and incorporated with the BSC. It also ensured that the chosen initiatives were clearly driven by the new strategic priorities.

Martin Fanghanel, Bolivia

Patt

erns

"Pattern in architecture is the idea of capturing architectural design ideas as archetypal and reusable descriptions."

Christopher Alexander, Architect

This section describes business models with similar characteristics, similar arrangements of business model Building Blocks, or similar behaviors. We call these similarities business model patterns. The patterns described in the following pages should help you understand business model dynamics and serve as a source of inspiration for your own work with business models.

We've sketched out five business model patterns built on important concepts in the business literature. We've "translated" these into the language of the Business Model Canvas to make the concepts comparable, easy to understand, and applicable. A single business model can incorporate several of these patterns.

Concepts upon which our patterns are based include Unbundling, the Long Tail, Multi-Sided Platforms, FREE, and Open Business Models. New patterns based on other business concepts will certainly emerge over time.

Our goal in defining and describing these business model patterns is to recast well-known business concepts in a standardized format—the Business Model Canvas—so that they are immediately useful in your own work around business model design or invention.

Patterns

56   Unbundling Business Models

66   The Long Tail

76   Multi-Sided Platforms

88   FREE as a Business Model

108   Open Business Models

Un-
Bundling
Business
Models

Def_Pattern No. 1

The concept of the "unbundled" corporation holds that there are three fundamentally
different types of businesses: Customer Relationship businesses, product innovation businesses, and infrastructure businesses. • Each
type has different economic, competitive, and
cultural imperatives. • The three types may
co-exist within a single corporation, but ideally
they are "unbundled" into separate entities in
order to avoid conflicts or undesirable trade-offs.

[REF·ER·ENCES]

1 • "Unbundling the
Corporation." *Harvard
Business Review*. Hagel,
John, Singer, Marc.
March–April 1999.
2 • *The Discipline of Market
Leaders: Choose Your
Customers, Narrow Your
Focus, Dominate Your
Market*. Treacy, Michael,
Wiersema, Fred. 1995.

[EX·AM·PLES]

mobile telecom industry,
private banking industry

1 John Hagel
and Marc Singer, who coined
the term "unbundled corporation,"
believe that companies are composed of three
very different types of businesses with different
economic, competitive, and cultural imperatives:
Customer Relationship businesses, product innovation
businesses, and infrastructure businesses. Similarly,
Treacy and Wiersema suggest that companies
should focus on one of three value disciplines:
operational excellence, product leadership, or customer intimacy.

Bundled

2 Hagel and Singer
describe the role of Customer
Relationship businesses as finding and
acquiring customers and building relationships
with them. Similarly, the role of product innovation
businesses is to develop new and attractive products and
services, while the role of infrastructure businesses is to build
and manage platforms for high volume, repetitive tasks. Hagel
and Singer argue that companies should separate these
businesses and focus on only one of the three internally.
Because each type of business is driven by different
factors, they can conflict with each other or
produce undesirable trade-offs within the
same organization.

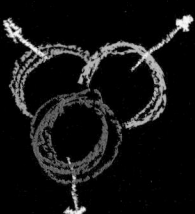

Unbundling

3 On the
following pages we
show how the idea of unbundling
applies to business models. In the first
example, we describe the conflicts and
undesirable trade-offs created by a "bundled"
business model within the private banking
industry. In the second example we show
how mobile telecom operators are
unbundling and focusing on new
core businesses.

Unbundled!

THREE CORE BUSINESS TYPES

	Product Innovation	Customer Relationship Management	Infrastructure Management
Economics	Early market entry enables charging premium prices and acquiring large market share; speed is key	High cost of customer acquisition makes it imperative to gain large wallet share; economies of scope are key	High fixed costs make large volumes essential to achieve low unit costs; economies of scale are key
Competition	Battle for talent; low barriers to entry; many small players thrive	Battle for scope; rapid consolidation; a few big players dominate	Battle for scale; rapid consolidation; a few big players dominate
Culture	Employee centered; coddling the creative stars	Highly service oriented; customer-comes-first mentality	Cost focused; stresses standardization, predictability, and efficiency

Source: Hagel and Singer, 1999.

Private Banking: Three Businesses in One

Swiss private banking, the business of providing banking services to the very wealthy, was long known as a sleepy, conservative industry. Yet over the last decade the face of the Swiss private banking industry changed considerably. Traditionally, private banking institutions were vertically integrated and performed tasks ranging from wealth management to brokerage to financial product design. There were sound reasons for this tight vertical integration. Outsourcing was costly, and private banks preferred keeping everything in-house due to secrecy and confidentiality concerns.

But the environment changed. Secrecy became less of an issue with the demise of the mystique surrounding Swiss banking practices, and outsourcing became attractive with the breakup of the banking value chain due to the emergence of specialty service providers such as transaction banks and financial product boutiques. The former focus exclusively on handling banking transactions, while the latter concentrate solely on designing new financial products.

Zurich-based private banking institution Maerki Baumann is an example of a bank that has unbundled its business model. It spun off its transaction-oriented platform business into a separate entity called Incore Bank, which offers banking services to other banks and securities dealers. Maerki Baumann now focuses solely on building Customer Relationships and advising clients.

On the other hand, Geneva-based Pictet, the largest Swiss private bank, has preferred to remain integrated. This 200-year-old institution develops deep Customer Relationships, handles many client transactions, and designs its own financial products. Though the bank has been successful with this model, it has to carefully manage trade-offs between three fundamentally different types of businesses.

The figure opposite depicts the traditional private banking model, describes trade-offs, and unbundles it into three basic businesses: relationship management, product innovation, and infrastructure management.

Trade Offs

1 The bank serves two different markets with very different dynamics. Advising the wealthy is a long-term, relationship-based business. Selling financial products to private banks is a dynamic, fast-changing business.

2 The bank aims to sell its products to competing banks in order to increase revenues—but this creates a conflict of interest.

3 The bank's product division pressures advisors to sell the bank's own products to clients. This conflicts with client interest in neutral advice. Clients want to invest in the best products on the market, regardless of origin.

4 The cost- and efficiency-focused transaction platform business conflicts with the remuneration-intensive advisory and financial products business, which needs to attract costly talent.

5 The transaction platform business requires scale to drive down costs, which is difficult to achieve within a single bank.

6 The product innovation business is driven by speed and quick market entry, which is at odds with the long-term business of advising the wealthy.

The Private Banking Model

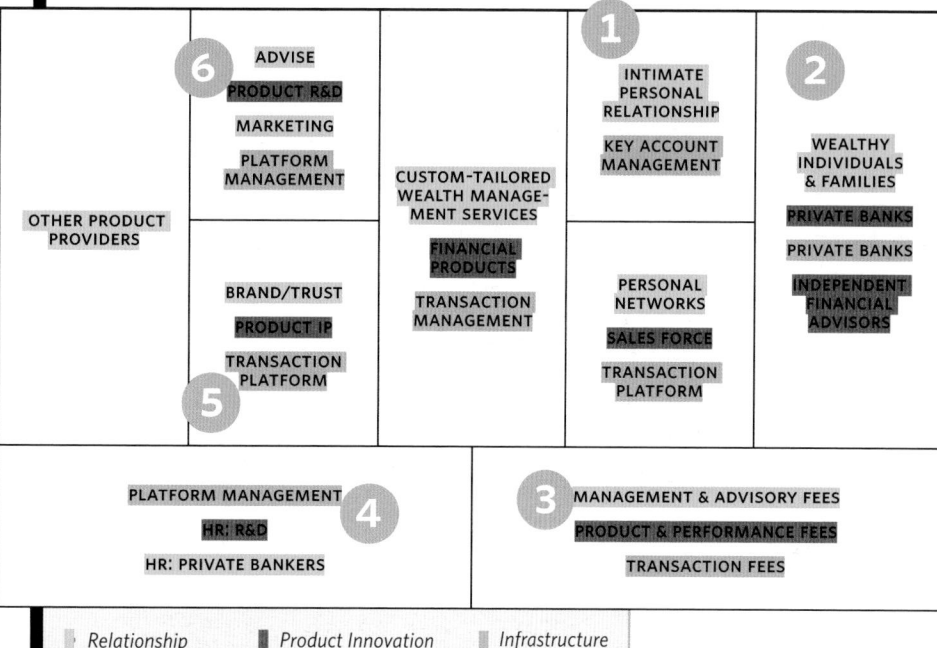

Unbundling the Mobile Telco

Mobile telecommunication firms have started unbundling their businesses. Traditionally they competed on network quality, but now they are striking network sharing deals with competitors or outsourcing network operations altogether to equipment manufacturers. Why? Because they realize that their key asset is no longer the network—it is their brand and their Customer Relationships.

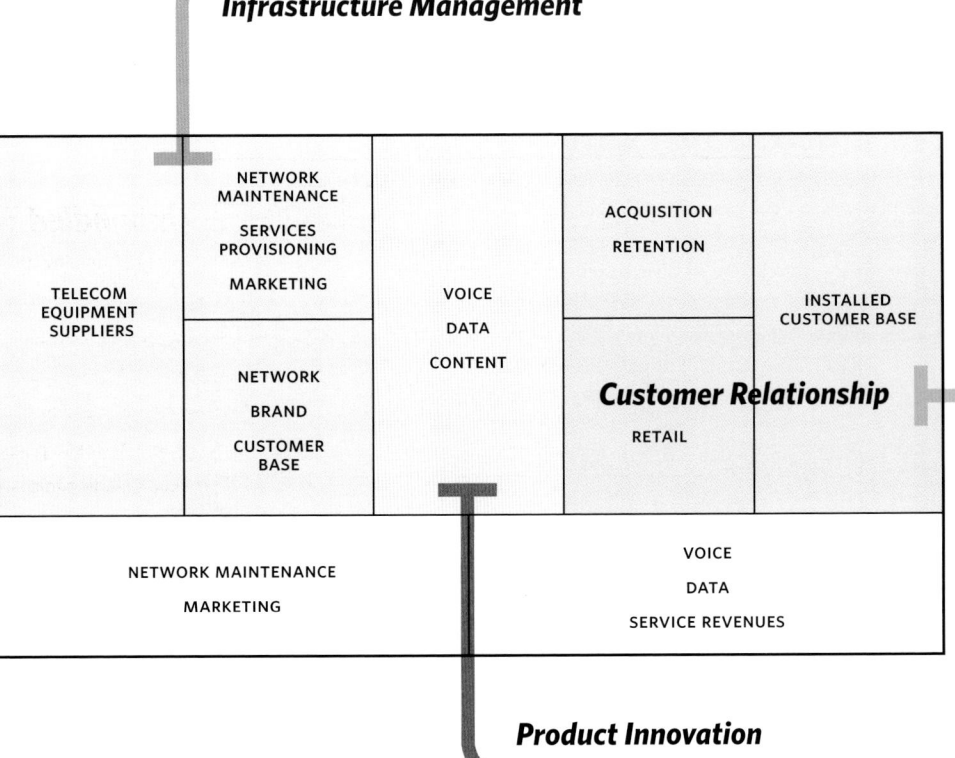

Equipment Manufacturers

Telcos such as France Telecom, KPN, and Vodafone have outsourced operation and maintenance of some of their networks to equipment manufacturers such as Nokia Siemens Networks, Alcatel-Lucent, and Ericsson. Equipment manufacturers can run the networks at lower cost because they service several telcos at a time and thus benefit from economies of scale.

Unbundled Telco

After unbundling its infrastructure business, a telco can sharpen its focus on branding and segmenting customers and services. Customer relationships comprise its key asset and its core business. By concentrating on customers and increasing share of wallet with current subscribers, it can leverage investments made over the years acquiring and retaining customers. One of the first mobile telcos to pursue strategic unbundling was Bharti Airtel, now one of India's leading telcos. It outsourced network operations to Ericsson and Nokia Siemens Networks and IT infrastructure to IBM, allowing the company to focus on its core competency: building Customer Relationships.

Content Providers

For product and service innovation, the unbundled telco can turn to smaller, creative firms. Innovation requires creative talent, which smaller and more dynamic organizations typically do a better job of attracting. Telcos work with multiple third-parties that assure a constant supply of new technologies, services, and media content such as mapping, games, video, and music. Two examples are Mobilizy of Austria and Sweden's tat. Mobilizy focuses on location-based service solutions for smartphones (it developed a popular mobile travel guide), and tat concentrates on creating advanced mobile user interfaces.

Unbundled Patterns

×3

Everything in this model is tailored to understanding and serving customers, or building strong Customer Relationships

Product and service innovation, infrastructure acquired from THIRD PARTIES

KEY ASSETS and RESOURCES are the customer base and subscriber trust acquired over time

KP — PRODUCT + SERVICE INNOVATION / INFRASTRUCTURE MANAGEMENT

KA — CUSTOMER ACQUISITION + RETENTION

KR — INSTALLED CUSTOMER BASE

VP — HIGHLY SERVICE ORIENTED

CR — STRONG RELATIONSHIP, ACQUISITION + RETENTION

CH — STRONG CHANNELS

CS — CUSTOMER FOCUSED

C$ — HIGH COSTS OF CUSTOMER ACQUISITION

R$ — LARGE SHARE OF WALLET

KP

C$

Customer acquisition and retention comprise main COSTS, which include branding and marketing expenses

This model aims at generating revenues with a broad scope of products built upon customer trust—the goal is to win a large "share of wallet"

ACTIVITY is focused on leveraging research and development to bring new products and services to market

Products and services can be brought to market directly, but are usually delivered through B2B intermediaries focused on CUSTOMER RELATIONSHIPS

The ACTIVITIES and offer are focused on delivering infrastructure services

Services are usually delivered to BUSINESS CUSTOMERS

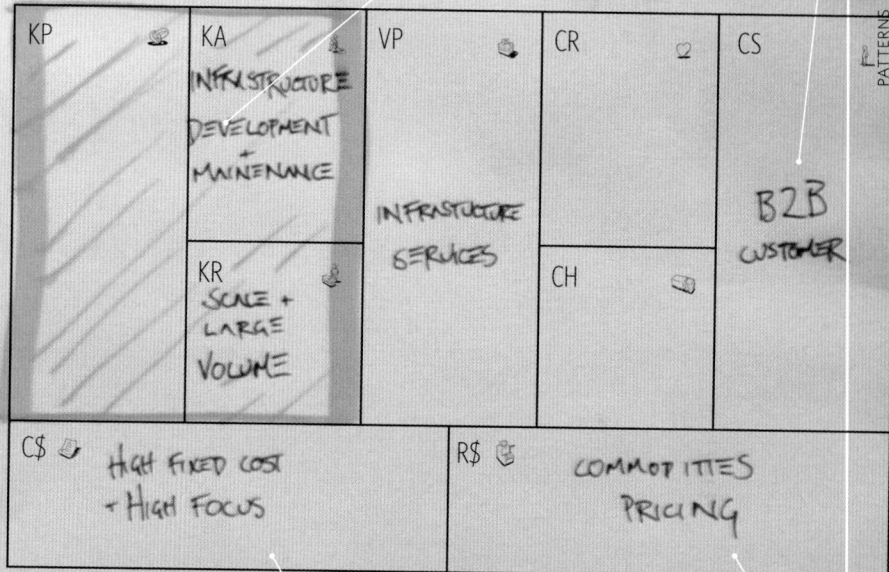

High COST base due to the battle over creative talent, the KEY RESOURCE in this model

High PREMIUM CHARGEABLE because of novelty factor

Platform is characterized by HIGH FIXED COSTS, which are leveraged through scale and large volume

REVENUES are based on low margins and high volume

Left canvas (sketch):

VP — PRODUCT + SERVICE INNOVATION
CR
CS — B2C / B2B
CH
...NANCE R+D
...TRACTING ...LENT
...STRONG ...ENT POOL
...MPLOYEE ...S
R$ — PREMIUM PRICING

Right canvas (sketch):

KP
KA — INFRASTRUCTURE DEVELOPMENT + MAINTENANCE
KR — SCALE + LARGE VOLUME
VP — INFRASTRUCTURE SERVICES
CR
CH
CS — B2B CUSTOMER
C$ — HIGH FIXED COST + HIGH FOCUS
R$ — COMMODITIES PRICING

The Long Tail

Def_Pattern No. 2

LONG TAIL BUSINESS MODELS are about selling less of more: They focus on offering a large number of niche products, each of which sells relatively infrequently. • Aggregate sales of niche items can be as lucrative as the traditional model whereby a small number of bestsellers account for most revenues. • Long Tail business models require low inventory costs and strong platforms to make niche content readily available to interested buyers.

[REF·ER·ENCES]

1 • *The Long Tail: Why the Future of Business Is Selling Less of More.* Anderson, Chris. 2006.

2 • "The Long Tail." *Wired Magazine.* Anderson, Chris. October 2004.

[EX·AM·PLES]

Netflix, eBay, YouTube, Facebook, Lulu.com

# of Sales

TOP 20%
Focus on a small number of products, each selling in high volume

The Long Tail concept was coined by Chris Anderson to describe a shift in the media business from selling a small number of "hit" items in large volumes toward selling a very large number of niche items, each in relatively small quantities. Anderson described how many infrequent sales can produce aggregate revenues equivalent to or even exceeding revenues produced by focusing on "hit" products.

Anderson believes three economic triggers gave rise to this phenomenon in the media industry:

1. Democratization of tools of production: Falling technology costs gave individuals access to tools that were prohibitively expensive just a few years ago. Millions of passionate amateurs can now record music, produce short films, and design simple software with professional results.

2. Democratization of distribution: The Internet has made digital content distribution a commodity, and dramatically lowered inventory, communications, and transaction costs, opening up new markets for niche products.

3. Falling search costs to connect supply with demand: The real challenge of selling niche content is finding interested potential buyers. Powerful search and recommendation engines, user ratings, and communities of interest have made this much easier.

LONG TAIL Focus on a large number of products, each selling in low volumes

Anderson's research focuses primarily on the media industry. For example, he showed how online video rental company Netflix moved toward licensing a large number of niche movies. While each niche movie is rented relatively infrequently, aggregate revenue from Netflix's vast niche film catalog rivals that from the rental of blockbuster movies.

But Anderson demonstrates that the Long Tail concept applies outside the media industry as well. The success of online auction site eBay is based on a huge army of auctioneers selling and buying small quantities of "non-hit" items.

# of Products

The Transformation of the Book Publishing Industry

Old Model

We've all heard about aspiring authors who carefully craft and submit manuscripts to publishing houses in the hope of seeing their work in print—and face constant rejection. This stereotypical image of publishers and authors holds much truth. The traditional book publishing model is built on a process of selection whereby publishers screen many authors and manuscripts and select those that seem most likely to achieve minimum sales targets. Less promising authors and their titles are rejected because it would be unprofitable to copyedit, design, print, and promote books that sell poorly. Publishers are most interested in books they can print in quantity for sale to large audiences.

	CONTENT ACQUISITION PUBLISHING SALES PUBLISHING KNOWLEDGE CONTENT	BROAD CONTENT (IDEALLY "HITS")	- RETAIL NETWORK	BROAD AUDIENCE
PUBLISHING / MARKETING			WHOLESALE REVENUES	

A New Model

Lulu.com turned the traditional bestseller-centric publishing model on its head by enabling anyone to publish. Lulu.com's business model is based on helping niche and amateur authors bring their work to market. It eliminates traditional entry barriers by providing authors the tools to craft, print, and distribute their work through an online marketplace. This contrasts strongly with the traditional model of selecting "market-worthy" work. In fact, the more authors Lulu.com attracts, the more it succeeds, because authors become customers. In a nutshell, Lulu.com is a multi-sided platform (see p. 76) that serves and connects authors and readers with a Long Tail of user-generated niche content. Thousands of authors use Lulu.com's self-service tools to publish and sell their books. This works because books are printed only in response to actual orders. The failure of a particular title to sell is irrelevant to Lulu.com, because such a failure incurs no costs.

	PLATFORM DEVELOPMENT LOGISTICS	SELF-PUBLISH-ING SERVICES	COMMUNITIES OF INTEREST ONLINE PROFILE	NICHE AUTHORS
-	PLATFORM PRINT-ON-DEMAND INFRASTRUC-TURE	MARKETPLACE FOR NICHE CONTENT	LULU.COM	NICHE AUDIENCES
PLATFORM MANAGEMENT & DEVELOPMENT			SALES COMMISSIONS (LOW) PUBLISHING SERVICE FEES	

LEGO®'s New Long Tail

The Danish toy company LEGO started manufacturing its now famous interlocking bricks in 1949. Generations of children have played with them, and LEGO has released thousands of kits around a variety of themes, including space stations, pirates, and the Middle Ages. But over time, intensifying competition in the toy industry forced LEGO to seek innovative new paths to growth. It started licensing the rights to use characters from blockbuster movies such as *Star Wars*, *Batman*, and *Indiana Jones*. While such licensing is expensive, it proved to be an impressive revenue generator.

In 2005 LEGO started experimenting with user-generated content. It introduced LEGO Factory, which allows customers to assemble their very own LEGO kits and order them online. Using software called LEGO Digital Designer, customers can invent and design their own buildings, vehicles, themes, and characters, choosing from thousands of components and dozens of colors. Customers can even design the box containing the customized kit. With LEGO Factory, LEGO turned passive users into active participants in the LEGO design experience.

This requires transforming the supply chain infrastructure, and because of low volumes LEGO has not yet fully adapted its support infrastructure to the new LEGO Factory model. Instead, it simply tweaked existing resources and activities.

In terms of a business model, though, LEGO took a step beyond mass customization by entering Long Tail territory. In addition to helping users design their own LEGO sets, LEGO Factory now sells user-designed sets online. Some sell well; some sell poorly or not at all. What's important for LEGO is that the user-designed sets expand a product line previously focused on a limited number of best-selling kits. Today this aspect of LEGO's business accounts for only a small portion of total revenue, but it is a first step towards implementing a Long Tail model as a complement—or even alternative—to a traditional mass-market model.

LEGO

+

LEGO users can make
their own designs
and order them online

=

LEGO Factory

+

LEGO allows users
to post and sell their
designs online

=

LEGO Users Catalog

LEGO Factory: Customer-Designed Kits

KP	KA	VP	CR	CS
	LEGO has to provide and manage the platform and logistics that allow packaging and delivery of custom-made LEGO sets	LEGO Factory substantially expands the scope of the off-the-shelf kit offering by giving LEGO fans the tools to build, showcase, and sell their own custom-designed kits	LEGO Factory builds a Long Tail community around customers who are truly interested in niche content and want to go beyond off-the-shelf retail kits	Thousands of new, customer-designed kits perfectly complement LEGO's standard sets of blocks. LEGO Factory connects customers who create customized designs with other customers, thus becoming a customer match-making platform and increasing sales
Customers who build new LEGO designs and post them online become key partners generating content and value	KR		CH	
	LEGO has not yet fully adapted its resources and activities, which are optimized primarily for the mass market		LEGO Factory's existence depends heavily on the Web channel	

C$	R$
LEGO Factory leverages production and logistics costs already incurred by its traditional retail model	LEGO Factory aims to generate small revenues from a large number of customer-designed items. This represents a valuable addition to traditional high-volume retail revenues

Long Tail
Pattern

Niche content providers (professional and/or user-generated) are the KEY PARTNERS in this pattern.

The VALUE PROPOSITION of a Long Tail business model is characterized by offering a wide scope of "non-hit" items that may co-exist with "hit" products. Long Tail business models may also facilitate and build on user-generated content.

Long Tail business models focus on niche CUSTOMERS.

A Long Tail business model can serve both professional and amateur content producers, and may create a multi-sided platform (see p. 76) catering to users and producers alike.

The KEY RESOURCE is the platform; KEY ACTIVITIES include platform development and maintenance and niche content acquisition and production.

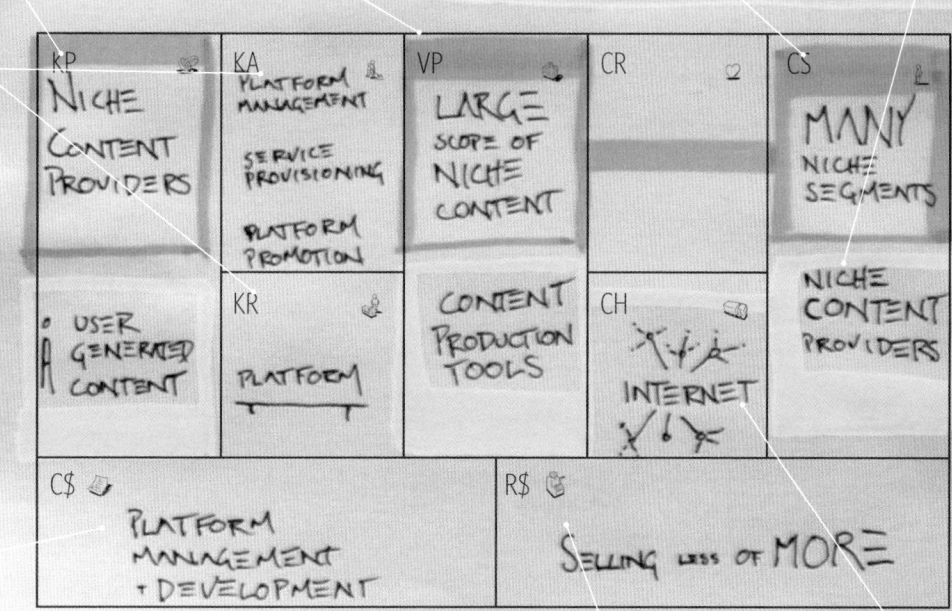

KP	KA	VP	CR	CS
NICHE CONTENT PROVIDERS	PLATFORM MANAGEMENT / SERVICE PROVISIONING / PLATFORM PROMOTION	LARGE SCOPE OF NICHE CONTENT		MANY NICHE SEGMENTS
USER GENERATED CONTENT	KR — PLATFORM	CONTENT PRODUCTION TOOLS	CH — INTERNET	NICHE CONTENT PROVIDERS

C$	R$
PLATFORM MANAGEMENT + DEVELOPMENT	SELLING LESS OF MORE

The main COSTS incurred cover platform development and maintenance

This model is based on aggregating small revenues from a large number of items. REVENUE STREAMS vary; they may come from advertising, product sales, or subscriptions.

Long Tail business models usually rely on the Internet as a CUSTOMER RELATIONSHIP and/or TRANSACTION CHANNEL.

Multi-Sided Platforms

Def_Pattern No. 3

MULTI-SIDED PLATFORMS bring together two or more distinct but interdependent groups of customers. • Such platforms are of value to one group of customers *only* if the other groups of customers are also present. • The platform creates value by *facilitating interactions* between the different groups. • A multi-sided platform grows in value to the extent that it attracts more users, a phenomenon known as the *network effect.*

[REF·ER·ENCES]

1 • "Strategies for Two-Sided Markets." *Harvard Business Review*. Eisenmann, Parker, Van Alstyne. October 2006.

2 • *Invisible Engines: How Software Platforms Drive Innovation and Transform Industries*. Evans, Hagiu, Schmalensee. 2006.

3 • "Managing the Maze of Multisided Markets." *Strategy & Business*. Evans, David. Fall 2003.

[EX·AM·PLES]

Visa, Google, eBay, Microsoft Windows, *Financial Times*

Multi-sided platforms, known by economists as multi-sided markets, are an important business phenomenon. They have existed for a long time, but proliferated with the rise of information technology. The Visa credit card, the Microsoft Windows operating system, the *Financial Times*, Google, the Wii game console, and Facebook are just a few examples of successful multi-sided platforms. We address them here because they represent an increasingly important business model pattern.

What exactly are multi-sided platforms? They are platforms that bring together two or more distinct but interdependent groups of customers. They create value as intermediaries by connecting these groups. Credit cards, for example, link merchants with cardholders; computer operating systems link hardware manufacturers, application developers, and users; newspapers link readers and advertisers; video gaming consoles link game developers with players. The key is that the platform must attract and serve all groups simultane-

ously in order to create value. The platform's value for a particular user group depends substantially on the number of users on the platform's "other sides." A video game console will only attract buyers if enough games are available for the platform. On the other hand, game developers will develop games for a new video console only if a substantial number of gamers already use it. Hence multi-sided platforms often face a "chicken and egg" dilemma.

One way multi-sided platforms solve this problem is by subsidizing a Customer Segment. Though a platform operator incurs costs by serving all customer groups, it often decides to lure one segment to the platform with an inexpensive or free Value Proposition in order to subsequently attract users of the platform's "other side." One difficulty multi-sided platform operators face is understanding which side to subsidize and how to price correctly to attract customers.

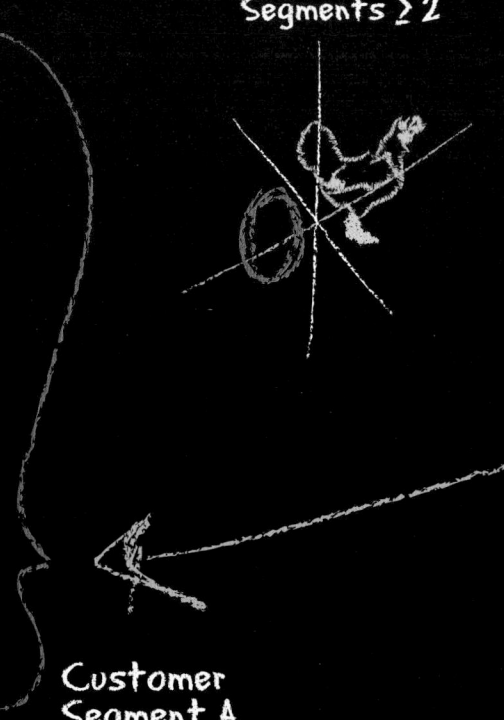

Segments ≥ 2

Customer
Segment A

Segment B

FACILITATE INTERACTION

etc.

etc.

Segment N

One example is *Metro*, the free daily newspaper that originated in Stockholm and can now be found in many large cities worldwide. It launched in 1995 and immediately attracted a large readership because it was distributed free of charge to urban commuters in train and bus stations throughout Stockholm. This allowed it to attract advertisers and rapidly become profitable. Another example is Microsoft, which gave its Windows software development kit (SDK) away for free to encourage development of new applications for its operating system. The larger number of applications attracted more users to the Windows platform and increased Microsoft's revenues. Sony's Playstation 3 game console, on the other hand, is an example of a multi-sided platform strategy that backfired. Sony subsidized each console purchased in hopes of later collecting more game royalties. This strategy performed poorly because fewer Playstation 3 games sold than Sony initially estimated.

Operators of multi-sided platforms must ask themselves several key questions: Can we attract sufficient numbers of customers for each side of the platform? Which side is more price sensitive? Can that side be enticed by a subsidized offer? Will the other side of the platform generate sufficient revenues to cover the subsidies?

The following pages outline three examples of multi-sided platform patterns. First, we sketch Google's multi-sided platform business model. Then we show how Nintendo, Sony, and Microsoft compete with slightly different multi-sided platform patterns. Finally, we describe how Apple has slowly evolved into an operator of a powerful multi-sided platform.

Google's Business Model

The heart of Google's business model is its Value Proposition of providing extremely targeted text advertising globally over the Web. Through a service called AdWords, advertisers can publish advertisements and sponsored links on Google's search pages (and on an affiliated content network as we will later see). The ads are displayed alongside search results when people use the Google search engine. Google ensures that only ads relevant to the search term are displayed. The service is attractive to advertisers because it allows them to tailor online campaigns to specific searches and particular demographic targets. The model only works, though, if many people use Google's search engine. The more people Google reaches, the more ads it can display and the greater the value created for advertisers.

Google's Value Proposition to advertisers depends heavily on the number of customers it attracts to its Web site. So Google caters to this second group of consumer customers with a powerful search engine and a growing number of tools such as Gmail (Web based e-mail), Google maps, and Picasa (an online photo album) among others. To extend its reach even further, Google designed a third service that enables its ads to be displayed on other, non-Google Web sites. This service, called AdSense, allows third parties to earn a portion of Google's advertising revenue by showing Google ads on their own sites. AdSense automatically analyzes a participating Web site's content and displays relevant text and image ads to visitors. The Value Proposition to these third party Web site owners, Google's third Customer Segment, is to enable them to earn money from their content.

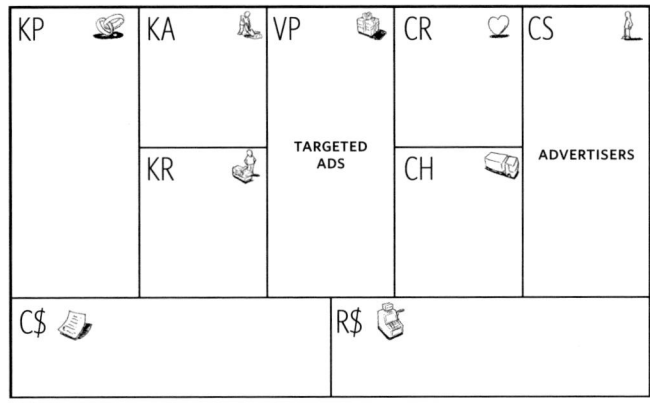

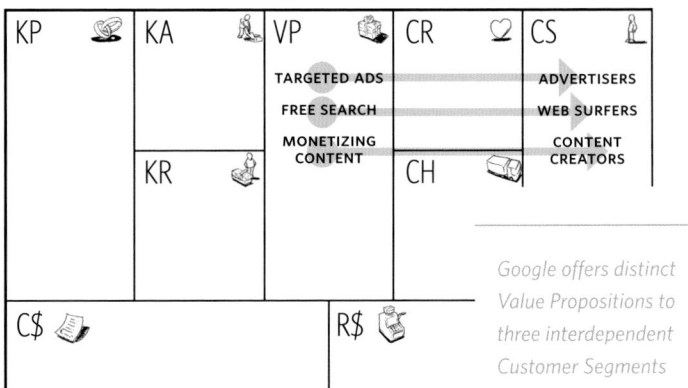

Google offers distinct Value Propositions to three interdependent Customer Segments

As a multi-sided platform Google has a very distinct revenue model. It makes money from one Customer Segment, advertisers, while subsidizing free offers to two other segments: Web surfers and content owners. This is logical because the more ads it displays to Web surfers, the more it earns from advertisers. Increased advertising earnings, in turn, motivates even more content owners to become AdSense partners. Advertisers don't directly buy advertising space from Google. They bid on ad-related keywords associated with either search terms or content on third party Web sites. The bidding occurs through an AdWords auction service: the more popular a keyword, the more an advertiser has to pay for it. The substantial revenue that Google earns from AdWords allows it to continuously improve its free offers to search engine and AdSense users.

Google's Key Resource is its search platform, which powers three different services: Web search (Google.com), advertising (AdWords), and third-party content monetization (AdSense). These services are based on highly complex proprietary search and matchmaking algorithms supported by an extensive IT infrastructure. Google's three Key Activities can be defined as follows: (1) building and maintaining the search infrastructure, (2) managing the three main services, and (3) promoting the platform to new users, content owners, and advertisers.

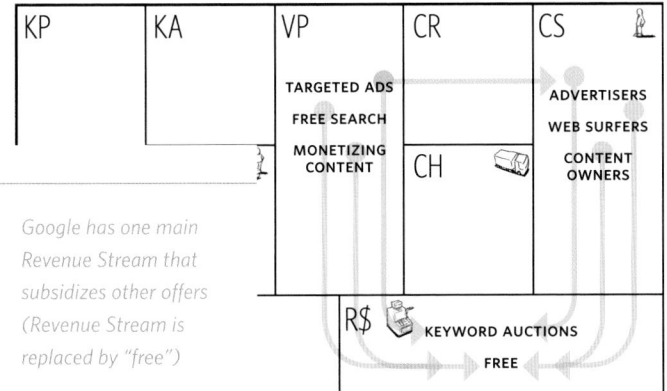

Google has one main Revenue Stream that subsidizes other offers (Revenue Stream is replaced by "free")

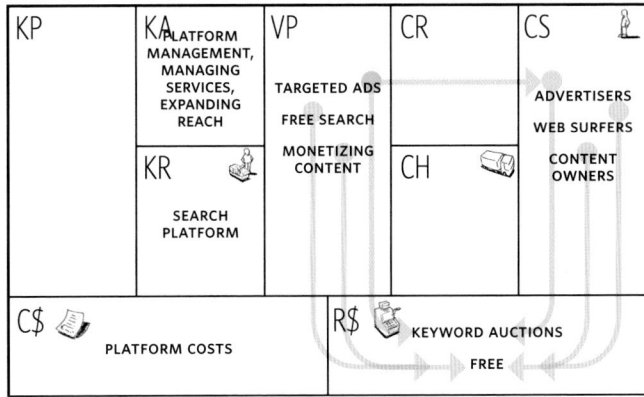

Wii versus PSP/Xbox Same Pattern, Different Focus

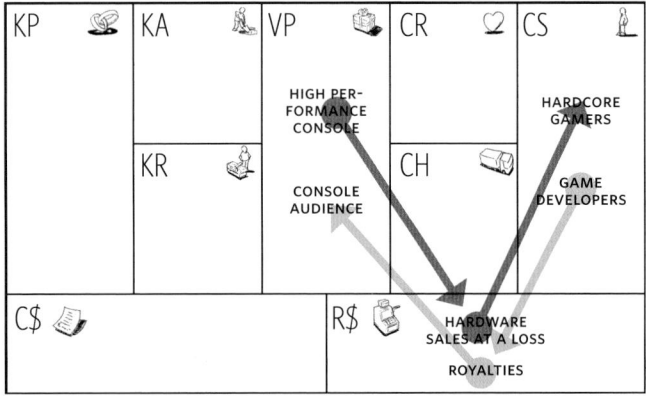

PSP/Xbox Focus

Video game consoles, today a multi-billion dollar business, provide good examples of double-sided platforms. On one hand, a console manufacturer has to draw as many players as possible to attract game developers. On the other hand, players only buy the hardware if there is a sufficient number of interesting games available for that console. In the game industry, this has led to a fierce battle between three main competitors and their respective devices: the Sony Playstation series, the Microsoft Xbox series, and the Nintendo Wii. All three are based on double-sided platforms, but there are substantial differences between the Sony/Microsoft business model and Nintendo's approach, demonstrating that there is no "proven" solution for a given market.

Sony and Microsoft dominated the game console market until Nintendo's Wii swept the sector with a fresh approach to technology and an astonishingly different business model. Before launching the Wii, Nintendo was spiraling downward, rapidly losing market share, and teetering on the edge of bankruptcy. The Wii console changed all that and catapulted the company to the market leader position.

Traditionally, video console manufacturers targeted avid gamers and competed on console price and performance. For this audience of "hardcore gamers" graphics and game quality and processor speed were the main selection criteria. As a consequence, manufacturers developed extremely sophisticated and expensive consoles and sold them at a loss for years, subsidizing the hardware with two other revenue sources.

First, they developed and sold their own games for their own consoles. Second, they earned royalties from third party developers who paid for the right to create games for specific consoles. This is the typical pattern of a double-sided platform business model: one side, the consumer, is heavily subsidized to deliver as many consoles as possible to the market. Money is then earned from the other side of the platform: game developers.

*Same pattern, but
different business model:
Nintendo's Wii*

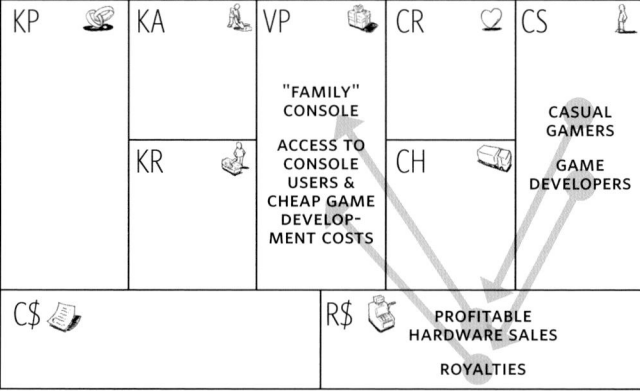

Wii Focus

Nintendo's Wii changed all this. Like its competitors, the Wii is based on a double-sided platform business, but with substantially different elements. Nintendo aimed its consoles at the huge audience of casual gamers rather than the smaller "traditional" market of avid gamers. It won the hearts of casual gamers with relatively inexpensive machines equipped with a special remote control device that allows players to control the action with physical gestures. The novelty and fun of motion-controlled games such as Wii Sports, Wii Music, and Wii Fit attracted enormous numbers of casual gamers. This differentiator is also the basis for the new type of double-sided platform that Nintendo created.

Sony and Microsoft competed with costly, proprietary, state-of-the-art technology aimed at avid gamers and subsidized it in order to gain market share and keep hardware prices affordable. Nintendo, on the other hand, focused on a market segment that was far less sensitive to technological performance. Instead, it lured customers with its motion-controlled "fun factor." This was a much cheaper technological innovation compared to new, more powerful chipsets. Thus, the Nintendo Wii was less costly to produce, allowing the company to forego commercialization subsidies. This is the main difference between Nintendo and rivals Sony and Microsoft: Nintendo earns money from both sides of its double-sided Wii platform. It generates profits on each console sold to consumers and pockets royalties from game developers.

To summarize, three interlinked business model factors explain the commercial success of the Wii: (1) low-cost differentiation of the product (motion control), (2) focus on a new, untapped market that cares less about technology (casual gamers), and (3) a double-sided platform pattern that generates revenues from both "sides" of the Wii. All three represent clean breaks from past game sector traditions.

Apple's Evolution into a Platform Operator

The evolution of Apple's product line from the iPod to the iPhone high-lights the company's transition to a powerful platform business model pattern. The iPod was initially a stand-alone device. The iPhone, on the contrary, evolved into a powerful multi-sided platform for which Apple controls third party applications through its App Store.

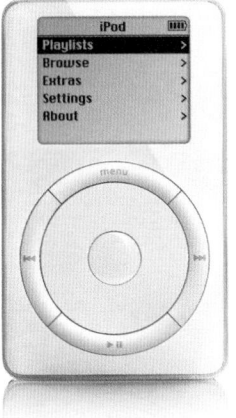

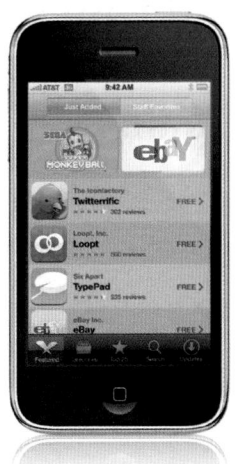

| IPOD | *Switch to multi-sided platform business model* | IPOD & ITUNES | *Consolidation of platform business model* | IPHONE & APPSTORE |

2001   2003   2008

Apple introduced the iPod in 2001 as a stand-alone product. Users could copy their CDs and download music from the Internet onto the device. The iPod represented a technology platform for storing music from various sources. At this point, though, Apple was not exploiting the platform aspect of the iPod in its business model.

In 2003 Apple introduced the iTunes Music Store, which was closely integrated with the iPod. The store allowed users to buy and download digital music in an extremely convenient way. The store was Apple's first attempt at exploiting platform effects. iTunes essentially connected "music rightsholders" directly with buyers. This strategy catapulted Apple to its position today as the world's largest online music retailer.

In 2008 Apple consolidated its platform strategy by launching its App Store for the highly popular iPhone. The App Store allows users to browse, buy, and download applications directly from the iTunes Store and install them on their iPhones. Application developers must channel sales of all applications through the App Store, with Apple collecting a 30 percent royalty on each application sold.

Multi-Sided Platform Pattern

The VALUE PROPOSITION usually creates value in three main areas: First, attracting user groups (i.e. Customer Segments); Second, matchmaking between Customer Segments; Third, reducing costs by channeling transactions through the platform.

Business models with a multi-sided platform pattern have a distinct structure. They have two or more CUSTOMER SEGMENTS, each of which has its own Value Proposition and associated Revenue Stream. Moreover, one Customer Segment cannot exist without the others.

The KEY RESOURCE required for this business model pattern is the platform. The three Key Activities are usually platform management, service provisioning, and platform promotion.

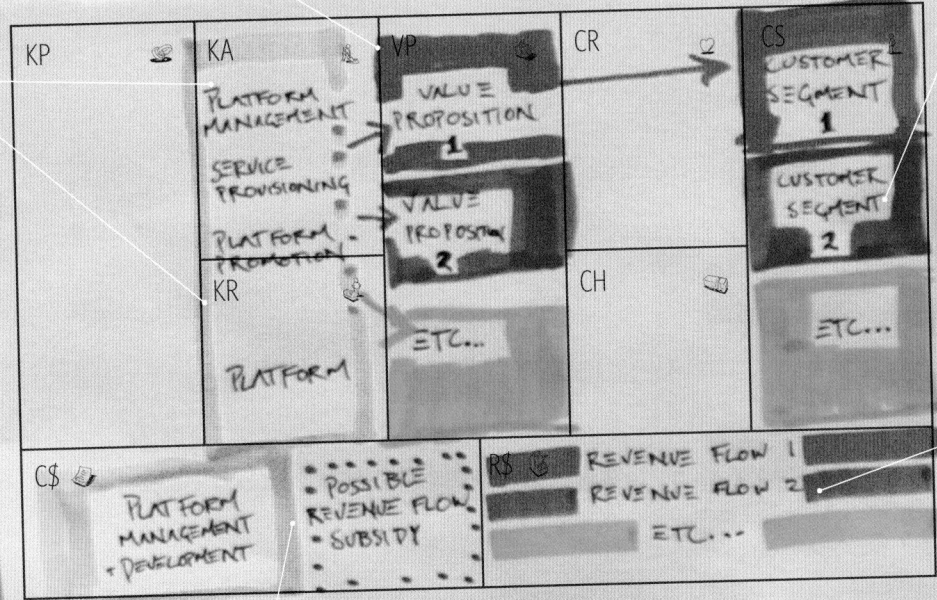

KP | KA | VP | CR | CS

PLATFORM MANAGEMENT
SERVICE PROVISIONING
PLATFORM PROMOTION

VALUE PROPOSITION 1
VALUE PROPOSITION 2

CUSTOMER SEGMENT 1
CUSTOMER SEGMENT 2

KR — PLATFORM

CH — ETC...

ETC...

C$ — PLATFORM MANAGEMENT + DEVELOPMENT

POSSIBLE REVENUE FLOW = SUBSIDY

R$ — REVENUE FLOW 1 / REVENUE FLOW 2 / ETC...

The main COSTS incurred under this pattern relate to maintaining and developing the platform.

Each Customer Segment produces a different REVENUE STREAM. One or more segments may enjoy free offers or reduced prices subsidized by revenues from other Customer Segments. Choosing which segment to subsidize can be a crucial pricing decision that determines the success of a multi-sided platform business model.

FREE as a Business Model

Def_Pattern No. 4

FREE • In the *FREE* business model *at least one* substantial Customer Segment is able to *continuously benefit* from a free-of-charge offer. • *Different patterns* make the free offer possible. • Non-paying customers are financed by another part of the business model or by another Customer Segment.

[REF·ER·ENCES]

1 • "Free! Why $0.00 is the Future of Business." *Wired Magazine.* Anderson, Chris. February 2008.

2 • "How about Free? The Price Point That Is Turning Industries on Their Heads." *Knowledge@ Wharton.* March 2009.

3 • *Free: The Future of a Radical Price.* Anderson, Chris. 2008.

[EX·AM·PLES]

Metro (free paper), Flickr, Open Source, Skype, Google, Free Mobile Phones

Receiving something free of charge has always
been an attractive Value Proposition. Any marketer or
economist will confirm that the demand generated at a price of zero
is many times higher than the demand generated at one cent or any other price
point. In recent years free offers have exploded, particularly over the Internet. The question, of course, is how can you systematically offer something for free and still earn substantial
revenues? Part of the answer is that the cost of producing certain giveaways, such as online data storage
capacity, has fallen dramatically. Yet to make a profit, an organization offering free products or services must
still generate revenues somehow.

There are several patterns that make integrating free products and services into a business model possible. Some of the traditional FREE patterns are well known, such as advertising, which is based on the previously discussed pattern of multi-sided
platforms (see p. 76). Others, such as the so-called freemium model, which provides basic services free of charge and premium
services for a fee, have become popular in step with the increasing digitization of goods and services offered via the Web.

Chris Anderson, whose Long Tail concept we discussed previously (see p. 66), has helped the concept of FREE gain widespread
recognition. Anderson shows that the rise of new free-of-charge offers is closely related to the fundamentally different economics of digital products and services. For example, creating and recording a song costs an artist time and money, but the cost of
digitally replicating and distributing the work over the Internet is close to zero. Hence, an artist can promote and deliver music
to a global audience over the Web, as long as he or she finds other Revenue Streams, such as concerts and merchandising, to cover costs. Bands and artists who have experimented successfully with free music include Radiohead and Trent
Reznor of Nine Inch Nails.

In this section we look at three different patterns that make FREE a viable business model option. Each
has different underlying economics, but all share a common trait: at least one Customer Segment
continuously benefits from the free-of-charge offer. The three patterns are (1) free offer based
on multi-sided platforms (advertising-based), (2) free basic services with optional
premium services (the so-called "freemium" model), (3) and the "bait &
hook" model whereby a free or inexpensive initial offer lures
customers into repeat purchases.

(How) can you set it free?

Advertising: A Multi-Sided Platform Model

Advertising is a well-established revenue source that enables free offers. We recognize it on television, radio, the Web, and in one of its most sophisticated forms, in targeted Google ads. In business model terms, FREE based on advertising is a particular form of the multi-sided platform pattern (see p. 76). One side of the platform is designed to attract users with free content, products, or services. Another side of the platform generates revenue by selling space to advertisers.

One striking example of this pattern is *Metro*, the free newspaper that started in Stockholm and is now available in dozens of cities around the world. The genius of *Metro* lies in how it modified the traditional daily newspaper model. First, it offered the paper for free. Second, it focused on distributing in high-traffic commuter zones and public transport networks by hand and with self-service racks. This required *Metro* to develop its own distribution network, but enabled the company to quickly achieve broad circulation. Third, it cut editorial costs to produce a paper just good enough to entertain younger commuters during their short rides

to and from work. Competitors using the same model soon followed, but *Metro* kept them at bay with a couple of smart moves. For example, it controlled many of the news racks at train and bus stations, forcing rivals to resort to costly hand distribution in important areas.

Minimizes costs by cutting editorial team to produce a daily paper just "good enough" for a commute read

Assures high circulation through free offer and by focusing on distributing in high-traffic commuter zones and public transport networks

Metro

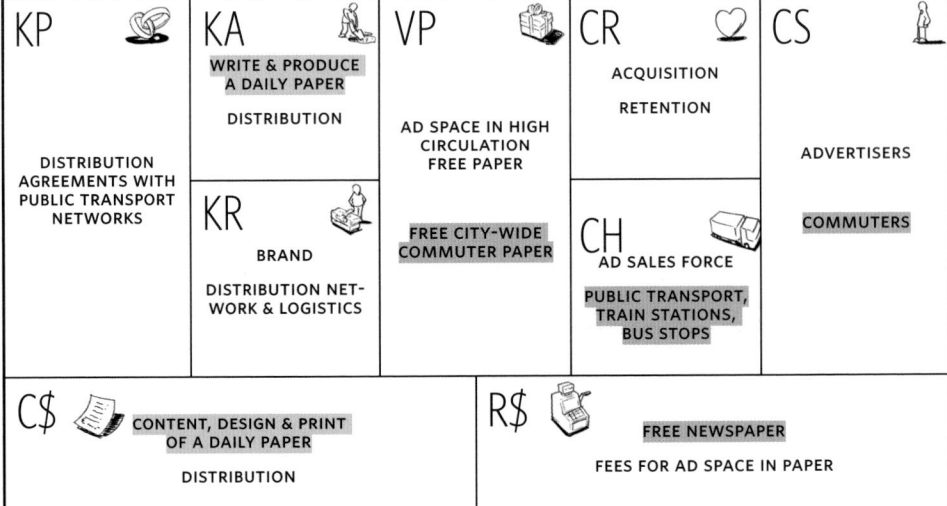

Mass ≠ automatic ad $

A large number of users does not automatically translate into an El Dorado of advertising revenues, as the social networking service Facebook has demonstrated. The company claimed over 200 million active users as of May 2009, and said more than 100 million log on to its site daily. Those figures make Facebook the world's largest social network. Yet users are less responsive to Facebook advertising than to traditional Web ads, according to industry experts. While advertising is only one of several potential Revenue Streams for Facebook, clearly a mass of users does not guarantee huge advertising revenues. At this writing, privately held Facebook did not disclose revenue data.

Facebook

AD SPACE ON HIGH TRAFFIC SOCIAL NETWORK	MASS CUSTOMIZED	ADVERTISERS
FREE SOCIAL NETWORK	AD SALES FORCE	GLOBAL WEB AUDIENCE
	FACEBOOK.COM	
FREE ACCOUNTS		
FEES FOR AD SPACE ON FACEBOOK		

Newspapers: Free or Not Free?

One industry crumbling under the impact of FREE is newspaper publishing. Sandwiched between freely available Internet content and free newspapers, several traditional papers have already filed for bankruptcy. The U.S. news industry reached a tipping point in 2008 when the number of people obtaining news online for free outstripped those paying for newspapers or news magazines, according to a study by the Pew Research Center.

Traditionally, newspapers and magazines relied on revenues from three sources: newsstand sales, subscription fees, and advertising. The first two are rapidly declining and the third is not increasing quickly enough. Though many newspapers have increased online readership, they've failed to achieve correspondingly greater advertising revenues. Meanwhile, the high fixed costs that guarantee good journalism—news gathering and editorial teams—remained unchanged.

Several newspapers have experimented with paid online subscriptions, with mixed results. It is difficult to charge for articles when readers can view similar content for free on Web sites such as CNN.com or MSNBC.com. Few newspapers have succeeded in motivating readers to pay for access to premium content online.

On the print side, traditional newspapers are under attack from free publications such as *Metro*. Though *Metro* offers a completely different format and journalistic quality and focuses primarily on young readers who previously ignored newspapers, it is ratcheting up the pressure on fee-for-service news providers. Charging money for news is an increasingly difficult proposition.

Some news entrepreneurs are experimenting with novel formats focused on the online space. For example, news provider True/Slant (trueslant.com) aggregates on one site the work of over 60 journalists, each an expert in a specific field. The writers are paid a share of the advertising and sponsorship revenues generated by True/Slant. For a fee, advertisers can publish their own material in pages paralleling the news content.

Free Advertising: Pattern of Multi-Sided Platforms

With the right PRODUCT OR SERVICE and high traffic, the platform becomes interesting to advertisers, which in turn allows CHARGING fees to subsidize free products and services.

Main COSTS relate to developing and maintaining the platform; traffic-generation and retention costs may also arise.

Free products or services generate high platform traffic and increase attractiveness to advertisers.

KP	KA	VP	CR	CS
	PLATFORM DEVELOPMENT + MAINTENANCE	AD SPACE + HIGH FREQUENTATION		ADVERTISERS
	KR	PRODUCT OR SERVICE	CH	~~CLIENTS~~ CUSTOMERS
	PLATFORM			

C$		R$		
PLATFORM COSTS	CUSTOMER ACQUISITION COSTS	AD FEES		
		FREE		

Freemium: Get the Basics for Free, Pay for More

Flickr

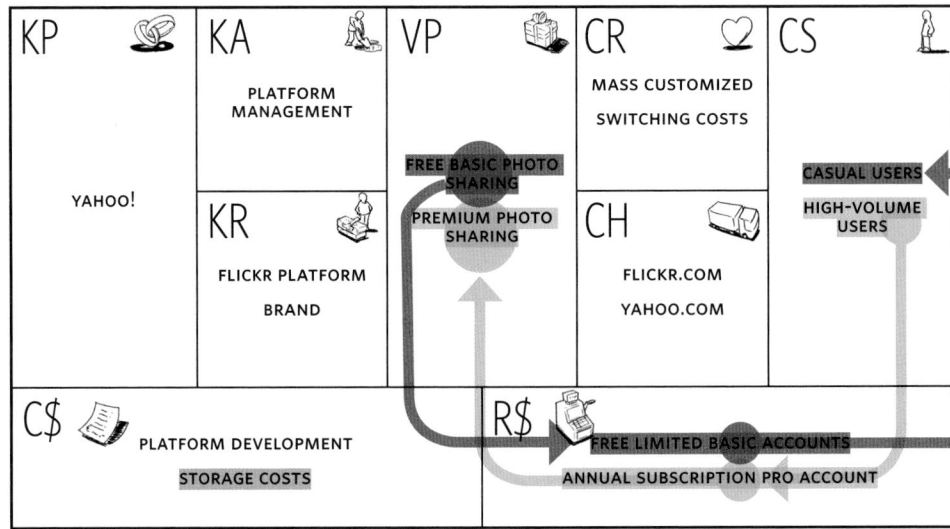

The term "freemium" was coined by Jarid Lukin and popularized by venture capitalist Fred Wilson on his blog. It stands for business models, mainly Web-based, that blend free basic services with paid premium services. The freemium model is characterized by a large user base benefiting from a free, no-strings-attached offer. Most of these users never become paying customers; only a small portion, usually less than 10 percent of all users, subscribe to the paid premium services. This small base of paying users subsidizes the free users. This is possible because of the low marginal cost of serving additional free users. In a freemium model, the key metrics to watch are (1) the average cost of serving a free user, and (2) the rates at which free users convert to premium (paying) customers.

Flickr, the popular photo-sharing Web site acquired by Yahoo! in 2005, provides a good example of a freemium business model. Flickr users can subscribe for free to a basic account that enables them to upload and share images. The free service has certain constraints, such as limited storage space and a maximum number of uploads per month. For a small annual fee users can purchase a "pro" account and enjoy unlimited uploads and storage space, plus additional features.

Fixed and sunk costs related to platform development

Variable cost depending on number of photos stored

Large base of basic accounts for casual users

Small base of paying "pro" users

Open Source: Freemium with a Twist

Business models in the enterprise software industry are usually characterized by two traits: First, the high fixed cost of supporting an army of expert software developers who build the product; Second, a revenue model based on selling multiple per-user licenses and regular upgrades of the software.

Red Hat, a U.S. software company, turned this model upside down. Rather than creating software from scratch, it builds its product on top of so-called open source software developed voluntarily by thousands of software engineers around the world. Red Hat understood that companies were interested in robust, licensing fee-free open source software, but were reluctant to adopt it due to concerns that no single entity was legally responsible for providing and maintaining it. Red Hat filled this gap by offering stable, tested, service-ready versions of freely available open source software, particularly Linux.

Each Red Hat release is supported for seven years. Customers benefit from this approach because it allows them to enjoy the cost and stability advantages of open source software,

while protecting them from the uncertainties surrounding a product not officially "owned" by anyone. Red Hat benefits because its software kernel is continuously improved by the open source community free of charge. This substantially reduces Red Hat's development costs.

Naturally, Red Hat also has to earn money. So rather than charging clients for each major

new release—the traditional software revenue model—it sells subscriptions. For an annual fee, each client enjoys continuous access to the latest Red Hat release, unlimited service support, and the security of interacting with the legal owner of the product. Companies are willing to pay for these benefits despite the free availability of many versions of Linux and other open source software.

Red Hat

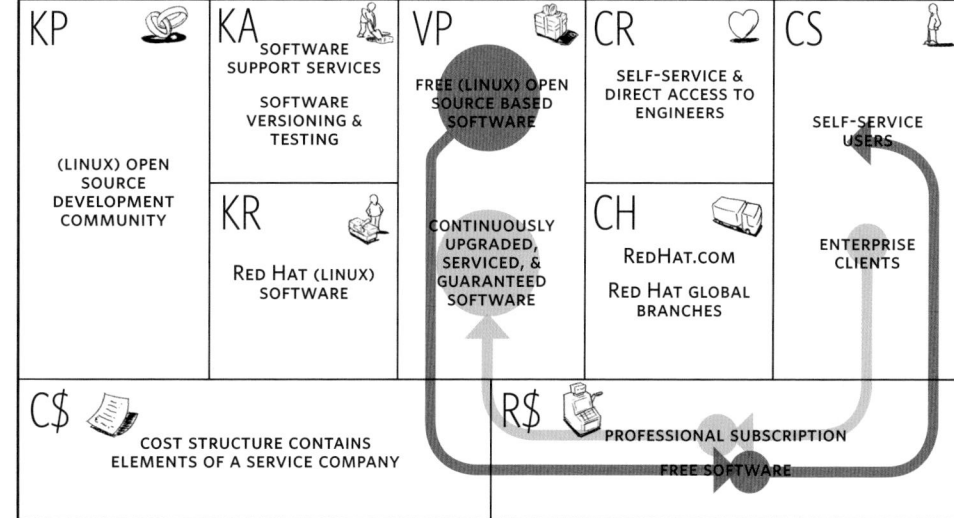

Skype

Skype offers an intriguing example of a free-mium pattern that disrupted the telecommunications sector by enabling free calling services via the Internet. Skype developed software by the same name that, when installed on computers or smartphones, enables users to make calls from one device to another free of charge. Skype can offer this because its Cost Structure is completely different from that of a telecom carrier. Free calls are fully routed through the Internet based on so-called peer-to-peer technology that employs user hardware and the Internet as communications infrastructure. Hence, Skype does not have to manage its own network like a telco and incurs only minor costs to support additional users. Skype requires very little of its own infrastructure besides backend software and the servers hosting user accounts.

Users pay only for calling landlines and mobile phones through a premium service called SkypeOut, which offers very low rates. In fact, users are charged only slightly more than the termination costs that Skype itself incurs for calls routed through wholesale carriers such as iBasis and Level 3, which handle the company's network traffic.

Skype

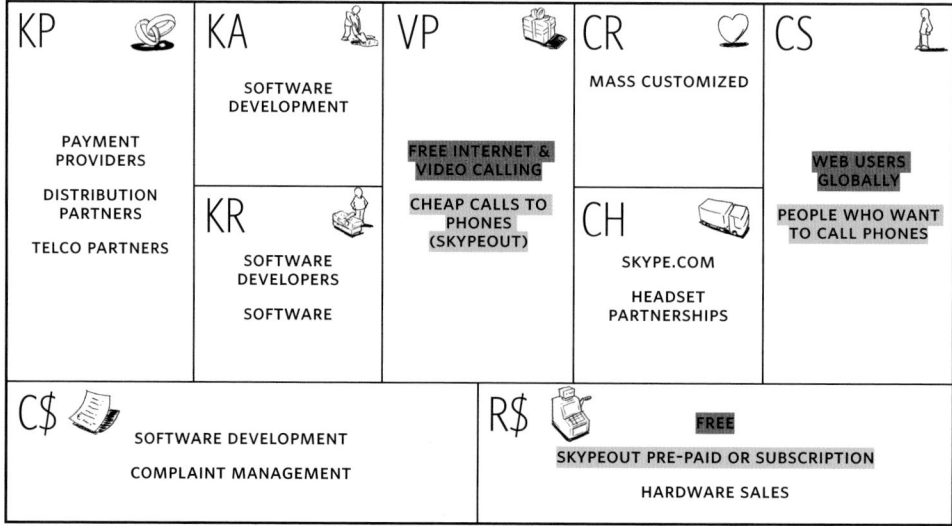

Skype claims it has over 400 million registered users who have made more than 100 billion free calls since the company was founded in 2004. Skype reported revenues of U.S. $550 million in 2008, though the company and its owner, eBay, do not release detailed financial data including information on profitability. We may soon know more as eBay has announced plans to list Skype through an initial public offering (IPO).

Over 90 percent of Skype users subscribe to the free service

Paid SkypeOut calls account for less than 10 percent of total usage

5+ years old
400 million+ users
100 billion+ free
* calls generated*
2008 revenues of
* U.S. $550 million*

Skype disrupted the telecommunications industry and helped drive voice communication costs close to zero. Telecom operators initially didn't understand why Skype would offer calls for free and didn't take the company seriously. What's more, only a tiny fraction of the traditional carriers' customers used Skype. But over time more and more customers decided to make their international calls with Skype, eating into one of the most lucrative carrier revenue sources. This pattern, typical of a disruptive business model, severely affected the traditional voice communication business, and today Skype is the world's largest provider of cross-border voice communication services, according to telecommunications research firm Telegeography.

Skype versus Telco

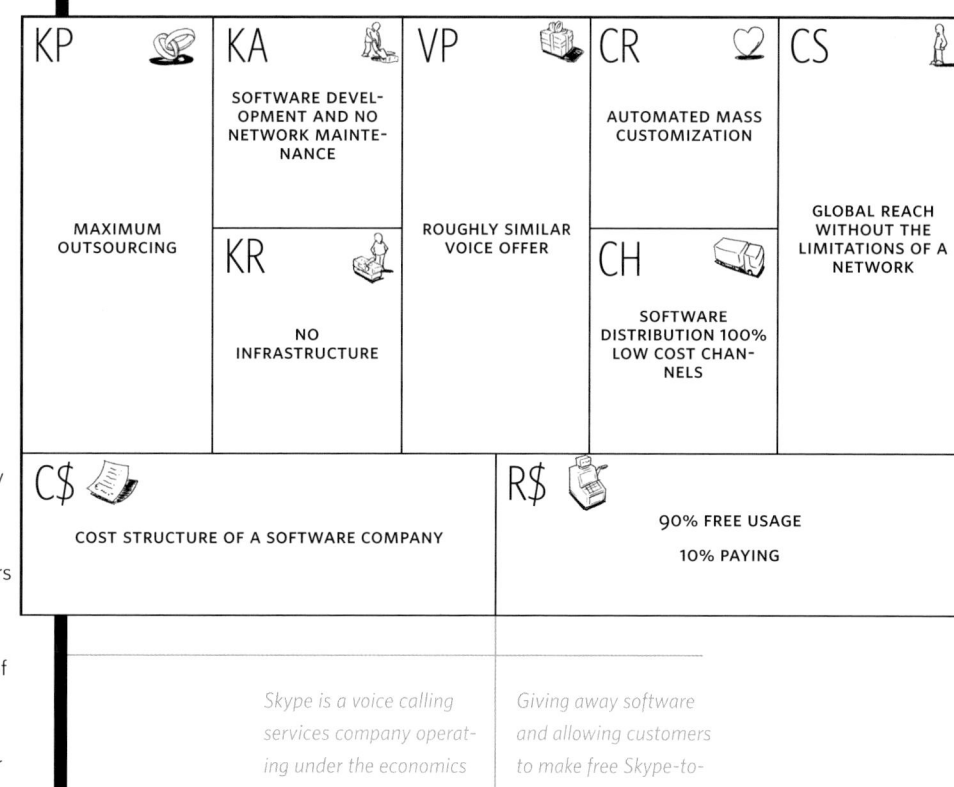

KP	KA	VP	CR	CS
	SOFTWARE DEVELOPMENT AND NO NETWORK MAINTENANCE		AUTOMATED MASS CUSTOMIZATION	
MAXIMUM OUTSOURCING	KR	ROUGHLY SIMILAR VOICE OFFER	CH	GLOBAL REACH WITHOUT THE LIMITATIONS OF A NETWORK
	NO INFRASTRUCTURE		SOFTWARE DISTRIBUTION 100% LOW COST CHANNELS	

C$	R$
COST STRUCTURE OF A SOFTWARE COMPANY	90% FREE USAGE 10% PAYING

Skype is a voice calling services company operating under the economics of a software company

Giving away software and allowing customers to make free Skype-to-Skype calls costs the company little

The Insurance Model: Freemium Upside Down

In the freemium model a small base of customers paying for a premium service subsidizes a large base of non-paying customers. The insurance model is actually the opposite—it's the freemium model turned on its head. In the insurance model, a large base of customers pay small regular fees to protect themselves from unlikely—but financially devastating—events. In short, a large base of paying customers subsidizes a small group of people with actual claims—but any one of the paying customers could at any time become part of the beneficiary group.

Let's look at REGA as an example. REGA is a Swiss non-profit organization that uses helicopters and airplanes to transport medical staff to the scene of accidents, notably in the mountainous areas of Switzerland. Over two million so-called "patrons" finance the organization. In return, patrons are exempt from paying any costs arising from being rescued by REGA. Mountain rescue operations can be extremely expensive, so REGA patrons find the service attractive in protecting them against the high cost of accidents during skiing vacations, summer hikes, or mountain drives.

REGA

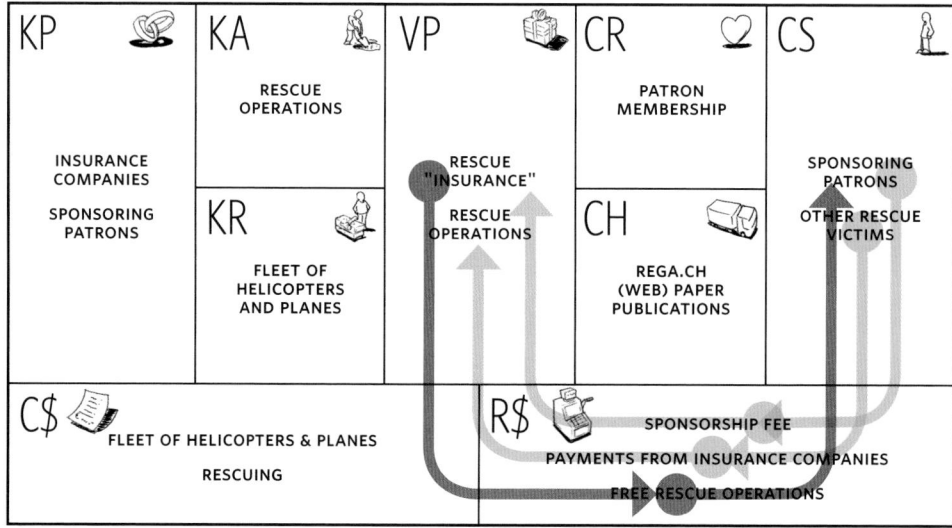

Many paying users cover the costs of a few claims

"Every industry that becomes digital eventually becomes free."

— *Chris Anderson*
Editor-in-Chief, Wired Magazine

"We can no longer stand by and watch others walk off with our work under misguided legal theories."

— *Dean Singleton*
Chairman, Associated Press

"The demand you get at a price of zero is many times higher than the demand you get at a very low price."

— *Kartik Hosanagar*
Assistant Professor, Wharton

"Google's not a real company. It's a house of cards."

— *Steve Ballmer*
CEO, Microsoft

Freemium Pattern

The platform is the most important ASSET in the freemium pattern, because it allows free basic services to be offered at low marginal cost.

The COST STRUCTURE of this pattern is tripartite: usually with substantial fixed costs, very low marginal costs for services to free accounts, and (separate) costs for premium accounts

CUSTOMER RELATIONSHIP must be automated and low cost in order to handle large numbers of free users.

An IMPORTANT METRIC to follow is the rate at which free accounts convert to premium accounts

USERS describes how many users a company with a freemium business model can attract

FIXED COSTS a company incurs to run its business model (e.g. systems costs)

The freemium model is characterized by a large base of free service users subsidized by a small base of paying users.

Users enjoy a free basic service and can pay for a premium service that offers additional benefits.

COST OF SERVICE
indicates the average cost the company incurs to deliver a free or premium service to a free or premium user.

GROWTH & CHURN RATE
specifies how many users defect/respectively join the user base.

CUSTOMER ACQUISITION COSTS
total expenses a company incurs to acquire new users.

PERCENT OF PREMIUM & FREE USERS
specifies how many of all users are premium paying users or free users.

PRICE OF PREMIUM SERVICE
indicates the average cost the company incurs to deliver a premium service to a premium paying user.

operating profit period	income	cost of service	fixed costs	customer acquisition costs	operating profit
month 1	$2,116,125	$391,500	$1,100,000	$650,000	-$25,3
month 2	$2,151,041	$397,960	$1,100,000	$650,000	$3,081
month 3	$2,186,533	$404,526	$1,100,000	$650,000	$32,007
month 4	$2,222,611	$411,201	$1,100,000	$650,000	$6
month 5	$2,259,284	$417,986	$1,100,000	$650,000	
month 6	$2,296,562	$424,882	$1,100,000	$650,000	
month 7	$2,334,456	$431,893			
month 8	$2,372,974				
month 9	$2,4				

cost of service period	users	% of free users	cost of service free users	users	% of premium users	cost of service premium users	cost of service to all users
month 1	9,000,000	0.95	$0.03	9,000,000	0.05	$0.30	$391,500
	9,148,500	0.95	$0.03	9,148,500	0.05	$0.30	$397,960
		0.95	$0.03	9,299,450	0.05	$0.30	$404,526
				9,152,891	0.05	$0.30	$411,201
					0.05	$0.30	$417,986

income period	users	% of premium users	price of premium service/month	growth rate	churn rate	income
month 1	9,000,000	0.05	$4.95	1.07	0.95	$2,116,125
month 2	9,148,500	0.05	$4.95	1.07	0.95	$2,151,041
month 3	9,299,450	0.05	$4.95	1.07	0.95	$2,186,533
month 4	9,452,891	0.05	$4.95	1.07	0.95	$2,222,611
month 5	9,608,864	0.05	$4.95	1.07	0.95	$2,259,284
month 6	9,767,410	0.05	$4.95	1.07	0.95	$2,296,562
month 7	9,928,572	0.05	$4.95	1.07	0.95	$2,334,456
month 8	10,092,394	0.05	$4.95	1.07	0.95	$2,372,974
	10,258,918	0.05	$4.95	1.07	0.95	$2,412,128
	191	0.05	$4.95	1.07	0.95	$2,451,928
		0.05	$4.95	1.07	0.95	$2,492,385
		0.05	$4.95	1.07	0.95	$2,533,509

$$INCOME = \left\{ USERS \times \%\,OF\,PREMIUM\,USERS \times PRICE\,OF\,PREMIUM\,SERVICE \right\} \times GROWTH\,RATE \times CHURN\,RATE$$

$$COST\,OF\,SERVICE = \left\{ USERS \times \%\,OF\,FREE\,USERS \times COST\,OF\,SERVICE\,TO\,FREE\,USERS \right\} + \left\{ USERS \times \%\,OF\,PREMIUM\,USERS \times COST\,OF\,SERVICE\,TO\,PREMIUM\,USERS \right\}$$

$$OPERATING\,PROFIT = INCOME - COST\,OF\,SERVICE - FIXED\,COSTS - CUSTOMER\,ACQUISITION\,COSTS$$

Bait & Hook

"Bait & hook" refers to a business model pattern characterized by an attractive, inexpensive, or free initial offer that encourages continuing future purchases of related products or services. This pattern is also known as the "loss leader" or "razor & blades" model. "Loss leader" refers to a subsidized, even money-losing initial offer with the intention of generating profits from subsequent purchases. "Razor & blades" refers to a business model popularized by an American businessman, King C. Gillette, inventor of the disposable razor blade (see p. 105). We use the term bait & hook pattern to describe the general idea of luring customers with an initial offering, while earning from follow-up sales.

The mobile telecommunications industry provides a good illustration of the bait & hook pattern with a free offer. It is now standard practice for mobile network operators to offer free telephone handsets bundled with service subscriptions. Operators initially lose money by giving away mobile phones for free, but they easily cover the loss through subsequent monthly service fees. Operators provide instant gratification with a free offer that later generates recurring income.

Bait & Hook of Free Mobile Phones

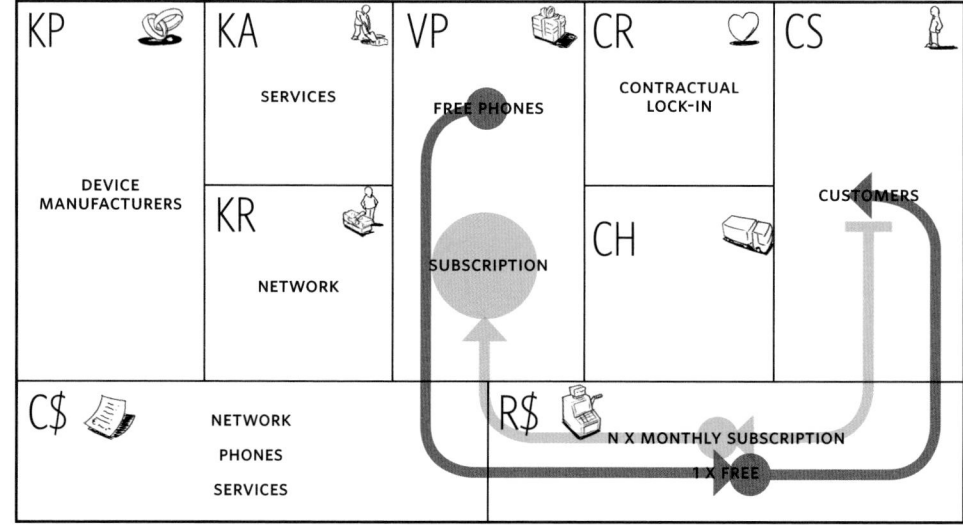

Razor & Blades : Gillette

The form of the bait & hook pattern known as the razor and blades model derives from the way the first disposable razors were sold. In 1904 King C. Gillette, who commercialized the first disposable razor blade system, decided to sell razor handles at a steep discount or even give them away with other products in order to create demand for his disposable blades. Today Gillette is still the preeminent brand in shaving products. The key to this model is the close link between the inexpensive or free initial product and the follow-up item—usually disposable—on which the company earns a high margin. Controlling the "lock-in" is crucial to this pattern's success. Through blocking patents, Gillette ensured that competitors couldn't offer cheaper blades for the Gillette razor handles. In fact, today razors are among the world's most heavily patented consumer products, with more than 1,000 patents covering everything from lubricating strips to cartridge-loading systems.

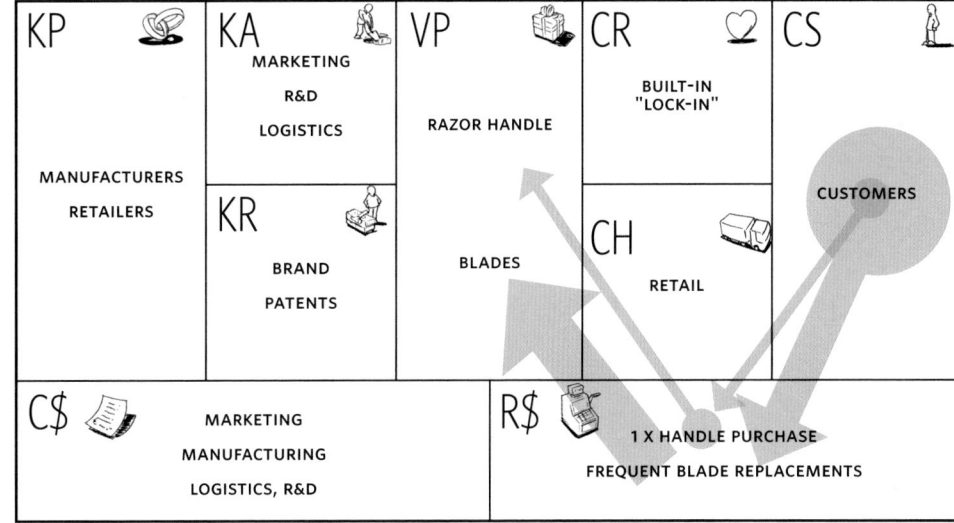

KP	KA	VP	CR	CS
	MARKETING R&D LOGISTICS	RAZOR HANDLE	BUILT-IN "LOCK-IN"	CUSTOMERS
MANUFACTURERS RETAILERS	KR		CH	
	BRAND PATENTS	BLADES	RETAIL	
C$ MARKETING MANUFACTURING LOGISTICS, R&D		R$ 1 X HANDLE PURCHASE FREQUENT BLADE REPLACEMENTS		

This pattern is popular in the business world and has been applied in many sectors, including inkjet printers. Manufacturers such as HP, Epson, and Canon typically sell printers at very low prices, but they generate healthy margins on subsequent sales of ink cartridges.

Bait & Hook Pattern

This pattern is characterized by a tight link or "LOCK-IN" between the initial product and the follow-up products or services.

CUSTOMERS are attracted by the instant gratification of a cheap or free initial product or service.

Cheap or free "bait" LURES customers—and is closely linked to a (disposable) follow-up item or service.

The initial one-time purchase generates little or no REVENUE, but is made up for through repeat follow-up purchases of high-margin products or services.

Focuses on DELIVERY of follow-up products or services.

Bait & hook patterns usually require a strong BRAND.

Important COST STRUCTURE elements include subsidization of the initial product and the costs of producing follow-up products or services.

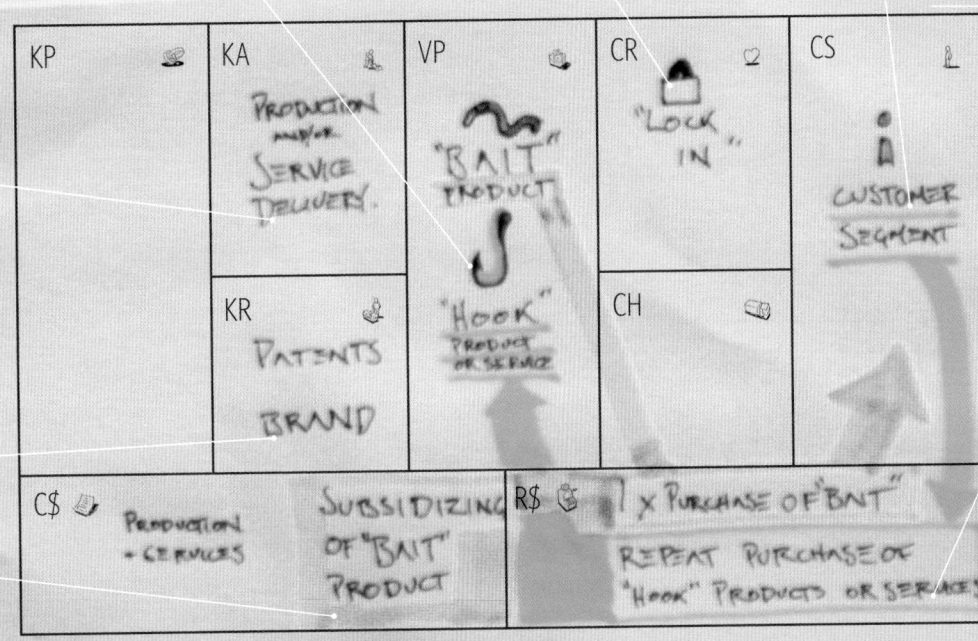

Open Business Models

Def_Pattern No. 5

OPEN BUSINESS MODELS can be used by companies to create and capture value by systematically *collaborating with outside partners.* • This may happen from the *"outside-in"* by exploiting external ideas within the firm, or from the *"inside-out"* by providing external parties with ideas or assets lying idle within the firm.

[REF·ER·ENCES]

1 • *Open Business Models: How to Thrive in the New Innovation Landscape.* Chesbrough, Henry. 2006.

2 • "The Era of Open Innovation." *MIT Sloan Management Review.* Chesbrough, Henry. Nº 3, 2003.

[EX·AM·PLES]

P&G, GlaxoSmithKilne, Innocentive

Other firm's market

Our NEW market

Our CURRENT market

Internal Technology Base

External Technology Base

Open innovation and open business models are two terms coined by Henry Chesbrough. They refer to opening up a company's research process to outside parties. Chesbrough argues that in a world characterized by distributed knowledge, organizations can create more value and better exploit their own research by integrating outside knowledge, intellectual property, and products into their innovation processes. In addition, Chesbrough shows that products, technologies, knowledge, and intellectual property lying idle inside a company can be monetized by making them available to outside parties through licensing, joint ventures, or spin-offs. Chesbrough distinguishes between "outside-in" innovation and "inside-out" innovation. "Outside-in" innovation occurs when an organization brings external ideas, technology, or intellectual property into its development and commercialization processes. The table opposite illustrates how companies increasingly rely on outside sources of technology to strengthen their business models. "Inside-out" innovation occurs when organizations license or sell their intellectual property or technologies, particularly unused assets. In this section we describe the business model patterns of firms that practice open innovation.

PRINCIPLES OF INNOVATION

Closed	Open
The smart people in our field work for us.	We need to work with smart people both inside and outside our company.
To profit from research and development (R&D), we must discover it, develop it, and ship it ourselves.	External R&D can create significant value; internal R&D is needed to claim some portion of that value.
If we conduct most of the best research in the industry, we will win.	We don't have to originate the research to benefit from it.
If we create the most or the best ideas in the industry, we will win.	If we make the best use of internal and external ideas, we will win.
We should control our innovation process, so that competitors don't profit from our ideas.	We should profit from others' use of our innovations, and we should buy others' intellectual property (IP) whenever it advances our own interests.

Source: Adapted from Chesbrough, 2003 and Wikipedia, 2009.

Procter & Gamble: Connect & Develop

In June of 2000, amid a continuing slide in Procter & Gamble's share price, longtime P&G executive A.G. Lafley got the call to become the consumer product giant's new CEO. To rejuvenate P&G, Lafley resolved to put innovation back at the company's core. But instead of boosting R&D spending, he focused on structuring a new innovation culture: one that moved from an internally focused R&D approach to an open R&D process. A key element was a "Connect & Develop" strategy aimed at exploiting internal research through outside partnerships. Lafley set an ambitious goal: create 50 percent of P&G's innovations with outside partners at a time when that figure was closer to 15 percent. The company surpassed that goal in 2007. Meanwhile, R&D productivity had soared 85 percent, even though R&D spending was only modestly higher compared to when Lafley took over as CEO.

In order to link its internal resources and R&D activities with the outside world, Procter & Gamble built three "bridges" into its business model: technology entrepreneurs, Internet platforms, and retirees.

❶ Technology entrepreneurs are senior scientists from P&G business units who systematically develop relationships with researchers at universities and other companies. They also act as "hunters" who scan the outside world for solutions to internal P&G challenges.

❷ Through Internet platforms, P&G connects with expert problem-solvers around the world. Platforms such as InnoCentives (see p. 114) allow P&G to expose some of its research problems to non-P&G scientists around the globe. Respondents earn cash prizes for developing successful solutions.

❸ P&G solicits knowledge from retirees through YourEncore.com, a platform the company launched specifically to serve as an open innovation "bridge" to the outside world.

Outside-In

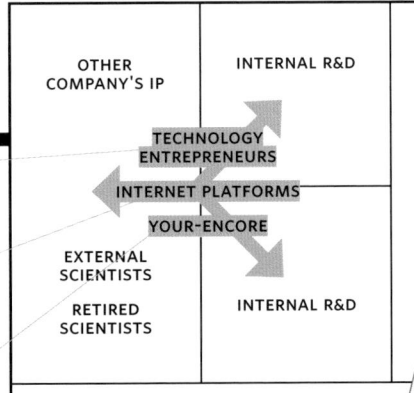

OTHER COMPANY'S IP

INTERNAL R&D

TECHNOLOGY ENTREPRENEURS

INTERNET PLATFORMS

YOUR-ENCORE

EXTERNAL SCIENTISTS

RETIRED SCIENTISTS

INTERNAL R&D

LEVERAGING INTERNAL R&D

GlaxoSmithKline's Patent Pools

The inside-out approach to open innovation ordinarily focuses on monetizing unused internal assets, primarily patents and technology. In the case of GlaxoSmithKline's "patent pool" research strategy, though, the motivation was slightly different. The company's goal was to make drugs more accessible in the world's poorest countries and to facilitate research into understudied diseases. One way to achieve this was to place intellectual property rights relevant to developing drugs for such diseases into a patent pool open to exploration by other researchers. Since pharmaceutical companies focus mainly on developing blockbuster drugs, intellectual property related to less-studied diseases often lies idle. Patent pools aggregate intellectual property from different rights-holders and makes it more accessible. This helps prevent R&D advances from being blocked by a single rights-holder.

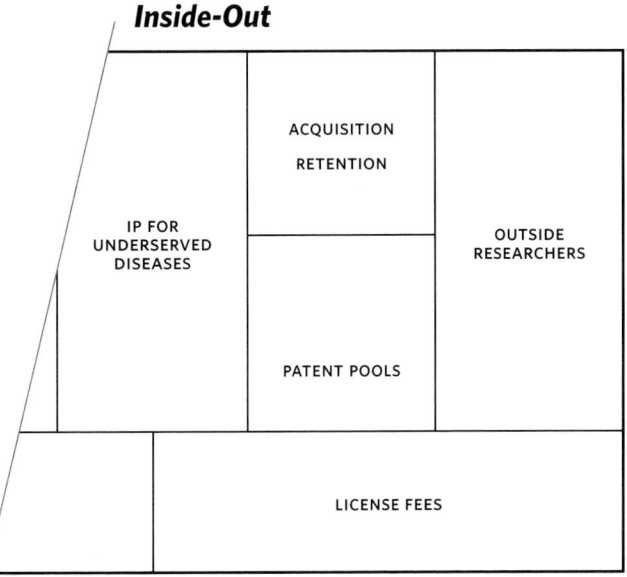

Inside-Out

IP FOR UNDERSERVED DISEASES

ACQUISITION RETENTION

OUTSIDE RESEARCHERS

PATENT POOLS

LICENSE FEES

Unused internal ideas, R&D, and intellectual property related to diseases in poor nations have substantial value when "pooled"

The Connector: Innocentive

Companies seeking insights from external researchers incur substantial costs when trying to attract people or organizations with knowledge that could solve their problems. On the other hand, researchers who want to apply their knowledge outside their own organizations also incur search costs when seeking attractive opportunities. That is where a company called InnoCentive saw opportunity.

InnoCentive provides connections between organizations with research problems to solve and researchers from around the world who are eager to solve challenging problems. Originally part of drug maker Eli Lilly, InnoCentive now functions as an independent intermediary listing non-profits, government agencies, and commercial organizations such as Procter & Gamble, Solvay, and the Rockefeller Foundation. Companies who post their innovation challenges on InnoCentive's Web site are called "seekers." They reward successful problemsolvers with cash prizes that can range from $5,000 to $1,000,000. Scientists who attempt to find solutions to listed problems are called "solvers." InnoCentive's Value Proposition lies

Innocentive

in aggregating and connecting "seekers" and "solvers." You may recognize these qualities as characteristic of the multi-sided platform business model pattern (see p. 76). Companies with open business model patterns often build on such platforms to reduce search costs.

"Open Innovation is fundamentally about operating in a world of abundant knowledge, where not all the smart people work for you, so you better go find them, connect to them, and build upon what they can do."

— *Henry Chesbrough*
Executive Director, Center for Open Innovation
Haas School of Business, UC Berkeley

"Long known for a preference to do everything in-house, we began to seek out innovation from any and all sources, inside, outside the company."

— *A.G. Lafley*
Chairman & CEO, P&G

"Nestlé clearly recognizes that to achieve its growth objective it must extend its internal capabilities to establish a large number of strategic partnering relationships. It has embraced open innovation and works aggressively with strategic partners to co-create significant new market and product opportunities."

— *Helmut Traitler*
Head of Innovation Partnerships, Nestlé

Outside-In Pattern

EXTERNAL ORGANIZATIONS, sometimes from completely different industries, may be able to offer valuable insights, knowledge, patents, or ready-made products to internal R&D groups.

Building on external knowledge requires dedicated **ACTIVITIES** that connect external entities with internal business processes and R&D groups.

Taking advantage of outside innovation requires specific **RESOURCES** to build gateways to external networks.

It **COSTS** money to acquire innovation from outside sources. But by building on externally-created knowledge and advanced research programs, a company can shorten time-to-market and increase its internal R&D productivity.

Established companies with strong brands, strong Distribution Channels, and strong Customer Relationships are well suited to an outside-in open business model. They can leverage existing Customer Relationships by building on outside sources of innovation.

Inside-Out Pattern

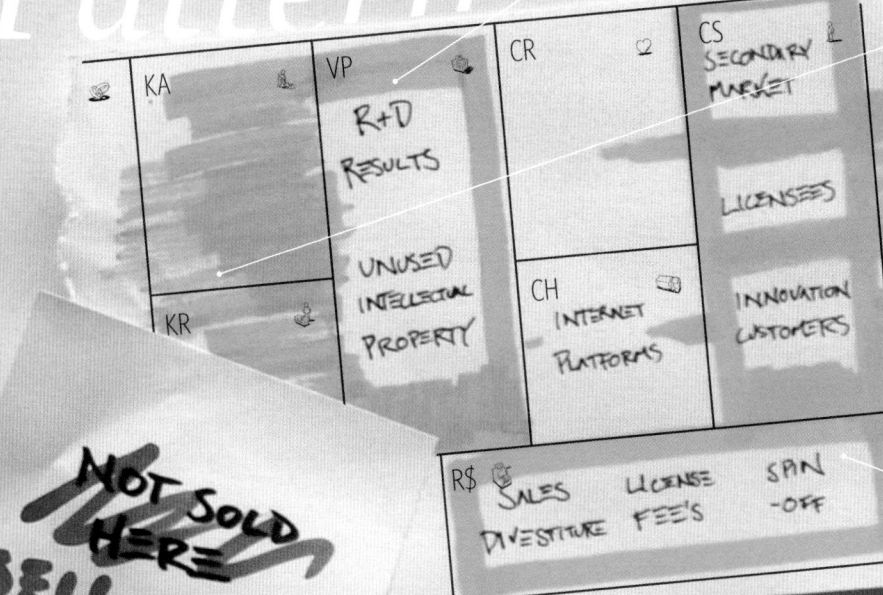

Some R&D outputs that are unusable internally—for strategic or operational reasons—may be of high VALUE to organizations in other industries.

Organizations with substantial internal R&D operations typically possess much unutilized knowledge, technology, and intellectual property. Due to sharp focus on core businesses, some of these otherwise valuable intellectual assets sit idle. Such businesses are good candidates for an "inside-out" open business model.

By enabling others to exploit unused internal ideas, a company adds "easy" additional REVENUE STREAMS.

Patterns Overview

	Unbundling Business Models	**The Long Tail**
CONTEXT (BEFORE)	An integrated model combines infrastructure management, product innovation, and Customer Relationships under one roof.	The Value Proposition targets only the most profitable clients.
CHALLENGE	Costs are too high. Several conflicting organizational cultures are combined in a single entity, resulting in undesirable trade-offs.	Targeting less profitable segments with specific Value Propositions is too costly.
SOLUTION (AFTER)	The business is unbundled into three separate but complementary models dealing with • Infrastructure management • Product innovation • Customer relationships	The new or additional Value Proposition targets a large number of historically less profitable, niche Customer Segments—which in aggregate are profitable.
RATIONALE	IT and management tool improvements allow separating and coordinating different business models at lower cost, thus eliminating undesirable trade-offs.	IT and operations management improvements allow delivering tailored Value Propositions to a very large number of new customers at low cost.
EXAMPLES	Private Banking Mobile Telco	Publishing Industry (Lulu.com) LEGO

Multi-Sided Platforms	FREE as a Business Model	Open Business Models
One Value Proposition targets one Customer Segment.	A high-value, high-cost Value Proposition is offered to paying customers only.	R&D Resources and Key Activities are concentrated in-house: • Ideas are invented "inside" only • Results are exploited "inside" only
Enterprise fails to acquire potential new customers who are interested in gaining access to a company's existing customer base (e.g. game developers who want to reach console users)	The high price dissuades customers.	R&D is costly and/or productivity is falling.
A Value Proposition "giving access" to a company's existing Customer Segment is added (e.g. a game console manufacturer provides software developers with access to its users)	Several Value Propositions are offered to different Customer Segments with different Revenue Streams, one of them being free-of-charge (or very low cost).	Internal R&D Resources and Activities are leveraged by utilizing outside partners. Internal R&D results are transformed into a Value Proposition and offered to interested Customer Segments.
An intermediary operating a platform between two or more Customer Segments adds Revenue Streams to the initial model.	Non-paying Customer Segments are subsidized by paying customers in order to attract the maximum number of users.	Acquiring R&D from external sources can be less expensive, resulting in faster time-to-market. Unexploited innovations have the potential to bring in more revenue when sold outside.
Google Video game consoles from Nintendo, Sony, Microsoft Apple iPod, iTunes, iPhone	Advertising and newspapers *Metro* Flickr Open Source Red Hat Skype (versus Telco) Gillette Razor and blades	Procter & Gamble GlaxoSmithKline Innocentive

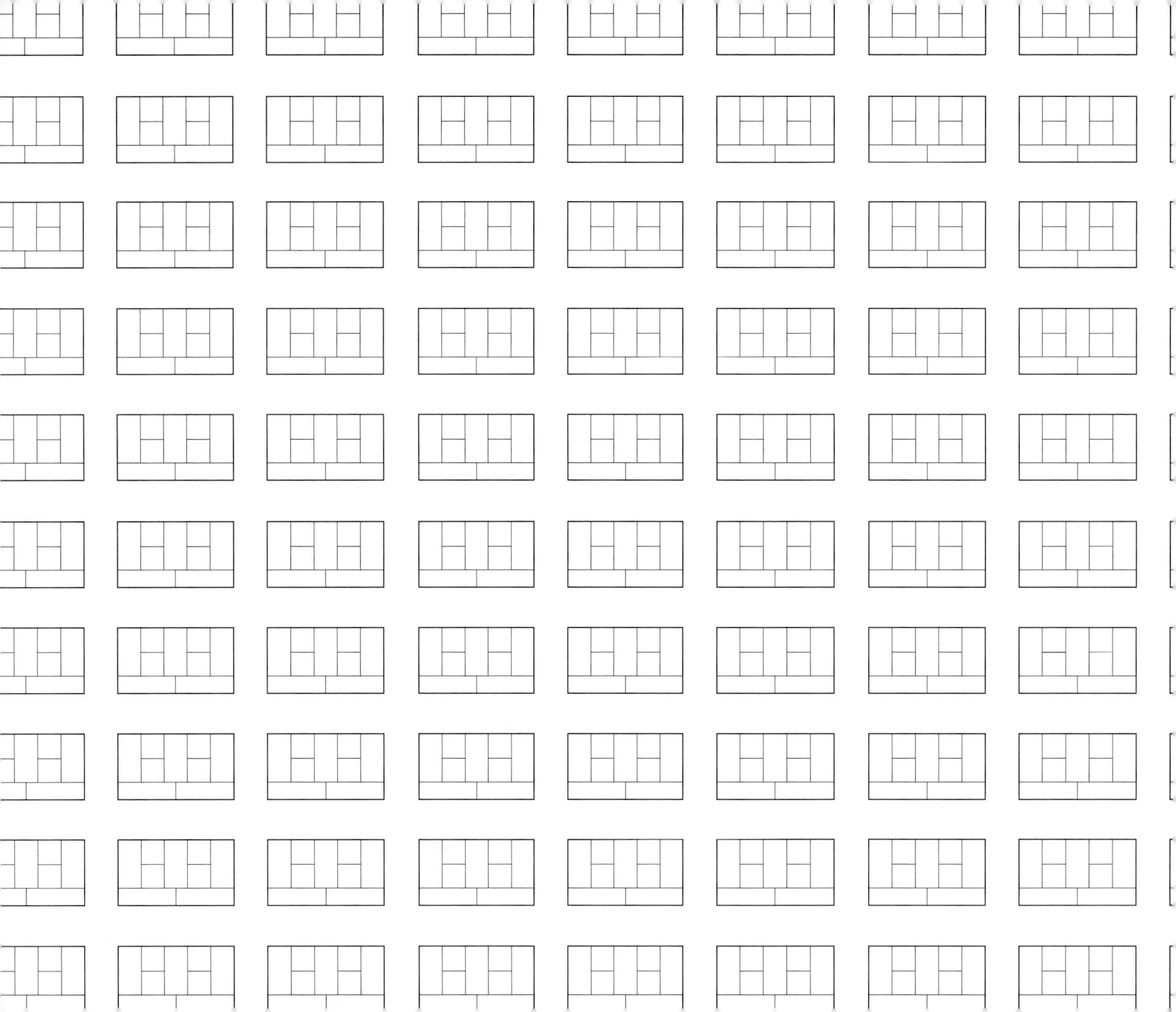

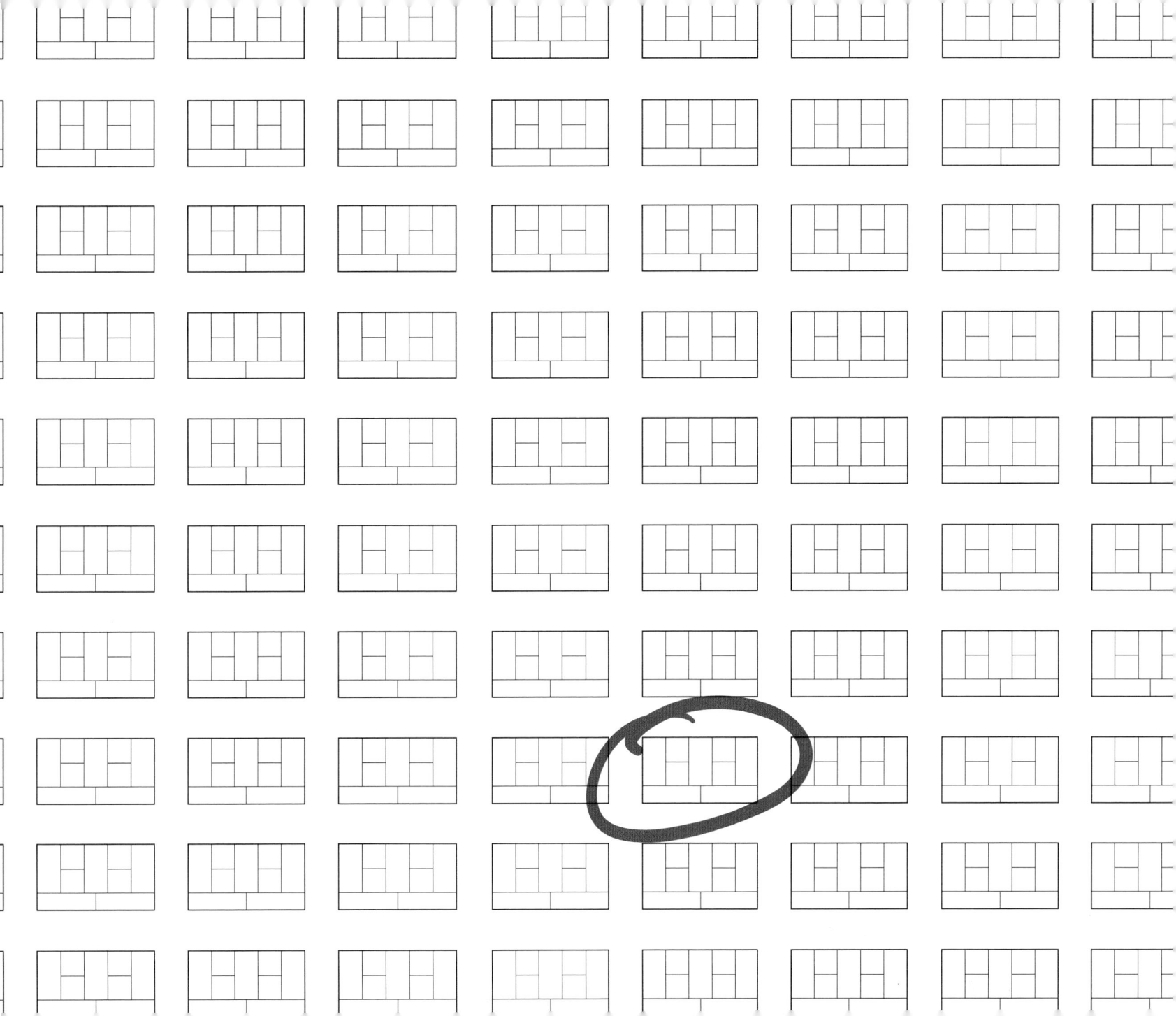

Des

ign

"Businesspeople don't just need to understand designers better; they need to become designers."

Roger Martin, Dean, Rotman School of Management

This section describes a number of techniques and tools from the world of design that can help you design better and more innovative business models. A designer's business involves relentless inquiry into the best possible way to create the new, discover the unexplored, or achieve the functional. A designer's job is to extend the boundaries of thought, to generate new options, and, ultimately, to create value for users. This requires the ability to imagine "that which does not exist." We are convinced that the tools and attitude of the design profession are prerequisites for success in the business model generation.

Businesspeople unknowingly practice design every day. We design organizations, strategies, business models, processes, and projects. To do this, we must take into account a complex web of factors, such as competitors, technology, the legal environment, and more. Increasingly, we must do so in unfamiliar, uncharted territory. This is precisely what design is about. What businesspeople lack are design tools that complement their business skills.

The following pages explore six business model design techniques: Customer Insights, Ideation, Visual Thinking, Prototyping, Storytelling, and Scenarios. We introduce each technique with a story, then demonstrate how the technique applies to business model design. Here and there we've added exercises and suggestions for workshop activities that show you specifically how the design technique can be applied. Book references are provided at the end for those interested in exploring each technique in more depth.

Design

126 Customer Insights

134 Ideation

146 Visual Thinking

160 Prototyping

170 Storytelling

180 Scenarios

Technique_No. 1

Customer Insights

Outside an office building on the outskirts of Oslo, four Norwegian teenagers wearing American-style "letter" jackets and baseball caps are engaged in a lively discussion with a man in his 50s...

... The teenagers are young, hip snowboarders answering questions posed by Richard Ling, a senior sociologist working for Telenor, the world's seventh largest mobile operator. Ling is interviewing the group as part of a study to gain insights into the use of photos and photo sharing over social networks. Now that nearly every mobile phone sports a camera, photo sharing is of keen interest to cellular operators. Ling's research will help Telenor capture the "big picture" of photo sharing. He focuses not just on existing and potential new mobile photo sharing services, but on broader issues, such as the role photo-sharing plays with respect to trust, secrecy, group identity, and the social fabric linking these young men. Ultimately, his work will enable Telenor to design and deliver better services.

Building Business Models on Customer Insights

128

Companies invest heavily in market research, yet often wind up neglecting the customer perspective when designing products, services—and business models. Good business model design avoids this error. It views the business model through customers' eyes, an approach that can lead to the discovery of completely new opportunities. This does not mean that customer thinking is the only place from which to start an innovation initiative, but it does mean that we should include the customer perspective when evaluating a business model. Successful innovation requires a deep understanding of customers, including environment, daily routines, concerns, and aspirations.

Apple's iPod media player provides an example. Apple understood that people were uninterested in digital media players per se. The company perceived that consumers wanted a seamless way to search, find, download, and listen to digital content, including music, and were willing to pay for a successful solution. Apple's view was unique at a time when illegal downloading was rampant and most companies argued that nobody would be willing to pay for digital music online. Apple dismissed these views and created a seamless music experience for customers, integrating the iTunes music and media software, the iTunes online store, and the iPod media player. With this Value Proposition as the kernel of its business model, Apple went on to dominate the online digital music market

The challenge is to develop a sound understanding of customers on which to base business model design choices. In the field of product and service design, several leading companies work with social scientists to achieve this understanding. At Intel, Nokia, and Telenor, teams of anthropologists and sociologists work to develop new and better products and services. The same approach can lead to new or better business models.

Many leading consumer companies organize field trips for senior executives to meet customers, talk to sales teams, or visit outlets. In other industries, particularly those involving heavy capital investments, talking to customers is part of the daily routine. But the challenge of innovation is developing a deeper understanding of customers rather than just asking them what they want.

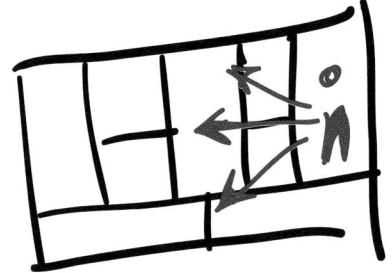

«

Adopting the customer perspective is a guiding principle for the entire business model design process. Customer perspectives should inform our choices regarding Value Propositions, Distribution Channels, Customer Relationships, and Revenue Streams.

As pioneering automaker Henry Ford once said, "If I had asked my customers what they wanted, they would have told me 'a faster horse.'"

Another challenge lies in knowing which customers to heed and which customers to ignore. Sometimes tomorrow's growth segments wait at the periphery of today's cash cows. Therefore business model innovators should avoid focusing exclusively on existing Customer Segments and set their sights on new or unreached segments. A number of business model innovations have succeeded precisely because they satisfied the unmet needs of new customers. For example, Stelios Haji-Ioannou's easyJet made air travel available to lower- and middle-income customers who rarely flew. And Zipcar allowed city dwellers to eliminate the hassles of metropolitan car ownership. Instead, customers who pay an annual fee can rent automobiles by the hour. Both are examples of new business models built on Customer Segments located at the periphery under incumbent models: traditional air travel and traditional car rentals.

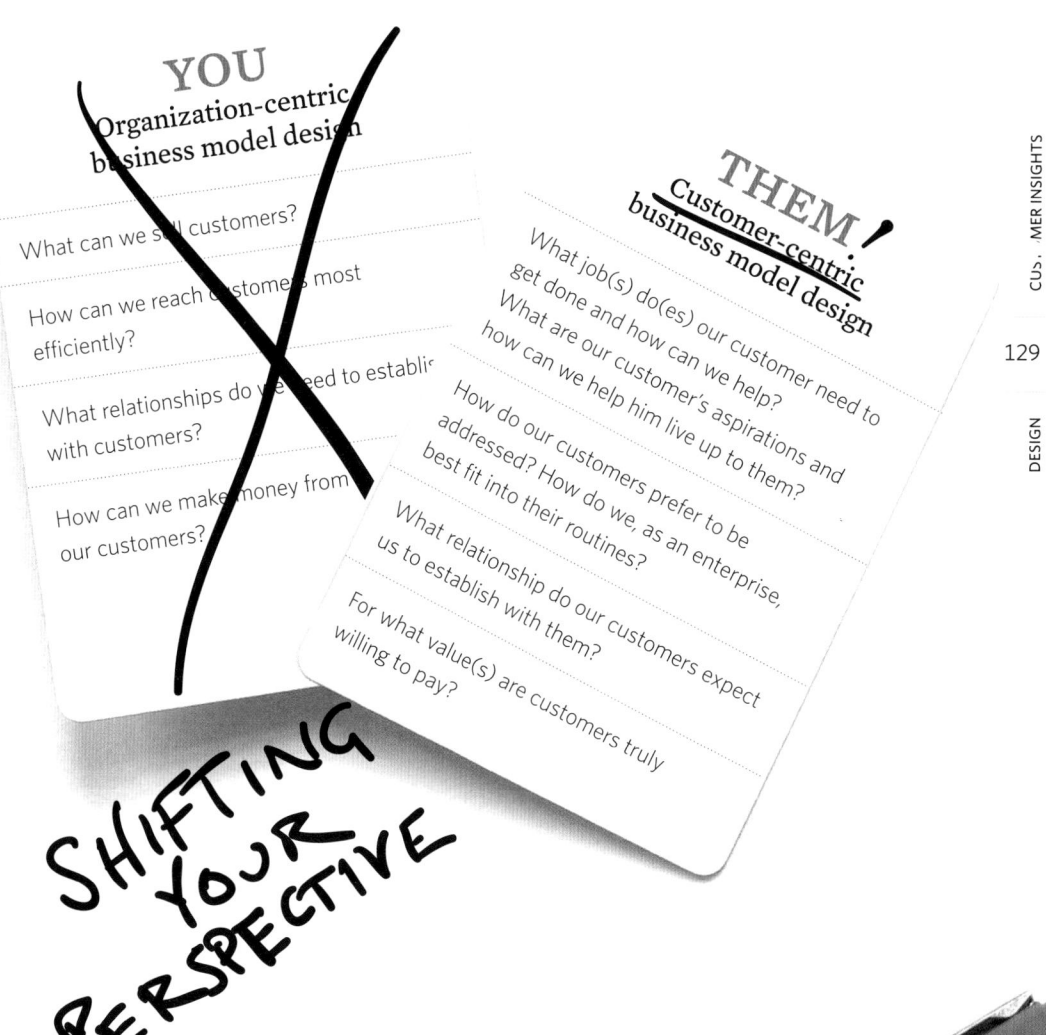

YOU
Organization-centric business model design

What can we sell customers?

How can we reach customers most efficiently?

What relationships do we need to establish with customers?

How can we make money from our customers?

THEM!
Customer-centric business model design

What job(s) do(es) our customer need to get done and how can we help?

What are our customer's aspirations and how can we help him live up to them?

How do our customers prefer to be addressed? How do we, as an enterprise, best fit into their routines?

What relationship do our customers expect us to establish with them?

For what value(s) are customers truly willing to pay?

SHIFTING YOUR PERSPECTIVE

What does she
THINK AND FEEL?
what really counts
major preoccupations
worries & aspirations

What does she
HEAR?
what friends say
what boss says
what influencers say

What does she
SEE?
environment
friends
what the market offers

What does she
SAY AND DO?
attitude in public
appearance
behavior toward others

PAIN
fears
frustrations
obstacles

GAIN
wants/needs
measures of success

Source : Adapted from XPLANE

The Empathy Map

Few of us enjoy the services of a full team of social scientists, but anybody examining a business model can sketch profiles of the Customer Segments addressed therein. A good way to start is by using the Empathy Map, a tool developed by visual thinking company XPLANE. This tool, which we also like to call the "really simple customer profiler," helps you go beyond a customer's demographic characteristics and develop a better understanding of environment, behavior, concerns, and aspirations. Doing so allows you to devise a stronger business model, because a customer profile guides the design of better Value Propositions, more convenient ways to reach customers, and more appropriate Customer Relationships. Ultimately it allows you to better understand what a customer is truly willing to pay for.

How to Use the (Customer) Empathy Map

Here's how it works. First, brainstorm to come up with all the possible Customer Segments that you might want to serve using your business model. Choose three promising candidates, and select one for your first profiling exercise.

Start by giving this customer a name and some demographic characteristics, such as income, marital status, and so forth. Then, referring to the diagram on the opposite page, use a flipchart or whiteboard to build a profile for your newly-named customer by asking and answering the following six questions:

1

WHAT DOES SHE SEE?

DESCRIBE WHAT THE CUSTOMER SEES IN HER ENVIRONMENT

- *What does it look like?*
- *Who surrounds her?*
- *Who are her friends?*
- *What types of offers is she exposed to daily (as opposed to all market offers)?*
- *What problems does she encounter?*

2

WHAT DOES SHE HEAR?

DESCRIBE HOW THE ENVIRONMENT INFLU-ENCES THE CUSTOMER

- *What do her friends say? Her spouse?*
- *Who really influences her, and how?*
- *Which media Channels are influential?*

3

WHAT DOES SHE REALLY THINK AND FEEL?

TRY TO SKETCH OUT WHAT GOES ON IN YOUR CUSTOMER'S MIND

- *What is really important to her (which she might not say publicly)?*
- *Imagine her emotions. What moves her?*
- *What might keep her up at night?*
- *Try describing her dreams and aspirations.*

4

WHAT DOES SHE SAY AND DO?

IMAGINE WHAT THE CUSTOMER MIGHT SAY, OR HOW SHE MIGHT BEHAVE IN PUBLIC

- *What is her attitude?*
- *What could she be telling others?*
- *Pay particular attention to potential conflicts between what a customer might say and what she may truly think or feel.*

5

WHAT IS THE CUSTOMER'S PAIN?

- *What are her biggest frustrations?*
- *What obstacles stand between her and what she wants or needs to achieve?*
- *Which risks might she fear taking?*

6

WHAT DOES THE CUSTOMER GAIN?

- *What does she truly want or need to achieve?*
- *How does she measure success?*
- *Think of some strategies she might use to achieve her goals.*

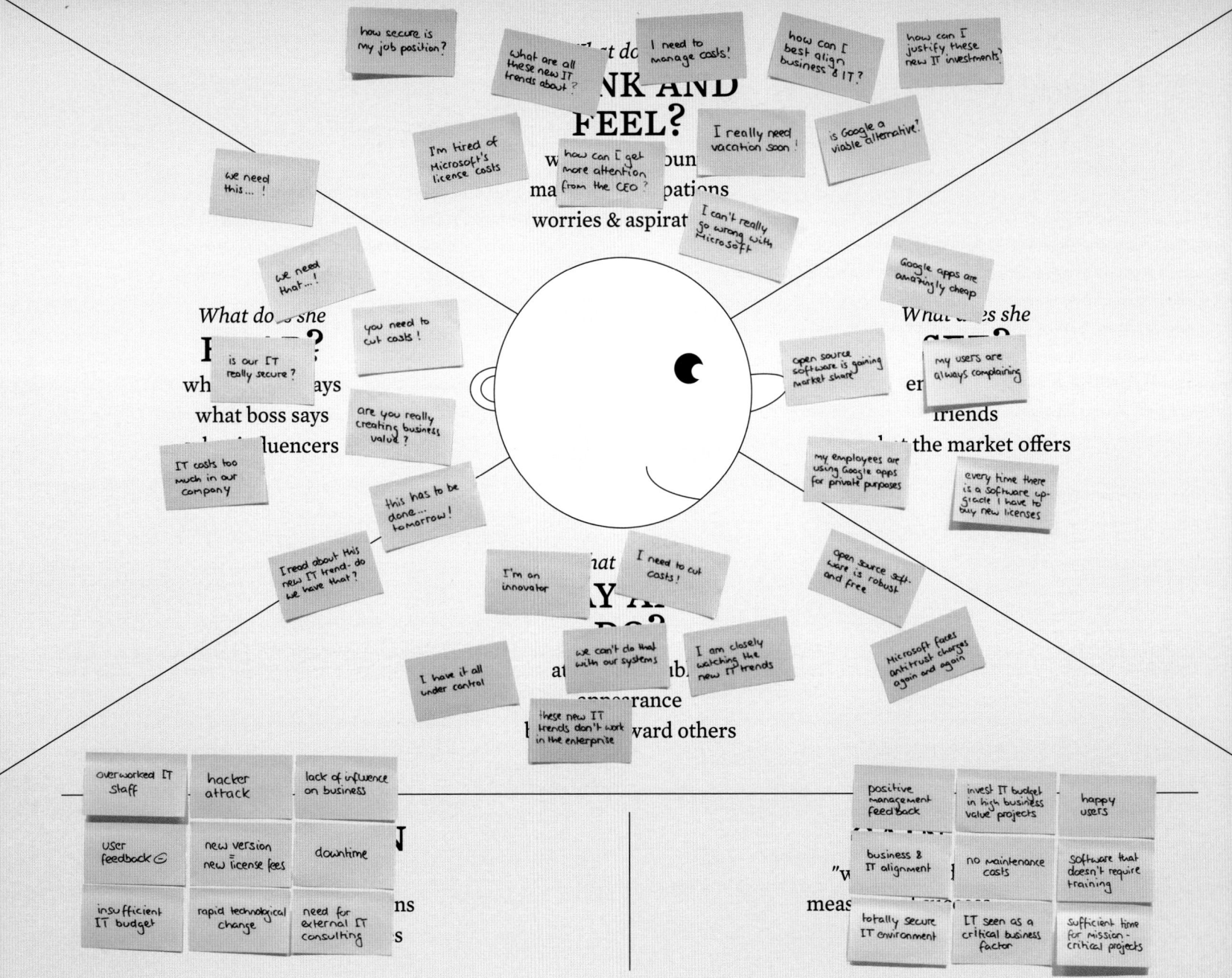

Source : Adapted from XPLANE

Understanding a B2B customer using the Empathy Map

In October 2008, Microsoft announced plans to provide its entire suite of Office applications online. According to the announcement, customers will eventually be able to use Word, Excel, and all other Office applications through browsers. This will require Microsoft to significantly reengineer its business model. One starting point for this business model renovation could be to create a customer profile for a key buying segment: chief information officers (CIO), who define IT strategy and make overarching purchasing decisions. What might a CIO customer profile look like?

The goal is to create a customer viewpoint for continuously questioning your business model assumptions. Customer profiling enables you to generate better answers to questions such as: Does this Value Proposition solve real customer problems? Would she really be willing to pay for this? How would she like to be reached?

Ideation

MARCH, 2007

Elmar Mock is listening carefully as Peter elaborates excitedly on an idea amid a sea of Post-it™ notes smothering the walls...

IDEATION

135

DESIGN

... Peter works for a pharmaceutical group that has hired Elmar's innovation consultancy, Creaholic, to help with a breakthrough product. The two men are part of a six-person innovation team holding a three-day offsite meeting.

The group is deliberately heterogeneous, a pastiche of different experience levels and backgrounds. Though all members are accomplished specialists, they joined the group not as technicians, but as consumers unsatisfied with the current state of affairs. Creaholic instructed them to leave their expertise at the door and carry it with them only as a "backpack" of distant memories.

For three days the six form a consumer microcosm and unleash their imaginations to dream up potential breakthrough solutions to a problem, unbridled by technical or financial constraints. Ideas collide and new thinking emerges, and only after generating a multitude of potential solutions are they asked to recall their expertise and pin down the three most promising candidates.

Elmar Mock boasts a long track record of breakthrough innovation. He is one of two inventors of the legendary Swatch watch. Since then, he and his team at Creaholic have helped companies such as BMW, Nestlé, Mikron, and Givaudan innovate successfully.

Elmar knows how difficult it is for established companies to innovate. Such firms require predictability, job descriptions, and financial projections. Yet real innovations emerge from something better described as systematic chaos. Creaholic has found a way to master that chaos. Elmar and his team are obsessed by innovation.

Generating New
Business Model Ideas

—

Mapping an existing business model is one thing; designing a new and innovative business model is another. What's needed is a creative process for generating a large number of business model ideas and successfully isolating the best ones. This process is called ideation. Mastering the art of ideation is crucial when it comes to designing viable new business models.

Traditionally, most industries were characterized by a dominant business model. This has changed radically. Today we enjoy many more choices when designing new business models. Today, different business models compete in the same markets, and boundaries between industries are blurring—or disappearing altogether.

One challenge we face when trying to create new business model options is ignoring the status quo and suspending concerns over operational issues so that we can generate truly new ideas.

Business model innovation is not about looking back, because the past indicates little about what is possible in terms of future business models. Business model innovation is not about looking to competitors, since business model innovation is not about copying or benchmarking, but about creating new mechanisms to create value and derive revenues. Rather, business model innovation is about challenging orthodoxies to design original models that meet unsatisfied, new, or hidden customer needs.

To come up with new or better options, you must dream up a grab bag of ideas before narrowing them down to a short list of conceivable options. Thus, ideation has two main phases: idea generation, where quantity matters, and synthesis, in which ideas are discussed, combined, and narrowed down to a small number of viable options. Options do not necessarily have to represent disruptive business models. They may be innovations that expand the boundaries of your current business model to improve competitiveness.

You can generate ideas for innovative business models from several different starting points. We will look at two: epicenters of business model innovation using the Business Model Canvas, and "what if" questions.

GENERATION | SYNTHESIS

Ignore the status quo
Forget the past
Stop focusing on competitors
Challenge orthodoxies

Epicenters of Business Model Innovation

Ideas for business model innovation can come from anywhere, and each of the nine business model building blocks can be a starting point. Transformative business model innovations affect multiple building blocks. We can distinguish four epicenters of business model innovation: *resource-driven, offer-driven, customer-driven, and finance-driven.*

Each of the four epicenters can serve as the starting point for a major business model change, and each can have a powerful impact on the other eight building blocks. Sometimes, business model innovation can emerge from several epicenters. Also, change often originates in areas identified through a SWOT analysis: an investigation of a business model's strengths, weaknesses, opportunities, and threats (see p. 216).

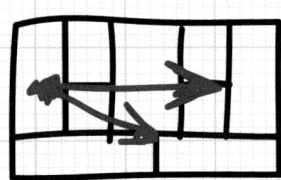

RESOURCE-DRIVEN

RESOURCE-DRIVEN INNOVATIONS ORIGINATE FROM AN ORGANIZATION'S EXISTING INFRASTRUCTURE OR PARTNERSHIPS TO EXPAND OR TRANSFORM THE BUSINESS MODEL.

Example: Amazon Web Services was built on top of Amazon.com's retail infrastructure to offer server capacity and data storage space to other companies.

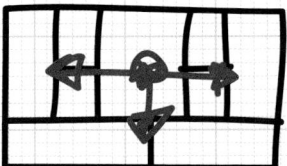

OFFER-DRIVEN

OFFER-DRIVEN INNOVATIONS CREATE NEW VALUE PROPOSITIONS THAT AFFECT OTHER BUSINESS MODEL BUILDING BLOCKS.

Example: When Cemex, a Mexican cement maker, promised to deliver poured cement to job sites within four hours rather than the 48 hour industry standard, it had to transform its business model. This innovation helped change Cemex from a regional Mexican player into the world's second largest cement producer.

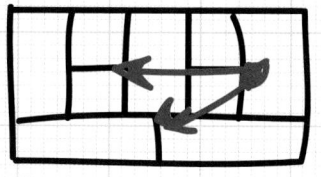

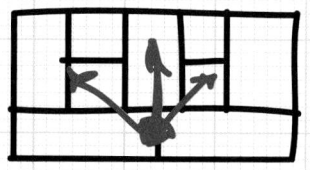

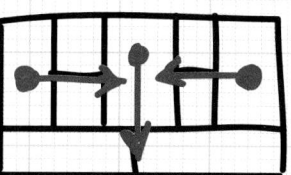

CUSTOMER-DRIVEN

CUSTOMER-DRIVEN INNOVATIONS ARE BASED ON CUSTOMER NEEDS, FACILITATED ACCESS, OR INCREASED CONVENIENCE. LIKE ALL INNOVATIONS EMERGING FROM A SINGLE EPICENTER, THEY AFFECT OTHER BUSINESS MODEL BUILDING BLOCKS.

FINANCE-DRIVEN

INNOVATIONS DRIVEN BY NEW REVENUE STREAMS, PRICING MECHANISMS, OR REDUCED COST STRUCTURES THAT AFFECT OTHER BUSINESS MODEL BUILDING BLOCKS.

MULTIPLE-EPICENTER DRIVEN

INNOVATIONS DRIVEN BY MULTIPLE EPICENTERS CAN HAVE SIGNIFICANT IMPACT ON SEVERAL OTHER BUILDING BLOCKS.

Example: 23andMe brought personalized DNA testing to individual clients—an offer previously available exclusively to health professionals and researchers, This had substantial implications for both the Value Proposition and the delivery of test results, which 23andMe accomplishes through mass-customized Web profiles.

Example: When Xerox invented the Xerox 914 in 1958—one of the first plain paper copiers—it was priced too high for the market. So Xerox developed a new business model. It leased the machines at $95 per month, including 2,000 free copies, plus five cents per additional copy. Clients acquired the new machines and started making thousands of copies each month.

Example: Hilti, the global manufacturer of professional construction tools, moved away from selling tools outright and toward renting sets of tools to customers. This was a substantial change in Hitli's Value Proposition, but also in its Revenue Streams, which shifted from one-time product revenues to recurring service revenues.

The Power of "What If" Questions

We often have trouble conceiving innovative business models because we are held back in our thinking by the status quo. The status quo stifles imagination. One way to overcome this problem is to challenge conventional assumptions with "what if" questions. With the right business model ingredients, what we think of as impossible might be just doable. "What if" questions help us break free of constraints imposed by current models. They should provoke us and challenge our thinking. They should disturb us as intriguing, difficult-to-execute propositions.

Managers of a daily newspaper might ask themselves: What if we stopped our print edition and went to entirely digital distribution, through Amazon's Kindle e-book reader or through the Web? This would allow the newspaper to drastically reduce production and logistics costs, but would require making up lost print advertising revenues and transitioning readers to digital Channels.

"What if" questions are merely starting points. They challenge us to discover the business model that could make their suppositions work. Some "what if" questions may remain unanswered because they are too provocative. Some may simply need the right business model to become reality.

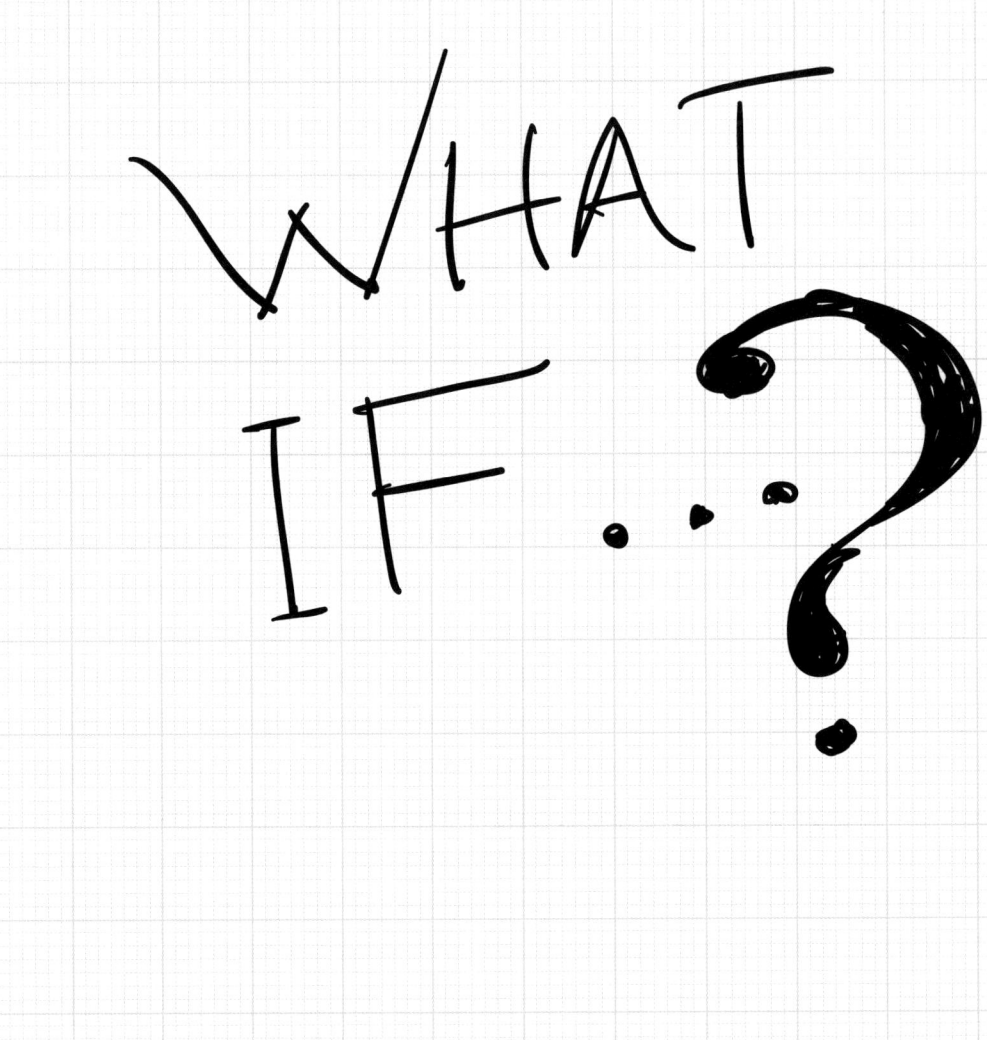

... furniture buyers picked up components in flat pack form from a large warehouse and assembled the products themselves in their homes? What is common practice today was unthinkable until IKEA introduced the concept in the 1960s.

... airlines didn't buy engines for their airplanes, but paid for every hour an engine runs? That is how Rolls-Royce transformed itself from a money-losing British manufacturer into a service firm that today is the world's second biggest provider of large jet engines.

... voice calls were free worldwide? In 2003 Skype launched a service that allowed free voice calling via the Internet. After five years Skype had acquired 400 million registered users who collectively had made 100 billion free calls.

... car manufacturers didn't sell cars, but provided mobility services? In 2008 Daimler launched car2go, an experimental business in the German city of Ulm. Car2go's fleet of vehicles allows users to pick up and drop off cars anywhere in the city, paying by-the-minute fees for mobility services.

... individuals could lend money to each other rather than borrowing from banks? In 2005, U.K.-based Zopa launched a peer-to-peer lending platform on the Internet.

... every villager in Bangladesh had access to a telephone? That is what Grameenphone set out to achieve under a partnership with micro-finance institution Grameen Bank. At the time, Bangladesh still had the world's lowest tele-density. Today Grameenphone is Bangladesh's largest taxpayer.

The Ideation Process

The ideation process can take several forms. Here we outline a general approach to producing innovative business model options:

1. TEAM COMPOSITION

KEY QUESTION: IS OUR TEAM SUFFICIENTLY DIVERSE TO GENERATE FRESH BUSINESS MODEL IDEAS?

Assembling the right team is essential to generating effective new business model ideas. Members should be diverse in terms of seniority, age, experience level, business unit represented, customer knowledge, and professional expertise.

2. IMMERSION

KEY QUESTION: WHICH ELEMENTS MUST WE STUDY BEFORE GENERATING BUSINESS MODEL IDEAS?

Ideally the team should go through an immersion phase. which could include general research, studying customers or prospects, scrutinizing new technologies, or assessing existing business models. Immersion could last several weeks or could be as short as a couple of workshop exercises (e.g. the Empathy Map).

3. EXPANDING

KEY QUESTION: WHAT INNOVATIONS CAN WE IMAGINE FOR EACH BUSINESS MODEL BUILDING BLOCK?

During this phase the team expands the range of possible solutions, aiming to generate as many ideas as possible. Each of the nine business model building blocks can serve as a starting point. The goal of this phase is quantity, not quality. Enforcing brainstorming rules will keep people focused on generating ideas rather than on critiquing too early in the process (see p. 144).

4. CRITERIA SELECTION

KEY QUESTION: WHAT ARE THE MOST IMPORTANT CRITERIA FOR PRIORITIZING OUR BUSINESS MODEL IDEAS?

After expanding the range of possible solutions, the team should define criteria for reducing the number of ideas to a manageable few. The criteria will be specific to the context of your business, but could include things such as estimated implementation time, revenue potential, possible customer resistance, and impact on competitive advantage.

5. "PROTOTYPING"

KEY QUESTION: WHAT DOES THE COMPLETE BUSINESS MODEL FOR EACH SHORTLISTED IDEA LOOK LIKE?

With criteria defined, the team should be able to reduce the number of ideas to a prioritized shortlist of three to five potential business model innovations. Use the Business Model Canvas to sketch out and discuss each idea as a business model prototype (see p. 160).

Assemble a Diverse Team

The task of generating new ideas should not be left exclusively to those typically considered to be "creative types." Ideation is a team exercise. In fact, by its very nature business model innovation requires the participation of people from across the entire organization. Business model innovation is about seeking to create value by exploring new business model building blocks and forging innovative links between blocks. This can involve all nine blocks of the canvas, whether Distribution Channels, Revenue Streams, or Key Resources. Thus it requires input and ideas from people representing multiple areas.

That's why assembling the right task force is a critical prerequisite for generating new business model ideas. Thinking about business model innovation should not be confined to the R&D unit or the strategic planning office. Business model innovation teams should have a diverse membership. The diversity will help you generate, discuss, and select new ideas. Consider adding outsiders, or even children. Diversity works. But make sure to teach people how to listen actively, and consider engaging a neutral facilitator for key meetings.

A diverse business model innovation team has members...

- *from various business units*
- *of different ages*
- *with different areas of expertise*
- *of differing levels of seniority*
- *with a mixture of experiences*
- *from different cultural backgrounds*

Brainstorming Rules

Successful brainstorming requires following a set of rules. Enforcing these rules will help you maximize the number of useful ideas generated.

Stay focused

Start with a well-honed statement of the problem at hand. Ideally, this should be articulated around a customer need. Don't let the discussion stray too far; always bring it back to the problem statement.

Enforce rules

Clarify the brainstorming rules upfront and enforce them. The most important rules are "defer judgment," "one conversation at a time," "go for quantity," "be visual," and "encourage wild ideas." Facilitators should enforce the rules.

Think visually

Write ideas down or sketch them out on a surface everyone can see. A good way to collect ideas is to jot them down on Post-it™ notes and stick these to a wall. This allows you to move ideas around and regroup them.

Prepare

Prepare for brainstorming with some sort of immersion experience related to the problem at hand. This could be a field trip, discussions with customers, or any other means of immersing the team in issues related to your problem statement.

Adapted from an interview with Tom Kelley of IDEO in *Fast Company* magazine: "Seven Secrets to Good Brainstorming"

Warm-Up:
The Silly Cow Exercise

To get your team's creative juices flowing, it can be helpful to start an ideation session with a warm-up such as the Silly Cow exercise. Here's how it works: Instruct participants to sketch out three different business models using a cow. Ask them to first define some characteristics of a cow (produces milk, eats all day, makes a mooing sound, etc.). Tell them to use those characteristics to come up with an innovative business model based on a cow. Give them three minutes.

Keep in mind that this exercise can backfire, as it is indeed quite silly. But it has been tested with senior executives, accountants, risk managers, and entrepreneurs, and usually is a great success. The goal is to take people out of their day-to-day business routines and show them how readily they can generate ideas by disconnecting from orthodoxies and letting their creativity flow.

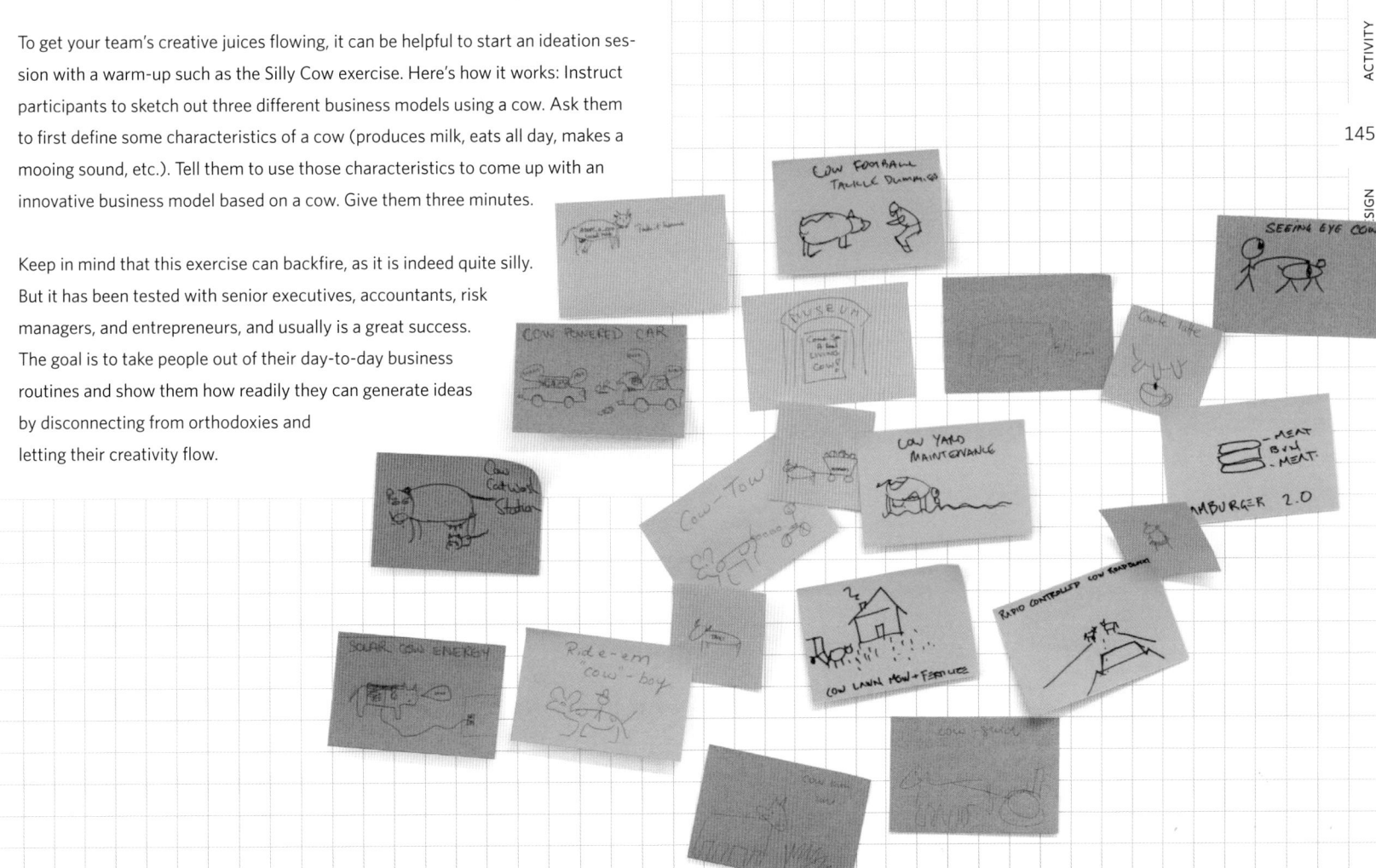

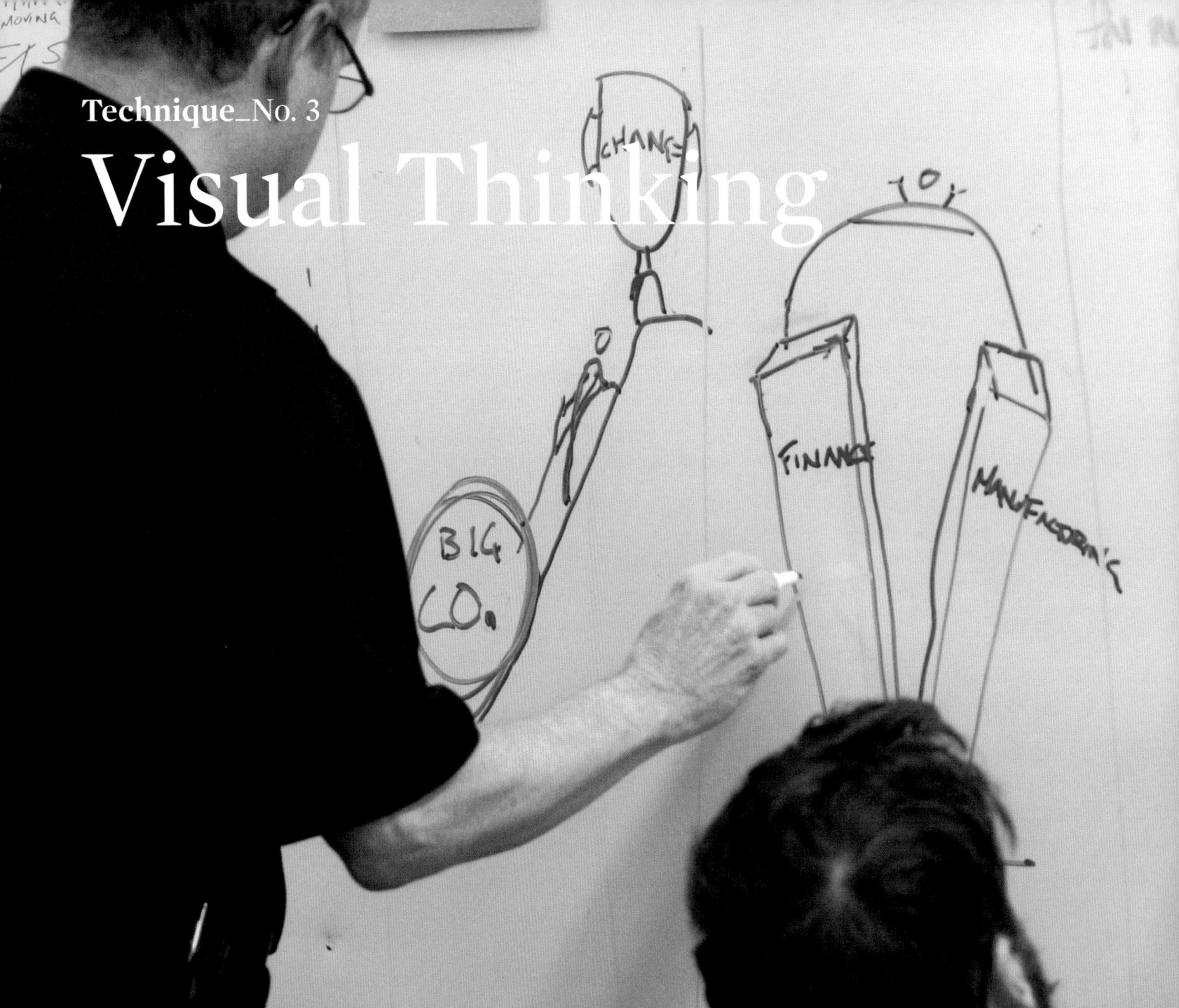

Technique_No. 3

Visual Thinking

The meeting room walls are plastered with large posters on which a group of 14 people are assiduously sketching drawings and pasting Post-it™ notes. Though the scene almost has the atmosphere of an art class, it's taking place at the headquarters of Hewlett-Packard, the technology products and services giant …

… The 14 participants hail from throughout HP, but all are involved in information management. They've gathered here for a one-day workshop to literally draw a picture of how a global enterprise should manage information flows.

Dave Gray, founder and chairman of consultancy XPLANE, is facilitating the meeting. XPLANE uses visual thinking tools to help clients clarify problems involving everything from corporate strategy to operational implementations. Together with an XPLANE artist, Dave helps the 14 HP specialists gain a better understanding of the big picture of information sharing in a global enterprise. The group uses the posted sketches to discuss information sharing, to identify relationships between elements, to fill in missing pieces, and to develop a joint understanding of multiple issues.

With a knowing smile, Dave talks about a common misconception: that one shouldn't draw something until one understands it. On the contrary, he explains, sketches—however rudimentary or amateurish—help people better describe, discuss, and understand issues, particularly those of a complex nature. For the 14 Hewlett-Packard collaborators, XPLANE's visualization approach has worked beautifully. They gathered as 14 specialists with deeply individual understandings, but parted with a simple one-page image of how a global enterprise should manage information. XPLANE's client roster, which reads like a who's who of the world's most successful companies, testifies to the growing number of organizations that understand the value of this type of visual thinking.

The Value of
Visual Thinking

—

Visual thinking is indispensable to working with business models. By visual thinking we mean using visual tools such as pictures, sketches, diagrams, and Post-it™ notes to construct and discuss meaning. Because business models are complex concepts composed of various building blocks and their interrelationships, it is difficult to truly understand a model without sketching it out.

A business model really is a system where one element influences the other; it only makes sense as a whole. Capturing that big picture without visualizing it is difficult. In fact, by visually depicting a business model, one turns its tacit assumptions into explicit information. This makes the model tangible and allows for clearer discussions and changes. Visual techniques give "life" to a business model and facilitate co-creation.

Sketching a model transforms it into a persistent object and a conceptual anchor to which discussions can always return. This is critical because it shifts discourse from the abstract toward the concrete and greatly improves the quality of debate. Typically, if you aim to improve an existing business model, visually depicting it will unearth logical gaps and facilitate their discussion. Similarly,

if you are designing a completely new business model, drawing it will allow you to discuss different options easily by adding, removing, or moving pictures around.

Businesses already make frequent use of visual techniques such as diagrams and charts. Such elements are used extensively to clarify messages within reports and plans. But visual techniques are used less frequently to discuss, explore, and define business issues. When was the last time you attended a meeting where executives were drawing on the walls? Yet it is in the strategic process where visual thinking can add tremendous value. Visual thinking enhances strategic inquiries by making the abstract concrete, by illuminating relationships between elements, and by simplifying the complex. In this section we describe how visual thinking can help you throughout the process of defining, discussing, and changing business models.

We refer to two techniques: the use of Post-it™ notes and the use of sketches in combination with the Business Model Canvas. We also discuss four processes improved by visual thinking: understanding, dialogue, exploration, and communication.

Visualizing with Post-it™ Notes

A set of Post-it™ notes is an indispensable tool that everyone reflecting on business models should keep handy. Post-it™ notes function like idea containers that can be added, removed, and easily shifted between business model building blocks. This is important because during business model discussions, people frequently do not immediately agree on which elements should appear in a Business Model Canvas or where they should be placed. During exploratory discussions, some elements might be removed and replaced multiple times to explore new ideas.

Here are three simple guidelines: (1) use thick marking pens, (2) write only one element per Post-it™ note, and (3) write only a few words per note to capture the essential point. Using thick markers is more than a detail: it prevents you from putting too much information on a single Post-it™, and makes for easier reading and overview.

Keep in mind, too, that the discussion leading to the final business model picture created by all the Post-it™ notes is just as important as the outcome. Discussion around which notes to place on or remove from the Canvas and debate over how one element influences others give participants a deep understanding of the business model and its dynamics. Consequently, a Post-it™ note becomes more than just a piece of sticky paper representing a business model building block; it becomes a vector for strategic discussion.

Visualizing with Drawings

Drawings can be even more powerful than Post-it™ notes because people react more strongly to images than to words. Pictures deliver messages instantly. Simple drawings can express ideas that otherwise require many words.

It's easier than we think. A stick figure with a smiling face conveys emotion. A big bag of money and a small bag of money convey proportions. The problem is that most of us think we can't draw. We're embarrassed lest our sketches appear unsophisticated or childish. The truth is that even crude drawings, sincerely rendered, make things tangible and understandable. People interpret simple stick figures far more easily than abstract concepts expressed in text.

Sketches and drawings can make a difference in several ways. The most obvious one is explaining and communicating your business model based on simple drawings, something we explain how to do at the end of this chapter. Another is sketching out a typical client and her environment to illustrate one of your Customer Segments. This will trigger a more concrete, intensive discussion compared to outlining that person's characteristics in writing. Finally, sketching out a Customer Segment's needs and jobs-to-get-done is a powerful way to exploit visual techniques.

Such drawings will likely trigger constructive discussion from which new business model ideas will emerge. Now let's examine four processes improved by visual thinking.

Understand the Essence

VISUAL GRAMMAR

The Business Model Canvas poster is a conceptual map that functions as a visual language with corresponding grammar. It tells you which pieces of information to insert in the model, and where. It provides a visual and text guide to all the information needed to sketch out a business model.

CAPTURING THE BIG PICTURE

By sketching out all the elements of the Canvas you immediately give viewers the big picture of a business model. A sketch provides just the right amount of information to allow a viewer to grasp the idea, yet not too much detail to distract him. The Business Model Canvas visually simplifies the reality of an enterprise with all its processes, structures, and systems. In a business model like Rolls-Royce's, where jet engine units are leased by the hour rather than sold, it is the big picture, rather than the individual pieces, that is compelling.

SEEING RELATIONSHIPS

Understanding a business model requires not only knowing the compositional elements, but also grasping the interdependencies between elements. This is easier to express visually than through words. This is even more true when several elements and relationships are involved. In describing the business model of a low-cost airline, for example, drawings can effectively show why a homogenous fleet of airplanes is crucial to keeping maintenance and training costs low.

Enhance Dialogue

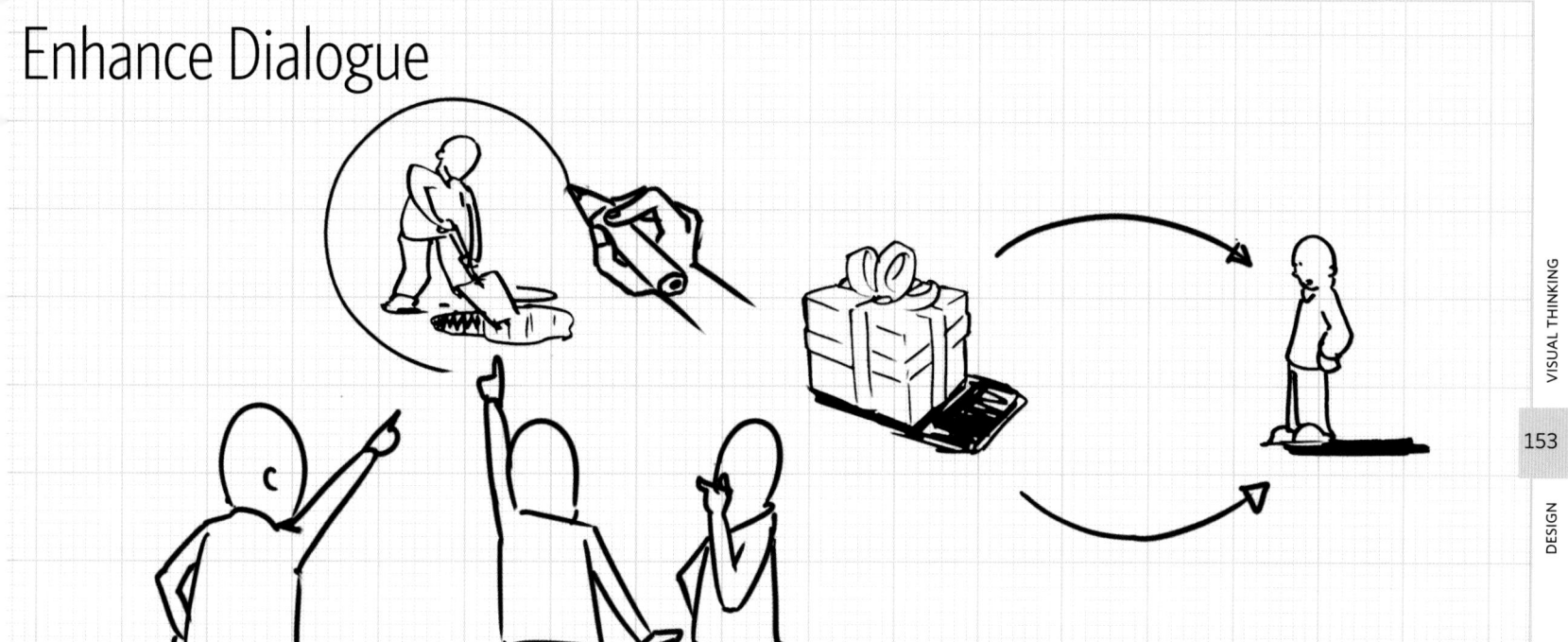

COLLECTIVE REFERENCE POINT

We all hold tacit assumptions in our heads, and posting an image that turns those implicit assumptions into explicit information is a powerful way to improve dialogue. It makes a business model into a tangible and persistent object, and provides a reference point to which participants can always return. Given that people can hold only a limited number of ideas in short-term memory, visually portraying business models is essential to good discussion. Even the simplest models are composed of several building blocks and interrelationships.

SHARED LANGUAGE

The Business Model Canvas is a shared visual language. It provides not only a reference point, but also a vocabulary and grammar that helps people better understand each other. Once people are familiar with the Canvas, it becomes a powerful enabler of focused discussion about business model elements and how they fit together. This is particularly valuable in organizations with matrix reporting structures where individuals in a working group or task force may know little about each other's functional areas. A shared visual business model language powerfully supports idea exchange and increases team cohesiveness.

JOINT UNDERSTANDING

Visualizing business models as a group is the most effective way to achieve shared understanding. People from different parts of an organization may deeply understand parts of a business model but lack a solid grasp of the whole. When experts jointly draw a business model, everybody involved gains an understanding of the individual components and develops a shared understanding of the relationships between these components.

Explore Ideas

IDEA TRIGGER

The Business Model Canvas is a bit like an artist's canvas. When an artist starts painting, he often has a vague idea—not an exact image—in mind. Rather than starting in one corner of a canvas and executing sequentially, he starts wherever his muse dictates and builds the painting organically. As Pablo Picasso said, "I begin with an idea and then it becomes something else." Picasso saw ideas as nothing more than points of departure. He knew they would evolve into something new during their explication.

Crafting a business model is no different. Ideas placed in the Canvas trigger new ones. The Canvas becomes a tool for facilitating the idea dialogue—for individuals sketching out their ideas and for groups developing ideas together.

PLAY

A visual business model also provides opportunity for play. With the elements of a model visible on a wall in the form of individual Post-it™ notes, you can start discussing what happens when you remove certain elements or insert new ones. For example, what would happen to your business model if you eliminated the least profitable Customer Segment? Could you do that? Or do you need the unprofitable segment to attract profitable customers? Would eliminating unprofitable customers enable you to reduce resources and costs and improve services to profitable customers? A visual model helps you think through the systemic impact of modifying one element or another.

Improve Communication

CREATE COMPANY-WIDE UNDERSTANDING

When it comes to communicating a business model and its most important elements, a picture is truly worth a thousand words. Everybody in an organization needs to understand its business model, because everybody can potentially contribute to its improvement. At the very least, employees need a shared understanding of the model so they can move in the same strategic direction. Visual depiction is the best way to create such a shared understanding.

SELLING INTERNALLY

In organizations, ideas and plans often must be "sold" internally at various levels to garner support or obtain funding. A powerful visual story reinforcing your pitch can increase your chances of winning understanding and backing for your idea. Using images rather than just words to tell the story makes your case even stronger, because people identify immediately with images. Good imagery readily communicates your organization's current status, what needs doing, how it can be done, and what the future might look like.

SELLING EXTERNALLY

Just as employees must "sell" ideas internally, entrepreneurs with plans based on new business models must sell them to other parties, such as investors or potential collaborators. Strong visuals substantially increase chances of success.

Different Types of Visualization for Different Needs

Visual representations of business models call for different levels of detail depending on one's goal. The sketch of Skype's business model on the right drives home the key differences between its business model and that of a traditional telecommunications carrier. The goal is to point out the striking differences between Skype's business model building blocks and those of a traditional carrier, even though both offer similar services.

The right-hand page sketch depicting the young Dutch company Sellaband has a different goal and is therefore more detailed. It aims to paint the big picture of a completely new music industry business model: that of a platform enabling crowd-funding of independent musical artists. Sellaband uses the drawing to explain its innovative business model to investors, partners, and employees. Sellaband's combination of images and text has proven to be far more effective than words alone at accomplishing this task.

- *Skype's Key Resources and Activities resemble those of a software company, because its service is based on software that uses the Internet to carry calls. Given its 400 million+ user base, the company enjoys very low infrastructure costs. In fact, it does not own or operate a telecommunications network at all.*

- *From day one, Skype was a global voice carrier because its service is delivered through the Internet, unrestricted by traditional telecommunications networks. Its business is highly scalable.*

- *Though it provides a telecommunications service, Skype's business model features the economics of a software company rather than a telecommunications network operator.*

- *Ninety percent of Skype users never pay. Only an estimated 10 percent of users are paying customers. Unlike traditional telecommunication carriers, Skype's Channels and Relationships are highly automated. They require almost no human intervention and are therefore relatively inexpensive.*

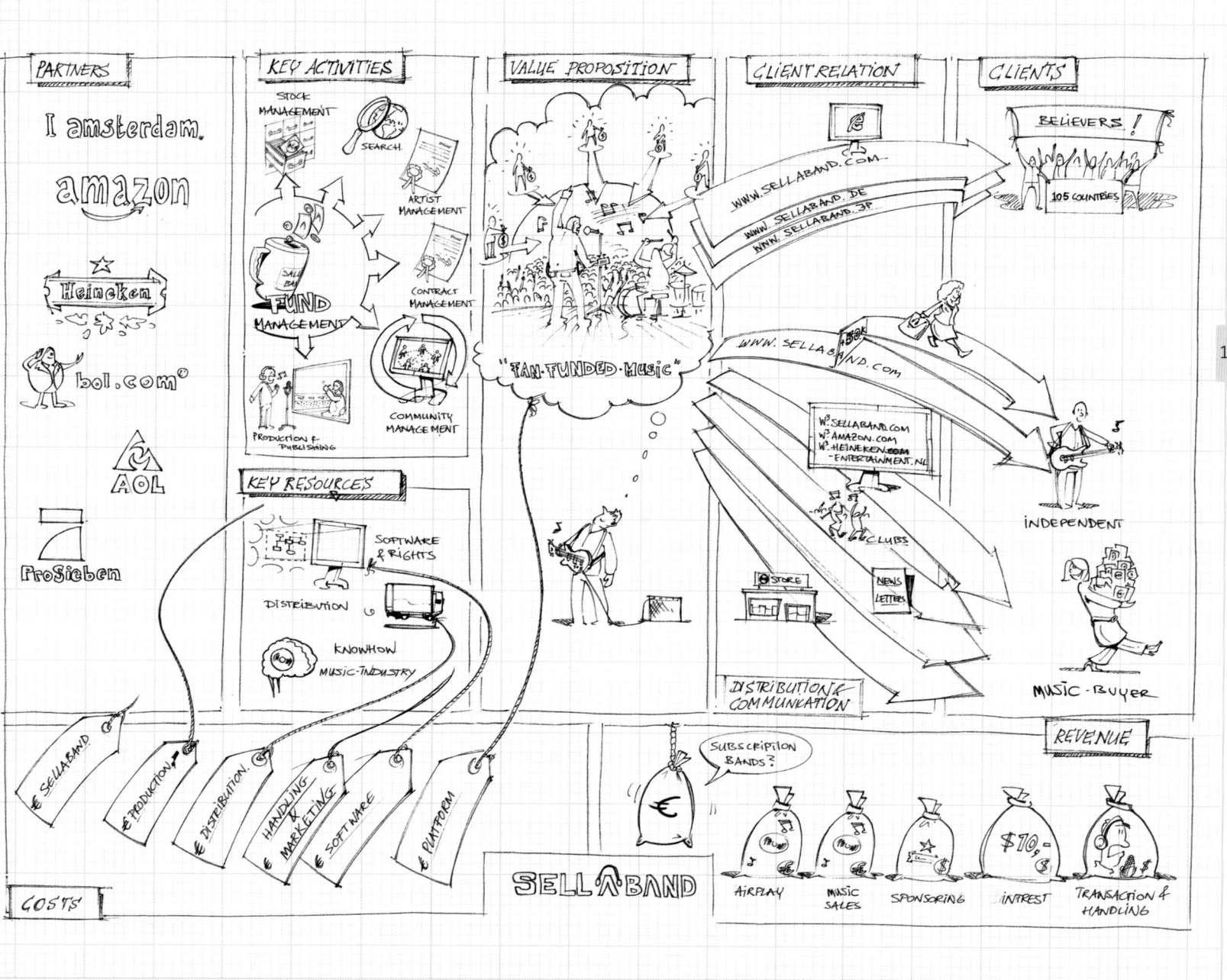

Telling a Visual Story

A powerful way to explain a business model is to tell a story one image at a time. Presenting a full description within the Business Model Canvas can overwhelm an audience. It's better to introduce the model piece by piece. You could do this by drawing one piece after another, or by using PowerPoint. An appealing alternative is to pre-draw all the elements of a business model on Post-it™ notes, then put them up one after another as you explain the model. It allows the audience to follow the build-up of the model, and the visuals complement your explanation.

Visual Storytelling Activity

MAP YOUR BUSINESS MODEL

- *Begin by mapping out a simple, text-based version of your business model.*

- *Write each business model element on an individual Post-it™ note.*

- *Mapping can be done individually or with a group.*

DRAW EACH BUSINESS MODEL ELEMENT

- *One at a time, take each Post-it™ note and replace it with a drawing representing the content.*

- *Keep the images simple: omit detail.*

- *Drawing quality is unimportant as long as the message is conveyed.*

DEFINE THE STORYLINE

- *Decide which Post-it™ notes you will put up first when telling your story.*

- *Try different paths. You might start with Customer Segments, or maybe the Value Proposition.*

- *Basically, any starting point is possible if it effectively supports your story.*

TELL THE STORY

- *Tell your business model story one drawn Post-it™ picture at a time.*

  Note: Depending on the context and your personal preferences, you may want to use PowerPoint or Keynote. Slideware, though, is unlikely to produce the positive surprise effect of the Post-it™ approach.

Technique_No. 4

Prototyping

With a look bordering on panic, Weatherhead School of Management Professor Richard Boland Jr. watched as Matt Fineout, an architect with Gehry & Associates, casually tore up plans for a new school building …

... Boland and Fineout had been struggling for two full days to remove some 5,500 square feet from the floor plan designed by star architect Frank Gehry, while leaving room needed for meeting spaces and office equipment.

At the end of the marathon planning session, Boland had breathed a sigh of relief. "It's finally done," he thought. But at that very moment, Fineout rose from his chair, ripped the document apart, and tossed the scraps into a trash bin, not bothering to retain a single trace of the pair's hard labor. He responded to Professor Boland's shocked expression with a gentle shrug and a soft remark. "We've shown we *can* do it; now we need to think of *how* we want to do it."

Looking back, Boland describes the incident as an extreme example of the relentless approach to inquiry he experienced while working with the Gehry group on the new Weatherhead building. During the design phase, Gehry and his team made hundreds of models with different materials and of varying sizes, simply to explore new directions. Boland explains that the goal of this prototyping activity was far more than the mere testing or proving of ideas. It was a methodology for exploring different possibilities until a truly good one emerged. He points out that prototyping, as practiced by the Gehry group, is a central part of an inquiry process that helps participants gain a better sense of what is missing in the initial understanding of a situation. This leads to completely new possibilities, among which the right one can be identified. For Professor Boland, the experience with Gehry & Associates was transformative. He now understands how design techniques, including prototyping, contribute to finding better solutions for the entire spectrum of business problems. Together with fellow professor Fred Collopy and other colleagues, Boland is now spearheading the concept of Manage by Designing: the integration of design thinking, skills, and experiences into Weatherhead's MBA curriculum. Here, students use tools of design to sketch alternatives, follow through on problem situations, transcend traditional boundaries, and prototype ideas.

Prototyping's Value

—

Prototyping is a powerful tool for developing new, innovative business models. Like visual thinking, it makes abstract concepts tangible and facilitates the exploration of new ideas. Prototyping comes from the design and engineering disciplines, where it is widely used for product design, architecture, and interaction design. It is less common in business management because of the less tangible nature of organizational behavior and strategy. While prototyping has long played a role at the intersection of business and design, for example in manufactured product design, in recent years it has gained traction in areas such as process design, service design, and even organization and strategy design. Here we show how prototyping can make an important contribution to business model design.

Although they use the same term, product designers, architects, and engineers all have different understandings of what constitutes a "prototype." We see prototypes representing potential future business models: as tools that serve the purpose of discussion, inquiry, or proof of concept. A business model prototype can take the form of a simple sketch, a fully thought-through concept described with the Business Model Canvas, or a spreadsheet that simulates the financial workings of a new business.

It is important to understand that a business model prototype is not necessarily a rough picture of what the actual business model will actually look like. Rather, a prototype is a thinking tool that helps us explore different directions in which we could take our business model. What does it mean for the model if we add another client segment? What are the consequences of removing a costly resource? What if we gave away something for free and replaced that Revenue Stream with something more innovative? Making and manipulating a business model prototype forces us to address issues of structure, relationship, and logic in ways unavailable through mere thought and discussion. To truly understand the pros and cons of different possibilities, and to further our inquiry, we need to construct multiple prototypes of our business model at different levels of refinement. Interaction with prototypes produces ideas far more readily than discussion. Prototype business models may be thought-provoking—even a bit crazy—and thus help push our thinking. When this happens, they become signposts pointing us in as-yet unimagined directions rather than serving as mere representations of to-be-implemented business models. "Inquiry" should signify a relentless search for the best solution. Only after deep inquiry can we effectively pick a prototype to refine and execute—after our design has matured.

Businesspeople are likely to display one of two reactions to this process of business model inquiry. Some might say, "Well, that is a nice idea, if we only had the time to explore different options." Others might say that a market research study would be an equally good way to come up with new business models. Both reactions are based on dangerous preconceptions.

The first supposes that "business as usual" or incremental improvements are sufficient to survive in today's competitive environment. We believe this path leads to mediocrity. Businesses that fail to take the time to develop and prototype new, ground-breaking business model ideas risk being sidelined or overtaken by more dynamic competitors—or by insurgent challengers appearing, seemingly, from nowhere.

The second reaction assumes that data is the most important consideration when designing new strategic options. It is not. Market research is a single input in the long and laborious process of prototyping powerful new business models with the potential to outperform competitors or develop entirely new markets.

Where do you want to be? At the top of the game, because you've taken the time to prototype powerful new business models? Or on the sidelines, because you were too busy sustaining your existing model? We're convinced that new, game-changing business models emerge from deep and relentless inquiry.

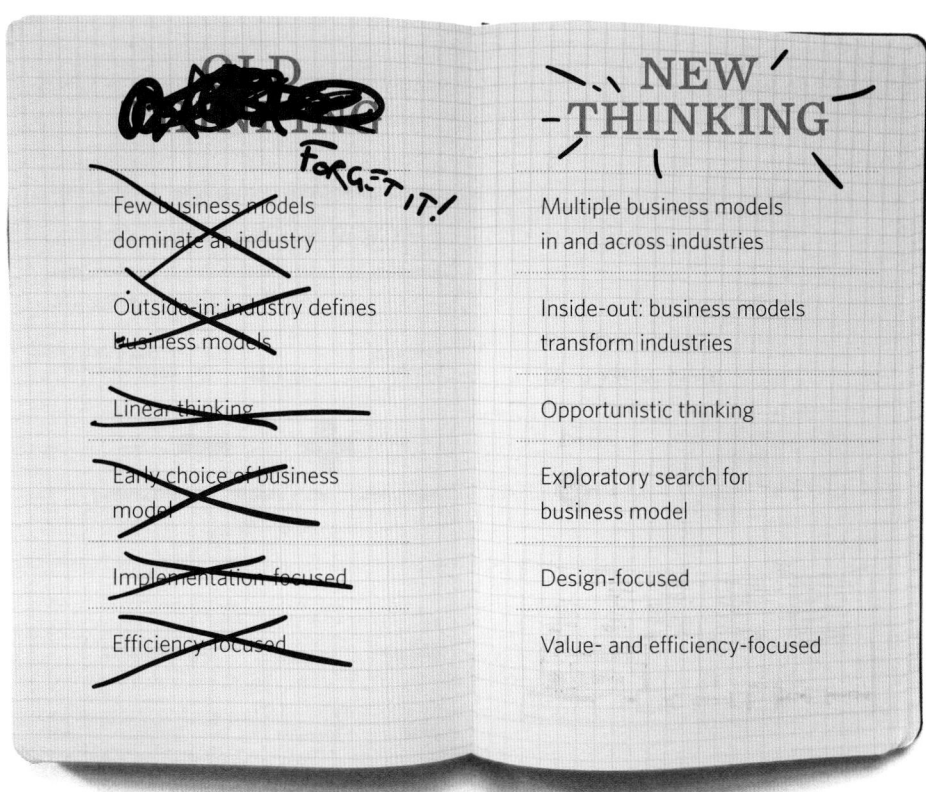

OLD ~~THINKING~~ FORGET IT!	NEW THINKING
~~Few business models dominate an industry~~	Multiple business models in and across industries
~~Outside-in: industry defines business models~~	Inside-out: business models transform industries
~~Linear thinking~~	Opportunistic thinking
~~Early choice of business model~~	Exploratory search for business model
~~Implementation-focused~~	Design-focused
~~Efficiency-focused~~	Value- and efficiency-focused

Design Attitude

"If you freeze an idea too quickly, you fall in love with it.
If you refine it too quickly, you become attached to it
and it becomes very hard to keep exploring, to keep
looking for better. The crudeness of the early models
in particular is very deliberate."

Jim Glymph, Gehry Partners

As businesspeople, when we see a prototype we tend to focus on its physical form or its representation, viewing it as something that models, or encapsulates the essence of, what we eventually intend to do. We perceive a prototype as something that simply needs to be refined. In the design profession, prototypes do play a role in pre-implementation visualization and testing. But they also play another very important role: that of a tool of inquiry. In this sense they serve as thinking aids for exploring new possibilities. They help us develop a better understanding of what could be.

This same design attitude can be applied to business model innovation. By making a prototype of a business model we can explore particular aspects of an idea: novel Revenue Streams, for example. Participants learn about the elements of a prototype as they construct and discuss

it. As previously discussed , business model prototypes vary in terms of scale and level of refinement. We believe it is important to think through a number of basic business model possibilities before developing a business case for a specific model. This spirit of inquiry is called design attitude, because it is so central to the design professions, as Professor Boland discovered. The attributes of design attitude include a willingness to explore crude ideas, rapidly discard them, then take the time to examine multiple possibilities before choosing to refine a few—and accepting uncertainty until a design direction matures. These things don't come naturally to businesspeople, but they are requirements for generating new business models. Design attitude demands changing one's orientation from making decisions to creating options from which to choose.

Prototypes at Different Scales

In architecture or product design, it is easy to understand what is meant by prototyping at different scales, because we are talking about physical artifacts. Architect Frank Gehry and product designer Philippe Starck construct countless prototypes during a project, ranging from sketches and rough models to elaborate, full-featured prototypes. We can apply the same scale and size variations when prototyping business models, but in a more conceptual way. A business model prototype can be anything from a rough sketch of an idea on a napkin to a detailed Business Model Canvas to a field-testable business model. You may wonder how all of this is any different from simply sketching out business ideas, something any businessperson or entrepreneur does. Why do we need to call it "prototyping"?

There are two answers. First, the mindset is different. Second, the Business Model Canvas provides structure to facilitate exploration.

Business model prototyping is about a mindset we call "design attitude." It stands for an uncompromising commitment to discovering new and better business models by sketching out many prototypes —both rough and detailed—representing many strategic options. It's not about outlining only ideas you really plan to implement. It's about exploring new and perhaps absurd, even impossible ideas by adding and removing elements of each prototype. You can experiment with prototypes at different levels.

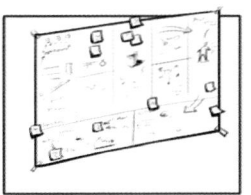

NAPKIN SKETCH	ELABORATED CANVAS	BUSINESS CASE	FIELD-TEST
OUTLINE AND PITCH A ROUGH IDEA	**EXPLORE WHAT IT WOULD TAKE TO MAKE THE IDEA WORK**	**EXAMINE THE VIABILITY OF THE IDEA**	**INVESTIGATE CUSTOMER ACCEPTANCE AND FEASIBILITY**
DRAW A SIMPLE BUSINESS MODEL CANVAS. DESCRIBE THE IDEA USING ONLY KEY ELEMENTS.	DEVELOP A MORE ELABORATE CANVAS TO EXPLORE ALL THE ELEMENTS NEEDED TO MAKE THE BUSINESS MODEL WORK.	TURN THE DETAILED CANVAS INTO A SPREADSHEET TO ESTIMATE YOUR MODEL'S EARNING POTENTIAL.	YOU'VE DECIDED ON A POTENTIAL NEW BUSINESS MODEL, AND NOW WANT TO FIELD-TEST SOME ASPECTS.

NAPKIN SKETCH:
- *Outline the idea*
- *Include the Value Proposition*
- *Include the main Revenue Streams*

ELABORATED CANVAS:
- *Develop a full Canvas*
- *Think through your business logic*
- *Estimate the market potential*
- *Understand the relationships between Building Blocks*
- *Do some basic fact-checking*

BUSINESS CASE:
- *Create a full Canvas*
- *Include key data*
- *Calculate costs and revenues*
- *Estimate profit potential*
- *Run financial scenarios based on different assumptions*

FIELD-TEST:
- *Prepare a well-justified business case for the new model*
- *Include prospective or actual customers in the field test*
- *Test the Value Proposition, Channels, pricing mechanism, and/or other elements in the marketplace*

Eight Business Model Prototypes
for Publishing a Book

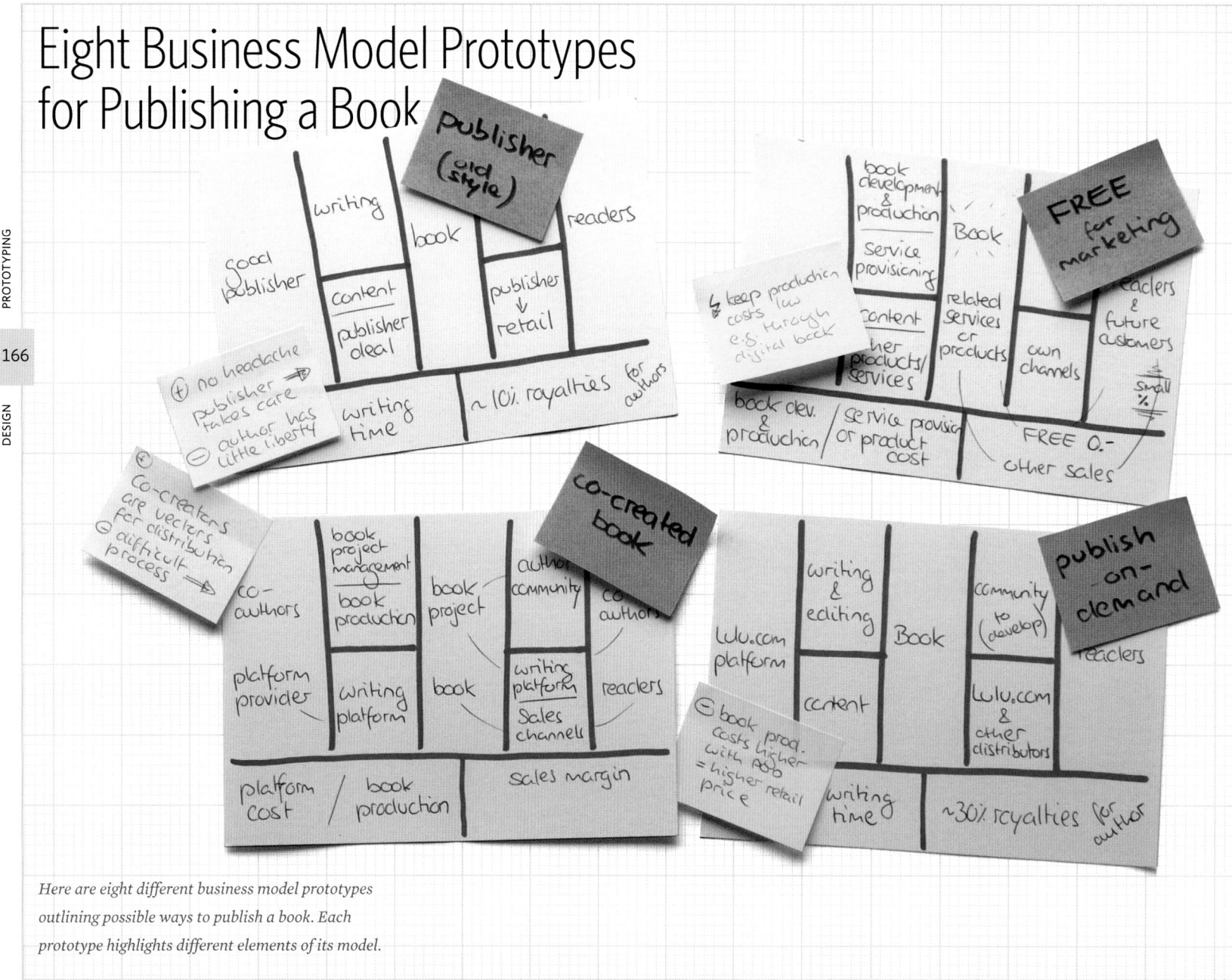

*Here are eight different business model prototypes
outlining possible ways to publish a book. Each
prototype highlights different elements of its model.*

A prototype rarely describes all the elements of a "real" business model. It focuses instead on illuminating particular aspects of the model and thus indicating new directions for exploration.

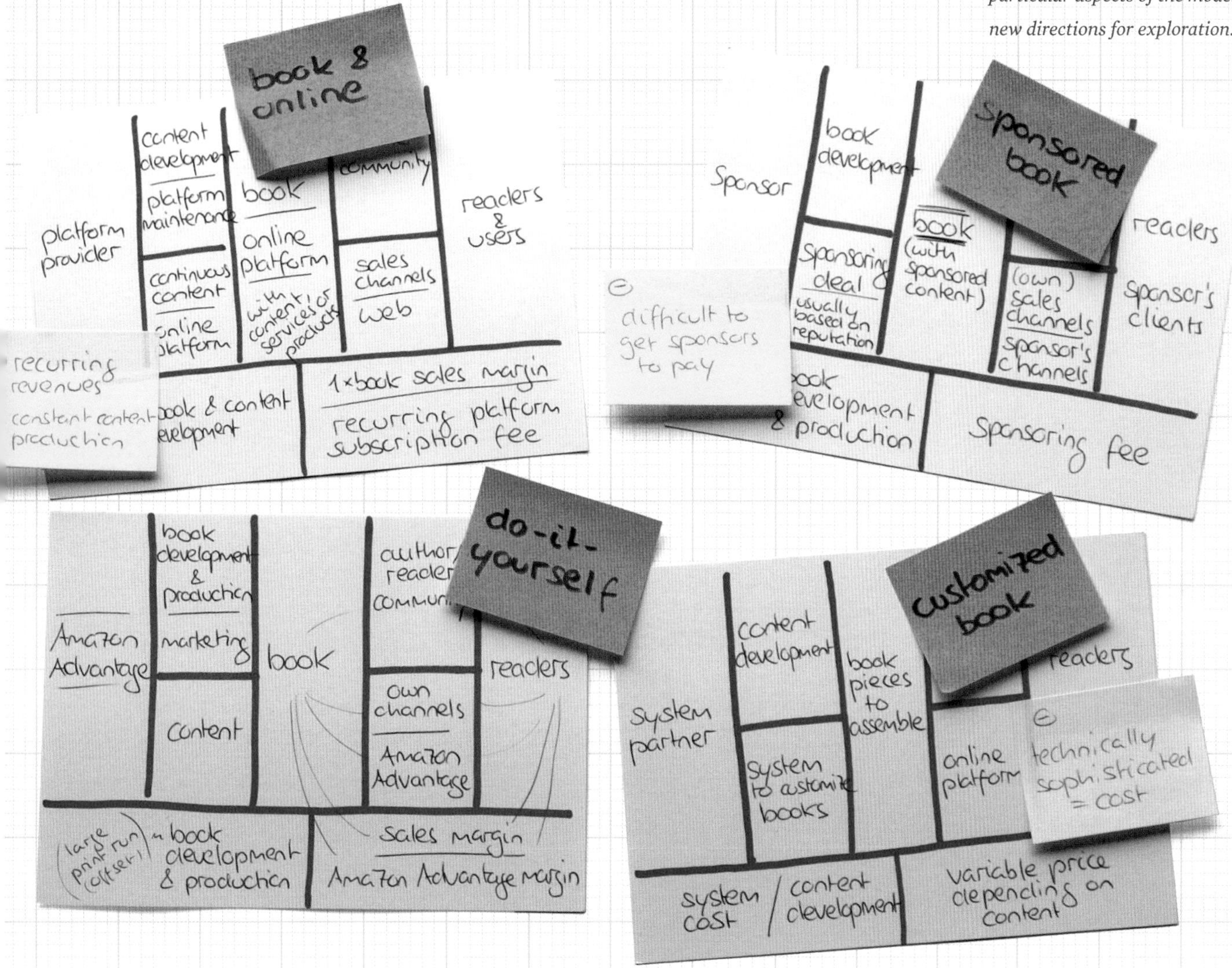

design   *prototype*

DECIDE   INQUIRY   EXECUTE

provoke

Wanted: A New Consulting Business Model

John, 55
Founder & CEO
Strategy Consultancy
210 employees

John Sutherland needs your help. John is the founder and CEO of a midsized global consulting firm that focuses on advising companies on strategy and organizational issues. He is looking for a fresh, outside perspective on his company because he believes that his business needs to be re-envisioned.

John built his company over two decades and now employs 210 people worldwide. The focus of his consultancy is helping executives develop effective strategies, improve their strategic management, and realign their organizations. He competes directly with McKinsey, Bain, and Roland Berger. One problem he faces is being smaller than his top-tier competitors, yet much larger than the typical niche-focused strategy consultancy. But John is not preoccupied with this issue, since his company is still doing reasonably well. What really troubles him is the strategic consulting profession's poor reputation in the marketplace, and growing client perception that the prevalent hourly and project-based billing model is outdated. Though his own firm's reputation remains good, he has heard from several clients that they think consultants overcharge, under-deliver, and show little genuine commitment to client projects.

Such comments alarm John, because he believes his industry employs some of the brightest minds in business. After much thought, he has concluded that this reputation results from an outdated business model, and he now wants to transform his own company's approach. John aims to make hourly and project billing a thing of the past, but isn't quite sure how to do so.

Help John by providing him with some fresh perspectives on innovative consulting business models.

1

OUTLINE BIG ISSUES

- *Think of a typical strategy-consulting client.*
- *Pick the Customer Segment and industry of your choice.*
- *Describe five of the biggest issues related to strategy consulting. Refer to the Empathy Map (see p. 131).*

2

GENERATE POSSIBILITIES

- *Take another close look at the five customer issues you selected.*
- *Generate as many consulting business model ideas as you can.*
- *Pick the five ideas you think are best (not necessarily the most realistic). Refer to the Ideation Process (see p. 134).*

3

PROTOTYPE THE BUSINESS MODEL

- *Choose the three most diverse ideas of the five generated.*
- *Develop three conceptual business model prototypes by sketching the elements of each idea on different Business Model Canvases.*
- *Annotate the pros and cons of each prototype.*

It is already far past midnight as Anab Jain watches the latest video footage she shot during the day …

… She's working on a series of small films for Colebrook Bosson Saunders, a designer and manufacturer of award-winning office furniture accessories. Anab is a storyteller and designer, and the films she is working on are part of a project to help Colebrook Bosson Saunders make sense of how the future of work and the work-place could look. To make this future tangible, she invented three protagonists and projected them into 2012. She gave them new jobs based on research into new and emerging technologies and the impact of demographics and environmental risks on our future lives. The films then show this near future. But rather than describing 2012, Anab takes the role of the storyteller, visiting this future environment and interviewing the three protagonists. They each explain their work and show objects they use. The films are real enough to cause viewers to suspend their disbelief and become intrigued by the different environment. That is exactly what companies that hire Anab Jain, like Microsoft and Nokia, are looking for: stories to make potential futures tangible.

Storytelling's Value

—

As parents, we read stories to our kids, sometimes the same ones we heard as children ourselves. As colleagues, we share the latest organizational gossip. And as friends, we tell one another stories of our personal lives. Somehow, it is only in our roles as business-people that we avoid using stories. This is unfortunate. When was the last time you heard a story used to introduce and discuss a business issue? Storytelling is an undervalued and underused art in the world of business. Let's examine how storytelling can serve as a powerful tool to make new business models more tangible.

By their very nature, new or innovative business models can be difficult to describe and understand. They challenge the status quo by arranging things in unfamiliar ways. They force listeners to open their minds to new possibilities. Resistance is one likely reaction to an unfamiliar model. Therefore, describing new business models in a way that overcomes resistance is crucial.

Just as the Business Model Canvas helps you sketch and analyze a new model, storytelling will help you effectively communicate what it is all about. Good stories engage listeners, so the story is the ideal tool to prepare for an in-depth discussion of a business model and its underlying logic. Storytelling takes advantage of the explanatory power of the Business Model Canvas by suspending disbelief in the unfamiliar.

Why Storytelling?

Introducing the New

New business model ideas can pop up anywhere in an organization. Some ideas may be good, some may be mediocre, and some may be, well, completely useless. But even outstanding business model ideas can have a tough time getting past layers of management and finding their way into an organization's strategy. So effectively pitching your business model ideas to management is crucial. This is where stories can help. Ultimately, managers are interested in numbers and facts, but having the right story can win their attention. A good story is a compelling way to quickly outline a broad idea before getting caught up in the details.

Pitching to Investors

If you are an entrepreneur, chances are you will pitch your idea or business model to investors or other potential shareholders (and you already know that investors stop listening the instant you tell them how you will become the next Google). What investors and other shareholders want to know is: How will you create value for customers? How will you make money doing so? That's the perfect setting for a story. It's the ideal way to introduce your venture and business model before getting into the full business plan.

Engaging Employees

When an organization transitions from an existing business model to a new business model, it must convince collaborators to follow. People need a crystal clear understanding of the new model and what it means for them. In short, the organization needs to powerfully engage its employees. That is where traditional text-based Power-Point presentations usually fail. Introducing a new business model through an engaging story-based presentation (delivered with PowerPoint, drawings, or other techniques) is far more likely to connect with listeners. Capturing people's attention and curiosity paves the way for in-depth presentations and discussions of the unfamiliar.

Make the New Tangible

Explaining a new, untested business model is like explaining a painting with words alone. But telling a story of how the model creates value is like applying bright colors to canvas. It makes things tangible.

Clarification

Telling a story that illustrates how your business model solves a customer problem is a clear way to introduce listeners to the idea. Stories give you the "buy-in" needed to subsequently explain your model in detail.

Engaging People

People are moved more by stories than by logic. Ease listeners into the new or unknown by building the logic of your model into a compelling narrative.

Making Business Models Tangible?

The goal of telling a story is to introduce a new business model in an engaging, tangible way. Keep the story simple and use only one protagonist. Depending on the audience, you can use a different protagonist with a different perspective. Here are two possible starting points.

STORYTELLING

174

DESIGN

COMPANY
perspective

Employee Observer

Explain the business model in the form of a story told from an employee's perspective. Use the employee as the protagonist who demonstrates why the new model makes sense. This may be because the employee frequently observes customer problems that the new business model solves. Or it may be that the new model makes better or different use of resources, activities, or partnerships compared to the old model (e.g. cost reduction, productivity improvement, new revenue sources, etc.). In such a story, the employee embodies the inner workings of an organization and its business model and shows the reasons for transitioning to a new model.

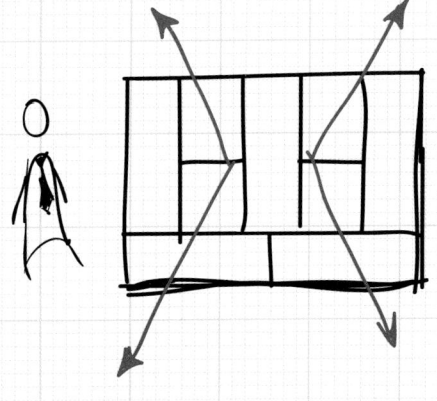

CUSTOMER
perspective

Customer Jobs

The customer perspective provides a powerful starting point for a story. Cast a customer as the protagonist and tell the tale from her point of view. Show the challenges she faces and which jobs she must get done. Then outline how your organization creates value for her. The story can describe what she receives, how it fits into her life, and what she is willing to pay for. Add some drama and emotion to the story, and describe how your organization is making her life easier. Ideally, weave in how your organization gets these jobs done for the customer, with which resources and through which activities. The biggest challenge with stories told from a customer perspective is keeping them authentic and avoiding a facile or patronizing tone.

Making the Future Tangible

Stories offer a wonderful technique for blurring the lines separating reality and fiction. Thus stories provide a powerful tool for imparting tangibility to different versions of the future. This can help you challenge the status quo or justify adopting a new business model.

CURRENT BUSINESS MODEL

WHAT FUTURE BUSINESS MODEL?

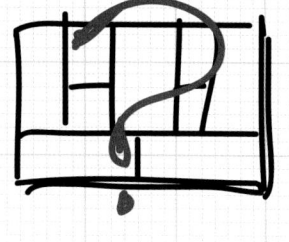

PLANNED FUTURE BUSINESS MODEL

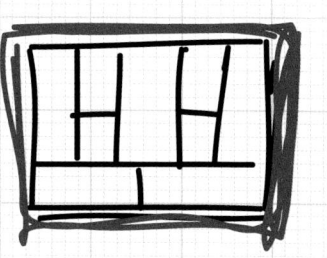

Provoke Ideas

Sometimes a story's sole purpose is to challenge the organizational status quo. Such a story must bring vividly to life a future competitive environment in which the current business model is severely challenged or even obsolete. Telling a story like this blurs the lines between reality and fiction and catapults listeners into the future. This suspends disbelief, instills a sense of urgency, and opens the audience's eyes to the need to generate new business models. Such a story can be told from either an organization or a customer perspective.

Justify Change

Sometimes an organization has strong ideas about how its competitive landscape will evolve. In this context, a story's purpose is to show how a new business model is ideally suited to help an organization compete in the new landscape. Stories temporarily suspend disbelief and help people imagine how the current business model should evolve to remain effective in the future. The story's protagonist could be a customer, an employee, or a top manager.

Developing the Story

The goal of telling a story is to introduce a new business model in an engaging, tangible way. Keep the story simple and use only one protagonist. Depending on the audience, you can use a different protagonist with a different perspective. Here are two possible starting points.

Company Perspective

Ajit, 32, Senior IT Manager, Amazon.com

Ajit has worked for Amazon.com as an IT manager for the past nine years. He and his colleagues have pulled countless all-nighters over the years to deliver the world-class IT infrastructure that serves and maintains the company's e-commerce business.

Ajit is proud of his work. Along with its fulfillment excellence (1, 6), Amazon.com's powerful IT infrastructure and software development capabilities (2, 3) form the heart of its success at selling everything from books to furniture online (7). Amazon.com (8) delivered over half a billion page impressions to online shoppers (9) in 2008, and spent over a billion dollars for technology and content (5), notably to run its e-commerce operations.

But now Ajit is even more excited, because Amazon.com is traveling far beyond its traditional retail offers. It's in the process of becoming one of the most important infrastructure providers in e-commerce.

With a service called Amazon Simple Storage Systems (Amazon S3) (11) the company is now using its own IT infrastructure to provide online storage to other companies at rock-bottom prices. This means that an online video hosting service can store all customer videos on Amazon's infrastructure rather than buying and

maintaining its own servers. Similarly, Amazon Elastic Computing Cloud (Amazon EC2) (11) offers Amazon.com's own computing capability to outside clients.

Ajit knows that outsiders might view such services as distracting Amazon.com from its core retail operations. From the inside, though, the diversification makes perfect sense.

Ajit remembers that four years ago, his group spent much time coordinating the efforts of the network engineering groups, which managed IT infrastructure, and the applications programming groups, which managed Amazon.com's many Web sites. So they decided to build so-called application programming interfaces (APIs) (12) between these two layers, which would allow the latter to easily build on the former. Ajit also remembers exactly when they started to realize that this would be useful to external as well as internal customers. So under Jeff Bezos's leadership, Amazon.com decided to create a new business with the potential to generate a significant revenue source for the company. Amazon.com opened up its infrastructure APIs to provide what it calls Amazon Web Services to outside parties on a fee-for-service basis (14). Since Amazon.com had to design, create, implement, and maintain this infrastructure anyway, offering it to third parties was hardly a distraction.

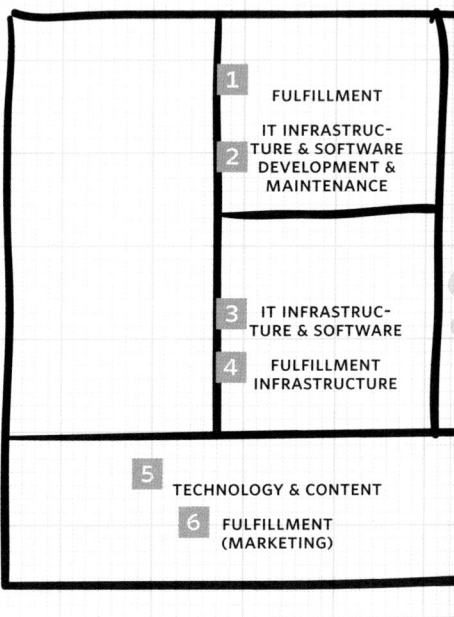

1 FULFILLMENT
2 IT INFRASTRUCTURE & SOFTWARE DEVELOPMENT & MAINTENANCE
3 IT INFRASTRUCTURE & SOFTWARE
4 FULFILLMENT INFRASTRUCTURE
5 TECHNOLOGY & CONTENT
6 FULFILLMENT (MARKETING)

E-commerce

9 CONSUMER MARKET

7 NLINE RETAIL SHOP

AMAZON.COM **8**

10 SALES MARGINS

Infrastructure NEW

AMAZON WEB ERVICES: S3, EC2, QS, OTHER WEB SERVICES **11**

APIs **12**

COMPANIES AND DEVELOPERS **13**

UTILITY COMPUTING FEES

14

Customer Perspective
Randy, 41, Web Entrepreneur
Randy is a passionate Web entrepreneur. After 18 years in the software industry he is now running his second startup, providing enterprise software through the Web. He spent 10 years of his career in large software companies and eight years in start-ups.

Throughout his career, one constant struggle has been getting infrastructure investments right. To him, running servers to provide services was basically a commodity business, but a tricky one due to the enormous costs involved. Tight management was crucial; when you're running a start-up you can't invest millions in a server farm.

But when serving the enterprise market, you'd better have a robust IT infrastructure in place. That's why Randy was intrigued when a friend at Amazon.com told him about the new IT infrastructure services his company was launching. That was the answer to one of Randy's most important in-house jobs: running his services on a world-class IT infrastructure, being able to scale quickly, and all the while paying only for what his company was actually using. That was exactly what Amazon's Web Services (**11**) promised. With Amazon Simple Storage Systems (Amazon S3), Randy could plug into Amazon's infrastructure through a so-called application programming interface (API)(**12**) and store all the data and applications for his own services on Amazon.com's servers. The same went for Amazon's Elastic Computing Cloud (Amazon EC2). Randy didn't have to build and maintain his own infrastructure to crunch the numbers for his enterprise application service. He could simply plug into Amazon and use its computing power in return for hourly usage fees (**14**).

He immediately understood why the value was coming from the giant e-tailer rather than from IBM or Accenture. Amazon.com was providing and maintaining IT infrastructure (**2**, **3**, **5**) to serve its online retail business (**7**) every day on a global scale. This was its core competency. Taking the step to offer the same infrastructure services to other companies (**9**) was not much of a stretch. And since Amazon.com was in retail, a business with low margins (**11**), it had to be extremely cost-efficient (**5**), which explained the rock-bottom prices of its new Web Services.

Techniques

Telling an engaging story can be done in different ways. Each technique has advantages and disadvantages and is better suited for certain situations and audiences. Choose a suitable technique after you understand who your audience will be and the context in which you will present.

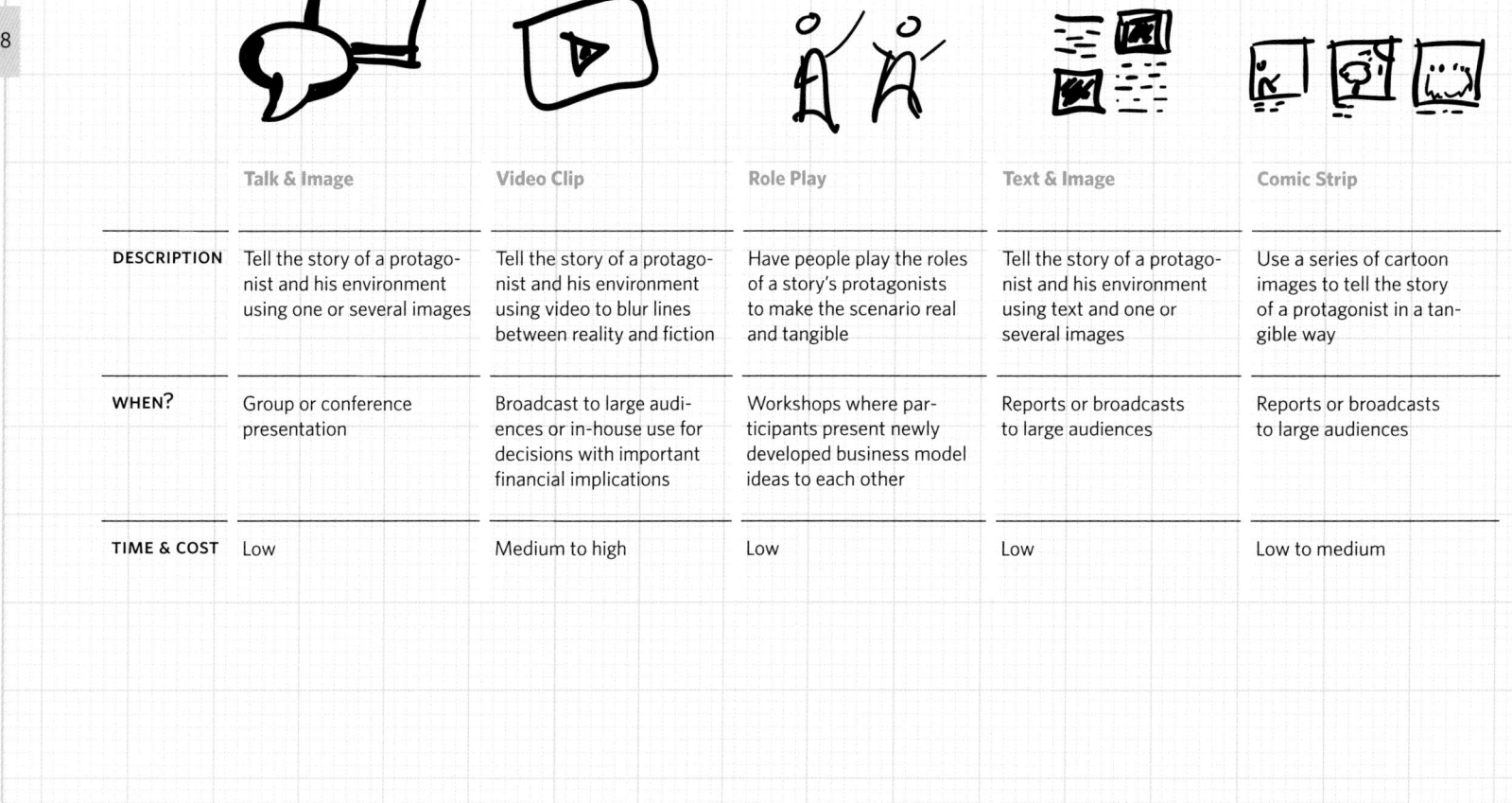

	Talk & Image	**Video Clip**	**Role Play**	**Text & Image**	**Comic Strip**
DESCRIPTION	Tell the story of a protagonist and his environment using one or several images	Tell the story of a protagonist and his environment using video to blur lines between reality and fiction	Have people play the roles of a story's protagonists to make the scenario real and tangible	Tell the story of a protagonist and his environment using text and one or several images	Use a series of cartoon images to tell the story of a protagonist in a tangible way
WHEN?	Group or conference presentation	Broadcast to large audiences or in-house use for decisions with important financial implications	Workshops where participants present newly developed business model ideas to each other	Reports or broadcasts to large audiences	Reports or broadcasts to large audiences
TIME & COST	Low	Medium to high	Low	Low	Low to medium

SuperToast, Inc. Business Model

Start practicing your business model storytelling skills with this simple, slightly silly exercise: The business model of SuperToast, Inc. outlined in the Canvas below. You can start anywhere you like: with Customers, the Value Proposition, Key Resources, or elsewhere. Invent your own story. The only constraints are the nine images that outline SuperToast Inc.'s business model. Try telling the story several times, starting from different Building Blocks. Each starting point will give the story a slightly different twist and emphasize different aspects of the model.

By the way, this is a wonderful approach to introducing the Business Model Canvas to the "uninitiated" in a simple and engaging way—with a story.

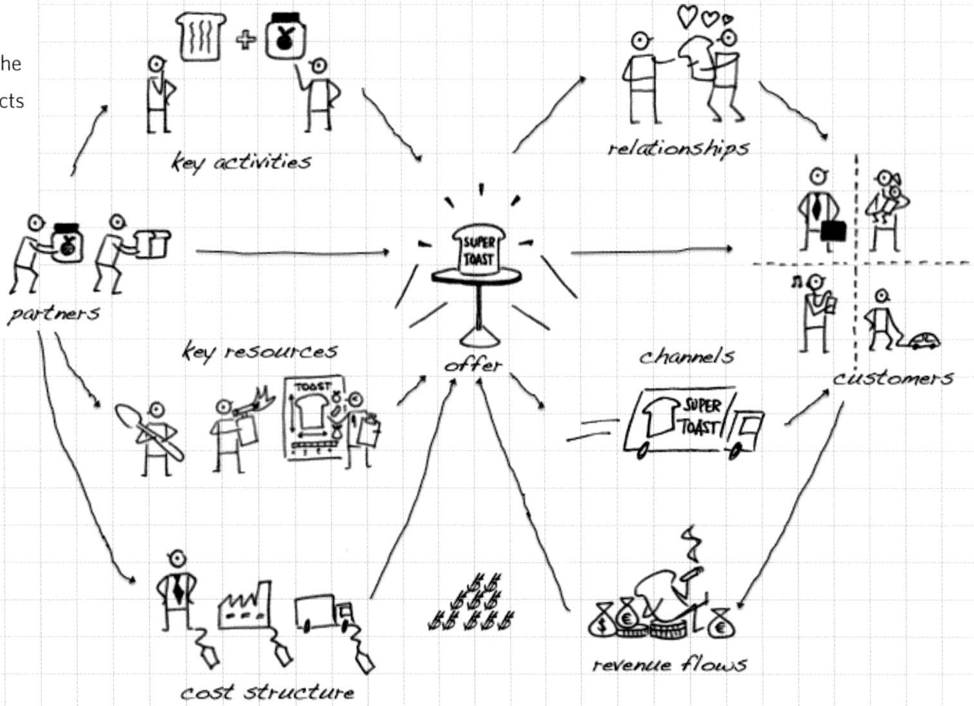

key activities
relationships
partners
SUPER TOAST
offer
customers
key resources
TOAST
channels
SUPER TOAST
cost structure
revenue flows

XPLANATIONS™ by XPLANE™

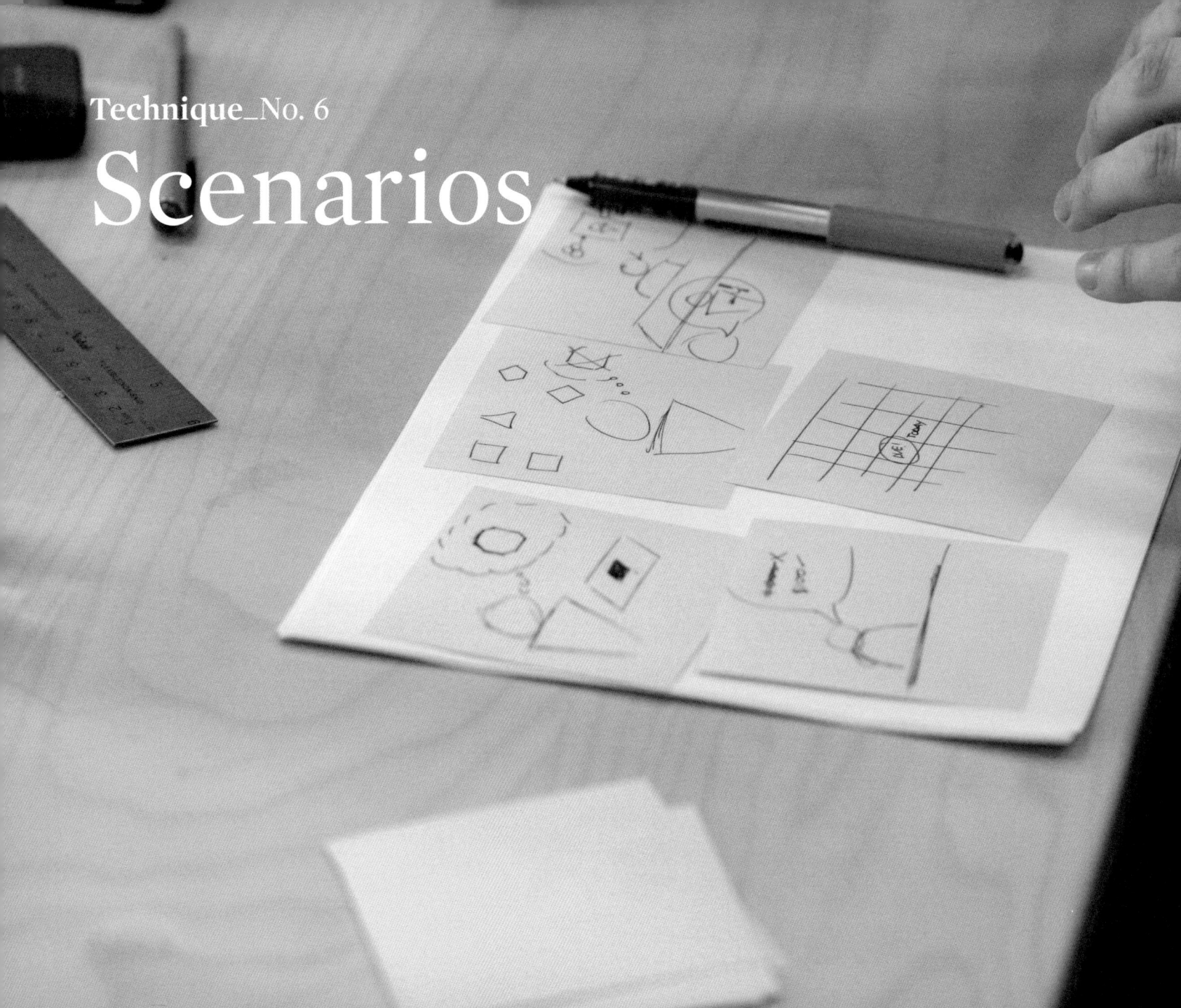

Technique_No. 6
Scenarios

Professor Jeffrey Huang and Muriel Waldvogel seem lost in thought as they ponder scale models of the Swisshouse, the new Swiss consulate facility to be built in Boston, Massachusetts ...

... Huang and Waldvogel were brought in to conceive the architectural design of the building, which, rather than issuing visas, will serve as a networking and knowledge exchange hub. The two are studying several scenarios of how people will use the Swisshouse, and have constructed both physical models and screenplay-like texts designed to make tangible the purpose of this unprecedented government facility.

One scenario describes Nicolas, a brain surgeon who has just moved to Boston from Switzerland. He visits the Swisshouse to meet likeminded scientists and other members of the Swiss-American community. A second scenario tells the story of a Professor Smith, who uses the Swisshouse to present his MIT Media Lab research to Boston's Swiss community and to academics at two Swiss universities, using a high-speed Internet connection.

These scenarios, while simple, are the result of intensive research into roles the new type of consulate might play. The stories illustrate the Swiss government's intentions and serve as thinking tools to guide the building's design. Ultimately, the new facility effectively accommodated the applications imagined and fulfilled its objectives.

Today, almost a decade after its conception, the Swisshouse enjoys an outstanding reputation for helping build stronger international ties in greater Boston's science and technology communities. Under the banner of the Swiss Knowledge Network, or swissnex, the Swisshouse has inspired "colleague" facilities in Bangalore, San Francisco, Shanghai, and Singapore.

Scenario-Guided Business Model Design

—

Scenarios can be useful in guiding the design of new business models or innovating around existing models. Like visual thinking (p. 146), prototyping (p. 160), and storytelling (p. 170), scenarios render the abstract tangible. For our purposes, their primary function is to inform the business model development process by making the design context specific and detailed.

Here we discuss two types of scenarios. The first describes different customer settings: how products or services are used, what kinds of customers use them, or customer concerns, desires, and objectives. Such scenarios build on customer insights (p. 126), but go a step further by incorporating knowledge about customers into a set of distinct, concrete images. By describing a specific situation, a customer scenario makes customer insights tangible.

A second type of scenario describes future environments in which a business model might compete. The goal here is not to predict the future, but rather to imagine possible futures in concrete detail. This exercise helps innovators reflect on the most appropriate business model for each of several future environ-

ments. The strategy literature discusses this practice in detail under the topic of "scenario planning." Applying scenario planning techniques to business model innovation forces reflection on how a model might have to evolve under certain conditions. This sharpens understanding of the model, and of potentially necessary adaptations. Most important, it helps us prepare for the future.

Directions

INFORMED
DESIGN

Explore Ideas

Customer scenarios guide us during business model design. They help us address issues such as which Channels are most appropriate, which relationships would be best to establish, and which problem solutions customers would be most willing to pay for. Once we've generated scenarios for different Customer Segments, we can ask ourselves whether a single business model is sufficient to serve them all—or if we need to adapt the model to each segment.

Here are three different scenarios describing location-based services that make use of Global Positioning Systems (GPS). They inform the business model design, but are deliberately left open to allow for specific questions around the Value Proposition, Distribution Channels, Customer Relationships, and Revenue Streams. The scenarios are written from the standpoint of a mobile telephone service operator working to develop innovative new business models.

THE HOME DELIVERY SERVICE

Tom has always dreamed of running his own small business. He knew it would be difficult, but earning a living by living his passion was definitely worth working more and earning less.

Tom is a film buff whose knowledge of movies is encyclopedic, and that's what customers of his home-delivery DVD movie service appreciate. They can query him about actors, production techniques, and just about anything else film-related before ordering movies for delivery to their doorsteps.

Given the formidable online competition, it's hardly an easy business. But Tom's been able to boost his productivity and improve customer service with a new GPS-based delivery planner acquired from his mobile phone operator. For a small fee he equipped his phone with software that easily integrated with his Customer Relationship management program. This software won back much of Tom's time by helping him better plan delivery routes and avoid traffic. It even integrated with the cell phones used by two aides who help out on weekends when demand for his service peaks. Tom knows his little business will never make him rich, but wouldn't trade his situation for any corporate job.

THE TOURISTS

Dale and Rose are traveling to Paris for an extended weekend. They are excited because they haven't visited Europe since their honeymoon 25 years ago. The couple organized this mini-escape from everyday work and family life just two weeks before departure, leaving their three kids with parents back in Portland. Lacking time and energy to plan the trip in detail, they decided to "wing it." As a consequence, they were intrigued to read an article in the inflight magazine about a new GPS-based tourist service that uses mobile phones. Dale and Rose, both technology fans, rented the recommended handset upon arrival at Charles de Gaulle airport. Now they're happily strolling around Paris on a customized tour proposed by the compact device—all without having consulted a single traditional tourist guide. They particularly appreciate the built-in audio guide that suggests various story and background information options as they approach particular sites. On the return flight, Dale and Rose muse about relocating to Paris after retiring. Laughing to themselves, they wonder whether the handy device would be enough to help them adapt to French culture.

THE WINE FARMER

Alexander inherited vineyards from his father, who in turn inherited them from Alexander's grandfather, who emigrated from Switzerland to California to grow wine. Carrying on this family history is hard work, but Alexander enjoys adding small innovations to his family's long wine-growing tradition.

His latest discovery is a simple land management application that now resides on his mobile phone. Though not aimed at vintners, it was designed in such a way that Alexander was easily able to customize it for his own particular needs. The application integrates with his task list, which means he now has a GPS-based to-do list that reminds him when and where to check soil or grape quality. Now he's pondering how to share the application with all of his managers. After all, the tool makes sense only if everyone on the management team updates the soil and grape quality database.

THE TOURISTS

- Should the service be based on a proprietary device or on an application that can be downloaded to customer handsets?
- Could airlines serve as Channel partners to distribute the service/device?
- Which prospective content partners would be interested in being part of the service?
- Which Value Propositions would customers be most willing to pay for?

THE HOME DELIVERY SERVICE

- Is the value added sufficient to motivate delivery services to pay monthly fees?
- Through which Channels could such Customer Segments most easily be reached?
- With what other devices and/or software would this service need to be integrated?

THE WINE FARMER

- Is the value added sufficient to motivate a landowner to pay a monthly service fee?
- Through which Channels could such Customer Segments most easily be reached?
- With what other devices and/or software would this service need to be integrated?

QUESTIONS REGARDING THE BUSINESS MODEL

Could one model serve all three Customer Segments?

Does each segment need a separate, specific Value Proposition?

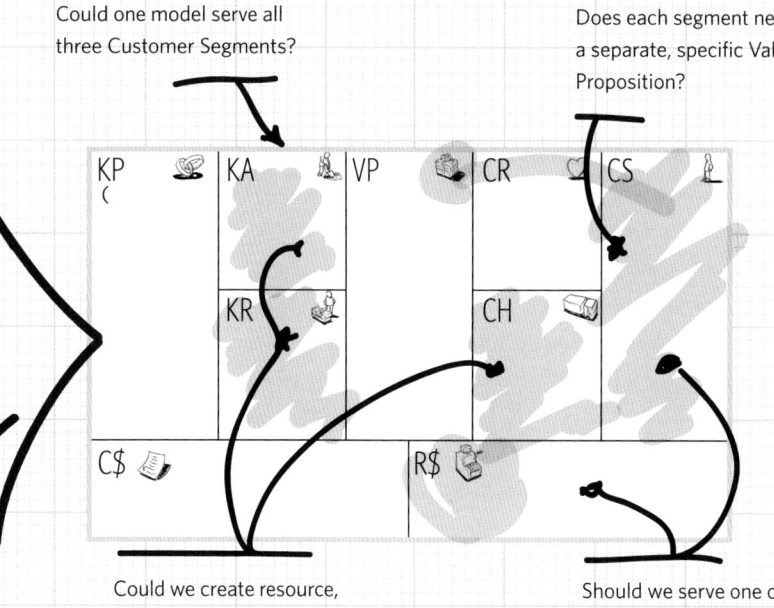

Could we create resource, activity, or Channel synergies by simultaneously serving all three Customer Segments?

Should we serve one or more Customer Segments at low or no cost in order to attract other, high-value customers?

Future Scenarios

The scenario is another thinking tool that helps us reflect on business models of the future. Scenarios kick-start our creativity by providing concrete future contexts for which we can invent appropriate business models. This is usually easier and more productive than free brainstorming about possible future business models. It does require, however, developing several scenarios, which can be costly depending on their depth and realism.

One sector under strong pressure to devise innovative new business models is the pharmaceutical industry. There are a number of reasons for this. Major player research productivity has declined in recent years, and these companies face enormous challenges discovering and marketing new blockbuster drugs—traditionally the core of their businesses. At the same time, patents on many of their cash cow drugs are expiring. This means revenues from those drugs are likely to be lost to generic drug manufacturers. This combination of empty product pipelines and evaporating revenue are just two headaches plaguing incumbent pharmaceutical makers.

In this turbulent context, combining business model brainstorming with the development of a set of future scenarios can be a powerful exercise. The scenarios help trigger out-of-the-box thinking, which is not always easy when trying to develop innovative business models. Here's an overview of how such an exercise might be conducted.

First, we must devise a set of scenarios that paint pictures of the future of the pharmaceutical industry. This is best left to scenario planning specialists equipped with the right tools and methodology. To illustrate, we developed four bare bones scenarios based on two criteria that may shape the evolution of the pharma industry over the next decade. There are, of course, several other drivers and many different scenarios that could be crafted based on deeper research into the industry.

The two drivers we've selected are (1) the emergence of personalized medicine and (2) the shift from treatment toward prevention. The former is based on advances in pharmacogenomics, the science of identifying underlying causes of diseases based on a person's DNA structure. Someday, this may result in completely personalized treatment, using customized drugs based on a person's genetic structure. The shift from treatment to prevention is driven in part by pharmacogenomics, in part by advances in diagnostics, and in part by renewed cost-consciousness amid growing awareness that prevention is less expensive than hospitalization and treatment. These two drivers suggest trends that may or may not materialize and thus provide four scenarios illustrated in the figure opposite. These are:

- BUSINESS AS USUAL: Personal medicine fails to materialize despite its technological feasibility (e.g. for privacy reasons, etc.) and treatment remains the core revenue generator.

- MY.MEDICINE: Personal medicine materializes, but treatment remains the core revenue generator.

- THE HEALTHY PATIENT: The shift toward preventive medicine continues, but personal medicine remains a fad despite technological feasibility.

- REINVENTING PHARMA: Personal and preventive medicine comprise the new growth areas of the drug industry.

Pharma Business Models
of the Future

C) The Healthy Patient:

- *What kind of Customer Relationship does effective preventive medicine require?*

- *Who are the main partners we should involve in developing our business model for preventive medicine?*

- *What does the shift toward preventive medicine imply about the relationship between doctors and our salespeople?*

D) Reinventing pharma:

- *What does our Value Proposition look like in this new landscape?*

- *What roles will Customer Segments play under our new business model?*

- *Should we develop relevant activities, such as bioinformatics and gene sequencing, in-house or through partnerships?*

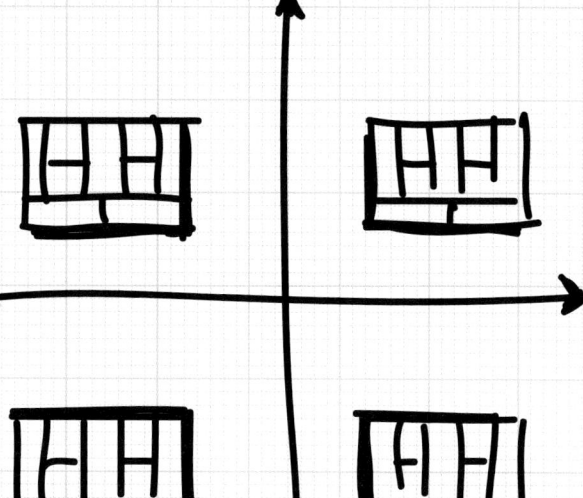

PREVENTION BECOMES THE MAIN
REVENUE GENERATOR

PERSONALIZED MEDICINE
REMAINS A FAD

PERSONALIZED MEDICINE BECOMES
A MARKET MAINSTAY

TREATMENT REMAINS THE MAIN
REVENUNE GENERATOR

A) Business as Usual

- *How will our business model look in the future if these two drivers don't change?*

B) My.medicine

- *What kinds of relationships will we have to establish with patients?*

- *Which Distribution Channels are most appropriate for personalized medicine?*

- *Which resources and activities, such as bioinformatics and gene sequencing, do we need to develop?*

Scenario D: Reinventing Pharma

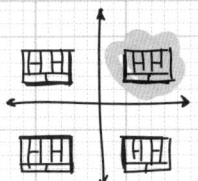

The landscape of the pharmaceutical industry has completely changed. Pharmacogenomic research has fulfilled its promise and is now a core part of the industry. Personalized drugs tailored to individual genetic profiles account for a large portion of industry revenues. All this has increased the importance of prevention—and is partially replacing treatment, thanks to substantially improved diagnostic tools and a better understanding of the links between diseases and individual genetic profiles.

These two trends—the rise of personalized drugs and the increasing importance of prevention—have completely transformed the traditional pharmaceutical manufacturing business model. The twin trends have had a dramatic impact on pharma's Key Resources and Activities. They've transformed the way drug makers approach customers and provoked substantial changes in how revenue is generated.

The new pharma landscape has taken a heavy toll on incumbents. A number were unable to adapt quickly enough and disappeared or were acquired by more agile players. At the same time, upstarts with innovative business models were able to acquire significant market share. Some were themselves acquired and integrated into the operations of larger but less nimble companies.

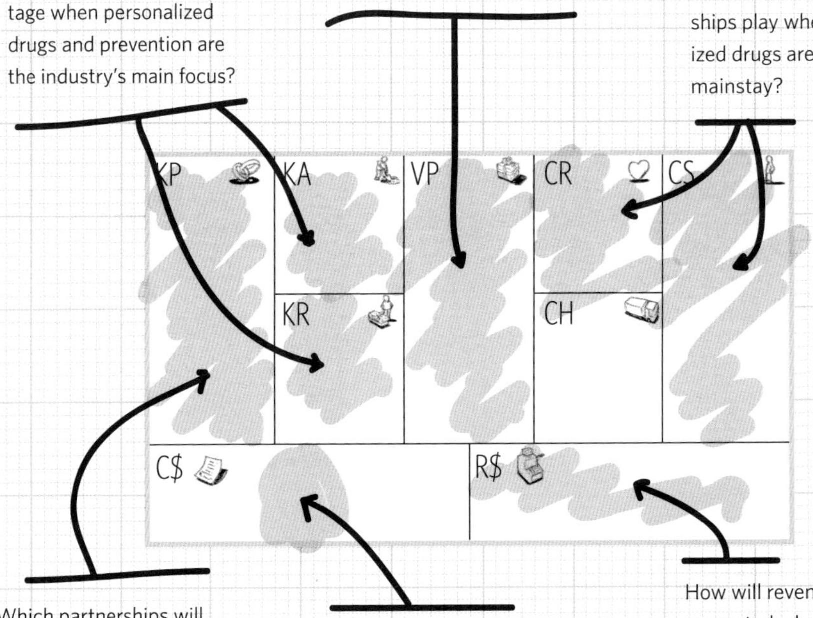

What new Key Resources and Key Activities will provide a competitive advantage when personalized drugs and prevention are the industry's main focus?

What are the attributes of a competitive Value Proposition under the new landscape?

What roles will Customers and Customer Relationships play when personalized drugs are an industry mainstay?

KP · KA · VP · CR · CS

KR · CH

C$ · R$

Which partnerships will maximize the effectiveness of a drug company's new business model?

How will the Cost Structure of a pharmaceutical company's business model change under this new landscape?

How will revenues be generated when the focus is on personalized drugs and prevention?

Future Scenarios and New Business Models

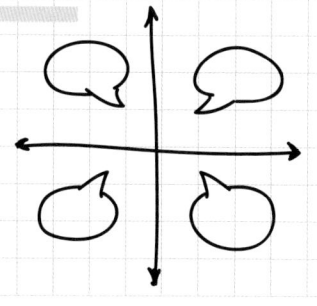

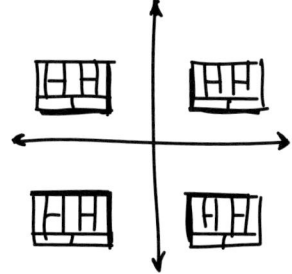

1 DEVELOP A SET OF FUTURE SCENARIOS BASED ON TWO OR MORE MAIN CRITERIA.

2 DESCRIBE EACH SCENARIO WITH A STORY THAT OUTLINES THE MAIN ELEMENTS OF THE SCENARIO

3 WORKSHOP

DEVELOP ONE OR MORE APPROPRIATE BUSINESS MODELS FOR EACH SCENARIO

The goal of combining scenarios with business model innovation efforts is to help your organization prepare for the future. This process engenders meaningful discussion about a difficult topic, because it forces participants to project themselves into concrete "futures" underpinned by hard (though assumed) facts. When participants describe their business models they must be able to make a clear case for their choices within the context of the specific scenario.

Scenarios should be developed before the business model workshop begins. The sophistication of the "screenplays" will vary depending on your budget. Keep in mind that once you develop scenarios, they may be usable for other purposes as well. Even simple scenarios help jumpstart creativity and project participants into the future.

Ideally you should develop between two and four different scenarios based on two or more criteria in order to run a good business model scenario workshop. Each scenario should be titled and described with a short, specific narrative outlining the main elements.

Begin the workshop by asking participants to review the scenarios, then develop an appropriate business model for each. If your objective is to maximize a group's understanding of all the potential futures, you might want everyone to participate in a single group and let them collectively develop different business models for each scenario. If you are more interested in generating a set of very diverse future business models, you might decide to organize participants into different groups that work in parallel on separate solutions for the various scenarios.

Further Reading on Design and Business

Design Attitude

Managing as Designing
by Richard Boland Jr. and Fred Collopy
(Stanford Business Books, 2004)

A Whole New Mind: Why Right-Brainers Will Rule the Future
by Daniel H. Pink (Riverhead Trade, 2006)

The Ten Faces of Innovation: Strategies for Heightening Creativity
by Tom Kelley (Profile Business, 2008)

Customer Insights

Sketching User Experiences: Getting the Design Right and the Right Design
by Bill Buxton (Elsevier, 2007)

Designing for the Digital Age: How to Create Human-Centered Products and Services
by Kim Goodwin (John Wiley & Sons, Inc. 2009)

Ideation

The Art of Innovation: Lessons in Creativity from IDEO, America's Leading Design Firm
by Tom Kelley, Jonathan Littman, and Tom Peters (Broadway Business, 2001)

IdeaSpotting: How to Find Your Next Great Idea
by Sam Harrison (How Books, 2006)

Visual Thinking

The Back of the Napkin: Solving Problems and Selling Ideas with Pictures
by Dan Roam (Portfolio Hardcover, 2008)

Brain Rules: 12 Principles for Surviving and Thriving at Work, Home, and School
by John Medina (Pear Press, 2009)
(pp. 221–240)

Prototyping

Serious Play: How the World's Best Companies Simulate to Innovate
by Michael Schrage (Harvard Business Press, 1999)

Designing Interactions
by Bill Moggridge (MIT Press, 2007) (ch. 10)

Storytelling

The Leader's Guide to Storytelling: Mastering the Art and Discipline of Business Narrative
by Stephen Denning (Jossey-Bass, 2005)

Made to Stick: Why Some Ideas Survive and Others Die
by Chip Heath and Dan Heath (Random House, 2007)

Scenarios

The Art of the Long View: Planning for the Future in an Uncertain World
by Peter Schwartz (Currency Doubleday, 1996)

Using Trends and Scenarios as Tools for Strategy Development
by Ulf Pillkahn (Publicis Corporate Publishing, 2008)

191

Do you have the guts to start from scratch?

WHAT STANDS IN YOUR WAY?

194

In my work with non-profit organizations, the biggest obstacles to business model innovation are **1.** inability to understand the existing business model, **2.** lack of a language to talk about business model innovation, and **3.** counterproductive constraints on imagining the design of new business models.
Jeff De Cagna, United States

The management of an SME (wood manufacturing industry-WMI) did not begin changing its business model until the bank no longer wanted to give them credit. The biggest obstacle to business model innovation (in the WMI case and likely every case) is the people who resist any changes until problems appear and need corrective actions.
Danilo Tic, Slovenia

EVERYONE LOVES INNOVATION UNTIL IT AFFECTS THEM.

The biggest obstacle to business model innovation is not technology: it is we humans and the institutions we live in. Both are stubbornly resistant to experimentation and change.
Saul Kaplan, United States

I have found that the management and key employees in many SME companies lack a common framework and language for discussing business model innovation. They do not have the theoretical background, but they are essential to the process because they are the ones who know the business.
Michael N. Wilkens, Denmark

METRICS OF SUCCESS:

They can direct the scope and ambition of behavior. At best they can allow for the agility that brings truly disruptive innovation; at worst they reduce vision to near term iterative cycles of evolution that fail to take opportunity from changing environments.
Nicky Smyth, U.K.

Fear to take risks. As a CEO you need courage to take a business model innovation decision. In 2005, Dutch telecom provider KPN decided to migrate proactively to IP and thus to cannibalize its traditional business. KPN is now internationally recognized as an outperformer in the telco industry.
Kees Groeneveld, Netherlands

In my experience with a large archive, the biggest hurdle was to make them understand that even an archive has a business model. We overcame this by starting a small project and showed them this would affect their current model.
Harry Verwayen, Netherlands

GET EVERYBODY INVOLVED

and keep up the speed of change. For our disruptive meeting concept Seats-2meet.com we trained the staff almost daily for a period of four months just on communicating this new business model to all stakeholders.
Ronald van Den Hoff, Netherlands

1. Organizational antibodies that attack a project as resources drawn from their area conflict with their business objectives. **2.** Project management processes that can't deal with risks/uncertainties associated with bold ideas so leaders decline or claw ideas back to existing comfort zones.
John Sutherland, Canada

The biggest obstacle is a belief that models must contain every detail—experience shows that clients ask for a lot but settle for simplicity once they have insight into their business.
David Edwards, Canada

1. Not knowing: What is a business model? What is business model innovation? **2.** Not able: How to innovate a business model? **3.** Not willing: Why should I innovate my business model? Is there a sense of urgency? **4.** Combinations of the above.

Ray Lai, Malaysia

In my experience, the biggest obstacle is failure to change the thinking process from the traditional linear way to holistic and systemic.

Entrepreneurs need to make a concerted effort to develop the capability to envision the model as a system whose parts interact with each other and affect each other in a holistic and non-linear manner.

Jeaninne Horowitz Gassol, Spain

As an Internet marketer for 15 years I've seen new business models live and die.

The key for the winners was that the major stakeholders completely understood and advanced the model.

Stephanie Diamond, United States

THE MENTAL MODELS
of executives and the board.

The lack of candor and fear of deviating from the status quo sets in groupthink. Executives are comfortable with exploit phase and not 'explore' phase, which is unknown and hence risky.

Cheenu Srinivasan, Australia

In my experience as an Internet entrepreneur and investor, the biggest obstacles are lack of vision and bad governance. Without good vision and governance a company will miss the emerging industry paradigm and avoid reinventing the business model in time.

Nicolas De Santis, U.K.

Within large multinationals it is key to create cross-functional understanding and synergies. Business model innovation does not hold itself to the organizational constraints that the people in it experience. For successful execution it is key to have all disciplines on board and interconnected!

Bas van Oosterhout, Netherlands

FUG: FEAR, UNCERTAINTY & GREED

of the people vested in the current business model…

Frontier Service Design, LLC, United States

A lack of entrepreneurship in the organization.

Innovation is about taking risks, wisely. If there is no room for creative insights or if people can't think and act outside the boundaries of the existing model, don't even try to innovate: you will fail.

Ralf de Graaf, Netherlands

On an organizational level, the biggest obstacle for a large, successful company is a reluctance to risk doing anything that may jeopardize their current model. On a leader/personal level, **their very success was likely a product of the current business model...**

Jeffrey Murphy, United States

"If it ain't broke, don't fix it"

thinking. Established companies stick to current ways of doing business until it is obvious that the customers want something else.

Ola Dagberg, Sweden

STRENGTH OF LEADERSHIP

can be an obstacle. Risk management and due diligence color the perceived purpose of many boards. Where innovation is assessed as a risk issue it's easy to relegate it to tokenism, especially within cultural institutions that tend not to have championing cultures. Here innovation often dies the death of a thousand cuts inflicted by entrenched critical business processes, instead of being placed front and center as the fuel for future strategy.

Anne McCrossan, U.K.

Oftentimes, companies design an innovative business model, but do a poor job of constructing a compensation structure that is properly aligned with the model and its objectives.

Andrew Jenkins, Canada

CURRENT SUCCESS

prevents companies from asking themselves how their business model could be innovated. Organizational structures are not typically designed for new business models to emerge.

Howard Brown, United States

The companies that are the most successful in continuously improving the efficiency of their current business model often get blinded by

"this is the way things are done in our business"

and fail to see the emergence of innovative business models.

Wouter van der Burg, Netherlands

Stra

tegy

"There's not a single business model . . . There are really a lot of opportunities and a lot of options and we just have to discover all of them."

Tim O'Reilly, CEO, O'Reilly

In previous sections we taught you a language for describing, discussing, and designing business models, described business model patterns, and explained techniques that facilitate the design and invention of new business models. This next section is about re-interpreting strategy through the lens of the Business Model Canvas. This will help you constructively question established business models and strategically examine the environment in which your own business model functions.

The following pages explore four strategic areas: the Business Model Environment, Evaluating Business Models, a Business Model Perspective on Blue Ocean Strategies, and how to Manage Multiple Business Models within an enterprise.

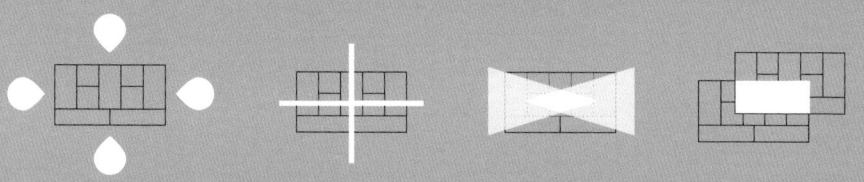

Strategy

200 Business Model
Environment

212 Evaluating Business
Models

226 Business Model
Perspective on Blue
Ocean Strategy

232 Managing Multiple
Business Models

BUSINESS MODEL ENVIRONMENT: CONTEXT, DESIGN DRIVERS, AND CONSTRAINTS

BUSINESS MODELS ARE DESIGNED AND EXECUTED IN SPECIFIC ENVIRONMENTS. Developing a good understanding of your organization's environment helps you conceive stronger, more competitive business models.

Continuous environmental scanning is more important than ever because of the growing complexity of the economic landscape (e.g. networked business models), greater uncertainty (e.g. technology innovations) and severe market disruptions (e.g. economic turmoil, disruptive new Value Propositions). Understanding changes in the environment helps you adapt your model more effectively to shifting external forces.

You may find it helpful to conceive of the external environment as a sort of "design space." By this we mean thinking of it as a context in which to conceive or adapt your business model, taking into account a number of design drivers (e.g. new customer needs, new technologies, etc.) and design constraints (e.g. regulatory trends, dominant competitors, etc.). This environment should in no way limit your creativity or predefine your business model. It should, however, influence your design choices and help you make more informed decisions. With a breakthrough business model, you may even become a shaper and transformer of this environment, and set new standards for your industry.

To get a better grasp on your business model "design space," we suggest roughly mapping four main areas of your environment. These are (1) market forces, (2) industry forces, (3) key trends, and (4) macroeconomic forces. If you'd like to deepen your analysis of the landscape beyond the simple mapping we propose, each of these four areas is backed by a large body of literature and specific analytical tools.

In the following pages, we describe the key external forces that influence business models and categorize them using the four areas just mentioned. The pharmaceutical industry, introduced in the previous chapter, is used to illustrate each external force. The pharma sector is likely to undergo substantial transformation in coming years, though it is unclear how the changes will play out. Will biotechnology companies, which are currently copying the pharmaceutical sector's blockbuster drug model, come up with new, disruptive business models? Will technological change lead to transformation? Will consumers and market demand force changes?

We strongly advocate mapping your own business model environment and reflecting on what trends mean for the future of your enterprise. A good understanding of the environment will allow you to better evaluate the different directions in which your business model might evolve. You may also want to consider creating scenarios of future business model environments (see p. 186). This can be a valuable tool for jumpstarting business model innovation work or simply preparing your organization for the future.

REGULATORY TRENDS

SOCIETAL AND CULTURAL TRENDS

TECHNOLOGY TRENDS

SOCIOECONOMIC TRENDS

KEY TRENDS

SUPPLIERS AND OTHER VALUE CHAIN ACTORS

MARKET SEGMENTS

STAKEHOLDERS

NEEDS AND DEMANDS

INDUSTRY FORCES

MARKET FORCES

COMPETITORS (INCUMBENTS)

MARKET ISSUES

NEW ENTRANTS (INSURGENTS)

SWITCHING COSTS

SUBSTITUTE PRODUCTS AND SERVICES

REVENUE ATTRACTIVENESS

KP	KA	VP	CR	CS
	KR		CH	
C$			R$	

MACRO-ECONOMIC FORCES

GLOBAL MARKET CONDITIONS

ECONOMIC INFRASTRUCTURE

CAPITAL MARKETS

COMMODITIES AND OTHER RESOURCES

201

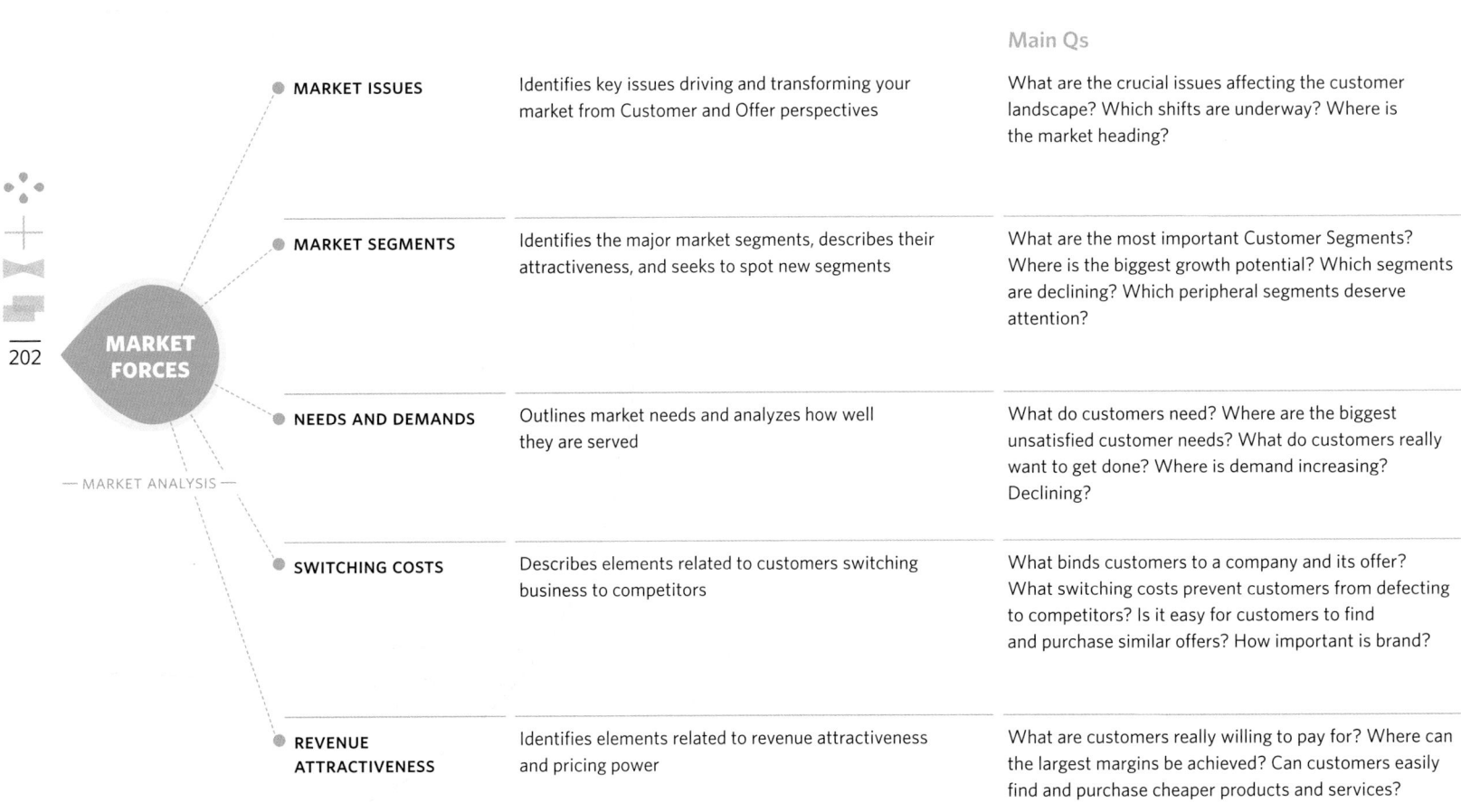

MARKET FORCES

— MARKET ANALYSIS —

Main Qs

MARKET ISSUES	Identifies key issues driving and transforming your market from Customer and Offer perspectives	What are the crucial issues affecting the customer landscape? Which shifts are underway? Where is the market heading?
MARKET SEGMENTS	Identifies the major market segments, describes their attractiveness, and seeks to spot new segments	What are the most important Customer Segments? Where is the biggest growth potential? Which segments are declining? Which peripheral segments deserve attention?
NEEDS AND DEMANDS	Outlines market needs and analyzes how well they are served	What do customers need? Where are the biggest unsatisfied customer needs? What do customers really want to get done? Where is demand increasing? Declining?
SWITCHING COSTS	Describes elements related to customers switching business to competitors	What binds customers to a company and its offer? What switching costs prevent customers from defecting to competitors? Is it easy for customers to find and purchase similar offers? How important is brand?
REVENUE ATTRACTIVENESS	Identifies elements related to revenue attractiveness and pricing power	What are customers really willing to pay for? Where can the largest margins be achieved? Can customers easily find and purchase cheaper products and services?

Pharmaceutical Industry Landscape

- Skyrocketing healthcare costs
- Emphasis shifting from treatment to prevention
- Treatments, diagnostics, devices, and support services are converging
- Emerging markets becoming more important

- Doctors and healthcare providers
- Governments/regulators
- Distributors
- Patients
- Strong potential in emerging markets
- U.S. remains the predominant global market

- Strong, with dispersed need for niche treatments
- Need to manage exploding cost of health care
- Large, unsatisfied health care needs in emerging markets and developing countries
- Consumers are better informed

- Monopoly on patent-protected drugs
- Low switching costs for patent-expired drugs replaceable by generic versions
- Growing amount of quality information available online
- Deals with governments, large-scale healthcare providers increase switching costs

- High margins on patent-protected drugs
- Low margins on generic drugs
- Healthcare providers, governments enjoy growing influence over prices
- Patients continue to have little influence over prices

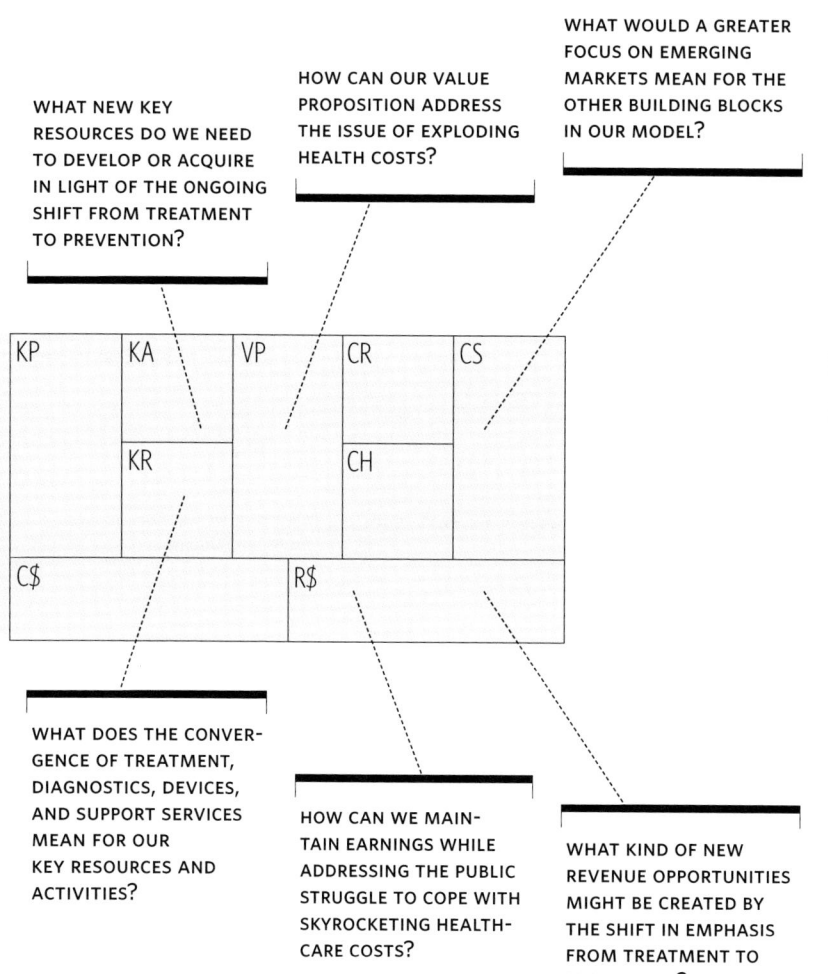

WHAT NEW KEY RESOURCES DO WE NEED TO DEVELOP OR ACQUIRE IN LIGHT OF THE ONGOING SHIFT FROM TREATMENT TO PREVENTION?

HOW CAN OUR VALUE PROPOSITION ADDRESS THE ISSUE OF EXPLODING HEALTH COSTS?

WHAT WOULD A GREATER FOCUS ON EMERGING MARKETS MEAN FOR THE OTHER BUILDING BLOCKS IN OUR MODEL?

WHAT DOES THE CONVERGENCE OF TREATMENT, DIAGNOSTICS, DEVICES, AND SUPPORT SERVICES MEAN FOR OUR KEY RESOURCES AND ACTIVITIES?

HOW CAN WE MAINTAIN EARNINGS WHILE ADDRESSING THE PUBLIC STRUGGLE TO COPE WITH SKYROCKETING HEALTHCARE COSTS?

WHAT KIND OF NEW REVENUE OPPORTUNITIES MIGHT BE CREATED BY THE SHIFT IN EMPHASIS FROM TREATMENT TO PREVENTION?

INDUSTRY FORCES

COMPETITORS (INCUMBENTS)

Identifies incumbent competitors and their relative strengths

Who are our competitors? Who are the dominant players in our particular sector? What are their competitive advantages or disadvantages? Describe their main offers. Which Customer Segments are they focusing on? What is their Cost Structure? How much influence do they exert on our Customer Segments, Revenue Streams, and margins?

NEW ENTRANTS (INSURGENTS)

Identifies new, insurgent players and determines whether they compete with a business model different from yours

Who are the new entrants in your market? How are they different? What competitive advantages or disadvantages do they have? Which barriers must they overcome? What are their Value Propositions? Which Customer Segments are they focused on? What is their Cost Structure? To what extent do they influence your Customer Segments, Revenue Streams, and margins?

SUBSTITUTE PRODUCTS AND SERVICES

Describes potential substitutes for your offers—including those from other markets and industries

Which products or services could replace ours? How much do they cost compared to ours? How easy it is for customers to switch to these substitutes? What business model traditions do these substitute products stem from (e.g. high-speed trains versus airplanes, mobile phones versus cameras, Skype versus long-distance telephone companies)?

SUPPLIERS AND OTHER VALUE CHAIN ACTORS

Describes the key value chain incumbents in your market and spots new, emerging players

Who are the key players in your industry value chain? To what extent does your business model depend on other players? Are peripheral players emerging? Which are most profitable?

STAKEHOLDERS

Specifies which actors may influence your organization and business model

Which stakeholders might influence your business model? How influential are shareholders? Workers? The government? Lobbyists?

Pharmaceutical Industry Landscape

- Several large and medium size players compete in pharma
- Most players are struggling with empty product pipelines and low R&D productivity
- Growing trend toward consolidation through mergers and acquisitions
- Major players acquire biotech, specialty drug developers to fill product pipeline
- Several players starting to build on open innovation processes

- Little disruption of the pharmaceutical industry over the last decade
- Main new entrants are generic drug companies, particularly from India

- To a certain extent, prevention represents a substitution for treatment
- Patent-expired drugs replaced by low-cost generics

- Increasing use of research contractors
- Biotech firms and specialty drug developers as important new product generators
- Doctors and healthcare providers
- Insurance companies
- Bioinformatics providers growing in importance
- Laboratories

- Shareholder pressure forces drug companies to focus on short term (quarterly) financial results
- Governments/regulators have a strong stake in the actions of pharmaceutical companies because of their pivotal role in healthcare services
- Lobbyists, social enterprise groups and/or foundations, particularly those pursuing agendas such as low-cost treatments for developing countries
- Scientists, who represent the core talent of the drug manufacturing industry

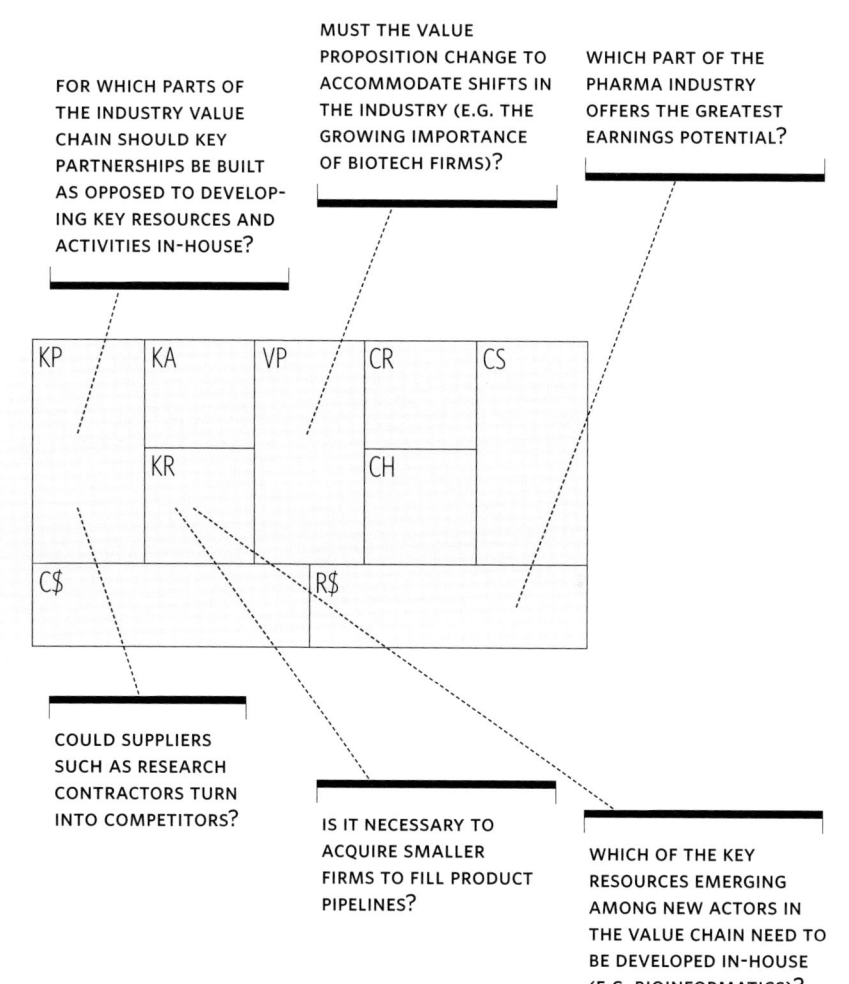

FOR WHICH PARTS OF THE INDUSTRY VALUE CHAIN SHOULD KEY PARTNERSHIPS BE BUILT AS OPPOSED TO DEVELOPING KEY RESOURCES AND ACTIVITIES IN-HOUSE?

MUST THE VALUE PROPOSITION CHANGE TO ACCOMMODATE SHIFTS IN THE INDUSTRY (E.G. THE GROWING IMPORTANCE OF BIOTECH FIRMS)?

WHICH PART OF THE PHARMA INDUSTRY OFFERS THE GREATEST EARNINGS POTENTIAL?

COULD SUPPLIERS SUCH AS RESEARCH CONTRACTORS TURN INTO COMPETITORS?

IS IT NECESSARY TO ACQUIRE SMALLER FIRMS TO FILL PRODUCT PIPELINES?

WHICH OF THE KEY RESOURCES EMERGING AMONG NEW ACTORS IN THE VALUE CHAIN NEED TO BE DEVELOPED IN-HOUSE (E.G. BIOINFORMATICS)?

KEY TRENDS

— FORESIGHT —

Main Qs

TECHNOLOGY TRENDS

Identifies technology trends that could threaten your business model—or enable it to evolve or improve

What are the major technology trends both inside and outside your market? Which technologies represent important opportunities or disruptive threats? Which emerging technologies are peripheral customers adopting?

REGULATORY TRENDS

Describes regulations and regulatory trends that influence your business model

Which regulatory trends influence your market? What rules may affect your business model? Which regulations and taxes affect customer demand?

SOCIETAL AND CULTURAL TRENDS

Identifies major societal trends that may influence your business model

Describe key societal trends. Which shifts in cultural or societal values affect your business model? Which trends might influence buyer behavior?

SOCIOECONOMIC TRENDS

Outlines major socioeconomic trends relevant to your business model

What are the key demographic trends? How would you characterize income and wealth distribution in your market? How high are disposable incomes? Describe spending patterns in your market (e.g. housing, health-care, entertainment, etc.). What portion of the population lives in urban areas as opposed to rural settings?

Pharmaceutical Industry Landscape

- Emergence of pharmacogenomics, declining cost of gene sequencing, and the imminent rise of personalized medicine
- Major advances in diagnostics
- Use of pervasive computing and nanotechnology for the injection/delivery of drugs

- Heterogeneous global regulatory landscape in the pharmaceutical industry
- Many countries prohibit drug companies from marketing directly to consumers
- Regulatory agency pressure to publish data on unsuccessful clinical trials

- Generally unfavorable image of big drug makers
- Growing social consciousness among consumers
- Customers increasingly conscious of global warming, sustainability issues, prefer "green" purchases
- Customers are better informed about drug maker activity in developing countries (e.g. HIV/AIDS drugs)

- Aging society in many mature markets
- Good but costly healthcare infrastructure in mature markets
- Growing middle class in emerging markets
- Large, unsatisfied healthcare needs in developing countries

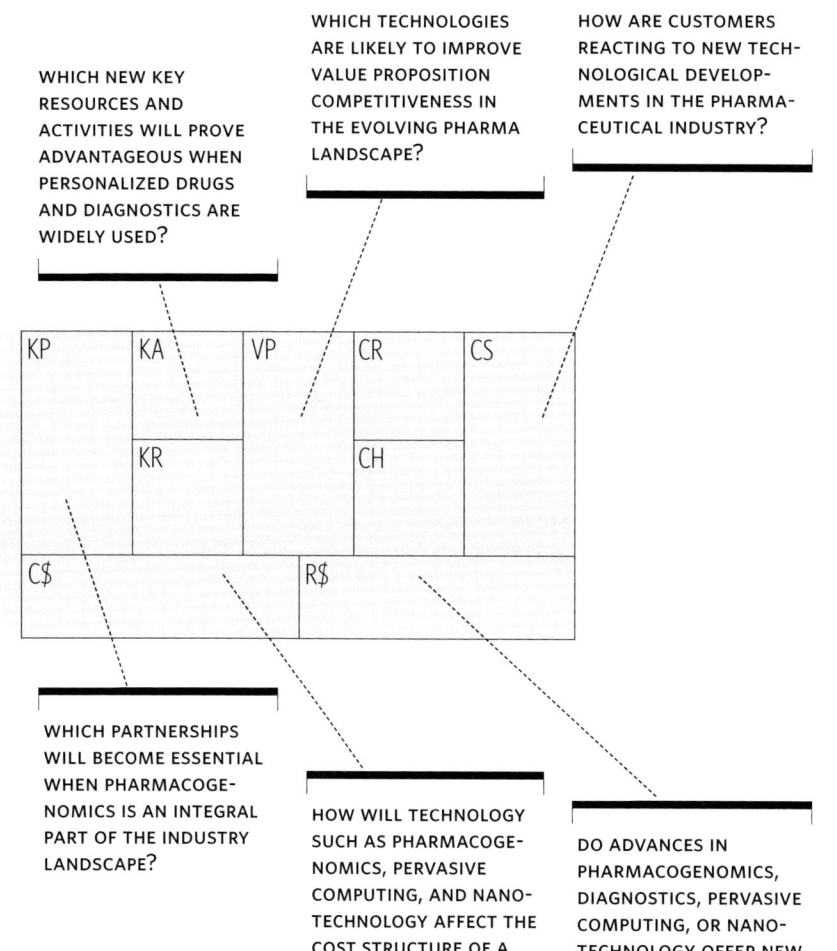

WHICH NEW KEY RESOURCES AND ACTIVITIES WILL PROVE ADVANTAGEOUS WHEN PERSONALIZED DRUGS AND DIAGNOSTICS ARE WIDELY USED?

WHICH TECHNOLOGIES ARE LIKELY TO IMPROVE VALUE PROPOSITION COMPETITIVENESS IN THE EVOLVING PHARMA LANDSCAPE?

HOW ARE CUSTOMERS REACTING TO NEW TECHNOLOGICAL DEVELOPMENTS IN THE PHARMACEUTICAL INDUSTRY?

WHICH PARTNERSHIPS WILL BECOME ESSENTIAL WHEN PHARMACOGENOMICS IS AN INTEGRAL PART OF THE INDUSTRY LANDSCAPE?

HOW WILL TECHNOLOGY SUCH AS PHARMACOGENOMICS, PERVASIVE COMPUTING, AND NANOTECHNOLOGY AFFECT THE COST STRUCTURE OF A DRUG MAKER'S BUSINESS MODEL?

DO ADVANCES IN PHARMACOGENOMICS, DIAGNOSTICS, PERVASIVE COMPUTING, OR NANOTECHNOLOGY OFFER NEW REVENUE OPPORTUNITIES?

208

— MACROECONOMICS —

MACRO-ECONOMIC FORCES

			Main Qs
●	**GLOBAL MARKET CONDITIONS**	Outlines current overall conditions from a macroeconomic perspective	Is the economy in a boom or bust phase? Describe general market sentiment. What is the GDP growth rate? How high is the unemployment rate?
●	**CAPITAL MARKETS**	Describes current capital market conditions as they relate to your capital needs	What is the state of the capital markets? How easy is it to obtain funding in your particular market? Is seed capital, venture capital, public funding, market capital, or credit readily available? How costly is it to procure funds?
●	**COMMODITIES AND OTHER RESOURCES**	Highlights current prices and price trends for resources required for your business model	Describe the current status of markets for commodities and other resources essential to your business (e.g. oil prices and labor costs). How easy is it to obtain the resources needed to execute your business model (e.g. attract prime talent)? How costly are they? Where are prices headed?
●	**ECONOMIC INFRASTRUCTURE**	Describes the economic infrastructure of the market in which your business operates	How good is the (public) infrastructure in your market? How would you characterize transportation, trade, school quality, and access to suppliers and customers? How high are individual and corporate taxes? How good are public services for organizations? How would you rate the quality of life?

Pharmaceutical Industry Landscape

- Global recession
- Negative GDP growth in Europe, Japan, and the United States
- Slower growth rates in China and India
- Uncertainty as to when recovery will occur

- Tight capital markets
- Credit availability restricted due to banking crisis
- Little venture capital available
- Risk capital availability extremely limited

- Fierce "battles" for prime talent
- Employees seek to join pharmaceutical companies
  with positive public image
- Commodity prices rising from recent lows
- Demand for natural resources likely to pick up with
  economic recovery
- Oil prices continue to fluctuate

- Specific to the region in which a company operates

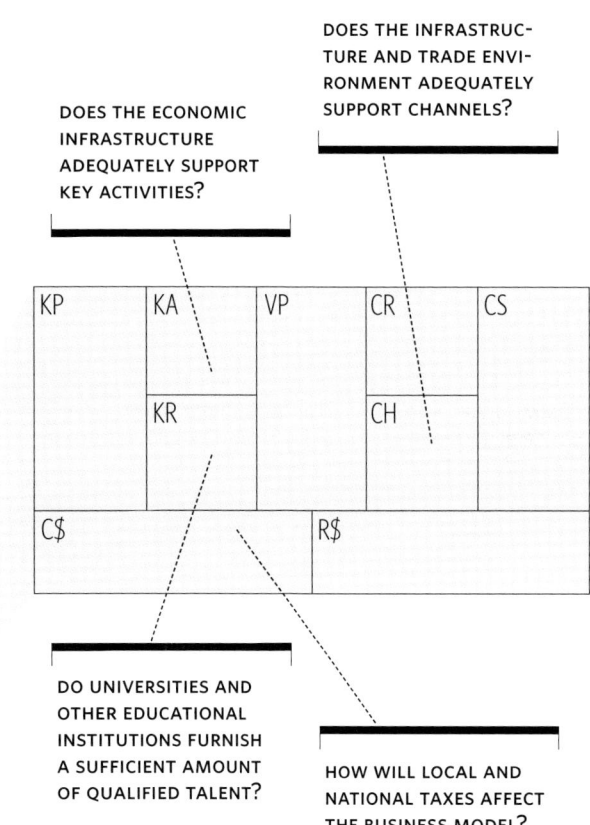

DOES THE ECONOMIC INFRASTRUCTURE ADEQUATELY SUPPORT KEY ACTIVITIES?

DOES THE INFRASTRUCTURE AND TRADE ENVIRONMENT ADEQUATELY SUPPORT CHANNELS?

DO UNIVERSITIES AND OTHER EDUCATIONAL INSTITUTIONS FURNISH A SUFFICIENT AMOUNT OF QUALIFIED TALENT?

HOW WILL LOCAL AND NATIONAL TAXES AFFECT THE BUSINESS MODEL?

HOW SHOULD YOUR BUSINESS MODEL EVOLVE IN LIGHT OF A CHANGING ENVIRONMENT?

A competitive business model that makes sense in today's environment might be outdated or even obsolete tomorrow. We all have to improve our understanding of a model's environment and how it might evolve. Of course we can't be certain about the future, because of the complexities, uncertainties, and potential disruptions inherent in the evolving business environment. We can, however, develop a number of hypotheses about the future to serve as guidelines for designing tomorrow's business models. Assumptions about how market forces, industry forces, key trends, and macroeconomic forces unfold give us the "design space" to develop potential business model options or prototypes (see p. 160) for the future. The role of business model scenarios (see p. 186) in forecasting should also be evident by now. Painting pictures of the future makes it much easier to generate potential business models. Depending on your own criteria (e.g. acceptable level of risk, growth potential sought, etc.) you may then select one option over another.

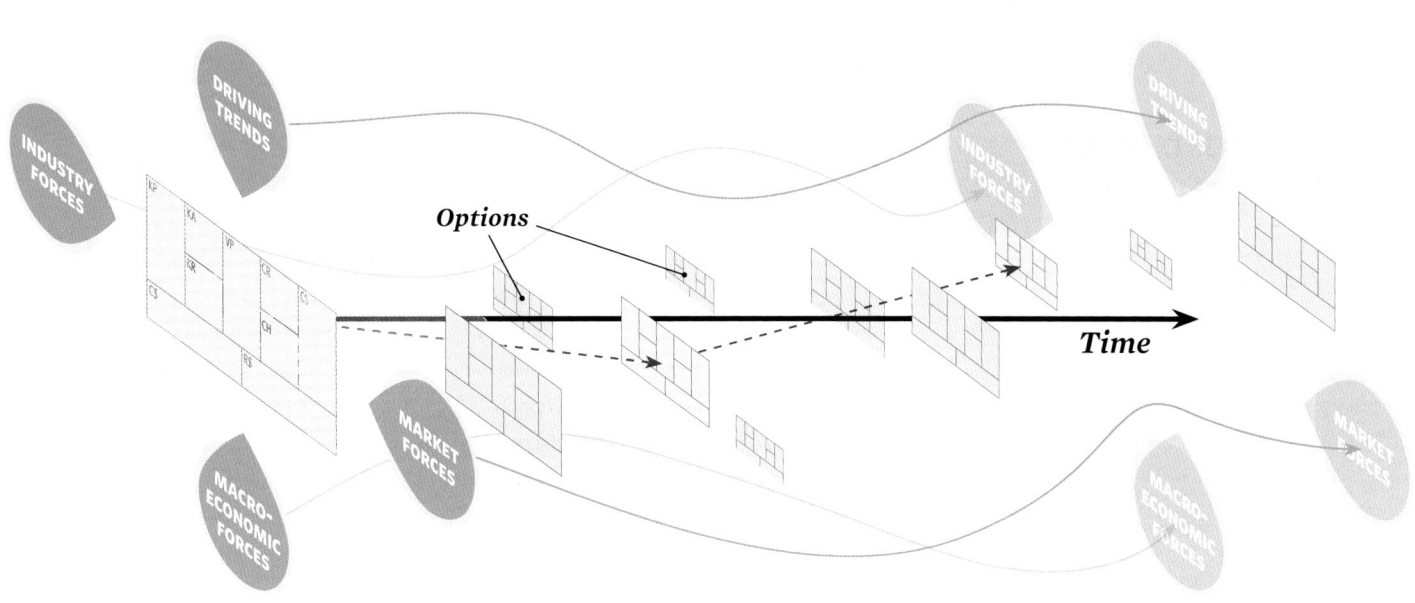

Options

Time

— PRESENT ENVIRONMENT —

— PROJECTED ENVIRONMENT —

EVALUATING BUSINESS MODELS

LIKE SEEING THE DOCTOR FOR AN ANNUAL EXAM, REGULARLY ASSESSING a business model is an important management activity that allows an organization to evaluate the health of its market position and adapt accordingly. This checkup may become the basis for incremental business model improvements, or it might trigger a serious intervention in the form of a business model innovation initiative. As the automobile, newspaper, and music industries have shown, failing to conduct regular checkups may prevent early detection of business model problems, and may even lead to a company's demise.

In the previous chapter on the business models environment (see p. 200), we evaluated the influence of external forces. In this chapter, we adopt the point of view of an existing business model and analyze external forces from the inside out.

The following pages outline two types of assessment. First, we provide a big picture assessment of Amazon.com's online retailing model circa 2005 and describe how the company has built strategically on that model since. Second, we provide a set of checklists for assessing your business model's strengths, weaknesses, opportunities, and threats (SWOT) and to help you evaluate each Building Block. Keep in mind that assessing a business model from a big picture perspective and assessing it from a Building Block perspective are complementary activities. A weakness in one Building Block, for example, may have consequences for one or several other Building Blocks—or for the entire model. Business model assessment, therefore, alternates between individual elements and overall integrity.

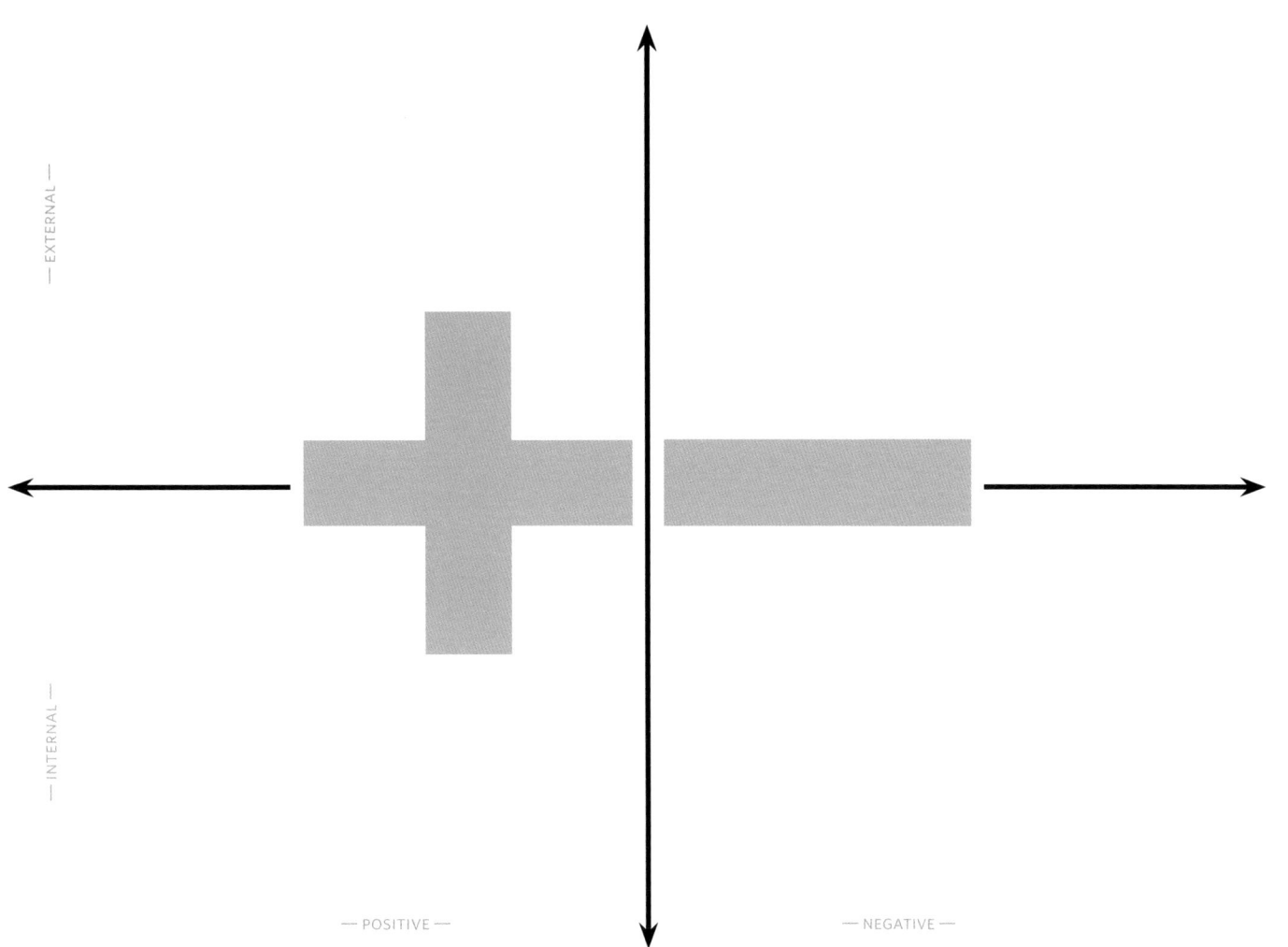

POSITIVE

NEGATIVE

BIG PICTURE ASSESSMENT: AMAZON.COM

Amazon.com's main strengths and weaknesses in 2005:

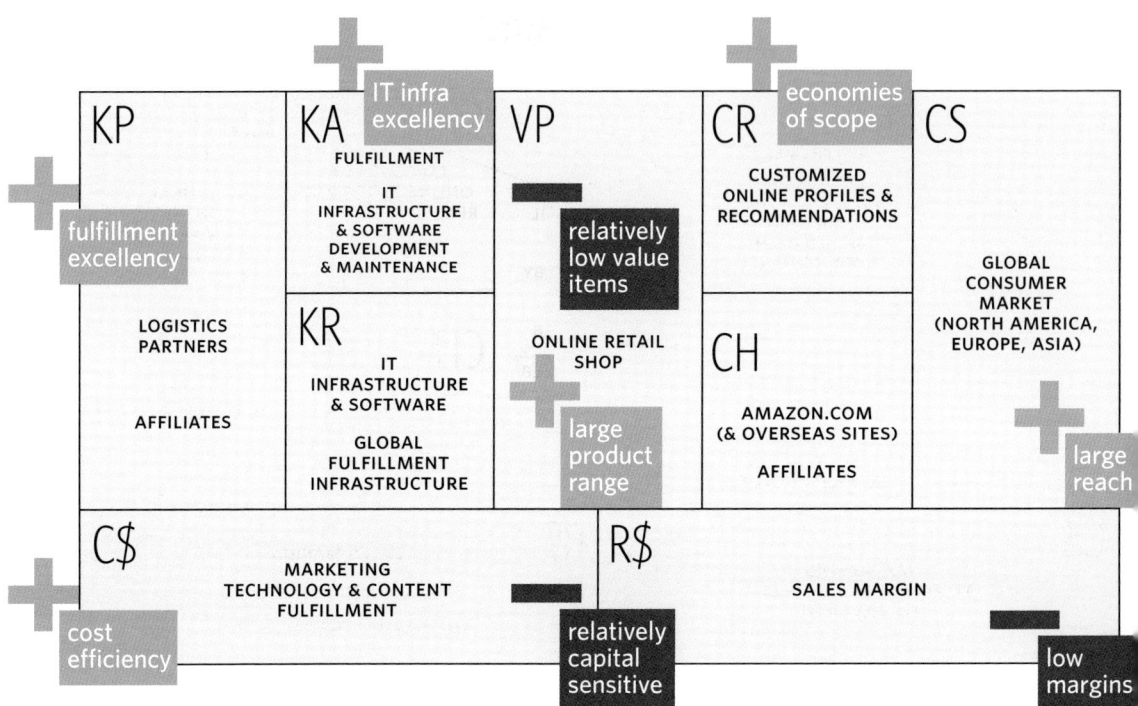

Amazon.com provides a powerful illustration of implementing business model innovation based on an analysis of strengths and weaknesses. We've already described why it made sense for Amazon.com to launch a series of new service offers under the moniker Amazon Web Services (see p. 176). Now let's examine how those new offers launched in 2006 related to Amazon.com's strengths and weaknesses the previous year.

Assessing the strengths and weaknesses of Amazon.com's business model circa 2005 reveals an enormous strength and a dangerous weakness. Amazon.com's strength was its extraordinary customer reach and huge selection of products for sale. The company's main costs lay in the activities in which it excelled, namely fulfillment ($745 million, or 46.3 percent of operating expenses) and technology and content ($451 million, or 28.1 percent of operating expenses). The key weakness of Amazon.com's business model was weak margins, the result of selling primarily low-value, low-margin products such as books, music CDs, and DVDs. As an online retailer, Amazon.

com recorded sales of $8.5 billion in 2005 with a net margin of only 4.2 percent. At the time, Google enjoyed a net margin of 23.9 percent on sales of $6.1 billion while eBay achieved a net margin of 23.7 percent on sales of $4.6 billion.

Looking to the future, founder Jeff Bezos and his management team took a two-pronged approach to building on Amazon.com's business model. First, they aimed to grow the online retail business through a continuing focus on customer satisfaction and efficient fulfillment. Second, they began growth initiatives in new areas. Management was clear on the requirements for these new initiatives. They had to (1) target underserved markets, (2) be scalable with potential for significant growth, and (3) leverage existing Amazon.com capabilities to bring strong customer-facing differentiation to that marketplace.

Opportunities Amazon.com explored in 2006:

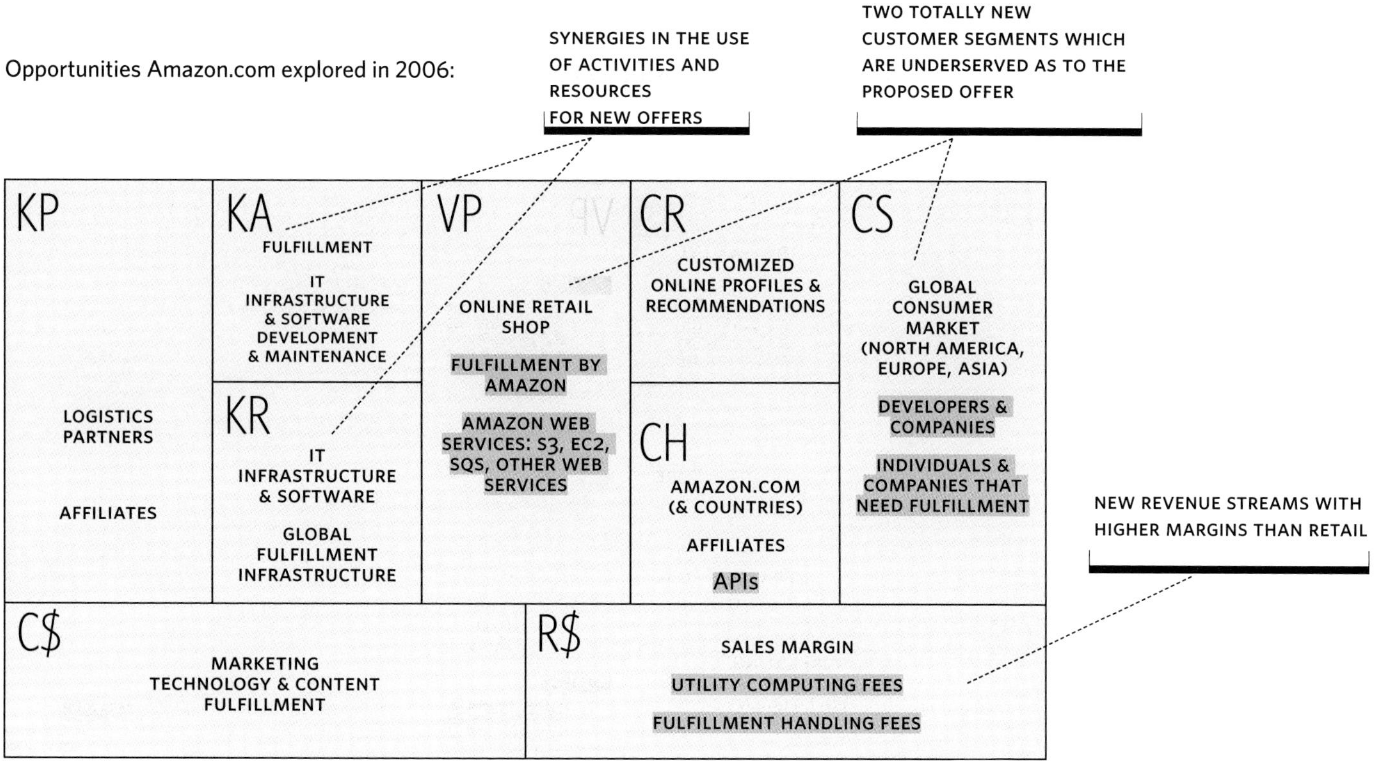

SYNERGIES IN THE USE OF ACTIVITIES AND RESOURCES FOR NEW OFFERS

TWO TOTALLY NEW CUSTOMER SEGMENTS WHICH ARE UNDERSERVED AS TO THE PROPOSED OFFER

NEW REVENUE STREAMS WITH HIGHER MARGINS THAN RETAIL

KP	KA	VP	CR	CS
	FULFILLMENT		**CUSTOMIZED ONLINE PROFILES & RECOMMENDATIONS**	
	IT INFRASTRUCTURE & SOFTWARE DEVELOPMENT & MAINTENANCE	**ONLINE RETAIL SHOP**		**GLOBAL CONSUMER MARKET (NORTH AMERICA, EUROPE, ASIA)**
LOGISTICS PARTNERS		**FULFILLMENT BY AMAZON**		
	KR	**AMAZON WEB SERVICES: S3, EC2, SQS, OTHER WEB SERVICES**	**CH**	**DEVELOPERS & COMPANIES**
AFFILIATES	**IT INFRASTRUCTURE & SOFTWARE**		**AMAZON.COM (& COUNTRIES)**	**INDIVIDUALS & COMPANIES THAT NEED FULFILLMENT**
	GLOBAL FULFILLMENT INFRASTRUCTURE		**AFFILIATES** **APIs**	

C$	R$
MARKETING TECHNOLOGY & CONTENT FULFILLMENT	**SALES MARGIN** **UTILITY COMPUTING FEES** **FULFILLMENT HANDLING FEES**

In 2006 Amazon.com focused on two new initiatives that satisfied the above requirements and which promised to powerfully extend the existing business model. The first was a service called Fulfillment by Amazon, and the second was a series of new Amazon Web Services. Both initiatives built on the company's core strengths—order fulfillment and Web IT expertise—and both addressed underserved markets. What's more, both initiatives promised higher margins than the company's core online retailing business.

Fulfillment by Amazon allows individuals and companies to use Amazon.com's fulfillment infrastructure for their own businesses in exchange for a fee. Amazon.com stores a seller's inventory in its warehouses, then picks, packs, and ships on the seller's behalf when an order is received. Sellers can sell through Amazon.com, their own Channels, or a combination of both.

Amazon Web Services targets software developers and any party requiring high-performance server capability by offering on-demand storage and computing capacity.

Amazon Simple Storage Systems (Amazon S3) allows developers to use Amazon.com's massive data center infrastructure for their own data storage needs. Similarly, Amazon Elastic Compute Cloud (EC2), allows developers to "rent" servers on which to run their own applications. Thanks to its deep expertise and unprecedented experience scaling an online shopping site, the company can offer both at cutthroat prices, yet still earn higher margins compared to its online retail operations.

Investors and investment analysts were initially skeptical about these new long-term growth strategies. Unconvinced that the diversification made sense, they contested Amazon.com's investments in even more IT infrastructure. Eventually, Amazon.com overcame their skepticism. Nonetheless, the true returns from this long-term strategy may not be known for several more years—and after even more investment in the new business model.

DETAILED SWOT
ASSESSMENT OF EACH
BUILDING BLOCK

Assessing your business model's overall integrity is crucial, but looking at its components in detail can also reveal interesting paths to innovation and renewal. An effective way to do this is to combine classic strengths, weaknesses, opportunities, and threats (SWOT) analysis with the Business Model Canvas. SWOT analysis provides four perspectives from which to assess the elements of a business model, while the Business Model Canvas provides the focus necessary for a structured discussion.

SWOT analysis is familiar to many businesspeople. It is used to analyze an organization's strengths and weaknesses and identify potential opportunities and threats. It is an attractive tool because of its simplicity, yet its use can lead to vague discussions because its very openness offers little direction concerning which aspects of an organization to analyze. A lack of useful outcomes may result, which has lead to a certain SWOT-fatigue among managers. When combined with the Business Model Canvas, though, SWOT enables a focused assessment and evaluation of an organization's business model and its Building Blocks.

SWOT asks four big, simple questions. The first two—what are your organization's strength and weaknesses?—assess your organization internally. The second two—what opportunities does your organization have and what potential threats does it face?—assess your organization's position within its environment. Of these four questions, two look at helpful areas (strengths and opportunities) and two address harmful areas. It is useful to ask these four questions with respect to both the overall business model and each of its nine Building Blocks. This type of SWOT analysis provides a good basis for further discussions, decision-making, and ultimately innovation around business models.

The following pages contain non-exhaustive sets of questions to help you assess the strengths and weaknesses of each of your business model Building Blocks. Each set can help jumpstart your own assessments. Results from this exercise can become the foundation for business model change and innovation in your organization.

What are your business model's ...

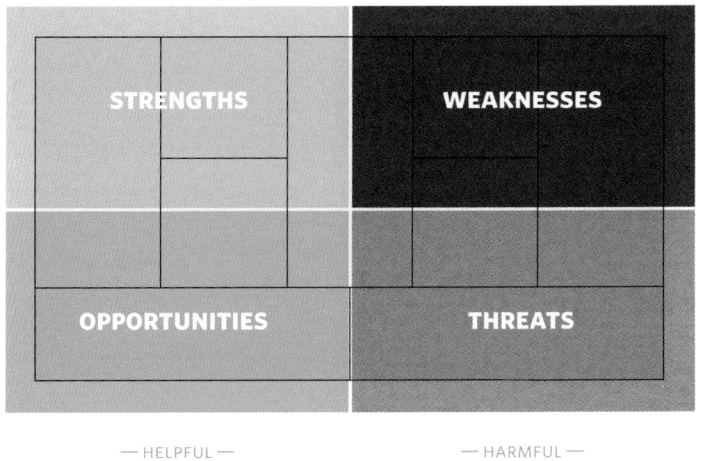

— INTERNAL —

— EXTERNAL —

STRENGTHS

WEAKNESSES

OPPORTUNITIES

THREATS

— HELPFUL —   — HARMFUL —

Value Proposition Assessment

IMPORTANCE TO MY B.M. 1–10	Statement (+)	5 4 3 2 1	1 2 3 4 5	Statement (−)	CERTAINTY OF EVALUATION 1–10
	Our Value Propositions are well aligned with customer needs	⑤④③②①	①②③④⑤	Our Value Propositions and customer needs are misaligned	
	Our Value Propositions have strong network effects	⑤④③②①	①②③④⑤	Our Value Propositions have no network effects	
	There are strong synergies between our products and services	⑤④③②①	①②③④⑤	There are no synergies between our products and services	
	Our customers are very satisfied	⑤④③②①	①②③④⑤	We have frequent complaints	

Cost/Revenue Assessment

IMPORTANCE TO MY B.M. 1–10	Statement (+)	5 4 3 2 1	1 2 3 4 5	Statement (−)	CERTAINTY OF EVALUATION 1–10
	We benefit from strong margins	⑤④③②①	①②③④⑤	Our margins are poor	
	Our revenues are predictable	⑤④③②①	①②③④⑤	Our revenues are unpredictable	
	We have recurring Revenue Streams and frequent repeat purchases	⑤④③②①	①②③④⑤	Our revenues are transactional with few repeat purchases	
	Our Revenue Streams are diversified	⑤④③②①	①②③④⑤	We depend on a single Revenue Stream	
	Our Revenue Streams are sustainable	⑤④③②①	①②③④⑤	Our revenue sustainability is questionable	
	We collect revenues before we incur expenses	⑤④③②①	①②③④⑤	We incur high costs before we collect revenues	
	We charge for what customers are really willing to pay for	⑤④③②①	①②③④⑤	We fail to charge for things customers are willing to pay for	
	Our pricing mechanisms capture full willingness to pay	⑤④③②①	①②③④⑤	Our pricing mechanisms leave money on the table	
	Our costs are predictable	⑤④③②①	①②③④⑤	Our costs are unpredictable	
	Our Cost Structure is correctly matched to our business model	⑤④③②①	①②③④⑤	Our Cost Structure and business model are poorly matched	
	Our operations are cost-efficient	⑤④③②①	①②③④⑤	Our operations are cost-inefficient	
	We benefit from economies of scale	⑤④③②①	①②③④⑤	We enjoy no economies of scale	

Infrastructure Assessment

IMPORTANCE TO MY B.M. 1-10

CERTAINTY OF EVALUATION 1-10

Our Key Resources are difficult for competitors to replicate	⑤④③②① ①②③④⑤	Our Key Resources are easily replicated
Resource needs are predictable	⑤④③②① ①②③④⑤	Resource needs are unpredictable
We deploy Key Resources in the right amount at the right time	⑤④③②① ①②③④⑤	We have trouble deploying the right resources at the right time

We efficiently execute Key Activities	⑤④③②① ①②③④⑤	Key Activity execution is inefficient
Our Key Activities are difficult to copy	⑤④③②① ①②③④⑤	Our Key Activities are easily copied
Execution quality is high	⑤④③②① ①②③④⑤	Execution quality is low
Balance of in-house versus outsourced execution is ideal	⑤④③②① ①②③④⑤	We execute too many or too few activities ourselves

We are focused and work with partners when necessary	⑤④③②① ①②③④⑤	We are unfocused and fail to work sufficiently with partners
We enjoy good working relationships with Key Partners	⑤④③②① ①②③④⑤	Working relationships with Key Partners are conflict-ridden

IMPORTANCE TO MY B.M. 1–10

CERTAINTY OF EVALUATION 1–10

	+	−	
Customer churn rates are low	5 4 3 2 1	1 2 3 4 5	Customer churn rates are high
Customer base is well segmented	5 4 3 2 1	1 2 3 4 5	Customer base is unsegmented
We are continuously acquiring new customers	5 4 3 2 1	1 2 3 4 5	We are failing to acquire new customers

	+	−	
Our Channels are very efficient	5 4 3 2 1	1 2 3 4 5	Our Channels are inefficient
Our Channels are very effective	5 4 3 2 1	1 2 3 4 5	Our Channels are ineffective
Channel reach is strong among customers	5 4 3 2 1	1 2 3 4 5	Channel reach among prospects is weak
Customers can easily see our Channels	5 4 3 2 1	1 2 3 4 5	Prospects fail to notice our Channels
Channels are strongly integrated	5 4 3 2 1	1 2 3 4 5	Channels are poorly integrated
Channels provide economies of scope	5 4 3 2 1	1 2 3 4 5	Channels provide no economies of scope
Channels are well matched to Customer Segments	5 4 3 2 1	1 2 3 4 5	Channels are poorly matched to Customer Segments

	+	−	
Strong Customer Relationships	5 4 3 2 1	1 2 3 4 5	Weak Customer Relationships
Relationship quality correctly matches Customer Segments	5 4 3 2 1	1 2 3 4 5	Relationship quality is poorly matched to Customer Segments
Relationships bind customers through high switching costs	5 4 3 2 1	1 2 3 4 5	Customers switching costs are low
Our brand is strong	5 4 3 2 1	1 2 3 4 5	Our brand is weak

219

ASSESSING THREATS

We've described how business models are situated within specific environments, and shown how external forces such as competition, the legal environment, or technology innovation can influence or threaten a business model (see p. 200). In this section we look at threats specific to each business model Building Block, and provide a non-exhaustive set of questions to help you think about ways to address each threat.

Value Proposition Threats

	Are substitute products and services available?	① ② ③ ④ ⑤
	Are competitors threatening to offer better price or value?	① ② ③ ④ ⑤

Cost/Revenue Threats

	Are our margins threatened by competitors? By technology?	① ② ③ ④ ⑤
	Do we depend excessively on one or more Revenue Streams?	① ② ③ ④ ⑤
	Which Revenue Streams are likely to disappear in the future?	① ② ③ ④ ⑤
	Which costs threaten to become unpredictable?	① ② ③ ④ ⑤
	Which costs threaten to grow more quickly than the revenues they support?	① ② ③ ④ ⑤

Infrastructure Threats

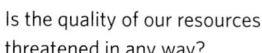

Could we face a disruption in the supply of certain resources?	① ② ③ ④ ⑤
Is the quality of our resources threatened in any way?	① ② ③ ④ ⑤

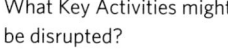

What Key Activities might be disrupted?	① ② ③ ④ ⑤
Is the quality of our activities threatened in any way?	① ② ③ ④ ⑤

Are we in danger of losing any partners?	① ② ③ ④ ⑤
Might our partners collaborate with competitors?	① ② ③ ④ ⑤
Are we too dependent on certain partners?	① ② ③ ④ ⑤

Customer Interface Threats

Could our market be saturated soon?	① ② ③ ④ ⑤
Are competitors threatening our market share?	① ② ③ ④ ⑤
How likely are customers to defect?	① ② ③ ④ ⑤
How quickly will competition in our market intensify?	① ② ③ ④ ⑤

Do competitors threaten our Channels?	① ② ③ ④ ⑤
Are our Channels in danger of becoming irrelevant to customers?	① ② ③ ④ ⑤

Are any of our Customer Relationships in danger of deteriorating?	① ② ③ ④ ⑤

ASSESSING OPPORTUNITIES

As with threats, we can assess the opportunities that may lie within each business model Building Block. Here's a non-exhaustive set of questions to help you think about opportunities that could emerge from each of the Building Blocks in your business model.

Value Proposition Opportunities

Could we generate recurring revenues by converting products into services?	① ② ③ ④ ⑤
Could we better integrate our products or services?	① ② ③ ④ ⑤
Which additional customer needs could we satisfy?	① ② ③ ④ ⑤
What complements to or extensions of our Value Proposition are possible?	① ② ③ ④ ⑤
What other jobs could we do on behalf of customers?	① ② ③ ④ ⑤

Cost/Revenue Opportunities

Can we replace one-time transaction revenues with recurring revenues?	① ② ③ ④ ⑤
What other elements would customers be willing to pay for?	① ② ③ ④ ⑤
Do we have cross-selling opportunities either internally or with partners?	① ② ③ ④ ⑤
What other Revenue Streams could we add or create?	① ② ③ ④ ⑤
Can we increase prices?	① ② ③ ④ ⑤

Where can we reduce costs?	① ② ③ ④ ⑤

Infrastructure Opportunities

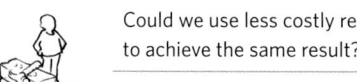 Could we use less costly resources to achieve the same result? ① ② ③ ④ ⑤

Which Key Resources could be better sourced from partners? ① ② ③ ④ ⑤

Which Key Resources are under-exploited? ① ② ③ ④ ⑤

Do we have unused intellectual property of value to others? ① ② ③ ④ ⑤

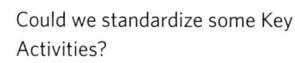 Could we standardize some Key Activities? ① ② ③ ④ ⑤

How could we improve efficiency in general? ① ② ③ ④ ⑤

Would IT support boost efficiency? ① ② ③ ④ ⑤

 Are there outsourcing opportunities? ① ② ③ ④ ⑤

Could greater collaboration with partners help us focus on our core business? ① ② ③ ④ ⑤

Are there cross-selling opportunities with partners? ① ② ③ ④ ⑤

Could partner Channels help us better reach customers? ① ② ③ ④ ⑤

Could partners complement our Value Proposition? ① ② ③ ④ ⑤

Customer Interface Opportunities

 How can we benefit from a growing market? ① ② ③ ④ ⑤

Could we serve new Customer Segments? ① ② ③ ④ ⑤

Could we better serve our customers through finer segmentation? ① ② ③ ④ ⑤

 How could we improve channel efficiency or effectiveness? ① ② ③ ④ ⑤

Could we integrate our Channels better? ① ② ③ ④ ⑤

Could we find new complementary partner Channels? ① ② ③ ④ ⑤

Could we increase margins by directly serving customers? ① ② ③ ④ ⑤

Could we better align Channels with Customer Segments? ① ② ③ ④ ⑤

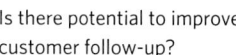 Is there potential to improve customer follow-up? ① ② ③ ④ ⑤

How could we tighten our relationships with customers? ① ② ③ ④ ⑤

Could we improve personalization? ① ② ③ ④ ⑤

How could we increase switching costs? ① ② ③ ④ ⑤

Have we identified and "fired" unprofitable customers? If not, why not? ① ② ③ ④ ⑤

Do we need to automate some relationships? ① ② ③ ④ ⑤

USING SWOT ASSESSMENT ANALYSIS RESULTS TO DESIGN NEW BUSINESS MODEL OPTIONS

A structured SWOT assessment of your business model yields two results. It provides a snapshot of where you are now (strengths and weaknesses) and it suggests some future trajectories (opportunities and threats). This is valuable input that can help you design new business model options toward which your enterprise can evolve. SWOT analysis is thus a significant part of the process of designing both business model prototypes (see p. 160) and, with luck, a new business model that you will eventually implement.

Future Model(s)

Current Model

— SWOT PROCESS —

225

BUSINESS MODEL PERSPECTIVE ON BLUE OCEAN STRATEGY

IN THIS SECTION WE BLEND OUR BUSINESS MODEL TOOLS WITH THE Blue Ocean Strategy concept coined by Kim and Mauborgne in their million-selling book of the same name. The Business Model Canvas is a perfect extension of the analytical tools presented by Kim and Mauborgne. Together they provide a powerful framework for questioning incumbent business models and creating new, more competitive models.

Blue Ocean Strategy is a potent method for questioning Value Propositions and business models and exploring new Customer Segments. The Business Model Canvas complements Blue Ocean by providing a visual "big picture" that helps us understand how changing one part of a business model impacts other components.

In a nutshell, Blue Ocean Strategy is about creating completely new industries through fundamental differentiation as opposed to competing in existing industries by tweaking established models. Rather than outdoing competitors in terms of traditional performance metrics, Kim and Mauborgne advocate creating new, uncontested market space through what the authors call value innovation. This means increasing value for customers by creating new benefits and services, while simultaneously reducing costs by eliminating less valuable features or services. Notice how this approach rejects the traditionally accepted trade-off between differentiation and lower cost.

To achieve value innovation, Kim and Mauborgne propose an analytical tool they call the Four Actions Framework. These four key questions challenge an industry's strategic logic and established business model:

1. Which of the factors that the industry takes for granted should be eliminated?
2. Which factors should be reduced well below the industry standard?
3. Which factors should be raised well above the industry standard?
4. Which factors should be created that the industry has never offered?

In addition to value innovation, Kim and Mauborgne propose exploring non-customer groups to create Blue Oceans and tap untouched markets.

Blending Kim and Mauborgne's value innovation concept and Four Actions Framework with the Business Model Canvas creates a powerful new tool. In the Business Model Canvas the right-hand side represents value creation and the left-hand side represents costs. This fits well with Kim and Mauborgne's value innovation logic of increasing value and reducing costs.

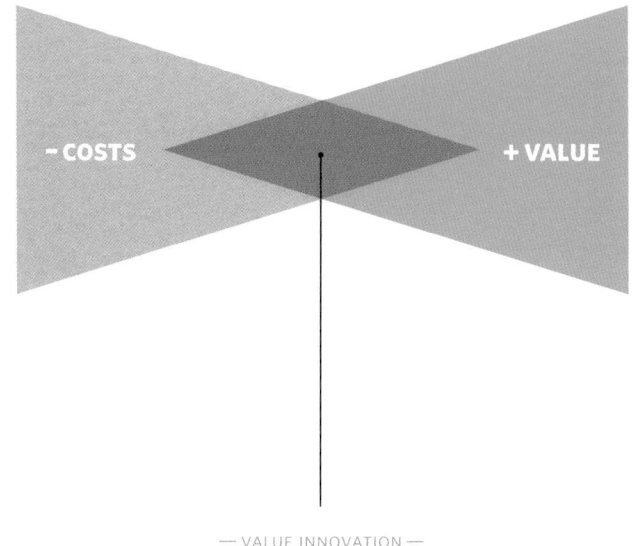

- COSTS

+ VALUE

— VALUE INNOVATION —

ELIMINATE	RAISE
WHICH FACTORS CAN YOU ELIMINATE THAT YOUR INDUSTRY HAS LONG COMPETED ON?	WHICH FACTORS SHOULD BE RAISED WELL ABOVE THE INDUSTRY'S STANDARD?
REDUCE	**CREATE**
WHICH FACTORS SHOULD BE REDUCED WELL BELOW THE INDUSTRY'S STANDARD?	WHICH FACTORS SHOULD BE CREATED THAT THE INDUSTRY HAS NEVER OFFERED?

— FOUR ACTIONS FRAMEWORK —

Source: Adapted from Blue Ocean Strategy.

BLENDING THE BLUE OCEAN STRATEGY FRAMEWORK WITH THE BUSINESS MODEL CANVAS

Business Model Canvas

Value innovation

Blending approaches

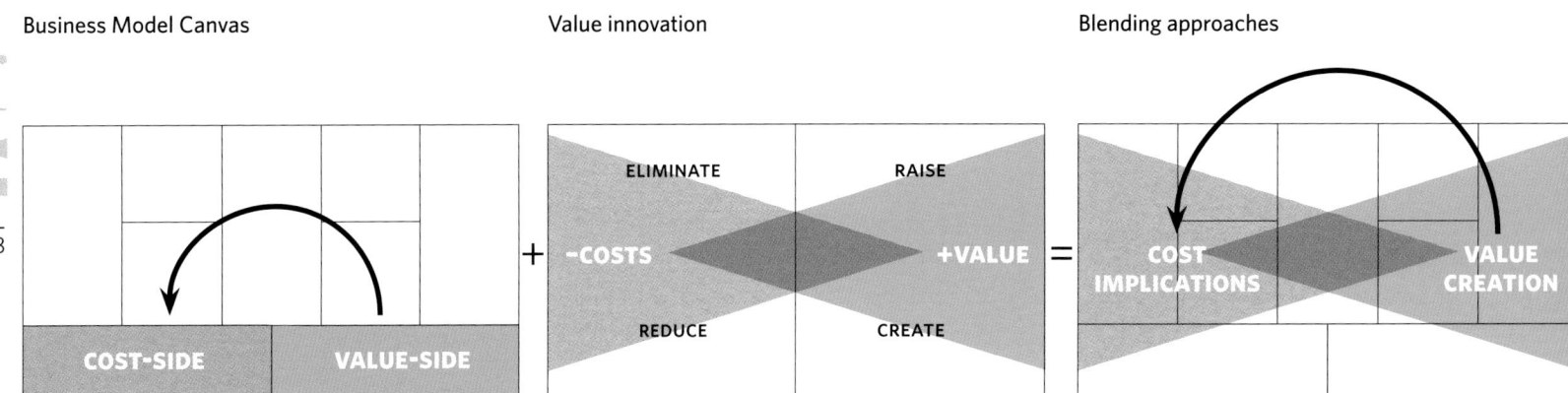

The Business Model Canvas consists of a right-hand value and customer-focused side, and a left-hand cost and infrastructure side, as descibed earlier (see p. 49). Changing elements on the right-hand side has implications for the left-hand side. For example, if we add to or eliminate parts of the Value Proposition, Channels, or Customer Relationship Building Blocks, this will have immediate implications for Resources, Activities, Partnerships, and Costs.

Blue Ocean Strategy is about simultaneously increasing value while reducing costs. This is achieved by identifying which elements of the Value Proposition can be eliminated, reduced, raised, or newly created. The first goal is to lower costs by reducing or eliminating less valuable features or services. The second goal is to enhance or create high-value features or services that do not significantly increase the cost base.

Blending Blue Ocean Strategy and the Business Model Canvas lets you systematically analyze a business model innovation in its entirety. You can ask the Four Actions Framework questions (eliminate, create, reduce, raise) about each business model Building Block and immediately recognize implications for the other parts of the business model, (e.g. what are the implications for the cost side when we make changes on the value side? and vice versa).

CIRQUE DU SOLEIL

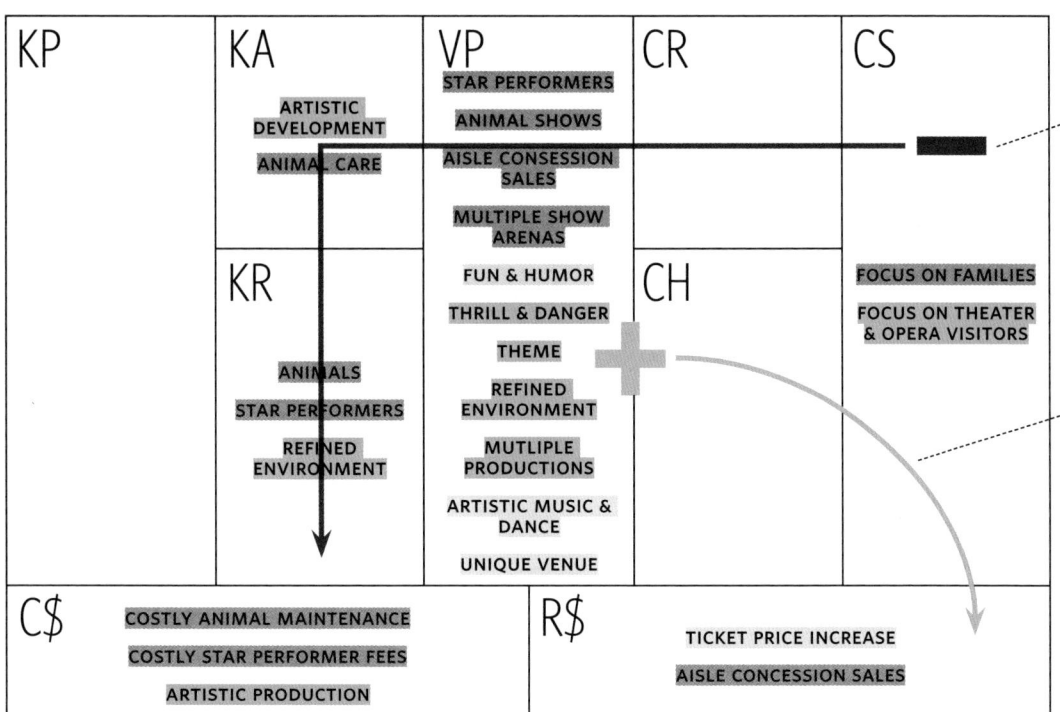

KP	KA	VP	CR	CS
	ARTISTIC DEVELOPMENT	STAR PERFORMERS		
	ANIMAL CARE	ANIMAL SHOWS		
		AISLE CONSESSION SALES		
		MULTIPLE SHOW ARENAS		

ADDING THE ARTISTIC ELEMENT TO THE VALUE PROPOSITION CHANGES ACTIVITIES & COSTS

ELIMINATING ANIMALS FROM THE SHOW SUBSTANTIALLY REDUCES COSTS

THE VALUE PROPOSITION COMBINES ELEMENTS FROM CIRCUS, THEATER & OPERA, WHICH ALLOWS CATERING TO HIGHER END CUSTOMERS WHO PAY HIGHER TICKET PRICES

KR — ANIMALS, STAR PERFORMERS, REFINED ENVIRONMENT

VP — FUN & HUMOR, THRILL & DANGER, THEME, REFINED ENVIRONMENT, MUTLIPLE PRODUCTIONS, ARTISTIC MUSIC & DANCE, UNIQUE VENUE

CH

CS — FOCUS ON FAMILIES, FOCUS ON THEATER & OPERA VISITORS

C$ — COSTLY ANIMAL MAINTENANCE, COSTLY STAR PERFORMER FEES, ARTISTIC PRODUCTION

R$ — TICKET PRICE INCREASE, AISLE CONCESSION SALES

229

Cirque du Soleil features prominently among Blue Ocean Strategy examples. Next we apply the blended Blue Ocean and Business Model Canvas approach to this intriguing and highly successful Canadian business.

First, the Four Actions Framework shows how Cirque du Soleil "played" with the traditional elements of the circus business Value Proposition. It eliminated costly elements, such as animals and star performers, while adding other elements, such as theme, artistic atmosphere, and refined music. This revamped Value Proposition allowed Cirque du Soleil to broaden its appeal to theatergoers and other adults seeking sophisticated entertainment, rather than the traditional circus audience of families.

As a consequence, it was able to substantially raise ticket prices. The Four Actions Framework, outlined in blue and gray in the business model canvas above, illustrates the effects of changes in the Value Proposition.

ELIMINATE

STAR PERFORMERS
ANIMAL SHOWS
AISLE CONCESSION SALES
MULTIPLE SHOW ARENAS

REDUCE

FUN & HUMOR
THRILL & DANGER

RAISE

UNIQUE VENUE

CREATE

THEME
REFINED ENVIRONMENT
MULTIPLE PRODUCTIONS
ARTISTIC MUSIC & DANCE

Source: Adapted from Blue Ocean Strategy.

NINTENDO'S Wii

KP	KA	VP	CR	CS
GAME DEVELOPERS	STATE OF THE ART CHIP DEVELOPMENT	HIGH END CONSOLE PERFORMANCE & GRAPHICS		NAROW MARKET OF "HARDCORE" GAMERS
OFF-THE-SHELF HARDWARE COMPONENT MANUFACTURERS	**KR**	MOTION CONTROLLED GAMES	**CH**	LARGE MARKET OF CASUAL GAMERS & FAMILIES
	NEW PROPRIETARY TECHNOLOGY	FUN FACTOR & GROUP (FAMILY) EXPERIENCE	RETAIL DISTRIBUTION	GAME DEVELOPERS
	MOTION CONTROL TECHNOLOGY			

| ELIMINATE |
| REDUCE |
| CREATE |
| UNCHANGED |

C$	R$
CONSOLE PRODUCTION PRICE	PROFIT ON CONSOLE SALES
TECHNOLOGY DEVELOPMENT COSTS	CONSOLE SUBSIDIES
CONSOLE SUBSIDIES	ROYALTIES FROM GAME DEVELOPERS

We've discussed Nintendo's successful Wii game console as an example of a multi-sided platform business model pattern (see p. 76). Now we look at how Nintendo differentiated itself from competitors Sony and Microsoft from the standpoint of Blue Ocean Strategy. Compared to Sony's PlayStation 3 and Microsoft's Xbox 360, Nintendo pursued a fundamentally different strategy and business model with Wii.

The heart of Nintendo's strategy was the assumption that consoles do not necessarily require leading-edge power and performance. This was a radical stance in an industry that traditionally competed on technological performance, graphic quality, and game realism: factors valued primarily by diehard gaming fans. Nintendo shifted its focus to providing a new form of player interaction targeted at a wider demographic than the traditional avid gamer audience. With the Wii, Nintendo brought to market a console that technologically underperformed rival machines, but boosted the fun factor with new motion control technology. Players could control games through a sort of "magic wand," the Wii Remote, simply through physical movement. The console was an instant success with casual gamers, and outsold rival consoles focused on the traditional market of "hardcore" gamers.

Nintendo's new business model has the following characteristics: A shift in focus from "hardcore" to casual gamers, which allowed the company to reduce console performance and add a new element of motion control that created more fun; elimination of state-of-the-art chip development and increased use of off-the-shelf components, reducing costs and allowing lower console prices; elimination of console subsidies resulting in profits on each console sold.

QUESTIONING YOUR CANVAS WITH THE FOUR ACTIONS FRAMEWORK

The combination of Blue Ocean Strategy tools and the Business Model Canvas provide a solid foundation upon which to question your business model from value creation, customer, and Cost Structure perspectives. We propose that three different perspectives—the Customer Segment perspective, the Value Proposition perspective, and the cost perspective—provide ideal starting points from which to start questioning your business model using the Four Actions Framework. Changes to each starting point then allow you to analyze impacts on other areas of the Business Model Canvas (see also innovation epicenters on p. 138).

Cost Impact Exploration

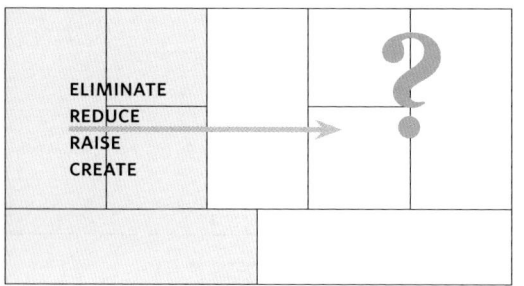

Identify the highest cost infrastructure elements and evaluate what happens if you eliminate or reduce them. What value elements disappear, and what would you have to create to compensate for their absence? Then, identify infrastructure investments you may want to make and analyze how much value they create.

- Which activities, resources, and partnerships have the highest costs?
- What happens if you reduce or eliminate some of these cost factors?
- How could you replace, using less costly elements, the value lost by reducing or eliminating expensive resources, activities, or partnerships?
- What value would be created by planned new investments?

Exploring Value Proposition Impact

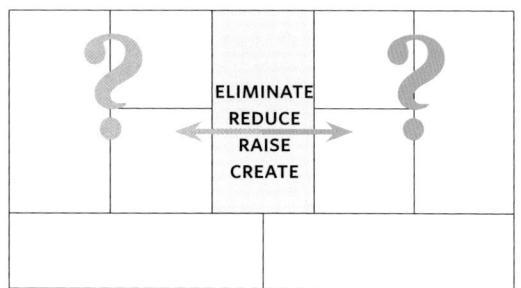

Begin the process of transforming your Value Proposition by asking the Four Actions Framework questions. Simultaneously, consider the impact on the cost side and evaluate what elements you need to (or could) change on the value side, such as Channels, Relationships, Revenue Streams, and Customer Segments.

- What less-valued features or services could be eliminated or reduced?
- What features or services could be enhanced or newly created to produce a valuable new customer experience?
- What are the cost implications of your changes to the Value Proposition?
- How will changes to the Value Proposition affect the customer side of the model?

Exploring Customer Impact

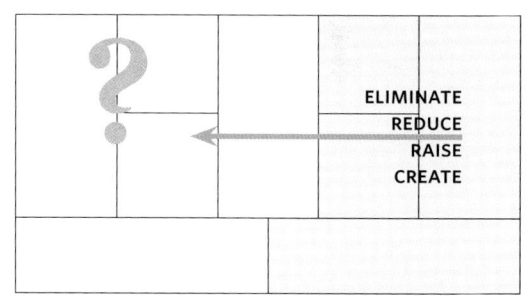

Ask yourself the Four Actions Framework questions about each business model Building Block on the customer side of the Canvas: Channels, Relationships, and Revenue Streams. Analyze what happens to the cost side if you eliminate, reduce, raise, or create value side elements.

- Which new Customer Segments could you focus on, and which segments could you possibly reduce or eliminate?
- What jobs do new Customer Segments really want to have done?
- How do these customers prefer to be reached and what kind of relationship do they expect?
- What are the cost implications of serving new Customer Segments?

MANAGING MULTIPLE BUSINESS MODELS

VISIONARIES, GAME CHANGERS, AND CHALLENGERS ARE GENERATING innovative business models around the world—as entrepreneurs and as workers within established organizations. An entrepreneur's challenge is to design and successfully implement a new business model. Established organizations, though, face an equally daunting task: how to implement and manage new models while maintaining existing ones.

Business thinkers such as Constantinos Markides, Charles O'Reilly III, and Michael Tushman have a word for groups that successfully meet this challenge: ambidextrous organizations. Implementing a new business model in a longstanding enterprise can be extraordinarily difficult because the new model may challenge or even compete with established models. The new model might require a different organizational culture, or it might target prospective customers formerly ignored by the enterprise. This begs a question: How do we implement innovative business models within long-established organizations?

Scholars are divided on the issue. Many suggest spinning off new business model initiatives into separate entities. Others propose a less drastic approach and argue that innovative new business models can thrive within established organizations, either as-is or in separate business units. Constantinos Markides, for example, proposes a two-variable framework for deciding on how to manage new and traditional business models simultaneously. The first variable expresses the severity of conflict between the models, while the second expresses strategic similarity. Yet, he also shows that success depends not only on the correct choice—integrated versus standalone implementation—but also on *how* the choice is implemented.

Synergies, Markides claims, should be carefully exploited even when the new model is implemented in a standalone unit.

Risk is a third variable to consider when deciding whether to integrate or separate an emerging model. How big is the risk that the new model will negatively affect the established one in terms of brand image, earnings, legal liability, and so forth?

During the financial crisis of 2008, ING, the Dutch financial group, was nearly toppled by its ING Direct unit, which provides online and telephone retail banking services in overseas markets. In effect, ING treated ING Direct more as a marketing initiative than as a new, separate business model that would have been better housed in a separate entity.

Finally, choices evolve over time. Markides emphasizes that companies may want to consider a phased integration or a phased separation of business models. e.Schwab, the Internet arm of Charles Schwab, the U.S. retail securities broker, was initially set up as a separate unit, but later was integrated back into the main business with great success. Tesco.com, the Internet branch of Tesco, the giant U.K. retailer, made a successful transition from integrated business line into standalone unit.

In the following pages we examine the issue of integration versus separation with three examples described using the Business Model Canvas. The first, Swiss watch manufacturer SMH, chose the integration route for its new Swatch business model in the 1980s. The second, Swiss foodmaker Nestlé, chose the separation route for bringing Nespresso to the marketplace. As of this writing, the third, German vehicle manufacturer Daimler, has yet to choose an approach for its car2go vehicle rental concept.

— SIMILARITY OF NINE
BUILDING BLOCKS —

— POTENTIAL
FOR SYNERGIES —

— POTENTIAL
FOR CONFLICTS —

CREATE SYNERGIES AMONG THE SEPARATED
BUSINESS MODELS AND COORDINATE
BETWEEN THEM AS NECESSARY

++ ++ − −

INTEGRATION

++ + − − −

AUTONOMY

− − + − ++

SEPARATION

AVOID CONFLICTS BETWEEN THE
INTEGRATED BUSINESS MODELS AND
ALLOW FOR NECESSARY AUTONOMY

SMH'S AUTONOMOUS MODEL FOR SWATCH

In the mid-seventies the Swiss watch industry, which had historically dominated the timepiece sector, found itself in deep crisis. Japanese and Hong Kong watch manufacturers had dislodged the Swiss from their leadership position with cheap quartz watches designed for the low-end market. The Swiss continued to focus on traditional mechanical watches for the mid- and high-end markets, but all the while Asian competitors threatened to intrude on these segments as well.

In the early 1980s competitive pressure intensified to the point that most Swiss manufacturers, with the exception of a handful of luxury brands, were teetering on collapse. Then Nicolas G. Hayek took over the reigns of SMH (later renamed Swatch Group). He completely restructured a newly formed group cobbled together from companies with roots in the two biggest ailing Swiss watchmakers.

Hayek envisioned a strategy whereby SMH would offer healthy, growing brands in all three market segments: low, mid, and luxury. At the time, Swiss firms dominated the luxury watch market with a 97 percent share. But the Swiss owned only 3 percent of the middle market and were non-players in the low end, leaving the entire segment of inexpensive timepieces to Asian rivals.

Launching a new brand at the bottom end was provocative and risky, and triggered fears among investors that the move would cannibalize Tissot, SMH's middle-market brand. From a strategic point of view, Hayek's vision meant nothing less than combining a high-end luxury business model with a low-cost business model under the same roof, with all the attending conflicts and trade-offs. Nevertheless, Hayek insisted on this three-tiered strategy, which triggered development of the Swatch, a new type of affordable Swiss watch priced starting at around U.S. $40.

The specifications for the new watch were demanding: inexpensive enough to compete with Japanese offers yet providing Swiss quality, plus sufficient margins and the potential to anchor a larger product line. This forced engineers to entirely rethink the very idea of a timepiece and its manufacture; they were essentially deprived of the ability to apply their traditional watchmaking knowledge.

The result was a watch made with far fewer components. Manufacturing was highly automated: molding replaced screws, direct labor costs were driven down to less than 10 percent, and the watches were produced in large quantities. Innovative guerrilla marketing concepts were used to bring the watch to market under several different designs. Hayek saw the new product communicating a lifestyle message, rather than just telling time on the cheap.

Thus the Swatch was born: high quality at a low price, for a functional, fashionable product. The rest is history. Fifty-five million Swatches were sold in five years, and in 2006 the company celebrated aggregate sales of over 333 million Swatches.

SMH's choice to implement the low end Swatch business model is particularly interesting in light of its potential impact on SMH's higher end brands. Despite a completely different organizational and brand culture, Swatch was launched under SMH and not as a standalone entity.

SMH, though, was careful to give Swatch and all its other brands near-complete autonomy regarding product and marketing decisions, while centralizing everything else. Manufacturing, purchasing, and R&D were each regrouped under a single entity serving all of SMH's brands. Today, SMH maintains a strong vertical integration policy in order to achieve scale and defend itself against Asian competitors.

CENTRALIZED — DECENTRALIZED

SMH

KP	KA	VP	CR	CS
	PRODUCTION & QUALITY CONTROL R&D HR, FINANCE, ETC.	BLANCPAIN, OMEGA, LONGINES, RADO		HIGH END AND LUXURY SEGMENT
	KR	TISSOT, CERTINA, HAMILTON, MIDO	CH	MID SEGMENT
		SWATCH, FLIK FLAK		MASS MARKET
	MANUFACTURING PLANTS			
	BRAND PORTFOLIO			

SMH is vertically integrated and centralized with respect to production, R&D, sourcing and HR.

Each SMH brand enjoys autonomy regarding product, design, and marketing communication decisions.

Swatch

KP	KA	VP	CR	CS	R$
SMH AS PRODUCTION PARTNER	PRODUCT DESIGN MARKETING & COMMUNICATION	TRENDY LOW-COST LIFESTYLE (SECOND) WATCH	LIFESTYLE MOVEMENT	MASS-MARKET	WATCH SALES
	KR SWATCH DESIGN SWATCH BRAND		CH SWATCH SHOPS RETAIL LIFESTYLE EVENTS GUERRILLA MARKETING		

C$	R$
MANUFACTURING PAYMENTS TO SMH MARKETING	WATCH SALES

235

THE NESPRESSO SUCCESS MODEL

1976
FIRST PATENT
FILED FOR
NESPRESSO
SYSTEM

1982
FOCUS ON
THE OFFICE
MARKET

1986
SEPARATE
COMPANY
CREATED

1988
NEW CEO
OVERHAULS
STRATEGY

1991
NESPRESSO
IS LAUNCHED
INTERNA-
TIONALLY

1997
FIRST AD
CAMPAIGNS
LAUNCHED

1998
FOCUS ON
INTERNET
WITH WEB
SITE REDESIGN

2006
GEORGE
CLOONEY
RETAINED
AS SPOKES-
MAN FOR
NESPRESSO

2000–2008
AVERAGE
ANNUAL
GROWTH OF
OVER 35%

236

Another ambidextrous organization is Nespresso, part of Nestlé, the world's largest food company with 2008 sales of approximately U.S. $101 billion.

Nespresso, which each year sells over U.S.$1.9 billion worth of single-serve premium coffee for home consumption, offers a potent example of an ambidextrous business model. In 1976, Eric Favre, a young researcher at a Nestlé research lab, filed his first patent for the Nespresso system. At the time Nestlé dominated the huge instant coffee market with its Nescafé brand, but was weak in the roast and ground coffee segments. The Nespresso system was designed to bridge that gap with a dedicated espresso machine and pod system that could conveniently produce restaurant-quality espresso.

An internal unit headed by Favre was set up to eliminate technical problems and bring the system to market. After a short, unsuccessful attempt to enter the restaurant market, in 1986 Nestlé created Nespresso SA, a wholly-owned subsidiary that would start marketing the system to offices in support of another Nestlé joint venture with a coffee machine manufacturer already active in the office segment. Nespresso SA was completely independent of Nescafé, Nestlé's established coffee business. But by 1987 Nespresso's sales had sagged far below expectations and it was kept alive only because of its large remaining inventory of high-value coffee machines.

In 1988 Nestlé installed Jean-Paul Gaillard as the new CEO of Nespresso. Gaillard completely overhauled the company's business model with two drastic changes. First, Nespresso shifted its focus from offices to high-income households and started selling coffee capsules directly by mail. Such a strategy was unheard of at Nestlé, which traditionally focused on targeting mass markets through retail Channels (later on Nespresso would start selling online and build high-end retail stores at premium locations such as the Champs-Élysées, as well as launch its own in-store boutiques in high-end

department stores). The model proved successful, and over the past decade Nespresso has posted average annual growth rates exceeding of 35 percent.

Of particular interest is how Nespresso compares to Nescafé, Nestlé's traditional coffee business. Nescafé focuses on instant coffee sold to consumers indirectly through mass-market retailers, while Nespresso concentrates on direct sales to affluent consumers. Each approach requires completely different logistics, resources, and activities. Thanks to the different focus there was no risk of direct cannibalization. Yet, this also meant little potential for synergy between the two businesses. The main conflict between Nescafé and Nespresso arose from the considerable time and resource drain imposed on Nestlé's coffee business until Nespresso finally became successful. The organizational separation likely kept the Nespresso project from being cancelled during hard times.

The story does not end there. In 2004 Nestlé aimed to introduce a new system, complementary to the espresso-only Nespresso devices, that could also serve cappuccino and lattes. The question, of course, was with which business model and under which brand should the system be launched? Or should a new company be created, as with Nespresso? The technology was originally developed at Nespresso, but cappuccinos and lattes seemed more appropriate for the mid-tier mass market. Nestlé finally decided to launch under a new brand, Nescafé Dolce Gusto, but with the product completely integrated into Nescafé's mass-market business model and organizational structure. Dolce Gusto pods sell on retail shelves alongside Nescafé's soluble coffee, but also via the Internet—a tribute to Nespresso's online success.

NESTLÉ'S PORTFOLIO OF COFFEE BUSINESS MODELS

Nescafé

KP	KA	VP	CR	CS
	PRODUCTION MARKETING	DOLCE GUSTO: MULTI-BEVERAGE MACHINE & PODS	RETAIL ONLINE SHOP	
RETAILERS				MASS MARKET
	KR MANUFACTURING PLANTS BRAND PORTFOLIO	NESCAFÉ: QUALITY INSTANT COFFEE	**CH** RETAIL	

C$	R$
MARKETING & SALES PRODUCTION	SALES THROUGH RETAIL (LOWER MARGIN)

Nespresso

KP	KA	VP	CR	CS
	MARKETING PRODUCTION LOGISTICS		NESPRESSO CLUB	
COFFEE MACHINE MANUFACTURERS	**KR** DISTRIBUTION CHANNELS PATENTS ON SYSTEM BRAND PRODUCTION PLANTS	HIGH-END RESTAURANT QUALITY ESPRESSO AT HOME	**CH** NESPRESSO.COM NESPRESSO BOUTIQUES CALL CENTER RETAIL (MACHINES ONLY) MAIL ORDER	HOUSEHOLDS OFFICE MARKET

C$	R$
MANUFACTURING MARKETING DISTRIBUTION & CHANNELS	MAIN REVENUES: CAPSULES OTHER: MACHINES & ACCESSORIES

high-end
(Nespresso)

mid-tier
(Dolce Gusto)

mass-market
(Nescafé)

DAIMLER'S CAR2GO BUSINESS MODEL

Market introduction of car2go

| CONCEPT DEVELOPMENT | INTERNAL PILOT | EXTENDED INTERNAL PILOT | ULM PUBLIC PILOT | AUSTIN INTERNAL PILOT | AUSTIN PUBLIC PILOT | → | WHICH ORGANIZATIONAL FORM? |

Our final example is still emerging as of this writing. Car2go is a new concept in mobility created by German vehicle manufacturer Daimler. Car2go provides an example of a business model innovation that complements the parent company's core model of manufacturing, selling, and financing vehicles ranging from luxury cars to trucks and buses.

Daimler's core business generates annual revenue exceeding U.S. $136 billion through sales of more than two million vehicles. Car2go, on the other hand, is a startup business offering city dwellers mobility on demand using a citywide fleet of *smart* cars (*smart* is Daimler's smallest and lowest-priced vehicle brand). The service is currently being tested in the German city of Ulm, one of Daimler's key operational bases. The business model was developed by Daimler's Business Innovation Department, which is tasked with developing new business ideas and supporting their implementation.

Here's how car2go works: a fleet of *smart* "fortwo" two-person vehicles is made available throughout the city, serving as a vehicle pool accessible by customers at any time. Following a one-time registration process, customers can rent fortwo cars on the spot (or reserve them in advance) then use them for as long as they like. Once a trip is completed, the driver simply parks the car somewhere within the city limits.

Rentals cost the equivalent $0.27 per minute, all-inclusive, or $14.15 per hour with a maximum of $70 per day. Customers pay monthly. The concept resembles popular car-sharing companies such as Zipcar in North America and the U.K. Distinctive characteristics of car2go include freedom from the obligation to use an assigned parking place, on-the-spot rental for as long as one likes, and a simple pricing structure.

Daimler launched car2go in response to the accelerating global trend toward urbanization, and saw the service as an intriguing complement to its core business. As a pure service model, car2go naturally has completely different dynamics compared to Daimler's traditional business, and revenues will likely remain comparatively small for some years. But Daimler clearly has high hopes for car2go over the long term.

In the pilot phase, launched in October of 2008, 50 fortwo cars were made available to some 500 employees of the Daimler Research Center in Ulm. These 500, plus 200 family members, participated as initial customers. The aim was to test the technical systems, gather data on user acceptance and behavior, and give the service an overall "road test." In February 2009, the pilot was extended to include employees of Mercedes-Benz sales and service outlets and other Daimler subsidiaries, with the number of vehicles increased to 100. At the end of March, a public test was initiated with 200 vehicles and car2go was made available to all 120,000 of Ulm's residents and visitors.

At the same time, Daimler announced a U.S. pilot in Austin, Texas, a city with 750,000 residents. As in the first phase of the German test, car2go will begin with a limited user group, such as city employees, then be opened to the public. These pilots can be seen as prototypes of a business model (see p. 160). Now, car2go's business model prototype is being fixed into organizational form.

As of this writing, Daimler had not yet decided whether to internalize car2go or spin it off as a separate company. Daimler chose to start with business model design, then test the concept in the field, and defer decisions regarding organizational structure until it could assess car2go's relationship to its long-established core business.

Daimler

239

Daimler's phased approach to business model innovation:

PHASE 1: Business model design within Daimler Innovation Department
PHASE 2: Field test of the concept run by Daimler Innovation
PHASE 3: Decision on organizational structure of new business model (integration versus separation) vis-à-vis relationship to established core business

KP	KA	VP	CR	CS
CAR PARTS MANUFACTURERS	MANUFACTURING / DESIGN	CARS, TRUCKS, VANS, BUSES, FINANCIAL SERVICES (E.G. MERCEDES BRANDS)	MAINLY HIGH-END BRANDS	MASS MARKET
	KR VEHICLE PLANTS / INTELLECTUAL PROPERTY / BRANDS		**CH** DEALERS / SALES FORCE	

C$	R$
MARKETING & SALES / MANUFACTURING / R&D	VEHICLE SALES / VEHICLE FINANCING

car2go

KP	KA	VP	CR	CS
CITY MANAGEMENT	**KA** FLEET MANAGEMENT / TELEMATICS MANAGEMENT / CLEANING	INDIVIDUAL URBAN MOBILITY WITHOUT CAR OWNERSHIP	ONE-OFF SIGN-UP	CITY DWELLERS
	KR SERVICE TEAM / TELEMATIC SYSTEMS / SMART FORTWO CAR FLEET		**CH** CAR2GO.COM / MOBILE PHONE / CAR2GO PARKING LOTS / CAR2GO SHOPS / PICK-UP/DROP-OFF ANYWHERE	

C$	R$
SYSTEMS MANAGEMENT / FLEET MANAGEMENT	PAY PER MINUTE—$0.27 (ALL INCLUSIVE)

improve

invent

Pro

cess

Business Model Design Process

In this chapter we tie together the concepts and tools from the book to simplify the task of setting up and executing a business model design initiative. We propose a generic business model design process adaptable to your organization's specific needs.

Every business model design project is unique, and presents its own challenges, obstacles, and critical success factors. Every organization starts from a different point and has its own context and objectives when it begins addressing an issue as fundamental as its business model. Some may be reacting to a crisis situation, some may be seeking new growth potential, some may be in startup mode, and still others may be planning to bring a new product or technology to market.

The process we describe provides a starting point upon which just about any organization can customize its own approach. Our process has five phases: Mobilize, Understand, Design, Implement, and Manage. We describe each of these phases in a general way, then revisit them from the perspective of the established organization, as business model innovation in enterprises already executing on one or more existing business models requires taking additional factors into account.

Business model innovation results from one of four objectives: (1) to satisfy existing but unanswered market needs, (2) to bring new technologies, products, or services to market, (3) to improve, disrupt, or transform an existing market with a better business model, or (4) to create an entirely new market.

In longstanding enterprises, business model innovation efforts typically reflect the existing model and organizational structure. The effort usually has one of four motivations: (1) a crisis with the existing business model (in some cases a "near death" experience), (2) adjusting, improving, or defending the existing model to adapt to a changing environment, (3) bringing new technologies, products, or services to market, or (4) preparing for the future by exploring and testing completely new business models that might eventually replace existing ones.

Business Model Design and Innovation

Satisfy market: Fulfill an unanswered market need *(e.g. Tata car, NetJets, GrameenBank, Lulu.com)*

Bring to market: Bring a new technology, product, or service to market or exploit existing intellectual property (IP) *(e.g. Xerox 914, Swatch, Nespresso, Red Hat)*

Improve market: Improve or disrupt an existing market *(e.g. Dell, EFG Bank, Nintendo Wii, IKEA, Bharti Airtel, Skype, Ryanair, Amazon.com retail, better place)*

Create market: Create an entirely new type of business *(Diners Club, Google)*

CHALLENGES

- Finding the right model
- Testing the model before a full-scale launch
- Inducing the market to adopt the new model
- Continuously adapting the model in response to market feedback
- Managing uncertainty

Factors Specific to Established Organizations

Reactive: Arising out of a crisis with the existing business model *(e.g. IBM in the 1990s, Nintendo Wii, Rolls Royce jet engines)*

Adaptive: Adjusting, improving, or defending the existing business model *(Nokia "comes with music," P&G open innovation, Hilti)*

Expansive: Launching a new technology, product, or service *(e.g. Nespresso, Xerox 914 in the 1960s, iPod/iTunes)*

Pro-active/explorative: Preparing for the future *(e.g. car2go by Daimler, Amazon Web Services)*

CHALLENGES

- Developing an appetite for new models
- Aligning old and new models
- Managing vested interests
- Focusing on the long term

245

Design Attitude

Business model innovation rarely happens by coincidence. But neither is it the exclusive domain of the creative business genius. It is something that can be managed, structured into processes, and used to leverage the creative potential of an entire organization.

The challenge, though, is that business model innovation remains messy and unpredictable, despite attempts to implement a process. It requires the ability to deal with ambiguity and uncertainty until a good solution emerges. This takes time. Participants must be willing to invest significant time and energy exploring many possibilities without jumping too quickly to adopt one solution. The reward for time invested will likely be a powerful new business model that assures future growth.

We call this approach design attitude, which differs sharply from the decision attitude that dominates traditional business management. Fred Collopy and Richard Boland of the Weatherhead School of Management eloquently explain this point in their article "Design Matters" in the book *Managing as Designing.* The decision attitude, they write, assumes that it is easy to come up with alternatives but difficult to choose between them. The design attitude, in contrast, assumes that it is difficult to design an outstanding alternative, but once you have, the decision about which alternative to select becomes trivial (see p. 164).

This distinction is particularly applicable to business model innovation. You can do as much analysis as you want yet still fail to develop a satisfactory new business model. The world is so full of ambiguity and uncertainty that the design attitude of exploring and prototyping multiple possibilities is most likely to lead to a powerful new business model. Such exploration involves messy, opportunistic bouncing back and forth between market research, analysis, business model prototyping, and idea generation. Design attitude is far less linear and uncertain than decision attitude, which focuses on analysis, decision, and optimization. Yet a purposeful quest for new and competitive growth models demands the design approach.

Damien Newman of the design firm Central eloquently expressed the design attitude in an image he calls the "Design Squiggle." The Design Squiggle embodies the characteristics of the design process: Uncertain at the outset, it is messy and opportunistic, until it focuses on a single point of clarity once the design has matured.

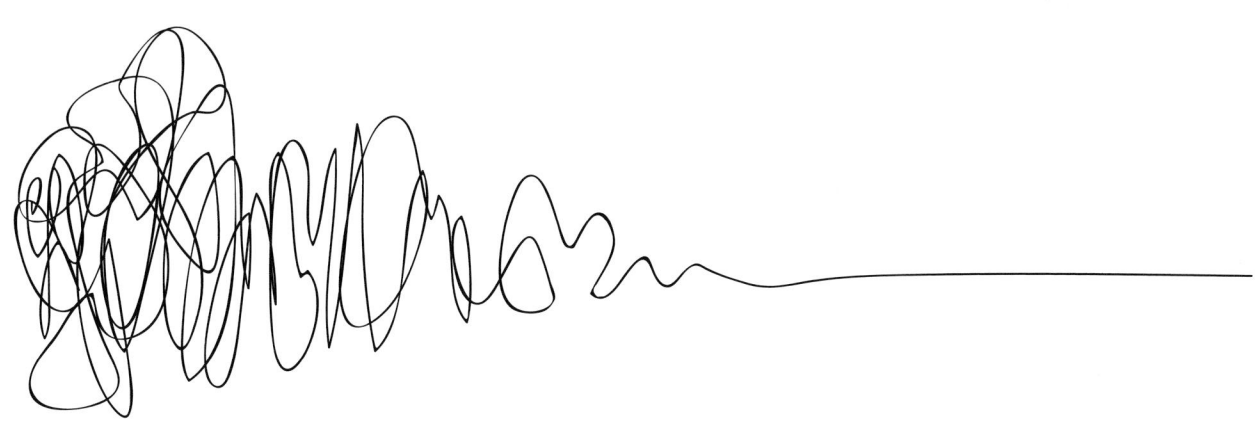

247

research   design business   implement business
& understand   model prototypes   model design

Source: Adapted from Damien Newman, Central

5 Phases

The business model design process we propose has five phases: Mobilize, Understand, Design, Implement, and Manage. As previously mentioned, the progression through these phases is rarely as linear as depicted in the table on the right. In particular, the Understanding and Design phases tend to proceed in parallel. Business model prototyping can start early in the Understanding phase, in the form of sketching preliminary business model ideas. Similarly, prototyping during the design phase may lead to new ideas requiring additional research—and a revisiting of the Understand phase.

Finally, the last phase, Manage, is about continuously managing your business model(s). In today's climate, it's best to assume that most business models, even successful ones, will have a short lifespan. Considering the substantial investment an enterprise makes in producing a business model, it makes sense to extend its life through continuous management and evolution until it needs complete rethinking. Management of the model's evolution will determine which components are still relevant and which are obsolete.

For each process phase we outline the objective, the focus, and which content in *Business Model Generation* supports that phase. Then we outline the five phases in more detail, and explain how the circumstances and focus can change when you are working with an existing business model in an established organization.

248

OBJECTIVE

FOCUS

DESCRIPTION

BOOK SECTIONS

			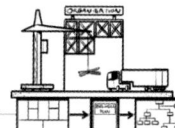	
Mobilize	**Understand**	**Design**	**Implement**	**Manage**
Prepare for a successful business model design project	Research and analyze elements needed for the business model design effort	Generate and test viable business model options, and select the best	Implement the business model prototype in the field	Adapt and modify the business model in response to market reaction
Setting the stage	**Immersion**	**Inquiry**	**Execution**	**Evolution**
Assemble all the elements for successful business model design. Create awareness of the need for a new business model, describe the motivation behind the project, and establish a common language to describe, design, and analyze and discuss business models.	You and the business model design team immerse yourselves in relevant knowledge: customers, technology, and environment. You collect information, interview experts, study potential customers, and identify needs and problems.	Transform the information and ideas from the previous phase into business model prototypes that can be explored and tested. After an intensive business model inquiry, select the most satisfactory business model design.	Implement the selected business model design.	Set up the management structures to continuously monitor, evaluate, and adapt or transform your business model.
• Business Model Canvas (p. 44) • Storytelling (p. 170)	• Business Model Canvas (p. 44) • Business Model Patterns (p. 52) • Customer Insights (p. 126) • Visual Thinking (p. 146) • Scenarios (p. 180) • Business Model Environment (p. 200) • Evaluating Business Models (p. 212)	• Business Model Canvas (p. 44) • Business Model Patterns (p. 52) • Ideation (p. 134) • Visual Thinking (p. 146) • Prototyping (p. 160) • Scenarios (p. 180) • Evaluating Business Models (p. 212) • Business Model Perspective on Blue Ocean Strategy (p. 226) • Managing Multiple Business Models (p. 232)	• Business Model Canvas (p. 44) • Visual Thinking (p. 146) • Storytelling (p. 170) • Managing Multiple Business Models (p. 232)	• Business Model Canvas (p. 44) • Visual Thinking (p. 146) • Scenarios (p. 180) • Business Model Environment (p. 200) • Evaluating Business Models (p. 212)

Mobilize

Prepare for a successful business
model design project

ACTIVITIES	CRITICAL SUCCESS FACTORS	KEY DANGERS
• Frame project objectives	• Appropriate people, experience, and knowledge	• Overestimating value of initial idea(s)
• Test preliminary business ideas		
• Plan		
• Assemble team		

The main activities of this first phase are framing the project objectives, testing preliminary ideas, planning the project, and assembling the team.

How objectives are framed will vary depending on the project, but this usually covers establishing the rationale, project scope, and main objectives. Initial planning should cover the first phases of a business model design project: Mobilize, Understand, and Design. The Implementation and Management phases depend heavily on the outcome of these first three phases—namely the business model direction—and therefore can only be planned later.

Crucial activities in this first phase include assembling the project team and gaining access to the right people and information. While there are no rules about training the perfect team—again, each project is unique—it makes sense to seek a mix of people with broad management and industry experience, fresh ideas, the right personal networks, and a deep commitment to business model innovation. You may want to start doing some preliminary testing of the basic business idea during the mobilization phase. But since the potential of a business idea depends heavily on the choice of the right business model, this is easier said than done. When Skype launched its business, who would have imagined it would become the world's largest long-distance call carrier?

In any case, establish the Business Model Canvas as the shared language of the design effort. This will help you structure and present preliminary ideas more effectively and improve communications. You may also want to try weaving your business model ideas into some stories to test them.

One clear danger in the Mobilization phase is that people tend to overestimate the potential of initial business model ideas. This can lead to a closed mindset and limited exploration of other possibilities. Try to mitigate this risk by continuously testing the new ideas with people from varied backgrounds. You may also want to consider organizing a so-called kill/thrill session in which all participants are tasked first with brainstorming for 20 minutes on reasons why the idea won't work (the "kill" portion), then spend 20 minutes brainstorming exclusively on why the idea will fly (the "thrill" portion). It's a powerful way to challenge an idea's fundamental worth.

Working from the Established Company Perspective

● *Project legitimacy* Building project legitimacy is a critical success factor when working within established organizations. Since business model design projects affect people across organizational boundaries, a strong and visible commitment by the board and/or top management is indispensable to obtaining cooperation. A straightforward way to create legitimacy and visible sponsorship is to directly involve a respected member of top management from the very beginning.

● *Manage vested interests* Take care to identify and manage vested interests throughout the organization. Not everybody in an organization is interested in reinventing the current business model. In fact, the design effort may threaten some people.

● *Cross-functional team* As described previously (see p. 143), the ideal business model task force is composed of people from across the organization, including different business units, business functions (e.g. marketing, finance, IT), levels of seniority and expertise, and so forth. Different organizational perspectives help generate better ideas, and increase the likelihood that the project will succeed. A cross-functional team helps identify and overcome potential obstacles to reinvention early in the game and encourages buy-in.

● *Orienting decision makers* You should plan on spending a considerable amount of time orienting and educating decision makers on business models, their importance, and the design and innovation process. This is critical to gaining buy-in and overcoming resistance to the unknown or not-yet-understood. Depending on your organization's management style you may want to avoid overemphasizing the conceptual aspects of business models. Stay practical and deliver your message with stories and images rather than concepts and theory.

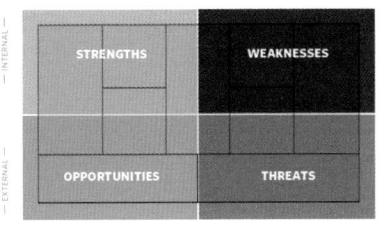

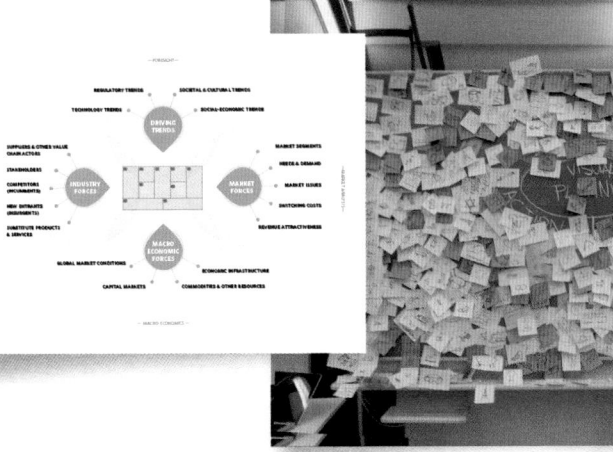

Understanding

Research and analyze the elements needed
for the business model design effort

ACTIVITIES

- Scan environment

- Study potential customers

- Interview experts

- Research what has already been
  tried (e.g. examples of failures and
  their causes)

- Collect ideas and opinions

CRITICAL SUCCESS FACTORS

- Deep understanding of potential
  target markets

- Looking beyond the traditional
  boundaries defining target markets

KEY DANGERS

- Over-researching: disconnect
  between research and objectives

- Biased research because of precom-
  mitment to a certain business idea

This second phase consists of developing a good understanding
of the context in which the business model will evolve.

Scanning the business model environment is a mix of activities,
including market research, studying and involving customers,
interviewing domain experts, and sketching out competitor business
models. The project team should immerse itself in the necessary
materials and activities to develop a deep understanding of the
business model "design space."

Scanning, though, is inevitably accompanied by the risk of over-
researching. Make your team aware of this risk at the outset and
ensure that everyone agrees to avoid excessive researching. "Analysis
paralysis" can also be avoided by prototyping business models early
on (see Prototyping, p. 160). This has the added benefit of allowing you
to quickly collect feedback. As mentioned earlier, research, understanding, and designing go hand in hand, and the boundaries separating them are often unclear.

During research, one area that deserves careful attention is developing deep knowledge of the customer. This sounds obvious, but it
is often neglected, particularly in technology-focused projects.
The Customer Empathy Map (see p. 131) can serve as a powerful tool
to help you structure customer research. One common challenge is
that the Customer Segment is not necessarily clear from the outset.
A technology "still in search of a problem to solve" may be applicable
in several different markets.

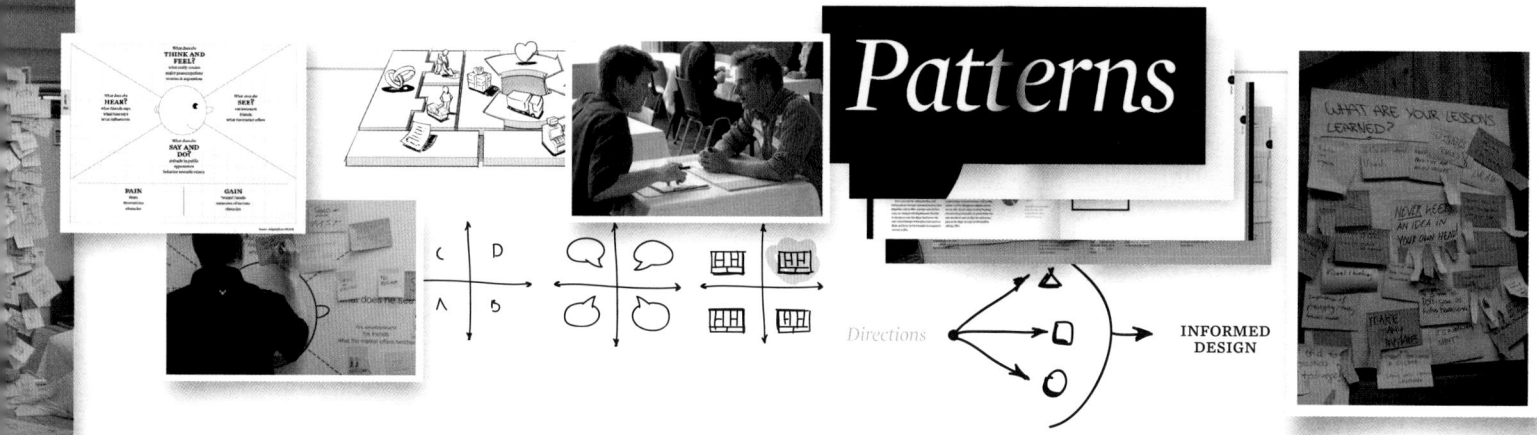

A critical success factor in this phase is questioning industry assumptions and established business model patterns. The game console industry was building and selling cutting edge subsidized consoles until the Nintendo Wii overturned commonly accepted assumptions (see p. 82). Questioning assumptions includes exploring the potential of "the low end" of established markets, as Scott Anthony points out in *The Silver Lining*. As you scan the environment and assess trends, markets, and competitors, remember that the seeds of business model innovation can be found just about anywhere.

During the Understanding phase you should also actively seek input from varied sources, including customers. Start testing preliminary business model directions early by soliciting feedback on Business Model Canvas sketches. Bear in mind, though, that breakthrough ideas may encounter strong resistance.

Working from the Established Company Perspective

● *Mapping/assessing existing business models* Established organizations start with existing business models. Ideally, mapping and assessing your current business model should be done in separate workshops involving people throughout the organization, at the same time ideas and opinions for new business models are being collected. This will provide multiple perspectives on the strengths and weaknesses of your business model, and provide the first ideas for new models.

● *Looking beyond the status-quo* It is particularly challenging to see beyond the current business model and business model patterns. Because the status quo is usually the result of a successful past, it is deeply embedded in organizational culture.

● *Searching beyond the existing client base* Searching beyond your existing client base is critical when seeking lucrative new business models. Tomorrow's profit potential may well lie elsewhere.

● *Demonstrate progress* Excessive analysis risks losing senior management support due to a perceived lack of productivity. Demonstrate your progress by describing customer insights or showing a series of business model sketches based on what you've learned from research.

Canvas *Patterns* *Design* *Strateg*

Design

Adapt and modify the business model
in response to market response

ACTIVITIES

- Brainstorm
- Prototype
- Test
- Select

CRITICAL SUCCESS FACTORS

- Co-create with people from across the organization
- Ability to see beyond status quo
- Taking time to explore multiple business model ideas

KEY DANGERS

- Watering down or suppressing bold ideas
- Falling in love with ideas too quickly

The key challenge during the Design phase is to generate and stick with bold new models. Expansive thinking is the critical success factor here. In order to generate breakthrough ideas, team members must develop the ability to abandon the status quo (current business models and patterns) during ideation. An inquiry-focused design attitude is also crucial. Teams must take the time to explore multiple ideas, because the process of exploring different paths is most likely to yield the best alternatives.

Avoid "falling in love" with ideas too early. Take the time to think through multiple business model options before selecting the one you want to implement. Experiment with different partnership models, seek alternative revenue streams, and explore the value of multiple distribution channels. Try out different business model patterns (see p. 52) to explore and test new possibilities.

To test potential business models with outside experts or prospective clients, develop a narrative for each and seek feedback on your telling of each model's "story." This is not to imply that you need to modify your model based on each and every comment. You will hear feedback such as "this won't work, customers don't need it," "that's not doable, it goes against industry logic," or "the marketplace just isn't ready." Such comments indicate potential roadblocks ahead but should not be considered showstoppers. Further inquiry may well enable you to successfully refine your model.

Iqbal Quadir's quest to bring mobile telephony to poor rural villagers in Bangladesh in the late 1990s provides a powerful example. Most industry experts rejected his idea, saying poor villagers were pressed by more basic needs and wouldn't pay for mobile telephones. But seeking feedback and developing contacts outside the telecommunications

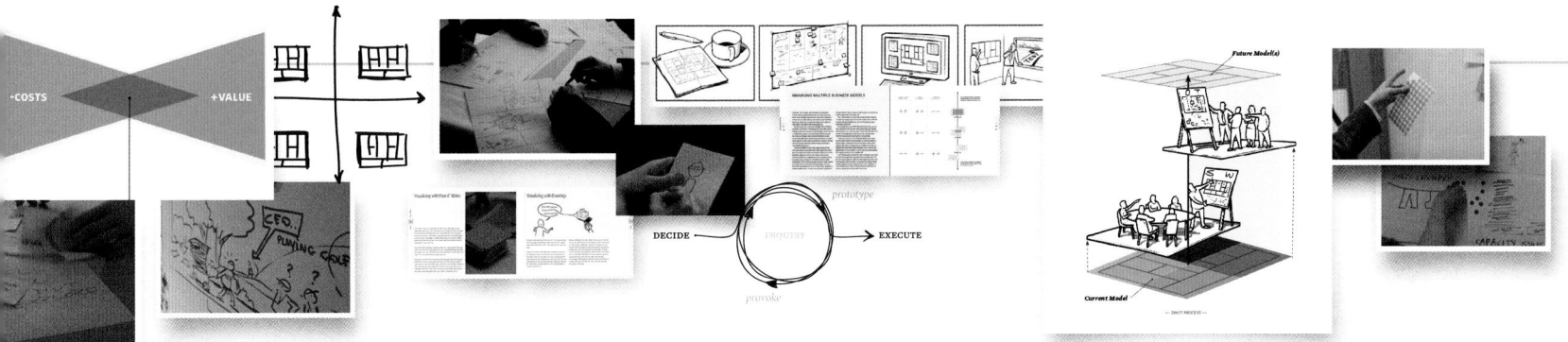

industry led to a partnership with microfinance institution Grameen Bank, which became the cornerstone of Grameenphone's business model. Contrary to expert opinion, poor villagers were indeed willing to pay for mobile connectivity, and Grameenphone became Bangladesh's leading telecommunications provider.

Working from the Established Company Perspective

● *Prevent taming of bold ideas* Established organizations tend to water down bold business model ideas. Your challenge is to defend their boldness —while assuring that they won't face overwhelming obstacles if implemented.

To achieve this tricky balance it can be helpful to draw a risk/reward profile of each model. The profile could include questions such as, What is the profit/loss potential? Describe potential conflicts with existing business units. How might this affect our brand? How will existing customers react? This approach can help you clarify and address the uncertainties in each model. The bolder the model, the higher the level of

uncertainty. If you clearly define the uncertainties involved (e.g. new pricing mechanisms, new Distribution Channels), you can prototype and test them in the market to better predict how the model will perform when launched full-scale.

● *Participatory design* Another way to improve the likelihood of having bold ideas adopted and subsequently implemented is to be especially inclusive when assembling the design team. Co-create with people from different business units, different levels of the organizational hierarchy, and different areas of expertise. By integrating comments and concerns from across the organization, your design can anticipate and possibly circumvent implementation roadblocks.

● *Old versus new* One big design question is whether the old and new business models should be separated or integrated into one. The right design choice will greatly affect chances of success (see Managing Multiple Business Models, p. 232).

● *Avoid short-term focus* One limitation to avoid is a short-term focus on ideas with large first-year revenue potential. Big corporations, in particular, can experience huge absolute growth. A company with annual sales of U.S. $5 billion, for example, generates $200 million in new revenues by growing at the modest rate of four percent. Few breakthrough business models can achieve such revenues during their first year (doing so would require acquiring 1.6 million new customers, each paying an annual fee of $125). Therefore, a longer-term perspective is required when exploring new business models. Otherwise, your organization is likely to miss out on many future growth opportunities. How much do you imagine Google earned in its first year?

Implement

Implement the business model
prototype in the field

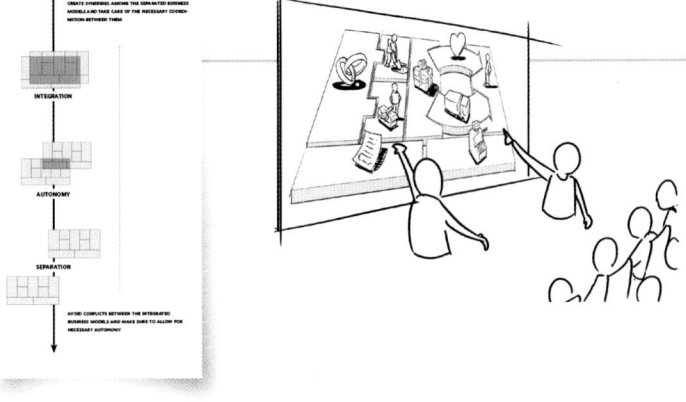

ACTIVITIES	CRITICAL SUCCESS FACTORS	KEY DANGERS
• Communicate and involve	• Best practice project management	• Weak or fading momentum
• Execute	• Ability and willingness to rapidly adapt the business model	
	• Align "old" and "new" business models	

Business Model Generation focuses on understanding and developing innovative business models, but we'd also like to offer some suggestions on implementing new business models, particularly within established organizations.

Once you've arrived at a final business model design, you will start translating this into an implementation design. This includes defining all related projects, specifying milestones, organizing any legal structures, preparing a detailed budget and project roadmap, and so forth. The implementation phase is often outlined in a business plan and itemized in a project management document.

Particular attention needs to be paid to managing uncertainties. This implies closely monitoring how risk/reward expectations play out against actual results. It also means developing mechanisms to quickly adapt your business model to market feedback.

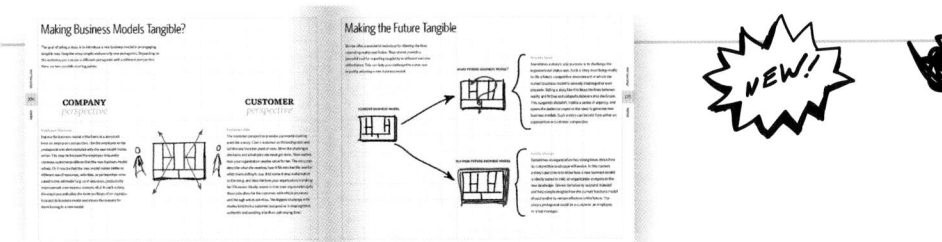

For example, when Skype started becoming successful and was signing up tens of thousands of new users each day, it had to immediately develop mechanisms to cost-effectively handle user feedback and complaints. Otherwise, skyrocketing expenses and user dissatisfaction would have brought the company to its knees.

Working from the Established Company Perspective

● *Proactively managing "roadblocks"* The single element that most increases the likelihood of a new business model's success is in place long before actual implementation. By this we are referring to the participation of people from throughout the organization during the Mobilization, Understanding, and Design phases. Such a participatory approach will have already established buy-in and uncovered obstacles before the imple-

mentation of the new model is even planned. Deep, cross-functional participation allows you to directly address any concerns regarding the new business model before drawing the roadmap for its implementation.

● *Project sponsorship* A second success element is the sustained and visible support of your project sponsor, something that signals the importance and legitimacy of the business model design effort. Both elements are crucial to keeping vested interests from undermining the successful implementation of a new business model.

● *Old versus new business model* A third element is creating the right organizational structure for your new business model (see Managing Multiple Business Models, p. 232). Should it be a standalone entity or a business unit within the parent organization? Will it draw on resources shared with an existing business model? Will it inherit the parent's organizational culture?

● *Communication campaign* Finally, conduct a highly visible, multi-channel internal communication campaign announcing the new business model. This will help you counter "fear of the new" in your organization. As outlined earlier, stories and visualizations are powerful, engaging tools that help people understand the logic of and rationale for the new business model.

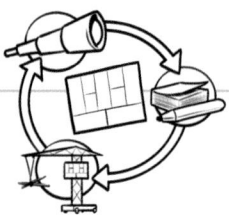

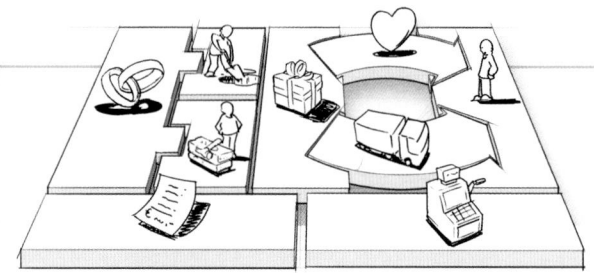

Canvas

Manage

Adapt and modify the business model in response to market reaction

ACTIVITIES

- Scan the environment
- Continuously assess your business model
- Rejuvenate or rethink your model
- Align business models throughout the enterprise
- Manage synergies or conflicts between models

CRITICAL SUCCESS FACTORS

- Long-term perspective
- Proactiveness
- Governance of business models

KEY DANGERS

- Becoming a victim of your own success, failing to adapt

For successful organizations, creating a new business model or rethinking an existing one is not a one-time exercise. It's an activity that continues beyond implementation. The Manage phase includes continuously assessing the model and scanning the environment to understand how it might be affected by external factors over the long term.

At least one person on the organizational strategy team—if not a new team—should be assigned responsibility for business models and their long-term evolution. Consider organizing regular workshops with cross-functional teams to evaluate your business model. This will help you judge whether a model needs minor adjustments or a complete overhaul.

Ideally, improving and rethinking the organization's business model should be every employee's obsession rather than something that preoccupies only top management. With the Business Model Canvas you now have a formidable tool with which to make business models clear to everybody throughout the enterprise. New business model ideas often emerge from unlikely places within an organization.

Proactive response to market evolutions is also increasingly important Consider managing a "portfolio" of business models. We live in the business model generation, a time when the shelf life of successful business models is shrinking quickly. As with traditional product life-

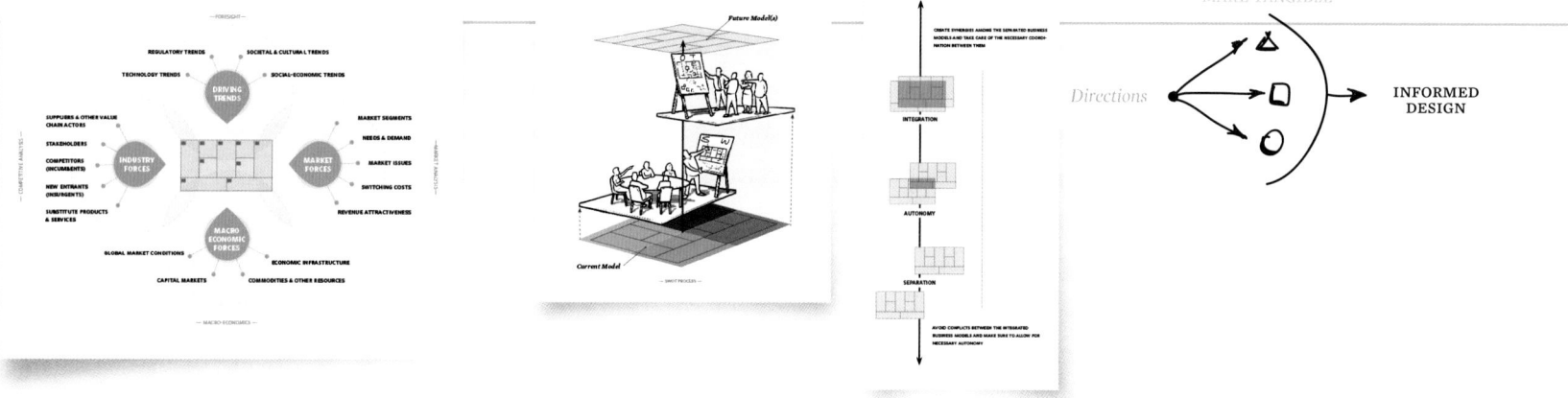

cycle management, we all need to start thinking about replacing our current cash-generating business models with growth models for tomorrow's marketplace.

Dell disrupted the PC industry when it introduced the build-to-order format and direct online sales. Over the years, Dell grew so successfully that it established itself as the industry leader. But the company failed to fully rethink its once disruptive business model. Now that the industry landscape has changed, Dell risks remaining stuck in a commoditized PC market, while growth and profits, generated elsewhere, lie outside its reach.

Working from the Established Company Perspective

● *Business Model Governance* Consider establishing a "business model governance" authority to help better manage business models across the enterprise. This group's role would be to orchestrate business models, engage stakeholders, launch innovation or redesign projects, and track the overall evolution of the organization's business models. It should also manage the "master" business model that describes the entire organization. This master template could serve as the starting point for each business model project within the organization. The master business model would also help different functional groups, such as operations, manufacturing, or sales align with the organization's overarching goals.

● *Manage synergies and conflicts* One of the business model governance authority's main tasks would be to align business models with each other to exploit synergies and avoid or manage conflicts. A Canvas document describing each business model in the organization would help illuminate the big picture and achieve better alignment.

● *Business model portfolio* Successful, established companies should proactively manage a "portfolio" of business models. Many formerly successful companies in the music, newspaper, and automotive industries failed to proactively examine their business models and slid into crisis as a result. A promising approach to avoiding this fate is to develop a portfolio of business models whereby cash-generating businesses finance business model experiments for the future.

● *A beginner's mindset* Maintaining a beginner's mindset helps keep us from becoming victims of our own successes. We all need to constantly scan the landscape and continuously assess our own business models. Take a fresh look at your model regularly. You may need to overhaul a successful model sooner than you thought.

WHAT ELSE?

Prototyping is potentially the most important part of the book and tools provided.

My reasoning is based upon the stress and resistance that established organizations are facing in the process of innovating their own business models. Therefore a very potent strategy is prototyping—in order to create buy-in processes needed.

Terje Sand, Norway

Typically when an organization looks at improving their business model, it is as a result of gaps. Visualizing your current business model can demonstrate the logical gaps that exist and make them tangible as action items.

Ravila White, United States

In established companies, there are often ample physical "product ideas" that never get serious consideration because they don't immediately fit the prevailing business model.

Gert Steens, Netherlands

Do not get too attached to the first idea or implementation. Build in feedback loops and monitor early warning signals to explicitly challenge your original concept and be willing and able to completely change it if required.

Erwin Fielt, Australia

The freemium business model as the reverse of insurance—insightful! Makes me want to turn other models upside down!

Victor Lombardi, United States

A business model is the **"CORE CONTENT"** *or the* **"SHORT STORY"** of the company (actual or prospective). A business plan is the "guideline for the action" or the "full story."

Fernando Saenz-Marrero, Spain

When I work with non-profits the first thing I tell them is that they in fact have a "business" (model) in that they must create and capture value, whether that value comes from donations, subscriptions, and so on.

Kim Korn, United States

Begin with the end in mind while taking the end client perspective.

Karl Burrow, Japan

It's one thing to map out a Business Model Canvas. But for creating a business model that in itself is a breakthrough innovation, it is helpful to use tools used to create breakthrough innovation in other industries, such as in design.
Ellen Di Resta, United States

Aravind uses the Freemium Business Model to enable FREE eye surgery for the poor in India. Business model innovation can really make a difference!
Anders Sundelin, Sweden

I find that although most managers understand strategy concepts, they have a tough time applying these concepts at their level of the organization.
However, discussions about business models connect the high-level concepts to day-to-day decision-making. It's a great middle ground.
Bill Welter, United States

Personas, Scenarios, Visualization, Empathy maps, and so on are techniques that I have used since the late 1990s in user experience type projects. In the last few years I have seen that they are incredibly effective at a strategy/business level.
Eirik V Johnsen, Norway

If solving humanity's current problems requires rethinking how value is generated and for whom, then business model innovation is the premier tool to organize, communicate, and implement that new thinking.
Nabil Harfoush, Canada

I'm interested in hearing how people are integrating technology ideas into their models using the Canvas. We've explored adding it as a separate layer (above or below financial) but have now settled on integrating it as notes on each of the 9 key areas. From this we then step back and develop a separate integrated technology plan.
Rob Manson, Australia

YOUR BUSINESS MODEL IS **NOT** YOUR BUSINESS

It's a method of inquiry to help you understand what to do next. Testing and iteration is key.
Matthew Milan, Canada

Multi-sided platforms are actually rather easy at the business model level; the difficulty comes in execution: attracting the "subsidized side," pricing on both sides, vertical or horizontal integration, how to change the business model in step with the size of the market on each side.
Hampus Jakobsson, Sweden

BUSINESS MODEL INNOVATION COMBINES *creativity* WITH A *structured approach*—THE BEST OF BOTH WORLDS.
Ziv Baida, Netherlands

Many of my clients do not have a holistic view of their business model and tend to focus on trying to address the immediate problem. The Business Model Canvas provides a framework that helps clarify the why, who, what, when, where, and how.
Patrick van Abbema, Canada

I love the idea of using these tools to design businesses and to tinker under the hood of the engine of an organization.
Michael Anton Dila, Canada

There are **thousands of business models to be investigated** and many **thousands of people who are interested** in them.
Steven Devijver, Belgium

Simplicity is very important to explain the patterns and to trigger the non-professional's involvement in business innovation.
Gertjan Verstoep, Netherlands

We have been working too long and too hard for companies with bad or improper business models.
Lytton He, China

The term business model is thrown around a lot and more frequently than not to mean an incomplete understanding of what makes a business a business (mostly just the financial/revenue aspect).
Livia Labate, United States

Business model innovation is one of the

LEAST USED & **MOST POWERFUL**

ways to create sustainable profit growth, economic development and create new 'markets' and 'industries'.
Deborah Mills-Scofield, United States

261

Outlook

We hope we've shown you how visionaries, game changers, and challengers can tackle the vital issue of business models. We hope we've provided you with the language, the tools and techniques, and the dynamic approach needed to design innovative and competitive new models. But much remains to be said. So here we touch on five topics, each of which might well merit its own book.

The first examines business models beyond profit: how the Canvas can drive business model innovation in the public and non-profit sectors. The second suggests how computer-aided business model design might leverage the paper-based approach and allow for complex manipulation of business model elements. The third discusses the relationship between business models and business plans. The fourth addresses issues that arise when implementing business models in either new or existing organizations. The final topic examines how to better achieve business model and IT alignment.

Beyond-Profit Business Models

The application of the Canvas is in no way limited to for-profit corporations. You can easily apply the technique to non-profit organizations, charities, public sector entities, and for-profit social ventures.

Every organization has a business model, even if the word "business" is not used as a descriptor. To survive, every organization that creates and delivers value must generate enough revenue to cover its expenses. Hence it has a business model. The difference is merely a matter of focus: the for-profit business's goal is to maximize earnings, while the organizations discussed in the following pages have strong non-financial missions focused on ecology, social causes, and public service mandates. We find useful entrepreneur Tim Clark's suggestion that the term "enterprise model" be applied to such organizations.

We distinguish between two categories of beyond-profit models: third-party funded enterprise models (e.g. philanthropy, charities, government) and so-called triple bottom line business models with a strong ecological and/or social mission ("triple bottom line" refers to the practice of accounting for environmental and social, as well as financial, costs). It is mainly the source of revenue that distinguishes these two, but as a direct consequence they have two very different business model patterns and drivers. Many organizations are experimenting with blending the two models in order to exploit the best of both.

donors to Oxfam, a large U.K. non-profit organization, help finance its efforts to end poverty and social injustice. Third parties rarely expect to receive direct economic benefits from the exchange, unlike advertisers—who are players in for-profit business models which also feature third party financing.

One risk of the third-party enterprise model is that value creation incentives can become misaligned. The third-party financer becomes the main "customer," so to speak, while the recipient becomes a mere receiver. Since the very existence of the enterprise depends on contributions, the incentive to create value for donors may be stronger than the incentive to create value for recipients.

All this is not to say that third-party funded enterprise models are bad and recipient-funded business models are good. Conventional businesslike selling of products and services doesn't always work: education, healthcare, and utility services are clear examples. There are no simple answers to the questions raised by third-party financed enterprise models and the resulting risks of misaligned incentives. We must explore which models make sense, then strive to design optimal solutions.

Third-Party Funded Models

In this type of enterprise model, the product or service recipient is not the payer. Products and services are paid for by a third party, which might be a donor or the public sector. The third party pays the organization to fulfill a mission, which may be of a social, ecological, or public service nature. For example, government (and indirectly, taxpayers) pays schools to deliver education services. Likewise,

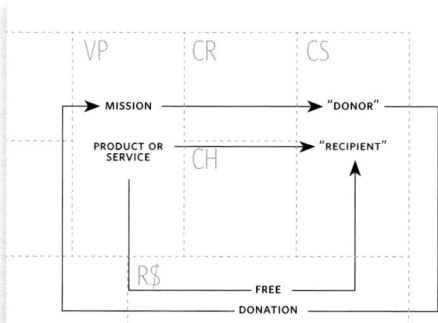

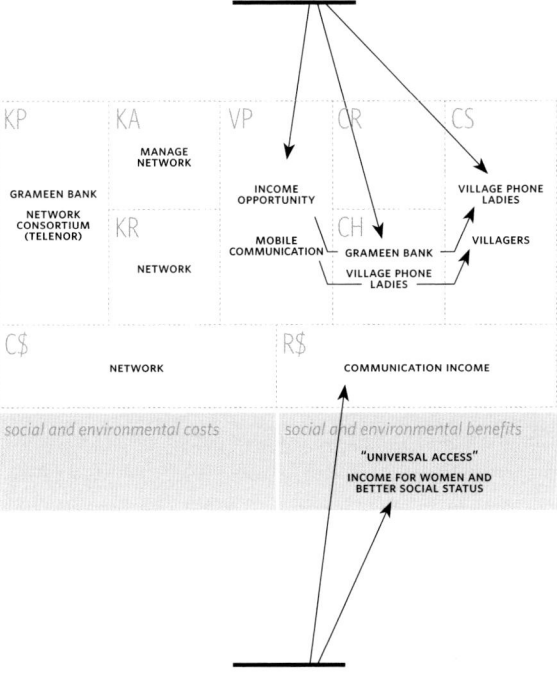

Villagers in Bangladesh were too poor to afford phones, so Grameenphone partnered with Grameen Bank, the microfinance institution, to provide local women with microloans to purchase mobile phones. The women sold calling services in their villages, repaid the loans, earned income, and thereby improved their social status.

Grameenphone went beyond establishing near universal access to telephone service and earning a profit. It also had substantial social impact by providing "village phone ladies" with earning opportunities and improved social status.

Solving the big issues of
our generation requires
bold new business models

Triple Bottom Line Business Models

Earlier we shared the story of how Iqbal Quadir, an investment banker in New York, set out to build Grameenphone. His goal was to provide universal access to telecommunications services in remote, rural areas of his home country of Bangladesh. He achieved his aim with a for-profit model that had a profound, positive impact on rural Bangladesh. Grameenphone eventually provided over 200,000 women in rural areas with income-earning opportunities, raised their social status, connected 60,000 villages to a mobile phone network, reached 100 million people, turned a profit, and became the Bangladeshi government's biggest taxpayer.

To accommodate triple bottom line business models, we can extend the Canvas with Blocks illustrating two outcomes: (1) the social and environmental costs of a business model (i.e. its negative impact), and (2) the social and environmental benefits of a business model (i.e. its positive impact). Just as earnings are increased by minimizing financial costs and maximizing income, the triple bottom line model seeks to minimize negative social and environmental impacts and maximize the positive.

265

Computer-Aided Business Model Design

Improving the process

Mike, a senior business analyst with a large financial group, wraps up the first of a two-day workshop he is facilitating with a group of 24 executives. He collects the business model prototypes and ideas that participants sketched on large Canvas posters and hurries to his office.

There, Mike and his team enter the ideas into a collaborative computer-aided business model design program to further develop the prototypes. Other business analysts working overseas add resource and activity cost estimates, as well as calculations of potential Revenue Streams. The software then spits out four different financial scenarios, with business model data and prototype diagrams for each plotted on large posters. The following morning Mike presents the results to the executives, who have gathered for the second day of their workshop to discuss the potential risks and rewards of each prototype.

This scenario doesn't yet describe reality, but that is changing rapidly. A Business Model Canvas printed on a large poster and a big box of Post-it notes will always be a very powerful tool for triggering creativity and generating innovative business model ideas. However, we extended this paper-based approach with the help of the computer, the Internet, and the iPad. Turning a prototype business model into a spreadsheet is time-consuming, and each change to the prototype usually requires a manual modification of the spreadsheet. Therefore we developed the Business Model Toolbox, Web and iPad-based platform that combines the speed of a napkin sketch with the smarts of a spreadsheet.

Scratching the Surface: a Prototype

The Business Model Toolbox makes the creation, storage, manipulation, tracking, and communication of business models far easier. The toolbox also supports collaborative work on business models for geographically disparate teams. With this software our aim is to bring the same computer support to business models than what we take for granted when we design, simulate, and build airplanes or develop software across continents. Inventing innovative business models certainly requires human creativity, but computer-aided systems can help us manipulate business models in more sophisticated and complex ways.

Try our prototype of computer aided business model editor free at www.businessmodeltoolbox.com

CAD's Influence Past, Present and Future

An example from the field of architecture is helpful in illustrating the power of computer-aided design. In the 1980s so-called Computer-Aided Design (CAD) systems started becoming more affordable and slowly were adopted by architectural firms. CAD made it much easier and cheaper for architects to create threedi-mensionalmodels and prototypes. They brought speed, integration, improved collaboration, simulation, and better planning to architec-ture practices, Cumbersome manual tasks, such as constant redraw-ing and blueprint sharing, were eliminated, and a whole new world of opportunity, such as rapid visual 3-D exploration and prototyping, opened up. Today paper-based sketching and CAD happily co-exist, each method retaining its own strengths and weaknesses.

In the realm of business models, too, computer-aided systems could make many tasks easier and quicker, while revealing as-yet unseen opportunity. At the least, CAD systems could help visualize, store, manipulate, track, annotate, and communicate business models just as the Business Model Toolbox does.

More complex functions could involve manipulating layers or business model versions, or moving business model elements dynamically and evaluating the impact in real-time. Systems might facilitate business model critiquing, provide a repository of business model patterns and off-the-shelf building blocks,simulate models, or integrate with other enterprise systems (e.g. ERP or business process management).

Computer-aided business model design systems like the Business Model Toolbox will likely evolve in step with interface improvements. Manipulating business models on wall-sized touch screens would bring computer-aided design closer to the intuitive paper-based approach and improve usability.

	Paper-based	**Computer-aided**
Advantages	• Paper or poster-based Canvases can be easily created and used just about anywhere • Paper and poster-based Canvases impose few barriers: no need to learn a specific computer application • Very intuitive and engaging in group settings • Fosters creativity, spurs ideation when used on large surfaces	Easy to create, store, manipulate, and track business models • Enable remote collaboration • Quick, comprehensive financial, other simulations • Provide business model design guidance (critiquing systems, business model database, pattern ideas, control mechanisms)
Applications	• Napkin sketches to draw, understand, or explain business models • Collaborative brainstorming sessions to develop business model ideas • Collaborative assessment of business models	• Collaborative business model design with remote teams • Complex manipulations of business models (navigation, business model layers, merging models) • Deep, comprehensive analysis

The purpose of a business plan is to describe and communicate a for-profit or non-profit project and how it can be implemented, either inside or outside an organization. The motivation behind the business plan may be to "sell" a project, either to potential investors or internal organizational stakeholders. A business plan may also serve as an implementation guide.

In fact, the work you may have done designing and thinking through your own business model is the perfect basis for writing a strong business plan. We suggest giving business plans a five-section structure: The Team, The Business Model, Financial Analysis, External Environment, Implementation Roadmap, and Risk Analysis.

The Team

One business plan element that venture capitalists particularly emphasize is the management team. Is the team experienced, knowledgeable, and connected enough to accomplish what they propose? Do the members have successful track records? Highlight why your team is the right one to successfully build and execute the business model you propose.

The Business Model

This section showcases the attractiveness of the business model. Use the Canvas to provide readers with an immediate visual portrait of your model. Ideally, illustrate the elements with drawings. Then, describe the Value Proposition, show evidence of customer need, and explain how you will reach the market. Use stories. Highlight the attractiveness of your target segments to pique the reader's interest. Finally, describe the Key Resources and Activities needed to build and execute the business model.

Financial Analysis

This is traditionally an important business plan component that attracts much attention. You can make pro forma calculations based on your Canvas Building Blocks and estimate how many customers can be acquired. Include elements such as breakeven analysis, sales scenarios, and operating costs. The Canvas can also help with capital spending calculations and other implementation cost estimates. Total cost, revenue, and cash flow projections determine your funding requirements.

External Environment

This section of the business plan describes how your business model is positioned with respect to the external environment. The four external forces covered earlier (see p. 201) provide the basis for this description. Summarize your business model's competitive advantages.

Implementation Roadmap

This section shows the reader what it will take to implement your business model and how you will do it. Include a summary of all projects and the overarching milestones. Outline the implementation agenda with a project roadmap that includes Gantt charts. Projects can be derived directly from your Canvas.

Risk Analysis

In closing, describe limiting factors and obstacles, as well as critical success factors. These can be derived from a SWOT analysis of your business model (see p. 216).

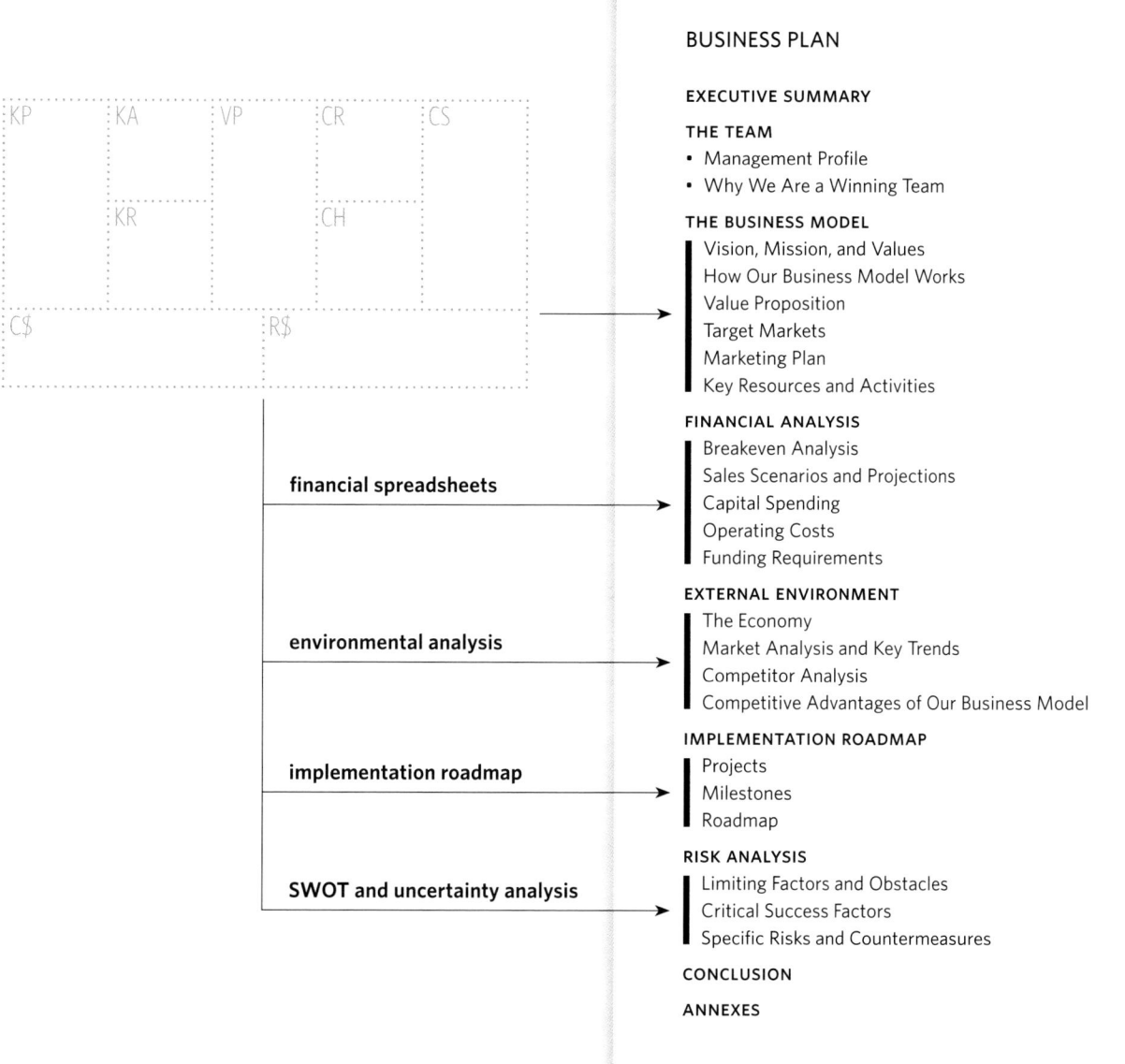

KP | KA | VP | CR | CS
KR | CH
C$ | R$

financial spreadsheets

environmental analysis

implementation roadmap

SWOT and uncertainty analysis

BUSINESS PLAN

EXECUTIVE SUMMARY

THE TEAM
- Management Profile
- Why We Are a Winning Team

THE BUSINESS MODEL
Vision, Mission, and Values
How Our Business Model Works
Value Proposition
Target Markets
Marketing Plan
Key Resources and Activities

FINANCIAL ANALYSIS
Breakeven Analysis
Sales Scenarios and Projections
Capital Spending
Operating Costs
Funding Requirements

EXTERNAL ENVIRONMENT
The Economy
Market Analysis and Key Trends
Competitor Analysis
Competitive Advantages of Our Business Model

IMPLEMENTATION ROADMAP
Projects
Milestones
Roadmap

RISK ANALYSIS
Limiting Factors and Obstacles
Critical Success Factors
Specific Risks and Countermeasures

CONCLUSION

ANNEXES

269

We've laid out the fundamentals of business model innovation, explained the dynamics of different patterns, and outlined techniques for inventing and designing models. Naturally there is much more to say about the implementation that is critical to a business model's success.

We've already addressed the question of how to manage multiple business models (see p. 232). Now let's turn to another aspect of implementation: turning your business model into a sustainable enterprise, or implementing it in an existing organization. To illustrate, we've combined the Canvas with Jay Galbraith's Star Model to suggest aspects of organizational design you may want to consider when executing a business model.

Galbraith specifies five areas that should be aligned in an organization: Strategy, Structure, Processes, Rewards, and People. We place the business model in the middle of the star as a "center of gravity" that holds the five areas together.

Strategy

Strategy drives the business model. Do you want to grow 20 percent in new market segments? Then that should be reflected in your business model in terms of new Customer Segments, Channels, or Key Activities.

Structure

The characteristics of a business model determine the optimal organizational structure for its execution. Does your business model call for a highly centralized or decentralized organizational structure? If you will implement the model in an established business, should the new operation be integrated or spun off (see p. 233)?

Processes

Each business model demands different processes. Operations run under a low-cost business model should be lean and highly automated. If the model calls for selling high-value machines, quality processes must be exceptionally rigorous.

Rewards

Different business models require different reward systems. A reward system must use appropriate incentives to motivate workers to do the right things. Does your model require a direct sales force to acquire new customers? Then your reward system should be highly performance oriented. Does your model depend heavily on customer satisfaction? Then your reward system must reflect that commitment.

People

Certain business models call for people with particular mindsets. For example, some business models call for particularly entrepreneurial mechanisms to bring products and services to market. Such models must give employees significant leeway, which means hiring proactive, but dependable, free-thinkers.

270

Direction

What are your strategic goals? How do they drive the business model?

Skills/mindset

What kinds of people with what skills does your business model require? What type of mindset is needed?

Power

What type of organizational structure does your business model require?

Motivation

What reward system does your business model require? How can you motivate your people?

Information

What information flows, processes, and workflows does your business model require?

strategy

people

structure

rewards

processes

271

Aligning IT with Business

Aligning information systems and business goals is fundamental to the success of an enterprise. Chief executives officers ask their chief information officers (CIOs), Do we have the right IT? How do we know? How can we best align our business with our technology systems?

Information technology research and advisory firm Gartner highlights this issue in a report called "Getting the Right IT: Using Business Models." Gartner asserts that the Business Model Canvas is a powerful tool that helps CIOs quickly grasp how a business works without getting bogged down in operational details. Gartner recommends that CIOs use the Business Model Canvas to align IT and key business processes. This helps them align business and IT decisions without diving too deeply into tactical issues.

We find it useful to pair the Canvas with an Enterprise Architecture approach. Many of the various Enterprise Architecture concepts describe the enterprise from three perspectives: the business perspective, the applications perspective, and the technology perspective. We recommend using the Canvas to guide the business perspective, then align the business with the applications and technology perspectives.

In the application perspective, you describe the portfolio of applications that leverage aspects of your business model (e.g. recommendation systems, supply chain management applications, etc.) and you describe all the business model's information requirements (e.g. customer profiles, warehousing, etc.). In the technology perspective you describe the technology infrastructure that drives your business model (e.g. server farms, data storage systems, etc.).

Authors Weill and Vitale propose another interesting way to explore IT alignment. They pair categories of IT infrastructure service with business models. Weill and Vitale propose aligning business models with application infrastructure, communications management, data management, IT management, security, IT architecture, channel management, IT research and development, and IT training and education.

On the opposite page we've brought these elements together in a graphic to help you pose some fundamental questions regarding business and IT alignment.

KP | KA | VP | CR | CS
KR | | | CH |
C$ | | R$ | |

strategy
business model
operational models

Business

Applications

Technology

How can IT support the processes and workflows required by my business models?

What information do I need to capture, store, share, and manage to improve my business model?

How does my application portfolio leverage the specific dynamics of my business model?

How will IT architecture, standards, and interface choices limit or leverage my business model?

Which technology infrastructure is required and crucial to the success of my business model (e.g. server farms, communications, and so on)?

Where in my business model does security play an important role and how does that influence my IT?

Do I need to invest in IT training and education to leverage my business model?

Could investments in IT research and development improve my business model in the future?

273

WHERE DID THIS BOOK COME FROM?

CONTEXT

2004: Alexander Osterwalder completes a Ph.D. dissertation on the topic of business model innovation with Professor Yves Pigneur at HEC Lausanne, Switzerland. Fast forward. **2006:** The approach outlined in the dissertation starts being applied around the world based on Alexander's business model blog, notably in companies such as 3M, Ericsson, Deloitte, and Telenor. During a workshop in the Netherlands Patrick van der Pijl asks **"why is there no book accompanying the method?"** Alexander and Yves take up the challenge. **But how does one stand out in a market where countless strategy and management books are published every year?**

INNOVATING THE MODEL

Alexander and Yves decide **they can't credibly write a book about business model innovation without an innovative business model.** They ditch publishers and launch the Hub, an online platform to share their writings from day one. Anybody with an interest in the topic can join the platform for a fee (initially U.S. $24, which is gradually raised to U.S. $243 to keep the platform exclusive). That this and other innovative Revenue Streams finance the book production in advance itself is an innovation as well. It breaks the format of conventional strategy and management books in order to create more value for readers: it is co-created highly visual, and complemented by exercises and workshop tips.

KEY AUDIENCE
visionary and game changing ... entrepreneurs / consultants / executives

MADE IN…

Written: **Lausanne, CH**
Designed: **London, UK**
Edited: **Portland, USA**
Photographed: **Toronto, CA**
Produced: **Amsterdam, NL**
Events: **Amsterdam & Toronto**

PROCESS

The core team, consisting of Alexander, Yves, and Patrick start the project with a number of meetings to sketch out the business model of the book. The Hub is launched to co-create the book with business model innovation practitioners throughout the world. Creative Director Alan Smith of The Movement hears about the project and puts his company behind it. Finally, Hub member Tim Clark joins the core team after recognizing the need for an editor. The group is completed by JAM, a company that uses visual thinking to solve business problems. An engagement cycle is started to pump fresh "chunks" of content out to the Hub community for feedback and contributions. The writing of the book becomes completely transparent. Content, design, illustrations, and structure are constantly shared and thoroughly commented upon by Hub members worldwide. The core team responds to every comment and integrates the feedback back into the book and design. A "soft launch" of the book is organized in Amsterdam, Netherlands, so members of the Hub can meet in person and share their experiences with business model innovation. Sketching out participant business models with JAM becomes the core exercise of the day. Two hundred special limited edition prototypes of the (unfinished) book go to print and a video of the writing process is produced by Fisheye Media. After several more iterations the first print run is produced.

TOOLS USED

STRATEGY:
- Environmental Scanning
- Business Model Canvas
- Customer Empathy Map

CONTENT AND R&D:
- Customer Insights
- Case Studies

OPEN PROCESS:
- Online Platform
- Co-Creation
- Access to Unfinished Work
- Commenting & Feedback

DESIGN:
- Open Design Process
- Moodboards
- Paper Mockups
- Visualization
- Illustration
- Photography

THE NUMBERS

9
years of research and practice

470
co-authors

19
book chunks

8
prototypes

200
copies of a messed up test print

77
forum discussions

287
Skype calls

1,360
comments

45
countries

137,757
views of method online before book publishing

13.18
GB of content

28,456
Post-it™ notes used

4,000+
hours of work

521
photos

REFERENCES

Boland, Richard Jr., and Collopy, Fred. *Managing as Designing.* Stanford: Stanford Business Books. 2004.

Buxton, Bill. *Sketching User Experience, Getting the Design Right and the Right Design.* New York: Elsevier. 2007.

Denning, Stephen. *The Leader's Guide to Storytelling: Mastering the Art and Discipline of Business Narrative.* San Francisco: Jossey-Bass. 2005.

Galbraith, Jay R. *Designing Complex Organizations.* Reading: Addison Wesley. 1973.

Goodwin, Kim. *Designing for the Digital Age: How to Create Human-Centered Products and Services.* New York: John Wiley & Sons, Inc. 2009.

Harrison, Sam. *Ideaspotting: How to Find Your Next Great Idea.* Cincinnati: How Books. 2006.

Heath, Chip, and Heath, Dan. *Made to Stick: Why Some Ideas Survive and Others Die.* New York: Random House. 2007.

Hunter, Richard, and McDonald, Mark, "Getting the Right IT: Using Business Models." *Gartner EXP CIO Signature report,* October 2007.

Kelley, Tom, et. al. *The Art of Innovation: Lessons in Creativity from IDEO, America's Leading Design Firm.* New York: Broadway Business. 2001.

Kelley, Tom. *The Ten Faces of Innovation: Strategies for Heightening Creativity.* New York: Profile Business. 2008.

Kim, W. Chan, and Mauborgne, Renée. *Blue Ocean Strategy: How to Create Uncontested Market Space and Make Competition Irrelevant.* Boston: Harvard Business School Press. 2005.

Markides, Constantinos C. *Game-Changing Strategies: How to Create New Market Space in Established Industries by Breaking the Rules.* San Francisco: Jossey-Bass. 2008.

Medina, John. *Brain Rules: 12 Principles for Surviving and Thriving at Work, Home, and School.* Seattle: Pear Press. 2009.

Moggridge, Bill. *Designing interactions.* Cambridge: MIT Press. 2007.

O'Reilly, Charles A., III, and Michael L. Tushman. "The Ambidextrous Organization." *Harvard Business Review* 82, no. 4 (April 2004): 74–81.

Pillkahn, Ulf. *Using Trends and Scenarios as Tools for Strategy Development.* New York: John Wiley & Sons, Inc. 2008.

Pink, Daniel H. *A Whole New Mind: Why Right-Brainers Will Rule the Future.* New York: Riverhead Trade. 2006.

Porter, Michael. *Competitive Strategy: Techniques for Analyzing Industries and Competitors.* New York: Free Press. 1980.

Roam, Dan. *The Back of the Napkin: Solving Problems and Selling Ideas with Pictures.* New York: Portfolio Hardcover. 2008.

Schrage, Michael. *Serious Play: How the World's Best Companies Simulate to Innovate.* Boston: Harvard Business School Press. 1999.

Schwartz, Peter. *The Art of the Long View: Planning for the Future in an Uncertain World.* New York: Currency Doubleday. 1996.

Stabell, Charles and Fjeldstad, Øystein, "Configuring Value for Competitive Advantage: on Chain, Shops, and Networks," *Strategic Management Journal*, no.19, 1998: 413–437.

Weill, Peter, and Vitale, Michael. *Place to Space: Migrating to Ebusiness Models.* Boston: Harvard Business School Press. 2001.

MARKET RESPONSE

The market response to *Business Model Generation* has been extremely gratifying. The first print run of 5,000 books sold out in two months, with no marketing budget and without the support of a traditional publisher. News about the book spread exclusively by word-of-mouth, blogs, Web sites, e-mail, and Twitter. Most gratifying of all, local meetups, where readers and Hub followers got together to discuss *Business Model Generation*'s content, formed spontaneously worldwide.

#BMGEN

@business_design Three steps to effective use of "Business Model Generation": 1) Buy book 2) Test live 3) Be amazed ;-) http://bit.ly/OzZh0
@Acluytens

Excitement! Business Model Generation book arrived! It's going to be an "I'm reading weekend," sorry darling! :-) #bmgen
@tkeppins

Still quiet in the house this sunday morning. Enjoying a cappuccino and reading Business Model Generation.
@hvandenbergh

I have a dilemma now: to catch up on class reading or have fun with Business Model Generation by @business_design...
@vshamanov

Just got my copy of Business Model Generation by @business_design designed by @thinksmith Even more beautiful than I imagined #bmgen
@remarkk

Heading over to #ftjco to visit @ryantaylor and borrow his copy of #bmgen tonight. Exciting evening all-around!
@bgilham

I'm SO tempted to write all over my copy of #bmgen, but it's too beautiful to destroy. Think I need 2 copies. #bmgento
@skanwar

Just got my copy of Business Model Generation - looks to be as beautifully made as it is useful. Congrats!
@francoisnel

@business_design I am BLOWN AWAY by the stuff I've learned from #bmgen!! I can't thank you guys enough for writing it!
@will_lam

Is reading Business Model Generation... This is perhaps the neatest and most innovative book I have ever read!
@jhemlig

I am so in love with my copy! Thanks @business_design #bmgen
@evelynso

Just got my copy of Business Model Generation.. Too good!! The new age of innovation in book-writing
@Neerumarya

Just received my copy of the book 'Business Model Generation'. It's a musthave for entrepreneurs who think out of the box
@Peter_Engel

Business model generatiom really is a stunning book. Feeling like a kid at Christmas with it in my hands. #bmgen
@mrchrisadams

my edition of http://www .businessmodelgeneration.com has arrived! This is the coolest business book ever! WOW! #bmgen
@snuikas

278

Is it me or is everybody in Toronto picking up a copy of Business Model Generation? #bmgen
@will_iam

The Business Model Generation book will bring a lot more depth to current, often superficial BM discussions #bmgen http://pic.gd/6671ef
@provice

Reading Business Model Generation over a lonely dinner in London. The book is exquisitely designed. Once you see it, there's no going back.
@roryoconnor

Excited to have participated in the Business Model Generation book. Now published!!
@pvanabbema

giddy as a little kid. just received my copy of Business Model Generation http://tinyurl.com/l847fj awesome book design.
@santiago_rdm

Reading Business Model Generation by Alex Osterwalder and Yves Pigneur: best mngt book in a long time
@JoostC

your big experiment just arrived in Japan. First printing of "Business Model Generation." Electrifying hands-on book.
@CoCreatr

My Business Model Generation by @business_design & Yves Pigneur arrived! So awesome to have been a TINY part.
@jaygoldman

@thinksmith @business_design @ patrickpijl Guys, I am happy! Insane. What a wonderful result.
@dulk

Got my hands on the #bmgen book a few days ago, very nice! Great job, @business_design, @thinksmith et al!
@evangineer

It was so amazing to experience 40+ people all embracing business model gen thinking in Toronto #bmgento - this city is exploding!
@davidfeldt

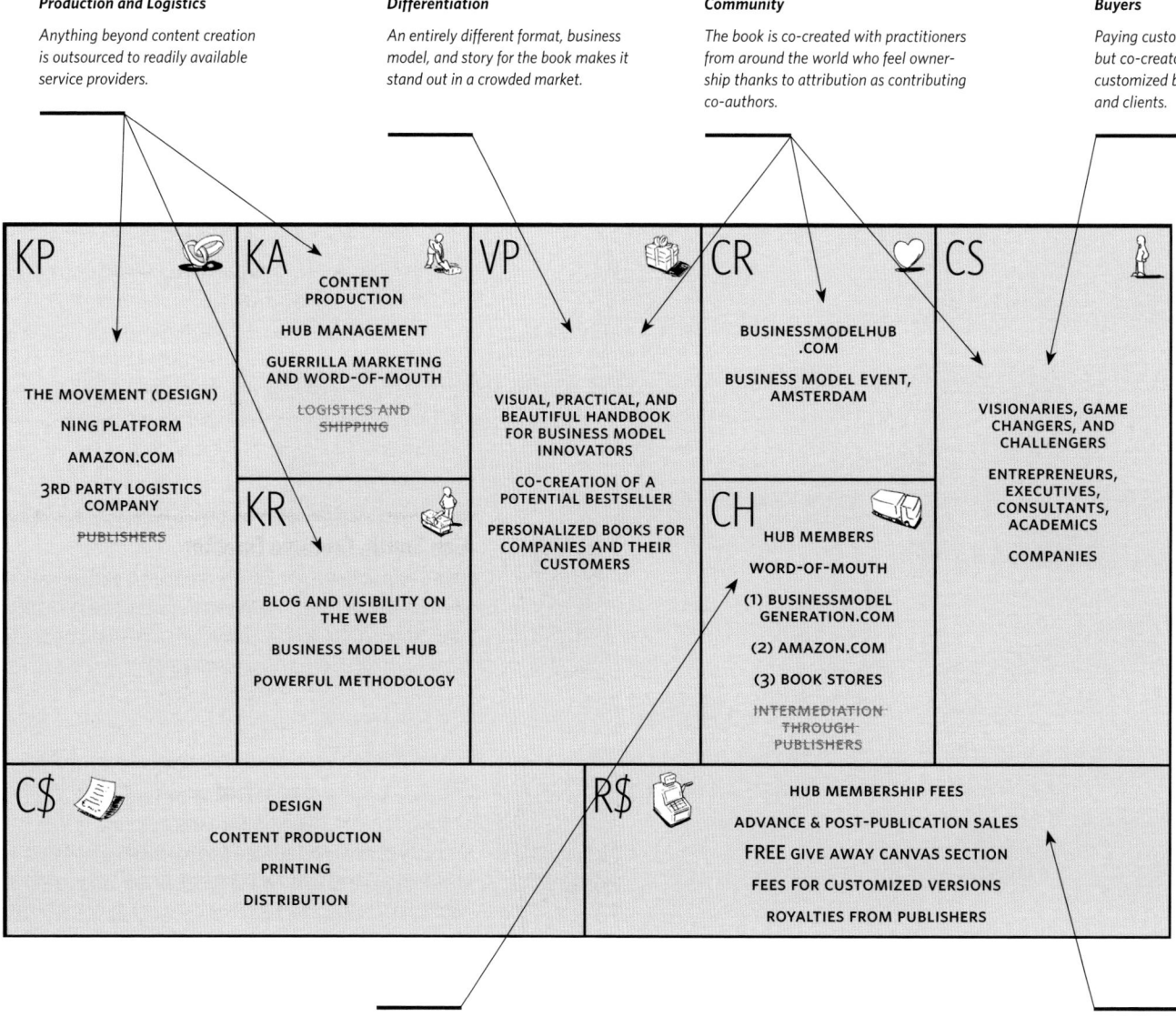

Production and Logistics

Anything beyond content creation is outsourced to readily available service providers.

Differentiation

An entirely different format, business model, and story for the book makes it stand out in a crowded market.

Community

The book is co-created with practitioners from around the world who feel owner-ship thanks to attribution as contributing co-authors.

Buyers

Paying customers are not only readers, but co-creators and companies that want customized books for their employees and clients.

KP

THE MOVEMENT (DESIGN)

NING PLATFORM

AMAZON.COM

3RD PARTY LOGISTICS COMPANY

~~PUBLISHERS~~

KA

CONTENT PRODUCTION

HUB MANAGEMENT

GUERRILLA MARKETING AND WORD-OF-MOUTH

~~LOGISTICS AND SHIPPING~~

KR

BLOG AND VISIBILITY ON THE WEB

BUSINESS MODEL HUB

POWERFUL METHODOLOGY

VP

VISUAL, PRACTICAL, AND BEAUTIFUL HANDBOOK FOR BUSINESS MODEL INNOVATORS

CO-CREATION OF A POTENTIAL BESTSELLER

PERSONALIZED BOOKS FOR COMPANIES AND THEIR CUSTOMERS

CR

BUSINESSMODELHUB .COM

BUSINESS MODEL EVENT, AMSTERDAM

CH

HUB MEMBERS

WORD-OF-MOUTH

(1) BUSINESSMODEL GENERATION.COM

(2) AMAZON.COM

(3) BOOK STORES

~~INTERMEDIATION THROUGH PUBLISHERS~~

CS

VISIONARIES, GAME CHANGERS, AND CHALLENGERS

ENTREPRENEURS, EXECUTIVES, CONSULTANTS, ACADEMICS

COMPANIES

C$

DESIGN

CONTENT PRODUCTION

PRINTING

DISTRIBUTION

R$

HUB MEMBERSHIP FEES

ADVANCE & POST-PUBLICATION SALES

FREE GIVE AWAY CANVAS SECTION

FEES FOR CUSTOMIZED VERSIONS

ROYALTIES FROM PUBLISHERS

THE CANVAS OF *BUSINESS MODEL* GENERATION

Reach

A mix of direct and indirect Channels and a phased approach optimizes reach and margins. The story of the book lends itself well to viral marketing and word-of-mouth promotion.

Revenues

The book was financed through advance sales and fees paid by co-creators. Additional revenues come from custom-ized versions for companies and their clients.

Alex Osterwalder, Author

Dr. Osterwalder is an author, speaker, and adviser on the topic of business model innovation. His practical approach to designing innovative business models, developed together with Dr. Yves Pigneur, is practiced in multiple industries throughout the world by companies including 3M, Ericsson, Capgemini, Deloitte, Telenor, and many others. Previously he helped build and sell a strategic consulting firm, participated in the development of a Thailand-based global nonprofit organization combating HIV/AIDS and malaria, and did research at the University of Lausanne, Switzerland.

Yves Pigneur, Co-Author

Dr. Pigneur has been a Professor of Management Information Systems at the University of Lausanne since 1984, and has held visiting professorships at Georgia State University in Atlanta and at the University of British Columbia in Vancouver. He has served as the principal investigator for many research projects involving information system design, requirements engineering, information technology management, innovation, and e-business.

Alan Smith, Creative Director

Alan is a big scale thinker who loves the details just as much. He's a co-founder at the aptly named change agency: The Movement. There he works with inspired clients to blend community knowledge, business logic, and design thinking. The resulting strategy, communications, and interactive projects feel like artifacts from the future but always connect to the people of today. Why? Because he designs like he gives a damn—every project, every day.

Tim Clark, Editor and Contributing Co-Author

A teacher, writer, and speaker in the field of entrepreneurship, Tim's perspective is informed by his experience founding and selling a marketing research consultancy that served firms such as Amazon.com, Bertelsmann, General Motors, LVMH, and PeopleSoft. Business model thinking is key to his *Entrepreneurship for Everyone* approach to personal and professional learning, and central to his doctoral work on international business model portability. *Business Model Generation* is his fourth book.

Patrick van der Pijl, Producer

Patrick van der Pijl is the founder of Business Models, Inc., an international business model consultancy. Patrick helps organizations, entrepreneurs, and management teams discover new ways of doing business by envisioning, evaluating, and implementing new business models. Patrick helps clients succeed through intensive workshops, training courses, and coaching.

Testing
Business
Ideas

ISBN 9781119551447 (Paperback)
ISBN 9781119551423 (ePDF)
ISBN 9781119551416 (ePub)

Cover Design and Front Cover Illustration: © Alan Smith
Back Cover Illustrations by Owen D. Pomery

SKY10029158_081721

You're holding a field guide for rapid experimentation.
Use the 44 experiments inside to find your path to scale.
Systematically win big with small bets by...

Testing
Business
Ideas

strategyzer.com/test

WRITTEN BY
David J. Bland
Alex Osterwalder

DESIGNED BY
Alan Smith
Trish Papadakos

WILEY

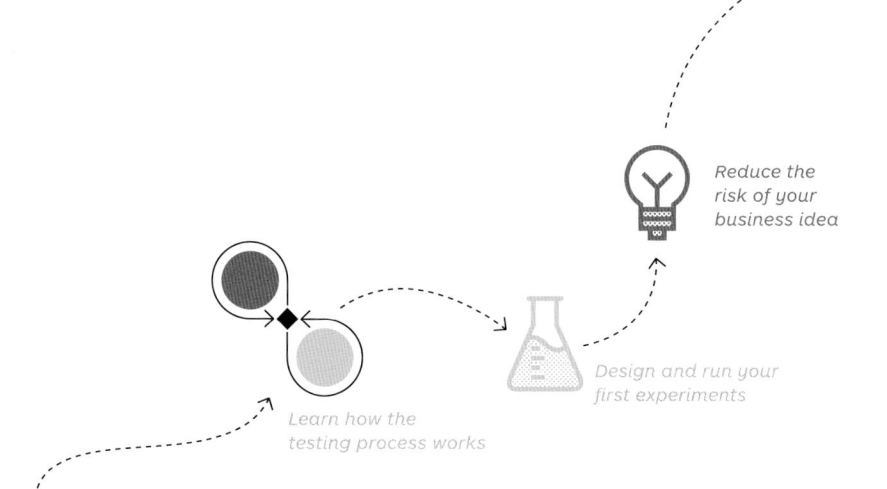

Reduce the
risk of your
business idea

Learn how the
testing process works

Design and run your
first experiments

This book will help you Start Testing
Business Ideas

You are relatively new to the concept of Testing
Business Ideas. Maybe you've read the leading books
in the domain by Steve Blank and Eric Ries, maybe
you haven't. However, you do know that you want to
get started. You are eager to test your ideas.

Fine-tune your testing process

Discover an extensive experiment library that goes beyond interviews, surveys, and minimum viable products

Bullet-proof your business ideas with stronger evidence than you've ever gathered before.

Learn about experimentation ceremonies.

Be able to share an extensive testing library with all your teams.

Reduce risk and uncertainty of new ideas across your organization.

V

Boost your Testing Skills

You are very familiar with the process of Testing Business Ideas. You have read all of the books that cover the topic. You have run several projects and built minimum viable products. Now you want to up your game and boost your testing skills.

Scale Testing in Your Organization

You are tasked with systematizing and scaling testing activities in your organization. You are experienced with the topic and are looking for state-of-the-art practical thinking to bring to teams throughout your organization.

This book was made for **Corporate Innovators**, **Startup Entrepreneurs**, and **Solopreneurs**.

Which best describes you?

☐ **Corporate Innovator** who is challenging the status quo and who is building new business ventures within the constraints of a large organization.

☐ **Startup Entrepreneur** who wants to test the building blocks of your business model to avoid wasting the time, energy, and money of the team, cofounders, and investors.

☐ **Solopreneur** who has a side hustle or an idea that isn't quite yet a business.

Which of the following resonates with you?

☐ I am seeking to find new ways to experiment, instead of always relying on focus groups, interviews, and surveys.

☐ I want to succeed at creating new growth but don't want to accidentally damage my company's brand in the testing process.

☐ I understand that to be truly disruptive, I need a dedicated team who owns the work and is capable of creating their own evidence.

☐ I know the perils of prematurely scaling a company that isn't quite ready yet, so I want to test my business model to produce evidence that shows I am on the right track.

☐ I know that I need to allocate limited resources wisely and make decisions based on strong evidence.

☐ I want to fall asleep at night knowing we've spent our frantic day working on the most important things that matter to our startup's success.

☐ I am mindful that we need to show evidence of progress to justify current and future investment rounds.

☐ I don't have the resources of a funded startup, let alone a corporation.

☐ I haven't necessarily tried any of this before, so I want to make these late nights and weekends worth it.

☐ I eventually want to devote all of my time to this idea, but it all seems so risky. In order to make the leap, I'll need the evidence that I'm onto something big.

☐ I have read a few books on entrepreneurship, but need guidance on how to test my ideas and what types of experiments to run.

How to Get from a Good Idea to a Validated Business

Too many entrepreneurs and innovators execute ideas prematurely because they look great in presentations, make excellent sense in the spreadsheet, and look irresistible in the business plan... only to learn later that their vision turned out to be a hallucination.

Systematically applying Customer Development and Lean Startup

This book builds on the seminal work by Steve Blank whose Customer Development methodology and the concept of "getting out of the building" to test business ideas launched the Lean Startup movement and Eric Ries who coined the term Lean Startup.

Don't make the mistake of executing business ideas without evidence: test your ideas thoroughly, regardless of how great they may seem in theory.

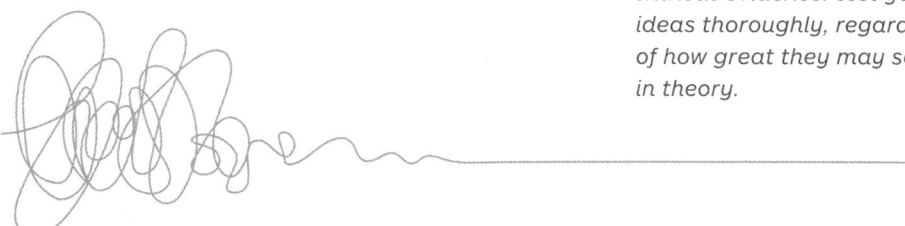 

Idea　　Search & Testing　　Execution　　**Business**

*"No business plan survives
first contact with customers."*

STEVE BLANK

*Inventor of Customer Development and
Godfather of the Lean Startup Movement*

Navigate the Experiment Library in This Book to Make Your Ideas Bulletproof

Testing is the activity of reducing the risk of pursuing ideas that look good in theory, but won't work in reality. You test ideas by conducting rapid experiments that allow you to learn and adapt.

This book outlines the most extensive testing library on the market to help you make your ideas bulletproof with evidence. Test extensively to avoid wasting time, energy, and resources on ideas that won't work.

The entrepreneur's and innovator's #1 task is to reduce risk and uncertainty.

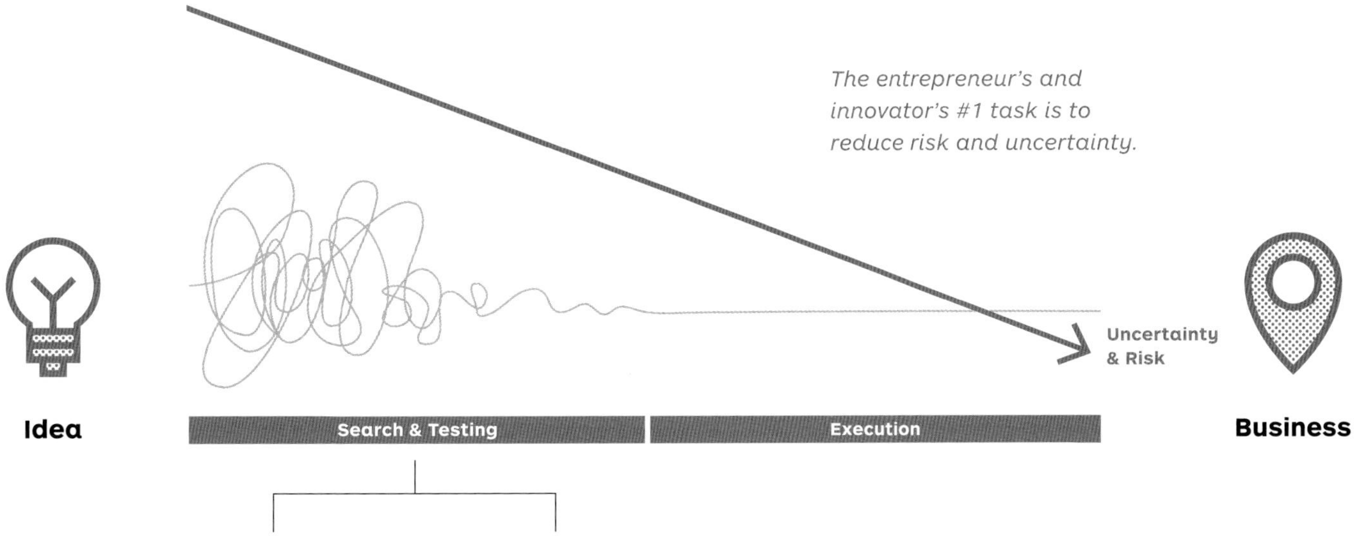

Idea

Uncertainty & Risk

Business

| Search & Testing | Execution |

Discovery
Discover if your general direction is right. Test basic assumptions. Get first insights to course correct rapidly.

Validation
Validate the direction you've taken. Confirm with strong evidence that your business idea is very likely to work.

In this book we use the discovery and validation phases from Steve Blank's The Startup Owner's Manual *as the foundation of our process. We heavily build on his original work.*

The Iterative Process

Business Concept Design

Design is the activity of turning vague ideas, market insights, and evidence into concrete value propositions and solid business models. Good design involves the use of strong business model patterns to maximize returns and compete beyond product, price, and technology.

The risk is that a business can't get access to key resources (technology, IP, brand, etc.), can't develop capabilities to perform key activities, or can't find key partners to build and scale the value proposition.

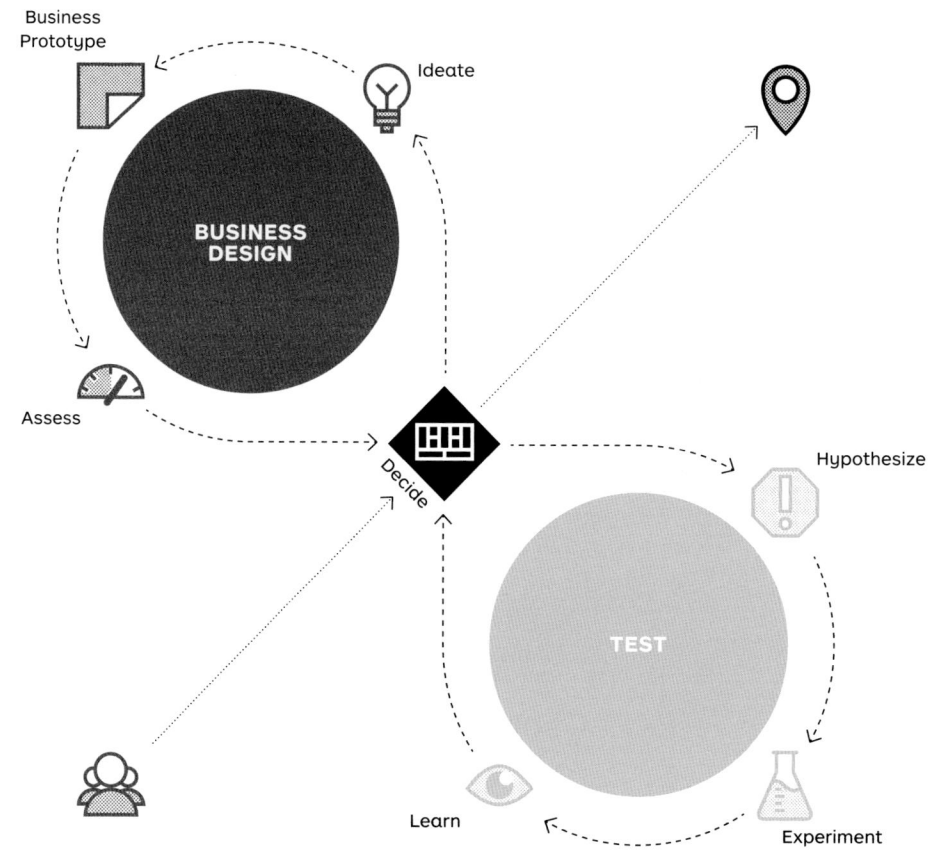

Business Prototype

Ideate

BUSINESS DESIGN

Assess

Decide

Hypothesize

TEST

Learn

Experiment

 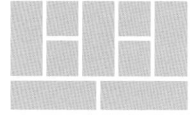  

Idea + **Business Model** + **Value Proposition** =

x

Testing and reducing risk

To test a big business idea you break it down into smaller chunks of testable hypotheses. These hypotheses cover three types of risk. First, that customers aren't interested in your idea (desirability). Second, that you can't build and deliver your idea (feasibility). Third, that you can't earn enough money from your idea (viability).

You test your most important hypotheses with appropriate experiments. Each experiment generates evidence and insights that allow you to learn and decide. Based on the evidence and your insights you either adapt your idea, if you learn you were on the wrong path, or continue testing other aspects of your idea, if the evidence supports your direction.

Key Hypotheses + **Experiments** + **Key Insights** = **Reducing Uncertainty & Risk**

Desirability risk
Customers aren't interested

The risk is that the market a business is targeting is too small; that too few customers want the value proposition; or that the company can't reach, acquire, and retain targeted customers.

Feasibility risk
We can't build and deliver

The risk is that a business can't get access to key resources (technology, IP, brand, etc.), can't develop capabilities to perform key activities, or can't find key partners to build and scale the value proposition.

Viability risk
We can't earn enough money

The risk is that a business can't generate successful revenue streams, that customers are unwilling to pay (enough), or that the costs are too high to make a sustainable profit.

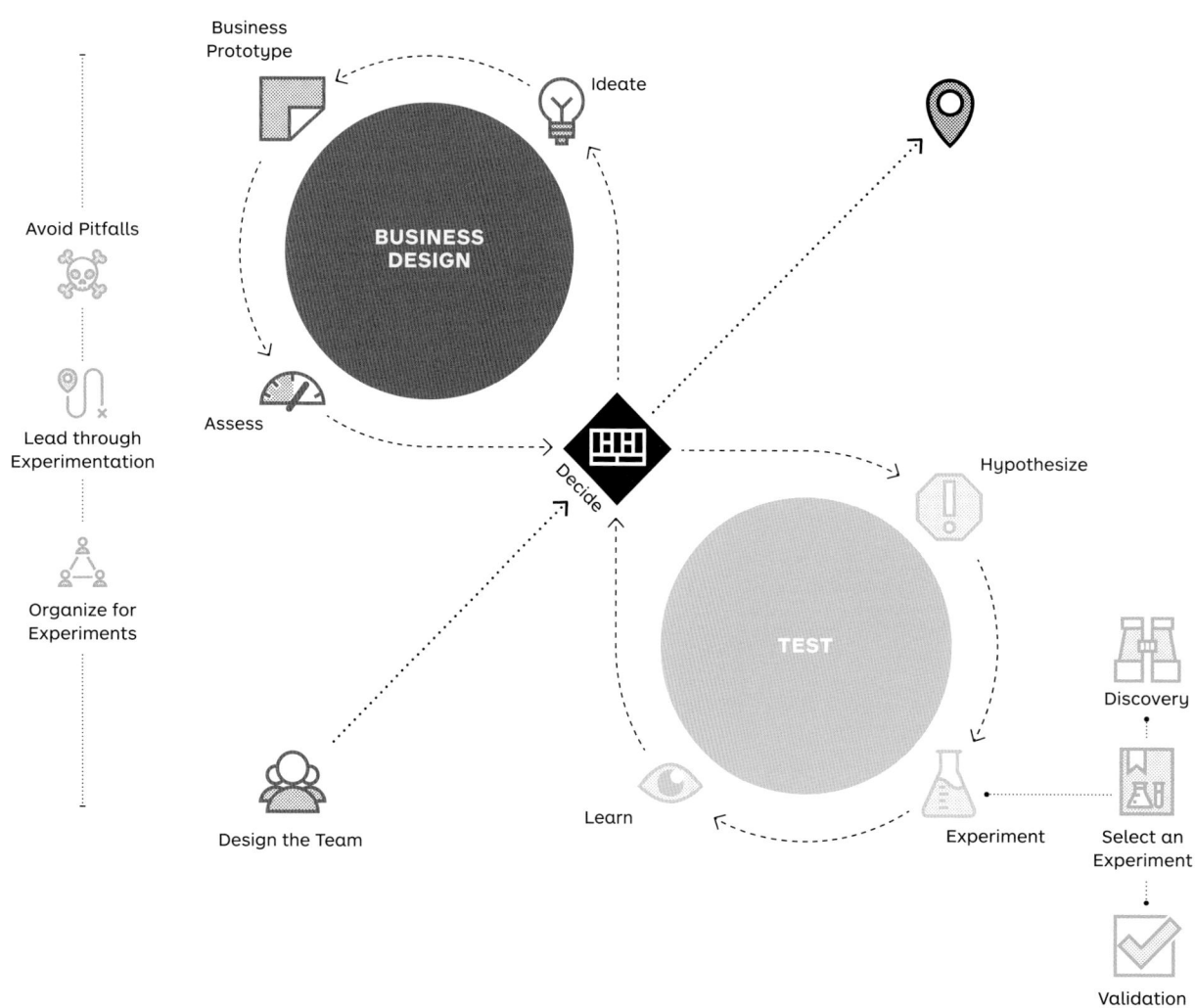

1

Design

Design the Team
p. 3

Shape the Idea
p. 15

2

Test

Hypothesize
p. 27

Experiment
p. 41

Learn
p. 49

Decide
p. 59

Manage
p. 65

3

Experiments

Select an Experiment
p. 91

Discovery
p. 101

Validation
p. 231

4

Mindset

Avoid Experiment Pitfalls
p. 313

Lead through Experimentation
p. 317

Organize for Experiments
p. 323

AFTERWORD
p. 329

Des

ign

"The strength of the team
is each individual member.
The strength of each member
is the team."

———————

Phil Jackson
Former NBA Coach

SECTION 1 — DESIGN

1.1 — DESIGN THE TEAM

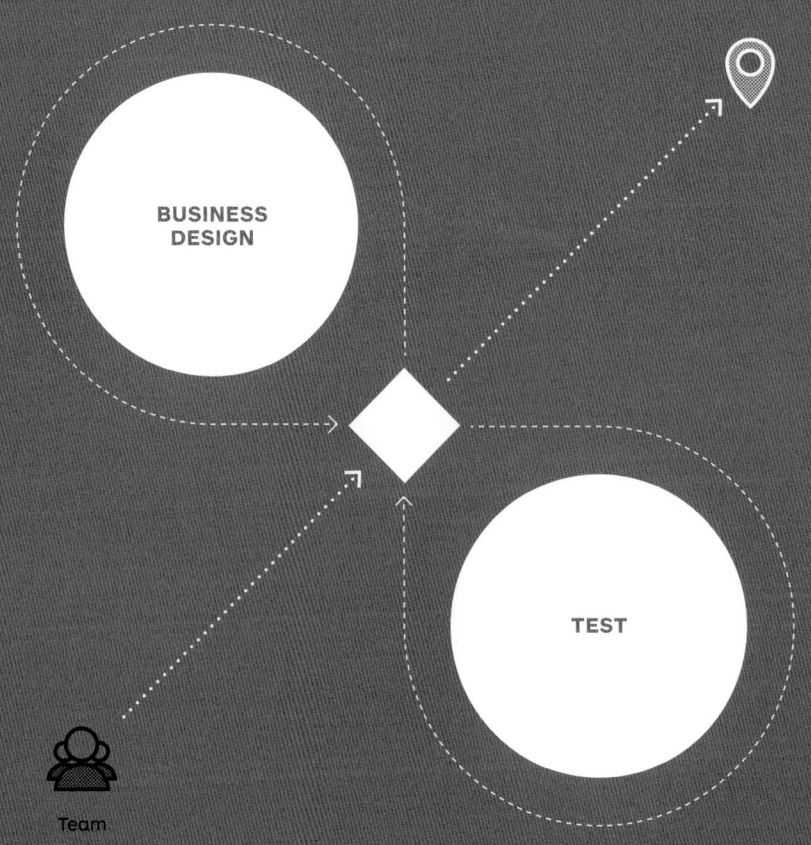

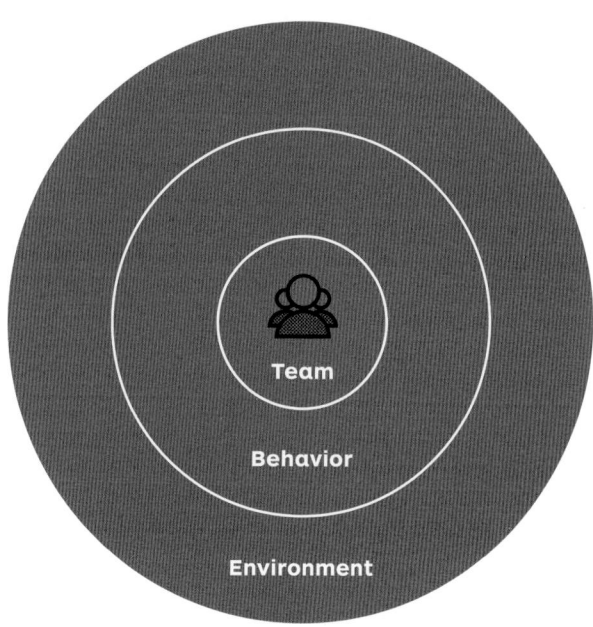

Team

Behavior

Environment

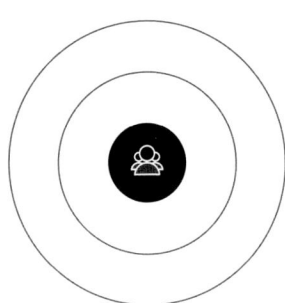

SYNOPSIS

Team Design

What kind of team do we need to create our business?

Having worked with teams all around the world, we have learned that behind every successful new venture is a great team. If you are at a startup, the founding team is the glue that holds it all together. If you are in a corporation, you'll still need a solid team to create a new business venture. If you are a solopreneur, the team you eventually bring in will make or break your business.

Commonly Required Skills to Test Business Ideas

- Design
- Sales
- Product
- Marketing
- Tech
- Research
- Legal
- Finance
- Data

Cross-Functional Skillset

A cross-functional team has all the core abilities needed to ship the product and learn from customers. A common basic example of a cross-functional team consists of design, product, and engineering.

Adapted from Jeff Patton.

Access to Missing Skillsets

If you do not have all of the skills needed or are unable to partner with external team members, then evaluate technological tools to fill the void.

Testing Tools

There are new tools coming on to the market every day that allow you to:

- Create landing pages
- Design logos
- Run online ads
- And more...

All with little or no expertise needed.

Entrepreneurial Experience

It's not a coincidence that successful businesses benefit from those who already have entrepreneurial experience.

Many entrepreneurs needed several attempts before finding success. Rovio's hit game, Angry Birds, was preceded by six years and 51 failed games.

Diversity

Team member diversity means they vary in aspects such as race, ethnicity, gender, age, experience, and thought. Now, more than ever, new businesses have real world impact on people and society. If the people who make up your team all have similar life experiences, thoughts, and appearance, then it can make it very difficult to navigate uncertainty.

A lack of diverse experiences and perspectives on a team will result in baking your biases right into the business.

When forming your team, keep diversity top of mind, rather than as an afterthought. Lead by example, by having a diverse leadership team. The issues that arise from having a homogeneous team are very difficult to rectify later.

SYNOPSIS

Team Behavior

How does our team need to act?

Team design is necessary, but not sufficient. You can have entrepreneurial experience, but how you interact with your team needs to exhibit entrepreneurial characteristics as well. Team behavior can be unpacked into six categories that are leading indicators of team success.

Successful Teams Exhibit Six Behaviors

1. Data Influenced

You do not have to be data driven, but you need to be data influenced. Teams no longer have the luxury of burning down a product backlog of features. The insights generated from data shape the backlog and strategy.

2. Experiment Driven

Teams are willing to be wrong and experiment. They are not only focused on the delivery of features, but also craft experiments to learn about their riskiest assumptions. Match experiments to what you are trying to learn over time.

3. Customer Centric

To create new businesses today, teams have to know "the why" behind the work. This begins with being constantly connected to the customer. This should not be limited to the new customer experience, and expands to both inside and outside of the product.

4. Entrepreneurial

Move fast and validate things. Teams have a sense of urgency and create momentum toward a viable outcome. This includes creative problem-solving at speed.

5. Iterative Approach

Teams aim for a desired result by means of a repeated cycle of operations. The iterative approach assumes you may not know the solution, so you iterate through different tactics to achieve the outcome.

6. Question Assumptions

Teams have to be willing to challenge the status quo and business as usual. They aren't afraid to test out a disruptive business model that will lead to big results, as compared to always playing it safe.

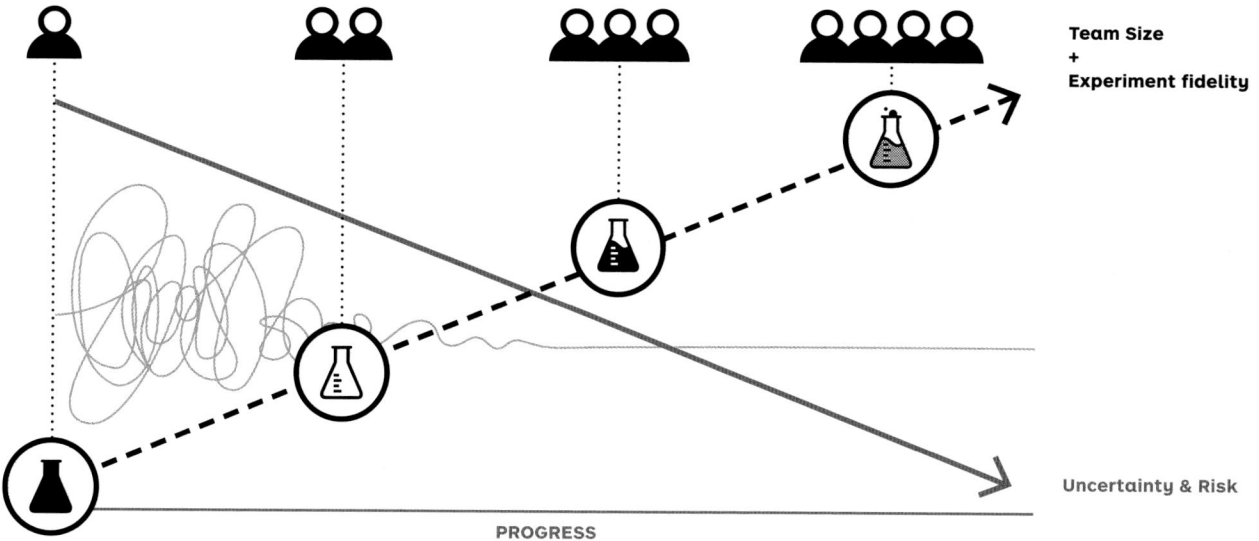

Team Size
+
Experiment fidelity

Uncertainty & Risk

PROGRESS

Growing the Team

You can begin this journey without a team, but as experiments get more complicated over time, chances are you'll be adding to your team. Expect to grow and evolve your team configuration over time, as you eventually find product/market fit, build the right way, and scale.

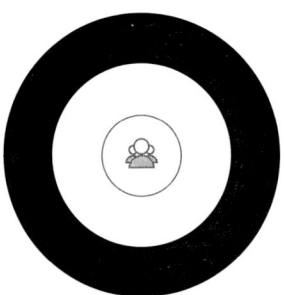

SYNOPSIS

Team Environment

How can you design an environment for your team to thrive?

Teams need a supportive environment to explore new business opportunities. They cannot be held to a standard where failure is not an option. Failure will occur, but failure isn't the goal. The goal is to learn faster than the competition and put that learning into action. Leaders need to intentionally design an environment where this can occur, otherwise even an ideal team configuration with the right behaviors will eventually stall out and give up.

The Team Needs to be...

Dedicated

Teams need an environment in which they can be dedicated to the work. Multitasking across several projects will silently kill any progress. Small teams who are dedicated to the work make more progress than large teams who are not dedicated.

Funded

It's unrealistic to expect these teams to function without a budget or funding. Experiments cost money. Incrementally fund the teams using a venture-capital style approach, based on the learnings they share during stakeholder reviews.

Autonomous

Teams need to be given space to own the work. Do not micromanage them to the extent where it slows down their progress. Instead, give them space to give an accounting of how they are making progress toward the goal.

The Company Needs to Provide...

Support

Leadership

Teams need an environment that has the right type of leadership support. A facilitative leadership style is ideal here because you do not know the solution. Lead with questions, not answers, and be mindful that the bottleneck is always at the top of the bottle.

Coaching

Teams need coaching, especially if this is their first journey together. Coaches, either internal or external, can help guide the teams when they are stuck trying to find the next experiment to run. Teams that have only used interviews and surveys can benefit from coaches who've seen a wide range of experiments.

Access

Customers

Teams need access to customers. The trend over the years has been to isolate teams from the customer, but in order to solve customer problems, this can no longer be the case. If teams keep getting pushback on customer access, they'll eventually just guess and build it anyway.

Resources

Teams need access to resources in order to be successful. Constraints are good, but starving a team will not yield results. They need enough resources to make progress and generate evidence. Resources can be physical or digital in nature, depending on the new business idea.

Direction

Strategy

Teams need a direction and strategy, or it'll be very difficult to make informed pivot, persevere, or kill decisions on the new business idea. Without a clear coherent strategy, you'll mistake being busy with making progress.

Guidance

Teams need constraints to focus their experimentation. Whether it's an adjacent market or creating a new one, to unlock new revenue teams need direction on where they will play.

KPIs

Teams need key performance indicators (KPIs) to help everyone understand whether they are making progress toward a goal. Without signposts along the way, it may be challenging to know if you should invest in the new business.

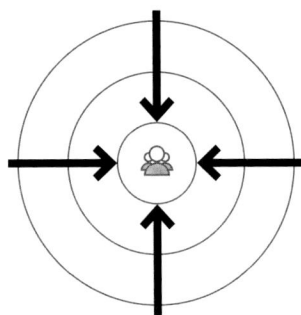

Team Alignment

How can you ensure your team members are aligned?

Teams often lack a shared goal, context, and language when being formed. This can be devastating later on, if not resolved during the team formation and kickoff.

   The Team Alignment Map, created by Stefano Mastrogiacomo, is a visual tool that allows participants to prepare for action: hold more productive meetings and structure the content of their conversations. It can help teams have more productive kickoffs, with better engagement and increased business success.

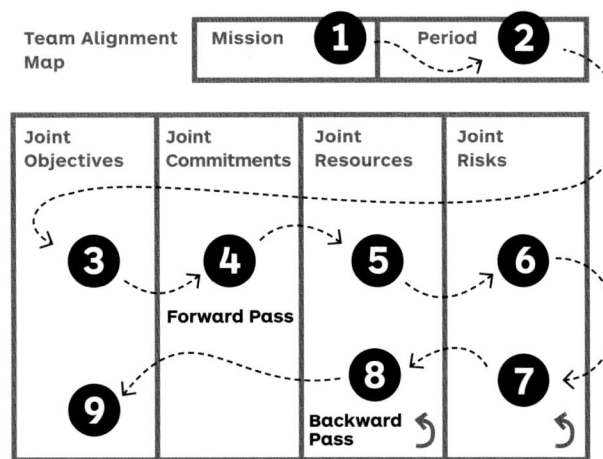

Each building block illustrates essential information to be discussed with your team. Identifying perception gaps early on can prevent you from being misaligned without even knowing it.

1. Define the mission.

2. Define the time box for the agreement.

3. Create joint team objectives.
   Joint Objectives
   What do we intend to achieve together?

4. Identify commitment levels for team members.
   Joint Commitments
   Who does what?

5. Document joint resources needed to succeed.
   Joint Resources
   What resources do we need?

6. Write down the biggest risks that could arise.
   Joint Risks
   What can prevent us from succeeding?

7. Describe how to address the biggest risks by creating new objectives and commitments.

8. Describe how to address resource constraints.

9. Set joint dates and validate.

   To learn more about the Team Map visit www.teamalignment.co.

Team Alignment Map

Mission:

Period:

Joint Objectives

What do we intend to achieve together?

Joint Commitments

Who does what?

Joint Resources

What resources do we need?

Joint Risks

What can prevent us from succeeding?

DESIGNED BY: Stefano Mastrogiacomo

teamalignment.co

"Generating ideas
is not a problem."

———————

Rita McGrath
Professor of Management
Columbia Business School

SECTION 1 — DESIGN

1.2 — SHAPE THE IDEA

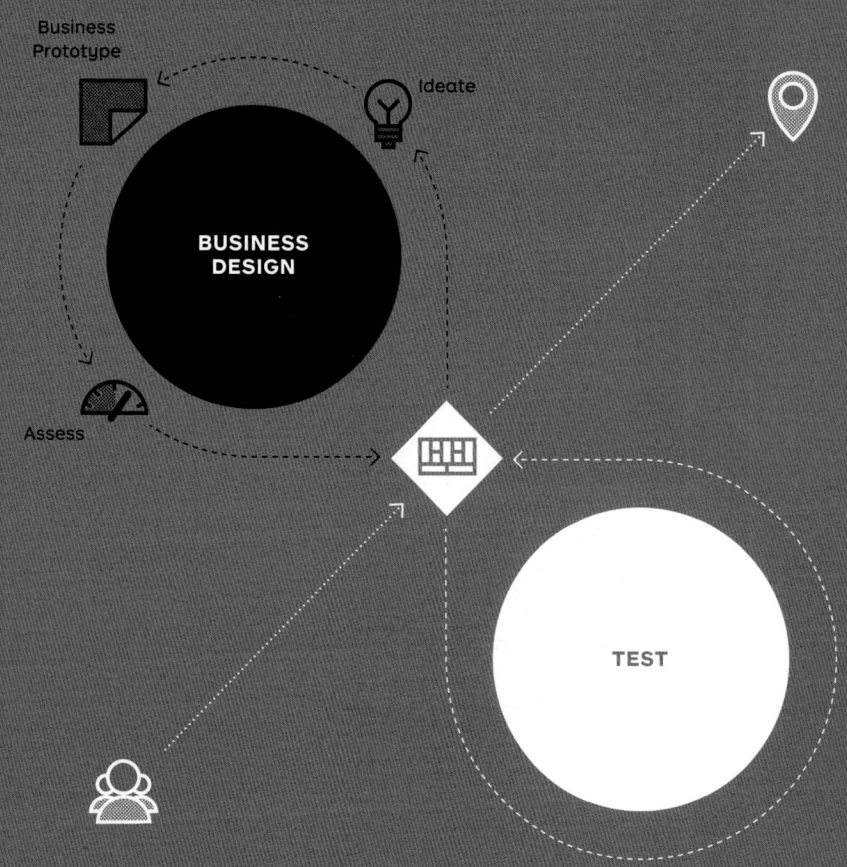

Business
Prototype

Ideate

**BUSINESS
DESIGN**

Assess

TEST

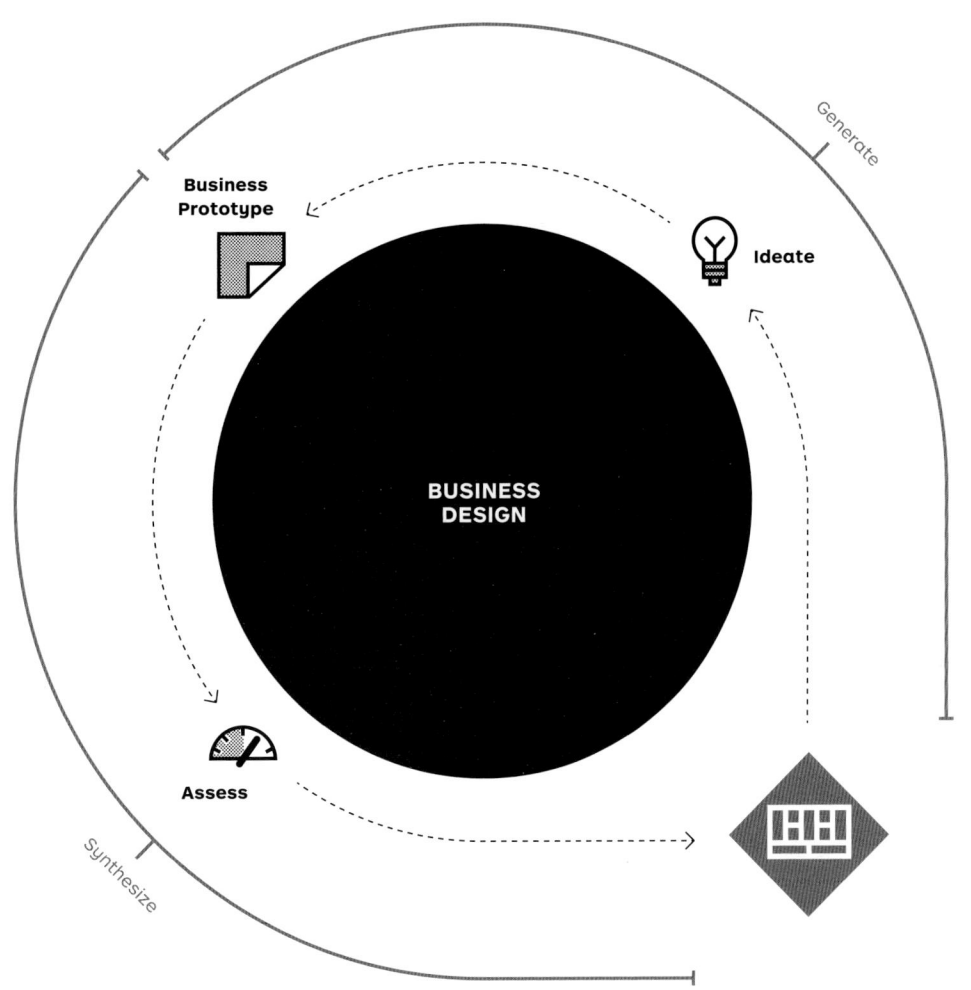

Business Design

In the design loop you shape and reshape your business idea to turn it into the best possible value proposition and business model. Your first iterations are based on your intuition and starting point (product idea, technology, market opportunity, etc.). Subsequent iterations are based on evidence and insights from the testing loop.

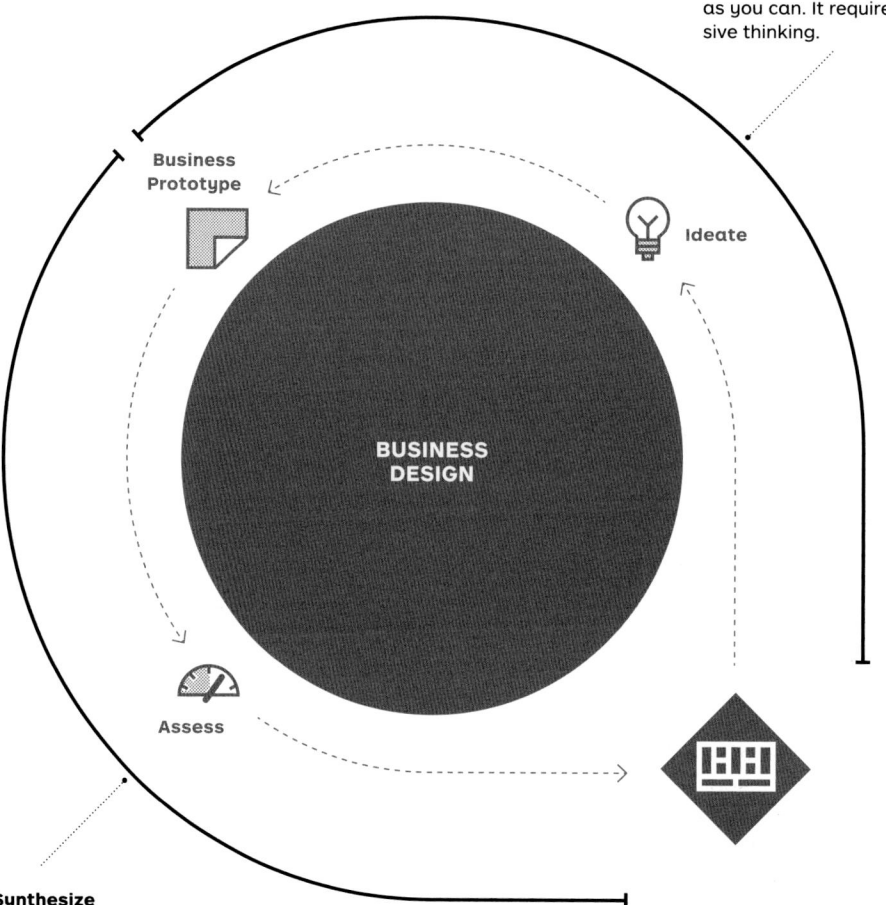

Generate

The first phase of the design loop is about generating as many possibilities and ideas as you can. It requires expansive thinking.

Business Prototype

Ideate

BUSINESS DESIGN

Assess

Synthesize

The second phase of the design loop is about synthesizing possibilities and narrowing the options down to the most promising opportunity.

The design loop has three steps.

1. **Ideate**
   In this first step you try to come up with as many alternative ways as possible to use your initial intuition or insights from testing to turn your idea into a strong business. Don't fall in love with your first ideas.

2. **Business Prototype**
   In this second step you narrow down the alternatives from ideation with business prototypes. When you start out you might use rough prototypes like napkin sketches. Subsequently, use the Value Proposition Canvas and Business Model Canvas to make your ideas clear and tangible. In this book we use these two tools to break ideas into smaller testable chunks. You will constantly improve your business prototypes with insights from testing in future iterations.

3. **Assess**
   In this last step of the design loop you assess the design of your business proto-types. You ask questions like "Is this the best way to address our customers' jobs, pains, and gains?," or, "Is this the best way to monetize our idea?," or, "Does this best take into account what we have learned from testing?" Once you are satisfied with the design of your business prototypes you start testing in the field or go back to testing, if you are working on subsequent iterations.

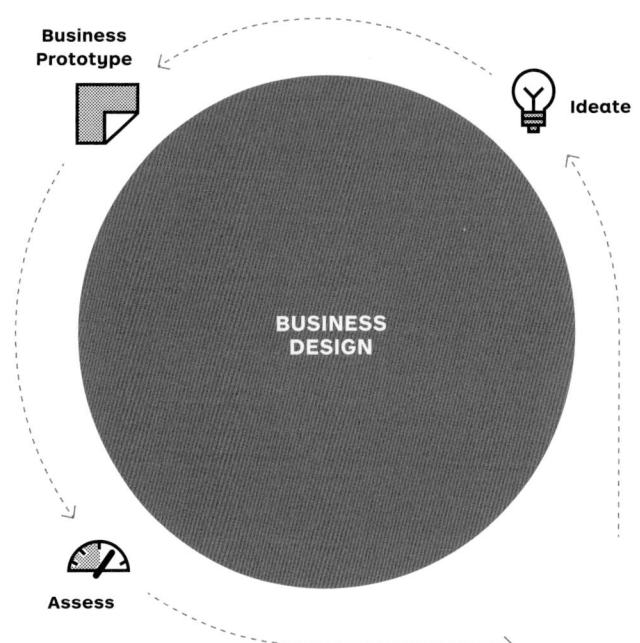

Business Prototype

Ideate

BUSINESS DESIGN

Assess

Caveat

This book focuses on Testing Business Ideas and provides you with a library of experiments to test your ideas and business prototypes. If you want to learn more about business design, we suggest you read *Business Model Generation* (Wiley, 2010) and *Value Proposition Design* (Wiley, 2014) or download the free online material.

SYNOPSIS

The Business Model Canvas

You don't have to be a master of the Business Model Canvas to use this book, but you can use it to shape ideas into a business model so you can define, test, and manage risk. In this book, we use the Business Model Canvas to define the desirability, feasibility, and viability of an idea. If you'd like to go deeper than the synopsis of the Business Model Canvas, we recommend reading *Business Model Generation* or go online to learn more.

Customer Segments

Describe the different groups of people or organizations you aim to reach and serve.

Value Propositions

Describe the bundle of products and services that create value for a specific customer segment.

Channels

Describe how a company communicates with and reaches its customer segments to deliver a value proposition.

Customer Relationships

Describe the types of relationships a company establishes with specific customer segments.

Revenue Streams

Describe the cash a company generates from each customer segment.

Key Resources

Describe the most important assets required to make a business model work.

Key Activities

Describe the most important things a company must do to make its business model work.

Key Partners

Describe the network of suppliers and partners that make the business model work.

Cost Structure

Describe all costs incurred to operate a business model.

To learn more about the Business Model Canvas visit strategyzer.com/books/business-model-generation.

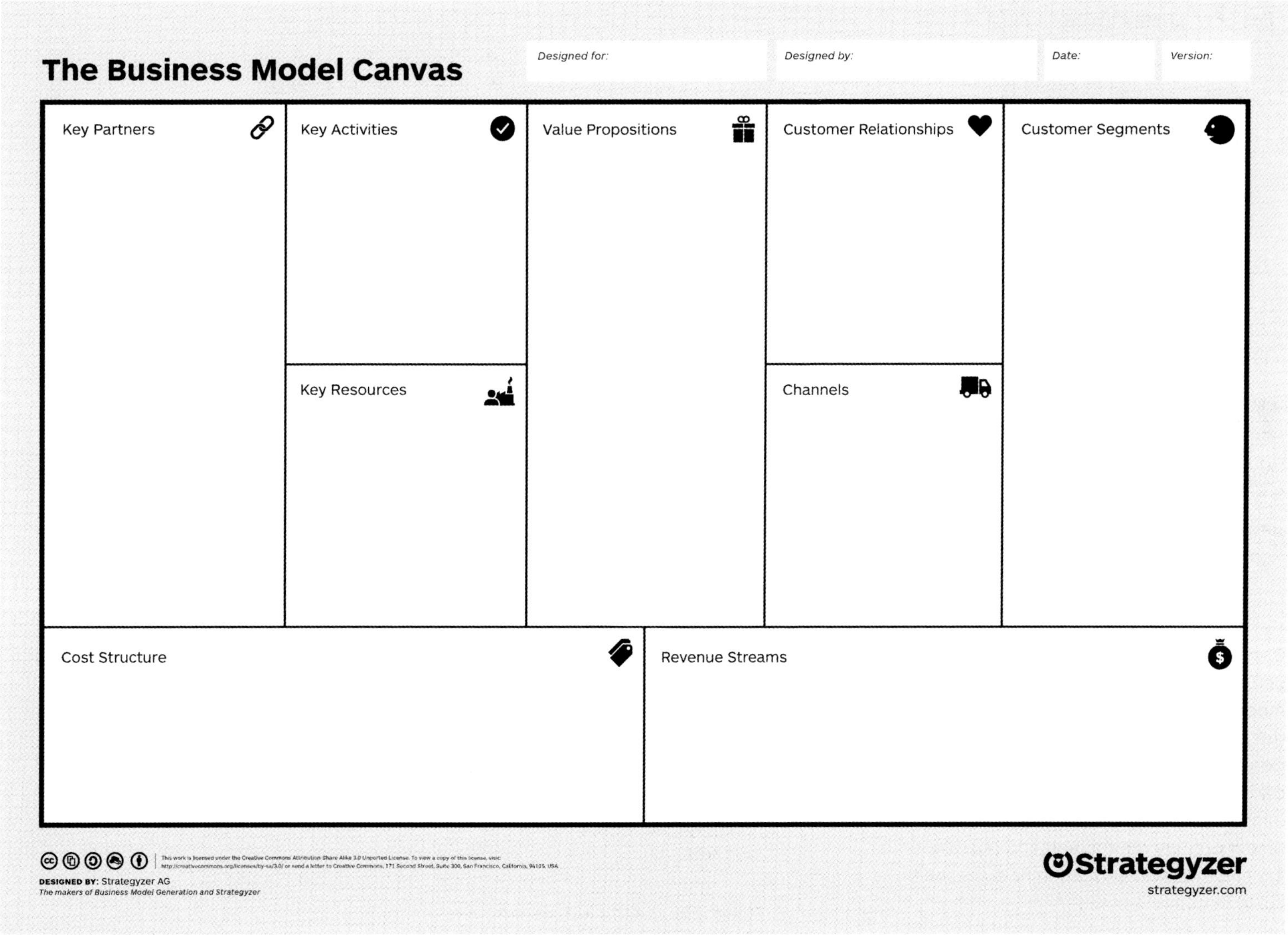

The Business Model Canvas
Designed for:
Designed by:
Date:
Version:
Key Partners
Key Activities
Key Resources
Value Propositions
Customer Relationships
Channels
Customer Segments
Cost Structure
Revenue Streams
This work is licensed under the Creative Commons Attribution Share Alike 3.0 Unported License. To view a copy of this license, visit: http://creativecommons.org/licenses/by-sa/3.0/ or send a letter to Creative Commons, 171 Second Street, Suite 300, San Francisco, California, 94105, USA.
DESIGNED BY: Strategyzer AG
The makers of Business Model Generation and Strategyzer
Strategyzer
strategyzer.com

SYNOPSIS

The Value Proposition Canvas

Much like the Business Model Canvas, the same goes for the Value Proposition Canvas. You'll get value from this book without having a proficiency in using it, but we do reference it for framing your experimentation, especially with regard to understanding the customer and how your products and services create value. If you'd like to go deeper than the synopsis of the Value Proposition Canvas, we recommend reading *Value Proposition Design* or go online to learn more.

Value Map

Describes the features of a specific value proposition in your business model in a structured and detailed way.

Customer Profile

Describes a specific customer segment in your business in a structured and detailed way.

Products and Services

List the products and services your value proposition is built around.

Customer Jobs

Describe what customers are trying to get done in their work and in their lives.

Gain Creators

Describe how your products and services create customer gains.

Gains

Describe the outcomes customers want to achieve or the concrete benefits they are seeking.

Pain Relievers

Describe how your products and services alleviate customer pains.

Pains

Describe the bad outcomes, risk, and obstacles related to customer jobs.

To learn more about the Value Proposition Canvas visit strategyzer.com/books/value-proposition-design.

The Value Proposition Canvas

Value Proposition

Customer Segment

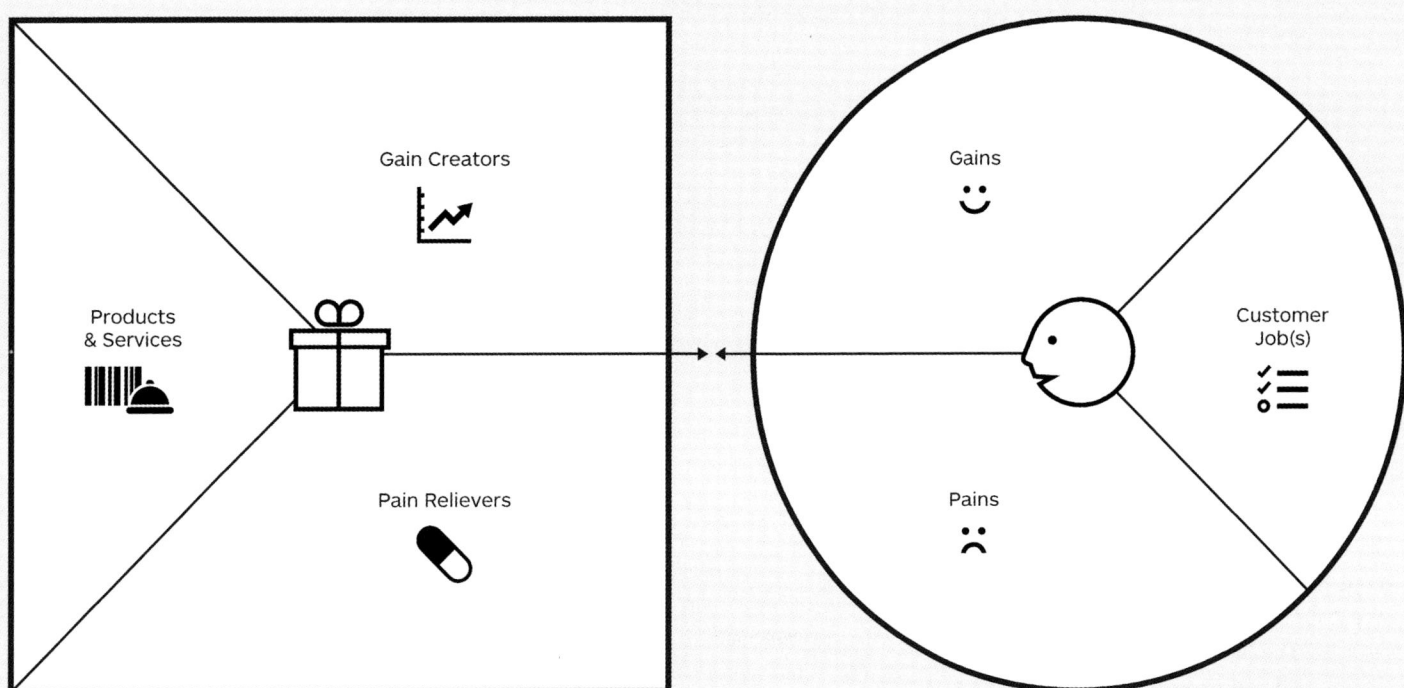

Gain Creators

Products & Services

Pain Relievers

Gains

Customer Job(s)

Pains

⊛Strategyzer

strategyzer.com

Te

st

"A founding vision for a startup
is similar to a scientific hypothesis."

————

Rashmi Sinha
Founder, Slideshare

SECTION 2 — TEST

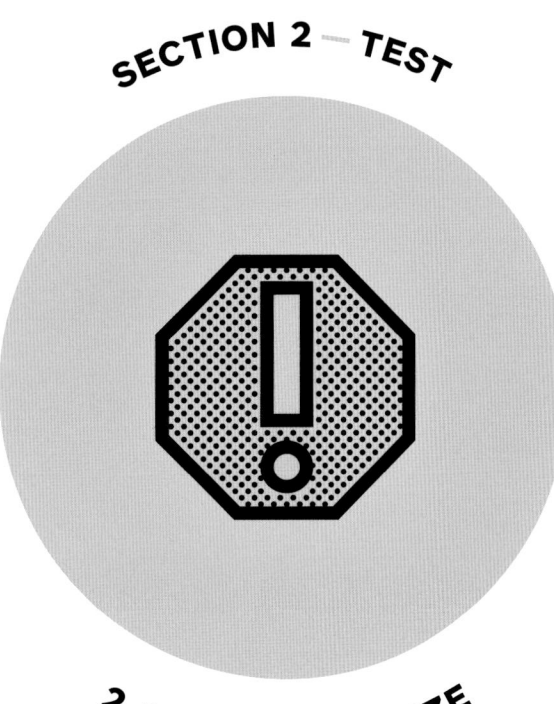

2.1 — HYPOTHESIZE

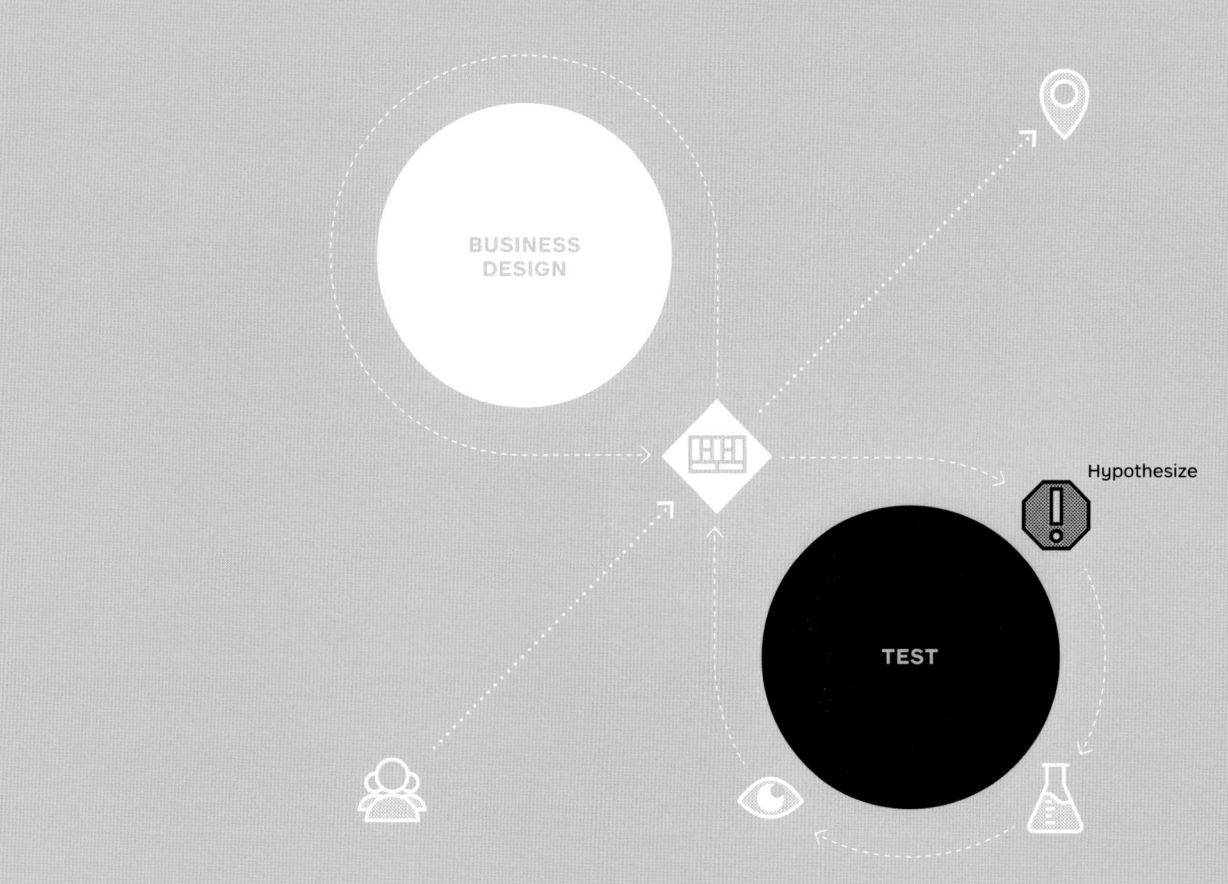

BUSINESS
DESIGN

TEST

Hypothesize

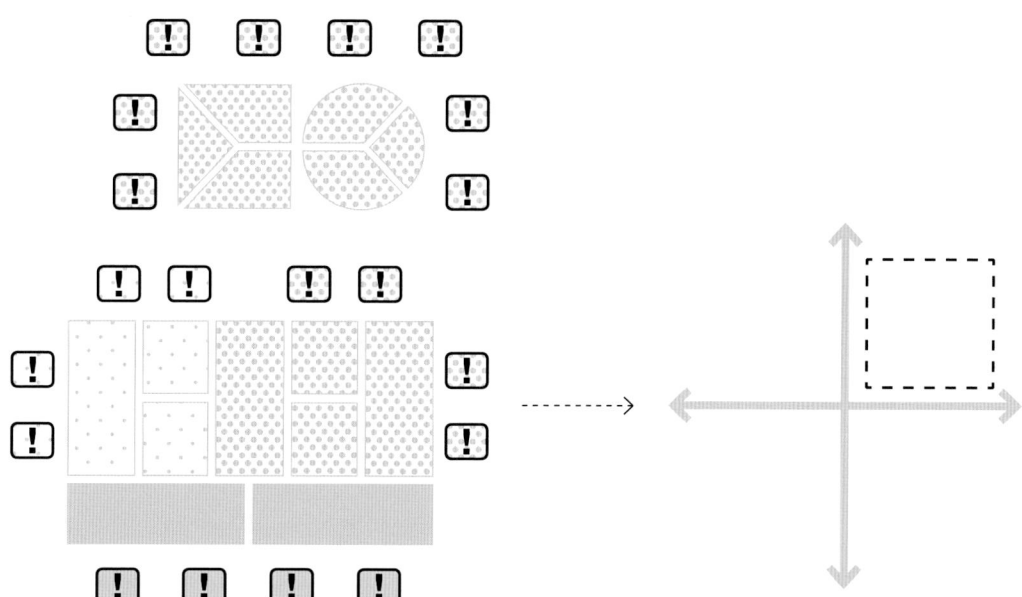

1. **Identify the Hypotheses Underlying Your Idea**
   To test a business idea you first have to make explicit all the risks that your idea won't work. You need to turn the assumptions underlying your idea into clear hypotheses that you can test.

2. **Prioritize Most Important Hypotheses**
   To identify the most important hypotheses to test first, you need to ask two questions. First, "What is the most important hypothesis that needs to be true for my idea to work?" Second, "For which hypotheses do I lack concrete evidence from the field?"

DEFINITION

Hypothesis

The hypothesis has its roots in ancient civilization. The English word "hypothesis" comes from the Greek word hypothesis *which means "to suppose." Some even refer to a hypothesis as an educated guess. Hypotheses are instruments you use to prove or refute your assumptions.*

For the purposes of Testing Business Ideas, we focus on your business hypothesis, which is defined as:

- an assumption that your value proposition, business model, or strategy builds on.
- what you need to learn about to understand if your business idea might work.

Creating a good business hypothesis

When creating hypotheses you believe to be true for your business idea, begin by writing the phrase "We believe that…"

"We believe that millennial parents will subscribe to monthly educational science projects for their kids."

Be mindful that if you create all of your hypotheses in the "We believe that…" format, you can fall into a confirmation bias trap. You'll be constantly trying to prove what you believe, instead of trying to refute it. In order to prevent this from occurring create a few hypotheses that try to disprove your assumptions.

"We believe that millennial parents won't subscribe to monthly educational science projects for their kids."

You can even test these competing hypotheses at the same time. This is especially helpful when team members cannot agree on which hypothesis to test.

Characteristics of a good hypothesis

A well-formed business hypothesis describes a testable, precise, and discrete thing you want to investigate. With that in mind, we can continue to refine and unpack our hypotheses about the science project subscription business.

	✕	✓
Testable Your hypothesis is testable when it can be shown true (validated) or false (invalidated), based on evidence (and guided by experience).	– We believe millennial parents prefer craft projects.	☐ We believe millennial parents prefer curated science projects that match their kids' education level.
Precise Your hypothesis is precise when you know what success looks like. Ideally, it describes the precise what, who, and when of your assumptions.	– We believe millennials will spend a lot on science projects.	☐ We believe millennial parents with kids ages 5–9 will pay $15 a month for curated science projects that match their kids' education level.
Discrete Your hypothesis is discrete when it describes only one distinct, testable, and precise thing you want to investigate.	– We believe we can buy and ship science project boxes at a profit.	☐ We believe we can purchase science project materials at wholesale for less than $3 a box. ☐ We believe we can ship science project materials domestically for less than $5 a box.

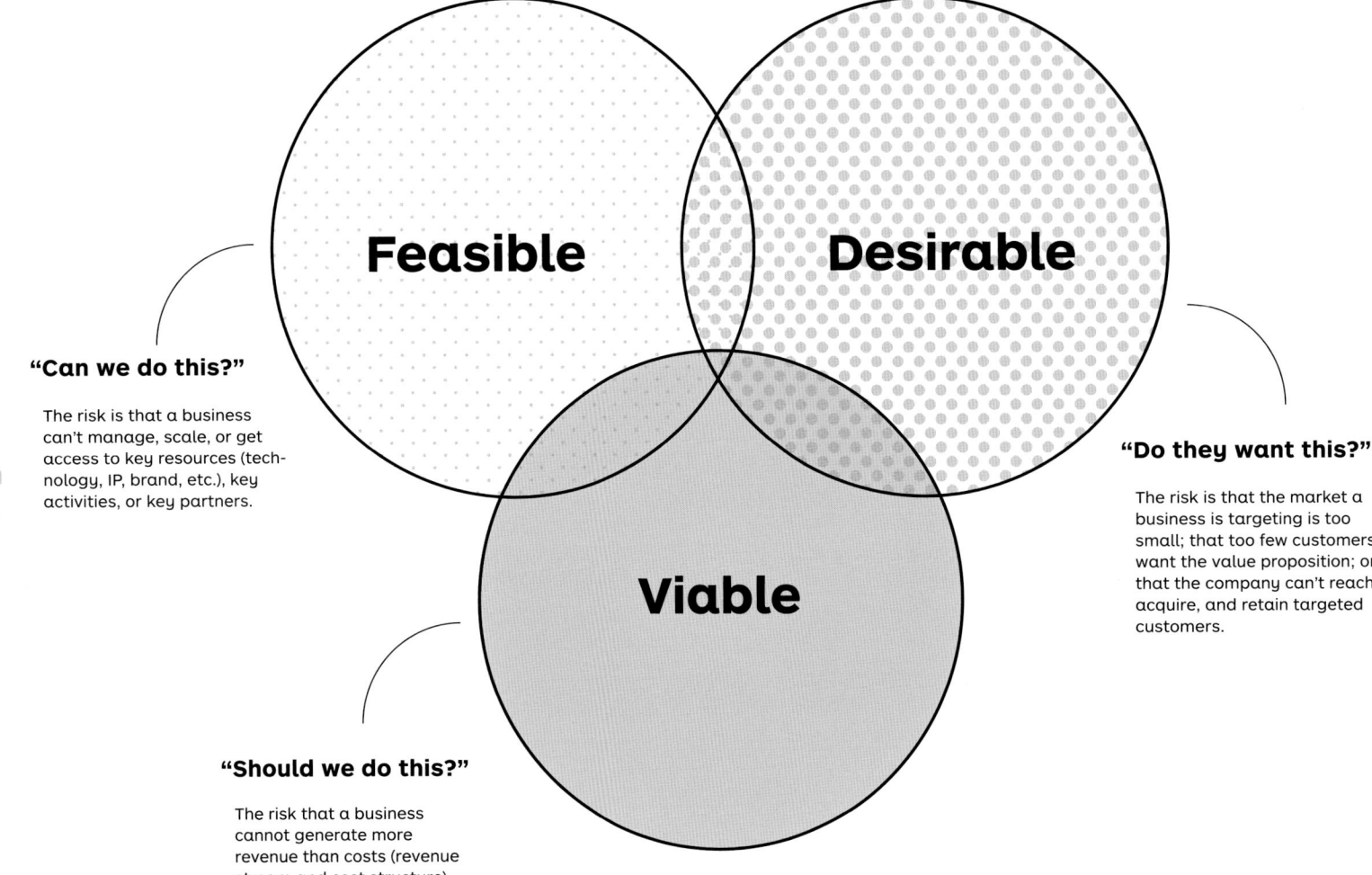

"Can we do this?"

The risk is that a business can't manage, scale, or get access to key resources (technology, IP, brand, etc.), key activities, or key partners.

"Do they want this?"

The risk is that the market a business is targeting is too small; that too few customers want the value proposition; or that the company can't reach, acquire, and retain targeted customers.

"Should we do this?"

The risk that a business cannot generate more revenue than costs (revenue stream and cost structure).

Types of Hypotheses

Adapted from Larry Keeley, Doblin Group and IDEO.

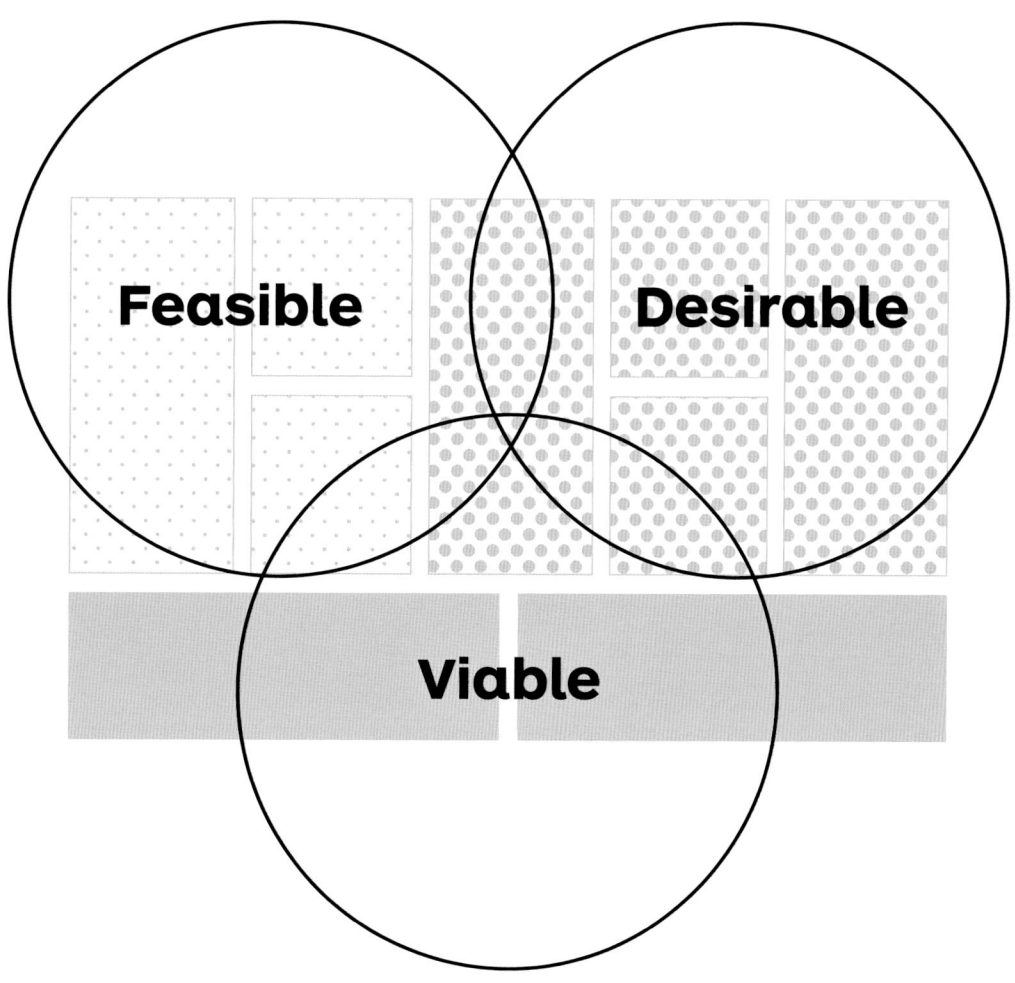

Types of Hypotheses on the Business Model Canvas

Desirability Hypotheses
Explore first

The Value Proposition Canvas contains market risk in both the Value Map and Customer Profile. Identify the desirability hypotheses you are making in:

The Business Model Canvas contains market risk in the value proposition, customer segment, channel, and customer relationship components. Identify the desirability hypotheses you are making in:

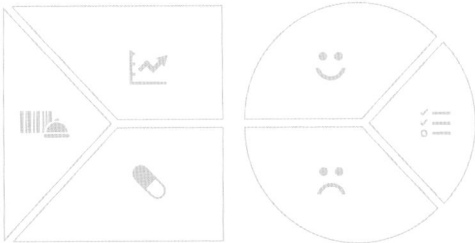

Customer Profile
We believe that we...

- are addressing jobs that really matter to customers.
- are focused on pains that really matter to customers.
- are focused on gains that really matter to customers.

Value Map
We believe...

- our products and services really solve high-value customer jobs.
- our products and services relieve top customer pains.
- our products and services create important customer gains.

Customer Segments
We believe...

- we are targeting the right customer segments.
- the segments we are targeting actually exist.
- the segments we are targeting are big enough.

Value Propositions
We believe...

- we have the right value propositions for the customer segments we are targeting.
- our value proposition is unique enough to replicate.

Channels
We believe...

- we have the right channels to reach and acquire our customers.
- we can master the channels to deliver value.

Customer Relationships
We believe...

- we can build the right relationships with customers.
- it is difficult for customers to switch to a competitor's product.
- we can retain customers.

Feasibility Hypotheses
Explore second

The Business Model Canvas contains infrastructure risk in the key partners, key activities, and key resources components. Identify the feasibility hypotheses you are making in:

Key Activities

We believe that we...

- can perform all activities (at scale) and at the right quality level that is required to build our business model.

Key Resources

We believe that we...

- can secure and manage all technologies and resources (at scale) that are required to build our business model, including intellectual property and human, financial, and other resources.

Key Partners

We believe that we...

- can create the partnerships required to build our business.

Viability Hypotheses
Explore third

The Business Model Canvas contains financial risk in the revenue stream and cost structure. Identify the viability hypotheses you are making in:

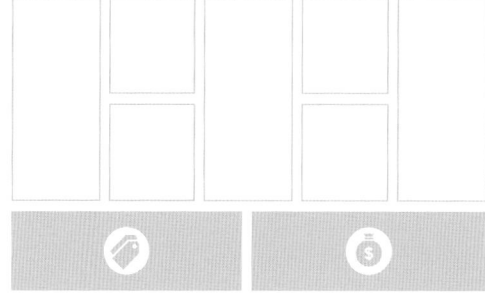

Revenue Streams

We believe that we...

- can get customers to pay a specific price for our value propositions.
- can generate sufficient revenues.

Cost Structure

We believe that we...

- can manage costs from our infrastructure and keep them under control.

Profit

We believe that we...

- can generate more revenues than costs in order to make a profit.

How to Facilitate

DEFINITION

Assumptions Mapping

A team exercise where desirability, viability, and feasibility hypotheses are made explicit and prioritized in terms of importance and evidence.

Every radically new idea, product, service, value proposition, business model, or strategy requires a leap of faith. If proven false, these important and yet unproven aspects of your idea can make or break your business. The Assumptions Mapping exercise is designed to help you make all risks explicit in the form of hypotheses, so you can prioritize them and focus your near-term experimentation.

Adapted from Gothelf & Seiden, Lean UX

Core team

The core team consists of individuals who are going to be dedicated to making this new business endeavor a success. They are cross-functional. This means they have product, design, and technology skills needed to ship and learn rapidly in the market with real customers. At a minimum, the core team needs to be present when mapping out the assumptions from your Business Model Canvas.

Supporting team

The supporting team consists of individuals who are not necessarily dedicated to the business endeavor but who are needed for it to be a success. People from legal, safety, compliance, marketing, and user research will be required for testing assumptions where the core team lacks the domain knowledge and know-how.

Without a strong supporting team, the core members may lack evidence and make uninformed decisions about what's important.

Identify Hypotheses
Step 1

Use a sticky note to write down each:

- desirability hypothesis and put it on your canvases.
- feasibility hypothesis and put it on your canvases.
- viability hypothesis and put it on your canvases.

Best Practices

- Use different color sticky notes for desirability, feasibility, and viability hypotheses.
- Your hypotheses should be as specific as possible, to the best of your knowledge, based on what you know today.
- Every hypothesis should be a single sticky note. Don't use bullet points; that makes it easier to prioritize your hypotheses.
- Keep your hypotheses short and precise. No blah blah blah.
- Discuss and agree as a team when writing.

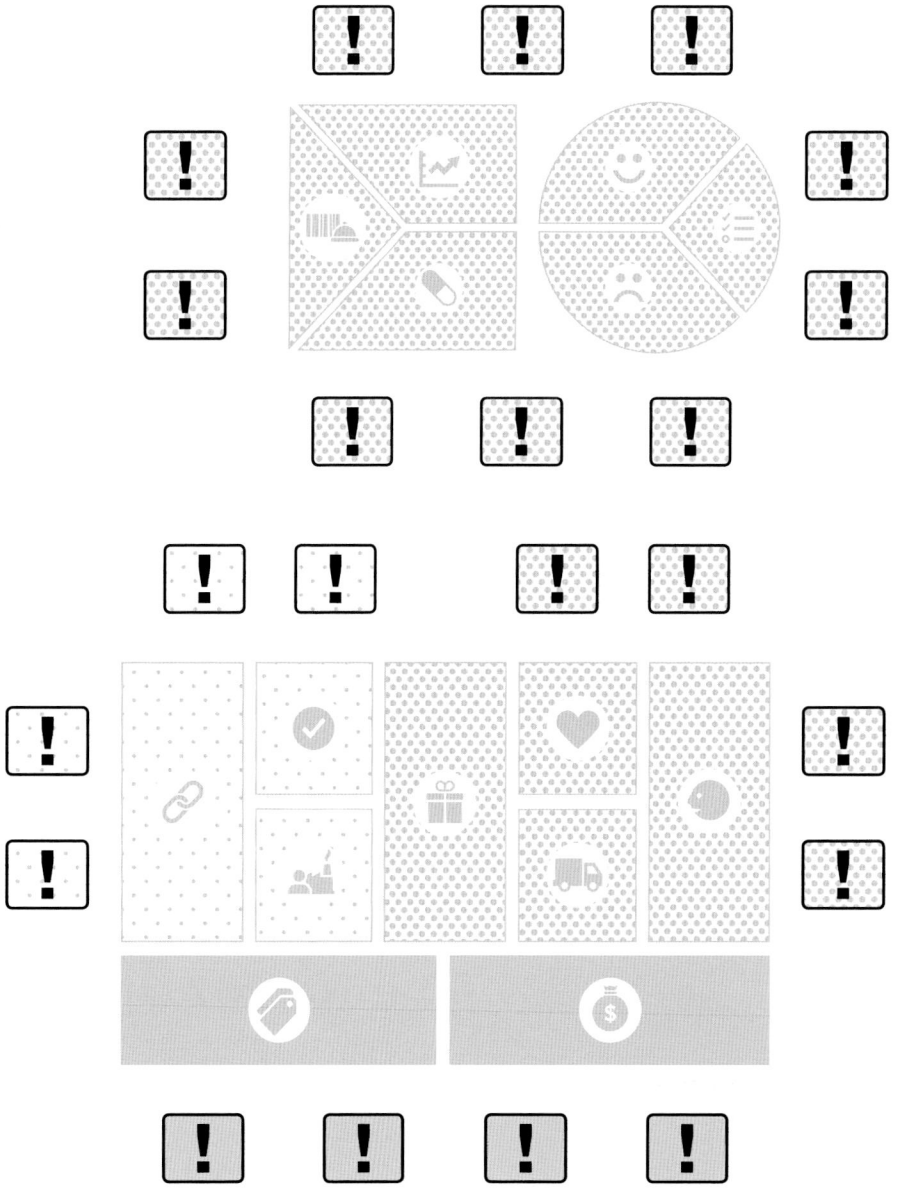

Prioritize Hypotheses
Step 2

Use the Assumptions Map to prioritize all your hypotheses in terms of importance and existence or absence of evidence that supports different types of hypotheses.

x-Axis: Evidence
On the x-axis you place all your hypotheses positioned to show how much evidence you have or don't have to support or refute a specific hypothesis. You place a hypothesis on the left if you are able to produce relevant, observable, and recent evidence to support a hypothesis. You place a hypothesis on the right if you do not have evidence and therefore will need to generate it.

y-Axis: Importance
On the y-axis you place all your hypotheses in terms of importance. Position a hypothesis at the top if it is absolutely critical for your business idea to succeed. In other words, if that hypothesis is proven wrong, your business idea will fail and all other hypotheses become irrelevant. You place a hypothesis at the bottom if it is not one of the first things you'd go out and test.

Top Left

Share

Check the top left quadrant against your evidence and share it with the team. Do these hypotheses really have observable evidence to back them up? Challenge the evidence to make sure it's good enough. Keep track of these hypotheses in your plan going forward.

Top Right

Experiment

Focus on the top right quadrant to identify which hypotheses to test first. This defines your near-term experimentation. Create experiments to address these high-risk themes in your business.

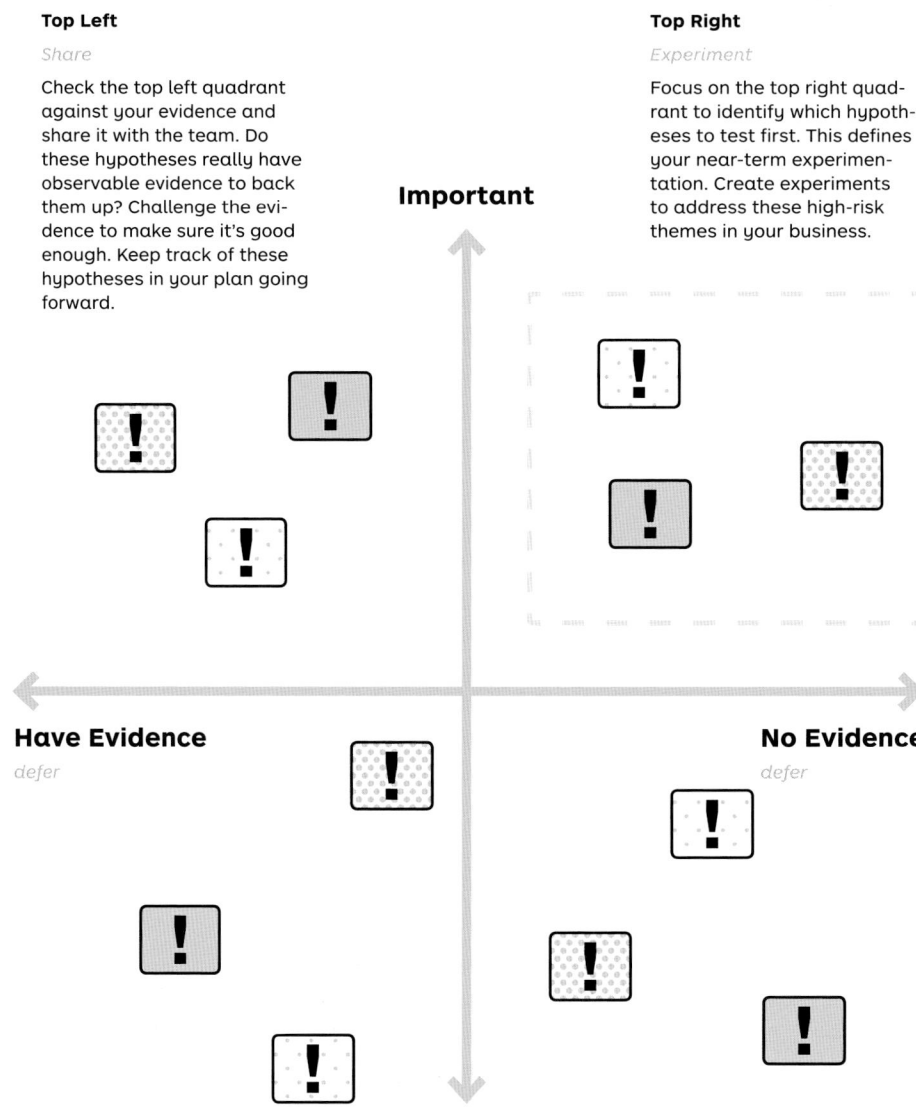

TEST

Identify and Prioritize Riskiest Hypotheses
Step 3

For the purposes of this book, the major focus will be on how to test the top right quadrant of your Assumptions Map: experiments with important hypotheses and with light evidence. These assumptions, if proven false, will cause your business to fail.

Prioritize Desirability Hypotheses
As a team, pull over each desirability hypothesis and place it on the Assumptions Map.

Prioritize Feasibility Hypotheses
Next, pull over each feasibility hypothesis and place it on the Assumptions Map.

Prioritize Viability Hypotheses
Then pull over each viability hypothesis and place it on the Assumptions Map.

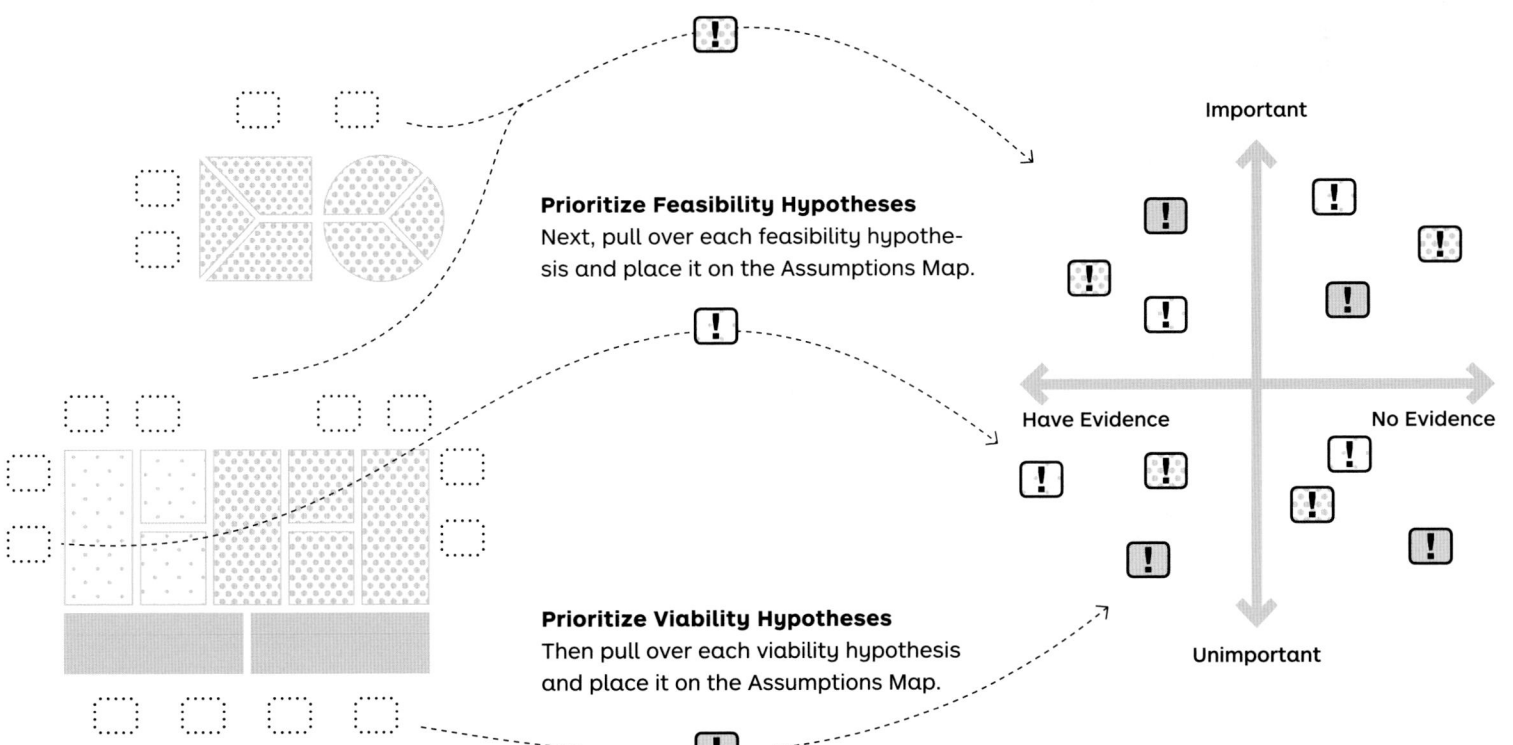

HYPOTHESIZE

"It doesn't matter how beautiful
your theory is, it doesn't matter
how smart you are. If it doesn't
agree with experiment, it's wrong."
———————
Richard Feynman
American theoretical physicist

SECTION 2 — TEST

2.2 — EXPERIMENT

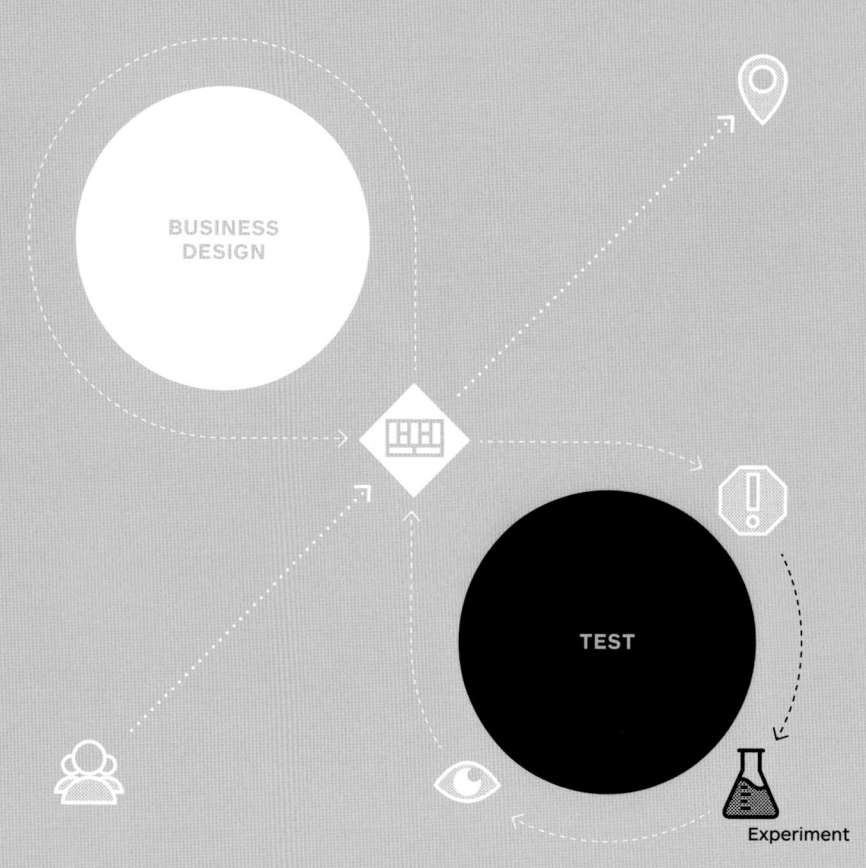

BUSINESS
DESIGN

TEST

Experiment

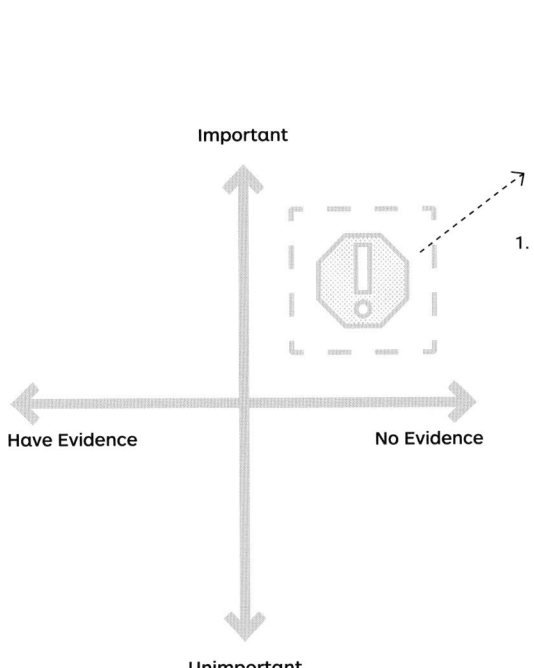

Important

Have Evidence   No Evidence

Unimportant

1. Design Experiment

To get started with testing your business idea, you turn your most important hypotheses into experiments. You should start with cheap and fast experiments to learn quickly. Every experiment will reduce the risk that you'll spend time, energy, and money on ideas that won't work.

2. Run Experiment

Every experiment has a specific run time to generate sufficient evidence that you can learn from. Make sure you run your experiments almost like a scientist, so that your evidence is clean and not misleading.

Experiment

Experiments are the means to reduce the risk and uncertainty of your business idea.

The experiment is at the core of scientific method. Like the hypothesis, it can be traced back through history to everything from how the vision works with the eye to measuring time.

What has remained consistent over time is that the scientific method is a valuable method for generating insights.

Children naturally experiment and iterate their way through problems. Once they begin to progress through traditional schooling, experimentation gradually becomes less and less of a practice outside of science class. The way students are graded, judged, and tested means they have to find the single right answer. In life, as it is in business, there is rarely a single right answer. So over time people optimize for being right, instead of making progress, because they're accustomed to being penalized for being wrong.

It's no surprise that children raised in this style of educational system become adults who often struggle with the idea of being wrong. The culture of rewarding who is right and penalizing who is wrong extends into their businesses. They've been conditioned to look for that one right answer.

As you read this book and learn how to test your business ideas, you will find there is often not one path forward, but many.

As you experiment, think back to what it felt like to be in kindergarten and preschool: when you were allowed to try to fit the square peg into the round hole. Experimentation is about structured creativity. Tap into that energy within yourself and with your teams.

For the purposes of Testing Business Ideas, the focus is on business experiments, which:

- are procedures to reduce the risk and uncertainty of a business idea.
- produce weak or strong evidence that supports or refutes a hypothesis.
- can be fast/slow and cheap/expensive to conduct.

What is a good experiment?

A good experiment is precise enough so that team members can replicate it and generate usable and comparable data.

- Defines the "who" precisely (test subject)
- Defines the "where" precisely (test context)
- Defines the "what" precisely (test elements)

What are the components of an experiment?

A well-formed business experiment is made up of four components:

1. Hypothesis
The most critical hypothesis from the top right quadrant of your Assumptions Map.

2. Experiment
The description of the experiment you will run to support or refute the hypothesis.

3. Metrics
The data you will measure as part of the experiment.

4. Criteria
The success criteria for your experiment metrics.

Call-to-Action Experiment

A specific type of experiment that prompts a test subject to perform an observable action. Used in an experiment in order to test one or more hypotheses.

Create multiple experiments for your hypothesis

We've yet to work with a team who created just one experiment, had a major break-through, and then went on to create a multibillion dollar business from it. In reality, it takes a series of experiments to generate the possibility of a successful business. Use the Test Cards and the experiment library to create well-formed experiments to test your business hypotheses.

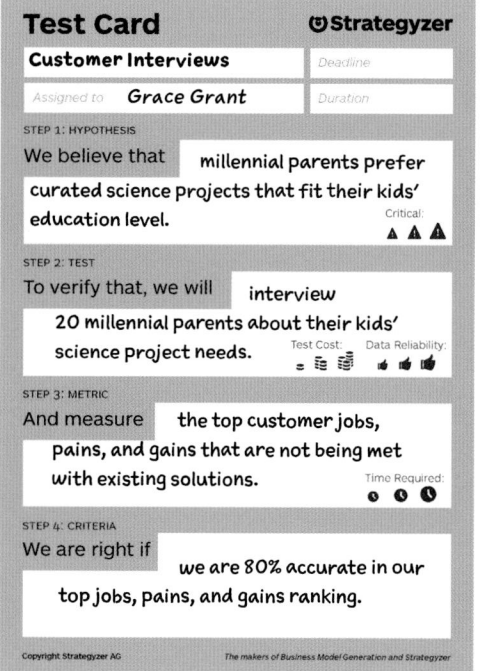

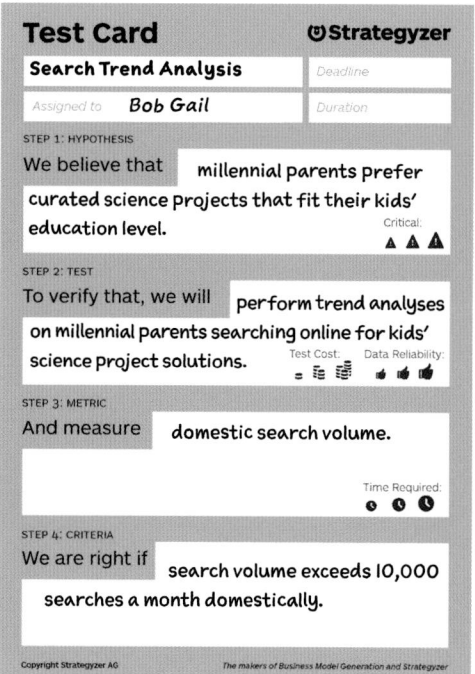

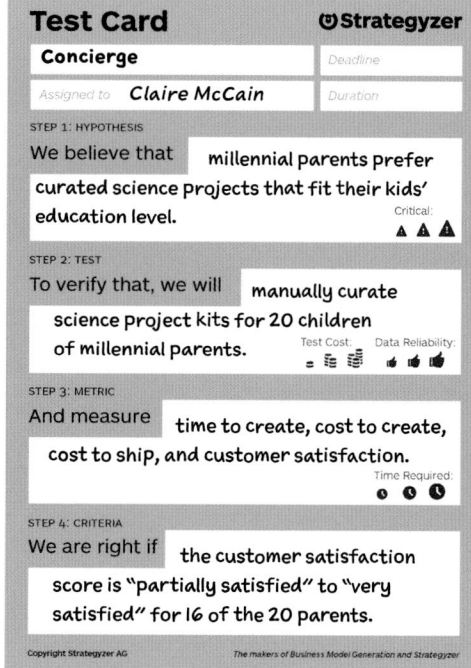

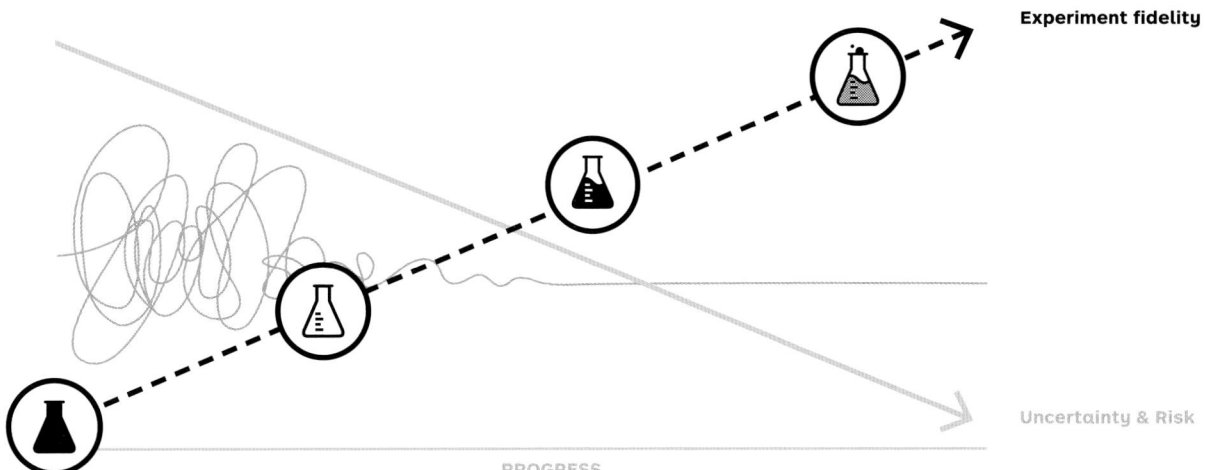

Experiment fidelity

Uncertainty & Risk

PROGRESS

Experiments Reduce the Risk of Uncertainty

As you read through *Testing Business Ideas*, you'll begin to understand how experiments can help you rapidly reduce the risk of uncertainty. Instead of building internally for long periods in a customer-free zone, you'll learn how to incrementally reduce your risk over time. This allows you to build at the right time and at the right fidelity.

"Anyone who isn't embarrassed
by who they were last year
probably isn't learning enough."
————
Alain de Botton
Philosopher

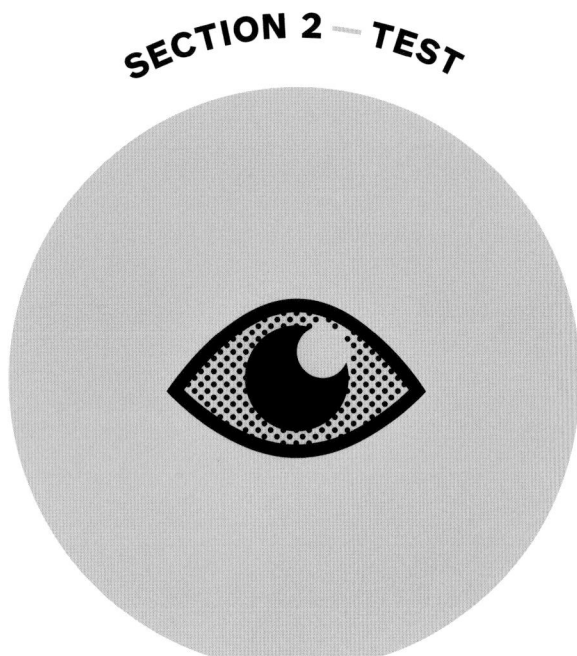

SECTION 2 — TEST

2.3 — LEARN

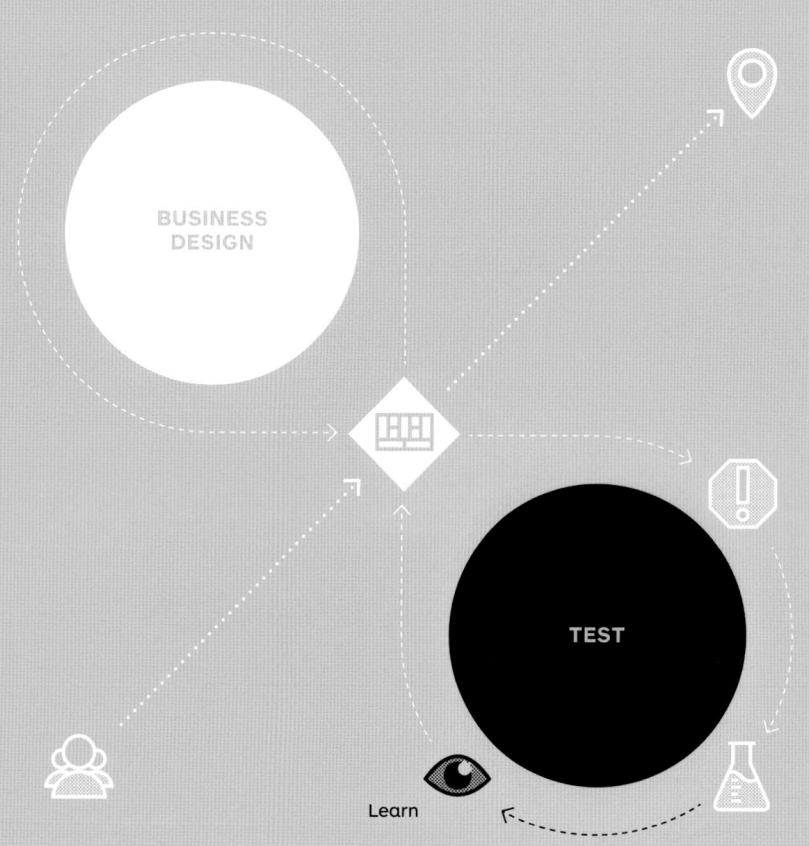

BUSINESS
DESIGN

TEST

Learn

Test Card ⦿ **Strategyzer**

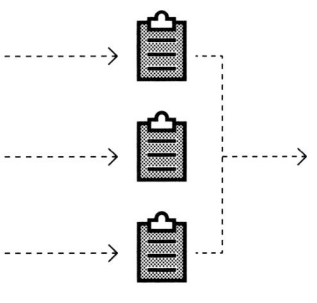

Learning Card ⦿ **Strategyzer**

1. **Analyze the Evidence**

   Evidence does not speak on its own. Gather the evidence you have from different experiments for a specific hypothesis and analyze it. Make sure you distinguish between strong and weak evidence.

2. **Gain Insights**

   Insights are key learnings you get from analyzing the data. They allow you to support or refute the hypotheses you've been testing. Your insights help you understand how likely your idea is to work.

Strength of Evidence

The strength of a piece of evidence determines how reliably the evidence helps support or refute a hypothesis. You can evaluate the strength of evidence by checking four areas. Is the evidence based on...

Evidence

What is Evidence?

Evidence is what you use to support or refute the hypotheses underlying your business idea. It is data that you get from research or generate from business experiments. Evidence can come in many different forms, ranging from weak to strong evidence.

For the purposes of Testing Business Ideas, we focus on your business experiment evidence which we define as:

- data generated from an experiment or collected in the field.
- facts that support or refute a hypothesis.
- possibly of different nature (e.g., quotes, behaviors, conversion rates, orders, purchases...); can be weak/strong.

52

TEST

Weak Evidence		Strong(er) Evidence
1. **Opinions (beliefs)** When people say things like "I would...," "I think _____ is important," "I believe...," or "I like..."		**Facts (events)** When people say things like "Last week I _____," "In that situation I usually _____," or "I spent _____ on."
2. **What people say** What people say in an interview or survey is not necessarily what they do in real life or will do in the future.		**What people do** Observable behavior is generally a good predictor of how people act and what people might do in the future.
3. **Lab settings** When people are aware that you are testing something, they may behave differently than in a real world setting.		**Real world settings** The most reliable predictor of future behavior is what you observe people doing when they are not aware they are being tested.
4. **Small investments** Signing up by email to be informed about an upcoming product release is a small investment and relatively weak evidence of interest.		**Large investments** Pre-purchasing a product or putting one's professional reputation on the line is an important investment and strong evidence of real interest.

Different experiments create different evidence

Customer Interviews

Test Card — ⊌ Strategyzer

Customer Interviews *Deadline*
Assigned to **Grace Grant** *Duration*

STEP 1: HYPOTHESIS
We believe that **millennial parents prefer curated science projects that fit their kids' education level.**
Critical: ▲ ▲ ▲

STEP 2: TEST
To verify that, we will **interview 20 millennial parents about their kids' science project needs.**
Test Cost: Data Reliability:

STEP 3: METRIC
And measure **the top customer jobs, pains, and gains that are not being met with existing solutions.**
Time Required:

STEP 4: CRITERIA
We are right if **we are 80% accurate in our top jobs, pains, and gains ranking.**

Copyright Strategyzer AG   The makers of Business Model Generation and Strategyzer

Transcripts & Quotes

 ● ○ ○ ○ ○
EVIDENCE STRENGTH

"We want our child to have a unique science fair project that stands out, not the same one as every other kid."

"It has to be appropriate for her grade level. The one we tried stated 2nd grade but was way too difficult."

"Many of the kits we find for free online have missing or confusing instructions."

"I'd pay to have a science project kit with everything we need all in a box."

Search Trend Analysis

Test Card — ⊌ Strategyzer

Search Trend Analysis *Deadline*
Assigned to **Bob Gail** *Duration*

STEP 1: HYPOTHESIS
We believe that **millennial parents prefer curated science projects that fit their kids' education level.**
Critical: ▲ ▲ ▲

STEP 2: TEST
To verify that, we will **perform trend analyses on millennial parents searching online for kids' science project solutions.**
Test Cost: Data Reliability:

STEP 3: METRIC
And measure **domestic search volume.**
Time Required:

STEP 4: CRITERIA
We are right if **search volume exceeds 10,000 searches a month domestically.**

Copyright Strategyzer AG   The makers of Business Model Generation and Strategyzer

Search Volume Data

 ● ● ● ○ ○
EVIDENCE STRENGTH

Month of February:

"science fair ideas" had 5k–10k searches.

"kindergarten science fair ideas" had 10k–15k searches.

"first grade science fair ideas" had 1k–5k searches.

"second grade science fair ideas" had less than 1k searches.

"third grade science fair ideas" had less than 1k searches.

Concierge

Test Card — ⊌ Strategyzer

Concierge *Deadline*
Assigned to **Claire McCain** *Duration*

STEP 1: HYPOTHESIS
We believe that **millennial parents prefer curated science projects that fit their kids' education level.**
Critical: ▲ ▲ ▲

STEP 2: TEST
To verify that, we will **manually curate science project kits for 20 children of millennial parents.**
Test Cost: Data Reliability:

STEP 3: METRIC
And measure **time to create, cost to create, cost to ship, and customer satisfaction.**
Time Required:

STEP 4: CRITERIA
We are right if **the customer satisfaction score is "partially satisfied" to "very satisfied" for 16 of the 20 parents.**

Copyright Strategyzer AG   The makers of Business Model Generation and Strategyzer

Concierge Data

 ● ● ● ● ●
EVIDENCE STRENGTH

Time to Create = 2 hours for each kit

Cost to Create = $10–$15

Cost to Ship = $5–$8

Parent Customer Satisfaction Score = Partially Satisfied

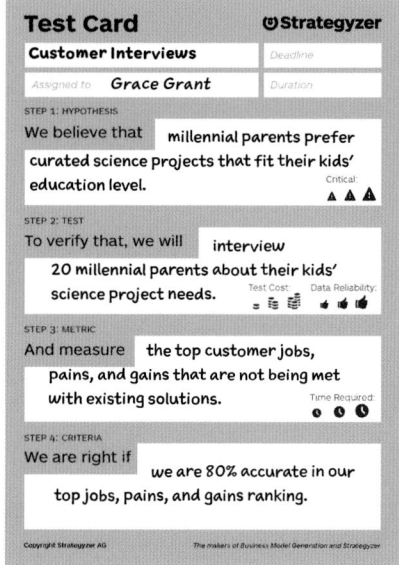

DEFINITION

Insights

What are insights?

There is a difference between looking at something and looking for something. Evidence on its own will not help you reduce risk in your business idea; therefore, we recommend gleaning insights from the evidence your experiments generate.

For the purposes of Testing Business Ideas, business insights are defined as:

- what you learn from studying the evidence.
- learning related to the validity of a hypothesis and potential discovery of new directions.
- the foundation to make informed business decisions and take action.

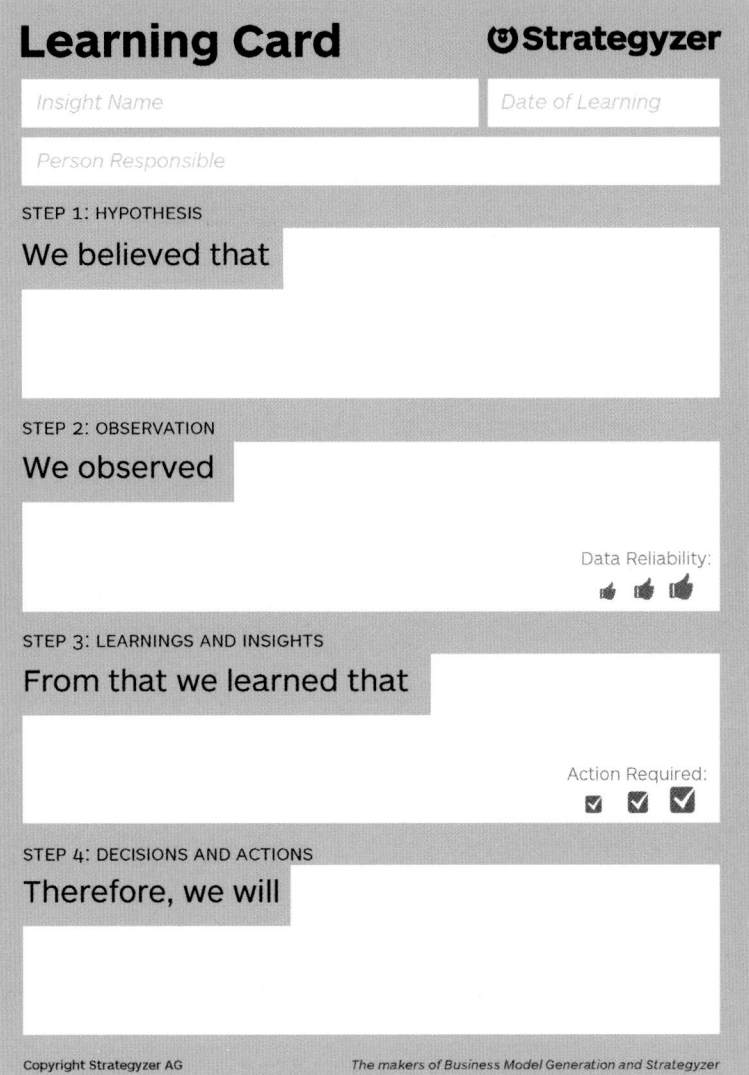

Learning Card   ⓦ **Strategyzer**

| Insight Name | Date of Learning |

| Person Responsible |

STEP 1: HYPOTHESIS

We believed that

STEP 2: OBSERVATION

We observed

Data Reliability:
👍 👍 👍

STEP 3: LEARNINGS AND INSIGHTS

From that we learned that

Action Required:
☑ ☑ ☑

STEP 4: DECISIONS AND ACTIONS

Therefore, we will

Copyright Strategyzer AG   *The makers of Business Model Generation and Strategyzer*

Customer Interviews

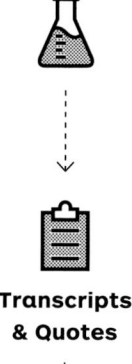

Test Card ⓦStrategyzer

→ **Transcripts & Quotes**

Search Trend Analysis

Test Card ⓦStrategyzer

→ **Search Volume Data**

Concierge

Test Card ⓦStrategyzer

→ **Concierge Data**

Learning Card ⓦStrategyzer

Customer Interviews | *Date of Learning*

Person Responsible | **Grace Grant**

STEP 1: HYPOTHESIS
We believed that **millennial parents prefer curated science projects that fit their kids' education level.**

STEP 2: OBSERVATION
We observed **millennial parents want their kids to have a unique project with clear instructions that matches their ability.** Data Reliability: 👍 👍 👍

STEP 3: LEARNINGS AND INSIGHTS
From that we learned that **uniqueness was a top job that we had previously not emphasized.** Action Required: ☑ ☑ ☑

STEP 4: DECISIONS AND ACTIONS
Therefore, we will **use the unique customer language in our upcoming landing page's value proposition.**

Copyright Strategyzer AG The makers of Business Model Generation and Strategyzer

---

Learning Card ⓦStrategyzer

Search Trend Analysis | *Date of Learning*

Person Responsible | **Bob Gail**

STEP 1: HYPOTHESIS
We believed that **millennial parents prefer curated science projects that fit their kids' education level.**

STEP 2: OBSERVATION
We observed **millennial parents are searching online for science fair ideas.** Data Reliability: 👍 👍 👍

STEP 3: LEARNINGS AND INSIGHTS
From that we learned that **kindergarten grade level yielded the most search volume.** Action Required: ☑ ☑ ☑

STEP 4: DECISIONS AND ACTIONS
Therefore, we will **dive deeper into the parents of kindergarteners to better understand their needs.**

Copyright Strategyzer AG The makers of Business Model Generation and Strategyzer

---

Learning Card ⓦStrategyzer

Concierge | *Date of Learning*

Person Responsible | **Claire McCain**

STEP 1: HYPOTHESIS
We believed that **millennial parents prefer curated science projects that fit their kids' education level.**

STEP 2: OBSERVATION
We observed **overall feedback was positive, but time and cost for creating the kits exceeded our target price point.** Data Reliability: 👍 👍 👍

STEP 3: LEARNINGS AND INSIGHTS
From that we learned that **even though parents are satisfied, we have to find ways to bring the time and cost down.** Action Required: ☑ ☑ ☑

STEP 4: DECISIONS AND ACTIONS
Therefore, we will **explore wholesale suppliers and find optimized steps to assemble the kits.**

Copyright Strategyzer AG The makers of Business Model Generation and Strategyzer

Confidence Level

Your confidence level indicates how much you believe that your evidence is strong enough to support or refute a specific hypothesis.

Not all evidence and insights are equal. You should be more confident about your insights when you've run several experiments with increasingly strong evidence for a specific hypothesis. For example, you might start with interviews to gain some first insights into your customers' jobs, pains, and gains. Then you might run a survey to test your insights on a larger scale with more customers. Finally, you might continue with a simulated sale to generate the strongest type of evidence for customer interest.

There are three dimensions to help you determine your confidence level:

1. **Type and strength of evidence**
   Different types of evidence have different strengths. A quote from an interview is a relatively weak indicator of future behavior. A purchase in a simulated sale is a very strong indicator of future behavior. The type of evidence you've collected for a specific hypothesis will influence how confident you can be about the reliability of your insights.

2. **Number of data points per experiment**
   The more data points you have, the better. Five quotes from personal customer interviews is obviously weaker than 100 quotes. However, those same quotes are likely to be more accurate than 100 data points in an anonymous customer survey.

Type of Test	Strength of Evidence	Number of Data Points	Resulting Evidence Quality
CUSTOMER INTERVIEWS	●○○○○	10 PEOPLE	WEAK
DISCOVERY SURVEY	●●○○○	500 PEOPLE	WEAK
MOCK SALES	●●●●○	250 PEOPLE	VERY STRONG

Hypothesis Confidence Level

How confident are you that you can support or refute a specific hypothesis based on experiments, evidence, and insights?

Very Confident

You can be very confident if you've run several experiments of which at least one is a call-to-action test that produced very strong evidence.

Somewhat Confident

You can be somewhat confident if you've run several experiments that produce strong evidence or a particularly strong call-to-action experiment.

Not Really Confident

You need to run more and stronger experiments if you've only done interviews or surveys in which people say what they will do. They might behave differently in reality.

Not Confident at All

You need to experiment more if you've only run one experiment that produces weak evidence, such as an interview or survey.

3. **Number and type of experiments conducted for the same hypothesis**

Your confidence level should rise with the number of experiments you conduct to test the same hypothesis. Three interview series are better than one. Conducting interviews, surveys, and simulated sales to test the same hypothesis is even better. You achieve the best results when you conduct experiments with increasing strength of evidence, and the more you learn.

"Have a bias toward action—
let's see something happen now.
You can break that big plan into
small steps and take the first step
right away."

———

Indira Gandhi
Former Prime Minister of India

2.4 — DECIDE

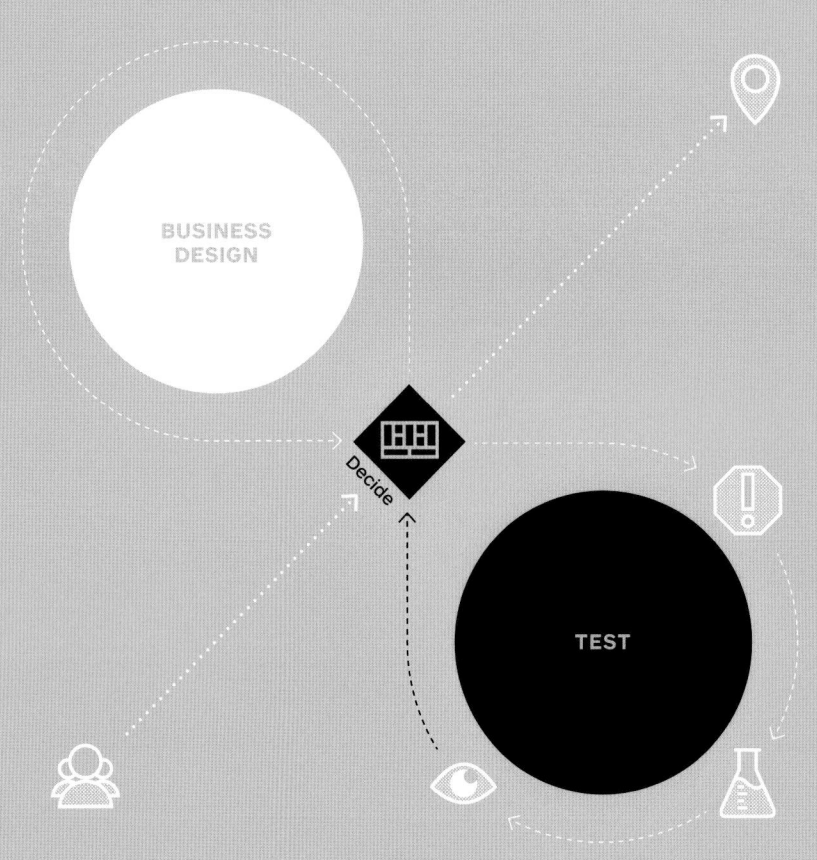

BUSINESS
DESIGN

Decide

TEST

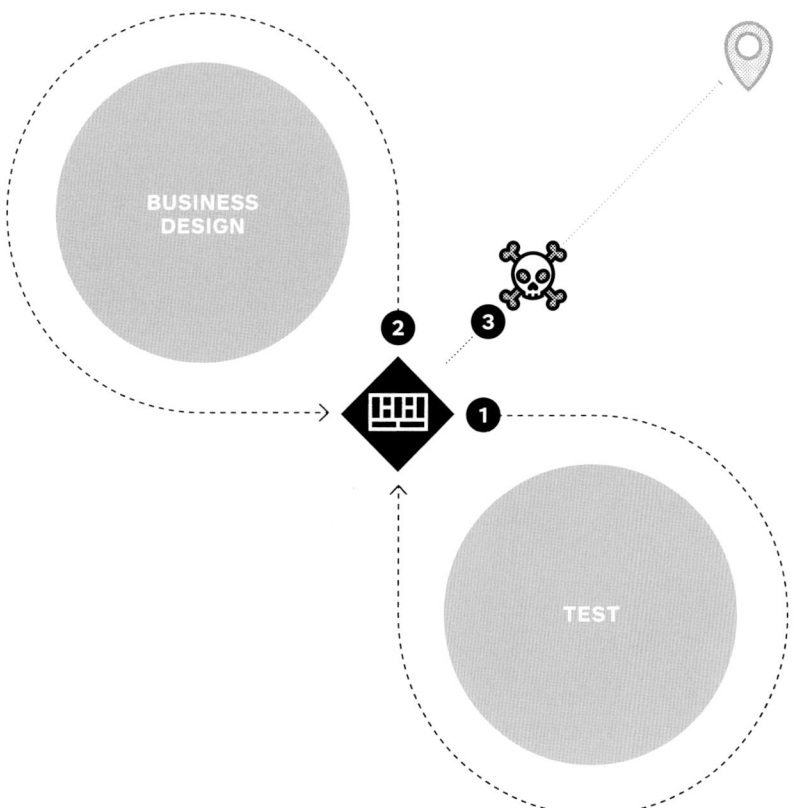

BUSINESS
DESIGN

TEST

1. **Perservere**

   The decision to continue
   testing an idea based on
   evidence and insights. You
   persevere by further testing
   the same hypothesis with
   a stronger experiment, or
   by moving on to your next
   important hypothesis.

2. **Pivot**

   The decision to make a
   significant change to one
   or more elements of your
   ideas, value proposition,
   or business model. A pivot
   often means that some
   of your earlier evidence
   may be irrelevant to your
   new trajectory. It usually
   requires retesting elements
   of your business model that
   you've already tested.

3. **Kill**

   The decision to kill an idea
   based on evidence and
   insights. The evidence
   might show that an idea
   won't work in reality or
   that the profit potential is
   insufficient.

DEFINITION

Decide

Turning insights into action

Learning faster than everyone else is no longer enough. You need to put that learning into action, because what you've learned has an expiration date. If you feel like this is happening faster than any time in recorded history, you may be correct. People today are exposed to more information in a year than those in the early 1900s experienced in a lifetime. Both markets and technology move so quickly that the insights you've gained can expire within months, weeks, or even days.

   For the purposes of Testing Business Ideas, we define action as:

- next steps to make progress with testing and de-risking a business idea.
- informed decisions based on collected insights.
- decisions to abandon, change, and/or continue testing a business idea.

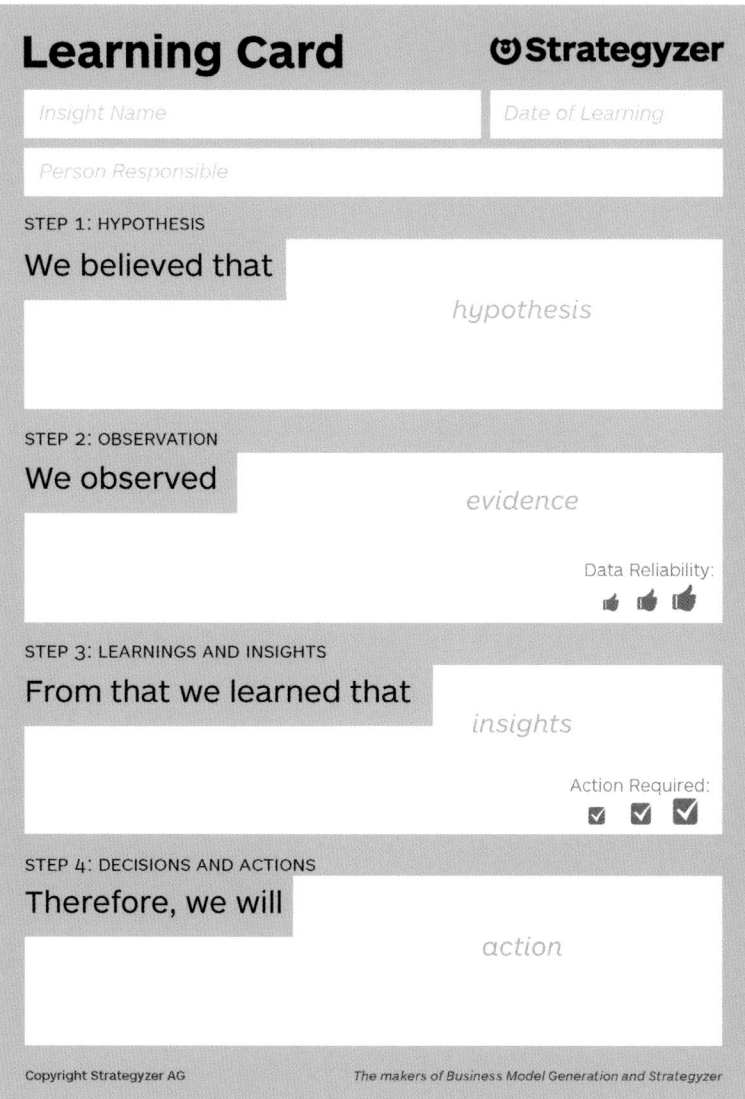

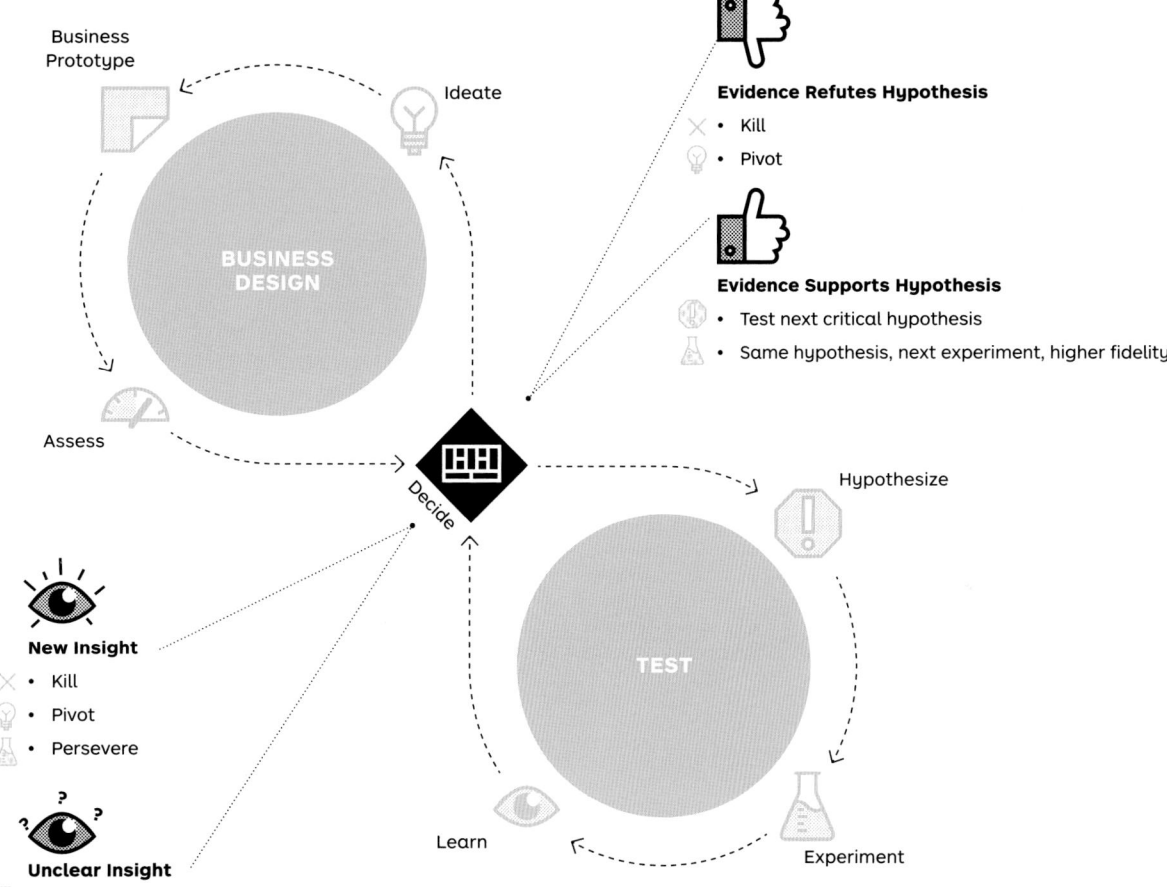

Business
Prototype

Ideate

Evidence Refutes Hypothesis
✕ • Kill
💡 • Pivot

BUSINESS
DESIGN

Evidence Supports Hypothesis
• Test next critical hypothesis
• Same hypothesis, next experiment, higher fidelity

Assess

Decide

Hypothesize

New Insight
✕ • Kill
💡 • Pivot
🧪 • Persevere

TEST

Unclear Insight
🧪 • Continue testing

Learn

Experiment

"The single biggest problem
in communication is the illusion
that it has taken place."
————
George Bernard Shaw
Irish playwright and political activist

SECTION 2 — TEST

2.5 — MANAGE

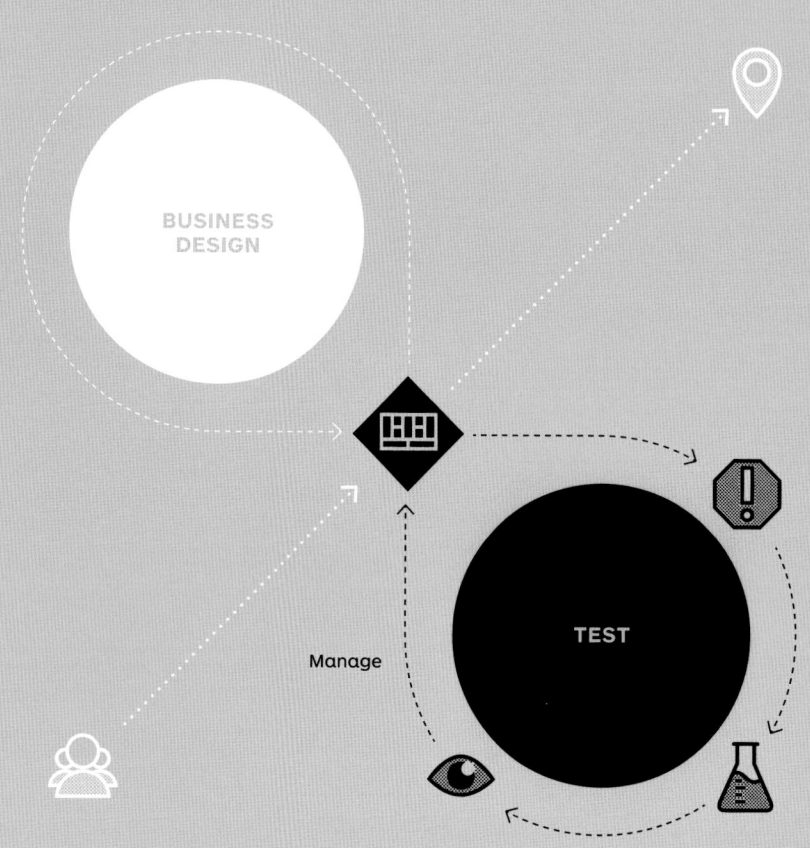

BUSINESS
DESIGN

TEST

Manage

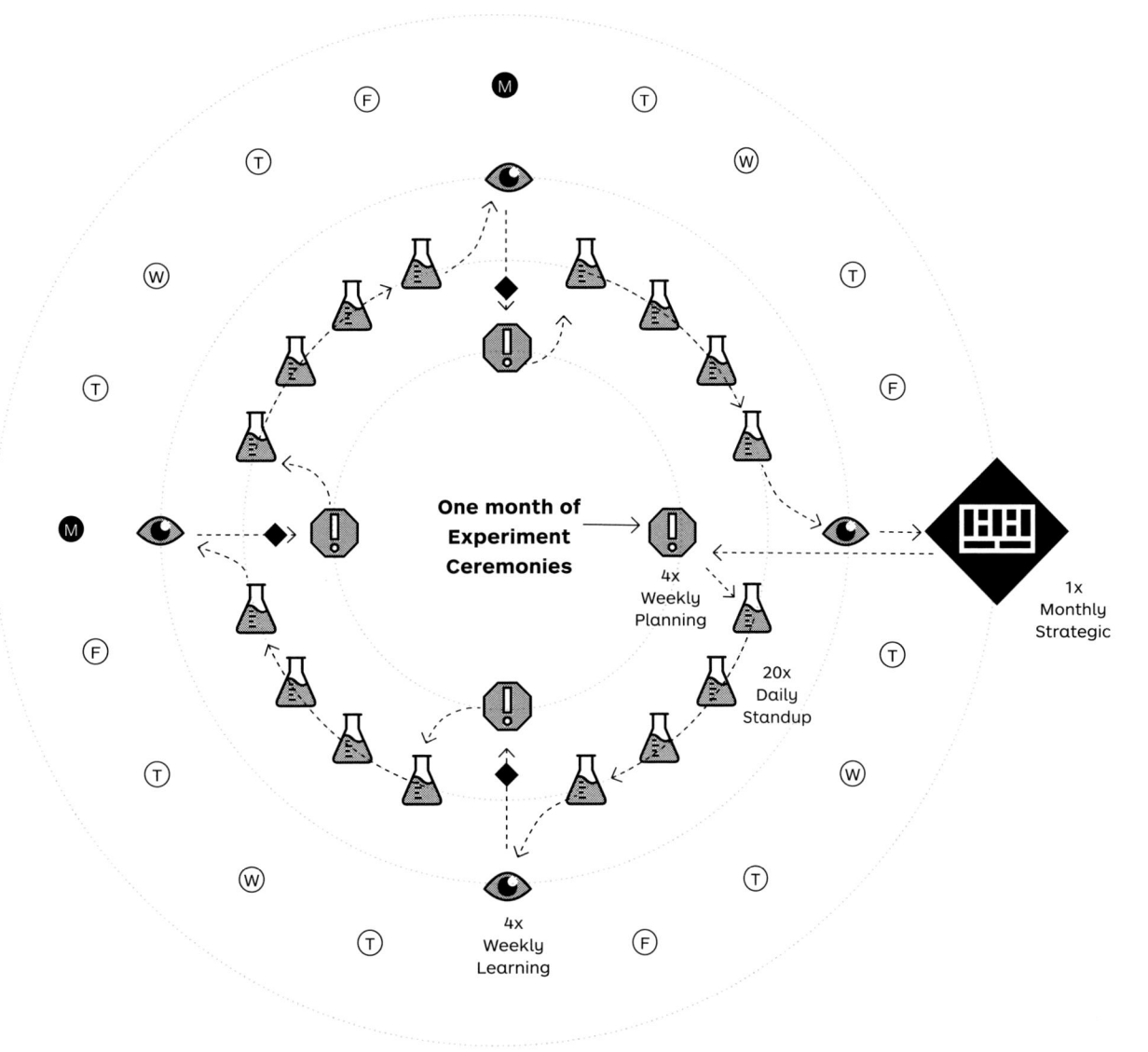

Experiment Ceremonies

Ceremonies help us collaborate and it is no different for experimentation. If your goal is to create a successful new business, you'll need more than one experiment to find your way. This is why we recommend a series of ceremonies to create a repeatable process. Each ceremony informs its connecting ceremony, creating a system.

This series of experiment ceremonies is a result of years of experience working with teams who've made business experimentation a repeatable process. We draw inspiration from agile design thinking and lean methodologies.

Meeting Type	Time		Attendees	Agenda
Planning	60 minutes Weekly		Core Team	• Learning goal • Prioritization • Tasking
Standup	15 minutes Daily		Core Team	• Learning goal • Blockers • Help
Learning	60 minutes Weekly		Extended Team Core Team	• Synthesize evidence • Insights • Actions
Retros	30 minutes Biweekly		Core Team	• Went well • To fix • To try
Deciding	60 minutes Monthly		Stakeholders Extended Team Core Team	• Learnings • Blockers • Decisions

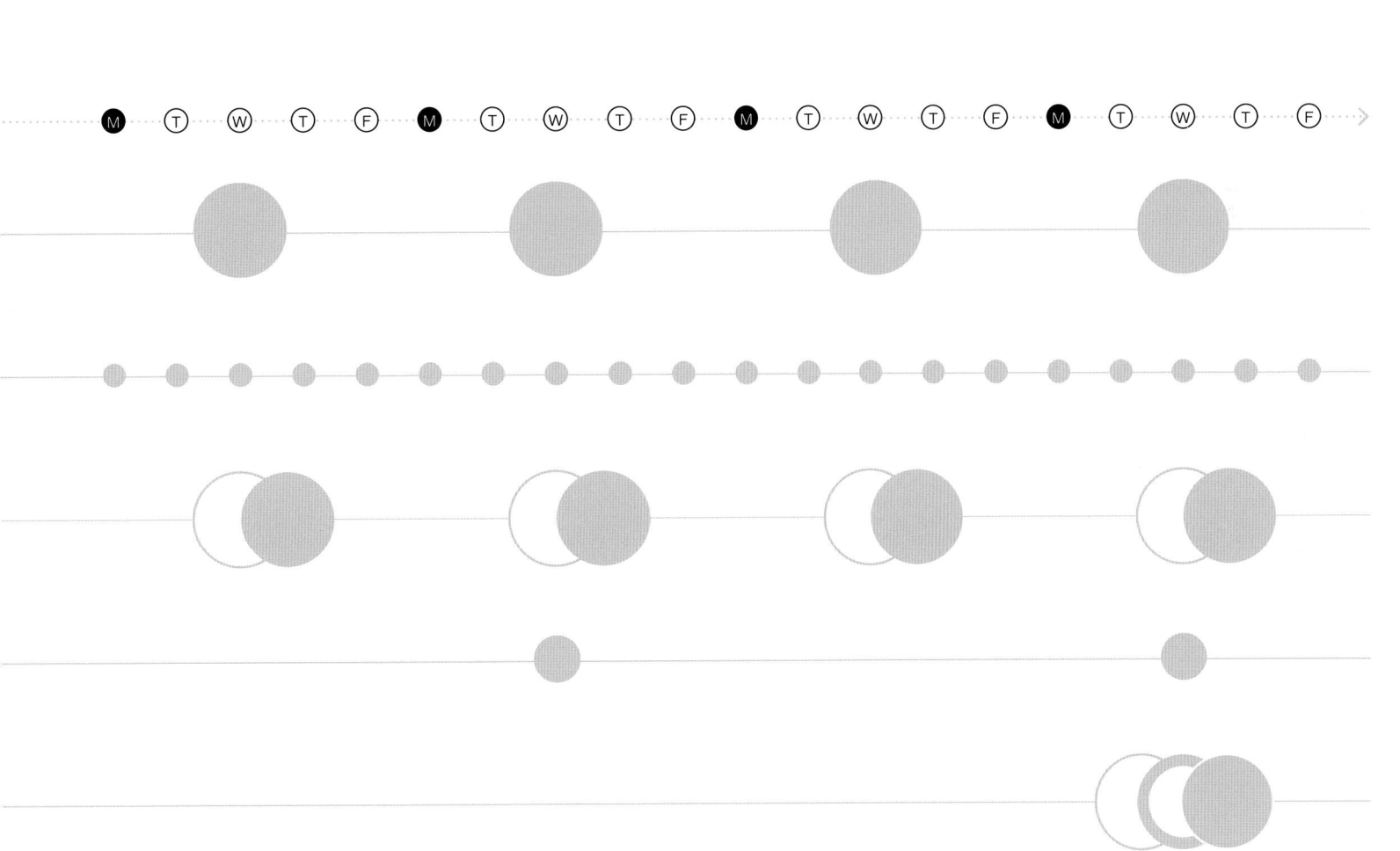

Co-Located or Distributed?

In this rapidly evolving technical world of work, it's no longer a prerequisite that teams need to sit in the same room to be highly effective. Whether you are co-located or distributed, we've witnessed teams adopt these Experiment Ceremonies to help propel their new business ideas.

Co-Located Teams

For Co-Located Teams, we recommend having a space that is semiprivate. It can be difficult to secure a conference room for all of these ceremonies, and it would mean bringing your artifacts in every time if they are physically printed out.

Many teams we've coached pick a wall or have a pod setup that allows them to quickly collaborate and then get back to work.

Distributed Teams

For Distributed Teams, we strongly recommend video chat whenever possible. It's important to make a connection to your team members and be able to see their body language. Luckily for you there are ample options to choose from in video chat.

When reviewing artifacts or conducting exercises, try to use software that shows people editing and moving things in real time. This will prevent confusion and duplication from attendees.

Time Commitment

Based on a 40-hour week, the volume of cermonies can seem overwhelming for your team. In reality, the commitment outside of actually running the experiments is quite modest, and appropriately shouldered by the core team.

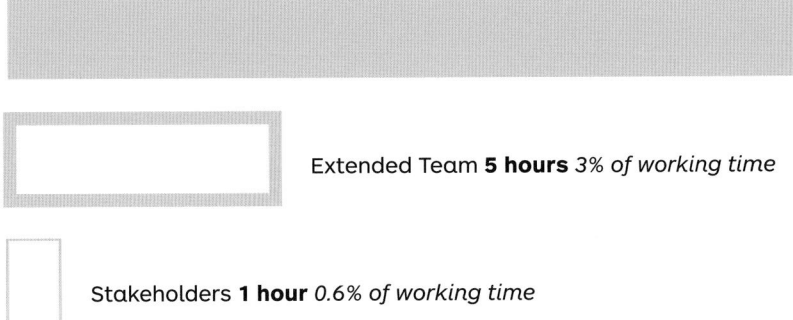

Core Team **15.25 hours** *9% of working time*

Extended Team **5 hours** *3% of working time*

Stakeholders **1 hour** *0.6% of working time*

Time
30–60 minutes
Once a week
After Weekly Learning

Attendees
Core Team

Weekly Planning

Plan and task out the experiments for the upcoming week. While the plan may change, the planning that goes into it is still a valuable exercise.

Agenda

1. Hypotheses to Test
Identify and revisit the hypotheses you are testing. Choose at least one of your important hypotheses to test for the upcoming week.

2. Experiment Prioritization
Once you've defined your hypotheses, prioritize the experiments you'll need to run in order to learn about the hypotheses. Use our experiment library to identify which experiment is best suited for testing desirability, viability, and feasibility.

3. Experiment Tasking
After the experiments have been prioritized, task out the top experiments you've selected to run for the upcoming week. Remember that complex experiments take longer and often require sequential tasks.

Corporate Team

Core members of the Corporate Team.
Extended Team members are optional, unless you anticipate that their expertise will be needed for the upcoming week. Then they are recommended.

Startup Team

Core members of the Startup Team.
Even if it's only two of you, get into a habit of explaining what's bouncing around your head, so that you can prioritize the most important work.

External contractors are optional, unless you anticipate that their expertise will be needed for the upcoming week. Then they are recommended.

Solopreneur

Solopreneurs benefit from Weekly Planning, even if you are not coordinating with external contractors.

The ritual of planning your work every week will help you keep a cadence and establish a sense of accomplishment.

If you are using external contractors then their attendance is optional, unless you anticipate that their expertise will be needed for the upcoming week's experiments. Then it is recommended.

Time
15 minutes
Every weekday
Morning, same time

Attendees
Core Team

Daily Standups

Stay aligned and focus on your daily work. Many experiments require a series of tasks to complete, and Daily Standups help coordinate your day-to-day work.

Agenda

1. What's the Daily Goal?

Create a daily goal. If your goal is to get an experiment out the door, then it's important to align your tasks to achieve that goal. Remember that daily goals feed into your larger, more ambitious goals for the overall business.

2. How to Achieve That Goal?

Identify the tasks needed to achieve the daily goal and plan your day.

3. What's in the Way?

Identify any blockers that would prevent you from completing experiment tasks for the day or achieving the goal. Some of these can be addressed within the standup if it is quick, otherwise meet after the standup to work through it.

TEST

Corporate Team

Core members of the Corporate Team.

Have the Daily Standup in a location where others can see you planning your day. It's a great way to socialize your process to the rest of the organization.

Startup Team

Core members of the Startup Team.

You'll still benefit from Daily Standups. Startups move fast and you can get out of sync rather quickly. This will help you stay aligned and focused on your goals over time.

Solopreneur

Yes, even Solopreneurs need to plan out your day. Daily Standups help you stay organized and aligned with your bigger goals, even if you are not coordinating with external contractors.

Time
30–60 minutes
Once a week
Before Weekly planning

Attendees
Extended Team
Core Team

Weekly Learning

Have a conversation to interpret the evidence and turn it into action. Remember that what you've learned from experiments should inform your overall strategy.

Agenda

1. Gather Evidence

Gather up the evidence your experiments have generated. This includes both qualitative and quantitative types of evidence.

2. Generate Insights

Look for patterns and insights from your evidence. Even qualitative evidence can be quickly themed using techniques such as affinity sorting. Try to keep an open mind. You may find unexpected insights that lead you to new paths to revenue.

3. Revisit Your Strategy

Take the new insights you have and revisit your Business Model Canvas, Value Proposition Canvas, and Assumptions Map. Make any updates needed so that they reflect your current state of learning. This is a crucial step in using what you've learned to inform your strategy. If it feels awkward, don't worry, it's a normal part of being an entrepreneur.

Corporate Team

Core members of the Corporate Team.

Extended Team members are optional, unless you anticipate that their expertise will be needed for synthesizing the learning. Then they are recommended.

Startup Team

Core members of the Startup Team.

External contractors are optional, unless you anticipate that their expertise will be needed for synthesizing the learning. Then they are recommended.

Solopreneur

If you are using external contractors, they are optional to attend, unless you anticipate that their expertise will be needed for synthesizing the learning. Then they are recommended.

Time
30–60 minutes
Biweekly
After Weekly
Learning / Before
Weekly Planning

Attendees
Core Team

Biweekly Retrospective

Take a step back, breathe, and talk about how you can improve the way you work. In our opinion, this is the most important ceremony. When you stop reflecting, you stop learning and improving.

Agenda

1. What's Going Well

Take five minutes to silently write down what's going well. This gets the retrospective off to a good start as people have space to speak positively about team members and how they are working together.

2. What Needs Improvement

Take five minutes to silently write down what needs improvement. These are things that aren't going well or could be doing better. It's important to frame these items as an opportunity to improve, rather than as a personal attack against a team member.

3. What to Try Next

Come up with three things you'd like to try. It can be one of the items you've previously discussed, or something completely new. This gives you a chance to try out a new way of working that isn't simply rooted in what needs improvement.

Tip
There are plenty of additional retrospective options, such as Speed Boat, Start — Stop — Keep, *and* Keep — Drop — Add.
We recommend trying out a few different formats to see what works best for you.

Corporate Team

Core members of the Corporate Team.

For Corporate Teams, it's important to detail what you can control inside the team and what may be outside your sphere of influence in the organization.

After the retrospective is completed, have a designated team member communicate any external issues upstream to get help.

If you cannot get them resolved, try to find creative ways to mitigate their impact on the team.

Startup Team

Core members of the Startup Team.

For Startup Teams, keep in mind that as you incorporate improvements into the way you work, it can help build the culture you want to create in your startup.

Cofounders who exhibit the willingness to inspect and adapt how they work will eventually attract employees who want to work that way.

Solopreneur

For Solopreneurs, it can sometimes feel like an isolating experience. Take the time to reflect on how you are working, even if it's only you during the ceremony.

If you are unable to achieve the results you are aiming for, then it's a good idea to try new ways of working to break through.

If you are using external contractors then they are optional to attend, unless you want to check in with them and improve how you are collaborating.

Time
60–90 minutes
Once a month

Attendees
Stakeholders
Extended Team
Core Team

Monthly Stakeholder Reviews

Keep stakeholders in the loop on how you are pivoting, persevering, or killing the idea.

Agenda

1. What You've Learned
Provide an executive summary of what you've learned over the past month. This includes each Weekly Learning Goal and any additional insights generated from experiments. It's important not to overwhelm the attendees with detailed breakdowns of every experiment. Have the information in the appendix to dive deeper if needed.

2. What's Blocking Progress
This is the time to review any impediments that Stakeholders can assist in removing. This includes items from previous Retrospectives that fall outside your influence or control. These should be clearly communicated as requests for assistance.

3. Pivot / Persevere / Kill Decision
Make your recommendation to Stakeholders on whether you should pivot, persevere, or kill the new business idea. This should be based not only on what you've learned, but also what you see as a path forward in your strategy.

Tip
The three major types of pivots we witness are based on the customer, problem, and solution. You can stick with the customer, pivot on the problem. You can stick with the problem and pivot on customer. You can stick with customer and problem, and pivot on the solution.

Corporate Team

Core members of the Corporate Team and Stakeholders.

For Corporate Teams, continue to communicate the progress on what you've learned to Stakeholders. Walk a balance between showing how you are working differently and making progress.

If the Stakeholders take the form of a funding committee, then decisions will be made during the session on whether to fund the effort going forward.

Startup Team

Core members of the Startup Team and Stakeholders.

For Startup Teams, you want to keep investors in the loop on how you are making progress, even if that means sharing your struggles. Great investors realize it's not a linear path to a success. Balaji Srinivasan affectionally calls this the "Idea Maze."

You can choose to communicate this via an email or video update, if your Investors are not physically nearby.

Solopreneur

Solopreneur and an Advisor.

Get on a video call or have coffee with your advisor and share what you've learned and what you're recommending. Although your advisor is not likely an investor, it's still helpful to get an outside opinion on your strategy.

To learn more about the "Idea Maze" visit
spark-public.s3.amazonaws.com/startup/lecture_slides/lecture5-market-wireframing-design.pdf.

Principles of Experiment Flow

Running one experiment is great, but the goal is to reduce the uncertainty in your business. This means running several experiments over time. You want your experiment process to flow, generating the evidence needed to make informed investment decisions.

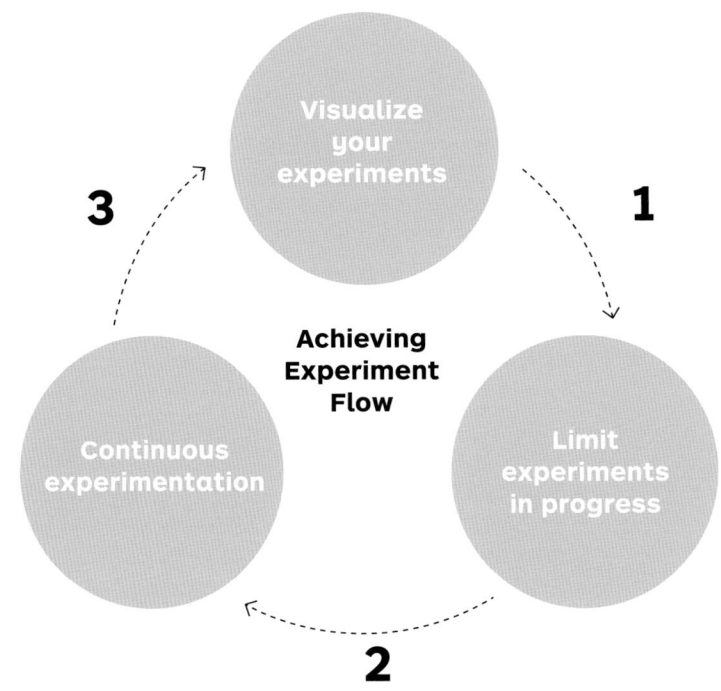

Visualize Your Experiments

*Make your work visible
to yourself and others.*

We've found inspiration from the lean and kanban movements, particularly on this principle. If you keep all this work in your head, you'll never be able to achieve flow. Not only are your teammates unable to read your mind, but much of flow requires you to visualize your work.

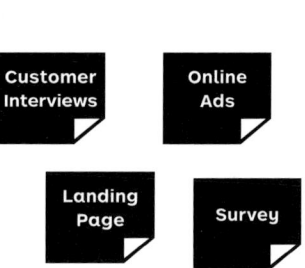

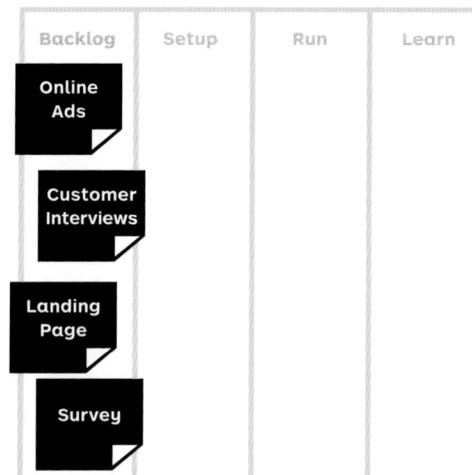

1. Write down your experiments

We recommend only one experiment per sticky, to keep things organized. You don't have to write down hundreds of experiments — only the ones you feel you'll be running over the upcoming weeks.

2. Draw a simple experiment board

This is one of the simplest forms of an experiment board you can create. We've been playing with this format for quite some time and used to like the "Validate" column, which we got originally from Eric Ries. Over time, we've started to back off a bit on that language because teams will set the bar so low on their hypotheses that they'll artificially validate them and move on too quickly. We prefer "Learn" over "Validate."

3. Add your experiments to the Backlog column

Rank your experiments from top to bottom, where the top is the one you are going to do next. Pull them across as you begin to work on each, moving from Setup, to Run, to Learn.

Limit Experiments in Progress

Multitasking too many experiments can often lead to trouble.

Teams inherently underestimate how much work it is to run experiments, especially if they've never run them before. So it should come as no surprise that they often pull all the experiments over at once and try to do them all in parallel. This results in slowing the entire process down. It's also difficult to extract insights from a previous experiment to inform your next one.

84

TEST

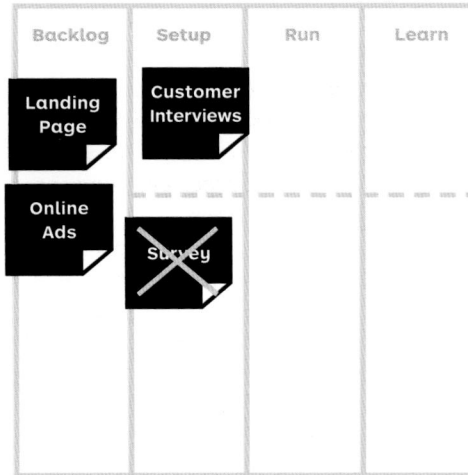

Define work in progress limits for your experiments.

For example, start with a limit of 1 for Setup, Run, and Learn columns. This will prevent the team from pulling a second experiment over until the first is moved to the next column and finally archived.

In this example, the team runs the customer interviews before the survey, instead of trying to do both at once (and slowing everything down). The experiments flow, using what you've learned to inform your next experiment.

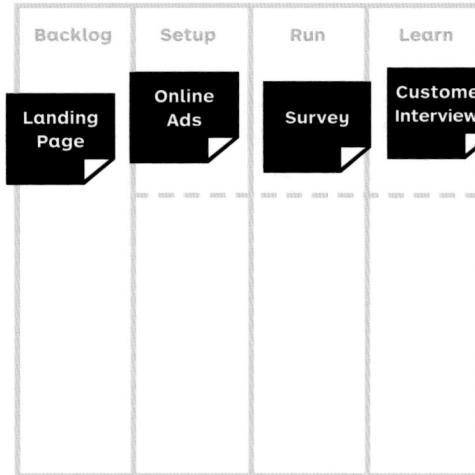

Continuous Experimentation
Continue to experiment over time.

The last principle, which also finds its roots in lean and kanban, is the idea of continuous experimentation. A team that starts with the previous board to achieve flow will eventually outgrow it. You don't want the board to artificially constrain the team from growing and maturing over time. As we recommend in the section on ceremonies (see page 80 and following), have a retrospective every two weeks. This applies to your experiment flow, which can yield interesting artifacts for improvement.

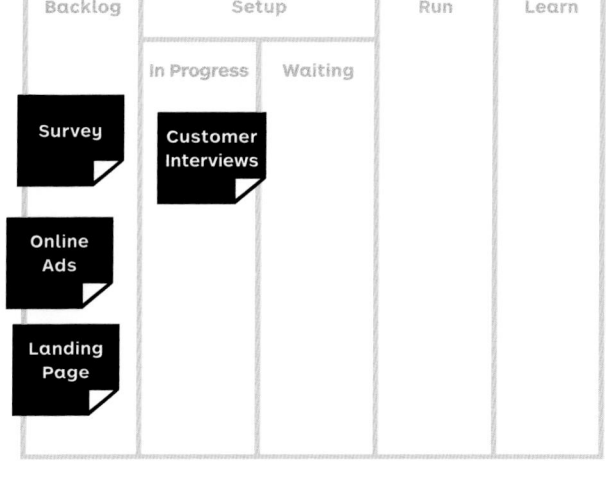

● = Blocked

Blocker Experiment

As an example, is that the team is trying to line up customer interviews, but the research department won't let them. They state that it's against company policy to talk to customers. That is a "blocker" that's preventing you from making progress on that experiment.

It's a good idea to identify and visualize these, which will help you communicate progress to stakeholders as to why things are slowing down. It's hard to achieve flow when you are blocked.

Splitting Columns Experiment

Another example is that the team has outgrown the initial board and is frustrated that the Setup column doesn't capture the nuances of experimentation.

There is work setting up an experiment, but then you have to run it, and if the team is at capacity the experiment may sit around for a long time waiting to be run. When we talk about the board, it would be great to see which ones are ready to be run and which experiments are still being set up.

Ethics in Experimentation

Are you experimenting with your customers or on them?

This book is about helping you determine if your business idea is desirable, viable, and feasible. What it is *not* is a reason to scam people out of their money. Vaporware was a term that became popular during the late 1980s and much of the 1990s. It described products that never launched, but never really canceled either. Vaporware products managed to get people hyped up, often promising unrealistic expectations. In more severe cases, people even used the lure of vaporware to scam people out of real money. Our goal isn't to recreate the vaporware environment of the 1990s. This is especially important in the era of fake news, when techniques can be weaponized as propaganda to influence entire nations. Context is important when using experiments to de-risk your business. In short, don't be evil.

Experiment Guidelines

Poor communication can destroy any experiment cadence you try to create. You can address this by clearly communicating the details and "the why" behind the experimentation. Teams who've done this repeatedly, over time, find that they are repeating themselves quite a bit. To make things a bit more efficient, they've crafted experiment guidelines to help communicate with those outside of the team. This is particularly effective when working with legal, safety, and compliance departments.

Experiment Guidelines Sample

1. *Our customer segment is _____.*
2. *The total number of customers involved in our experiment is estimated to be _____.*
3. *Our experiment will run from _____ to _____.*
4. *The information currency we are collecting is _____.*
5. *The branding we'll use for the experiment is _____.*
6. *The financial exposure of the experiment is _____.*
7. *We can turn off the experiment by using _____.*

Experi

ments

"The problem happens when you
don't put that first note down.
Just start!"
———————
Herbie Hancock
Jazz musician, composer, and actor

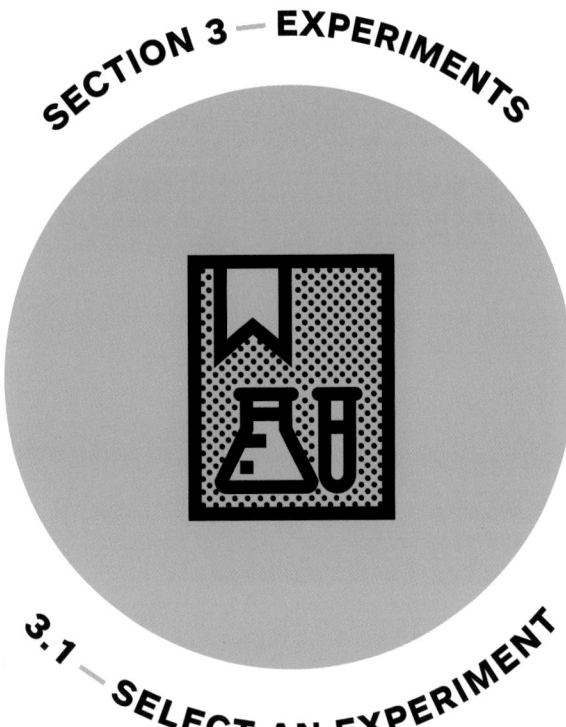

SECTION 3 — EXPERIMENTS

3.1 — SELECT AN EXPERIMENT

Experiment Selection

Pick the right experiment by asking these three questions:

1. Type of hypothesis: What type of hypothesis are you testing?
Pick experiments based on your major learning objective. Some experiments produce better evidence for desirability, some work better for feasibility, and some are more appropriate for viability.

2. Level of uncertainty: How much evidence do you already have (for a specific hypothesis)?
The less you know, the less you should waste time, energy, and money. When you know little, your only goal is to produce evidence that points you in the right direction. Quick and cheap experiments are most appropriate for that goal, despite the generally weak evidence. The more you know, the stronger the evidence should become, which is usually achieved by more costly and lengthier experiments.

3. Urgency: How much time do you have until the next major decision point or until you run out of money?
The selection of the right experiment may depend on the time and money you have available. If you have a major meeting with decision makers or investors coming up, you might need to use quick and cheap experiments to quickly generate evidence on multiple aspects of your idea. When you are running out of money, you need to pick the right experiments to convince decision-makers and investors to extend funding.

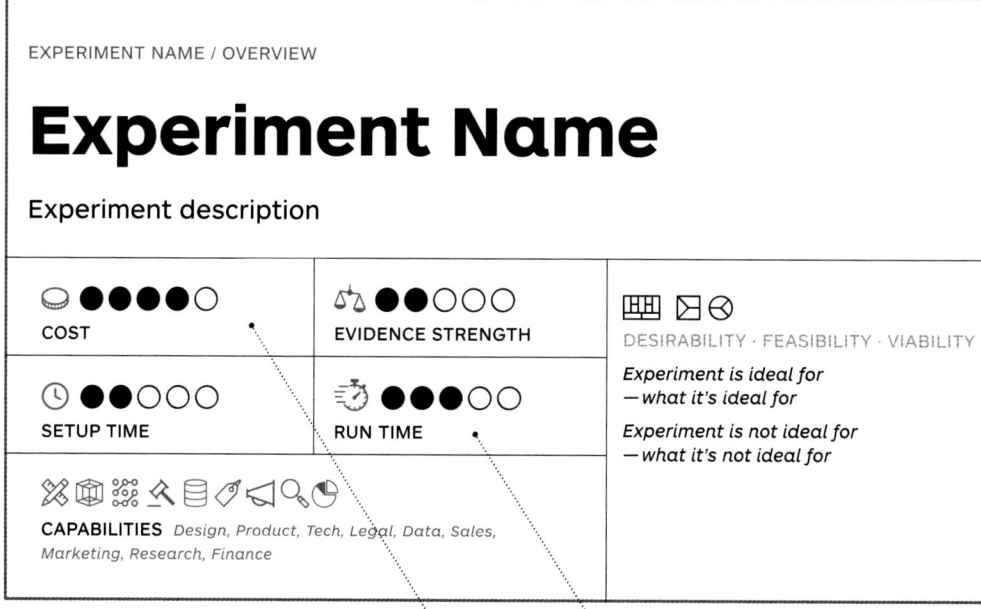

EXPERIMENT NAME / OVERVIEW

Experiment Name

Experiment description

COST ●●●●○
EVIDENCE STRENGTH ●●○○○
DESIRABILITY · FEASIBILITY · VIABILITY

SETUP TIME ●●○○○
RUN TIME ●●●○○

Experiment is ideal for
— what it's ideal for

Experiment is not ideal for
— what it's not ideal for

CAPABILITIES Design, Product, Tech, Legal, Data, Sales, Marketing, Research, Finance

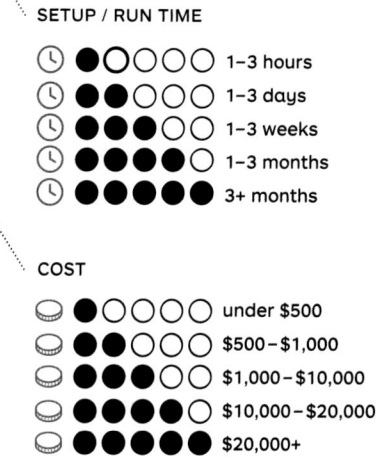

SETUP / RUN TIME

●○○○○ 1–3 hours
●●○○○ 1–3 days
●●●○○ 1–3 weeks
●●●●○ 1–3 months
●●●●● 3+ months

COST

●○○○○ under $500
●●○○○ $500–$1,000
●●●○○ $1,000–$10,000
●●●●○ $10,000–$20,000
●●●●● $20,000+

Rules of thumb

1. **Go cheap and fast at the beginning.**
   Early on, you generally know little. Stick to cheap and quick experiments to pinpoint the right direction. You can afford starting out with weaker evidence, because you will test more later. Ideally, you select an experiment that is cheap, fast, and still produces strong evidence.

2. **Increase the strength of evidence with multiple experiments for the same hypothesis.**
   Run several experiments to support or refute a hypothesis. Try to learn about a hypothesis as fast as possible, then run more experiments to produce stronger evidence for confirmation. Don't make important decisions based on one experiment or weak evidence.

3. **Always pick the experiment that produces the strongest evidence given your constraints.**
   Always select and design the strongest experiment you can, while respecting the context. When uncertainty is high you should go fast and cheap, but that doesn't necessarily mean you can't produce strong evidence.

4. **Reduce uncertainty as much as you can before you build anything.**
   People often think they need to build something to start testing an idea. Quite the contrary. The higher the costs to build something, the more you need to run multiple experiments to show that customers actually have the jobs, pains, and gains you think they have.

Our work on experiments in the discovery and validation phases heavily build on Steve Blank's foundational work in "The Four Steps to the Epiphany and "The Startup Owner's Manual." We strongly recommend both as essential reading.

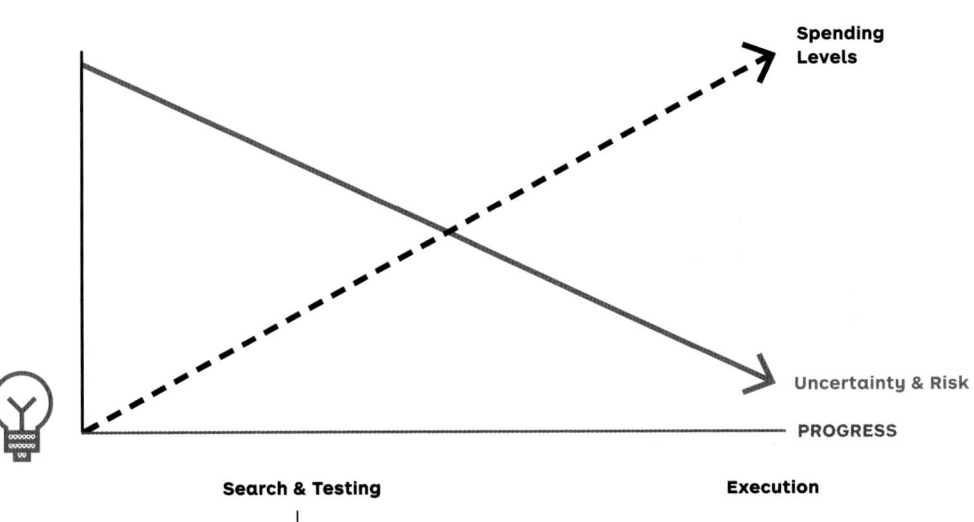

- Spending Levels
- Uncertainty & Risk
- PROGRESS

Search & Testing

Execution

Discovery
Weak evidence is sufficient to discover if your general direction is right. You get first insights into your most important hypotheses.

Validation
Strong evidence is required to validate the direction you've taken. You aim to confirm the insights you've gotten for your most important hypotheses.

Discovery Experiments

Ask these three questions

1. **What type of hypothesis are you testing?**
2. **How much evidence do you already have (for a specific hypothesis)?**
3. **How much time do you have until the next major decision point or until you run out of money?**

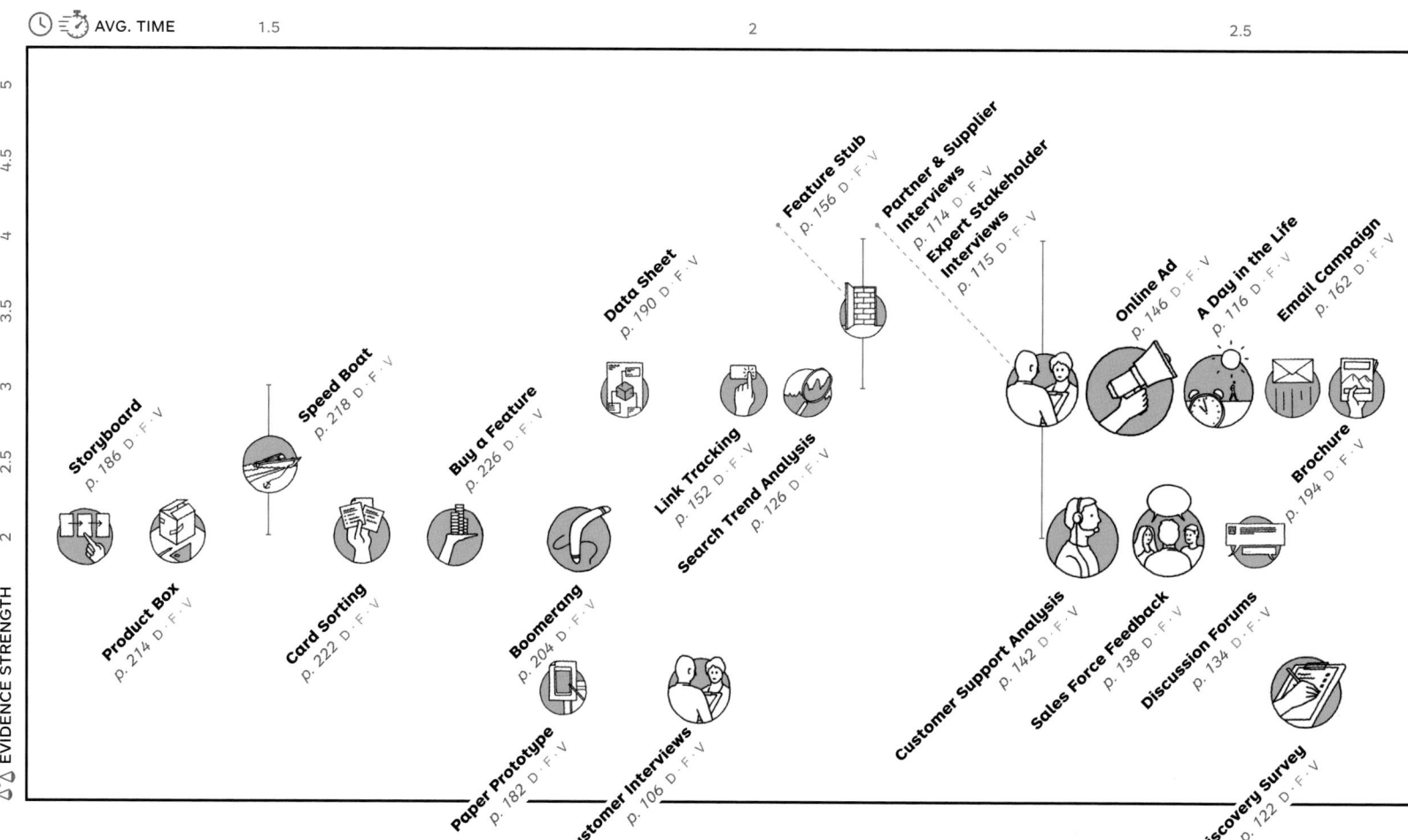

AVG. TIME   1.5   2   2.5

EVIDENCE STRENGTH

EXPERIMENTS

94

Storyboard p. 186 D · F · V

Product Box p. 214 D · F · V

Speed Boat p. 218 D · F · V

Card Sorting p. 222 D · F · V

Buy a Feature p. 226 D · F · V

Boomerang p. 204 D · F · V

Paper Prototype p. 182 D · F · V

Customer Interviews p. 106 D · F · V

Data Sheet p. 190 D · F · V

Link Tracking p. 152 D · F · V

Search Trend Analysis p. 126 D · F · V

Feature Stub p. 156 D · F · V

Partner & Supplier Interviews p. 114 D · F · V

Expert Stakeholder Interviews p. 115 D · F · V

Customer Support Analysis p. 142 D · F · V

Sales Force Feedback p. 138 D · F · V

Discussion Forums p. 134 D · F · V

Discovery Survey p. 122 D · F · V

Online Ad p. 146 D · F · V

A Day in the Life p. 116 D · F · V

Email Campaign p. 162 D · F · V

Brochure p. 194 D · F · V

Rules of thumb

1. **Go cheap and fast early on in your journey.**

2. **Increase the strength of evidence with multiple experiments for the same hypothesis.**

3. **Always pick the experiment that produces the strongest evidence, given your constraints.**

4. **Reduce uncertainty as much as you can before you build anything.**

3   3.5   4

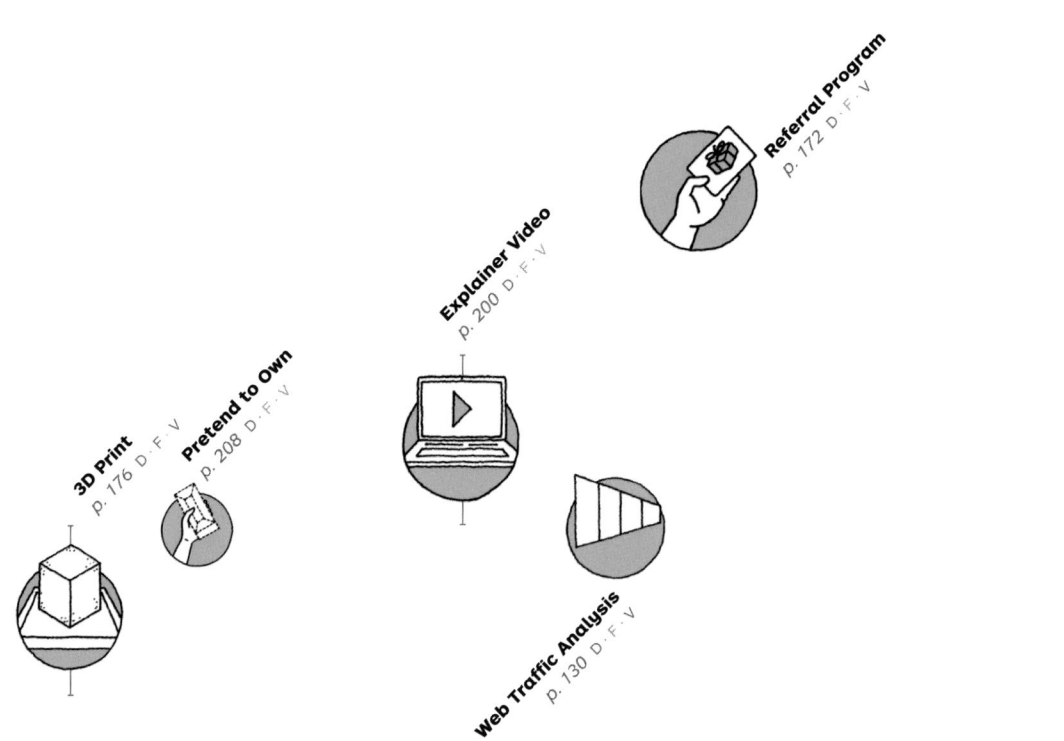

3D Print P. 176 D. F. V

Pretend to Own P. 208 D. F. V

Explainer Video P. 200 D. F. V

Web Traffic Analysis P. 130 D. F. V

Referral Program P. 172 D. F. V

Social Media Campaign P. 168 D. F. V

Validation Experiments

Ask these three questions

1. **What type of hypothesis are you testing?**
2. **How much evidence do you already have (for a specific hypothesis)?**
3. **How much time do you have until the next major decision point or until you run out of money?**

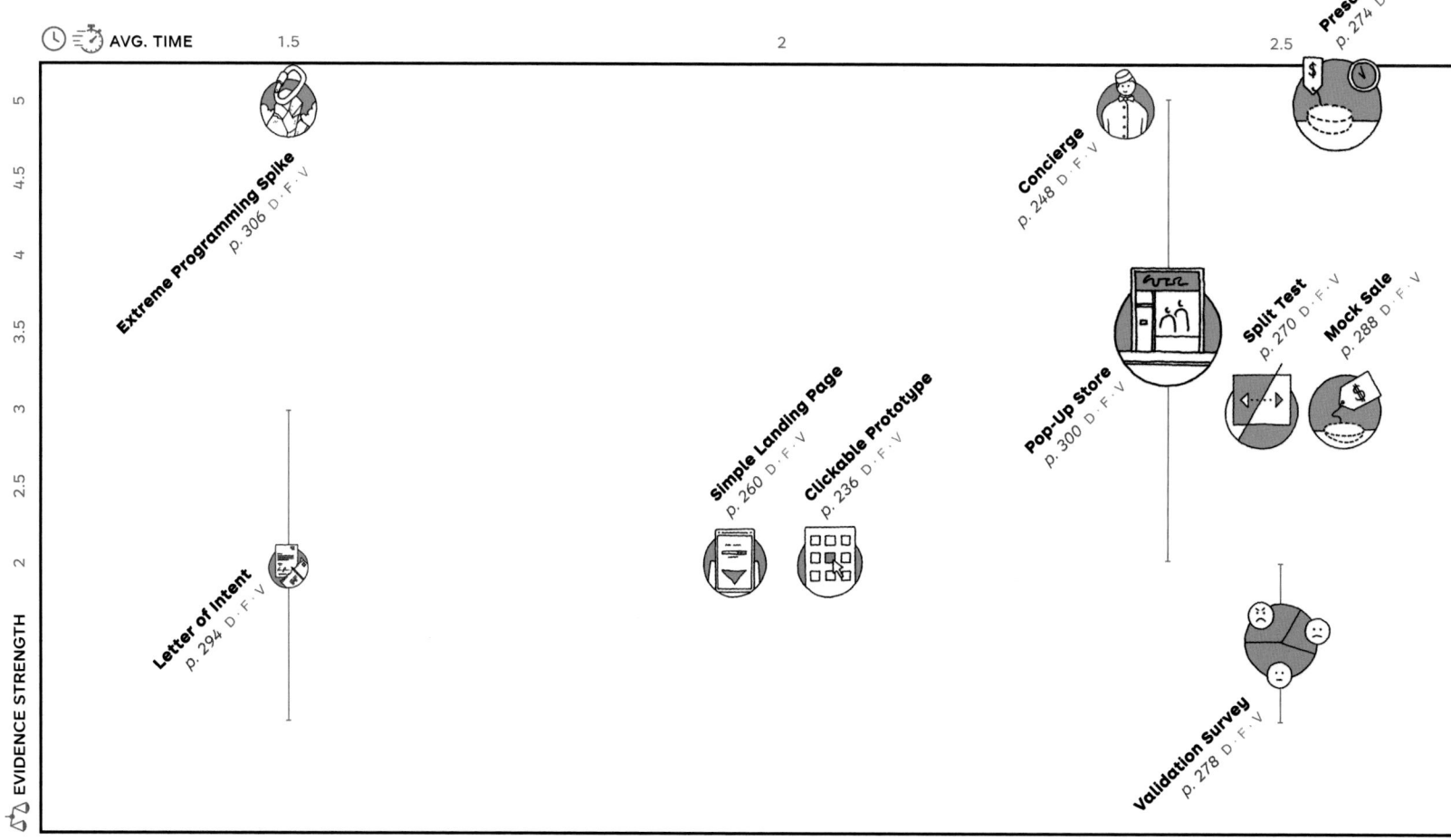

EXPERIMENTS

96

🕐 ⏱ AVG. TIME   1.5   2   2.5

EVIDENCE STRENGTH   2   2.5   3   3.5   4   4.5   5

Extreme Programming Spike p. 306 D . F . V

Letter of Intent p. 294 D . F . V

Simple Landing Page p. 260 D . F . V

Clickable Prototype p. 236 D . F . V

Concierge p. 248 D . F . V

Presale p. 274 D . F . V

Pop-Up Store p. 300 D . F . V

Split Test p. 270 D . F . V

Mock Sale p. 288 D . F . V

Validation Survey p. 278 D . F . V

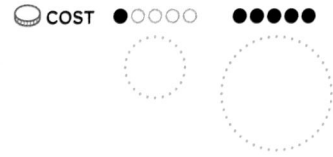

Rules of thumb

1. **Go cheap and fast early on in your journey.**

2. **Increase the strength of evidence with multiple experiments for the same hypothesis.**

3. **Always pick the experiment that produces the strongest evidence, given your constraints.**

4. **Reduce uncertainty as much as you can before you build anything.**

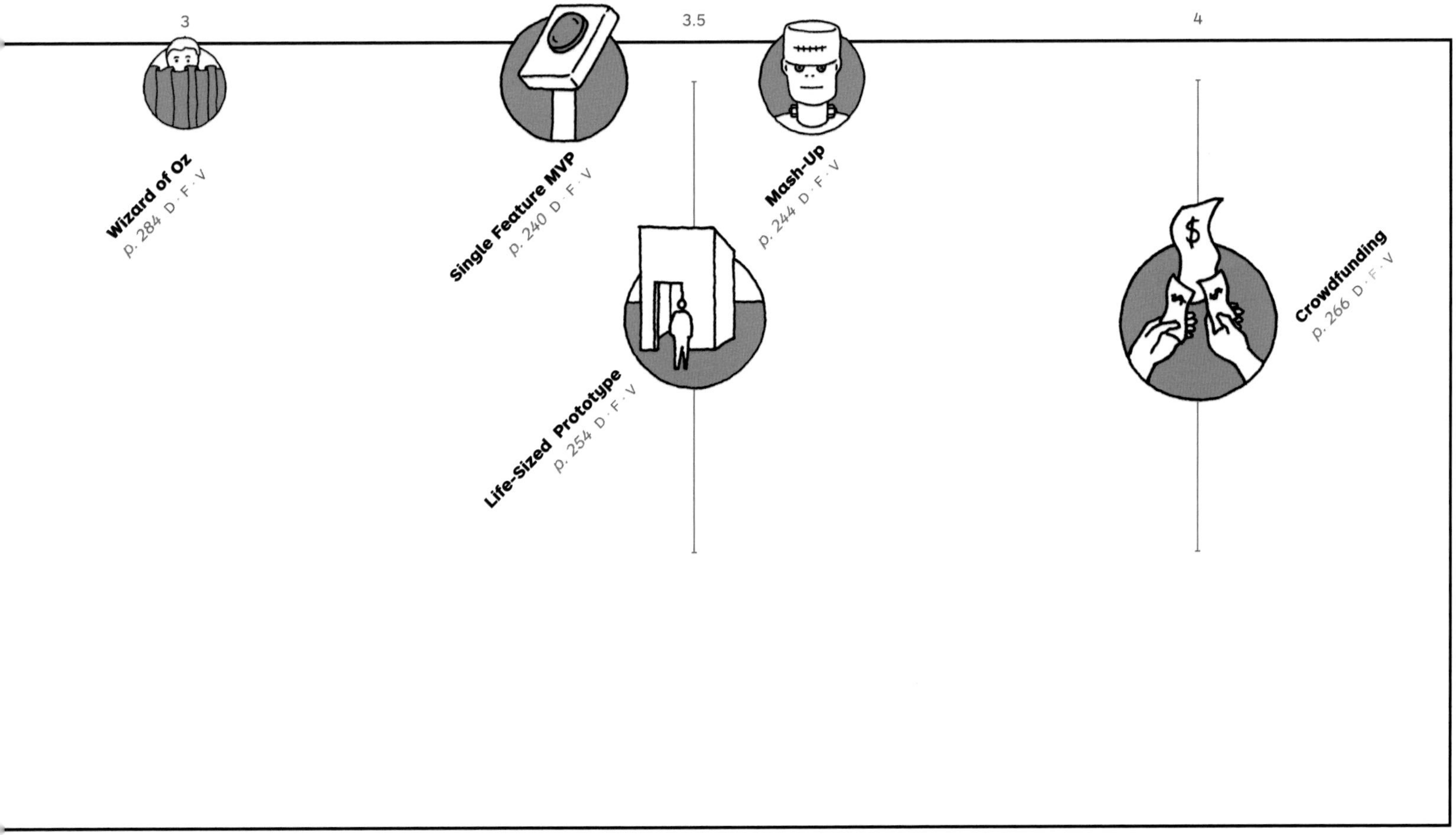

3

Wizard of Oz
P. 284 D · F · V

Single Feature MVP
P. 240 D · F · V

3.5

Mash-Up
P. 244 D · F · V

Life-Sized Prototype
P. 254 D · F · V

4

Crowdfunding
P. 266 D · F · V

Experiment Sequences

Go beyond pairing with experimentation sequences.

Once you've turned your insights into action, it's time to move on and throw the experiment away, correct? Well, not necessarily. As illustrated in the pairings for each experiment, there are experiments you can run before, during, and after. But what about a sequence of experiments? Great teams are able to gain momentum and build up stronger evidence over time with a series of experiments.

B2B Hardware Sequence

B2B hardware companies search for evidence of customers already hacking together their own solutions to a problem. They use this to inform their design to do the job even better. Then they test it out quickly by integrating standard components with potential customers and crowdfunding it if the signal is strong.

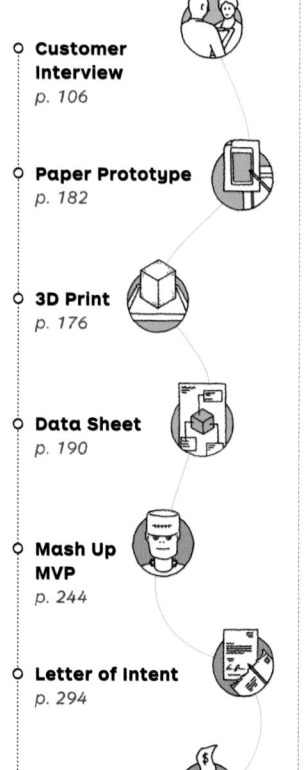

- **Customer Interview** p. 106
- **Paper Prototype** p. 182
- **3D Print** p. 176
- **Data Sheet** p. 190
- **Mash Up MVP** p. 244
- **Letter of Intent** p. 294
- **Crowdfunding** p. 266

B2B Software Sequence

B2B software companies look for opportunities where employees are mandated to use subpar software. Many have disrupted incumbents simply by observing where their deficiencies exist and then designing a better experience that solves for a high value customer job, using modern technology.

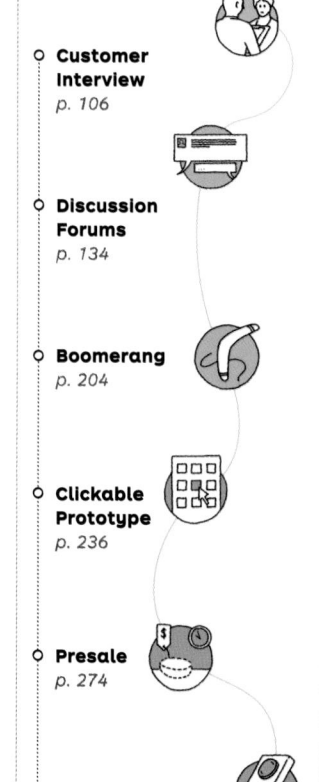

- **Customer Interview** p. 106
- **Discussion Forums** p. 134
- **Boomerang** p. 204
- **Clickable Prototype** p. 236
- **Presale** p. 274
- **Single Feature MVP** p. 240

B2B Services Sequence

B2B services companies often interview stakeholders to research the cost of poorly designed processes and services. They analyze customer support data to see if this is reflected in other areas within the company. Afterward, they create a brochure to communicate the improvement and then deliver the service manually to a handful of customers before scaling.

- **Expert Stakeholder Interviews** p. 115
- **Customer Support Analysis** p. 142
- **Brochure** p. 194
- **Presale** p. 274
- **Concierge** p. 248

B2C Hardware Sequence

Consumer hardware companies have more options now than ever before. They can create Explainer Videos on how their new product will solve an existing problem, then rapidly build using standard hardware components. They can eventually crowdfund the build and distribute to the customer through retail or direct.

- **Customer Interview** p. 106
- **Search Trend Analysis** p. 126
- **Paper Prototype** p. 182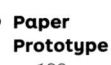
- **3D Print** p. 176
- **Explainer Video** p. 200
- **Crowdfunding** p. 266
- **Pop-Up Store** p. 300

B2C Software Sequence

The rise of the Internet, open source software, and tools have catapulted new software companies into global markets. Smart B2C companies use the words of their customers in their content to increase conversions. They rapidly prototype experiences and even deliver the value manually before building the product.

- **Customer Interview** p. 106
- **Online Ad** p. 146
- **Simple Landing Page** p. 260
- **Email Campaign** p. 162
- **Clickable Prototype** p. 236
- **Mock Sale** p. 288
- **Wizard of Oz** p. 284

B2C Services Sequence

B2C services companies start in a specific region by interviewing customers and looking for search volume to determine interest. They can quickly launch ads that drive regional customers to their landing page, then follow it up with an email campaign. Once they've conducted a few presales, B2C services can deliver the value manually to refine it before scaling.

- **Customer Interview** p. 106
- **Search Trend Analysis** p. 126
- **Online Ad** p. 146
- **Simple Landing Page** p. 260
- **Email Campaign** p. 162
- **Presale** p. 274
- **Concierge** p. 248

B2B2C with B2C Experimentation Sequence

B2B2C companies are in a unique position to use experimentation to inform the supply chain. Many companies we work with go directly to the consumer with their experiments, generate evidence, and then use it in negotiations with their B2B partners. The presence of evidence helps provide leverage, instead of circular conversations based only on opinion.

- **Customer Interview** p. 106
- **Online Ad** p. 146
- **Simple Landing Page** p. 260
- **Explainer Video** p. 200
- **Presale** p. 274
- **Concierge** p. 248
- **Buy a Feature** p. 226
- **Data Sheet** p. 190
- **Partner & Supplier Interview** p. 114
- **Letter of Intent** p. 294
- **Pop-Up Store** p. 300

Highly Regulated Sequence

Contrary to popular belief, highly regulated companies can also use experimentation. They need to do so within the constraints of the system and be mindful that not all testing activities involve a catastrophic degree of risk. Companies carve out the extremely high risk areas they are not willing to experiment on and then go after the places in which they can experiment.

- **A Day in the Life** p. 116
- **Validation Survey** p. 278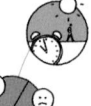
- **Customer Support Analysis** p. 142
- **Sales Force Feedback** p. 138
- **Storyboard** p. 186
- **Explainer Video** p. 200
- **Brochure** p. 194
- **Partner & Supplier Interview** p. 114
- **Data Sheet** p. 190
- **Presale** p. 274

"Knowing your customer
inside and out is mission-critical,
and it takes time."

————

Sallie Krawcheck
Founder, Ellevest

SECTION 3 — EXPERIMENTS

3.2 — DISCOVERY

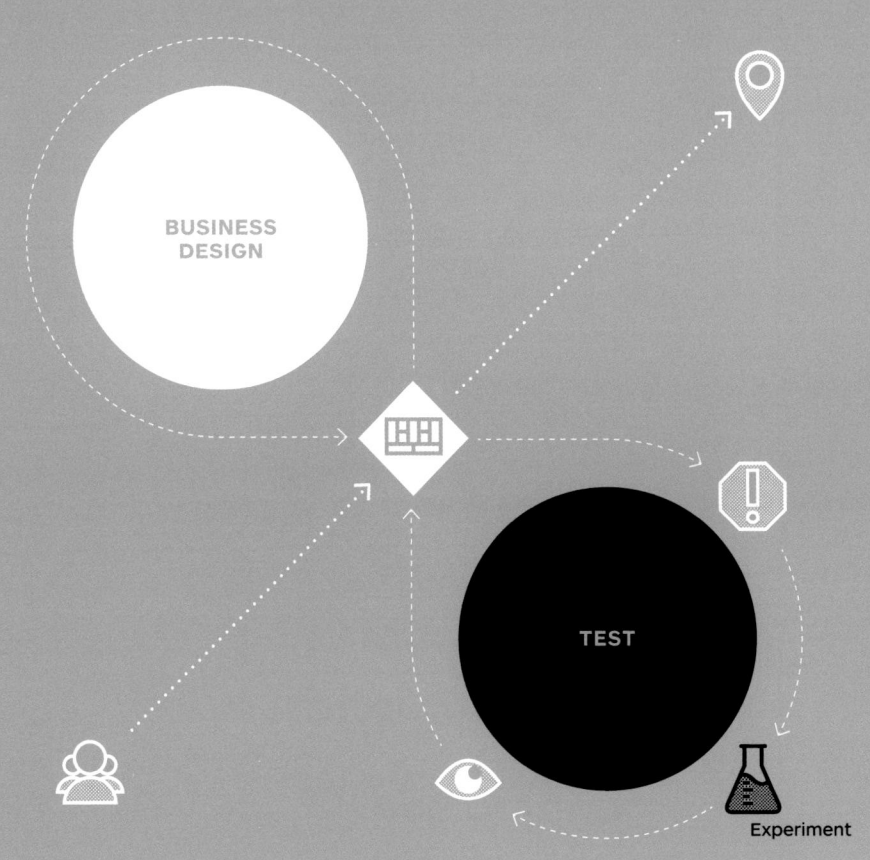

BUSINESS
DESIGN

TEST

Experiment

Idea

Business

Search & Testing	Execution

Discovery
Discover if your general direction is right. Test basic hypotheses. Get first insights to course-correct rapidly.

Validation
Validate the direction you've taken. Confirm with strong evidence that your business idea is very likely to work.

The discovery and validation phases in this book build on Steve Blank's seminal work "The Four Steps to the Epiphany." Steve and Bob Dorf elaborated on these phases in "The Startup Owner's Manual." Both these books are essential reading and landmarks in the development of modern thinking about entrepreneurship.

Discovery Experiments

TYPE	EXPERIMENT
Exploration	Customer Interview *p. 106* Expert Stakeholder Interviews *p. 115* Partner & Supplier Interviews *p. 114* A Day in the Life *p. 116* Discovery Survey *p. 122*
Data Analysis	Search Trend Analysis *p. 126* Web Traffic Analysis *p. 130* Discussion Forums *p. 134* Sales Force Feedback *p. 138* Customer Support Analysis *p. 142*
Interest Discovery	Online Ad *p. 146* Link Tracking *p. 152* 404 Test *p. 160* Feature Stub *p. 156* Email Campaign *p. 162* Social Media Campaign *p. 168* Referral Program *p. 172*
Discussion Prototypes	3D Print *p. 176* Paper Prototype *p. 182* Storyboard *p. 186* Data Sheet *p. 190* Brochure *p. 194* Explainer Video *p. 200* Boomerang *p. 204* Pretend to Own *p. 208*
Preference & Prioritization Discovery	Product Box *p. 214* Speed Boat *p. 218* Card Sorting *p. 222* Buy a Feature *p. 226*

COST	SETUP TIME	RUN TIME	EVIDENCE STRENGTH	THEME
●●○○○	●●○○○	●●○○○	●○○○○	DESIRABILITY · FEASIBILITY · VIABILITY
●●○○○	●●○○○	●●●○○	●●○○○	DESIRABILITY · FEASIBILITY · VIABILITY
●●○○○	●●○○○	●●●○○	●●●●○	DESIRABILITY · **FEASIBILITY** · VIABILITY
●●○○○	●●○○○	●●●○○	●●●○○	DESIRABILITY · FEASIBILITY · VIABILITY
●●○○○	●●○○○	●●●○○	●○○○○	DESIRABILITY · FEASIBILITY · VIABILITY
●○○○○	●●○○○	●●○○○	●●●○○	DESIRABILITY · FEASIBILITY · VIABILITY
●●○○○	●●○○○	●●●○○	●●○○○	DESIRABILITY · FEASIBILITY · VIABILITY
●○○○○	●●○○○	●●●○○	●●○○○	DESIRABILITY · FEASIBILITY · VIABILITY
●●○○○	●●○○○	●●○○○	●●○○○	DESIRABILITY · FEASIBILITY · VIABILITY
●●○○○	●●○○○	●●●○○	●●○○○	DESIRABILITY · FEASIBILITY · VIABILITY
●●●○○	●●○○○	●●●○○	●●●○○	DESIRABILITY · FEASIBILITY · VIABILITY
●○○○○	●○○○○	●●●○○	●●●○○	DESIRABILITY · FEASIBILITY · VIABILITY
●○○○○	●○○○○	●○○○○	●●●○○	DESIRABILITY · FEASIBILITY · VIABILITY
●○○○○	●●○○○	●●○○○	●●●●○	DESIRABILITY · FEASIBILITY · VIABILITY
●○○○○	●●○○○	●●●○○	●●●○○	DESIRABILITY · FEASIBILITY · VIABILITY
●●○○○	●●●○○	●●●●●	●●●○○	DESIRABILITY · FEASIBILITY · VIABILITY
●●●○○	●●○○○	●●●●●	●●●●○	DESIRABILITY · FEASIBILITY · VIABILITY
●●●○○	●●●○○	●●●○○	●●○○○	DESIRABILITY · FEASIBILITY · VIABILITY
●○○○○	●●○○○	●●○○○	●○○○○	DESIRABILITY · FEASIBILITY · VIABILITY
●●○○○	●●○○○	●○○○○	●●○○○	DESIRABILITY · FEASIBILITY · VIABILITY
●○○○○	●●○○○	●●○○○	●●●○○	DESIRABILITY · FEASIBILITY · VIABILITY
●○○○○	●●●○○	●●○○○	●●●○○	DESIRABILITY · FEASIBILITY · VIABILITY
●●●○○	●●●○○	●●●●○	●●●○○	DESIRABILITY · FEASIBILITY · VIABILITY
●●○○○	●●○○○	●●○○○	●●○○○	DESIRABILITY · FEASIBILITY · VIABILITY
●○○○○	●●○○○	●●●●○	●●○○○	DESIRABILITY · FEASIBILITY · VIABILITY
●●○○○	●●○○○	●○○○○	●●○○○	DESIRABILITY · FEASIBILITY · VIABILITY
●●○○○	●●○○○	●○○○○	●●●○○	DESIRABILITY · FEASIBILITY · VIABILITY
●●○○○	●●○○○	●○○○○	●●○○○	DESIRABILITY · FEASIBILITY · VIABILITY
●●○○○	●●○○○	●○○○○	●●○○○	DESIRABILITY · FEASIBILITY · VIABILITY

DISCOVERY / EXPLORATION

Customer Interview

An interview that is focused on exploring customer jobs, pains, gains, and willingness to pay.

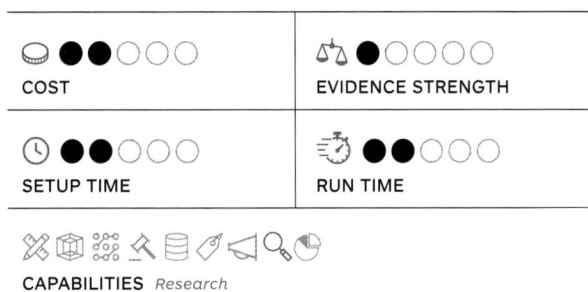

○ ●●○○○
COST

⚖ ●○○○○
EVIDENCE STRENGTH

🕐 ●●○○○
SETUP TIME

 ●●○○○
RUN TIME

✂🧊⚙⚒🗄🏷📢🔍🥧
CAPABILITIES *Research*

▦ ▷ ◑
DESIRABILITY · FEASIBILITY · VIABILITY

Customer Interviews are ideal for gaining qualitative insights into the fit between your value proposition and the customer segment. It's also a good starting point for price testing.

Customer Interviews are not ideal as a substitute for what people will do.

Prepare

☐ Write a script to learn about:

- customers jobs, pains, and gains.

- customers' willingness to buy.

- unmet needs between product and solution.

☐ Find Interviewees.

☐ Select a time frame for your analysis.

Execute

☐ Interviewer asks questions from the script and dives deeper when required.

☐ Scribe takes notes with exact phrasing and notes on body language.

☐ Repeat for 15–20 interviews.

Analyze

☐ Do a 15-minute debrief while impressions are fresh in mind.

☐ Affinity sort the notes.

☐ Perform a ranking analysis.

☐ Update your Value Proposition Canvas.

Cost

Cost is relatively low as customers may not even need to be compensated. In general, remote interviews over video have a lower compensation than scheduled in-person interviews. B2B interviews are typically more expensive than B2C interviews, because the sample size is smaller and may have less free time.

Setup Time

Setup time for customer interviews can be very short or take a few weeks, depending on where your customers are and how accessible. You'll need to create a script, find your customers, and schedule the interviews.

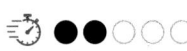

Run Time

Run time for customer interviews is relatively short: they only take 15–30 minutes each. You'll need to have a 15-minute buffer in between each one to recap your findings and make any edits you need to the script.

Evidence Strength

Customer jobs
Customer pains
Customer gains

80% average accuracy ranking on top-3 customer jobs, pains, and gains. You want to be really dialed into your customer segment, so set the bar high.

●○○○○

Customer feedback

Customer jobs, pains, and gains that were not originally in your Customer Profile, but were offered up by your interviewee.

●○○○○

Interview referrals

Referrals are an added bonus. It's a good sign if they occur and it'll save you on acqui-sition costs for more interviews.

Customer Interviews are relatively weak evidence: it's only what people say and not necessarily what they'll do. However, they are great for qualitative insights to inform your value proposition and customer jobs, pains, and gains for future testing.

Capabilities

Research

While customer interviews can be decep-tively difficult to do well, the good news it that almost anyone can do them with practice. It helps if you have a research background, but it isn't required. You'll need to write the script, source candidates, conduct the interview, and synthesize results. A partner makes this all so much easier — otherwise you'll have to record all of the interviews and watch them again.

Requirements

Target Customer

Customer Interviews work best when you are focused on a narrow target audience. Without a customer in mind, you'll end up getting very mixed results and conflicting feedback. It takes much longer to interview everyone, then back your way into a niche customer segment. Instead, we recommend you focus on a niche customer segment before running any customer interviews.

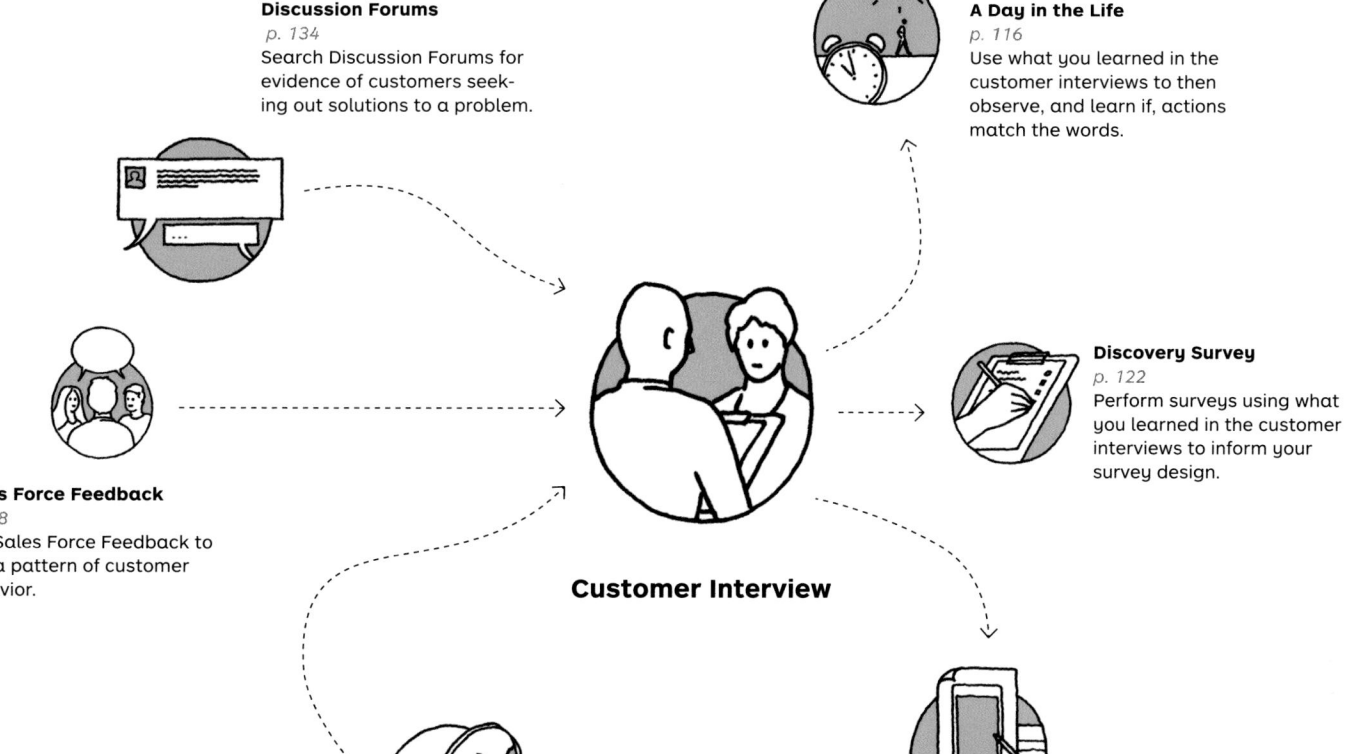

Discussion Forums
p. 134
Search Discussion Forums for evidence of customers seeking out solutions to a problem.

A Day in the Life
p. 116
Use what you learned in the customer interviews to then observe, and learn if, actions match the words.

Sales Force Feedback
p. 138
Use Sales Force Feedback to find a pattern of customer behavior.

Discovery Survey
p. 122
Perform surveys using what you learned in the customer interviews to inform your survey design.

Customer Interview

Search Trend Analysis
p. 126
Search online for volume around a specific job, pain, or gain.

Paper Prototype
p. 182
Sketch out what the solution to the customer jobs, pains, and gains could look like on paper.

CUSTOMER INTERVIEW

EXPLORATION

109

Writing a Script

Scripts are a key part of conducting effective customer interviews, otherwise they often turn into conversations that wander and rarely extract the learning. You need to de-risk your idea. We recommend building your script after you've created your Value Proposition Canvas and ranked the top three customer jobs, pains, and gains.

Sample Script

1. Introduction & Context

"Hello, I am [name] doing research on [idea]"

"No pressure to make a purchase."

"Not going to sell you anything."

2. Have Them Tell a Story

"When was the last time you experienced [pain or job]?"

"What motivated you to do [action]?"

"How did you solve it?"

"If not, why?"

3. Ranking Customer Jobs, Pains, and Gains

List the top three customer jobs, pains, and gains.

Interviewee ranks them based on personal experiences.

"Are there any others you expected to be on the list?"

4. Thanks & Wrap Up

"What question should I have asked you?"

"Can you refer me to someone else?"

"May we contact you in the future?"

"Thanks!"

Finding Interviewees

B2C Segment

We recommend creating a Value Proposition Canvas for your B2C segment and then brainstorming where you can find them online and offline. Vote as a team where you want to focus your search.

B2B Segment

Same exercise applies to B2B interviewee candidates, although it may be harder to brainstorm where to find them. Luckily there are online and offline locations that, in general, work well for finding B2B interviewees.

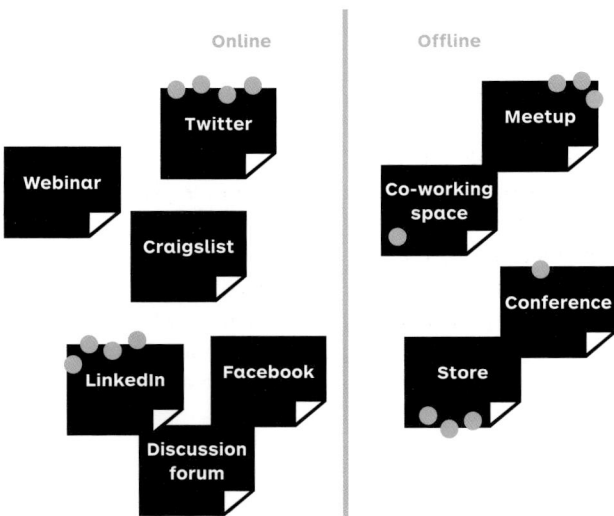

Vetting Interviewees

Vetting interview candidates isn't fail-safe, but overall it'll save you time by screening out those who do not qualify for the interview process. One or two less-than-ideal candidates will always slip through, but it's still better than not qualifying people at all. One way to do so is a simple screener survey to qualify people before scheduling anything.

Screening on Craigslist

Craigslist is a popular website for posting things to buy and sell, but it's also a gold mine for finding customers to interview. Simply go to the Community → Volunteers section of Craigslist and post your research request. In the description, include a survey link for those who are interested in participating. The survey should include qualifying and disqualifying questions.

For example, if you are looking for people who own a bicycle, ask: *"How many bicycles do you own—0, 1, 2, or 3+?"*

If people answer 0, then it saves you from interviewing those who do not own a bicycle. If people answer 3+, they also might not be ideal candidates because they own so many bicycles. Simple screener questions like this will save you and your interviewees hours.

Screening in-person

The offline version of this is very similar, although you'd simply ask these questions in person before diving into the entire interview. If they don't qualify, thank them for their time and move on.

Roles & Responsibilities

We recommend not doing these on your own if at all possible, whether your customer interview is online or in person. It's very difficult and time-consuming to ask the question, actively listen, note body language and response, and then ask the next question. If you get permission to record the interview, it'll take twice as long because you'll need to watch and listen to it all again. Instead, we recommend conducting interviews in pairs.

Scribe

- Takes notes.
- Writes exact quotes when possible without paraphrasing.
- Describes body language.

Interviewer

- Asks questions from script.
- Delves deeper when needed by asking why.
- Thanks and wrap up.

Interviewee

- Answers questions.

15-Minute Debrief

Immediately after each interview is concluded, take 15 minutes to debrief with your partner to quickly recap what you learned and if anything needs to be revised.

Debrief Topics

- What went well with that interview?
- What did we learn from body language?
- Did we bias the candidate in any way?
- Is there anything we want to quickly revise in the script?

Synthesizing Feedback

In addition to the 15-minute debrief, the team should synthesize their notes and update the Value Proposition Canvas to help inform your strategy. One quick way to sort through a lot of qualitative feedback is a technique called Affinity Sorting.

Affinity Sorting

As a team, set aside 30–60 minutes and bring your notes.

- Make sure there is plenty of wall space if meeting in person.
- Write one quote per sticky note.
- Write one insight per sticky note.
- Place the interviewee name or initials on the bottom of the sticky note.
- Place all stickies on the wall.
- Sort them into similar themes.

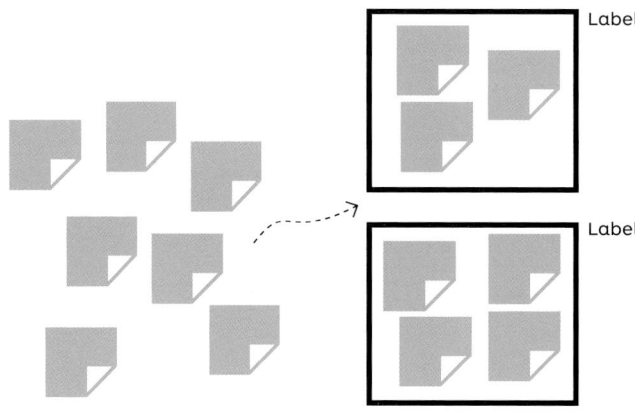

Ranking Analysis

Ranking isn't a perfect science, but it'll give you a sense of how close you are to the ranking in your Customer Profile. The drawback of having interviewees rank is that on its own, you don't know how much they feel the job, pain, or gain, relatively, compared to others. This is why it's important to ask follow-up questions and pick up on body language.

If you've interviewed 10 customers that match your Customer Profile, then ideally you want the customer jobs, pains, and gains ranking from your Customer Profile to be at the 80%+ accuracy rate. Which means 8 out of 10 ranked job 1 as #1, job 2 as #2, job 3 as #3, and so on.

Updating Your Canvas

After you've synthesized the qualitative feedback and analyzed rankings from your first batch of customer interviews, go back to your Value Proposition Canvas and make any edits needed. It's important that your testing inform your strategy.

☐ Ask for permission before recording.

☐ Qualify the candidate so that you don't waste each other's time.

☐ Adopt a beginner's mind.

☐ Listen more than you talk.

☐ Get facts, not opinions.

☐ Ask "why" to get real motivations.

☐ Ask for permission to follow up.

☐ Ask for referrals to interview.

☐ Ask if there is anything you should have asked, but didn't.

✖

– Talk more than you listen.

– Pitch the solution.

– Be thinking of the next question to ask, instead of actively listening to the response.

– Nod your head yes or no while the interviewee is speaking.

– Ask only closed ended questions.

– Schedule the interviews back to back, without any time in between to debrief.

– Forget to update your Value Proposition Canvas with your findings.

CUSTOMER INTERVIEW

EXPLORATION

113

114

DISCOVERY / EXPLORATION

Partner & Supplier Interviews

Partner & Supplier Interviews are similar to Customer Interviews, but you are focused on whether you can feasibly run the business. You'll be sourcing and interviewing Key Partners to supplement the Key Activities and Key Resources that you cannot do, or do not want to do, in-house.

DESIRABILITY · FEASIBILITY · VIABILITY

 ●●○○○
COST

 ●●○○○
SETUP TIME

●●●○○
RUN TIME

 ●●○○○

Evidence Strength
●●●●○

# of key partner bids

Response rate = number of partner interviews divided by the number of partner bids provided to you.

Key Partner bids are strong evidence that Key Partners are interested, although many details need to be agreed upon before it is a binding contract.

●●○○○

Key partner feedback

Key Partner quotes and feedback from the interviews.

When Key Partners state what they can deliver, it's relatively strong evidence as long as they check out.

Expert Stakeholder Interviews

Stakeholder Interviews are similar to Customer Interviews, but are focused on getting "buy-in" from key players inside your organization.

DESIRABILITY · FEASIBILITY · VIABILITY

Evidence Strength

Expert stakeholder feedback

Expert Stakeholder quotes and feedback from the interviews.

When stakeholders state what they wish to see strategically out of the initiative, it's moderately strong evidence. They need to back up their words with actions for it to be stronger.

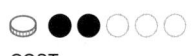

COST

SETUP TIME

RUN TIME

INTERVIEWS

115

EXPLORATION

DISCOVERY / EXPLORATION

A Day in the Life

A method of qualitative research that uses customer ethnography to better understand customer jobs, pains, and gains.

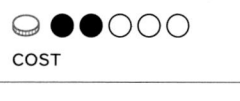 ●●○○○
COST

⚖ ●●●○○
EVIDENCE STRENGTH

🖩 ⧎ ◉
DESIRABILITY · FEASIBILITY · VIABILITY

🕐 ●●○○○
SETUP TIME

⏱ ●●●○○
RUN TIME

A Day in the Life is relatively cheap. You may need to compensate people for their time if you decide to work alongside or observe them for the entire day.

CAPABILITIES *Research*

1. Prepare

☐ In teams of 2–3, define where and how you plan to observe. Clear your calendar so that you can commit several hours. Identify how to take notes and set the ground rules for not biasing the participants.

2. Permission

☐ Get consent from those who you'd like to observe. Explain the "why" behind the request.

3. Observe

☐ Using the Day in the Life worksheet, capture the customer time, activity, jobs, pains, gains, and notes on what you think. Do not interview or interact with the participants while observing.

4. Analyze

☐ Once the session is over, meet with your team to sort through the notes. Update your Value Proposition Canvas to reflect the latest findings to help inform future experiments.

Cost

A Day in the Life is relatively cheap. You may need to compensate people for their time if you decide to work alongside or observe them for the entire day.

Setup Time

Setup time for A Day in the Life is relatively short. You'll need to define and obtain consent from the participants you observe for the day.

Run Time

Run time for A Day in the Life is a bit longer than other methods, in that you need to spend several hours each day observing customer behavior. This can extend over several days or weeks at a time, depending on the number of participants.

Evidence Strength

Customer jobs
Customer pains
Customer gains

Notes and activities on observed customer jobs, pains, and gains throughout the day.

The grouping and ranking output of A Day in the Life is weak evidence, although it's stronger than inviting people into a lab setting because it's observed behavior in the real world.

Customer quotes

Take note of additional quotes from the customers that are not limited to jobs, pains, and gains.

Customer quotes are relatively weak, but helpful for context and qualitative insights for upcoming experiments.

Capabilities

Research

Almost anyone can use A Day in the Life. It will help if you have research abilities so that you can collect and document the data properly. It's recommended that you have a partner when doing so to compare notes.

Requirements

Consent

A Day in the Life ideally requires consent from those you are observing. It also requires you to coordinate with management and security at the locations in which you observe. For example, if you are going to hang out at a retail store and observe patterns, then speak to the manager first to get permission. If you wish to observe someone who made a purchase, ask them for permission before doing so. Otherwise this can become creepy and you may be escorted out by security.

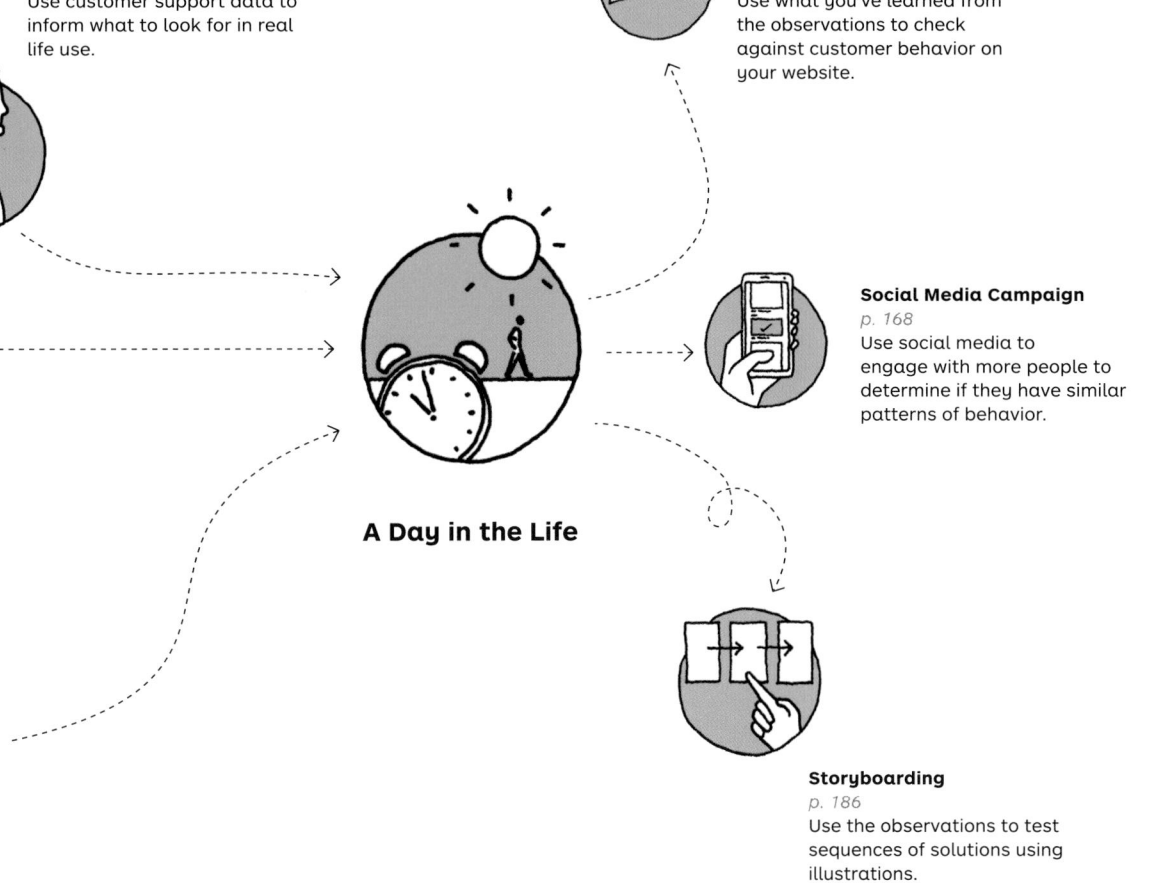

Customer Support Analysis
p. 142
Use customer support data to inform what to look for in real life use.

Web Traffic Analysis
p. 130
Use what you've learned from the observations to check against customer behavior on your website.

Discussion Forums
p. 134
Search through Discussion Forums to identify unmet customer needs and observe if they occur in real life.

Social Media Campaign
p. 168
Use social media to engage with more people to determine if they have similar patterns of behavior.

A Day in the Life

Storyboarding
p. 186
Use the observations to test sequences of solutions using illustrations.

Search Trend Analysis
p. 126
Use what you've found people searching for online and observe if this is happening in day-to-day usage.

A DAY IN THE LIFE

119

EXPLORATION

A DAY IN THE LIFE

Closing the Say/Do Gap
Intuit's Follow-Me-Home Program

Intuit creates financial, accounting, and tax preparation solutions for small businesses, accountants, and individuals, such as TurboTax, Quick-Books, and Mint.com. Intuit is located in the heart of Silicon Valley (Mountain View, California) and is well known for pushing the boundaries of customer-centric problem solving.

Can you give us a brief explanation of the Follow-Me-Home Program at Intuit?
The Follow-Me-Home is one technique from Intuit's "Design for Delight" program, that teaches our employees the skills required to create awesome products for our customers. Design for Delight includes three core principles: Deep Customer Empathy, Go Broad to Go Narrow, and Rapid Experimentation with Customers. The Follow-Me-Home is the most powerful technique from the Design for Delight principle, Deep Customer Empathy. There is nothing more effective than observing a customer when and where they are actually experiencing the pain and problems we are trying to solve.

We teach the Follow-Me-Home technique to each and every employee in the company, and each new person who joins Intuit learns the technique as part of their onboarding process. In fact, each new hire conducts at least two Follow-Me-Homes within the first few weeks of starting their career at Intuit, regardless of their function or level of seniority. From new engineers, to seasoned HR personnel, to product managers, to our most senior leaders, everyone is expected to learn how do to a Follow-Me-Home.

How did it get started?
Intuit's founder, Scott Cook, was inspired by a similar technique used by Toyota. In the early days of Intuit, Scott suspected he could use this technique to improve Intuit's products, and so he began testing the Follow-Me-Home approach while building our early products such as Quicken and QuickBooks. In those days software was installed on a physical computer via floppy discs (sounds crazy), so Scott and our product teams asked real customers if they could watch them install the software after it was purchased.

Through observation, product teams uncovered new insights, and complete surprises about how customers actually used our software in the real world. These insights often led to product improvements, so the Follow-Me-Home principles were codified, then shared with our employees. The Follow-Me-Home technique continues to evolve with the times, but the spirit remains the same—go observe customers where they are experiencing the pain or problems about which you need to learn.

What's your role in the program?
My team reports to Diego Rodriguez, Intuit's Chief Product and Design Officer. Our mission is to nurture Intuit's culture of innovation, through programs such as Design for Delight, our network of expert Innovation Catalyst Coaches, and high-impact training. Our job is to ensure each and every employee has the opportunity to learn and apply the most effective innovations skills to their daily work, such as Follow-Me-Homes, and we continuously improve these skills as the world changes.

We partner with other organizations such as HR, Learning and Development, and functional communities to achieve this goal, but our team's specialty is ensuring Intuit's innovation flame always burns bright. I work with an amazing team who are all dedicated to this goal, so my job is to simply continue learning and improving as a team. There are always ways we can get better.

What do you find most challenging about training employees in this technique?
Techniques like Follow-Me-Home can be learned by anyone, but just like any new skill, it takes consistent practice to master. In the early stages of learning people often misunderstand the details of how to execute a Follow-Me-Home, and it takes time for best practice to become second nature.

For example, one VERY important aspect of a great Follow-Me-Home is the focus on observation, versus traditional interviewing—i.e., talking. We teach people to focus first on what they observe a customer actually doing in a real situation, using their real tools, rather than overly scripting a simulation, or asking questions. Once observation is complete, only then should you ask interview-like questions, and when you ask questions focus on the "why" behind the observed behaviors, not speculation or opinions. When people first learn how to conduct a Follow-Me-Home, they typically ask way too many questions, and do not focus on simply observing the behaviors in question. That's just one example.

We also know that not everyone is comfortable "getting outside the building" to speak with people who are complete strangers. It does take a bit of courage to go try a Follow-Me-Home the first few times, so getting people over their initial reluctance is something we focus on, as well as encouraging them to practice often. The good news is that the vast majority of people tell us Follow-Me-Homes are transformative, and they often begin doing Follow-Me-Homes on their own. They end up loving the technique.

How do you see programs like this evolving in the future?
We've already improved our approach to Follow-Me-Homes over the years, and we'll continue to do so as the world around us evolves. For example, Intuit has an increasing number of customers all over the world. We've adapted the Follow-Me-Home so we can conduct them remotely, using video camera and screen share technology. We've also tweaked the approach to ensure we respect the cultures and traditions of the locations we visit. As the world continues to get flatter, and technology changes, we'll continue to adapt our approach. However, the spirit remains the same. Go observe for yourself.

What advice would you give readers who'd like to try this at their organization?
The simple answer is to just try it. Start small, trying it yourself on a few projects so you can learn what works and what does not work in the context of your organization. Then you build on what you learned to scale a formal program, or just continue using the technique yourself. You just might become the most effective person in your organization.

People who read this book are familiar with innovation best practices, so I simply suggest you apply these best practices to your future Follow-Me-Home program as if it is a "new product." Remember that Follow-Me-Homes are just one of the many skills required to be an effective innovator, so Follow-Me-Homes won't make you successful in a vacuum. You will likely need to develop supporting programs, and a culture which embraces these types of techniques. The good news is Follow-Me-Homes and the related skills are extremely fast to execute, flexible, and much cheaper than a failed product launch. Get out there and try it.

— Bennett Blank
Innovation Leader, Intuit Inc.

DISCOVERY / EXPLORATION

Discovery Survey

An open-ended questionnaire used in the collection of information from a sample of customers.

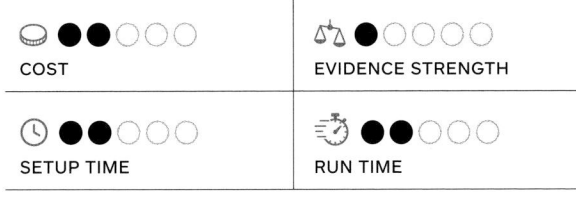

COST

EVIDENCE STRENGTH

SETUP TIME

RUN TIME

CAPABILITIES *Product / Marketing / Research*

DESIRABILITY · FEASIBILITY · VIABILITY

Discovery Survey is ideal for uncovering your value proposition and customer jobs, pains, and gains.

Discovery Survey is not ideal for determining what people will do, only what they say they'll do.

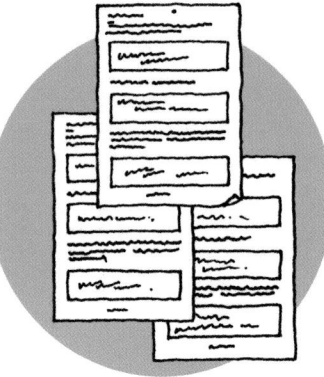

Sample Survey Questions

- *When was the last time you have [insert scenario here]?*
- *Can you explain what happened and how it impacted you?*
- *What other options did you explore? Why?*
- *If you could wave a magic wand, what would you have liked to have happened?*
- *What question do you wish we would have asked you?*

Prepare

☐ Define your goal for the survey and what you are trying to learn.

☐ Identify your target audience for the survey.

☐ Assuming a 10–20% response rate and calculate how many people should receive the survey.

☐ Set a start and stop date for the survey.

☐ Create your survey.

Execute

☐ Send your survey to customers.

Analyze

☐ Use Affinity Sorting to cluster responses into themes. Don't label before you sort; allow the labels to emerge from the sorting.

☐ Use word clouds or a text analyzer to quickly visualize which words and phrases customers use most frequently.

☐ Review the themes and quotes with your team and dot vote on the 1–3 themes you want to explore in more detail in upcoming experiments.

☐ Update your Value Proposition Canvas based on your findings.

Cost

Discovery surveys are not very expensive and there are several free and low-cost services that you can use to send them to your customers. Much of the cost comes from reaching the target audience. It gets more expensive if you are targeting professionals or are in the B2B space. Your sample size gets smaller; therefore you may end up spending time and money to reach your audience.

Setup Time

Discovery surveys do not take very long to set up and configure. Many of the questions are open-ended. It should only take a few hours to a day at most.

Run Time

Much of the run time on a discovery survey depends on the size of your customer pool and how easy it is to reach them. It shouldn't take more than a few days, but could take longer if you aren't able to get enough results.

Evidence Strength

●○○○○

# of free text answer responses

Insights

Look for repeating patterns in the responses to the survey. By the fifth survey response with a similar target customer, you should start seeing the same thing written in different ways.

●○○○○

 # people willing to be contacted after the survey

Valid Emails

Ideally you have a small percentage, around 10%, who want to be contacted in the future.

Capabilities

Product / Marketing / Research

Discovery surveys require the ability to write open-ended survey questions without a negative tone. You'll also need to be able to identify the audience and interpret the results by Affinity Sorting or using word clouds to find patterns in the feedback.

Requirements

Qualitative Source Material

Surveys are generally more impactful when you already have qualitative insights from other methods that don't scale. Use that material to inform your survey design.

Access to an Audience

Getting in front of the right audience is just as important as your survey design. If you have an existing site with lots of traffic, then you can leverage that to get to your audience. If you do not have this luxury or are going after a new market, then brainstorm channels to use before designing your survey.

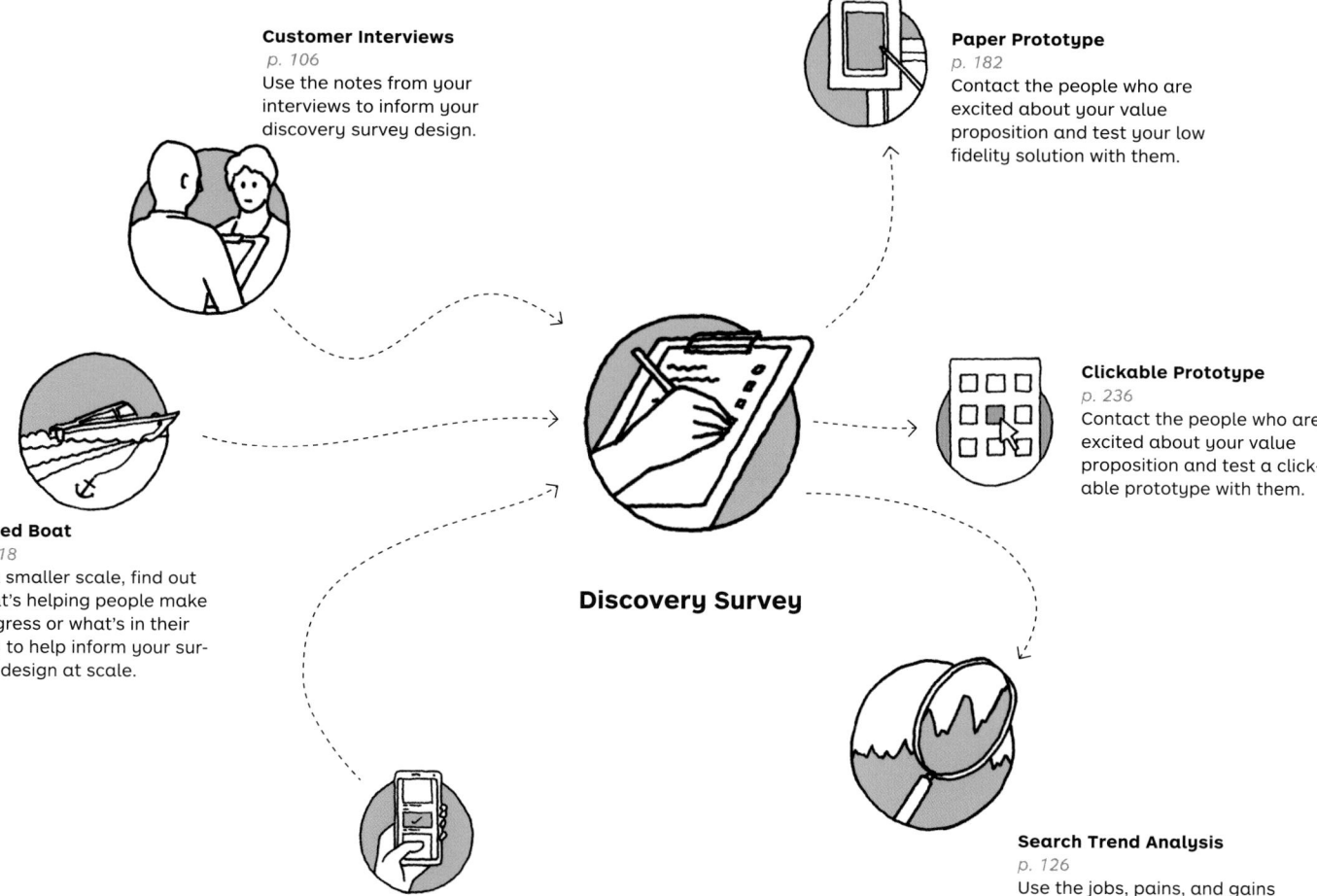

Customer Interviews
p. 106
Use the notes from your interviews to inform your discovery survey design.

Paper Prototype
p. 182
Contact the people who are excited about your value proposition and test your low fidelity solution with them.

Speed Boat
p. 218
At a smaller scale, find out what's helping people make progress or what's in their way to help inform your survey design at scale.

Clickable Prototype
p. 236
Contact the people who are excited about your value proposition and test a click-able prototype with them.

Discovery Survey

Social Media Campaign
p. 168
Use social media to acquire an audience for your discovery survey.

Search Trend Analysis
p. 126
Use the jobs, pains, and gains people listed to find out if these are popular search trends online.

DISCOVERY / DATA ANALYSIS

Search Trend Analysis

The use of search data to investigate particular interactions among online searchers, the search engine, or the content during searching episodes.

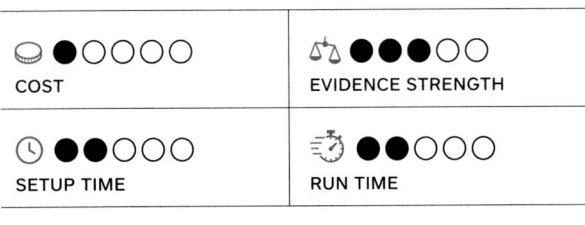

○● ○○○○
COST

⚖ ●●●○○
EVIDENCE STRENGTH

🕐 ●●○○○
SETUP TIME

⏱ ●●○○○
RUN TIME

CAPABILITIES *Marketing / Research / Data*

DESIRABILITY · FEASIBILITY · VIABILITY

Search Trend Analysis is ideal for performing your own market research, especially on newer trends, instead of relying on third party market research data.

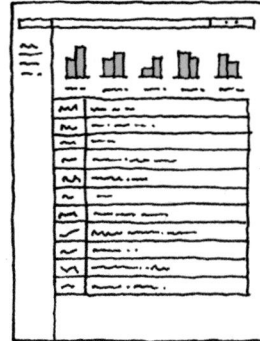

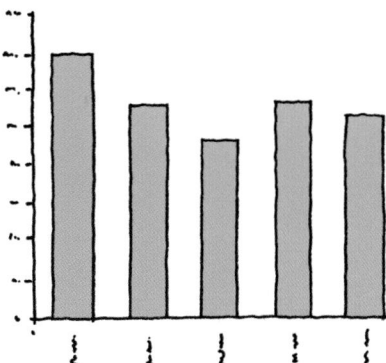

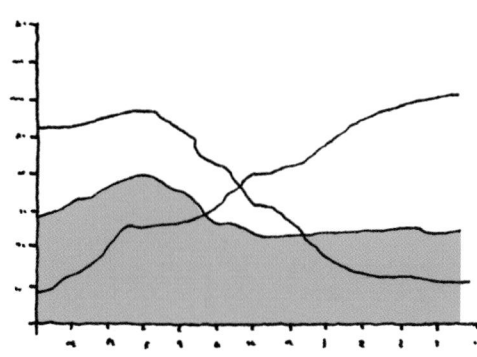

Prepare

☐ Identify what tools to use (Google Trends, Google Keyword Planner, etc.)

☐ Define a geographical area for your search.

☐ List the topics you want to explore such as:

- people trying to solve for customer jobs.

- individuals needing to address a customer pain.

- people wanting to create a customer gain.

- customers who are unhappy with an existing solution.

Execute

☐ Search for phrases related to your topics.

☐ Take screenshots and export your results.

☐ Write down notes alongside your research on what surprised you.

Analyze

☐ Gather your findings.

☐ Consider focusing on problem size over market size. What has the highest search volume on a typical problem? Would that be a meaningful business opportunity for you?

☐ Select the top 1–3 volume searches you want to explore in more detail in upcoming experiments.

Cost

The cost of performing your own Search Trend Analysis is relatively cheap, since there are existing free and low-cost tools. Both Google Trends and Google Keyword Planner are currently free to use.

Setup Time

Setup Time to perform Search Trend Analysis is relatively short, from a few minutes to a few hours. You'll need to define the criteria for your search and choose a tool.

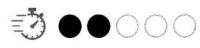

Run Time

Run Time to perform Search Trend Analysis is also relatively short, from a few hours to a few days. It largely depends on the number of topics and geographic locations you are exploring. The more you have, the longer it'll take to do well.

Evidence Strength

Search Volume

# of searches for keyword within a certain period of time

Search Volume varies across geographic location, time, and industry. You'll want to compare your results against the others to get an overall feel for the level of interest.

Related Queries

Queries that users also searched for, in addition to the one you entered

If conducted properly, strength of evidence on search volume and related queries can be stronger than other smaller qualitative research methods.

Capabilities

Marketing / Research / Data

Search Trend Analysis can be performed by almost anyone who is willing to learn online trend analysis tools. Most of them, such as Google Trends and Google Keyword Planner, will have contextual help to walk you through the process. You'll still need to be able to interpret the results, so having a marketing, research, and data background will be beneficial.

Requirements

Online Customers

Search Trend Analysis can be a powerful way to uncover customer jobs, pains, gains, and even their willingness to pay for a solution. However, they must have performed searches online to generate this evidence. If you are targeting a niche, B2B, or mainly offline customer, your searches are not going to return any significant volume.

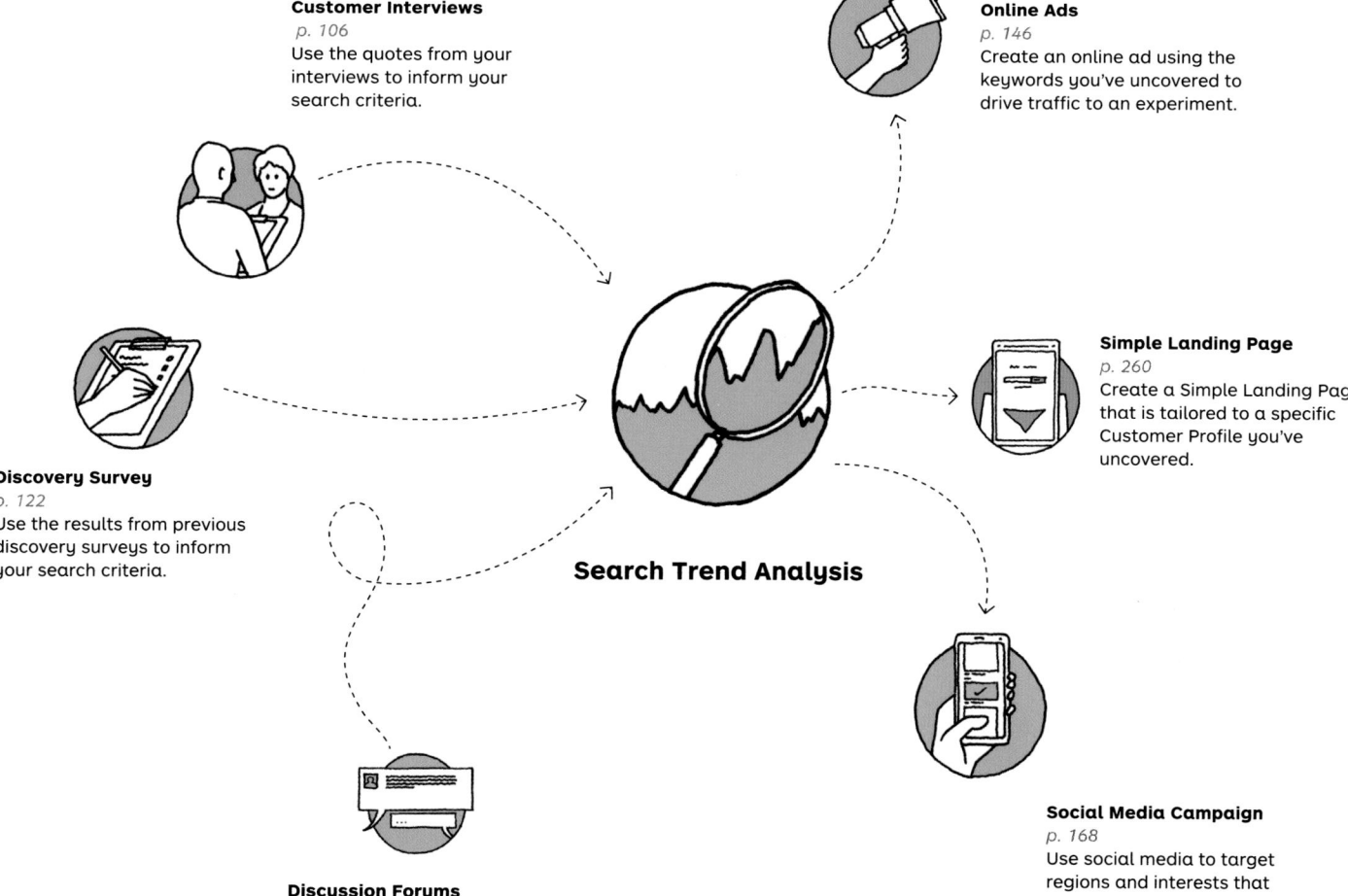

Customer Interviews
p. 106
Use the quotes from your interviews to inform your search criteria.

Online Ads
p. 146
Create an online ad using the keywords you've uncovered to drive traffic to an experiment.

Discovery Survey
p. 122
Use the results from previous discovery surveys to inform your search criteria.

Simple Landing Page
p. 260
Create a Simple Landing Page that is tailored to a specific Customer Profile you've uncovered.

Search Trend Analysis

Discussion Forums
p. 134
Use what you've learned from browsing discussion forums to better inform your search criteria to determine problem size.

Social Media Campaign
p. 168
Use social media to target regions and interests that you've analyzed through Search Trend Analysis.

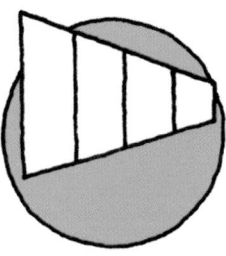

DISCOVERY / DATA ANALYSIS

Web Traffic Analysis

The use of website data collection, reporting, and analysis to look for customer behavior patterns.

COST ● ● ○ ○ ○

EVIDENCE STRENGTH ● ○ ○ ○ ○

SETUP TIME ● ● ○ ○ ○

RUN TIME ● ● ● ○ ○

CAPABILITIES *Technology / Data*

DESIRABILITY · FEASIBILITY · VIABILITY

The use of website data collection, reporting, and analysis to look for customer behavior patterns.

Prepare

☐ Create your focus area and what customer event it applies to:

- Increasing signups.

- Increasing downloads.

- Increasing # of purchases.

☐ Identify the steps leading up to that event.

☐ Select a time frame for your analysis.

Execute

☐ Using your web analytics software, run your analysis on the defined path.

☐ Note the drop-off points and percentages of each.

Analyze

☐ What are the biggest drop-offs in your flow?

☐ What experiments can you run to improve that number?

Cost

The cost of performing web traffic analysis is relatively cheap, especially if you use a free tool like Google Analytics. If you require more in-depth, event-level tracking and want to pay for a tool, they can vary widely in cost. Some start out very cheap, but as your customer traffic scales the cost can increase with it. If you are looking for heat map analysis of how people use the pages, there are low-cost options for that as well.

Setup Time

Setup time to perform web traffic analysis is relatively short, from a few hours to a few days. You'll need to integrate the tool into your website and log into the dashboard to view the data. Depending on the tool, it may take a day or more for the data to appear.

Run Time

Run time to perform web traffic analysis is unfortunately rather long, typically from weeks to months. It largely depends on the amount of traffic you have, but essentially you don't want to make large risky decisions based on a few days' worth of data.

Evidence Strength

●○○○○

# of sessions

Number of interactions with your website within a given time frame, for a specific user. Usually within a 30-minute period.

●●○○○

# of drop-offs

Drop-offs occur when a user drops out of the flow you've defined. You'll want to analyze the percent of drop-offs at which step and whether they left the site entirely.

How many customers you have on the site and where they are dropping off is relatively strong evidence, as it is measuring what they do. You don't know why they are doing it until you ask them.

●●●●○

Amount of attention

Attention can be a number of different user actions, usually including time spent on page and where they clicked. Users don't always click on buttons and links, so having heat map data can give you amazing insights into how you are gaining or losing attention in your site.

Attention is also relatively strong evidence, and yet, like session and drop-offs, it only tells you the "what" and not the "why."

Capabilities

Technology / Data

The learning curve on web traffic analysis can get steep rather quickly, especially once you go beyond the basics of user behavior. We suggest having the technical capability to integrate the analytics software and the data awareness of being able to analyze the results. For example, the heat map data will show you where people clicked, but you'll want to slice that data by source to see if people coming from online ads click differently than those who come from an email campaign.

Requirements

Traffic

Web traffic analysis requires an existing website with active users, otherwise you won't be able to collect any evidence. Similar to the simple landing page, we recommend driving traffic to your site using:

- Online ads
- Social media campaigns
- Email campaigns
- Word of mouth
- Discussion forums

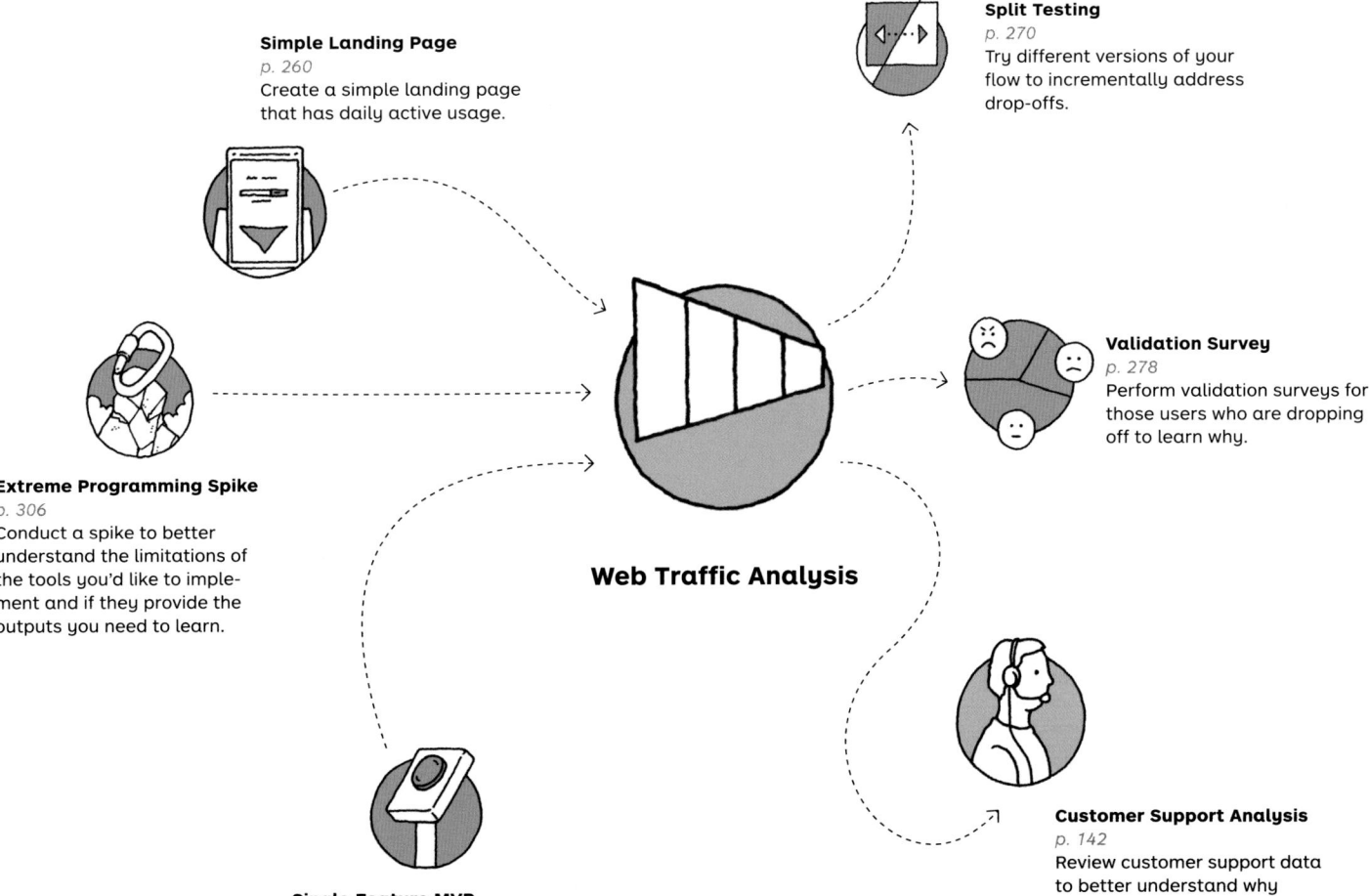

Simple Landing Page
p. 260
Create a simple landing page that has daily active usage.

Split Testing
p. 270
Try different versions of your flow to incrementally address drop-offs.

Extreme Programming Spike
p. 306
Conduct a spike to better understand the limitations of the tools you'd like to implement and if they provide the outputs you need to learn.

Validation Survey
p. 278
Perform validation surveys for those users who are dropping off to learn why.

Web Traffic Analysis

Customer Support Analysis
p. 142
Review customer support data to better understand why customers may be behaving this way on your website.

Single Feature MVP
p. 240
Build a single feature MVP in your website to better understand onboarding flow and getting customers to use it.

WEB TRAFFIC ANALYSIS

133

DATA ANALYSIS

DISCOVERY / DATA ANALYSIS

Discussion Forums

The use of discussion forums to uncover unmet jobs, pains, and gains in a product or service.

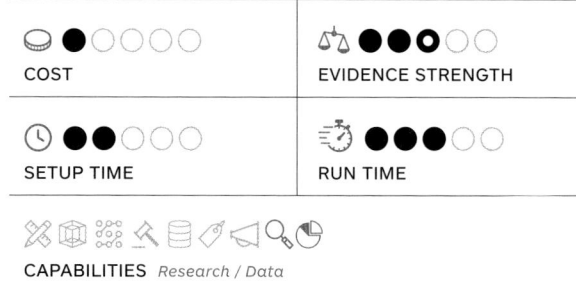

COST

EVIDENCE STRENGTH

SETUP TIME

RUN TIME

CAPABILITIES *Research / Data*

DESIRABILITY · FEASIBILITY · VIABILITY

Discussion Forums are ideal for finding unmet needs in your existing product or a competitor's product.

Execute

☐ Search for phrases related to your questions on discussion forums.

☐ Take screenshots and export your results.

☐ Write down notes about sense of urgency and tone in the forum threads.

Analyze

☐ Update your Value Proposition Canvas based on your findings.

☐ Contact the forum posters in direct messages to learn if they'll speak to you in more detail.

☐ If yes, then run experiments with them to help close the gap.

Prepare

☐ Identify what discussion forums you want to use for your analysis (internal vs. external).

☐ Define the questions you want to answer such as, is there evidence that:

• you are not solving for top customer jobs?

• you are not addressing major customer pains?

• you are not creating customer gains?

• customers are creating their own work-around solutions to address your product deficiencies?

Cost

Cost is relatively cheap, since you are basically analyzing online discussion forums to find unmet needs. If it's your own discussion forum, this should be relatively cost effective and analytics may even be already built into your software. If you are analyzing a competitor's or other community discussion boards, you'll likely be web scraping them with low-cost tools or just doing it manually yourself. You'll save on the cost by manually doing so but it might take much longer.

Setup Time

Setup time to analyze discussion forums is relatively short. It'll require you to define the questions you want to answer and identify which discussion forums to analyze.

Run Time

Run time for analyzing discussion forums is also relatively short. It takes a bit longer if you decide not to use a web scraping tool, so we'd recommend automating it if possible to shorten run time. You'll want to look for patterns of unmet customer jobs, pains, and gains.

Evidence Strength

Types of work-arounds

Look for a pattern of work-arounds or ways to hack the product to get it to do what people need. This can provide insights into improvements.

Similar to Steve Blank's "built a solution to solve the problem," it's strong evidence if people are hacking together their own methods to solve problems the product doesn't fully address.

Types of feature requests

Look for a pattern in the top three features requested on the discussion forums and what pains and underlying jobs they could solve.

Feature requests are relatively weak evidence, in that you'll need to perform more experiments around the underlying job or pain the proposed feature is intended to solve.

Capabilities

Research / Data

You'll need to be able to identify discussion forums, gather data, and analyze it. In doing so, it'll help to be able to understand how to scrape online websites and what questions you'll want to answer from looking through the data. It'll help if you have data and research capabilities when doing so.

Requirements

Discussion Forum Data

The most important requirement for analyzing discussion forum data is having existing discussion forums to analyze the questions you need to answer. If you feel there are unmet needs in a competitor's product, go to community and support forums where their customers post topics. If you have your own discussion forums, they should also be a great source of data.

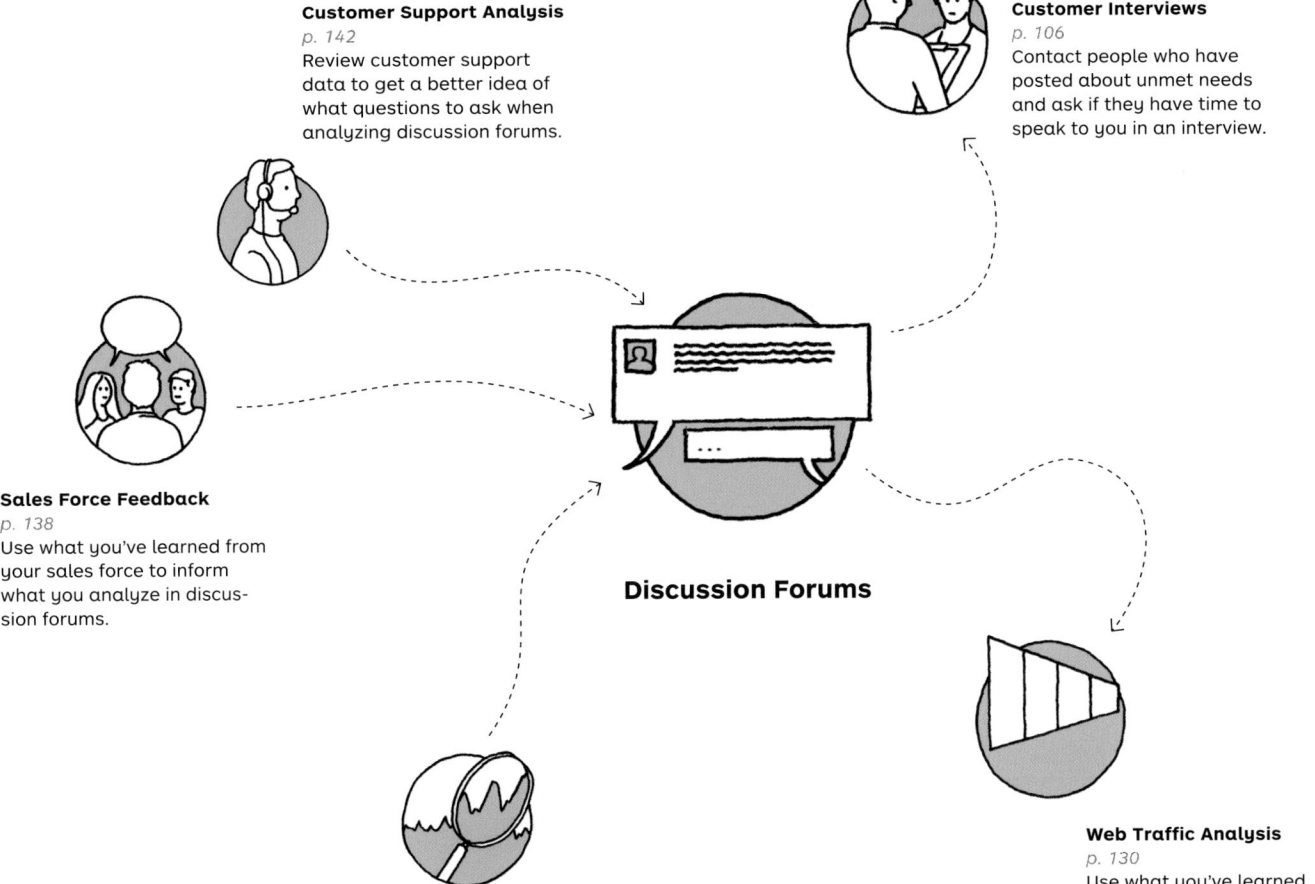

Customer Support Analysis
p. 142
Review customer support data to get a better idea of what questions to ask when analyzing discussion forums.

Customer Interviews
p. 106
Contact people who have posted about unmet needs and ask if they have time to speak to you in an interview.

Sales Force Feedback
p. 138
Use what you've learned from your sales force to inform what you analyze in discussion forums.

Discussion Forums

Search Trend Analysis
p. 126
Search the web to see how people are responding to your product or a competitor's product.

Web Traffic Analysis
p. 130
Use what you've learned from the discussion forums to check against customer behavior on your website.

DISCOVERY / DATA ANALYSIS

Sales Force Feedback

The use of sales force feedback to uncover unmet jobs, pains, and gains in your product or service.

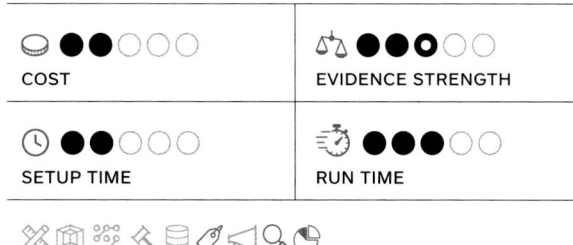

COST ●●○○○

EVIDENCE STRENGTH ●●◐○○

SETUP TIME ●●○○○

RUN TIME ●●●○○

CAPABILITIES *Sales / Research / Data*

DESIRABILITY · FEASIBILITY · VIABILITY

Sales force feedback is ideal for businesses that use a group of people to conduct sales.

Prepare

☐ Identify the questions you'd like answered from your sales force:

• Are you are solving for top customer jobs?

• Are you addressing major customer pains?

• Are you creating customer gains?

☐ If you have a complex B2B business, then segment your questions into the additional roles of:

• decision makers.

• economic buyers.

• recommenders.

• influencers.

☐ Schedule sessions with your sales force to answer the questions.

Execute

☐ Discuss with your sales force their thoughts on these questions.

☐ Have them bring up any evidence to support their answers from sales calls, dashboards, emails, and so on.

☐ Thank them for their time to help improve the experience.

Analyze

☐ Update your Value Proposition Canvas based on your findings.

☐ Use what you've learned to identify experiments to improve fit.

Cost

Cost is relatively cheap, with much of it focused around collecting the data in a usable way from your existing sales force. The analysis of the sale force feedback data can be done without expensive software or consultants.

Setup Time

Setup time to sort through sales force feedback is relatively short. You'll need to define the time period you'll analyze and what you are specifically looking for in the feedback.

Run Time

Run time for analyzing sales force feedback is also relatively short once you set it up. You'll want to look for patterns of unmet jobs, pains, and gains.

Evidence Strength

# of near misses
Near miss feedback

When your sales group has successfully closed, what almost prevented the sale from occurring? You'll want to log how many sales were almost lost and what customers had to say about what "almost prevented them from purchasing" to better understand fit.

Customer feedback on why they almost didn't purchase, but ultimately did, is a gold mine of relatively strong evidence. It's stronger than most feedback because they've just converted.

Types of feature requests

Look for a pattern in the top three features requested in the sales process and what pains and underlying jobs they could solve.

Feature requests are relatively weak evidence, in that you'll need to perform more experiments around the underlying job or pain the proposed feature is intended to solve.

Capabilities

Research / Data

You'll need to be able to gather, sort, and analyze sales force feedback. In doing so, it'll help to be able to understand how sales operate and what questions you'll want to answer.

Requirements

Sales Force Data

The most important requirement for analyzing sales force feedback is having an engaged sales force that can either provide feedback to you in verbal form or through the customer relationship management (CRM) software.

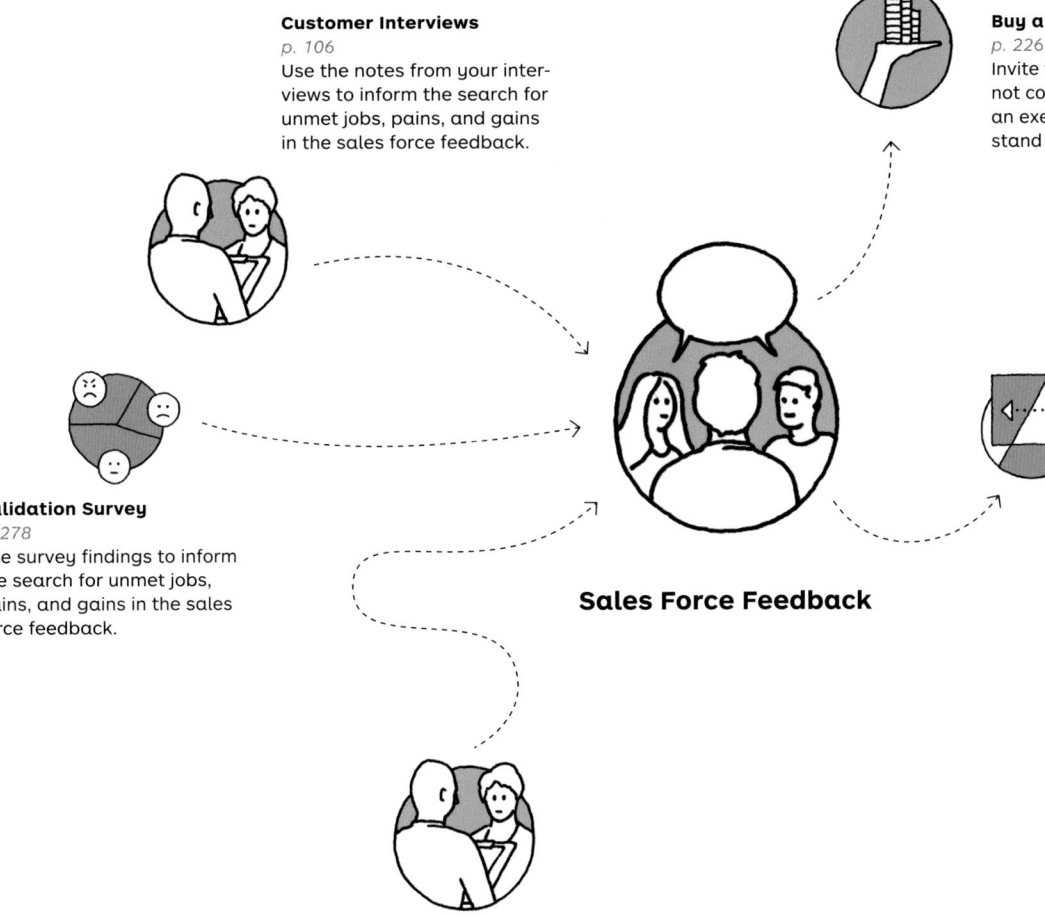

Customer Interviews
p. 106
Use the notes from your interviews to inform the search for unmet jobs, pains, and gains in the sales force feedback.

Buy a Feature
p. 226
Invite those people who did not convert to participate in an exercise to better understand the features they need.

Validation Survey
p. 278
Use survey findings to inform the search for unmet jobs, pains, and gains in the sales force feedback.

Split Test
p. 270
Run a Split Test in your sales process to test out different versions of your value proposition to customers.

Sales Force Feedback

Expert Stakeholder Interviews
p. 115
Use the notes from stakeholders to better understand if their needs translate into sales.

DISCOVERY / DATA ANALYSIS

Customer Support Analysis

The use of customer support data to uncover unmet jobs, pains, and gains in your product or service.

◔ ●●○○○
COST

⚖ ●●○○○
EVIDENCE STRENGTH

🕐 ●●○○○
SETUP TIME

⏱ ●●●○○
RUN TIME

CAPABILITIES *Sales / Marketing / Research / Data*

▦ ▶ ◑
DESIRABILITY · FEASIBILITY · VIABILITY

Customer support analysis is ideal for businesses that already have a substantial amount of existing customers.

Prepare

☐ Identify the questions you'd like answered from your customer support data:

- Are you are solving for top customer jobs?
- Are you addressing major customer pains?
- Are you creating customer gains?

☐ Schedule sessions with your customer support team to answer these questions.

Execute

☐ Discuss with your customer support team — their thoughts on these questions.

☐ Have them bring up any evidence to support their answers from customer support calls, dashboards, emails, and so on.

☐ Thank them for their time to help improve the experience.

Analyze

☐ Update your Value Proposition Canvas based on your findings.

☐ Use what you've learned to identify experiments to improve fit.

Cost

Cost is relatively cheap, in that most of the cost is incurred by simply gathering the customer data over time. The analysis of that data can be done without expensive software or consultants.

Setup Time

Setup time for customer support analysis is relatively short once you have the data. You'll need to define the time period you'll analyze and what you are specifically looking for in the data.

Run Time

Run time for customer support analysis is also relatively short once you have the data and have defined what you are looking for in the data. You'll want to look for patterns of unmet jobs, pains, and gains.

Evidence Strength

Customer feedback

Customer quotes during customer support calls that refer to jobs they are trying to accomplish, pains they feel aren't addressed, and unmet gains.

Customer feedback in customer support data is relatively weak evidence on its own, but can be used to inform future experiments.

Types of feature requests

Look for a pattern in the top three features requested and what pains and underlying jobs they could solve.

Feature requests are relatively weak evidence, in that you'll need to perform more experiments around the underlying job or pain the proposed feature is intended to solve.

Capabilities

Research / Marketing / Sales / Data

You'll need to be able to gather, sort, and analyze customer support data. In doing so, it'll help to be able to understand how sales operates, how your product is marketed, and what questions you'll want to answer from looking at the data.

Requirements

Customer Support Data

The most important requirement for customer support analysis is already having customer support data to analyze. This can be in many forms, whether it is recorded calls from your support team to emails or bug/feature requests submitted. The data you analyze should consist of more than one-off, anecdotal conversations with a handful of customers.

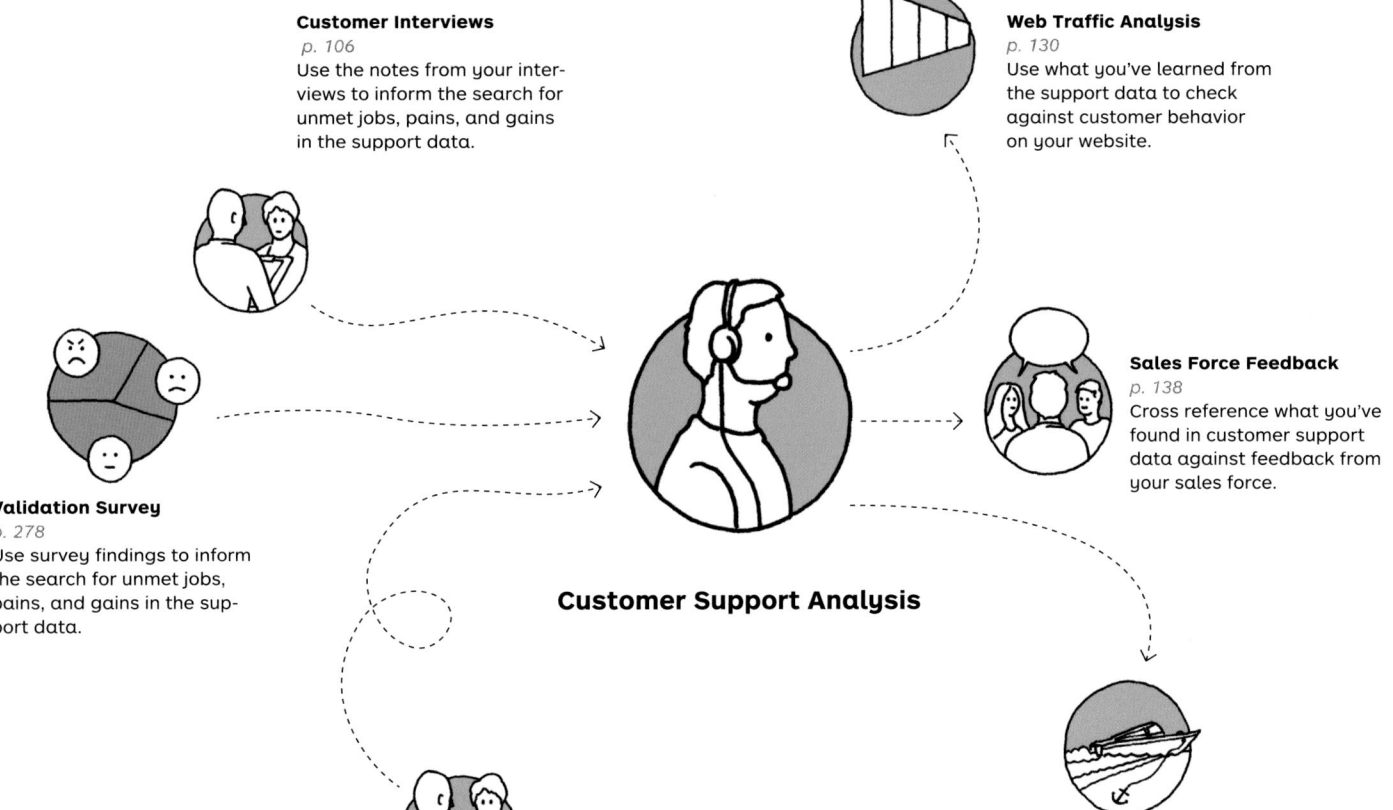

Customer Interviews
p. 106
Use the notes from your interviews to inform the search for unmet jobs, pains, and gains in the support data.

Web Traffic Analysis
p. 130
Use what you've learned from the support data to check against customer behavior on your website.

Validation Survey
p. 278
Use survey findings to inform the search for unmet jobs, pains, and gains in the support data.

Sales Force Feedback
p. 138
Cross reference what you've found in customer support data against feedback from your sales force.

Customer Support Analysis

Expert Stakeholder Interviews
p. 115
Use the notes from stakeholders to better understand if their needs translate to what you are hearing from customers.

Speed Boat
p. 218
Rather than have customers simply point out what they feel the product lacks, invite them in for a speed boat exercise to better understand what helps them go faster and what slows them down in regard to the product.

CUSTOMER SUPPORT ANALYSIS

145

DATA ANALYSIS

Online Ad

An online advertisement that clearly articulates a value proposition for a targeted customer segment with a simple call to action.

⊘ ●●●○○
COST

⚖ ●●●○○
EVIDENCE STRENGTH

🕐 ●●○○○
SETUP TIME

⏱ ●●●○○
RUN TIME

DESIRABILITY · FEASIBILITY · VIABILITY

Online ads are ideal for quickly testing your value proposition at scale with customers online.

CAPABILITIES *Design / Product / Marketing*

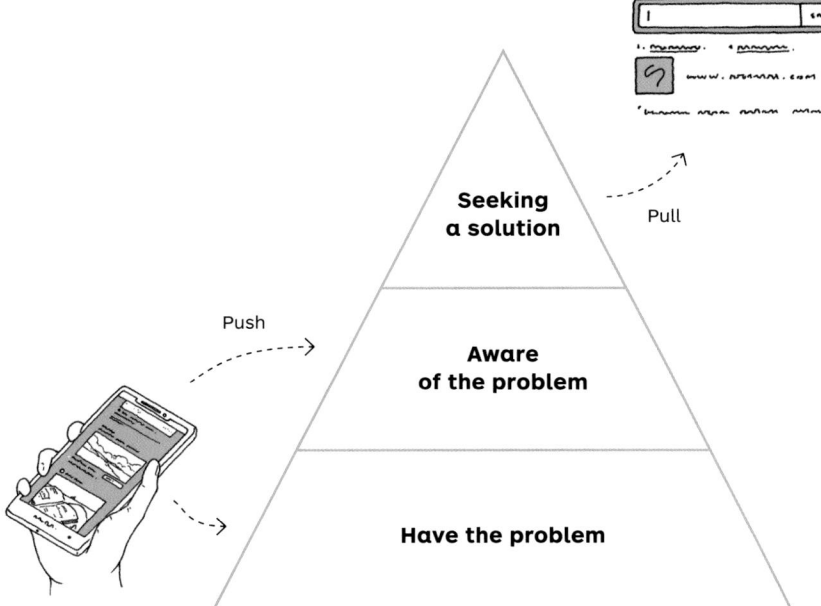

This tool was inspired by Steve Blank's Earlyvangelist Characteristics in Chapter 3 of The Four Steps to the Epiphany, *page 47, figure 3.1.*

Finding Target Customers

Finding target customers online can be challenging, but it is possible with creativity and resilience. You can start thinking about this early, even before your experiment design.

For example, when creating your Value Proposition Canvas, take time to brainstorm different places to find your target customers online. Then as a team, vote on the ones you'd like to test first.

What Stage Are Your Customers?

After prioritizing places to find your target customers, you'll want to customize your approach based on the state of the customer. You can use Steve Blank's model to help inform your strategy for engaging with customers.

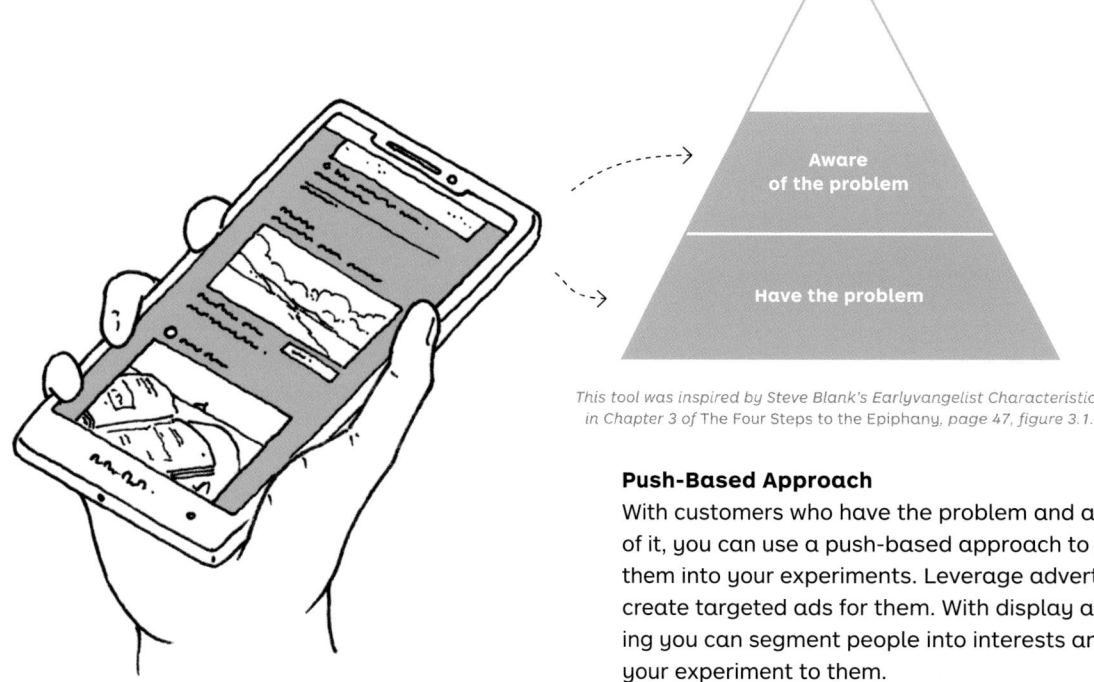

This tool was inspired by Steve Blank's Earlyvangelist Characteristics in Chapter 3 of The Four Steps to the Epiphany, *page 47, figure 3.1.*

Aware
of the problem

Have the problem

Push-Based Approach

With customers who have the problem and are aware of it, you can use a push-based approach to getting them into your experiments. Leverage advertising to create targeted ads for them. With display advertising you can segment people into interests and "push" your experiment to them.

SOCIAL MEDIA AD

Prepare

☐ Define on which social media platforms you'll run the ad.

☐ Create your target audience, ad campaign length, and budget.

☐ Choose CPC (cost per click) option.

☐ Include your business name and logo.

☐ Craft a value statement from your Value Proposition Canvas to properly communicate your offering.

☐ Create a compelling image that reinforces your value statement.

☐ Include the destination URL that directs to a landing.

Execute

☐ Once approved, run your social media ad.

☐ Monitor how it performs daily with:

• ad spend.

• impressions.

• click through rate.

• comments and shares.

Analyze

☐ Analyze your ad performance daily.

☐ If you are spending a large amount of money for a very low click through rate, pause the campaign, iterate on your text and images, then run the campaign again.

Prepare

☐ Define on which search platforms you'll run the ad.

☐ Create your target audience, ad campaign length,
and budget.

☐ Choose CPC (cost per click)
option.

☐ Craft a value statement
from your Value Proposition
Canvas to properly commu-
nicate your offering.

☐ Include the destination URL
that directs to a landing
page.

☐ Craft a shorter version of
your value statement as a
value headline.

☐ Submit your ad for
approval.

Execute

☐ Once approved, run your
search only ad.

☐ Monitor how it performs
daily with:

• ad spend.

• impressions.

• click through rate.

Analyze

☐ Analyze your ad perfor-
mance daily.

☐ If you are spending a large
amount of money for a
very low click through
rate, pause the campaign,
iterate on your text and
images, then run the cam-
paign again.

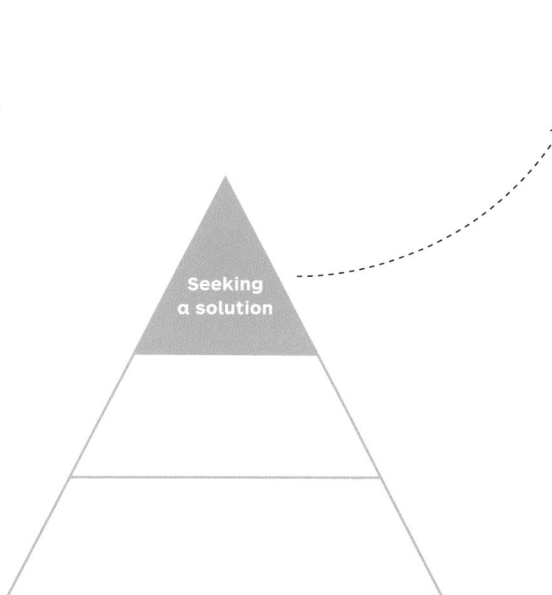

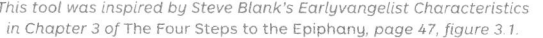

*This tool was inspired by Steve Blank's Earlyvangelist Characteristics
in Chapter 3 of* The Four Steps to the Epiphany, *page 47, figure 3.1.*

Pull-Based Approach

In contrast to push-based acquisition, you can take a
slightly different approach for those already seeking
a solution to the problem. You will need to get in front
of them when they are seeking it.

Pull-based acquisition means ensuring your experiment is displayed when people go online to search
for a solution to their problems. Using online search
advertising you can narrow in on the key search terms
and "pull" them to your value proposition as they
actively seek a solution.

Cost

Online ads can vary in cost, depending on whether you are doing display versus search, the keywords, and the average cost per click for your industry. Overall you should stay away from very expensive online ads early on in your journey. You don't want to get addicted to paid acquisition and have trouble scaling your business later on.

Setup Time

If your ad is text only, you can create it in a few minutes. If your ad contains imagery, it might take longer to find and create the right image for the ad.

Run Time

Depending on the platform, it may take 1–3 days for your ad to be approved. Once it's approved, you'll usually run your ad for at least a week to see how it performs day-to-day.

Evidence Strength

# of unique views
# of clicks

Click through rate = clicks that your ad receives divided by the number of times your ad is shown. CTR varies per industry, so research online to see what a comparable CTR is for your product.

Users clicking ads is a relatively weak strength of evidence, but it it necessary to test acquisition channels. It can also be combined with conversions on a simple landing page to make the evidence stronger overall.

Capabilities

Design / Product / Marketing

Running online ads is much easier than it used to be, mostly because online ad platforms give you a step-by-step experience for managing them. You'll still need to be able to design an ad that conveys your value proposition well, with the right call to action and target audience. This means you'll need product, marketing, and design skills—otherwise your ads will not convert.

Requirements

Destination

You are going to need a destination for the target audience to visit once they click the ad. Most of the time this is some type of landing page. Platforms have become more restrictive over the years, so the page will need to match the overall value proposition of the ad and meet the site's ad destination requirements. Be sure to review these before running your ads, otherwise they'll get rejected in the approval process.

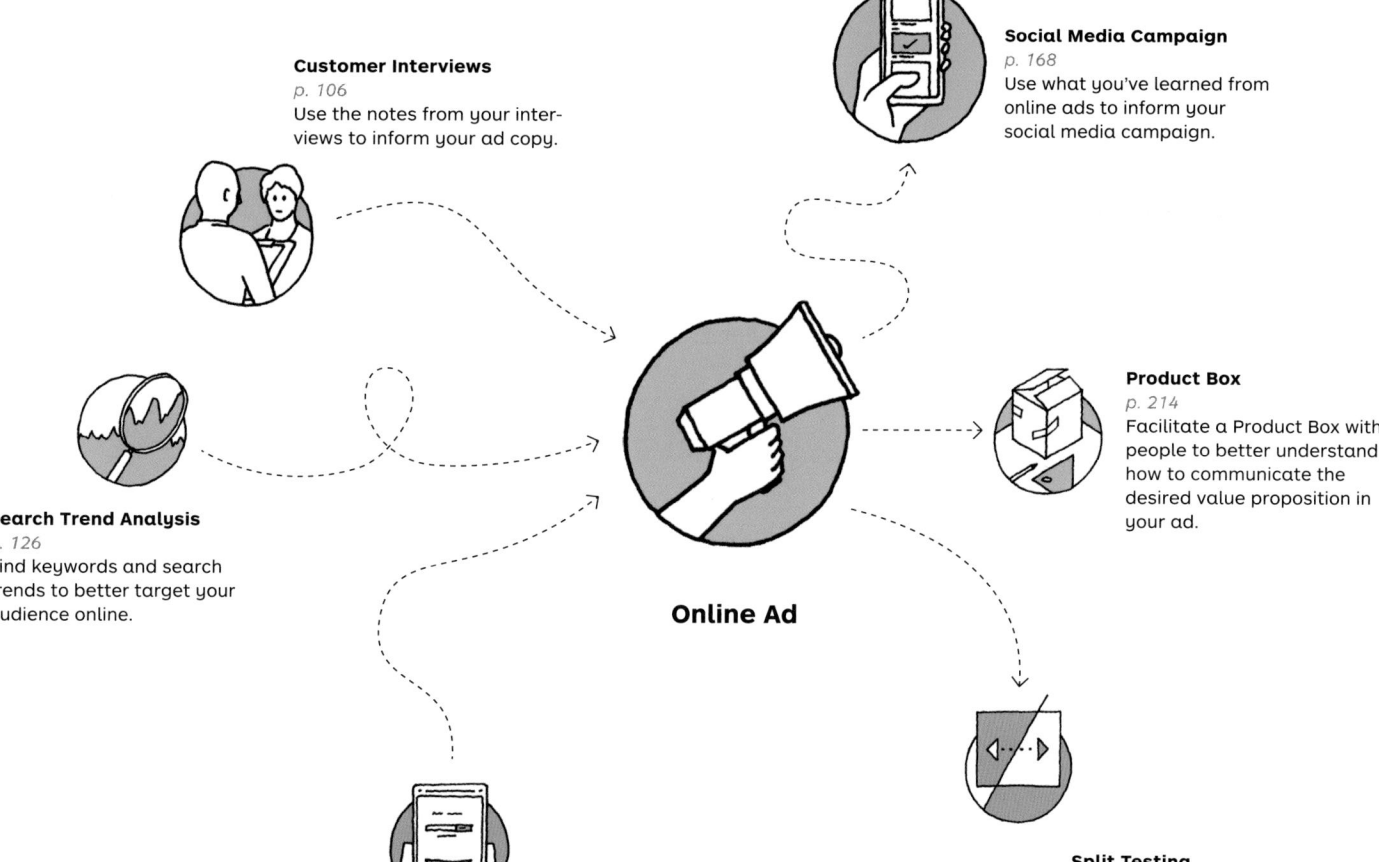

Customer Interviews
p. 106
Use the notes from your interviews to inform your ad copy.

Social Media Campaign
p. 168
Use what you've learned from online ads to inform your social media campaign.

Search Trend Analysis
p. 126
Find keywords and search trends to better target your audience online.

Product Box
p. 214
Facilitate a Product Box with people to better understand how to communicate the desired value proposition in your ad.

Online Ad

Simple Landing Page
p. 260
Create a simple landing page to act as your destination for your ads.

Split Testing
p. 270
Try different versions of your ads to see what resonates best with customers.

EXPERIMENTS

DISCOVERY / INTEREST DISCOVERY

Link Tracking

A unique, trackable hyperlink to gain more detailed information about your value proposition.

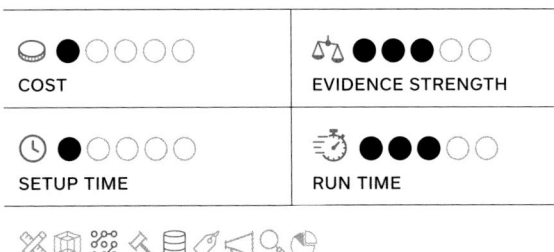

COST

EVIDENCE STRENGTH

SETUP TIME

RUN TIME

CAPABILITIES Technology / Data

DESIRABILITY · FEASIBILITY · VIABILITY

Link tracking is ideal for testing customer actions to gather quantitative data.

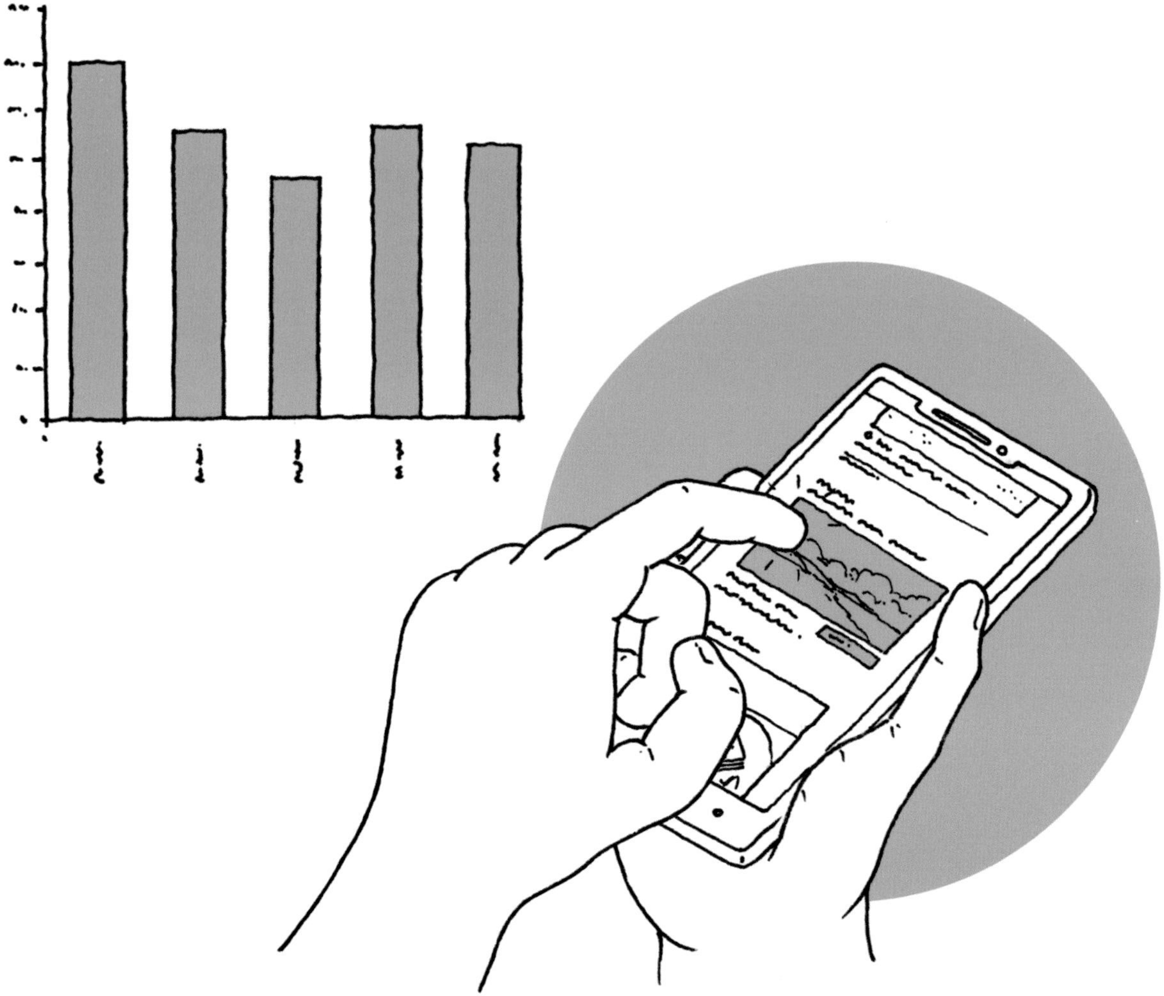

Prepare

☐ Define where you are going to include the link.

☐ Create a clear call to action for the link.

☐ Integrate analytics to track the link views and clicks.

☐ Create the destination that will load once the customer clicks the link.

Execute

☐ Make your link live and give it to customers.

☐ Run it for several days or weeks to give people time to click.

Analyze

☐ Calculate conversion on the link click rate.

☐ Compare it to the behavior on your destination.

☐ Use what you've learned to refine and split test your link copy.

LINK TRACKING

153

INTEREST DISCOVERY

Cost

Link tracking is relatively cheap. Most online web analytics, online ad, and email software provide the ability to track unique URL links.

Setup Time

The setup time for link tracking is relatively short if you use existing software. You'll need to create the links for your different digital media formats.

Run Time

The run time for link tracking is usually over a few weeks. It'll take time for people to view it and decide to click, or not.

Evidence Strength

# of unique views

Click rate = percentage of people who viewed your link divided by the number of people who clicked on your link.

Click rates vary by industry. Use industry guidelines to determine what the average is for your experiment.

Link clicks are an average strength of evidence. You'll learn what they do, but you won't know why unless you talk to them.

Capabilities

Technology / Data

Link tracking doesn't require deep expertise, as most software already has it included. You'll need to be able to create links with tracking and interpret the results.

Requirements

Call to Action

Link tracking isn't going to be very success-ful without a clear call to action and value proposition. You'll want to clearly communi-cate this in your content and imagery, while providing a link that brings the customer to a web page.

Customer Interviews
p. 106
Gather email addresses from
your customer interviews to
send a follow-up email with
link tracking.

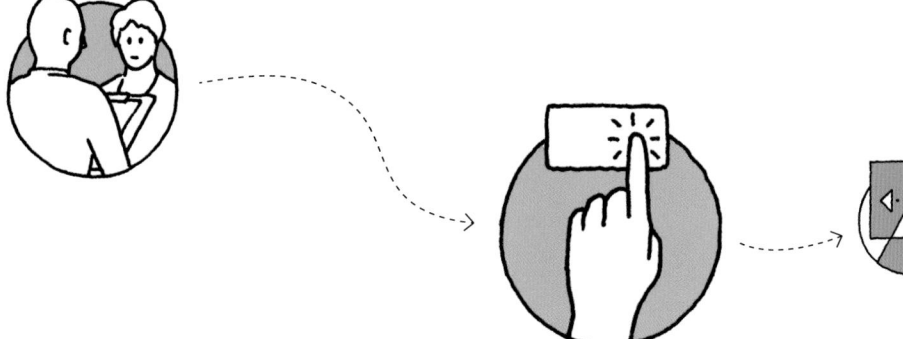

Split Test
p. 270
Use link tracking analysis
to create different version
to Split Test.

Link Tracking

Online Ad
p. 146
Create an online ad with
clickable links to track click
through rate (CTR).

Simple Landing Page
p. 260
Include link tracking in your
landing page to understand
how customers who clicked
online ads converted on your
page.

Email Campaign
p. 162
Include link tracking to
understand how many people
clicked the links in your email
campaign.

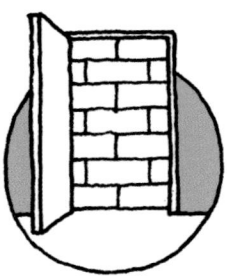

DISCOVERY

EXPERIMENTS

156

Feature Stub

A small test of an upcoming feature that includes the very beginning of the experience, usually in the form of a button.

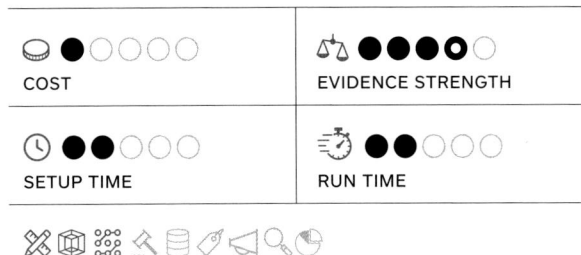

COST ● ○ ○ ○ ○
COST

⚖ ● ● ● ◐ ○
EVIDENCE STRENGTH

🕐 ● ● ○ ○ ○
SETUP TIME

⏱ ● ● ○ ○ ○
RUN TIME

CAPABILITIES *Design / Product / Technology*

DESIRABILITY · FEASIBILITY · VIABILITY

Feature Stub is ideal for rapidly testing the desirability of a new feature of an already existing offering.

Feature Stub is not ideal for testing mission critical functionality for your product.

Prepare

☐ Decide where you are going to include the Feature Stub: preferably in the part of your product where your customers would need it most in the workflow.

☐ Define the length and schedule for the Feature Stub.

☐ Create the Feature Stub, using the same visual styling as the rest of the product.

☐ When clicked, launch a popup that states the feature isn't completed yet.

☐ Include a "learn more" link to determine if people are interested enough to click again. Optionally, it can display a survey that asks how interested and has an email signup.

☐ Integrate analytics to track views and clicks.

☐ Implement a feature toggle that allows you to quickly turn it on and off. This is a very important step!

Execute

☐ Toggle your Feature Stub on.

☐ Monitor the activity usage of the link very closely, by the hour.

☐ Toggle the Feature Stub off once you've reached the end of the schedule.

Analyze

☐ Calculate conversion rates on your button, learn more, and surveys. Did these reach your success criteria?

☐ Review the findings with your team to determine whether the feature is still worth pursuing.

Cost

Feature Stubs are usually very cheap, since you are not building out an entire feature but merely the entry point for it.

Setup Time

It should only take few hours to set up a Feature Stub in your existing product or service. If it takes longer than that, you may need to rethink your architecture when it comes to implementing experiments.

Run Time

Feature Stubs should never be run for more than 1–3 days. They are designed as a short experiment to quickly gather evidence.

Anything longer will frustrate your customers, since they'll continue to expect it to work.

Evidence Strength

# of unique views
# of button clicks
Button % Conversion Rates

You can calculate the conversion rate by taking the number of unique views divided by button clicks = conversion rate. Aim for a 15% conversion on button click.

Button views and clicks are relatively weak evidence, although they do signal interest in the feature.

of "learn more" clicks
Learn More % Conversion Rates

You can calculate the conversion rate by taking the number of unique "learn more" views divided by link clicks = conversion rate. Aim for a 5% conversion on learn more click.

Clicking to learn more is a bit stronger than simply closing the popup.

# of surveys completed
Survey Feedback

You can calculate the conversion rate by taking the number of unique learn more clicks divided by completions = conversion rate. Aim for a 3% conversion on survey completion.

Filling out the survey from the learn more link is a bit stronger than closing the popup. You can learn valuable insights from people voluntarily clicking on and filling out a survey on a feature they'd love to see in the product.

Capabilities

Design / Product / Technology

You'll need to be able design a button that fits into the existing product. You'll also need the button to launch a window stating that the feature isn't ready yet and optionally asks the customer to fill out a survey. Analytics will be important—you'll need to measure its performance.

Requirements

Existing Product

Feature Stubs require a product that already has daily active users. If you don't already have one with a steady stream of users, it will be difficult to gauge customer interest. They have to see it in the context of the product for the evidence to be believable.

Integration and Analytics

Feature Stubs need to be toggled off and on at a moment's notice. Make sure you have this capability and that it works before launching one. In addition, you'll need analytics to measure feature interest.

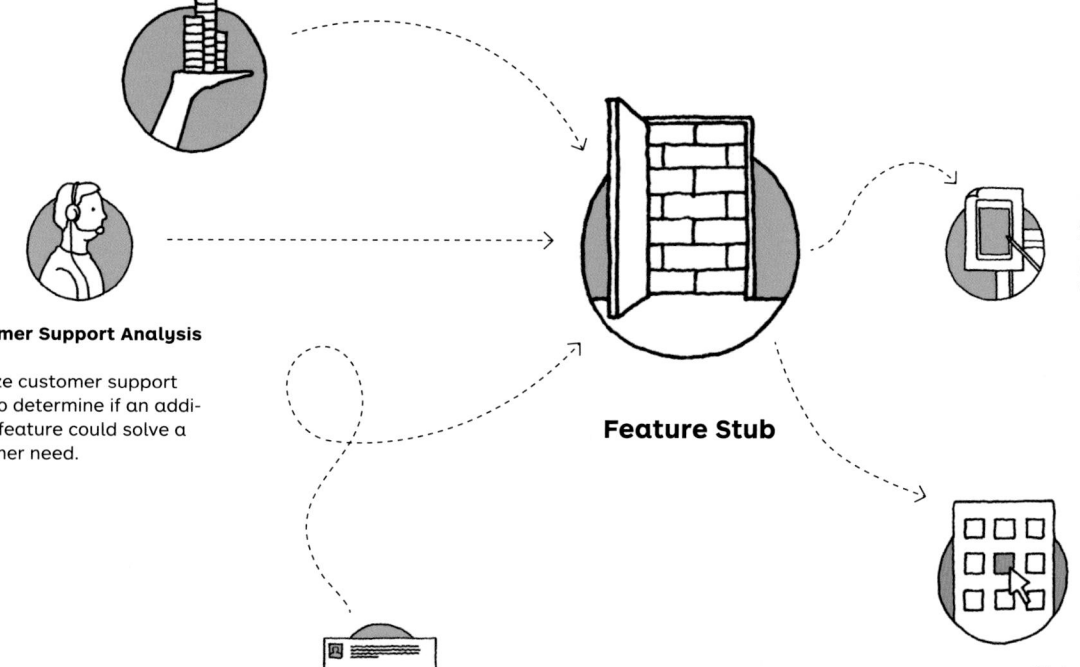

Buy a Feature
p. 226
Facilitate an exercise with customers to decide if the feature would even be a priority for them.

Customer Support Analysis
p. 142
Analyze customer support data to determine if an additional feature could solve a customer need.

Feature Stub

Paper Prototype
p. 182
Test low fidelity versions of how the feature could function with customers.

Discussion Forums
p. 134
Search through discussion forums to see if customers are using creative work-arounds to address your product deficiencies.

Clickable Prototype
p. 236
Test clickable prototypes of how the feature could work with customers.

DISCOVERY / INTEREST DISCOVERY

404 Test

Another faster, and somewhat riskier, variation of a Feature Stub is the 404 test. It is very similar, except you do not put anything behind the button or link whatsoever. Hence, the 404 test name, as it generates 404 errors each time it is clicked. To learn if a feature is desirable, you simply count the number of 404 errors generated.

This variant has trade-offs since, on one hand, you can test something as quickly as possible at scale with customers. On the other hand, it gives the impression that your product is broken.

When running a 404 test, do not run it for more than a few hours.

COST

SETUP TIME

RUN TIME

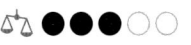
EVIDENCE STRENGTH

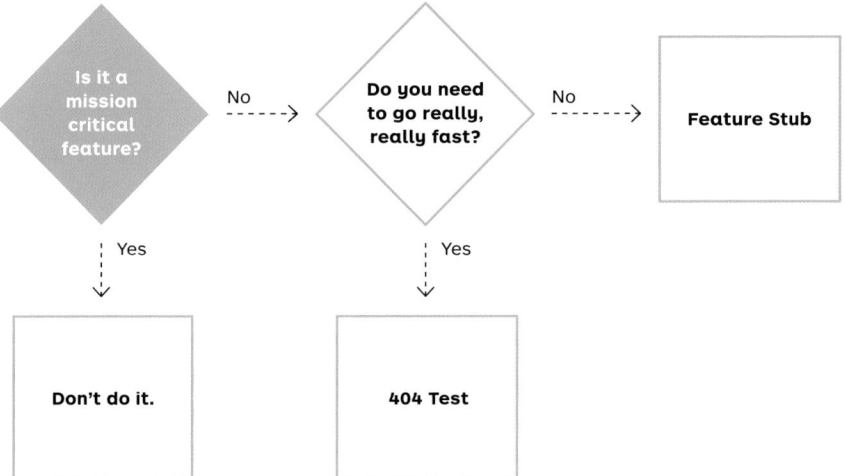

The flowchart reads:

- **Is it a mission critical feature?**
  - Yes → **Don't do it.**
  - No → **Do you need to go really, really fast?**
    - Yes → **404 Test**
    - No → **Feature Stub**

The notion of doing a quick test, solves umpteen meetings' worth of powerful debate and logical argument.

—Stephen Kaufer, CEO of TripAdvisor

Endless Meetings

Have you ever been in a meeting where team members debated over whether a feature would be a good idea to build for your customers?

Without evidence, the conversation goes in circles, using only opinions for decision-making.

A Feature Stub will generate data to help you gauge demand.

What if the test is a wild success and customers reach out to you asking when they can use the feature? It then helps break the circular meetings of opinion on the feature.

What if the test is a dud and no one even clicks on it? Then it also helps move the conversation forward.

It's not so much about being right and able to gloat in the meeting to your peers that your prediction was correct, but instead to use data to help move the conversation forward. Making progress is far more important than being correct in these scenarios, and a Feature Stub is a great way to make progress.

DISCOVERY / INTEREST DISCOVERY

Email Campaign

Email messages that are deployed across a specific period of time to customers.

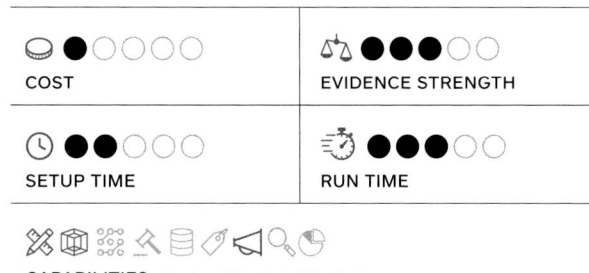

◎ ●○○○○	⚖ ●●●○○
COST	EVIDENCE STRENGTH
◷ ●●○○○	⏱ ●●●○○
SETUP TIME	RUN TIME

CAPABILITIES *Design / Product / Marketing*

DESIRABILITY · FEASIBILITY · VIABILITY

Email campaigns are ideal for quickly testing your value proposition with a customer segment.

Email campaigns are not ideal as a replacement for face-to-face customer interaction.

Prepare

- ☐ Define your email campaign goal.
- ☐ Create your series of "drip emails" to incrementally deliver value to the customer over a period of days or weeks.
- ☐ Send test emails internally to review content and images.

Execute

- ☐ Run your email campaign with customers.
- ☐ Be responsive to customers who reply.

Analyze

- ☐ Analyze which emails are performing best.
- ☐ What type of content is driving the most opens?
- ☐ What type of content is driving the most clicks?
- ☐ What type of content is driving the most reply emails?
- ☐ Recap with your team and decide what revisions you'd like to make for your next campaign.

Cost

Email campaigns are relatively cheap: there are several services that make it cost effective to manage the creation, distribution, and analysis of emails across large numbers of subscribers.

Setup Time

Using today's email tools, it only takes minutes to a few hours to craft an email campaign. You can create auto-drip emails to send on a schedule over time without manually having to intervene.

Run Time

Depending on the nature of the email campaign, it can take 1–2 days or 3–4 weeks.

Evidence Strength

Opens

Clicks

Bounces

Unsubscribes

Open rate = unique clicks divided by the number of unique opens.

Click rate = percentage of people who clicked on at least one link in your email message.

Open and click rates vary by industry. Use industry guidelines to determine what the average is for your experiment. They can be found in most email service tools as part of the reports package.

   Email opens and clicks are an average strength of evidence.

Capabilities

Design / Product / Marketing

Email campaigns are relatively easy to create and manage now that many dedicated tools and services exist. You'll still need to be able to write clear, coherent copy with compelling images and a strong call to action. Much of the formatting can be taken care of by online templates.

Requirements

Subscriber List

Email campaigns require subscribers before you can effectively use them. You can acquire subscribers from a number of different sources including:

- Social media campaigns
- Website signup
- Blog posts with email signup
- Word of mouth
- Discussion forums

Campaign Goal

Email campaigns need a goal, otherwise you can't be confident that it's helping you make progress. Goals can vary from driving traffic to a page for conversions, onboarding new customers, building trust, and learning customers needs to re-engaging existing or lost customers. Create a goal before putting in the effort to create the email campaign.

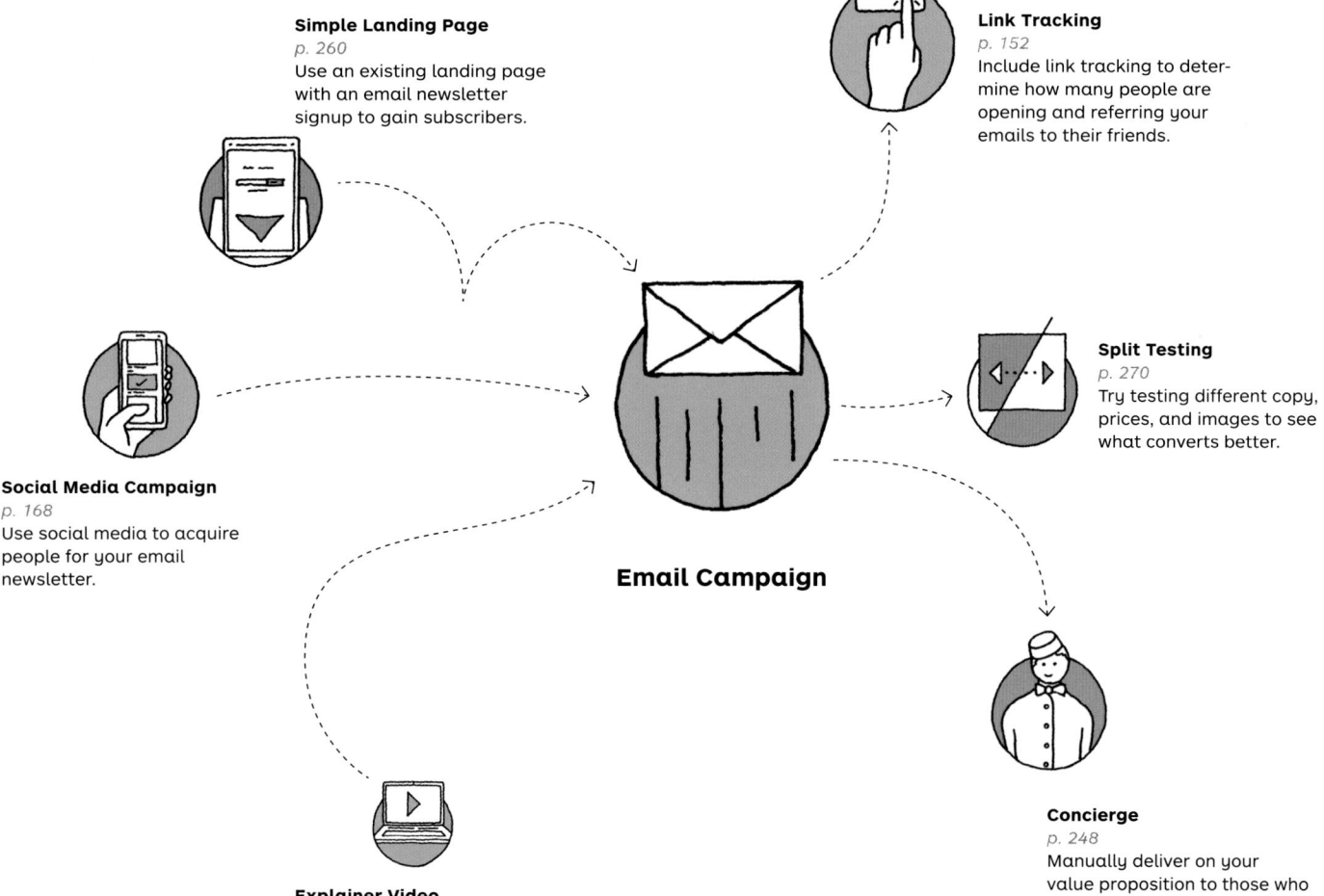

Simple Landing Page
p. 260
Use an existing landing page
with an email newsletter
signup to gain subscribers.

Link Tracking
p. 152
Include link tracking to determine how many people are
opening and referring your
emails to their friends.

Social Media Campaign
p. 168
Use social media to acquire
people for your email
newsletter.

Email Campaign

Split Testing
p. 270
Try testing different copy,
prices, and images to see
what converts better.

Explainer Video
p. 200
Have an email signup at
the beginning of your video
as currency to watch it.

Concierge
p. 248
Manually deliver on your
value proposition to those who
show interest and respond to
your email campaign.

EMAIL CAMPAIGN
Share, Discover, Discuss New Products
Product Hunt

Product Hunt is a website that lets users share and discover new products. The website has grown tremendously over the years since it's inception in 2013. Product Hunt has become the place to launch your new product, but curiously enough it all started off in a Philz Coffee as a 20-minute experiment by Ryan Hoover, mainly using email.

Hypothesis

Ryan believed that product people would join an online community to share, discover, and discuss new and interesting products.

Experiment

Creating the first version of Product Hunt as an email campaign.

In only 20 minutes, Ryan created a group on Linkydink, a link-sharing tool built by the folks over at Makeshift. At the time, it allowed people to share links with a group and send them out as a daily email. He then invited a few of his startup friends to contribute to the group. To promote it, Ryan announced the experiment on Quibb (a technology focused, online community) and Twitter.

Evidence

Opens, clicks and shares.

Within two weeks, over 200 people had subscribed to product discoveries from 30 hand-picked contributors, consisting of startup founders, venture capitalists, and prominent bloggers.

Ryan also received several unsolicited emails and in-person conversations expressing their love and support of the project.

Insights

There is a there, there.

The response was overwhelmingly positive and unlike most email that is opened and clicked (or not), Ryan had an audience openly contributing and sharing links over email. He had built up a network over the years of hungry entrepreneurs and product people. Clearly there was an unmet need of a community for product enthusiasts, based on the sheer volume of activity from his email list.

Actions

Turning user behavior from email into a platform.

Ryan used what he learned from the experiment to inform the design and technology of Product Hunt as a community platform.

Since then, Product Hunt graduated from Y Combinator (YC S14) and was acquired by AngelList for a reported $20 million in 2016. It's become the place where makers and startups launch their new product to a global community of founders, journalists, investors, and enthusiastic people in technology.

DISCOVERY / INTEREST DISCOVERY

Social Media Campaign

Social media messages that are deployed across a specific period of time to customers.

COST

EVIDENCE STRENGTH

SETUP TIME

RUN TIME

CAPABILITIES *Design / Marketing*

DESIRABILITY · FEASIBILITY · VIABILITY

Social media campaigns are ideal for acquiring new customers, increasing brand loyalty, and driving sales.

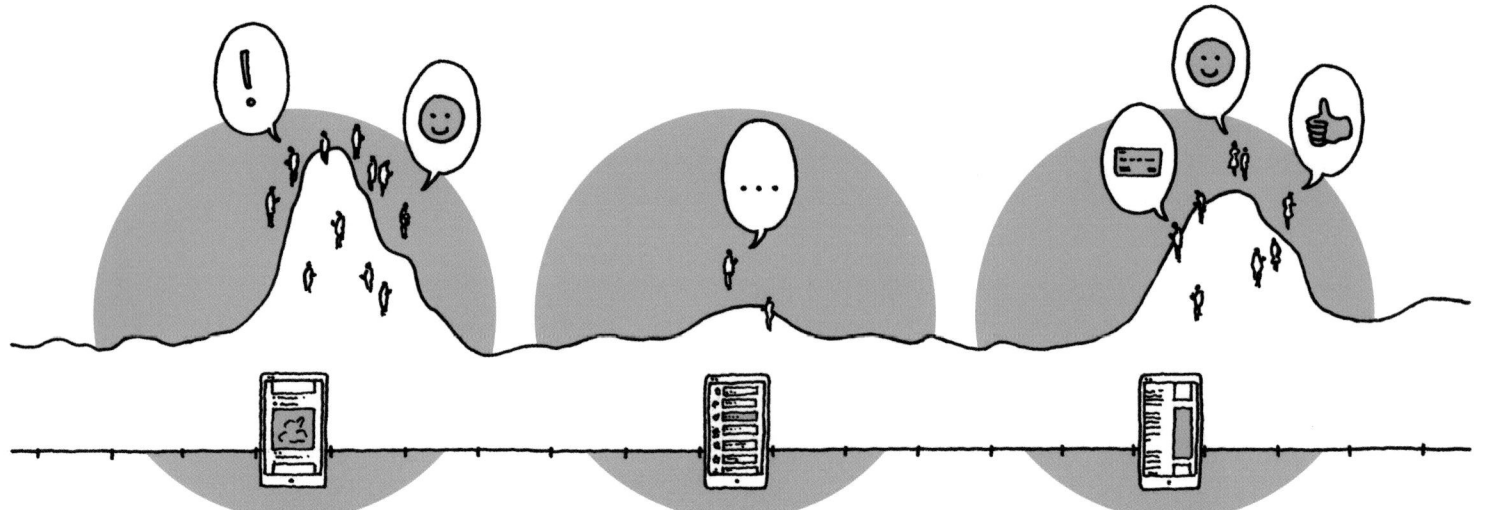

Prepare

☐ Define your social media campaign goal.

☐ Identify the platforms to use for your campaign.

☐ Create your content calendar and schedule.

☐ Create your social media content.

Execute

☐ Post your content across platforms per your schedule.

☐ Monitor, respond, and engage with those who comment.

Analyze

☐ Analyze which posts and platforms are performing best.

☐ What type of content is driving the most shares?

☐ What type of content is driving the most clicks?

☐ What type of content is driving the most comments?

☐ What type of content is driving the most conversions?

☐ Recap with your team and decide what revisions you'd like to make for your next campaign.

Cost

Social media campaigns are moderately cheap to produce if you are doing the work yourself and not paying for social media ads. However, costs can go up rather quickly ($5k to $20k a month), if you are paying people to manage and create content.

Setup Time

Setup time for a social media campaign can take days or weeks, depending on how much content you need to create. Setup time increases as well if you are running it across multiple platforms.

Run Time

Run Time for a social media campaign is long, usually several weeks or months. You'll need time to post, read, and respond over social media. You'll also need to measure the effectiveness it has toward your business goals.

Evidence Strength

●●○○○

# of views
# of shares
# of comments

Engagement is how customers are viewing, sharing, and commenting on your social media posts.

Social media engagement is rather weak evidence. You can learn qualitative insights from the comments to inform your value proposition.

●●●○○

# of clicks

Click through rate is the number of views your social media post receives divided by the number who clicked.

●●●●○

# of conversions

Conversion rate is the number who clicked on the social media link divided by the number who used it to sign up or make a purchase.

Conversions are strong evidence and can help you determine what social media platform works best for driving business.

Capabilities

Design / Marketing

Social media campaigns require a great deal of marketing and design: marketing to create, respond, and manage social media across multiple platforms; design to help shape and visualize the content before it is posted.

Requirements

Content

Social media campaigns are not simply posting here and there, they are about scheduling content over weeks and months. Without content, your campaign will not be successful. Make sure you have a plan and the resources to create the content before jumping into your campaign.

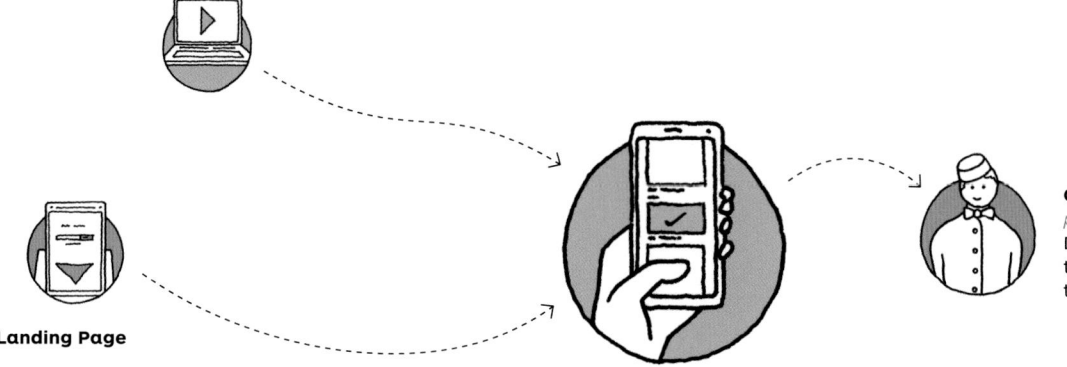

Explainer Video
p. 200
Use the social media
campaign to drive traffic
to your video.

Concierge
p. 248
Deliver value manually to
those who converted from
the social media campaign.

Simple Landing Page
p. 260
Use a landing page for as
the destination for your social
media links.

Social Media Campaign

DISCOVERY / INTEREST DISCOVERY

Referral Program

A method of promoting products or services to new customers through referrals, by word of mouth, or through digital codes.

⬭ ●●●○○	⚖ ●●●●○
COST	EVIDENCE STRENGTH
🕐 ●●○○○	⏱ ●●●●●
SETUP TIME	RUN TIME

CAPABILITIES *Design / Product / Marketing*

DESIRABILITY · FEASIBILITY · VIABILITY

Referral programs are ideal for testing with customers how to organically scale your business.

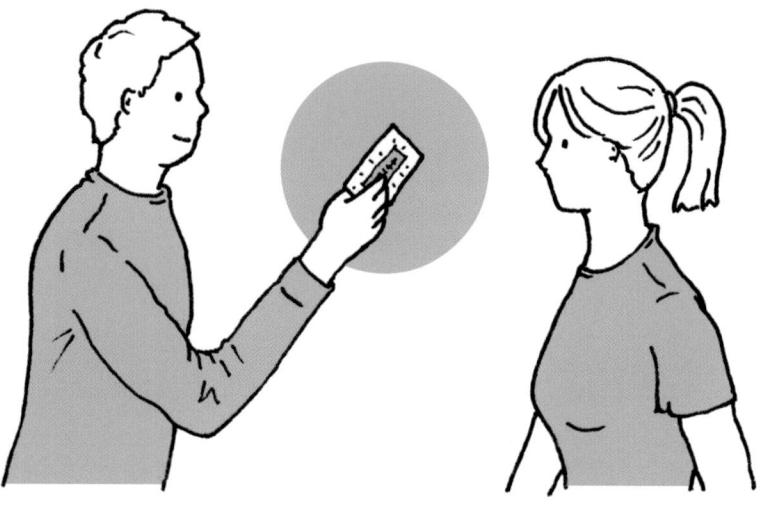

Prepare

☐ Define your referral program conversion goal.

☐ Identify the advocates you'll send the referral codes to.

☐ Create the unique codes and integrate analytics.

Execute

☐ Provide your advocates with the referral codes.

☐ Run it for several weeks to give friends time to consider and click.

Analyze

☐ Calculate advocate share rate.

☐ Calculate friend click through rate.

☐ Calculate friend conversion rate.

☐ Compare the conversion rate to your previously defined goal.

☐ Use what you've learned to refine and Split Test the referral program.

Cost

Referral programs are moderately cheap. You'll need to incentivize customers (advocates) for making referrals, which will incur cost in the way of discounts for both the advocate and the customer (friend) being referred. Low cost software can help you manage referrals, so that you have analytics on how the program is performing.

Setup Time

Setup time for a referral program is short. You'll need to configure your referral codes and choose which advocates to send them to.

Run Time

Run time for a referral program is long, usually several weeks or months. You'll need time for advocates to refer and for their friends to decide whether or not to act on the referral.

Evidence Strength

# of advocates
# of advocate shares

Advocates are the customers you provide referral codes to for sharing. The number of shares is how many customers actively shared the code with friends.

Advocate share rate is the number of advocates who received a code divided by the number who shared it with a friend. Target 15%–20%.

Advocates agreeing to accept and share a code is relatively strong evidence. They are acting to refer friends to your product.

# of friends
# of friend clicks
# of friend conversions

Friends are the people who received the code from the advocate.

Friend click through rate is the number of friends who received the code divided by the number who clicked on it. Percent varies by channel. Target 50%–80%.

Friend conversion rate is the number who clicked on the code divided by the number who used it to sign up or make a purchase. Target 5%–15%.

Friends accepting the referral code and converting is strong evidence. They are acting on a referral for an incentive, so it remains to be seen if they will stay over time.

Capabilities

Design / Product / Marketing

Referral programs mostly require product and marketing capabilities. You'll need to clearly communicate why you are offering the discount and how your friends would benefit from it. You'll need design skills if you have custom emails, social media posts, or landing pages dedicated to the program.

Requirements

Passionate Customers

Customers usually do not start out passionate about your product. It takes time for them to be satisfied and grow into passionate customers. Therefore, we recommend that you gauge this before randomly sending out referral codes. You'll want to give codes to those who you think will actually refer their friends to your product and speak to it in a positive light.

Link Tracking
p. 152
Have link tracking already in place to determine which customers are the most active.

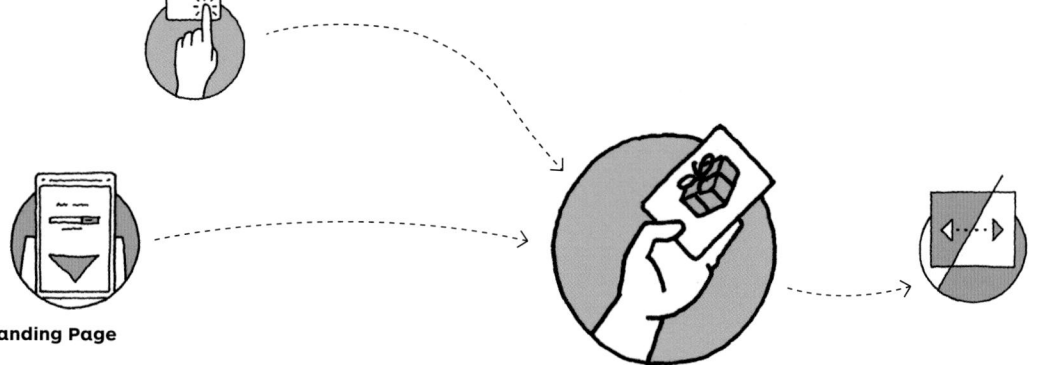

Simple Landing Page
p. 260
Use a landing page for testing the demand of your referral program.

Split Test
p. 270
Use analytics to Split Test different discount codes and determine which media converts better with friends.

Referral Program

Email Campaign
p. 162
Use email to distribute your referral program to advocates.

Social Media Campaign
p. 168
Use social media to distribute your referral program.

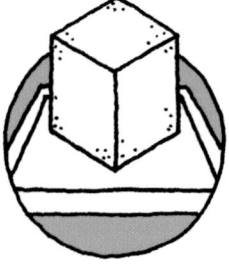

DISCOVERY / DISCUSSION PROTOTYPES

3D Print

Rapidly prototyping a physical object from a three-dimensional digital model by using a 3D printer.

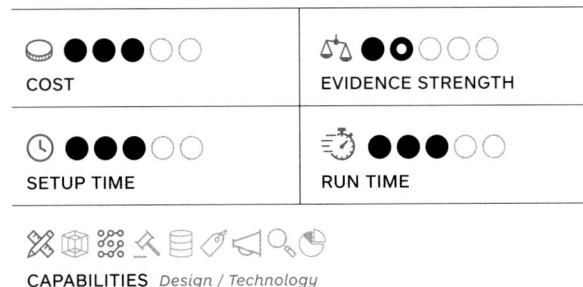

◯ ●●●◯◯
COST

⚖ ●●◑◯◯◯
EVIDENCE STRENGTH

🕐 ●●●◯◯
SETUP TIME

⏱ ●●●◯◯
RUN TIME

CAPABILITIES *Design / Technology*

DESIRABILITY · FEASIBILITY · VIABILITY

3D print is ideal for rapidly testing iterations of your physical solution with customers.

Prepare

☐ Gather your previous low fidelity evidence to support the 3D print.

☐ Model the print in 3D modeling software.

☐ Create a 3D print using a printer.

☐ Source customers and schedule the interactive session.

Execute

☐ Show the 3D print to customers.

☐ One person on the team conducts the interview.

☐ Another person on the team takes notes on customer quotes, jobs, pains, gains, and body language.

☐ Wrap up the interview by asking if it is ok to contact them in the future with higher fidelity solutions.

Analyze

☐ Review your notes with the team.

☐ Update your Value Proposition Canvas based on what you've learned.

☐ Use what you've learned to refine and iterate on your 3D print for the next round of testing.

Cost

3D prints are moderately cheap. If you are printing small basic prototypes to test with customers, it can be less expensive. The more complex and larger the 3D print, the more costly it will be.

Setup Time

The setup time for a 3D print can take days or weeks, depending on your ability to model it out and your access to a printer.

Run Time

Run time for a 3D print is relatively short. You'll want customers interacting with the prototype to better understand the fit between your value proposition and customer jobs, pains, and gains.

Evidence Strength

●●○○○

Customer jobs
Customer pains
Customer gains
Customer jobs, pains, and gains and how the prototype could solve for them.

The evidence is relatively weak evidence—they need to suspend belief and imagine using it in real world scenarios.

●○○○○

Customer feedback
Customer Quotes
Take note of additional quotes from the customers that are not limited to customer jobs, pains, and gains.

Customer quotes are relatively weak, but helpful for context and qualitative insights for upcoming experiments.

Capabilities
Design / Technology

You'll need to be able to model the 3D print in software, then create it using a 3D printer. Some software is easier to learn that others, but the learning curve can be quite steep if you don't have a design background. We suggest getting help from a 3D modeling expert. With regards to 3D printers, don't rush out and purchase one. Maker spaces and workshops usually allow members to rent time for creating 3D prints.

Requirements
Sketches to Model

Before planning to create a 3D print, make sure you've spent time testing faster, lower fidelity experiments. For example, you should have at least placed paper prototypes in front of customers to receive feedback. That feedback should help inform your design and solution. It doesn't necessarily mean you make all of the changes customers requested.

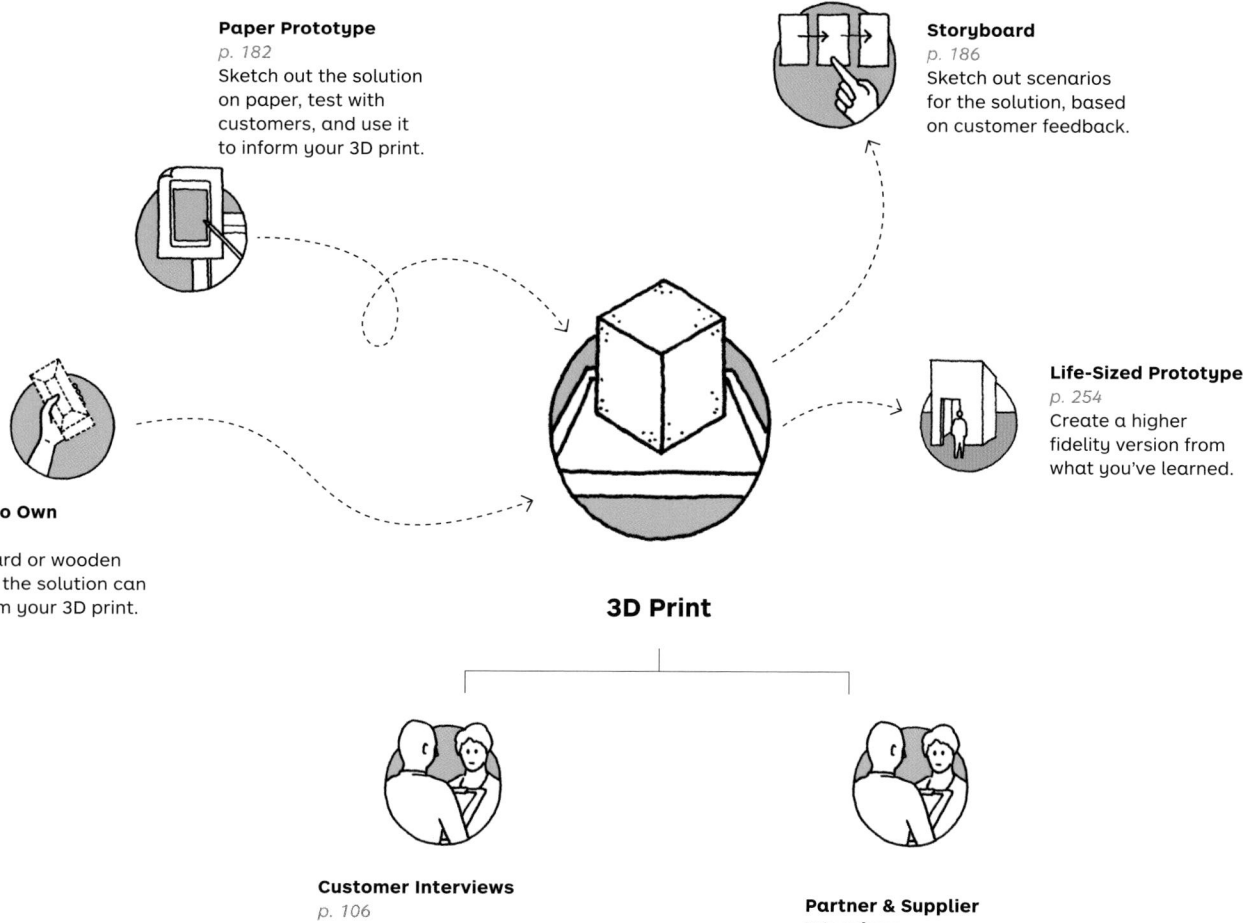

Paper Prototype
p. 182
Sketch out the solution
on paper, test with
customers, and use it
to inform your 3D print.

Storyboard
p. 186
Sketch out scenarios
for the solution, based
on customer feedback.

Life-Sized Prototype
p. 254
Create a higher
fidelity version from
what you've learned.

Pretend to Own
p. 208
A cardboard or wooden
version of the solution can
help inform your 3D print.

3D Print

Customer Interviews
p. 106
Interview your customers
while they interact with the 3D
print to learn about customer
jobs, pains, and gains.

**Partner & Supplier
Interviews**
p. 114
Interview your partners and
suppliers to get feedback on
the feasibility of your solution.

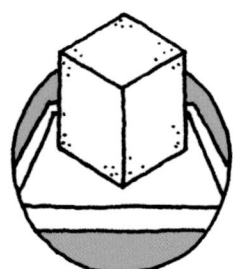

3D PRINT
3D Printing with CubeSats
The National Security Agency

The National Security Agency (NSA) is a world leader in cryptology (the art and science of making and breaking codes) that helps protect sensitive national security information, even in space! If you're like most people, the word "satellite" conjures up images of a bus-sized object weighing several tons and costing hundreds of millions of dollars orbiting the Earth for several years.

CubeSats, on the other hand, are a newer type of satellite that measure only 10 cm × 10 cm × 11.35 cm, weigh less than 2 kg, and utilize commercial off-the-shelf components. An Innovation Corps (I-Corps) team from NSA's Cybersecurity Solutions Group had an idea for creating a new type of cryptographic device to secure uplink and downlink communications from CubeSats. Their solution had dramatically smaller size, weight, power, and price characteristics as compared to existing products designed and certified for use with those expensive bus-sized satellites.

Hypothesis
The NSA team believed that...
Resisting the urge to start building an early version of their encryption device, these intrapreneurs "got out of the building" to validate the desirability of their product. Finding broad demand for CubeSat encryption by external customers, they sought to determine if they could get the "buy-in" of some key internal stakeholders who unfortunately didn't see the need for a new solution. If we can help them see the need, thought the entrepreneurs, then they will authorize and fund our project.

Experiment
The team set out to devise a way to help these stakeholders quickly and unequivocally see the need for a new solution. After a few failed attempts, the team and their coach wondered if using a 3D-printer to create a life-sized mockup of the CubeSat might help them see it. They were ready the next day!

Evidence
The stakeholders immediately saw the need for a new solution after seeing how the currently certified encryption product simply wouldn't fit in the 3D printed mock-up!

Actions
The team was resourced, and they confidently began building their solution that will be tested in orbit in 2019.

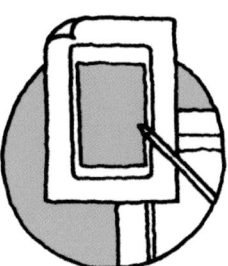

DISCOVERY / DISCUSSION PROTOTYPES

Paper Prototype

Sketched interface on paper, manipulated by another person
to represent the software's reactions to the customer interaction.

○●○○○○
COST

⚖●○○○○
EVIDENCE STRENGTH

🕐●●○○○
SETUP TIME

⏱●●○○○
RUN TIME

 ▥ ◧ ◑
DESIRABILITY · FEASIBILITY · VIABILITY

*Paper prototypes are ideal for rapidly testing the concept
of your product quickly with customers.*

*Paper prototypes are not ideal as a replacement for proper
usability with customers.*

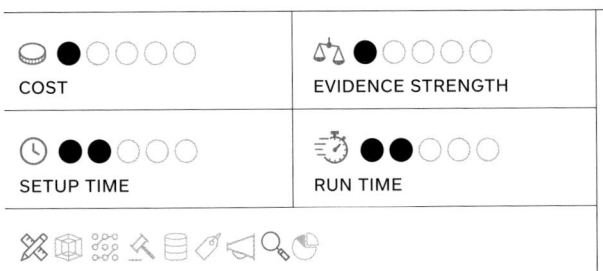

CAPABILITIES *Design / Research*

Prepare

- ☐ Define the goals of your paper prototype experiment
- ☐ Determine the target audience to test with, preferably a group that isn't cold and has context for your offering.
- ☐ Write your script.
- ☐ Create your paper prototype sketches.
- ☐ Test it internally to make sure the flow works.
- ☐ Schedule your Paper Prototype experiments with target customers.

Execute

- ☐ Explain to the customers that this is an exercise to get their feedback on what you are planning to deliver. Make sure they understand that you value their input.
- ☐ Have one person conduct the interviews and interact with the customer.
- ☐ Have another person write notes and act as a scribe.
- ☐ Wrap up and thank the participants.

Analyze

- ☐ Place the paper prototypes on the wall and place your notes, observations, and quotes around them.
- ☐ Where did they get stuck or confused?
- ☐ What did they get excited about?
- ☐ Use this feedback to inform your next higher fidelity experiment of the experience.

Cost

Paper prototypes are very cheap. You are sketching out what the solution could be and simulating the experience with paper. Your paper prototype should not be an expensive endeavor. If you purchase stencils or apps to assist in the process it can add a small amount of cost.

Setup Time

Setup time for a paper prototype is relatively short. It should only take a few hours to a few days to create your paper prototype. It'll most likely take you longer to find customers to test with than to create the paper prototype itself.

Run Time

Run time for a paper prototype is also a few days to a week. You'll want to rapidly test the paper prototype with target customers, to get feedback on the value proposition and flow of the solution.

Evidence Strength

●○○○○

Task completion
Task completion percentage
Time to complete tasks

Manual task completion is not necessarily strong evidence, but it will provide glimpses into where customers could get confused.

●○○○○

Customer feedback

Customer quotes on the value proposition and usefulness of the imagined solution.

Customer quotes on paper prototypes are relatively weak, but can be helpful to inform your higher fidelity experiments.

Capabilities

Design / Research

In addition to an imagination, you'll need some design skills to sketch out the product. You'll also want to write a coherent script and record the sessions.

Requirements

An Imagined Product

Paper prototyping requires a great deal of imagination and creativity. You'll need to be able to sketch out the flow of the product and manually replicate customer interactions. This will require you to think through the experience first, before putting it in front of potential customers.

DISCOVERY

184

EXPERIMENTS

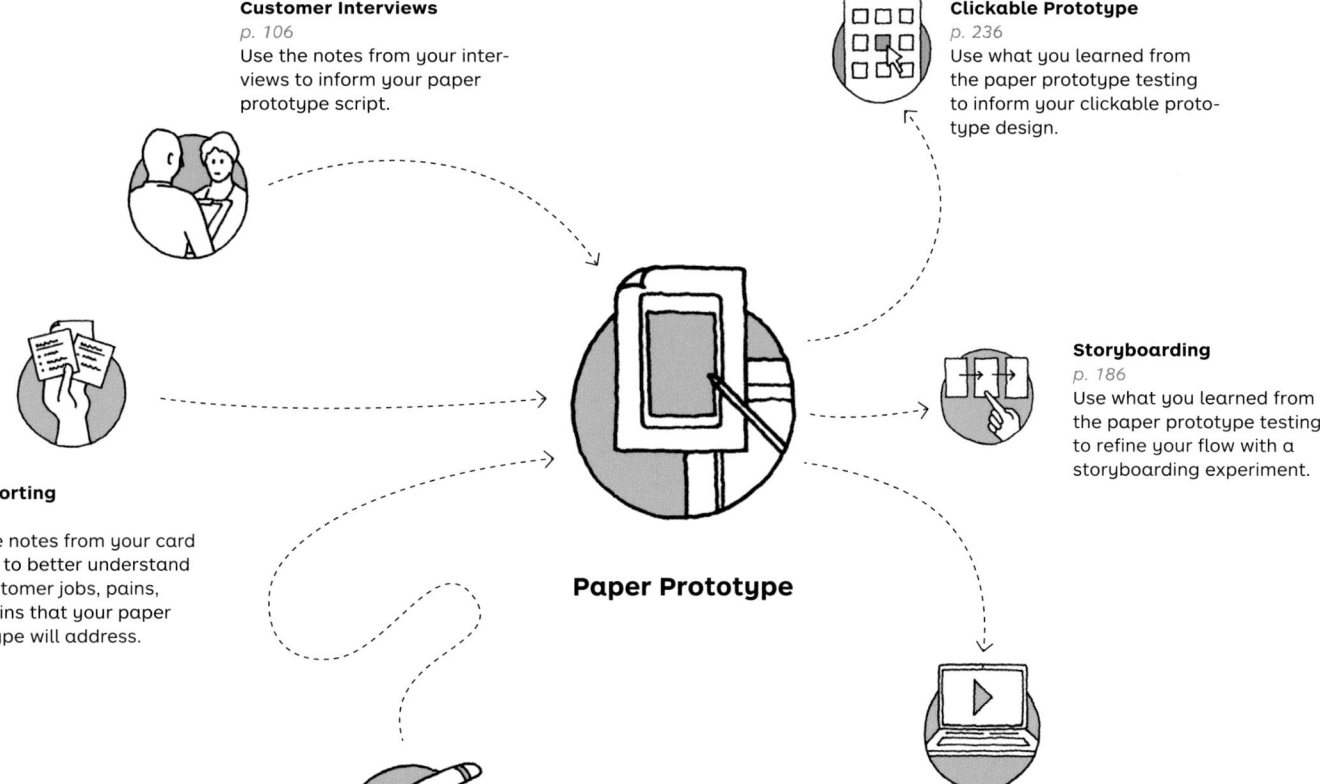

Customer Interviews
p. 106
Use the notes from your interviews to inform your paper prototype script.

Clickable Prototype
p. 236
Use what you learned from the paper prototype testing to inform your clickable prototype design.

Card Sorting
p. 222
Use the notes from your card sorting to better understand the customer jobs, pains, and gains that your paper prototype will address.

Storyboarding
p. 186
Use what you learned from the paper prototype testing to refine your flow with a storyboarding experiment.

Paper Prototype

Explainer Video
p. 200
Use the notes from your paper prototype testing to inform your higher fidelity Explainer Video.

Boomerang
p. 204
Use the notes from your Boomerang testing to shape how the paper prototype can address unmet needs.

PAPER PROTOTYPES

185

DISCUSSION PROTOTYPES

DISCOVERY / DISCUSSION PROTOTYPES

Storyboard

Illustrations displayed in sequence for the purpose of visualizing
an interactive experience.

🪙 ●●○○○ **COST**	⚖️ ●●○○○ **EVIDENCE STRENGTH**
🕐 ●●○○○ **SETUP TIME**	⏱️ ●○○○○ **RUN TIME**

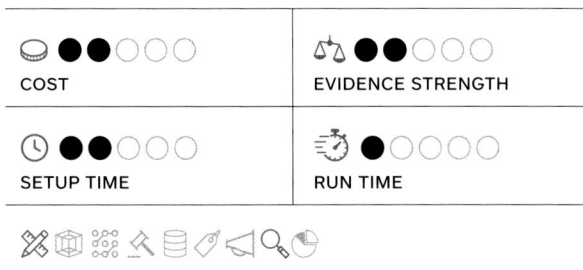
CAPABILITIES *Design / Research*

DESIRABILITY · FEASIBILITY · VIABILITY

*Storyboards are ideal for brainstorming scenarios of different
value propositions and solutions with customers.*

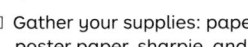

Prepare

☐ Gather your supplies: paper, poster paper, sharpie, and sticky notes.

☐ Book a room with lots of wall and table space.

☐ Define the customer segment and overall value proposition.

☐ Invite your team members and schedule the interactive session.

Execute

☐ Have the team members brainstorm 8–12 alternative value propositions.

☐ Sketch out storyboards on poster paper that describe how the customer will experience the value proposition.

☐ Take notes on customer quotes, the jobs, pains, and gains mentioned for each scenario.

☐ Have an illustrator help visualize the customer experiences as a single illustration for each scenario.

Analyze

☐ Review your notes with the team.

☐ Update your Value Proposition Canvas or create new ones based based on what you've learned.

☐ Use your sketches in customer interviews.

Cost

Storyboarding is relatively cheap. If you are facilitating it in person, you'll need a lot of wall space, markers, and poster paper. If you are facilitating it remotely over video, you'll need low cost or free, virtual white-boarding software.

Setup Time

Setup time for storyboarding is relatively short. You'll need to gather the supplies and recruit customers.

Run Time

Run time for storyboarding is a few hours. You'll be facilitating it with customers to illustrate value propositions and scenarios.

Evidence Strength

●●○○○

Customer jobs
Customer pains
Customer gains

Illustrations of customer scenarios as to how they'd experience different value propositions.
Top three ranked jobs, pains, and gains.
Themes of jobs, pains, and gains.

The illustrations are relatively weak evidence, in that it's a lab environment. However, these can help inform higher fidelity feature experiments that focus on action.

●●○○○

Customer feedback
Customer Quotes

Take note of additional quotes from the customers that are not limited to jobs, pains, and gains.

Customer quotes are relatively weak, but helpful for context and qualitative insights for upcoming experiments.

Capabilities

Design / Research

Almost anyone can facilitate storyboarding with some practice. It will help if you have design and research abilities on your team.

Requirements

Customer Segment

Storyboarding works best if you already have a specific customer segment in mind. It's meant to help you visualize various interactive experiences, but they can be too wide if you don't narrow in on a customer segment first.

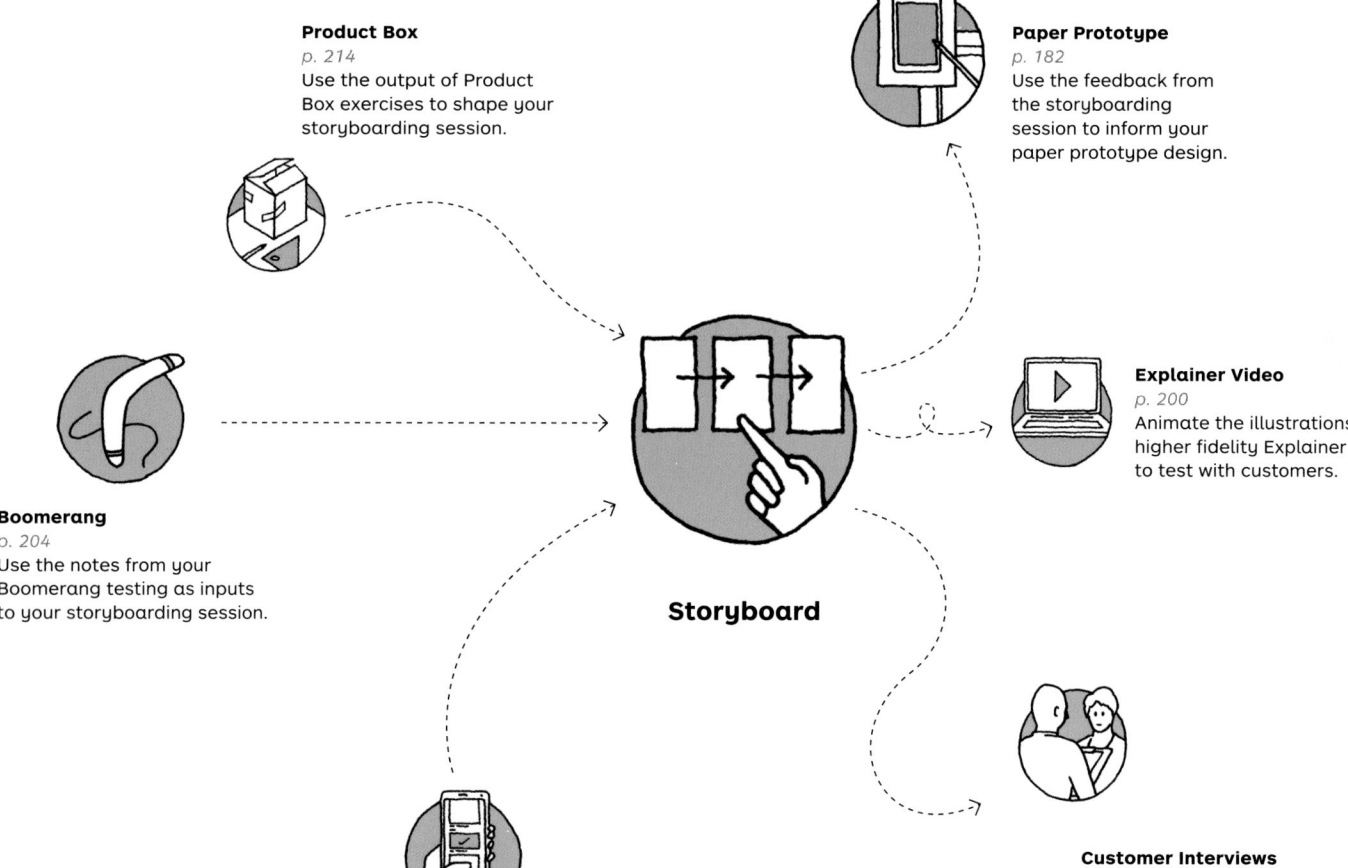

Product Box
p. 214
Use the output of Product Box exercises to shape your storyboarding session.

Paper Prototype
p. 182
Use the feedback from the storyboarding session to inform your paper prototype design.

Explainer Video
p. 200
Animate the illustrations as a higher fidelity Explainer Video to test with customers.

Boomerang
p. 204
Use the notes from your Boomerang testing as inputs to your storyboarding session.

Storyboard

Customer Interviews
p. 106
Use the sketches from your storyboarding in customer interviews.

Social Media Campaign
p. 168
Use social media to recruit people for your storyboarding session.

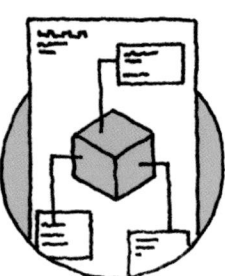

DISCOVERY / DISCUSSION PROTOTYPES

Data Sheet

One page physical or digital sheet with specifications
of your value proposition.

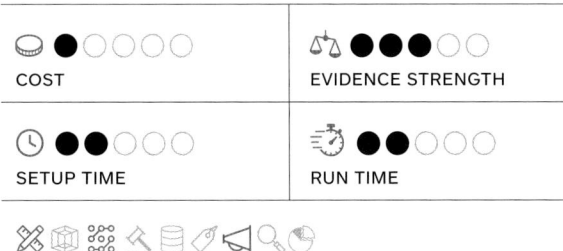

COST ● ○ ○ ○ ○ ○

SETUP TIME ● ● ○ ○ ○

CAPABILITIES *Design / Technology / Marketing*

EVIDENCE STRENGTH ● ● ● ○ ○

RUN TIME ● ● ○ ○ ○

DESIRABILITY · FEASIBILITY · VIABILITY

*Data sheets are ideal for distilling down your specifications
into a single page for testing with customers and key partners.*

Prepare

- ☐ Define your value proposition and solution specifications.
- ☐ Create your data sheet.
- ☐ Source customers and key partners and schedule the interviews.

Execute

- ☐ Show the data sheet to customers.
- ☐ One person on the team conducts the interview.
- ☐ Another person on the team takes notes on customer quotes, jobs, pains, gains, and body language.
- ☐ Wrap up the interview by asking if it is okay to contact them in the future with higher fidelity solutions or the opportunity to buy.

Analyze

- ☐ Review your notes with the team.
- ☐ Update your Value Proposition Canvas based on what you've learned.
- ☐ Use what you've learned to refine and inform your higher fidelity experiments.

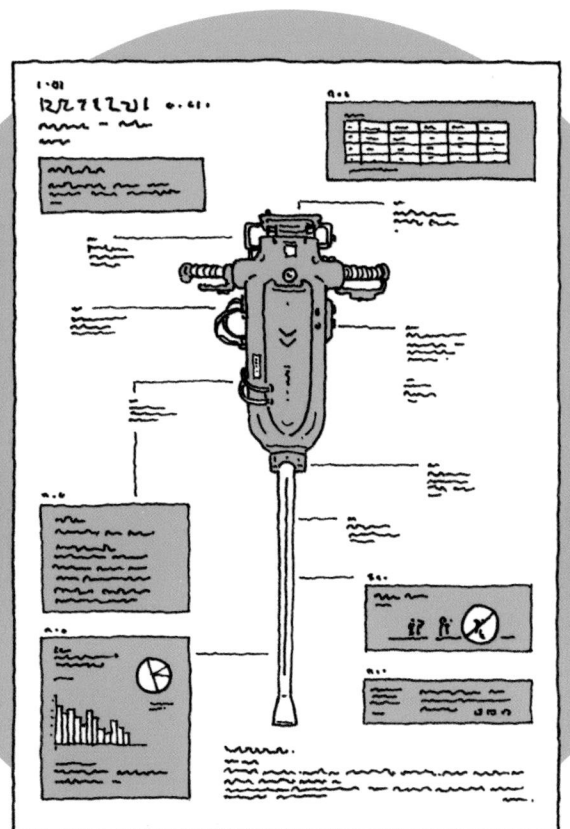

Connections

- Use the value proposition from your Value Map as your title.
- Include the product/service from your Value Map.
- Expand on the product/ service specifications and illustrate details.
- Include the top three gain creators from your Value Map.
- Include the top three pain relievers from your Value Map.

DATA SHEET

191

DISCUSSION PROTOTYPES

Cost

A data sheet is very cheap. If it's physical, you'll need basic word processor or office software to create the physical one page document and print it. If it's digital, you'll need basic web software to include the specifications in your web page or email.

Setup Time

Setup time for a data sheet is a few hours to a day to set up and create. This includes the time needed to gather your specifications and properly format them. You'll need to recruit customers and key partners if you are planning on showing it in person.

Run Time

Testing your data sheet with customers and key partners is generally quick and only takes about 15 minutes each.

Evidence Strength

Customer feedback

Partner feedback

Customer and partner quotes when reviewing the data sheet.

Feedback is weak but generally good for qualitative insights.

Capabilities

Design / Research

Data sheets require basic design skills to effectively convey the information about the value proposition and technical specifications. You'll need to include your value proposition and the technical specifications of the solution as well as source customers and/or key partners.

Requirements

A data sheet will require you to have specifications and a specific value proposition. You'll want to think through how it performs technically and what the benefits are, before creating a data sheet. You'll also need a target customer or key partner to have in mind for testing purposes.

Product Box
p. 214
Inform your data sheet by facilitating a Product Box exercise with your potential customers.

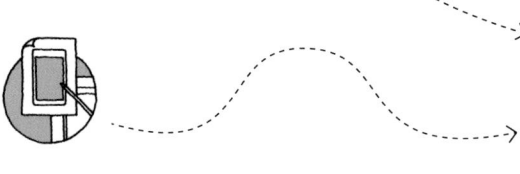

3D Print
p. 176
Create a 3D print of your solution based on what you learned from testing the data sheet.

Paper Prototype
p. 182
Use the feedback from a paper prototype to inform your data sheet.

Presale
p. 274
Conduct presales with the people who showed interest in the data sheet.

Data Sheet

Customer Interviews
p. 106
Share your data sheet in customer interviews to get feedback on how it solves for jobs, pains, and gains.

Partner & Supplier Interviews
p. 114
Interview your key partners and suppliers to get feedback on the feasibility of your data sheet.

Simple Landing Page
p. 260
Include the data sheet in your landing page to clearly communicate the detailed specifications of your solution.

DATA SHEET

193

DISCUSSION PROTOTYPES

DISCOVERY / DISCUSSION PROTOTYPES

Brochure

Mocked up physical brochure of your imagined value proposition.

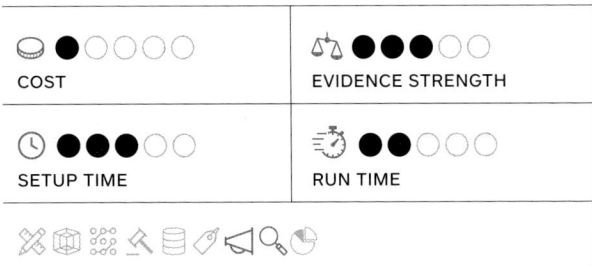

COST ○●○○○○

EVIDENCE STRENGTH ●●●○○

SETUP TIME ●●●○○

RUN TIME ●●○○○

CAPABILITIES *Marketing / Research*

DESIRABILITY · FEASIBILITY · VIABILITY

Physical brochures are ideal for testing your value proposition in person with customers who are difficult to find online.

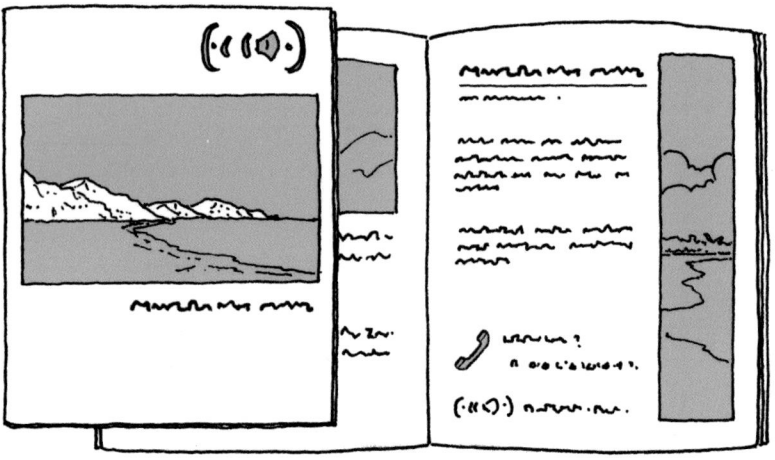

Prepare

☐ Design your brochure, using the connections from your Value Proposition Canvas.

☐ Create your plan on where to find target customers.

Execute

☐ Show the brochure to customers.

☐ One person on the team conducts the interview.

☐ Another person on the team takes notes on customer quotes, jobs, pains, gains, and body language.

☐ Count how many viewed the brochure and how many accepted it.

☐ Wrap up the interview stating that if they want to learn more or purchase to contact you using the information on the brochure.

Analyze

☐ Review your notes with the team.

☐ Update your Value Proposition Canvas based on what you've learned.

☐ Keep track of how many people contact you from the brochure information.

☐ Use what you've learned to refine and inform your higher fidelity experiments.

Connections

• The value proposition comes from your Value Map.

• The solution comes from the Value Map product and service. Position this under the value proposition so that customers understand how you are going to deliver.

• Pains come from your Customer Profile. Take the top three voted pains from the canvas and include them in the inside of the brochure.

BROCHURE

195

DISCUSSION PROTOTYPES

Cost

Physical brochure costs are low if you can use a word processor and have basic design skills. The costs increase if you decide to outsource the creation of the physical brochure to a professional agency or designer.

Setup Time

If you have the skills, a brochure should only take 1–2 days to set up and create. This includes the time needed to define the brochure hypothesis, pull in concepts from your Value Proposition Canvas, write the content, and include the graphics. If you do not have the skills, it can take 1–2 weeks instead.

Run Time

Testing your brochure with customers is generally quick and only takes about 15 minutes. Your brochures can be used with interviews wherever your customers are located physically, whether that be on the street, a cafe, or at a conference.

Evidence Strength

# of brochure views

# of brochures taken

# of interviews

# of people who contact you

Email % Conversion Rates

Phone % Conversion Rates

You can calculate the conversion rate by taking the number people given a brochure divided by number who took action = conversion rate.

Brochure conversion rates vary by industry and segment; however, if you target a very specific segment for your brochure, you should look for a strong signal of 15% or more on the call-to-action conversion.

When customers take action to reach out, it's a good signal that you are on the right path. This is different than a landing page where people are giving up their email. On a brochure with a call to action, it takes more initiative on the customer's side to take the brochure home, read through it, and then call or email you to find out more about the value proposition you are offering.

Capabilities

Marketing / Research

Brochures require design skills to create a compelling visual experience, with high quality images and styling. If you are unable to do so, you may get false negatives in your testing—people won't believe your value proposition is real. The other important aspect of the brochure is the copy and content. You'll need to be able to write clear, concise sentences that resonate with your customers.

Requirements

Acquisition Plan

Brochures are different than online digital experiments—you need to physically interact with people to distribute them. Have a plan about what you are trying to achieve and where to find your customers before finalizing a brochure. Brainstorm locations to visit, such as:

- Conferences.
- Meetups.
- Events.
- Cafes.
- Stores.
- Door-to-door.

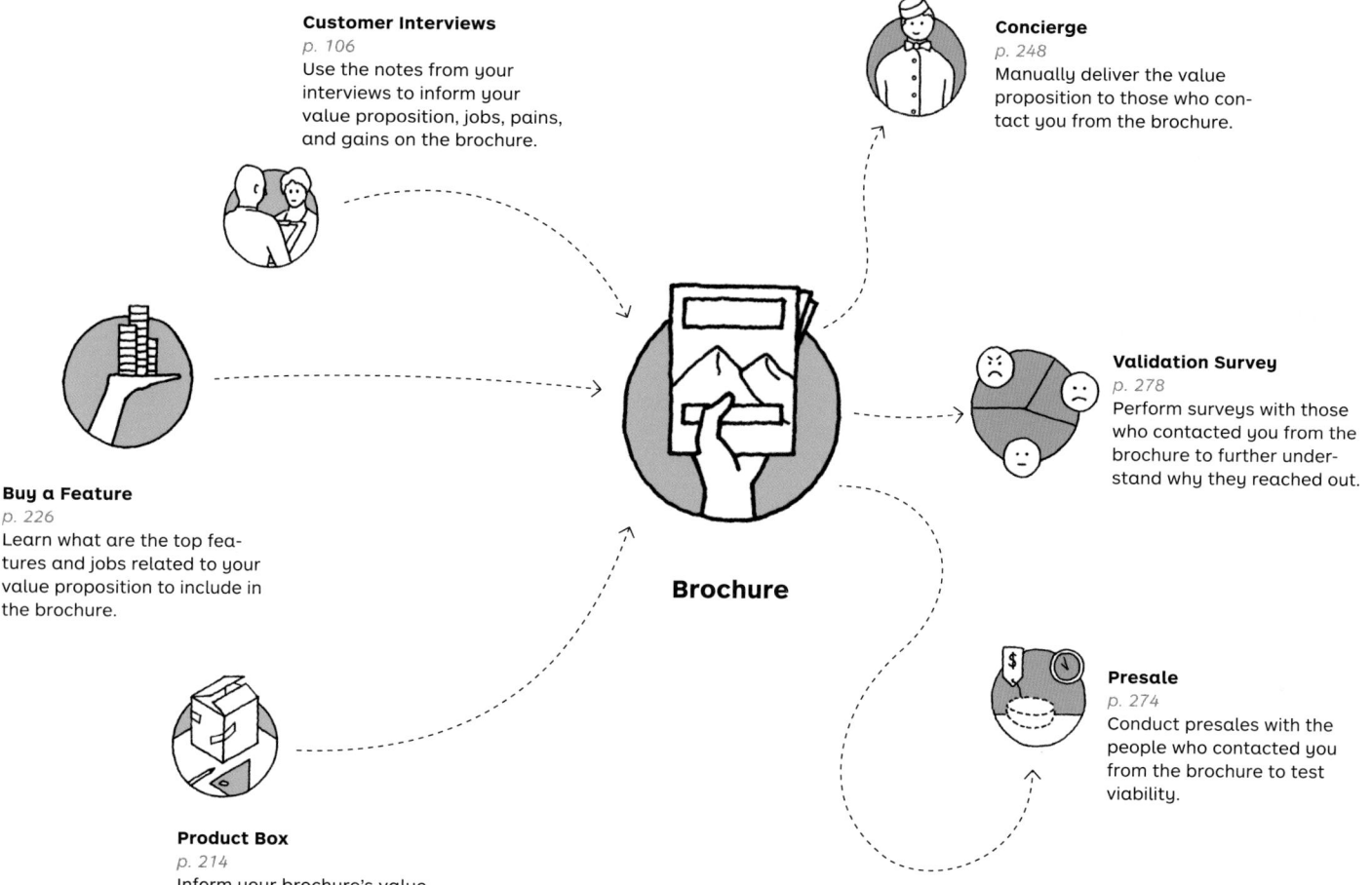

Customer Interviews
p. 106
Use the notes from your interviews to inform your value proposition, jobs, pains, and gains on the brochure.

Concierge
p. 248
Manually deliver the value proposition to those who contact you from the brochure.

Buy a Feature
p. 226
Learn what are the top features and jobs related to your value proposition to include in the brochure.

Validation Survey
p. 278
Perform surveys with those who contacted you from the brochure to further understand why they reached out.

Brochure

Product Box
p. 214
Inform your brochure's value proposition by first facilitating a Product Box exercise with your potential customers.

Presale
p. 274
Conduct presales with the people who contacted you from the brochure to test viability.

BROCHURE
A New Type of Insurance
Farm and Ranch Insurance

American Family Insurance is a private mutual company that focuses on property, casualty, and auto insurance. As an insurance company, they understand risk very well and do not want to build complex insurance offerings that no one will buy. In this example, the Commercial Farm Ranch division was searching for fit for new market risk protection offerings.

In the past, this team had used Facebook/Google Ads to drive traffic to a landing page, which is a great combination but it was difficult to target farmers online, and the team wasn't getting enough qualitative insights. So they decided to go analog and face-to-face at a large farmer convention.

Hypothesis
The Farm and Ranch team believed that...
We believe that farmers desire a new type of financial/insurance risk protection offering.

Experiment
Going analog with physical brochures.
The team went to a farming trade show in Missouri and handed out professional physical marketing brochures with a clearly articulated value proposition and solution. They had a call to action of getting in touch with the team via a phone call or email for more information.

The team screened for small/mid-sized cattle and corn farmers.

Their target metric was that 20% of the target farmers (small/mid sized cattle or corn farmers) would take initiative and call or email.

Evidence
Conversions using a brochure.
15% target farmers who received the brochure called or emailed requesting more info.

Qualitative learnings talking to the farmers and getting reaction to the brochure in face-to-face conversations.

Insights
Segmenting different types of farmers for a stronger value proposition.
Cattle farmers' pain points seemed greater based on metrics and emotion in conversations compared to corn farmers.

The farmers' current way to solve the problem was to go to a bank and get another loan/line of credit but that felt risky to them.

Several farmer focused banks/credit unions were interested in the the concept. The team could explore this as a channel.

Actions
Narrowing in on cattle farmers.
The team refined the value proposition and marketing to be more cattle-farmer specific. Next they reran the experiment to see if focusing on a more niche customer segment would get a more decisive validation signal.

DISCOVERY / DISCUSSION PROTOTYPES

Explainer Video

A short video that focuses on explaining a business idea in a simple, engaging, and compelling way.

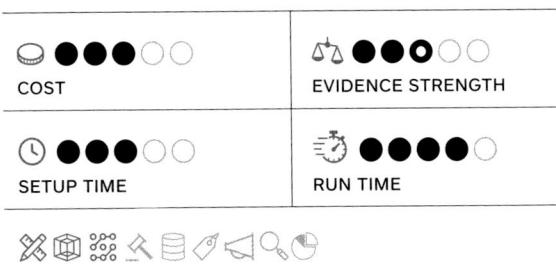

● ●●●○○
COST

⚖ ●●●○○○
EVIDENCE STRENGTH

🕐 ●●●○○
SETUP TIME

⏱ ●●●●○
RUN TIME

DESIRABILITY · FEASIBILITY · VIABILITY

An Explainer Video is ideal for quickly explaining your value proposition at scale with customers.

CAPABILITIES *Design / Product / Technology*

Prepare

☐ Write a script for your Explainer Video.

☐ Use the connections from your Value Proposition Canvas to inform the script and visuals.

☐ Create your Explainer Video.

☐ Upload it on a social media platform, video platform, email, or landing page.

☐ Test that the video analytics and CTA links work.

Execute

☐ Make your video live to the public.

☐ Drive traffic to your video.

☐ If comments are enabled, engage with the public on questions they have about the solution.

Analyze

☐ How many views and shares does the video receive?

☐ What is your click through rate?

☐ Are people that land on your destination from the video converting?

☐ Use what you've learned to tailor the video content. It's quite common to have different versions of the video depending on your target customer and platform.

Connections

• Lead with the top pain from your Customer Profile.

• Introduce your solution to the pain from your Value Map.

• Illustrate the gain from the Customer Profile you receive from solving the pain.

• Close with a call-to-action link to gauge desirability.

Cost

The cost of running an Explainer Video is relatively cheap, but can get expensive quickly depending on the production value. There are many products that'll enable you to create an Explainer Video that looks good enough, but if you want to stand out, it'll likely cost you for professional videography. You should also consider how you'll drive traffic to the Explainer Video as part of the cost.

Setup Time

Good Explainer Videos take a few days or weeks to set up. You'll need to think through how to clearly convey your value proposition, write a script, and do multiple takes and edits.

Run Time

Run time for Explainer Videos is relatively long, from several weeks to months, unless it goes viral. While viral videos get a lot of buzz, they tend to be the outliers. Many Explainer Videos require a great deal of work to drive traffic to them, both with paid advertising and social media.

Evidence Strength

●●○○○

# of unique views

How many unique views you receive and from what referral source.

# of shares

How many shares of the video there are and via what platform.

Views and shares are relatively weak evidence.

●●●○○

# of clicks

Click through rate = clicks that your video receives divided by the number of views.

Clicks are stronger evidence in that people are clicking to learn more.

●●○○○

Comments

Viewer comments on the video with regard to availability, price, and how it works.

Comments are relatively weak evidence but at times good for qualitative insights.

Capabilities

Design / Product / Technology

You'll need to be able to write a script for a compelling Explainer Video, create the video, edit it, and then share and promote it to your target audience. The Explainer Video will need a clear call to action, usually at the end, to encourage your audience to click and learn more.

Requirements

Traffic

Explainer Videos need traffic to generate evidence, regardless whether they exist on a video hosting platform or a landing page. Drive traffic to your Explainer Video using:

- Online ads.
- Social media campaigns.
- Email campaigns.
- Redirecting existing traffic.
- Word of mouth.
- Discussion forums.

Data Sheet
p. 190
Create a data sheet that explains the performance and specifications of your proposed solution.

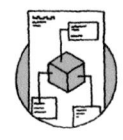

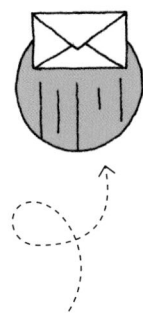

Email Campaign
p. 162
Contact the people who signed up and interview them to learn why they liked the video.

Storyboarding
p. 186
Test out different sequences of events using illustrations to inform your Explainer Video.

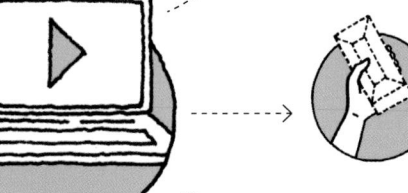

Pretend to Own
p. 208
Create a nonfunctioning prototype of your solution and see if you have the desire to use it in real world situations.

Explainer Video

Simple Landing Page
p. 260
Create a simple landing page as a destination for the call-to-action link at the end of your Explainer Video.

Card Sorting
p. 222
Facilitate a card sorting exercise to better understand different sequences to solve for customer needs.

EXPLAINER VIDEO

203

DISCUSSION PROTOTYPES

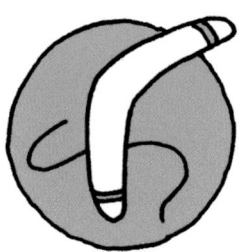

Boomerang

Performing a customer test on an existing competitor's product to gather insights on the value proposition.

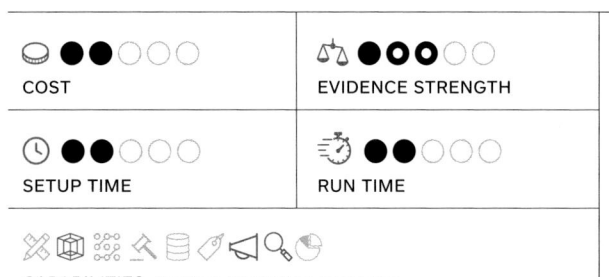

COST	EVIDENCE STRENGTH
◎ ●●○○○○	⚖ ●○○○○○

SETUP TIME	RUN TIME
🕐 ●●○○○	⏱ ●●○○○

CAPABILITIES *Product / Marketing / Research*

DESIRABILITY · FEASIBILITY · VIABILITY

Boomerang is ideal for finding unmet needs with potential customers in an existing market, without building anything.

Boomerang is not ideal for stripping away branding and testing a product as if it's your own.

Prepare

☐ Identify a product to test that has unmet needs related to your idea.

☐ Create a script for customer testing.

☐ Recruit customers who agree to test the product and be recorded.

☐ Schedule the Boomerang sessions.

☐ Prepare the Boomerang location with a competitor's product.

Execute

☐ Share the script and explain the goal.

☐ Record the session and take notes on what they say, where they get stuck, and how long it takes them to complete tasks.

☐ Wrap up and thank the participants.

Analyze

☐ Review your notes with the team.

• Which tasks were unfinished? Took the longest? Caused the most frustration?

☐ Create a Value Proposition Canvas for the competition indicating where they are misaligned.

☐ Use this information to inform your upcoming experiments to learn more.

Perils of Rebranding Competitor Products as Yours

Over time we've observed Boomerang tests and variants of it, sometimes called Imposter Judo. While, at times, these techniques vary widely in definition, we have come to a consensus that it is too risky to rebrand a competitor's product entirely for customer testing purposes.

The technique usually involves creating a clone of the competitor's, stripping away the branding and replacing it with your branding, or a fabricated brand.

This has legal and ethical implications which we advise against, especially for established corporations or those operating in heavily regulated environments.

Interestingly enough, we've seen both corporations and startups use Boomerang testing with branding intact to get an idea of unmet needs.

Corporations have pointed their Boomerang testing at a hot up-and-coming startup.

Startups have pointed their Boomerang testing at entrenched established corporations.

BOOMERANG

DISCUSSION PROTOTYPES

205

Cost

Boomerang is a low cost experiment involving pointing people to your competitor's product and not building anything. Any incurred costs would be associated with sourcing people to test with and recording the sessions.

Setup Time

Setup time for a Boomerang is short, in that you only need to find and schedule people to participate in the test.

Run Time

Run time for a Boomerang is short, as the sessions should not last more than 30 minutes each. Even if you schedule several of these, it should only take a few days to complete.

Evidence Strength

●●●○○

Task completion
Time to complete the task

Task completion rate = tasks completed divided by tasks attempted.

Average time to complete a task.

In the evidence you are looking for unmet gaps and needs when it comes to the espoused value proposition versus what it really takes for an average customer.

Evidence for measuring tasks in existing competitors' products is relatively strong—you are measuring actual behavior in the product.

●○○○○

Customer feedback
Customer quotes with regards to ease of use and unmet needs.
Look for gaps in what the customer wants and expects the product to do versus what it does in reality.

Customer feedback is relatively weak evidence, but it is helpful in determining unmet needs to explore.

Capabilities

Product / Marketing / Research

Boomerang capabilities include the ability to select an applicable product, craft a script, recruit an audience to test with, record the sessions, and synthesize the results. Many of these capabilities reside within product and marketing and research. Like interviews, these are best performed in pairs when possible.

Requirements

Existing Product

Before you schedule a Boomerang experiment, you'll need to identify the existing product to use for the testing. It needs to be a product from which you can extract learning to inform your new idea, otherwise the feedback you'll collect will not be useful.

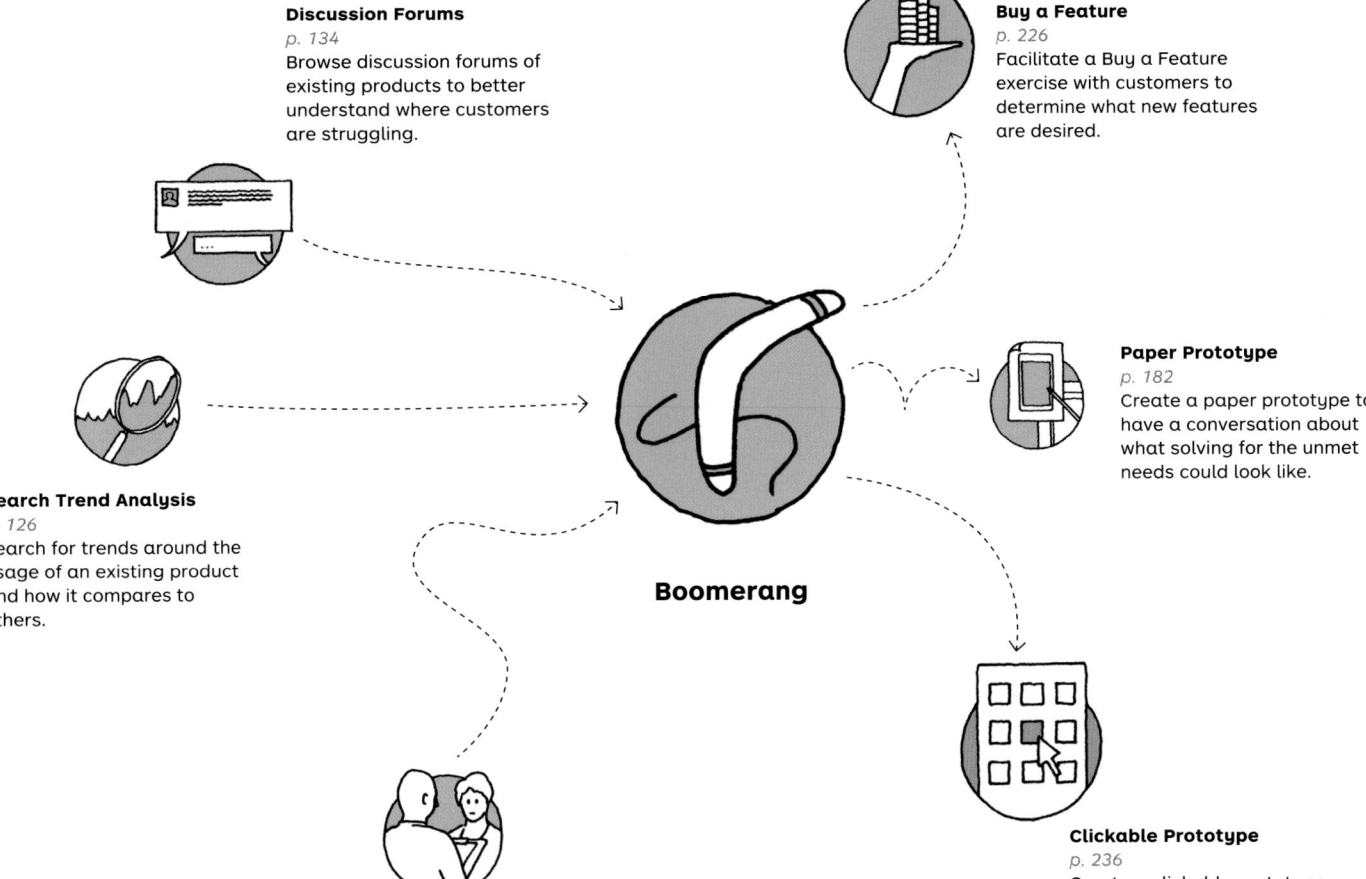

Discussion Forums
p. 134
Browse discussion forums of
existing products to better
understand where customers
are struggling.

Buy a Feature
p. 226
Facilitate a Buy a Feature
exercise with customers to
determine what new features
are desired.

Search Trend Analysis
p. 126
Search for trends around the
usage of an existing product
and how it compares to
others.

Paper Prototype
p. 182
Create a paper prototype to
have a conversation about
what solving for the unmet
needs could look like.

Boomerang

Customer Interviews
p. 106
Perform customer interviews
on people who are already
using the competitor's
product.

Clickable Prototype
p. 236
Create a clickable prototype
that simulates customers'
expectations.

BOOMERANG

207

DISCUSSION PROTOTYPES

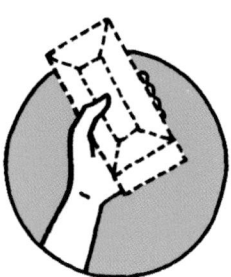

DISCOVERY / INTERACTION PROTOTYPES

Pretend to Own

Creating a nonfunctioning, low fidelity prototype of the solution to determine whether it fits into the day-to-day life of the customer. Sometimes called a Pinocchio experiment.

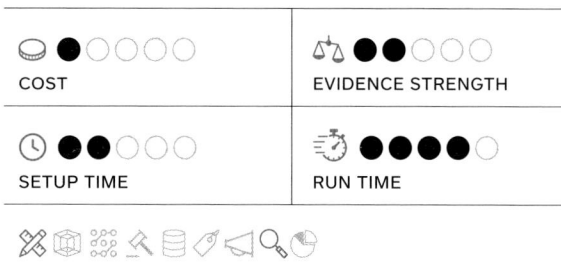

COST

EVIDENCE STRENGTH

SETUP TIME

 RUN TIME

CAPABILITIES *Design / Research*

DESIRABILITY · FEASIBILITY · VIABILITY

Pretend to Own is ideal for generating your own evidence on the potential usefulness of an idea.

 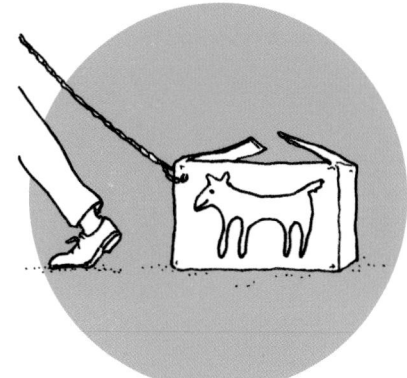 

Prepare

☐ Sketch out the product idea on a piece of paper.

☐ Gather the materials you'd need to make a Pretend to Own experiment of the product.

☐ Time box the amount of time to create it so that you do not over-iterate internally.

☐ Create your Pretend to Own product.

☐ Create an experiment log to track your metrics.

Execute

☐ Run your Pretend to Own experiment, acting as though it was a functioning product.

☐ Track your usage in an experiment log.

Analyze

☐ Review your log for events:

• How many times did you engage with it?

• Were there certain aspects of it that made it difficult or cumbersome?

☐ Use your findings to inform your higher fidelity experiment.

Cost

Cost of Pretend to Own is very cheap, in that you are using readily available material such as wood and paper. Cost can increase with size and complexity.

Setup Time

Setup time for Pretend to Own is a few minutes to a few hours. You don't want to iterate on the design internally very much at all, but instead have the bare bones shape and user interface.

Run Time

Run time for Pretend to Own can be several weeks to several months, depending on the nature of your idea. You'll want to test it over time, in order to forget that it isn't real (almost).

Evidence

When do you use it?

Engagement Logbook

Keep a spreadsheet that tracks the amount of time it was available and the number of occurrences in which you thought it would be of use to you.

Document the types of uses and in what scenarios they occurred. Overall engagement is a relatively weak strength of evidence, but you'll learn firsthand insights that can help shape the idea and value proposition.

Capabilities

Design / Research

Basic design and research skills are helpful when running a Pretend to Own experiment. You'll need to be able to create a rough replica and then log your activities over time.

Requirements

Pretend to Own doesn't require a great deal to get started: simply an idea that you want to validate and some creativity on how to create a nonfunctioning replica of it.

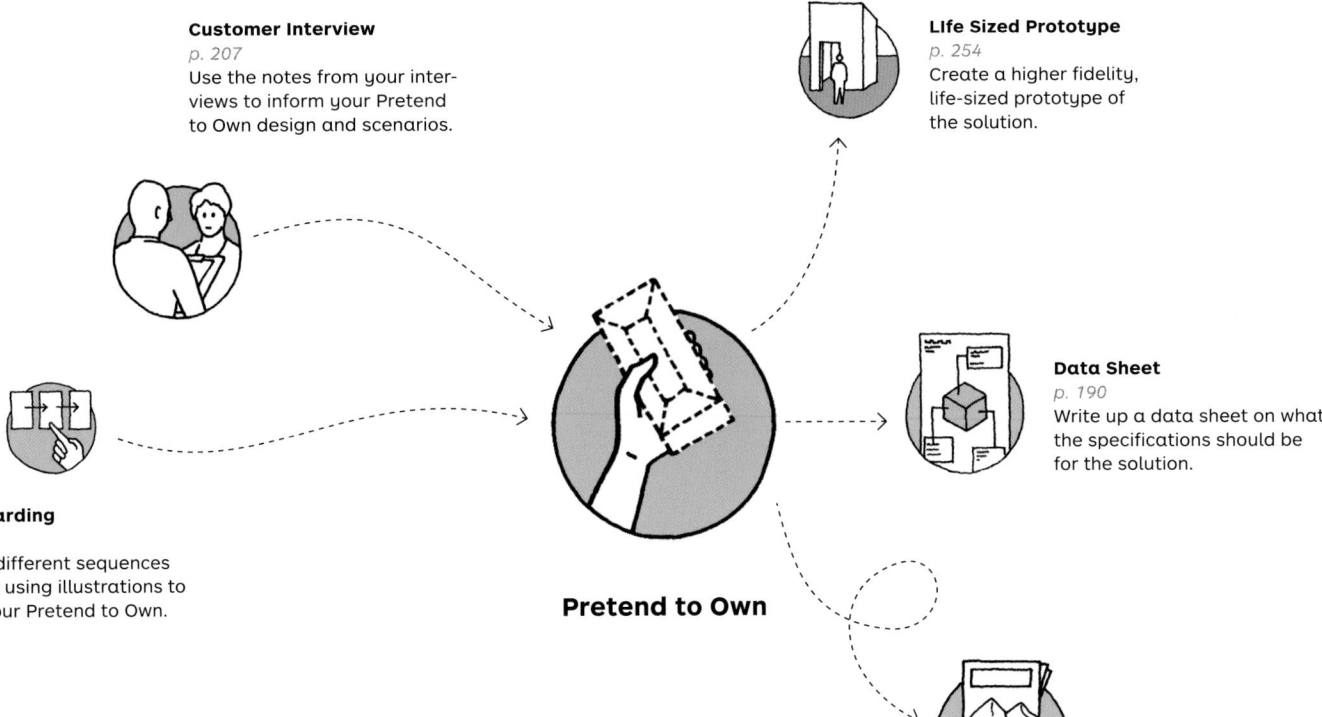

Customer Interview
p. 207
Use the notes from your interviews to inform your Pretend
to Own design and scenarios.

Storyboarding
p. 186
Test out different sequences
of events using illustrations to
inform your Pretend to Own.

Life Sized Prototype
p. 254
Create a higher fidelity,
life-sized prototype of
the solution.

Data Sheet
p. 190
Write up a data sheet on what
the specifications should be
for the solution.

Pretend to Own

Brochure
p. 194
Create a brochure that
conveys the value proposition
of the solution to test with
customers.

PRETEND TO OWN

211

DISCUSSION PROTOTYPES

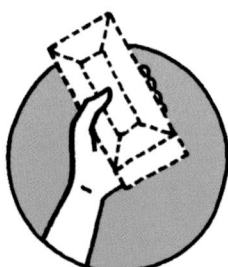

PRETEND TO OWN
Wooden Palm Pilot
Palm

Before the Palm Pilot was created, Jeff Hawkins wanted to gauge the desirability of the product. He had seen personal digital assistants in the past that were feasible, but not desirable. These ultimately led to large expensive failures.

Jeff Hawkins cut a block of wood to fit the overall size of the envisioned product and printed out a simple user interface, like the one he envisioned. He taped the printout over the wooden block and used a wooden chopstick as the stylus. This was rough enough that it only took hours to create. He then carried it around in his pocket at work for months to determine the desirability of the value proposition in the real world.

When someone asked for a meeting or email, he would pull the wood block out of his pocket, tap on it with the chopstick and then put it away.

After several instances when he felt it would've been useful to have the real product, only then did he decide to go forward with the product development of the Palm Pilot.

Evidence
Palm Pilot Engagement Logbook

- Carried the device in my pocket 95% of the time
- Pulled it out to use it an average of 12 times
- For scheduling appointments: 55% of the time
- To look up phone numbers or addresses: 25% of the time
- To add to or check a to-do list: 15% of the time
- To take notes: 5% of the time

Adapted from The Right It *by Alberto Savoia*

✓
- ☐ *Create your nonfunctioning replica as soon as possible in the design process.*
- ☐ *Be thrifty and use low cost, commonly available craft materials.*
- ☐ *Use your creative inspiration to pretend it functions in real life.*
- ☐ *Keep a logbook of your interactions, whether they be physical or digital.*

✗
- – *Spend a lot of money and time creating the replica.*
- – *Choose extremely large and expensive products for this technique.*
- – *Be embarrassed to carry it around in real world scenarios.*
- – *Forget to have fun in the process.*

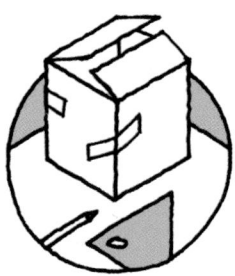

DISCOVERY / PREFERENCE & PRIORITIZATION

Product Box

A facilitation technique used with customers to visualize value propositions, main features, and key benefits in the physical form of a box.

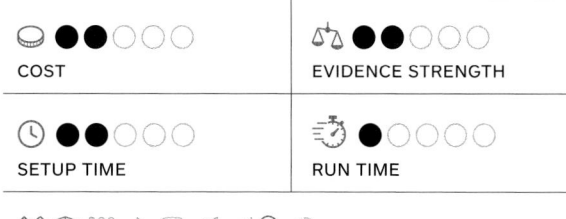

COST

EVIDENCE STRENGTH

SETUP TIME

 RUN TIME

CAPABILITIES *Design / Product / Research*

DESIRABILITY · FEASIBILITY · VIABILITY

Product Box is ideal for refining your value proposition and narrowing in on key features to your solution.

Prepare

☐ Recruit 15–20 target customers.

☐ Set up the room with boxes and supplies for each table.

Execute

☐ Set the stage by defining the area to explore.

☐ Have each table design a box for a product idea they would buy.

☐ Have them include messaging, features, and benefits of the imaginary product.

☐ Each team has to imagine selling the imaginary product at a trade show. Have them take turns pitching the product to you, a skeptical customer.

☐ Take notes during the pitches on key messaging, features, benefits.

Analyze

☐ Debrief with your team. What aspects did the teams emphasize over others?

☐ Use what you've learned to update your Value Proposition Canvas. This can be the basis of future experiments.

To learn more about Product Box we highly recommend reading Innovation Games *by Luke Hohmann.*

PRODUCT BOX

215

PREFERENCE & PRIORITIZATION

Cost

Running a Product Box experiment is relatively cheap. The materials you need are low cost and widely available at craft stores. You'll need cardboard boxes and supplies to decorate the box, colored markers, paper, and stickers.

Setup Time

Setup time for Product Box is relatively short, in that you'll need to recruit customers to participate. You'll need to purchase the supplies and set up the room.

Run Time

Run time for Product Box is very short. You can facilitate it in less than 1 hour.

Evidence Strength

●●○○○

Value propositions
Customer jobs
Customer pains
Customer gains

Collect and organize the key customer jobs, pains, and gains offered up by the participants. Highlight the top three of each.

Take note of the messaging of the value propositions from the participants, as these can inform your own messaging.

Artifacts produced by Product Box are relatively weak evidence, but they can be used to shape and inform your upcoming experiments.

●●○○○

Customer feedback
Customer Quotes

Take note of additional quotes from the customers that are not limited to jobs, pains, and gains.

Customer quotes are relatively weak evidence, but helpful for context and qualitative insights for upcoming experiments.

Capabilities

Design / Product / Research

Almost anyone can facilitate a Product Box with some practice. It will help though if you have design, research, and product abilities—you'll want to assess the outputs and provide inspiration when needed.

Requirements

Idea and Target Customer

Product Box requirements are not expansive, although ideally you'll want to have an idea and target customer in mind. Without this, the session will likely go very wide and the results will be difficult to interpret.

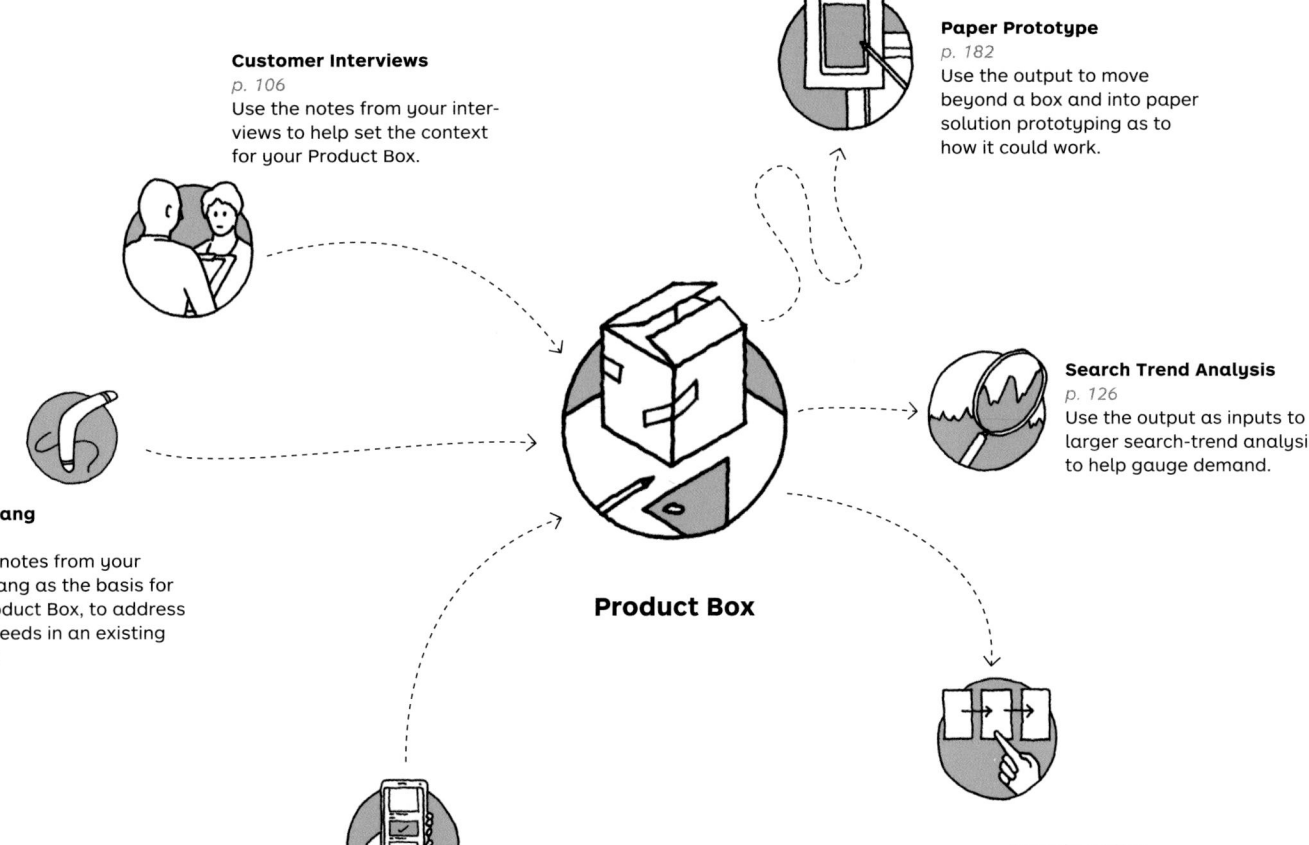

Customer Interviews
p. 106
Use the notes from your interviews to help set the context for your Product Box.

Paper Prototype
p. 182
Use the output to move beyond a box and into paper solution prototyping as to how it could work.

Boomerang
p. 204
Use the notes from your Boomerang as the basis for your Product Box, to address unmet needs in an existing product.

Search Trend Analysis
p. 126
Use the output as inputs to larger search-trend analysis to help gauge demand.

Product Box

Social Media Campaign
p. 168
Use social media to recruit people for your Product Box session.

Storyboarding
p. 186
Use the output to test sequences of solutions using illustrations.

Speed Boat

A visual game technique used with customers to identify what's inhibiting progress.

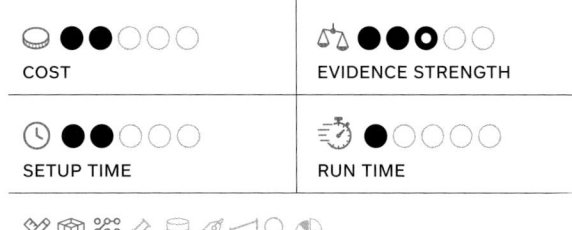

COST	EVIDENCE STRENGTH
SETUP TIME	RUN TIME

CAPABILITIES *Design / Product / Technology*

DESIRABILITY · FEASIBILITY · VIABILITY

Speed Boat is ideal for going beyond conversations and having a visual representation of what's slowing your customers down and learning how it impacts feasibility.

1. Recruit

☐ Recruit 15–20 customers who use your existing product for the exercise.

2. Prepare

☐ If it's in person, you'll want a picture of a speed boat and cards. If it's remote, then you'll need to set up a virtual whiteboard that has a speed boat and virtual cards which customers can write on digitally.

3. Facilitate

☐ Give each customer a few minutes to think before writing down anchors. After they've placed them near the speed boat, note their location. Anchors that are in groups, repeating the same thing in different ways, are clustered together. If they are deeper below the speed boat, then it means they are slowing things down more so than others. Be mindful to review each card with the group, but refrain from trying to solve or provide feedback. Doing so will bias the group and the exercise.

4. Analyze

☐ Once Speed Boat has concluded and the customers have left, assign a severity and urgency to each anchor as a team. Some you may want to address right away while others you may ignore entirely. These results, after you've processed the anchors, should be inputs into your upcoming experiments.

To learn more about Speed Boat we highly recommend reading Innovation Games *by Luke Hohmann.*

DISCOVERY

EXPERIMENTS

Cost

Running a Speed Boat experiment is relatively cheap. The materials you need are a picture of a speed boat, writing utensils, and note cards. If you choose to run this remotely, then you'll need to use a virtual product, which could slightly increase cost.

Setup Time

Setup time for Speed Boat is relatively short, in that you'll need to recruit customers to participate. You'll also want to review any existing support data that could help inform what to look for during the experiment.

Run Time

Run time for Speed Boat is very short. It takes 1–2 hours to facilitate with multiple customers involved.

Evidence

# of anchors
Severity
Urgency
# of severe and urgent anchors

The higher number of severe and urgent anchors, the bigger gap you have between your Value Map and your Customer Profile.

Artifacts produced by Speed Boat are still relatively weak evidence, but it's stronger than simply talking to customers. You are unpacking what specifically is keeping your product from living up to its value proposition.

Customer feedback
Customer Quotes

In addition to the anchors, you'll want to collect customer quotes to better understand their context when struggling with the product.

Customer quotes are relatively weak evidence, but helpful for context and qualitative insights on your product.

Capabilities

Design / Product / Technology

In addition to facilitation capabilities, which are not necessarily role specific, you'll need the right people in the room to assign severity and urgency to the anchors. Not all anchors are created equal, and some you'll want to fix right away while others you may ignore entirely.

Requirements

Facilitation Skills

Speed Boat requires some degree of facilitation skills, especially with a group of customers who are about to complain about your product. You'll need to check your ego at the door and have the skills to extract the specific anchors. If you feel you are unable to do so because you are too close to the product, then we recommend bringing in a neutral third-party facilitator to lead the session.

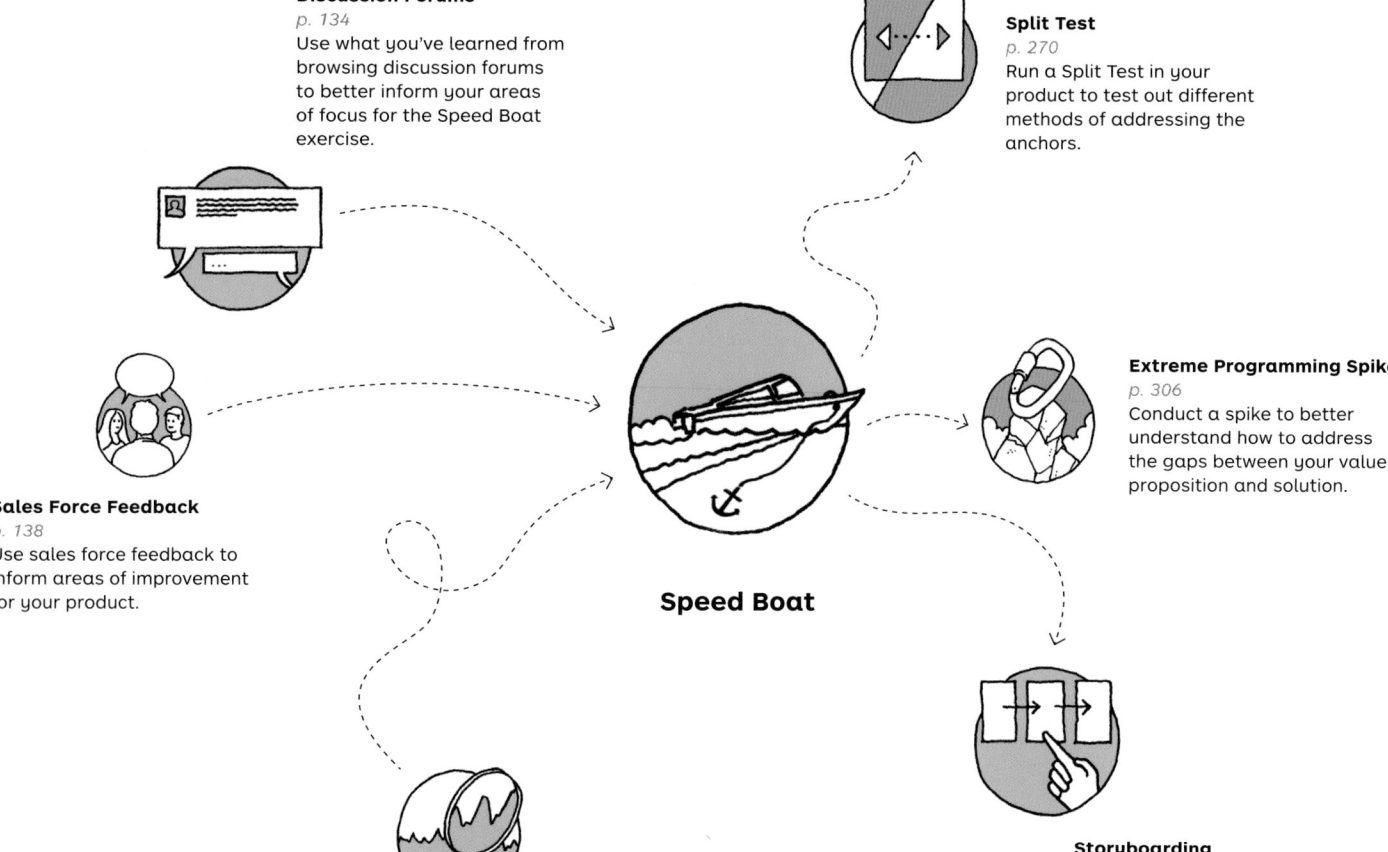

Discussion Forums
p. 134
Use what you've learned from browsing discussion forums to better inform your areas of focus for the Speed Boat exercise.

Split Test
p. 270
Run a Split Test in your product to test out different methods of addressing the anchors.

Sales Force Feedback
p. 138
Use sales force feedback to inform areas of improvement for your product.

Extreme Programming Spike
p. 306
Conduct a spike to better understand how to address the gaps between your value proposition and solution.

Speed Boat

Storyboarding
p. 186
Test out different sequences of solutions using storyboarding to design solutions to the anchors.

Search Trend Analysis
p. 126
Search online for volume of customers who are complaining about your product.

DISCOVERY / DISCUSSION PROTOTYPES

Card Sorting

A technique in user experience design in which a person uses cards
with customers to generate insights.

◯ ●●◯◯◯
COST

⚖ ●●◯◯◯
EVIDENCE STRENGTH

🕐 ●●◯◯◯
SETUP TIME

⏱ ●◯◯◯◯
RUN TIME

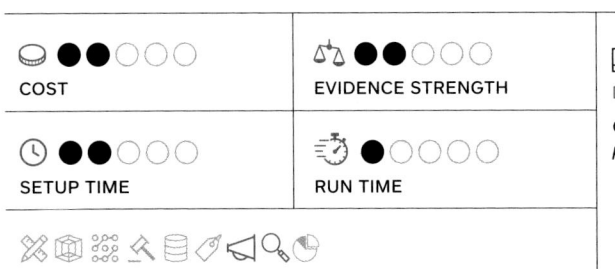

CAPABILITIES *Marketing / Research*

DESIRABILITY · FEASIBILITY · VIABILITY

*Card sorting is ideal for getting insights into customer jobs,
pains, gains, and value propositions.*

1. Recruit

☐ Recruit 15–20 existing or target customers for the card sorting session.

2. Prepare

☐ If it's in person, you'll need cards you've created for customer jobs, pains, and gains as well as blank cards for customers to fill out. If it's remote, then you'll need to set up a virtual whiteboard that has cards you've already created as well as blank ones.

3. Facilitate

☐ Explain the categories of customer jobs, pains, and gains that you've witnessed in the market. Have the participants map the existing cards to each category and rank them. Encourage them to talk out loud as they do so. Ask if there are any missing and, if so, have the participants write them down and include them in the ranking. Have an additional person take notes on your side during the session for qualitative insights.

4. Analyze

☐ Once card sorting is concluded, identify any themes you've found and calculate how the participants have ranked the top three jobs, pains, and gains. Update or create your Value Proposition Canvas to reflect the latest findings to help inform future experiments.

Cost

Running a card sorting experiment is relatively cheap. If you are facilitating it in person, then the only materials you need are note cards. If you are facilitating it remotely over video, then you'll need low-cost or free virtual white-boarding software.

Setup Time

Setup time for card sorting is relatively short. You'll need to define the content of the cards and recruit customers.

Run Time

Run time for card sorting is very short. You can facilitate it in less than 1 hour.

Evidence

Customer jobs
Customer pains
Customer gains
Top three ranked jobs, pains, and gains.
Themes of jobs, pains, and gains.

The grouping and ranking output of card sorting is relatively weak evidence, in that it's a lab environment. However it can help inform higher fidelity feature experiments that focus on action.

Customer feedback
Customer Quotes

Take note of additional quotes from the customers that are not limited to jobs, pains, and gains.

Customer quotes are relatively weak evidence, but helpful for context and qualitative insights for upcoming experiments.

Capabilities

Marketing / Research

Almost anyone can facilitate a card sorting session with some practice. It will help if you have marketing and research abilities, in that you'll want to recruit the right customers and analyze the categories and rankings created.

Requirements

Target Customer

Card sorting works best with existing customers, but it can also be used for learning about a potential niche customer as well. Both will require you to put thought into customer jobs, pains, and gains so that the output can be used to inform your Value Proposition Canvas and future experiments.

Sales Force Feedback
p. 138
Use sales force feedback to inform what cards to include in card sorting.

Storyboarding
p. 186
Create a storyboard to define a solution that address the customer jobs, pains, and gains.

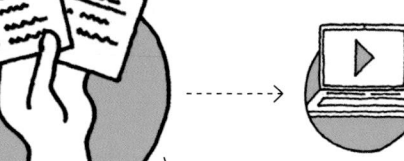

Explainer Video
p. 200
Create an Explainer Video that tells the story of how your solution addresses customer jobs, pains, and gains.

Customer Support Analysis
p. 142
Use customer support data to inform what cards to include in card sorting.

Card Sorting

Discussion Forums
p. 134
Search through discussion forums to see what unmet needs customers have to inform your cards.

Paper Prototype
p. 182
Create a paper prototype of how the solution could address the customer jobs, pains, and gains.

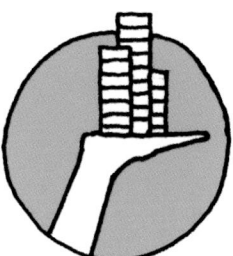

DISCOVERY / DISCUSSION PROTOTYPES

Buy a Feature

A technique where people use pretend currency to buy the features
that they would like to be available for a given product.

◯●●◯◯◯	⚖ ●●◯◯◯
COST	EVIDENCE STRENGTH
🕐 ●●◯◯◯	⏱ ●◯◯◯◯
SETUP TIME	RUN TIME

⚒ 📦 ⬚ ⚒ 🗄 🏷 📢 🔍 🥧

CAPABILITIES *Product / Research / Finance*

DESIRABILITY · FEASIBILITY · VIABILITY

*Buy a Feature is ideal for prioritizing features and refining
customer jobs, pains, and gains.*

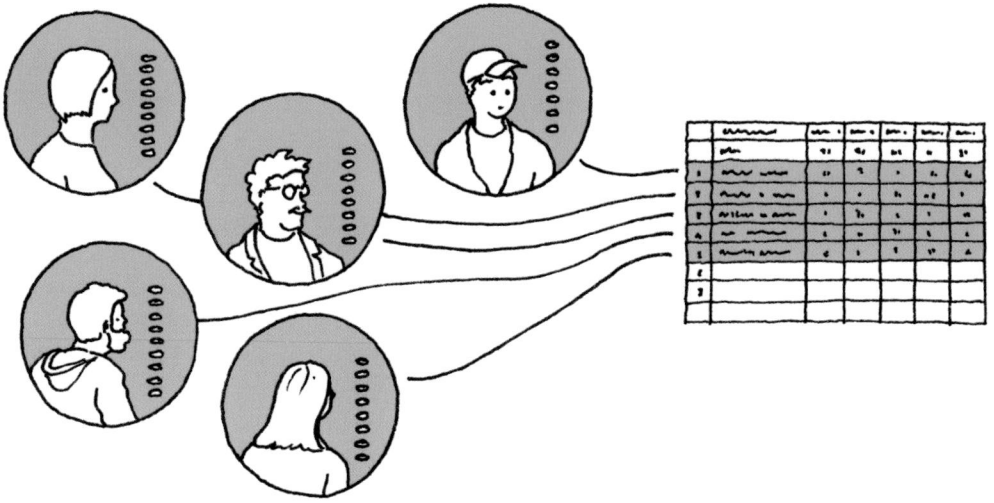

1. Recruit

☐ Recruit 15–20 target customers.

2. Prepare

☐ Set up the room with play money, note cards, and grid paper.

3. Design

☐ Explain that this is a hypothetical setting. Share the list of 15–30 features and available play money budget.

4. Buy

☐ Each customer allocates their budget to the features they want. They can collaborate with others to receive more features. It's important not to bias customers by providing feedback as they choose features.

5. Analyze

☐ Calculate on grid paper which features received the most play money.

To learn more about Buy a Feature we highly recommend reading Innovation Games *by Luke Hohmann.*

Cost

Running a Buy a Feature experiment is relatively cheap. If you are facilitating it in person, then the only materials you need are play money, note cards, and grid paper. If you are facilitating it remotely over video, then you'll need low-cost or free virtual white-boarding software.

Setup Time

Setup time for Buy a Feature can take a few days. You'll need to recruit customers, purchase supplies, and setup the room. Most of your time will be spent defining and pricing the features for the session.

Run Time

Run time for Buy a Feature is very short. You can facilitate it in less than one hour.

Evidence

Feature ranking
Customer jobs
Customer pains
Customer gains

Top three features that were purchased the most by customers.

Take note of any customer jobs, pains, and gains mentioned that are driving the customers' prioritizations.

Buy a Feature is relatively weak evidence—it's a lab environment. However, it can help inform higher fidelity feature experiments that focus on action.

Customer feedback
Customer Quotes

Take note of additional quotes from the customers that are not limited to customer jobs, pains, and gains.

Customer quotes are relatively weak evidence, but helpful for context and qualitative insights for upcoming experiments.

Capabilities

Product / Research / Finance

Almost anyone can facilitate a Buy a Feature with some practice. It will help, however, if you have design, research, and product abilities—you'll want to assess the outputs and provide inspiration when needed.

Requirements

Feature List and Target Customer

Buy a Feature requires you to put significant thought into what features you'd like to include in your product. It also requires customers to have a bit of context about the product, otherwise their rankings will not be very useful to you.

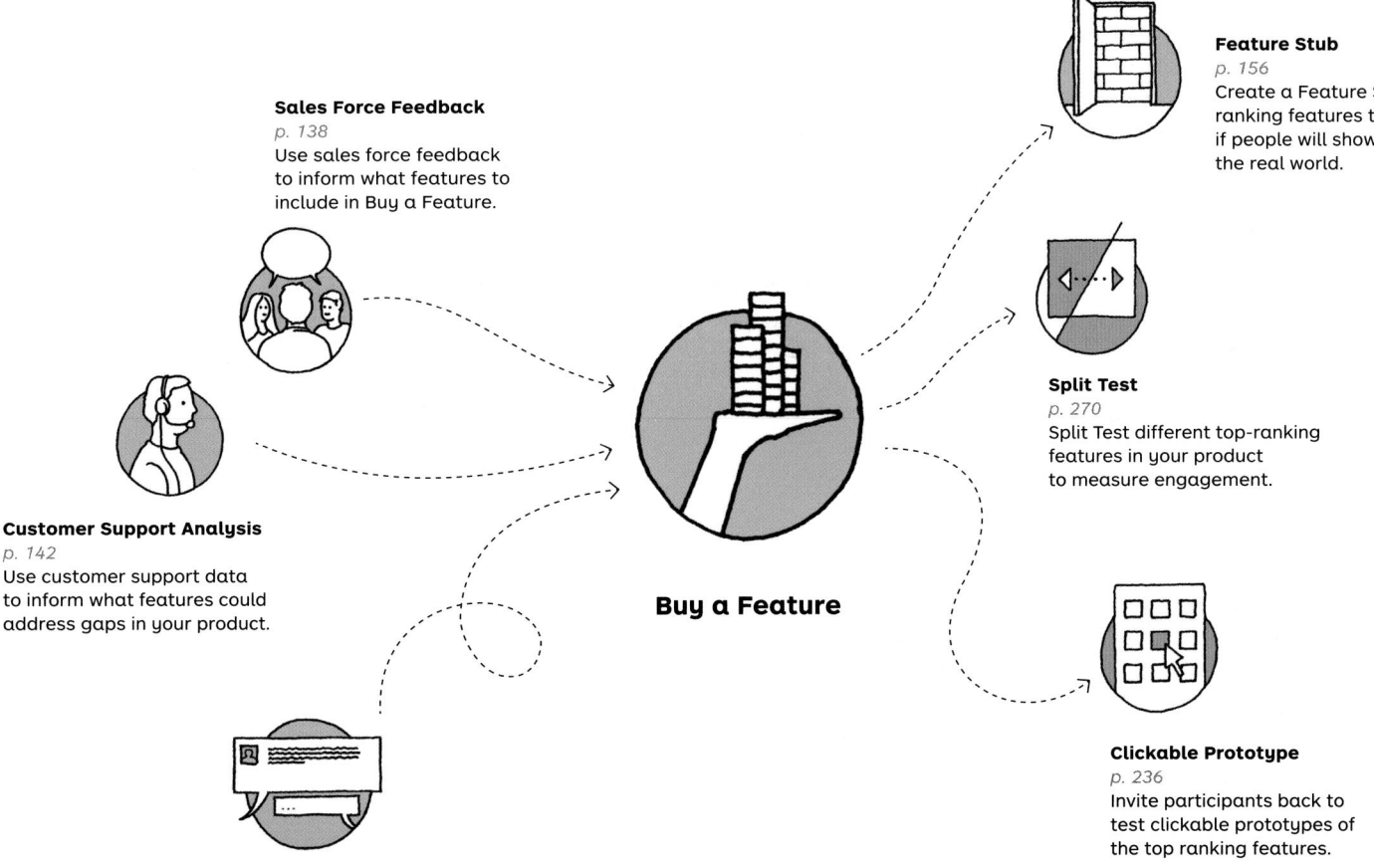

Sales Force Feedback
p. 138
Use sales force feedback
to inform what features to
include in Buy a Feature.

Feature Stub
p. 156
Create a Feature Stub for top
ranking features to determine
if people will show interest in
the real world.

Customer Support Analysis
p. 142
Use customer support data
to inform what features could
address gaps in your product.

Split Test
p. 270
Split Test different top-ranking
features in your product
to measure engagement.

Buy a Feature

Clickable Prototype
p. 236
Invite participants back to
test clickable prototypes of
the top ranking features.

Discussion Forums
p. 134
Search through discussion
forums to see what unmet
needs customers have to
inform your feature list.

BUY A FEATURE

DISCUSSION PROTOTYPES

"Invention is not disruptive.
Only customer adoption
is disruptive."

———————

Jeff Bezos
Entrepreneur and philanthropist,
founder of Amazon.com

SECTION 3 — EXPERIMENTS

3.3 — VALIDATION

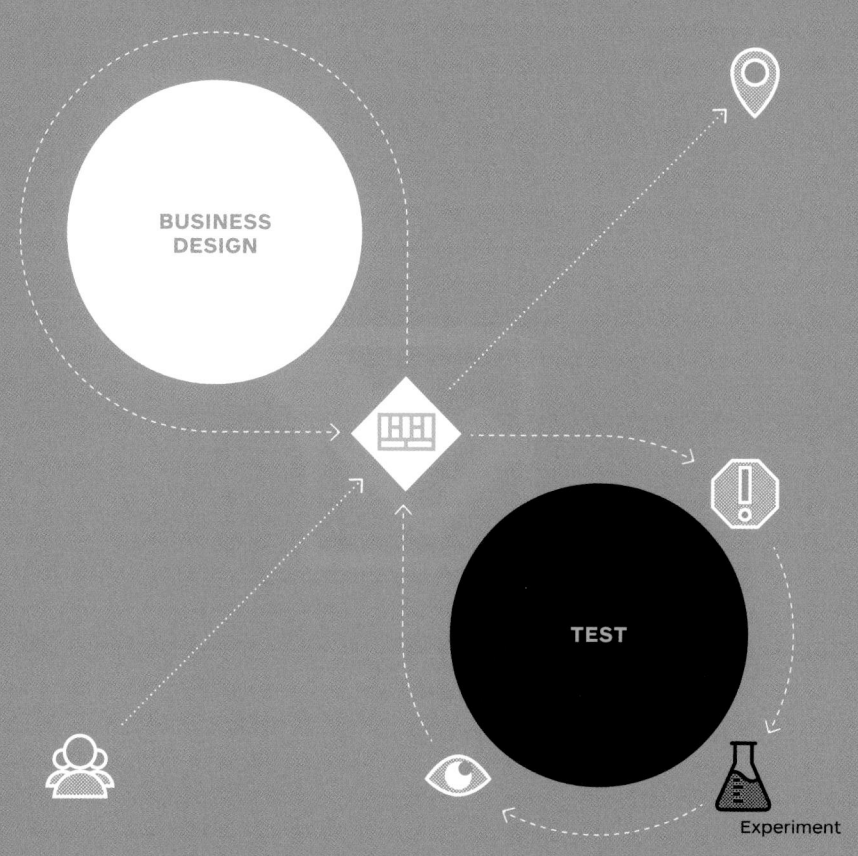

BUSINESS DESIGN

TEST

Experiment

Idea

Business

Search & Testing	Execution

Discovery
Discover if your general direction is right. Test basic hypotheses. Get first insights to course-correct rapidly.

Validation
Validate the direction you've taken. Confirm with strong evidence that your business idea is very likely to work.

The discovery and validation phases in this book build on Steve Blank's seminal work "The Four Steps to the Epiphany," and elaborated on in "The Startup Owner's Manual." Both these books are essential reading and landmarks in the development of modern thinking about entrepreneurship.

Validation Experiments

TYPE	EXPERIMENT
Interaction Prototypes	Clickable Prototype *p. 236* Single Feature MVP *p. 240* Mash-Up *p. 244* Concierge *p. 248* Life-Sized Prototype *p. 254*
Call to Action	Simple Landing Page *p. 260* Crowdfunding *p. 266* Split Test *p. 270* Presale *p. 274* Validation Survey *p. 278*
Simulation	Wizard of Oz *p. 284* Mock Sale *p. 288* Letter of Intent *p. 294* Pop-Up Store *p. 300* Extreme Programming Spike *p. 306*

⊖ COST	🕐 SETUP TIME	⏱ RUN TIME	⚖ EVIDENCE STRENGTH	THEME
●●○○○	●●○○○	●●○○○	●●○○○	DESIRABILITY · FEASIBILITY · VIABILITY
●●●●○	●●●○○	●●●●○	●●●●●	DESIRABILITY · FEASIBILITY · VIABILITY
●●●○○	●●●○○	●●●●○	●●●●●	DESIRABILITY · FEASIBILITY · VIABILITY
●○○○○	●●○○○	●●●○○	●●●●●	DESIRABILITY · FEASIBILITY · VIABILITY
●●●●●	●●●●○	●●●○○	●●○○○	DESIRABILITY · FEASIBILITY · VIABILITY
●●○○○	●●○○○	●●●○○	●●○○○	DESIRABILITY · FEASIBILITY · VIABILITY
●●●●●	●●●●○	●●●●○	●●○○○	DESIRABILITY · FEASIBILITY · VIABILITY
●●○○○	●●○○○	●●●○○	●●●○○	DESIRABILITY · FEASIBILITY · VIABILITY
●●●○○	●●○○○	●●●○○	●●●●●	DESIRABILITY · FEASIBILITY · VIABILITY
●●○○○	●●○○○	●●●○○	●○○○○	DESIRABILITY · FEASIBILITY · VIABILITY
●●○○○	●●●○○	●●●○○	●●●●●	DESIRABILITY · FEASIBILITY · VIABILITY
●○○○○	●○○○○	●●●○○	●●●○○	DESIRABILITY · FEASIBILITY · VIABILITY
●○○○○	●○○○○	●●○○○	●●●○○	DESIRABILITY · FEASIBILITY · VIABILITY
●●●●○	●●●○○	●●○○○	●●○○○	DESIRABILITY · FEASIBILITY · VIABILITY
●●○○○	●○○○○	●●○○○	●●●●●	DESIRABILITY · FEASIBILITY · VIABILITY

235

VALIDATION / INTERACTION PROTOTYPES

Clickable Prototype

Digital interface representation with clickable zones to simulate
the software's reactions to customer interaction.

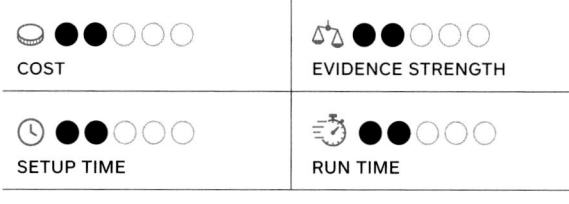

◷ ●● ○ ○ ○
COST

⚖ ●● ○ ○ ○
EVIDENCE STRENGTH

🕐 ●● ○ ○ ○
SETUP TIME

⏱ ●● ○ ○ ○
RUN TIME

CAPABILITIES *Design / Product / Technology / Research*

DESIRABILITY · FEASIBILITY · VIABILITY

*Clickable prototype is ideal for rapidly testing the concept of your
product quickly with customers at a higher fidelity than paper.*

*Clickable prototype is not ideal as a replacement for proper
usability with customers.*

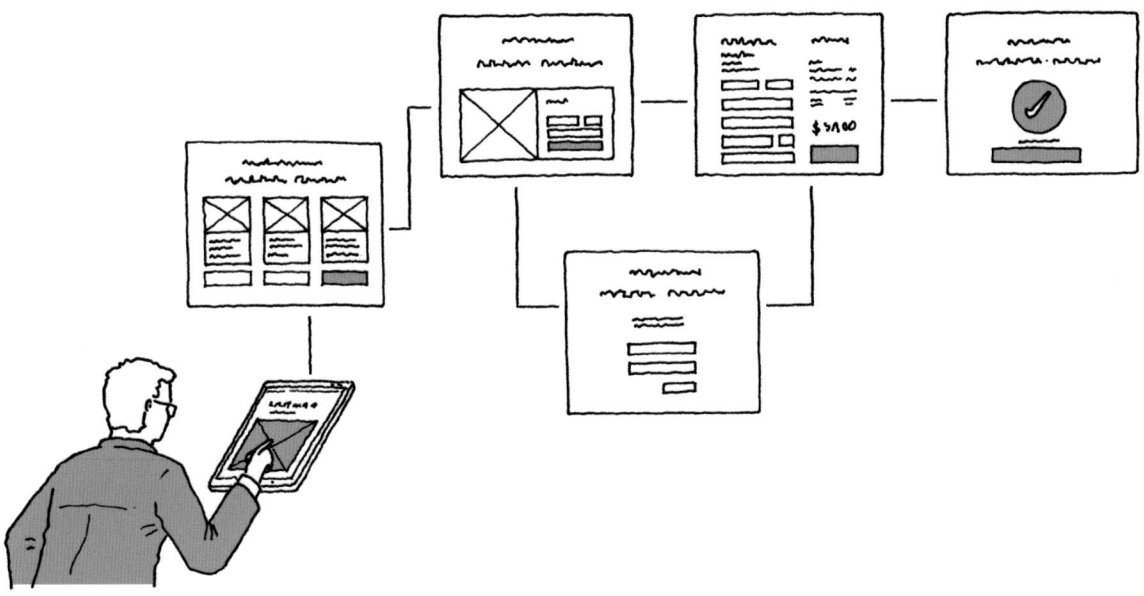

Prepare

- ☐ Define the goals of your clickable prototype experiment.
- ☐ Determine the target audience to test with, preferably a group that isn't cold and has no context for your offering.
- ☐ Write your script.
- ☐ Create your clickable prototype screens with hot zones.
- ☐ Test it internally to make sure that the interaction works.
- ☐ Schedule your clickable prototype experiments with target customers.

Execute

- ☐ Explain to the customers how this is an exercise to get their feedback on what you are planning to deliver. Make sure they understand that you value their input.
- ☐ Have one person conduct the interviews and interact with the customer.
- ☐ Have another person write notes and act as a scribe.
- ☐ Wrap up and thank the participants.

Analyze

- ☐ Place the sketches on the wall and place your notes, observations, and quotes around them.
- ☐ Where did they get stuck or confused?
- ☐ What did they get excited about?
- ☐ Use this feedback to inform your next experiment of the experience.

Cost

Clickable prototypes are a little more expensive than paper prototypes, but still relatively cheap. There are many tools and templates that allow you to quickly create a clickable prototype without having to create it from scratch yourself.

Setup Time

Setup time for a clickable prototype is relatively short. It should only take a day or two to create your clickable prototype.

Run Time

Run time for a clickable prototype is also short, as in a few days to a week. You'll want to rapidly test the clickable prototype with target customers, to get feedback on the Value Proposition and flow of the solution.

Evidence

●●○○○

Task completion

Task completion percentage.
Time to complete tasks.

Manual task completion is not necessarily strong evidence, but it is a bit stronger than using paper and will provide glimpses into where customers could get confused.

●●○○○

Customer feedback

Customer quotes on the Value Proposition and usefulness of the imagined solution.

Customer quotes on clickable prototypes are relatively weak evidence, but stronger than feedback on paper prototype experiments.

Capabilities

Design / Product / Technology / Research

In addition to a digital product idea, you'll need design skills to create the appearance of the product in a prototype tool or template. It'll require you to create hot zones that link to other mocked up screens once clicked. You'll also want to write a script and have the sessions recorded.

Requirements

A Digital Product Idea

Clickable prototyping requires that your idea be digital in nature, since your audience will be clicking through a digital experience on a screen. At the point at which you're considering a clickable prototype, you should have a strong opinion on what the flow of the product should look like, but still be open to it being wrong.

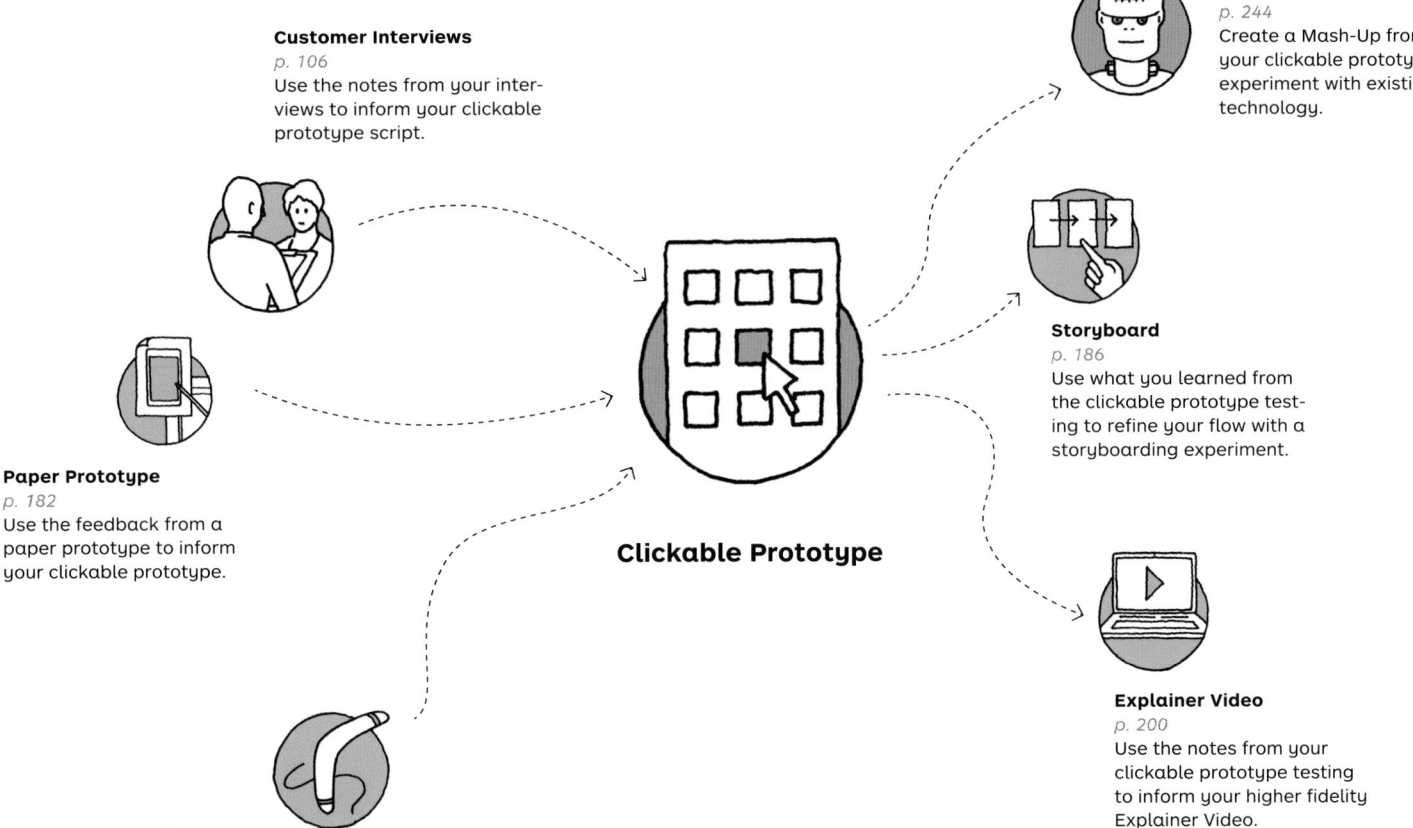

Customer Interviews
p. 106
Use the notes from your interviews to inform your clickable prototype script.

Paper Prototype
p. 182
Use the feedback from a paper prototype to inform your clickable prototype.

Boomerang
p. 204
Use the notes from your Boomerang testing to shape how the clickable prototype can address unmet needs.

Clickable Prototype

Mash-Up
p. 244
Create a Mash-Up from your clickable prototype experiment with existing technology.

Storyboard
p. 186
Use what you learned from the clickable prototype testing to refine your flow with a storyboarding experiment.

Explainer Video
p. 200
Use the notes from your clickable prototype testing to inform your higher fidelity Explainer Video.

CLICKABLE PROTOTYPE

239

INTERACTION PROTOTYPES

VALIDATION / INTERACTION PROTOTYPES

Single Feature MVP

A functioning minimum viable product with the single feature
needed to test your assumption.

⬭ ●●●●○ **COST**	⚖ ●●●●● **EVIDENCE STRENGTH**
🕐 ●●●○○ **SETUP TIME**	⏱ ●●●●○ **RUN TIME**

⚒ ⬡ ⠿ ⚒ 🗄 🏷 📢 🔍 📊
CAPABILITIES *Design / Product / Tech / Legal / Marketing / Finance*

▦ ▷ ◐

DESIRABILITY · FEASIBILITY · VIABILITY

*Single Feature MVP is ideal for learning if the core promise
of your solution resonates with customers.*

Prepare

☐ Design the smallest version of your feature that solves for a high impact customer job.

☐ Test it out internally first to make sure it works.

☐ Acquire customers for your Single Feature MVP.

Execute

☐ Conduct the Single Feature MVP experiment with customers.

☐ Gather satisfaction feedback from the customers.

Analyze

☐ Review your customer satisfaction feedback.

☐ How many customers converted?

☐ What did it cost you to operate this solution?

SINGLE FEATURE MVP

241

INTERACTION PROTOTYPES

Cost

Single Feature MVPs are a bit more expensive then low fidelity experiments, because you're creating a higher fidelity version that delivers value to the customer.

Setup Time

Setting up a Single Feature MVP can take 1–3 weeks. You'll need to design, create, and test it out internally before involving customers. You are likely going to charge for this version, so it'll need to do one thing really well.

Run Time

Running a Single Feature MVP experiment can take several weeks or months. You'll want to run it long enough to analyze qualitative and quantitative feedback before prematurely optimizing or trying to scale.

Evidence

●●●●●

Customer satisfaction

Customer quotes and feedback on how satisfied they were after receiving the output from your Single Feature MVP.

Customer satisfaction evidence is strong in this case because you are asking for feedback after the value was delivered to the customer, instead of a hypothetical situation.

●●●●●

# of purchases

Customer purchases from using the Single Feature MVP.

Payments are strong evidence, even if it's only a single feature customers are purchasing.

●●●●●

Cost

How much does it cost to design, create, deliver, and maintain a Single Feature MVP?

The cost it takes you to deliver a Single Feature MVP is strong evidence and a leading indicator of what it'll take to create a viable business in the future.

Capabilities

Design / Product / Technology / Legal / Marketing / Finance

You'll need all of the capabilities to create and deliver the feature to the customer. This is very context specific, depending on whether you are delivering a physical or digital product or service to the end customer.

Requirements

Evidence of Niche Customer Need

This is a longer, more expensive experiment with a higher transaction cost. Before considering a Single Feature MVP, you'll need to have worked through a series of lower fidelity experiments to inform the feature. You should have clear evidence of a specific customer need that the feature will address.

Customer Interviews
p. 106
Interview the people who used the feature to better understand how it satisfied their needs.

Concierge
p. 248
Use what you've learned from the Concierge experiment to inform the design of your feature.

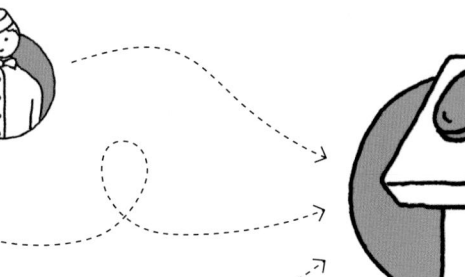

Validation Survey
p. 278
Survey the people who used the feature to better understand how it satisfied their needs.

Wizard of Oz
p. 284
Use what you've learned from the Wizard of Oz experiment to inform the design of your feature.

Single Feature MVP

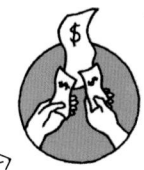

Crowdfunding
p. 266
Create a crowdfunding campaign to fund what it would take to scale beyond a single feature.

Simple Landing Page
p. 260
Create a simple landing page to collect interest in your Single Feature MVP experiment.

SINGLE FEATURE MVP

243

INTERACTION PROTOTYPES

VALIDATION / INTERACTION PROTOTYPES

Mash-Up

A functioning minimum viable product that consists of combining multiple existing services to deliver value.

◯ ●●●◯◯
COST

⚖ ●●●●●
EVIDENCE STRENGTH

DESIRABILITY · FEASIBILITY · VIABILITY

Mash-Up is ideal for learning if the solution resonates with customers.

🕐 ●●●◯◯
SETUP TIME

⏱ ●●●●◯
RUN TIME

CAPABILITIES *Design / Product / Tech / Legal / Marketing / Finance*

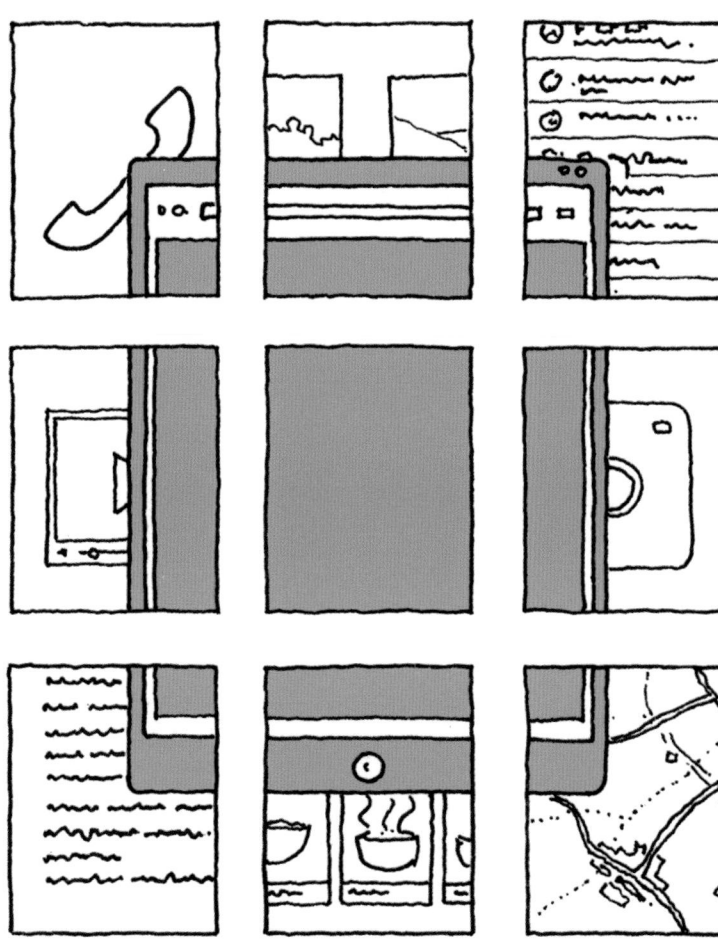

Prepare

☐ Map out the process flow needed to create the customer value.

☐ Assess the market for existing technology products that can be integrated to complete the process.

☐ Integrate the technology pieces and test the output.

☐ Acquire customers for the Mash-Up.

Execute

☐ Conduct the Mash-Up experiment with customers.

☐ Gather satisfaction feedback from customers.

Analyze

☐ Review your customer satisfaction feedback.

☐ How many customers made it through the process and purchased?

☐ Where did they abandon the process?

☐ Are there any gaps where the existing technology fell short of customer expectations?

☐ Only consider building custom solutions as a result, if the experience was unsatisfactory or if the cost of using these solutions doesn't scale.

MASH-UP MVP

245

INTERACTION PROTOTYPES

Cost

Mash-Ups are a bit more expensive then low fidelity experiments, since you need to piece together multiple existing technological components to deliver an overall solution. The costs incurred will be paying for the existing technology and the effort to wire it all together.

Setup Time

Setting up a Mash-Up can take 1–3 weeks. You'll need to evaluate and piece together existing technology.

Run Time

Running a Mash-Up experiment can take several weeks or months. You'll want to run it long enough to analyze qualitative and quantitative feedback before prematurely optimizing or trying to scale.

Evidence

●●●●●
Customer satisfaction

Customer quotes and feedback on how satisfied they were after receiving the output from your Mash-Up.

Customer satisfaction evidence is strong in this case because you are asking for feedback after the value was delivered to the customer, instead of a hypothetical situation.

●●●●●
# of purchases

Customer purchases from using the Mash-Up.

Payments are strong evidence, even if they don't realize it's pieced together behind the scenes with existing technology.

●●●●●
Cost

How much does it cost to design, create, deliver, and maintain a Mash-Up?

The cost it takes you to deliver a Mash-Up is strong evidence and a leading indicator of what it'll take to create a viable business in the future.

Capabilities

Design / Technology / Product / Marketing / Legal / Finance

You'll need to be able assess existing technology, choose the right components, and integrate them together into a solution that can deliver the needed value to customers. It doesn't necessarily mean you need to know how all the technology works, but you'll need to know enough to put it all together behind the scenes. In addition, the Mash-Up will need all of the other characteristics of a legitimate product.

Requirements

A Process to Automate

This is another longer, more expensive experiment with a higher transaction cost. Before considering a Mash-Up, you'll need to have run enough lower fidelity experiments to have an idea of the process you'll need to deliver value to the customer. Use that process knowledge to begin the assessment of what existing technology you could piece together to deliver that value.

VALIDATION

EXPERIMENTS

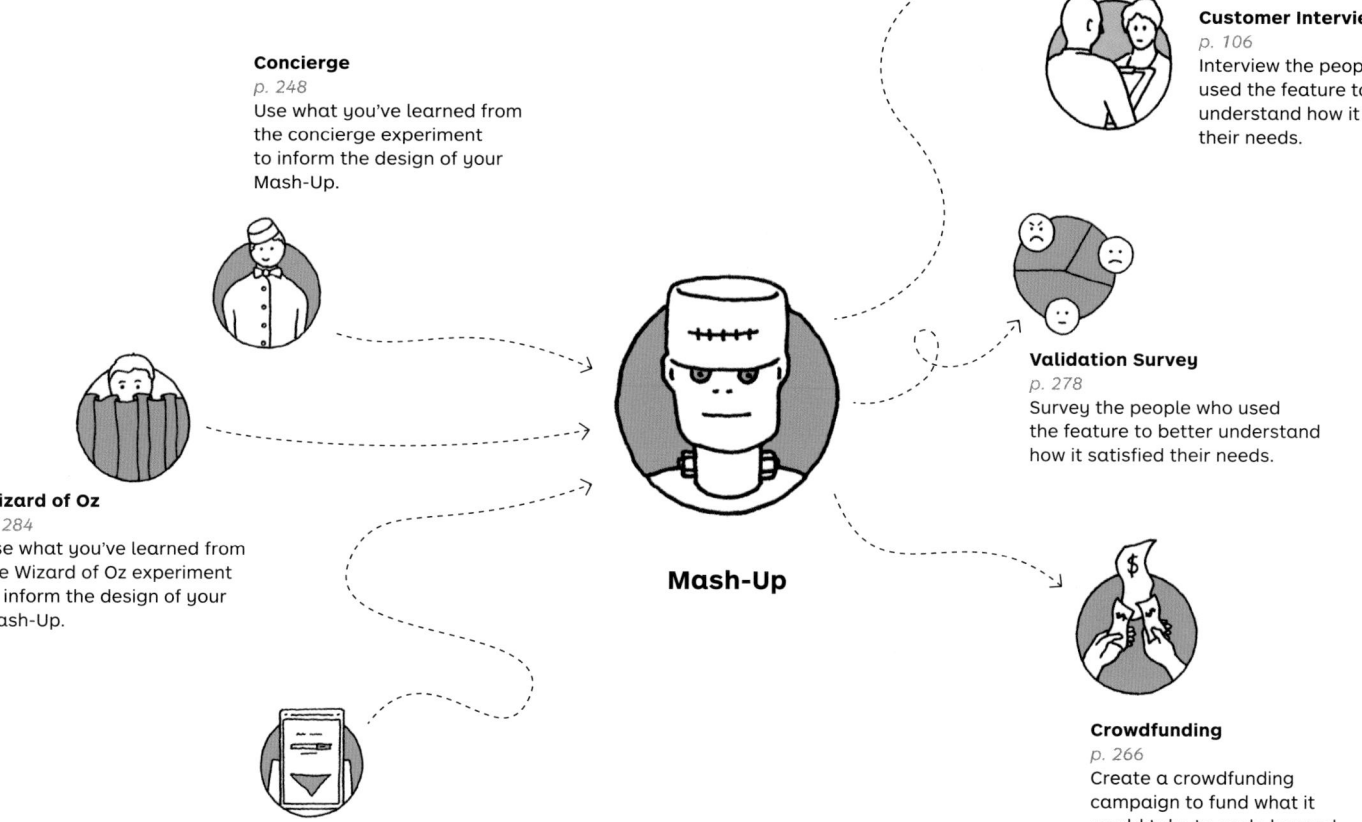

Concierge
p. 248
Use what you've learned from
the concierge experiment
to inform the design of your
Mash-Up.

Customer Interviews
p. 106
Interview the people who
used the feature to better
understand how it satisfied
their needs.

Validation Survey
p. 278
Survey the people who used
the feature to better understand
how it satisfied their needs.

Wizard of Oz
p. 284
Use what you've learned from
the Wizard of Oz experiment
to inform the design of your
Mash-Up.

Mash-Up

Crowdfunding
p. 266
Create a crowdfunding
campaign to fund what it
would take to scale beyond
a Mash-Up.

Simple Landing Page
p. 260
Create a simple landing page
to collect interest in your
Mash-Up experiment.

VALIDATION / INTERACTION PROTOTYPES

Concierge

Creating a customer experience and delivering value manually, with people instead of using technology. Unlike Wizard of Oz, the people involved are obvious to the customer.

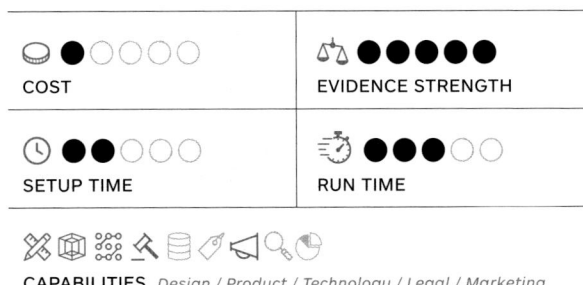

○ ● ○ ○ ○ ○
COST

⚖ ● ● ● ● ●
EVIDENCE STRENGTH

⏱ ● ● ● ○ ○
RUN TIME

🕐 ● ● ○ ○ ○
SETUP TIME

DESIRABILITY · FEASIBILITY · VIABILITY

Concierge is ideal for learning firsthand about steps needed to create, capture, and deliver value to a customer.

Concierge is not ideal for scaling a product or business.

CAPABILITIES *Design / Product / Technology / Legal / Marketing*

Prepare

☐ Plan the steps of creating the product manually.

☐ Create a board to track the orders and steps needed.

☐ Test the steps with someone first to make sure they work.

☐ If taking orders on the web, make sure analytics are integrated. Otherwise, document the numbers on grid paper or excel.

Execute

☐ Receive orders for the concierge experiment.

☐ Conduct the concierge experiment.

☐ Document how long it takes to complete the tasks.

☐ Gather feedback from customers with interviews and surveys.

Analyze

☐ Review your customer feedback.

☐ Review your metrics for:

• Length of time for task completion.

• Where you experienced delays in the process.

• How many purchased.

☐ Use these findings to improve your next concierge experiment and to help inform where to automate the process.

CONCIERGE

249

INTERACTION PROTOTYPES

Cost

As long as you keep the concierge experiments small and simple, they are cheap to run, mostly because you are doing all of the work manually with little to no technology involved. If you try to scale the experiment or make it overly complex, it'll increase the cost.

Setup Time

Setting up a concierge experiment takes a bit longer than other rapid prototyping techniques, because you have to manually plan out all of the steps and acquire customers for it.

Run Time

Running a concierge experiment can take days to weeks, depending on how complex the process is and how many customers you involve in the experiment. It generally takes longer than other rapid prototyping techniques.

Evidence

Customer satisfaction

Customer quotes and feedback on how satisfied they were after receiving the output from your experiment.

Customer satisfaction evidence is strong in this case because you are asking for feedback after the value was delivered to the customer, instead of a hypothetical situation.

# of purchases

Customer purchases from the concierge experiment. What are they willing to pay for a manual experience?

Payments are strong evidence, even if you are manually delivering value.

●●●●●

Time it takes to complete the process

Lead time is the total time measured from customer request to when the order was delivered.

Cycle time is the amount of time spent working on the request. It does not include the time the request sits idle before action was taken on it.

The time it takes for you to complete the concierge experiment is very strong, in that it gives you firsthand knowledge of the steps needed to receive a request and deliver value to a customer.

Capabilities

Design / Technology / Product / Marketing / Legal

You'll need all of the capabilities to manually create and deliver the product to the customer. This is very context specific, depending on whether you are delivering a physical or digital product or service to the end customer.

Requirements

Time

The biggest requirement for a concierge test is time. Your time. The team's time. If you do not make time to run this experiment, it will be frustrating for both you and the customer. Be sure to plan when you will run the Concierge experiment and clear your schedule so that you can give it the attention it will need.

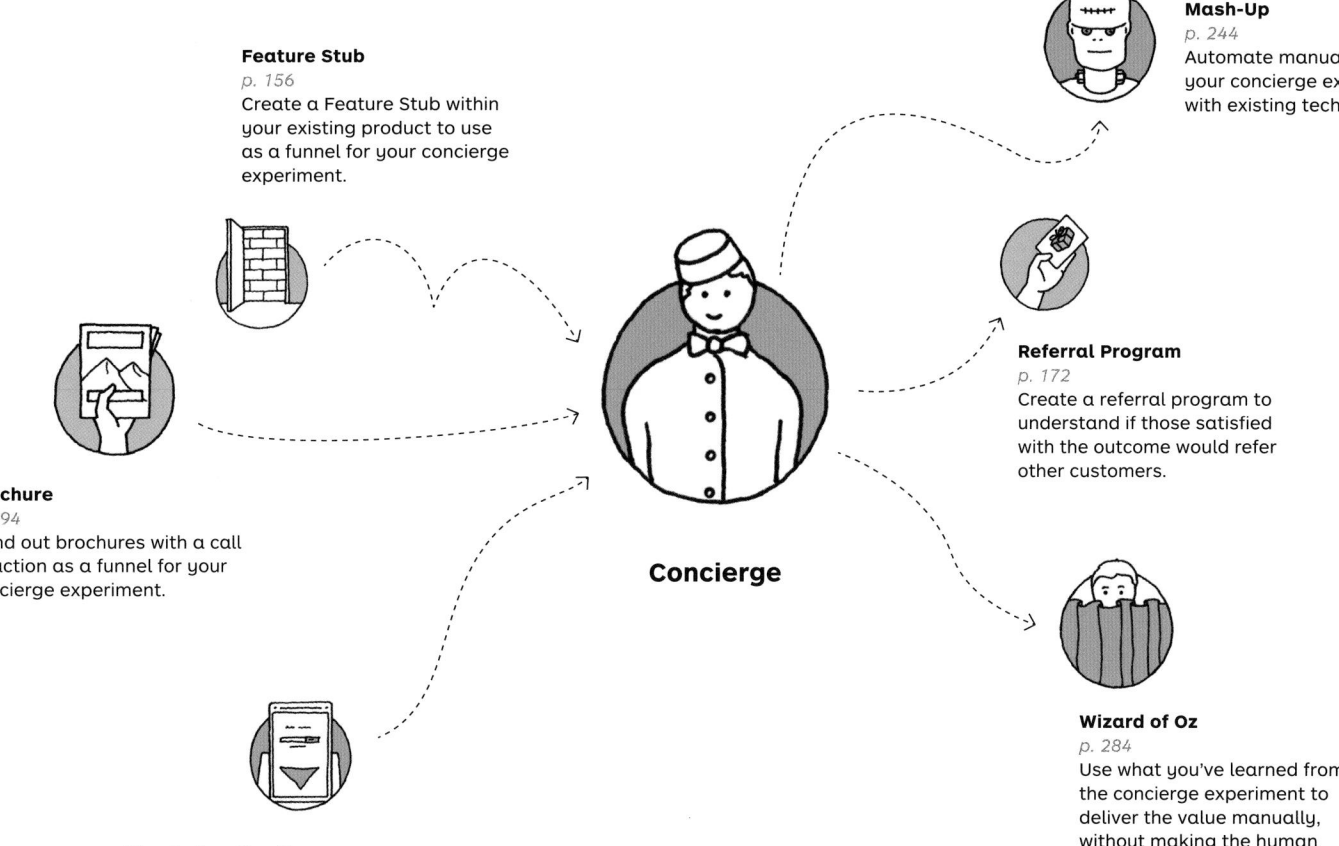

Feature Stub
p. 156
Create a Feature Stub within your existing product to use as a funnel for your concierge experiment.

Mash-Up
p. 244
Automate manual steps from your concierge experiment with existing technology.

Brochure
p. 194
Hand out brochures with a call to action as a funnel for your concierge experiment.

Referral Program
p. 172
Create a referral program to understand if those satisfied with the outcome would refer other customers.

Concierge

Simple Landing Page
p. 260
Create a simple landing page to collect interest in your concierge experiment.

Wizard of Oz
p. 284
Use what you've learned from the concierge experiment to deliver the value manually, without making the human steps visible to the end customer.

VALIDATION

252

EXPERIMENTS

CONCIERGE
Buying and Selling a Home
Realtor.com

Realtor.com is a real estate listings web-site operated by Move, Inc. out of Santa Clara, California. It provides buyers and sellers with the information, tools and professional expertise they need throughout the home journey.

As realtor.com teams spoke with people who were looking to sell their home, one of the problems commonly heard was the struggle with timing the process of selling a house with buying a new one. When people move, they end up moving to another zip code or other cities or even other states.

The idea was to aggregate and show the market insights for them with the two markets side by side. Would that be useful for them? Would we extend that into a real feature?

Hypothesis
The realtor.com team believed that sellers on their site who are looking to sell within the next year will also be buying at the same time.

Experiment
Concierge delivery of PDF insights.
The team did a simple concierge experiment that was triggered by a call to action. When clicked, the modal window highlighting a value proposition for insights on timing your ability to buy and sell at the same time appeared. Users would then click through a series of questions. Once complete, Dave Masters (the product manager) manually created the output by piecing together insights from other parts found throughout Realtor.com into a PDF.

Dave would then individually email these PDFs out to the users who signed up. Additionally in his email to them, Dave added a meeting link to further connect to these users in hopes to learn more and see how we could help.

Evidence
80 signups in just a few minutes.
It surpassed expectations quite quickly. Based on site statistical data, the team had estimated that it would generate 30 signups within 3 hours. It generated more than 80 signups in a few minutes, faster than they could even shut it off.

Insights
Hypothesis validated — audience has problem. The team learned that a reasonably large pool of people within their site that had the buying and selling problem.

The team also learned about the challenge with concierge testing. High volume could be a good sign but might require you to do a lot more manual work than you initially set out to do. It's probably worth noting that this type of work requires your ability to execute for these users. When dual-tracking work, you have to anticipate and set aside appropriate time to deliver on this promise and really aim to learn. With the copious amounts of work you might have in your day-to-day, it can be hard to manage it all.

Actions
Persevere by testing in app features.
Knowing the audience mix was roughly the size anticipated, the team felt confident in moving forward with more experiments targeting these users within this app. In fact, the very next experiment was a feature stub that included a link to a nonexistent tab for "Selling-Tools"—a place that the team would begin to put Seller specific features and tests.

VALIDATION / INTERACTION PROTOTYPES

Life-Sized Prototype

Life-sized prototypes and real-world replicas of service experiences.

◎ ●●●●●
COST

⚖ ●●○○○
EVIDENCE STRENGTH

🕐 ●●●●○
SETUP TIME

⏱ ●●●○○
RUN TIME

CAPABILITIES *Design / Product*

DESIRABILITY · FEASIBILITY · VIABILITY

Life-sized prototypes are ideal for testing higher fidelity solutions with customers at a small sample size, before deciding to scale your solution.

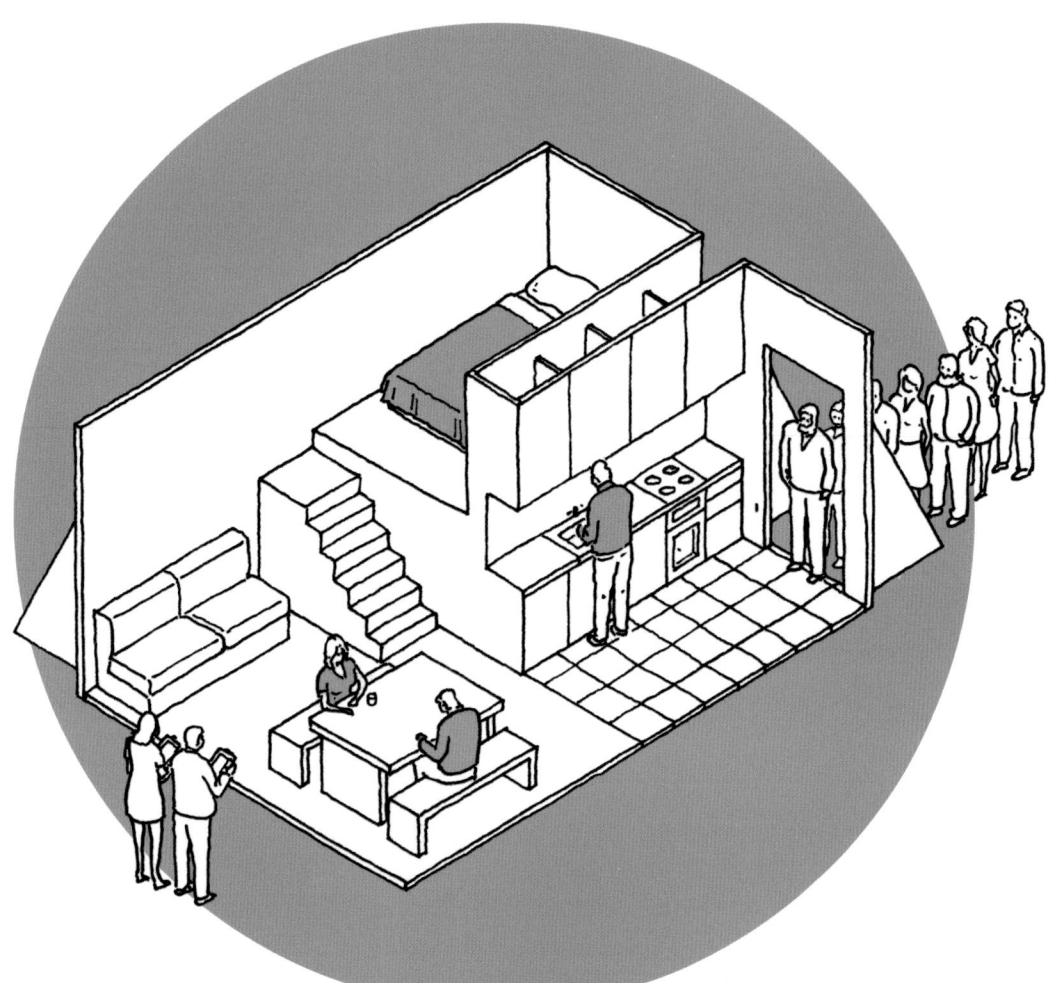

Prepare

☐ Gather your previous evidence to support the solution.

☐ Create your life-sized prototype, which is a replica of your proposed solution.

☐ Source customers and schedule the interactive session.

Execute

☐ Show the life-sized prototype to customers.

☐ One person on the team conducts the interview.

☐ Another person on the team takes notes on customer quotes, jobs, pains, gains, and body language.

☐ Wrap up the interview with a call to action or mock sale, to get beyond what the customer says and into what they would do.

Analyze

☐ Review your notes with the team.

☐ Update your Value Proposition Canvas based on what you've learned.

☐ Calculate conversion on mock sales and call to action.

☐ Use what you've learned to refine and iterate on your prototype for the next round of testing.

LIFE-SIZED PROTOTYPE

255

INTERACTION PROTOTYPES

Cost

Life-sized prototypes can be moderately expensive. They need to have a believable level of polish and the bigger the size, the greater the expense.

Setup Time

The setup time for a life-sized prototype can be quite long, depending on the size and complexity of your solution. It may take several weeks or months to create a high fidelity replica.

Run Time

Run time for a life-sized prototype is relatively short. You'll want customers interacting with the prototype to better understand the fit between your Value Proposition and their customer jobs, pains, and gains.

Evidence

●●●●○

Customer jobs
Customer pains
Customer gains
Customer feedback

Customer jobs, pains, and gains and how the prototype could solve for them.

Take note of additional quotes from the customers that are not limited to customer jobs, pains, and gains.

The evidence is relatively weak evidence— they need to suspend belief and imagine using it in real world scenarios.

# of successful mock sales

You can calculate the mock sale conversion rate by taking the number people who view the price divided by the number of people who filled out payment information.

Payment information submission is very strong evidence.

# of email signups

Conversion rate on people who you interviewed who provided their email address to be contacted when the solution is available.

Customer emails are rather weak evidence, but good for future experiments.

Capabilities

Design / Product

You'll need mostly product and design capabilities to create the life-sized prototype. It doesn't need to be fully operational or have all of the bells and whistles, but it needs to be at a high enough fidelity to interact with customers.

Requirements

Evidence of a Solution

Before considering a life-sized prototype, you'll want to have a significant amount of evidence that a solution is needed. This means you've gathered and generated evidence of unmet customer jobs, pains, and gains in the market that warrant testing a high fidelity experiment with customers.

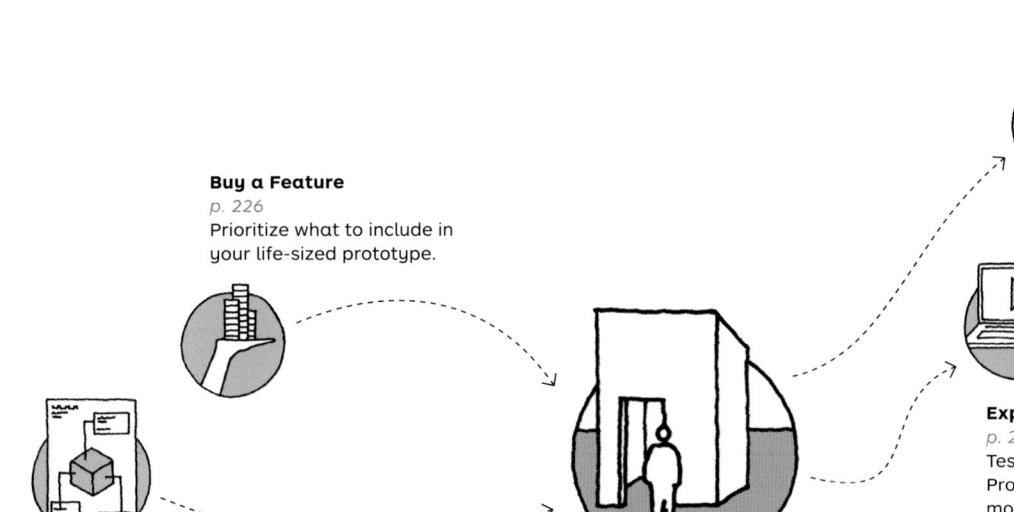

Buy a Feature
p. 226
Prioritize what to include in your life-sized prototype.

Data Sheet
p. 190
Visualize the specifications to include in your life-sized prototype.

Crowdfunding
p. 266
Generate demand and further validate desirability and viability at a bigger scale.

Explainer Video
p. 200
Test a video of your Value Proposition and solution with more customers.

Life-Sized Prototype

Mock Sales
p. 288
Learn if your customers are willing to pay for the solution while they interact with the prototype.

Customer Interviews
p. 106
Interview your customers while they interact with the prototype to learn about customer jobs, pains, and gains.

LIFE-SIZED PROTOTYPE

257

INTERACTION PROTOTYPES

LIFE-SIZED PROTOTYPE
Validating a Physical Space
Zoku

Zoku is a hive of smart lofts and friendly spaces based in Amsterdam and is viewed by experts as the next evolution of Airbnb. They provide a home base for traveling professionals who are living and working in a city for periods from a few days to a few months. As is the case any time you create a new market, the Zoku team has risky assumptions about their business that need testing.

Hypothesis

The Zoku team believed that traveling pro-
fessionals would like to stay for weeks and
months in a micro-apartment of only 25m²
(around 250 square feet).

Experiment

Testing living spaces with customers.
The team built a Life-Sized prototype of
the micro-apartment to test with traveling
professionals to determine if they'd stay
for weeks and months. They sourced 150
traveling professionals, shuttling them over
from their workplaces, to interact with the
Life-Sized Prototype.

Travelers toured and stayed in the Life-
Sized Prototype. The Zoku team interviewed
them while they interacted with the physical
space, learning about what worked and
what didn't in the design.

Evidence

Gathering qualitative feedback on
the space.
People were the most enthusiastic about
staying when the space used stacking,
eliminating internal walls and circulation.
If the stairs are in, there is more living space;
if the stairs are out it becomes circulation
space for the sleeping area. This evidence
especially came out when they tested with
groups of 4–5 people at once.

Insights

The experience of the space means more
than the size of the space.
The experiment helped the Zoku team
understand nuances about the prototype.
When stacked all the normal home elements
(sleeping area, storage area, bathroom and
kitchen) on to each other like Tetris/Lego, it
resulted in a distinction between secondary
space (functional elements) and primary
space (living space to move around and put
your loose furniture).

During the course of all the validation
rounds they learned that "the experience
of space" is different from the amount of
square feet and can be positively influenced
by clear sight lines through the furniture
(the shutters in the sleeping area), large
windows, and smart lighting.

Actions

Testing space flow with cleaning services.
Using what they had learned from the
Life-Sized Prototype testing, the team ran
another round of testing with cleaning
services for the unit. This helped them learn
about the service challenges, specifically
with the raised sleeping platform.

VALIDATION / CALL TO ACTION

Simple Landing Page

A simple, digital web page that clearly illustrates your
Value Proposition with a call to action.

○ ●●○○○
COST

⚖ ●●○○○
EVIDENCE STRENGTH

🕐 ●●○○○
SETUP TIME

⏱ ●●●○○
RUN TIME

DESIRABILITY · FEASIBILITY · VIABILITY

*A simple landing page is ideal for determining if your
Value Proposition resonates with your customer segment.*

CAPABILITIES *Design / Product / Technology*

Prepare

- ☐ Choose a template or layout that supports your industry.
- ☐ Find high quality, royalty-free photos to use for your design.
- ☐ Purchase a short, memorable domain name that reinforces your brand. If your preferred brand is taken already, which many domains are by now, use a verb in front of the name such as "try" or "get."
- ☐ Include a Value Proposition statement above the fold in large font, preferably header sized.
- ☐ Place your call-to-action email signup above the fold, below your Value Proposition statement.
- ☐ Include customer pains, your solution, and the customer gains below the call-to-action.
- ☐ Integrate analytics and confirm they are working.
- ☐ Don't forget website requirements such as logo, brand, contact, terms of service, and cookie and privacy policy information.

Execute

- ☐ Make your landing page live on the web.
- ☐ Drive traffic to your page.

Analyze

- ☐ Review your analytics on how many people:
  - • viewed your landing page.
  - • signed up with their email address.
  - • spent time or engaged with the page by clicking and scrolling.
- ☐ How did different traffic sources convert? For example, if a specific social media ad or email campaign causes more customers to sign up, you may want to replicate it across other platforms.
- ☐ Use these findings to refine your Value Proposition and contact those who signed up for interviews.

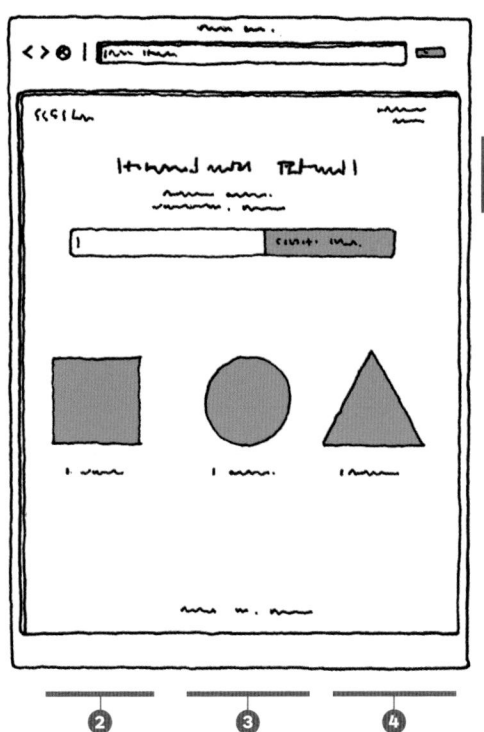

Connections

1 **Value propositions** come from your Value Map. Do not create your Value Proposition in a vacuum or neglect the work that you've already done. The Value Map contains hypotheses and your landing page value proposition test is a great way to prove or disprove those hypotheses.

2 **Customer pains** come from your Customer Profile. Take the top three voted customer pains from the canvas and include them in the pains description at the bottom left of the landing page.

3 **Solution** comes from the Value Map product and service. The visitor needs to know how you are delivering the Value Proposition in a real tangible way. The product and services in the middle column of the page should reflect this.

4 **Gains** come from the customer profile. Take the top three voted customer gains from the canvas and include them in the gains description at the bottom right of the landing page.

Cost

Landing pages are relatively cheap to produce, mostly due to the fact that digital tools have evolved and are much easier to use. It's one of the cheapest ways you can test your Value Proposition at scale with potential customers.

Setup Time

Landing pages can be deceptively difficult to do, mostly because you are distilling down all the customer jobs, pains, and gains into short easy-to-understand statements. Still, it shouldn't take more than a few days at most to design a landing page.

Run Time

Run time takes a few weeks, although it is largely depending on the amount of traffic you can drive to the landing page. If the daily traffic is low (i.e., less than 100 unique visitors), then you'll need to run the test for a longer period of time to gather sufficient information.

Evidence

Unique Views
Time Spent on Page
Email Signups

You can calculate the conversion rate by taking the number views divided by actions = conversion rate. Email conversion rates vary widely by industry but on average it's between 2%–5%. For early stage validation we recommend 10%–15% in that you want to be better than average, otherwise why create something new?

Email is a rather weak strength of evidence, in that everyone has email and they give it out freely if even mildly interested. It's not difficult to unsubscribe or send unwanted email to a junk folder.

Capabilities

Design / Product / Technology

Landing pages need to communicate the value clearly and succinctly in the language of the customer. You'll need the ability to do this well, otherwise it has the risk of generating false negatives. If you do not have these abilities yourself, then don't despair because you are in luck. There are many landing page services that have professional-looking templates that allow you to create landing pages using drag-and-drop technology.

Requirements

Traffic

Landing pages need traffic to generate evidence, generally about 100 unique visitors a day. The good news is that there are many ways you can drive traffic to your landing page, including:

- Online ads.
- Social media campaigns.
- Email campaigns.
- Redirecting existing traffic.
- Word of mouth.
- Discussion forums.

Online Ads
p. 146
Create the smallest form of your Value Proposition as an online ad to test with customers.

Customer Interviews
p. 106
Contact the people who signed up and interview them to learn why they signed up.

Customer Interviews
p. 106
Use the notes from interviews to inform your Value Proposition, jobs, pains, and gains on the landing page.

Simple Landing Page

Validation Survey
p. 278
Perform surveys with those who signed up to understand why they signed up.

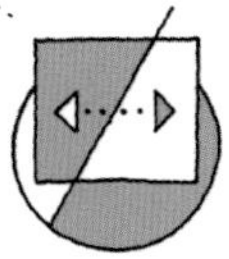

Split Testing
p. 270
Try widely different versions of your Value Proposition to see what resonates best with customers.

Wizard of Oz
p. 284
Behind the scenes, manually create the Value Proposition for the customers who signed up on the landing page.

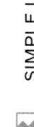

SIMPLE LANDING PAGE

263

CALL TO ACTION

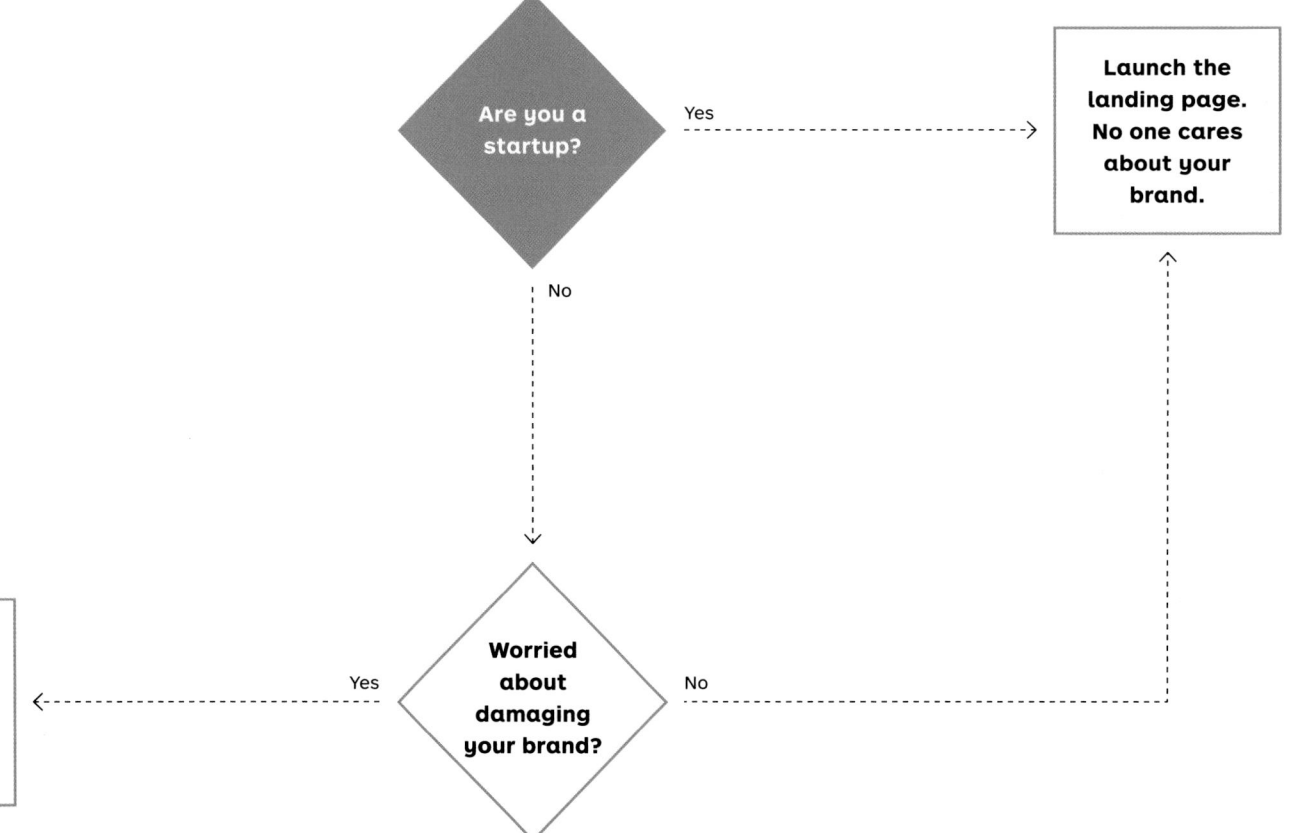

Branding Concerns

Branding the landing page can become a hand-wringing decision if you are part of a larger corporation. Startups have the luxury of testing without drawing attention, based on their brand alone. They can launch a landing page and when people sign up, it's rarely because of the startup's brand. Instead, people sign up because the idea stands on its own merit as a solution that can solve a problem for them.

If corporations keep the landing page on-brand, with the corporate logo front-and-center, it can make things harder for the team. Branding and marketing reviews will usually slow down the process by weeks, if not months. People will visit the page just to check it out because of the branding. It can be difficult to sift through all of the traffic noise to see who is really interested in the Value Proposition.

Create a sub-brand or new company to test the business idea. It allows you to go faster, without the endless meetings around branding and what happens if people sign up. A side effect of this approach is that you won't be able to leverage existing acquisition channels for the brand. This means you'll need to do your own customer acquisition by running ads, talking to people, and using social media to drive traffic.

✓

☐ *Use the words from customer interviews in your headline.*

☐ *Contact the people who signed up and ask if they are available for customer interviews.*

☐ *Use high quality photos and videos.*

☐ *Use a short domain name.*

✗

– *Don't include fake testimonials to generate conversions.*

– *Don't label products as "sold out" when you've not yet created them.*

– *Don't make unrealistic claims for your product.*

– *Don't use a negative or harsh tone.*

SIMPLE LANDING PAGE

265

CALL TO ACTION

VALIDATION / CALL TO ACTION

Crowdfunding

Funding a project or venture by raising many small amounts of money from a large number of people, typically via the Internet.

⬭ ●●●●●
COST

⚖ ●●○○○
EVIDENCE STRENGTH

🕐 ●●●●○
SETUP TIME

⏱ ●●●●○
RUN TIME

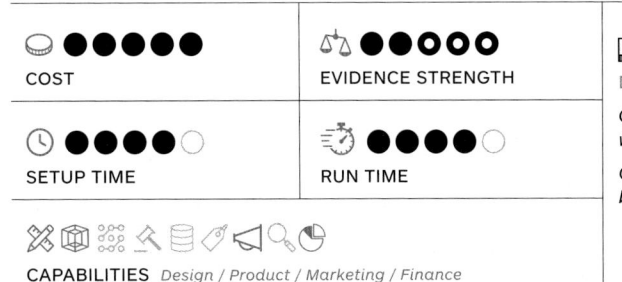

CAPABILITIES *Design / Product / Marketing / Finance*

DESIRABILITY · FEASIBILITY · VIABILITY

Crowdfunding is ideal for funding your new business venture with customers who believe in your Value Proposition.

Crowdfunding is not ideal for determining whether your new business venture is feasible.

Prepare

☐ Define the dollar amount for your funding target goal. Be pragmatic and specific on how the money will be used for each activity needed to create the product.

☐ Choose an existing crowdfunding platform or create your own, custom crowdfunding website.

☐ Create your crowdfunding video. It should be high quality and draw the user in to convince them to fund your product.

☐ Include a Value Proposition statement below your video in large font, preferably header sized.

☐ Place your call to action for funding the product to the right of the video in clear language.

☐ Include customer pains, your solution, and the customer gains below the Value Proposition.

☐ Include different pledge amounts and desirable perks.

Execute

☐ Make your crowdfunding campaign live to the public.

☐ Drive traffic to your page.

☐ Be active on social media and your campaign page by responding to comments and answering questions as they come in.

Analyze

☐ Review how many pledges were received, the amount for each, and if you reached your funding target goal.

☐ If you did not achieve your goal, use what you've learned to iterate on the campaign.

☐ If you did achieve your goal, then keep actively responding on your progress to backers through social media and email.

☐ How did different traffic sources convert? For example, if a specific social media ad or email campaign causes more customers to pledge, you may want to keep that in mind for customer acquisition once the product is live and for sale.

Connections

❶
Your video should tell a story, leading with the greatest hits. Show how your solution solves for the top customer job, pain, and gain for the customer segment in your **customer profile**.

❷
Pains come from your Customer Profile. Take the top three voted customer pains and include them in the pains description at the bottom left of the crowdfunding campaign page.

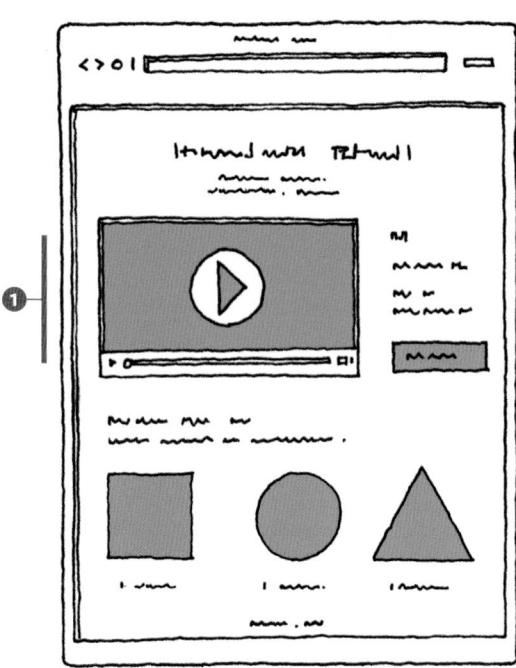

❸
Solution comes from the Value Map product and service. Your potential crowdfunding backers should understand the solution, which is next to the pain on the crowdfunding campaign page.

❹
Gains come from the Customer Profile. Take the top three voted customer gains and include them in the gains description at the bottom right of the crowdfunding campaign page.

✓

☐ *Account for the commission percentage crowdfunding platforms take as a fee from your campaign.*

☐ *Refund those who contributed if you didn't meet your goal.*

☐ *Be specific and transparent on how the funds you are raising will be used, including a cost breakdown of the activities.*

✗

– *Include so may perks that you spend all of your time fulfilling them instead of building the product.*

– *Be greedy and raise more than you need for your product build.*

– *Cut corners on the production quality of your video.*

– *Make unrealistic claims on the benefits of your product.*

Cost

Crowdfunding costs are typically focused around the video production, marketing, logistics, and length of campaign. Even though there are crowdfunding platforms available, the fidelity needs to be high or you will not garner interest from customers.

Setup Time

Crowdfunding campaigns can take a few weeks to a few months to put together. It's not trivial to produce a compelling, high quality video, create content that conveys the Value Proposition, and structure the pricing tiers and perks for your customers.

Run Time

Run time typically takes 30–60 days for a crowdfunding campaign to run its course. This isn't to say you won't be wildly successful and fund it in less — just be aware that those funded in a few days are the exceptions.

Evidence Strength

●●○○○

Referrers
# of unique views
# of comments
# of social media shares

Where your visitors are coming from online and how they interact with your campaign.

Views, comments, and shares are all relatively weak evidence but good for qualitative insights.

●●●●●

# of pledges
Pledge amount

How your viewers are converting to pledges. At least 6% of your pledges come from direct traffic. At least 2% of your pledges come from targeted online ads.

Percent funded. Ideally this is 100% and your idea gets funded.

Viewers pledging their money to make your crowdfunding campaign a success is very strong evidence. They are voting with their wallets, not just their words.

Capabilities

Design / Product / Marketing / Finance

Crowdfunding's popularity has created a rise in crowdfunding platforms, which means you don't need an entire development team to create a campaign anymore. You'll still need to create an authentic campaign with interesting perks, while building awareness in the market. Design plays a big role here in that it needs to look professional, otherwise you may get false negatives on your Value Proposition. Finance plays a bigger role, in that you need to correctly spec out your pricing tiers and perks in hopes that you can build a sustainable business from the campaign.

Requirements

Value Proposition and Customer Segment

Before jumping into a crowdfunding campaign, you'll need a clear Value Proposition that you can turn into a high quality video and a target customer segment. Crowdfunding campaigns without videos are few and far between and their success rate is quite low. You'll also want to know how you are targeting the customer, otherwise it'll be very difficult to drive people to it.

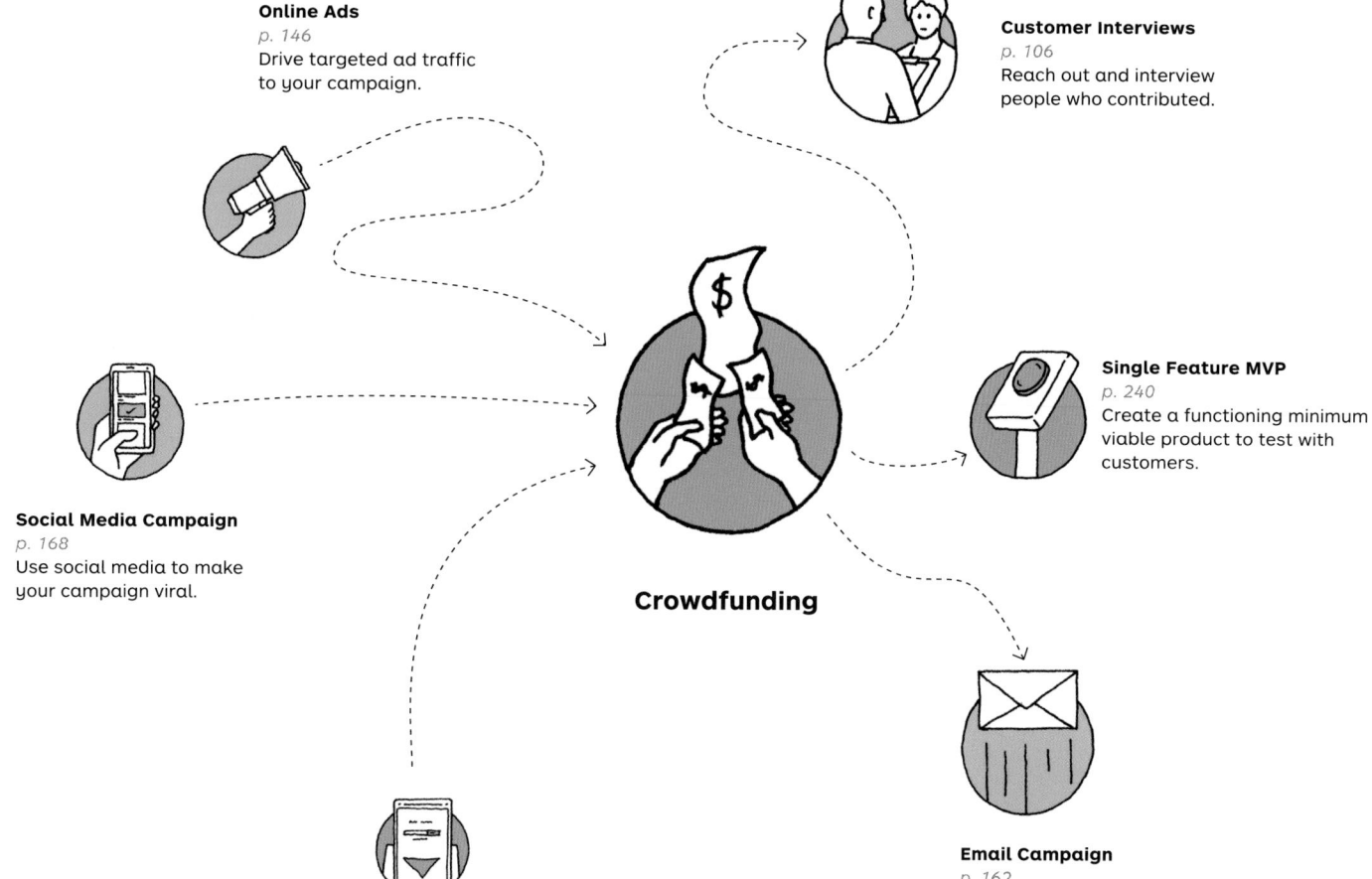

Online Ads
p. 146
Drive targeted ad traffic
to your campaign.

Customer Interviews
p. 106
Reach out and interview
people who contributed.

Single Feature MVP
p. 240
Create a functioning minimum
viable product to test with
customers.

Social Media Campaign
p. 168
Use social media to make
your campaign viral.

Crowdfunding

Simple Landing Page
p. 260
Create a landing page to
drive traffic to your campaign.

Email Campaign
p. 162
Keep contributors in the loop
on what is happening after
the campaign.

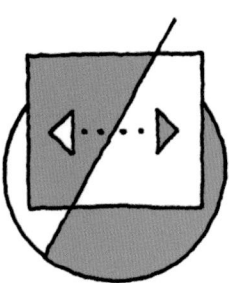

VALIDATION / CALL TO ACTION

Split Test

Split Test is a method of comparing two versions, control A against variant B, and determining which which one performs better.

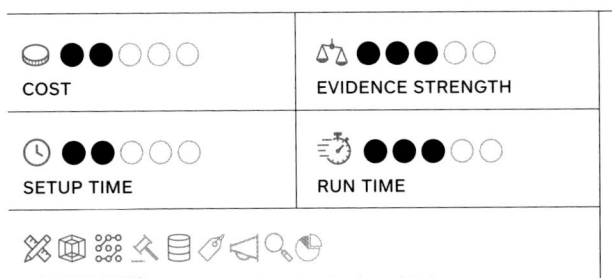

◒ ●●○○○○
COST

⚖ ●●●○○
EVIDENCE STRENGTH

🕐 ●●○○○
SETUP TIME

 ●●●○○
RUN TIME

⊞ ▷ ◉
DESIRABILITY · FEASIBILITY · VIABILITY

Split Test is ideal for testing different versions of Value Propositions, prices, and features to see what resonates best with customers.

✂ ▣ ⋇ ⌂ 🗄 🏷 📢 🔍 📊
CAPABILITIES *Design / Product / Technology / Data*

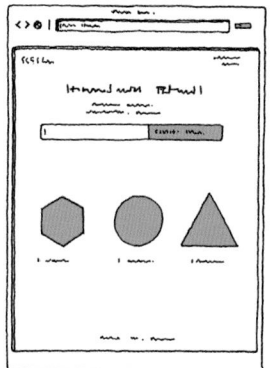

Prepare

- ☐ Identify the customer behavior you wish to improve (i.e., progressing through a funnel).
- ☐ Create your Control A.
- ☐ Baseline your Control A and write it down.
- ☐ Create your Variant B.
- ☐ Define the measurable improvement percentage you wish to observe in Variant B.
- ☐ Identify your customer sample size and percent confidence level.

Prepare

- ☐ Run your Split Test by randomly driving 50% of your traffic to Control A and 50% of your traffic to Variant B.

Analyze

- ☐ Review your results once the sample size is met and if it met your confidence level.
- ☐ Did you meet your confidence level?
  - • If so, consider replacing Control A with your Variant B as a static element.
  - • If not, run another Split Test with a different Variant B.

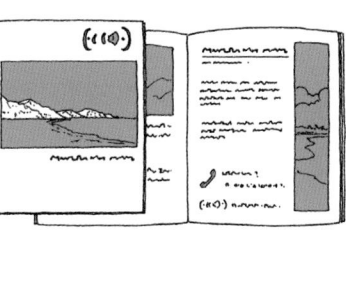

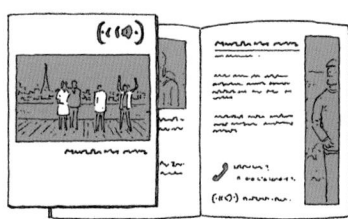

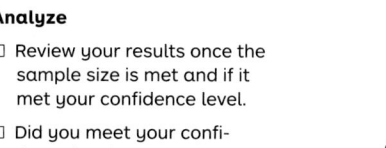

✔

- ☐ *Use quotes from customer interviews to Split Test your Value Propositions.*
- ☐ *Contact the people who converted to understand why.*
- ☐ *Use a Split Test calculator to determine the sample size needed to reach your confidence level.*
- ☐ *Split Test radically different ideas, especially early on. It'll yield more insights than small incremental tests.*

✘

- – *Stop your Split Tests early because you like or dislike the preliminary results.*
- – *Forget to keep measuring KPIs that you don't want to go down.*
- – *Run too many Split Tests all at once or in conjunction with other experiments.*
- – *Give up if your first Split Test doesn't yield amazing results.*

SPLIT TEST

271

CALL TO ACTION

Cost

Split Tests are relatively cheap and online digital tools allow you to perform them without having to know much about programming. You can copy and paste a script into your page or app, then log into the product and configure the Split Tests. It resembles using a word processor, by dragging, dropping, and typing. Split Tests become more expensive if you are building customized hardware or printing out mailers, since you have to physically make two different versions to test with customers.

Setup Time

The setup time for Split Tests is relatively short, especially with digital products where you can use existing Split Testing tools. Setup time can be a bit longer if you are physically making two different versions.

Run Time

The run time for Split Tests usually spans several days to weeks. You'll want to have statistically significant data to gain insights into which one performed better.

Evidence Strength

Traffic
Control A behavior
Control A Conversion Rate

Conversion rate is the number of people who are routed into the Control A test divided by number of actions. Use previous data if possible to predict what the control conversion rate is for a baseline.

Variant B behavior
Variant B Conversion Rate

Conversion rate is the number of people who are routed into the Variant B divided by number of actions. Define what measurable impact you'd like Variant B to have on the conversion percentage.

Evidence strength is moderate—customers aren't aware they are participating in the Split Test. You'll want to have, at the very least, an 80% confidence level in the results. Ideally you'd want 98% confidence level, but it can vary depending on what you are testing. Use an online Split Test calculator to help guide you through the process.

Capabilities

Design / Product / Technology / Data

You'll need the capabilities required to define what you'll be testing, the expected baseline for Control A, and the needed improvement from Variant B. You'll want to design it visually to fit the overall theme, otherwise you'll receive false negatives. It'll require some degree of technology to integrate if it's software. Lastly, you'll need to be able to analyze the results to help inform your next experiment.

Requirements

Significant Traffic

Split Tests need a significant amount of traffic to generate believable evidence. Your traffic will be randomized to display either Control A or Variant B to the customer. If you have little to no traffic, it'll take entirely too much time to come to a conclusion that one performs better than the other.

Email Campaign
p. 162
Test email subject lines, copy, and images to determine what causes readers to open and click.

Simple Landing Page
p. 260
Test different Value Propositions and call to actions to see what improves conversion.

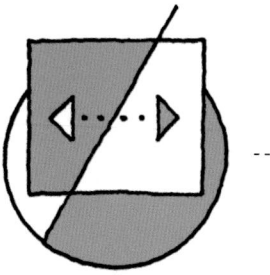

Customer Interviews
p. 106
Interview your customers and find out why they converted.

Customer Interviews
p. 106
Use quotes from your interviews to Split Test what converts better.

Split Test

Online Ads
p. 146
Test different images or copy for your online ad to see what improves click through rate.

Brochure
p. 194
Test different images and Value Propositions to determine what converts best on the contact call to action.

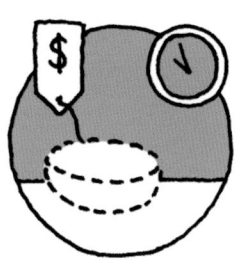

VALIDATION / CALL TO ACTION

Presale

A sale held before an item is made available for purchase. Unlike mock sale, you are processing a financial transaction when it ships.

○ ●●●○○
COST

⚖ ●●●●●
EVIDENCE STRENGTH

🕐 ●●○○○
SETUP TIME

 ●●●○○
RUN TIME

CAPABILITIES *Design / Sales / Finance*

DESIRABILITY · FEASIBILITY · VIABILITY

Presale is ideal for gauging market demand at a smaller scale before you launch to the public.

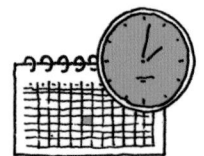

Prepare

☐ Create a simple landing page.

☐ Insert your price options.

☐ On a price option click, show a "we're not available to the public yet" pop-up with a payment information form. Cards will not be billed until you ship the product.

☐ Integrate and verify web analytics are working correctly.

Execute

☐ Make your page live to the public.

☐ Drive traffic to your page.

Analyze

☐ Review your analytics on how many people:

- viewed your price options.

- clicked on a price option.

- added in their payment information.

- clicked on pre-order to be billed when it ships.

- dropped out of the flow (i.e., web analytics funnel).

- converted on your page, based on traffic source.

☐ Use these findings to gauge viability and refine your Value Proposition and price options.

Connections

- Price options come from your revenue stream in your Business Model Canvas.

Cost

Presales are relatively cheap, but unlike mock sales you have the additional costs of processing the transaction and shipping the product. If you are using a point of sale system, then you may need to purchase hardware or software. In addition, most payment systems take a percentage of your sales (2%–3%) and may charge a monthly fee on top of that.

Setup Time

Setup time for a presale is relatively short. Once you are close to shipping your product, it requires the setup of accepting and processing financial information.

Run Time

Run time for a presale is a few days or weeks. You'll want to target a specific audience with your solution and give them enough time to consider a purchase. Presales aren't usually very long—payment providers may require you to ship product within 20 days of purchase.

Evidence

# of unique views
# of purchases

You can calculate the purchase conversion rate by taking the number people who view the price divided by the number of purchases.

Purchases are strong evidence. Customers are paying for your solution before it is generally available to the public.

# of abandons

Mostly associated with online shopping carts, if people are beginning the purchase process and then leaving, they are abandoning the sale.

You can calculate the abandonment rate by dividing the total number of completed purchases by the number of people who entered the purchase process.

People dropping out of the purchase process is strong evidence, albeit a bad sign. It means something is incorrect with your process, misconfigured, or the purchase price is not appropriate.

Capabilities

Design / Sales / Finance

Conducting a presale will require defining your price options. You'll also need to design the sale in such a way that it is the right fidelity for your target audience. Finally, you'll need sales capability, especially if you are conducting these in person in the physical world.

Requirements

Ability to Fulfill

Presales are different than mock sales: you are collecting and processing payment information, conducting an actual sale. This means you should be close to the final solution or at the very least have a minimum viable product to deliver. Do not rush ahead and conduct several presales without having the ability to fulfill your promise to customers.

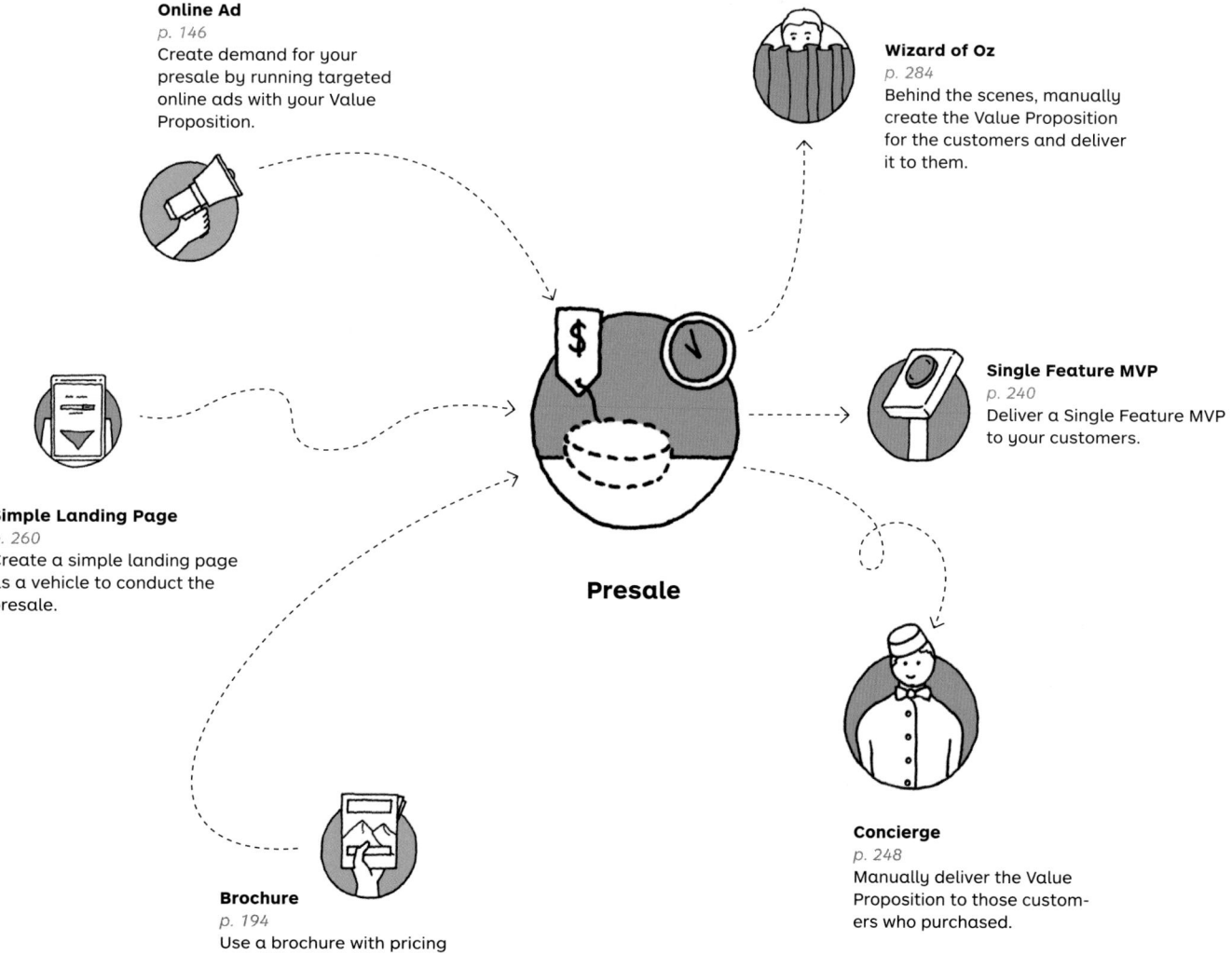

Online Ad
p. 146
Create demand for your
presale by running targeted
online ads with your Value
Proposition.

Wizard of Oz
p. 284
Behind the scenes, manually
create the Value Proposition
for the customers and deliver
it to them.

Single Feature MVP
p. 240
Deliver a Single Feature MVP
to your customers.

Simple Landing Page
p. 260
Create a simple landing page
as a vehicle to conduct the
presale.

Presale

Concierge
p. 248
Manually deliver the Value
Proposition to those customers who purchased.

Brochure
p. 194
Use a brochure with pricing
to use as material for your
presale.

278

VALIDATION / CALL TO ACTION

Validation Survey

A closed-ended questionnaire used in the collection of information from a sample of customers about a specific topic.

⊖ ●●○○○
COST

⚖ ●●○○○
EVIDENCE STRENGTH

🕐 ●●○○○
SETUP TIME

⏱ ●●●○○
RUN TIME

▦ ✉ ◈
DESIRABILITY · FEASIBILITY · VIABILITY

A validation survey is ideal for getting insights into whether customers will be disappointed if your product went away or if they'll refer other customers.

✂🔲 ⠿ ⚒ 🗄 ✎ 📢 🔍 🥧
CAPABILITIES *Product / Marketing / Research*

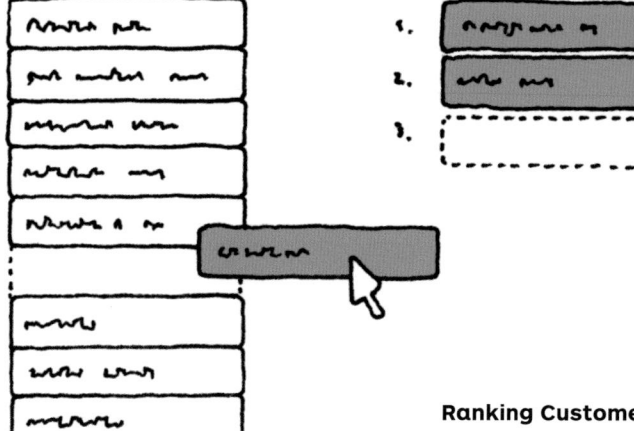

Discovering Missing Customer Jobs, Pains, and Gains

In addition to ranking, you can take inspiration from the discovery survey and include an open-ended question after each ranking, just in case you are missing out on those you didn't think of:

- What job do you wish we would have asked you about that wasn't on this list? Why?
- What pain do you wish we would have asked you about that wasn't on this list? Why?
- What gain do you wish we would have asked you about that wasn't on this list? Why?

Other Types of Validation Surveys

Validation surveys are, in general, very simple with closed-ended feedback responding to a single question. With that in mind, you can apply that to other types of assumptions you wish to validate with your customers such as:

- CSAT (customer satisfaction).
- CES (consumer effort score).
- Brand awareness.

Ranking Customer Jobs, Pains, and Gains

Another popular type of validation survey is validating the importance ranking of the jobs, pains, and gains in your Customer Profile in the Value Proposition Canvas. Most teams take their best guess at this ranking in a workshop setting, but need to quickly get feedback from outside the building to see how close they are to the real world. You can easily do this in most survey software today by creating two boxes, one for the list and next to it one for the customer ranking.

Sean Ellis Test
"How disappointed would you be if you could no longer use this product?"

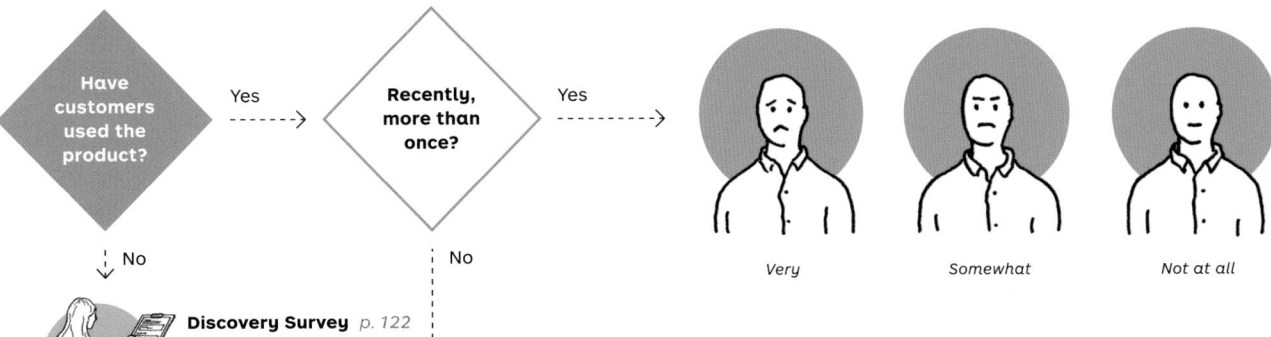

Very   Somewhat   Not at all

Discovery Survey *p. 122*

Sean Ellis Test

One type of survey is called the Sean Ellis Test, which is named after it's creator and growth-hacking expert Sean Ellis. His approach is to gauge desirability through scarcity.

The Sean Ellis Test keys in on one important question: *"How disappointed would you be if you could no longer use this product? Very disappointed, somewhat disappointed, or not disappointed?"*

It can be argued that you've not achieved product/market fit until a score of 40% is reached. If customers are apathetic and do not care if your product goes away, then you have a desirability problem. It doesn't make sense to scale before you have fit, otherwise you can waste a lot of money scaling things that no one wants.

Context is important when running a Sean Ellis Test. If you run it as soon as the customer experiences the Value Proposition, it can feel very out of place and return skewed data because they've yet to really experience the product. Who is going to genuinely be disappointed if they've never really used it?

On the flip side, if you show this survey to someone who hasn't used the product in six months, then there's a good chance they're long gone and won't even take the survey at this point.

The recommendation is to show this survey to gauge desirability with customers who have experienced the core of your product at least twice in the past two weeks.

Net Promoter Score (NPS)
"How likely is it that you would recommend this product to a friend or colleague?"

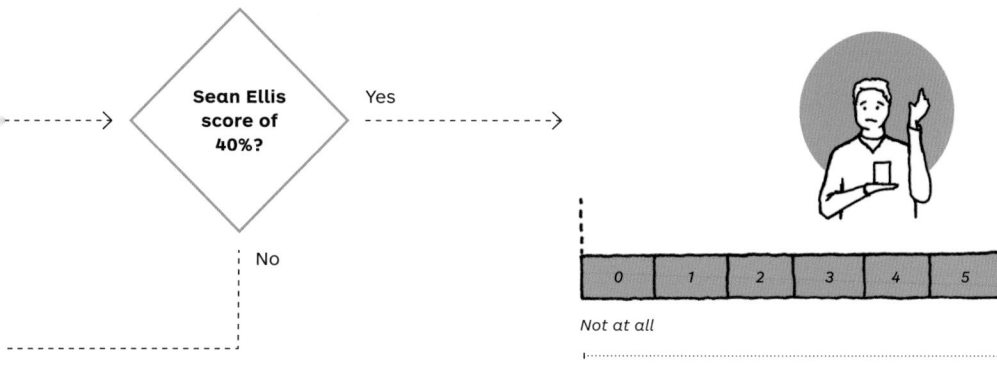

Sean Ellis score of 40%? — Yes

No

NPS

Net promoter score (NPS) is one of the most common types of surveys and is widely adopted by organizations around the world.

The key question for a NPS survey is: *"How likely is it that you would recommend this product to a friend or colleague? 0 (not at all) to 10 (extremely likely)"*

You can calculate NPS score using the following formula:

% PROMOTERS - % DETRACTORS = NPS

Much like the Sean Ellis test, the context of when you show this to your customer matters. They need to have completed something meaningful in your product before they would be willing to recommend it to a friend or colleague. While interesting, it's not enough for customers to want to recommend before they've used it. Likewise, it'll be tough to believe customers who say they'll recommend if they've used it, but wouldn't be disappointed if it went away entirely. Use the NPS after they've answered the Sean Ellis test.

You want to avoid prematurely scaling a business based on hypothetical referrals, from people who'd not be disappointed if your product went away.

Cost

Validation surveys are inexpensive because you should already have a channel to reach them. There are many tools and services today to help you intercept active customers on your website through a pop-up or email, if they trigger a specific action.

Setup Time

Setting up a validation survey is relatively quick and should take you a few hours or a day to configure.

Run Time

If you have sufficient validation survey distribution channels, a survey may only take 1–3 days to get thousands of responses. If you have a difficult time reaching your audience, it may take a few weeks to get enough responses.

Evidence

●●○○○

How disappointed would you be?
% Disappointed.

More than 40% disappointed is an ideal score before you worry about scaling your business. Otherwise, you'll churn out people as fast as you sign them up.

Survey data is rather weak, but hinting that the product could go away will solicit a better response.

●○○○○

How likely would you be to refer?
% Likely to Refer

More than 0% is considered good, although these can vary by industry. You'll want to search online for industry benchmarks.

NPS survey data is weaker than a Sean Ellis test. You are getting answers to a hypothetical referral situation.

●●○○○

Jobs / Pains / Gains ranking
% Accuracy When Compared to Customer Profile

Aim for 80%, since being wrong on this has ripple effects in your entire strategy.

Rather weak strength but an important step before moving to more involved testing.

Capabilities

Product / Marketing / Research

Validation surveys require the ability to carefully craft questions and have the correct tone and structure. Because validation surveys target existing customers, you'll need to be able to identify specific segments and sub-segments to help reduce noise in the data.

Requirements

Quantitative Source Material

Validation surveys are meant to have customers respond to a situation, price, or feature. You'll need to have something for them to respond to so that you can quantitatively measure their responses.

Channel to an Existing Customer

Validation surveys are meant for existing customers, which means you need to confirm you can leverage the existing channel to reach them, whether that is online via the website, by email, or offline via direct mail or a handout.

VALIDATION

EXPERIMENTS

Simple Landing Page
p. 260
Use an existing landing page to hang your survey off of to reach your audience in the moment.

Referral Program
p. 172
Use what you learn from the survey results to inform your referral program design.

Single Feature MVP
p. 240
Deliver value repeatedly to customers before asking them validation survey questions.

Discovery Survey
p. 122
Perform discovery surveys if the scores are low, to better understand unmet customer needs.

Validation Survey

Wizard of Oz
p. 284
Behind the scenes, manually deliver the value to customers before asking them validation survey questions.

Customer Interviews
p. 106
Contact the people who scored low and interview them to learn about unmet needs.

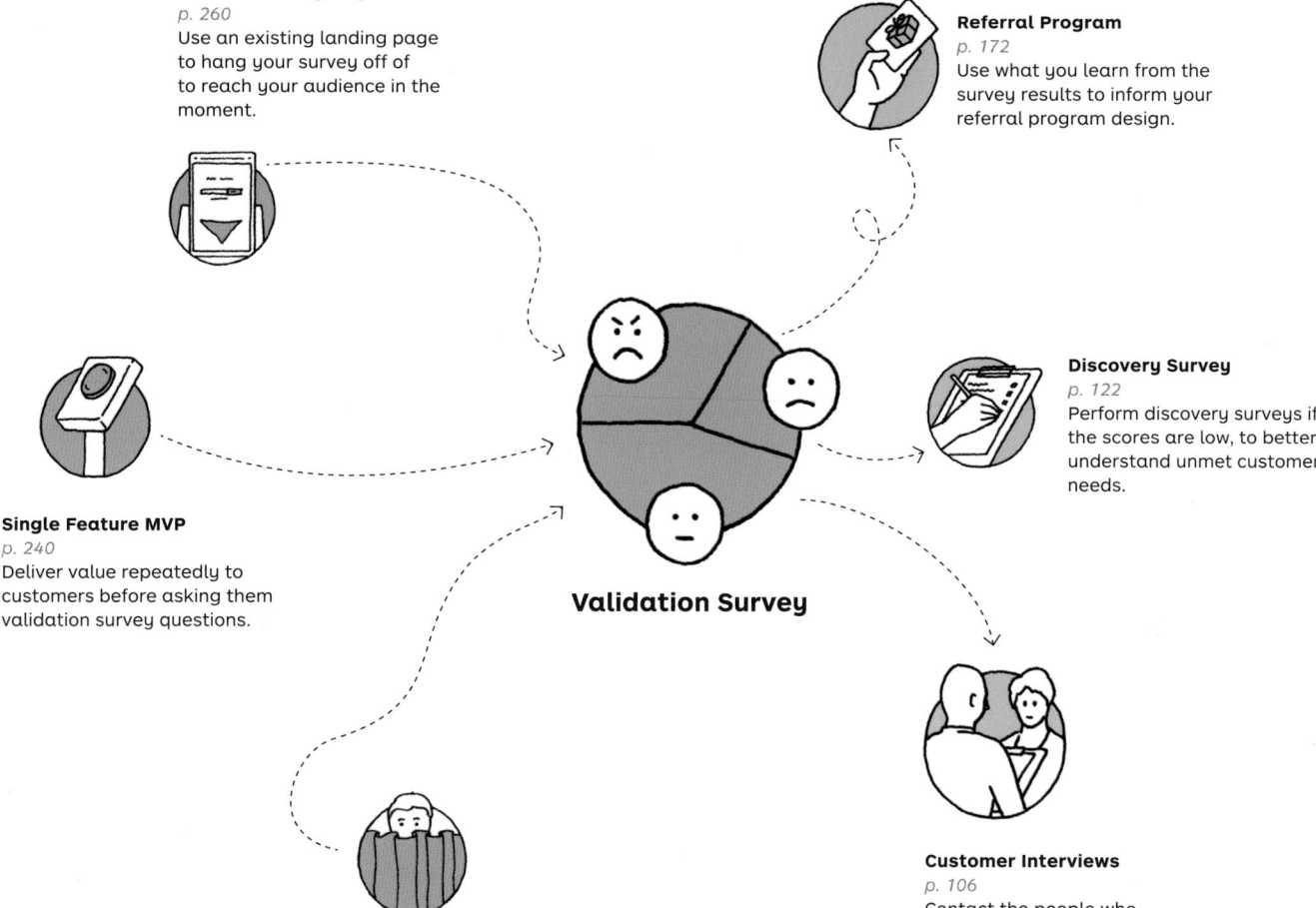

VALIDATION SURVEY

283

CALL TO ACTION

VALIDATION / SIMULATION

Wizard of Oz

Creating a customer experience and delivering value manually, with people instead of solely using technology. The name Wizard of Oz is derived from the movie, where you have a request that is handled by a person. Unlike Concierge, the people involved aren't visible to the customer.

⊖ ●●○○○
COST

⚖ ●●●●●
EVIDENCE STRENGTH

🕐 ●●●○○
SETUP TIME

⏱ ●●●○○
RUN TIME

DESIRABILITY · FEASIBILITY · VIABILITY

Wizard of Oz is ideal for learning manually, firsthand about steps needed to create, capture, and deliver value to a customer.

Wizard of Oz is not ideal for scaling a product or business.

CAPABILITIES *Design / Product / Technology / Legal / Marketing*

Drawing a Line in the Sand

Wizard of Oz is one way to address the issue of prematurely scaling a solution. We recommend drawing a line in the sand where automation of the manual Wizard of Oz tasks makes sense.

If it takes you 15 minutes to manually create the value for the end customer, ask yourself:

1. How many customer requests could we perform manually each day?
2. What is the cost to deliver each one (cost structure)?
3. What is the most customers will pay (revenue streams)?
4. At what volume is it more cost effective to automate these tasks?

We've witnessed entrepreneurs rush to automate the solution and, in turn, prematurely scale. When you draw a line in the sand to manually deliver the value, then you don't have to scale until that threshold is exceeded. Some entrepreneurs exceed it and and then turn to automation. Others may never hit the threshold. For those who never hit it, we recommend taking a step back and re-evaluating the strategy.

WIZARD OF OZ

285

SIMULATION

Prepare

☐ Plan the steps of creating the product manually.

☐ Create a board to track all of the orders and steps needed.

☐ Test the steps with someone internally first to make sure it works.

☐ Integrate and verify web analytics are working correctly.

Execute

☐ Receive orders for the Wizard of Oz experiment.

☐ Conduct the Wizard of Oz experiment.

☐ Update your board with the steps for each order. Document how long it took to complete the tasks.

☐ Gather satisfaction feedback from the customers with interviews and surveys.

Analyze

☐ Review your customer satisfaction feedback.

☐ Review your board metrics for:

  • length of time for task completion.

  • where you experienced delays in the process.

  • how many purchased.

☐ Use these findings to improve on your next Wizard of Oz experiment and to help inform where to automate the process.

VALIDATION

286

EXPERIMENTS

Cost

As long as you keep the Wizard of Oz experiments small and simple, they are cheap to run, mostly because you are doing all of the work manually with little to no technology involved. If you try to scale the experiment or make it overly complex, it'll increase the cost.

Setup Time

Setting up a Wizard of Oz experiment takes a bit longer than other rapid prototyping techniques, because you have to manually plan out all of the steps and acquire customers for it.

Run Time

Running a Wizard of Oz experiment can take days to weeks, depending on how complex the process is and how many customers you involve in the experiment. It generally takes longer than other rapid prototyping techniques.

Evidence

Customer satisfaction

Customer quotes and feedback on how satisfied they were after receiving the output from your experiment.

Customer satisfaction evidence is strong in this case because you are asking for feedback after the value was delivered to the customer, instead of a hypothetical situation.

●●●●●

# of purchases

Customer purchases from the Wizard of Oz experiment. What are they willing to pay for a manual experience?

Payments are strong evidence, even if you are manually delivering value.

Time it takes to complete the process

Lead time is the total time measured from customer request to when the order was delivered.

Cycle time is the amount of time spent working on the request. It does not include the time the request sits idle before action is taken on it.

The time it takes for you to complete the Wizard of Oz experiment is very strong—it gives you firsthand knowledge of the steps needed to receive a request and deliver value to a customer.

Capabilities

Design / Product / Tech / Legal / Marketing

You'll need all of the capabilities to manually create and deliver the product to the customer. This is very context specific, depending on whether you are delivering a physical or digital product or service to the end customer.

Requirements

Time

The biggest requirement for a Wizard of Oz experiment is time, closely followed by a digital curtain. Like the Concierge experiment, you'll need quite a bit of time to perform the testing but in addition to this, you'll need a curtain to hide the people performing the tasks from the customer. This can take many forms, but the most common is a simple landing page or digital interface where the customer requests and receives the value.

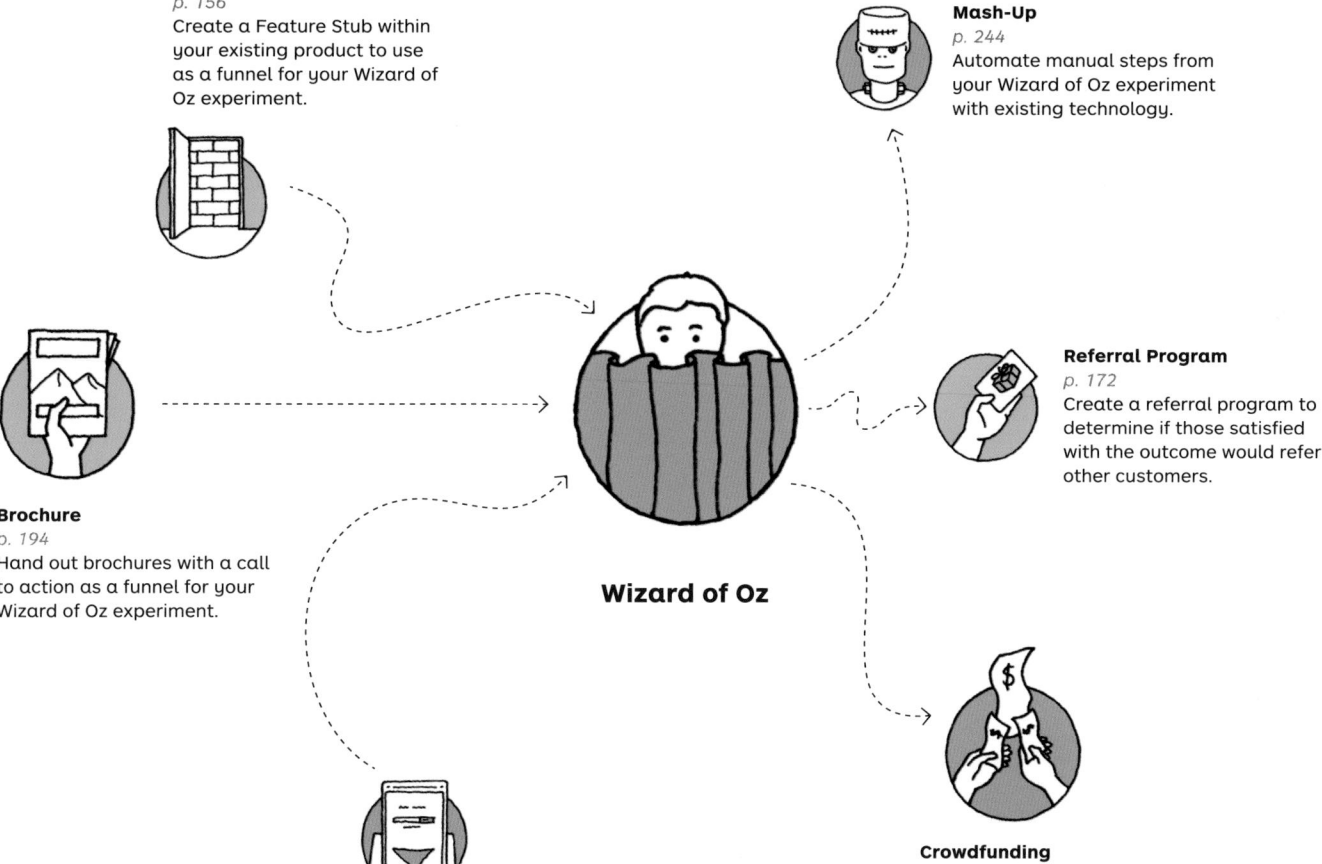

Feature Stub
p. 156
Create a Feature Stub within your existing product to use as a funnel for your Wizard of Oz experiment.

Mash-Up
p. 244
Automate manual steps from your Wizard of Oz experiment with existing technology.

Brochure
p. 194
Hand out brochures with a call to action as a funnel for your Wizard of Oz experiment.

Referral Program
p. 172
Create a referral program to determine if those satisfied with the outcome would refer other customers.

Wizard of Oz

Simple Landing Page
p. 260
Create a simple landing page to collect interest in your Wizard of Oz experiment.

Crowdfunding
p. 266
Create a crowdfunding campaign to fund what it would take to automate all of the steps as a scalable product.

VALIDATION / SIMULATION

Mock Sale

Presenting a sale for your product without processing
any payment information.

⊖ ●●○○○
COST

⚖ ●●●●○
EVIDENCE STRENGTH

🕐 ●●○○○
SETUP TIME

⏱ ●●●○○
RUN TIME

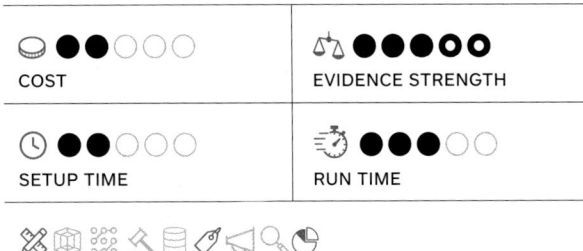
CAPABILITIES *DESIGN / SALES / FINANCE*

▦ ✉ ◔

DESIRABILITY · FEASIBILITY · VIABILITY

*Mock sale is ideal for determining different price points
for your product.*

ONLINE WITH EMAIL SIGNUP

PREPARE

☐ Create a simple landing page.

☐ Insert your price options.

☐ On price option click, show a "we're not ready yet" pop-up with email signup form.

☐ Integrate and verify web analytics are working correctly.

Execute

☐ Make your page live to the public.

☐ Drive traffic to your page.

Analyze

☐ Review your analytics on how many people:

- viewed your price options.
- clicked on a price option.
- signed up with their email address.
- dropped out of the flow (i.e., web analytics funnel).
- converted on your page, based on traffic source.

☐ Use these findings to gauge viability and refine your Value Proposition and price options.

Connections

- Price options come from your revenue stream in your Business Model Canvas.

OFFLINE RETAIL

PREPARE

☐ Create a high fidelity physical prototype of your product.

☐ Communicate the length and nature of the experiment with store managers and personnel so that employees involved understand what's going on.

Execute

☐ Strategically place the prototype on the desired shelf in the store.

☐ Observe and document who views the product, picks it up, and places it in the basket.

☐ Before or at time of customer purchase, intercept and explain that the product is not yet available.

☐ Get feedback from the customer on whether they want to be contacted when it's available and why they picked it up for purchase compared to other products.

☐ Compensate customer with a gift card for the inconvenience.

Analyze

☐ Review your customer feedback notes.

☐ Review your activity log of how many:

- viewed the product.
- put it in the basket.
- wanted to purchase.
- provided contact information for when the product launches.

☐ Use your findings to improve the Value Proposition and product design.

Cost

Mock sale is relatively cheap: you are price testing your product without building all of it. You'll need a believable level of fidelity for your target audience, so there is some cost in presenting your solution digitally or physically.

Setup Time

Setup time for a mock sale is relatively short, meaning you can create a believable platform for your Value Proposition in a few hours or a few days.

Run Time

Run time for a mock sale is a few days or weeks. You'll want to target a specific audience with your solution and give them enough time to consider a purchase.

Evidence

●●○○○

# of unique views
# of purchase clicks

You can calculate the purchase conversion rate by taking the number of people who view the price divided by the number of purchase clicks.

Purchase clicks are relatively strong, although not as strong as subsequent email and payment submissions.

●●●○○

# of purchase email signups

You can calculate the purchase email conversion rate by taking the number of people who view the price divided by the number of email signups.

Email signups after purchase clicks are relatively strong, although not as strong as payment submissions.

●●●●●

# of purchase payment
Information submitted

You can calculate the purchase payment conversion rate by taking the number of people who view the price divided by the number who filled out payment information.

Payment info submissions are very strong evidence.

Capabilities

Design / Sales / Finance

Conducting a mock sale will require financial modeling skills to inform the price options. You'll also need to design the sale in such a way that it is the right fidelity for your target audience. Finally, you'll need sales capability, especially if you are conducting these in person in the physical world.

Requirements

Pricing Strategy

Mock sale does require some thought and number crunching before you conduct the experiment. This isn't a scenario where you simply ask people how much they'll pay. Customers are notoriously bad at answering that question. Instead, you'll need to be able to present a sale price or multiple prices to have them respond. If you test a ridiculously low price, then you'll receive false positives on something you won't be able to deliver. Therefore, spend time thinking through the cost structure to make the mock sale evidence worthwhile.

Online Ad
p. 146
Create demand for your mock
sale by running targeted
online ads with your Value
Proposition.

Customer Interviews
p. 106
Contact the people who
showed interest in purchasing
the product to better understand their needs.

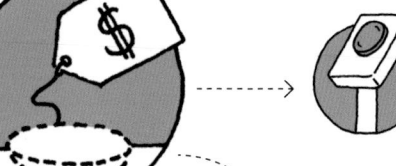

Single Feature MVP
p. 240
Create a single feature
minimum viable product to
test with customers.

Simple Landing Page
p. 260
Create a simple landing page
as a vehicle to conduct the
mock sale.

Mock Sale

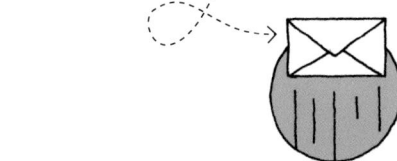

Brochure
p. 194
Use a brochure with pricing as
material for your mock sale.

Email Campaign
p. 162
Keep those who were interested in the loop when you
launch the product.

MOCK SALE
They will come, when you build it.
Buffer

When Joel Gascoigne, cofounder of Buffer, started the company from his bedroom nine years ago, he wasn't certain if people would even pay for his social media scheduling service.

At the time, social media managers were still manually logging into multiple social media platforms and posting their content. They used calendars and reminders to tell them the perfect moment to log in and post across time zones. This wasn't ideal, especially when it occurred in the middle of the night.

The Buffer application would solve that problem, beginning with a scheduling service for Twitter, before expanding to additional social media platforms. Joel decided to lightly test the desirability of the Buffer app by adding a "Plans and Pricing" button to his simple landing page. When clicked, it displayed a message about not being ready yet with an email signup to be notified.

After a few people submitted their email, Joel determined there was initial interest but wanted to collect more evidence.

Hypothesis

Joel believed that people would pay a monthly fee to schedule their social media posts on Twitter.

It wasn't enough that people would enter their email without any pricing information. Joel needed to know if it was viable.

Experiment

Price testing different monthly fees to gauge viability.

Joel decided to test viability by adding three different payment tier options to the landing page. Free = $0/month for 1 tweet a day and 5 tweets in your buffer queue. Standard = $5/month for 10 tweets a day and 50 tweets in your buffer queue. Max = $20/month for unlimited tweets a day and unlimited tweets in your buffer queue. These options appeared once people clicked the "Plans and Pricing" button. Once people clicked

an option, an email signup form appeared stating Buffer wasn't quite yet ready for launch. Each option in the page had analytics integrated, so Joel could analyze who was signing up based on the selected price.

Evidence

A $5/month signal.

The evidence showed that the $5/month plan was the clear winner in this initial test. This option generated the most email signups when he compared it to the $0 and $20 options.

Insights

People were interested in paying.

With the data showing the $5/month plan being the most popular, it started to become clear how people valued Buffer. They didn't need to only schedule one tweet a day, because they could simply log in and do that. On the other hand, they didn't need unlimited tweets because social media managers don't want to overwhelm their audience and be perceived as spam. The sweet spot seemed to be 5 tweets per day, where it was enough of a hassle that people would pay a $5/month fee to address.

Actions

Evidence that Buffer should be built.

After generating evidence and insights into the demand of Buffer, Joel decided to build the application. He used this learning to help shape his price points for launch. Joel also kept it lean and manually processed the payments for each customer early on. Today Buffer is used by hundreds of thousands of customers around the world and has a monthly recurring revenue of $1.54 million.

VALIDATION / SIMULATION

Letter of Intent

Short, written contract that is simple to read and not legally binding.

◯ ●◯◯◯◯
COST

⚖ ●●◯◯◯
EVIDENCE STRENGTH

🕐 ●◯◯◯◯
SETUP TIME

⏱ ●●◯◯◯
RUN TIME

✂📦 ▦ ⚒ 🗄 🏷 📢 🔍 📊
CAPABILITIES *Product / Technology / Legal / Finance*

▦ ▨ ◕
DESIRABILITY · FEASIBILITY · VIABILITY

Letter of intent is ideal for evaluating key partners and B2B customer segments.

Letter of intent is not ideal for B2C customer segments.

Prepare

- ☐ Define your the letter of intent target audience, preferably one that already has knowledge of your business.
- ☐ Research what legal Letter of Intent format best suits your business. (i.e., B2B customer vs. B2B key partner).
- ☐ Create your letter of intent template.

Execute

- ☐ Show the letter of intent to your target audience.
- ☐ One person on the team conducts the interview.
- ☐ Another person on the team takes notes on customer quotes, jobs, pains, gains, and body language.

Analyze

- ☐ Review your notes with the team.
- ☐ How many were sent, viewed, and signed?
- ☐ Follow up with those who signed to continue the conversation and push your business idea forward.

Basic LOI Sample

[Your Name]

[Title]

[Business Name]

[Business Address]

[Date]

[To Name]

[Title]

[Business Name]

[Business Address]

Dear [Name]

We hereby submit a non-binding letter of intent to [insert terms of partnership here].

Sincerely,

[Your Name]

LETTER OF INTENT

295

SIMULATION

Cost

Letter of intent contracts are relatively cheap to produce as they are usually 1 or 2 pages long. You can find free LOI templates online or spend a little money to have a lawyer help you properly craft one.

Setup Time

Setup time for a letter of intent is only a few hours or potentially 1 day if you involve legal help.

Run Time

Run time for a letter of intent is short in that your recipients either accept it or not.

Evidence

# of LOIs sent
# of LOI views
# of LOI signatures

LOI ccceptance rate = # of LOIs sent divided by the # of LOIs signed.

Letter of Intent signatures are not legally binding, but stronger than people merely saying they'll partner or buy.

●○○○○

Customer feedback
Partner feedback
Customer and Partner Quotes

Feedback is weak but generally good for qualitative insights.

Capabilities
Product / Technology / Legal / Finance

To create a letter of intent it helps to have basic legal understanding, even though it's a non-legal document. If using it with partners, you'll need to be able to articulate the key activity or key resource needed in detail. For B2B customers, you'll need to be able to speak clearly about your value proposition and pricing structure.

Requirements
Warm Leads

Unless you have warm leads, meaning there is a basic understanding of your perceived Value Proposition and business, then we don't recommend using a letter of intent. It would be poor form to cold email your LOIs to people, resulting in a dismal conversion rate. Instead, have the LOI ready for scheduled conversations so that you can present it during or shortly after the meeting.

**Partner & Supplier
Interviews**
p. 114
Interview partners and suppliers to better understand their
capabilities before creating
the LOI.

Single Feature MVP
p. 240
Create a Single Feature MVP
with your LOI partners or
customers.

Presales
p. 274
Conduct a presale of the
solution to your customers
before it is made available
to the public.

Customer Interviews
p. 106
Use the notes from your interviews to inform the shape of
your LOI.

Letter of Intent

Life-sized Prototype
p. 254
Create a life-sized prototype
to test with your customer
segment.

LETTER OF INTENT

SIMULATION

LETTER OF INTENT
Using LOIs with Landscapers
Thrive Smart Systems

Thrive Smart Systems is a company set on empowering people with the latest in irrigation technology. Their wireless system saves you time and money, providing smarter irrigation.

The cofounders, Seth Bangerter and Grant Rowberry, wanted to know if people would buy their product before they completed product development. Many people, landscapers in particular, expressed so much interest that when they asked them how many they would buy they would respond with "a ton" or "as many as you can give me." While this was exciting to hear, Seth and Grant wanted to get a firm number on how many these customers were willing to purchase.

The Thrive team chose to have interested customers write a letter of intent to purchase. The idea was to allow people to write down, in numbers, precisely what they wanted. Seth and Grant decided to make a template to include vital elements that a letter of intent should have. When a potential customer stated they are willing to buy x amount of Thrive's product, then x amount was to be placed on the letter of intent.

Thrive called this template their letter of intent form.

Hypothesis
Seth and Grant believed that they could generate $25,000 during the test phase through 20 LOIs.

Experiment
Asking customers to write an LOI.
They began to test this hypothesis by asking interested customers to write a Letter of Intent for how many units they were willing to purchase.

After receiving a few, they created a LOI template to pass out to each person that expresses interest in buying the product.

Evidence
Generating over $50k in purchases.
The Thrive team found that with no advertising and by just asking potential customers to fill out a form, they could generate over $50,000 in projected revenue.

Insights
Expectations versus reality.
They also learned that the number of units people say they will purchase is much more than they are willing to put into writing.

Those who said they would buy 1000 units only wrote down that they will buy 300 units. A few who said they would buy 100 only wrote down that they will buy 15–20. From this, Seth and Grant gained insights into how to formalize their purchasing process. Even though the LOI is non-binding, when a potential customer puts pen to paper they have more skin in the game.

Actions
Iterating on the LOI approach.
From the LOI experiments, Seth and Grant refined their LOIs to two different flavors. One being a "pledge of purchase" for those who want to buy the end product. The other flavor being a "testing agreement" for those who want to participate in the beta test.

VALIDATION / SIMULATION

Pop-Up Store

A retail store that is opened temporarily to sell goods,
usually a trendy or seasonal product.

◯ ●●●●◯
COST

⚖ ●●◯◯◯
EVIDENCE STRENGTH

🕐 ●●●◯◯
SETUP TIME

⏱ ●●◯◯◯
RUN TIME

DESIRABILITY · FEASIBILITY · VIABILITY

*A pop-up store is ideal for testing face-to-face interactions
with customers to see if they'll really make a purchase.*

*A pop-up store is not ideal for B2B businesses: consider
a booth at a conference instead.*

CAPABILITIES *Design / Product / Legal / Sales / Marketing*

Prepare

☐ Find a location.

☐ Get the required lease, license, permits, and insurance.

☐ Design the experience.

☐ Plan the logistics of how it will operate.

☐ Promote the dates it'll be open to customers.

Execute

☐ Open your pop-up store.

☐ Gather evidence you need from customers.

☐ Close your pop-up store.

Analyze

☐ Review your notes with the team:
- What did people get excited about?
- What made them skeptical?

☐ Review how many meaning-ful interactions took place:
- Did you collect any emails from customers?
- Did you perform any successful mock sales, presales, or actual sales?

☐ Use what you've learned to iterate on the experience before running another pop-up store.

POP-UP STORE

☑

301

SIMULATION

Cost

Pop-up stores are generally small, but will still cost more money than low fidelity experiments. Much of the cost is leasing the space and advertising, which can vary depending on the location and access to the store. You can bring costs down if you can find an owner to give you extra space in their existing store for the experiment. Additional costs may include licenses, permits, and insurance required in order to conduct business transactions.

Setup Time

Setup time for a pop-up store can take days or weeks, depending on what locations are available. It'll need to look professional, which requires having the right people and appearance for the store. You'll also need to create demand using ads, unless it is a very high traffic area with your target customers.

Run Time

Run time for a pop-up store is generally short, from a few hours to a few days. The intent here is to learn quickly, synthesize the results, and move on.

Evidence

●●○○○

# of customer visits
# of email signups

Conversion rate on people who visited and provided their email addresses.

Customer Feedback

Customer quotes provided in the feedback to you.

Customer visits, emails, and feedback are rather weak evidence, but good for qualitative insights.

●●●●●

# of presales
# of mock sales
# of sales

Conversion rate on people who are willing to pay or paid for the product.

Sales are strong evidence that customers want your product.

Capabilities

Design / Product / Legal / Sales / Marketing

To set up and run a pop-up store, you'll need legal expertise to determine licensing, permits, lease, and insurance contracts. You'll need online marketing skills to promote the store and sales experience to staff it for customer interaction.

Requirements

Traffic

Pop-up stores thrive on the idea of a niche, limited-time offer for customers. In order to create that demand, you'll need to advertise and create buzz for your shop via:

- online ads.
- social media campaigns.
- email campaigns.
- word of mouth.

VALIDATION

EXPERIMENTS

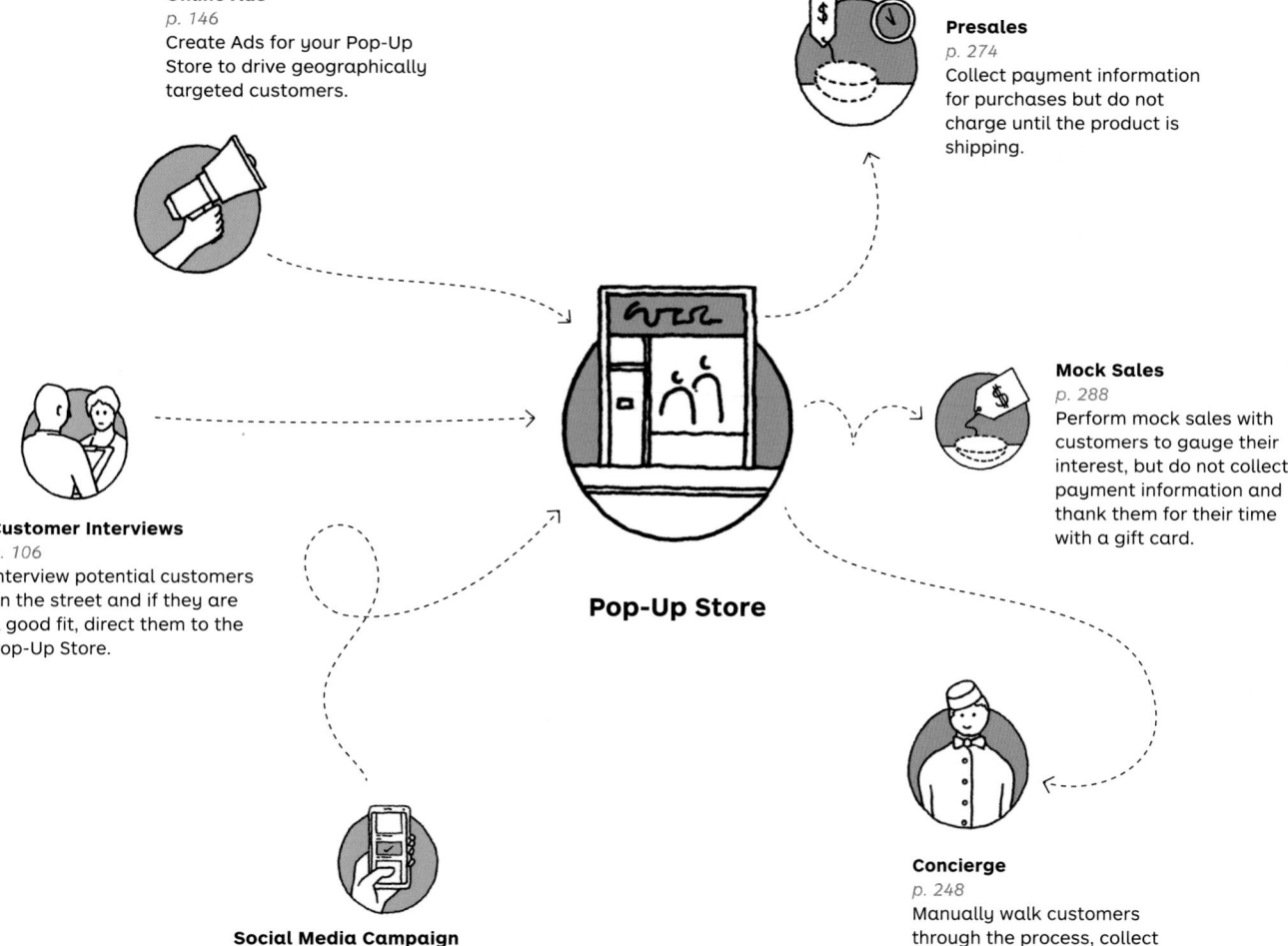

Online Ads
p. 146
Create Ads for your Pop-Up
Store to drive geographically
targeted customers.

Presales
p. 274
Collect payment information
for purchases but do not
charge until the product is
shipping.

Customer Interviews
p. 106
Interview potential customers
on the street and if they are
a good fit, direct them to the
Pop-Up Store.

Mock Sales
p. 288
Perform mock sales with
customers to gauge their
interest, but do not collect
payment information and
thank them for their time
with a gift card.

Pop-Up Store

Social Media Campaign
p. 168
Use social media to drive
people to your Pop-Up Store.

Concierge
p. 248
Manually walk customers
through the process, collect
payment, and deliver the
product to them.

POP-UP STORE

303

SIMULATION

VALIDATION

304

EXPERIMENTS

Learning Through Temporary Retail
Topology Eyewear

Topology Eyewear aims to solve the problem of poorly fitting glasses, by making custom-tailored glasses that are sized and styled via an augmented reality app. Customers can take a selfie, see how different glasses look on their faces, and then purchase custom glasses that are specifically sculpted to fit their unique dimensions. As with any new innovation, there are risky hypotheses that need to be tested.

Even though the technology worked, the team needed to test for any barriers to adoption with customers.

Hypothesis

The Topology team believed that many people would identify with the problem of poor glasses fit, and would welcome the high-tech approach as a potential solution.

Experiment

Getting out of the building with a pop-up store.

The team rented a partially empty storefront on San Francisco's Union Street for a Friday and created a temporary company name—Alchemy Eyewear—and commissioned posters and flyers to make it feel exclusive and exciting. Chris Guest, the marketing lead, went out onto the street to cold approach strangers, ask about their eyewear, summarize the pitch, and encourage them to visit the pop-up store. When customers entered the store, Topology staff would first ask them about the problems they experience with their eyewear, taking note of how they describe the problem in their own words. Then they would introduce our solution and note their response and what questions they asked about it. They would then demo the app using a default face model and note their responses and questions. They would then seek their permission to take a face scan so they could

try it for themselves. When loaded, they would guide them how to scan themselves and noted and answered their questions. On selecting a chosen design, they would ask if we could get their email address so we could save the design and send it to them.

Evidence

Finding early adopters off of the street.

Despite humble expectations, after 2 hours, they sold 4 pairs of glasses at an average price of about $400.

The conversion rates on email signups were too small to be meaningful in the absolute sense, but they were helpful to see where the biggest drop-off occurred in the the process.

Insights

People knew their glasses didn't fit, but weren't sure why.

Even though the team sold 4 pairs of glasses, it was the qualitative insights that were the most valuable.

The team noticed noticed that people seemed to be "symptom aware" but not "problem aware." That is, when asked if they had a problem with fit, most people would say no. But when asked if their glasses slid down their nose, pinched, created red marks etc, most people would say yes. They understood the symptoms of bad fit, but nobody thought of it as being due to bad fit. This directed marketing messages for years afterwards.

Actions

Using the voice of the customer.

The customer quotes inspired the company purpose and vision, becoming central to the branding.

The team used what they learned to run more pop-up stores to test the Value Proposition, positioning, and marketing, eventually talking to over a thousand customers face to face.

VALIDATION / SIMULATION

Extreme Programming Spike

A simple program to explore potential technical or design solutions. The term spike is derived from rock climbing and railroads. It's a necessary task to stop and perform so that you can feasibly continue to make progress.

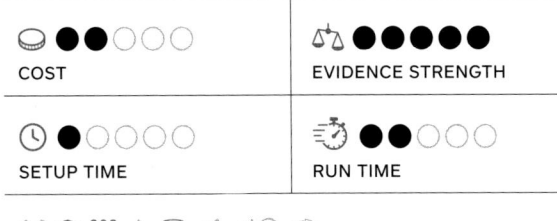

COST	EVIDENCE STRENGTH
○ ●● ○○○	⚖ ●●●●●

SETUP TIME	RUN TIME
○ ●○○○○	⏱ ●●○○○

CAPABILITIES *Product / Technology / Data*

DESIRABILITY · **FEASIBILITY** · VIABILITY

The Extreme Programming Spike is ideal for quickly evaluating whether or not your solution is feasible, usually with software.

The Extreme Programming Spike is not ideal for scaling the solution, as it is typically thrown away and re-created afterwards.

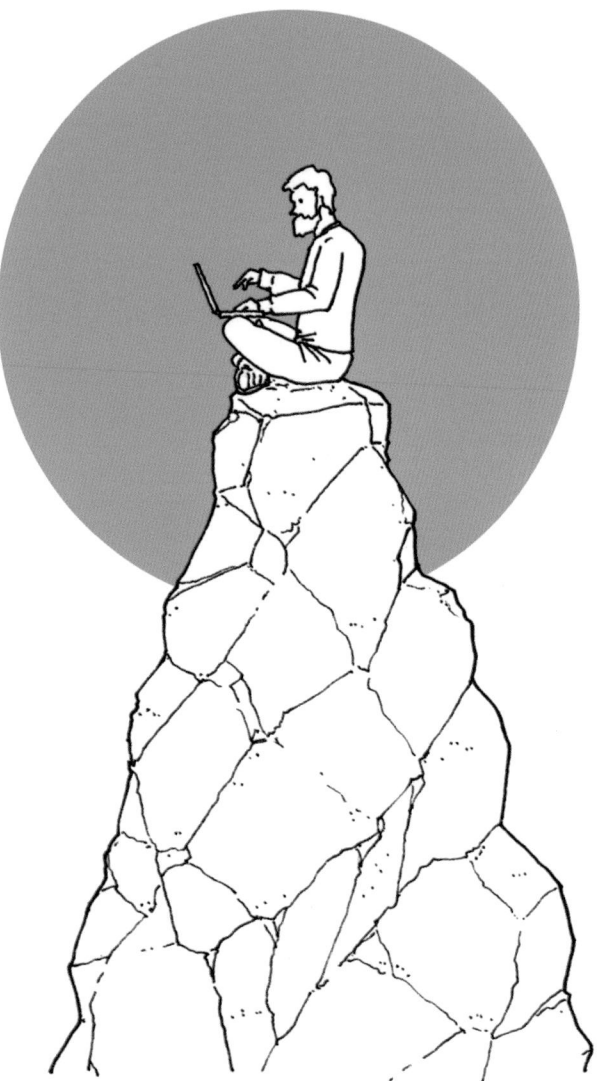

☑

307

Prepare

☐ Define your acceptance criteria.

☐ Define your time box for the spike.

☐ Plan your start and end date.

Execute

☐ Write the code to achieve the acceptance criteria.

☐ Strongly consider pairing programming with another person to help navigate the code and create any needed tests.

Analyze

☐ Share what you've found with regards to:

  • performance.

  • level of complexity.

  • outputs.

☐ Determine if the acceptance criteria were successfully met.

☐ Use what you've learned to build, borrow, or buy the necessary solution.

Cost

Cost is relatively cheap and much more inexpensive than building the entire solution—only to find out at the end if it is feasible.

Setup Time

Setup time for an Extreme Programming Spike is usually about one day. This is the time needed to research what methods are available and usually done by someone that already has technical expertise.

Run Time

Run time for an Extreme Programming Spike is typically from 1 day to 2 weeks. It is aggressively time boxed for a reason— you are laser focused on testing feasibility for a specific solution.

Evidence

Acceptance criteria

The acceptance criteria defined for the spike was sufficiently met. Did the code perform the task and generate the output required?

Recommendation

The people working on the spike provide their recommendation on how steep of a learning curve it is to use the software and if it is fit for your purpose in creating the solution.

Spikes generate strong evidence: you are working with code that is representative of the bigger solution.

Capabilities

Product / Technology / Data

You'll need product capabilities to clearly communicate how the solution creates the Value Proposition. This includes answering any questions from the team and customer expectations with regard to speed and quality. Data capabilities are also helpful if there is any visualization or analytics aspect to the spike. The most important capability you'll need is technology and software, since the spike is usually working with code to produce a signal on the next course of action.

Requirements

Acceptance Criteria

Before performing a spike, clearly define the acceptance criteria and time box so that everyone is clear on the goal before getting started. These can turn into never-ending research projects if left unchecked.

Partner & Supplier Interviews
p. 114
Interview partners and suppliers to better understand their capabilities before building it yourself.

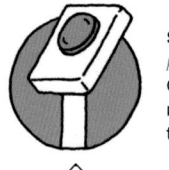

Single Feature MVP
p. 240
Create a single feature minimum viable product to test with customers.

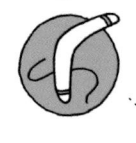

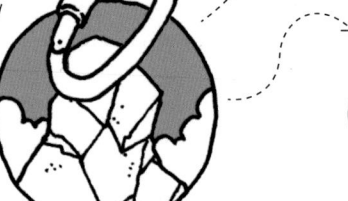

Data Sheet
p. 190
Create a data sheet on what specifications the solution should contain.

Boomerang
p. 204
Use competitor solutions and research how they perform and what technology stack they are using.

**Extreme
Programming Spike**

EXTREME PROGRAMMING SPIKE

309

SIMULATION

Mind

set

"The more success you've had in the past, the less critically you examine your own assumptions."

————

Vinod Khosla
Venture capitalist

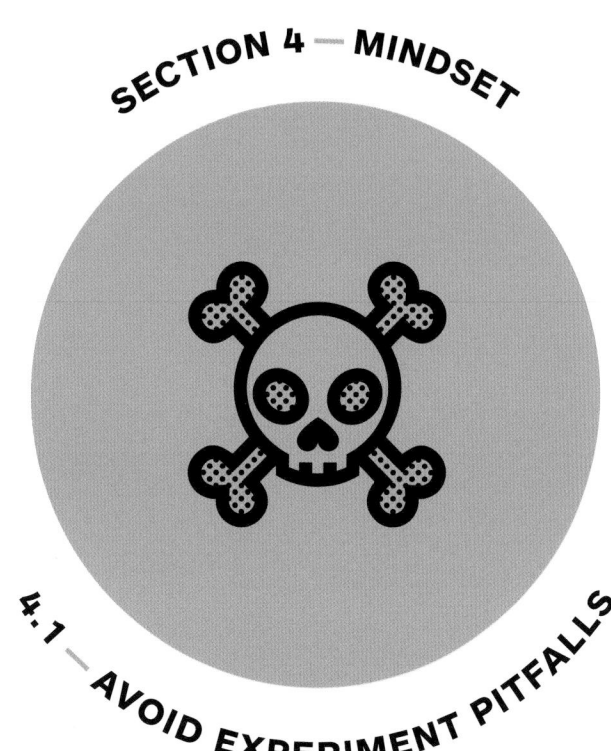

SECTION 4 — MINDSET

4.1 — AVOID EXPERIMENT PITFALLS

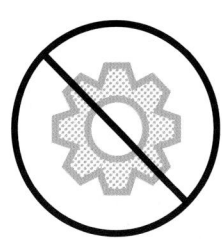

Experiment Pitfalls

The best plans for experimentation don't always come through. We've learned this in working with teams to design, run, and analyze experiments over the years. Part of learning this process is becoming more proficient at quickly running experiments. We have found common pitfalls that you can identify early on and benefit from our mistakes.

Time Trap

Not dedicating enough time.

✗
- You get what you invest. Teams that don't put in enough time to test business ideas won't get great results. Too often, teams underestimate what it takes to conduct multiple experiments and test ideas well.

✓
- ☐ Carve out dedicated time every week to test, learn, and adapt.
- ☐ Set weekly goals in regard to what you'd like to learn about your hypotheses.
- ☐ Visualize your work so that it becomes clear when tasks are stalled or blocked.

Analysis Paralysis

Overthinking things that you should just test and adapt.

✗
- Good ideas and concepts are important, but too many teams overthink and waste time, rather than getting out of the building to test and adapt their ideas.

✓
- ☐ Time box your analysis work.
- ☐ Differentiate between reversible and irreversible decisions. Act fast on the former. Take more time for the latter.
- ☐ Avoid debates of opinion. Conduct evidence-driven debates followed by decisions.

Incomparable Data/Evidence

Messy data that are not comparable.

✗
- Too many teams are sloppy in defining their exact hypothesis, experiment, and metrics. That leads to data that are not comparable (e.g., not testing with the exact same customer segment or in wildly different contexts).

✓
- ☐ Use the Test Card.
- ☐ Make test subject, experiment context, and precise metrics explicit.
- ☐ Make sure everybody involved in running the experiment is part of the design.

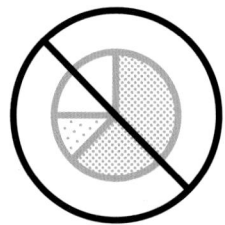

Weak Data/Evidence

Only measure what people say, not what they do.

Confirmation Bias

Only believing evidence that agrees with your hypothesis.

Too Few Experiments

Conduct only one experiment for your most important hypothesis.

Failure to Learn and Adapt

When you don't take time to analyze the evidence to generate insights and action.

Outsource Testing

When you outsource what you should be doing and learning yourself.

✖

– Often teams are happy with running surveys and interviews and they fail to go deeper into how people act in real life situations.

☐ Don't just believe what people say.

☐ Run call-to-action experiments.

☐ Generate evidence that gets as close as possible to the real world situation you are trying to test.

✖

– Sometimes teams discard or underplay evidence that conflicts with their hypothesis. They prefer the illusion of being correct in their prediction.

☐ Involve others in the data synthesis process to bring in different perspectives.

☐ Create competing hypotheses to challenge your beliefs.

☐ Conduct multiple experiments for each hypothesis.

✖

– Few teams realize how many experiments they should conduct to validate a hypothesis. They make decisions on important hypotheses based on one experiment with weak evidence.

☐ Conduct multiple experiments for important hypotheses.

☐ Differentiate between weak and strong evidence.

☐ Increase the strength of evidence with decreasing uncertainty.

✖

– Some teams get so deep into testing that they forget to keep their eyes on the prize. The goal is not to test and learn. The goal is to decide, based on evidence and insights, to progress from idea to business.

☐ Set aside time to synthesize your results, generate insights, and adapt your idea.

☐ Always navigate between detailed testing process and big picture idea: which patterns that matter are you observing?

☐ Create rituals to keep your eyes on the prize: ask if you're making progress from idea to business.

✖

– Outsourcing testing is rarely a wise idea. Testing is about rapid iterations between testing, learning, and adapting an idea. An agency can't make those rapid decisions for you and you risk wasting time and energy by outsourcing.

☐ Shift resources you reserved for an agency to internal team members.

☐ Build up a team of professional testers.

"It takes humility to realize
we don't know everything,
not to rest on our laurels,
and to know that we must keep
learning and observing.
If we don't, we can be sure
some startup will be there
to take our place."

—————

Cher Wang
Cofounder HTC

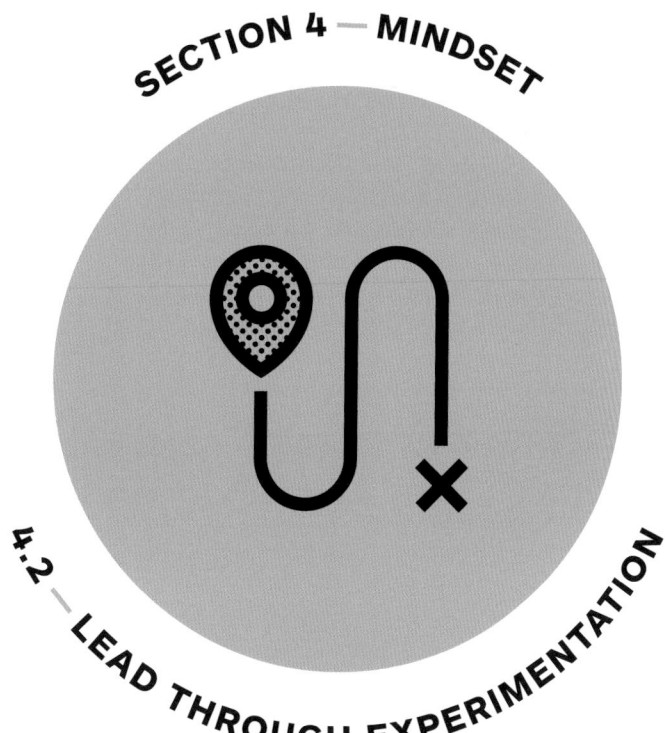

Improving Business Models

Language

Leaders who are improving existing business models need to be aware of their language and tone. Chances are you have evolved into a leader over time because you are an expert with knowledge and experience.

As you lead teams through experimenting on a known business model, be mindful of the fact that overuse of your words can unintentionally disempower the teams. They may feel as though their decision-making authority is taken away, even if you are merely giving your opinion. They'll simply wait for you to assign them experiments, which is not ideal.

Accountability

Accountability often has a negative connotation in today's organizations, but it doesn't need to. Teams do not always need to be "held accountable" to hitting dates and releasing features. While features are important, they are outputs, not outcomes. Remember to focus on business outcomes, not just the features and dates.

Your teams need the opportunity to give an account on how they are experimenting and making progress toward business outcomes. As a leader, it's your job to create an environment for these opportunities to occur.

Facilitation

How you interact with teams while improving business models is also important. As you grow into a leader at higher levels of the organization, you'll realize that facilitation skills are imperative.

We recommend taking courses on facilitation to level up your leadership game. There might be many different options to improve the business and instead of choosing one, use facilitation to select multiple experiments. Have the evidence shape what approach works best for your business.

✔

☐ "We, Us, Our"

☐ "How would you achieve this business outcome?"

☐ "Can you think of 2–3 additional experiments?"

✘

– "I, Me, Mine"

– "Deliver this feature by release date."

– "This is the only experiment we should run."

*Allow your intuition to guide
you to a conclusion, no matter
how imperfect—this is the
"strong opinion" part. Then—
and this is the "weakly held"
part—prove yourself wrong.*
— Paul Saffo

Inventing Business Models

Strong Opinions, Weakly Held

Inventing new business models requires experimentation and openness to the idea of being wrong. One way to think about this is from Paul Saffo's "strong opinions, weakly held" approach. It means you start out with a hypothesis, but be open for it to be proven wrong. If you are merely trying to prove that you are right, then you become susceptible to your cognitive biases.

For example, when attending a stakeholder review, teams will be sharing what they tested and where they want to go. If you lead with answers and ignore all of the data that contradict your opinion, it'll be a very frustrating meeting for everyone. It'll essentially unravel the experimentation culture you are trying to build.

✔

☐ "What is your learning goal?"

☐ "What obstacles can I remove to help you make progress?"

☐ "How else might we approach this problem?"

☐ "What learning has surprised you so far?"

✘

– "I don't trust the data."

– "I still think it's a good idea and we should build it anyway."

– "You need to talk to 1,000 customers before it means anything."

– "This has to be a $15 million dollar business by the end of next year."

Steps Leaders Can Take

Create an Enabling Environment: Processes, Metrics, and Culture

Leadership's key role in helping test business ideas is to create the right environment. Give people enough time and resources to test ideas iteratively. Leaders need to abolish business plans and establish appropriate testing processes and metrics that differ from execution processes and metrics. They need to give teams the autonomy to make decisions, move fast, and then get out of the way.

Make Sure Evidence Trumps Opinion: Change Decision-Making

Leaders are used to deciding based on their often deep experience and extensive track record. Yet, in innovation and entrepreneurship, past experience might actually prevent an individual from seeing and adapting to the future. Here evidence from testing trumps opinion. The leader's role is to push a team to make a compelling case for an idea based on evidence, not based on the leader's preferences.

Remove Obstacles and Open Doors: Access to Customers, Brand, IP, and Other Resources

Leaders can remove obstacles when teams that are testing business ideas encounter internal roadblocks, like lack of access to internal expertise or specialized resources. Leaders can open doors to customers when required. It's surprising how few corporate innovation and growth teams have easy access to customers to test new ideas.

Ask Questions Rather Than Provide Answers: Help Teams Grow and Adapt Their Ideas

Leaders need to up their questioning skills to push teams to develop better value propositions and business models that can succeed in the real world. They need to relentlessly inquire about experiments, evidence, insights, and patterns on which teams build Value Propositions and business model ideas.

SYNOPSIS

Create More Leaders

Meet Your Teams One-Half Step Ahead

Leaders need to bring their teams along for the journey, instead of inadvertently leaving them behind. Think of where you eventually want team members to be, then look backward. How will they get here? What steps will they have to take? It's a small cognitive trick but it works. Leaders need a sense of where their teams are today and how to nudge them down that path. Find opportunities to guide them to take that first step, whether it be in scheduled one-on-ones, retrospectives, or in hallway conversations.

Understand Context Before Giving Advice

Leaders need to actively listen and understand the context before giving advice to team members. Practice letting team members speak until they are finished. Once there is a pause in the conversation, ask clarifying questions to make sure you understand the context before giving advice. Don't get too excited and interrupt team members while they are speaking because you've already thought of an answer. You may prematurely provide advice and connected dots where none exist.

Say "I Don't Know."

These three simple words can strike fear into the heart of leaders. "I don't know." We often ask leaders when was the last time they uttered these three words in front of their employees. The answers range from "Why, just yesterday!" to "Never!" It's the latter answer that is concerning. Imagine feeling the pressure of leading an organization and always having the answers. There's a good chance that you don't have them. When building a culture of innovation and entrepreneurship, acting like you have all the answers can be disastrous. Teams will quickly see through the veil once they learn how to run experiments and generate their own evidence. Worse yet, you'll feel like you have undermined your position of leadership by being proven wrong. Instead, we strongly recommend that you practice saying these three words, "I don't know," when you are in a situation where you don't know. It will help your teams begin to understand that you don't have all of the answers, nor should you. Follow it up with "How would you approach this?" or "What do you think we should do?" Saying "I don't know" will help you model the behavior the leaders you create will embrace.

"A bad system will beat
a good person every time."

———

W. Edwards Deming
Professor and author

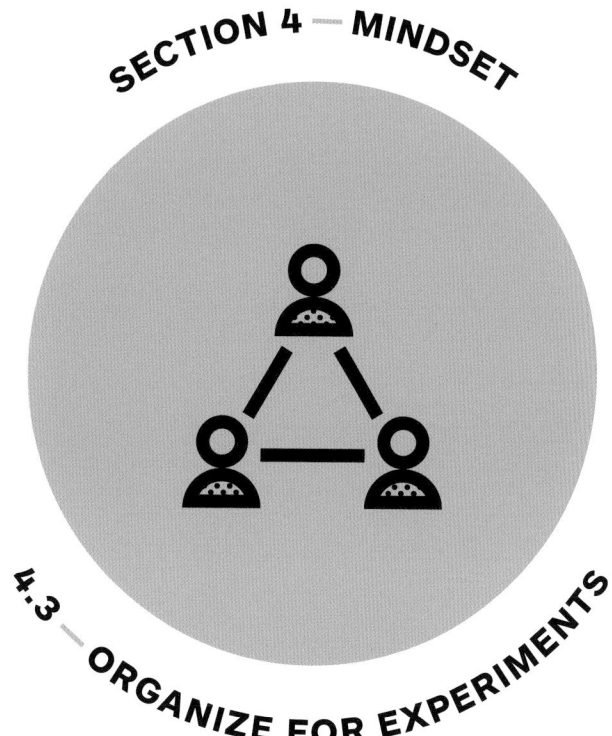

SECTION 4 — MINDSET

4.3 — ORGANIZE FOR EXPERIMENTS

Silos vs. Cross-Functional Teams

Much of how we've structured organizations today is based on the Industrial Era. Back then, you would create a factory to assemble a product, such as an automobile. You'd break the creation of an automobile into tasks, create an assembly line, and have workers complete the same task over and over. This works if you know the solution, since you can analyze your way to efficiently create the solution. Today's corporations are, not coincidentally, modeled the same way. We create projects, break them down into tasks, and assign them across functions. Organizing by function can work if you truly know the problem and the solution—and nothing changes.

We've learned over the last few decades of work that rarely do we know the solution, especially in software. Things change fast. Really fast. So the idea that the solution is known and nothing changes is becoming less and less common in today's market. This is why there has been a shift from traditional, functionally siloed organization models to more agile, cross-functional team approaches. When testing out new business ideas, speed and agility are imperative. cross-functional teams can adapt more quickly than functionally siloed teams. In many organizations, small, dedicated, cross-functional teams can outperform large, siloed project teams.

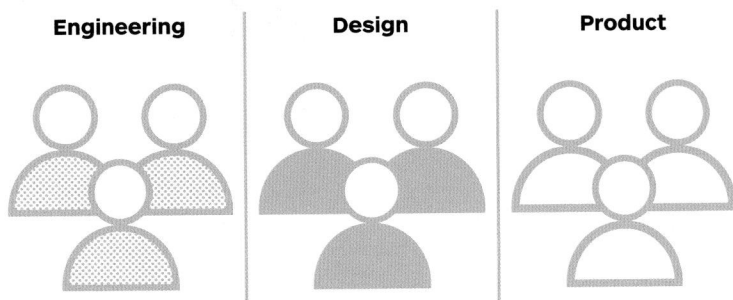

Engineering   **Design**   **Product**

Functional Silos

Cross-Functional Teams

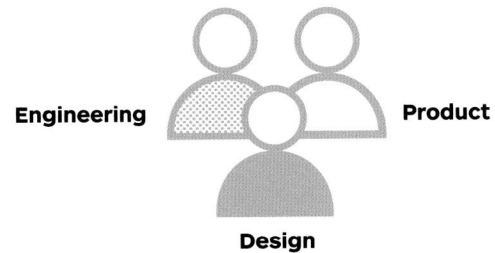

Engineering   **Product**

Design

Thinking Like a Venture Capitalist

Another outdated model we observe in organizations pertains to funding. Many organizations still adhere to the big bang, annual funding style of the past. This severely limits the agility of the organization and incentivizes bad behavior. For example, if your department doesn't spend all of its budget, then it is likely your budget for the upcoming fiscal year will be decreased. Therefore, budget is spent not on the most impactful activities, but those that will ensure there will be no money left at the end of the cycle. Annual funding also limits your at-bats, in that instead of taking one big home run swing, you're much better off taking several base hit level swings. This is where organizations can learn from the Venture Capital community. Unfortunately, the level of patience and willing-ness to give teams space is somewhat limited in organizations, as we illustrate below.

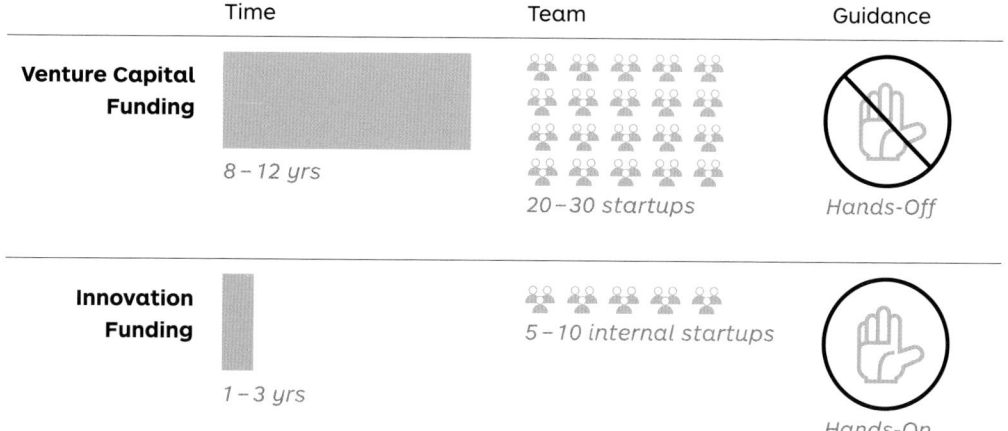

	Time	Team	Guidance
Venture Capital Funding	8 – 12 yrs	20 – 30 startups	Hands-Off
Innovation Funding	1 – 3 yrs	5 – 10 internal startups	Hands-On

Innovation Portfolio

In contrast to the annual budgeting, organizations are adopting a more venture capitalist-style approach. This helps leaders invest incrementally in a series of business ideas and double down on the ones that are successful. It greatly increases your at-bats and your chance at finding a unicorn, instead of placing 1–2 large bets.

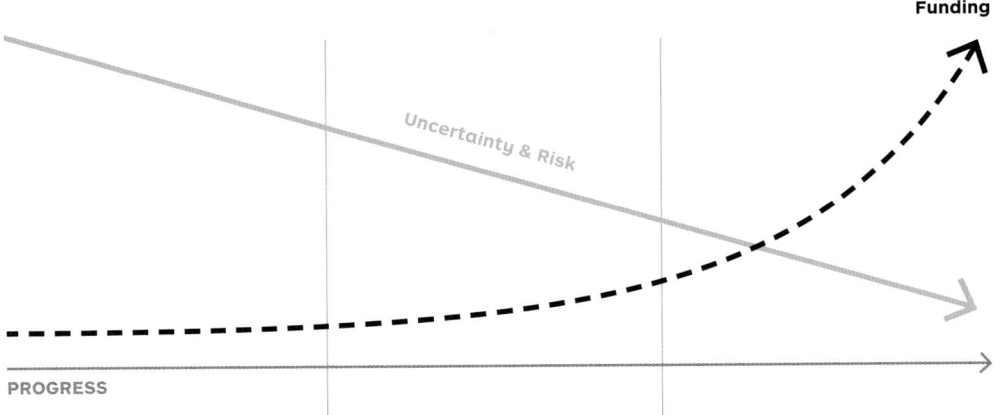

Funding

Uncertainty & Risk

PROGRESS

	Seed	Launch	Growth
Funding	Less than $50,000	$50,000 – $500,000	$500,000+
Team Size	1–3	2–5	5+
Time per Team Member	20–40%	40–80%	100%
Number of Projects	High	Medium	Low
Objectives	Customer understanding, context, and willingness to pay	Proven interest and indications of profitability	Proven model at limited scale
KPIs	• Market size • Customer evidence • Problem/solution fit • Opportunity size	• Value Proposition evidence • Financial evidence • Feasibility evidence	• Product/market fit • Acquisition and retention evidence • Business model fit
Experiment Themes	50–80% 0–10% 10–30%	30–50% 10–40% 20–50%	10–30% 40–50% 20–50%

DESIRABILITY
FEASIBILITY
VIABILITY

Investment Committees

Another important aspect of funding in a venture capitalist-style method is having a small investment committee that consists of leadership to usher the process along. These leaders in the organization need to have decision-making authority when it comes to budget, because they'll be helping the teams navigate from seed, launch, and growth stages. These funding decisions typically take place in the Stakeholder Review Ceremony (see page 80). While we recommend stakeholder reviews to occur every month, the investment decisions usually take place at 3–6 month intervals, depending on your business venture. Here are some guidelines when it comes to creating your investment committee.

Designing the Committee

- *3–5 members:* Keep the committee relatively small in size so that you can make decisions and run fast.

- *External member:* Consider adding an external member or entrepreneur in residence (EIR) who can help bring a fresh perspective to the portfolio.

- *Decision-making authority:* Include members who can make decisions with regard to approval and budget.

- *Entrepreneurial:* While members do not necessarily have to have a history of entrepreneurship, they need to be willing to challenge the status quo. Too many conservative members will prematurely stunt the growth of new innovations.

Create a Working Agreement

Once assembled, create a working agreement for the committee before inviting teams to present their recommendations. As a team, write down and agree upon rules such as:

- *Be on time:* Members have busy schedules, but they have to prioritize the stakeholder review ceremonies, otherwise teams will be left wondering if their initiatives are important.

- *Make decisions in the meeting:* Teams should not leave the review wondering if they can move forward. Decide with the teams present before adjourning.

- *Leave ego at the door:* Have an opinion in the review but be willing to be swayed by evidence. The teams will be bringing what experiments they ran and how to move forward. It is your job to listen, not talk over them.

Foster an Environment

This committee is in part responsible for fostering the team environment we introduced on page 10.

Without your help, the teams will not be able to sustain over time even if they are cross-functional and exhibit the right behaviors.

As a committee, have a plan to revisit how you are helping the team with obstacles centered on:

- Time.
- Multitasking.
- Funding.
- Support.
- Access.
- Direction.

After

word

Glossary

Action
Next step to progress with testing and de-risking a business idea; informed decision to abandon, pivot, iterate, or continue testing.

Affinity sorting
An exercise used to organize ideas and data in which ideas are sorted into groups or themes based on their relationships.

Assumption
A statement or fact that we believe to be true; a statement in which we take something for granted without any evidence to support it.

Assumptions mapping
A team exercise where desirability, viability, and feasibility assumptions are explicitly written down and then decided upon.

Business Model
Rationale of how an organization creates, delivers, and captures value.

B2B
Business to business; exchange of products or services between businesses.

B2C
Business to consumer; exchange of products or services between businesses and consumers.

Business Model Canvas
Strategic management tool to design, test, build, and manage (profitable and scalable) business models.

Call to action (CTA)
Prompts a subject to perform an action; used in an experiment in order to test one or more hypotheses.

Conversion
When a customer interacts with your ad and then takes an action that is valuable to your business.

CSAT
Short for customer satisfaction.

Customer development
Four-step process invented by Steve Blank to reduce risk and uncertainty in entrepreneurship by continuously testing the hypotheses underlying a business model with customers and stakeholders.

Customer gains
Outcomes and benefits customers must have, expect, desire, or dream to achieve.

Customer insight
Minor or major breakthrough in your customer understanding helping you design better value propositions and business models.

Customer pains

Bad outcomes, risks, and obstacles that customers want to avoid, notably because they prevent them from getting a job done (well).

Customer Profile

Business tool that constitutes the right-hand side of the Value Proposition Canvas. Visualizes the jobs, pains, and gains of a customer segment (or stakeholder) for whom you intend to create value.

Daily Standup

A short, daily organizational meeting meant to make the team aware of the project status; derived from the Agile Method.

Desirability

Do your customers want your product or service? Having evidence that customers desire a solution to the problem your value proposition is targeting.

Distributed team

A team that is spread across geographical locations; remote.

Dot voting

Participants vote by placing a "dot" or a sticker next to the options they prefer, using a limited number of stickers (dotmocracy or multi-voting).

Environment map

Strategic foresight tool to map the context in which you design and manage value propositions and business models.

Ethnography

The study of people in everyday life and practice.

Evidence

Data generated from an experiment or collected in the field. Proves or disproves a (business) hypothesis, customer insight, or belief about a value proposition, business model, or the environment.

Experiment

A procedure to validate or invalidate a value proposition or business model hypothesis that produces evidence. A procedure to reduce risk and the uncertainty of a business idea.

Feasibility

Can you build your product or service? Having the resources and infrastructure to build your product or service.

Fidelity

The degree to which the prototype accurately reproduces the product or service. Level of detail and functionality within the prototype.

Fit

When the elements of your Value Map meet relevant jobs, pains, and gains of your customer segment and a substantial number of customers "hire" your value proposition to satisfy those jobs, pains, and gains.

Gain creators

Describes how products and services create gains and help customers achieve the outcomes and benefits they require, expect, desire, or dream of by getting a job done (well).

Hypothesis

A belief drawn from a strategy, business model, or value proposition that needs to be true for your idea to work partially or fully but that hasn't been validated yet.

Iterative approach

The process of repeating a cycle in order to bring a result closer to discovery with every repetition.

Ideation

The process of generating and communicating ideas in a group session.

Jobs to be done

What customers need, want, or desire to get done in their work and in their lives.

KPIs (Key Performance Indicators)
Measurable value that demonstrates how effectively you are achieving your targets for success.

Lean Startup
Approach by Eric Ries based on the Customer Development process to eliminate waste and uncertainty from product development by continuously building, testing, and learning in an iterative fashion.

Learning Card
Strategic learning tool to capture insights from research and experiments.

Metrics
A quantifiable measurement used to track and assess.

Minimum Viable Product (MVP)
A model of a value proposition designed specifically to validate or invalidate one or more hypotheses.

Pain Relievers
Describes how products and services alleviate customer pains by eliminating or reducing bad outcomes, risks, and obstacles that prevent customers from getting a job done (well).

Products and Services
The items that your value proposition is based on that your customers can see in your shop window — metaphorically speaking.

Progress Board
Strategic management tool to manage and monitor the business model and value proposition design process and track progress towards a successful value proposition and business model.

Prototyping (low/high fidelity)
The practice of building quick, inexpensive, and rough study models to learn about the desirability, feasibility, and viability of alternative value propositions and business models.

Solopreneur
Abbreviation for Solo Entrepreneur (building a business on your own.

Stakeholder
Someone with a legitimate interest, can affect or be affected by your business.

Team Map
A visual tool created by Stefano Mastrogiacomo to boost alignment among team members for more effective meetings and conversations.

Test Card
Strategic testing tool to design and structure your research and experiments.

Time Box
A set period of time in which a task must be completed, derived from the Agile Method.

Validate
To confirm that a hypothesis is legitimate, well-grounded, or justifiable.

Value Map
Business tool that constitutes the left-hand side of the Value Proposition Canvas. Makes explicit how your products and services create value by alleviating pains and creating gains.

Value Proposition
Describes the benefits customers can expect from your products and services.

Value Proposition Canvas
Strategic management tool to design, test, build, and manage products and services. Fully integrates with the Business Model Canvas.

Value Proposition Design
The process of designing, testing, building, and managing value propositions over their entire lifecycle.

Viability
Can we make a profit from our product or service? Having evidence that you can generate more revenue than costs from your product or service.

Acknowledgments

This book would have been impossible to create without the love and support of my wife, Elizabeth. She's been my rock throughout the years and continues to provide encouragement for me on this journey. Our kids have been amazing during this writing process, providing me with love and time to focus. So to Catherine, Isabella, and James: I thank you for cheering me on. I'm lucky to be a father to such amazing kids.

I want to thank my coauthor Alex Osterwalder. He provided excellent guidance and insights throughout the entire book. It has been my pleasure and honor to have him be a part of this ambitious endeavor. I'd also like to thank Alan Smith and the entire Strategyzer team for putting in long hours and weekends creating such a beautifully designed book.

Testing Business Ideas is written from the viewpoint that we are standing on the shoulders of giants. To all of those who have influenced my thinking over the years, in small ways and in large, it is only because of you that this book exists. You were brave enough to put your thoughts out there for others to see.

I want to thank all of you who continue to push these ideas forward in practice: Eric Ries, Steve Blank, Jeff Gothelf, Josh Seiden, Giff Constable, Janice Fraser, Jason Fraser,

Ash Maurya, Laura Klein, Christina Wodtke, Brant Cooper, Patrick Vlaskovits, Kate Rutter, Tendayi Viki, Barry O'Reilly, Melissa Perri, Jeff Patton, Sam McAfee, Teresa Torres, Marty Cagan, Sean Ellis, Tristan Kromer, Tom Looy, and Kent Beck.

A book can feel like a very large batch waterfall process. We did our best to test our content as we iterated along the way. I want to thank everyone who helped proofread and provided feedback early on. Your insights helped shape the book into what it is today.

— David J. Bland 2019

I particularly want to thank Steve Blank, one of the seminal modern thinkers on entrepreneurship, and a good friend and mentor. Without Steve's Customer Development process, his founding of the entire Lean Startup movement, and his personal encouragement, my books would have remained a modern version of the business plan — great in concept, not grounded in reality. Steve's thinking, experience, and writing on the topic of "getting out of the building" and testing ideas with customers, became the foundation of much of my own thinking. Many of the ideas in this book emerged from long conversations with Steve, on walks at his beautiful ranch.

— Alexander Osterwalder 2019

334

AUTHOR
David J. Bland
Founder, Advisor, Speaker

COAUTHOR
Alex Osterwalder
Founder, Speaker, Business Thinker

DESIGN LEAD
Alan Smith
Founder, Explorer, Designer

David J. Bland is an advisor, author and founder who lives in the San Francisco Bay Area. In 2015, he created Precoil to help companies find product market fit using lean startup, design thinking and business model innovation. He has helped validate new products and services at companies all around the world. Prior to advising, David spent over 10 years of his career scaling technology startups. He continues to give back to the startup community by teaching at several startup accelerators in Silicon Valley.

@davidjbland
precoil.com

In 2015 Alex won the strategy award by Thinkers50, called the "Oscars of Management Thinking" by the FT, and currently ranks #7 among the leading business thinkers of the world.

   He is a frequent keynote speaker at Fortune 500 companies and has held guest lectures in top universities around the world, including Wharton, Stanford, Berkeley, IESE, MIT, KAUST, and IMD. Alex works regularly with senior executives from leading companies such as Bayer, Bosch, WL Gore, and Fortune 500 companies such as Mastercard on projects related to strategy and innovation.

@AlexOsterwalder
strategyzer.com/blog

Alan uses his curiosity and creativity to ask questions and turn the answers into simple, visual, practical tools. He believes that the right tools give people confidence to aim high and build big meaningful things.

   He cofounded Strategyzer with Alex Osterwalder, where he works with an inspired team on product. Strategyzer's books, tools, and services are used by leading companies around the world.

strategyzer.com

DESIGN LEAD
Trish Papadakos
Designer, Photographer, Creator

Trish holds a Masters in Design from Central St. Martins in London and a Bachelor of Design from the York Sheridan Joint Program in Toronto.

She has taught design at her alma mater, worked with award-winning agencies, launched several businesses, and is collaborating for the fourth time with the Strategyzer team.

@trishpapadakos

ADDITIONAL DESIGN
Chris White
Editorial Designer

Alan and Trish would like to thank Chris for hopping on and providing significant extra muscle near the finish line to help make this project a success.

ILLUSTRATION
Owen Pomery
Narrative illustration

Deep thanks to Owen for his patience and willingness to iterate to communicate the right ideas.

owenpomery.com

ICON DESIGN
b Farias
Contributor

Icons: team, light bulb, report abuse, flask, visible, gear, telescope, checkbox, cross bones, destination, paper note, dashboard, like, clipboard, charty pie, chemistry book, map pin, trophy, and graduate hat by b farias from the Noun Project.

thenounproject.com/bfarias

Strategyzer uses the best of technology and coaching to support your transformation and growth challenges.

Discover what we can do for you at Strategyzer.com

TRANSFORMATION
Create Change
*Skill building at the Strategyzer
Cloud Academy course library.*

Build value for customers, value for
your business, testing your ideas,
and an in-depth experiment library.

GROWTH
Create Growth
*Systematize and scale your
growth efforts.*

Growth strategy, innovation
readyness assessment, innovation
funnel design, sprints, and metrics.

Index

A

Abandonment rate, 276
Access to customers, for teams, 11
Accountability, 318
Action(s). *See also* Behaviors
    attention as, 132
    of customers, testing, 152
    defined, 62
    turning insights into, 62–63
Advisors, for solopreneurs, 81
Advocates, 174
Advocate share rate, 174
Affinity Sorting, 112
Alchemy Eyewear, 305
Alignment, on teams, 12–13
American Family Insurance, 198–199
Analysis paralysis, 314
Anchors, 220
AngelList, 167
Angry Birds, 7
Assessment, in design loop, 19
Assumptions, questioning, 8
Assumptions Mapping, 36–39
Attention, 132
Autonomous teams, 10
Avoiding experiment pitfalls, 313–315

B

Bangerter, Seth, 299

Behaviors. *See also* Action(s)
    of customers, 130
    of teams, 8–9
Bezos, Jeff, 230
Bi-weekly retrospective meetings, 68–69, 78–79
Blank, Bennett, 121
Blank, Steve, 136, 147
Blocker experiments, 85
Boomerang, 204–207
    details of, 206
    function of, 204
    overview of, 205
    pairings for, 207
Branding, landing pages and, 265
Brochures, 194–199
    American Family Insurance case study,
      198–199
    details of, 196
    function of, 194
    overview of, 195
    pairings for, 197
B2B companies:
    Customer Interviews with, 110
    hardware companies, 98
    letters of intent for, 294
    sequence of experiments for, 98
    services companies, 98
    software companies, 98
B2B with B2C experimentation sequence, 99
B2C companies:
    Customer Interviews with, 110
    sequence of experiments for, 99
    services companies, 99
    software companies, 99
Buffer, 292–293

Business concept design, x
Business design, 18–19
Business experiments, 44. *See also* Experiment(s)
Business hypotheses, 30. *See also* Hypotheses
Business ideas, *see* Ideas
Business Model Canvas, 20–21
    financial risk in, 35
    infrastructure risk in, 35
    market risk in, 34
Business Model Generation, 19, 20
Business models:
    improving, 318
    inventing, 319
Business prototype, in design loop, 19
Button views, 158
Buy a Feature, 226–229
    details of, 228
    function of, 226
    overview of, 227
    pairings for, 229

C

Call to action experiments, 234–235, 260–277
    brochures, 196
    crowdfunding, 266–269
    function of, 45
    presale, 274–277
    simple landing page, 260–265
    Split Test, 270–273
Card sorting, 222–225
    details of, 224
    function of, 222

overview of, 223
pairings for, 225
Ceremonies, 68–69. *See also* Experiment
   ceremonies
Clickable prototypes, 236–239
   details of, 238
   function of, 236
   overview of, 237
   pairings for, 239
Click rates, 154, 164
Click through rate (CTR), 150, 170, 202
Coaching, for teams, 11
Cognitive biases, 319
Co-Located Teams, experiment ceremonies
   for, 70
Communication, 87. *See also* experiment
   ceremonies
   active listening, 321
   of experiment purpose and details, 87
   impact of language and tone, 318
   saying "I don't know," 321
Concierge, 248–253
   details of, 250
   evidence from, 53
   function of, 248
   learning from, 55
   overview of, 249
   pairings for, 251
   realtor.com case study, 252–253
Confidence levels, 56–57
Confirmation bias, 315
Constraints, for teams, 11
Continuous experimentation, 82, 85
Conversion rates:
   brochures, 196

Feature Stubs, 158
landing pages, 262
life-sized prototypes, 256
pop-up stores, 302
social media campaigns, 170
Split Tests, 272
Cook, Scott, 120
Core teams, 36
   bi-weekly retrospectives for, 78–79
   daily standups for, 74–75
   monthly stakeholder reviews for, 80–81
   weekly learning meetings for, 76–77
   weekly planning meetings for, 72–73
Corporate Team:
   bi-weekly retrospectives for, 79
   daily standups for, 75
   monthly stakeholder reviews for, 81
   weekly learning meetings for, 77
   weekly planning meetings for, 73
Cost:
   discovery experiments, 105
   validation experiments, 235
Craigslist, 111
Creating more leaders, 321
Cross-functional teams:
   silos vs., 324
   skillsets on, 6
Crowdfunding, 266–269
   details of, 268
   function of, 266
   overview of, 267
   pairings for, 269
Cryptology, 180–181
CTR, *see* Click through rate
CubeSats, 180–181

Customers:
   stage of, 147
   target, 147
   teams' access to, 11
Customer-centric behaviors, 8
Customer Interviews, 106–113
   details of, 108, 110–113
   evidence from, 53
   function of, 106
   learning from, 55
   overview of, 107
   pairings for, 109
Customer Profile, 22
Customer support analysis, 142–145
   details of, 144
   function of, 142
   overview of, 143
   pairings for, 145
Cycle time, 250, 286

D

Daily standup meetings, 68–69, 74–75
Data:
   and confidence level, 57
   incomparable, 314
   weak, 315
Data analysis experiments, 104–105, 126–145
   customer support analysis, 142–145
   Discussion Forums, 134–137
   sales force feedback, 138–141
   Search Trend Analysis, 126–129
   web traffic analysis, 130–133

Data-influenced behaviors, 8
Data points, number of, 57
Data sheets, 190–193
    details of, 192
    function of, 190
    overview of, 191
    pairings for, 193
A Day in the Life, 116–121
    details of, 118
    Intuit case study, 120–121
    overview of, 117
    pairings for, 119
De Botton, Alain, 48
Decision making, 59–63
    evidence vs. opinion in, 320
    by investment committees, 327
    monthly stakeholder reviews, 68–69, 80–81
    teams' authority in, 318
    for turning insights into action, 62–63
    types of decisions, 61
Dedicated teams, 10
Deming, W. Edwards, 322
Design:
    business concept, x
    of experiments, 43
    shaping ideas, 15–23
    of teams, 3–13
Design for Delight program (Intuit), 120
Design loop, 18–19
Desirability hypotheses, 32–34, 39
Desirability risk, xi
Direction, for teams, 11
Discovery experiments, 94–95, 101–229
    Boomerang, 204–207
    brochures, 194–199
    Buy a Feature, 226–229
    card sorting, 222–225

Customer Interviews, 106–113
customer support analysis, 142–145
data analysis, 104–105, 126–145
data sheets, 190–193
A Day in the Life, 116–121
Discovery Survey, 122–125
Discussion Forums, 134–137
discussion prototypes, 104–105, 162–213
email campaigns, 162–167
Expert Stakeholder Interviews, 115
Explainer Videos, 200–203
exploration, 104–125
Feature Stub, 156–159
404 test, 160–161
interest discovery, 104–105, 146–175
link tracking, 152–155
online ads, 146–151
paper prototypes, 182–185
Partner & Supplier Interviews, 114
preference and prioritization, 104–105, 218–229
Pretend to Own, 208–213
Product Box, 214–217
referral programs, 172–175
sales force feedback, 138–141
Search Trend Analysis, 126–129
selecting, 94–95
social media campaigns, 168–171
Speed Boat, 218–221
storyboards, 186–189
3D print, 176–181
types of, 94–95, 104–105
web traffic analysis, 130–133
Discovery Survey, 122–125
    details of, 124
    function of, 122
    overview of, 123

pairings for, 125
Discrete hypotheses, 31
Discussion Forums, 134–137
    details of, 136
    function of, 134
    overview of, 135
    pairings for, 137
Discussion prototypes, 104–105, 162–213
    Boomerang, 204–207
    brochures, 194–199
    data sheets, 190–193
    Explainer Videos, 200–203
    paper prototypes, 182–185
    Pretend to Own, 208–213
    storyboards, 186–189
    3D print, 176–181
Distributed Teams, experiment ceremonies for, 70
Diversity, on teams, 7

E

Ellis, Sean, 280–281
Email campaigns, 162–167
    details of, 164
    function of, 162
    overview of, 163
    pairings for, 165
    Product Hunt case study, 166–167
Engagement, 170, 210
Entrepreneurs, 7. See also Solopreneurs
Entrepreneurial iterative approach, 8
Entrepreneurship, of investment committee members, 327

Environment:
  creating, 320
  investment committee impact on, 327
  of teams, 10–11
Ethics, 86
Ethnography, 116
Evidence:
  analyzing, 51
  on Assumptions Map, 38
  confidence level in, 56–57
  defined, 52
  from different experiments, 53
  incomparable, 314
  insights from, 51, 54–55
  opinion vs., 320
  quality of, 57
  sales force feedback, 140
  social media campaigns, 170
  strength of, See Evidence strength
  3D print, 178
  type of, 57
  weak, 315
Evidence strength, 52–53, 57
  and confidence level, 57
  discovery experiments, 105
  and selection of experiments, 93
  validation experiments, 235
Execution of business ideas, premature, viii
Experiment(s), 41–47
  avoiding pitfalls in, 313–315
  blocker, 85
  components of, 45
  confidence level and number of, 57
  designing, 43
  discovery, 94–95. See also Discovery
    experiments
  ethics in, 86

  guidelines for, 87
  leading through, 317–321
  organizing for, 323–327
  principles of experiment flow, 82–85
  to reduce risk of uncertainty, 47
  running, 43
  selecting, 91–93
  sequences of, 98–99
  splitting-columns, 85
  Test Cards for, 45, 46
  too few, 315
  validation, 96–97. See also Validation
    experiments
Experiment boards, 83–85
Experiment ceremonies, 67–81
  bi-weekly retrospective, 78–79
  for Co-Located Teams, 70
  daily standups, 74–75
  for Distributed Teams, 70
  monthly stakeholder reviews, 80–81
  time commitment for, 71
  weekly learning, 76–77
  weekly planning, 72–73
Experiment-driven behaviors, 8
Experiment flow principles, 82–85
  continuous experimentation, 82, 85
  limit experiments in progress,
    82, 84
  visualize experiments, 82, 83
Experiment pitfalls, 313–315
Experiment sequences, 98–99
Expert Stakeholder Interviews, 115
Explainer Videos, 200–203
  details of, 202
  function of, 200
  overview of, 201
  pairings for, 203

Exploration experiments, 104–125
  Customer Interviews, 106–113
  A Day in the Life, 116–121
  Discovery Survey, 122–125
  Expert Stakeholder Interviews, 115
  Partner & Supplier Interviews, 114
Extended team:
  monthly stakeholder reviews for, 80–81
  weekly learning meetings for, 76–77
Extreme Programming Spike, 306–309
  details of, 308
  function of, 306
  overview of, 307
  pairings for, 309

F

Facilitation, 318
Facilitative leadership style, 11
Failure to learn and adapt, 315
Fake news, 86
Farm and ranch insurance, 198–199
Feasibility hypotheses, 32, 33, 39
Feasibility risk, xi
Feature Stub, 156–159
  details of, 158
  function of, 156
  overview of, 157
  pairings for, 159
Feynman, Richard, 40
Financial risk, 35
Follow-Me-Home program (Intuit), 120–121
404 test, 160–161
Friends, 174
Friend click through rate, 174

Friend conversion rate, 174
Functional silos, 324
Funding:
    crowdfunding, 266–269
    innovation approach to, 325
    in selecting experiments, 92
    for teams, 10
    venture capital approach to, 325–327

G

Gandhi, Indira, 58
Gascoigne, Joel, 292–293
Generation, in design loop, 18
Guest, Chris, 305

H

Hancock, Herbie, 90
Hawkins, Jeff, 212–213
Highly regulated companies, experiment
        sequence for, 99
Hohmann, Luke, 215, 219, 227
Hoover, Ryan, 166–167
Hypotheses, 27–39
    Assumptions Mapping, 36–39
    characteristics of, 31
    confidence level for, 56–57
    creating, 30
    creating multiple experiments for, 46
    identifying, 29, 37, 39
    prioritizing, 29, 38, 39
    in selecting experiments, 92
    types of, 32–35

I

Ideas:
    commonly required skills for testing, 6
    identifying, 29
    premature execution of, viii
    shaping, 15–23
Idea Maze, 81
Ideation, in design loop, 19
Importance:
    on Assumptions Map, 38
    ranking, 279
Imposter Judo, 205. See also Boomerang
Incomparable data/evidence, 314
Infrastructure risk, 35
Innovation Corps (I-Corps), 181
Innovation funding, 325
Innovation Games (Hohmann), 215, 219, 227
Innovation portfolio, 326
Insights:
    defined, 51
    from evidence, 51, 54–55
    generating, 44
    turned into action, 62–63
Interaction prototypes, 234–259, 278–283
    clickable prototypes, 236–239
    Concierge, 248–253
    life-sized prototypes, 254–259
    Mash-Up, 244–247
    Single Feature MVP, 240–243
    validation surveys, 278–283
Interest discovery experiments, 104–105,
        146–175
    email campaigns, 162–167
    Feature Stub, 156–159
    404 test, 160–161
    link tracking, 152–155
    online ads, 146–151
    referral programs, 172–175
    social media campaigns, 168–171
Interviews:
    Customer Interviews, 106–113
    Expert Stakeholder Interviews, 115
    Partner & Supplier Interviews, 114
Intuit, 120–121
Investment committees, 327
Iterative process, x

J

Jackson, Phil, 2

K

Kaufer, Stephen, 161
Key Partners, 114
Key performance indicators (KPIs), 11
Khosla, Vinod, 312
Kill, decision to, 61, 80
KPIs (key performance indicators), 11
Krawcheck, Sallie, 100

L

Landing page, see Simple landing page
Language, impact of, 318
Leaders:
    creating, 321
    role in working with teams, 318–321

team environment design by, 10
venture capitalist approach by,
325–327
Leading through experimentation,
317–321
creating more leaders, 321
improving business models, 318
inventing business models, 319
steps to take in, 320
Lead time, 250, 286
Learning, 49–57
and confidence level, 56–57
from evidence, 52–53
failure to learn, 315
gleaning insights from evidence, 54–55
Learning Cards, 54–55, 62
Learning meetings, weekly, 68–69, 76–77
Letters of intent (LOIs), 294–299
details of, 296
function of, 294
overview of, 295
pairings for, 297
Thrive Smart Systems case study, 298–299
Life-sized prototypes, 254–259
details of, 256
function of, 254
overview of, 255
pairings for, 257
Zoku case study, 258–259
Limiting experiments in progress, 82, 84
Link tracking, 152–155
details of, 154
function of, 152
overview of, 153
pairings for, 155
LOIs, see Letters of intent
Lynkydink, 167

M

McGrath, Rita, 14
Makeshift, 167
Managing, 65–87
ethics in experimentation, 86
experiment ceremonies, 67–81
guidelines for experiments, 87
principles of experiment flow,
82–85
Market research, 126
Market risk, 34
Mash-Up, 244–247
details of, 246
function of, 244
overview of, 245
pairings for, 247
Masters, Dave, 253
Mastrogiacomo, Stefano, 12
Meetings, 161. See also Experiment
ceremonies
Mindset:
avoid experiment pitfalls, 313–315
lead through experimentation,
317–321
organize for experiments, 323–327
Mock sale, 288–293
Buffer case study, 292–293
details of, 290
function of, 288
overview of, 289
pairings for, 291
Monthly stakeholder reviews, 68–69,
80–81
Move, Inc., 252
Multi-tasking, 84

N

National Security Agency (NSA), 180–181
Net promoter score (NPS), 281

O

Online ads, 146–151
details of, 150
function of, 146
overview of, 147–149
pairings for, 151
Open rates, 164
Organizing for experiments, 323–327
innovation portfolio, 326
investment committees, 327
silos vs. cross-functional teams, 324
thinking like a venture capitalist, 325
Outsourcing of testing, 315

P

Palm Pilot, wooden, 212–213
Paper prototypes, 182–185
details of, 184
function of, 182
overview of, 183
pairings for, 185
Partner & Supplier Interviews, 114
Persevere, decision to, 61, 80
Pinocchio experiment, see Pretend to Own
Pivot, decision to, 61, 80

Planning meetings, weekly, 68–69, 72–73
Pop-up store, 300–305
    details of, 302
    function of, 300
    overview of, 301
    pairings for, 303
    Topology Eyewear case study, 304–305
Precise hypotheses, 31
Preference and prioritization experiments,
        104–105, 218–229
    Buy a Feature, 226–229
    card sorting, 222–225
    Product Box, 214–217
    Speed Boat, 218–221
Premature execution of business ideas, viii
Presale, 274–277
    details of, 276
    function of, 274
    overview of, 275
    pairings for, 277
Pretend to Own, 208–213
    details of, 210
    function of, 208
    overview of, 209
    pairings for, 211
    wooden Palm Pilot case study, 212–213
Price testing, 106, 288
Prioritization:
    of features, 226
    of hypotheses, 29, 38, 39
Product Box, 214–217
    details of, 216
    function of, 214
    overview of, 215
    pairings for, 217
Product Hunt, 166–167
Prototypes:
    business, 19
    clickable, 236–239
    discussion, 104–105, 162–213
    interaction, 234–259, 278–283
    life-sized, 254–259
    paper, 182–185
    rapid prototyping, 176–181
Pull-based customer acquisition, 149
Purchase conversion rate, 276, 290
Push-based customer acquisition, 148

Q

Questioning assumptions, 8

R

Ranking:
    with card sorting, 224
    with Customer Interviews, 113
    with validation surveys, 279
Rapid prototyping, 176–181
Realtor.com, 252–253
Rebranding competitor products, 205
Referral programs, 172–175
    details of, 174
    function of, 172
    overview of, 173
    pairings for, 175
Resources, teams' access to, 11
Retrospective meetings, bi-weekly, 68–69,
        78–79
Ries, Eric, 83

Risk:
    desirability, xi
    feasibility, xi
    financial, 35
    infrastructure, 35
    market, 34
    reducing, xi, 47, 93
    of uncertainty, 47, 93
    viability, xi
Rodriguez, Diego, 120
Rowberry, Grant, 299
Run time, 43
    discovery experiments, 105
    validation experiments, 235

S

Saffo, Paul, 319
Sales force feedback, 138–141
    details of, 140
    function of, 138
    overview of, 139
    pairings for, 141
Scaling:
    organic, 172
    premature, 285
Sean Ellis Test, 280–281
Search only ads, 149
Search Trend Analysis, 126–129
    details of, 128
    evidence from, 53
    function of, 126
    learning from, 55
    overview of, 127
    pairings for, 129

Selecting experiments, 91–93
    questions to ask in, 92
    rules of thumb for, 93
Sequences of experiments, 98–99
Setup time:
    discovery experiments, 105
    validation experiments, 235
Shaping ideas, 15–23
    business design, 18–19
    Business Model Canvas, 20–21
    Value Proposition Canvas, 22–23
Shares, number of, 202, 268
Shaw, George Bernard, 64
Silos, cross-functional teams vs., 324
Simple landing page, 260–265
    considerations with, 264–265
    details of, 262
    function of, 260
    overview of, 261
    pairings for, 263
Simulations, 234–235, 284–309
    Extreme Programming Spike, 306–309
    letter of intent, 294–299
    mock sale, 288–293
    pop-up store, 300–305
    Wizard of Oz, 284–287
Single Feature MVP, 240–243
    details of, 242
    function of, 240
    overview of, 241
    pairings for, 243
Sinha, Rashmi, 26
Skillsets, 6
Social media ads, 148
Social media campaigns, 168–171
    details of, 170
    function of, 168

overview of, 169
    pairings for, 171
Solopreneurs:
    bi-weekly retrospectives for, 79
    daily standups for, 75
    monthly stakeholder reviews for, 81
    weekly learning meetings for, 77
    weekly planning meetings for, 73
Speed Boat, 218–221
    details of, 220
    function of, 218
    overview of, 219
    pairings for, 221
Split Test, 270–273
    details of, 272
    function of, 270
    overview of, 271
    pairings for, 273
Splitting columns experiments, 85
Srinivasan, Balaji, 81
Stakeholder reviews:
    Expert Stakeholder Interviews, 115
    and investment decisions, 327
    monthly, 68–69, 80–81
Standup meetings, daily, 68–69, 74–75
Startup Team:
    bi-weekly retrospectives for, 79
    daily standups for, 75
    monthly stakeholder reviews for, 81
    weekly learning meetings for, 77
    weekly planning meetings for, 73
Storyboards, 186–189
    details of, 188
    function of, 186
    overview of, 187
    pairings for, 189
Strategy, team, 11

Strong evidence, 52–53. *See also* Evidence
    strength
"Strong opinions, weakly held" approach,
    319
Sub-brands, 265
Support, for teams, 11
Supporting team, 36
Synthesis, in design loop, 18

T

Target customers, finding, 147
Task completion, 184, 206, 238
Team(s), 3–13
    alignment on, 12–13
    behaviors of, 8–9
    bi-weekly retrospectives for, 78–79
    Co-Located, 70
    core, 36. *See also* Core teams
    cross-functional, 6, 324
    daily standups for, 74–75
    design of, 6–7
    Distributed, 70
    diversity on, 7
    environment of, 10–11, 327
    growing, 9
    leaders' role with, 318–321
    monthly stakeholder reviews for, 80–81
    siloed, 324
    supporting, 36
    weekly learning meetings for, 76–77
    weekly planning meetings for, 72–73
Team Alignment Map, 12–13
Testable hypotheses, 31
Test Cards, 45–46

Testing, ix, xi–xii
    commonly required skills for, 6
    decide phase in, 59–63
    experiment phase in, 41–47
    hypothesize phase in, 27–39
    learn phase in, 49–57
    manage phase in, 65–87
    outsourcing of, 315
    to reduce risk, xi
    tools for, 7
Themes:
    discovery experiments, 105
    validation experiments, 235
3D print, 176–181
    CubeSats case study, 180–181
    details of, 178
    function of, 176
    overview of, 177
    pairings for, 179
Thrive Smart Systems, 298–299
Time commitment:
    for experiment ceremonies, 68, 71
    in selecting experiments, 92
Time trap, 314
Topology Eyewear, 304–305
Toyota, 120

U

Uncertainty:
    reducing, 47, 93
    in selecting experiments, 92
Urgency, in selecting experiments, 92

V

Validation experiments, 96–97, 231–309
    call to action, 260–277
    clickable prototypes, 236–239
    Concierge, 248–253
    crowdfunding, 266–269
    Extreme Programming Spike, 306–309
    interaction prototypes, 236–259,
        278–283
    letter of intent, 294–299
    life-sized prototypes, 254–259
    Mash-Up, 244–247
    mock sale, 288–293
    pop-up store, 300–305
    presale, 274–277
    selecting, 96–97
    simple landing page, 260–265
    simulation, 284–309
    Single Feature MVP, 240–243
    Split Test, 270–273
    types of, 96–97, 234–235
    validation surveys, 278–283
    Wizard of Oz, 284–287
Validation surveys, 278–283
    details of, 282
    function of, 278
    overview of, 279–281
    pairings for, 283
    types of, 279
Value Map, 22
Value Proposition Canvas, 22–23, 34
Value Proposition Design, 19, 22
Vaporware, 86
Venture capital funding approach, 325–327
Viability hypotheses, 32, 33, 39
Viability risk, xi
Views, number of, 202, 268, 290
Viewer comments, 202, 268
Visualizing experiments, 82, 83

W

Wang, Cher, 316
Weak data, 315
Weak evidence, 52–53, 315. *See also* Evidence
    strength
Web traffic analysis, 130–133
    details of, 132
    function of, 130
    overview of, 131
    pairings for, 133
Weekly meetings:
    learning, 68–69, 76–77
    planning, 68–69, 72–73
Wizard of Oz, 284–287
    details of, 286
    function of, 284
    overview of, 285
    pairings for, 287
Wooden Palm Pilot, 212–213

Z

Zoku, 258–259

High-Impact Tools for Teams

Published by John Wiley & Sons, Inc., Hoboken, New Jersey.
Published simultaneously in Canada.

For general information on our other products and services or for technical support, please contact our Customer Care Department within the United States at (800) 762-2974, outside the United States at (317) 572-3993 or fax (317) 572-4002.

Wiley publishes in a variety of print and electronic formats and by print-on-demand. Some material included with standard print versions of this book may not be included in e-books or in print-on-demand. If this book refers to media such as a CD or DVD that is not included in the version you purchased, you may download this material at http://booksupport.wiley.com. For more information about Wiley products, visit www.wiley.com.

Library of Congress Cataloging-in-Publication Data:
ISBN 9781119602385 (Paperback)
ISBN 9781119602804 (ePDF)
ISBN 9781119792024 (ePDF Print Replica)
ISBN 9781119724490 (ePub Fixed format)

Cover illustration: Blexbolex
Cover design: Alan Smith

10 9 8 7 6 5 4 3 2 1

You're holding a powerful toolkit to create alignment, build trust, and get results fast. Rediscover the joy of teamwork with these five...

High-Impact Tools for Teams

strategyzer.com/teams

Written by
Stefano Mastrogiacomo
Alex Osterwalder

Designed by
Alan Smith
Trish Papadakos

WILEY

"Management is about human beings. Its task is to make people capable of joint performance."

Peter Drucker, Management Thinker

Contents

Foreword
p. viii

Seven Great Thinkers
Who Inspired This Book
p. x

Meet the
Strategyzer Series
p. xii

Essentials
What makes teams
underperform and how
to get better results
p. 1

1

Discover the Team Alignment Map
What it is and how it works

1.1
Getting Started: The Four Pillars
of the Team Alignment Map p. 34

1.2
Planning Who Does What
with the Team Alignment Map
(Planning Mode) p. 72

1.3
Keeping Team Members on
Track (Assessment Mode) p. 90

2

Put the Map into Action
How to use the
Team Alignment Map

2.1
The Team Alignment Map
for Meetings p. 114

2.2
The Team Alignment Map
for Projects p. 132

2.3
The Team Alignment Map
for Organizational Alignment p. 154

3

Trust Among Team Members
Four tools to create a high-trust
climate and increased
psychological safety

3.1
The Team Contract p. 184

3.2
The Fact Finder p. 204

3.3
The Respect Card p. 220

3.4
The Nonviolent Requests Guide
p. 236

4

Dive Deeper
Discover the science behind
the tools and the book

4.1
Mutual Understanding
and Common Ground p. 258

4.2
Trust and Psychological Safety p. 266

4.3
Relationship Types p. 274

4.4
Face and Politeness p. 282

Foreword

Amy Edmondson

If you are leading a team – or plan to any-time soon – you'll want to keep this book close at hand. Most leaders today recognize that their organizations are deeply dependent on teams to accelerate innovation and digitalization, address changing customer demands, and cope with sudden disruptive events such as the global pandemic, social unrest, and recession.

But just putting a team together does not ensure its success. Teams fail on a regular basis. Launched with a meaningful goal, the right people to accomplish it, and even sufficient resources, time and time again, teams nevertheless struggle to deliver on their undeniable potential. They get bogged down by coordination lapses, ineffective meetings, unproductive conflicts, and dysfunctional group dynamics – leading to frustration, delays, and flawed decisions. Researchers call these factors "process losses" – in an effort to explain the gap between inputs (skills, goals, and resources) and outcomes (team performance or member satisfaction). Even when teams seem to get work done, their performance may be suboptimal – conventional rather than

innovative, or come at a cost of high levels of overwork, stress, and disengagement.

It doesn't have to be this way.

Stefano Mastrogiacomo and Alex Osterwalder show us how teams can thrive by using simple practices that work. They offer a playbook any team can use to immediately put itself on a path to full participation, productive conflict, and steady progress. With its engaging illustrations, accessible tools, and thoughtful sequences of activities that teams can use to avoid (and recover from) predictable team problems of all sorts, this book is an invaluable resource. I have long believed that simple tools can bring synergy within reach by nudging team behavior in the right direction. And this book is full of such tools – activities and guidelines that will serve any team well.

Yet, what is particularly powerful about *High Impact Tools for Teams* is its emphasis on team process and the psychological climate. Most authors address one or the other – offering a step-by-step guide to manage a team project or else explaining the benefits of a psychologically safe climate that allows teams to learn and innovate.

This book offers simple tools to do both. When speaking up in a team is thwarted by a poor climate, innovation suffers, problems fester and sometimes turn into major failures. But creating psychological safety can sound like an elusive goal, especially for team leaders under pressure to deliver results. Drawing from my research, and that of so many others whose work underpins this terrific resource, Stefano and Alex demystify the quest for a healthy team culture – and walk us through how to create it. For this reason alone, I'm excited about this book. It injects new energy – and new tools – into the quest to build teams that can thrive in the 21st century by fully engaging the energy and expertise of all who work in them.

Even if teamwork will always be challenging, leaders now have access to practical, easy-to-use tools to help teams work well. Leaders who adopt them with passionate intent will be poised to build the kind of teams that companies need and employees want.

– Amy C. Edmondson
Harvard Business School, Cambridge, MA

Seven Great Thinkers Who Inspired This Book

Herbert Clark

Herbert H. Clark is a psycholinguist and professor of psychology at Stanford University. The very foundations of this book lie in his works on language use in human coordination. The design of the **Team Alignment Map** is inspired by his research on mutual understanding and the coordination of joint activities.

Alan Fiske

Alan Page Fiske is professor of psychological anthropology at the University of California, Los Angeles. His works on the nature of human relationships and cross-cultural variations have disrupted our understanding of what "social" means and resulted in the actual design of the **Team Contract**.

Yves Pigneur

Yves Pigneur is professor of management and information systems at the University of Lausanne, Switzerland. His work in design thinking and tool design helped us bridge the difficult gap between theory and practice. Without his conceptual support and guidance, this book and all the tools it contains would simply not exist.

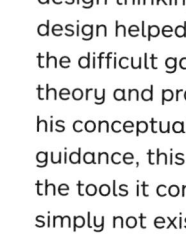

Amy Edmondson

Amy Edmondson is professor of leadership and management at the Harvard Business School. The integration of the four add-ons has been influenced by her work on trust in teams, in particular the notion of psychological safety among team members. Her research provided us with great insight in understanding the impact of trust in cross-functional teamwork and on innovation.

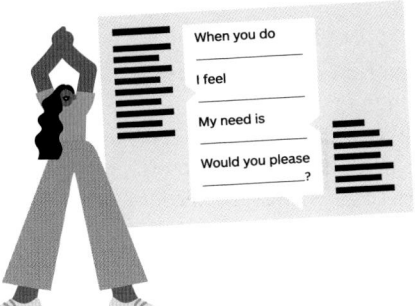

Steven Pinker

Steven Pinker is professor of psychology at Harvard. His works on psycholinguistics and social relations, in particular the use of indirect language and polite requests in cooperative games, inspired the design of the **Respect Card**. His recent works on common knowledge shape our future developments.

Françoise Kourilsky

Françoise Kourilsky is a psychologist and coach specializing in change management. She pioneered the introduction of systemics and brief therapy techniques to manage change in organization, working directly with Paul Watzlawick of the Mental Research Institute, Palo Alto, California. We owe her the **Fact Finder**, which is a new interpretation of her "language compass."

Marshall Rosenberg

Marshall Rosenberg was a psychologist, mediator, and author. He founded the Center for Nonviolent Communication and worked worldwide as a peacemaker. His work on the language of conflict resolution and empathetic communication inspired the design of the **Nonviolent Requests Guide**.

Meet the Strategyzer Series

We believe that simple, visual, practical tools can transform the effectiveness of a person, a team, and their organization. While new business ideas fail, existing businesses are under constant threat of disruption and obsolescence. Unacceptable amounts of time and money are lost each year due to lack of clarity and alignment on fundamental business issues. Each of our books has a set of purpose-built tools and processes to tackle specific challenges. These challenges are interconnected, so we've meticulously designed the tools to stand on their own and integrate with each other to create the world's most integrated strategy and innovation toolkit. Get one or get them all, either way — you'll get results.

strategyzer.com/books

Business Model Generation

A handbook for visionaries, game changers, and challengers striving to defy outmoded business models and design tomorrow's enterprises. Adapt to harsh new realities and get out in front of your competitors with *Business Model Generation*.

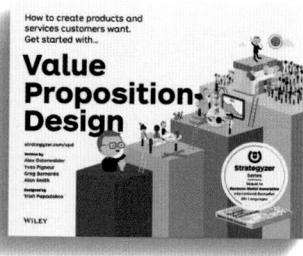

Value Proposition Design

Tackle the core challenge of every business — creating compelling products and services customers want to buy. Discover a repeatable process and the right tools to create products that sell.

Testing Business Ideas

Discover a library of 44 experiments to systematically test your business ideas. Combine the Business Model Canvas and Value Proposition Canvas with Assumptions Mapping and other powerful lean startup tools.

The Invincible Company

Become unstoppable by simultaneously managing a portfolio of existing businesses and exploring a pipeline of potential new growth engines. Discover practical and essential tools including the Business Portfolio Map, Innovation Metrics, the Culture Map, and a library of Business Model Patterns.

High-Impact Tools for Teams

Five powerful teamwork and change management tools to successfully implement new business models. Make every innovation project a success with the Team Alignment Map, the Team Contract, the Fact Finder, the Respect Card, and the Nonviolent Requests Guide.

Essentials

What makes teams underperform and how to get better results

"Talk is the technology
of leadership."

Jeanne Liedtka, Strategist

Our people are top-notch.

So, how come we have all these problems?

When was the last time you enjoyed contributing to a team?

50%

of meetings are considered unproductive and a waste of time.

Atlassian *

$37B

is the salary cost in USD of unnecessary meetings for U.S. businesses.

Atlassian *

29%

of projects are successful.

*Chaos Report,
The Standish Group, 2019*

75%

of cross-functional teams are dysfunctional.

Behnam Tabrizi, "75% of Cross-Functional Teams Are Dysfunctional,"

Harvard Business Review, 2015

10%

of team members
agree about who is on
their team (120 teams).

Diane Coutu, "Why Teams Don't Work,"
Harvard Business Review, 2009

66%

of U.S. workers are not
engaged or are actively
disengaged at work.

Jim Harter, Gallup, 2018 **

95%

of a company's
employees are
unaware of, or
do not understand,
its strategy.

Robert Kaplan and David Norton,
"The Office of Strategy Management,"
Harvard Business Review, 2005

1/3

of value-added
collaborations come
from only 3% to 5%
of employees.

Rob Cross, Reb Rebele, and
Adam Grant, "Collaborative
Overload," Harvard Business Review,
2016

* *"You Waste a Lot of Time at Work," Atlassian, www.atlassian.com/time-wasting-at-work-infographic*
** *"Employee Engagement on the Rise in the U.S.," Gallup, news.gallup.com/poll/241649/employee-engagement-rise.aspx*

What Makes Teams Underperform

Teams underperform when members work *around* each other and not *with* each other, something that happens when the team climate is unsafe and the team activities are poorly aligned.

Working around each other is an exhausting journey. Endless meetings and skyrocketing budgets for poor results usually occur in a poor team climate where most members work under high pressure and feel isolated and unhappy. This is the daily life of many team members, without caricaturing things as surveys illustrate.

We are capable of doing more than merely work around each other. We can work with each other, for real. When this happens we can accomplish the nearly impossible with passion. We may not necessarily realize it but in that moment, we are experiencing a "high-performing team." Something people coin in retrospect because good results gradually add up.

We have experienced both types of teams, and this book contains what we have learned over the past 20 years. Our key learning is that joint success and failure largely depend on how well we manage our day-to-day interactions, at two levels:

- The team activities: having an obsession for mutual clarity — what's the mission, who is doing what, is it clear for everyone?
- The team climate: carefully nurturing strong, trust-based relationships.

We believe in teams and we believe in tools. This is why we spent the past five years designing and revamping tools that do just that. Tools that help team members improve:

1. the team activities through better team alignment, and
2. the team climate by building psychologically safer work environments.

Only teams can tackle the complexity of the challenges brought by an interconnected world. We're going through a period of spectacular changes: game-changing technologies and unprecedented lockdowns are disrupting entire industries. Organizations are forced to innovate and deliver at an unprecedented pace, and teams are, for us, the building block. The need to revisit the way we work together has never been greater.

As the visionary Peter Drucker announced long ago: The critical question is not "How can I achieve?" but "What can I contribute?" We couldn't agree more. We hope the Team Alignment Map and the other tools presented in this book help you as much as they help us become better team contributors, every day.

Unsafe Team Climate
Signs of a poor team climate

- Lack of trust between colleagues and teams
- Internal competition
- Disengagement
- Lack of recognition
- Fear: it's difficult to speak up
- Over-collaboration
- Lost joy of working together

Misaligned Team Activities
Signs of poor alignment of team activities

- It's unclear who does what
- Invaluable time is lost in endless meetings
- Work is delivered too slowly
- Priorities keep changing and no one can figure out why
- Duplicate projects and projects overlap
- Team members work in silos
- A lot of work is done with poor results and little impact

Activities Get Stuck in Misaligned Teams

In concrete terms, alignment is communicating to create common ground, common knowledge, shared or mutual understanding (all used as synonyms in this book — Dive Deeper, p. 252). Common ground enables team members to anticipate the actions of others and act accordingly through aligned predictions. The richer a team's common ground, the better the mutual predictions between team members and the overall execution, thanks to a seamless division of labor and a consistent integration of the individual parts. Interestingly, conversation — face-to-face dialogue — is still the most effective technology on Earth to build relevant common ground.

Adapted from: Herbert H. Clark, Using Language (Cambridge University Press, 1996). Simon Garrod and Martin J. Pickering, "Joint Action, Interactive Alignment, and Dialogue," Topics in Cognitive Science 1, no. 2 (2009): 292–304.

How Team Alignment Works

Successful alignment
Anything teams achieve, from having a party to building an airplane, is a by-product of team alignment. Alignment is the process of making individual contributions converge to achieve a shared goal for mutual benefit. It transforms individuals going about their business into successful team contributors. Working in a team requires more effort than working alone; team members must constantly synchronize with each other in addition to doing their own part of the work. The payoff is achieving (greater) goals that can't be accomplished alone.

Cooperation for Mutual Outcome

Unsuccessful alignment
Expect only poor results from a misaligned team. Unsuccessful communication prevents the creation of relevant common ground; participants do not understand each other and mispredict each other's actions. This causes team members to carry out tasks with important perception gaps. The division of work and the integration of the individual parts goes off track and the lack of collaboration is inefficient and costly. The intended results are not achieved as expected.

Successful communication
Team members openly exchange relevant information.

Relevant common ground
Mutual understanding is established among team members; they are aligned on what needs to be achieved and how.

Effective coordination
Team members make successful predictions about each other; coordination is harmonious and individual contributions integrate successfully.

Mutual benefit

Communication
Information team members share verbally and non-verbally, synchronously and asynchronously.

Common Ground
Knowledge team members know they have in common, also known as common knowledge or mutual knowledge.

Coordination
Tasks team members need to perform to work together harmoniously.

Outcome

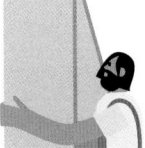

Unsuccessful communication
Team members do not exchange relevant information.

Low or irrelevant common ground
Perception gaps build up while team members execute their individual parts.

Coordination surprises
Individual contributions are not integrated with one another. Bad surprises accumulate due to inefficient coordination.

Mutual loss

An Unsafe Team Climate Undermines Innovation

I feel insecure: I don't want to look ignorant, incompetent, intrusive, or negative. Better to not take risks.

I stay silent and don't share crucial information

Adapted from Amy Edmondson, "Psychological Safety and Learning Behavior in Work Teams," *Administrative Science Quarterly* 44, no. 2 (1999): 350–383.

Psychologically unsafe environment

Team members protect themselves from embarrassment and other possible threats by remaining silent when the climate is psychologically unsafe. The team doesn't engage in collective learning behaviors and that results in poor team performance.

+
No learning behaviors

Low common ground
The team's common ground (or common knowledge) is not updated. Perception gaps increase between team members and the team relies on outdated information.
↓

Low team learning
Habitual or automatic behaviors keep being repeated, despite changes in context.
↓

Low team performance
Assumptions are not revised and plans are not corrected. The work performed is not in line with the actual situation and the delivered outcomes become inadequate.

↓

Status quo or worse

I am confident that errors won't be held against me. I respect and I feel respected by my team.

I speak up and share crucial information

Psychologically safe environment

Team members are not afraid to speak up when the climate is psychologically safe. Team members engage in a productive dialogue that fosters the proactive learning behaviors required to understand the environment and the clients and solve problems together efficiently.

+

Learning behaviors

Seeking feedback

Sharing info

Asking for help

Talking about errors

Experimenting

High common ground
The team's common ground (or common knowledge) is regularly updated with new and fresh information.
↓

High team learning
New information helps the team learn and adapt. Learning behaviors help the team make changes in assumptions and plans.
↓

High team performance
Open communications help the team coordinate effectively. Constant integration of learnings and adaptation to changes in the context result in relevant work.

↓

Complex problem-solving

The new hire will solve all our problems.

How Alignment and Safety Affect Team Impact

Today's challenges are too daunting for isolated talents working in pseudo teams. Complex problem solving requires real teamwork and that starts by building solid team alignment and a safe climate.

Low Effort Toward Mission

Low Ability to Achieve

× **Misaligned Activities**
× **Unsafe Climate**

Low Effort Toward Mission

High Ability to Achieve

× **Misaligned Activities**
√ **Safe Climate**

High Effort Toward Mission

Some Ability to Achieve

√ Aligned Activities
× Unsafe Climate

Best Effort Toward Mission

Best Ability to Achieve

√ Aligned Activities
√ Safe Climate

Impact

The Team Alignment Map Solution

Increase alignment and trust in your teams with the Team Alignment Map (TAM) and its four add-ons. They're simple, practical, and easy to implement.

Clarify and align every team member's contribution to the TAM in planning mode. A simple two-step process (named the forward pass and backward pass) facilitates planning and helps reduce risks.

Also use the TAM in assessment mode, for rapidly assessing teams and projects. Assessments are performed on the same canvas by adding four scales on which the team can vote, think, and act.

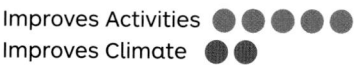

Improves Activities ●●●●●
Improves Climate ●●

Improve team activities

Use the Team Alignment Map to align the team activities

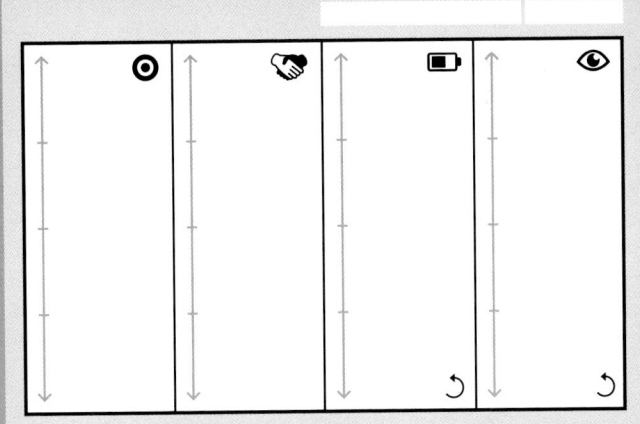

TAM – Planning Mode
Align together on the team mission and the objectives to be achieved by whom and how with the Team Alignment Map. Visually reduce fears and risks for higher chances of success. Use the TAM as a co-planning tool to engage people from the start and to build higher levels of buy-in and commitment (p. 72).

TAM – Assessment Mode
Don't let collaboration blind spots compromise your projects. TAM assessments are fast and reveal the unseen in a visual and neutral manner. Create genuine opportunities for productive dialogue, collective "aha" moments that do not stigmatize those who wish to speak up, and reinforce team learning behaviors (p. 90).

The Four Trust and Psychological Safety Add-Ons

Use the four add-ons to:

- Clarify the rules of the game with the Team Contract

- Ask good questions with the Fact Finder

- Demonstrate consideration for others with the Respect Card

- Manage conflict constructively with the Nonviolent Requests Guide

The Team Alignment Map and the Team Contract are co-creation tools. The Fact Finder, the Nonviolent Requests Guide, and the Respect Card are behavioral tools. They're used individually to improve everyday interactions.

Improves Activities ●●●●○
Improves Climate ●●●●●

Improve team climate

JOINT MISSION

Use the four trust add-ons to build a safer team climate

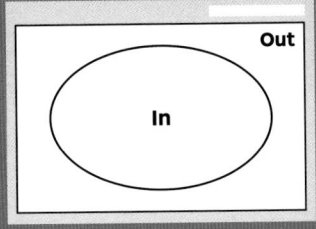

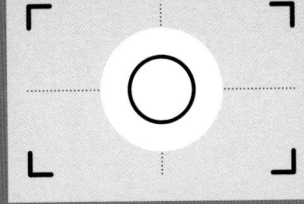

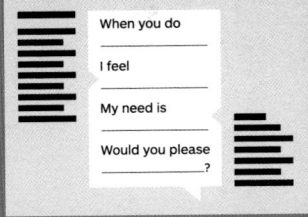

The Team Contract
Define team rules with the Team Contract. Address behaviors, values, decision-making, and communication, and frame expectations in terms of failure as a team. Create a transparent and fair environment that fosters team learning behaviors and harmony (see p. 184).

The Fact Finder
The Fact Finder proposes powerful questions that transform unproductive assumptions, judgments, limitations, and generalizations into observable facts and experiences. Inquire like a pro — restore clarity in discussions when you feel puzzled. Build more trust by demonstrating a genuine interest in what others are saying (see p. 204).

The Respect Card
The Respect Card suggests tips for being tactful and demonstrating consideration by (1) valuing others (2) demonstrating respect. This makes conversations less efficient from a task perspective but adds greatly to a safer team climate (see p. 220).

The Nonviolent Requests Guide
Don't make things worse by exploding emotionally; manage conflict constructively with the Nonviolent Requests Guide. Express legitimate negative feelings by using proper wording. Help others understand what's wrong and what should change in a nonaggressive manner and keep the team climate safe (see p. 236).

Common Challenges: The Team Alignment Map in Action

In Meetings

- Focus the team, p. 120
- Boost team members' engagement, p. 122
- Increase meeting impact, p. 124
- Make informed decisions, p. 126

In Projects

- Get projects off to a good start, p. 138
- Maintain alignment over time, p. 140
- Monitor tasks' progress, p. 144
- Reduce risks (while having fun) p. 148
- Align distributed teams, p. 150

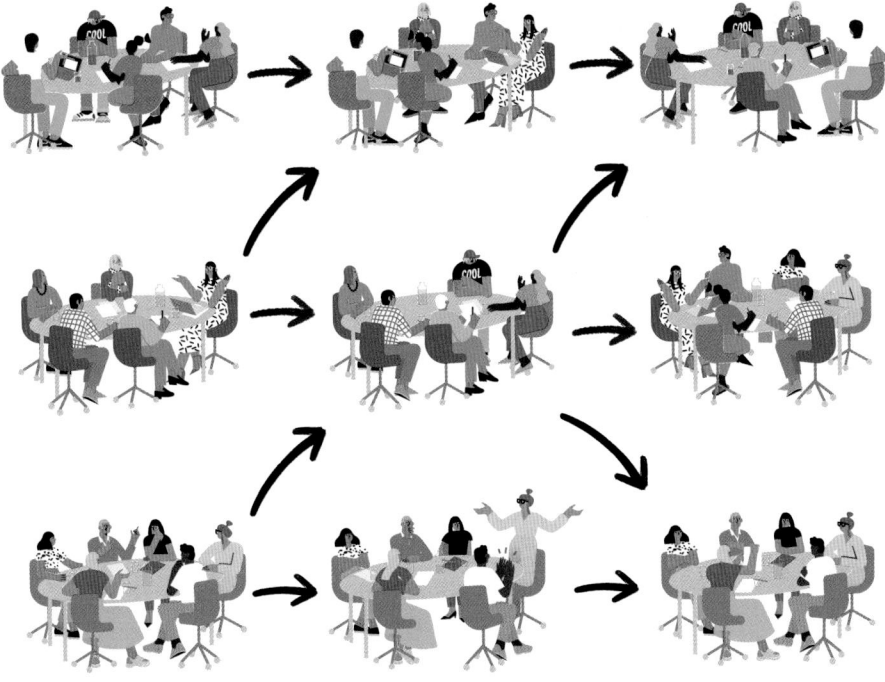

In Organizations

- Empower teams, p. 160
- Engage large groups, p. 162
- Facilitate collaboration across departments and functions, p. 164
- Negotiate and allocate resources, p. 166
- Integrate the TAM with strategy processes and tools, p. 168
- Assess the readiness of strategic initiatives, p. 170

What to Read First

Leaders of Organizations

You will benefit from reading the Essentials (p. 1), learning to De-silo organizations (p. 154). You can lead better conversations in your teams by getting a firm understanding of the Fact Finder (p. 204).

Entrepreneurs

You can start with the Essentials (p. 1) and learn how to use the TAM for Keeping projects on track (p. 132), and bring rules to a team by signing the Team Contract (p. 184).

Team Coaches

You should ensure that you know all about Aligning for successful team-work (p. 10–71) and understanding Are we still on track? (p. 90). Additionally, all of the add-on tools in Section 3 (p. 190) will be useful.

Project Leaders

You should thoroughly understand the Essentials (p. 1), and learn how to use the TAM for Keeping projects on track (p. 132). You can get rules in place on your team with the the Team Contract (p. 184).

Team Members

You can get a quick overview with Essentials (p. 1). You can then learn to Run move-to-action meetings (p. 118), and have better conversations with the Fact Finder (p. 204).

Educators

You must understand the Essentials (p. 1) first. You will find Aligning for successful team work (planning mode) (p. 72), and helping teams check: Are we still on track? (p. 90).

Discover the
Team Alignment Map

What it is and
how it works

"Working together itself takes work."

Herbert Clark, Psycholinguist

Overview

Understand the layout and content
of each column, plan and reduce risks,
and assess projects and teams.

1.1
Getting Started: The Four Pillars of the Team Alignment Map

How to describe joint objectives, team member commitments, required resources, and risks.

1.2
Planning Who Does What with the Team Alignment Map (Planning Mode)

Start with a forward pass (the plan), then make a backward pass (to lower any risks).

1.3
Keeping Team Members on Track (Assessment Mode)

Use the Team Alignment Map to assess team readiness or address ongoing problems.

1.1

Getting Started:
The Four Pillars of the
Team Alignment Map

How to describe joint objectives, team member
commitments, required resources, and risks.

The Workspace

The workspace is divided into two parts: the header area to frame the collaboration and the content area to guide meetings with regard to the four pillars. Each pillar covers a crucial aspect for any successful collaboration.

Joint Objectives
p. 40
What do we intend to achieve together, concretely?

Joint Commitments
p. 48
Who will do what?

Joint Resources
p. 56
What resources do we need?

Joint Risks
p. 64
What can prevent us from succeeding?

Dive Deeper
To discover the academic back-stage of the Team Alignment Map, please read p. 258: Mutual Understanding and Common Ground (in Psycholinguistics).

Mission
Give meaning and context by explaining the purpose of the meeting or the project (p. 38–39).

Period
Set a timeframe in days, months, or a deadline to start getting real (p. 38–39).

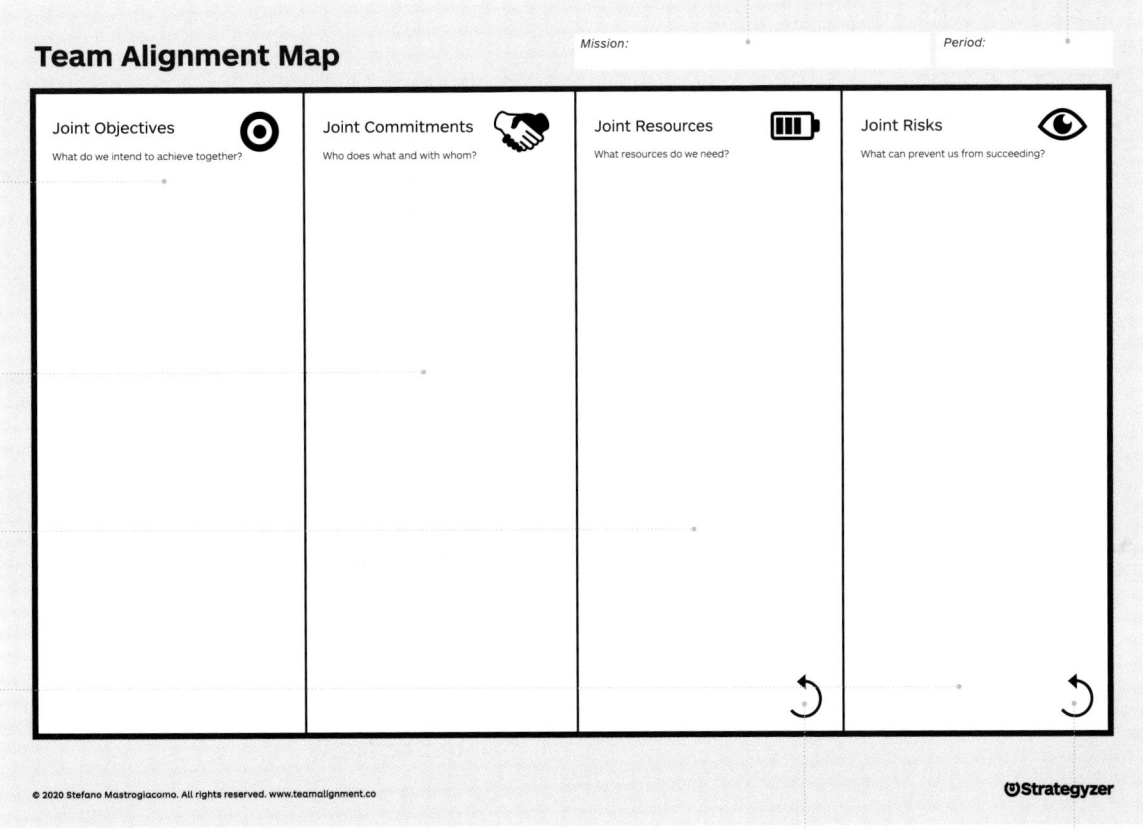

Team Alignment Map

Mission:

Period:

Joint Objectives	Joint Commitments	Joint Resources	Joint Risks
What do we intend to achieve together?	Who does what and with whom?	What resources do we need?	What can prevent us from succeeding?

© 2020 Stefano Mastrogiacomo. All rights reserved. www.teamalignment.co

Strategyzer

Content Area
Space to work.

Backward pass indicators
Visual reminders that risks must be addressed as a team (backward pass, p. 78–79).

Mission and Period

A mission is the starting point of any collaboration, the glue that brings everyone together. It helps everyone understand what's at stake and provides a rationale for personal engagement because:

- It is appealing, or
- Everyone feels concerned, or
- It is a necessary part of everyone's duties.

Participants constantly ask themselves "Why am I here?" when missions are unclear. Attention and participation drop, the conversation jumps from subject to subject, and dialogue becomes inconsistent, making participants feeling confused and often bored.

Periods set a time horizon for the team. Time limits are essential: they help remove exotic considerations in terms of goals and immerse everyone in the realm of concrete actions.

The header area helps participants simply understand why they are there and creates interest in listening and participating.

Describing Meaningful Missions

To benefit from higher levels of team buy-in and motivation, describe missions positively and from a participant's perspective. Respect these criteria as much as possible when writing down a mission: challenging, audacious, unique, unusual, or fun.

Example
- DO: Strengthen our profitability and secure our salaries for the next three years.
  [goal + benefit]
- DON'T: Reduce costs by 30%.

As described by Amy Edmondson, people must agree on and feel proud of their team's mission to motivate their personal efforts and overcome the relational and technical hurdles to succeed (Edmondson and Harvey 2017; Deci and Ryan 1985; Locke and Latham 1990).

Search keywords: mission statements; naming projects.

"Buy-In Check"

It's ideal for a mission to be validated using the following statement:

For the entire duration of the mission (M), every participant is able to give meaning to his or her personal contribution (X) by thinking:

"I am doing X because my group is doing M and requires my X, and that is meaningful for me."

Mission
What's the challenge?
What do we want to create
or improve?

Period
For how long?
Until when?

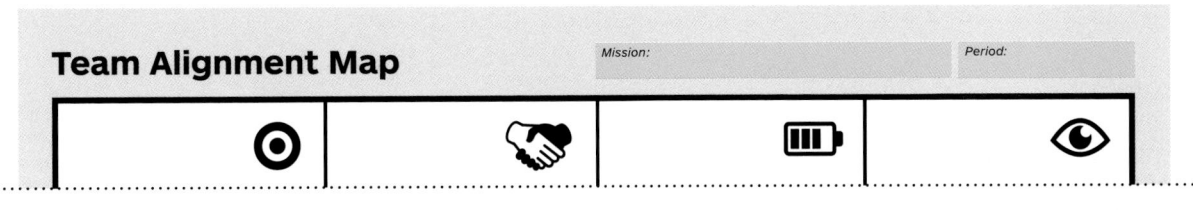

Team Alignment Map

| Mission: | Period: |

A mission can be described in various formats such as a purpose, challenge, problem, project name, and so on.

Any of these formats will work as long as the mission:
- Is crystal clear for all participants,
- Helps people project themselves in a positive outcome, and
- Generates a personal desire to contribute

Mission examples:

A period can be defined as:
- A duration: number of hours, days, weeks, or months.
- A deadline: a precise date or a range between two dates.

Period examples:

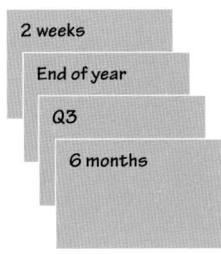

2 weeks

End of year

Q3

6 months

| Reduce time to market by 20% for all new products | Implement corporate social responsibility actions | Accelerate the onboarding of new colleagues | Annual Off-Site | Project X |

More
Clarity

More
Abstraction

Joint Objectives

What do we intend to achieve together, concretely?

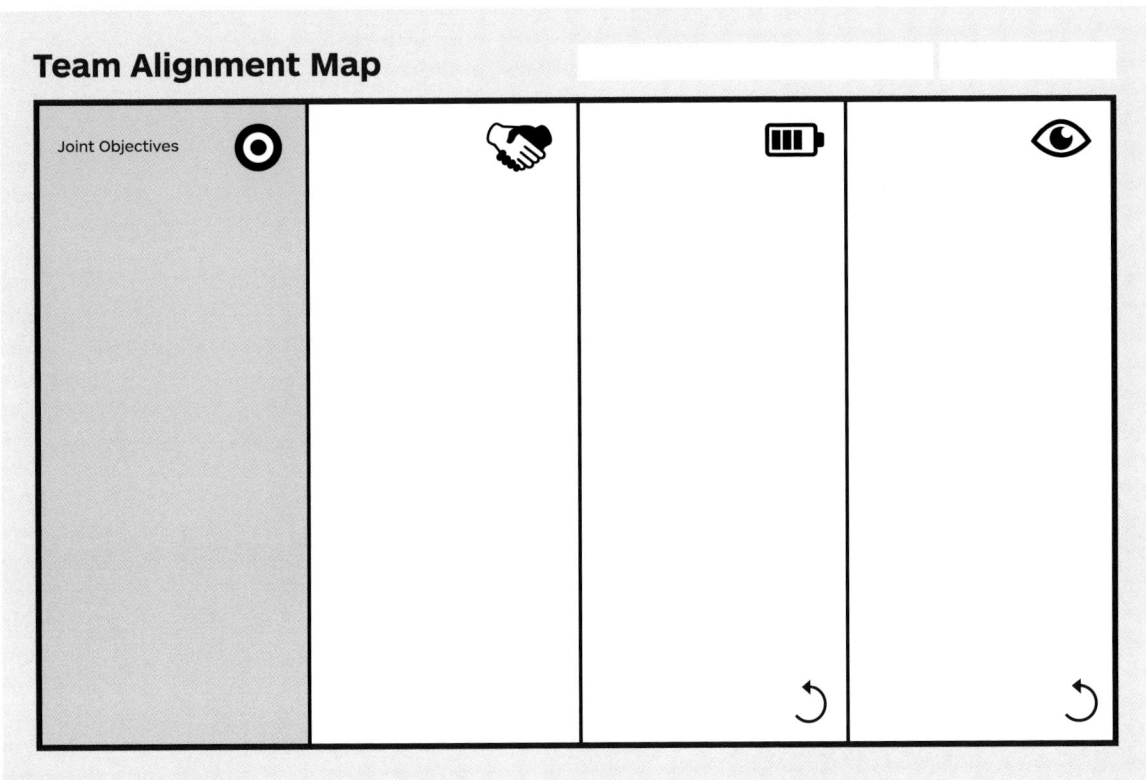

What Are Joint Objectives?

Clear joint objectives align participants' intentions on what needs to get done, expressed in terms of:

• Goals (intention to be achieved)
• Objectives (measurable goals)
• Activities (something to be done)
• Actions (pieces of activities)
• Tasks (pieces of actions)
• Work packages (work given to a person)
• Results (consequences of activities)
• Deliverables (synonym for results)
• Outcomes (synonym for results)
• Products, services (synonyms for results)

The TAM is a semi-structured tool. The key here is to agree on actionable work; however, it may be shaped. A typical TAM contains 3–10 joint objectives. If you have more than 10 objectives, ask the team if the mission is not too broad or ambiguous. You may be describing several projects at once. Consider splitting it into several TAMs if this is the case.

Setting joint objectives as a team
helps break down the mission
into actionable pieces of work.

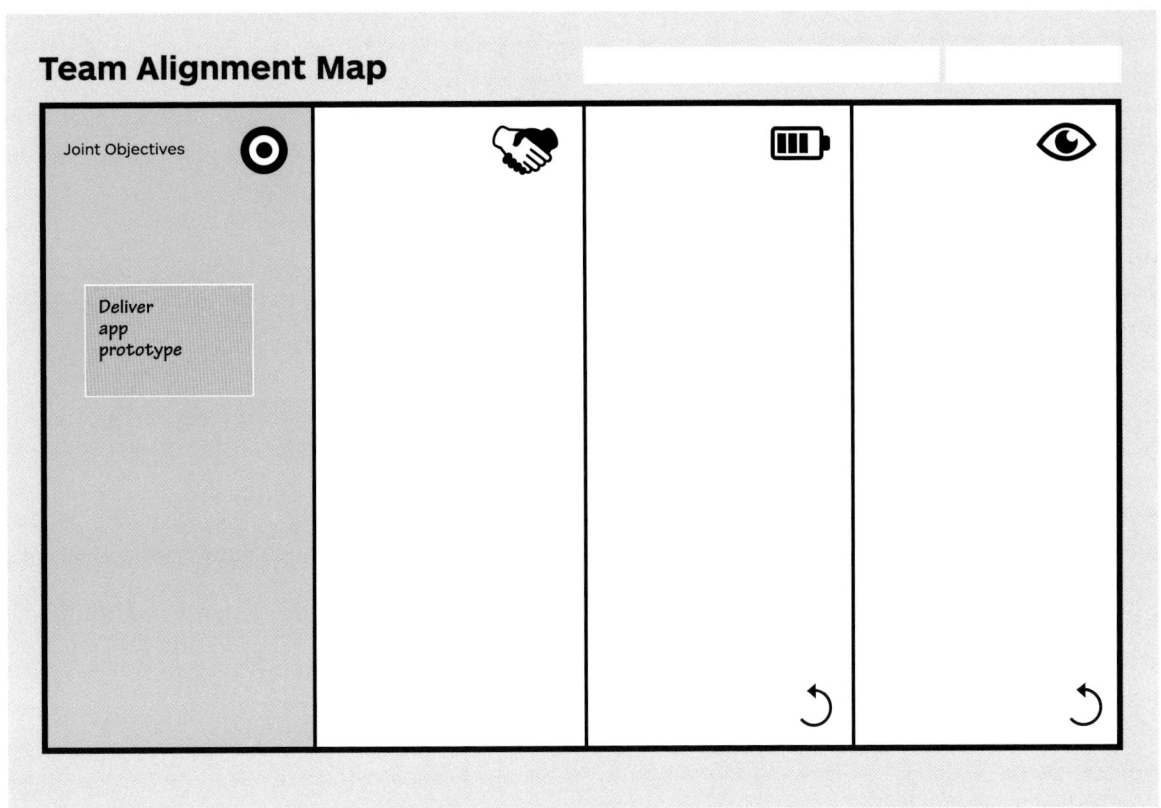

Team Alignment Map

Joint Objectives

Deliver
app
prototype

Ask
- What do we intend to achieve together, concretely?
- What do we have to do?
- What do we need to deliver?
- What work must be done?

Examples

| Create a plan | Hire a consultant | Amend contracts | Negotiate leasing | Update product backlog |
| Paint the interior | Grant access rights | Install electrical wires | Standardize onboarding process | |

Examples of Joint Objectives

Joint objectives can be described in more or less detail.
The tradeoff is between clarity and speed.

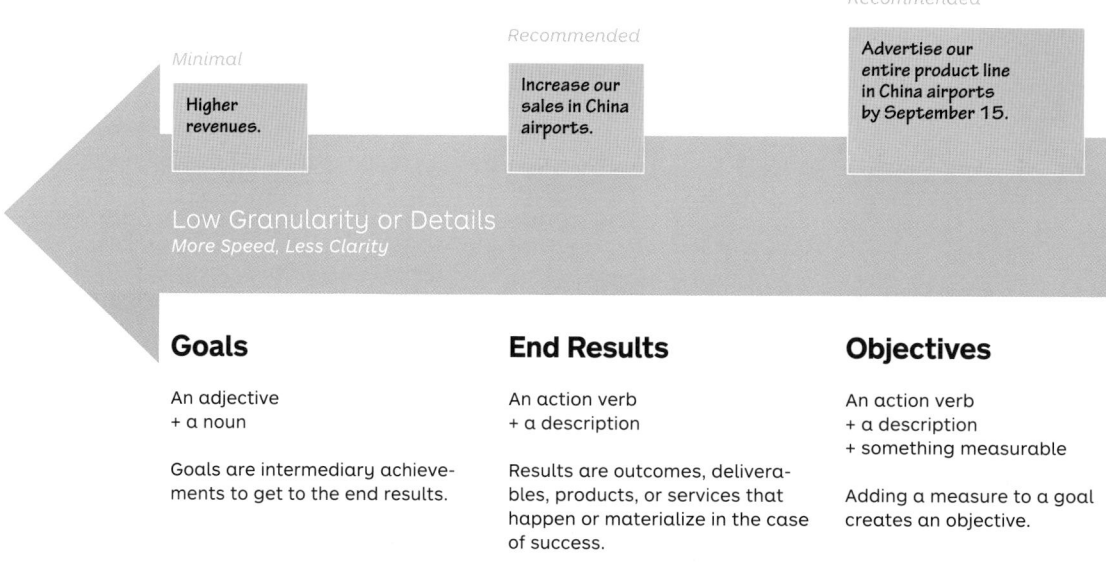

Minimal

Higher revenues.

Recommended

Increase our sales in China airports.

Recommended

Advertise our entire product line in China airports by September 15.

Low Granularity or Details
More Speed, Less Clarity

Goals

An adjective
+ a noun

Goals are intermediary achievements to get to the end results.

End Results

An action verb
+ a description

Results are outcomes, deliverables, products, or services that happen or materialize in the case of success.

Objectives

An action verb
+ a description
+ something measurable

Adding a measure to a goal creates an objective.

> As a market developer, I need an advertising budget, so that I can promote our product line in China airports.

> Grow market share in China.

> Grow market share by 20%, in China airports, for the entire product line, by the end of this fiscal year.

High Granularity or Details
Less Speed, More Clarity

User Stories

As a ‹ *role* ›,
I want ‹ *objectives* ›,
so that ‹ *reason* ›.

User stories are a technique to describe user requirements in agile software development. This approach is increasingly adopted by other industries to describe objectives from a user perspective.

Search: user story

OKR (Objectives and Key Results)

Goal + key results

OKR is a system to describe joint objectives, initially developed by Andy Grove while he was CEO of Intel. The method became famous after being adopted by Google. To write an OKR you have to specify measurable key results for each goal.

Search: OKR

SMART Objectives

SMART stands for specific, measurable, achievable, realistic, and time-bound. This way of describing objectives is usually associated with the popular concept of "management by objectives" presented by Peter Drucker in the 1950s.

It's of great use in situations where objectives do not change on a regular basis.

Search: SMART Objectives

+
Always start your TAM by clarifying the joint objectives

Work can't be directed and organized as a team if the joint objectives are unclear. It was Thomas Shelling's (game theory pioneer and Nobel Prize winner) insight that "joint actions are created from the goal backward. Two people realize they have common goals, realize their actions are interdependent, and work backward to find a way of coordinating their actions in a joint action that will reach those goals." In other words, regardless of its duration (for example, 3 weeks, 3 months, or 3 years), a plan has no value in terms of work if the objectives are unclear.

+
Objectives decomposition and granularity

The Team Alignment Map has not been designed for detailed task decomposition and tracking. The tool helps members align rapidly on key topics to collaborate more effectively. If higher levels of granularity are required, report and decompose the joint objectives in a project management tool after the team alignment session. Validate the decomposed list with the team afterwards.

Search keywords: work breakdown structure; backlog

Joint Commitments

Who will do what?

Team Alignment Map

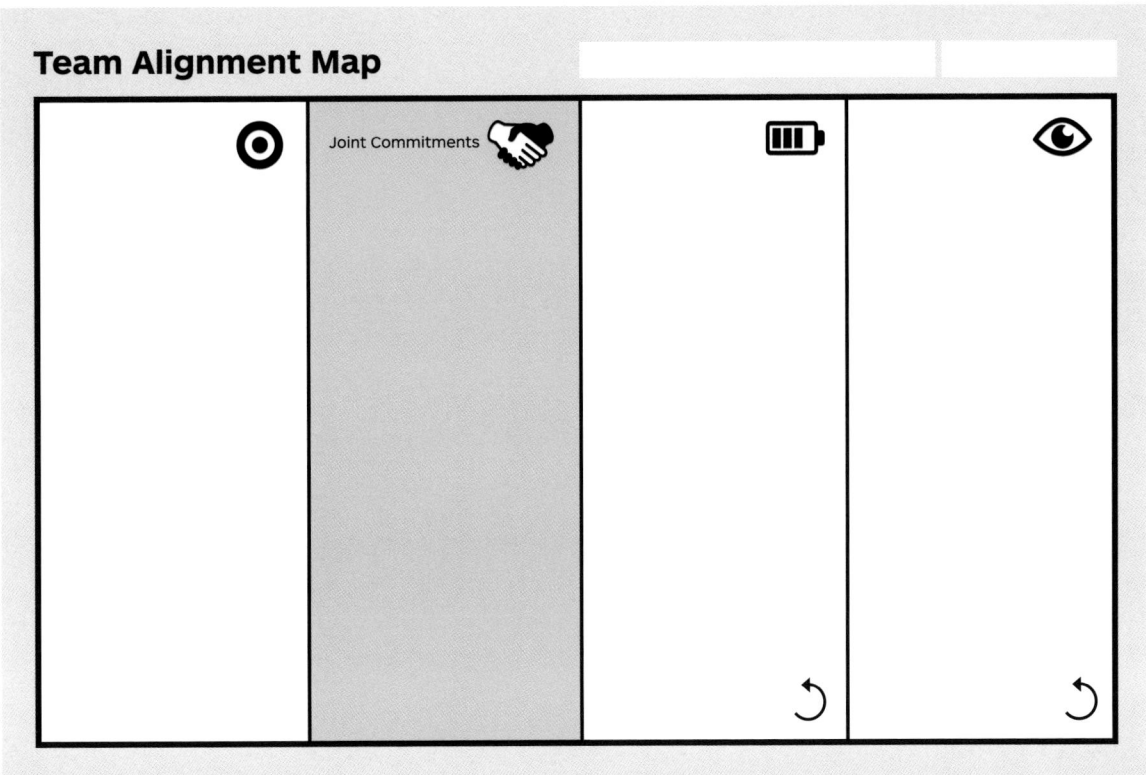

What Are Joint Commitments?

By establishing joint commitments, team members commit to take over and carry out one or more joint objectives. There is not much to write on the notes; names and high-level roles are usually enough. However, the ritual of each member committing in front of others plays an important role. This can be done in two ways:

- The team member writes his or her name next to the objectives he or she will be responsible for, or,
- The team member agrees by saying "okay," "I agree," "fine for me," or "I'll do it" if someone has placed their name on the TAM.

Ambiguous commitments result in a lack of accountability and occur mostly in teams where commitments are implicit, i.e. unspoken. Unspoken commitments create a gray zone in which participants can presuppose what the others will do at their convenience, which increases the likelihood of confusion and conflict. This can be reduced just by speaking clearly.

The Joint Commitment Ritual: Discover the Work of Margaret Gilbert

Margaret Gilbert is a British philosopher who investigated the notion of joint commitment for decades. She observed that to create pertinent joint commitments it is necessary and sufficient that team members express their readiness to be committed in front of others (Gilbert 2014). This makes commitments enter the team's common ground or common knowledge (see Dive Deeper, p. 252). Agreeing openly on joint commitments creates moral obligations and rights. Each team member who makes a commitment has the moral obligation to do his or her part, and in return the right to expect others to do their part. These rights and obligations bind team members and act as a powerful driving force.

Search: Margaret Gilbert philosophy

Joint commitments move participants from the status of individual to the status of active team member.

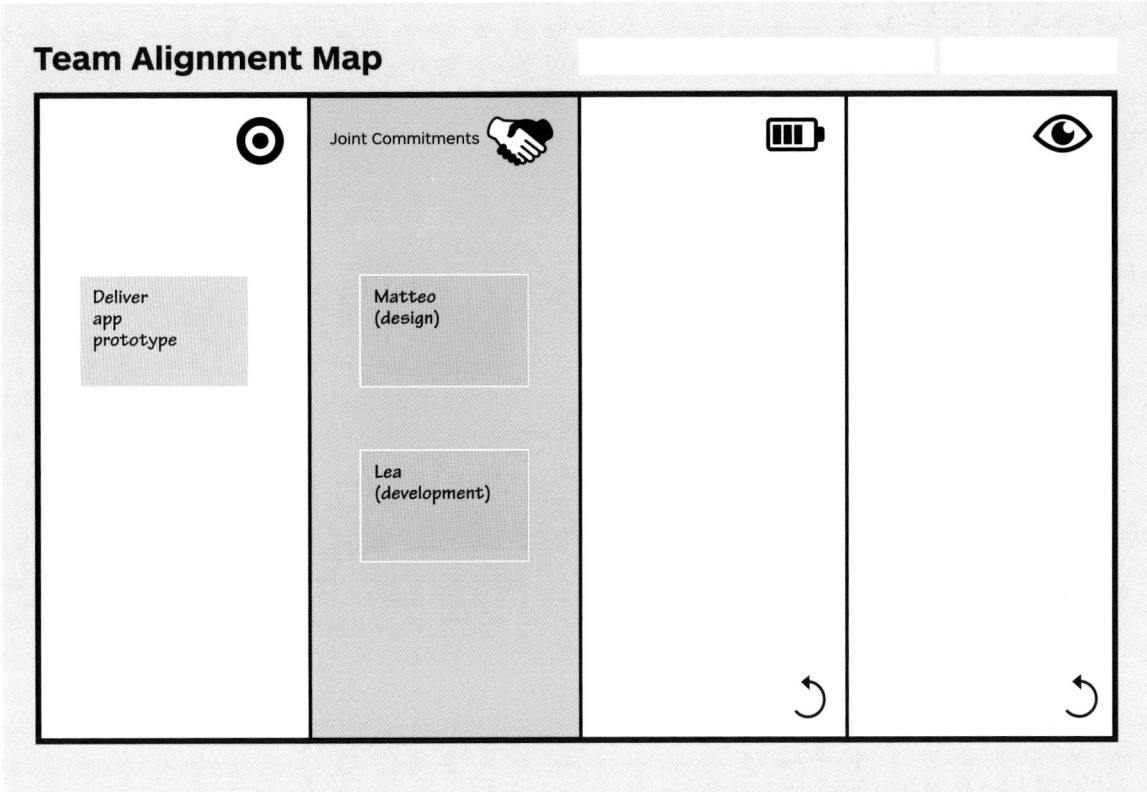

Ask
- **Who will do what?**
- Who commits to what?
- How will we work together?
- What's everyone's role?

Joint commitments are usually placed to the right of the related joint objective.

Examples of
Joint Commitments

Joint commitments can vary from a name to a name with a list of high-level tasks. What matters is that everyone understands who will do what and agrees.

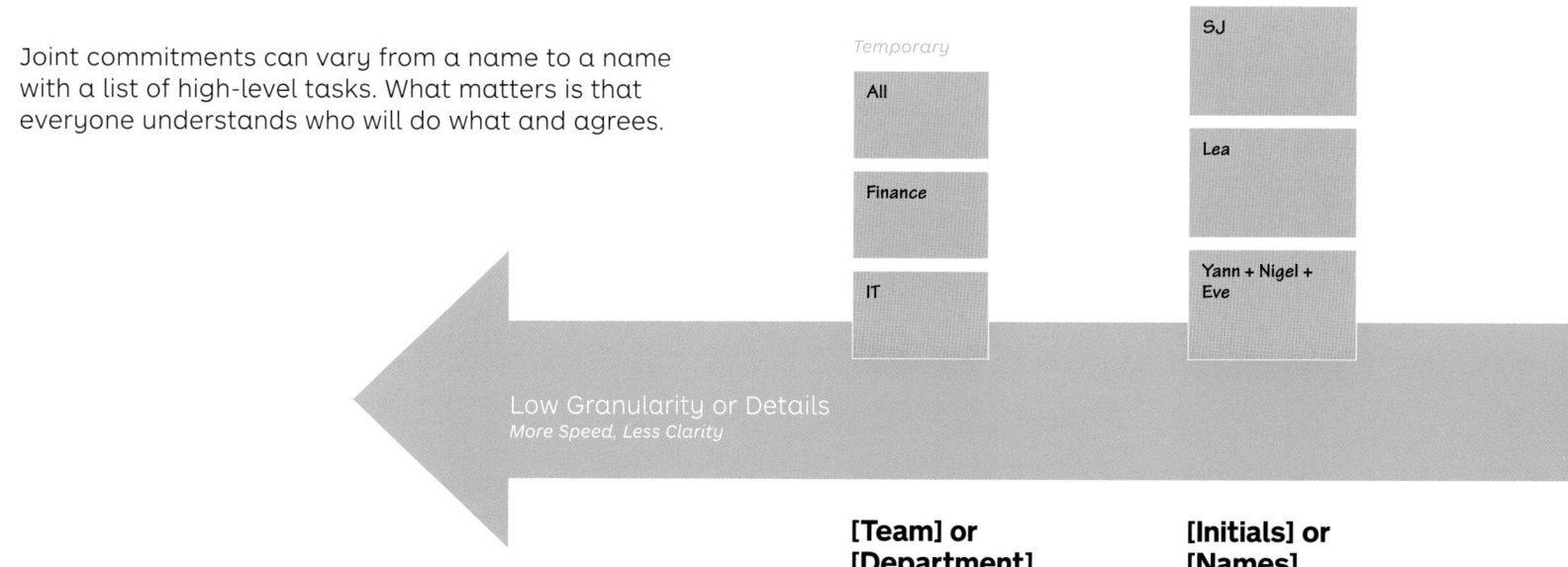

Temporary

All

Finance

IT

Minimal

SJ

Lea

Yann + Nigel + Eve

Low Granularity or Details
More Speed, Less Clarity

**[Team] or
[Department]**

A team's name is useful when not all commitments can be clarified right away. This is the quickest method, but commitments will need to be clarified rapidly to avoid misunderstandings.

**[Initials] or
[Names]**

Initials and first names are fast and useful for team members who are used to working together.

Lea
(development)

Matteo:
- Create paper version
- Design digital assets

Lea:
- Technical architecture
- Code and test

Matteo
(design)
Lea
(development)

High Granularity or Details

Less Speed, More Clarity

[Name] + [Role]

In addition to the name, describing each person's role or task concisely increases mutual clarity, while not slowing down the alignment session.

[Name] + [Main Tasks/Responsibilities]

High-level tasks can also be added. This longer approach is sometimes used by newly created teams. Beware of assigning subtasks that meet an objective in the Joint Objectives column to avoid confusing the team about what goes in each column.

Joint Resources

What resources do we need?

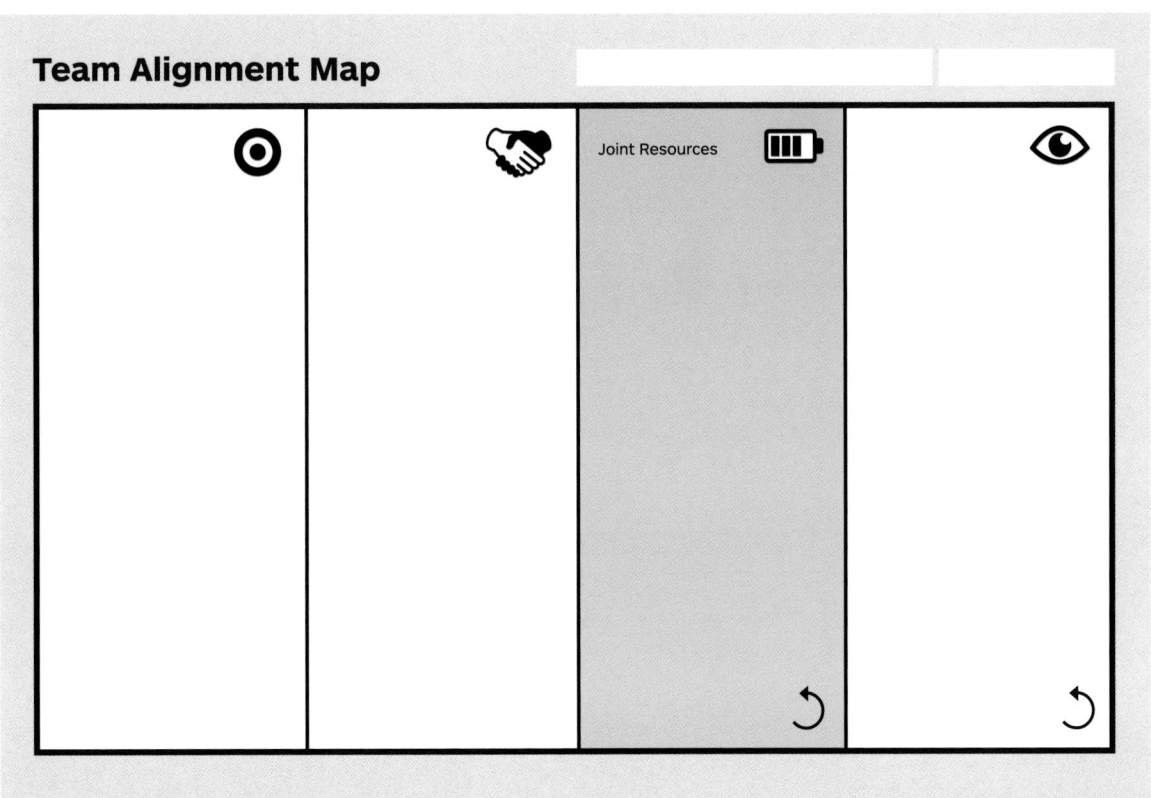

Team Alignment Map

		Joint Resources	

What Are Joint Resources?

All human activities require resources such as time, capital, or equipment. Describing the joint resources consists of estimating these requirements so that every team member can contribute successfully. This anchors the team in the real world by increasing the joint awareness of what is eventually needed to achieve the mission.

When resources are lacking, teams lose the ability to deliver because individuals get stuck. Workflows are interrupted and the proper achievement of the mission is compromised. Estimating and negotiating resources is key but insufficient. Resources must then be allocated, i.e. be made available for team members to perform. Do not hesitate to insist on this point in case of doubt.

+
Resource status

The status of a resource can be indicated as follows:

Available

Not available

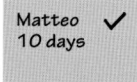

Don't know

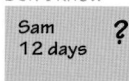

Joint resources help the team evaluate what is needed by each team member to do his or her part.

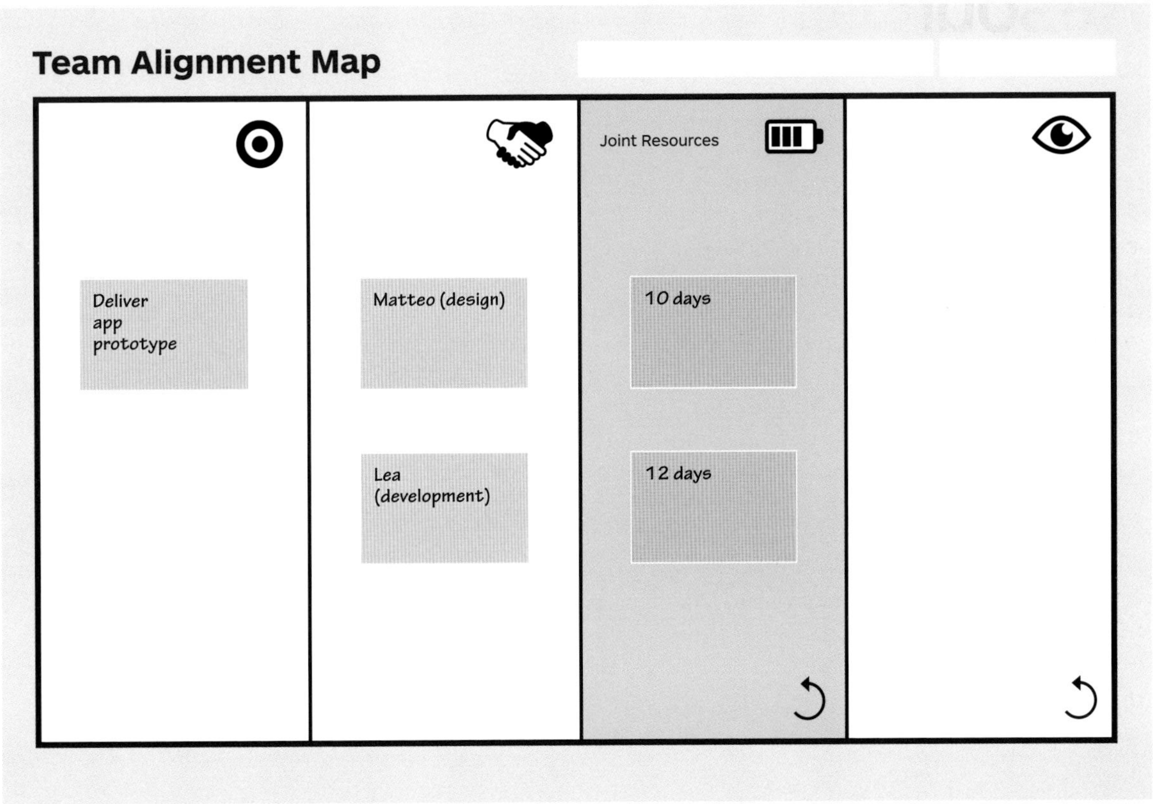

Team Alignment Map

🎯	🤝	Joint Resources 🔋	👁
Deliver app prototype	Matteo (design)	10 days	
	Lea (development)	12 days	

Ask

- **What resources do we need?**
- What should be made available or acquired?
- What is missing for everyone to contribute successfully?
- What are the necessary means to achieve our work?

Examples

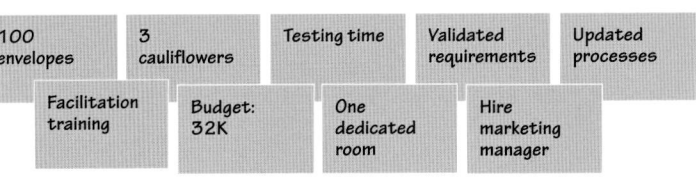

100 envelopes | 3 cauliflowers | Testing time | Validated requirements | Updated processes

Facilitation training | Budget: 32K | One dedicated room | Hire marketing manager

Examples of Joint Resources

If a team member needs something to do his or her work, then it's a resource! Resource needs can be described with more or less accuracy; the tradeoff is always between speed and clarity.

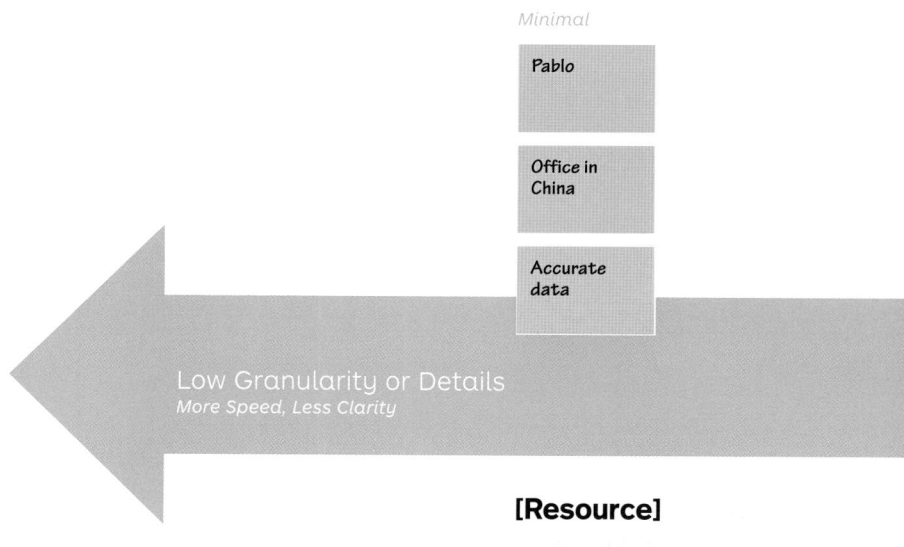

Minimal

Pablo

Office in China

Accurate data

Low Granularity or Details
More Speed, Less Clarity

[Resource]

Designating the resources can be a first step. That keeps the conversation moving in the right direction, i.e. identifying what is needed to get the job done.

☐ People: such as staffing, working hours, skills (technical, social), training, motivation

☐ Equipment and tools: such as office desks, meeting rooms, furniture, vehicles, machines

☐ Financial: such as budgets, cash, credit

☐ Materials: such as raw materials, supplies

☐ Technology: such as applications, computers, online services, network infrastructure needs

☐ Information: such as documents, data, access rights

☐ Legal: such as copyrights, patents, permits, contracts

☐ Organizational: such as processes, internal support, decisions

Recommended

Pablo – 10 days

Flyers – 100

Travel budget $20K

With constraints

Need Pablo for 10 days at a max. cost of $1.5K/day

Print 100 flyers (needed before June 3rd)

Validate $20K travel budget before the end of the week.

High Granularity or Details

Less Speed, More Clarity

[Resource] + [Estimated Quantity]

Naming and quantifying the resources creates a superior level of alignment and realism among team members. Suggest an interval or amount (1–10; $20–80K) when it's difficult to provide a single estimate.

[Verb] + [Estimated Quantity] + [Resource] + [Constraint]

This longer template can help align the team when high levels of accuracy are needed for critical resources. Used only in specific cases.

Joint Risks

What can prevent us from succeeding?

Team Alignment Map

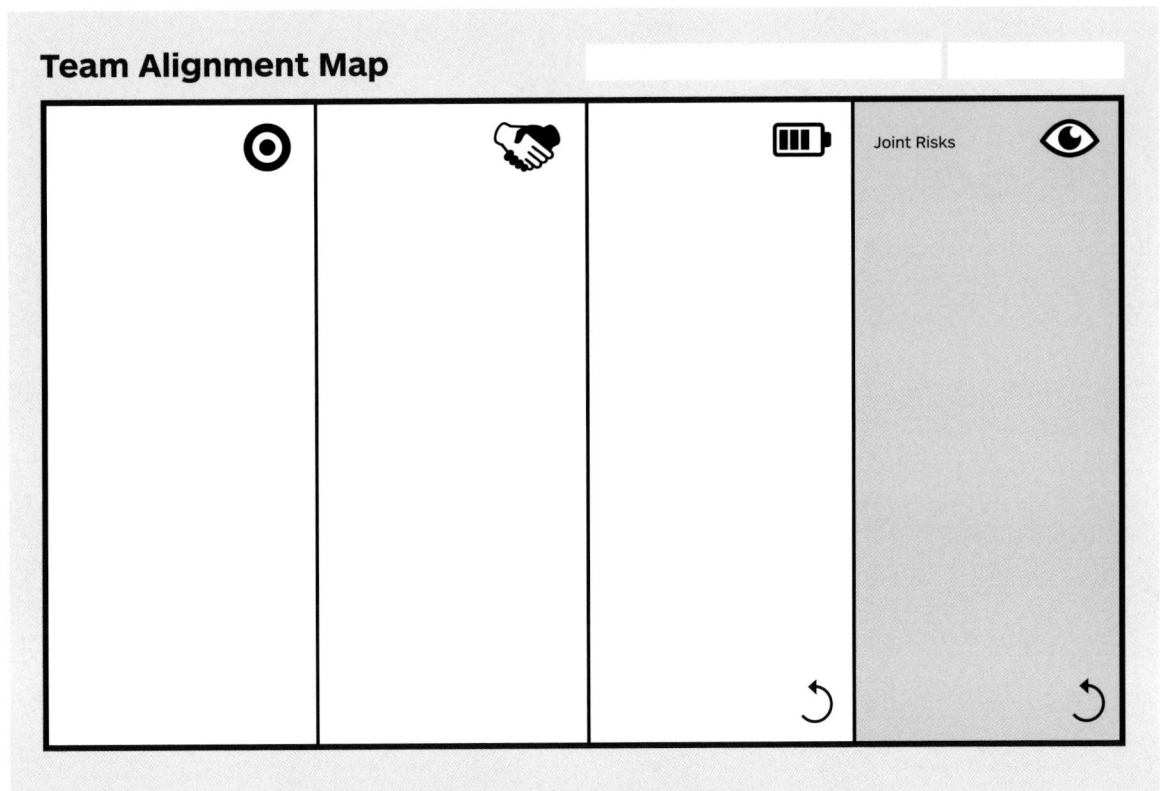

Joint Risks

I told you we were going too fast.

What Are Joint Risks?

Risk-free projects deliver... nothing. All projects carry risks related to their inherent degree of uncertainty. Risks are events that, if they occur, create unwanted obstacles. These obstacles make it more difficult for the team to achieve the mission. They can negatively impact the costs, the deadlines or quality of the deliverables, and even damage personal relationships. In the worst-case scenario, a risk that occurs can cause the entire project and team to fail.

The Team Alignment Map helps reduce project risk in three main steps:

1. Risk identification
   By filling in the joint risks column

2. Risk analysis
   By discussing the risk exposure of each entry

3. Risk mitigation
   By performing a backward pass
   (please read p. 74–75)

Risk management discussions matter: they increase the team's resilience — hence the likelihood of achieving the mission successfully.

+
Risk exposure

An easy technique is to mark risk exposure with a score or letter somewhere in the note.

For example: H = High, M = Medium, L = Low

(risk exposure = risk likelihood x risk impact)

+
Professional risk management

The TAM is designed for on-the-fly rapid risk management; it is not a substitute for in-depth risk analysis and management tools. Please refer to professional techniques in that case.

Search keywords: risk management, risk management process, risk management tools.

Joint risks help the team anticipate and fix potential problems proactively.

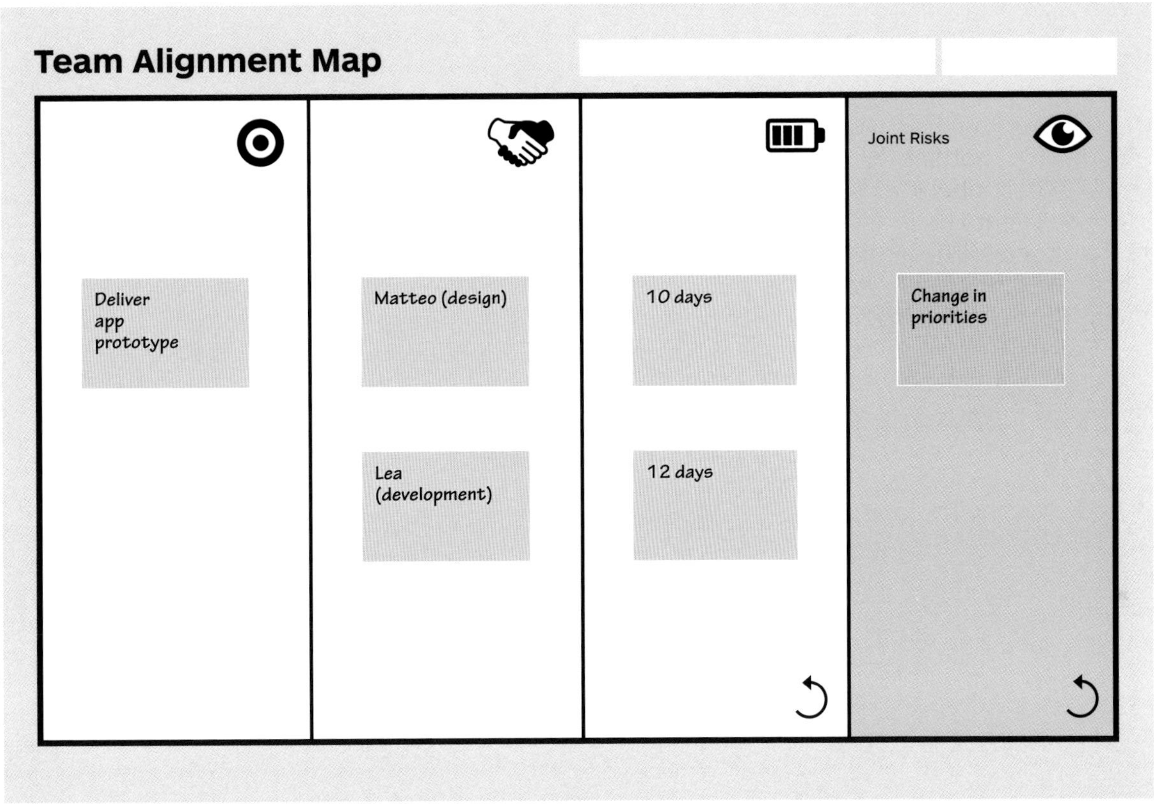

Team Alignment Map

🎯	🤝	🔋	Joint Risks 👁
Deliver app prototype	Matteo (design)	10 days	Change in priorities
	Lea (development)	12 days	

Ask

- **What can prevent us from succeeding?**
- What might go wrong?
- What's our worst-case scenario?
- What are problems/threats/dangers/ side effects in achieving our objectives?
- Are there any particular fears/objections?
- What would make us consider a plan B?

Examples

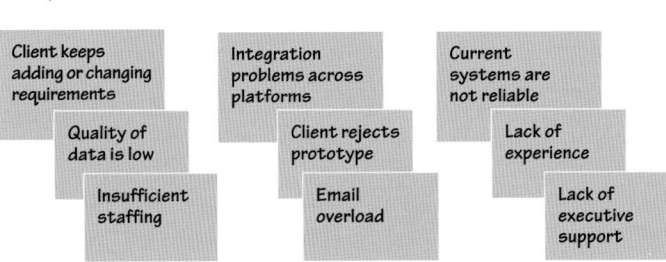

Client keeps adding or changing requirements

Quality of data is low

Insufficient staffing

Integration problems across platforms

Client rejects prototype

Email overload

Current systems are not reliable

Lack of experience

Lack of executive support

Examples of Joint Risks

When describing risks, pragmatism should prevail.

At one extreme, so many things can possibly go wrong that a team can spend more time describing risks accurately than working to achieve the mission. At the other extreme, overoptimism, doing nothing in terms of risk identification, may cause the project to fail for easily avoidable reasons. A compromise is to describe risks succinctly, and detail only those with the highest risk exposure.

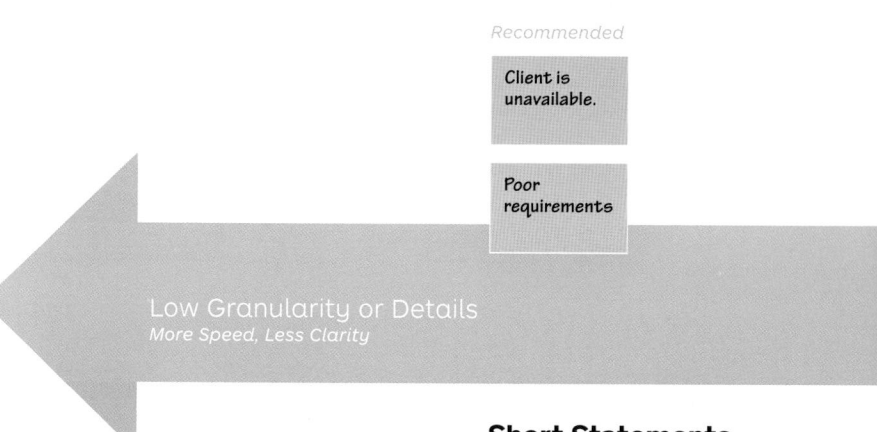

Recommended

Client is unavailable.

Poor requirements

Low Granularity or Details
More Speed, Less Clarity

Short Statements

A short statement is better than no risk identification at all. This is the spirit of assessing risks with the Team Alignment Map.

☐ Internal: such as risks caused by the team itself, mistakes, defects, lack of preparation, lack of skills, quality of deliverables, miscommunication, staffing, roles, conflict, etc.

☐ Equipment: such as risks caused by technical problems, products and services used by the team, insufficient quality of tools, building, etc.

☐ Organizational: such as risks caused by management and other teams in the same organization, lack of support, politics, logistics, funding, etc.

☐ External: such as risks caused by clients, end users, suppliers, regulatory problems, financial markets, weather conditions, etc.

With consequence

Client unavailability may cause severe delays.

Poor initial requirements may result in servers' downtime.

Detailed

Client unavailability caused by the time difference may result in a 6–12-month delay and a 40% increase in costs.

Poor initial requirements caused by systems engineers being overloaded may result in misconfigured servers and 30–60% downtime.

There is a risk that the client is not available because she lives in a different time zone, which could result in a 6–12-month delay and a 40% increase in costs.

There is a risk that we get poor initial requirements because systems engineers are overloaded, which could result in misconfigured servers and 30–60% downtime.

High Granularity or Details
Less Speed, More Clarity

[Risk] may [Consequence]

[Event] caused by [Cause/s] may result in [Quantifiable consequence/s on joint objectives]

There is risk that [Event] because [Cause/s], which could result in [Quantifiable consequence/s on joint objectives]

+

The templates on the right are more formal and describe risks in much more detail. They do, however, significantly increase the effort of alignment. To avoid discouraging the team, favor short statements such as presented on the left and use these detailed templates as additional guides for the discussion. If necessary, switch to professional risk management tools.

1.2
Planning Who Does What with the Team Alignment Map (Planning Mode)

Start with a forward pass to create the plan,
then make a backward pass to lower any risks.

Forward and Backward Pass

Planning with the Team Alignment Map is a two-step process.

1,2,3,4,5
The Forward Pass

The first part of the process, called the forward pass, consists of planning together. Participants describe what is needed to collaborate effectively by filling in each column in a logical order from left to right. This sets a big picture, both in terms of expectations and problems, on which participants can reflect to increase their chances of success.

The forward pass starts bringing everyone together as a real team. Team members jointly consider each other's contributions and needs, and common understanding develops.

6,7
The Backward Pass

The second part is called the backward pass and is aimed at reducing the level of execution risk. Practically speaking, this part consists of removing as much content as possible from the last two columns. This happens by creating, adapting, and removing content from the rest of the map. In other words, latent problems, such as missing resources and open risks, are transformed into new objectives and new commitments.

Fixing and removing problems visually, together, gives a sense of progression. Motivation and engagement increase as participants see that the risks they described disappear because they are properly addressed. This also allows confirmation of the mission and the period, at the very end of the backward pass.

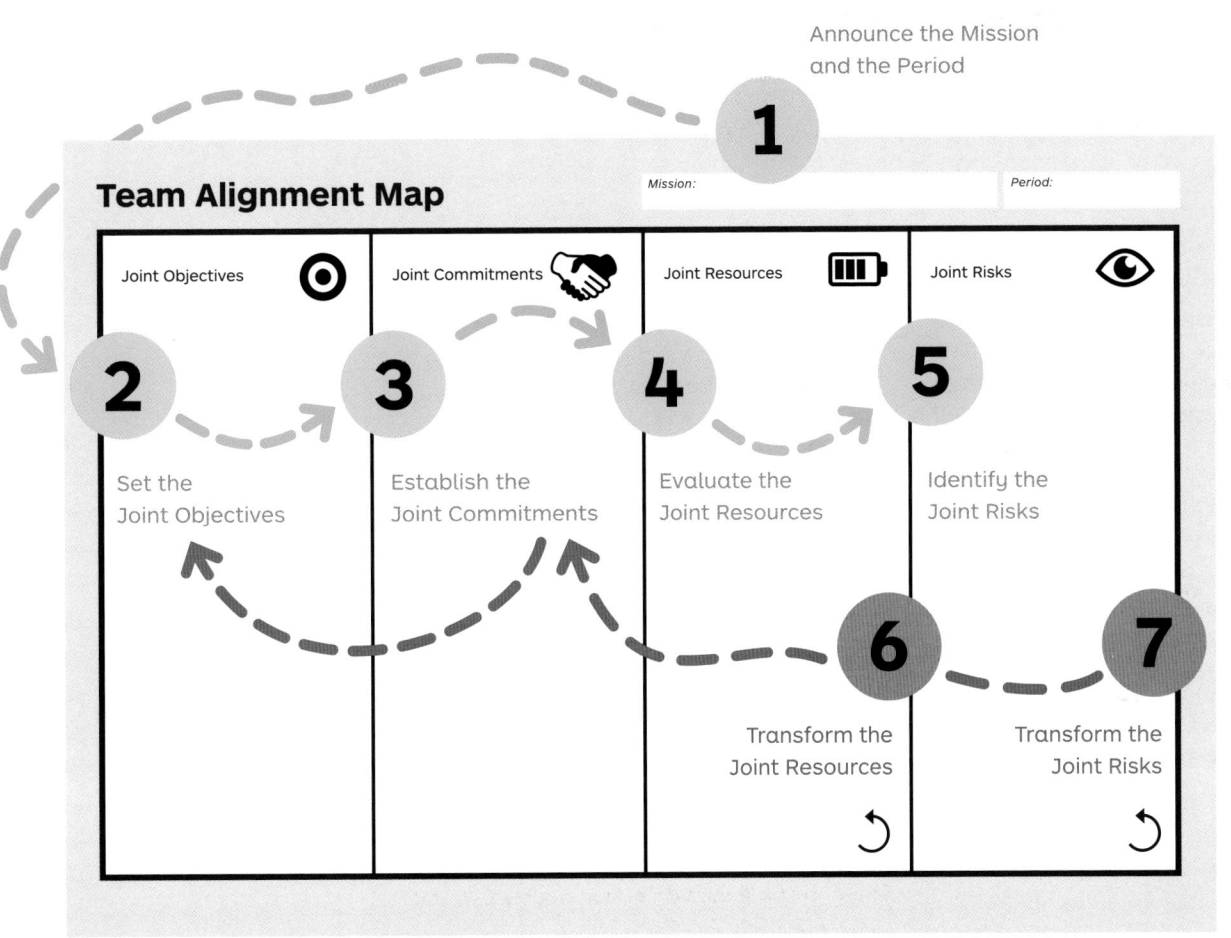

Announce the Mission and the Period

Team Alignment Map

Mission:

Period:

Joint Objectives	Joint Commitments	Joint Resources	Joint Risks
2 Set the Joint Objectives	**3** Establish the Joint Commitments	**4** Evaluate the Joint Resources	**5** Identify the Joint Risks
		6 Transform the Joint Resources	**7** Transform the Joint Risks

Example at Work

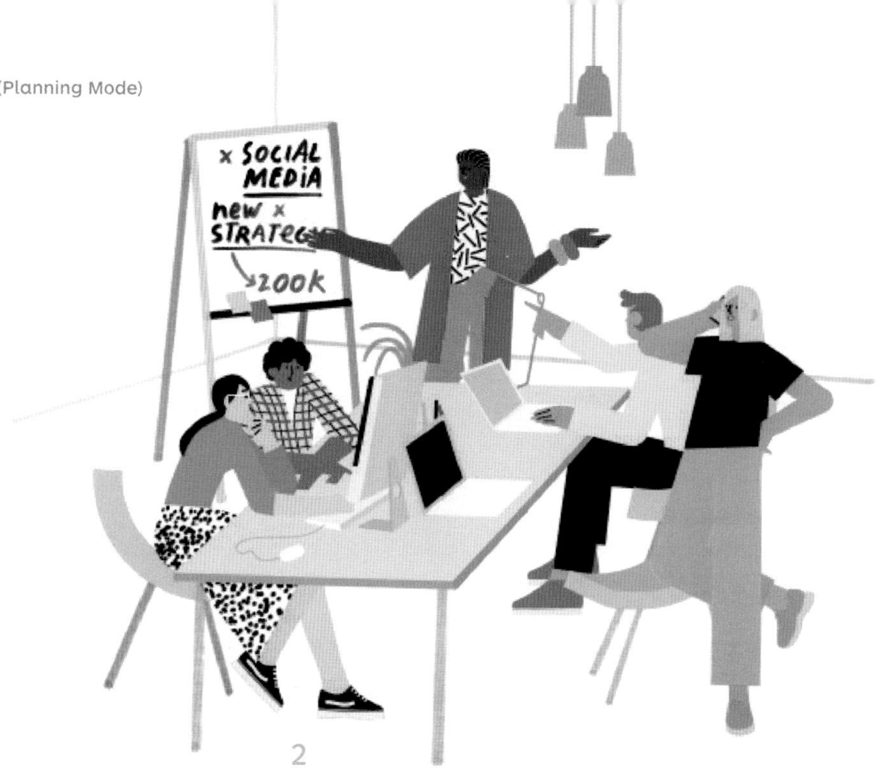

The Forward Pass
Develop a Social Media Strategy

Honora, Pablo, Matteo, Tess, and Lou work for a communications agency. Their mission is to develop a social media strategy for an important client in record time. They decide to align with the Team Alignment Map and here is the result of the forward and the backward pass.

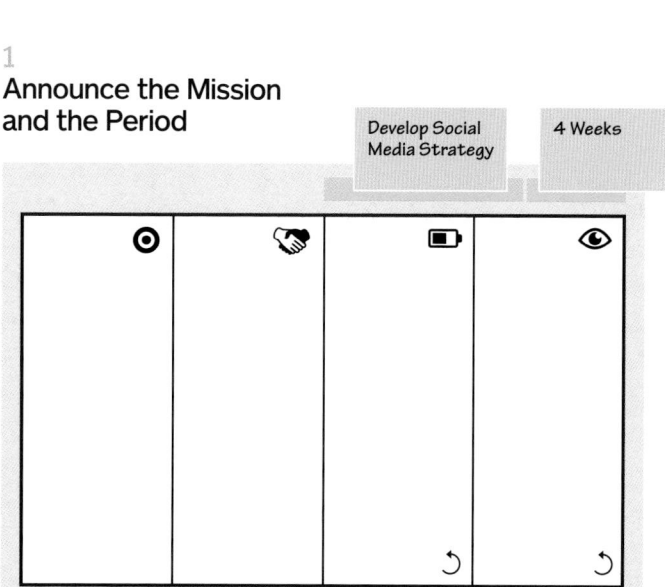

1
Announce the Mission and the Period

Develop Social Media Strategy

4 Weeks

2
Set the Joint Objectives

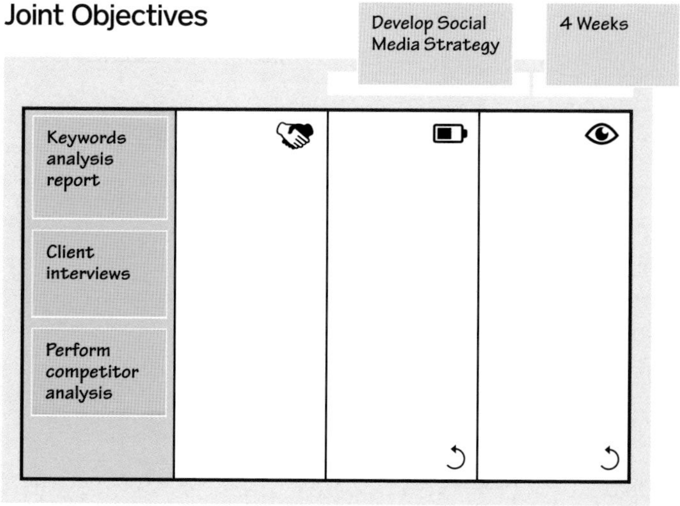

Develop Social Media Strategy

4 Weeks

Keywords analysis report

Client interviews

Perform competitor analysis

4
Evaluate the Joint Resources

| Develop Social Media Strategy | 4 Weeks |

Keywords analysis report	Honora: *analyze* Matteo: *write*	Analytics software	👁
Client interviews	All	Missing database access	
Perform competitor analysis	Pablo, Tess, Lou	Tess lacks time	↺
		↺	

3
Establish the Joint Commitments

| Develop Social Media Strategy | 4 Weeks |

Keywords analysis report	Honora: *analyze* Matteo: *write*	🔋	👁
Client interviews	All		
Perform competitor analysis	Pablo, Tess, Lou		
		↺	↺

5
Identify the Joint Risks

| Develop Social Media Strategy | 4 Weeks |

Keywords analysis report	Honora: *analyze* Matteo: *write*	Analytics software	Client is not available
Client interviews	All	Missing database access	Overreliance on data
Perform competitor analysis	Pablo, Tess, Lou	Tess lacks time	
		↺	↺

Example at Work

The Backward Pass
Develop a Social Media Strategy

6
Transform the Joint Resources

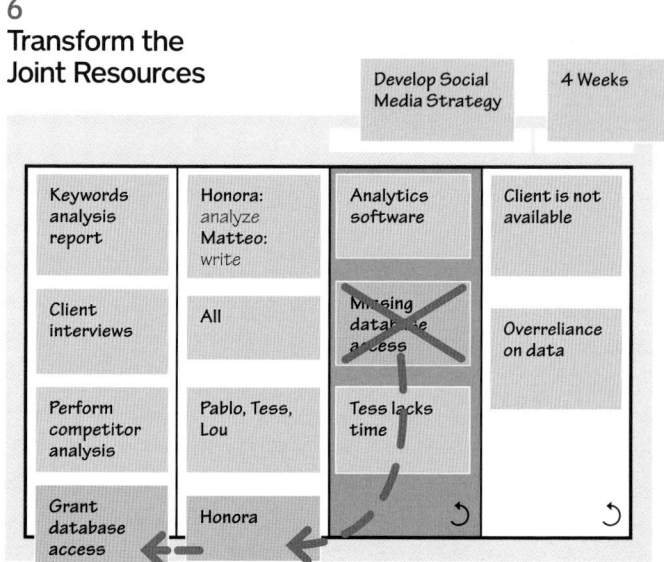

- Analytics software: The analytics software is available, the note is checked, and there's nothing special to do.
- Missing database access: Honora knows how to grant database access to the team, so she creates a new objective and a new commitment. The missing resource is removed from the column.
- Tess lacks time: A solution must still be found, so the element remains in this column.

7
Transform the Joint Risks

- Client is not available: There is a risk that the client is not available for the interviews, so Matteo commits to scheduling all meetings ahead of time. The risk is removed from the column.
- Overreliance on data: Nothing really can be done here except to keep that risk in mind. The team agrees to leave that risk as a reminder.

Team Validation

- The team agrees that work can start.
- A solution still needs to be found to free up time for Tess.
- Everyone knows it, which makes a big difference for her.

Example at Home

The Forward Pass
Successful Move to Geneva

Angela works for an international organization and she has just been relocated to its headquarters in Geneva, Switzerland. Together with her husband, Giuseppe, and their children, Renato, Manu, and Lydia, they decide to align to ensure a successful move. Here is what they discuss during the forward and the backward passes.

1
Announce the Mission and the Period

Successful move to Geneva	3 months

◎	🤝	🔋	👁
		↺	↺

2
Set the Joint Objectives

Successful move to Geneva	3 months

	🤝	🔋	👁
Find a new house in Geneva			
Pack the boxes			
Find a new doctor			
Find a moving company			
Buy a new car in Geneva		↺	↺

4
Evaluate the Joint Resources

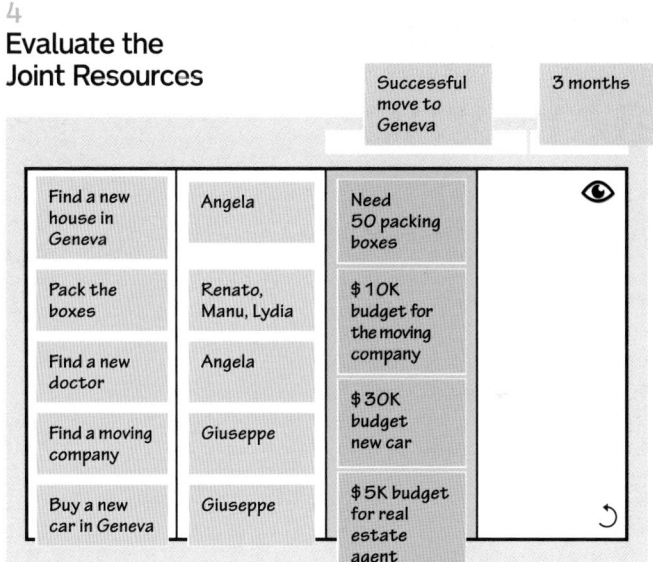

	Successful move to Geneva	3 months
Find a new house in Geneva	Angela	Need 50 packing boxes
Pack the boxes	Renato, Manu, Lydia	$10K budget for the moving company
Find a new doctor	Angela	$30K budget new car
Find a moving company	Giuseppe	
Buy a new car in Geneva	Giuseppe	$5K budget for real estate agent

3
Establish the Joint Commitments

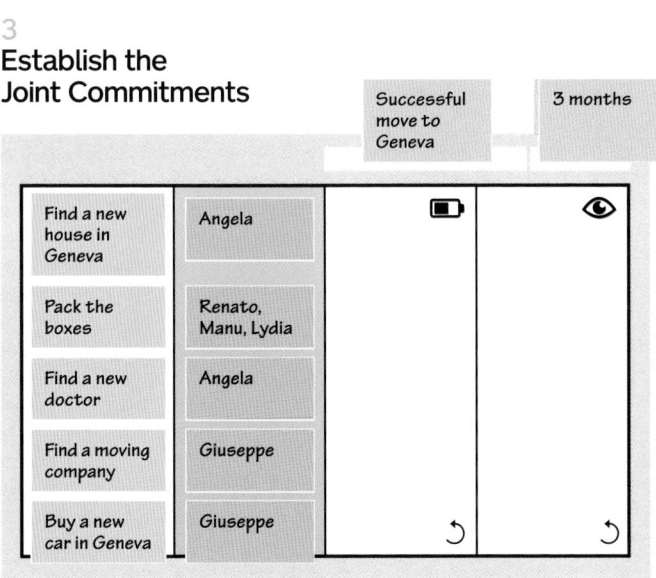

	Successful move to Geneva	3 months
Find a new house in Geneva	Angela	
Pack the boxes	Renato, Manu, Lydia	
Find a new doctor	Angela	
Find a moving company	Giuseppe	
Buy a new car in Geneva	Giuseppe	

5
Identify the Joint Risks

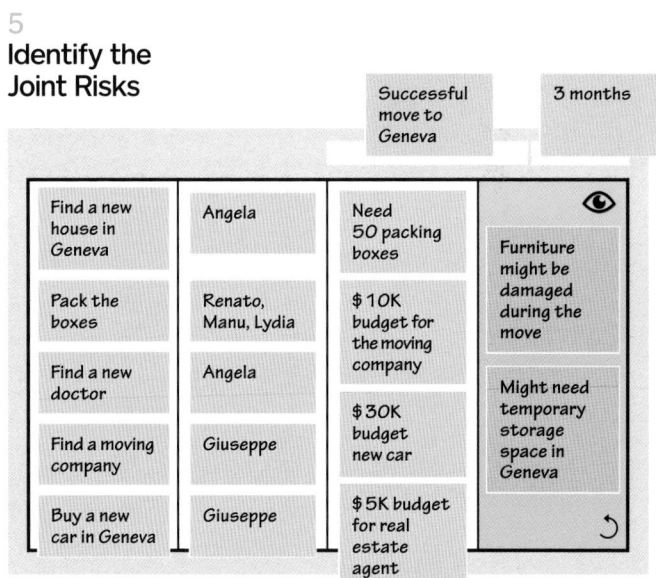

	Successful move to Geneva	3 months
Find a new house in Geneva	Angela	Need 50 packing boxes
Pack the boxes	Renato, Manu, Lydia	$10K budget for the moving company
Find a new doctor	Angela	$30K budget new car
Find a moving company	Giuseppe	
Buy a new car in Geneva	Giuseppe	$5K budget for real estate agent

Furniture might be damaged during the move

Might need temporary storage space in Geneva

Example at Home

The Backward Pass
Successful Move to Geneva

**6
Transform the
Joint Resources**

- Need 50 packing boxes: Angela will order the boxes today.
- $45K total budget (for the moving company, new car, real estate agent): Giuseppe will ensure that the money is available in the current bank account.

7
Transform the Joint Risks

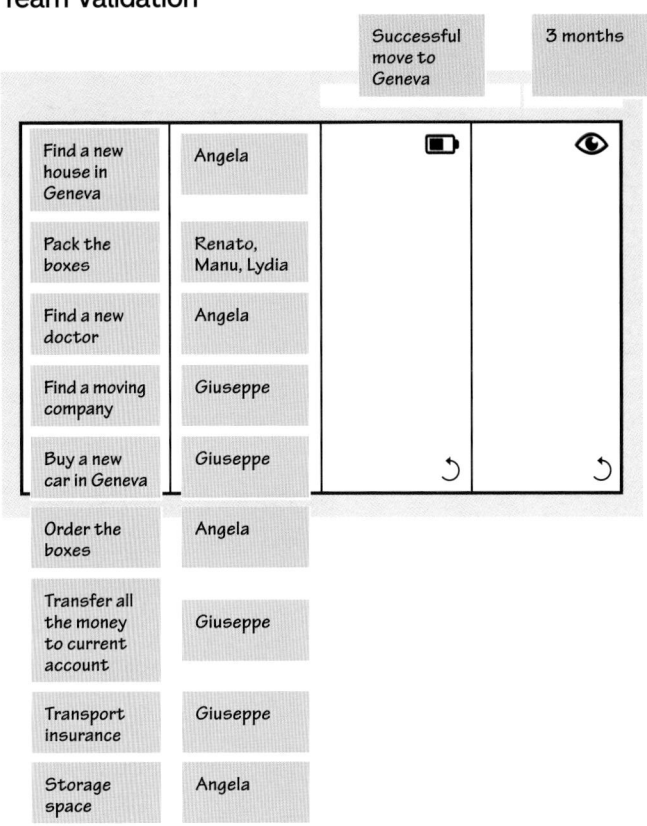

- Furniture might be damaged during transportation: Angela will take out transport insurance with their usual insurance company.
- Might need temporary storage space in Geneva: Giuseppe will contact the HR department for a recommendation and ensure that sufficient storage space is available.

Team Validation

- Everyone agrees and gets to work to make a successful move.

Example with Friends

The Forward Pass
A Great Birthday Party

Louise's birthday is approaching, and her parents, Mathilde and Bernard, want to organize a beautiful party. Her best friend, Thomas, also wants to help. Here is how they teamed up to do a forward and a backward pass.

1
Announce the Mission and the Period

Great Birthday Party	2 weeks

◎	🤝	🔋	👁
		↺	↺

2
Set the Joint Objectives

Great Birthday Party	2 weeks

	🤝	🔋	👁
Create guestlist			
Send the invitations			
Decorate the house			
Prepare the cakes and buy drinks		↺	↺

4
Evaluate the Joint Resources

Great Birthday Party | 2 weeks

		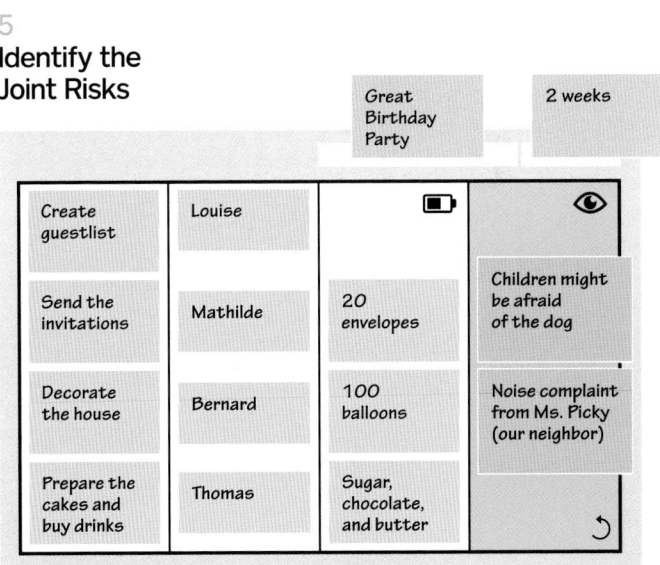 🔋	👁
Create guestlist	Louise		
Send the invitations	Mathilde	20 envelopes	
Decorate the house	Bernard	100 balloons	
Prepare the cakes and buy drinks	Thomas	Sugar, chocolate, and butter	↺

3
Establish the Joint Commitments

Great Birthday Party | 2 weeks

		🔋	👁
Create guestlist	Louise		
Send the invitations	Mathilde		
Decorate the house	Bernard		
Prepare the cakes and buy drinks	Thomas	↺	↺

5
Identify the Joint Risks

Great Birthday Party | 2 weeks

		🔋	👁
Create guestlist	Louise		
Send the invitations	Mathilde	20 envelopes	Children might be afraid of the dog
Decorate the house	Bernard	100 balloons	Noise complaint from Ms. Picky (our neighbor)
Prepare the cakes and buy drinks	Thomas	Sugar, chocolate, and butter	↺

Example with Friends

The Backward Pass
A Great Birthday Party

6
Transform the Joint Resources

- 20 envelopes and 100 balloons: Bernard will take care of this.
- Sugar, chocolate, and butter: Mathilde must go to the pharmacy and she will stop on the way back to buy the ingredients.

7
Transform the Joint Risks

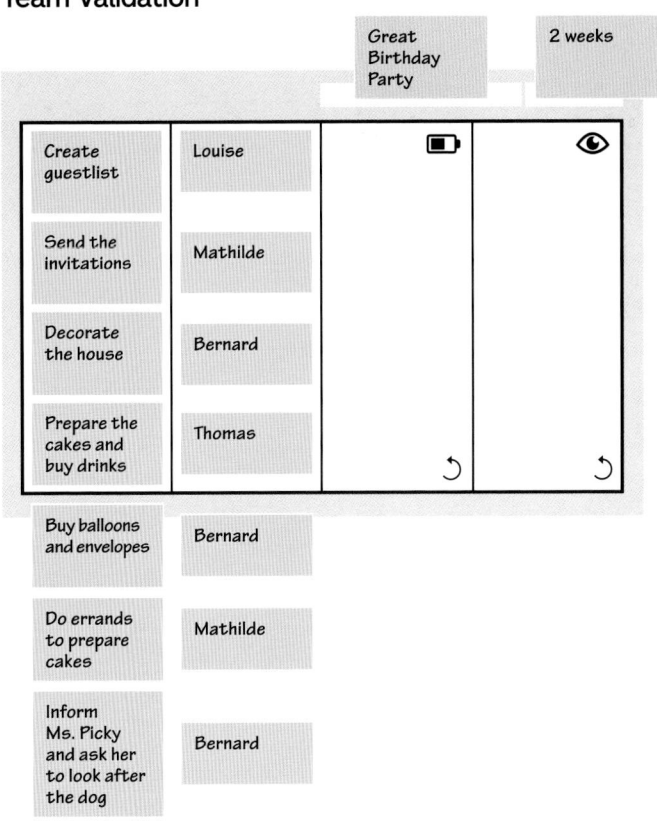

Create guestlist	Louise		🔋	👁
Send the invitations	Mathilde			~~Children might be afraid of the dog~~
Decorate the house	Bernard			~~Noise complaint from Ms. Picky (our neighbor)~~
Prepare the cakes and buy drinks	Thomas		↻	↻

Buy balloons and envelopes	Bernard
Do errands to prepare cakes	Mathilde
Inform Ms. Picky and ask her to look after the dog	Bernard

- Children might be afraid of the dog and Ms. Picky might complain about the noise: Bernard will inform Mrs. Picky immediately and ask her to keep the dog the afternoon of the party.

Team Validation

Create guestlist	Louise		🔋	👁
Send the invitations	Mathilde			
Decorate the house	Bernard			
Prepare the cakes and buy drinks	Thomas		↻	↻

Buy balloons and envelopes	Bernard
Do errands to prepare cakes	Mathilde
Inform Ms. Picky and ask her to look after the dog	Bernard

- Everyone agrees and they start preparing a great birthday party.

Pro Tips

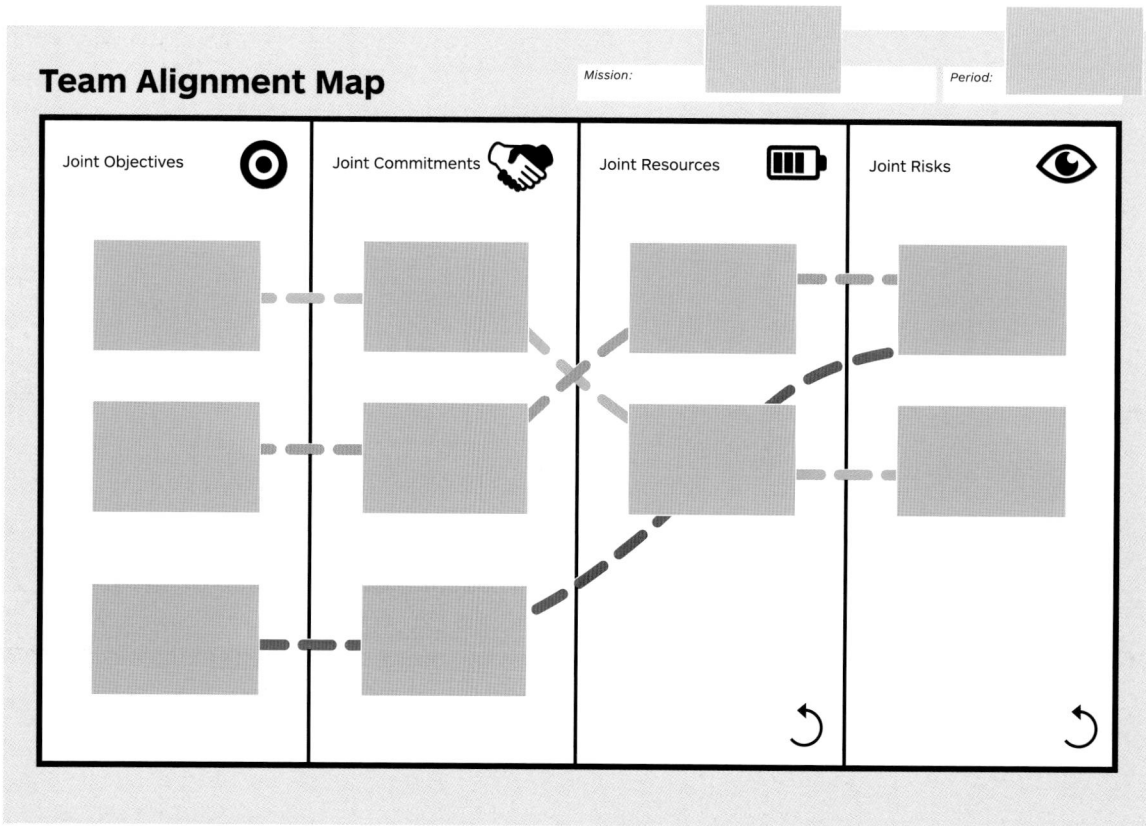

Visualizing Relationships
Simply draw lines to visualize relationships.

Removed Items

What to do with the joint risks and joint resources removed during the backward pass?

On the left: in front of the new objectives

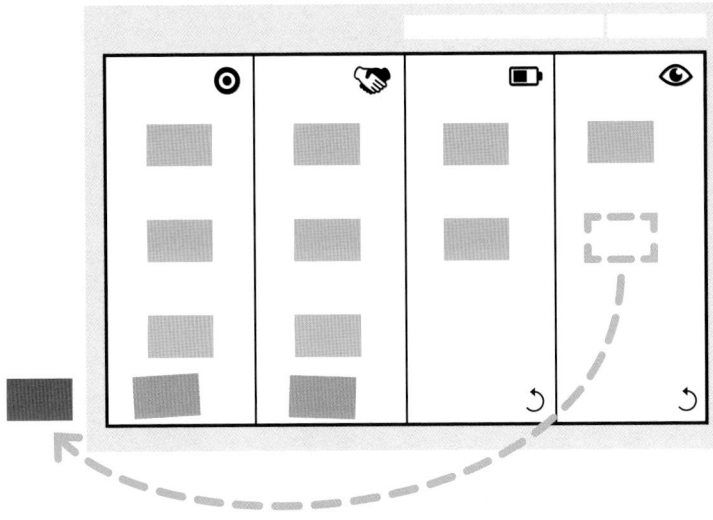

On the right on the wall

Trash

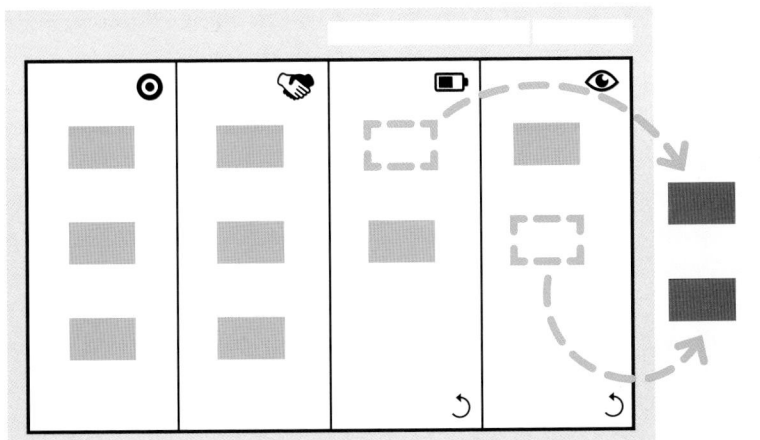

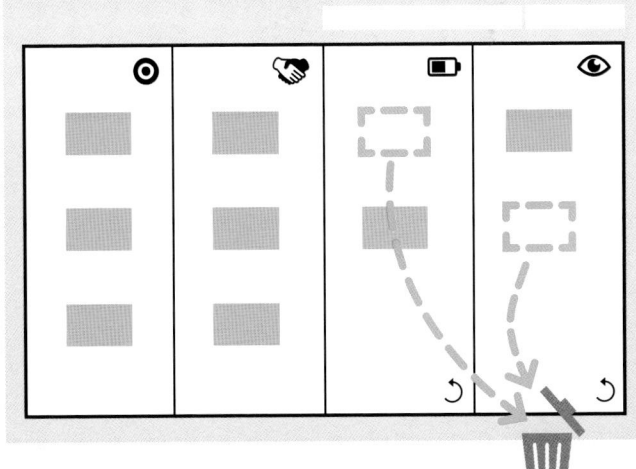

1.3
Keeping Team Members on Track (Assessment Mode)

Use the Team Alignment Map to assess team readiness or address ongoing problems.

How to Use the Team Alignment Map to Assess Projects and Teams

The Team Alignment Map can easily turn into an alert system that reveals blind spots and prevents the accumulation of small perception gaps from becoming big problems.

Rapid visual assessments with the TAM can help the team ensure that minimal success requirements are met:

- Initially, to have a good project start.
- Later on, to remain on the right track.

Too often we embark on projects where these minimal requirements are not met and collaborating turns into permanent crisis management. This happens when the team lacks preparation or when there are collaboration blind spots, i.e. when someone thinks he or she knows what others are thinking but is off base. Ensuring enough alignment from start to finish is essential to success, and with a rapid assessment the team can visualize the level of alignment and act early enough to avoid preventable problems.

Assessing consists of asking every team member if they think they can do their part successfully. This is done with a vote that can be anonymous if necessary. The image resulting from a vote is neutral, and is then interpreted as a team; repair actions are undertaken if the alignment is insufficient.

To start assessing, draw four horizontal sliders in each column and add the following values to each slider (starting from the bottom of the map) as illustrated in the figure on the next page:

1. Joint objectives: unclear, neutral, clear
2. Joint commitments: implicit, neutral, explicit
3. Joint resources: missing, neutral, available
4. Joint risks: underestimated, neutral, under control

Then follow by applying this basic three-step process:

1

Reveal
Participants vote individually and acknowledge the result collectively.

2

Reflect
Problem areas are identified and analyzed as a team.

3

Repair
Decisions are made to fix the problems and are validated together.

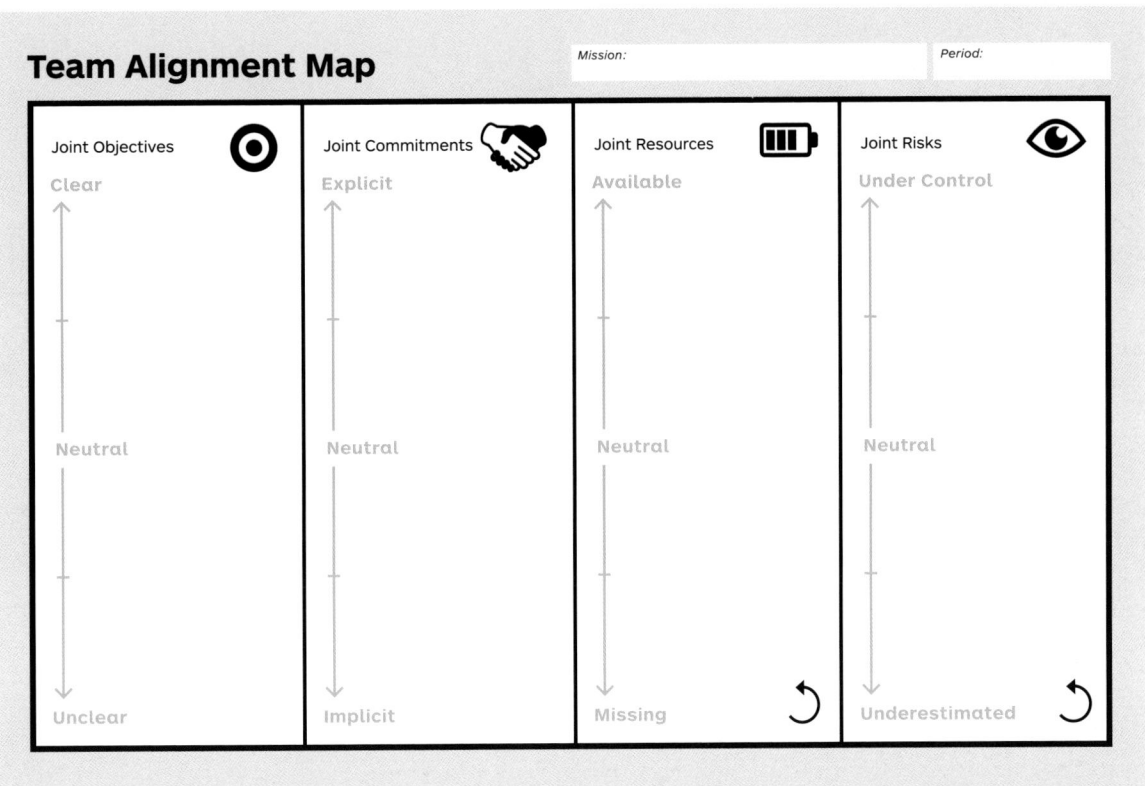

Step 1: Reveal

Team members vote to reveal whether they believe they can contribute successfully.

1
Announce the topic
What's the challenge?

Teresa   Luca   Jeremy   Mara

2
Vote individually
Do you think you can do your part?

Teresa thinks:

- Joint objectives: what we intend to achieve together is clear.

- Joint commitments: we have explicitly discussed each one of our role and commitments.

- Joint resources: we have the resources we need to do our jobs.

- Joint risks: the risks we face are under control.

Luca thinks:

- Joint objectives: what we intend to achieve together is clear.

- Joint commitments: our roles are implicit; mutual commitments have not been discussed.

- Joint resources: we miss critical resources to do our jobs.

- Joint risks: some risks are under control and some are underestimated.

Mara thinks:

- Joint objectives: some objectives are clear and some are not.
- Joint commitments: some commitments have been discussed and some are implicit.
- Joint resources: some resources are available but are not sufficient to do our jobs.
- Joint risks: some risks are under control and some are underestimated.

Jeremy thinks:

- Joint objectives: what we intend to achieve together is unclear; I'm confused.
- Joint commitments: our roles are implicit; mutual commitments have not been discussed.
- Joint resources: we miss critical resources to do our jobs.
- Joint risks: the risks we face are underestimated.

3
Acknowledge the result
What's the collective result?

Project X

The "aha" moment. The display of the vote triggers group awareness and problem recognition.

Step 2: Reflect

Identify perception gaps and discuss to understand the causes.

The vertical distribution of votes helps the team understand whether each member is in a position to contribute successfully and the level of alignment in the team, i.e. if team members share the same perception.

The ideal vote occurs when all votes are in the green zone. When a participant enters his or her entire vote into the green zone, he or she reports that:

1. Objectives are clear
2. Commitments have been explicitly agreed
3. Resources are available to do his or her work
4. Risks are under control

In other words, a vote in the green zone indicates that the minimum requirements are met for a successful personal contribution. When the whole team votes in the same way, team members are positively aligned and the team is likely on the path to success because everyone thinks they can successfully contribute.

The team can also be negatively aligned, when the majority of votes are concentrated at the bottom of the red zone. This means that all team members express that they

4
Interpret the vote
Surprised or not surprised?
Is it more positive or negative for us?
Where are the problems?

cannot contribute at all. Any other voting pattern in the red zone signals a problem for one or more members, that something is unclear or missing and that should be addressed rapidly.

To summarize, the vertical position of votes shows whether a requirement is met or not; the higher the position the better. A concentration of votes illustrates alignment

in the team, whereas dispersion indicates misalignment. The more votes are concentrated at the top, in the green zone, the higher the chances of success. The more votes are dispersed or concentrated at the bottom, in the red zone, the more problems are likely to appear while working together. In this case, better stop, talk, and take repair actions before it's too late.

Green zone

Higher likelihood of success

(all votes in the top third of the map)
It's okay when the majority of votes is in the green zone. The team is aligned and everyone is ready to perform. No need to discuss further; it's time to get back to work.

Red zone

Lower likelihood of success

(one or more votes in the bottom two-thirds of the sliders)
Problems are imminent when one or more votes are in the red zone. The requirements for a successful collaboration are not met for one or more team members. Better discuss to understand where the problems are and how to fix them before it's too late.

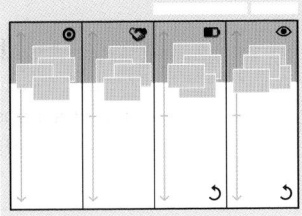

Example 1: Go ahead
This is the ideal vote. The team is positively aligned and confident that everyone can contribute successfully.

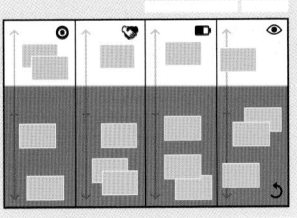

Example 2: Stop and talk
The four variables must be discussed and clarified. Some team members think that some requirements are okay (votes at the top), others that nothing is okay (votes at the bottom). This dispersion illustrates the highest level of misalignment.

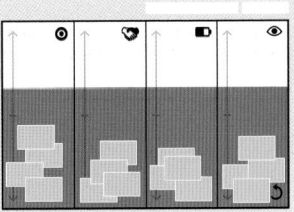

Example 3: Stop and talk
The four variables must be discussed. The team is negatively aligned: all members believe that nothing is okay.

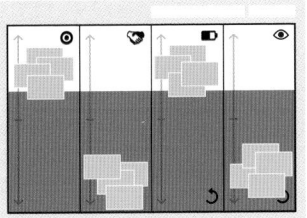

Example 4: Stop and talk
The team needs to discuss why commitments and risks are so low. For all team members, the joint commitments are unclear and joint risks are underestimated. Joint objectives appear clear and resources are available for the whole team.

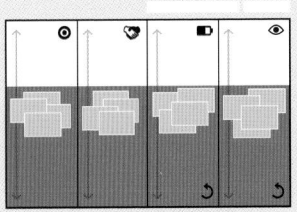

Example 5: Stop and talk
The four variables must be urgently discussed. All team members vote neutral. This is a typical vote for nonpriority projects or when participants are disengaged or prefer not to speak up.

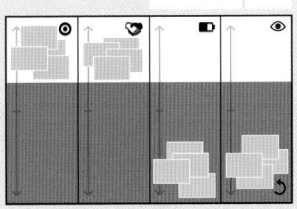

Example 6: Stop and talk
The last two variables must be discussed. Joint objectives and joint commitments are clear, but there is a critical lack of resources and risks are somehow underestimated. This is a typical vote for teams in startups. The last two variables must be discussed.

5

Analyze the problems

What's causing the problems?
What causes the perception gaps?
What prevents that requirement from being
in the green zone?

The objective of this step is to discuss the votes in the red zone and what causes the perception gaps—the trigger questions on the next page might help.

Discussion time may vary depending on the situation. For example, a problem with a missing resource, such as a software developer claiming three additional days of work, is quite simple to understand. Problems regarding unclear objectives, implicit commitments, or risks will need more time to be understood.

Trigger questions to analyze problems

These questions help spark collective thinking and dive deeper into possible issues. The following rule of thumb helps facilitate the analysis:

1. Ask a question
2. Listen to the answers
3. Summarize and share to validate understanding

High-level questions

What's your feeling about this vote?
What do you think is the problem?

Inquire deeper

Joint Objectives
- What are we supposed to achieve together, concretely?
- What will make our project a success?
- What are we supposed to deliver?
- What will the end result look like?
- What challenges do we have to address?
- What's the plan?

Joint Commitments
- Who will do what? With whom? For whom?
- What's everyone's role and responsibilities?
- What do we expect from each other, precisely?

Joint Resources
- What resources do we need?
- What is missing for everyone to do his or her part?

Joint Risks
- What can prevent us from succeeding?
- What's our worst-case scenario?
- What's our plan B?

Step 3: Repair

Repairing means taking concrete actions to ensure that the votes in the red zone are moved to the green zone in the next vote.

What causes problems is understood and it's time to redress the situation. Further explanations must be provided or decisions must be made. The resulting repair actions can vary considerably:

- Clarify or adapt something (mission, period, and the content of the four columns).
- Remove or add new content on the map.
- Make decisions outside the TAM, shift priorities, split the project into two or three projects, and so on.

As shown in 7, a final vote is conducted to validate the impact of the repair actions and to see if any problems remain. The assessment has been successful if the majority of votes is now in the green zone.

6

Decide and announce the repair actions

What concrete actions/measures should we take to redress the situation?
What can be done to get most of the votes in the green zone next time?

More questions for making decisions and acting

- So now what? What should we do, concretely?
- What actions must we take now? What's the priority?
- Where do we go from here? What do we decide?
- What are the immediate next steps?

+

Fixing the mission and period

- Clarify the mission
- Reframe the mission
- Review the scope
- Extend the period

+

Fixing the four variables

- Clarify
- Add
- Remove
- Adapt

+

Fixing outside the TAM

- Change priorities
- Split the project into sub-projects
- Assign to a different team, etc.

Team Validation

Do you think you can do your part now?

The new votes are in the green zone: great job! The situation is corrected, and everyone can get back to work.

Should some votes remain in the red zone: unfortunately, some problems still remain. In this case pragmatism prevails: the team and/or the team lead decide whether to resume an analysis cycle or move forward.

When to Assess

There are two types of assessments: when the project is kicked off (more frequent) and after (less frequent). The need for alignment is greatest at the beginning of projects and decreases over time as team members accumulate common ground (see Dive Deeper, p. 252). But changes in context and information can create dangerous blind spots that can be addressed by making rapid ad hoc validations.

	Readiness assessments "Are we having a good start?"	**Troubleshooting assessments** "Are we still on track?"
What?	• Are we ready to perform? • Will every member deliver optimally? • Shall we go or do we need to prepare more? • What are our chances of success?	• Can every member still deliver optimally? • Have any changes created harmful blind spots? • Are we still on the path to success?
When?	• Weekly coordination meetings (10 minutes before the end of the meeting) • Project initiation meetings (at the beginning or the middle of the meeting)	• Project execution meetings (10 minutes before the end of the meeting) • On-demand meetings (at the beginning of the meeting)
How many?	More frequent (until the actual kickoff) • Daily • Weekly • On-demand	Less frequent (after the actual kickoff) • Monthly • Quarterly • Every semester • On-demand

<u>Case study</u>
Healthcare company
500 employees

Will We Deliver on Time?

Simone is the regional boss of a mid-sized health-care company. Her project managers manage five projects on average and complain about their work overload. Rumors are flying around that the customer relationship management (CRM) project, which ranks high in terms of business priorities, will not be delivering on time. Is there anything Simone should worry about?

1
Reveal

Simone organizes an on-demand trouble-shooting assessment to understand whether the project will be delivered on time or not. The team of four is invited and they vote. Results illustrate that there is a problem with joint resources. All team members agree that there are not enough resources to complete the work as expected.

Adapted from S. Mastrogiacomo, S. Missonier, and R. Bonazzi,
"Talk Before It's Too Late: Reconsidering the Role of Conversation
in Information Systems Project Management." Journal of
Management Information Systems *31, no. 1 (2014): 47–78.*

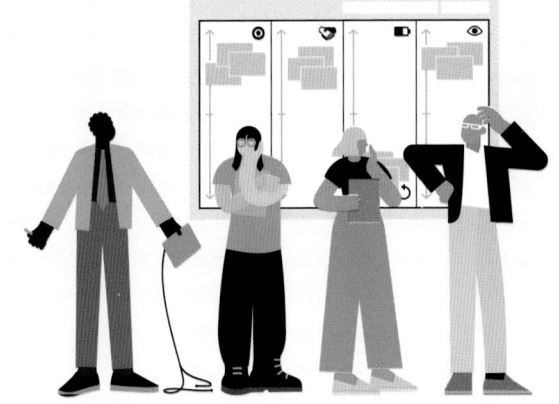

2
Reflect

The team reflects: members report high work overloads, which results in a persistent lack of time to complete all their tasks and their inability to maintain the deadline. Further investigation leads Simone to realize that some members are working on nonpriority tasks, out of the scope of this project, and beyond their responsibility.

There have been recent changes in the organization and somehow, this information didn't make it to this team. This is the turning point of the meeting: team members realize that they were unaware of these changes.

3
Repair

Simone explains that some activities are no longer to be performed by the team, since they will be externalized soon. She clarifies the new priorities and the objectives of the CRM project to the team. Team members are relieved and confirm with a new vote that under these new conditions everyone will be able to perform their parts on time.

The CRM project is eventually delivered on time.

Run Your First Assessment

1
Reveal

2
Reflect

Announce the mission, project, or subject
- What's the challenge?

Vote individually
- Do you think you can do your part?

Acknowledge the result
- What's the collective result?

Interpret the vote
- Surprised or not surprised? Is it more positive or negative for us?
- Where are the problems?

3
Repair

Analyze the problems
- What's causing the problems?
- What causes the perception gaps?
- What prevents that requirement from being in the green zone?

Decide and announce the repair actions
- What concrete actions/ measures should we take to redress the situation?
- What can be done to get most of the votes in the green zone next time?

Team validation
- Do you think you can do your part now?

Put the Map into Action

How to use the Team Alignment Map

"Information is a difference that makes a difference."

Gregory Bateson, Anthropologist

Overview

Starting with successful meetings as building blocks, learn techniques to apply the Team Alignment Map in <u>meetings</u>, in <u>projects</u> (add time), and in <u>organizations</u> (add time and teams).

2.1
The Team Alignment Map
for Meetings

Run more productive, move-to-action meetings.

2.2
The Team Alignment Map
for Projects

Lower project risk and reduce execution problems.

2.3
The Team Alignment Map
for Organizational Alignment

Get alignment between leaders, teams, and departments to break down internal silos.

2.1
The Team Alignment Map for Meetings

Run more productive, move-to-action meetings.

Shall we have another meeting?

Techniques to Run More Productive, Move-to-Action Meetings

Escape from conversations going around in endless loops. Use the TAM in your meetings to propel people from conversation to action, focus the team, and help everyone take action.

√

Recommended for taking action

Use the TAM to help the participants move to action, coordinate, and deliver as a team.

×

Not recommended for exploring

Do not use the TAM to brainstorm or debate. The tool has not been designed to support exploratory discussions.

Focus the team
p. 120
Structure the conversation and spend less time in confusing and boring meetings.

Boost team members' engagement
p. 122
Let every member be a driving force.

Increase meeting impact
p. 124
Less blah blah, more action.

Make informed decisions
p. 126
Reveal collaboration blind spots and issues with a neutral voice.

Focus the Team

Structure the conversation and spend less time in confusing and boring meetings.

The TAM can be used to close meetings and focus the team on concrete next steps. This encourages the organization of more effective meetings. Meetings have become unpopular and are considered a waste of time. But meetings are not the problem: face-to-face interaction is the best collaboration technology in the world (Dive Deeper, Impact of Communication Channels on Common Ground Creation, p. 264). The problem is what is discussed during meetings. The TAM can help by structuring the conversation in a logical order, making it easier for everyone to understand, participate, and agree on what's next.

Use the Team Alignment Map to

- Speed up interactions and save time
- Focus the discussion, reduce confusion

Timebox meetings with the TAM

1. Timebox your meeting (30, 60, 90 minutes)
2. Share the agenda
3. Discuss the topics
4. Conclude the meeting by performing a forward and a backward pass with the TAM to clarify who will do what
5. Share a photo of the TAM

The TAM can also be filled in progressively from the very beginning of the meeting. Topics are discussed and whenever a concrete action needs to be taken, a joint objective is created and a rapid forward and backward pass are performed.

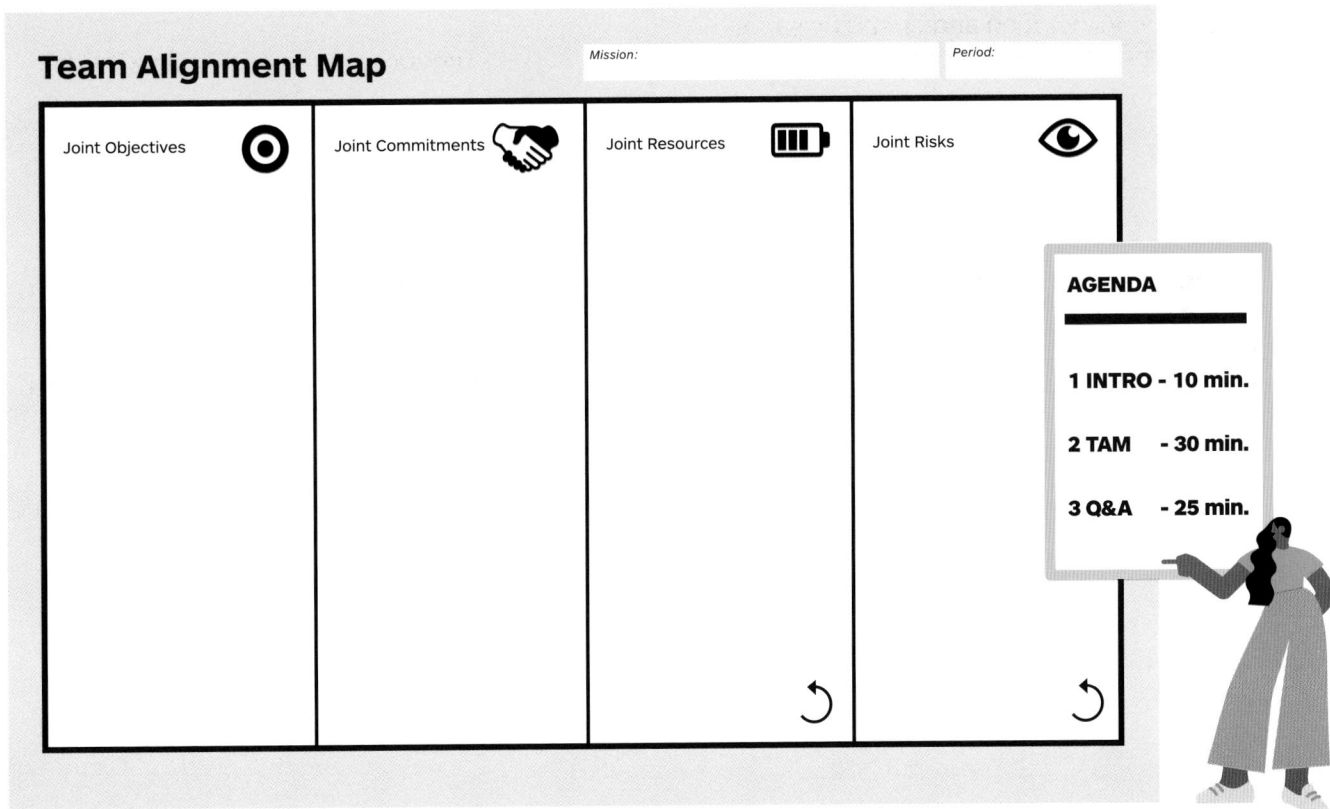

Team Alignment Map

Mission: _____ Period: _____

Joint Objectives ⦿	Joint Commitments 🤝	Joint Resources 🔋	Joint Risks 👁

AGENDA

1 INTRO - 10 min.

2 TAM - 30 min.

3 Q&A - 25 min.

Boost Team Members' Engagement

Tired of being the team's driving force?

Frame the mission as a compelling challenge for the whole team. Lack of engagement and ownership start with a lack of participation. Frame the mission as a challenging question and let every team member respond directly on the TAM. Responding together creates a higher level of participant engagement and energy. Allowing every participant to prepare and respond in 2, 3, or 5 minutes gives everyone (in particular, introverts) a voice and fosters creativity and the perception of fairness within the team.

Use the Team Alignment Map to

• Engage team members emotionally, create a we're-all-in-this-together mindset

• Bring the team together as a real team, align personal and collective goals

Frame the mission as a challenging question

1. Frame the mission as a question, a challenge, or a problem everyone understands. Start by "How will we…,?" "How can we…?," "How to…?"
2. Ensure that everyone understands the question.
3. Allow 5 minutes for individual preparation (forward pass).
4. Allocate 2 minutes per participant to present his or her forward pass.
5. Consolidate and perform the backward pass together.

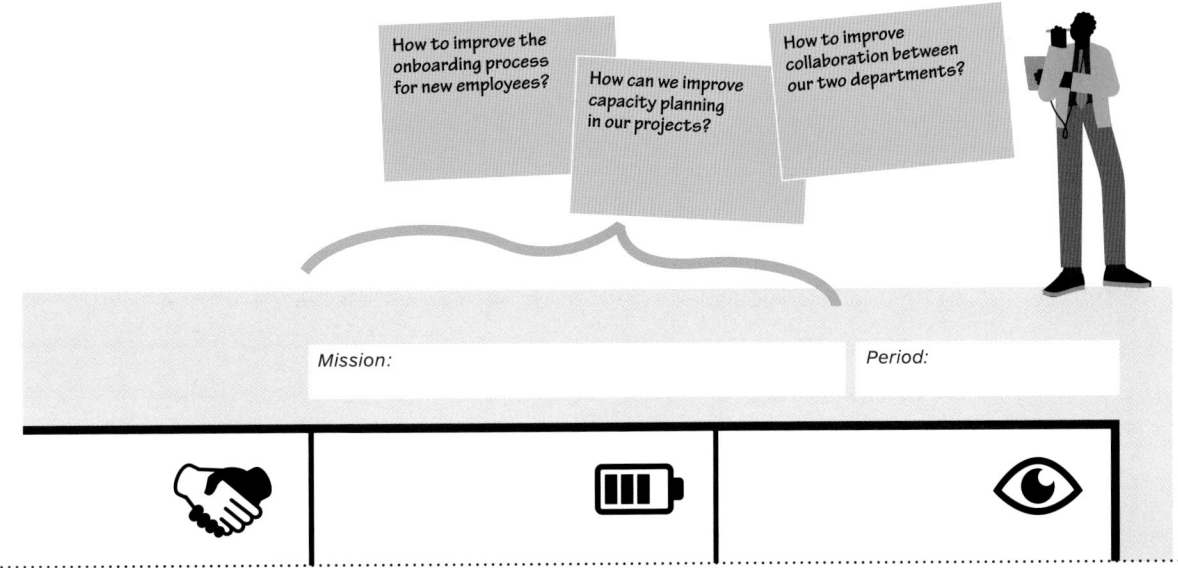

How to improve the onboarding process for new employees?

How can we improve capacity planning in our projects?

How to improve collaboration between our two departments?

Mission:

Period:

Increase Meeting Impact

Less blah blah, more action.

No one is in charge? The objective becomes a risk. Stop blah-blah and gossip by urging the team to agree on what needs to be done and by whom. Ensure that everyone's contribution is visible on the TAM and understood and agreed on by the other team members for maximum impact. Make everyone aware of the risk that the joint objectives nobody takes care of will result in… nothing.

Use the Team Alignment Map to

- Switch from talk to action, know who does what
- Stay grounded; objectives with no commitment are considered to be risks

Switch from talk to action with clear commitments

1. Perform a forward and backward pass.
2. Ensure that every joint objective has a joint commitment; add a deadline if necessary.
3. Move all the floating objectives (with no joint commitment) into joint risks (fourth column).
4. Share a photo of the TAM.

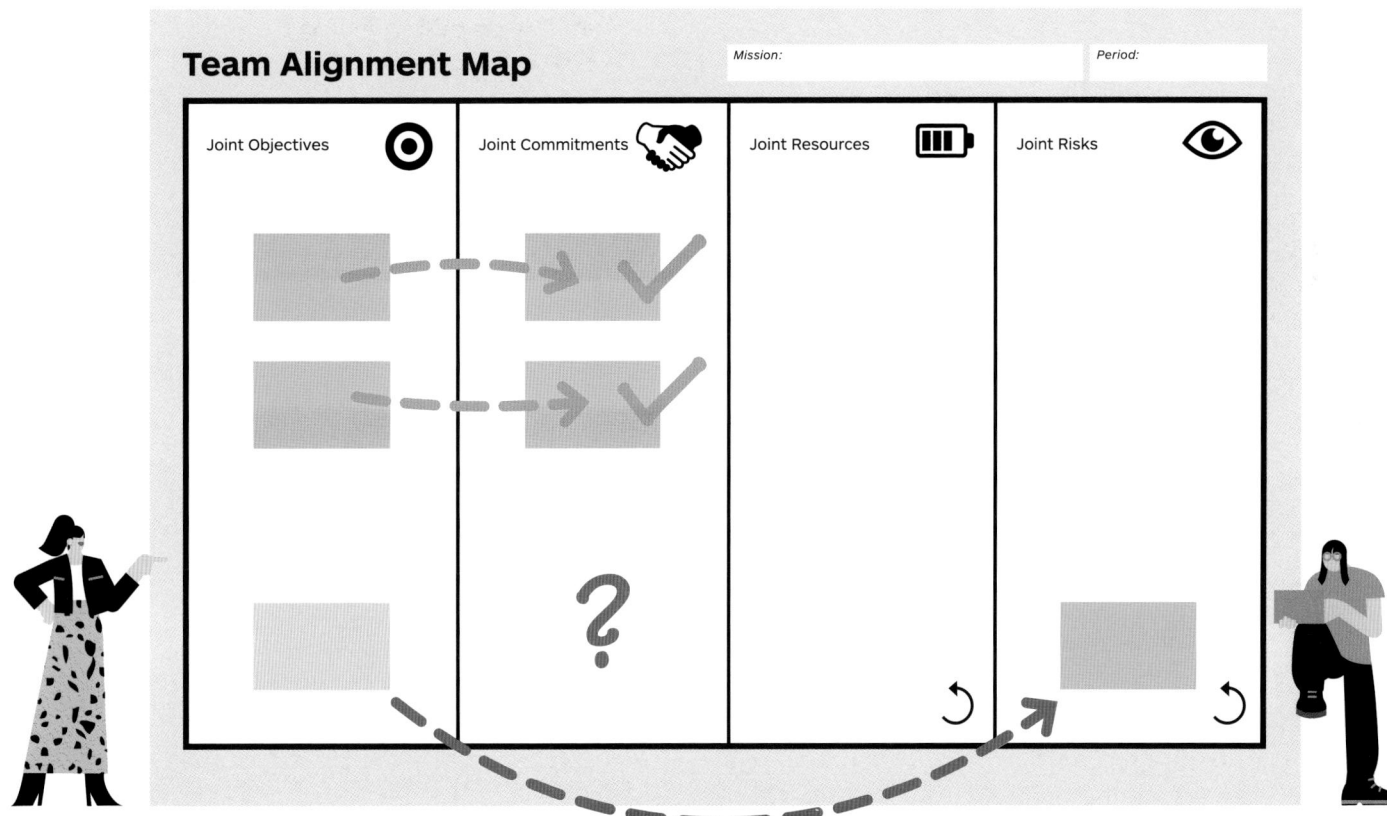

Make Informed Decisions

Reveal collaboration blind spots and issues and make better go/no go decisions.

A vote with the TAM in assessment mode can help team members to literally see their probability of success. Assessments reveal perception gaps and an aligned team will always be more likely to succeed than a misaligned team. Save your budget: assessments are fast, so don't miss an inexpensive opportunity to visualize alignment and decide whether to engage resources or if more preparation is required.

Use the Team Alignment Map to

- Proactively detect issues and reveal blind spots

- Make informed go/no go decisions, save budget

Assess team readiness and troubleshoot with the TAM

1. Run a TAM assessment (p. 90).
2. Use the vote to make a decision.

Tips

- Schedule another meeting quickly if time is short and problems can be solved reasonably fast. At the end of the second meeting, perform another assessment to confirm that issues have been addressed properly.

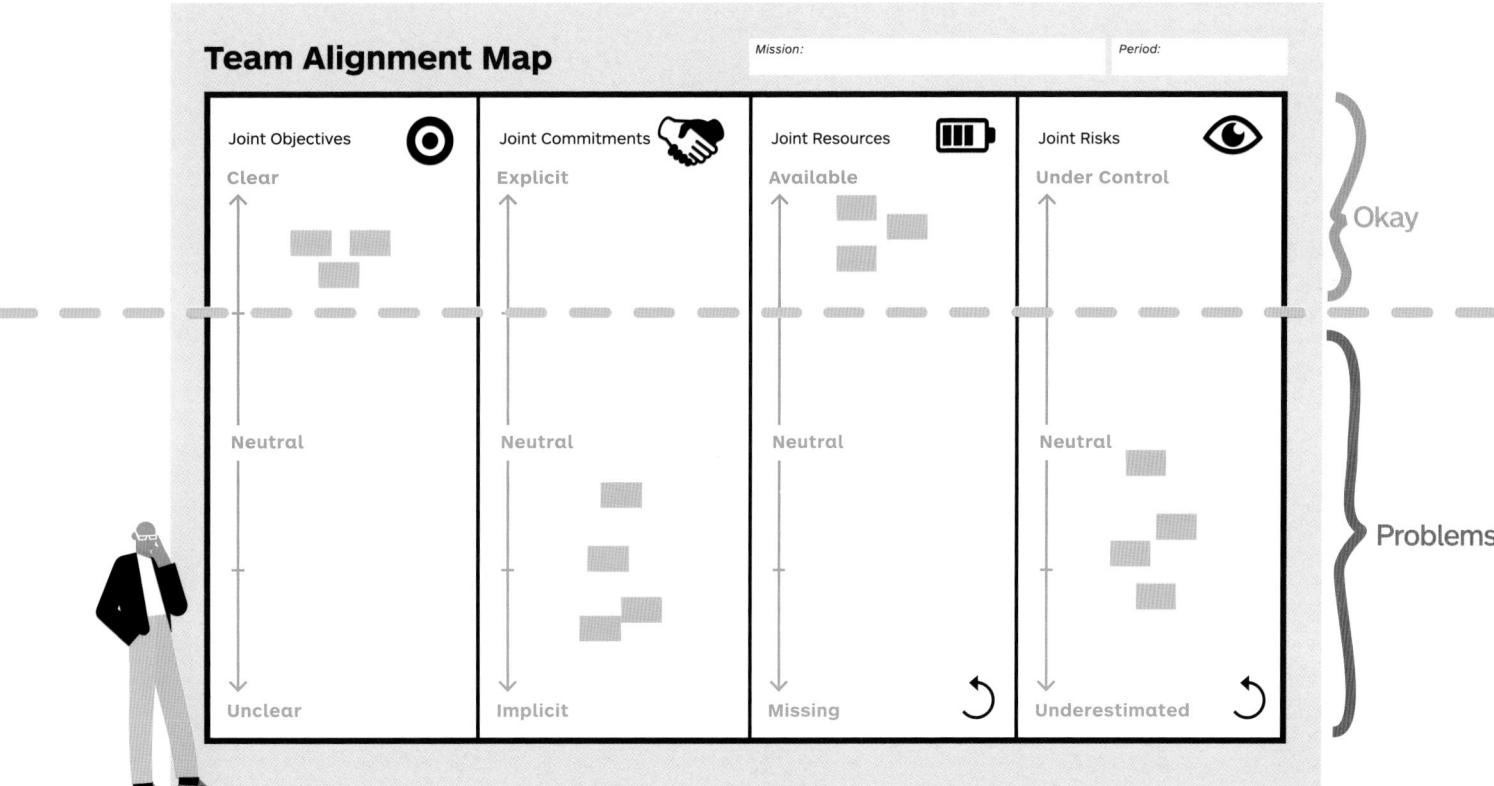

<u>Case study</u>
Humanitarian organization
36,000 employees

Do We Really Agree?

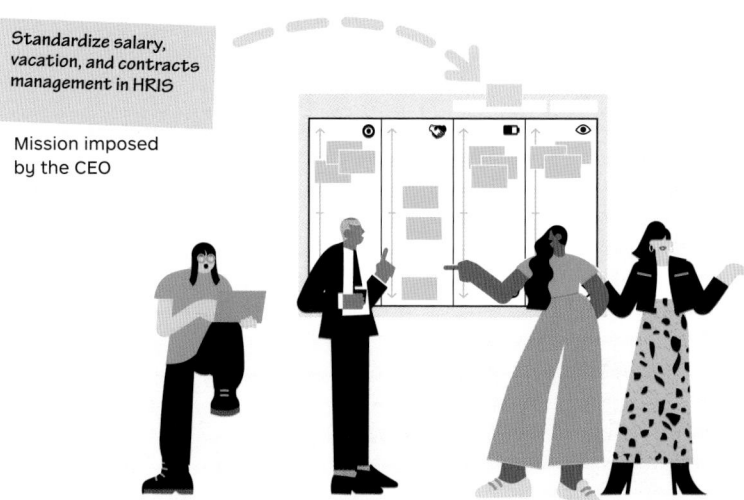

Standardize salary, vacation, and contracts management in HRIS

Mission imposed
by the CEO

Yasmine works in a humanitarian organization headquartered in Europe. She's in charge of standardizing the HR processes worldwide with a new HR Information System (HRIS). The mission has been assigned directly by the CEO and the project involves 13 participants from five different countries. Everyone seems to agree with the CEO, but Yasmine has doubts. She decides to assess the project team with a Team Alignment Map. Was her intuition right?

1
Reveal

The vote reveals that the participants seem positively aligned on joint objectives, joint resources, and joint risks, but joint commitments seem to be problematic.

S. Mastrogiacomo, Missonier, and R. Bonazzi, "Talk Before It's Too Late: Reconsidering the Role of Conversation in Information Systems Project Management." Journal of Management Information Systems 31, no. 1 (2014): 47–78.

Standardize salary, vacation, and contracts management in HRIS

2
Reflect

Perception gaps are discussed for the joint commitments column. The team rapidly notices that commitments are not the issue. The mission is ambiguous and everyone understands it differently, so the joint objectives are too high-level. Everyone had been committing to a different interpretation of the mission, which made the problem become visible.

3
Repair

The team decides to split the current mission into three submissions and projects by creating three new Team Alignment Maps. They perform a forward and a backward pass for each and organize three validation votes after that. The votes confirm that the team is aligned and confident about what will happen next. Françoise is clearly relieved.

Pro Tips

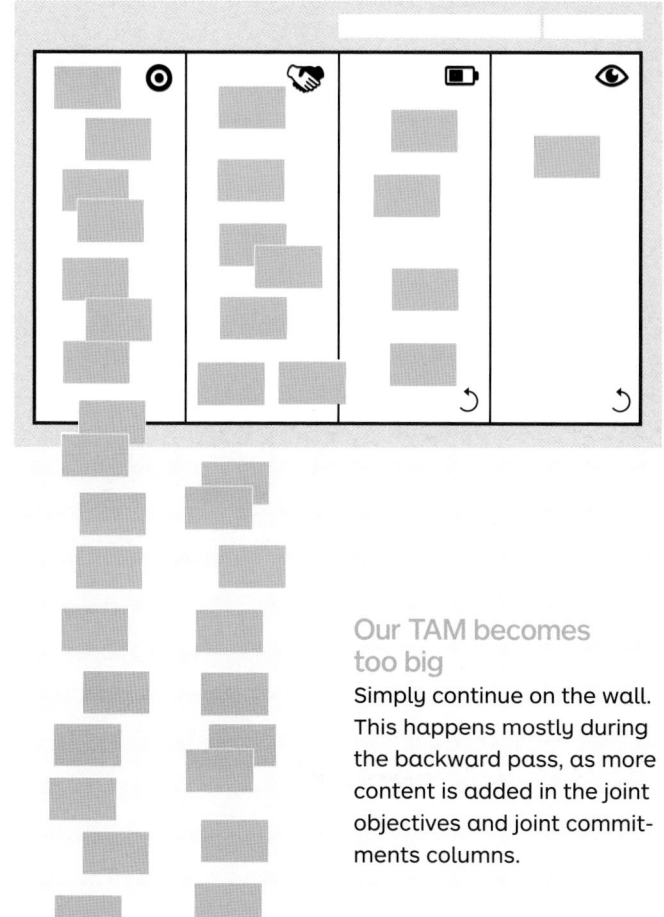

Dealing with disagreement and lack of clarity

Move unclear items to the joint risks column. The purpose of an alignment session is to create mutual clarity and agreement before people leave the meeting. When content on the TAM is perceived as ambiguous or there is disagreement in the meeting, place the item in the joint risks column for further discussion. Move it to the right column only when the content is perceived as clear and agreed on by the team.

Our TAM becomes too big

Simply continue on the wall. This happens mostly during the backward pass, as more content is added in the joint objectives and joint commitments columns.

How to manage missing stakeholders and latecomers

Take a few minutes to update briefly all latecomers so they can jump into the discussion and contribute. Team success springs from the team's common ground. Organize one-on-one update meetings when key stakeholders are missing meetings; keeping them in the loop is crucial for the team's success.

Risk identification: consider emotions as KPIs

Use fears, objections, and any emotional reactions as triggers to identify problems. We're biologically programmed to anticipate problems: fear, anger, sadness, and disgust can signal possible hidden risks. The Fact Finder (see p. 204) can help ask good questions and reveal the problems hidden behind negative emotions.

2.2
The Team Alignment Map for Projects

Lower project risk and reduce execution problems.

Do you think we can still make it?

Techniques to Lower Project Risk and Reduce Execution Problems

Significant energy and resources are lost in projects when key stakeholders are insufficiently aligned. Information flows poorly and execution problems spiral into cost and time overruns, poor quality, or lack of client satisfaction. Creating a shared initial view of what needs to be done and maintaining a high level of alignment over time should be a priority for any project leader or manager, just as it is the duty of any stakeholder to stay informed and share new information.

√

Recommended for projects

For any project team, new or experienced. These techniques can be used independently or to complement your preferred project management tools whether you're following waterfall or agile project management principles.

×

Not recommended for operations

Not of real use for operational teams, i.e. for teams running stable, high-volume, recurring activities, unless a project is in sight.

Get Projects Off to a Good Start
p. 138
Structure the conversation and spend less time in confusing and boring meetings.

Maintain Alignment over Time
p. 140
Staying in sync throughout the project lifecycle.

Monitor Tasks' Progress
p. 144
Align and track progress on a single poster with the Team Alignment Kanban.

Reduce Risks (While Having Fun)
p. 148
Mitigate risks visually as a team.

Align Distributed Teams
p. 150
Overcome the distance barrier using online boards.

Get Projects Off to a Good Start

It costs less than having a bad start.

The TAM can help create an initial big picture rapidly where each participant must find his or her place, whether your team is engaging in a project plan (waterfall) or a release plan (agile).

Building strong initial alignment requires additional effort, but the benefits will be tangible throughout the entire project.

Neglecting initial alignment is never a good idea. The need for coordination and crisis committees rapidly explodes in those teams that jump immediately into work with misaligned members. Nothing beats a good start when engaging in a project.

Use the Team Alignment Map to

- Give alignment an initial boost and increase the chances of success
- Gain more peace and control over the execution phases

Start projects with a TAM session

1. Create or validate alignment on who's doing what with the TAM before moving to action.
2. When initiating projects, run a TAM session. Experience tells us that it's wiser to postpone the kickoff until enough alignment is reached.

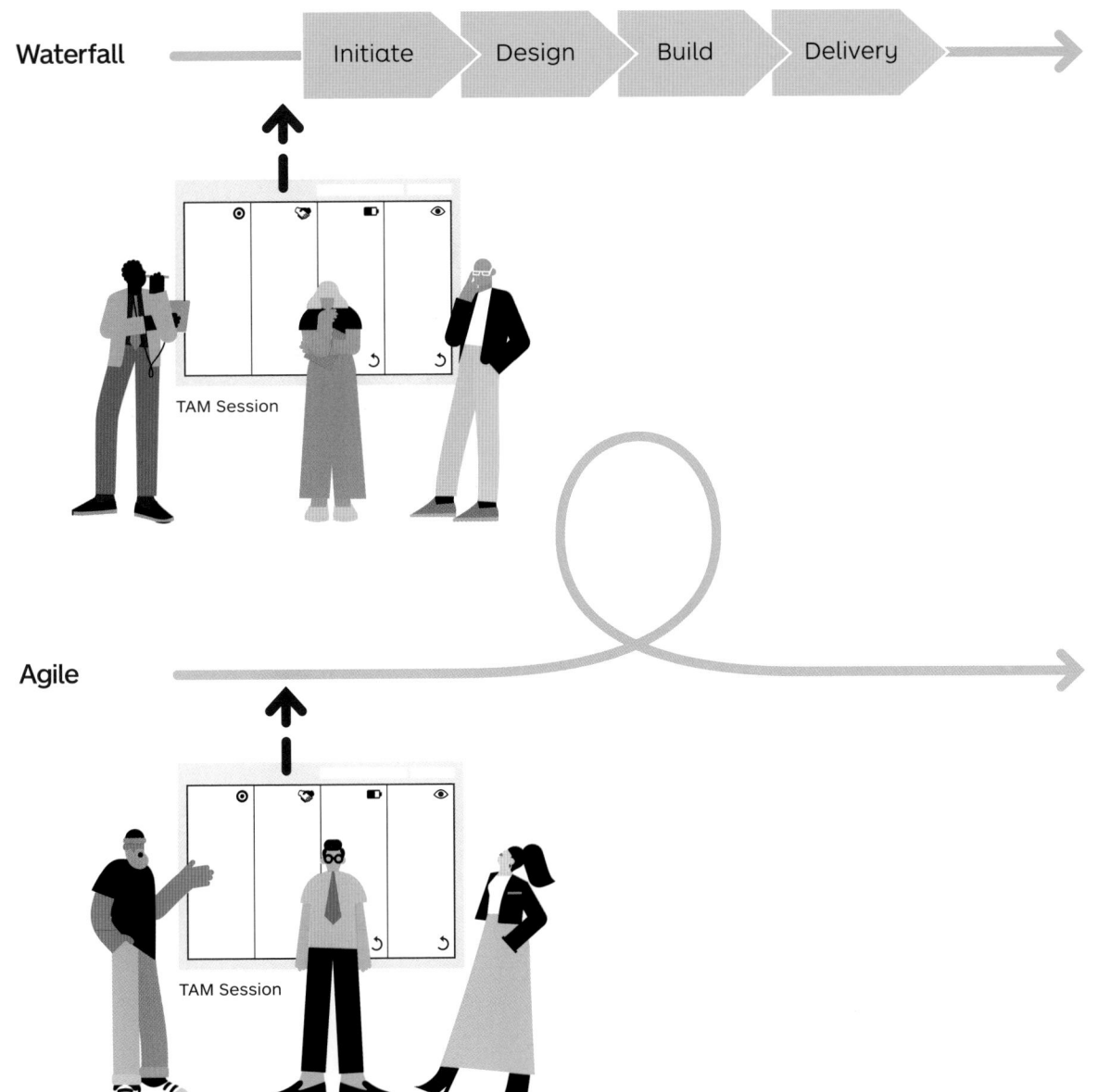

Waterfall

Initiate · Design · Build · Delivery

TAM Session

Agile

TAM Session

139

Maintain Alignment over Time

Staying in sync throughout the project lifecycle

Are alignment efforts similar throughout the entire project? No: in teams that have good initial alignment, the alignment efforts decrease over time — unlike teams that start projects with misaligned members and experience growing problems due to perception gaps.

Use the Team Alignment Map to

- Invest the right alignment effort at the right moment
- Avoid overcollaboration

Start projects with a TAM session

1. **Waterfall projects**: use the TAM weekly or monthly during the initiation and planning phase, and then only if required in the execution and delivery phases.
2. **Agile projects**: use a rapid TAM session at the beginning of each sprint. Sessions will become shorter over time.

Needs for alignment in Waterfall projects

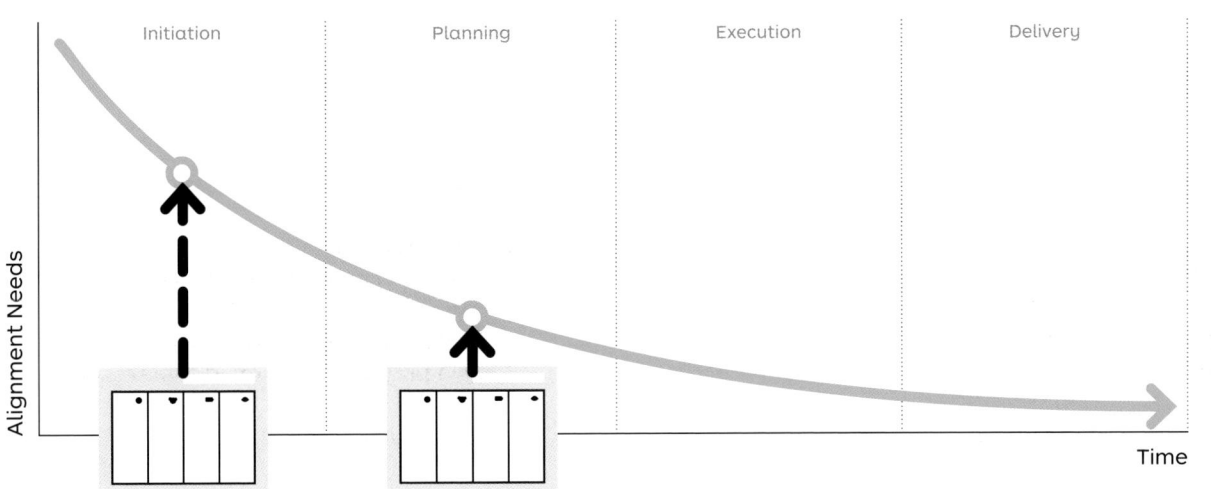

Needs for alignment in Agile projects

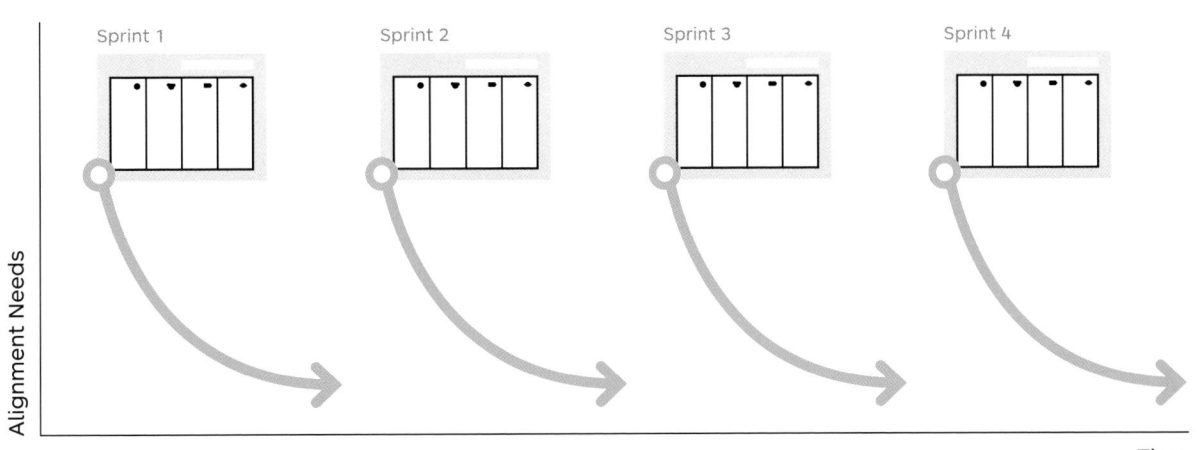

Four Easy Ways to Maintain Alignment with the TAM

Meeting 1
Plan

Meeting 2
Plan

Meeting N
Plan

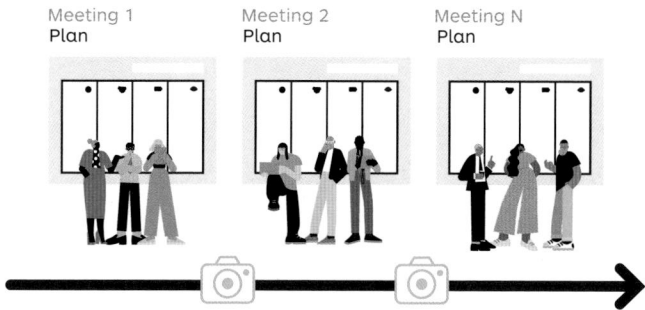

Meeting 1
Plan

Meeting 2
Assess (Check)

Meeting N
Assess (Check)

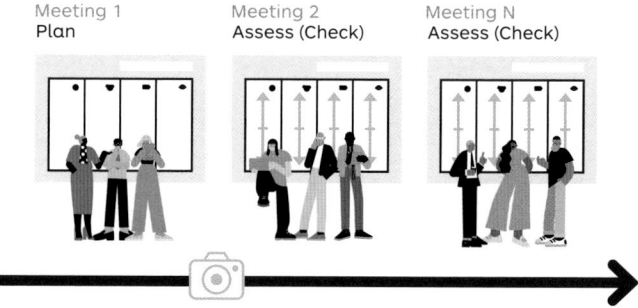

Weekly

Create an initial TAM and share a picture with all the team members. At the next session, create a new TAM for the next period by referring to the picture of the previous TAM.

Initially and with checks

Hold just one TAM session at the beginning and share a picture with the team.
Perform only rapid assessments to confirm that things are on track at the end of subsequent meetings. Update the initial TAM if necessary.

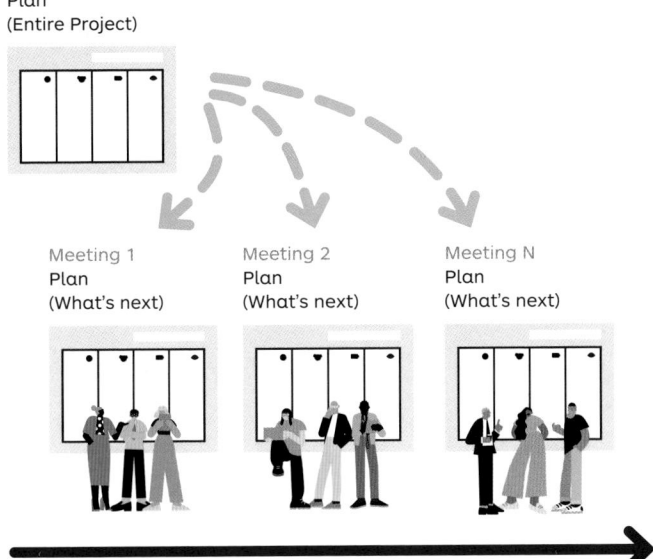

Plan
(Entire Project)

Meeting 1
Plan
(What's next)

Meeting 2
Plan
(What's next)

Meeting N
Plan
(What's next)

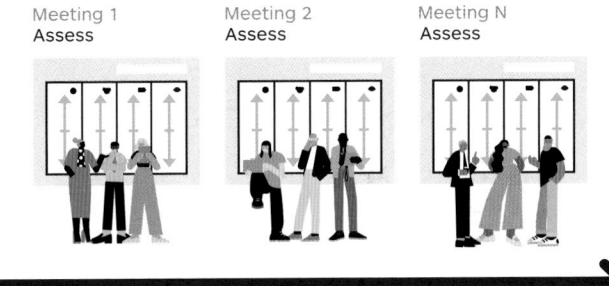

Meeting 1
Assess

Meeting 2
Assess

Meeting N
Assess

Entire project and weekly

A TAM is created that covers the entire project. New TAMs are created every week that cover only one week of work.

Rapid checks

For teams working with other project management tools and methods, rapid checks can be performed with the TAM at the end of key meetings.

Monitor Tasks' Progress

How to use the TAM Kanban-style to align and track work on a single wall.

Team alignment and task tracking are two different activities, and tasks are usually tracked using project management platforms. There is a low-cost solution that works for small and medium-sized projects: put a TAM on the wall and add three simple columns to simulate a Kanban board.

→

Use the Team Alignment Map to

- Align and monitor progress on a single wall

- Benefit from an easy and low-cost solution

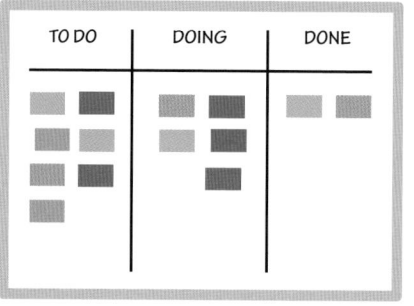

A Kanban Board offers a simple and powerful structure to monitor progress. Tasks (the colored notes) are moved between three columns: **To Do** contains the work agreed on and pending, **Doing** the tasks team members are working on, and **Done** the work that has been completed.

The **Backlog** column is an "inbox" to store ideas and objectives not yet discussed and validated as a team.

When combined, the joint objectives and joint commitments columns contain the **To Do** of a traditional Kanban Board.

Rest of the Kanban Board.

Monitor progress with a Team Alignment Map Kanban-style

1. Set the mission.
2. Enter new ideas and objectives in the Backlog column.
3. Perform a forward and backward pass for priority items.
4. Start moving the joint objectives combined with joint commitments (to do's) into the Doing and Done columns as team members start doing and completing their work.

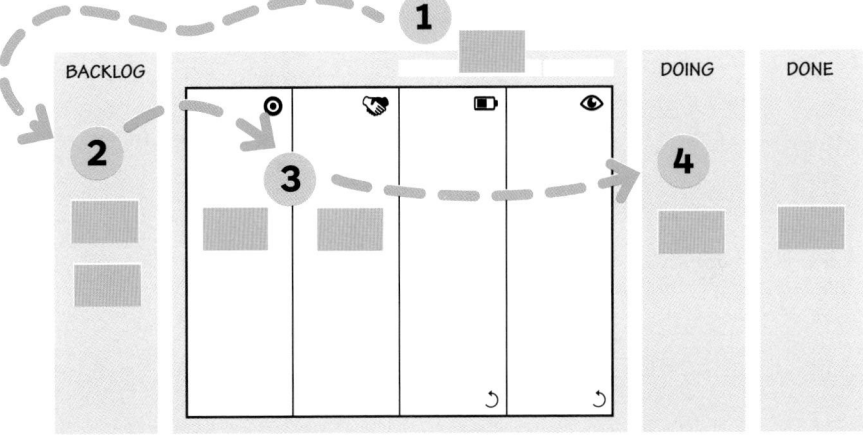

The TAM Kanban-style in Practice

Organize the wall in three main areas: Buffer, Clarify, and Track.

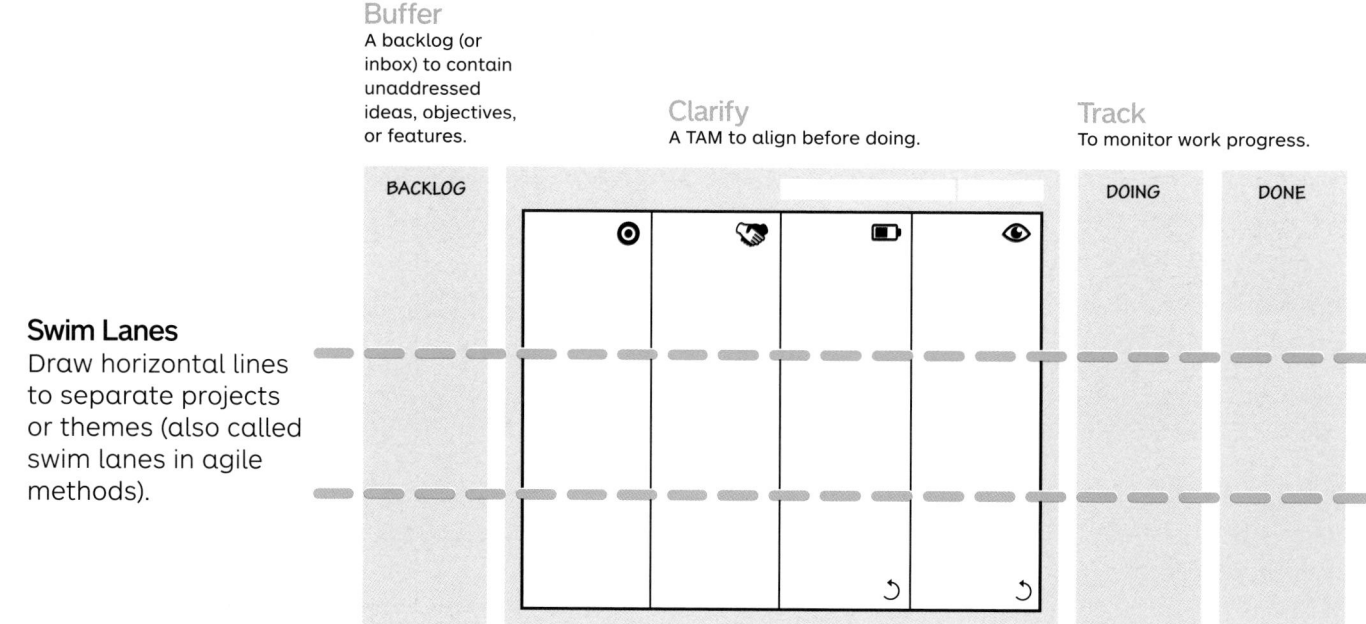

Buffer
A backlog (or inbox) to contain unaddressed ideas, objectives, or features.

Clarify
A TAM to align before doing.

Track
To monitor work progress.

Swim Lanes
Draw horizontal lines to separate projects or themes (also called swim lanes in agile methods).

BACKLOG

DOING

DONE

Example

1. The team's mission is to grow online market share. One of the pending ideas is to redesign the online store.

2. Pedro commits to improving the online store if a budget of $30K is allocated to buy the necessary licenses (forward pass).

3. Carmen, the Head of Marketing, commits to finding the budget rapidly (backward pass).

4. Carmen announces that the budget is okay and Pedro starts working on the redesign. They move their joint commitments (to do's) into the Doing and Done columns.

5. The Doing and Done columns show at any moment who's working on what and what has been completed.

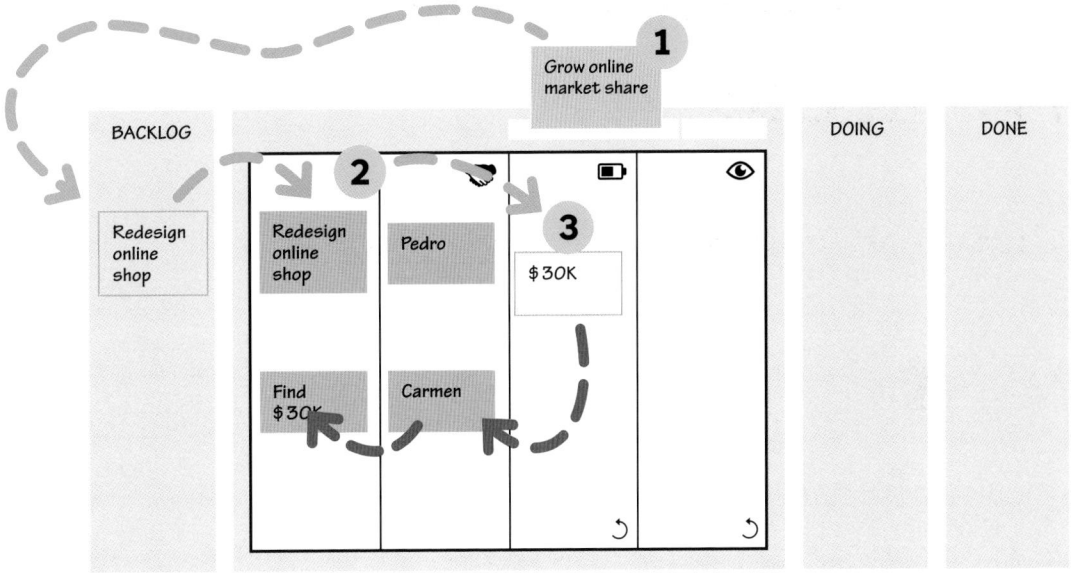

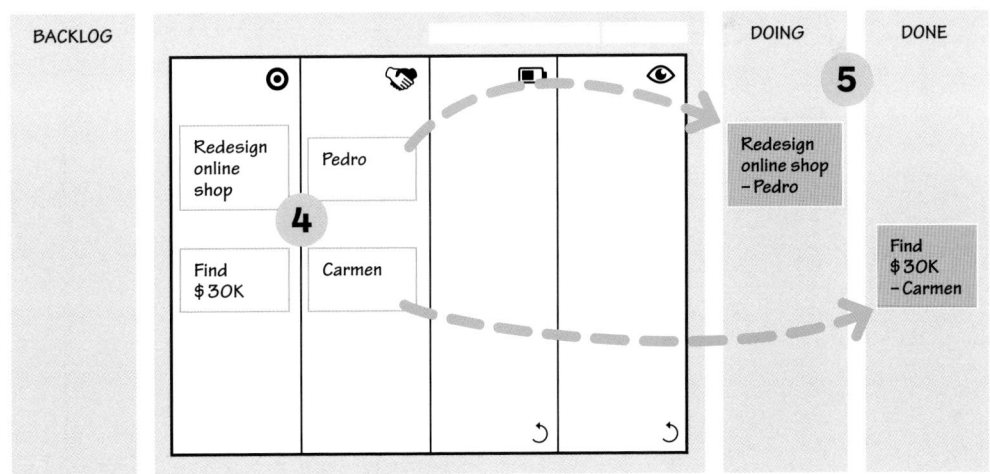

Reduce Risks (While Having Fun)

Mitigate risks visually as a team.

Project teams can neglect risk management. It's true that spending long hours filling in a projected spreadsheet line by line can be perceived as an unpleasant activity.

That exercise can become more enjoyable if done together visually during an alignment session; it's the raison d'être of the backward pass. Removing Post-it notes is removing problems — it demonstrates a tangible progression and motivates the team.

Use the Team Alignment Map to

- Mitigate project risks seamlessly
- Increase the team's accountability for risk management

Perform and emphasize the backward pass

1. Perform a forward and a backward pass for the project.
2. Insist on the backward pass: ensure that the last two columns are properly emptied and do not contain critical elements.
3. Schedule an additional meeting if you run out of time.
4. Validate as a team with a vote; share a photo of the TAM and the vote.

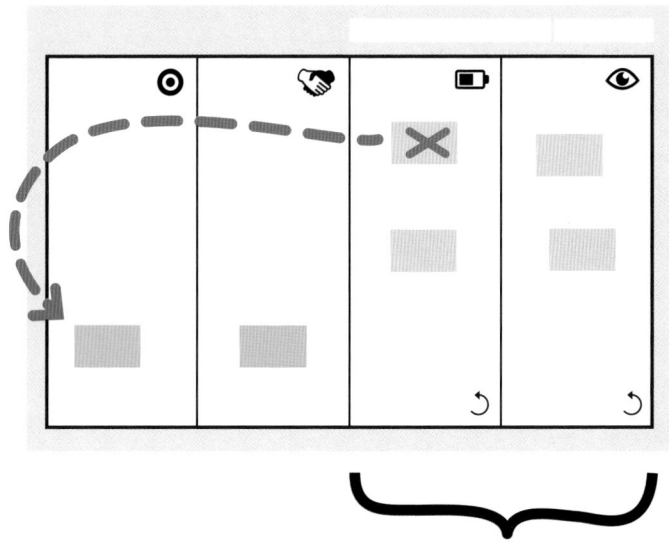

Challenge the team to empty these two columns completely.

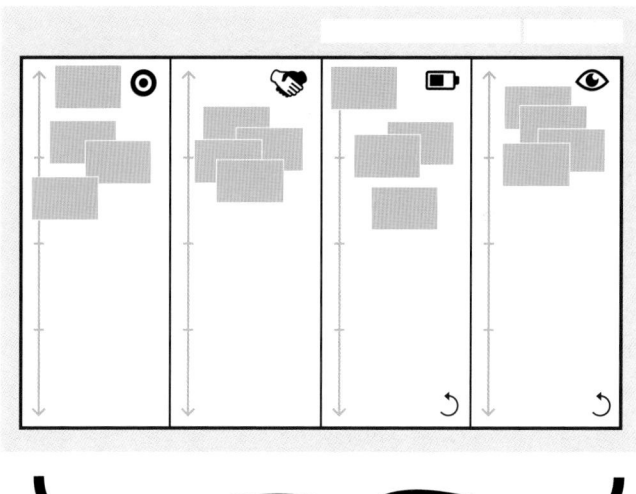

Conclude with a validation vote (the best possible validation vote is shown here).

Align Distributed Teams

Overcome the distance barrier using online boards.

Distributed teams can align remotely using online boards like Miro or Mural and benefit from great features such as:

- An infinite canvas, removing all physical constraints

- Synchronous and asynchronous collaboration

- Chat and video conferencing

- The ability to append videos and documents, add comments

On-site teams can also benefit from these features in addition to summaries of updates, version history, archiving, and integration with powerful project management tools.

→

Use the Team Alignment Map to

- Create a template in your preferred online board

- Create and maintain alignment remotely

Use an image of the TAM as background

1. Create a template of a TAM in your preferred online board.
2. Create and maintain alignment remotely.

+

Tips

- Use video conferencing in the first alignment session; it conveys nonverbal information

- Create a Team Alignment Map Kanban-style to align and monitor progress on a single board (p. 144).

- Online surveys, rather than online boards, are preferable for running TAM assessments.

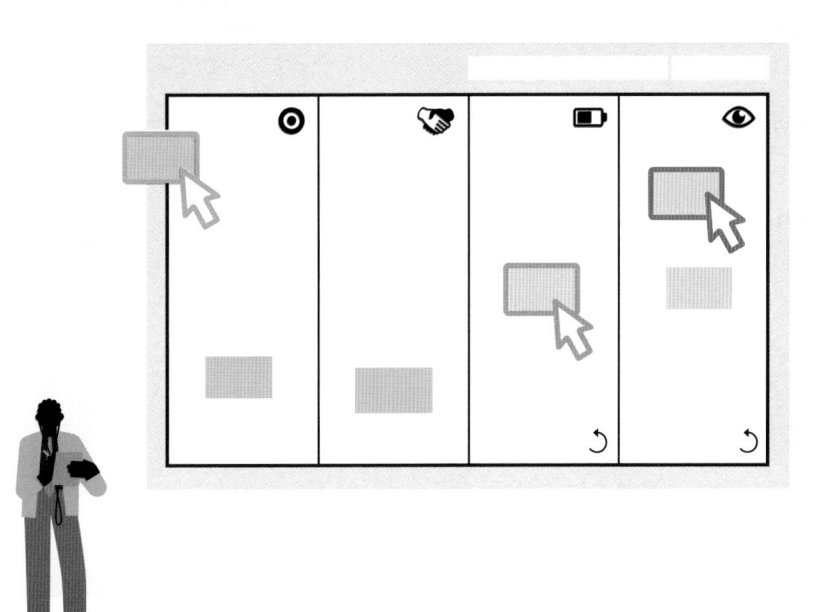

Pro Tips

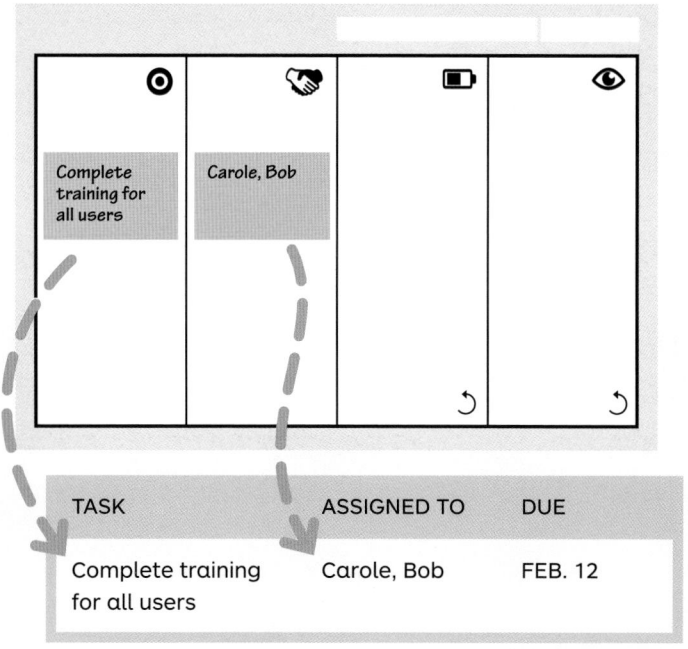

Tracking tasks with online tools

Translate objective-commitment pairs into tasks and assignments. Joint resources and joint risks can also be transferred and assigned using the same approach.

Adding delivery dates and milestones

Dates and durations can be added directly on the joint objectives or joint commitments notes. Add any milestones as joint objectives, in the first column.

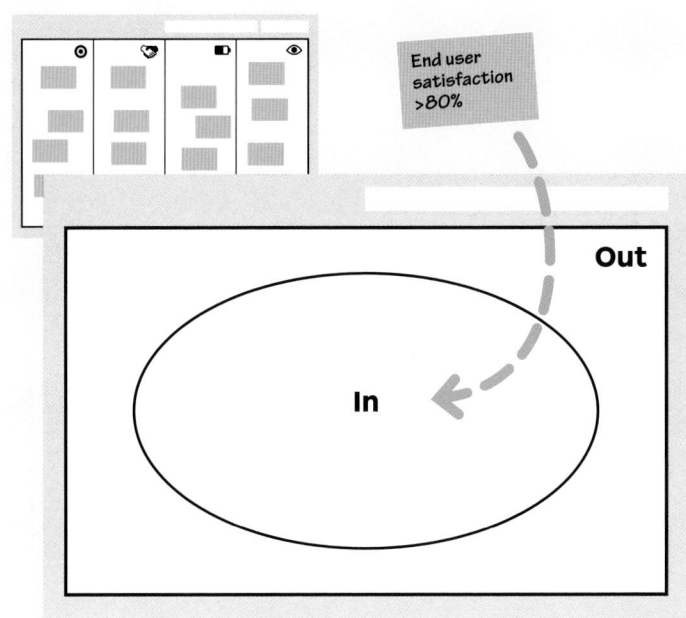

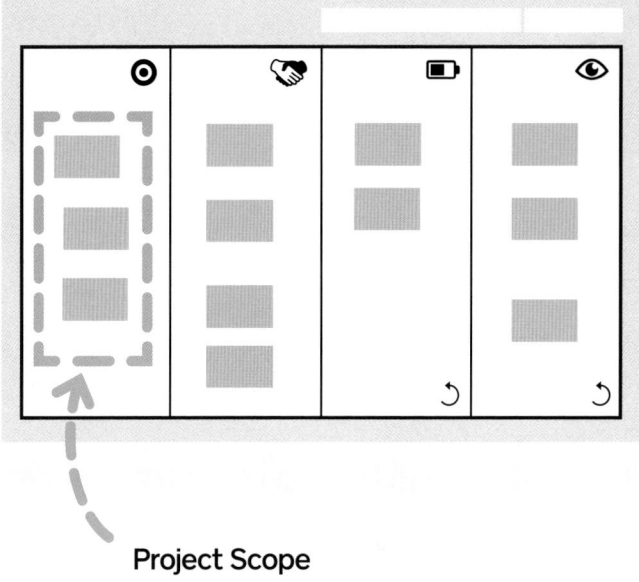

Project Scope

Adding success criteria

Use the Team Contract to discuss and hold success criteria (see p. 184). The TAM focuses on aligning on joint activities, while the Team Contract is dedicated to the rules of the game.

What if some objectives are not on the Team Alignment Map?

They are simply out of scope for that mission.

2.3
The Team Alignment Map for Organizational Alignment

Get alignment between leaders, teams, and departments to break down internal silos.

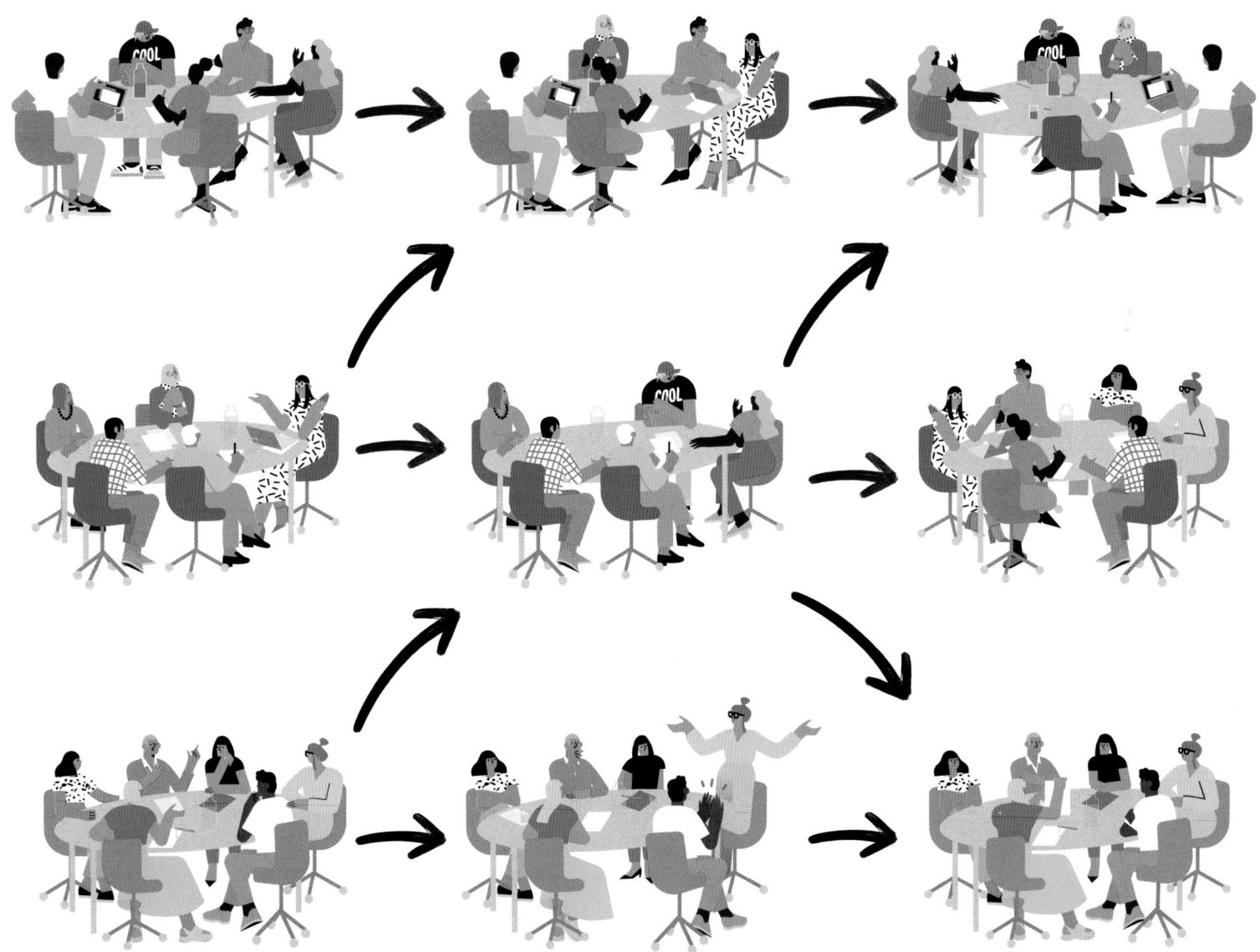

Techniques to Get Alignment Across Teams

High-caliber individuals and teams isolated in functional towers can't implement new business models, new client experiences, new products, and new services based on new processes. Complex challenges can only be addressed through effective cross-functional collaboration and participants who understand how the strategy translates into concrete, daily actions at the personal level.

Use these techniques to complement your strategy process or when launching new strategic initiatives to infuse organic alignment, facilitate cross-functional work, and engage at scale.

√

Recommended for organic change management

Create organic change by establishing a shared process and language, by empowering teams and by improving dialogue between teams and with leadership.

×

Not recommended without executive sponsorship

Make sure you are within your perimeter of legitimacy before gathering teams. The more cross-functional the initiative, the higher the level of sponsorship must be to avoid political backfires.

Empower Teams
p. 160
Escape from the role of the exhausted superhero.

Engage Large Groups
p. 162
Engaging dozens and hundreds of people.

**Facilitate Collaboration Across
Departments and Functions**
p. 164
Help cross-functional teams be more successful.

Negotiate and Allocate Resources
p. 166
Negotiate resources, peer-to-peer and with
leadership.

**Integrate the TAM with Strategy Processes
and Tools**
p. 168
Integrate the TAM with the
Business Model Canvas.

Assess the Readiness of Strategic Initiatives
p. 170
Assess readiness with hundreds of stakeholders.

Empower Teams

Escape from the role of the exhausted superhero.

Teams can seriously underperform when (1) the team members can't make informed decisions because they don't understand the strategic direction and (2) the conditions/resources required for each to do their work are missing.

As a team leader, a TAM empowerment session can help you act on these two problems. You set and explain the direction (mission), the team works independently on the how (forward pass), risks are mitigated, and resources are negotiated together (backward pass).

This approach is comparable to what is coined "aligned autonomy" at Spotify, the music streaming company. Teams are empowered using this basic formula: autonomy = authority x alignment (Henrik Kniberg 2014). The mission is set by leadership (authority), the team is accountable for the how (forward and backward pass), and all this happens in a constant dialogue (alignment).

Use the Team Alignment Map to

- Delegate work efficiently
- Help teams self-organize, increase autonomy

Empower teams with the TAM

Roles and Responsibilities
Leaders — the what and why
- Communicate the mission: what challenge must be addressed or what problem must be solved and for what reason.
- Set short-term objectives.
- Allocate the resources required by the team.

Team(s) — the how
- Find the best solution to the problem. Optimize resource utilization.
- Collaborate with other teams if necessary.

Fast empowerment meetings with the TAM (60 minutes)

1. Mission (5 minutes): the leader assigns a clear mission to the team (what and why) and sets short-term objectives (joint objectives). The leader leaves the room and comes back for step 3.
2. Forward pass (30 minutes): the team performs a forward pass independently; accountability increases when teams self-define the "how."
3. Presentation (5 minutes): the leader is back and the team presents the forward pass.
4. Backward pass (20 minutes): performed by the team and the leader: resources are negotiated/allocated and risks are mitigated together by adding, adapting, and removing content for the TAM.
5. Validation: joint validation of the TAM by leader and team.

+
Tips

- Frame the mission as a challenge to create even more engagement (Section 2, Boost Team Members' Engagement, p. 122).
- Use the Team Contract to define "how we will collaborate" in terms of rules, process, tools, and validation points (p. 184).

Team   Leader

Engage Large Groups

How to mobilize large teams

Engagement comes from participation. Period. Mobilizing large teams requires significant energy and time, particularly if several alignment sessions are required. But it's worth every penny because the larger the group or the initiative, the greater the financial risk and the likelihood of failure. Strong initial alignment is necessary to avoid significant budget overruns and other execution disasters.

So book a large venue, divide people into subgroups, run parallel sessions to give each participant a voice, consolidate and share the results before making decisions, and move to action.

Use the Team Alignment Map to

• Increase participants' buy-in and engagement

• Reduce financial risk

Mobilizing large groups

1. Split (5 minutes): split participants in groups of 4–8.
2. Align in subteams (30 minutes): run parallel TAM sessions by assigning groups the same global mission or submissions.
3. Present (5 minutes per subteam): each group presents its TAM to all the other groups.
4. Consolidate (after the meeting): if applicable, a facilitator aggregates the results into a single TAM.
5. Share (after the meeting): consolidated results are sent to all participants, usually with a list of decisions made and for what reason.

Additional iterations are performed until enough alignment is reached. Online TAM assessments can help confirm the level alignment in large groups.

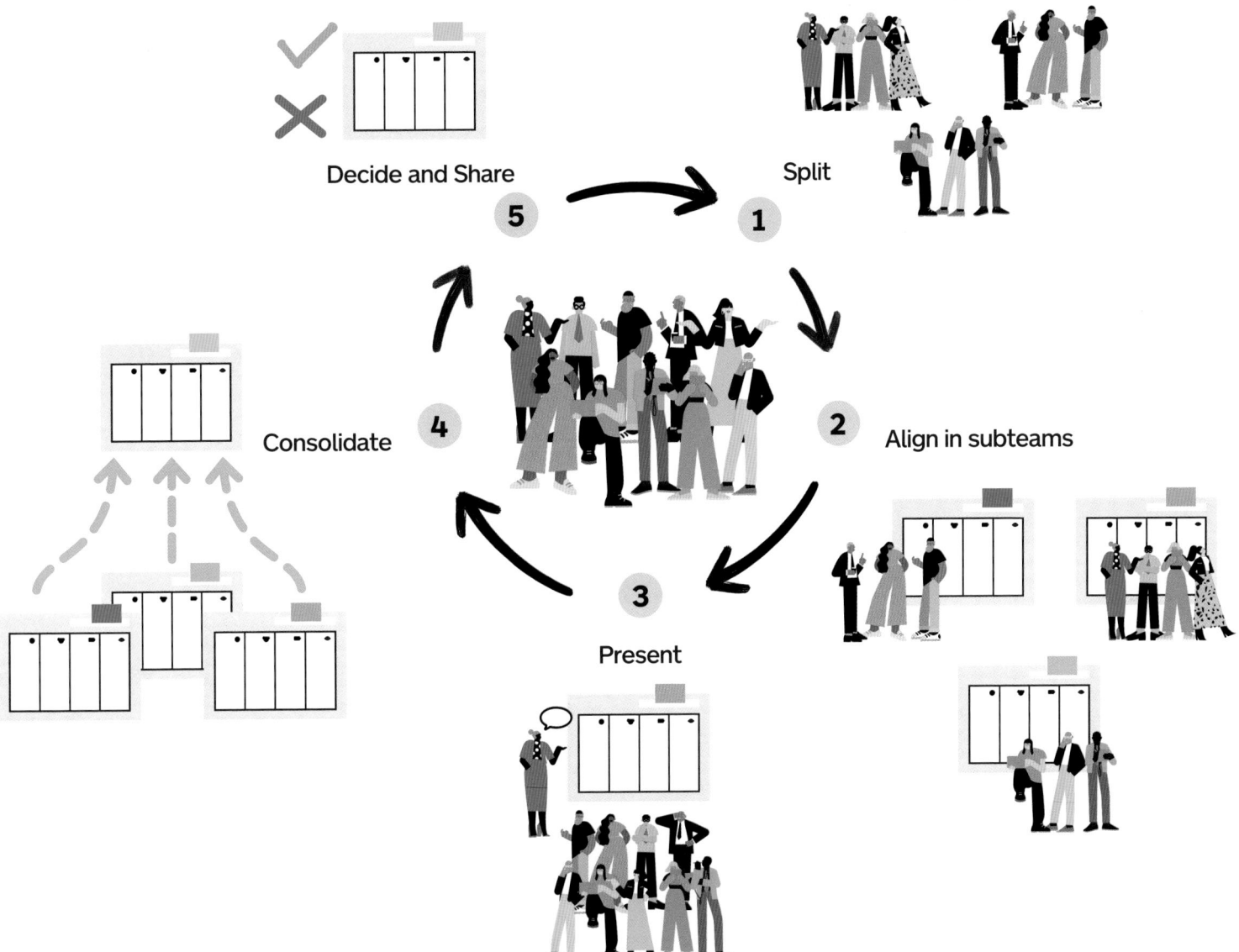

Decide and Share ⑤

Split ①

Consolidate ④

Align in subteams ②

Present ③

Facilitate Collaboration Across Departments and Functions

Help cross-functional teams be more successful.

When missions and objectives are misaligned within the organization, cross-functional teams get easily bogged down in unmanageable dependencies and political fights to grasp internal resources. Creating a supportive context for cross-functional work delivery starts by aligning the missions of all the impacted teams, assigning common short-term objectives, and allowing teams to discuss and negotiate shared objectives. This can be done with the TAM during alignment workshops by focusing on aligning missions and objectives with leaders and from team to team.

Use the Team Alignment Map to

- Create a shared language and process, set common goals
- Evolve the culture, implement new collaborative practices

Support Cross-Functional Work with the TAM

3 hours, up to 6 hours

1. **Mission** (10 minutes): leaders set and explain a clear global mission to the teams (what and why) and may add common joint objectives. Leaders leave the room and come back for step 3.
2. **Forward pass** (1 hour): the teams define how they will contribute to the global mission directly or by defining a sub-mission and perform a forward pass independently.
3. **Presentations** (5 minutes per team): leaders are back and each team presents the forward pass to all the other teams, which improves the awareness of who will do what. Leaders validate the submissions, if any, and the TAMs.
4. **Backward pass and negotiation** (1 hour): resources are negotiated/allocated and risks are mitigated team to team by adding, adapting, and removing content from the TAMs. Adding new objectives can trigger a new forward and backward pass! Leaders move from group to group, clarify understanding, and take the requests.
5. **Recap and next step**: leaders recap and announce the next meeting for the feedback and decisions.

+

Tips

- Establish one or more Team Contracts to clarify or change the rules of the game (see p 184).

Aligning Missions and Goals

Leaders

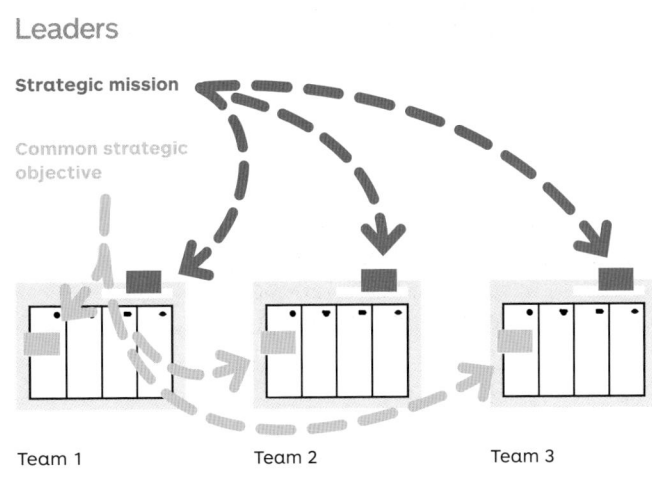

Teams

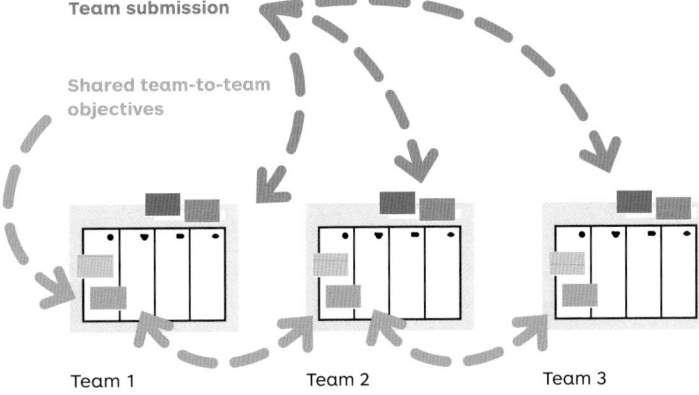

Negotiate and Allocate Resources

How to Integrate the TAM with the Business Model Canvas.

Resource negotiation is key for all projects. Whether this happens between teams or with a leader, the basic two principles remain the same:

- Gain the missing resource by explaining the relationship between the resource, the joint objectives, and the mission;

- If unsuccessful, the linked joint objective is removed or adapted.

Use the Team Alignment Map to

- Gain more resources with consistent storytelling

- Make the mission and the joint objectives more realistic

Negotiation with leadership

- **A forward and a backward pass** are performed by the team. A presentation is scheduled with leadership to negotiate any missing resources.

- **A presentation and negotiation with leaders**: The TAM is presented in logical order to provide context. Missing resources are discussed and negotiated, and when unavailable the linked objectives are adapted or removed.

Negotiation Team-to-Team

- **A forward and a backward pass** are per-formed by the teams on separate TAMs.
- **Negotiation criteria** are discussed, agreed, and prioritized between the teams before negotiating.
Criteria can be measured qualitatively (H, M, L) or quantitatively (1–5) and be equal or weighted (50%, 30%, 20%).
- **Presentation and negotiation**: teams mutually present their TAMs and tradeoffs are made team to team according to the criteria.

+

Which criteria are given the top priority?

Urgency, impact, client value, contribution to the strategy, etc. This helps avoid going around in circles and to make meaningful tradeoffs.

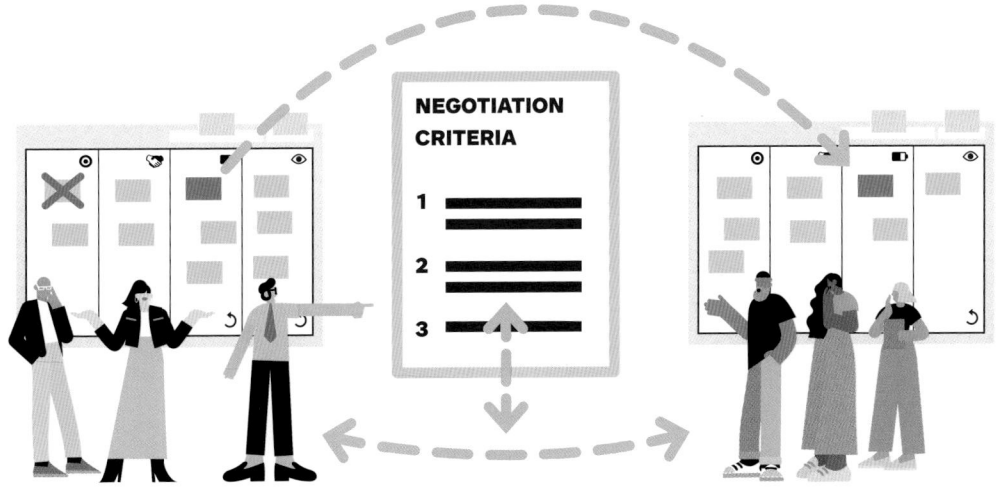

Integrate the TAM with Strategy Processes and Tools

Negotiate resources, peer-to-peer and with leadership.

The Team Alignment Map beautifully integrates with the Business Model Canvas (BMC) — a framework and tool to design business strategies. The strategy is operationalized by moving elements from one canvas to the other and by letting teams self-organize. This allows future contributors to feel part of the process and understand what's at stake; it also increases teams' buy-in.

Use the Team Alignment Map to

- Operationalize the strategy
- Easily integrate with the Business Model Canvas

Search keywords: business model canvas, business model generation, Alex Osterwalder

Integrate with the Business Model Canvas

1. Design the strategy with the BMC.
2. Operationalize key strategic objectives with the Team Alignment Map by:
   - Assigning missions (example: team 1)
   - Assigning objectives (example: team 2)
   - Assigning cross-cut objectives (example: teams 3 and 4)
3. Let the teams self-organize by performing a forward and a backward pass, possibly during implementation workshops where all the impacted teams are present and interact.

Additional iterations are performed until enough alignment is reached. Online TAM assessments can confirm the level alignment.

Tips

- Discuss the Key Activities of your BMC first; it's a good starting point
- Browse the rest of the canvas, looking for strategic goals to be executed

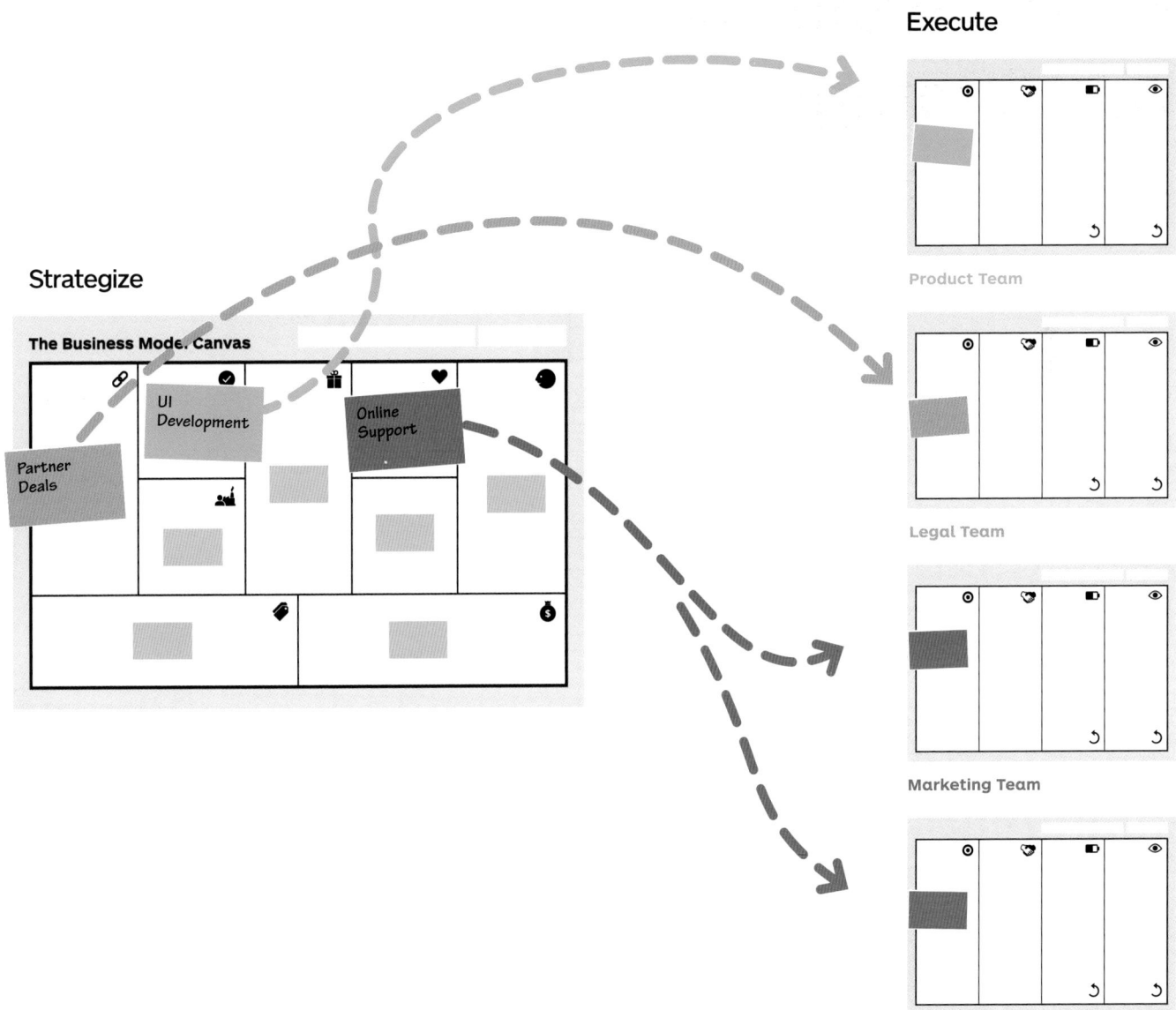

169

Assess the Readiness of Strategic Initiatives

How to assess initiatives' chances of success with hundreds of stakeholders.

Is our strategic initiative well positioned to succeed? Should we better prepare? Are any immediate decisions and actions needed?

It's not easy to capture the heartbeat of a strategic initiative with hundreds of stakeholders involved. Fast online assessments with the TAM can be run to ask hundreds of stakeholders if they think they can contribute successfully. The aggregated result gives an indication of the initiative's chances of success. It's not rocket science, but it may save your company millions. Such an assessment can be performed live with a voting platform during large coordination events, or via email using a survey tool.

Use the Team Alignment Map to

* Reduce execution risk
* Let everyone vote freely through anonymous votes

Assess online with the TAM

Run an online assessment implementing the following template in an online survey tool:

As a contributor of < *Initiative Name* >,
I find personally that the:
* Joint objectives are clear (1–5)
* Joint commitments have been defined; people and teams' roles are clear (1–5)
* Joint resources are available (1–5)
* Joint risks are under control (1–5)

1 = strongly disagree
5 = strongly agree

Online tools use horizontal sliders, so the TAM must be rotated right by 90 degrees.

Tips

* To conduct assessments by theme or group: run multiple votes, by strategic themes, by "tracks," by projects, or by teams, for a more refined assessment.

* Anonymous votes take courage: votes may reveal unexpected surprises.

Difference between paper-based and online assessments

Paper

Input

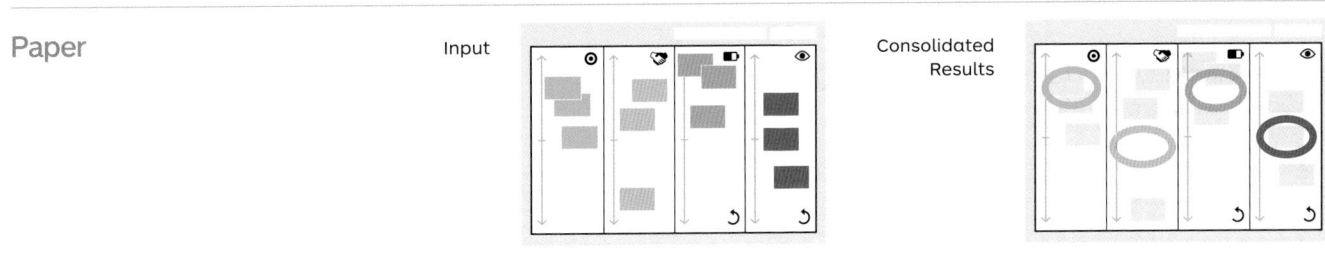

Consolidated
Results

Online

Input

Consolidated
Results

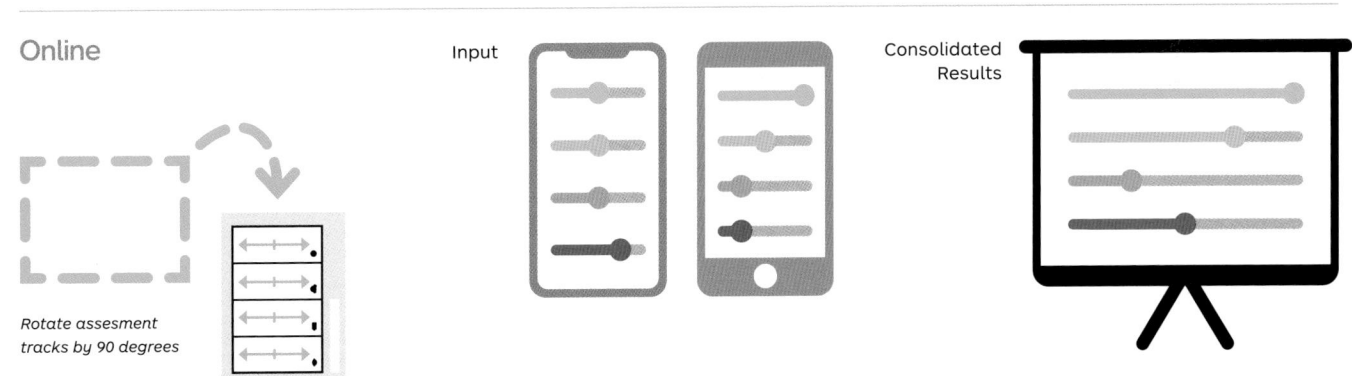

*Rotate assesment
tracks by 90 degrees*

<u>Case study</u>
Insurance group
71,000 employees

Are We Ready to Launch Our Strategic Initiative?

1
Reveal

The vote reveals a high level of misalignment for each variable, which is the worst-case scenario. The leadership team is surprised by the magnitude of the perception gaps.

Olivier heads an ambitious transformation program in an insurance group. The mission is to reduce costs by automating and delocalizing operational activities. The program is organized into four strategic tracks, each containing several projects. The budget is double-digits in millions. Olivier, the CEO, and the project committee fear that teams may not be ready to implement such drastic changes. Shortly before the launch of the program, they agree to assess the program readiness with 300 stakeholders.

Was the fear confirmed?

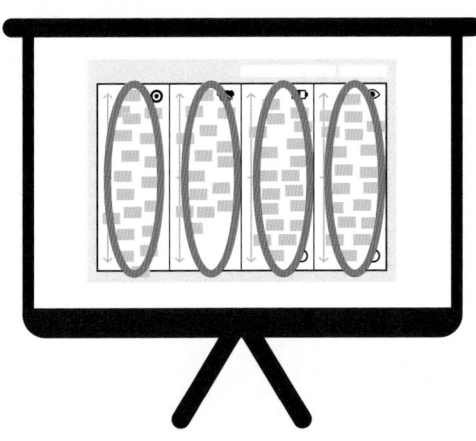

2
Reflect

The analysis discussion reveals that key parts of the program are not ready to start at all and that affects the whole vote.

3
Repair

The launch of the whole program is postponed to an unknown date. Parallel workshops are organized to work on the problematic parts. The decision is made not to launch the program until the key problems have been solved.

The good news is that the budget is still in their hands and that significant resources haven't gone up in smoke for nothing.

Pro Tips

Successful transformation initiatives

The successful transformation programs we've experienced have these three criteria in common:

√ **Good start**: objectives are clear and key stakeholders are onboarded properly.

√ **Consistent momentum**: dates are blocked in the agendas and alignment is actively maintained.

√ **Leadership support**: there is C-level sponsorship and commitment.

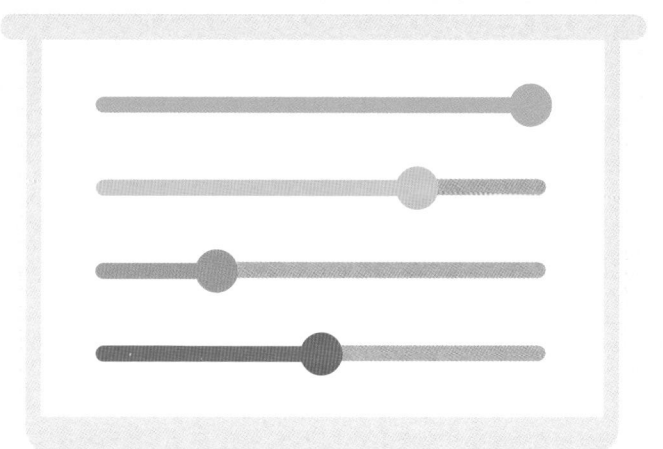

Performing assessments with large groups is easier and faster with online survey tools

Trust Among Team Members

Four tools to create a high-trust climate and increased psychological safety

"In human relations, all prediction is connected in one way or another with the phenomenon of trust."

Paul Watzlawick, Psychologist

Overview

This part introduces four add-ons to build more <u>psychological safety</u> and <u>trust</u> and create a safer team climate.

Trust and Psychological Safety Among Team Members: The Energy That Fuels the Team Alignment Map

Can a team of talents who are suspicious of each other solve complex problems together and innovate? The answer, simply, is no. Trust is a precondition for alignment.

The team doesn't engage in collective learning behaviors when people protect themselves from embarrassment and other possible threats by remaining silent. That results in poor team performance and an inability to innovate collectively. To innovate together, team members need to feel that they can talk openly and candidly to each other without fear of judgment or reprisals. Such climates are described as psychologically safe environments.

Simply put, psychological safety is a variation of trust: "The belief that the team is safe for interpersonal risk taking. That one will not be punished or humiliated for speaking up with ideas, questions, concerns, or mistakes." The term and definition were coined by Amy Edmonson, Professor of Leadership and Management at the Harvard Business School over 20 years ago in her seminal paper "Psychological Safety and Learning Behavior in Work Teams."

To learn more about Amy Edmondson's work: Dive Deeper, Trust and Psychological Safety, see p. 266

3.1
The Team Contract

Define how we work together, the principles everyone needs to know, and the behaviors that need to be respected.

3.2
The Fact Finder

Ask good questions for improving team communications, inquire like a pro to reduce perception gaps.

3.3
The Respect Card

Tips to demonstrate consideration for others.

3.4
The Nonviolent Requests Guide

Address latent conflicts and manage disagreement constructively.

3.1
The Team Contract

Define team behaviors and how we work together.

Shouldn't we have some rules in place?

Some team members
may systematically
arrive late...

...or criticize the work
of others without
suggesting alternatives.

Unspoken resentments and frustrations can accumulate and escalate into unnecessary conflict.

The Team Contract helps define the
rules of the game.

The Team Contract

What are the rules and behaviors we want to abide by in our team?

The Team Contract is a simple poster used to negotiate and establish team behavior and rules, both in general or temporarily. Psychological safety is increased and potential conflict reduced by:
- Aligning relationships on appropriate and inappropriate behaviors, making the team values explicit.
- Creating a cultural base to work in harmonious conditions.
- Allowing legitimate measures in case of noncompliance.
- Preventing a sense of inequity and injustice from developing within the team.

The poster presents two trigger questions to help participants position in terms of ins — what is accepted — and outs — what should not be accepted:
1. What are the rules and behaviors we want to abide by in our team?
2. As individuals, do we have preferences for working in a certain way?

This includes topics such as team behaviors and values, decision-making rules, how to coordinate and communicate, and framing expectations in case of failure. By helping clarify expected behaviors in advance, the Team Contract offers a big payoff for a small investment of time.

The Team Contract helps:

Make values explicit — share ideas, principles, and shared beliefs as tangible behaviors.
Set the rules of the game — set clear expectations by applying a fair process.
Minimize conflict — prevent unnecessary conflict and a reference point in case of noncompliance.

→

Dive Deeper
To discover the academic backstage of the Team Contract, please read:
- Mutual Understanding and Common Ground (in Psycholinguistics), p. 258
- Relationship Types (in Evolutionary Anthropology), p. 274
- Trust and Psychological Safety (in Psychology), p. 266

The Team Contract

What are the rules and behaviors that we want to abide by in our team?
As individuals, do we have preferences for working in a certain way?

Team:

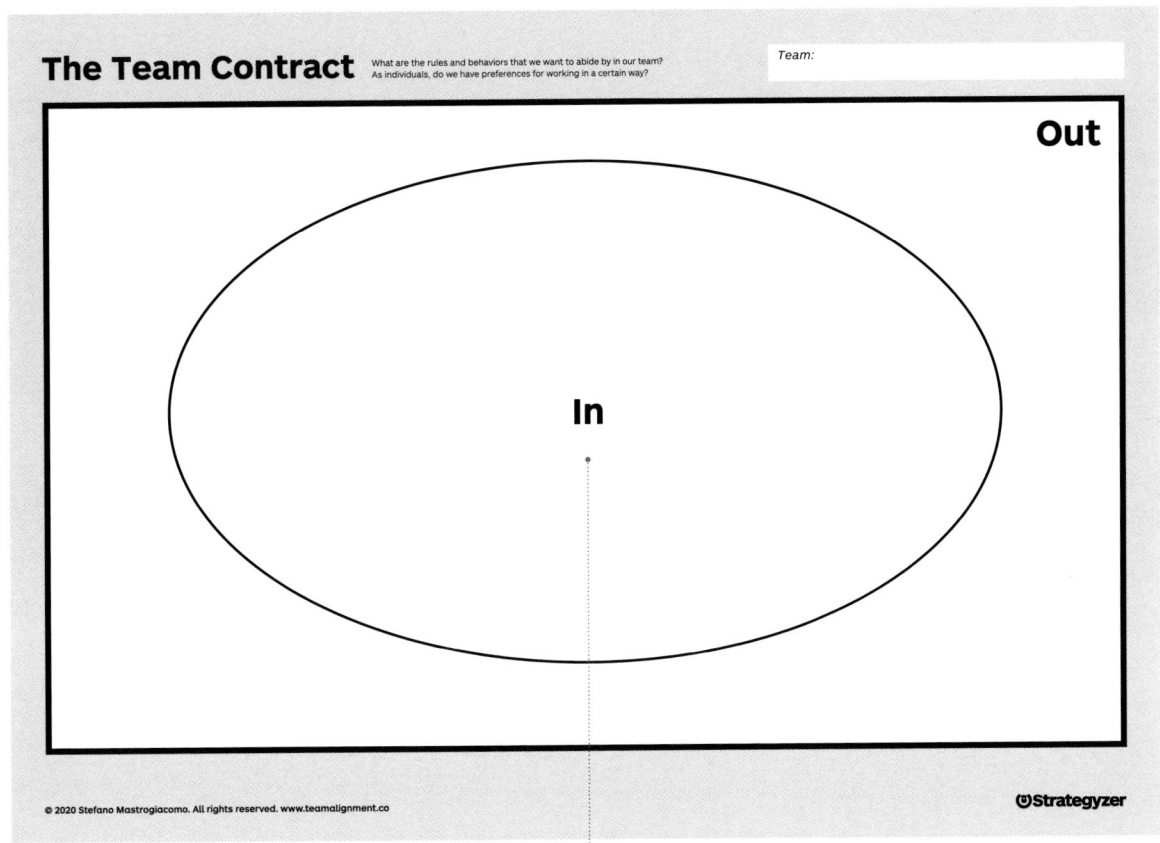

Out

In

© 2020 Stefano Mastrogiacomo. All rights reserved. www.teamalignment.co

Ⓢ Strategyzer

Out
The behaviors
the team wants
to avoid.

In
The rules and
behaviors the team
wants to abide by.

The Team Contract What's (Typically) In and Out?

Team Contracts are unique for each team. Expect a variety of answers as the trigger questions invite team members to position on topics covering:

- attitudes and behaviors,
- decision-making (priorities management, governance, responsibilities),
- communication (in particular, meeting management),
- the use of common tools and methods,
- disagreement and conflict management,
- relationships with other teams and departments, and so forth.

The team may also include the rewards in case of success, or the sanctions in case of noncompliance.

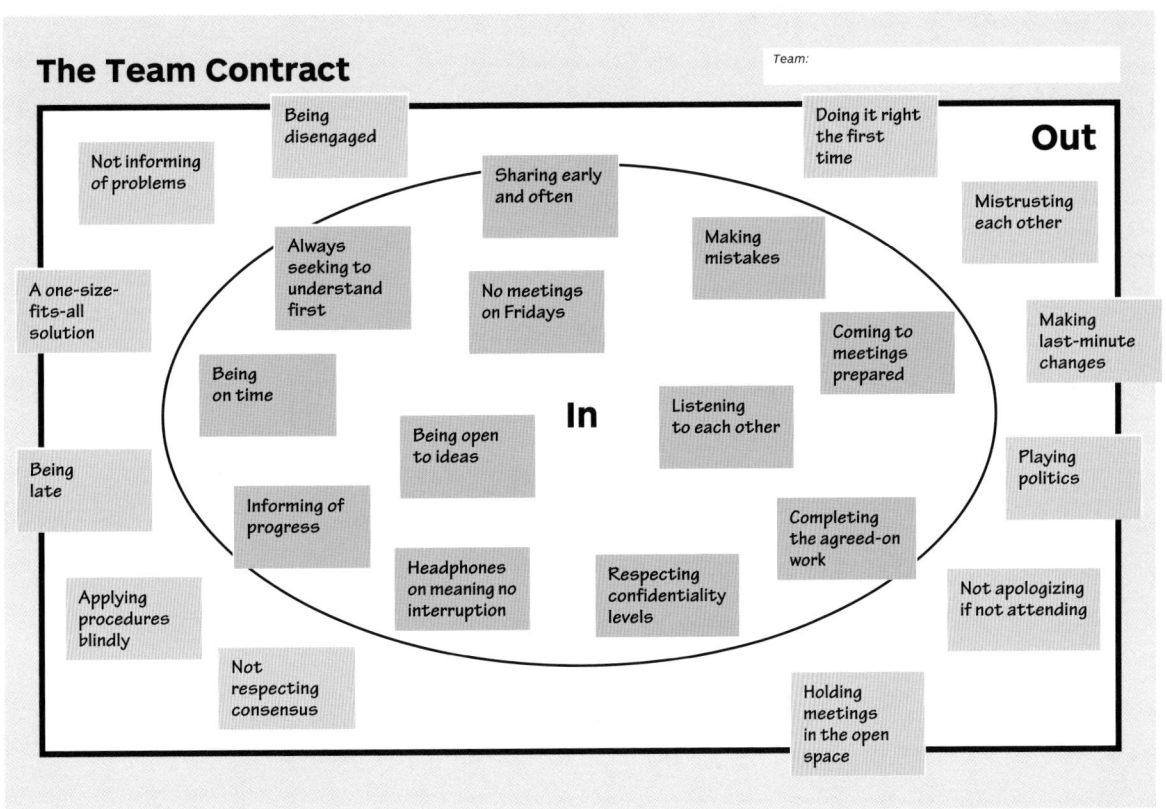

The Team Contract

Team:

Out

In

- Being disengaged
- Not informing of problems
- Doing it right the first time
- Sharing early and often
- Always seeking to understand first
- Making mistakes
- Mistrusting each other
- A one-size-fits-all solution
- No meetings on Fridays
- Coming to meetings prepared
- Making last-minute changes
- Being on time
- Listening to each other
- Being open to ideas
- Being late
- Playing politics
- Informing of progress
- Completing the agreed-on work
- Applying procedures blindly
- Headphones on meaning no interruption
- Respecting confidentiality levels
- Not apologizing if not attending
- Not respecting consensus
- Holding meetings in the open space

Light versus Heavy Conventions

The Team Contract is a light tool to set team conventions; it binds the team morally and not legally. It can evolve later into more substantial formal and legally binding documents.

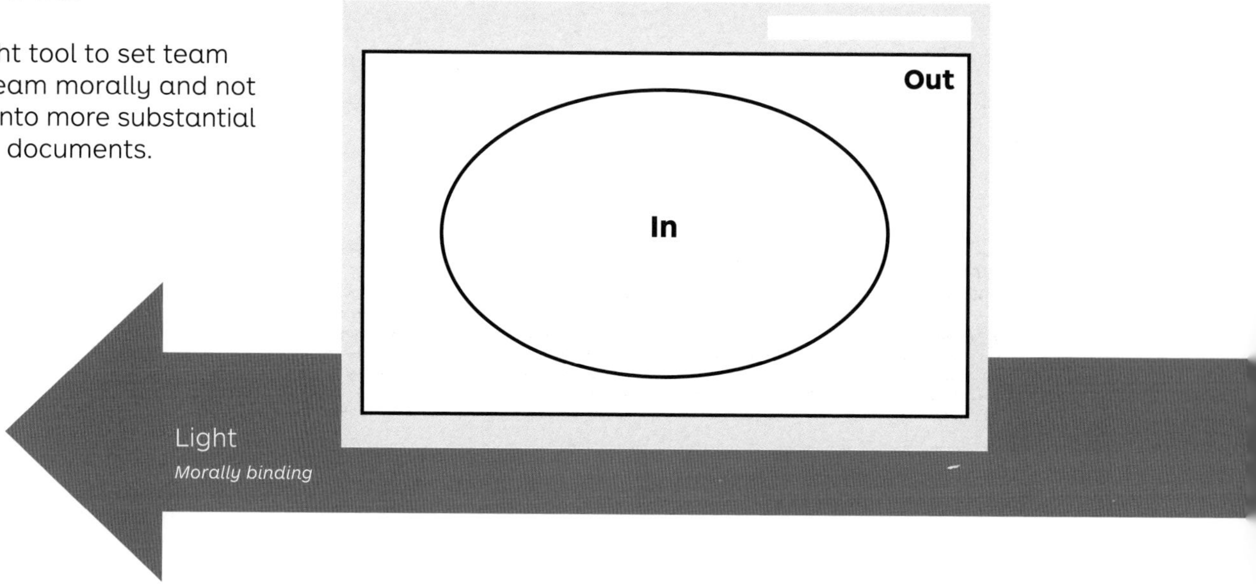

Out

In

Light
Morally binding

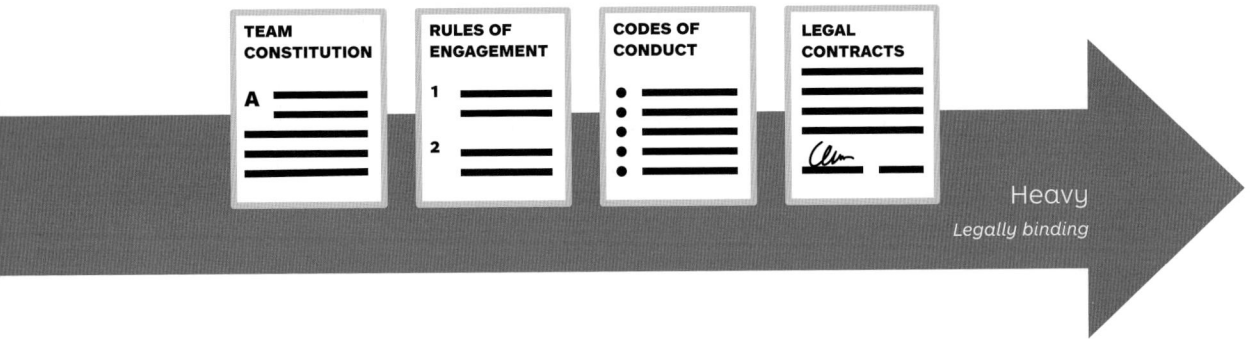

TEAM CONSTITUTION

A

RULES OF ENGAGEMENT

1

2

CODES OF CONDUCT

LEGAL CONTRACTS

Heavy
Legally binding

All the above documents formalize conventions between stakeholders in different contexts. *Conventions are recurring behaviors expected in recurring situations.*

How to Apply

Steps

Gather all the team members involved or all the key stakeholders in the case of a project. Place a Team Contract poster on the wall and:

1. Frame: announce the project and the period.
2. Prepare: ask every team member to respond individually to the two trigger questions in terms of possible ins and outs (5 minutes).
3. Share: allow each participant 3 minutes to present and share their answers on the poster.
4. Consolidate: open a team discussion to react, adapt, and consolidate all the content (approximately 20 minutes).
5. Validate: end the meeting when participants mutually agree on the Team Contract.

When?

As illustrated on the right, the TAM helps align everyone's contributions on a regular basis and usually requires frequent updates to reflect changes as the work is progressively delivered. The Team Contract helps establish agreements that span the entire period of the collaboration. Team Contracts are generally established at the beginning of projects, when new teams are formed, when new talents join an existing team, or when radical changes require the team to reboot its operating mode.

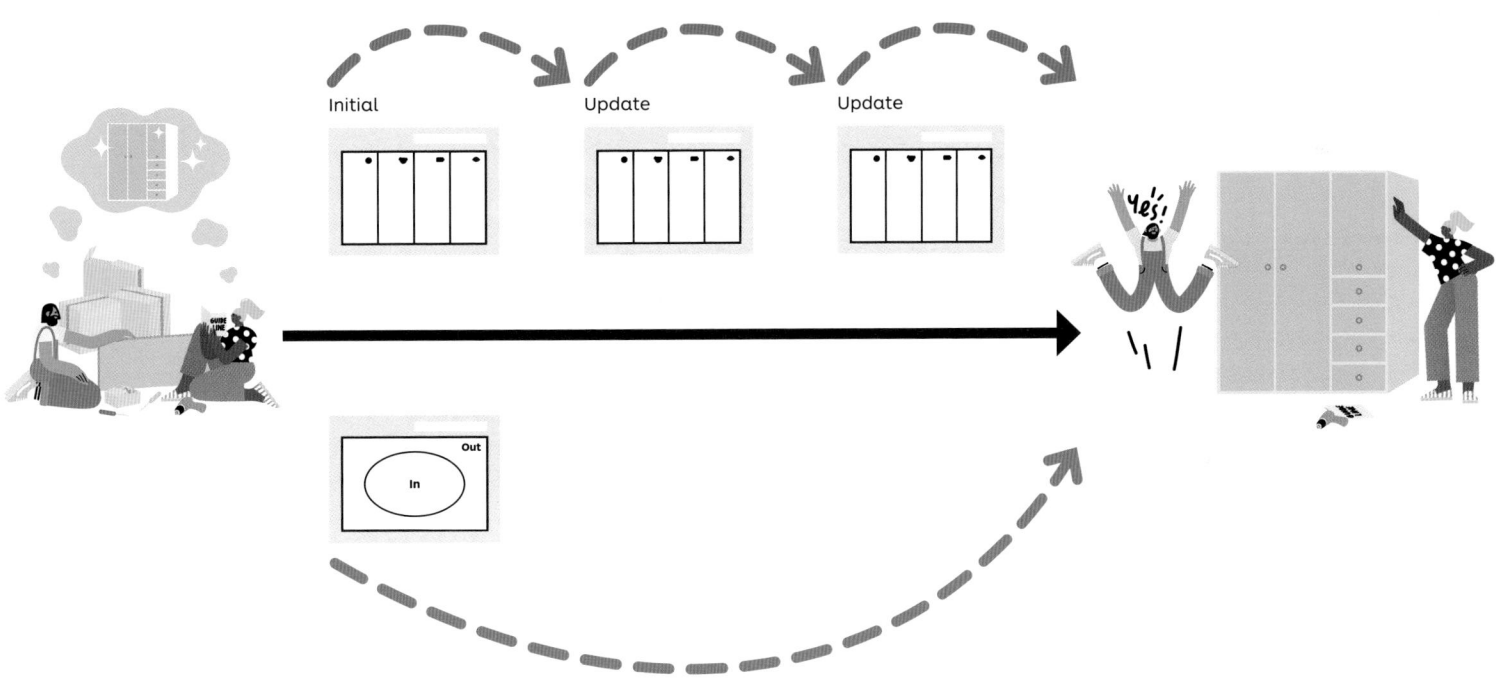

Short-term agreements
set regularly with the TAM

Initial   Update   Update

In   Out

Long-term agreements
formalized with the Team Contract

A Great Team Alignment Map (TAM) Companion

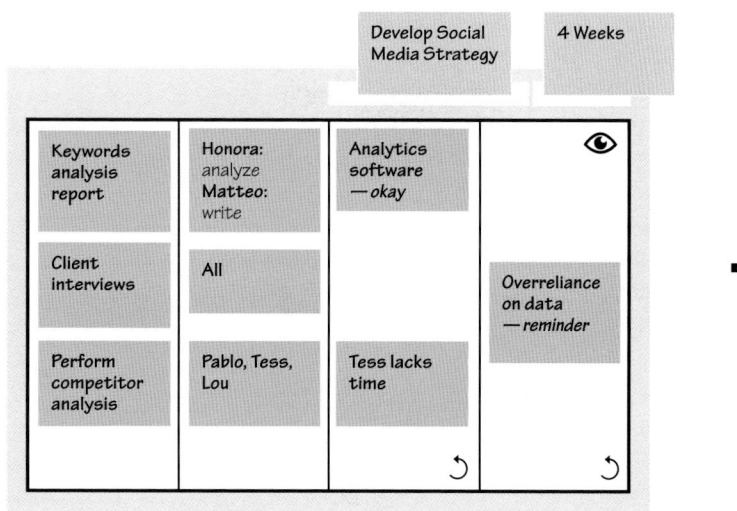

+

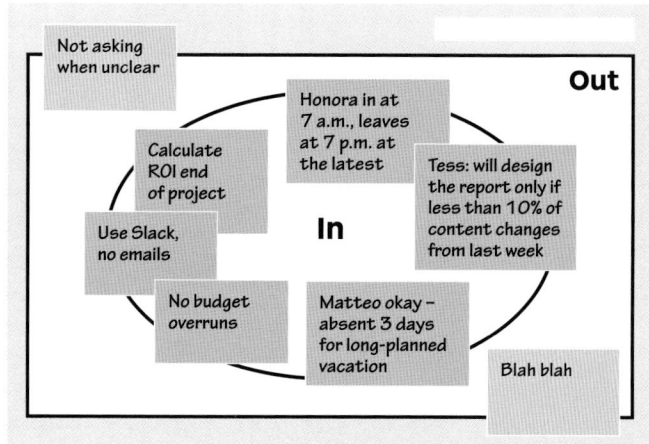

= More alignment + more psychological safety in the team

In Case of Noncompliance

Breaches of Team Contract

Inappropriate behaviors must be confronted if a Team Contract has been violated. Avoiding confronting issues increases resentment among members who play by the rules and can affect the work and the relationships of the entire team. As a rule of thumb, this three-step approach reduces discomfort in these (sometimes difficult) conversations:

1. Explain the problem factually and refer to the Team Contract.
2. Listen carefully to all the points of view.
3. Find an appropriate solution with all the parties involved.

Resolutions are considerably facilitated when behaviors have been specified beforehand on the Team Contract. It provides a reference point, a legitimate basis for turning the problem into a learning opportunity.

Sanctioning major violations

There are behaviors that put the entire team and organization at risk, and dismissing the offender might be the most productive response. As noted by Amy Edmondson, "psychological safety is reinforced rather then harmed by fair, thoughtful responses to potentially dangerous, harmful, or sloppy behavior" (Edmondson, 2018).

Being explicit beforehand makes it easier to turn behavioral problems into learning opportunities.

When the rules are explicit and clear, everyone has a chance to play fairly. Confronting inappropriate behaviors is perceived as legitimate.

Without any explicit rules, confronting cheaters' behaviors can be perceived as unfair and trigger vengeance.

Prevent contract breaches proactively

There are pros and cons as to whether to display consequences in case of noncompliance on the Team Contract itself.

Pros: things are transparent; everyone is informed and aware of the consequences in case of non-compliance.

Cons: visible sanctions can be negatively perceived, undermine trust, and affect cooperation from the start. Consider the Prenup Paradox in psychology (Fisk and Tetlock 1997; Pinker 2008): fiancé/ées don't like to think about their upcoming marriage in terms of a possible divorce. Most couples resist prenups for good reason: the very act of discussing penalties makes it more likely that they will be needed, and that breaks the atmosphere.

Recommended: it's more diplomatic to agree on the process; for example, that noncompliance will be treated on a case-by-case basis as a team.

Search keywords: difficult conversations; conflict resolution techniques; HR disciplinary actions

X Touchy

Out

In

If late to meetings, do not enter the room

Errors will have an impact on bonuses in case of noncompliance

Any offensive behavior will be reported to HR

Breaches will be discussed as a team

✓ Diplomatic

Framing Failure Accurately on the Team Contract

Failure must be approached differently for a team working in an innovation lab and for a team working at airport security. Amy Edmondson (2018) suggests ways to frame failure accurately in three different contexts:

1. high-volume repetitive work,
2. complex operations, and
3. innovation and research.

Each context has its own different requirements in terms of error management. The table on the right shows examples for each context.

	High-volume repetitive work	Complex operations	Innovation and research
Context	• Assembly plants • Fast-food restaurants • Logistics, etc.	• Hospitals • Financial institutions • Public services, etc.	• Creating a movie • Developing new sources of energy • New product design, etc.
Constructive attitude toward failure	**Minimize preventable failures** Caused by deviations from known processes due to deficient skills, attention, or behaviors.	**Analyze and fix complex failures** Caused by unexpected events, complex systems breakdowns, etc.	**Celebrate intelligent failures** Caused by uncertainty, experimentation, and risk taking.
Examples of expectations	Train *all* new hires Max. one defective delivery accepted per day	Weekly risk assessment meeting War room and task force setup for each system breakdown	Monthly failure party and award Revise design for each failed experiment

Adapted from Amy Edmonson (2018).

3.2
The Fact Finder

Ask good questions for improving team communications.

Deploy global transformational strategies!
Incubate wireless transparency and platforms!

Sometimes, it's difficult to understand other team members and follow their logic.

The Fact Finder helps bring clarity to the conversation.

Clarify with the Fact Finder

The Fact Finder suggests questions that bring clarity to the conversation. The questions give others a chance to reformulate their thinking more accurately and to be understood.

Dive Deeper
To discover the academic back-stage of the Fact Finder, please read:
- Mutual Understanding and Common Ground (in Psycholinguistics) p. 258
- Trust and Psychological Safety (in Psychology) p. 266

The tool is built on a straightforward principle: dialogue based on concrete facts is better than dialogue based on assumptions. Engaging in such dialogue requires training as we easily tend to omit or distort information. That distortion is a direct consequence of our three-level sense-making process (Kourilsky 2014):
1. Perception: we start by perceiving a situation or we have an experience.
2. Interpretation: we give this situation an interpretation or a meaning or we form a hypothesis.
3. Evaluation: finally, what we share about the perceived situation is an evaluation, a judgment, or even a rule we inferred.

Confusing these levels leads us directly into one (or several) of the five following communication traps:
1. Unclear facts or experiences: an absence of key information in the description.
2. Generalizations: when we turn a particular case into a universal law.

3. Assumptions: creative interpretations of an experience or situation.
4. Limitations: imaginary restrictions and obligations that narrow down options.
5. Judgments: subjective assessments of a thing, a situation, or a person.

These traps illustrate the difference between what psychologists call first-order reality and second-order realities:
A first-order reality is made up of the physically observable qualities — through our five senses — of a thing or a situation.
Second-order realities are personal interpretations of a first-order reality (judgments, hypotheses, assumptions, etc.).

For example, Ann can say "I'm hungry" (factual communication, a first-order reality) or loudly claim "we always eat too late," which is a judgment (a second-order reality) to express the fact that she's hungry. The second statement causes communication problems that can lead to conflicts,

blockages, and dead ends (Kourilsky 2014) and is mostly visible when we start arguing with each other.

By helping understand the facts (first-order reality) hidden behind ambiguous second-order statements (second-order realities), the Fact Finder makes the dialogue more productive and efficient.

The Fact Finder helps:

Inquire like a pro — identify and overcome common language traps.
Better information and decisions — clarify what is said: what others are saying and also what you are saying.
Save efforts — engage in shorter and more efficient dialogue.

The Fact Finder

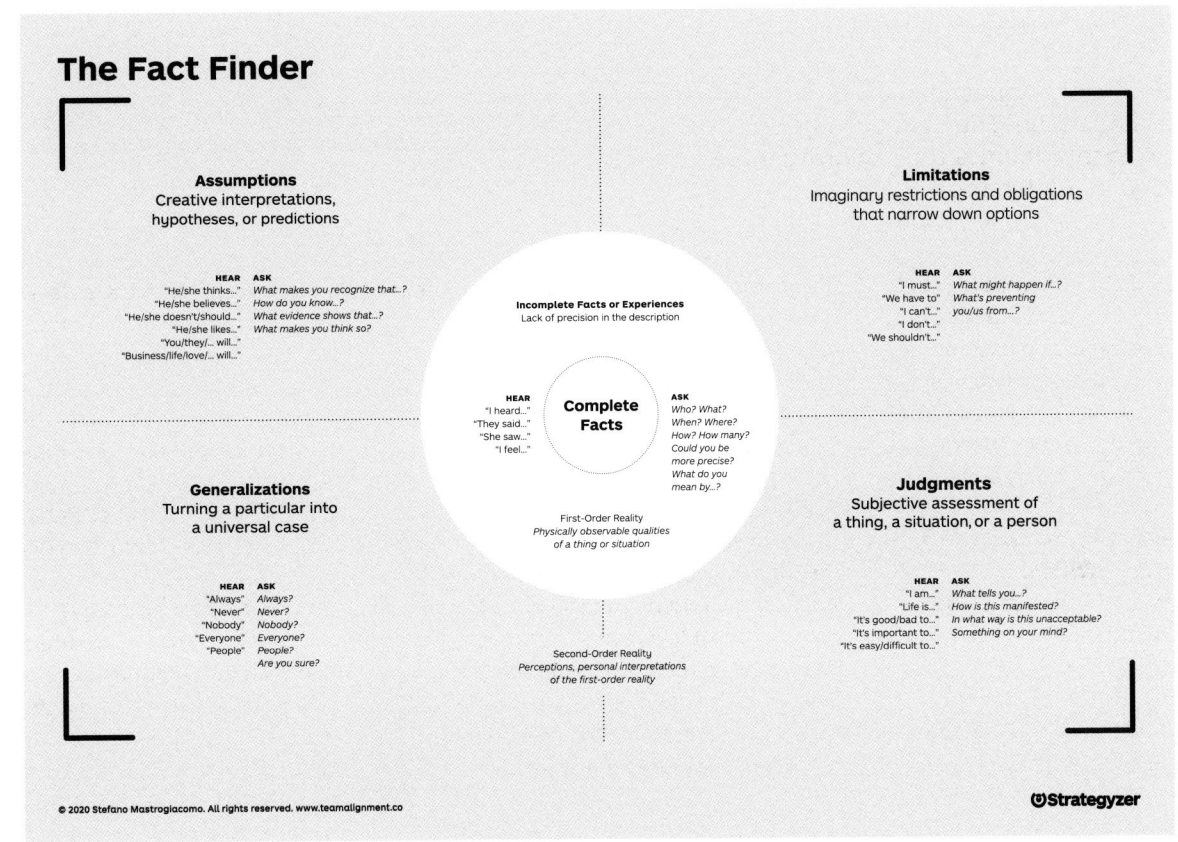

Assumptions
Creative interpretations, hypotheses, or predictions

HEAR
- "He/she thinks..."
- "He/she believes..."
- "He/she doesn't/should..."
- "He/she likes..."
- "You/they/... will..."
- "Business/life/love/... will..."

ASK
- *What makes you recognize that...?*
- *How do you know...?*
- *What evidence shows that...?*
- *What makes you think so?*

Limitations
Imaginary restrictions and obligations that narrow down options

HEAR
- "I must..."
- "We have to"
- "I can't..."
- "I don't..."
- "We shouldn't..."

ASK
- *What might happen if...?*
- *What's preventing you/us from...?*

Incomplete Facts or Experiences
Lack of precision in the description

HEAR
- "I heard..."
- "They said..."
- "She saw..."
- "I feel..."

Complete Facts

ASK
- *Who? What?*
- *When? Where?*
- *How? How many?*
- *Could you be more precise?*
- *What do you mean by...?*

First-Order Reality
Physically observable qualities of a thing or situation

Second-Order Reality
Perceptions, personal interpretations of the first-order reality

Generalizations
Turning a particular into a universal case

HEAR
- "Always"
- "Never"
- "Nobody"
- "Everyone"
- "People"

ASK
- *Always?*
- *Never?*
- *Nobody?*
- *Everyone?*
- *People?*
- *Are you sure?*

Judgments
Subjective assessment of a thing, a situation, or a person

HEAR
- "I am..."
- "Life is..."
- "It's good/bad to..."
- "It's important to..."
- "It's easy/difficult to..."

ASK
- *What tells you...?*
- *How is this manifested?*
- *In what way is this unacceptable?*
- *Something on your mind?*

Strategyzer

The Five Communication Traps Illustrated

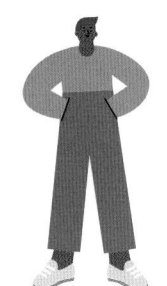

He can relate his experience factually.

"Yesterday I saw someone eating three burgers at the local fast-food restaurant."

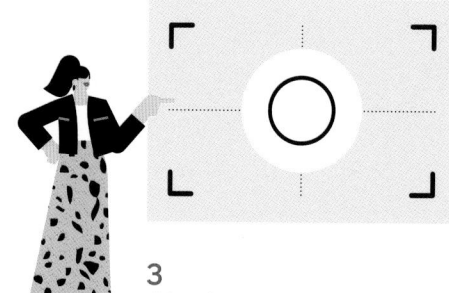

1
Original Situation
Ivan sees someone eating three burgers at the local fast-food restaurant.

3
Clarification Questions
Clarification questions help understand the facts and the experiences (first-order reality) behind the personal interpretations (second-order realities). This moves the conversation from the ambiguity and fuzziness of the gray area to the clarity of facts, i.e. to the central white area.

2
Communication Traps

Ivan can also fall into one of these traps
when relating his experience.

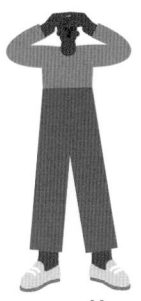

Assumptions

*"Yesterday I saw someone who
had not eaten for two weeks!"*

Generalizations

"People eat a lot."

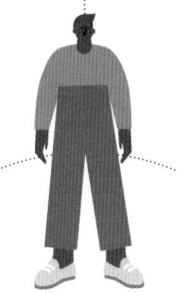

**Complete
Facts**

Incomplete Facts
or Experiences

*"Yesterday I saw
someone eating."*

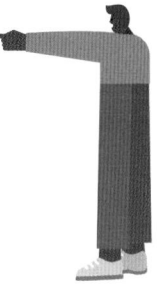

Limitations

"Burgers must be banned."

Judgments

"Eating three burgers is bad."

In Practice

Use of the Fact Finder occurs in two steps:

1. Hear: identify the trap: are you hearing an assumption, a limitation, a generalization, a judgment, or incomplete facts?
2. Ask: use one of the suggested clarifying questions to bring the conversation back to the center, i.e. complete facts and experiences.

Clarifying question are neutral — they do not convey any form of judgment — and open — they don't trigger closed binary responses (yes/no).

Clarify Incomplete Facts or Experiences
Questions help specify the facts further.

Hear
"I heard…"
"They said…"
"She saw…"
"I feel…"

Ask
Who? What?
When? Where?
How? How many?
Could you be more precise?
What do you mean by…?

The designers told me they need more time.

Could you be more precise?

Clarify Assumptions

Questions help disentangle the causal links.

Hear
"He/she thinks…"
"He/she believes…"
"He/she doesn't/should…"
"He/she likes…"
"You/they/… will…"
"Business/life/love/… will…"

Ask
What makes you recognize that…?
How do you know…?
What evidence shows that…?
What makes you think so?

I think if we receive the materials in two days the entire project will be delayed by two months.

How can two days cause a two-month delay?

Clarify Limitations

Questions help identify the cause or the consequences of the belief.

Hear
"I must..."
"We have to"
"I can't..."
"I don't..."
"We shouldn't..."

Ask
What might happen if...?
What's preventing you/us from...?

I can't, we never worked like this here, it's not in our DNA.

Sure, and if you did, what would happen?

Clarify Generalizations

Questions help reveal a counterexample.

Hear
"Always"
"Never"
"Nobody"
"Everyone"
"People"

Ask
Always?
Never?
Nobody?
Everyone?
People ?
Are you sure?

Risks are high, everyone is so demotivated.

Everyone?

Clarify Judgments

Questions help reveal the assessment criteria behind the judgment.

Hear
"I am..."
"Life is..."
"It's good/bad to..."
"It's important to..."
"It's easy/ difficult to..."

Ask
What tells you...?
How is this manifested?
In what way is this unacceptable?
Something on your mind?

It's important we achieve my objectives first.

Well, what tells you that?

215

In Summary

Communication traps
Clarification Questions Help...

Incomplete facts or experiences
Lack of precision in the description.
Specify the facts further.

Assumptions
Creative interpretations, hypotheses, or predictions.
Disentangle the causal links.

Generalizations
Turning a particular into a universal case.
Reveal a counterexample.

Limitations
Imaginary restrictions and obligations that
narrow down options.
Identify the cause or the consequences of the belief.

Judgments
Subjective assessment of a thing, a situation, or a person.
Reveal the assessment criteria.

Origins of the Fact Finder
The Fact Finder has its roots in
neuro-linguistic programming
(NLP), a therapeutic communication approach developed by
John Grinder and Richard Bandler.
They named their framework
the "metamodel." Implementing
the metamodel turned out to
be quite challenging and led
coach Alain Cayrol to develop
a more applicable version he
called the Language Compass.
The Language Compass has
been subsequently improved and
extended by Françoise Kourilsky,
a French psychologist who inspired
the design of the Fact Finder.

*Search keywords: NLP, meta-
model, powerful questions, clear
questions*

The Fact Finder

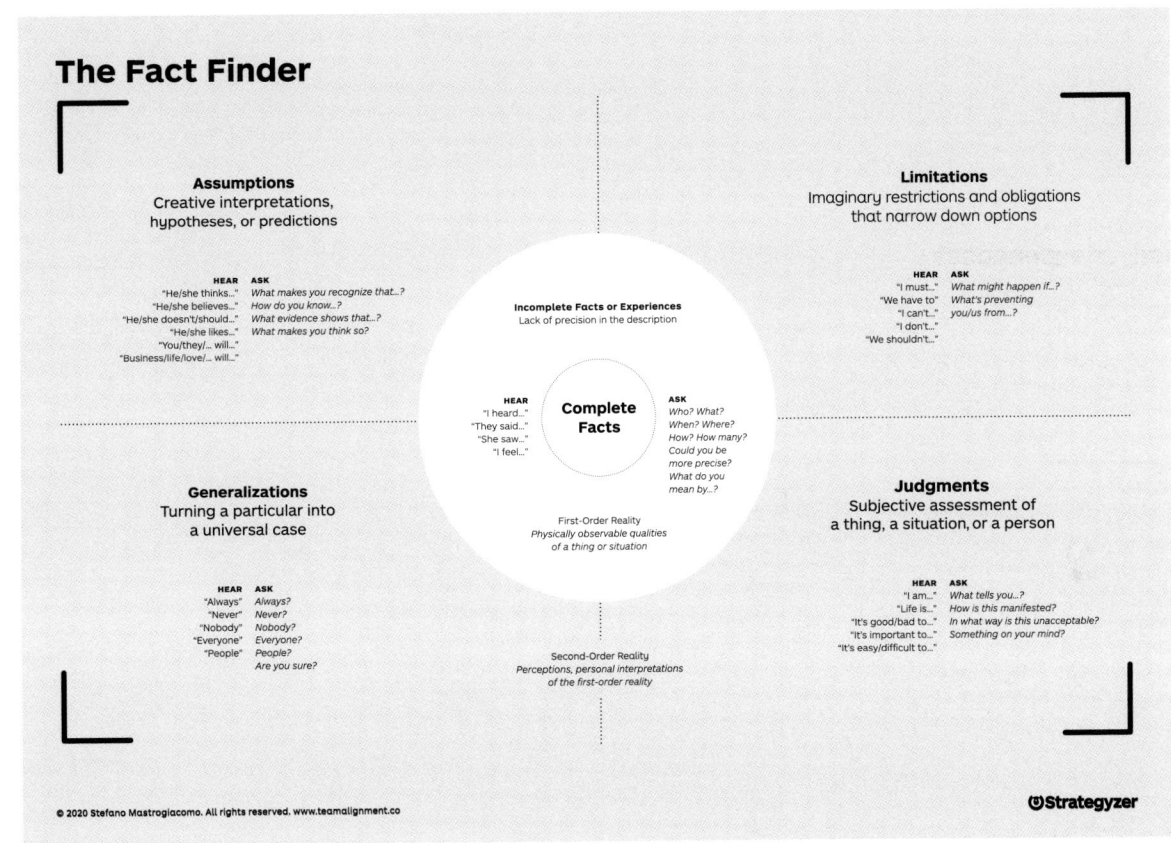

Assumptions
Creative interpretations, hypotheses, or predictions

HEAR
"He/she thinks..."
"He/she believes..."
"He/she doesn't/should..."
"He/she likes..."
"You/they/... will..."
"Business/life/love/... will..."

ASK
What makes you recognize that...?
How do you know...?
What evidence shows that...?
What makes you think so?

Limitations
Imaginary restrictions and obligations that narrow down options

HEAR
"I must..."
"We have to"
"I can't..."
"I don't..."
"We shouldn't..."

ASK
What might happen if...?
What's preventing you/us from...?

Incomplete Facts or Experiences
Lack of precision in the description

HEAR
"I heard..."
"They said..."
"She saw..."
"I feel..."

Complete Facts

ASK
Who? What?
When? Where?
How? How many?
Could you be more precise?
What do you mean by...?

First-Order Reality
Physically observable qualities of a thing or situation

Generalizations
Turning a particular into a universal case

HEAR
"Always"
"Never"
"Nobody"
"Everyone"
"People"

ASK
Always?
Never?
Nobody?
Everyone?
People?
Are you sure?

Judgments
Subjective assessment of a thing, a situation, or a person

HEAR
"I am..."
"Life is..."
"It's good/bad to..."
"It's important to..."
"It's easy/difficult to..."

ASK
What tells you...?
How is this manifested?
In what way is this unacceptable?
Something on your mind?

Second-Order Reality
Perceptions, personal interpretations of the first-order reality

Strategyzer

Pro Tips

Adapt the clarification questions

Adapt the wording to the context and situation to avoid being perceived as a robot. The Fact Finder has questions that may give the conversation an unnatural twist.

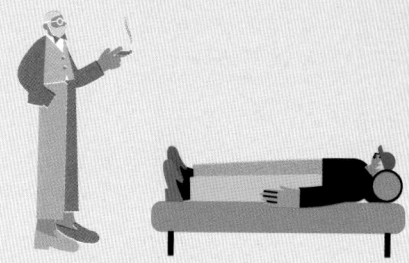

Don't
Repeat questions as they are

Do
Adapt to the context and situation

Stop justifying yourself and save energy

Stop justifying and ask a clarification question. Launching into long and visibly unconvincing justifications signals that it's time to use the Fact Finder. It will save everyone's energy and time.

Don't
Lose energy in justifications

Do
Ask a clarification question

Avoid closed-ended questions when inquiring

The Fact Finder contains only open-ended questions. Open-ended questions don't trigger a mere yes/no, which helps others develop their thinking.

Limits of the Fact Finder

Overuse of the Fact Finder will be perceived as intrusive and irritating. Use it mainly when you feel lost and find it difficult to understand the other person's logic.

Don't
Closed-ended questions don't help inquire

Do
Open-ended questions give access to the other's thoughts

Don't
Overusing the Fact Finder can make you look intrusive

Do
Use it primarily to clarify messages

3.3
The Respect Card

Demonstrate consideration for others by practicing basic politeness rules.

Lack of tact in interpersonal relationships makes teamwork slower and harder.

The Respect Card suggests ways to express consideration for others and maintain a respectful climate.

The Respect Card

The Respect Card gives tips for valuing others and expressing respect. Use it to prepare for meetings or when writing messages to people:
- You're not familiar with,
- With whom you feel less confident such as strangers, acquaintances, newcomers to the team, superiors, or
- With different cultural backgrounds.

The use of these hints demonstrates our ability to consider the identity and feelings of others (Brown 2015) and contributes to the creation of more psychological safety and harmony in teams.

The tool presents two checklists:
1. Tips for showing that you value and care for others (on the right)
2. Tips for demonstrating respect by minimizing requests and the likelihood of offending others (on the left)

The Respect Card is grounded in face and politeness theory; all tips present techniques to avoid causing others to lose face in public. The main focus is on language; the card presents only limited behaviors or good manners, such as not interrupting or not listening while someone is talking.

The Respect Card helps:
Get messages across with respect — challenge the status quo with respect.
Value others — by expressing consideration and gratitude.
Avoid unintentional gaffes — when dealing with strangers or power relationships.

Dive Deeper
To discover the academic backstage of the Respect Card, please read:
- Face and Politeness (in Psycholinguistics), p. 282
- Trust and Psychological Safety (in Psychology), p. 266

The Respect Card   Tips for tactful communication.

Need to be respected
Demonstrate Respect

Questioning rather than commanding
Will you...?

Express doubt
I don't suppose you might...?

Hedge the request
..., if possible.

Acknowledge the impingement
I'm sure you're busy, but...

Indicate reluctance
I normally wouldn't ask, but...

Apologize
I'm sorry to bother you, but...

Acknowledge a debt
I'd be grateful if you would...

Use honorifics
Mr., Mrs., Miss, Professor, Dr. etc...

Be indirect
I'm looking for a pen.

Request forgiveness
You must forgive me but...
Could I borrow your pen?

Minimize request
I just wanted to ask you if I could use your pen.

Pluralize the person responsible
*We forgot to tell you that you needed
to buy your plane ticket by yesterday.*

Hesitate
Can I, uh,...?

Impersonalize
Smoking is not permitted.

RISKY BEHAVIORS
Direct orders
Interrupt
Give warnings
Prohibit
Threaten
Suggestions
Reminders
Advice

Need to be valued
Demonstrate Recognition

Thank
A big thank you.

Wish
Be well, have a nice day.

Inquire
How are you? How is it going?

Compliment
Nice sweater.

Anticipate
You must be hungry.

Advice
Take care.

Endear
My friend, mate, buddy, pal, honey, dear, bro, guys.

Solicit agreement
You know?

Attend to others
*You must be hungry, it's been a long
time since breakfast. How about some lunch?*

Avoid disagreement
A: You don't like it?
B: Yes, yes I like it, um, I usually don't eat this but it's good.

Assume agreement
So, when are you coming to see us?

Hedge opinion
You really should sort of try harder.

RISKY BEHAVIORS
Embarrass
Disapprove
Ignore
Openly criticize
Contempt, ridicule
Speak only about yourself
Mention taboo topics
Insults, accusations, complaints

Strategyzer

Respect
Use these "social
breaks" to avoid gaffes
and express respect

Recognition
Use these "social
accelerators" to
value others.

How to Value Others

✓
Face is saved

The request is delivered by demonstrating appreciation.

✕
Face is not saved

The requests are presented as a criticism or a judgment.

How to

Use the Respect Card to prepare
for an oral or written communication

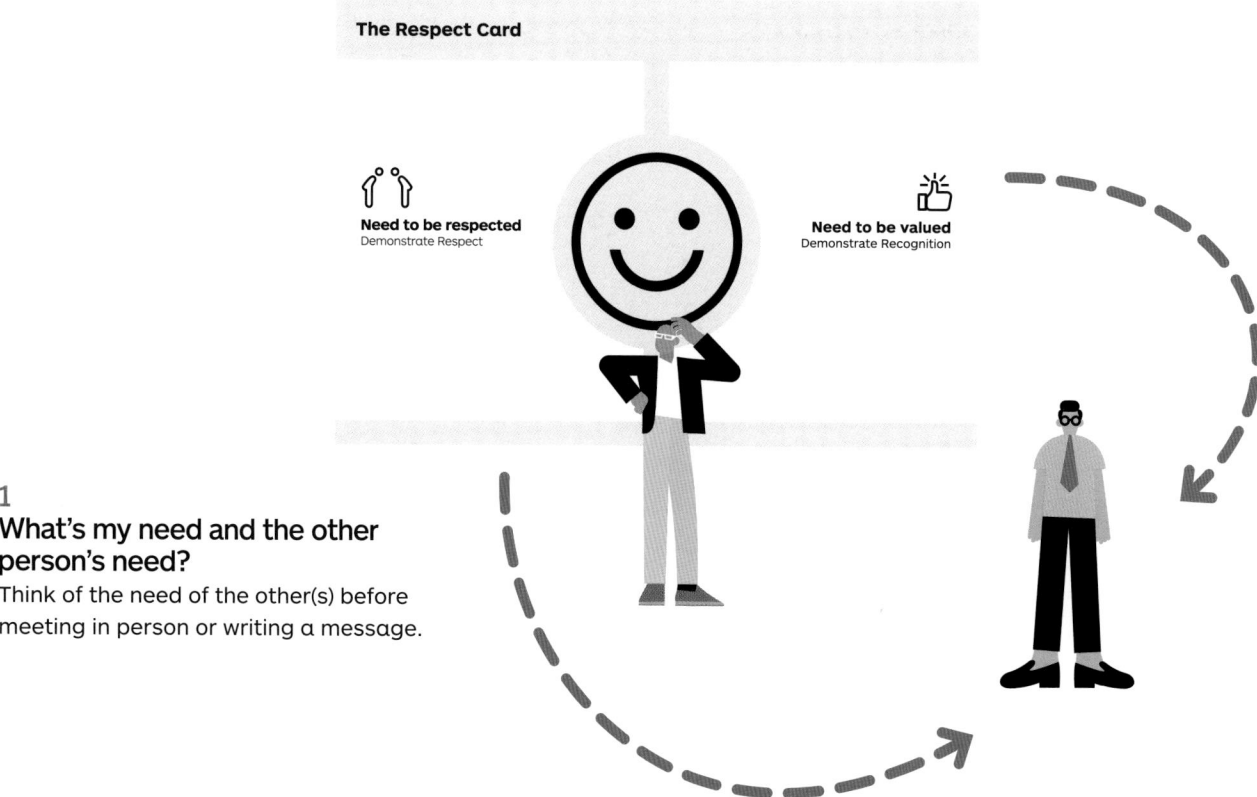

The Respect Card

Need to be respected
Demonstrate Respect

Need to be valued
Demonstrate Recognition

1
What's my need and the other person's need?
Think of the need of the other(s) before
meeting in person or writing a message.

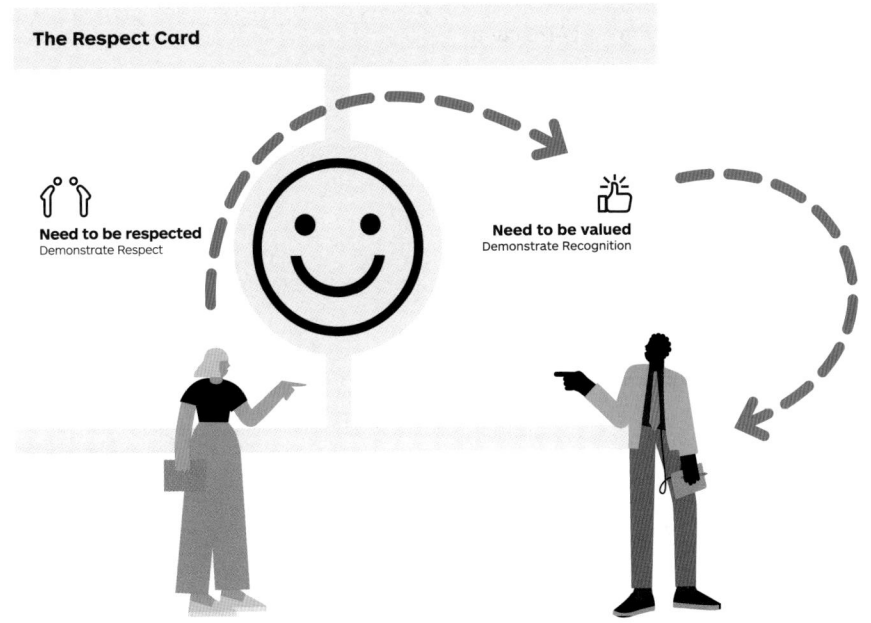

The Respect Card

Need to be respected
Demonstrate Respect

Need to be valued
Demonstrate Recognition

2
**Find ideas in the two checklists
for ideas before speaking or writing**
Browse the techniques to gain ideas;
pick and use the most appropriate.

Sarcasm
Thank you.

Public
I'm surprised!

The Respect Card is not for every situation
Urgent situations require direct instructions;
polite language is ambiguous and inefficient
for coordinating when things are urgent.

Direct request
Bring the extinguisher!

Indirect request
I was wondering if you might
possibly pass me the fire
extinguisher?

Impoliteness: extremes meet extremes
Being rude or overpolite are both perceived
as negative and inappropriate behaviors
(Locher and Watts 2008).

Rude
That's bad work.

Overly polite
Your highness, I would be
eternally grateful if you could
envision the possibility to
forgive me for daring asking
you an incredibly little favor.

The Nonviolent Requests Guide

The Nonviolent Requests Guide helps prepare and express discontent constructively. The guide presents a simplified version of the nonviolent communication (NVC) principles developed by psychologist Marshall Rosenberg. As he writes: "When we express our needs indirectly through the use of evaluations, interpretations, and images, others are likely to hear criticism. And when people hear anything that sounds like criticism, they tend to invest their energy in self-defense or counterattack" (Rosenberg 2003).

By suggesting a structure for making non-judgmental requests, disagreement can be expressed without making others feel personally attacked; this creates an opportunity for empathic dialogue and conflict resolution.

Nonviolent communication (NVC) is a powerful framework and one of the key tools behind Microsoft's cultural transformation and product renewal. When Satya Nadella became the company CEO, one of his first acts was to ask top executives to read Rosenberg's book (McCracken 2017).

The Nonviolent Requests Guide helps:

Express disagreement constructively — share your view without blaming or criticizing.

Resolve conflicts — create a win-win context.

Strengthen relationships — contribute to a safer team climate.

To discover the academic backstage of the Nonviolent Requests Guide, please read:

- Nonviolent Communication (in Psychology), p. 250
- Trust and Psychological Safety (in Psychology), p. 266

When you do

_____
OBSERVATION

I feel

_____
FEELING

My need is

_____
NEED

Would you please

_____?
REQUEST

Formulation Aids

The Request

In Practice

A nonviolent statement is composed of four consecutive parts (Rosenberg 2003):

The guide proposes a template to formulate the request and a list designed by the Center for Nonviolent Communication to convey feelings and needs more accurately.

How to formulate a nonviolent request?
1. **When you do [observation],**
2. **I feel [feeling].**
3. **My need is [need],**
4. **Would you please [request]?**

Example
"Do you ever say thank you?"

Nonviolent statement:
1. When you do [*compliment everyone in the team but me*],
2. I feel [*disappointed*].
3. My need is [*that my work is appreciated*],
4. Would you please [*help me understand if something is wrong with me*]?

Adapted from Rosenberg (2003).

The Nonviolent Requests Guide

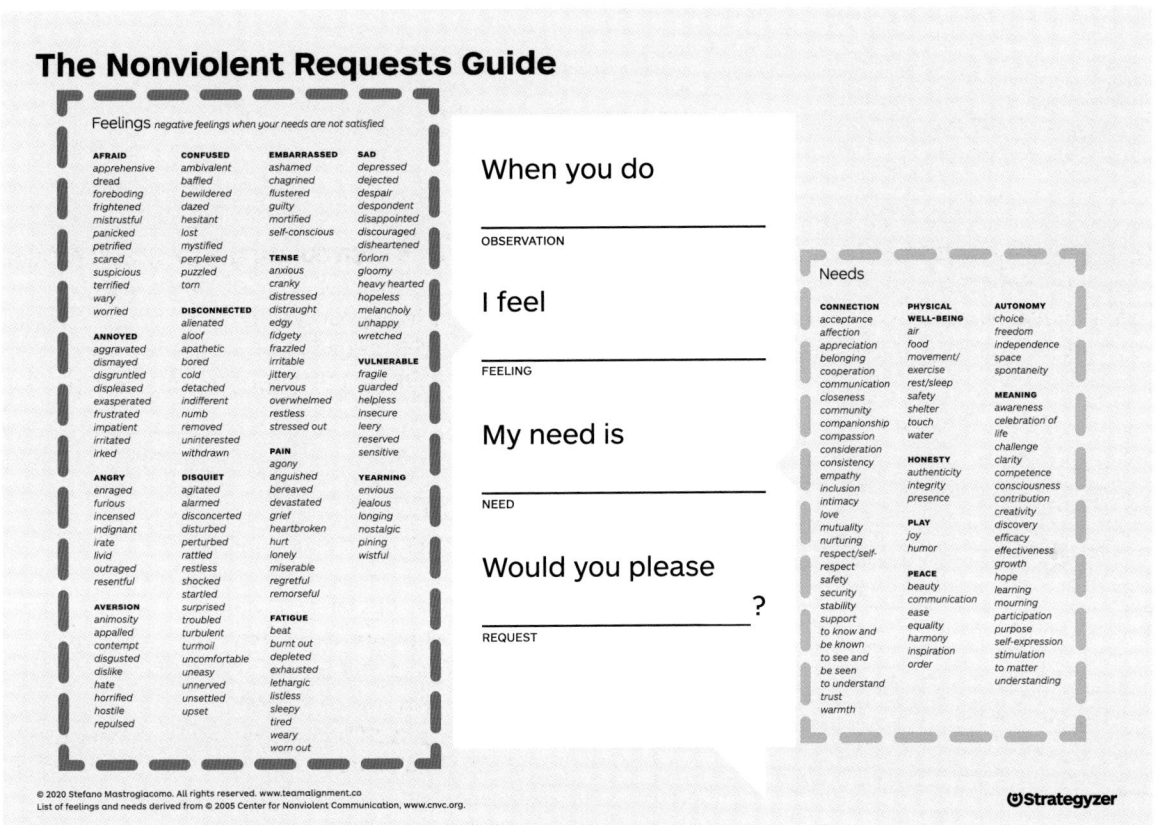

Feelings *negative feelings when your needs are not satisfied*

AFRAID	CONFUSED	EMBARRASSED	SAD
apprehensive	ambivalent	ashamed	depressed
dread	baffled	chagrined	dejected
foreboding	bewildered	flustered	despair
frightened	dazed	guilty	despondent
mistrustful	hesitant	mortified	disappointed
panicked	lost	self-conscious	discouraged
petrified	mystified		disheartened
scared	perplexed	**TENSE**	forlorn
suspicious	puzzled	anxious	gloomy
terrified	torn	cranky	heavy hearted
wary		distressed	hopeless
worried	**DISCONNECTED**	distraught	melancholy
	alienated	edgy	unhappy
ANNOYED	aloof	fidgety	wretched
aggravated	apathetic	frazzled	
dismayed	bored	irritable	**VULNERABLE**
disgruntled	cold	jittery	fragile
displeased	detached	nervous	guarded
exasperated	indifferent	overwhelmed	helpless
frustrated	numb	restless	insecure
impatient	removed	stressed out	leery
irritated	uninterested		reserved
irked	withdrawn	**PAIN**	sensitive
		agony	
ANGRY	**DISQUIET**	anguished	**YEARNING**
enraged	agitated	bereaved	envious
furious	alarmed	devastated	jealous
incensed	disconcerted	grief	longing
indignant	disturbed	heartbroken	nostalgic
irate	perturbed	hurt	pining
livid	rattled	lonely	wistful
outraged	restless	miserable	
resentful	shocked	regretful	
	startled	remorseful	
AVERSION	surprised		
animosity	troubled	**FATIGUE**	
appalled	turbulent	beat	
contempt	turmoil	burnt out	
disgusted	uncomfortable	depleted	
dislike	uneasy	exhausted	
hate	unnerved	lethargic	
horrified	unsettled	listless	
hostile	upset	sleepy	
repulsed		tired	
		weary	
		worn out	

When you do

_____

OBSERVATION

I feel

_____

FEELING

My need is

_____

NEED

Would you please

_____ ?

REQUEST

Needs

CONNECTION	PHYSICAL WELL-BEING	AUTONOMY
acceptance	air	choice
affection	food	freedom
appreciation	movement/	independence
belonging	exercise	space
cooperation	rest/sleep	spontaneity
communication	safety	
closeness	shelter	**MEANING**
community	touch	awareness
companionship	water	celebration of
compassion		life
consideration		challenge
consistency	**HONESTY**	clarity
empathy	authenticity	competence
inclusion	integrity	consciousness
intimacy	presence	contribution
love		creativity
mutuality	**PLAY**	discovery
nurturing	joy	efficacy
respect/self-	humor	effectiveness
respect		growth
safety	**PEACE**	hope
security	beauty	learning
stability	communication	mourning
support	ease	participation
to know and	equality	purpose
be known	harmony	self-expression
to see and	inspiration	stimulation
be seen	order	to matter
to understand		understanding
trust		
warmth		

Ⓢ **Strategyzer**

Attacks

You're always late!
I can't count on you!

Am I the only person
working here?

Are we done?
I have work to do.

Do it yourself!

Nobody cares here!

You're a bureaucrat...

Lack of context	**Motivation**	**Rules and procedures**

- When you do [*ask me to save their project*],
- I feel [*panicked because I already have a lot on my plate*].
- My need is [*clarity*],
- Would you please [*help me understand the big picture*]?

- When you do [*tell me that my project is abruptly abandoned*],
- I feel [*sad*].
- My need is [*to do meaningful work*],
- Would you please [*help me understand what motivates your decision*]?

- When you do [*ask me to respect time-consuming procedures*],
- I feel [*exhausted because I seriously lack time*].
- My need is [*efficacy*],
- Would you please [*help me understand why this is so important*]?

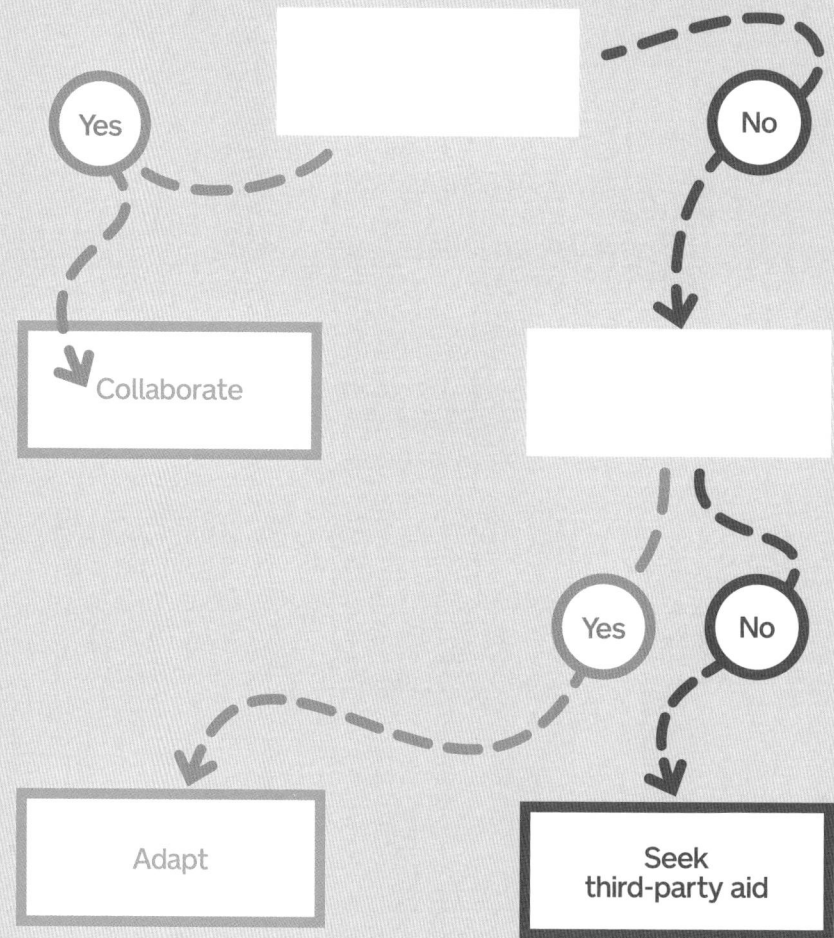

Collaborate

Adapt

Seek
third-party aid

Adapted from Kahane (2017).

Origins of the Nonviolent Requests Guide

A Revolutionary Approach to Nonviolent Interactions

Marshall Rosenberg (1934–2015) was an American psychologist who explored the causes of and what could be done to reduce violence. He observed that when we lack the emotional skills to describe our discontent, we tend to issue unproductive judgments and criticisms (called "evaluations" in NVC) perceived as an attack by the other. We might say, for example: "You lied to me" or "You're not accountable," both perceived as an attack, when what we really want to express is: "I am disappointed because you promised you would deliver this work today."

Rosenberg developed and used NVC to improve mediation and communication skills in public schools during the 1960s. He later founded the Center for Nonviolent Communication in 1984, an international peacemaking organization providing NVC training and support in over 60 countries across the world. To learn more about this powerful framework, go to the website for the Center for Nonviolent Communication, www.cnvc.org

List of feelings and needs © 2005 by Center for Nonviolent Communication

Feelings When Your Needs Are Not Satisfied

Afraid
apprehensive
dread
foreboding
frightened
mistrustful
panicked
petrified
scared
suspicious
terrified
wary
worried

Angry
enraged
furious
incensed
indignant
irate
livid
outraged
resentful

Annoyed
aggravated
dismayed
disgruntled
displeased
exasperated
frustrated
impatient
irritated
irked

Aversion
animosity
appalled
contempt
disgusted
dislike
hate
horrified
hostile
repulsed

Confused
ambivalent
baffled
bewildered
dazed
hesitant
lost
mystified
perplexed
puzzled
torn

Disconnected
alienated
aloof
apathetic
bored
cold
detached
distant
distracted
indifferent
numb
removed
uninterested
withdrawn

Disquiet
agitated
alarmed
discombobu-
lated
disconcerted
disturbed
perturbed
rattled
restless
shocked
startled
surprised
troubled
turbulent
turmoil
uncomfortable
uneasy
unnerved
unsettled
upset

Embarrassed
ashamed
chagrined
flustered
guilty
mortified
self-conscious

Fatigue
beat
burned out
depleted
exhausted
lethargic
listless

sleepy
tired
weary
worn out

Pain
agony
anguished
bereaved
devastated
grief
heartbroken
hurt
lonely
miserable
regretful
remorseful

Sad
depressed
dejected
despair
despondent
disappointed
discouraged
disheartened
forlorn
gloomy
heavy-hearted
hopeless
melancholy
unhappy
wretched

Tense
anxious
cranky
distressed
distraught
edgy
fidgety
frazzled
irritable
jittery
nervous
overwhelmed
restless
stressed out

Vulnerable
fragile
guarded
helpless
insecure
leery
reserved
sensitive
shaky

Yearning
envious
jealous
longing
nostalgic
pining
wistful

Feelings When Your Needs Are Satisfied

Affectionate
compassionate
friendly
loving
open-hearted
sympathetic
tender
warm

Engaged
absorbed
alert
curious
engrossed
enchanted
entranced
fascinated
interested
intrigued
involved
spellbound
stimulated

Hopeful
expectant
encouraged
optimistic

Confident
empowered
open
proud
safe
secure

Excited
amazed
animated
ardent
aroused
astonished
dazzled
eager
energetic
enthusiastic
giddy
invigorated
lively
passionate
surprised
vibrant

Grateful
appreciative
moved
thankful
touched

Inspired
amazed
awed
wonder

Joyful
amused
delighted
glad
happy
jubilant
pleased
tickled

Exhilarated
blissful
ecstatic
elated
enthralled
exuberant
radiant
rapturous
thrilled

Peaceful
calm
clear-headed
comfortable
centered
content
equanimous
fulfilled
mellow
quiet
relaxed
relieved
satisfied
serene
still
tranquil
trusting

Refreshed
enlivened
rejuvenated
renewed
rested
restored
revived

Inventory of Needs

Connection
acceptance
affection
appreciation
belonging
cooperation
communication
closeness
community
companionship
compassion
consideration
consistency
empathy
inclusion
intimacy
love
mutuality
nurturing
respect/
self-respect
safety
security
stability
support
to know and be
known
to see and be
seen
to understand
and be
understood
trust
warmth

**Physical
Well-Being**
air
food
movement/
exercise
rest/sleep
safety
shelter
touch
water

Honesty
authenticity
integrity
presence

Play
joy
humor

Peace
beauty
communion
ease
equality
harmony
inspiration
order

Autonomy
choice
freedom
independence
space
spontaneity

Meaning
awareness
celebration
of life
challenge
clarity
competence
consciousness
contribution
creativity
discovery
efficacy
effectiveness
growth
hope
learning
mourning
participation
purpose
self-expression
stimulation
to matter
understanding

Dive Deeper

Discover the science behind the tools and the book

Overview

The tools presented in this book are
the result of an <u>interdisciplinary</u> work.
Find out what body of <u>academic
research</u> lies behind each <u>tool.</u>

4.1
Mutual Understanding and Common Ground

What psycholinguistics reveals about how we understand each other.

4.2
Trust and Psychological Safety

Dive deeper into Amy Edmondson's work.

4.3
Relationship Types

The evolutionary anthropology perspective.

4.4
Face and Politeness

Face theory and the two key needs of mutual consideration.

The Science Behind the Tools

All the tools have been designed using a Lean UX cycle at the intersection of current management problems and possible conceptual solutions from social sciences, including psycholinguistics, evolutionary anthropology, and psychology. Translating theoretical concepts into actionable tools has required dozens of iterations and prototypes and chances are the tools will evolve further in the future.

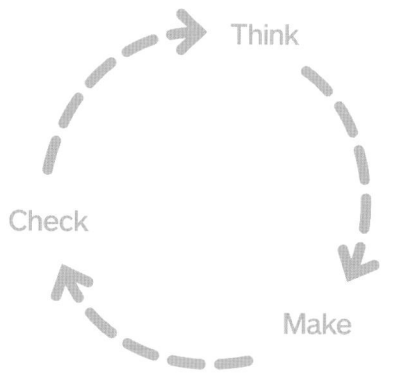

Lean UX Cycle

The Team Alignment Map

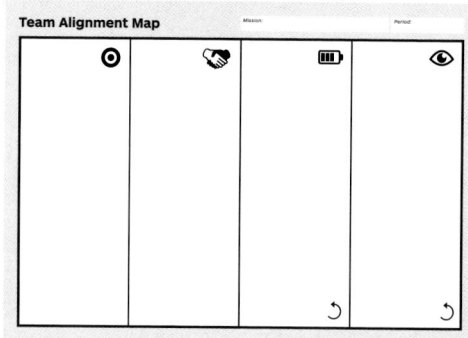

The Team Contract

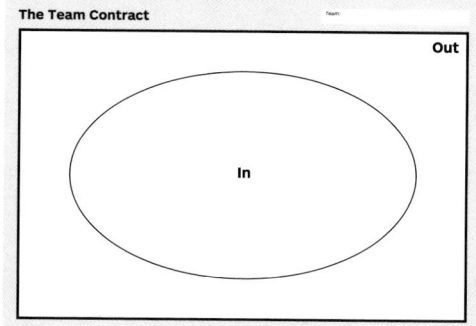

Mutual Understanding and Common Ground
(in Psycholinguistics), p. 258

Relationship Types
(in Evolutionary Anthropology), p. 274

Trust and Psychological Safety
(in Psychology), p. 266

The Fact Finder

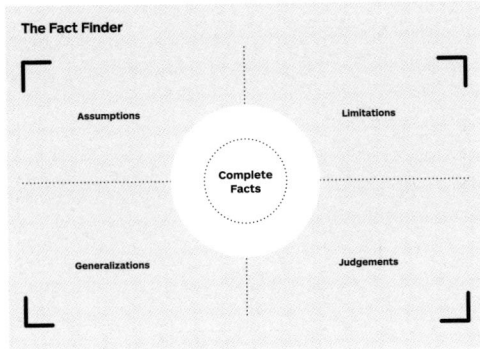

The Fact Finder

Assumptions

Limitations

Complete Facts

Generalizations

Judgements

The Respect Card

The Respect Card

Need to be respected
Demonstrate Respect

Need to be valued
Demonstrate Recognition

The Nonviolent Requests Guide

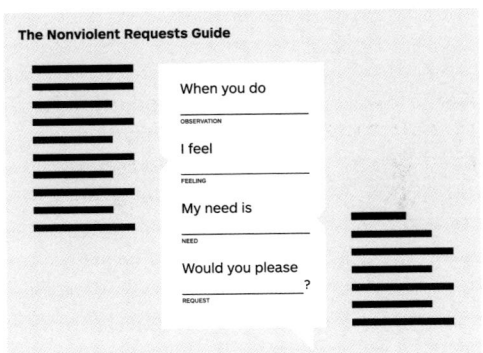

The Nonviolent Requests Guide

When you do

OBSERVATION

I feel

FEELING

My need is

NEED

Would you please

REQUEST

Face and Politeness
(in Psycholinguistics), p. 282

Nonviolent Communication
(in Psychology), p. 250

4.1
Mutual Understanding and Common Ground

What psycholinguistics reveals about how we understand each other.

What Is a Team's Common Ground?

Simply put, common ground is what every team member knows that the other team members know. The mechanics of common ground, common knowledge, shared or mutual understanding and so on, have been described by psycholinguist Herbert Clark and further developed psychologist Steven Pinker. People use language to coordinate joint activities. Team members are mutually dependent, as they need each other to be successful when working together. This interdependence forces everyone to solve coordination problems as everyone needs to constantly align his or her contribution with the contributions of others. As described by Clark, team members need to establish and maintain a sufficient level of common ground to carry out joint activities: a set of knowledge, beliefs, and suppositions shared by all. This matters for interpredictability reasons: team members must be able to successfully predict each others' actions and behaviors to coordinate and achieve what they intend to achieve as a team. How is a team's common ground created and maintained? Through language use and communication. From a Clarkian perspective, this is the raison d'être of communication — to put in place a device to create common ground

and help us coordinate with one another. When there is enough common ground, team members can predict one another's actions successfully and run into less coordination surprises. In other words, they experience less execution problems because their individual contributions are aligned. Coordination surprises occur each time team members see others do things that don't make sense in terms of their own beliefs. As noted by Klein (2005), these originate in common ground breakdowns, i.e. when there is confusion about what's going on and who does what — in other words, who knows what. Project failure factors such as incomplete requirements, lack of user involvement, unrealistic expectations, lack of support, or changing requirements can be interpreted as symptoms of common ground breakdowns, highlighting the importance of creating and maintaining enough common ground, common knowledge, or mutual understanding to ensure successful teamwork.

Successful Teamwork

Effective Coordination

Relevant Common Ground

Successful Conversations

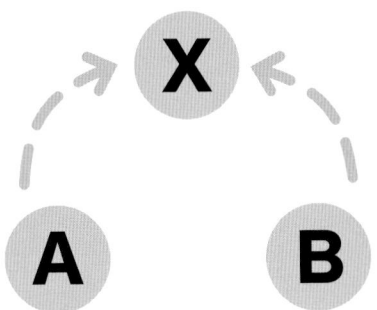

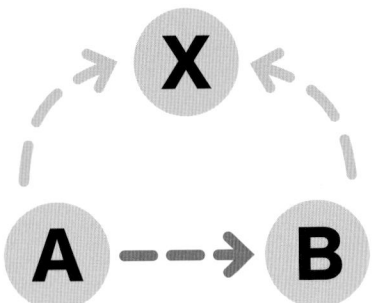

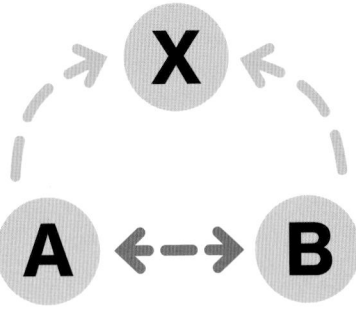

Private Knowledge

All know something, but
don't know that the others
know too.
- A knows X
- B knows X

Example
- Ann knows that there is a man
  walking in the street
- Bob knows that there is a man
  walking in the street
- Ann doesn't know that Bob
  knows it
- Bob doesn't know that Ann
  knows it

Shared Knowledge

All know something, but
only some know that the
others know.
- A knows X
- B knows X
- A knows that B knows X
- B doesn't know that A
  knows X

Example
- Ann knows that there is a man
  walking in the street
- Bob knows that there is a man
  walking in the street
- Ann knows that Bob knows it
- Bob doesn't know that Ann
  knows it

Common Ground, Common Knowledge, or Mutual Understanding

All know something, and
also know that all the others
know.
- A knows X
- B knows X
- A and B know that they
  both know X

Example
- Ann knows that there is a man
  walking in the street
- Bob knows that there is a man
  walking in the street
- Ann and Bob both know that
  they both know it

J. De Freitas, K. Thomas, P. DeScioli, and S. Pinker, "Common Knowledge, Coordination, and Strategic Mentalizing in Human Social Life," Proceedings of the National Academy of Sciences 116, no. 28 (2019): 13751–13758.

Building Up Common Ground

Common ground accumulates as the result of a social and cognitive process described as the "grounding process" by Herb Clark. This process allows two or more people to create and validate mutual understanding by signaling each other (1) that evidence of understanding is reached or (2) that misunderstanding is in the air and that further iterations are needed to be successful.

1 Signaling Understanding

Mutual understanding is achieved when people signal, verbally or nonverbally, signs of positive evidence of understanding.
In a conversation, positive signals include:
- Nodding: "uh-huh," "I see," "Mmm"
- Continuing: continuing the sentence of the other
- Answering: answering a question
- Examplifying: giving an example of what has just been said

This process of grounding unfolds in three co-occurring activities or levels that happen at the same time. Speakers and listeners must climb together a virtual ladder in this sequence:
1. **Attending**: speakers make sounds and gestures and listeners must attend to these sounds and gestures.
2. **Perceiving**: speakers must formulate messages with these sounds and gestures and listeners must identify those messages.
3. **Understanding**: speakers must mean something with these messages and listeners must make the right inferences to understand their meaning.

2 Signaling Misunderstanding

When things are unclear, the following signals illustrate misunderstanding, or negative evidence of understanding:
- Hesitating: "uh"
- Reformulating: "If I understand …," "You mean…," etc.
- Clarifying: ask good clarification questions, using the Fact Finder for example.

These repair mechanisms create new opportunities to build mutual understanding.

+
Ask. Listen. Repeat.
A simple method to boost mutual understanding is to validate our own understanding by repeating what the other person just told us.

The Grounding Process

Speaking and listening are themselves a joint activity, like dancing a waltz or playing a piano duet. The active participation of both parties is needed at each step to create common ground successfully.

Listening

Common Ground

Speaking

Understand meaning — **3. Understanding** — Mean something

Identify messages — **2. Perceiving** — Formulate messages

Attend to sounds and gestures — **1. Attending** — Make sounds and gestures

Impact of Communication Channels on Common Ground Creation

Not all communication channels have the same impact on common ground creation (Clark and Brennan, 1991). Face-to-face conversation remains the most effective technology followed by videoconferencing, which makes great progress in lowering the distance barrier and developing immersive experiences. Co-located task forces, war rooms, and crisis units still illustrate the importance of in-person meetings to create common knowledge rapidly when people need to be extremely effective.

All the other communication channels present communication obstacles compared to face-to-face interaction — for example, the lack of nonverbal and contextual infor-mation, bad signal, delays, or the inability to get an immediate explanation when receiving an ambiguous email. These obsta-cles can considerably reduce our ability to build common ground and coordinate as a team.

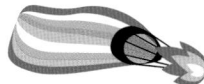

Synchronous Communication

Prefer face-to-face, video-conference, and conference calls when the team's common ground needs a strong boost, for example when:

- Initiating new activities and projects
- Solving problems
- Performing creative tasks

Asynchronous Communication

Use email, chat rooms, and other asynchronous media for incremental updates such as:

- Notifying of changes
- Co-editing documents
- Sharing updates
- Status reports

Communication Effectiveness
of Various Media Types

+
A face-to-face request is 34 times more successful than an email.

Vanessa K. Bohns, Harvard Business Review, April 2017

Adapted from Media Richness Theory, https://en.wikipedia.org/wiki/Media_richness_theory

Face-to-face conversation

Video conversation

Telephone conversation

Addressed letters, emails, reports

Short messages

Unaddressed spam, posters

4.2
Trust and Psychological Safety

Dive deeper into Amy Edmondson's work.

What Is Psychological Safety and How Does It Help Teams Perform Better?

According to Amy Edmondson, psychological safety is "the belief that the team is safe for interpersonal risk taking. That one will not be punished or humiliated for speaking up with ideas, questions, concerns, or mistakes." When the climate is psychologically safe, team members are not afraid to speak up; they engage in a productive dialogue that fosters the proactive learning behaviors required to understand the environment, the clients, and solve problems together effectively.

Solving complex problems is the bread and butter of any cutting-edge business, where constant experimentation is required: intense phases of trial and error until teams get things right, which by definition is the very basis of business innovation. Faced with uncertainty, psychologically safe teams are propelled into a performance spiral, where making mistakes is not considered a failure, but rather as experimentation and a learning opportunity. Creating safety is not about being nice to each other or reducing performance standards, but rather about creating a culture of openness where teammates can share learnings, be direct, take risks, admit they "screwed up," and are willing to ask for help when they're in over their head.

In Google's top-performing teams, people feel safe to speak up, collaborate, and experiment together. A large internal study conducted by their HR teams highlighted psychological safety as the key enabler of high-performance teamwork.

In a world characterized by Volatility, Uncertainty, Complexity, and Ambiguity (VUCA), creating and maintaining a psychologically safe climate must become a managerial priority for those who want to keep up in the global competitive race.

As noted by Edmondson, psychological safety is not about being nice or compromising performance standards. Conflict arises in every team, but psychological safety makes it possible to channel that energy into productive interactions, that is, constructive disagreement, an open exchange of ideas, and learning from different points of view. Similarly, psychological safety is not about creating a comfortable climate by relaxing performance standards and making people feel unaccountable at the individual level. Psychological safety and performance standards are two separate, equally important dimensions, and both are needed to achieve superior team performance (Edmondson 2018).

A. C. Edmondson, The Fearless Organization: Creating Psychological Safety in the Workplace for Learning, Innovation, and Growth (John Wiley & Sons, 2018).

Psychological Safety and Business Performance

Both high psychological safety and high performance standards are needed to enter the learning zone and achieve superior team performance.

Comfort Zone
Team members enjoy working together but are not challenged by work and don't see compelling reasons to engage in additional challenges.

Learning Zone
Everyone can collaborate, learn from each other, and get complex, innovative work done.

Apathy Zone
People are physically present but their mind is elsewhere. Significant energy is poured into making each other's life miserable.

Anxiety Zone
Maybe the worst area to work in, people must meet high standards and expectations mostly on their own, because they are suspicious and experience anxiety toward their colleagues.

Psychological Safety

Performance Standards

How to Rapidly Assess Psychological Safety

These seven questions help identify what works well and areas needing improvement. We recommend that this assessment be done between colleagues of the same hierarchical level to avoid biased responses.

1 Respond individually
Take two minutes individually to answer the seven questions and calculate your personal score.

2 Share the personal scores
Share the personal scores with your colleagues.

3 Discuss and investigate the gaps
Enter an open discussion to understand the different perceptions, question by question.

4 Agree on possible actions
If areas for improvement are identified, agree on appropriate solutions. The four add-ons presented on the next page can help.

		Strongly Disagree	Disagree	Somewhat Disagree	Neutral	Somewhat Agree	Agree	Strongly Agree	Your Scores
1 Learn from mistakes	If you make a mistake on this team, it is often held against you.	7	6	5	4	3	2	1	
2 Productive conflict	Members of this team are able to bring up problems and tough issues.	1	2	3	4	5	6	7	
3 Gain from diversity	People on this team sometimes reject others for being different.	7	6	5	4	3	2	1	
4 Foster exploration	It is safe to take a risk on this team.	1	2	3	4	5	6	7	
5 Mutual assistance	It is difficult to ask other members of this team for help.	7	6	5	4	3	2	1	
6 Strong partnership	No one on this team would deliberately act in a way that undermines my efforts.	1	2	3	4	5	6	7	
7 Optimal contributions	Working with members of this team, my unique skills and talents are valued and utilized.	1	2	3	4	5	6	7	

Total

+ As a rule of thumb, 40 and above can be considered a good total score.

Adapted from Amy Edmondson, 1999.

Differences Between Trust, Psychological Safety, and Similar Concepts

Psychological Safety

The belief held by members of a team that the team is safe for interpersonal risk taking, that one will not be punished or humiliated for speaking up with ideas, questions, concerns, or mistakes (Edmondson 1999).

Psychological safety describes a team climate and is experienced at the group level (Edmondson 2018); it captures the extent to which one believes that others will give them the benefit of the doubt when taking risks (Edmondson 2004). It involves but goes beyond trust.

Adapted from Frazier et al. (2017).

Empowerment

The motivational state employees feel when they have a sense of control over their work (Spreitzer 1995).

Engagement

The cognitive state describing individuals who invest their personal resources and energies into their work roles and tasks (Christian, Garza, and Slaughter 2011; Kahn 1990).

Trust

The willingness to be vulnerable to the actions of others (Mayer, Davis, and Schoorman 1995).

+

Trust is experienced at the interaction level, between two individuals. One might trust one colleague and not the other (Edmondson 2019).

4.3
Relationship Types

The evolutionary anthropology perspective.

Relationships:
The Four Playing Modes

When we work as a team we don't just work; we also manage our relationships with our colleagues. We constantly seek, make, sustain, repair, adjust, judge, construe, and sanction relationships. The anthropologist Alan Fiske brilliantly identified the "grammar" of human relationships in the form of four elementary types of bonds called relationship types. These four playing modes each organize a way of distributing resources between participants (adapted from Fiske 1992 and Pinker 2008).

The four modes are:
1. **Share**: "What's mine is yours, and vice versa." People are driven by a sense of belonging and decisions are made by consensus. Typical of communities such as couples, close friends, or allies.
2. **Authority**: "Who's in charge?" People are driven by power, rules and decisions are authoritative; one person is positioned above (gaining prestige) and the other is positioned below (gaining protection). Typical in hierarchical structures such as bosses and subordinates, soldiers and commanders, or professors and students.
3. **Reciprocate**: "To each the same." People are driven by equality, giving and taking in the same quantity, and decisions are made by voting (one person, one vote). Typical in peer groups such as clubs, carpools, and acquaintances: getting and giving presents, being invited and inviting in return, and so on.
4. **Bargain**: "To each in due proportion." People are driven by achievements; transactions are based on elements such as perceived utility, individual performance, and market price. Typical in for-profit businesses, stock markets, buyer and seller relationships.

What Fiske reveals is that when the two parties play in the same mode, things go pretty well. But if one plays in one mode and one in another—when there is a mode mismatch—things go wrong. To add more complexity, we never interact with one another using just one playing mode. We constantly switch modes depending on the context and the task at hand. The challenge is to navigate together successfully through the playing mode changes because the rules of the game change in each mode.

A. P. Fiske, "The Four Elementary Forms of Sociality: Framework for a Unified Theory of Social Relations," Psychological Review 99, no. 4 (1992): 689.
S. Pinker, M. A. Nowak, and J. J. Lee, "The Logic of Indirect Speech," Proceedings of the National Academy of Sciences 105, no. 3 (2008): 833–838.

What is your team's main playing mode, in what situation?

Understanding and aligning playing modes helps minimize unintentional gaffes; in each playing mode the rules of the game change and so do the expected behaviors.

Teamwork
Expectations

Playing Mode	Share *What's mine is yours*	Authority *Who's in charge?*	Reciprocate *Give and take*	Bargain *Pay in due proportion*
Appears in children by	Infancy	Age of 3	Age of 4	Age of 9
Primary motivation	Belonging • intimacy • altruism • generosity • kindness • caring	Belonging • power vs. protection • status, recognition vs. obedience, loyalty	Equality • equal treatment • strict fairness	Achievement • utility • benefits • profits
Examples	Families, close friends, clubs, ethnic groups, social movements, open-source communities	Subordinates and their bosses, soldiers and commanders, professors and students	Roommates (errands, rounds of beers), carpools, acquaintances (getting and giving presents, dinner parties, birthdays)	The business world: buyer and seller, get the best deal, make a profit, negotiate a contract, receive dividends
Organization	Community	Hierarchical	Peer group	Rationally structured
Contribution from members	Everyone contributes according to their personal abilities	Supervisors direct and control the work	Everyone does the same or equivalent work	Work is divided based on performance and productivity
Decision-making process	Consensus	Chain of authority	Voting, drawing lots	Arguments
Resource ownership	Owned by all, no bookkeeping	Increases with the hierarchical level	Divided in equal parts	In proportion to the contribution or the invested capital
Rewards	Common pool for rewards, no individual compensation	By rank and seniority	Same reward of same amount for everyone	By market value and individual performance

Crossing Playing Modes: Not a Good Idea

Emotions can run high when we assume that others are playing in the same mode we are, when in fact they aren't. The behaviors perceived as appropriate in one mode can be perceived as completely inappropriate in another one. Everyone is doing their best, but people offend each other involuntarily simply because they are operating in a different mode. That creates situations where the parties feel embarrassment, taboo, or even feel immoral (Pinker 2007).

Aligned Modes

A close friend
(Share = Share)

Take food from the plate of...

Misaligned Modes

A superior
(Share ≠ Authority)

S. Pinker, The Stuff of Thought: Language as a Window into Human Nature (Penguin, 2007).

A client
(Bargain = Bargain)

Make a profit from a sale to...

A parent
(Bargain ≠ Share)

At a restaurant
(Bargain = Bargain)

Pay for your dinner...

At your parents' house
(Bargain ≠ Share)

In teams, misaligned playing modes create awkward situations, can damage relationships, and can turn into conflict.

As an experienced professional, Tati tries to direct others, while they assume everyone should have an equal say.
(Authority ≠ Reciprocate)

The team is waiting for Antonio's directions, while he assumes he doesn't have to take responsibility because he's not being paid for that.
(Authority ≠ Bargain)

Susan thinks Ann is the most competent person to meet a client with her. Others think it's a matter of taking turns.
(Bargain ≠ Reciprocate)

Aligned Playing Modes: Crucial for Family Businesses

The risk of conflict is high in family businesses. Collaborating with family members in a business context creates a highly complex relational setting.

In a family business system, members often cumulate several roles (family member, owner, manager), which imply different value systems and interests. The more roles family members accumulate, the greater the likelihood of crossing the boundaries of each role and experience a playing mode mismatch with the other family members. Large family businesses address this challenge by designing their own family governance model to clarify the expectations and structure the responsibilities of each role. These are often compiled in a so-called family constitution, a document that formalizes the relationships in the family, thus minimizing unnecessary conflict due to the crossing of types.

Keywords: family business, family governance, family constitution

Kevin
Samantha's son, brother, student

Nina
Samantha's daughter, sister, manager in the family business

Bob
Samantha's dad, the grandfather, founder, retired, owner

Samantha
Nina and Kevin's mom, CEO and owner

Drafting a family constitution can require substantial effort, skills, and external resources. To preserve harmony, smaller family-owned businesses like shops, restaurants, and craft businesses can as a first step establish a Team Contract to define some basic rules of the game in the different roles.

Family Roles Overlap as a Source of Conflict

Bob (Share) — **Samantha** (Authority)
Despite a year of exceptional results, Bob keeps giving lengthy advice to Samantha on what he would have done in her place.

Kevin (Share) — **Samantha** (Bargain)
Kevin's upset because his sister Nina won't let him use her company car to go to a party.

Kevin (Reciprocate) — **Samantha** (Bargain)
Kevin is even angrier when he finds out that his sister got a financial bonus at work while he doesn't have enough pocket money.

Nina (Bargain) — **Samantha** (Authority)
Nina is angry at her mother because she promoted another person to a position she wanted.

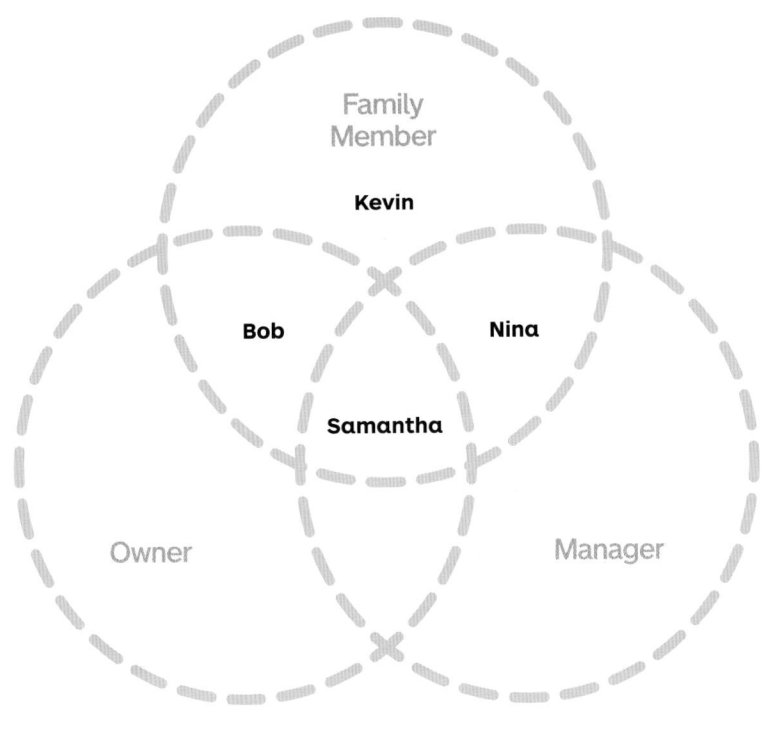

Source of the Three-Circle Model: R. Tagiuri and J. Davis, "Bivalent Attributes of the Family Firm," Family Business Review 9, no. 2 (Summer 1996), p. 200.

4.4
Face and Politeness

Face theory and two key needs of mutual consideration.

Politeness:
Our Two Key Social Needs

The anthropologists Penelope Brown and Stephen Levinson provided a unique description of mutual consideration in their book *Politeness: Some Universals in Language Usage*. They have developed a groundbreaking theory of politeness based on the concept of "face", from the expression "losing face" described by the sociologist Erving Goffmann as the positive social value that a person claims for him- or herself.

For Brown and Levinson, demonstrating consideration and being polite means doing "facework" by actively taking care of the face of each other. That is achieved by addressing two universally shared "social needs" (Brown and Levinson 1987):

- The need to be approved, or valued: when the actions and behaviors of others reflect a positive image of ourselves. That happens when we are thanked, expressed sympathy toward, recognized, and so forth, and it doesn't happen when we are ignored, disapproved of, or embarrassed in public.
- The need to be autonomous, or respected: the need to protect our freedom of action, not being impeded or trapped by others, that our private territory is not invaded. That happens when we are asked for permission to be interrupted, when we receive apologies in advance for an inconvenience, or when honorific titles such as Mrs., Mr., Dr., Prof., and so on are used to showcase our social status. That doesn't happen when we are prevented from having our morning coffee to hear complaints, when things are imposed on us, or when we receive warnings and summonses.

These (almost) antagonistic needs illustrate, according to psychologist Steven Pinker, the duality of social life: connection and autonomy, intimacy and power, solidarity and status. If I do whatever I want, my need to be respected is satisfied but I might not be valued by others. Wanting to be valued and respected constitutes our social DNA (Fiske, 1992) and we become very picky when these are threatened. Demonstrating mutual consideration, in Brown and Levinson's view, consists of doing what's right: choosing the right words and expressions to minimize the risk of making each other lose face. In other words, to be polite.

Search keywords: politeness theory, Brown and Levinson, theory of the strategic speaker, Steven Pinker, politeness

We value people who show us consideration by respecting our two social needs. We are less appreciative of those who don't. The same is true for the others.

Social need to be respected
Congratulations!

Social need to be valued
May I ask you to follow me?

What Is a Fair Process?

Valuing and respecting each other are the two key pillars of fairness. Fairness is a crucial foundation on which to grow teams and implement any diversity, equity, and inclusion initiative.

Implementing a fair process in a team or in an organization consists of making decisions so that everyone's needs to be valued and respected are equitably addressed. As illustrated by INSEAD's Cham Kim and Renée Mauborgne, this is achieved by adopting the three high-level principles of:

1. Engagement
2. Explanation
3. Expectation clarity

Research shows that people accept compromise and even sacrifice their personal interests when they believe that the process leading to important decisions and results is fair. Despite the evidence, some managers struggle to adopt a fair process approach because they fear their authority will be questioned and their power will decrease, which reveals a misunderstanding of the process: a fair process is not decision by consensus, or democracy in the workplace. Its goal is to nurture and pursue the best ideas.

The Three Principles of a Fair (Decision) Process

1
Engagement
Involving individuals in decisions by inviting their input and encouraging them to challenge one another's ideas.

Supported by:
- The Team Alignment Map
- The Team Contract

2
Explanation
Clarifying the thinking behind a final decision.

Supported by:
- The Team Alignment Map
- The Team Contract

3
Expectation Clarity
Stating the new rules of the game, including performance standards, penalties for failure, and new responsibilities.

Supported by:
- The Team Contract

Source: W. Kim and R. Mauborgne, "Fair Process," Harvard Business Review 75 (1997): 65–75.

Templates

Download the templates on teamalignment.co/downloads

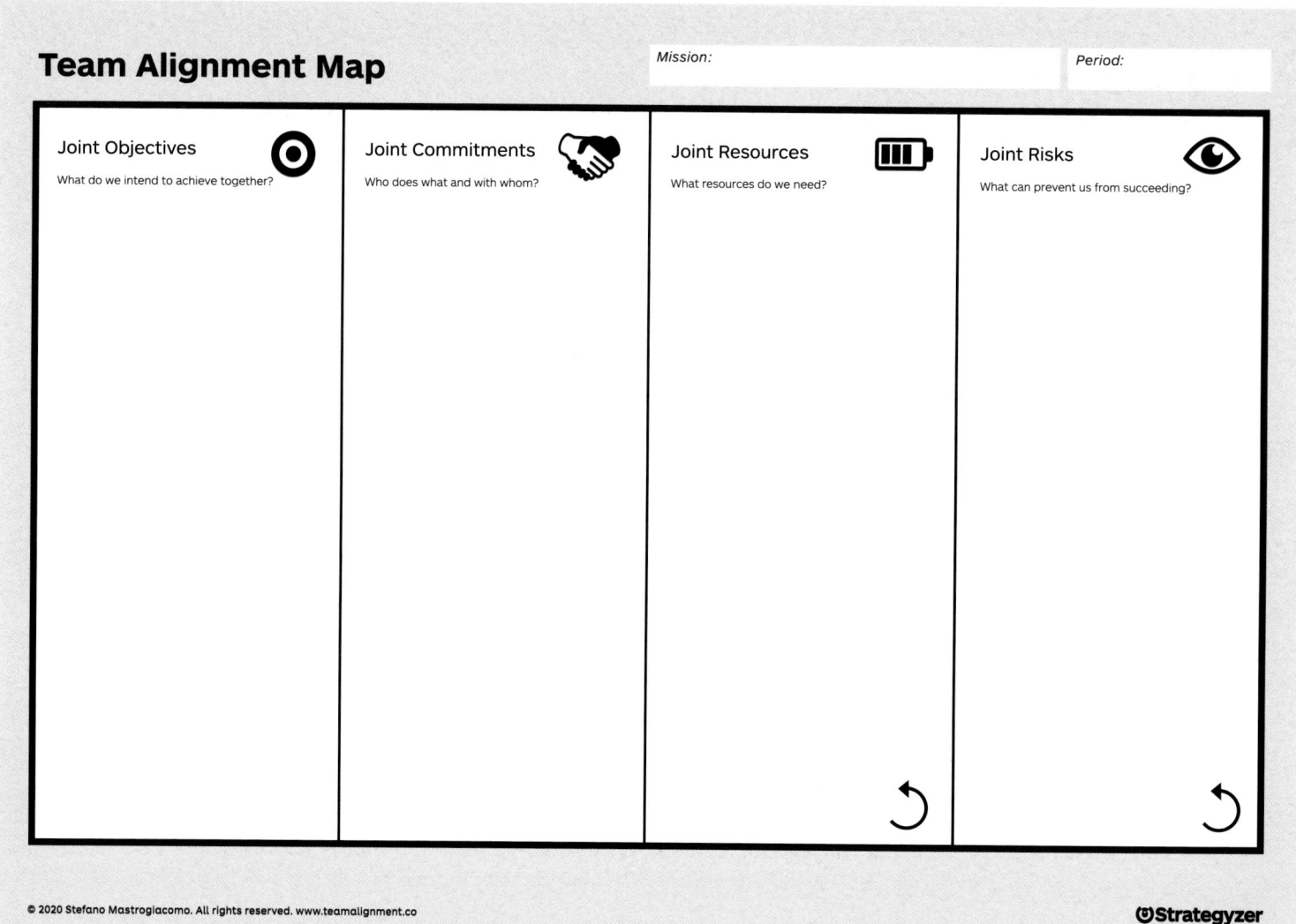

Team Alignment Map

Mission: _____ Period: _____

Joint Objectives
What do we intend to achieve together?

Joint Commitments
Who does what and with whom?

Joint Resources
What resources do we need?

Joint Risks
What can prevent us from succeeding?

Strategyzer

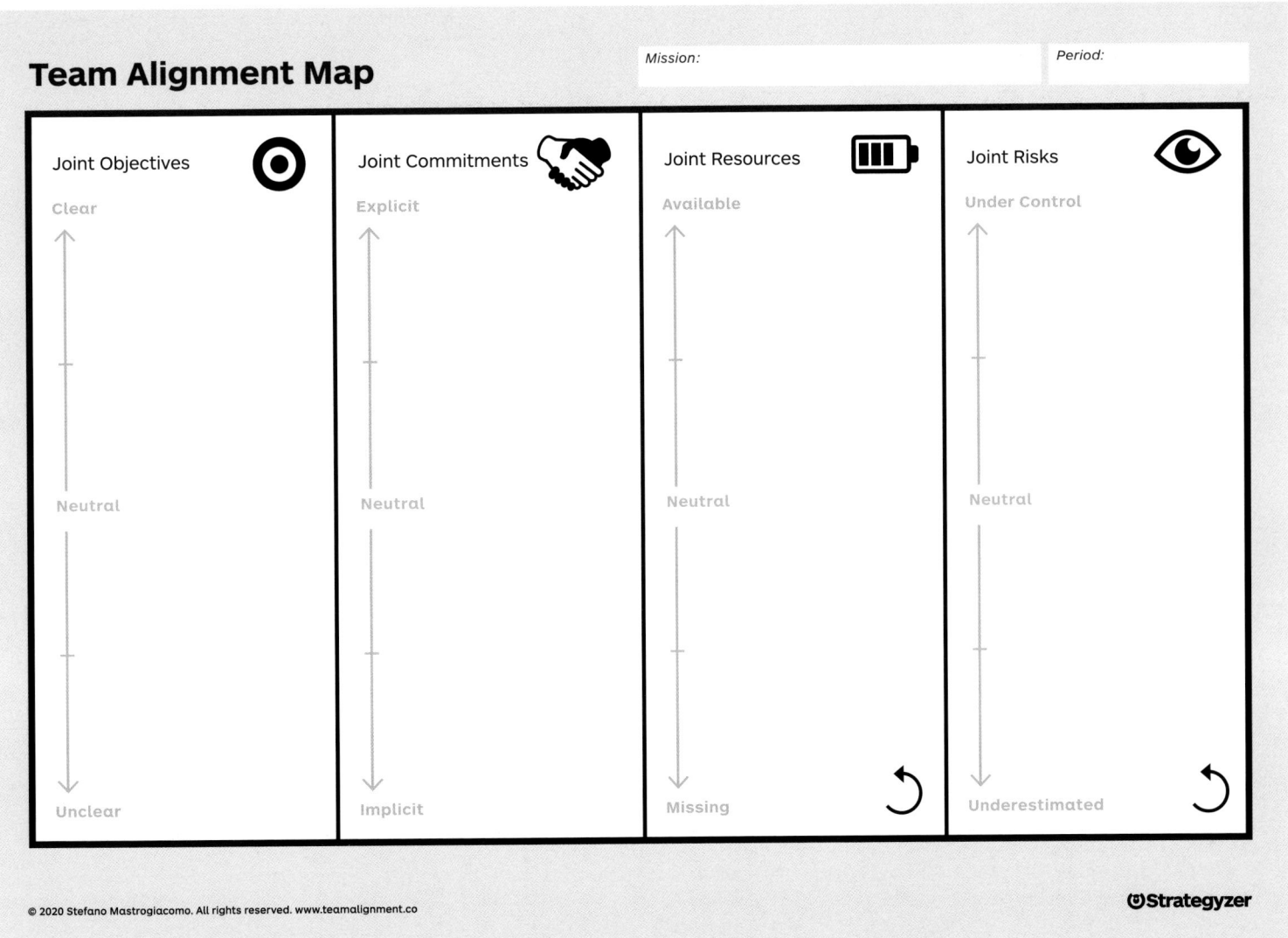

Team Alignment Map

Mission: _____   Period: _____

Joint Objectives
Clear
Neutral
Unclear

Joint Commitments
Explicit
Neutral
Implicit

Joint Resources
Available
Neutral
Missing

Joint Risks
Under Control
Neutral
Underestimated

Strategyzer

The Team Contract

What are the rules and behaviors that we want to abide by in our team?
As individuals, do we have preferences for working in a certain way?

Team:

Out

In

Strategyzer

The Fact Finder

Assumptions
Creative interpretations, hypotheses, or predictions

HEAR | **ASK**
"He/she thinks..." | *What makes you recognize that...?*
"He/she believes..." | *How do you know...?*
"He/she doesn't/should..." | *What evidence shows that...?*
"He/she likes..." | *What makes you think so?*
"You/they/... will..."
"Business/life/love/... will..."

Limitations
Imaginary restrictions and obligations that narrow down options

HEAR | **ASK**
"I must..." | *What might happen if...?*
"We have to" | *What's preventing you/us from...?*
"I can't..."
"I don't..."
"We shouldn't..."

Incomplete Facts or Experiences
Lack of precision in the description

HEAR
"I heard..."
"They said..."
"She saw..."
"I feel..."

Complete Facts

ASK
Who? What?
When? Where?
How? How many?
Could you be more precise?
What do you mean by...?

First-Order Reality
Physically observable qualities of a thing or situation

Generalizations
Turning a particular into a universal case

HEAR | **ASK**
"Always" | *Always?*
"Never" | *Never?*
"Nobody" | *Nobody?*
"Everyone" | *Everyone?*
"People" | *People?*
| *Are you sure?*

Judgments
Subjective assessment of a thing, a situation, or a person

HEAR | **ASK**
"I am..." | *What tells you...?*
"Life is..." | *How is this manifested?*
"It's good/bad to..." | *In what way is this unacceptable?*
"It's important to..." | *Something on your mind?*
"It's easy/difficult to..."

Second-Order Reality
Perceptions, personal interpretations of the first-order reality

Ⓤ Strategyzer

The Respect Card

Tips for tactful communication.

Need to be respected
Demonstrate Respect

Questioning rather than commanding
Will you...?

Express doubt
I don't suppose you might...?

Hedge the request
..., if possible.

Acknowledge the impingement
I'm sure you're busy, but...

Indicate reluctance
I normally wouldn't ask, but...

Apologize
I'm sorry to bother you, but...

Acknowledge a debt
I'd be grateful if you would...

Use honorifics
Mr., Mrs., Miss, Professor, Dr., etc...

Be indirect
I'm looking for a pen.

Request forgiveness
You must forgive me but...
Could I borrow your pen?

Minimize request
I just wanted to ask you if I could use your pen.

Pluralize the person responsible
*We forgot to tell you that you needed
to buy your plane ticket by yesterday.*

Hesitate
Can I, uh,...?

Impersonalize
Smoking is not permitted.

RISKY BEHAVIORS
Direct orders
Interrupt
Give warnings
Prohibit
Threaten
Suggestions
Reminders
Advice

Need to be valued
Demonstrate Recognition

Thank
A big thank you.

Wish
Be well, have a nice day.

Inquire
How are you? How is it going?

Compliment
Nice sweater.

Anticipate
You must be hungry.

Advice
Take care.

Endear
My friend, mate, buddy, pal, honey, dear, bro, guys.

Solicit agreement
You know?

Attend to others
*You must be hungry, it's been a long
time since breakfast. How about some lunch?*

Avoid disagreement
*A: You don't like it?
B: Yes, yes I like it, um, I usually don't eat this but it's good.*

Assume agreement
So, when are you coming to see us?

Hedge opinion
You really should sort of try harder

RISKY BEHAVIORS
Embarrass
Disapprove
Ignore
Openly criticize
Contempt, ridicule
Speak only about yourself
Mention taboo topics
Insults, accusations, complaints

Strategyzer

The Nonviolent Requests Guide

Feelings *negative feelings when your needs are not satisfied*

AFRAID
apprehensive
dread
foreboding
frightened
mistrustful
panicked
petrified
scared
suspicious
terrified
wary
worried

ANNOYED
aggravated
dismayed
disgruntled
displeased
exasperated
frustrated
impatient
irritated
irked

ANGRY
enraged
furious
incensed
indignant
irate
livid
outraged
resentful

AVERSION
animosity
appalled
contempt
disgusted
dislike
hate
horrified
hostile
repulsed

CONFUSED
ambivalent
baffled
bewildered
dazed
hesitant
lost
mystified
perplexed
puzzled
torn

DISCONNECTED
alienated
aloof
apathetic
bored
cold
detached
indifferent
numb
removed
uninterested
withdrawn

DISQUIET
agitated
alarmed
disconcerted
disturbed
perturbed
rattled
restless
shocked
startled
surprised
troubled
turbulent
turmoil
uncomfortable
uneasy
unnerved
unsettled
upset

EMBARRASSED
ashamed
chagrined
flustered
guilty
mortified
self-conscious

TENSE
anxious
cranky
distressed
distraught
edgy
fidgety
frazzled
irritable
jittery
nervous
overwhelmed
restless
stressed out

PAIN
agony
anguished
bereaved
devastated
grief
heartbroken
hurt
lonely
miserable
regretful
remorseful

FATIGUE
beat
burnt out
depleted
exhausted
lethargic
listless
sleepy
tired
weary
worn out

SAD
depressed
dejected
despair
despondent
disappointed
discouraged
disheartened
forlorn
gloomy
heavy hearted
hopeless
melancholy
unhappy
wretched

VULNERABLE
fragile
guarded
helpless
insecure
leery
reserved
sensitive

YEARNING
envious
jealous
longing
nostalgic
pining
wistful

When you do

_____
OBSERVATION

I feel

_____
FEELING

My need is

_____
NEED

Would you please

_____ ?
REQUEST

Needs

CONNECTION
acceptance
affection
appreciation
belonging
cooperation
communication
closeness
community
companionship
compassion
consideration
consistency
empathy
inclusion
intimacy
love
mutuality
nurturing
respect/self-respect
safety
security
stability
support
to know and be known
to see and be seen
to understand
trust
warmth

PHYSICAL WELL-BEING
air
food
movement/exercise
rest/sleep
safety
shelter
touch
water

HONESTY
authenticity
integrity
presence

PLAY
joy
humor

PEACE
beauty
communication
ease
equality
harmony
inspiration
order

AUTONOMY
choice
freedom
independence
space
spontaneity

MEANING
awareness
celebration of life
challenge
clarity
competence
consciousness
contribution
creativity
discovery
efficacy
effectiveness
growth
hope
learning
mourning
participation
purpose
self-expression
stimulation
to matter
understanding

⊕Strategyzer

Afterword

References

Section 1: Discover the
Team Alignment Map

Mission and Period

Deci, E. L., and R. M. Ryan. *(1985). Intrinsic Motivation and Self-Determination in Human Behavior*. Plenum Press.
Edmondson, A. C., and J. F. Harvey. 2017. *Extreme Teaming: Lessons in Complex, Cross-Sector Leadership*. Emerald Group Publishing.
Locke, E. A., and G. P. Latham. 1990. *A Theory of Goal Setting & Task Performance*. Prentice-Hall Inc.

Joint Objectives

Clark, H. H. 1996. *Using Language*. Cambridge University Press.
Klein, H. J., M. J. Wesson, J. R. Hollenbeck, and B. J. Alge. 1999. "Goal Commitment and the Goal-Setting Process: Conceptual Clarification and Empirical Synthesis." *Journal of Applied Psychology* 84 (6): 885.
Lewis, D. K. 1969. *Convention: A Philosophical Study*. Harvard University Press.

Locke, E. A., and G. P. Latham. 1990. *A Theory of Goal Setting & Task Performance*. Prentice-Hall.
Schelling, T. C. 1980. *The Strategy of Conflict*. Harvard University Press.

Joint Commitments

Clark, H. H. 2006. "Social Actions, Social Commitments." In *Roots of Human Sociality: Culture, Cognition and Human Interaction*, edited by Stephen C. Levinson and N. J. Enfield, 126–150. Oxford, UK: Berg Press.
Edmondson, A. C., and J. F. Harvey. 2017. *Extreme Teaming: Lessons in Complex, Cross-Sector Leadership*. Emerald Publishing.
Gilbert, M. 2014. *Joint Commitment: How We Make the Social World*. Oxford University Press.
Schmitt, F. 2004. *Socializing Metaphysics: The Nature of Social Reality*. Rowman & Littlefield.
Tuomela, R., and M. Tuomela. 2003. "Acting as a Group Member and Collective Commitment." *Protosociology* 18: 7–65.

Joint Resources

Corporate Finance Institute® (CFI). n.d. "What Are the Main Types of Assets"? https://corporatefinanceinstitute.com/resources/knowledge/accounting/types-of-assets/

Joint Risks

Aven, T. 2010. "On How to Define, Understand and Describe Risk." *Reliability Engineering & System Safety* 95 (6): 623–631.
Cobb, A. T. 2011. *Leading Project Teams: The Basics of Project Management and Team Leadership*. Sage.
Cohen, P. 2011. "An Approach for Wording Risks." http://www.betterprojects.net/2011/09/approach-for-wording-risks.html.
Lonergan, K. 2015. "Example Project Risks – Good and Bad Practice." https://www.pmis-consulting.com/example-project-risks-goodand-bad-practice.
Mar, A. 2015. "130 Project Risks" (List). https://management.simplicable.com/management/new/130-project-risks.

Power, B. 2014. "Writing Good Risk Statements." *ISACA* Journal. https://www.isaca.org/Journal/archives/2014/Volume-3/Pages/Writing-Good-Risk-Statements.aspx#f1.

Project Management Institute. 2013. *A Guide to the Project Management Body of Knowledge* (PMBOK® Guide). 5th ed.

Assessments

Avdiji, H., D. Elikan, S. Missonier, and Y. Pigneur. 2018. "Designing Tools for Collectively Solving Ill-Structured Problems." In *Proceedings of the 51st Hawaii International Conference on System Sciences* (January), 400–409.

Avdiji, H., S. Missonier, and S. Mastrogiacomo. 2015. "How to Manage IS Team Coordination in Real Time." In *Proceedings of the International Conference on Information Systems* (ICIS) 2015, December 2015, 13–16.

Mastrogiacomo, S., S. Missonier, and R. Bonazzi. 2014. "Talk Before It's Too Late: Reconsidering the Role of Conversation in Information Systems Project Management." *Journal of Management Information Systems* 31 (1): 47–78.

Section 2: Put the Map into Action

Corporate Rebels. "The 8 Trends." https://corporate-rebels.com/trends/.

Kaplan, R. S., and D. P. Norton. 2006. *Alignment: Using the Balanced Scorecard to Create Corporate Synergies*. Harvard Business School Press.

Kniberg, H. 2014. "Spotify Engineering Culture Part 1." Spotify Labs. https://labs.spotify.com/2014/03/27/spotifyengineering-culture-part-1/

Kniberg, H. 2014. "Spotify Engineering Culture Part 2." Spotify Labs. https://labs.spotify.com/2014/09/20/spotifyengineering-culture-part-2/

Larman, C., and B. Vodde. 2016. *Large-Scale Scrum: More with LeSS*. Addison-Wesley.

Leffingwell, D. 2018. SAFe 4.5 *Reference Guide: Scaled Agile Framework for Lean Enterprises*. Addison-Wesley.

Section 3: Trust Among Team Members

Psychological Safety

Christian M. S., A. S. Garza, and J. E. Slaughter. 2011. "Work Engagement: A Quantitative Review and Test of Its Relations with Task and Contextual Performance." *Personnel Psychology* 64: 89–136. http://dx.doi.org/10.1111/j.1744-6570.2010.01203.x

Duhigg, C. 2016. "What Google Learned from Its Quest to Build the Perfect Team." *New York Times Magazine*. February 25.

Edmondson, A. 1999. "Psychological Safety and Learning Behavior in Work Teams." *Administrative Science Quarterly* 44: 350–383. http://dx.doi.org/10.2307/2666999

Edmondson, A. C. 2004. "Psychological Safety, Trust, and Learning in Organizations: A Group-Level Lens." In *Trust and Distrust in Organizations: Dilemmas and Approaches*, edited by R. M. Kramer and K. S. Cook, 239–272. Russell Sage Foundation.

Edmondson, A. C. 2018. *The Fearless Organization: Creating Psychological Safety in the Workplace for Learning, Innovation, and Growth*. John Wiley & Sons.

Edmondson, A. C., and J. F. Harvey. 2017. *Extreme Teaming: Lessons in Complex, Cross-Sector Leadership*. Emerald Publishing.

Frazier, M. L., S. Fainshmidt, R. L. Klinger, A. Pezeshkan, and V. Vracheva. 2017. "Psychological Safety: A Meta-Analytic Review and Extension." *Personnel Psychology* 70 (1): 113–165.

Gallo, P. 2018. *The Compass and the Radar: The Art of Building a Rewarding Career While Remaining True to Yourself*. Bloomsbury Business.

Kahn, W. A. 1990. "Psychological Conditions of Personal Engagement and Disengagement at Work." *Academy of Management Journal* 33: 692–724. http://dx.doi.org/10.2307/256287

Mayer, R. C., J. H. Davis, and F. D. Schoorman. 1995. "An Integrative Model of Organizational Trust." *Academy of Management Review* 20: 709–734. http://dx.doi.org/10.5465/AMR.1995.9508080335

Schein, E. H., and W. G. Benni. 1965. *Personal and Organizational Change Through Group Methods: The Laboratory Approach*. John Wiley & Sons.

Spreitzer, G. M. 1995. "Psychological Empowerment in the Workplace: Dimensions, Measurement, and Validation." *Academy of Management Journal* 38: 1442–1465. doi: 10.2037/256865

The Team Contract

Edmondson, A. C. 2018. *The Fearless Organization: Creating Psychological Safety in the Workplace for Learning, Innovation, and Growth*. John Wiley & Sons.

Fiske, A. P., and P. E. Tetlock. 1997. "Taboo Trade-Offs: Reactions to Transactions That Transgress the Spheres of Justice." *Political Psychology* 18 (2): 255–297.

The Fact Finder

Edmondson, A. C. 2018. *The Fearless Organization: Creating Psychological Safety in the Workplace for Learning, Innovation, and Growth*. John Wiley & Sons.

Kourilsky, F. 2014. *Du désir au plaisir de changer: le coaching du changement*. Dunod.

Watzlawick, P. 1984. *The Invented Reality: Contributions to Constructivism*. W. W. Norton.

Zacharis, P. 2016. *La boussole du langage*. https://www.patrickzacharis.be/la-boussole-du-langage/

The Respect Card

Brown, P., and S. C. Levinson. 1987. *Politeness: Some Universals in Language Usage*. Vol. 4. Cambridge University Press.

Culpeper, J. 2011. "Politeness and Impoliteness." In *Pragmatics of Society*, edited by W. Bublitz, A. H. Jucker, and K. P. Schneider. Vol. 5, 393. Mouton de Gruyter.

Fiske, A. P. 1992. "The Four Elementary Forms of Sociality: Framework for a Unified Theory of Social Relations." *Psychological Review* 99 (4): 689.

Lee, J. J., and S. Pinker. 2010. "Rationales for Indirect Speech: The Theory of the Strategic Speaker." *Psychological Review* 117 (3): 785.

Locher, M. A., and R. J. Watts. 2008. "Relational Work and Impoliteness: Negotiating Norms of Linguistic Behaviour." In *Impoliteness in Language. Studies on its Interplay with Power in Theory and Practice*, edited by D. Bousfield and M. A. Locher, 77-99. Mouton de Gruyter.

Pinker, S. 2007. *The Stuff of Thought: Language as a Window into Human Nature*. Penguin.

Pinker, S., M. A. Nowak, and J. J. Lee. 2008. "The Logic of Indirect Speech." *Proceedings of the National Academy of Sciences* 105 (3): 833–838.

The Nonviolent Requests Guide

Hess, J. A. 2003. "Maintaining Undesired Relationships." In *Maintaining Relationships Through Communication: Relational, Contextual, and Cultural Variations*, edited by D. J. Canary and M. Dainton, 103–124. Lawrence Erlbaum Associates.

Kahane, A. 2017. *Collaborating with the Enemy: How to Work with People You Don't Agree with or Like or Trust*. Berrett-Koehler Publishers.

Marshall, R., and P. D. Rosenberg. 2003. *Nonviolent Communication: A Language of Life*. PuddleDancer Press.

McCracken, H. 2017. "Satya Nadella Rewrites Microsoft's Code." *Fast Company*. September 18.

Mutual Understanding and Common Ground

Clark, H. H. 1996. *Using Language*. Cambridge University Press.

Clark, H. H., and S. E. Brennan. 1991. "Grounding in Communication." Perspectives on Socially *Shared Cognition* 13: 127–149.

De Freitas, J., K. Thomas, P. DeScioli, and S. Pinker. 2019. "Common Knowledge, Coordination, and Strategic Mentalizing in Human Social Life." *Proceedings of the National Academy of Sciences* 116 (28): 13751–13758.

Klein, G., P. J. Feltovich, J. M. Bradshaw, and D. D. Woods. 2005. "Common Ground and Coordination in Joint Activity." In *Organizational Simulation*, edited by W. B. Rouse and K. R. Boff, 139–184. John Wiley & Sons.

Mastrogiacomo, S., S. Missonier, and R. Bonazzi. 2014. "Talk Before It's Too Late: Reconsidering the Role of Conversation in Information Systems Project Management." *Journal of Management Information Systems* 31 (1): 47–78.

"Media Richness Theory." Wikipedia. https://en.wikipedia.org/w/index.php?title=Media_richness_theory&oldid=930255670

Trust and Psychological Safety

Edmondson, A. 1999. "Psychological Safety and Learning Behavior in Work Teams." *Administrative Science Quarterly* 44 (2): 350–383.

Edmondson, A. C. 2018. *The Fearless Organization: Creating Psychological Safety in the Workplace for Learning, Innovation, and Growth*. John Wiley & Sons.

Edmondson, A. C. 2004. "Psychological Safety, Trust, and Learning in Organizations: A Group-Level Lens." In *Trust and Distrust in Organizations: Dilemmas and Approaches*, edited by R. M. Kramer and K. S. Cook, 239–272. Russell Sage Foundation.

Edmondson, A. C., and A. W. Woolley, A. W. 2003. "Understanding Outcomes of Organizational Learning Interventions." In *International Handbook on Organizational Learning and Knowledge Management*, edited by M. Easterby-Smith and M. Lyles, 185–211. London: Blackwell.

Tucker, A. L., I. M. Nembhard, and A. C. Edmondson. 2007. "Implementing New Practices: An Empirical Study of Organizational Learning in Hospital Intensive Care Units." *Management Science* 53 (6): 894–907.

Face and Politeness

Brown, P., and S. C. Levinson. 1987. *Politeness: Some Universals in Language Usage*. Vol. 4. Cambridge University Press.

Culpeper, J. 2011. "Politeness and Impoliteness." In *Pragmatics of Society*, edited by W. Bublitz, A. H. Jucker, and K. P. Schneider. Vol. 5, 393. Mouton de Gruyter.

Fiske, A. P. 1992. "The Four Elementary Forms of Sociality: Framework for a Unified Theory of Social Relations." *Psychological Review* 99 (4): 689.

Kim, W., and R. Mauborgne. 1997. "Fair Process." *Harvard Business Review* 75: 65–75.

Lee, J. J., and S. Pinker. 2010. "Rationales for Indirect Speech: The Theory of the Strategic Speaker." *Psychological Review* 117 (3): 785.

Locher, M. A., and R. J. Watts, R. J. 2008. "Relational Work and Impoliteness: Negotiating Norms of Linguistic Behaviour." In *Impoliteness in Language. Studies on its Interplay with Power in Theory and Practice*, edited by D. Bousfield and M. A. Locher, 77–99. Mouton de Gruyter.

Pless, N., and T. Maak. 2004. "Building an Inclusive Diversity Culture: Principles, Processes and Practice." *Journal of Business Ethics* 54 (2): 129–147.

Pinker, S. 2007. *The Stuff of Thought: Language as a Window into Human Nature*. Penguin.

Pinker, S., M. A. Nowak, and J. J. Lee. 2008. "The Logic of Indirect Speech." *Proceedings of the National Academy of Sciences* 105, (3): 833–838.

Index

A

Addressed letters, 265
Agile projects:
    about, 136, 138
    alignment in, 141
    in TAM sessions, 140
Aligned autonomy, 160
Aligned playing modes, 280–281
Alignment:
    in cross-functional teams, 164–165
    defining, 12
    initial, in projects, 138–141
    maintaining, with the TAM, 140, 142
    organizational (see Organizational
        alignment)
    successful, factors of, 12–13
    successful vs. unsuccessful, 12–13
    team impact affected by, 18–19
    throughout projects, 140–141
    unsuccessful, factors of, 12–13
Allocating resources, 166–167
Ambiguous commitments, 52
Anxiety zone, 269
Apathy zone, 269
Approval, need for, 284
Assessments:
    online, 170–171
    paper-based, 171

project, using TAM for, 92–93
    readiness, 103
    troubleshooting, 103
Assessment Mode (of TAM), 21, 90–107
    example, 103
    readiness vs. troubleshooting
        assessments in, 103
    Reflect (step 2), 96–99
    Repair (step 3), 100–101
    Reveal (step 1), 94–95
Assumptions, 210, 213, 214
Asynchronous communication, 264
Attacks, 246–247
Authority mode, of relationships, 276–277
Autonomy:
    aligned, 160
    need for, 251, 284

B

Backward pass:
    about, 74–75
    for cross-functional work, 165
    in empowerment meetings, 161
    example, 78–79, 82–83, 86–87
    negotiating resources with, 166–167
    for risk management in projects, 148–149
Bargain mode, of relationships, 276–277

BMC (Business Model Canvas), 166, 168–169
Breaches of Team Contract, 200–201
Brown, Penelope, 284
Budget, 126
Buffer (on Kanban board), 146
Business Model Canvas (BMC), 166, 168–169
Buy-in, team, 38, 162, 168

C

Center for Nonviolent Communication, xi,
    244, 250
Clarify (on Kanban board), 146
Clark, Herbert, x, 260, 262
Collaboration across departments and
    functions, 164–165
Comfort zone, 269
Commitments:
    ambiguous, 52
    joint (see Joint commitments)
Common ground:
    building up, 262–263
    communication channels impacting,
        264–265
    defining, 260–261
    high, 15
    importance of, in teams, 12
    irrelevant, 13

low, 13–14

in psychologically unsafe vs. safe
environments, 14–15

relevant, 13

relevant vs. irrelevant or low, 13

Common knowledge, 260–261

Communication:

asynchronous, 264

and communication channels,
264–265

effectiveness of media types for, 265

and face-to-face dialogue, 12, 264, 265

nonviolent, 242, 249

successful, 13

successful vs. unsuccessful, 13

synchronous, 264

traps of, 210, 212–213

unsuccessful, 13

using Respect Card for (see Respect
Card)

Complex failures, 203

Complex operations, failure in, 202–203

Conflict, managing, 268, 280. See also
Nonviolent Requests Guide

Coordination, effective, vs. coordination
surprises, 13

Coordination surprises, 13, 260

Cross-functional teams, 164–165

D

Decision making, informed, 126–127

Delivery dates, 152

Direct request, 229, 235

Disagreements, dealing with, 130

Drucker, Peter, 10, 47

E

Edmondson, Amy, x, 38, 200, 202, 268

Effective coordination, 13

Emails, 265

Emotions:

as KPIs, 131

and relationship modes, 278–279

when needs are not satisfied, 250

when needs are satisfied, 251

Empowerment, 160–161, 272

Empowerment meetings, 160–161

End results, defined, 46

Engagement:

in fair process, 286–287

and psychological safety, 273

team, 122–123

Evaluation, in Fact Finder, 210

Expectation clarity, in fair process,
286–287

Explanation, in fair process,
286–287

Expressing respect, 226–229

F

Face-to-face dialogue, 12, 264, 265

Fact Finder, 208–219

about, 22–23, 210–211

and communication traps, 212–213

in practice, 214–215

pro tips for, 218–219

template, 293

Failures:

and common ground, 260

complex, 203

framing, on Team Contract,
202–203

intelligent, 203

preventable, 203

Fair process, 286–287

Family businesses, 280–281

Family constitution, 280

Fear, as sign of unsafe team climate, 11

Fiske, Alan, x, 276

Forward pass:

about, 74–75

for cross-functional work, 165

in empowerment meetings, 161

example, 76–77, 80–81, 84–85

for resource negotiation,
166–167

G

Generalizations, 210, 213, 215

Gilbert, Margaret, 52

Goals, defined, 46

Google, 47, 268

Grounding process, 262–263

H

Harvard Business School, x

Harvard University, xi

Header area, 36–38

High common ground, 15

High-performance teams, 268

High team learning, 15

High team performance, 15

High-volume repetitive work, 203

I

Impoliteness, 235
Incomplete facts, 213–214
Indirect request, 229, 235
Informed decision making, 126–127
Initial alignment, in projects, 138–141
Initial TAM sessions, 142
Initiatives, transformation, 174–175
Inner dialogue, 249
Innovation:
    failure in, 203
    unsafe team climate undermining, 14–15
INSEAD, 286
Intelligent failures, 203
Interpretation, in Fact Finder, 210
Inventory of needs, 251
Irrelevant common ground, 13

J

Joint Commitment Ritual, 52
Joint commitments, 48–55
    analyzing, in Assessment Mode, 99
    defining, 52–53
    defining, in workspace, 36–37
    examples, 54–55
    in forward pass (example), 77, 81, 85
Joint objectives, 40–47
    analyzing, in Assessment Mode, 99
    defining, 44–45
    defining, in workspace, 36–37
    examples, 46–47
    in forward pass (example), 76, 80, 84
    negotiating and allocating resources
        for, 166

Joint resources, 56–63
    analyzing, in Assessment Mode, 99
    in backward pass (example), 78, 82, 86
    defining, 60–61
    defining, in workspace, 36–37
    examples, 62–63
    in forward pass (example), 77, 81, 85
Joint risks, 64–71
    analyzing, in Assessment Mode, 99
    in backward pass (example), 79, 83, 87
    defining, 68–69
    defining, in workspace, 36–37
    examples, 70–71
    in forward pass (example), 77, 81, 85
Judgments, 210, 213, 215

K

Kanban-stye TAM, 144–147
    about, 144–145
    in practice, 146–147
Kim, Cham, 286
Klein, G., 260
Kniberg, Henrik, 160
Kourilsky, Françoise, xi
KPIs, considering emotions as, 131

L

Lack of clarity, 130
Latecomers, managing, 131
Leaders:
    and cross-functional alignment, 165
    negotiating resources with, 166
    teams empowered by, 160
Lean UX cycle, 256

Learning, team, 14–15
Learning zone, 269
Letters, addressed, 265
Levinson, Stephen, 284
Limitations, 210, 213, 215
Low common ground, 13–14
Low team learning, 14
Low team performance, 14

M

Mauborgne, Renée, 286
Media types, for communication, 265
Meeting attendance, 246
Meetings, 118–131
    Assessment Mode for, 128–129
    boosting team engagement in, 122–123
    focusing the team in, 120–121
    increasing impact of, 124–125
    making informed decisions in, 126–127
    pro tips for, 130–131
    timebox, 120
    update, 131
    weekly TAM, 142–143
Mental Research Institute, xi
Microsoft, 242
Milestones, 152
Miro, 150
Misaligned relationship modes, 278–279
Misaligned team activities, signs of, 11
Missing stakeholders, managing, 131
Mission:
    describing your, 39
    in forward pass (example), 76, 80, 84
    importance of, 38
    repairing, 101

on TAM, 37
Misunderstanding, signaling, 262
Mobilizing large groups, 162–163
Motivation, 247
Mural, 150
Mutual understanding, 260–261

N

Nadella, Satya, 242
Needs:
    inventory of, 251
    satisfying, 250–251
    social, 284–285
Negotiation:
    in cross-functional teams, 165
    of resources, 166–167
    team-to-team, 167
Noncompliance with Team Contract, 200–201
Nonviolent communication (NVC), 242, 249
Nonviolent requests, 246–247
Nonviolent Requests Guide, 240–251
    about, 22–23, 242–243
    and attacks vs. nonviolent requests,
      246–247
    origins of, 250–251
    in practice, 244–245
    pro tips for, 248–249
    template, 295
NVC (nonviolent communication), 242, 249

O

Objective, defined, 46
Objectives, joint, see Joint objectives

OKR (objectives and key results), 47
Online assessments, 170–171
Online boards, 150–151
Online surveys, 150, 170
Online tools, 152, 170
Organizational alignment, 154–175
    assessing strategic initiative readiness,
      170–173
    within cross-functional teams,
      164–165
    empowering teams for, 160–161
    engaging large groups for, 162–163
    negotiating and allocating resources for,
      166–167
    pro tips for, 174–175
    using strategy processes and tools for,
      168–169
Overdue work, 246
Overly polite, 235

P

Paper-based assessments, 171
Perception, in Fact Finder, 210
Perception gaps, 140
Period(s):
    in forward pass (example), 76, 84
    repairing, 101
    setting the, 38–39
    on TAM, 37
Pigneur, Yves, x
Pinker, Steven, xi, 284
Planning Mode (of TAM), 21, 74–89
    backward pass (example), 78–79,
      82–83, 86–87
    backward pass in, 74

forward pass (example), 76–77, 80–81,
    84–85
    forward pass in, 74
    pro tips for, 88–89
Playing modes:
    about, 276–277
    aligned, for family businesses,
      280–281
    crossing, 278–279
Politeness, 234, 284–285
Politeness (Brown and Levinson), 284
Posters, 265
Prenup Paradox, 201
Preventable failures, 203
Private knowledge, 261
Professional risk management, 68
Project assessments, using TAM for,
    92–93
Projects, 132–153
    aligning distributed teams in,
      150–151
    having a good start with, 138–139
    maintaining alignment throughout,
      140–143
    pro tips for, 152–153
    reducing risks in, 148–149
    using Kanban board to track tasks in,
      144–147
Project scope, 153
Psychological safety, 15
    assessing, 270–271
    and breaches of Team Contract, 200
    defining, 268–269
    through Team Contracts, 190
    trust vs., 272–273
    using Add-ons to build, 22–23
Psychologically unsafe environments, 14

R

Rapid checks, 143

Readiness assessment, 103

Reciprocate mode, of relationships, 276–277

Reflect (Step 2 of Assessment Mode), 96–99
example, 105
for meetings (example), 129
with strategic initiatives, 173

Relationships, 276–281
crossing modes of, 278–279
and family businesses, 280–281
playing modes of, 276–277
unwanted, 249

Relevant common ground, 13

Repair (Step 3 of Assessment Mode), 100–101
example, 105
for meetings (example), 129
with strategic initiatives, 173

Repetitive work, high-volume, 203

Research, failure in, 203

Resources:
allocating, 166–167
joint (see Joint resources)

Respect:
expressing, 228–229
need for, 284

Respect Card, 220–235
about, 22–23, 226–227
expressing respect on, 226–229
how to use the, 232–233
pro tips for, 234–235
template, 294
valuing others on, 230–231

Reveal (Step 1 of Assessment Mode), 94–95
example, 104
for meetings (example), 128
with strategic initiatives, 172

Risks:
exposure to, 68
identification of, in meetings, 131
joint (see Joint risks)
management of, in projects, 148–149
and professional risk management, 68

Rosenberg, Marshall, xi, 242, 250

Rudeness, 235

Rules and procedures, 247

S

Safety:
psychological (see Psychological safety)
team impact affected by, 18–19

Sarcasm, 234

Sensitive topics, 234

Shared knowledge, 261

Share mode, of relationships, 276–277

Shelling, Thomas, 47

Short messages, 265

SMART objectives, defined, 47

Social needs, 284–285

Spam, unaddressed, 265

Spotify, 160

Stakeholders, managing missing, 131

Stanford University, x

Strategic initiative assessment, 170–173

Subteams, 162

Success criteria, 153

Successful alignment, factors of, 12–13

Successful communication, 13

Surprises, coordination, 13

Surveys, online, 150, 170

Swim lanes, for Kanban board, 146

Synchronous communication, 264

T

TAM, see Team Alignment Map

TAM Add-Ons:
about, 22–23
Fact Finder (see Fact Finder)
Nonviolent Requests Guide (see Nonviolent Requests Guide)
Respect Card (see Respect Card)
Team Contract (see Team Contract)

Team(s):
alignment and safety affecting impact of, 18–19
and cross-functional alignment, 165
empowerment through, 160
engagement in, 122–123
high-performance, 268
motivation of, importance of mission for, 38
performance of, in psychologically unsafe vs. safe environments, 14–15
underperforming, factors contributing to, 10–11, 160
using TAM to assess, 92–93
validation in (see Team validation)

Team activities:
importance of, 10
signs of misaligned, 11

Team Alignment Map (TAM):
about, 20–21
Add-ons (see TAM Add-Ons)

assessing projects and teams with, 92–93
joint commitments, 48–55
joint objectives, 40–47
joint resources, 56–63
joint risks, 64–71
for meetings (see Meetings)
mission and period on, 38–39
pillars of, 36–71
template, 290–291
workspace of, 38–39
Team buy-in, 38, 162, 168
Team climate:
    importance of, 10
    signs of poor, 11
Team Contract, 188–203
    about, 22–23, 190–191
    applying, 196–197
    framing failure on, 202–203
    Ins and Outs in, 192–193
    light vs. heavy conventions in, 194–195
    noncompliance of, 200–201
    as TAM companion, 198–199
    template, 292
Team learning, 14–15
Team-to-team negotiation, 167

Team validation:
    in backward pass (example), 79, 83, 87
    in Repair step of Assessment Mode, 101
Telephone conversations, 265
Third parties, in conflict management, 248
Timebox meetings, 134
Track (on Kanban board), 146
Transformation initiatives, 174–175
Troubleshooting assessments, 103
Trust:
    lack of, in teams, 11
    psychological safety vs., 272–273
    using Add-ons to build, 22–23

U

Unaddressed spam, 265
Unclear facts, 210
Underperforming teams, factors contributing to, 10–11, 160
Understanding, signaling, 262
University of California, x
University of Lausanne, x
Unsafe team climate:
    innovation undermined by, 14–15
    signs of, 11
Unspoken commitments, 52

Unsuccessful alignment, factors of, 12–13
Unsuccessful communication, 13
Unwanted relationships, 249
Update meetings, 131
User stories, defined, 47

V

Validation:
    in teams (see Team validation)
Validation, in empowerment meetings, 161
Valuing others, 230–231
Video conversations, 150, 265
VUCA (Volatility, Uncertainty, Complexity, and Ambiguity), 268

W

Waterfall projects:
    about, 139
    alignment in, 141
    TAM sessions in, 140
Watzlawick, Paul, xi
Weekly TAM meetings, 142–143
Work overload, 246
Workspace, 36–37

Acknowledgments

Book Team

This book is the result of a long journey involving a great many people and teams that helped us design, experiment, test, and improve the tools, and finally to design the content. We thank everyone for their individual contributions and patience during our endless workshops, repeated surveys, and rounds of unnecessary questions.

First, we thank the thousands of early adopters who used some of our early concepts and contributed to the evolution and refinement of the ideas we present here.

We are grateful to Stéphanie Missonier, Hazbi Avdiji, Yves Pigneur, Françoise Kourilsky, Adrian Bangerter, and Pierre Dillenbourg for the initial academic work and their unique contribution to the conceptual foundations of the tools. We thank many great field practitioners: Alain Giannattasio, Thomas Steiner, Yasmine Made, Renaud Litré, Antonio Carriero, Fernando Yepez, Jamie Jenkins, Gigi Lai, David Bland, Ivan Torreblanca, Sumayah Aljasem, Jose-Carlos Barbara, Eva Sandner, Koffi Kragba, and Julia van Graas for experimenting and helping improve our early prototypes and the manuscript. Thanks go to Pierre Sindelar, Tony Vogt, Monica Wagen, and Pascal Antoine for passionately challenging our ideas and findings, and to David Carroll for his great support when were struggling with the title.

We are indebted to our illustrators, Bernard Granger and Séverine Assous, for their dedication and the beauty of their artistic work, with a special thanks to Louise Ducatillon, who helped initiate this artistic collaboration, and to Trish Papadakos and Chris White, for the impressive design work they've accomplished. We are grateful to our publisher, Wiley, especially to Richard Narramore, Victoria Annlo, and Vicki Adang for the guidance and the improvements made to the manuscript. We also wish to thank all the great many collaborators at Strategyzer: Tom Philip, Jonas Baer, Federico Galindo, Przemek Kowalczyk, Mathias Maisberger, Kavi Guppta, Franziska Beeler, Niki Kotsonis, Jerry Steele, Tanja Oberst, Shamira Miller, Paweł Sułkowski, Aleksandra Czaplicka, Jon Friis, Frederic Etiemble, Matt Woodward, Silke Simons, Daniela Leutwyler, Gabriel Roy, Dave Thomas, Natlie Loots, Piotr Pawlik, Jana Stevanovic, Tendayi Viki, Janice Gallen, Andrew Martiniello, Lee Hockin, Laine McGarragle, Andrew Maffi, and Lucy Luo.

Finally, the book wouldn't be what it is without Honora Ducatillon, who relentlessly challenged, commented on, and encouraged each step of the editing process.

– Stefano, Alex, and Alan

Book Team

Lead Author
Stefano Mastrogiacomo

Stefano Mastrogiacomo is a management consultant, professor, and author. He has a passion for human coordination and he's the designer of the Team Alignment Map, the Team Contract, the Fact Finder, and the other tools presented in this book. He's been leading digital projects and advising project teams in international organizations for more than 20 years, while teaching and doing research at the University of Lausanne, Switzerland. His interdisciplinary work is anchored in project management, change management, psycholinguistics, evolutionary anthropology, and design thinking.

teamalignment.co

Author
Alex Osterwalder

Alex is a leading author, entrepreneur, and in-demand speaker whose work has changed the way established companies do business and how new ventures get started. Ranked No. 4 of the top 50 management thinkers worldwide, Alex also holds the Thinkers50 Strategy Award. Together with Yves Pigneur he invented the Business Model Canvas, the Value Proposition Canvas, and the Business Portfolio Map—practical tools that are trusted by millions of business practitioners.

@AlexOsterwalder
strategyzer.com/blog

Creative Lead
Alan Smith

Alan uses his curiosity and creativity to ask questions and turn the answers into simple, visual, practical tools. He believes that the right tools give people confidence to aim high and build big meaningful things. He cofounded Strategyzer with Alex Osterwalder, where he works with an inspired team to build great products. Strategyzer's books, tools, and services are used by leading companies around the world.

strategyzer.com

Design Lead
Trish Papadakos

Trish holds a Masters in Design from Central St. Martins in London and a Bachelor of Design from the York Sheridan Joint Program in Toronto.

She has taught design at her alma mater, worked with award-winning agencies, launched several businesses, and is collaborating for the seventh time with the Strategyzer team.

Designer
Chris White

Chris is a multidisciplinary designer who lives in Toronto. He has spent his time working on a number of business publications in various roles, most recently as Assistant Art Director at *The Globe and Mail*, focusing on presentation design for both print and online stories.

Illustrator
Severine Assous

Severine is a French illustrator based in Paris, working primarily on children's books, publications, and advertising. Her characters grace the pages of the book.

Illustrator
Blexbolex

Bernard Granger (Blexbolex) is an illustrator, comic book artist, and the 2009 recipient of the Golden Letter Award for best book design in the world. He created the image for the book's cover along with several pages throughout of humorous imaginings of contemporary office culture.

illustrissimo.fr

Strategyzer uses the best of technology and coaching to support your transformation and growth challenges.

Discover what we can do for you at Strategyzer.com

Create Growth Repeatedly

Systematize and scale your growth efforts, build an innovation culture, and broaden your pipeline of ideas and projects with Strategyzer Growth Portfolio.

Strategyzer is the global leader in growth and innovation services. We help companies around the world build new engines of growth based on our proven methodology and technology-enabled services.

Create Change at Scale

Build state-of-the-art business skills at scale with Strategyzer Academy and online coaching.

Strategyzer prides itself on designing the simplest and most applicable business tools. We help practitioners become more customer centric, design outstanding value propositions, find better business models, and align teams.